Distances and journey times

The mileage chart shows distances in miles between two towns along AA-recommended routes. Using motorways and other main roads this is normally the fastest route, though not necessarily the shortest.

The journey times, shown in hours and minutes, are average off-peak driving times along AA-recommended routes. These times should be used as a guide only and do not allow for unforeseen traffic delays, rest breaks or fuel stops.

For example, the 378 miles (608 km) journey between Glasgow and Norwich should take approximately 7 hours 28 minutes.

Journey times

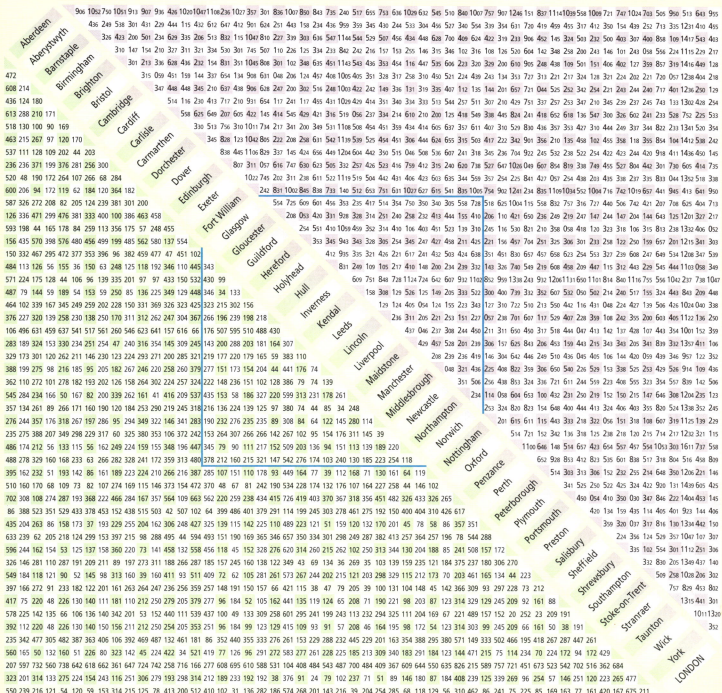

Distances in miles (one mile equals 1.6093 km)

GREAT BRITAIN ROAD ATLAS

2012

Atlas contents

Scale 1:200,000 or 3.16 miles to 1 inch

Map pages and distance times	inside front cover
Route planning	**2–20**
Route planner	2–7
Traffic signs	8–9
Channel hopping	10–11
Ferries to Ireland and the Isle of Man	12–13
Caravan and camping sites in Britain	14–17
Road safety cameras	18–19
Map pages	20
Road map symbols	**1**
Road maps	**2–173**
Britain 1:200,000 scale	**2–169**
Some islands are shown at slightly smaller scales.	
Ireland 1:1,000,000 scale	170–173
Motorways	**174–179**
Restricted junctions	174–177
M25 London Orbital	178
M6 Toll Motorway	179

Street map symbols	180
Towns, ports and airports	**181–231**
Town plans	182–228
Major airports	229–231
Channel Tunnel terminals	27
Central London	**232–247**
Central London street map	232–241
Central London index	242–247
District maps	**248–259**
London	248–251
Birmingham	252–253
Glasgow	254–255
Manchester	256–257
Newcastle	258–259
Index to place names	**260–308**
County, administrative area map	260
Place name index	261–308
Map pages and distance times	**inside back cover**

26th edition June 2011

© AA Media Limited 2011

Original edition printed 1986.

Cartography:
All cartography in this atlas edited, designed and produced by the Mapping Services Department of AA Publishing (A04648).

This atlas contains Ordnance Survey data © Crown copyright and database right 2011 and Royal Mail data © Royal Mail copyright and database right. All rights reserved. Licence number 100021153.

 Land & Property Services. This atlas is based upon Crown Copyright and is reproduced with the permission of Land and Property Services under delegated authority from the Controller of Her Majesty's Stationery Office, © Crown copyright and database rights 2011, Licence number 100,363. Permit No. 100161.

 Ordnance Survey Ireland Ireland's National Mapping Agency

© Ordnance Survey Ireland/Government of Ireland. Permit No. 8737.

Publisher's Notes:
Published by AA Publishing (a trading name of AA Media Limited, whose registered office is Fanum House, Basing View, Basingstoke, Hampshire RG21 4EA, UK. Registered number 06112600).

All rights reserved. No part of this publication may be reproduced, stored in a retrieval system, or transmitted in any form or by any means – electronic, mechanical, photocopying, recording or otherwise – unless the permission of the publisher has been given beforehand.

ISBN: 978 0 7495 6822 1 (leather bound hardback)
ISBN: 978 0 7495 6821 4 (standard hardback)

A CIP catalogue record for this book is available from The British Library.

Disclaimer:
The contents of this atlas are believed to be correct at the time of the latest revision, it will not contain any subsequent amended, new or temporary information including diversions and traffic control or enforcement systems. The publishers cannot be held responsible or liable for any loss or damage occasioned to any person acting or refraining from action as a result of any use or reliance on material in this atlas, nor for any errors, omissions or changes in such material. This does not affect your statutory rights.

The publishers would welcome information to correct any errors or omissions and to keep this atlas up to date. Please write to the Atlas Editor, AA Publishing, The Automobile Association, Fanum House, Basing View, Basingstoke, Hampshire RG21 4EA, UK. E-mail: roadatlasfeedback@theaa.com

Acknowledgements:
AA Publishing would like to thank the following for their assistance in producing this atlas:

RoadPilot® Information on fixed speed camera locations provided by and © 2011 RoadPilot® Driving Technology. Information on truckstops and transport cafés kindly provided by John Eden (www.transportcafe.co.uk). Crematoria data provided by the Cremation Society of Great Britain. Cadw, English Heritage, Forestry Commission, Historic Scotland, Johnsons, National Trust and National Trust for Scotland, RSPB, The Wildlife Trust, Scottish Natural Heritage, Natural England, The Countryside Council for Wales (road maps).

Crown copyright material (pages 8–9,18) reproduced under licence from the Controller of HMSO and the Driving Standards Agency.

Education Direct, Johnsons, The Post Office, Transport for London (Central London Map).

Nexus (Newcastle district map).

Printer:
Printed in China by Leo Paper Group on 113 gsm, FSC accredited paper.

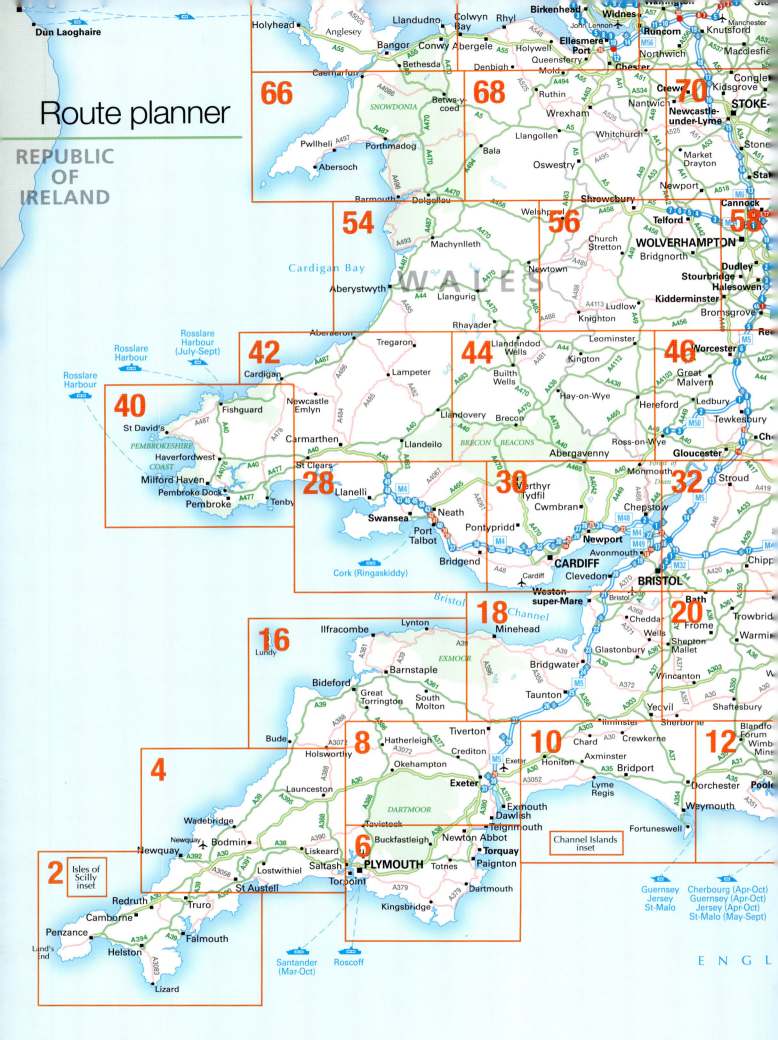

Route planner

REPUBLIC
OF
IRELAND

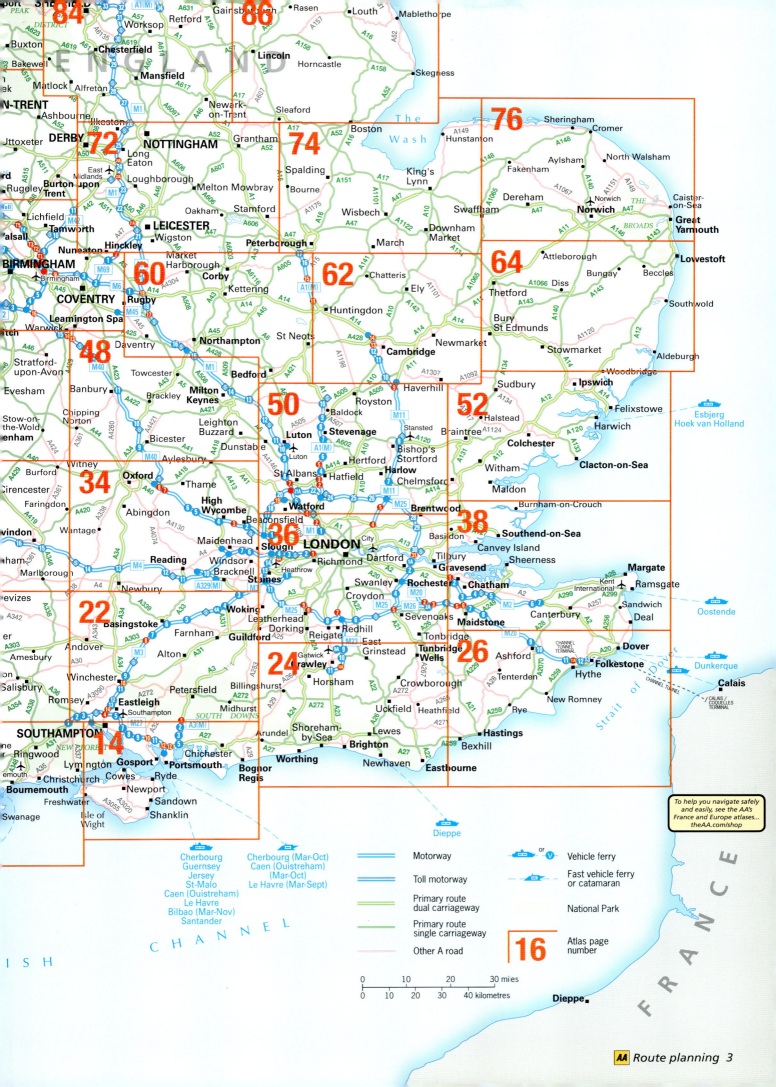

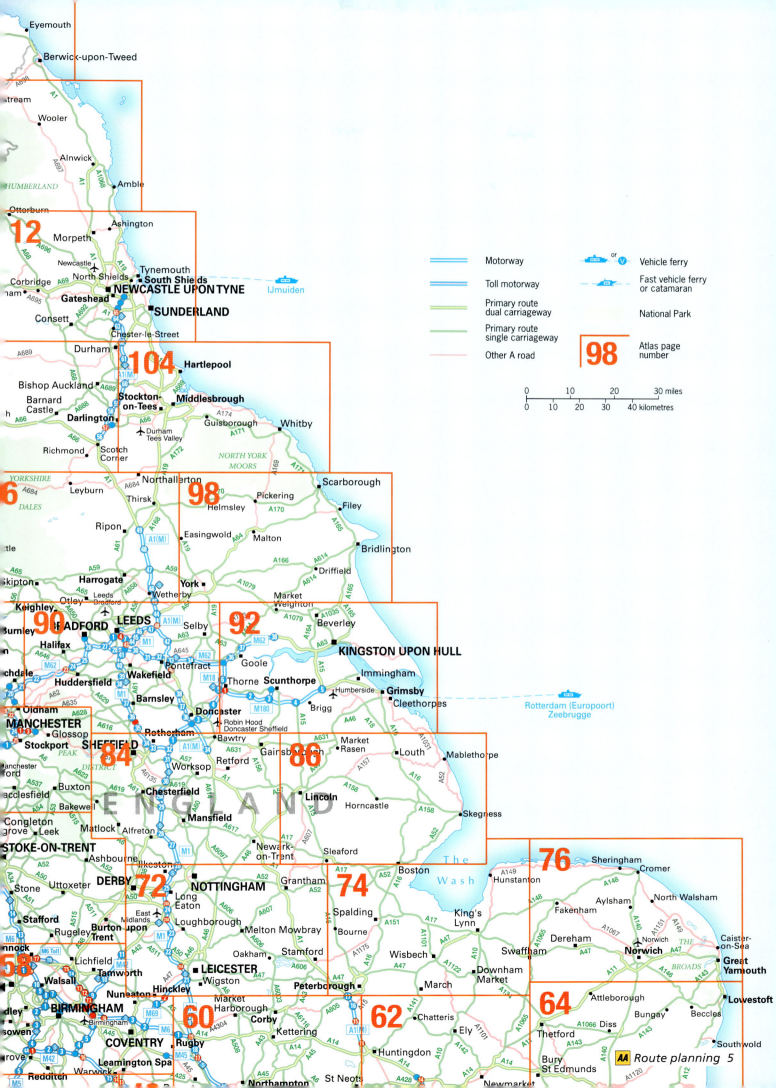

Map Legend

Motorway	Vehicle ferry
Toll motorway	Fast vehicle ferry or catamaran
Primary route dual carriageway	National Park
Primary route single carriageway	
Other A road	**98** Atlas page number

0 10 20 30 miles
0 10 20 30 40 kilometres

12
104
98
90
92
84
86
72
74
76
60
62
64

Eyemouth
Berwick-upon-Tweed
stream
Wooler
Alnwick
NORTHUMBERLAND
Ottburn
Amble
Ashington
Morpeth
Newcastle
Corbridge
North Shields
Tynemouth
South Shields
NEWCASTLE UPON TYNE
IJmuiden
Gateshead
SUNDERLAND
Consett
Chester-le-Street
Durham
Bishop Auckland
Hartlepool
Barnard Castle
Stockton-on-Tees
Middlesbrough
Darlington
Guisborough
Whitby
Richmond
Scotch Corner
Durham Tees Valley
NORTH YORK MOORS
YORKSHIRE DALES
Leyburn
Northallerton
Scarborough
Thirsk
Pickering
Filey
Ripon
Helmsley
Easingwold
Malton
Bridlington
Skipton
Harrogate
Driffield
Otley
Leeds Bradford
Wetherby
York
Market Weighton
Keighley
BRADFORD
LEEDS
Selby
Beverley
Burnley
Halifax
KINGSTON UPON HULL
Huddersfield
Wakefield
Goole
Rochdale
Barnsley
Thorne
Scunthorpe
Immingham
Oldham
Doncaster
Humberside
Grimsby
MANCHESTER
Robin Hood Doncaster Sheffield
Brigg
Cleethorpes
Glossop
Rotherham
Bawtry
Rotterdam (Europoort) Zeebrugge
Stockport
SHEFFIELD
Bawtry
Market Rasen
Louth
PEAK DISTRICT
Worksop
Retford
Gainsborough
Mablethorpe
Buxton
Chesterfield
Lincoln
Bakewell
Horncastle
Macclesfield
Matlock
Alfreton
Congleton
Leek
Mansfield
Skegness
STOKE-ON-TRENT
Ashbourne
Newark-on-Trent
Sleaford
ENGLAND
Ilkeston
Boston
The Wash
Sheringham
Cromer
Stone
DERBY
NOTTINGHAM
Grantham
Hunstanton
Uttoxeter
Long Eaton
North Walsham
Stafford
East Midlands
Loughborough
Melton Mowbray
Spalding
King's Lynn
Aylsham
Rugeley
Burton upon Trent
Bourne
Fakenham
Dereham
Norwich
Lichfield
Oakham
Stamford
Wisbech
Swaffham
THE BROADS
Walsall
Tamworth
LEICESTER
Downham Market
Caister-on-Sea
BIRMINGHAM
Nuneaton
Hinckley
Wigston
March
Peterborough
Great Yarmouth
Attleborough
Lowestoft
Market Harborough
Corby
Chatteris
Bungay
Beccles
COVENTRY
Rugby
Kettering
Ely
Thetford
Diss
Southwold
Huntingdon
Bury St Edmunds
Leamington Spa
Warwick
St Neots
Northampton
Newmarket
Redditch

AA *Route planning* 5

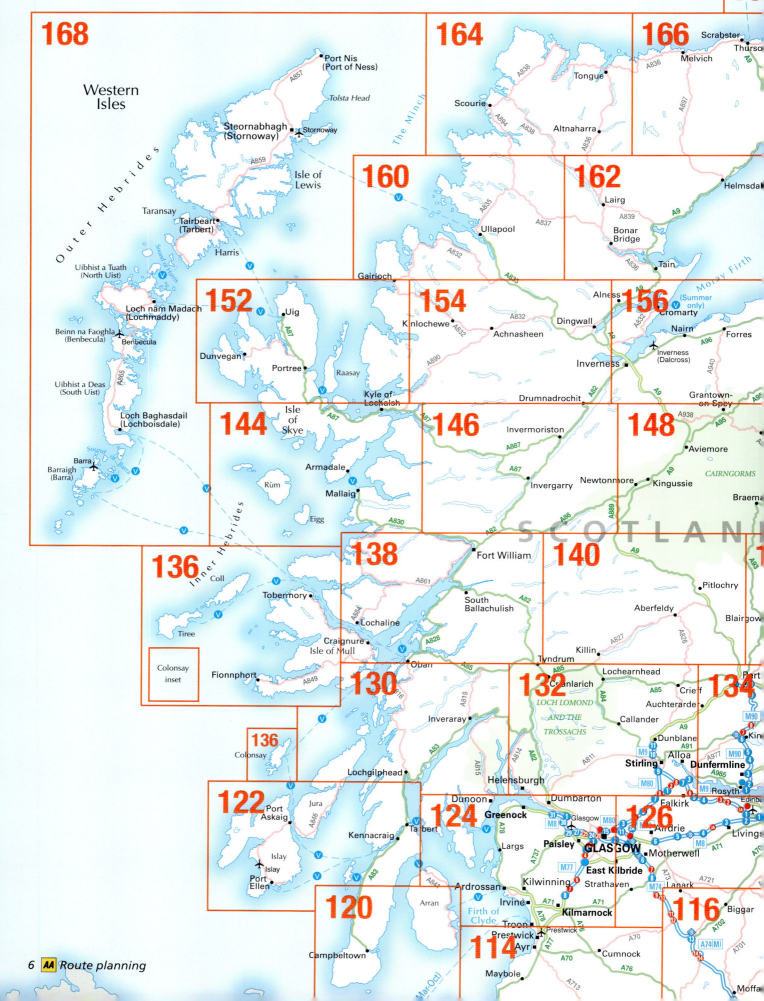

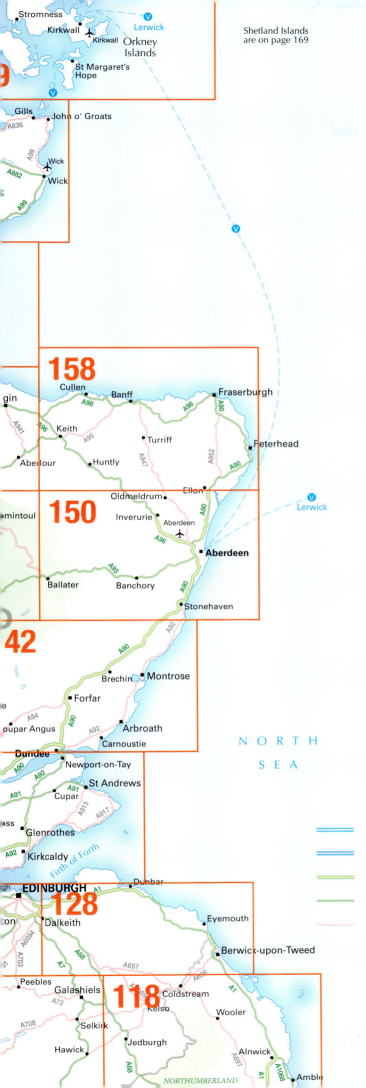

Shetland Islands
are on page 169

FERRY INFORMATION

Hebrides and west coast Scotland
calmac.co.uk · 0800 066 5000
skyeferry.co.uk · 01599 522 756
western-ferries.co.uk · 01369 704 452

Orkney and Shetland
jogferry.co.uk · 01955 611 353
northlinkferries.co.uk · 0845 6000 449
pentlandferries.co.uk · 01856 831 226
orkneyferries.co.uk · 01856 872 044
shetland.gov.uk/ferries · 01595 693 535

Isle of Man
steam-packet.com · 08722 992 992

Ireland
fastnetline.com · 0844 576 8831
irishferries.com · 08717 300 400
dfdsseaways.co.uk · 08715 229 955
poferries.com · 08716 642 020
stenaline.co.uk · 08705 70 70 70

North Sea (Scandinavia and Benelux)
dfdsseaways.co.uk · 08715 229 955
poferries.com · 08716 642 020
stenaline.co.uk · 08705 70 70 70

Isle of Wight
wightlink.co.uk · 0871 376 1000
redfunnel.co.uk · 0844 844 9988

Channel Islands
condorferries.co.uk · 0845 609 1024

Channel hopping (France and Belgium)
brittany-ferries.co.uk · 0871 244 0744
condorferries.co.uk · 0845 609 1024
eurotunnel.com · 08443 35 35 35
ldlines.co.uk · 0844 576 8836
dfdsseaways.co.uk · 08715 229 955
poferries.com · 08716 642 020
seafrance.com · 0871 423 7119
transeuropaferries.com · 01843 595 522
transmancheferries.co.uk · 0844 576 8836

Northern Spain
brittany-ferries.co.uk · 0871 244 0744
poferries.com · 08716 642 020

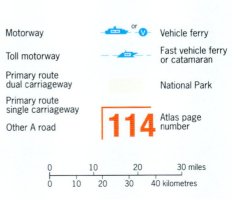

Motorway

Toll motorway

Primary route
dual carriageway

Primary route
single carriageway

Other A road

Vehicle ferry

Fast vehicle ferry
or catamaran

National Park

114 Atlas page
number

0   10   20   30 miles
0 10 20 30 40 kilometres

Traffic signs

Signs giving orders

Signs with red circles are mostly prohibitive. Plates below signs qualify their message.

Entry to 20mph zone

End of 20mph zone

Maximum speed

National speed limit applies

School crossing patrol

Stop and give way

Give way to traffic on major road

Manually operated temporary STOP and GO signs

No entry for vehicular traffic

No vehicles except bicycles being pushed

No cycling

No motor vehicles

No buses (over 8 passenger seats)

No overtaking

No towed caravans

No vehicles carrying explosives

No vehicle or combination of vehicles over length shown

No vehicles over height shown

No vehicles over width shown

Give priority to vehicles from opposite direction

No right turn

No left turn

No U-turns

No goods vehicles over maximum gross weight shown (in tonnes) except for loading and unloading

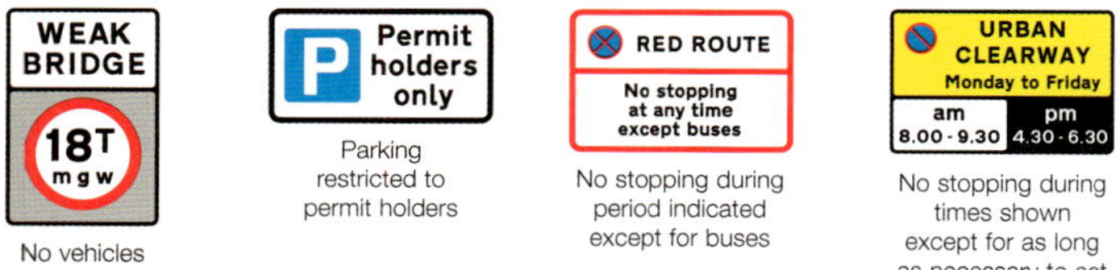

No vehicles over maximum gross weight shown (in tonnes)

Parking restricted to permit holders

No stopping during period indicated except for buses

No stopping during times shown except for as long as necessary to set down or pick up passengers

No waiting

No stopping (Clearway)

Signs with blue circles but no red border mostly give positive instruction.

Ahead only

Turn left ahead (right if symbol reversed)

Turn left (right if symbol reversed)

Keep left (right if symbol reversed)

Vehicles may pass either side to reach same destination

Mini-roundabout (roundabout circulation – give way to vehicles from the immediate right)

Route to be used by pedal cycles only

Segregated pedal cycle and pedestrian route

Minimum speed

End of minimum speed

Buses and cycles only

Trams only

Pedestrian crossing point over tramway

One-way traffic (note: compare circular 'Ahead only' sign)

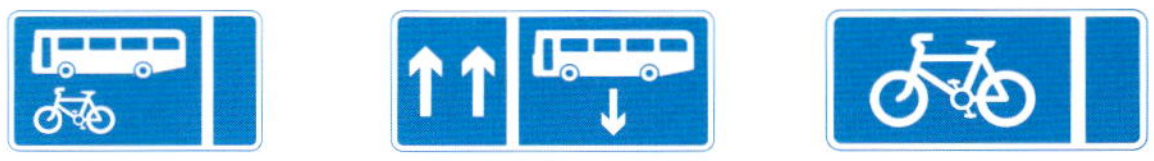

With-flow bus and cycle lane

Contraflow bus lane

With-flow pedal cycle lane

Warning signs

Mostly triangular

Distance to 'STOP' line ahead

Dual carriageway ends

Road narrows on right (left if symbol reversed)

Road narrows on both sides

Distance to 'Give Way' line ahead

Crossroads

Junction on bend ahead

T-junction with priority over vehicles from the right

Staggered junction

Traffic merging from left ahead

The priority through route is indicated by the broader line.

Double bend first to left (symbol may be reversed)

Bend to right (or left if symbol reversed)

Roundabout

Uneven road

Plate below some signs

Two-way traffic crosses one-way road

Two-way traffic straight ahead

Opening or swing bridge ahead

Low-flying aircraft or sudden aircraft noise

Falling or fallen rocks

Traffic signals not in use

Traffic signals

Slippery road

Steep hill downwards

Steep hill upwards

Gradients may be shown as a ratio i.e. 20% = 1:5

Tunnel ahead

Trams crossing ahead

Level crossing with barrier or gate ahead

Level crossing without barrier or gate ahead

Level crossing without barrier

Downward pointing arrows mean 'Get in lane'
The left-hand lane leads to a different destination from the other lanes.

Patrol

School crossing patrol ahead (some signs have amber lights which flash when crossings are in use)

Frail (or blind or disabled if shown) pedestrians likely to cross road ahead

No footway for 400 yds

Pedestrians in road ahead

Zebra crossing

Safe height 16'-6"

Overhead electric cable; plate indicates maximum height of vehicles which can pass safely

14'-6"   4.4 m

Available width of headroom indicated

The panel with the inclined arrow indicates the destinations which can be reached by leaving the motorway at the next junction

Signs on primary routes - green backgrounds

On approaches to junctions

Lampton Axtley A11   1 mile

At the junction

A 46 The SOUTH
Nottingham 17
Leicester 32
(M 1 South) 35

Route confirmatory sign after junction

TURPIN'S CROSSROADS
Biggleswick A 11
Lampton (M 11)
Dorfield A 123
Axtley B 1991
Steam railway

On approaches to junctions

Swansea Abertawe A 483

On approach to a junction in Wales (bilingual)

Blue panels indicate that the motorway starts at the junction ahead.
Motorways shown in brackets can also be reached along the route indicated.
White panels indicate local or non-primary routes leading from the junction ahead.
Brown panels show the route to tourist attractions.
The name of the junction may be shown at the top of the sign.
The aircraft symbol indicates the route to an airport.
A symbol may be included to warn of a hazard or restriction along that route.

Sharp deviation of route to left (or right if chevrons reversed)

STOP when lights show

Light signals ahead at level crossing, airfield or bridge

Red STOP
Green Clear
IF NO LIGHT - PHONE CROSSING OPERATOR

Miniature warning lights at level crossings

Port Lever Hartleby A 666
Ring road   Ring road
Maverton A 6604   Doncaster A 6604

Primary route forming part of a ring road

R

Signs on non-primary and local routes - black borders

Cattle

Wild animals

Wild horses or ponies

Accompanied horses or ponies

Cycle route ahead

Ice

Risk of ice

Queues likely

Traffic queues likely ahead

Humps for ½ mile

Distance over which road humps extend

Hidden dip

Other danger; plate indicates nature of danger

Soft verges for 2 miles

Soft verges

HANGMAN'S CROSSROADS
Axtley B 1234
(M 11) Lampton A 11   Townley A 11

On approaches to junctions

(A1(M)) 8
Barnes 10
Mackstone 2½
Elkington 1
A 404 (A 41)
Millington Green (A 4011) 3

Market Walborough B 486   7

At the junction

Side winds

Hump bridge

Ford

Worded warning sign

Quayside or river bank

Risk of grounding

Direction to toilets with access for the disabled

Green panels indicate that the primary route starts at the junction ahead.
Route numbers on a blue background show the direction to a motorway.
Route numbers on a green background show the direction to a primary route.

Direction signs

Mostly rectangular

Signs on motorways – blue backgrounds

Nottingham 23 M 1

At a junction leading directly into a motorway (junction number may be shown on a black background)

Nottingham A 52   25   ½ m

On approaches to junctions (junction number on black background)

M 1 The NORTH Sheffield 32 Leeds 59

Route confirmatory sign after junction

Channel Hopping

For business or pleasure, hopping on a ferry across to France, Belgium or the Channel Islands has never been easier.

The vehicle ferry routes shown on this map give you all the options, together with detailed port plans to help you navigate to and from the ferry terminals. Simply choose your preferred route, not forgetting the fast sailings; then check the colour-coded table for ferry operators, crossing times and contact details.

Bon voyage!

Fast ferry   Conventional ferry

E N G L I S H

ENGLISH CHANNEL FERRY CROSSINGS AND OPERATORS

To	From	Journey Time	Operator	Telephone	Website
Caen (Ouistreham)	Portsmouth	6 - 7 hrs	Brittany Ferries	0871 244 0744	brittany-ferries.co.uk
Caen (Ouistreham)	Portsmouth	3 hrs 45 mins (Mar-Oct)	Brittany Ferries	0871 244 0744	brittany-ferries.co.uk
Calais (Coquelles)	Channel Tunnel	35 mins	Eurotunnel	08443 35 35 35	eurotunnel.com
Calais	Dover	1 hr 30 mins	Sea France	0871 423 7119	seafrance.com
Calais	Dover	1 hr 30 mins	P&O Ferries	0871 664 2020	poferries.com
Cherbourg	Poole	2 hrs 15 mins (April-Oct)	Brittany Ferries	0871 244 0744	brittany-ferries.co.uk
Cherbourg	Portsmouth	3 hrs (Mar-Oct)	Brittany Ferries	0871 244 0744	brittany-ferries.co.uk
Cherbourg	Portsmouth	4 hrs 30 mins(day) 8 hrs(o/night)	Brittany Ferries	0871 244 0744	brittany-ferries.co.uk
Cherbourg	Portsmouth	5 hrs 30 mins (May-Sept)	Condor	0845 609 1024	condorferries.co.uk
Dieppe	Newhaven	4 hrs	Transmanche Ferries	0844 576 8836	transmancheferries.co.uk
Dunkerque	Dover	2 hrs	DFDS Seaways	0871 522 9955	dfdsseaways.co.uk
Guernsey	Poole	2 hrs 30 mins (April-Oct)	Condor	0845 609 1024	condorferries.co.uk
Guernsey	Portsmouth	7 hrs	Condor	0845 609 1024	condorferries.co.uk
Guernsey	Weymouth	2 hrs 10 mins	Condor	0845 609 1024	condorferries.co.uk
Jersey	Poole	3 hrs (April-Oct)	Condor	0845 609 1024	condorferries.co.uk
Jersey	Portsmouth	10 hrs 30 mins	Condor	0845 609 1024	condorferries.co.uk
Jersey	Weymouth	3 hrs 25 mins	Condor	0845 609 1024	condorferries.co.uk
Le Havre	Portsmouth	5 hrs 30 mins - 8 hrs	LD Lines	0844 576 8836	ldlines.co.uk
Le Havre	Portsmouth	3 hrs 15 mins (Mar-Sept)	LD Lines	0844 576 8836	ldlines.co.uk
Oostende	Ramsgate	4 hrs - 4 hrs 30 mins	Transeuropa	01843 595 522	transeuropaferries.com
Roscoff	Plymouth	6 - 8 hrs	Brittany Ferries	0871 244 0744	brittany-ferries.co.uk
St-Malo	Poole	4 hrs 35 mins (May-Sept)	Condor	0845 609 1024	condorferries.co.uk
St-Malo	Portsmouth	9 - 10 hrs 45 mins	Brittany Ferries	0871 244 0744	brittany-ferries.co.uk
St-Malo	Weymouth	5 hrs 15 mins	Condor	0845 609 1024	condorferries.co.uk

Portsmouth Harbour

Newhaven Harbour

Port of Dover

CHANNEL

Isle of Wight

Portsmouth

Newhaven

Folkestone

Dover

Ramsgate

Oostende

Calais

Dunkerque

Calais (Coquelles)

Dieppe

le Havre

Caen (Ouistreham)

Calais

Ferries to Ireland and the Isle of Man

With so many sea crossings to Ireland and the Isle of Man this map will help you make the right choice.

The vehicle ferry routes shown on this map give you all the options, together with detailed port plans to help you navigate to and from the ferry terminals. Simply choose your preferred route, not forgetting the fast sailings; then check the colour-coded table for ferry operators, crossing times and contact details.

 Fast ferry  Conventional ferry

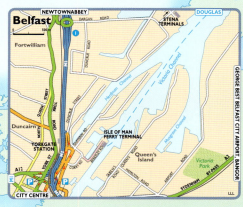

Belfast

Larne

Dún Laoghaire

Dublin Harbour

DUBLIN

Dún Laoghaire

Larne

BELFAST

Ringaskiddy

Rosslare Europort

Rosslare Harbour

Cork (Ringaskiddy)

IRISH SEA FERRY CROSSINGS AND OPERATORS

To	From	Journey Time	Operator	Telephone	Website
Belfast	Birkenhead	8 hrs	Stena Line	08705 70 70 70	stenaline.co.uk
Belfast	Douglas	2 hrs 55 mins (April-Sept)	Steam Packet Co	08722 992 992	steam-packet.com
Belfast	Stranraer *	2 hrs / 3 hrs	Stena Line	08705 70 70 70	stenaline.co.uk
Cork (Ringaskiddy)	Swansea	11 hrs	Fastnet Line	0844 576 8831	fastnetline.com
Douglas	Birkenhead	4 hrs 15 mins (Nov-Mar)	Steam Packet Co	08722 992 992	steam-packet.com
Douglas	Heysham	3 hrs 30 mins	Steam Packet Co	08722 992 992	steam-packet.com
Douglas	Liverpool	2 hrs 40 mins (Mar-Oct)	Steam Packet Co	08722 992 992	steam-packet.com
Dublin	Birkenhead	7 hrs	DFDS Seaways	0871 522 9955	dfdsseaways.co.uk
Dublin	Douglas	2 hrs 55 mins (April-Sept)	Steam Packet Co	08722 992 992	steam-packet.com
Dublin	Holyhead	1 hr 50 mins	Irish Ferries	08717 300 400	irishferries.com
Dublin	Holyhead	3 hrs 15 mins	Irish Ferries	08717 300 400	irishferries.com
Dublin	Holyhead	3 hrs 15 mins	Stena Line	08705 70 70 70	stenaline.co.uk
Dublin	Liverpool	8 hrs	P&O Ferries	08716 642 020	poferries.com
Dún Laoghaire	Holyhead	2 hrs	Stena Line	08705 70 70 70	stenaline.co.uk
Larne	Cairnryan	2 hrs	P&O Ferries	08716 642 020	poferries.com
Larne	Cairnryan	1 hr (Mar-Oct)	P&O Ferries	08716 642 020	poferries.com
Larne	Troon	2 hrs (Mar-Oct)	P&O Ferries	08716 642 020	poferries.com
Rosslare	Fishguard	2 hrs (July-Sept)	Stena Line	08705 70 70 70	stenaline.co.uk
Rosslare	Fishguard	3 hrs 30 mins	Stena Line	08705 70 70 70	stenaline.co.uk
Rosslare	Pembroke Dock	3 hrs 45 mins	Irish Ferries	08717 300 400	irishferries.com

* Sailings to new Loch Ryan Port from Autumn 2011. Phone for details.

Caravan and camping sites in Britain

These pages list the top 300 AA-inspected Caravan and Camping (C & C) sites in the Pennant rating scheme. Listings include addresses, websites and telephone numbers together with page and grid references to locate the sites in the atlas.

Available touring pitches are also included, abbreviated as follows: **C = Caravan   CV = Campervan   T = Tent**

To find out more about the AA's Pennant rating scheme and other rated caravan and camping sites visit *theAA.com*

ENGLAND

Abbey Farm Caravan Park
Dark Lane, Ormskirk,
L40 5TX
Tel: 01695 572686   **88 E9**
abbeyfarmcaravanpark.co.uk
Pitches: **C 46, CV 46, T 10**

Alders Caravan Park
Home Farm, Alne, York,
YO61 1RY
Tel: 01347 838722   **97 R7**
alderscaravanpark.co.uk
Pitches: **C 87, CV 6, T 5**

Andrewshayes Caravan Park
Dalwood, Axminster,
EX13 7DY
Tel: 01404 831225   **10 E5**
andrewshayes.co.uk
Pitches: **C 25, CV 5, T 15**

Appuldurcombe Gardens Holiday Park
Appuldurcombe Road,
Wroxall, Isle of Wight,
PO38 3EP
Tel: 01983 852597   **14 F10**
appuldurcombegardens.co.uk
Pitches: **C 70, CV 40, T 100**

Ayr Holiday Park
St Ives, Cornwall,
TR26 1EJ
Tel: 01736 795855   **2 E5**
ayrholidaypark.co.uk
Pitches: **C 40, CV 40, T 40**

Back of Beyond Touring Park
234 Ringwood Rd,
St Leonards, Dorset,
BH24 2SB
Tel: 01202 876968   **13 J4**
backofbeyondtouringpark.co.uk
Pitches: **C 80, CV 80, T 80**

Bagwell Farm Touring Park
Knights in the Bottom,
Chickerell, Weymouth,
DT3 4EA
Tel: 01305 782575   **11 N8**
bagwellfarm.co.uk
Pitches: **C 320, CV 320, T 170**

Bardsea Leisure Park
Priory Road, Ulverston,
LA12 9QE
Tel: 01229 584712   **94 F5**
bardsealeisure.co.uk
Pitches: **C 83, CV 83, T 0**

Barnstones C & C Site
Great Bourton, Banbury,
OX17 1QU
Tel: 01295 750289   **48 E6**
Pitches: **C 49, CV 49, T 49**

Beaconsfield Farm Caravan Park
Battlefield, Shrewsbury,
SY4 4AA
Tel: 01939 210370   **69 P11**
beaconsfield-farm.co.uk
Pitches: **C 60, CV 50, T 0**

Bingham Grange Touring & Camping Park
Melplash, Bridport,
DT6 3TT
Tel: 01308 488234   **11 K5**
binghamgrange.co.uk
Pitches: **C 111, CV 111, T 111**

Bo Peep Farm Caravan Park
Bo Peep Farm,
Aynho Road,
Banbury,
OX17 3NP
Tel: 01295 810605   **48 E8**
bo-peep.demon.co.uk
Pitches: **C 104, CV 104, T 40**

Broadhembury C & C Park
Steeds Lane, Kingsnorth,
Ashford,
TN26 1NQ
Tel: 01233 620859   **26 H4**
broadhembury.co.uk
Pitches: **C 60, CV 60, T 60**

Brokerswood Country Park
Brokerswood,
Westbury,
BA13 4EH
Tel: 01373 822238   **20 F4**
brokerswood.co.uk
Pitches: **C 69, CV 69, T 16**

Brompton Caravan Park
Brompton-on-Swale,
Richmond,
DL10 7EZ
Tel: 01748 824629   **103 N10**
bromptoncaravanpark.co.uk
Pitches: **C 177, CV 177, T 35**

Budemeadows Touring Park
Widemouth Bay, Bude,
EX23 0NA
Tel: 01288 361646   **16 C11**
budemeadows.com
Pitches: **C 145, CV 145, T 145**

Burrowhayes Farm C & C Site
West Luccombe, Porlock,
Minehead,
TA24 8HT
Tel: 01643 862463   **18 B5**
burrowhayes.co.uk
Pitches: **C 54, CV 54, T 66**

Cakes & Ale,
Abbey Lane, Theberton, Leiston,
IP16 4TE
Tel: 01728 831655   **65 N9**
cakesandale.net
Pitches: **C 50, CV 50, T 50**

Calloose C & C Park
Leedstown, Hayle,
TR27 5ET
Tel: 01736 850431   **2 F7**
calloose.co.uk
Pitches: **C 109, CV 20, T 80**

Carlton Meres Country Park
Rendham Road, Carlton,
Saxmundham,
IP17 2QP
Tel: 01728 603344   **65 M8**
carlton-meres.co.uk
Pitches: **C 96, CV 96, T 0**

Carlyon Bay C & C Park
Bethesda, Cypress Avenue,
Carlyon Bay,
PL25 3RE
Tel: 01726 812735   **3 R3**
carlyonbay.net
Pitches: **C 180, CV 180, T 180**

Carnevas Holiday Park & Farm Cottages
Carnevas Farm,
St Merryn,
PL28 8PN
Tel: 01841 520230   **4 D7**
carnevasholidaypark.co.uk
Pitches: **C 195, CV 195, T 195**

Carnon Downs C & C Park
Carnon Downs, Truro,
TR3 6JJ
Tel: 01872 862283   **3 L5**
carnon-downs-caravanpark.co.uk
Pitches: **C 120, CV 20, T 10**

Castlerigg Hall C & C Park
Castlerigg Hall,
Keswick,
CA12 4TE
Tel: 017687 74499   **101 J6**
castlerigg.co.uk
Pitches: **C 48, CV 48, T 120**

Channel View C & C Park
Manor Farm, Lynton,
EX35 6LD
Tel: 01598 753349   **17 N2**
channel-view.co.uk
Pitches: **C 76, CV 76, T 76**

Cheddar Bridge Touring Park
Draycott Rd, Cheddar,
BS27 3RJ
Tel: 01934 743048   **19 N4**
cheddarbridge.co.uk
Pitches: **C 45, CV 45, T 45**

Cheddar C & C Club Site
Townsend, Priddy, Wells,
BA5 3BP
Tel: 01749 870241   **19 P4**
campingandcaravanningclub.co.uk
Pitches: **C 90, CV 90, T 90**

Church Farm C & C Park
The Bungalow, Church Farm
High Street,
Sixpenny Handley,
Salisbury,
SP5 5ND
Tel: 01725 553005   **21 J11**
churchfarmcandcpark.co.uk
Pitches: **C 35, CV 35, T 35**

Claylands Caravan Park
Cabus, Garstang,
PR3 1AJ
Tel: 01524 791242   **95 K11**
claylands.com
Pitches: **C 30, CV 30, T 10**

Clippesby Hall, Hall Lane
Clippesby,
Great Yarmouth,
NR29 3BL
Tel: 01493 367800   **77 N9**
clippesby.com
Pitches: **C 70, CV 10, T 20**

Cofton Country Holidays
Starcross, Dawlish,
EX6 8RP
Tel: 01626 890111   **9 N8**
coftonholidays.co.uk
Pitches: **C 450, CV 450, T 450**

Colchester Holiday Park
Cymbeline Way, Lexden,
Colchester,
CO3 4AG
Tel: 01206 545551   **52 G6**
colchestercamping.co.uk
Pitches: **C 168, CV 168, T 168**

Constable Burton Hall Caravan Park
Constable Burton, Leyburn,
DL8 5LJ
Tel: 01677 450428   **97 J2**
Pitches: **C 40, CV 10, T 0**

Coombe Touring Park
Race Plain,
Netherhampton,
Salisbury,
SP2 8PN
Tel: 01722 328451   **21 L9**
coombecaravanpark.co.uk
Pitches: **C 50, CV 50, T 20**

Corfe Castle C & C Club Site
Bucknowle, Wareham,
BH20 5PQ
Tel: 01929 480280   **12 F8**
campingandcaravanningclub.co.uk
Pitches: **C 80, CV 80, T 80**

Cornish Farm Touring Park
Shoreditch, Taunton,
TA3 7BS
Tel: 01823 327746   **18 H10**
cornishfarm.com
Pitches: **C 50, CV 50, T 25**

Cosawes Park
Perranarworthal, Truro,
TR3 7QS
Tel: 01872 863724   **3 K6**
cosawestouringandcamping.co.uk
Pitches: **C 20, CV 20, T 30**

Cote Ghyll C & C Park
Osmotherley,
Northallerton,
DL6 3AH
Tel: 01609 883425   **104 E11**
coteghyll.com
Pitches: **C 77, CV 77, T 77**

Cotswold View Touring Park
Enstone Road,
Charlbury,
OX7 3JH
Tel: 01608 810314   **48 C10**
cotswoldview.co.uk
Pitches: **C 90, CV 90, T 35**

Dell Touring Park
Beyton Road, Thurston,
Bury St Edmunds,
IP31 3RB
Tel: 01359 270121   **64 C9**
thedellcaravanpark.co.uk
Pitches: **C 60, CV 15, T 15**

Diamond Farm C & C Park
Islip Road,
Bletchingdon,
OX5 3DR
Tel: 01869 350909   **48 F11**
diamondpark.co.uk
Pitches: **C 37, CV 37, T 25**

Dolbeare Park C & C
St Ive Road, Landrake,
Saltash,
PL12 5AF
Tel: 01752 851332   **5 P9**
dolbeare.co.uk
Pitches: **C 60, CV 60, T 30**

Dornafield
Dornafield Farm,
Two Mile Oak,
Newton Abbot,
TQ12 6DD
Tel: 01803 812732   **7 L5**
dornafield.com
Pitches: **C 135, CV 135, T 135**

East Fleet Farm Touring Park
Chickerell, Weymouth,
DT3 4DW
Tel: 01305 785768   **11 N9**
eastfleet.co.uk
Pitches: **C 400, CV 400, T 400**

Eden Valley Holiday Park
Lanlivery,
Nr Lostwithiel,
PL30 5BU
Tel: 01208 872277   **4 H10**
edenvalleyholidaypark.co.uk
Pitches: **C 56, CV 12, T 56**

Exe Valley Caravan Site
Mill House, Bridgetown,
Dulverton,
TA22 9JR
Tel: 01643 851432   **18 B8**
exevalleycamping.co.uk
Pitches: **C 41, CV 41, T 9**

Fallbarrow Park
Rayrigg Road,
Windermere,
LA23 3DL
Tel: 015394 44422   **101 M11**
slholidays.co.uk
Pitches: **C 38, CV 38, T 0**

Fernwood Caravan Park
Lyneal, Ellesmere,
SY12 0QF
Tel: 01948 710221   **69 N8**
fernwoodpark.co.uk
Pitches: **C 60, CV 60, T 0**

Fields End Water Caravan Park & Fishery
Benwick Road,
Doddington, March,
PE15 0TY
Tel: 01354 740199   **62 E2**
fieldsendfishing.co.uk
Pitches: **C 33, CV 33, T 20**

Flusco Wood Caravan Park
Flusco, Penrith,
CA11 0JB
Tel: 01768 480020   **101 N5**
fluscowood.co.uk
Pitches: **C 12, CV 12, T 0**

Forest Glade Holiday Park
Cullompton,
Kentisbeare,
EX15 2DT
Tel: 01404 841381   **10 C3**
forest-glade.co.uk
Pitches: **C 80, CV 80, T 80**

Gelderwood Country Park
Ashworth Road,
Rochdale,
OL11 5UP
Tel: 01706 364858   **89 N8**
ukparks.co.uk/gelderwood
Pitches: **C 34, CV 34, T 0**

Gill Head Farm C & C Park
Troutbeck, Penrith,
CA11 0ST
Tel: 017687 79652   **101 L5**
gillheadfarm.co.uk
Pitches: **C 25, CV 17, T 42**

Globe Vale Holiday Park
Radnor, Redruth,
TR16 4BH
Tel: 01209 891183   **3 J5**
globevale.co.uk
Pitches: **C 77, CV 19, T 58**

Golden Cap Holiday Park
Seatown, Chideock,
Bridport,
DT6 6JX
Tel: 01308 422139   **11 J6**
wdlh.co.uk
Pitches: **C 55, CV 53, T 159**

Golden Square Touring Caravan Park
Oswaldkirk, Helmsley,
YO62 5YQ
Tel: 01439 788269   **98 C5**
goldensquarecaravanpark.com
Pitches: **C 129, CV 129, T 129**

Golden Valley C & C Park
Coach Road, Ripley,
DE55 4ES
Tel: 01773 513881   **84 F10**
goldenvalleycaravanpark.co.uk
Pitches: **C 45, CV 45, T 120**

Goosewood Caravan Park
Sutton-on-the-Forest,
YO61 1ET
Tel: 01347 810829   **98 B8**
goosewood.co.uk
Pitches: **C 75, CV 75, T 0**

Greenacres Touring Park, Haywards Lane
Chelston, Wellington,
TA21 9PH
Tel: 01823 652844   **18 G10**
greenacres-wellington.co.uk
Pitches: **C 20, CV 20, T 0**

Gunvenna Caravan Park
St Minver, Wadebridge,
PL27 6QN
Tel: 01208 862405   **4 F6**
gunvenna.co.uk
Pitches: **C 75, CV 75, T 25**

Gwithian Farm Campsite
Gwithian Farm,
Gwithian, Hayle,
TR27 5BX
Tel: 01736 753127   **2 F5**
gwithianfarm.co.uk
Pitches: **C 40, CV 40, T 47**

Harbury Fields
Harbury Fields Farm, Harbury,
Nr Leamington Spa,
CV33 9JN
Tel: 01926 612457   **48 C2**
harburyfields.co.uk
Pitches: **C 30, CV 30, T 0**

Hawthorn Farm Caravan Park
Station Road, Martin Mill,
Dover,
CT15 5LA
Tel: 01304 852658   **27 P2**
keatfarm.co.uk
Pitches: **C 147, CV 147, T 100**

Heathfield Farm Camping
Heathfield Road,
Freshwater,
PO40 9SH
Tel: 01983 407822   **13 P7**
heathfieldcamping.co.uk
Pitches: **C 60, CV 60, T 60**

Heathland Beach Caravan Park
London Road, Kessingland,
NR33 7PJ
Tel: 01502 740337   **65 Q4**
heathlandbeach.co.uk
Pitches: **C 63, CV 63, T 63**

Hele Valley Holiday Park
Hele Bay, Ilfracombe,
North Devon,
EX34 9RD
Tel: 01271 862460   **17 J2**
helevalley.co.uk
Pitches: **C 4, CV 8, T 38**

Heyford Leys Camping Park
Camp Road, Upper Heyford,
Bicester,
OX25 5LX
Tel: 01869 232048   **48 F9**
heyfordleyspark.co.uk
Pitches: **C 16, CV 16, T 25**

Hidden Valley Park
West Down,
Ilfracombe,
EX34 8NU
Tel: 01271 813837   **17 J3**
hiddenvalleypark.com
Pitches: **C 115, CV 65, T 55**

Higher Chellew Holiday Park
Higher Trenowin, Nancledra,
Penzance,
TR20 8BD
Tel: 01736 364532   **2 D6**
higherchellewcamping.co.uk
Pitches: **C 5, CV 5, T 25**

Highfield Farm Touring Park
Long Road, Comberton,
Cambridge,
CB23 7DG
Tel: 01223 262308   **62 E9**
highfieldfarmtouring.co.uk
Pitches: **C 60, CV 60, T 60**

Highlands End Holiday Park
Eype, Bridport, Dorset,
DT6 6AR
Tel: 01308 422139 **11 K6**
wdlh.co.uk
Pitches: **C 60, CV 60, T 75**

High Moor Farm Park
Skipton Road, Harrogate,
HG3 2LT
Tel: 01423 563637 **97 K9**
highmoorfarmpark.co.uk
Pitches: **C 145, CV 15, T 0**

Hill Cottage Farm C & C Park
Sandleheath Road, Alderholt,
Fordingbridge,
SP6 3EG
Tel: 01425 650513 **13 K2**
hillcottagefarmcampingandcara
vanpark.co.uk
Pitches: **C 35, CV 35, T 60**

Hill Farm Caravan Park
Branches Lane,
Sherfield English, Romsey,
SO51 6FH
Tel: 01794 340402 **21 Q10**
hillfarmpark.com
Pitches: **C 70, CV 30, T 50**

Hillside Caravan Park
Canvas Farm,
Moor Road, Thirsk,
YO7 4BR
Tel: 01845 537349 **97 P3**
hillsidecaravanpark.co.uk
Pitches: **C 35, CV 35, T 0**

Hollins Farm C & C
Far Arnside, Carnforth,
LA5 0SL
Tel: 01524 701508 **95 J5**
holgates.co.uk
Pitches: **C 11, CV 11, T 65**

Homing Park
Church Lane, Seasalter,
Whitstable,
CT5 4BU
Tel: 01227 771777 **39 J9**
homingpark.co.uk
Pitches: **C 43, CV 43, T 43**

Honeybridge Park
Honeybridge Lane,
Dial Post, Horsham,
RH13 8NX
Tel: 01403 710923 **24 E7**
honeybridgepark.co.uk
Pitches: **C 112, CV 112, T 90**

Hurley Riverside Park
Park Office, Hurley,
Nr Maidenhead,
SL6 5NE
Tel: 01628 824493 **35 M8**
hurleyriversidepark.co.uk
Pitches: **C 138, CV 138, T 62**

Hutton-le-Hole Caravan Park
Westfield Lodge,
Hutton-le-Hole,
YO62 6UG
Tel: 01751 417261 **98 E3**
westfieldlodge.co.uk
Pitches: **C 38, CV 38, T 4**

Hylton Caravan Park
Eden Street, Silloth,
CA7 4AY
Tel: 016973 31707 **109 P10**
stanwix.com
Pitches: **C 90, CV 90, T 90**

Island Meadow Caravan Park
The Mill House,
Aston Cantlow,
B95 6JP
Tel: 01789 488273 **47 M3**
islandmeadowcaravanpark.co.uk
Pitches: **C 24, CV 24, T 10**

**Isle of Avalon Touring
Caravan Park**
Godney Road,
Glastonbury,
BA6 9AF
Tel: 01458 833618 **19 N7**
Pitches: **C 70, CV 70, T 50**

Jacobs Mount Caravan Park
Jacobs Mount,
Stepney Road,
Scarborough,
YO12 5NL
Tel: 01723 361178 **99 L3**
jacobsmount.com
Pitches: **C 144, CV 156, T 16**

Jasmine Caravan Park
Cross Lane, Snainton,
Scarborough,
YO13 9BE
Tel: 01723 859240 **99 J4**
jasminepark.co.uk
Pitches: **C 94, CV 94, T 20**

Juliot's Well Holiday Park
Camelford,
PL32 9RF
Tel: 01840 213302 **4 H5**
juliotswell.com
Pitches: **C 39, CV 39, T 39**

**Kennford International
Caravan Park**
Kennford, Exeter,
EX6 7YN
Tel: 01392 833046 **9 M7**
kennfordinternational.co.uk
Pitches: **C 96, CV 96, T 96**

Kloofs Caravan Park
Sandhurst Lane,
Bexhill,
TN39 4RG
Tel: 01424 842839 **26 B10**
kloofs.com
Pitches: **C 50, CV 50, T 50**

Kneps Farm Holiday Park
River Road, Stanah,
Thornton-Cleveleys,
Blackpool,
FY5 5LR
Tel: 01253 823632 **88 D2**
knepsfarm.co.uk
Pitches: **C 40, CV 5, T 15**

**Knight Stainforth Hall
Caravan & Campsite**
Stainforth, Settle,
BD24 0DP
Tel: 01729 822200 **96 B7**
knightstainforth.co.uk
Pitches: **C 50, CV 50, T 50**

**Ladycross Plantation Caravan
Park**
Egton, Whitby,
YO21 1UA
Tel: 01947 895502 **105 M9**
ladycrossplantation.co.uk
Pitches: **C 120, CV 10, T 0**

Lamb Cottage Caravan Park
Dalefords Lane, Whitegate,
Northwich,
CW8 2BN
Tel: 01606 882302 **82 D11**
lambcottage.co.uk
Pitches: **C 45, CV 28, T 0**

Larches Caravan Park
Mealsgate, Wigton,
CA7 1LQ
Tel: 016973 71379 **100 H2**
larchescaravanpark.co.uk
Pitches: **C 73, CV 73, T 73**

Lebberston Touring Park
Filey Road, Lebberston,
Scarborough,
YO11 3PE
Tel: 01723 585723 **99 M4**
lebberstontouring.co.uk
Pitches: **C 125, CV 50, T 0**

Lemonford Caravan Park
Bickington (near Ashburton),
Newton Abbot,
TQ12 6JR
Tel: 01626 821242 **7 K4**
lemonford.co.uk
Pitches: **C 82, CV 82, T 35**

Lickpenny Caravan Site
Lickpenny Lane,
Tansley, Matlock,
DE4 5GF
Tel: 01629 583040 **84 D9**
lickpennycaravanpark.co.uk
Pitches: **C 80, CV 80, T 0**

Lime Tree Park
Dukes Drive,
Buxton,
SK17 9RP
Tel: 01298 22988 **83 N10**
limetreeparkbuxton.co.uk
Pitches: **C 71, CV 22, T 35**

Lincoln Farm Park Oxfordshire
High Street, Standlake,
OX29 7RH
Tel: 01865 300239 **34 C4**
lincolnfarmpark.co.uk
Pitches: **C 75, CV 36, T 16**

Little Cotton Caravan Park
Little Cotton,
Dartmouth,
TQ6 0LB
Tel: 01803 832558 **7 M8**
littlecotton.co.uk
Pitches: **C 95, CV 15, T 20**

Little Lakeland Caravan Park
Wortwell,
Harleston,
IP20 0EL
Tel: 01986 788646 **65 K4**
littlelakeland.co.uk
Pitches: **C 38, CV 38, T 32**

Little Trevarrack Holiday Park
Laity Lane, Carbis Bay, St Ives,
TR26 3HW
Tel: 01736 797580 **2 E6**
littletrevarrack.co.uk
Pitches: **C 200, CV 200, T 200**

Lizard Lane C & C Site
Lizard Lane, South Shields,
NE34 7AB
Tel: 0191 454 4982 **113 N8**
Pitches: **C 45, CV 45, T 45**

Long Acre Caravan Park
Station Road, Old Leake, Boston,
PE22 9RF
Tel: 01205 871555 **87 L10**
longacres-caravanpark.co.uk
Pitches: **C 40, CV 40, T 15**

Lowther Holiday Park
Eamont Bridge, Penrith,
CA10 2JB
Tel: 01768 863631 **101 P5**
lowther-holidaypark.co.uk
Pitches: **C 144, CV 50, T 36**

Lytton Lawn Touring Park
Lymore Lane, Milford on Sea,
SO41 0TX
Tel: 01590 648331 **13 N6**
shorefield.co.uk
Pitches: **C 136, CV 136, T 83**

Manor Farm C & C Site
East Runton, Cromer,
NR27 9PR
Tel: 01263 512858 **76 H3**
manorfarmcaravansite.co.uk
Pitches: **C 100, CV 50, T 100**

**Manor Wood Country
Caravan Park**
Manor Wood,
Coddington, Chester,
CH3 9EN
Tel: 01829 782990 **69 N3**
cheshire-caravan-sites.co.uk
Pitches: **C 45, CV 45, T 45**

Maustin Caravan Park
Kearby with Netherby, Netherby,
LS22 4DA
Tel: 0113 288 6234 **97 M11**
maustin.co.uk
Pitches: **C 25, CV 25, T 25**

Mayfield Touring Park
Cheltenham Road,
Cirencester,
GL7 7BH
Tel: 01285 831301 **33 K3**
mayfieldpark.co.uk
Pitches: **C 36, CV 36, T 36**

Meadowbank Holidays
Stour Way, Christchurch,
BH23 2PQ
Tel: 01202 483597 **13 K6**
meadowbank-holidays.co.uk
Pitches: **C 41, CV 41, T 0**

Merley Court
Merley, Wimborne Minster,
BH21 3AA
Tel: 01590 648331 **12 H5**
shorefield.co.uk
Pitches: **C 160, CV 160, T 80**

**Middlewood Farm Holiday
Park**
Middlewood Lane, Fylingthorpe,
Robin Hood's Bay, Whitby,
YO22 4UF
Tel: 01947 880414 **105 P10**
middlewoodfarm.com
Pitches: **C 20, CV 20, T 80**

Minnows Touring Park
Holbrook Lane,
Sampford Peverell,
EX16 7EN
Tel: 01884 821770 **18 D11**
ukparks.co.uk/minnows
Pitches: **C 45, CV 45, T 5**

Moon & Sixpence
Newbourn Road, Waldringfield,
Woodbridge,
IP12 4PP
Tel: 01473 736650 **53 N2**
moonandsixpence.eu
Pitches: **C 65, CV 65, T 65**

Mosswood Caravan Park
Crimbles Lane, Cockerham,
LA2 0ES
Tel: 01524 791041 **95 K11**
mosswood.co.uk
Pitches: **C 25, CV 25, T 25**

Naburn Lock Caravan Park
Naburn,
YO19 4RU
Tel: 01904 728697 **98 C11**
naburnlock.co.uk
Pitches: **C 86, CV 86, T 14**

Newberry Valley Park
Woodlands, Combe Martin,
EX34 0AT
Tel: 01271 882334 **17 K2**
newberryvalleypark.co.uk
Pitches: **C 25, CV 25, T 95**

New House Caravan Park
Kirkby Lonsdale,
LA6 2HR
Tel: 01524 271590 **95 N5**
Pitches: **C 50, CV 50, T 0**

Newlands C & C Park
Charmouth, Bridport,
DT6 6RB
Tel: 01297 560259 **10 H6**
newlanasholidays.co.uk
Pitches: **C 140, CV 140, T 100**

Newperran Holiday Park
Rejerrah, Newquay,
TR8 5QJ
Tel: 01872 572407 **3 K3**
newperran.co.uk
Pitches: **C 357, CV 357, T 357**

Newton Mill Holiday Park
Newton Road, Bath,
BA2 9JF
Tel: 01225 333909 **20 D2**
newtonmillpark.co.uk
Pitches: **C 85, CV 66, T 116**

**Northam Farm Caravan &
Touring Park**
Brean, Burnham on Sea,
TA8 2SE
Tel: 01278 751244 **19 K3**
northamfarm.co.uk
Pitches: **C 350, CV 350, T 350**

Oakdown Holiday Park
Gatedown Lane, Sidmouth,
EX10 0PT
Tel: 01297 680387 **10 D6**
oakdown.co.uk
Pitches: **C 150, CV 150, T 150**

**Oathill Farm Touring and
Camping Site**
Oathill, Crewkerne,
TA18 8PZ
Tel: 01460 30234 **11 J3**
oathillfarmleisure.co.uk
Pitches: **C 13, CV 10, T 8**

Old Barn Touring Park
Cheverton Farm, Newport Road,
Sandown, PO36 9PJ
Tel: 01983 866414 **14 G10**
oldbarntouring.co.uk
Pitches: **C 60, CV 60, T 60**

Orchard Farm Holiday Village
Stonegate, Hunmanby,
YO14 0PU
Tel: 01723 891582 **99 N5**
orchardfarmholidayvillage.co.uk
Pitches: **C 85, CV 60, T 25**

Orchard Park
Frampton Lane,
Hubbert's Bridge, Boston,
PE20 3QU
Tel: 01205 290328 **74 E2**
orchardpark.co.uk
Pitches: **C 87, CV 87, T 87**

**Orchards Holiday Caravan
Park**
Main Road, Newbridge,
Yarmouth,
PO41 0TS
Tel: 01983 531331 **14 D9**
orchards-holiday-park.co.uk
Pitches: **C 171, CV 171, T 171**

Ord House Country Park
East Ord,
Berwick-upon-Tweed,
TD15 2NS
Tel: 01289 305288 **129 P9**
ordhouse.co.uk
Pitches: **C 70, CV 35, T 9**

Otterington Park
Station Farm, South Otterington,
Northallerton,
DL7 9JB
Tel: 01609 780656 **97 N3**
otteringtonpark.com
Pitches: **C 40, CV 40, T 0**

Oxon Hall Touring Park
Welshpool Road, Shrewsbury,
SY3 5FB
Tel: 01743 340868 **56 H2**
morris-leisure.co.uk
Pitches: **C 124, CV 124, T 124**

Padstow Touring Park
Padstow,
PL28 8LE
Tel: 01841 532061 **4 E7**
padstowtouringpark.co.uk
Pitches: **C 100, CV 100, T 100**

**Park Cliffe Camping &
Caravan Estate**
Birks Road, Tower Wood,
Windermere,
LA23 3PG
Tel: 01539 531344 **94 H2**
parkcliffe.co.uk
Pitches: **C 60, CV 60, T 100**

Parkers Farm Holiday Park
Higher Mead Farm,
Ashburton, Devon,
TQ13 7LJ
Tel: 01364 654869 **7 K4**
parkersfarm.co.uk
Pitches: **C 100, CV 100, T 100**

Pear Tree Holiday Park
Organford Road, Holton Heath,
Organford, Poole,
BH16 6LA
Tel: 01202 622434 **12 F6**
peartreepark.co.uk
Pitches: **C 145, CV 145, T 72**

Penrose Farm Touring Park
Goonhavern,
Truro,
TR4 9QF
Tel: 01872 573185 **3 K3**
penrosefarmtouringpark.com
Pitches: **C 100, CV 100, T 100**

Pilgrims Way C & C Park
Church Green Road,
Fishtoft, Boston,
PE21 0QY
Tel: 01205 366646 **74 G2**
pilgrimsway-caravanandcamp
ing.com
Pitches: **C 17, CV 13, T 22**

Polmanter Tourist Park
Halsetown, St Ives,
TR26 3LX
Tel: 01736 795640 **2 E6**
polmanter.com
Pitches: **C 240, CV 240, T 240**

Porlock Caravan Park
Porlock, Minehead,
TA24 8ND
Tel: 01643 862269 **18 A5**
porlockcaravanpark.co.uk
Pitches: **C 40, CV 40, T 40**

**Portesham Dairy Farm
Campsite**
Portesham, Weymouth,
DT3 4HG
Tel: 01305 871297 **11 N7**
porteshamdairyfarm.co.uk
Pitches: **C 90, CV 90, T 31**

Porth Beach Tourist Park
Porth, Newquay,
TR7 3NH
Tel: 01637 876531 **4 C9**
porthbeach.co.uk
Pitches: **C 200, CV 200, T 200**

Porthtowan Tourist Park
Mile Hill, Porthtowan, Truro,
TR4 8TY
Tel: 01209 890256 **2 H4**
porthtowantouristpark.co.uk
Pitches: **C 80, CV 80, T 80**

**Quantock Orchard Caravan
Park**
Flaxpool, Crowcombe, Taunton,
TA4 4AW
Tel: 01984 618618 **18 F7**
quantock-orchard.co.uk
Pitches: **C 31, CV 19, T 19**

Quarry Walk Park
Coppice Lane, Croxden
Common, Freehay, Cheadle,
ST10 1RQ
Tel: 01538 723412 **71 J6**
quarrywalkpark.co.uk
Pitches: **C 40, CV 40, T 40**

Quiet Waters Caravan Park
Hemingford Abbots,
Huntingdon,
PE28 9AJ
Tel: 01480 463405 **62 C6**
quietwaterscaravanpark.co.uk
Pitches: **C 20, CV 20, T 20**

Ranch Caravan Park
Station Road, Honeybourne,
Evesham,
WR11 7PR
Tel: 01386 830744 **47 M6**
ranch.co.uk
Pitches: **C 120, CV 120, T 0**

Ripley Caravan Park
Knaresborough Road, Ripley,
Harrogate,
HG3 3AU
Tel: 01423 770050 **97 L8**
ripleycaravanpark.com
Pitches: **C 75, CV 75, T 25**

River Dart Country Park
Holne Park, Ashburton,
TQ13 7NP
Tel: 01364 652511 **7 J5**
riverdart.co.uk
Pitches: **C 50, CV 67, T 67**

Riverside C & C Park
Marsh Lane, North Molton Road,
South Molton,
EX36 3HQ
Tel: 01769 579269 **17 N6**
exmoorriverside.co.uk
Pitches: **C 42, CV 42, T 42**

Riverside Caravan Park
High Bentham, Lancaster,
LA2 7FJ
Tel: 015242 61272 **6 E7**
riversidecaravanpark.co.uk
Pitches: **C 61, CV 61, T 0**

Riverside Caravan Park
Longbridge Road, Plymouth,
PL6 8LL
Tel: 01752 344122 **95 P7**
riversidecaravanpark.com
Pitches: **C 236, CV 236, T 60**

Riverside Holidays
21 Compass Point,
Ensign Way, Hamble,
SO31 4RA
Tel: 02380 453220 **14 E5**
riversideholidays.co.uk
Pitches: **C 77, CV 77, T 77**

Riverside Meadows Country Caravan Park
Ure Bank Top, Ripon,
HG4 1JD
Tel: 01765 602964 **97 M6**
flowerofmay.com
Pitches: **C 80, CV 5, T 10**

River Valley Holiday Park
London Apprentice, St Austell,
PL26 7AP
Tel: 01726 73533 **3 Q3**
cornwall-holidays.co.uk
Pitches: **C 45, CV 45, T 45**

Robin Hood C & C Park
Green Dyke Lane, Slingsby,
YO62 4AP
Tel: 01653 628391 **98 D6**
robinhoodcaravanpark.co.uk
Pitches: **C 32, CV 32, T 32**

Rosedale C & C Park
Rosedale Abbey, Pickering,
YO18 8SA
Tel: 01751 417272 **105 K11**
flowerofmay.com
Pitches: **C 30, CV 30, T 70**

Rose Farm Touring & Camping Park
Stepshort, Belton,
Nr Great Yarmouth,
NR31 9JS
Tel: 01493 780896 **77 P11**
rosefarmtouringpark.co.uk
Pitches: **C 80, CV 80, T 40**

Ross Park, Park Hill Farm
Ipplepen, Newton Abbot,
TQ12 5TT
Tel: 01803 812983 **7 L5**
rossparkcaravanpark.co.uk
Pitches: **C 110, CV 82, T 110**

Rudding Holiday Park
Follifoot, Harrogate,
HG3 1JH
Tel: 01423 870439 **97 M10**
ruddingpark.co.uk
Pitches: **C 141, CV 141, T 141**

Rutland C & C
Park Lane, Greetham, Oakham,
LE15 7FN
Tel: 01572 813520 **73 N8**
rutlandcaravanandcamping.co.uk
Pitches: **C 65, CV 65, T 70**

St Helens Caravan Park
Wykeham, Scarborough,
YO13 9QD
Tel: 01723 862771 **99 K4**
sthelenscaravanpark.co.uk
Pitches: **C 210, CV 210, T 40**

Scalby Close Park
Burniston Road, Scarborough,
YO13 0DA
Tel: 01723 365908 **99 L2**
scalbyclosepark.co.uk
Pitches: **C 42, CV 5, T 0**

Seaview International Holiday Park
Boswinger, Mevagissey,
PL26 6LL
Tel: 01726 843425 **3 P5**
seaviewinternational.com
Pitches: **C 189, CV 189, T 189**

Severn Gorge Park
Bridgnorth Road,
Tweedale, Telford,
TF7 4JB
Tel: 01952 684789 **57 N3**
severngorgepark.co.uk
Pitches: **C 10, CV 10, T 0**

Shamba Holidays
230 Ringwood Road,
St Leonards, Ringwood,
BH24 2SB
Tel: 01202 873302 **13 K4**
shambaholidays.co.uk
Pitches: **C 150, CV 150, T 150**

Shrubbery Touring Park
Rousdon,
Lyme Regis,
DT7 3XW
Tel: 01297 442227 **10 F6**
shrubberypark.co.uk
Pitches: **C 90, CV 10, T 20**

Silverbow Park
Perranwell,
Goonhavern,
TR4 9NX
Tel: 01872 572347 **3 K3**
chycor.co.uk/parks/silverbow
Pitches: **C 100, CV 100, T 100**

Silverdale Caravan Park
Middlebarrow Plain,
Cove Road, Silverdale,
Nr Carnforth,
LA5 0SH
Tel: 01524 701508 **95 K5**
holgates.co.uk
Pitches: **C 80, CV 80, T 6**

Skelwith Fold Caravan Park
Ambleside, Cumbria,
LA22 0HX
Tel: 015394 32277 **101 L10**
skelwith.com
Pitches: **C 75, CV 75, T 0**

Sleningford Watermill C & C Park
North Stainley, Ripon,
HG4 3HQ
Tel: 01765 635201 **97 L5**
sleningfordwatermill.co.uk
Pitches: **C 30, CV 10, T 45**

Somers Wood Caravan Park
Somers Road, Meriden,
CV7 7PL
Tel: 01676 522978 **59 K8**
somerswood.co.uk
Pitches: **C 48, CV 48, T 0**

Southfork Caravan Park
Parrett Works,
Martock,
TA12 6AE
Tel: 01935 825661 **19 M11**
southforkcaravans.co.uk
Pitches: **C 27, CV 27, T 5**

South Lytchett Manor
Dorchester Road,
Lytchett Minster, Poole,
BH16 6JB
Tel: 01202 622577 **12 G6**
southlytchettmanor.co.uk
Pitches: **C 120, CV 120, T 30**

Springfield Holiday Park
Tedburn St Mary,
Exeter,
EX6 6EW
Tel: 01647 24242 **9 K6**
springfieldholidaypark.co.uk
Pitches: **C 11, CV 3, T 11**

Stanmore Hall Touring Park
Stourbridge Road,
Bridgnorth,
WV15 6DT
Tel: 01746 761761 **57 N6**
morris-leisure.co.uk
Pitches: **C 131, CV 53, T 10**

Stowford Farm Meadows
Berry Down,
Combe Martin,
EX34 0PW
Tel: 01271 882476 **17 K3**
stowford.co.uk
Pitches: **C 600, CV 50, T 50**

Strawberry Hill Farm C & C Park
Old Cassop, Durham,
DH6 4QA
Tel: 0191 372 3457 **104 B2**
strawberry-hill-farm.co.uk
Pitches: **C 35, CV 35, T 10**

Stroud Hill Park
Fen Road, Pidley,
PE28 3DE
Tel: 01487 741333 **62 D5**
stroudhillpark.co.uk
Pitches: **C 60, CV 60, T 6**

Sun Haven Valley Holiday Park
Mawgan Porth, Newquay,
TR8 4BQ
Tel: 01637 860373 **4 D8**
sunhavenvalley.com
Pitches: **C 38, CV 38, T 61**

Sun Valley Holiday Park
Pentewan Road, St Austell,
PL26 6DJ
Tel: 01726 843266 **3 Q4**
sunvalleyholidays.co.uk
Pitches: **C 28, CV 28, T 29**

Swiss Farm Touring & Camping
Marlow Road,
Henley-on-Thames,
RG9 2HY
Tel: 01491 573419 **35 L8**
swissfarmcamping.co.uk
Pitches: **C 140, CV 140, T 100**

Tall Trees Park Homes
Old Mill Lane, Forest Town,
Mansfield,
NG19 0JP
Tel: 01623 626503 **85 J8**
jamesparkhomes.com
Pitches: **C 15, CV 15, T 15**

Tanner Farm Touring C & C Park
Tanner Farm,
Goudhurst Road,
Marden,
TN12 9ND
Tel: 01622 832399 **26 B3**
tannerfarmpark.co.uk
Pitches: **C 100, CV 100, T 100**

Tattershall Lakes Country Park
Sleaford Road, Tattershall,
LN4 4RL
Tel: 01526 348800 **86 H9**
tattershall-lakes.co.uk
Pitches: **C 186, CV 186, T 146**

The Grange Touring Park
Yarmouth Road,
Ormesby St Margaret,
Great Yarmouth,
NR29 3QG
Tel: 01493 730306 **77 Q9**
grangetouring.co.uk
Pitches: **C 70, CV 70, T 70**

The Inside Park
Down House Estate,
Blandford Forum,
DT11 9AD
Tel: 01258 453719 **12 E4**
theinsidepark.co.uk
Pitches: **C 125, CV 125, T 125**

The Old Brick Kilns
Little Barney Lane, Barney,
Fakenham,
NR21 0NL
Tel: 01328 878305 **76 E5**
old-brick-kilns.co.uk
Pitches: **C 65, CV 65, T 60**

The Old Oaks Touring Park
Wick Farm, Wick,
Glastonbury,
BA6 8JS
Tel: 01458 831437 **19 P7**
theoldoaks.co.uk
Pitches: **C 60, CV 20, T 20**

The Quiet Site
Ullswater, Watermillock,
CA11 0LS
Tel: 07768 727016 **101 M6**
thequietsite.co.uk
Pitches: **C 100, CV 100, T 100**

The Star C & C Park
Star Road, Cotton, Oakamoor,
Near Alton Towers,
ST10 3DW
Tel: 01538 702219 **71 K5**
starcaravanpark.co.uk
Pitches: **C 30, CV 30, T 60**

Tollgate Farm C & C Park
Budnick Hill, Perranporth,
TR6 0AD
Tel: 01872 572130 **3 K3**
tollgatefarm.co.uk
Pitches: **C 102, CV 102, T 102**

Townsend Touring Park
Townsend Farm,
Pembridge, Leominster,
HR6 9HB
Tel: 01544 388527 **45 M3**
townsendfarm.co.uk
Pitches: **C 60, CV 60, T 60**

Tregoad Park
St Martin, Looe,
PL13 1PB
Tel: 01503 262718 **5 M10**
tregoadpark.co.uk
Pitches: **C 150, CV 150, T 50**

Trencreek Holiday Park
Hillcrest, Higher Trencreek,
Newquay,
TR8 4NS
Tel: 01637 874210 **4 C9**
trencreekholidaypark.co.uk
Pitches: **C 194, CV 194, T 194**

Trethem Mill Touring Park
St Just-in-Roseland,
Nr St Mawes,
TR2 5JF
Tel: 01872 580504 **3 M6**
trethem.com
Pitches: **C 84, CV 84, T 35**

Trevalgan Touring Park
Trevalgan, St Ives,
TR26 3BJ
Tel: 01736 792048 **2 D5**
trevalgantouringpark.co.uk
Pitches: **C 40, CV 40, T 40**

Trevella Tourist Park
Crantock, Newquay,
TR8 5EW
Tel: 01637 830308 **4 C10**
trevella.co.uk
Pitches: **C 313, CV 313, T 313**

Truro C & C Park
Truro,
TR4 8QN
Tel: 01872 560274 **3 K4**
liskey.co.uk
Pitches: **C 51, CV 51, T 28**

Tudor C & C
Shepherds Patch,
Slimbridge, Gloucester,
GL2 7BP
Tel: 01453 890483 **32 D4**
tudorcaravanpark.com
Pitches: **C 75, CV 75, T 30**

Twin Willows
The Beeches, Penton, Carlisle,
CA6 5QD
Tel: 01228 577313 **110 H5**
twomills.co.uk
Pitches: **C 10, CV 10, T 10**

Two Mills Touring Park
Yarmouth Road, North Walsham,
NR28 9NA
Tel: 01692 405829 **77 K6**
twomills.co.uk
Pitches: **C 81, CV 81, T 70**

Ulwell Cottage Caravan Park
Ulwell Cottage,
Ulwell, Swanage,
BH19 3DG
Tel: 01929 422823 **12 H8**
ulwellcottagepark.co.uk
Pitches: **C 77, CV 77, T 77**

Vale of Pickering Caravan Park
Carr House Farm, Allerston,
Pickering,
YO18 7PQ
Tel: 01723 859280 **98 H4**
valeofpickering.co.uk
Pitches: **C 120, CV 120, T 120**

Virginia Lake Caravan Park
Smeeth Road,
St John's Fen End,
Wisbech,
PE14 8JF
Tel: 01945 430332 **75 K8**
virginialake.co.uk
Pitches: **C 50, CV 50, T 50**

Warcombe Farm C & C Park
Station Road, Mortehoe,
EX34 7EJ
Tel: 01271 870690 **16 H2**
warcombefarm.co.uk
Pitches: **C 250, CV 250, T 250**

Wareham Forest Tourist Park
North Trigon, Wareham,
BH20 7NZ
Tel: 01929 551393 **12 E6**
warehamforest.co.uk
Pitches: **C 200, CV 200, T 200**

Waren Caravan Park
Waren Mill, Bamburgh,
NE70 7EE
Tel: 01668 214366 **119 M4**
meadowhead.co.uk
Pitches: **C 120, CV 120, T 60**

Watergate Bay Touring Park
Watergate Bay, Tregurrian,
TR8 4AD
Tel: 01637 860387 **4 C9**
watergatebaytouringpark.co.uk
Pitches: **C 171, CV 171, T 171**

Waterrow Touring Park
Wiveliscombe, Taunton,
TA4 2AZ
Tel: 01984 623464 **18 E9**
waterrowpark.co.uk
Pitches: **C 38, CV 38, T 7**

Wayfarers C & C Park
Relubbus Lane,
St Hilary, Penzance,
TR20 9EF
Tel: 01736 763326 **2 F7**
wayfarerspark.co.uk
Pitches: **C 45, CV 5, T 15**

Wells Holiday Park
Haybridge, Wells,
BA5 1AJ
Tel: 01749 676869 **19 P5**
wellsholidaypark.co.uk
Pitches: **C 72, CV 54, T 30**

West End Farm
Salterns Way,
Great Carlton, Louth,
LN11 8BF
Tel: 01507 450949 **87 M4**
westendfarm.co.uk
Pitches: **C 15, CV 15, T 20**

Westwood Caravan Park
Old Felixstowe Road,
Bucklesham, Ipswich,
IP10 0BN
Tel: 01473 659637 **53 N3**
westwoodcaravanpark.co.uk
Pitches: **C 100, CV 100, T 100**

Whitefield Forest Touring Park
Brading Road, Ryde,
Isle of Wight,
PO33 1QL
Tel: 01983 617069 **14 H9**
whitefieldforest.co.uk
Pitches: **C 80, CV 80, T 80**

Whitemead Caravan Park
East Burton Road, Wool,
BH20 6HG
Tel: 01929 462241 **12 D7**
whitemeadcaravanpark.co.uk
Pitches: **C 95, CV 95, T 95**

Whitsand Bay Lodge & Touring Park
Millbrook, Torpoint,
PL10 1JZ
Tel: 01752 822597 **5 Q11**
whitsandbayholidays.co.uk
Pitches: **C 49, CV 49, T 0**

Widdicombe Farm Touring Park
Marldon, Paignton,
TQ3 1ST
Tel: 01803 558325 **7 M6**
widdicombefarm.co.uk
Pitches: **C 180, CV 180, T 20**

Widemouth Fields C & C Park
Park Farm, Poundstock,
Bude,
EX23 0NA
Tel: 01288 361351 **16 C11**
widemouthbaytouring.co.uk
Pitches: **C 156, CV 156, T 120**

Widend Touring Park
Berry Pomeroy Road,
Marldon, Paignton,
TQ3 1RT
Tel: 01803 550116 **7 M6**
widend.co.uk
Pitches: **C 207, CV 207, T 207**

Wild Rose Park
Ormside,
Appleby-in-Westmorland,
CA16 6EJ
Tel: 017683 51077 **102 C7**
wildrose.co.uk
Pitches: **C 240, CV 100, T 20**

Wilksworth Farm Caravan Park
Cranborne Road,
Wimborne Minster,
BH21 4HW
Tel: 01202 885467 **12 H4**
wilksworthfarmcaravanpark.co.uk
Pitches: **C 60, CV 60, T 25**

Willow Valley Holiday Park
Bush, Bude,
EX23 9LB
Tel: 01288 353104 **16 C10**
willowvalley.co.uk
Pitches: **C 41, CV 41, T 41**

Wolds Way Caravan and Camping
West Farm,
West Knapton, Malton,
YO17 8JE
Tel: 01944 728463 **98 H6**
rydalesbest.co.uk
Pitches: **C 30, CV 30, T 20**

Wooda Farm Holiday Park
Poughill, Bude,
EX23 9HJ
Tel: 01288 352069 **16 C10**
wooda.co.uk
Pitches: **C 100, CV 50, T 50**

Woodclose Caravan Park
High Casterton,
Kirkby Lonsdale,
LA6 2SE
Tel: 01524 271597 **95 N5**
woodclosepark.com
Pitches: **C 17, CV 17, T 12**

Wood Farm C & C Park
Axminster Road, Charmouth,
DT6 6BT
Tel: 01297 560697 **10 H6**
woodfarm.co.uk
Pitches: **C 175, CV 175, T 35**

Woodlands Grove C & C Park
Blackawton, Dartmouth,
TQ9 7DQ
Tel: 01803 712598 **7 L8**
woodlands-caravanpark.com
Pitches: **C 170, CV 25, T 30**

Woodlands Park
Wash Lane, Allostock,
Knutsford,
WA16 9LG
Tel: 01565 723429 **82 F10**
Pitches: **C 30, CV 10, T 10**

Woodovis Park
Gulworthy, Tavistock,
PL19 8NY
Tel: 01822 832968 **6 C4**
woodovis.com
Pitches: **C 50, CV 50, T 50**

Woolsbridge Manor Farm Caravan Park
Three Legged Cross,
Wimborne,
BH21 6RA
Tel: 01202 826369 **13 K4**
woolsbridgemanorcaravanpark.
co.uk
Pitches: **C 60, CV 60, T 60**

Yeatheridge Farm Caravan Park
East Worlington,
Crediton,
EX17 4TN
Tel: 01884 860330 **9 J2**
yeatheridge.co.uk
Pitches: **C 85, CV 85, T 85**

York Touring Caravan Site
Greystones Farm,
Towthorpe Moor Lane,
Towthorpe, York,
YO32 9ST
Tel: 01904 499275 **98 D9**
yorkcaravansite.co.uk
Pitches: **C 20, CV 20, T 20**

Zeacombe House Caravan Park
Blackerton Cross,
East Anstey, Tiverton,
EX16 9JU
Tel: 01398 341279 **17 R7**
zeacombeadultretreat.co.uk
Pitches: **C 50, CV 50, T 50**

SCOTLAND

Achindarroch Touring Park
Duror, PA38 4BS
Tel: 01631 740329 **138 H6**
achindarrochtp.co.uk
Pitches: **C 40, CV 40, T 19**

Aird Donald Caravan Park
London Road, Stranraer,
DG9 8RN
Tel: 01776 702025 **106 E5**
aird-donald.co.uk
Pitches: **C 50, CV 15, T 35**

Anwoth Caravan Site
Gatehouse of Fleet,
Castle Douglas,
DG7 2JU
Tel: 01557 814333 **108 C9**
auchenlarie.co.uk
Pitches: **C 28, CV 28, T 28**

Barrhill Holiday Park
Barrhill, Girvan,
KA26 0PZ
Tel: 01465 821355 **114 D11**
barrhillholidaypark.com
Pitches: **C 20, CV 20, T 10**

Beecraigs C & C Site
Beecraigs Country Park,
The Park Centre, Linlithgow,
EH49 6PL
Tel: 01506 844516 **127 J3**
beecraigs.com
Pitches: **C 36, CV 36, T 14**

Blair Castle Caravan Park
Blair Atholl, Pitlochry,
PH18 5SR
Tel: 01796 481263 **141 L4**
blaircastlecaravanpark.co.uk
Pitches: **C 190, CV 27, T 63**

Braids Caravan Park
Annan Road, Gretna,
DG16 5DQ
Tel: 01461 337409 **110 F7**
thebraidscaravanpark.co.uk
Pitches: **C 93, CV 93, T 0**

Brighouse Bay Holiday Park
Brighouse Bay, Borgue,
DG6 4TS
Tel: 01557 870267 **108 D11**
gillespie-leisure.co.uk
Pitches: **C 120, CV 120, T 70**

Camusdarach Campsite
Arisaig,
PH39 4NT
Tel: 01687 450221 **145 L10**
camusdarach.com
Pitches: **C 42, CV 42, T 42**

Castle Cary Holiday Park
Creetown,
Newton Stewart,
DG8 7DQ
Tel: 01671 820264 **107 N6**
castlecary-caravans.com
Pitches: **C 50, CV 50, T 50**

Craigtoun Meadows Holiday Park
Mount Melville,
St Andrews,
KY16 8PQ
Tel: 01334 475959 **135 M4**
craigtounmeadows.co.uk
Pitches: **C 55, CV 55, T 2**

Crossburn Caravan Park
Edinburgh Road, Peebles,
EH45 8ED
Tel: 01721 720501 **117 J2**
crossburncaravans.co.uk
Pitches: **C 45, CV 45, T 45**

Drum Mohr Caravan Park
Levenhall,
Musselburgh,
EH21 8JS
Tel: 0131 665 6867 **128 B5**
drummohr.org
Pitches: **C 45, CV 45, T 30**

East Bowstrips Caravan Park
St Cyrus,
Nr Montrose,
DD10 0DE
Tel: 01674 850328 **143 N4**
caravancampingsites.co.uk
Pitches: **C 27, CV 27, T 5**

Faskally Caravan Park
Pitlochry, Perthshire,
PH16 5LA
Tel: 01796 472007 **141 M5**
faskally.co.uk
Pitches: **C 300, CV 300, T 100**

Gart Caravan Park
The Gart, Callander,
FK17 8LE
Tel: 01877 330002 **133 J6**
theholidaypark.co.uk
Pitches: **C 128, CV 128, T 0**

Glen Nevis C & C Park
Glen Nevis,
Fort William,
PH33 6SX
Tel: 01397 702191 **139 L3**
glen-nevis.co.uk
Pitches: **C 250, CV 250, T 130**

Glendochart Holiday Park
Luib, Crianlarich,
FK20 8QT
Tel: 01567 820637 **132 F2**
glendochart-caravanpark.co.uk
Pitches: **C 28, CV 28, T 7**

Glenearly Caravan Park
Dalbeattie,
DG5 4NE
Tel: 01556 611393 **108 H8**
glenearlycaravanpark.co.uk
Pitches: **C 39, CV 39, T 39**

Hoddom Castle Caravan Park
Hoddom, Lockerbie,
DG11 1AS
Tel: 01576 300251 **110 C6**
hoddomcastle.co.uk
Pitches: **C 170, CV 170, T 40**

Huntly Castle Caravan Park
The Meadow, Huntly,
AB54 4UJ
Tel: 01466 794999 **158 D9**
huntlycastle.co.uk
Pitches: **C 66, CV 66, T 24**

Invercoe C & C Park
Glencoe, Ballachulish,
PH49 4HP
Tel: 01855 811210 **139 K6**
invercoe.co.uk
Pitches: **C 60, CV 60, T 60**

King Robert the Bruce's Cave
Cove Estate,
Kirkpatrick Fleming,
Gretna,
DG11 3AT
Tel: 01461 800285 **110 E6**
brucescave.co.uk
Pitches: **C 50, CV 10, T 15**

Linnhe Lochside Holidays
Corpach, Fort William,
PH33 7NL
Tel: 01397 772376 **139 K2**
linnhe-lochside-holidays.co.uk
Pitches: **C 63, CV 63, T 22**

Lomond Woods Holiday Park
Old Luss Road, Balloch,
Loch Lomond,
G83 8QP
Tel: 01389 755000 **132 D11**
holiday-parks.co.uk
Pitches: **C 100, CV 10, T 0**

Machrihanish Caravan Park
East Trodigal, Machrihanish,
Mull of Kintyre,
PA28 6PT
Tel: 01586 810366 **120 B7**
campkintyre.co.uk
Pitches: **C 32, CV 25, T 50**

Milton of Fonab Caravan Site
Bridge Road, Pitlochry,
PH16 5NA
Tel: 01796 472882 **141 M6**
fonab.co.uk
Pitches: **C 114, CV 15, T 25**

River Tilt Caravan Park
Blair Atholl, Pitlochry,
PH18 5TE
Tel: 01796 481467 **141 L4**
rivertilt.co.uk
Pitches: **C 37, CV 37, T 37**

Riverview Caravan Park
Marine Drive, Monifieth,
DD5 4NN
Tel: 01382 535471 **143 J11**
riverview.co.uk
Pitches: **C 40, CV 40, T 0**

Sands of Luce Holiday Park
Sands of Luce, Sandhead,
Stranraer, DG9 9JN
Tel: 01776 830456 **106 F7**
sandsofluceholidaypark.co.uk
Pitches: **C 25, CV 10, T 15**

Seaward Caravan Park
Dhoon Bay, Kirkudbright,
DG6 4TJ
Tel: 01557 870267 **108 E11**
gillespie-leisure.co.uk
Pitches: **C 20, CV 20, T 12**

Shieling Holidays
Craignure, Isle of Mull,
PA65 6AY
Tel: 01680 812496 **138 C10**
shielingholidays.co.uk
Pitches: **C 30, CV 30, T 60**

Silver Sands Leisure Park
Covesea, West Beach,
Lossiemouth,
IV31 6SP
Tel: 01343 813262 **157 N3**
travel.to/silversands
Pitches: **C 140, CV 140, T 140**

Skye C & C Club Site
Borve, Arnisort, Edinbane,
Isle of Skye,
IV51 9PS
Tel: 01470 582230 **152 E7**
skyecamp.com
Pitches: **C 105, CV 105, T 105**

Springwood Caravan Park
Kelso, TD5 8LS
Tel: 01573 224596 **118 D4**
springwood.biz
Pitches: **C 20, CV 20, T 0**

The Park of Brandedleys
Crocketford, Dumfries,
DG2 8RG
Tel: 01387 266700 **108 H6**
holgates.com
Pitches: **C 80, CV 40, T 40**

Thurston Manor Holiday Home Park
Innerwick, Dunbar,
EH42 1SA
Tel: 01368 840643 **129 J5**
thurstonmanor.co.uk
Pitches: **C 100, CV 10, T 20**

Trossachs Holiday Park
Aberfoyle,
FK8 3SA
Tel: 01877 382614 **132 G8**
trossachsholidays.co.uk
Pitches: **C 46, CV 46, T 20**

Witches Craig C & C Park
Blairlogie, Stirling,
FK9 5PX
Tel: 01786 474947 **133 N8**
witchescraig.co.uk
Pitches: **C 60, CV 60, T 60**

WALES

Barcdy Touring C & C Park
Talsarnau,
LL47 6YG
Tel: 01766 770736 **67 L7**
barcdy.co.uk
Pitches: **C 35, CV 5, T 40**

Bishops Meadow Caravan Park
Bishops Meadow,
Hay Road, Brecon,
LD3 9SW
Tel: 01874 610000 **44 F8**
bishops-meadow.co.uk
Pitches: **C 25, CV 25, T 32**

Bodnant Caravan Park
Nebo Road, Llanrwst,
Conwy Valley,
LL26 0SD
Tel: 01492 640248 **67 Q2**
bodnant-caravan-park.co.uk
Pitches: **C 38, CV 54, T 16**

Bron Derw Touring Caravan Park
Llanrwst,
LL26 0YT
Tel: 01492 640494 **67 P2**
bronderw-wales.co.uk
Pitches: **C 20, CV 20, T 0**

Bron-Y-Wendon Caravan Park
Wern Road, Llanddulas,
Colwyn Bay,
LL22 8HG
Tel: 01492 512903 **80 C9**
northwales-holidays.co.uk
Pitches: **C 120, CV 10, T 0**

Bryn Gloch C & C Park
Betws Garmon, Caernarfon,
LL54 7YY
Tel: 01286 650216 **67 J3**
bryngloch.co.uk
Pitches: **C 80, CV 80, T 80**

Caerfai Bay Caravan & Tent Park
Caerfai Bay, St David's,
Haverfordwest,
SA62 6QT
Tel: 01437 720274 **40 E6**
caerfaibay.co.uk
Pitches: **C 26, CV 18, T 78**

Cenarth Falls Holiday Park
Cenarth,
Newcastle Emlyn,
SA38 9JS
Tel: 01239 710345 **41 Q2**
cenarth-holipark.co.uk
Pitches: **C 30, CV 30, T 30**

Dinlle Caravan Park
Dinas Dinlle, Caernarfon,
LL54 5TW
Tel: 01286 830324 **66 G3**
thornleyleisure.co.uk
Pitches: **C 100, CV 20, T 50**

Eisteddfa, Eisteddfa Lodge
Pentrefelin, Criccieth,
LL52 0PT
Tel: 01766 522696 **67 J7**
eisteddfapark.co.uk
Pitches: **C 6, CV 27, T 70**

Erwlon C & C Park
Brecon Road, Llandovery,
SA20 0RD
Tel: 01550 721021 **43 Q8**
erwlon.co.uk
Pitches: **C 40, CV 10, T 20**

Hendre Mynach Touring C & C Park
Llanaber Road, Barmouth,
LL42 1YR
Tel: 01341 280262 **67 L11**
hendremynach.co.uk
Pitches: **C 60, CV 60, T 120**

Home Farm Caravan Park
Marian-Glas,
Isle of Anglesey,
LL73 8PH
Tel: 01248 410614 **78 H8**
homefarm-anglesey.co.uk
Pitches: **C 98, CV 10, T 20**

Hunters Hamlet Caravan Park
Sirior Goch Farm,
Betws-yn-Rhos, Abergele,
LL22 8PL
Tel: 01745 832237 **80 C10**
huntershamlet.co.uk
Pitches: **C 23, CV 23, T 0**

Islawrffordd Caravan Park
Tal-y-bont,
Barmouth,
LL43 2AQ
Tel: 01341 247269 **67 K10**
islawrffordd.co.uk
Pitches: **C 25, CV 25, T 120**

Pencelli Castle C & C Park
Pencelli, Brecon,
LD3 7LX
Tel: 01874 665451 **44 F10**
pencelli-castle.com
Pitches: **C 40, CV 40, T 60**

Pen-Y-Bont
Llangynog Road,
Bala,
LL23 7PH
Tel: 01678 520549 **68 B8**
penybont-bala.co.uk
Pitches: **C 59, CV 35, T 36**

Pont Kemys C & C Park
Chainbridge,
Abergavenny,
NP7 9DS
Tel: 01873 880688 **31 K3**
pontkemys.com
Pitches: **C 45, CV 45, T 20**

River View Touring Park
The Dingle, Llanedi,
Pontarddulais,
SA4 0FH
Tel: 01269 844876 **28 G3**
riverviewtouringpark.com
Pitches: **C 60, CV 10, T 30**

The Plassey Leisure Park
The Plassey, Eyton,
Wrexham,
LL13 0SP
Tel: 01978 780277 **69 L5**
plassey.com
Pitches: **C 30, CV 45, T 15**

Trawsdir Touring C & C Park
Llanaber,
Barmouth,
LL42 1RR
Tel: 01341 280999 **67 K11**
barmouthholidays.co.uk
Pitches: **C 70, CV 70, T 30**

Trefalun Park
Devonshire Drive,
St Florence, Tenby,
SA70 8RD
Tel: 01646 651514 **41 L10**
trefalunpark.co.uk
Pitches: **C 55, CV 5, T 30**

Tyddyn Isaf Caravan Park
Lligwy Bay, Dulas,
Anglesey,
LL70 9PQ
Tel: 01248 410203 **78 H7**
tyddynisaf.co.uk
Pitches: **C 6, CV 4, T 20**

Well Park C & C Site
Tenby,
SA70 8TL
Tel: 01834 842179 **41 M10**
wellparkcaravans.co.uk
Pitches: **C 40, CV 10, T 50**

White Tower Caravan Park
Llandwrog, Caernarfon,
LL54 5UH
Tel: 01286 830649 **66 H3**
whitetower.supanet.com
Pitches: **C 70, CV 29, T 5**

CHANNEL ISLANDS

Beuvelande Camp Site
Beuvelande,
St Martin, Jersey,
JE3 6EZ
Tel: 01534 853575 **11 c1**
campingjersey.com
Pitches: **C 0, CV 0, T 150**

Bleu Soleil Campsite
La Route de Vinchelez,
Leoville, St Ouen,
JE3 2DB
Tel: 01534 481007 **11 a1**
bleusoleilcamping.com
Pitches: **C 0, CV 55, T 55**

Fauxquets Valley Campsite
Castel, Guernsey,
GY5 7QL
Tel: 01481 236951 **10 b2**
fauxquets.co.uk
Pitches: **C 0, CV 0, T 120**

Rozel Camping Park
Summerville Farm,
St Martin, Jersey,
JE3 6AX
Tel: 01534 855200 **11 c1**
rozelcamping.co.uk
Pitches: **C 15, CV 15, T 100**

Road safety cameras

First, the advice you would expect from the AA - we advise drivers to always follow the signed speed limits – breaking the speed limit is illegal and can cost lives.

Both the AA and the Government believe that safety cameras ('speed cameras') should be operated within a transparent system. By providing information relating to road safety and speed hotspots, the AA believes that the driver is better placed to be aware of speed limits and can ensure adherence to them, thus making the roads safer for all users.

Most fixed cameras are installed at accident 'black spots' where four or more fatal or serious road collisions have occurred over the previous three years. It is the policy of both the police and the Department for Transport to make the location of cameras as well known as possible. By showing camera locations in this atlas the AA is identifying the places where extra care should be taken while driving. Speeding is illegal and dangerous and you MUST keep within the speed limit at all times.

Gatso™   Truvelo™   SPECS™   Traffipax™

There are currently more than 4,000 fixed cameras in Britain and the road mapping in this atlas identifies their on-the-road locations.

 This symbol is used on the mapping to identify **individual** camera locations - with speed limits (mph)

 This symbol is used on the mapping to identify **multiple** cameras on the same stretch of road - with speed limits (mph)

 This symbol is used on the mapping to highlight SPECS™ camera systems which calculate your **average speed** along a stretch of road between two or more sets of cameras - with speed limits (mph)

Mobile cameras are also deployed at other sites where speed is perceived to be a problem and mobile enforcement often takes place at the fixed camera sites shown on the maps in this atlas. Additionally, regular police enforcement can take place on any road.

Speed Limits	Built up areas*	Single carriageways	Dual carriageways	Motorways
Types of vehicle	MPH (km/h)	MPH (km/h)	MPH (km/h)	MPH (km/h)
Cars & motorcycles (including car derived vans up to 2 tonnes maximum laden weight)	30 (48)	60 (96)	70 (112)	70 (112)
 Cars towing caravans or trailers (including car derived vans and motorcycles)	30 (48)	50 (80)	60 (96)	60 (96)
 Buses, coaches and minibuses (not exceeding 12 metres (39 feet) in overall length)	30 (48)	50 (80)	60 (96)	70 (112)
Goods vehicles (not exceeding 7.5 tonnes maximum laden weight)	30 (48)	50 (80)	60 (96)	70[†] (112)
 Goods vehicles (exceeding 7.5 tonnes maximum laden weight)	30 (48)	40 (64)	50 (80)	60 (96)

* The 30mph (48km/h) limit usually applies to all traffic on all roads with street lighting unless signs show otherwise.
† 60mph (96km/h) if articulated or towing a trailer.

Read this before you use the atlas

Safety cameras and speed limits

The fixed camera symbols on the mapping show the maximum speed in mph that applies to that particular stretch of road and above which the camera is set to activate. The actual road speed limit however will vary for different vehicle types and you must ensure that you drive within the speed limit for your particular class of vehicle at all times.

The chart above details the speed limits applying to the different classes. Don't forget that mobile enforcement can take account of vehicle class at any designated site.

Camera locations

1 The camera locations were correct at the time of finalising the information to go to press.

2 Camera locations are approximate due to limitations in the scale of the road mapping used in this atlas.

3 In towns and urban areas camera locations are shown only on roads that appear on the road maps in this atlas.

4 Where two or more cameras appear close together, a special symbol is used to indicate multiple cameras on the same stretch of road.

5 Our symbols do not indicate the direction in which cameras point.

6 On the mapping we symbolise more than 4,000 fixed camera locations. Mobile laser device locations, roadwork cameras and 'fixed red light' cameras cannot be shown.

Be alert to accident black spots even before seeing the cameras

The AA brings you an iPhone® app that provides 'real-time' updates of safety camera locations

The AA Safety Camera app brings the latest safety camera location system to your iPhone®. It improves road safety by alerting you to the location of fixed and mobile camera sites and accident black spots.

The AA Safety Camera app ensures that you will always have the very latest data of fixed and mobile sites on your iPhone® without having to connect it to your computer. Updates are made available automatically.

Powered by **RoadPilot**®

Visual Countdown
To camera location

Your Speed
The speed you are travelling when approaching a camera. Dial turns red as an additional visual alert

Camera Types Located
Includes fixed cameras (Gatso, Specs etc.) and mobile cameras

Speed Limit at Camera

iPhone® Apps

Map pages

Orkney Islands

169
● Kirkwall

Shetland Islands

169
● Lerwick

Western Isles

168

● Steornabhagh (Stornoway)

164 165 166 167
Thurso ●
● Wick

160 161 162 163
Ullapool ●
● Gairloch
Tain ●

152 153 154 155 156 157 158 159
Uig ●
Portree ●
Dingwall ●
Elgin ●   Banff ●
Inverness ●   ● Peterhead

144 145 146 147 148 149 150 151
Kyle of Lochalsh ●
Mallaig ●
Aviemore ●
Aberdeen ●

136 137 138 139 140 141 142 143
Fort William ●
Pitlochry ●   Montrose ●
Oban ●   ● Dundee

130 131 132 133 134 135
Crianlarich ●   Perth ●
Stirling ●

122 123 254 255 128 129
124 Glasgow ● Edinburgh ●
125 126 127 Berwick-upon-Tweed ●

120 121
Campbeltown ●
Kilmarnock ●
Ayr ●

114 115 116 117 118 119
Galashiels ●   Alnwick ●
Moffat ●

Derry ●

Larne ●

Belfast ●

172   173

Sligo ●

Westport ●   Cavan ●   Newry ●

Galway ●   Athlone ●   DUBLIN ■

Limerick ●

170   171

Tralee ●
Killarney ●
Cork ●   Waterford ●   Rosslare Harbour ●

108 109 110 111 112 258 259 113
Stranraer ● Dumfries ●
106 107 Carlisle ●   Newcastle upon Tyne ●

100 101 102 103 104 105
Penrith ●   Durham ●
Brough ●   Middlesbrough ●

80
● Douglas
Isle of Man

94 95 96 97 98 99
Kendal ●   Thirsk ●   Scarborough ●
Lancaster ●   Skipton ●   York ●

88 89 256 90 91 92 93
Blackpool ● Burnley ● Leeds ● Kingston upon Hull ●
257 Liverpool ● Manchester ● Grimsby ●
82 83

78 79 80 81 84 85 86 87
Holyhead ●   Colwyn Bay ● Chester ● Sheffield ● Lincoln ●
Caernarfon ● Wrexham ● Newark-on-Trent ●
Nottingham ●

66 67 68 69 70 71 72 73 74 75 76 77
Dolgellau ●   Stoke-on-Trent ● Leicester ● King's Lynn ● Norwich ● Great Yarmouth ●
Stafford ●   Peterborough ●

54 55 56 57 58 252 253 59 60 61 62 63 64 65
Newtown ● Shrewsbury ● Birmingham Coventry ● Northampton ● Cambridge ● Bury St Edmunds ●
Aberystwyth ● Ludlow ● Stratford-upon-Avon ● Ipswich ●

42 43 44 45 46 47 48 49 50 51 52 53
Cardigan ● Hereford ● Worcester ● Milton Keynes ● Luton ● Chelmsford ●
Fishguard ● Brecon ● Gloucester ● Watford ●

40 41 28 29 30 31 32 33 34 35 36 37 38 39
Pembroke ● Swansea ● Cardiff ● Bristol ● Swindon ● Oxford ● LONDON Maidstone ●
Carmarthen ● Bath ● Reading ● 248 - 251 Dover ●
Guildford ● Folkestone ●

16 17 18 19 20 21 22 23 24 25 26 27
Barnstaple ● Taunton ● Yeovil ● Salisbury ● Basingstoke ● Brighton ● Hastings ●
Bude ● Southampton ● Newhaven ●

4 5 8 9 10 11 12 13 14 15
Bodmin ● Exeter ● Lyme Regis ● Weymouth ● Bournemouth ●
Truro ● Torquay ● Plymouth ●

2 3 6 7

Isles of Scilly
2

To help you navigate safely and easily, see the AA's Ireland atlases... theAA.com/shop

10-11
Channel Islands

To help you navigate safely and easily, see the AA's France and Europe atlases... theAA.com/shop

Road map symbols

Motoring information

M4	Motorway with number	⊙	Transport café	Toll →	Road toll, steep gradient (arrows point downhill)	50	Speed camera site (fixed location) with speed limit in mph
Toll T4	Toll motorway with toll station	BATH	Primary route destination	▼ 5 ▼	Distance in miles between symbols	40	Section of road with two or more fixed speed cameras, with speed limit in mph
11	Motorway junction with and without number	A1123	Other A road single/dual carriageway	🚢 or V	Vehicle ferry	60 ... 60	Average speed (SPECS™) camera system with speed limit in mph
3	Restricted motorway junctions	B2070	B road single/dual carriageway	⛴	Fast vehicle ferry or catamaran	V▶	Fixed speed camera site with variable speed limit
S Fleet	Motorway service area		Minor road more than 4 metres wide, less than 4 metres wide	- - - - -	Railway line, in tunnel	P+R	Park and Ride (at least 6 days per week)
	Motorway and junction under construction	⊕	Roundabout	—○—✕—	Railway station and level crossing		City, town, village or other built-up area
A3	Primary route single/dual carriageway	⊕	Interchange/junction	+++++++	Tourist railway	628 ▲ 637 Lecht Summit	Height in metres, mountain pass
1	Primary route junction with and without number		Narrow primary/other A/B road with passing places (Scotland)	✈ H F	Airport, heliport, international freight terminal		Sandy beach
3	Restricted primary route junctions		Road under construction	H	24-hour Accident & Emergency hospital		National boundary
S Grantham North	Primary route service area	⊨=====⊨	Road tunnel	C	Crematorium		County, administrative boundary

Touring information To avoid disappointment, check opening times before visiting.

	Scenic Route	❋	Garden	- - - - -	National trail		Air show venue
i	Tourist Information Centre	🌳	Arboretum	☀	Viewpoint		Ski slope (natural, artificial)
i	Tourist Information Centre (seasonal)	🍇	Vineyard	⁛	Hill-fort		National Trust property
V	Visitor or heritage centre		Country park	🐎	Roman antiquity		National Trust for Scotland property
♣	Picnic site	⚘	Agricultural showground		Prehistoric monument	#	English Heritage site
⛺	Caravan site		Theme park	✕ 1066	Battle site with year		Historic Scotland site
▲	Camping site	🚜	Farm or animal centre	🚂	Steam railway centre	⊕	Cadw (Welsh heritage) site
▲⛺	Caravan & camping site	🦌	Zoological or wildlife collection	⌒	Cave	★	Other place of interest
♱	Abbey, cathedral or priory	🐦	Bird collection	✠ ⚊	Windmill, monument	☐	Boxed symbols indicate attractions within urban areas
♰	Ruined abbey, cathedral or priory	🐟	Aquarium	⚑	Golf course	◉	World Heritage Site (UNESCO)
✗	Castle	RSPB	RSPB site	🏏	County cricket ground		National Park
🏛	Historic house or building		National Nature Reserve (England, Scotland, Wales)	⚽	Rugby Union national stadium		National Scenic Area (Scotland)
M	Museum or art gallery	🦆	Local nature reserve	🏃	International athletics stadium		Forest Park
⚒	Industrial interest		Wildlife Trust reserve	🐎🐎	Horse racing, show jumping		Heritage coast
⊓⊓	Aqueduct or viaduct	⋯⋯	Forest drive	🏁	Motor-racing circuit	⊞	Major shopping centre

Isles of Scilly

White Island
BRYHER
King Charles's
Cromwell's
Old Grimsby
ST.MARTIN'S
St Martin's Head
49
Old Blockhouse
Lizard Point
Higher Town
New Grimsby
Great Ganilly
Isles-of-Scilly Heritage Coast
TRESCO
Tresco
Tresco Abbey
Crow Bar
Crow Sound
Great Arthur
Pool
Bant's Carn Burial
Samson
Innisidgen Tomb
ST MARY'S
SV
Harry's Walls
A3111
Longstone
St Mary's Quay
Deep Point
North West Channel
Hugh Town
Porth Hellick Downs Tombs
Isles of Scilly (St Mary's)
Garrison Walls
Old Town
Annet
Peninnis Head
St Mary's Sound
Middle Town
Gugh
Broad Sound
ST.AGNES
Western Rocks
Horse Point

0 1 2 3 miles
0 1 2 3 4 5 kilometres

SW

SV

St Agnes Heritage Coast
ST AGNES HEAD
Wheal Coate
Goor
Porthtowan
Cambrose
Mav
South West Coast Path
Portreath
B3300
Godrevy-Porreath Heritage-Coast
No
Co
Godrevy Island
Navax Point
Godrevy Point
Illogan
Payner's Lane End
Coombe
Gwealavellan
South Tehidy
Tehidy Park Bottom
Carn Bre
Cornish Engines
Carn Brea
Reskadinnick
Tuckingmill
Pool
A3047
Carn Naun Point
Treveal
Gwithian
Treswithian
Roseworthy
60 60
Camborne
Penponds
Car
Zennor Head
Hellesveor
The Island or St Ives Head
Upton Towans
Kehelland
Trendrine
St Ives Bay
Connor Downs
Bolenowe
Fou
Lan
Gurnards Head
Zennor
Trendrine
St Ives
The Towans
Phillack
Angarrack
Barripper
Troon
B3280
Croft Mitchell
Burras
Farm Common
South West Coast Path
B3306
Halsetown
Carbis Bay
Hayle
Copperhouse
High Gwinear Lanes
Carnhell Green
Praze-an-Beeble
Porkel
Treen
Towednack
Brunnion
RSPB
Realwa
Rosewarne
Blackrock
B3297
Porthmeor
Cripplesease
Lelant
St Erth
Fraddam
Horsedown
B3303
Crowan
Lezerea
Lighthouse
B3306
14
Georgia
Nancledra
A30
Kerthen Wood
Leedstown
Releath
Penween
Pendeen Watch
Men-An-Tol
Carn Galver
Mulfra
Chysauster Ancient Village
Canonstown
Whitecross
St Erth
Townshend
Godolphin House
Trenwheal
Crowan
Nancegollan
Trenear
Poldar
Penwith Heritage Coast
Morvah
Mulfra Quoit
New Mill
Castle Gate
Cockwells
Crowlas
9
Godolphin Cross
Prospidnick
Wendron
A
Lower Boscaswell
Bojewyan
Boskednan
Badger's Cross
Ludgvan
Relubbus
St Hilary
Trescowe
Crowntown
Wendron Mining District
Levant Mine and Beam Engine
Pendeen Trewellard
Great Bosullow
Lanyon Quoit
Boswarthan
Penzance
Longrock
Marazion
Millpool
Balwest
Carleen
Sithney Green
Lower Coverack Town Bridges
Trewenn
Carnyorth
Trengwainton Garden
Madron
Trevarrack
Chyandour
Goldsithney
Newtown
Ashton
Sithney
Trevarno
Manhay
Botallack
St Just
A3071
Newbridge
Tremethick Cross
Heamoor
RSPB
Perranuthnoe
Germoe
Breage
A30
Helston
Tregeseal
Sellan
Penzance
St Michael's Mount
Rosudgeon
Kenneggy
Trew
Sithney
A3083
Cape Cornwall
Ballowall Barrow
B3306
Grumbla
Carn Euny Ancient Village
Sancreed
Drift
Trevedoe
Newlyn
13
Prussia Cove
Rinsey Croft
A394
Sithney Common
Mellangoose
Flambards
Bosavern
Kelynack
Catchall
Kerris
Paul
Cudden Point
Praa Sands
Rinsey
Rinsey Head
Trewavas Head
Higher Pentire
Trewennack
Nanquidno
Brane
A30
Crows-an-Wra
Sheffield
Mousehole
Chyvarloe
Garra
Whitesand Bay
Land's End
10
Escalls
Trevorgans
St Buryan
Raginnis
MOUNT'S BAY
Porthleven
Gunwalloe
Chyanvounder
White Cross
Sennen Cove
Sennen
The Merry Maidens
Lamorna
Castallack
Berepper
LAND'S END
Land's End
Trevescan
B3315
Bottoms
B3283
Boskenna
Lamorna Cove
Cury
Trewoon
Polgigga
Trethewey
Treen
Merthen Point
Angrouse
B3296
Porthcurno
Submarine Telegraphy
Cribba Head
Poldhu Point
Marconi Memorial
Mullion
Roskestal
Minack Open Air Theatre
St Levan
Mullion Cove
Mullion Island
R
M
Porthgwarra
Gwennap Head
Predannack Head
Predannack Wollas
Mount Hermon
Vellan Head
The Lizard Heritage Coast
South West Coast Path
Lizard Head
Kynance Cove
Lizar
LIZARD POINT

0 1 2 3 4 5 miles
0 1 2 3 4 5 6 7 8 kilometres

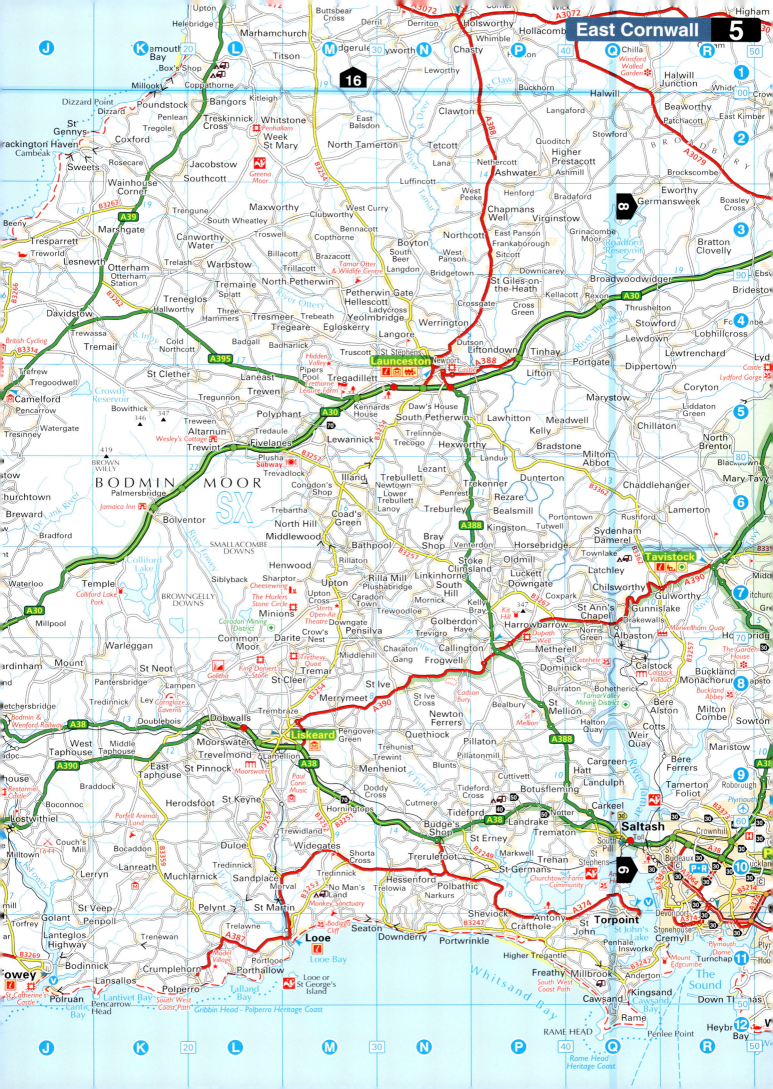

A B C D E F G H

Langore · Arrington
St Giles-on-the-Heath
Broadwoodwidger
Bridestowe
Lake
Okehampton
HIGH WILLHAYS
414 BUTTERN HILL
Wonson
Murchington
Gidleigh
Chagford

1
Launceston
Newport
Dutson
Liftondown
Tinhay
Stowford
Lewdown
Lobhillcross
Foxco
50
Teigncombe
Frenchbeer
Corndon

2
Daw's House
South Petherwin
Lifton
Lifton
Portgate
Dippertown
Lydford
Castle Lydford Gorge
Beardon
Willsworthy
DARTMOOR
568 GREAT KNEESET
605
602 WHITEHORSE HILL
Fernworthy Reservoir
Lettaford

Trelinnoe
Trecogo
Lawhitton
Kelly
Marystow
Chillaton
North Brenton
Coryton
Liddaton Green
16
Willsworthy
DARTMOOR
517 LYNCH TOR
538 SITTAFORD TOR
HA

Lezant
Newtown
Hexworthy
Bradstone
Milton Abbot
Blackdown
Mary Tavy
Horndon
Cudliptown
Godsworthy
501 COCKS HILL
F O R E S T
Postbridge
NATI
CORNDON TOR

3
Trebullett
Lower Trebullett
Treburley
Rezare
Bealsmill
Chaddlehanger
Lamerton
Peter Tavy
442 COXTOR
539 GREAT MIS TOR
Wistman's Wood
B3212 Clapper Bridge
Bellever
Cator Court
431

Bray Shop
A388
Kingston
Penrest
Tutwell
Portontown
Sydenham Damerel
Rushford
Townlake
Merrivale
8
Two Bridges
B3357
West Dart River
Huccaby
Babeny
Dartmeet
CORNDON TOR
Du
Poundsg

Stoke Climsland
Linkinhorne
South Hill
Venterdon
Coxpark
St Ann's Chapel
Tavistock
Merrivale
B3357
Moortown
Princetown
406 ROYAL HILL
Whiteworks
Hexworthy
516 RYDERS HILL
Michelcombe
Scorrite

4
Mornick
Kelly Bray
Oldmill
Luckett
Downgate
Chilsworthy
Gulworthy
Gunnislake
Drakewalls
Whitchurch
Grenofen
Sampford Spiney
Middlemore
Walkhampton
Venford Reservoir

Rilla Mill
Plush bridge
Golberdon
Haye
Trevigro
347 Kit Hill
Dupath Well
Harrowbarrow
Norris Green
Albaston
Morwellham Quay
The Garden House
Horrabridge
Dousland
Yelverton
Meavy
Burrator Reservoir
Sheepstor
480
Didworthy

5
Charaton Gang
Callington
Frogwell
Metherell
St Dominick
Calstock
Calstock Viaduct
Buckland Monachorum
Crapstone
Milton Combe
Hoo Meavy
Upper Plym Valley
Clearbrook
Goodameavy
471 SHELL TOP
SX

St Ive Cross
Newton Ferrers
Quethiock
Bealbury
Burraton
St Mellion
Bohetherick
Tamar Valley Mining District
Bere Alston
Sowton
Maristow
Dewerstone
Shaugh Prior
Bickleigh
Lee Moor
R Erme
Harbou

6
Trehunist
Trewint
Menh ot
Doddy Cross
ps
Pillaton
Pillatonmill
Blunts
Cuttivett
Botusfleming
Hatt
Landulph
Carkeel
Halton Quay
Weir Quay
Cotts
10
Tamerton Foliot
Roborough
Plymouth
Wotter
Lutton
Cornwood
BUTTERDON HILL
Harford
Aish
South Brent
Brent Mill

Cutmere
Tideford Cross
Tideford
A38
Landrake
Trematon
Trehan
Notter
Markwell
Cargreen
Bere Ferrers
Saltash
Toll
Crownhill
Boringdon
Dartmoor Wildlife Park
Hemerdon
Sparkwell
Venton
Ivybridge
Wrangaton
Cheston
Bittaford

7
Budge's Shop
60
St Erney
Trerulefoot
B3249
Hessenford
Trelowia
Polbathic
Narkurs
Sheviock
Antony
Crafthole
Churchtown Farm Community
South St Pill
St Budeaux
Devonport
Eggbuckland
Crownhill
PLYMOUTH
Colebrook
Plympton
Lee Mill
Woodland
A38
Keaton
Penquit
Ludbrook
Ugborou

Downderry
Portwrinkle
St John
Torpoint
Antony House
Cremyll
Stonehouse
Plymouth Dome
Saltram
Elburton
Brixton
Yealmbridge
Westward
Dunstone
Torr
Ford
Westlake
Worston
Ermington
Modbury
Brownston
East Leigh

8
Higher Tregantle
Freathy
Millbrook
Anderton
Kingsand
Turnchapel
Hooe
Spriddlestone
Staddiscombe
Yealmpton
Luson
Holbeton
Battisborough Cross
Ashford
St Ann's Chapel

South West Coast Path
Mount Edgcumbe
Cawsand
Cawsand Bay
The Sound
Down Thomas
West Wembury
Knighton
Newton Ferrers
B3186
Bridgend
Noss Mayo
Mothecombe
Kingston
Bigbury
Ringmore
Bridge End

9
RAME HEAD
Rame
Penlee Point
Heybrook Bay
Wembury
Wembury Bay
The Old Mill
Gara Point
Stoke Point
Beacon Point
Erme Mouth
Challaborough
Bigbury-on-Sea
Buckland
U

Rame Head Heritage Coast
Whitsand Bay

10
Santander (Mar-Oct)
Roscoff
Bigbury Bay
Burgh Island
Bantham
South Milton
Su
Thurlestone
South Huish
Galmpton

11
Hope
Bolt Tail
Bolberry

South Devon Heritage Coast

12

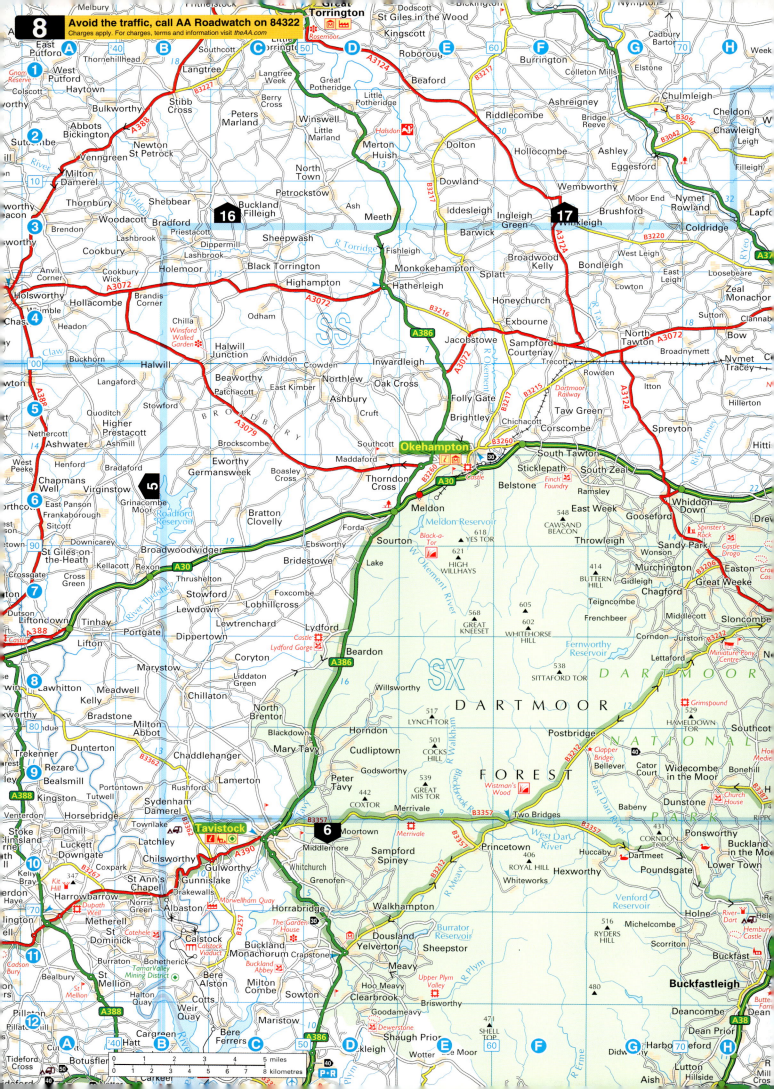

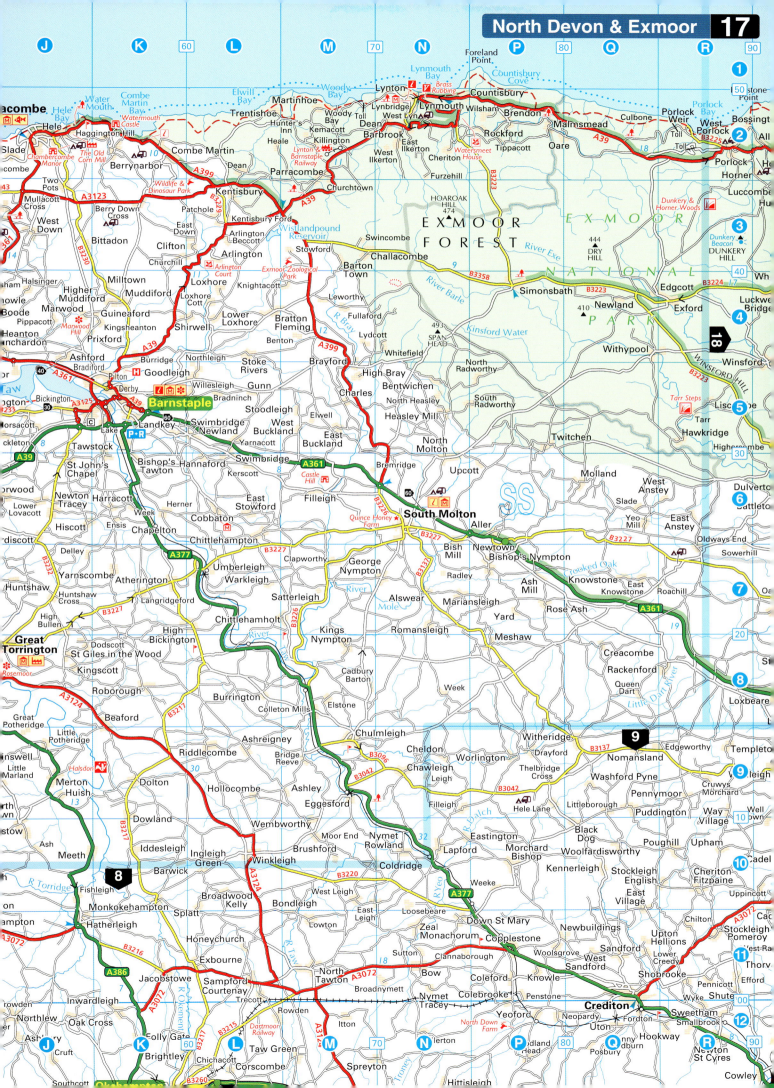

STRAIT OF DOVER

TR

Folkestone Terminal

0 ___ 400 yards
0 ___ 500 metres

Ashley Wood

Peene

Newington

Terminal Building

CHANNEL TUNNEL TERMINAL

BEACHBOROUGH CROSSROADS

Check-in

Police Station

Superstore

Cheriton Interchange

Cheriton

ASHFORD ROAD

ASHFORD ROAD

A20

A20

A20

M20

M20

1A

ASHFORD, MAIDSTONE, M15 & LONDON

DOVER, FOLKESTONE, CANTERBURY

12

| Departures to France follow | Arrivals from France follow |

Calais / Coquelles Terminal

Coquelles

0 ___ 400 yards
0 ___ 500 metres

Ibis Hotel

Etap Hotel

Novotel

Freight only

Cité de l'Europe

PASSENGER TERMINAL

Petrol Station

Check-in

Frontier Controls

Freight only

A16 (E402) ROCADE LITTORALE

A16 (E402) ROCADE LITTORALE

HGV Fuel Station

Eurotunnel Administration Headquarters

Parc d'activités les Terrasses

Freight Terminal

BOULOGNE

D243E

CALAIS

DUNKERQUE, A26 (PARIS)

D304

| Departures to England follow | Arrivals from England follow |

A '60 B C 70 D E 80 F G 90 H

1
2
40
3
4
30
5
20
6
7
8
10
9
'00
10
11
12

A '60 B C 70 D E 80 F G 90 H

SM

SR

STRUMBLE HEAD

Rosslare Harbour (July Sept)
Rosslare Harbour

Pen Brush
Pwll Deri
Pembrokeshire Coast Path
Trefasser
Goodwick
Llanv
Manorowen
St Nicholas
Panteg
Ynys Daullyn
Carreg Sampson
Granston
Abercastle
Llangloffan
Jordanston
A4
Porthgain
Trefin
Mathry
A487
Castle Morris
B4331
Abereiddy
Llanrhian
Square & Compass
Letterston
Berea
Croes-goch
Welsh Hook
Tretio
Treffynnon
B4330
St David's Head
Treleddyd-fawr
Carnhedryn
Treglemais
Cerbyd
Llandeloy
Pont-yr-hafod
Rhodiad-y-brenin
Caer Farchell
River Solva
Tancredston
Hayscastle Cross
Whitesand Bay
B4583
Whitchurch
Middle Mill
Treffgarne Owen
Hayscastle
Treffg
Bishop's Palace
St David's
Nine Wells
Solva
A487
Pen-y-cwn
178 DUDWELL MT
Leweston
Treff
RAMSEY ISLAND
RSPB
St David's Peninsula Heritage Coast
Newgale
16
Roch
Wolfsdale
PEMBROKESHIRE COAST NATIONAL PARK
Roch Gate
Camros
Simpson Cross
A487
Keeston
Pembrokes Cou
Rickets Head
Nolton Haven
Nolton
Pelcomb Cross
Pelcomb
Tangi
St Brides Bay Heritage Coast
Lambston
Pelcomb Bridge
Gla
Druidston
Sutton
St Brides Bay
Haroldston West
Portfield Gate
B4341
Broad Haven
Broadway
B4327
Dreen Hill
A407
Little Haven
Walton West
Solbury
Lov Freys
Fre
Pembrokeshire Coast Path
Talbenny
14
Tiers Cross
Joh
St Brides
Walwyn's Castle
SKOMER ISLAND
Wooltack Point
Hasguard
Thornton
A477
Marloes
B4327
Sandy Haven
Steynton
Martin's Haven
St Ishmael's
Herbrandston
Honeyborough
Waterston
Broad Sound
Hubberston
Hakin
Llanstadwell
Marloes and Dale Heritage Coast
Dale
Great Castle Head
Milford Haven (Aberdaugleddau)
Pembro Dock (Doc Pen
Westdale Bay
Dale Point
SKOKHOLM ISLAND
Milford Haven
Angle
Pwllcrochan
Rhoscrowther
St Anns Head
Angle Bay
Rosslare Harbour
Castlemartin Brook
B4320
Freshwater West
B4319
B4320
Castlemartin
Hur
Warren
Twy
Linney Head
Merrion
PEMBROKESHIRE COAS NATIONAL PARK
Bos
Pembrokeshire Coast Path

0 1 2 3 4 5 miles
0 1 2 3 4 5 6 7 8 kilometres

Port Plan: Pembroke Dock *p.13*

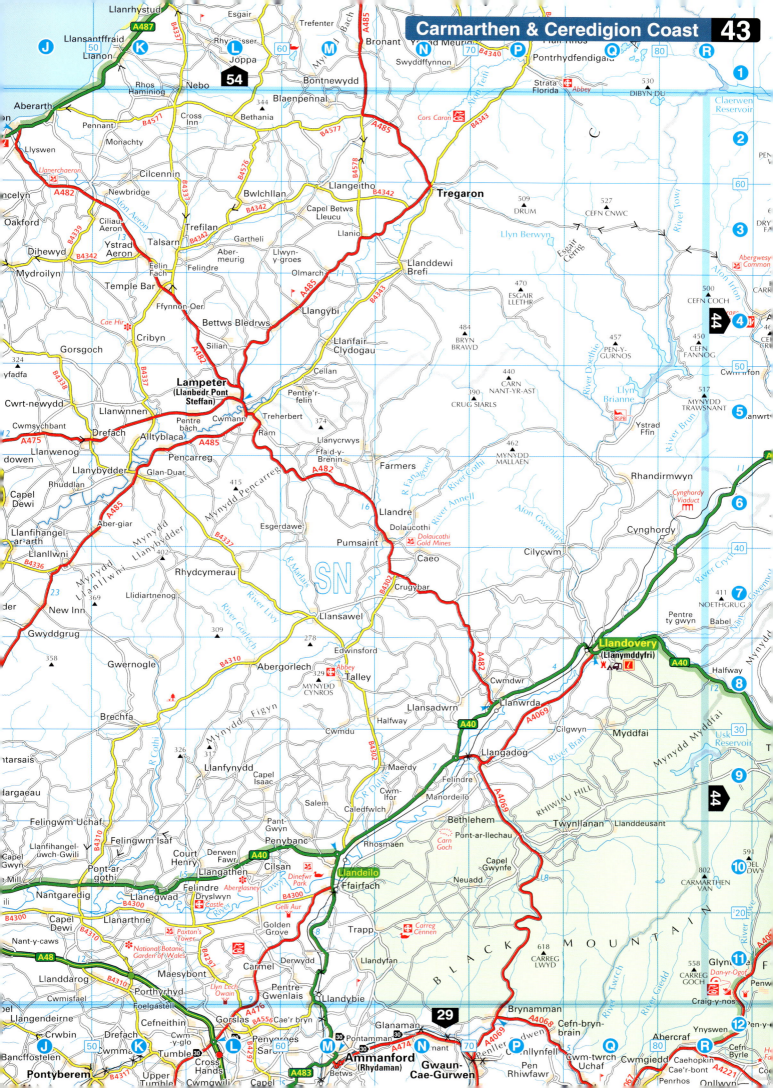

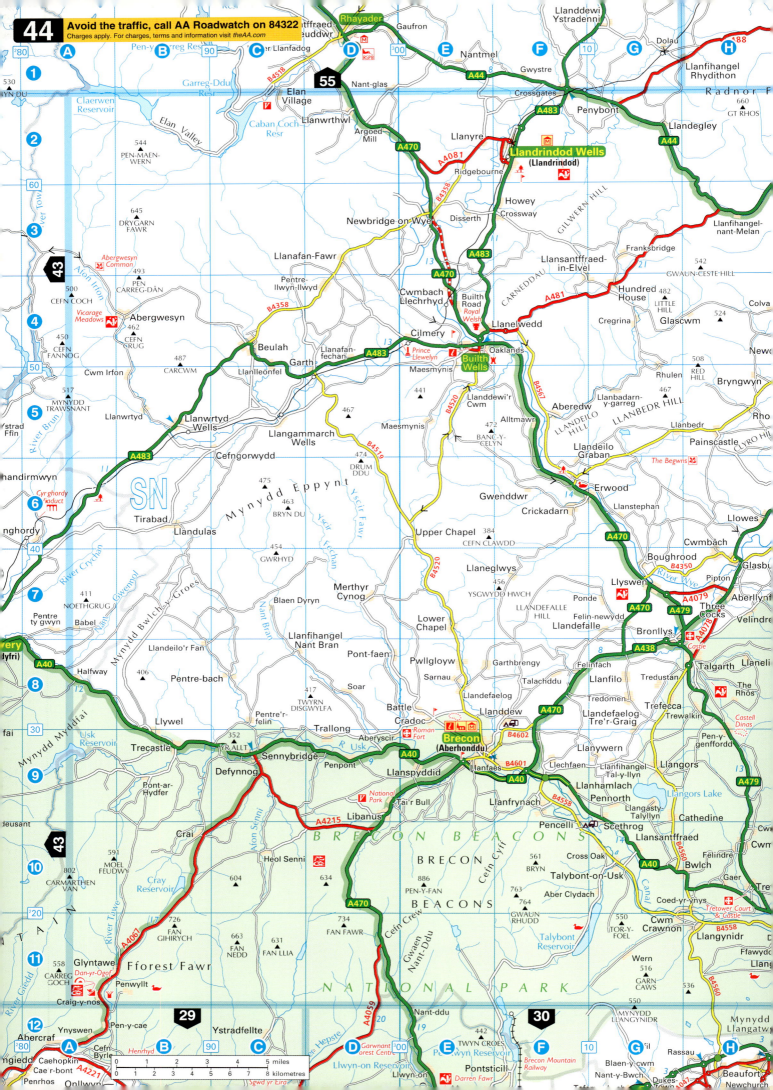

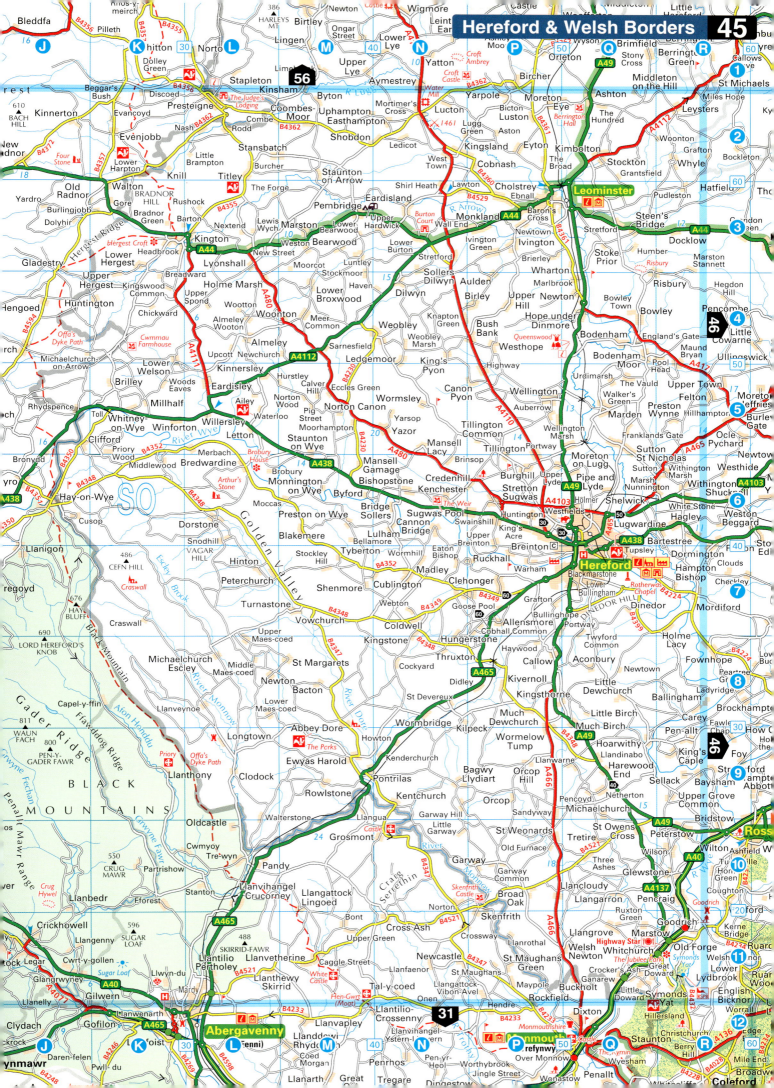

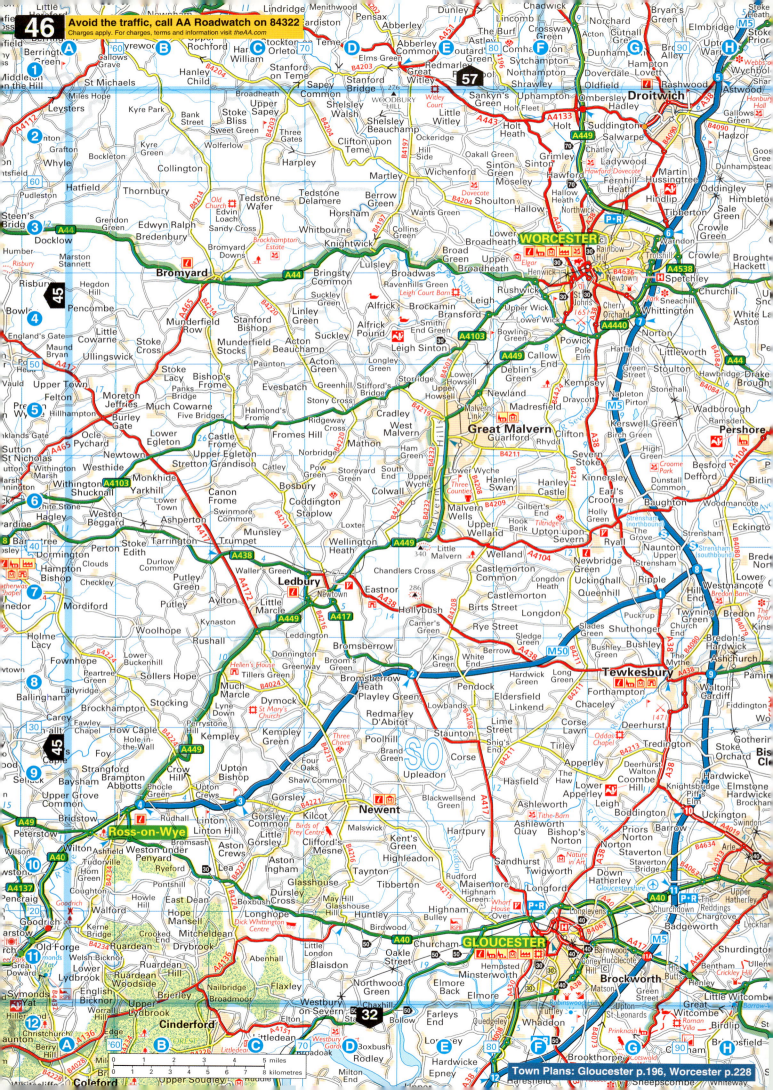

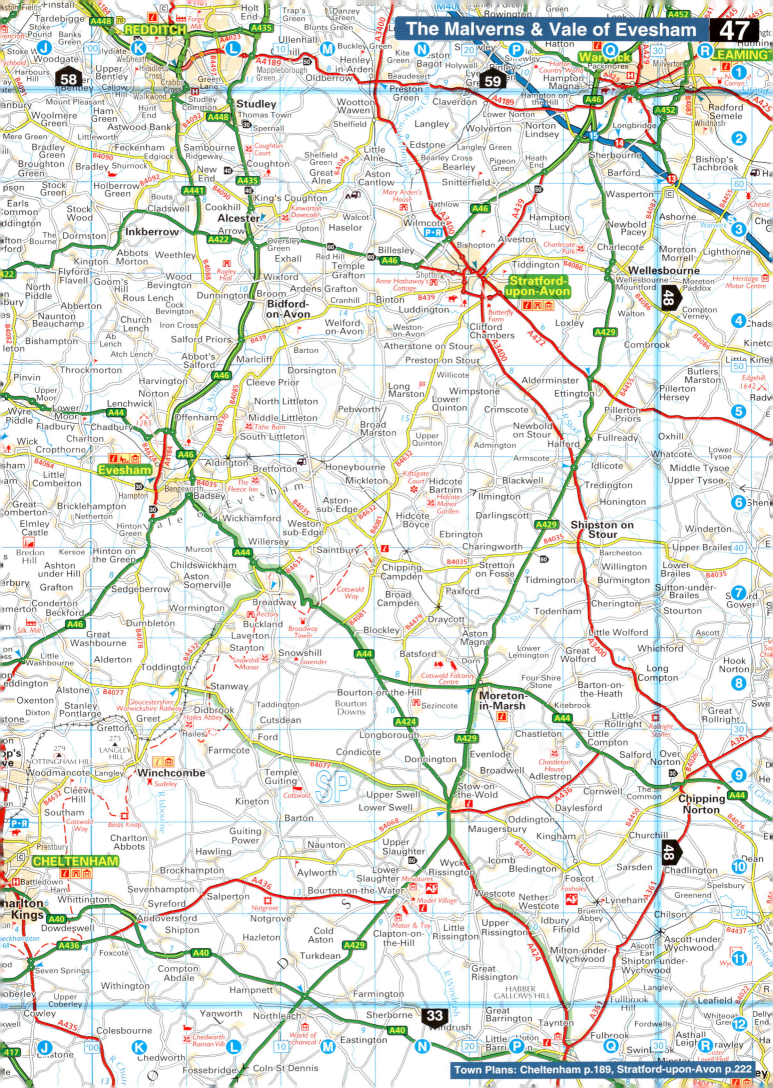

Town Plans: Luton p.205, Watford p.226

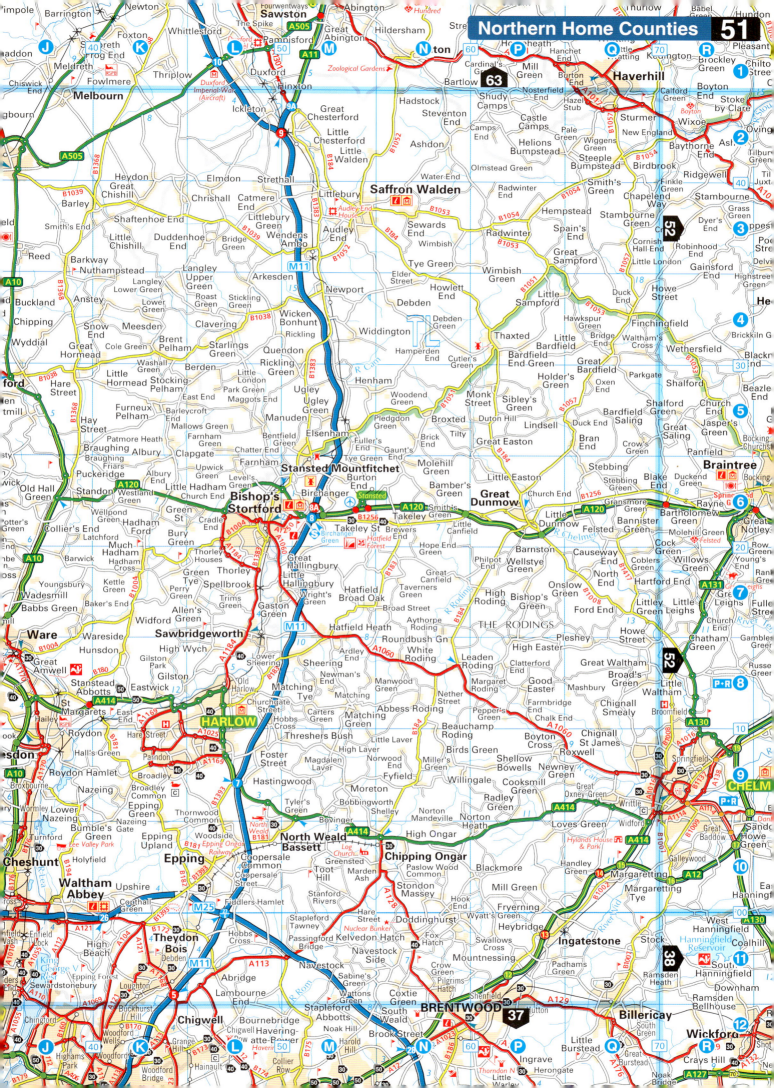

Harwich International Port

HARWICH INTERNATIONAL STATION

PASSENGER & CRUISE TERMINAL

CAR FERRY TERMINAL

CONTAINER TERMINAL

EAST DOCK ROAD

WEST DOCK ROAD

REFINERY ROAD

Parkeston

Harwich Industrial Estate

Superstore

PARKESTON ROUNDABOUT

ST NICHOLAS ROUNDABOUT

STATION ROAD

A120

HARWICH

IPSWICH COLCHESTER

PARKESTON ROAD

Dovercourt

MAIN ROAD

B1352

Upper Dovercourt

FRONK'S ROAD

FRYATT AVENUE

0   400 m

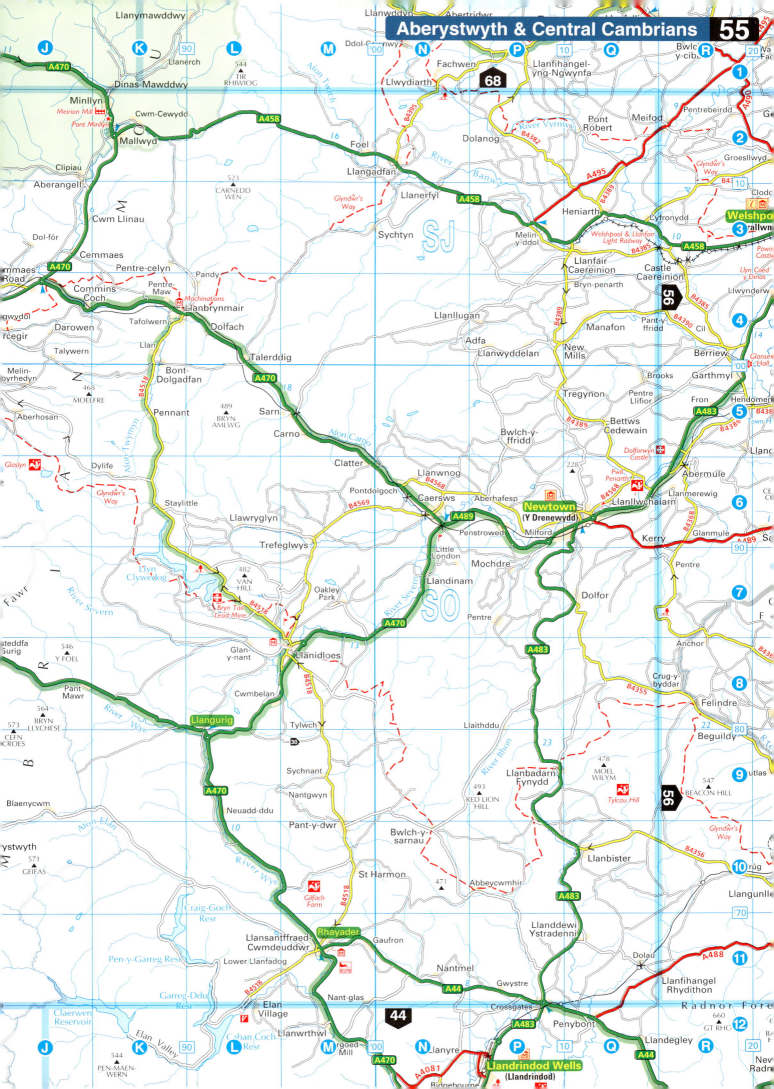

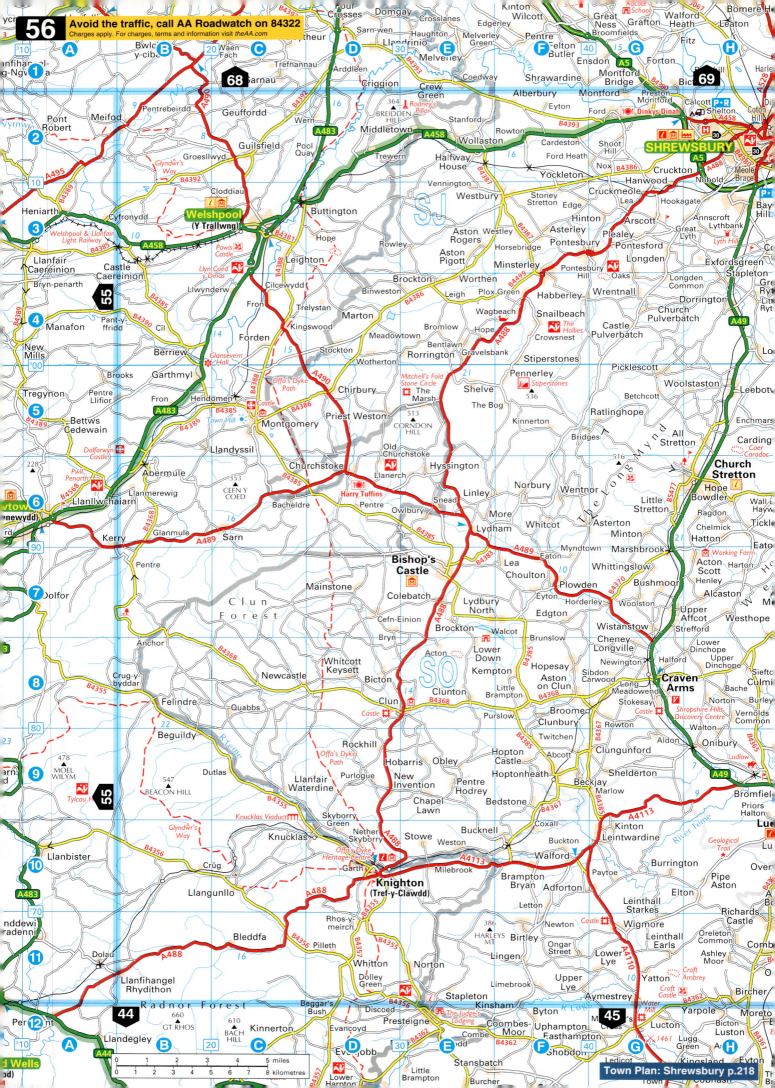

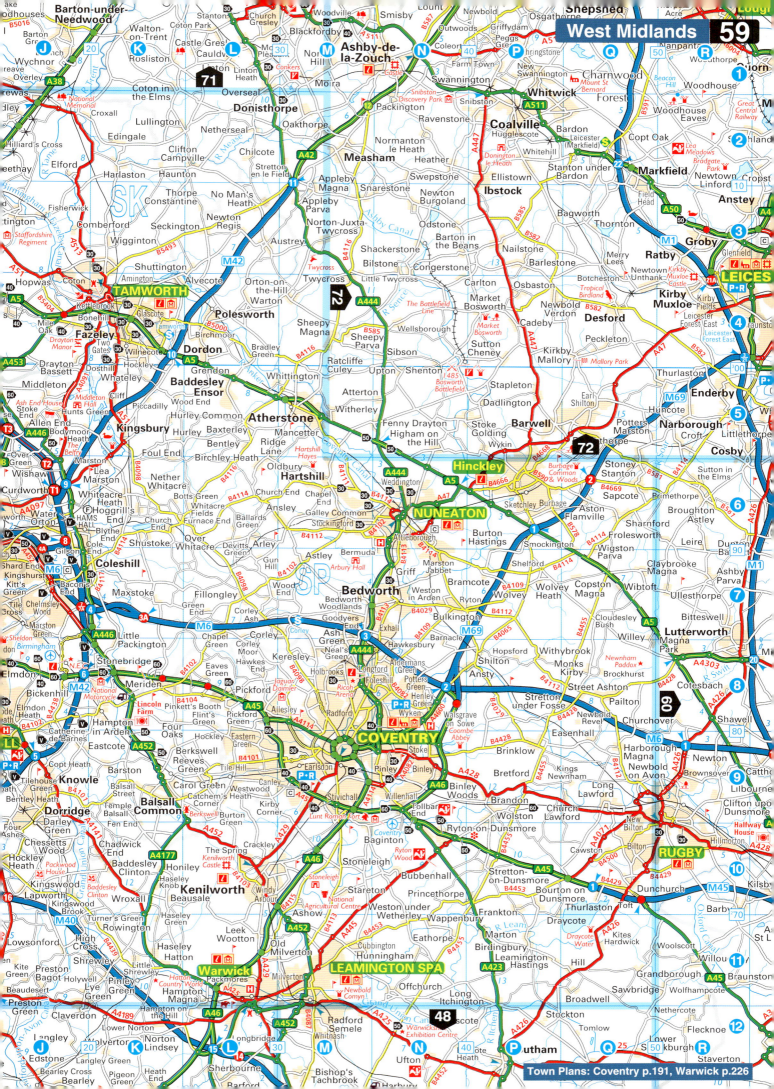

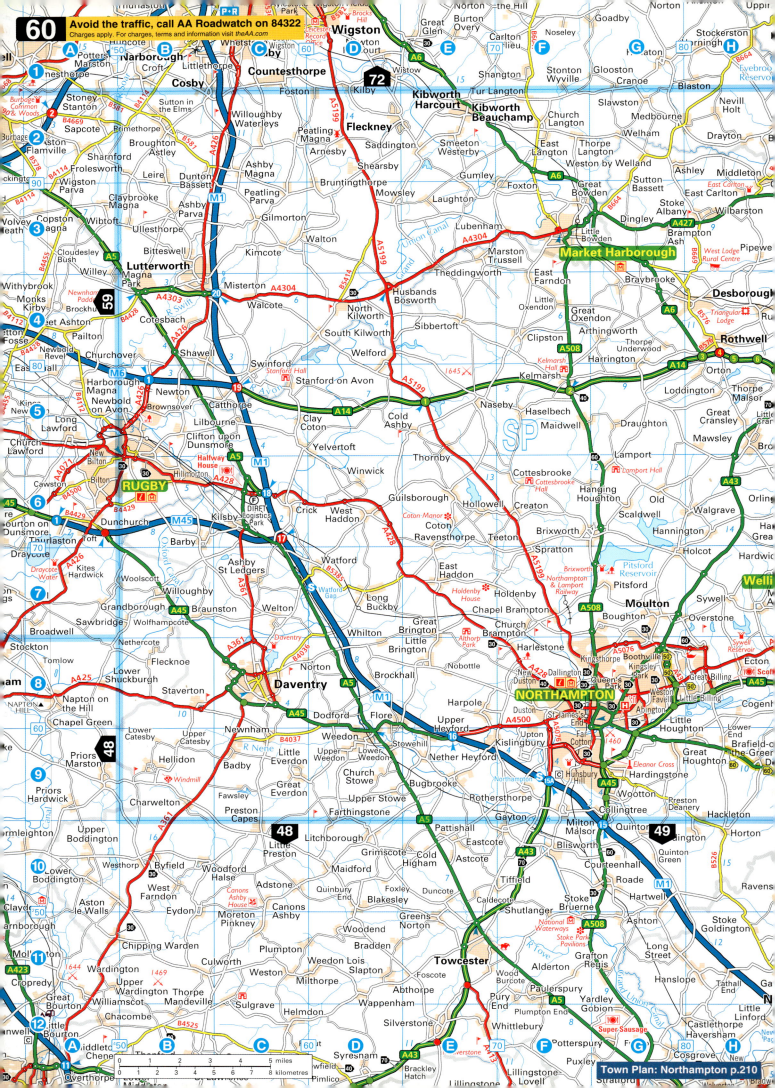

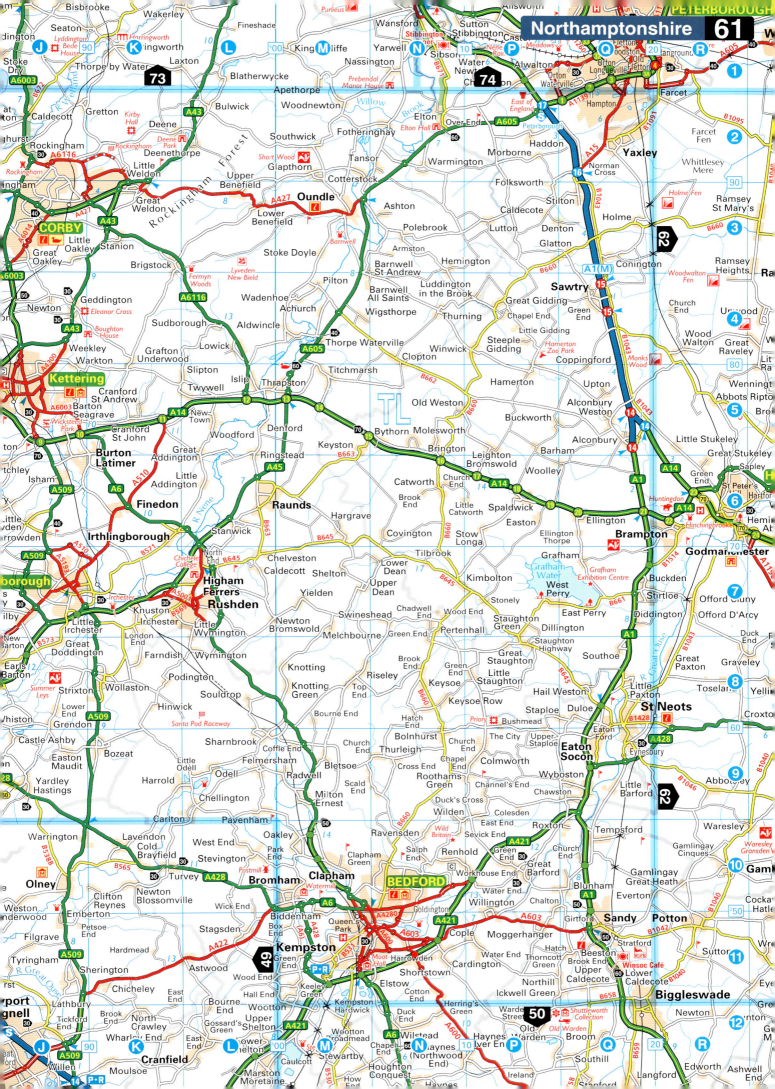

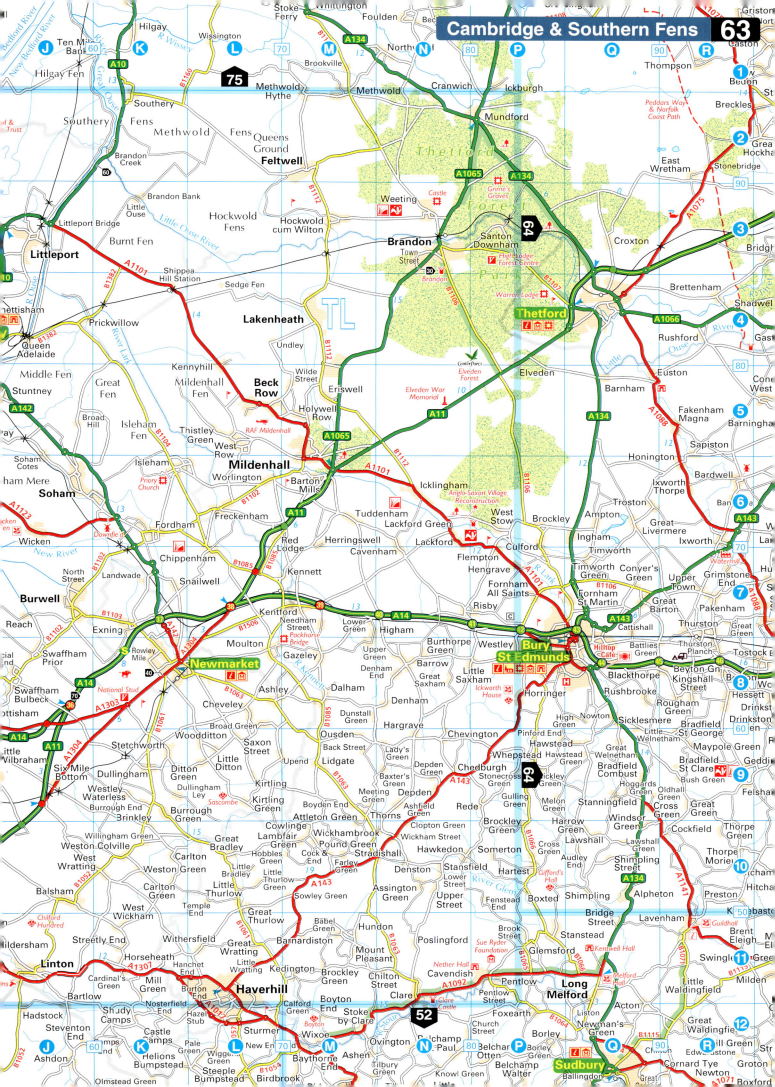

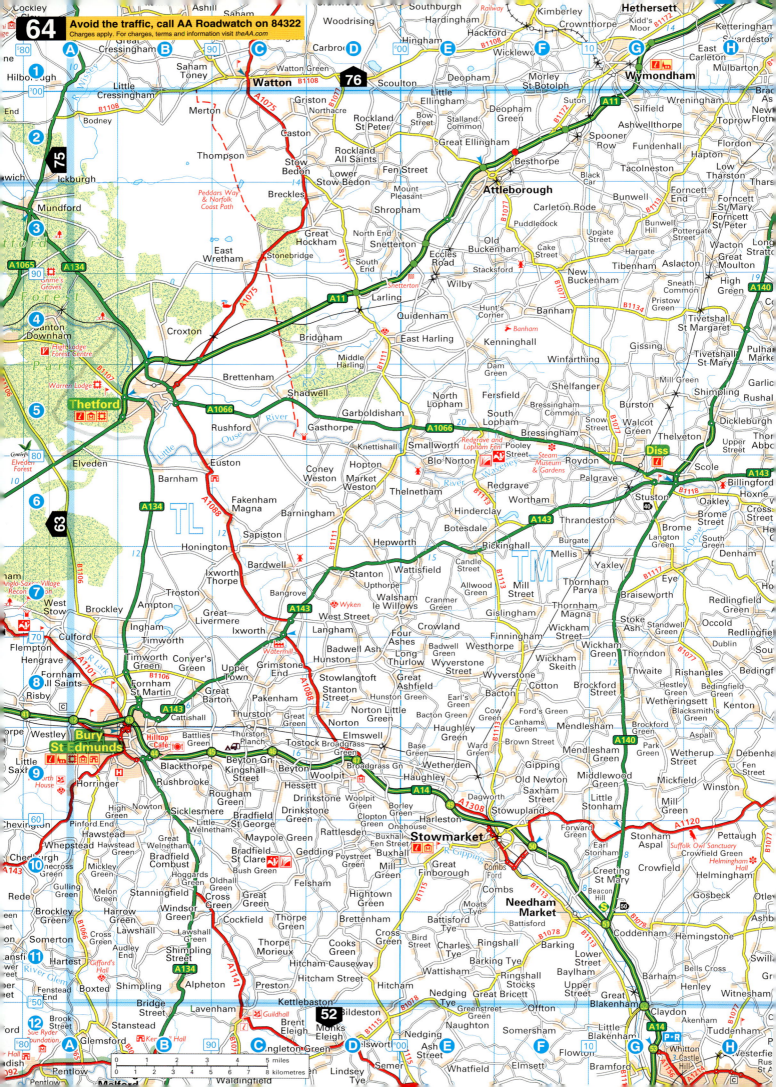

CAERNARFON

BAY

SH

LLEYN PENINSULA

BARDSEY ISLAND

St Mary's

Aberffraw
Llangadwaladr
Malltraeth
Hermon
Bodorgan
Llangaffo
Bodowyr Burial Chamber
B4421
B4419
Bryn...yn
Anglesey Circuit
A4080
Dwyran
Castell Bryn Gwyn
Caer...
Aberffraw Bay
Newborough
Pen-lôn
Anglesey Sea Zoo
Foel Farm Park
A487

Aberffraw Bay Heritage Coast
Malltraeth Bay
Caernarfon
Caernarfon Castle
Welsh Highland Railway
Wa...
A40...

Llanddwyn Island
Llanddwyn Bay
Abermenai Point
Forydd Bay
Airworld
Saron
Bont
Llanwn...

Morfa Dinlle
Dinas Dinlle
Llandwrog
Groeslon
Carmel
Glynllifon Slateworks
Penygroes
Nebo
Nasareth

Aberdesach
Pontllyfni
Llanllyfni
Capeluchaf
Pant Glas
A487

Clynnog-fawr
Gyrn-gôch
Y GYRN-DDU
522
Bryncir
Glan-Dwyfach
B4411

Lleyn Heritage Coast
Trefor
564
YR EIFL
Tre'r Ceiri
Llanaelhaearn
PENINSULA
St Cybi's Well
Llangybi
Rhoslan

Trwyn y Grolech
A499
20
21
Llithfaen
Pistyll
Llwyndyrys
Pencaenewydd

Carreg Ddu
Porth Nefyn
B4417
Fron
B4354
Y Ffor
B4354
Llanarmon
Llanystumdwy
Chwilog
13
M

Morfa Nefyn
Nefyn
Bodfuan
Rhos-fawr
Pennarth Fawr Medieval House

Porth Dinllaen
Groesffordd
Edern
A497
Llannor
Abererch

Porth Ysgaden
Rhos-y-llan
Dinas
371
Carn Fadrum
Efailnewydd
Denio
Pen-ychain

Tudweiliog
LLEYN
A499
7
Pwllheli

Porth Colman
Llaniestyn
Garnfadryn
Rhyd-y-clafdy
B4415
Penrhos

Pen-y-graig
Bryn-mawr
Meyllteyrn
B4417
14
Llanbedrog

Llangwnnadl
Sarn
Botwnnog
Nanhoron
Mynytho
B4413
Trwyn Llanbedrog

Bryncroes
Llandegwning
B4413
17

Rhydlios
Rhoshirwaun
Plas Yn Rhiw
Llangian
St Tudwal's Road

Anelog
Penycaerau
B4413
Y Rhiw
Llanengan
Abersoch

Uwchmynydd
Llanfaelrhys
Sarn Bach
St Tudwal's Island East

Aberdaron
Porth Ysgo
Bwlchtocyn
Marchros
St Tudwal's Island West

Bardsey Sound
Aberdaron Bay
Porth Neigwl or Hell's Mouth
Porth Geiriad

Lleyn Heritage Coast

78

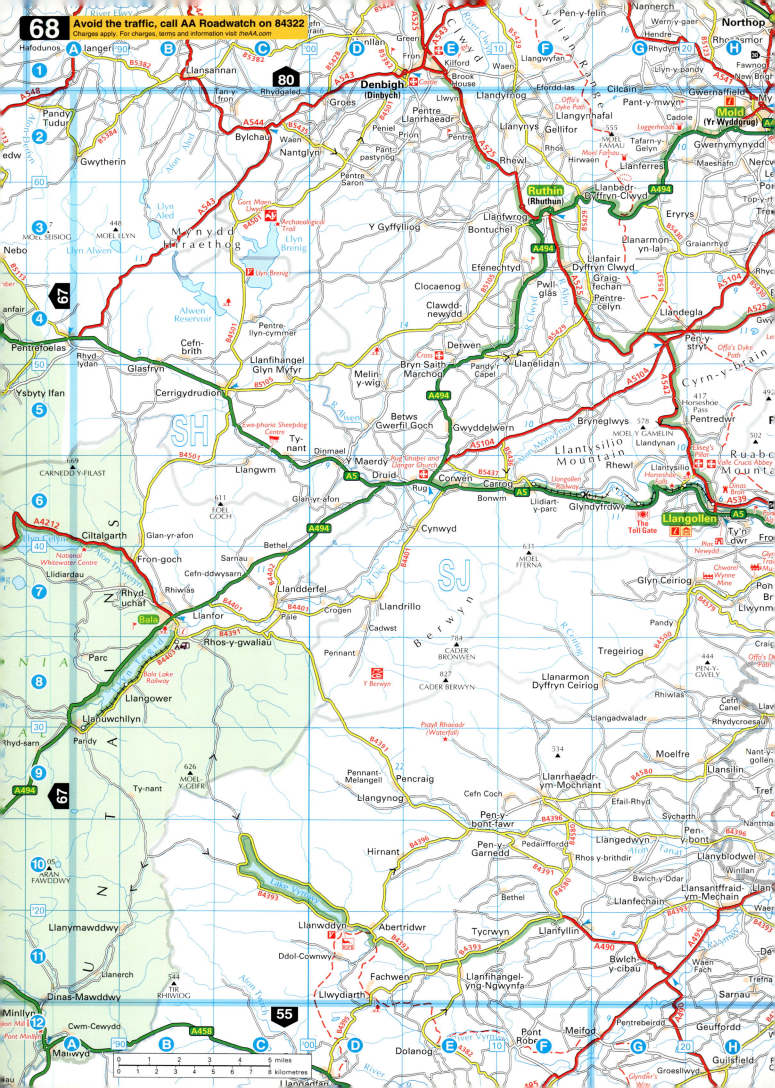

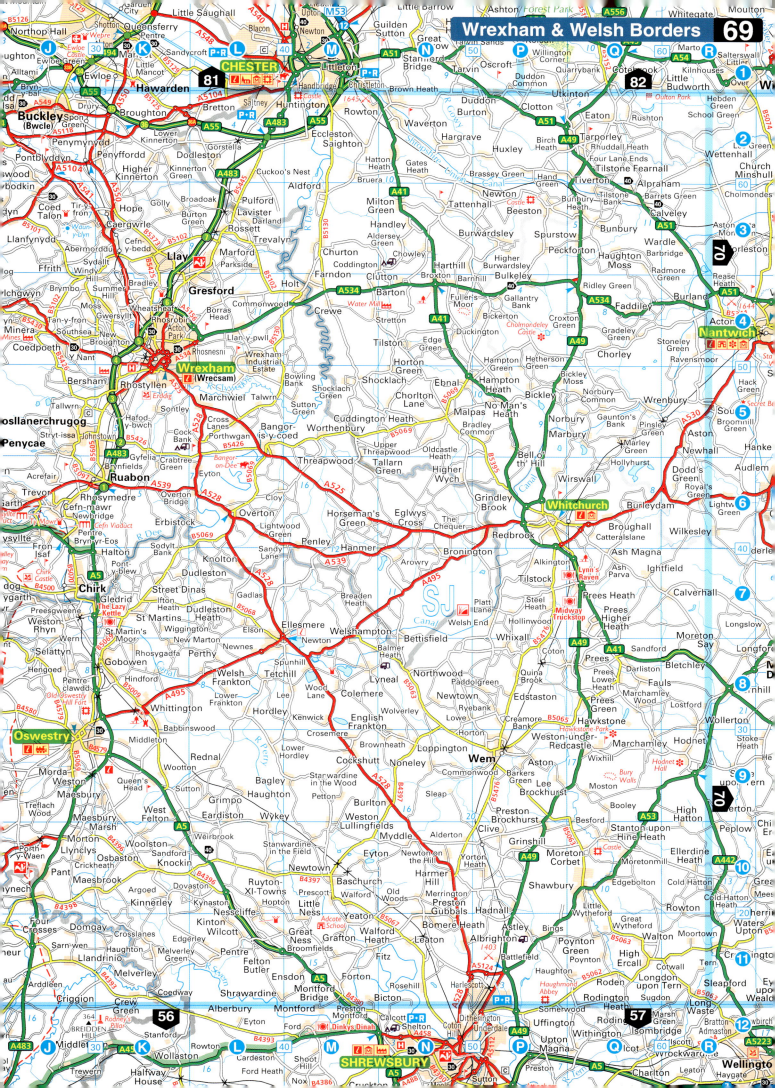

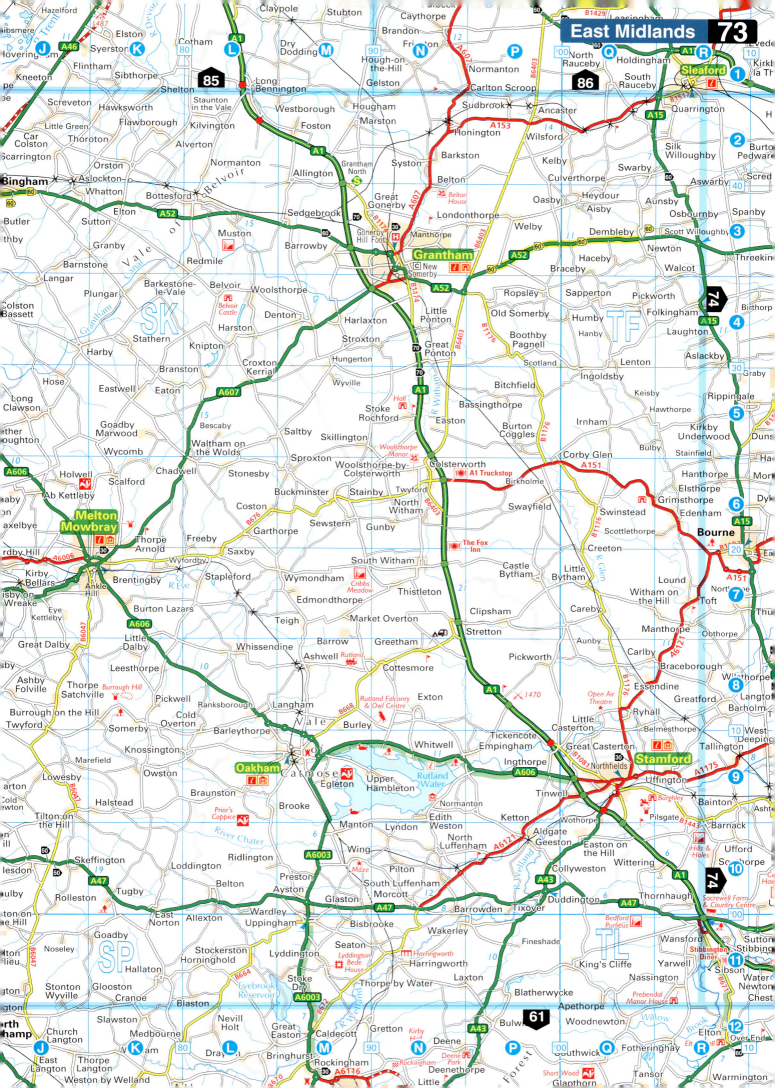

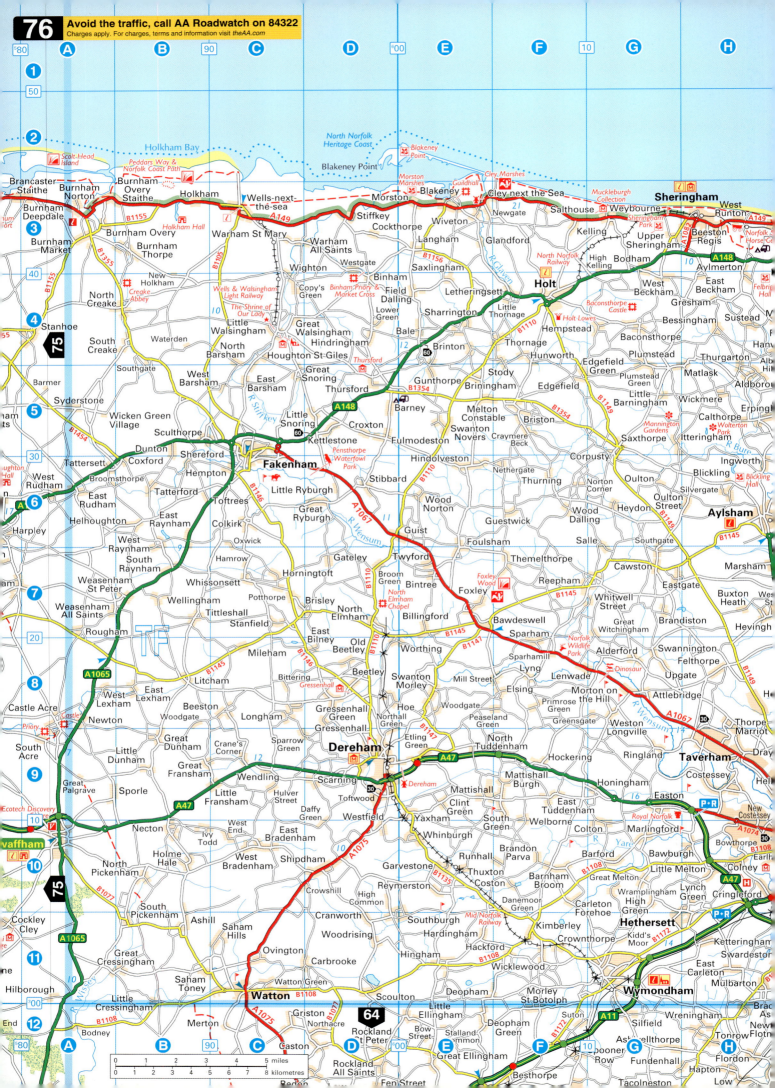

The Skerries

North Anglesey
Heritage Coast

Porth
Wen

Bull
Bay

Amlwch

Point Lyr

CARMEL HEAD

Wylfa
Head

Cemaes
Bay

Llanbadrig

Bull Bay

Llaneilian

Hen
Borth

Cemlyn
Bay

Cemaes

A5025

Burwen

Pentrefelin

Pengorffwysfa

Tregele

Rhosbeirio

Bodewryd

Penysarn

Nebo

Holyhead
Bay

Llanfairynghornwy

Llanfechell

Llanflewyn

Rhosgoch

Penysarn

Dulas

Church
Bay

Llanrhyddlad

Carreglefn

Gadfa

City
Dulas

Dublin

Llanfaethlu

Llanbabo

Llyn
Alaw

Rhosybol

Brynrefail

Rhos

Dublin
Dún Laoghaire

Porth
Tywynmawr

Llanddeusant

Gwredog

Capel
Parc

Din-Llgwy

Llandyfrydog

North Stack

Breakwater
Quarry

Llanfwrog

Stryd-y-
Facsen

Elim

Llantrisant

Llanerchymedd

Maenaddwyn

Gogarth
Bay

RSPB

Holyhead Mountain

Penrhos-
Feilw

Holyhead
(Caergybi)

Llanfachraeth

Llanfigael

Llyn
Llywenan

Llechcynfarwy

Hebron
Bachau

Capel
Coch

Brynteg

South Stack

Hut Group

Penrhos

Llanynghenedl

Pen-llyn

A N G L E S E Y

Tregaian

Holyhead Mountain
Heritage Coast

South
Stack

Kingsland

Trefignath

Valley

A5025

Bodedern

Trefor

Llangwyllog

Llanddy

Penrhyn Mawr

Porth
Dafarch

B4545

A55

Caergeiliog

Bryngwran

Llynfaes

Bodffordd

Ceini
Reservoir

Rhosmeirch

Trearddur Bay

Four Mile
Bridge

Llanfihangel
yn Nhowyn

Llechylched

Gwalchmai

Oriel
Ynys Mon

Ta

HOLY ISLAND

Llanfair-yn-Neubwll

Capel Gwyn

Heneglwys

A5

Llangefni

Rhoscolyn

Plas
Cymyran

RSPB

Dothan

Anglesey

A5114

Rhoscolyn
Head

Cymyran
Bay

Ty Newydd

Pencarnisiog

Cerrigceinwen

Llangristiolus

Pentre Berw

SH

Rhosneigr

A4080

Llanfaelog

Bryn Du

Dim Dryfol

Hen Blas

Gaerwen

Barclodiad
y Gawres

Bethel

Capel Mawr

Porth Trecastell

Trefdraeth

B4422

Llanddaniel Fab

Bodowyr
Burial Chamber

Aberffraw

Llangadwaladr

Malltraeth

Llangaffo

Caer Leb

Anglesey
Circuit

Hermon

A4080

Brynsiencyn

Bodorgan

Castell
Bryn Gwyn

Aberffraw
Bay

Newborough

Pen-lôn

Anglesey
Sea Zoo

Foel Farm
Park

Aberffraw Bay
Heritage Coast

Caernarfo

Malltraeth Bay

Llanddwyn Island

Llanddwyn
Bay

Caernarfo
Castle

Port Plan: Holyhead *p.13*

0   1   2   3   4   5 miles
0 1 2 3 4 5 6 7 8 kilometres

Llandudno

0   200 m

Great Orme
Tramway

Great Orme
Tramway

The Grand
Hotel

Llandudno
Bay

TABOR
HILL

Victoria
Station

War
Memorial

SOUTH PARADE

GLODDAETH AVENUE

DEGANWY

MOSTYN STREET

THE PARADE

A546

A546

B5115

Town
Hall

St John's

Our Lady Star
of the Sea

Holy
Trinity

Victoria

Medical
Centre

MOSTYN BROADWAY

CONWAY ROAD

CYLCH-TUDUR

Swimming
Pool

Venue
Cymru

St Paul's

Mostyn
Gallery

Parc Llandudno
Retail Park

Mostyn
Champneys
Retail Park

MOSTYN AVE

LLANDUDNO
STATION

Police
Station

Magistrates'
Court

Fire &
Ambulance
Station

Bowling
Alley

CLARENCE

CLARENCE DRIVE

CAE CLYD

Ysgol
Tudno

AVENUE

TRINITY

Superstore

CONWAY ROAD

B5115

A470

Ysgol Craig
Y Don

Ysgol
Ffordd
Dyffryn

Coach

Ysgol Morfa
Rhianedd

Ysgol John
Bright

Llandudno
FC

BETWS-Y-COED

SH

Seawatch Centre

Moelfre

Llanallgo

Marian-glas

Benllech

Red Wharf Bay

Red Wharf
Bay

Llanddona

Pentraeth

A5025

B5109

Penmon Priory,
Cross & Dovecote

Caim

Toll

Penmon

Puffin Island

Black Point

Llangoed

Llanfaes

Gaol & Courthouse

Beaumaris
Castle

Beaumaris

Llansadwrn

Llandegfan

A545

Menai
Bridge
(Porthaethwy)

Llanfair P G

Britannia
Bridge

Penrhos
garnedd

Capel-y-graig

Felinheli

Waen-wen

Glasinfryn

Pentir

Rhyd-y-
groes

Tregarth

Sling

Waen-pentir

Bethesda

Gerlan

Rachub

Llanllechid

Tal-y-
bont

Llandygai

Penrhyn

Bangor

A55

Abergwyngregyn

Aber
Waterfall

MOEL
WNION

Y DROSGL

757

FOEL-FRAS
942

Dolgarrog

Pont Dolgarrog

Llanbedr-y-Cennin

Tal-y-Bont

Caerhun

Castell

Ty'n-y-Groes

Rowen

TAL-Y-FAN
610

SNOWDONIA

NATIONAL

PARK

Dwygyfylchi

Penmaenmawr

Garizim

Penmaen

Nant-y-pandy

Gorddinog

Llanfairfechan

Conwy
Bay

GREAT ORMES HEAD

Great Orme
Heritage Coast

Little Ormes Head

Llandudno

Deganwy

Llanrhos

Penrhyn-
side

Penrhyn
Bay

Rhôs-on-Sea
Colwyn Bay
(Bae Colwyn)

Llandrillo
-yn-Rhos

Pydew

Esgyryn

Mochdre

Old
Colwyn

A55

A547

Llanelian-
yn-Rhos

Bryn-
y-Maen

Dolwen

Llysfaen

Conwy

Conwy
Castle

Tywyn

**Llandudno
Junction**

A470

A55

B5381

Llansanffraid
Glan Conwy

Henryd

Capelulo

Bodnant

Graig

Tal-y-Cafn

Eglwysbach

Pentre'r
Felin

B5106

B5113

Vale of Conwy

Maenan

Hafodunos

Trofarth

River Elwy

Llanddoget

Llyn
Eigiau

Afon Anafon

Afon Caseg

Afon Dulyn

Ogwen Bank

Mynydd
Llandygai

Rhiwlas

Penisarwaun

Rhiwen
Deiniolen

1062
CARNEDD
LLEWELYN

1044
CARNEDD
DAFYDD

923

Trefriw Woollen Mill

Llanrwst

Pentre-
tafarn-y-fedw

67

A5

80

Afon Ddu

A548

Llanddoget

Gwytherin

Melin-
continued to map references J K L M N P Q R with grid numbers 60 70 80 90

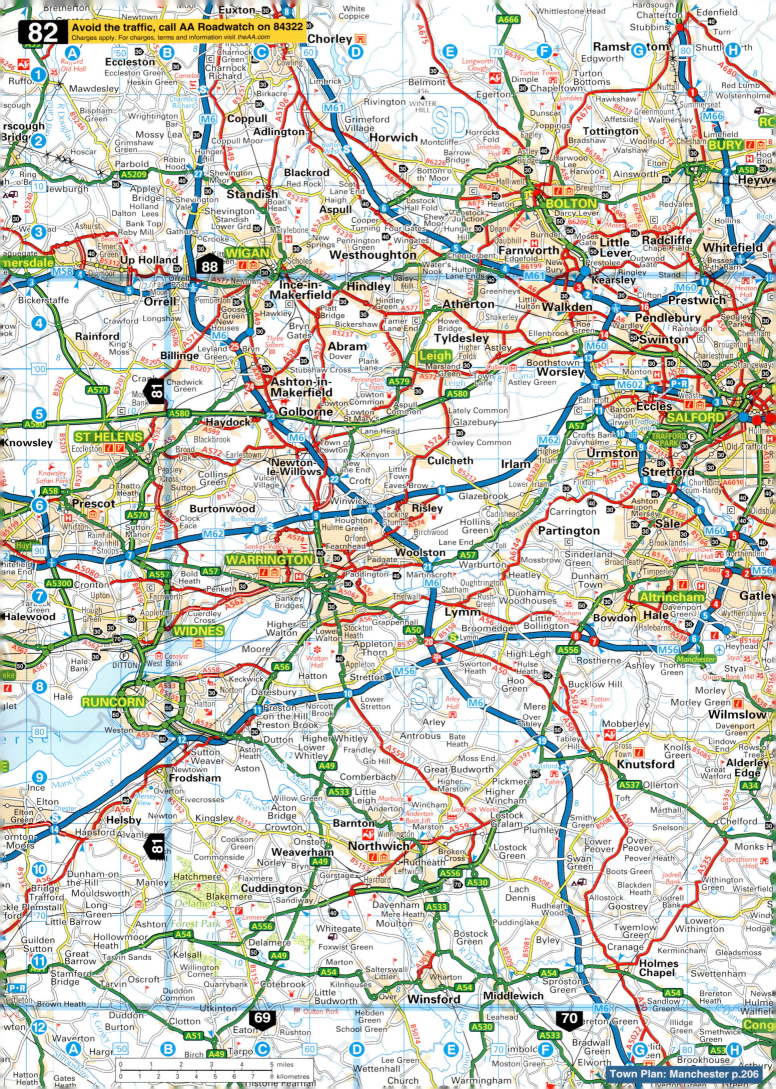

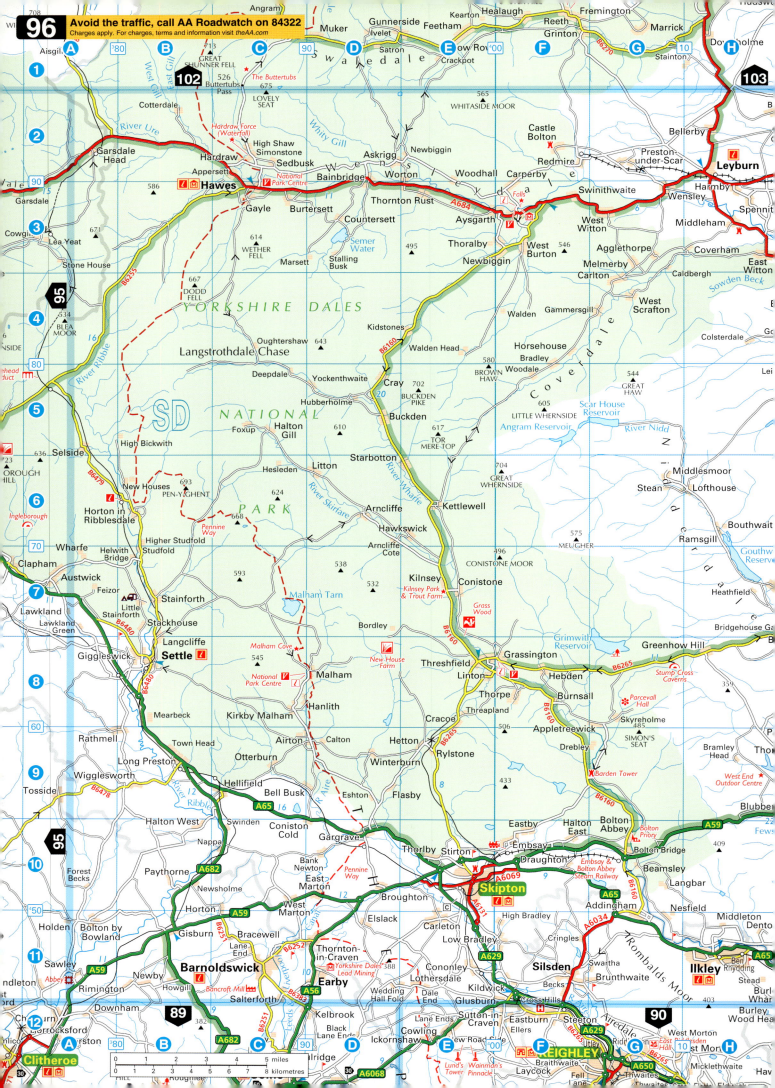

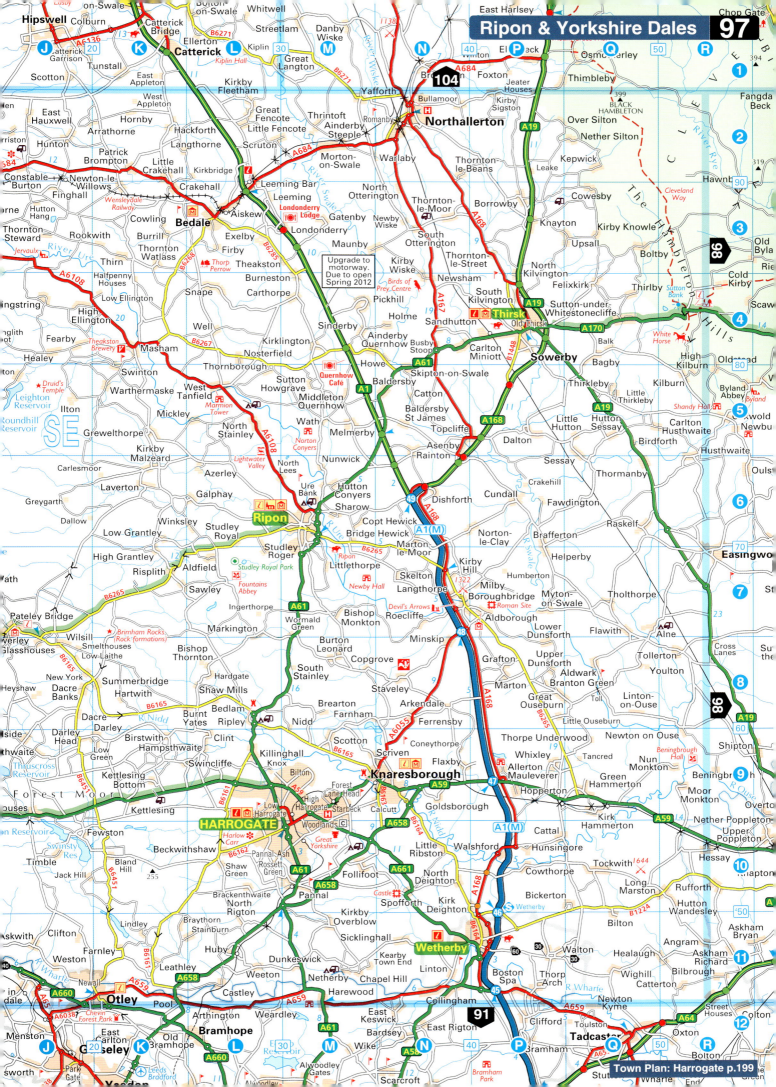

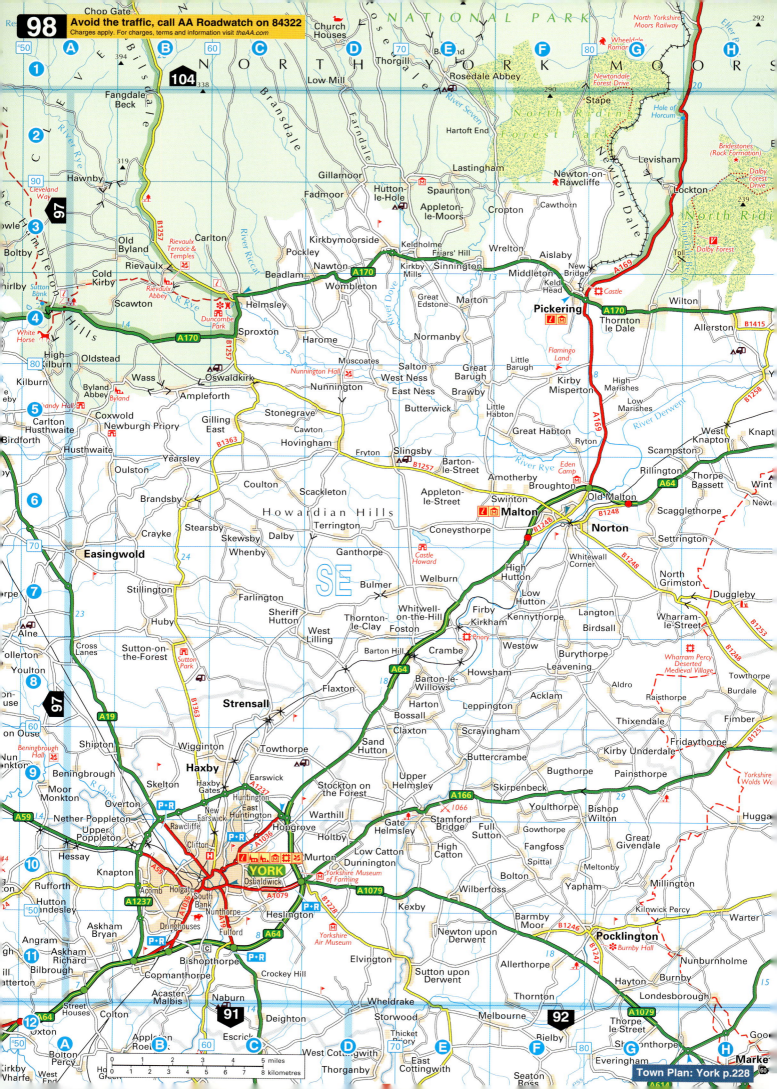

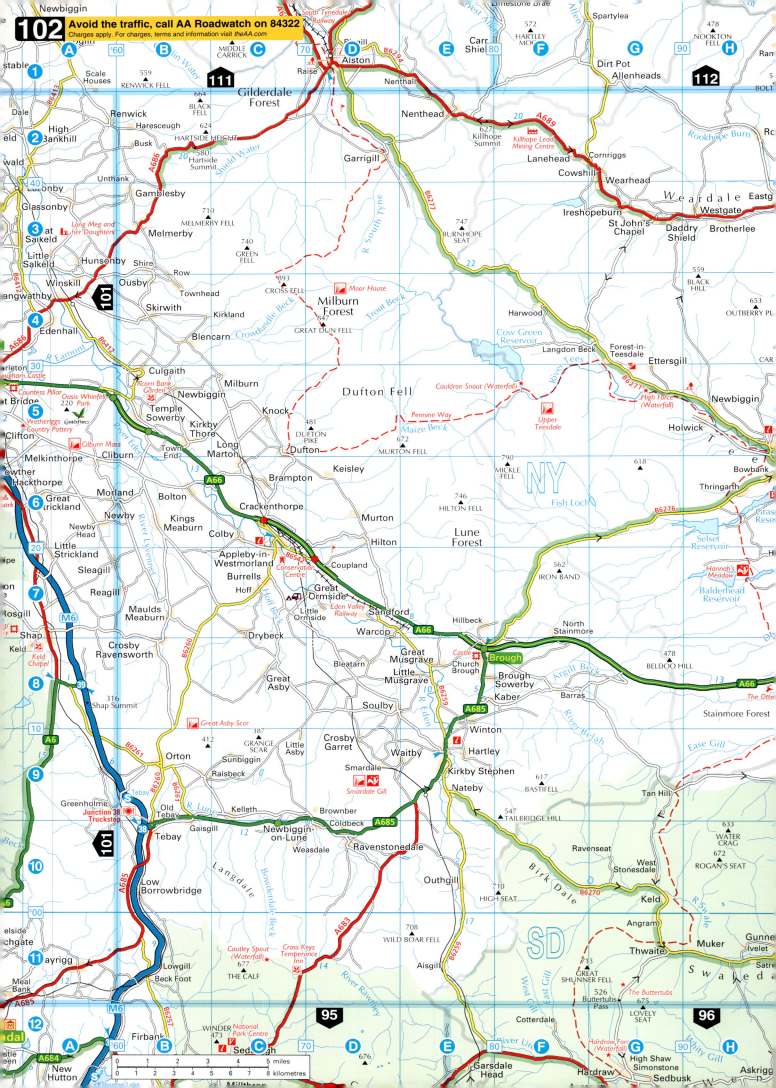

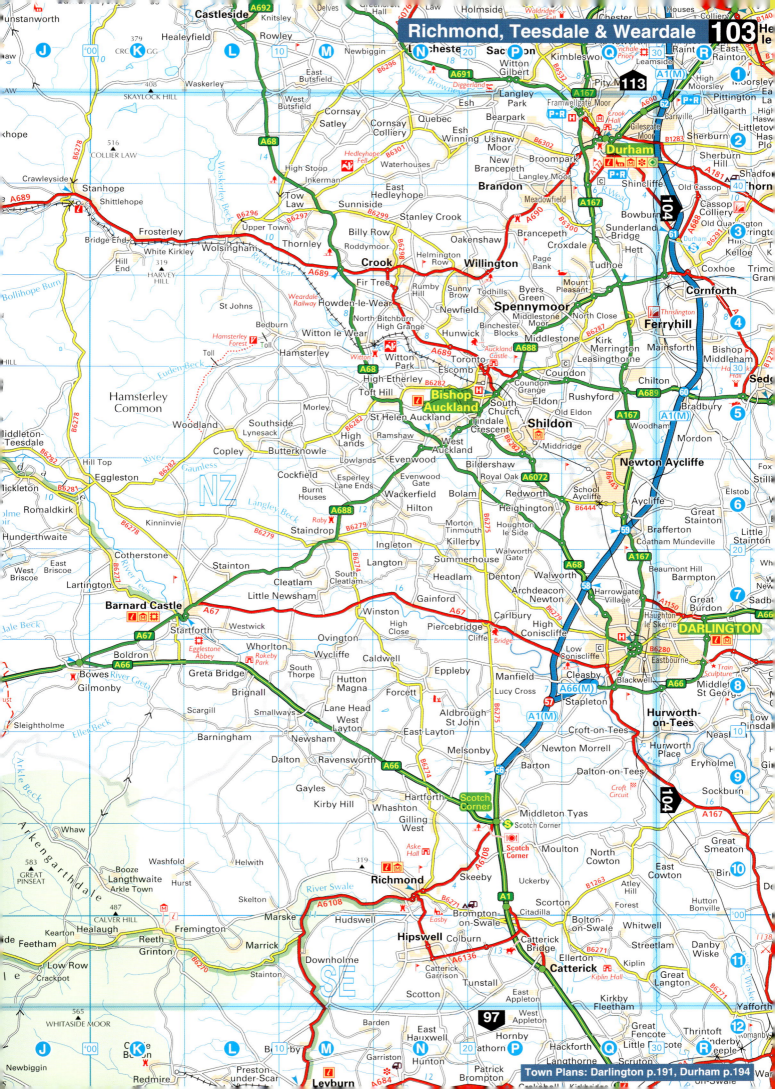

Saltburn-by-the-Sea
Saltburn Smugglers
Brotton
Skelton
New Brotton
New Skelton
North Skelton
Kilton
Lingdale
Kilton Thorpe
Stanghow
Woodhill
Liverton
A171
Moorsholm
Gerrick
Scaling
B1366
B1266
Carlin How
Skinningrove
Upton
Boulby
Loftus
Liverton Mines
Dalehouse
Easington
Staithes
Heritage Centre
Port Mulgrave
Hinderwell
Roxby
Newton Mulgrave
Runswick
Borrowby
Kettleness
Runswick Bay
Goldsborough
Ellerby
B1266
A174
Lythe
Overdale Wyke
Hummersea Scar
North Yorkshire and Cleveland Heritage Coast
NZ
Scaling Dam
Mickleby
West Barnby
East Barnby
Sandsend
Sandsend Wyke
Whitby
Raithwaite
Dunsley
Newholm
Abbey
Saltwick Bay
Ugthorpe
Hutton Mulgrave
A171
Ruswarp
Stainsacre
The Moors Centre
301
Danby
Stonegate
Aislaby
Briggswath
Sneaton
High Hawsker
Castleton
Ainthorpe
Lealholm Side
Egton
Sleights
Ugglebarnby
Low Hawsker
B1447
Ness Point or North Cheek
Lealholm
The Green
Iburndale
Sneatonthorpe
Robin Hood's Bay
River Esk
Glaisdale
Grosmont
Street
Egton Bridge
Key Green
Littlebeck
B1416
Raw
Fylingthorpe
Robin Hood's Bay
Vesterdale
Danby Bottom
Esk Dale
Old Peak or South Cheek
NORTH YORK MOORS
Beck Hole
A169
A171
Ravenscar
326
PIKE HILL
Goathland
369
20
Church Houses
NATIONAL PARK
North Yorkshire Moors Railway
292
Eller Beck
Staintondale
Shire Horse Centre
Hayburn Wyke
Rosedale
Low Bell End
Wheeldale Roman Road
Harwood Dale
Cloughton Newlands
Thorgill
ROSEDALE
Newtondale Forest Drive
Cloughton Wyke
w Mill
Rosedale Abbey
290
Stape
NORTH RIDING
Hole of Horcum
20
99
Cloughton
TA
Cromer Point
River Seven
rtoft End
LASTINGHAM
NEW
Levisham
MOORS
Bridestones (Rock Formation)
Bickley
Toll
Broxa
Silpho
Bur ton
Langdale
Hackness
Suffield
Cleveland Way

A '90 B C '00 D E 10 F G 20 H

1

80

Ballantrae
Heronsford
Water of Tig
Quisk River
Barr

114

Larne
Larne
Belfast
Belfast

2

Currarie Port
321
CARLOCK HILL
437
BENERAIRD
387
ALTIMEG HILL
305
BENBRAKE HILL

Milleur Point

Glen App

Southern Upland Way

3

Corsewall Point
Lady Bay
(Mar-Oct)
Barnhills
Portencalzie
Glenwhilly
Laggangairn Standing Stones

70

Kirkcolm
B738
Stena Line to relocate from Stranraer Autumn 2011
Cairnryan
17
Penwhirn Reservoir
Main Water of Luce
Cross Water of Luce

4

B738
Ervie
Low Barbeth
Loch Connell
A718
Beoch Burn
A77
Braid Fell
New Luce
271
ARTFIELD FELL

B998

THE

Low Salchrie

Knocknain
Leswalt
B7043
Loch Ryan
Innermessan
Black Loch
Castle Kennedy
White Loch
Chlenry
764
CRAIG FELL

5

60

RHINS

Balgracie
Castle of St John
Stranraer
Aird
A77
A751
A75
10
Castle Kennedy
Glenwhan
Dunragit
Glenluce Abbey
Glenluce
60

Auchnotteroch
Portslogan
B738
8
OF
Lochans
181
CAIRN PAT
Kildrochet House
Piltanton Burn
B7084
Whitecrook
Ringdoo Point
Milton

6

Broadsea Bay
Black Head
A77
14
B7077
A716
B7084
Stairhaven
A747

7

Portpatrick
Stoneykirk
B7042
North Milmain
18
19
B7084
Auchenmalg
Mull of Sinniness

50

GALLOWAY
Sandhead

8

Cairngarroch
Kirkmadrine Stones
Money Head
High Ardwell
Ardwell Bay
Ardwell House
Ardwell
Chapel Rossan
L U C E   B A

9

WAY
Drumbreddon
Balgowan
Logan

Port Logan Bay
A716

40

Port Logan
Garrochtrie
B7065
Kilstay

10

Clanyard Bay
Kirkmaiden
Drummore
Killiness Point

Laggantalluch Head
Barncorkrie
High Drummore
B7041
Maryport

11

Drumnaglaur
Cardryne
Cardrain
West Cairngaan
RSPB

30

MULL OF GALLOWAY

12

0 1 2 3 4 5 miles
0 1 2 3 4 5 6 7 8 kilometres

Port Plan: Stranraer Ferry Port *p.13*

NW

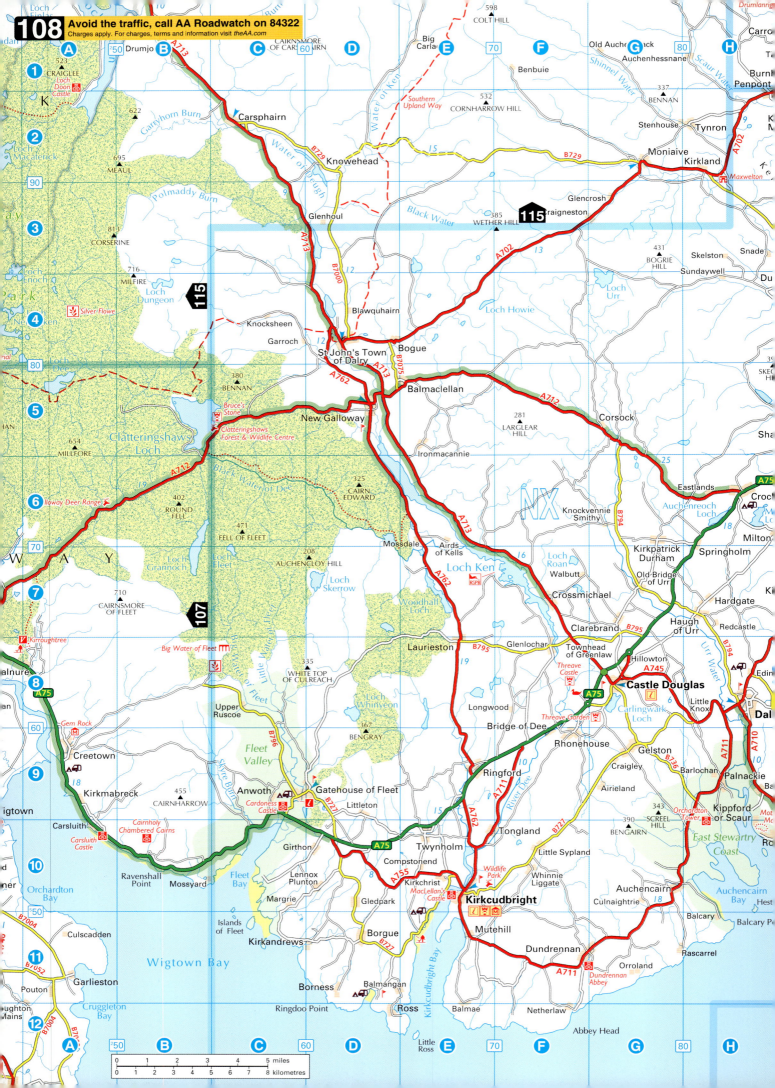

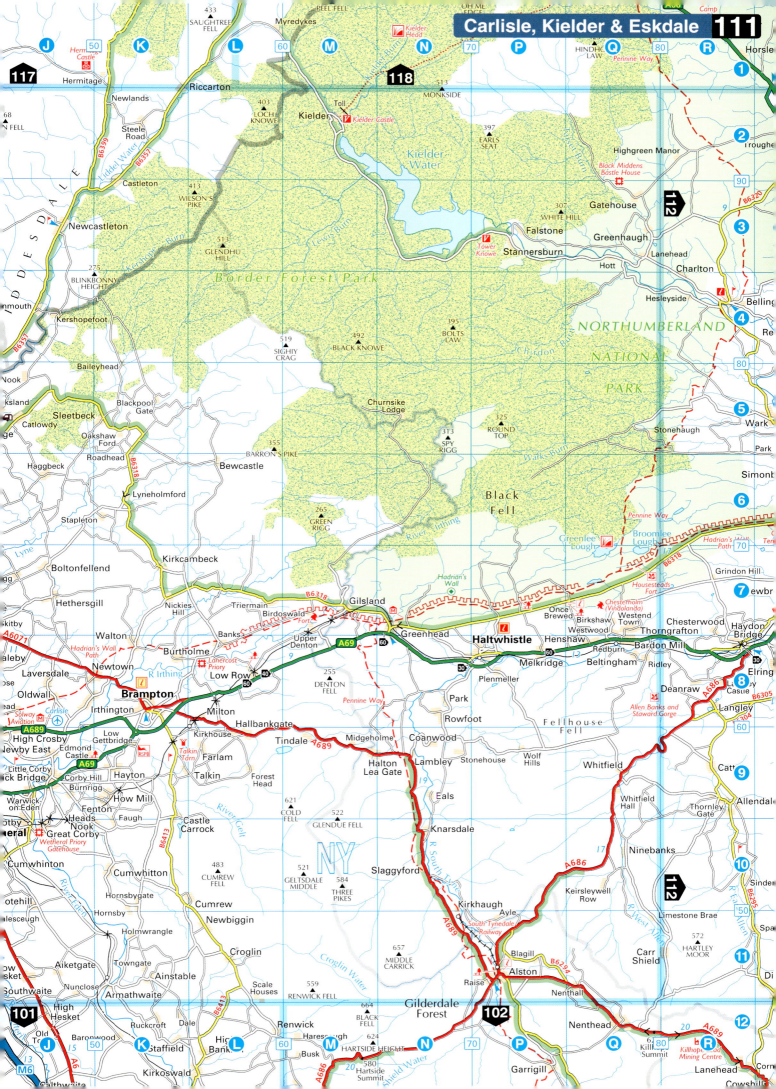

124

121

NS

NX

C A R R I C

Gallowa

Forest Pa

106

Margnaheglish

Holy Island

Kingscross
Knockenkelly

Whiting Bay

Largymore

Largybeg

Kingscross Head

Idonan

Barassie

Troon
Royal Troon

Loans

Monkton

Prestwick

New Prestwick

Whitletts

Ayr
Ayr Bay

Wallacetown

Doonfoot

Heads of Ayr
Heads of Ayr

Burns Cottage

Alloway

Burns Monument

Doonholm

Fisherton

Dunure

Drumshang

Croy Brae
(Electric Brae)

Knoweside

Culzean Bay

Culzean Castle
& Country Park

Pennyglen

Maidenhead Bay

Whitefaulds

Maidens

Maybole

Turnberry

Kirkoswald

Souter Johnnie's Cottage

Crossraguel Abbey

Turnberry Bay

Dipple

Wallacetown

Kilgrammie

Roan of Craigoch

Old Dailly

Dailly

Girvan

Dounepark

Penkill

Woodland

Pinminnoch

GREY HILL

Pinmore

Barr

Knockeen

Balloch

Dalquhairn

Balligmorrie

Lendalfoot

Bennane Head

Colmonell

Pinwherry

Muck Water

River Stinchar

Ballantrae

Heronsford

Water of Tig

Barrhill

Feoch Burn

Lochton

Glen Trool Lodge

Bruce Memorial

Glentrool Village

Bargrennan

Freebank

Drumlamford

Dundonald

Craigie

Symington

Bogend

Helenton

Wallace Monument Tower

Tarbolton

Mossblown

St Quivox

Annbank

Gadgirth

Belmont

Joppa

Coylton

Barbieston

Martnaham Loch

Hollybush

Minishant

Dalrymple

Culroy

Grimmet

Guiltreehill

Patna

Rankin

Kirkmichael

Threave

Crosshill

Straiton

KEIRS HILL

MARATZ HILL

GARLEFFIN FELL
Linfern Loch

Tallaminnock

Loch Bradan

POLMADDIE HILL

SHALLOCH ON MINNOCH

KIRRIEREOCH HILL

MERRICK

GARWALL HILL

Loch Moan

Loch Recar

Loch Trool

LAMACHAN HILL

CARLOCK HI

PENERAIRD

DRUMFAD HILL

Drumlamford

A scale bar reads: 0 to 5 miles / 0 to 8 kilometres

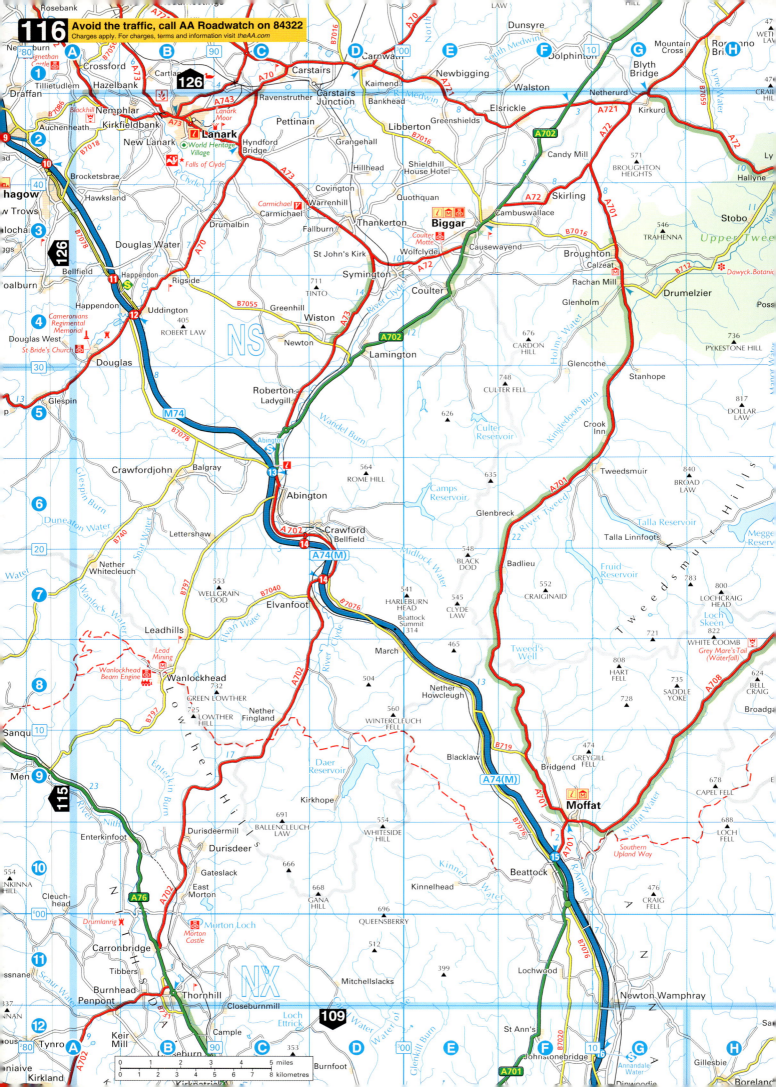

Spot

J K L M N P Q R

Eddleston
Fountainhall
Torquhan
Killochyett
Stow
Boon
Legerwo
127 **128**
651
BLACKHOPE SCAR
425
DUN LAW
B6362
Thir ne
1
MELDON
427
Cross Kirk (ruin)
Peebles
621
WHITEHOPE LAW
659
WINDLESTRAW LAW
Colquhar
Bowland
Nether Blainslie
West Morriston
2
A703
Kailzie
Kings Muir
Neidpath
Kirkburn
Cardrona
A72
Walkerburn
Blackhaugh
12
Torwoodlee
A72
Galashiels
Harmony and Priorwood Gardens
A68
Earlston
3
521
BLACK KNOWE
Borders railway due to open 2014
MEIGLE HILL
423
B6356
Redpath
Kirkton Manor
Castlehill
Robert Small's Printing Works
Innerleithen
River Tweed
Clovenfords
Caddonfoot
Langlee
Tweedbank
Gattonside
Abbey
B6360
Newstead
Scott's
Wall
Mon
Traquair
566
MINCHMUIR
NT
Fairnilee
THREE BRETHERN
464
A707
B7060
Darnick
Abbotsford
Melrose
422
Trimontium
Eildon and Lead
Dryburgh
Abbey
4
742
DUN RIG
426
PEAT LAW
Yarrowford
A7
EILDON HILLS
Newtown St Boswells
St Boswells
M
A708
Yarrow
Yarrow Water
Philiphaugh
B7039
A7
Selkirk
A699
Whitlaw Mosses
Bowden
Camieston
Longnev
5
696
BLACK LAW
629
Douglas Burn
Yarrow Feus
Bowhill
Aikwood Tower
B7009
Hartwoodmyres
A707
Midlem
Lilliesleaf
Riddell
Belses
B6453
B6359
Greenhouse
Bloomfiel
B64
Chesters
6
Cappercleuch
St Marys Loch
Gordon Arms Hotel
Sundhope
513
Ettrickbridge
E t t r i c k   F o r e s t
Ashkirk
B6400
Harelaw
276
MINTO
Newton
Tibbie Shiels Inn
Gilmanscleuch
B7009
15
A7
12
Clarilaw
Horsleyhill
B6359
B6405
20
Spittal-on-Rule
7
Chapelhope
Loch of the Lowes
B709
466
MOSSBRAE HEIGHT
Hellmoor Loch
Ale Water
Appletreehall
Denholm
Be
Tushielaw Inn
B717
Redfordgreen
Borthwickshiels
Roberton
Burnfoot
A698
A6088
Cauldmill
424
RUBERS LAW
Bonchester Bridge
8
BONCHE HILL
22
Birkhill
Ettrickhill
Hopehouse
Ettrick
Buccleuch
Borthwickbrae
Burnfoot
B711
Chisholme
Wilton Dean
Hawick
Whitlaw
Hobkirk
10
498
LAW KNEIS
Deanburnhaugh
Hoscote
Newmill
River Teviot
Stobs Castle
WOFFEE EAD
Crag
9
550
BLACK KNOWE
B709
443
THE PIKE
423
CRIB LAW
Borthwick Water
347
Teindside
392
BERRY FELL HILL
393
B6357
92
RICK EN
16
Falnash
417
T E V I O T
Caerlanrig
Teviothead
A7
THE PIKE
462
507
WINDBURGH HILL
118
10
Davington
White Esk
476
STOCK HILL
Rae Burn
23
20
00
Johnstone
Samye Ling Monastery
Fort
Mosspaul Hotel
594
WISP HILL
608
CAULDCLEUCH HEAD
433
SAUGHTREE FELL
Myred
11
Eskdalemuir
NY
Clerkhill
598
TUDHOPE HILL
Hermitage Castle
Riccarton
110 **111**
492
BROAD HEAD
Burnfoot
Hermitage
Newlands
60
yford
Castle O'er
Effgill
30
Georgefield
A7
Arkleton
21
ROAN FELL
568
Ste Roa
L0 KNOWE
12
J K E S L M N P Q R
Kirkstile
ARKLETON HILL
40
50
60

A B C D E F G H

1
Tarbert
Kilberry
GIGHA
Loch Ciaran
Loch Garasdale
Crossaig
Lochranza
Castle
Catacol

2
Ardminish
Achamore
Rhunahaorine Point
Cour Bay
Cour
Glen Catacol
North Ar

Tayinloan
Cara
Rhunahaorine
247
CRUACH MHIC GOUGAIN
264
CNOC-AN T-SAMHLAIDH
123
Grogport
Barmollack
Penrioch
Pirnmill
Loch Tanna

3
354
CRUACH NAN GABHAR
Whitefarland
715
BEINN BHARRAIN
Glen Iorsa

A83
Muasdale
Carradale Water
B842
39
Carradale
Imachar
Balliekine
Iorsa Water

4
Glenacardoch Point
Belloch
Bridgend
Dippen
B879
Carradale House
Carradale Point
A R R

Glenbarr
MacAlister Clan
454
BEINN-AN TUIRC
Torrisdale
Carradale Bay
Auchagallon Stone Circle
Machrie

5
Cleongart
319
408
BORD MOR
Saddell
Saddell Bay
Machrie Bay
Tormore
Machrie Moor Stone Circles
Moss Farm Road Stone Circle
Balmichae

Bellochantuy Bay
Bellochantuy
N
396
SGREADAN HILL
Balmichael

6
Tangy Loch
Glen Lussa
Peninver
Ugadale
Torbeg
Shiskine

I
Blackwaterfoot
Drumadoon Bay
Kilpatrick

7
Kilkenzie
A83
Kilmichael
B842
Ardnacross Bay
NR
Kilpatrick Dun
Brown Head

Machrihanish Bay
Campbeltown
Campbeltown
Campbeltown Loch
Island Davarr
Corriecravie
Slidde

8
Machrihanish
Drumlemble
B843
B842
6
Kilkerran
Kildalloig
352
BEINN GHUILEAN
Achinhoan
Torr a' Chaisteal Fort

Earadale Point
385
THE STATE

9
446
CNOC MOY
Ru Stafnish
Dalsmeran
Glen Breakevie
Conie Glen
Glen Kerran
B842
10
Strone Glen
Cattadale
Polliwilline Bay

10
BEINN NA LICE
428
Carskey
Southend
Macharioch
MULL OF KINTYRE
Dunaverty
Carskey Bay

11
Borgadalemore Point
Sanda Sound
Sheep Island
Sanda Island

12

A B C D E F G H

NU

Berwick-upon-Tweed

118

119

CAUSEWAY FLOODED AT HIGH TIDE

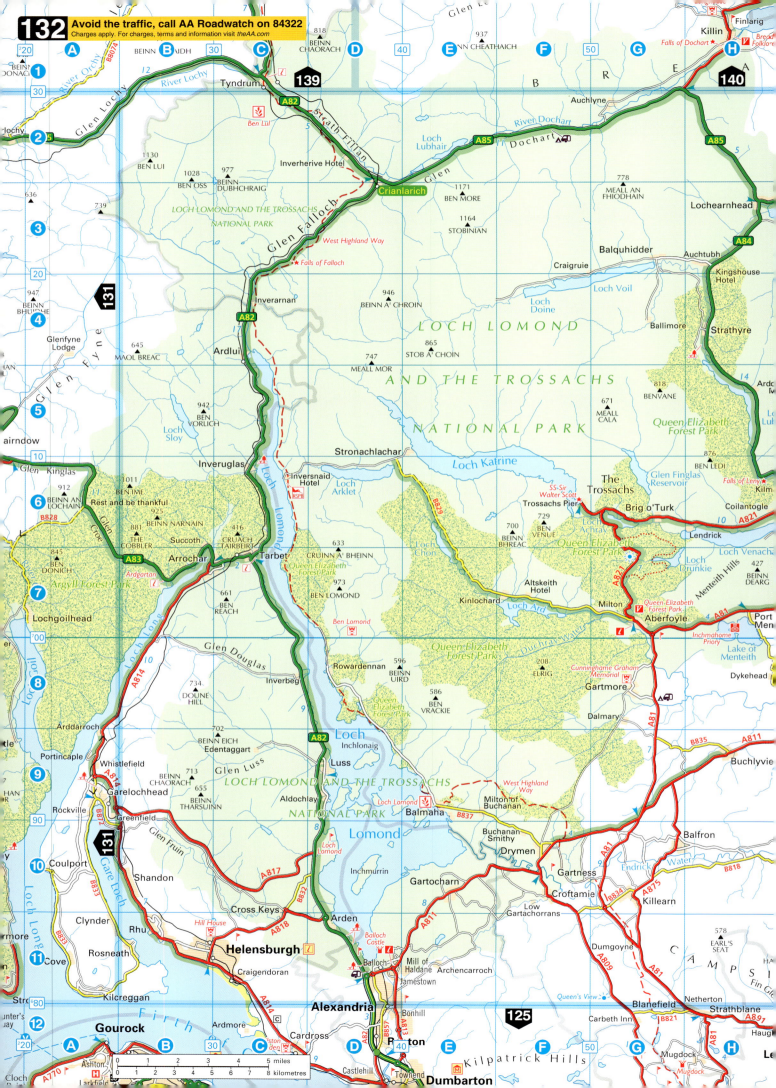

COLL

Eilean Mòr
Rudha Mòr
Rudha Sgor-innis
Bousd
Sorisdale
B8072
Cliad Bay
Arnabost
Grishipoll
Clabhach
Loch Cliad
B8071
Hogh Bay
Ballyhaugh
Arinagour
Totronald
Coll
Acha
B8070
Feall Bay
Arileod
Uig
Eilean Ornsay
RSPB
Loch Breachacha
Crossapol Bay
Rudha Fàsachd
Calgary Point
Gunna

NL

Rudha Port Bhiosd
Clachan Mor
Balephetrish Bay
Caoles
Rudha Dubh
B8069
Haugh Bay
Loch Bhasapoll
B8068
Ruaig
Ballevullin
Cornoigmore
Kenovay
Gott Bay
Kilkenneth
Tiree
B8068
B8065
Scarinish
Middleton
Moss
Heylipoll
Crossapoll
TIREE
Barrapoll
B8065
Hynish Bay
Loch a Phuill
B8067
Balemartine
Mannel
Rinn Thorbhais
Hynish
Balephuil Bay

Fladda
Lunga
TRESHNISH ISLES
Bac Mòr or Dutchmans Ca:
Bac Beag

Colonsay

NM

Eilean Dubh
Kiloran Bay
Balnahard
Rudh' a' Geodha
COLONSAY
Kiloran
Kilchattan
B8087
Colonsay - Oban
Scalasaig
B8086
Machrins
Colonsay
Colonsay - Port Askaig
NR
B8085
Garvard
Dubh Eilean
Oronsay
Rudha Bàn
ORONSAY
Eilean Ghurdmail

0 1 2 3 miles
0 1 2 3 4 5 kilometres

IONA
Iona Abbey & Nunnery
Baile Mòr
MacLean's Cross
Sound of Iona
Soa Island
Erraid

0 1 2 3 4 5 miles
0 1 2 3 4 5 6 7 8 kilometres

J   K   40   L   M   50   N   P   60   Q   R   70   Kir

Eilean
Rudha Aird
Druimnich
Ockle
Point

Morar, Moidart and
Ardnamurchan

Tiot
239
BEINN
BHREAC   **1**

Ardmolich

Sanna Point
Kilmory
Ockle
Ardtoe   D   70   reck

Sanna
Bay
Sanna Bay
Branault
356
BEINN
BHREAC
Kentra
Blain
Mingarrypar   **2**

Portuaik
Achnaha
Arevegaig
B8044

Achosnich
B8007   ARDNAMURCHAN   437
Acharacle

Ardnamurchan
Point
MEALL NAN CON   436
A861

342
BEINN
NA SEILG   Kilchoan   527
BEN
HIANT   19   Glenbeg   512
BEN
LAGA   B8007   Salen   **3**

Ormsaigmore
Mingary   Glenborrodale   Laga
RSPB   Loch   Su

GEARR CH   339

Ardslignish   Loch
Mudle

Carna   **138**   60

4

571
BEINN
LADAIN   M

Coll · Oban   V
Ardmore Point   V   Auliston
Point   Oronsay   Loch
Teacuis   Loch
Arienas   **5**

Quinish Point
Sorne
Point
Glengorm Castle   Drimnin   437
BEINN
BHUIDHE   Acha

Caliach Point   Tobermory   Calve
Island   550
SÌTHEAN NA RAPLAICH   G
Clagg   **6**

NM   292
'S AIRDE
BEINN   A848   B849
Larachbeg   A884

Calgary   5   Dervaig   Achnadrish House   Fuinary   Rar
Achn

Calgary Bay   B8073   6   444
SPEINNE MÒR   10   Aros   Lochaline   Loch
Aline   V

Treshnish Point
Ensay   342
CÀRN MÒR   Loch
Frisa   Glen Aros   Fishnish
Point   Fishnish Pier   **7**

Rudh' a' Chaoil   Burg   Glenaros House   Salen   A849   Scamastle Bay   40

Fanmore   390
CNOC AN DÀ CHINN   Killiechronan   B8035   2   408
BEINN
NAN LUS   Altcreich

Ballygown   Eas Fors (Waterfall)   333
BEINN
NAN CÀRN   Gruline   Macquarie
Mausoleum   636
BEINN
MHEADHON   Craignu   **8**

Loch Tuath   19   Oskamull   B8073   Glen
Forsa   11

Gometra   ULVA   Eorsa   591
BEINN A' GHRÀIG   Loch Bà   766
DUN DA
GHAOITHE

Little Colonsay   Inch Kenneth   Lochd   **9**
Inchkenneth Chapel
(ruin)   Loc

Staffa   **Loch na Keal,**   B8035   17   ISLE   A849   17
Isle of Mull   Balnahard   Strathcoil   30

Fingal's Cave   966
BEN
MORE   704
CRUACHAN
DEARG   OF   698
BEN CREACH   **10**

519
BEIN-NA
SRÈINE   MULL   Loch Uisg

491
CREACH BHEINN   Aird of
Kinloch   Glen More   717
BEN
BUIE   337
MAOL
BÀN   **11**

Fossil Tree
Burg   A849   Loch Fuaran   Lochbuie   Loch
Uisg

Rudha nan Cearc   Pennycross   Pennyghael   503
BEINN NA
CROISE   Lochbuie   **130**

Kintra   A849   14   Loch Scridain   Leidle Water   Loch Buie   377
DRUIM
FADA   FIRT   20

nphort   Aridhglas   376
CRUACHAN
MIN   376
BEINN
CHREAGACH   Carsaig   Rudha
Dubh   **12**

Columba
xhibition
Centre   Bunessan   Loch Assapol

ROSS OF MULL   Uisken

Ardchiavaig   Rudha nam
Braithrean   Malcolm's
Point

Rudha
Ardalanish

J   K   40   L   M   50   N   P   60   Q   R   70

'60 A 103 Druimindarroch Arìsaig Kinlochnanuagh B 70 C Polnish D Lochailort 80 E A830 14 F 90 Glen Finnan G Gleann Dubhlighe Gleann Fionnlighe H 796 SGURR AN UTHA Loch Beoriad 633

1 Sound of Arisaig 80 Rudha Choalais Ardnish Inverailort Loch Eilt 145 Glenfinnan Glenfinnan Visitor Centre Kinlocheil Loch Sta

2 Smearisary Glenuig 21 70 877 ROIS-BHEINN 712 664 BEINN GAIRE 882 BEINN ODHAR BHEAG Glen Shiel Scamodale 758 MEALL MÒR Glenfinnan Monument 718 MEALL NAM DAMH Glen Garvan Drimsallie Garvan Du

3 Loch Moidart Eilean Shona Tioram 239 BEINN BHREAC Ardmolich Kinlochmoidart Brunery Glen Moidart Glen Forsian MOIDART Loch Shiel 888 SGURR DHOMHNUILL 754 SGOR AN TARMACHAIN 888 MEALL MÒR Cona Glen Glen Scaddle

Moidart and namurchan Ardtoe Kentra 137 Shielfoot B8044 Blain Dalnabreck Mingarrypark Dalelia Pollach Loch Doilet SUNART

4 437 Arevegaig Acharacle A861 Claish Moss 846 BEINN RESIPOL Glen Hurich 888 SGURR DHOMHNUILL

5 Glenb BEN LAGA 512 B8007 Salen Resipole 12 Loch Sunart Glencripesdale 339 GEARR CHREAG Camasine Woodend Camasachoirce Anaheilt Strontian A861 Achnalea Glen Tarbert 884 GARBH BHEINN Ariundle Oakwood A861 13 Glen Gour Clovuli

nborrodale Laga 60 Carna RSPB

6 Loch Teacuis 437 BEINN BHUI A884 Liddesdale Ardnastang NM 620 GLAS BHEINN 853 CREACH BHEINN Inversanda Kent

7 550 SÌTHEAN NA RAPLAICH 50 Loch Arienas 571 BEINN LADAIN 522 MEALL A' CHOISE Glen Dubh 20 Lochuisge Lochuisge 651 BEINN NA CILLE B8043 Loch a' Choire LOCH LINNHE Cuil

8 Fuinary of Mull A884 Acharn Gleann Geal Claggan Larachbeg 339 MEALL DAMH Rannoch River Achranich 738 BEINN MHEADHOIN 568 SQURR A BHUIC Shuna Island 30 Portnacroish Appin Creagan Inn Glasdrum Wood Inver Hou

9 A849 Fishnish Point 137 Fishnish Pier Lochaline Loch Aline Loch Téarnait Port Ramsay Port Appin Inverfolla North Shian Eriska

10 408 BEINN AN LUS 40 Glen Forsa Altcreich Scallastle Bay 464 GLAIS BHEINN 514 AN SLEAGHOCH Rudha an Ridire LISMORE Clachan Eriska South Shian North Shian A828 Barcaldine Barcaldine B845 Scottish Sea Life Sanctuary Ardchattan Priory In

ISLE 636 BEINN MHEADHON 766 DUN DA GHAOITHE Craignure Duart Bay Duart Point Bernera Island Kilcheran B8045 Achnacroish Lynn of Lorne Kiel Crofts BENDERLOCH Benderloch Ledaig

11 OF MULL A849 17 Torosay Duart Lochdonhead Lochdon Gorten Loch Don Dunollie Castle Ardmucknish Bay Dunstaffnage Castle Dunstaffnage Chapel (ruin) North Connel Lynn of Lorne Connel Black Crofts Dunbeg Achaleven A85 Achnacloich

12 '60 7 BEN BUIE 698 BEN CREACH 130 Strathcoil Grass Point KERRERA Ganavan Bay McCaig's Tower Dunollie Castle Oban (An t-Oban) H F M River Glen Lonan Taynn

A B 70 C D 80 E Gallanachbeg Ariogan Gallanachmore F Loch Nell G 515 H

0 1 2 3 4 5 miles
0 1 2 3 4 5 6 7 8 kilometres

148

149

CAIRNGORMS

NATIONAL PARK

999 CARN EALAR

1006 AN SGARSOCH

P CARN BHAC

Q

SGOR MOR

R

Lodge

Glenshee Ski Area

814 SRON A' CHLEIRICH

1007 BEINN DEARG

897 BEINN A' CHART

1119 CÀRN NAN CABHAR

Tarf Water

River Tilt

Gleann Mòr

Loch Tilt

1050 GLAS TULAICHEAN

2 THE CAIRNWELL

93

861 CARN

3

1068

903 BEN VUIRICH

867 MEALL A' CHOIRE BHUIDHE

805 BEN GULABIN

Glen Lochsie

Spittal of Glenshee

A93

142

4

792 MEALL UAINE

70

DUC HIL

A9

491 CRAIG BHAGAILTEACH

Bruar Water

Glen Banvie

Glen Tilt

Glen Fender

CÀRN LIATH 973

River Tilt

Gleann Fearnach

Glen Shee

5

Calvine

Clan Donnachaidh

Blair Castle

Middlebridge

Struan

Pitagowan

Bridge of Tilt

B8079

Old Struan

Blair Atholl

Aldclune

B847

TULACH HILL

470

60

River Garry

Killiecrankie

840 BEN VRACKIE

Straloch

A924

Enochdhu

Milton

12

Tay Forest Park

River Ardle

Strath Ardle

13

Kirkmichael

B950

Blacklur

60

ERROCHTY

Tay Forest Park

Tressait

B8019

Killiecrankie

Tay Forest Park

Moulin

Kinnaird

622 CREAG DHUBA

Loch Broom

Ballintuim

A924

A93

6

Tummel Bridge

Queen's View

Loch Tummel

Frenich

Tay Forest Park

Foss

Daloist

Loch Tummel

Queen's View

Faskally Wayside Centre

Pitlochry (Baile Chloichridh)

Edradour Distillery

7

779 FARRAGON HILL

780 MEALL TAIRNEACHAN

Loch Derculich

Strathtay

Dunfallandy Stone

Dalcapon

5

561 CRAIG NAM MIAL

479

NO

Bridge of Cally

50

B846

780

Loch Glassie

Derculich

Grandtully

A827

A9

Ballinluig Truckstop

Tulliemet

Loch Ordie

Loch Benachally

ethertor

14

Edradynate

Balnaguard

Logierait

Ballinluig

B898

8

Coshieville

neyburn

Dull

Camserney

Weem

Menzies

Dewars

Aberfeldy

St Mary's

River Tay

532

GRANDTULLY HILL

Loch Skiach

Tay Forest Park

Kincraigie

B888

Kindallachan

Guay

Kincraigie

Dowally

509 DEUCHARY HILL

Blairgov

Kinloch

A923

9

The Crannog Centre

A827

Croftmoraig Stone Circle

616 MEALL DUBH

Loch Kennard

Ballinloan Burn

River Tay

Butterstone

Achalader

Concraigie

Craigie

Muirte Ardb

enmore

A826

Dunkeld Town

Cathedral

Loch of the Lowes

Lethendy

B9

N

Glen Quaich

River Quaich

Loch Freuchie

Trochry

Strath Braan

Glen Shee

Inver

Dunkeld

Little Dunkeld

Birnam

The Hermitage

60

Spittalfield

A984

Caputh

Gellyburn

Meikleour

142

10

864 SRON A' CHAOINEIDH

802 MEALL NAM FUARAN

Achnafauld

Amulree

A822

Meikle Obney

Obney

Waterloo

Bankfoot

B867

Balquharn

Murthly

A9

15

Kinclaven

Cargill

Balholmie

S

River Almond

666 MEALL REAMHAR

Airntully

Perthshire

B9099

Stanley

11

Guildtown

929 BEN CHONZIE

Harrietfield

B8063

Moneydie

Newmiln

Downhill

Luncarty

30

12

133

134

ntullich

Loch Turr

K

80

445 CNOC BEITHE

L

90

A822

M

Buchanty

River Almond

N

Dalcrue

P

Redgorton

Q

10

R

A93

Monzie

Methven

Pitcairngreen

Almondbank

Scone Palace

Scone

A9

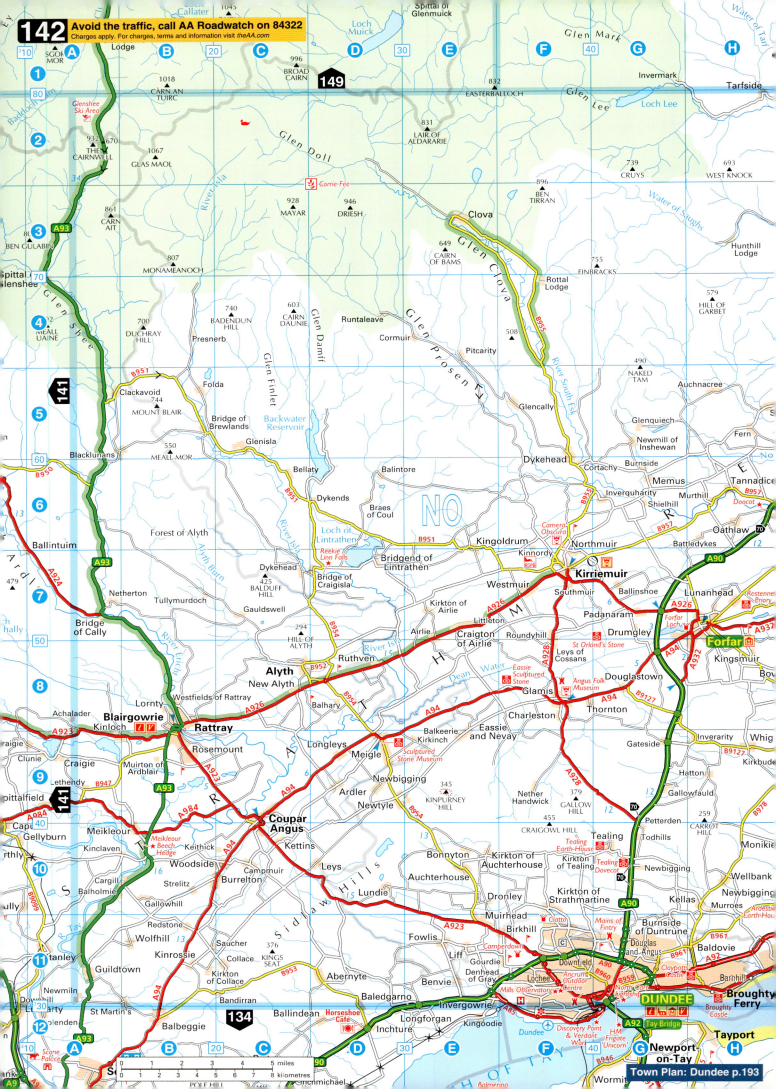

Fiskavaig

B8009

Fernilea

Drync

Carbost

369
ARNAVAL

Merkadale

Glen Drynoch

A863

152 Talisker
Bay

Talisker

Glen Eynort

Sligachan

A87

S · K · Y · E

ROINEVAL

BEN LEE
444

The Bracs

Peinchor

773
GLAMAIG

369
BEINN BHREAC

447
BEINN
BHREAC

Grula

Loch Eynort

965
SGURR NAN GILLEAN

The Cuillin Hills

434
AN CRUACHIN

974
SGURR
A' GHEADAIDH

Glenbrittle House

C u i l l i n   H i l l s

927
BLAVEN

Bualintur

1009
SGURR
ALASDAIR

Loch
Coruisk

Loch na
Crèitheach

Loch Brittle

225
CEANN NA BEINNE

894
GARS
BHEINN

Kirkibos

Rudh' an Dùnain

Soay Sound

139
BEINN
BHREAC

Loch
Scavaig

344
BEN
MEABOST

Mol-chlach

Elgol

Gla

SOAY

Rudh'
Aonghais

Strathair
Point

C U I L L I N   S O U N D

NG

CANNA

210
CÀRN A' GHAILL

Rudha
Shamhnan Insir

Garrisdale Point

A'Chill

Canna
Harbour

Sanday

Sound of Canna

302
MULLACH
MÒR

Rudha na Roinne

Kinloch

Loch
Scresort

A Bhrideanach

570
ORVAL

Oigh-sgeir

RÙM

810
ASKIVAL

763
SGÙRR NAN
GILLEAN

The Small Isles

Rudha nam
Meirleach

Sound of Rum

NM

Bay of
Laig

Cleadale

299
AN
CRUACHAN

Rudha an Fhasaidh

Laig

EIGG

Kildonnan

393
AN SGURR

Sandavore

Sound of Eigg

Eilean
nan Each

Eilean
Chathastail

MUCK

Port Mor

| 0 | 1 | 2 | 3 | 4 | 5 miles |
| 0 | 1 | 2 | 3 | 4 | 5 | 6 | 7 | 8 kilometres |

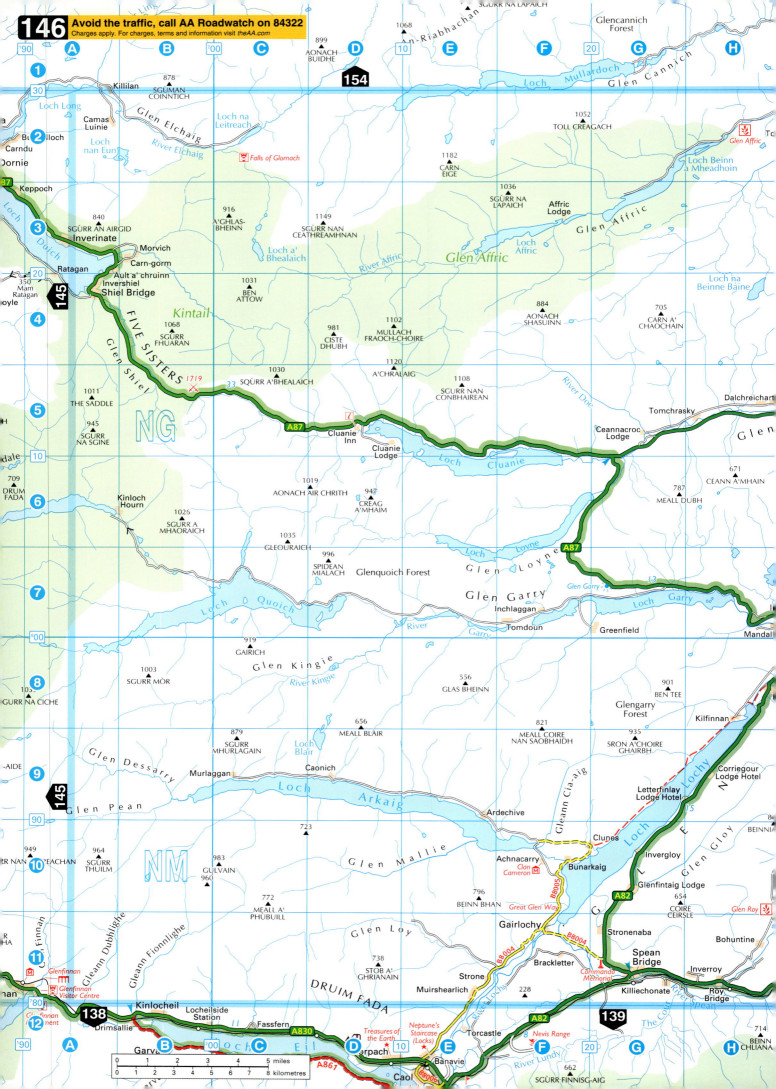

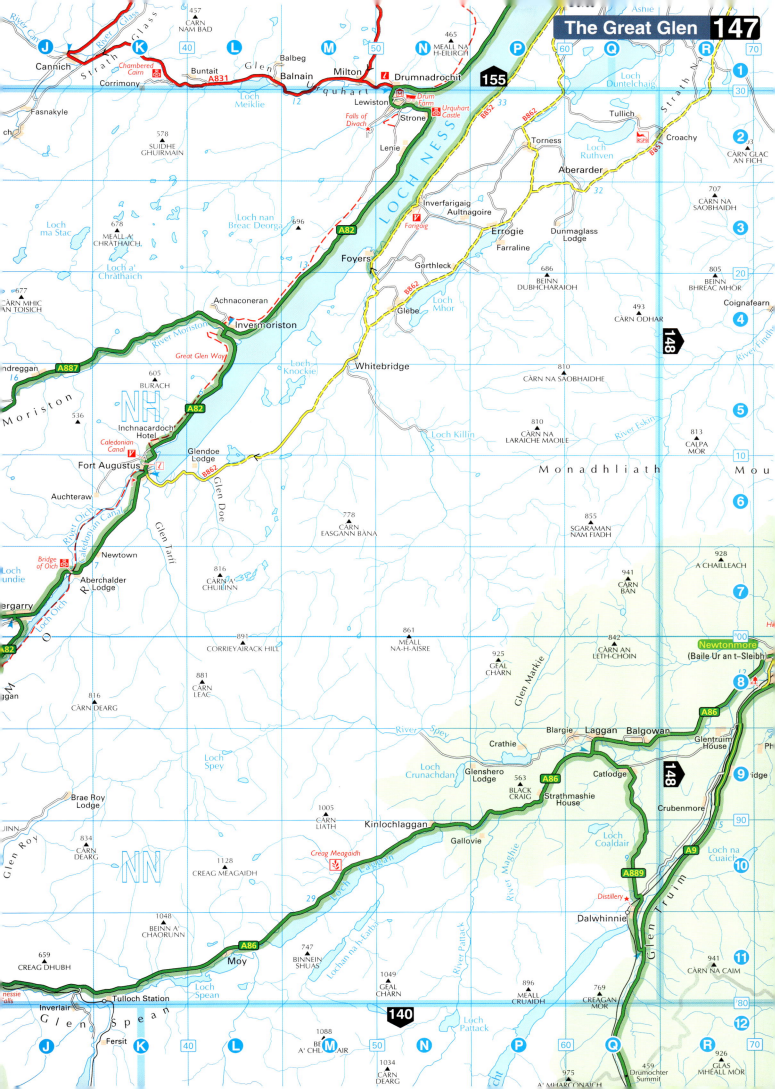

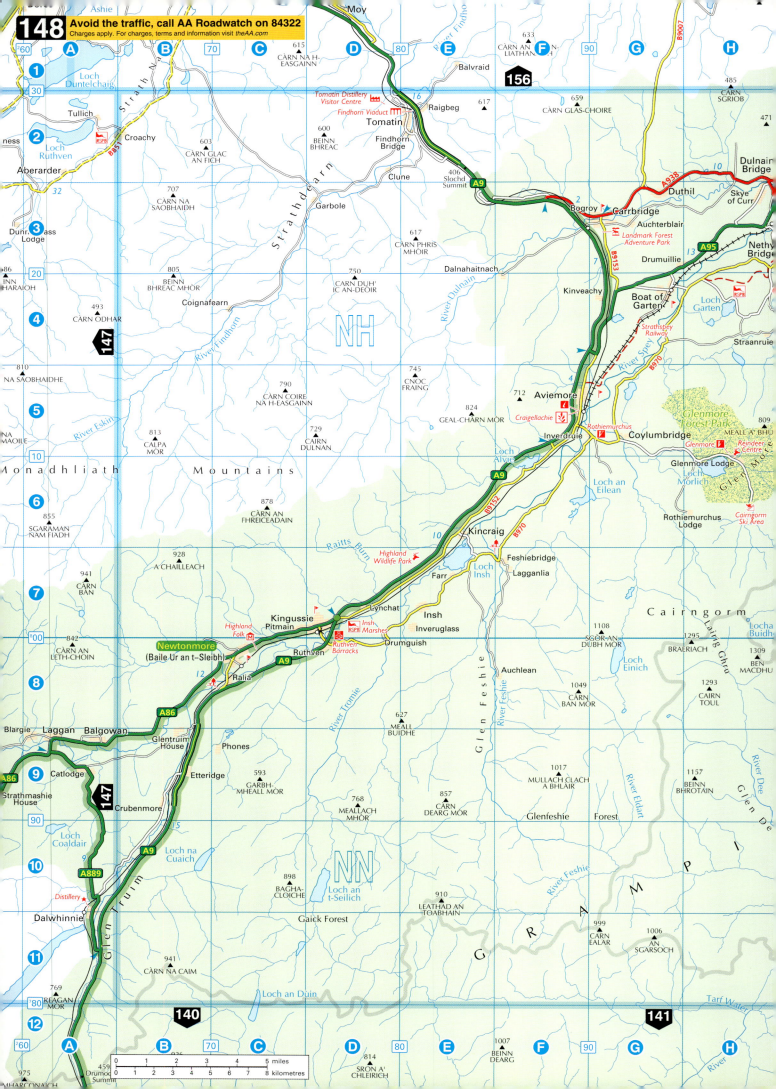

CNOC BREAC 293

Garden 13

Poolewe
Londubh
ALL NA

B8021

North Erradale

P 80

Q

R 90
250

1

Big Sand

160

Smithstown
Lonemore
Gairloch

Strath
A832
Auchtercairn
Heritage
Charlestown
MEALL AN DOIREIN 421

2

Longa Island

Loch Gairloch

Eilean Horrisdale

Loch Bad an Sgalaig

3

Port Henderson

B8056
Badachro
Opinan

South Erradale

Redpoint

Loch Ghobhainn
BEINN BHREAC 619
BAOSBHEINN 875
Loch a' Bhealaich
BEINN AN EOI 855
Talla 70

4

Red Point

NG

Loch Ghaineamhach

154

Loch na A-Oidho

Kilt Rock Waterfall
Ellishader

Valtos
Rudha nam Brathairean
Culnaknock

Loch a' Bhráige

Loch Torridon
Rudha na Fearn
Fearnmore

Craig River

BEINN ALLIGIN 985
BEINN DEARG 914
60

5

Tote
A855

RONA

Fearnbeg
Arrina
Kenmore
Ob Chuaig
Cuaig

Loch Diabaig
Lower Diabaig

Alligin Shuas
Inveralligin

LIATH

6

Loch Leathan

Eilean Tigh

Callakille

Lonbain

AN GARBH-MHEALL 492
CROIC-BHEINN 493

Ardheslaig
Loch Shieldaig

Torridon House
Upper Loch Torridon

Torr

7

Man Storr

Eilean Fladday

Manish Point
Loch Arnish
Torran
Arnish

Shieldaig
Annat

A896
Loch Damph

Wester Ross

Glenshieldaig Forest

902
50
DAMPH
MAC

8

Brochel

INNER SOUND

RAASAY

River Applecross

Loch Lundie

Loch Coultrie

312

SOUND OF RAASAY

Applecross Bay

Milton
Applecross

Camusteel

895
BEINN BHAN

730
SGURR A GHARAIDH

9

412
BEN TIANAVAIG

444
DUN CAAN

Camusterrach
Aird Dhubh
Culduie

626 Pass of the Cattle
774
SGURR A'CHAORACHAIN
Bealach-Na-Ba

Rassal Ashwood

Kishorn
Kirkton

A896
Lochcarron
40

Camastianavaig
Tianavaig Bay
Ollach

Oskaig
310
BEINN NA LEAC

Rudha na' Leac

Toscaig

Ardarroch
Achintraid
Loch Kishorn
Kishorn Island

154
Slumbay

10

Clachan
B883
Inverarish

e Braes
LEE

Peinchorran
Suisnish Point

Eyre Point

Eilean Meadhonach
Eilean Mòr

Caolas Mòr

River Toscaig

Caolas

Ardaneaskan

394
BAD A CHREAMHA
Strome

Stromeferry
Achmore

Ardnarff

A890

11

conser

773
GLAMAIG

Loch Ainort

396
MULLACH NA CARN

67 Longay

CROWLIN ISLANDS

SCALPAY

Loch Carron

Plockton
Port-an-Eorna
Drumbuie
Duirinish

447
BEINN RAIMH

15

30

12

564
GLAS BHEIN

A87

Dunan
L 60
K
L

M Pabay 70

2

145
Badicaul
Kyle of Lochalsh
N ol Loch Ailse
Skye Bridge
Kyleakin
A87

Balmacara
Auchtertyre

P 80
Lochalsh Woodland Garden

Q
Kirkton
Eilean Donan

Conchra
Nostie
Ardelve
Dornie
Carndu
Bundal
90

R

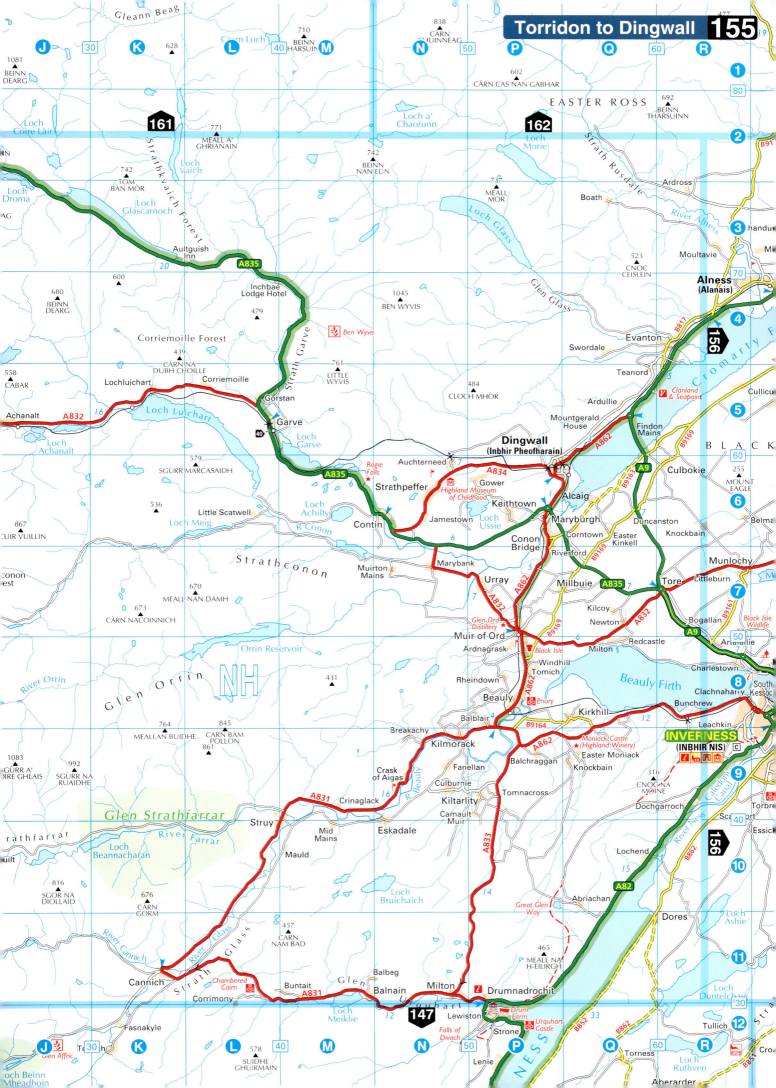

J K L M N P Q R

1
2
3
4
5
6
7
8
9
10
11
12

158
158
149

Lossiemouth
Branderburgh
Stotfield
B9040
Burnside
Hopeman
Burghead Well
Burghead
Duffus
Cummingston
St Peter's Kirk & Parish Cross
B9012
Roseisle
B9013
Duffus Castle
B9012
B9135
Loch Spynie
6
Spynie Palace
A941
Spey Bay
Tugnet Ice House
Moray Firth
Kingston on Spey
Stonewel's
Lochill
Viewfield
Innesmill
Garmouth
Nether Dallachy
Upper Dallachy
Buc
Buckpool
Portgor
College of Roseisle
Quarrywood
Newton
Bishopmill
Elgin
Calcots
Urquhart
Lhanbryde
The Lochs
Bogmoor
Newton
Stynie
Auchenhalrig
Bridge of Tynet
Broadley
Cloch
Culbin Sands
Findhorn
Hempriggs
B9089
Findhorn Bay
Kinloss
Kincorth House
Coltfield
Alves
A96
Glen Moray Distillery
New Elgin
Linkwood
Mosstodloch
Crofts of Dipple
B9015
B9104
Baxters Visitor Centre
Dipple
Fochabers
Braes o
264
WHITEASH HILL
MILL
B9011
Whiterow
Sueno's Stone
Grange Hall
Kilbuiack
Muir of Miltonduff
Clackmarras
Longmorn
B9103
Orbliston
Inchberry
Ordiequish
A96
Forgie
THIEF'S HILL
250
8
Aultn
Forg
Forres
Dallas Dhu Distillery
Califer
Barnhill
Pluscarden
Fogwatt
Millbuies
B9015
Cairnty
Sound Muir
Rafford
B9010
Kellas
Shougle
13
Glen of Rothes
A941
262
FINDLAY'S SEAT
Newlands of Dundurcas
Garbity
Auchroisk
B9103
Upper Mulben
Rumbler
7
B9
B9010
Branchill
Dallas
River Lossie
NJ
PIKEY HILL
355
Crofts
Glen Grant Distillery
Rothes
Deanshaugh
Tauchers
Mulben
Rosarie
50
Ei
Logie
371
MILL BUIE
365
CAIRN UISH
Speyside Way
12
HILL OF TOWie
338
Glenerney
Glen Lossie
400
CARN NA CAILLEICHE
369
HUNT HILL
471
BEN AIGAN
Arndilly House
Dandaleith
A95
KNOCKAN
372
Maggieknockater
A940
Dava Way
522
CARN KITTY
Archiestown
B9102
Cardhu
Ringorm
Craigellachie
A941
4
Glenfiddich Distillery
B9014
Drummuir
B9115
Dava
River Divie
515
Knockando
Carron
Speyview
Aberlour
Glenallachie
Dufftown
Balvenie Castle
9
Daugh of Kinermony
Milltown of Edinville
Dava Moor
543
LARIG HILL
STRATH SPEY
10
A95
Kirktown of Mortlach
Auchindoun Castle
10
Lettoch
548
CARN NA LOINE
Blacksboat
Marypark
Glenfarclas Distillery
Pitchroy
Ballindalloch
Bridge of Avon
Delnashaugh Inn
840
BEN RINNES
Glen Rinnes
Achnastank
Glen Fiddich
503
Hau of G
amerory
A939
Delliefure
A95
14
Mains of Dalvey
B9102
Advie
B9008
B9009
Drumin
19
Shenval
River Fiddich
Bridgend
11
rantown on-Spey
Cromdale
Hills of Cromdale
L
Glenlivet Distillery
Glenlivet
Auchbreck
149
766
CORRYHABBIE HILL
571
ROUND HILL
Cabrach
12
raggan
River Spey
River Avon
rath Avon
Tomnavoulin
M
N
P
Q
Aldivalloch
Aldunie
R

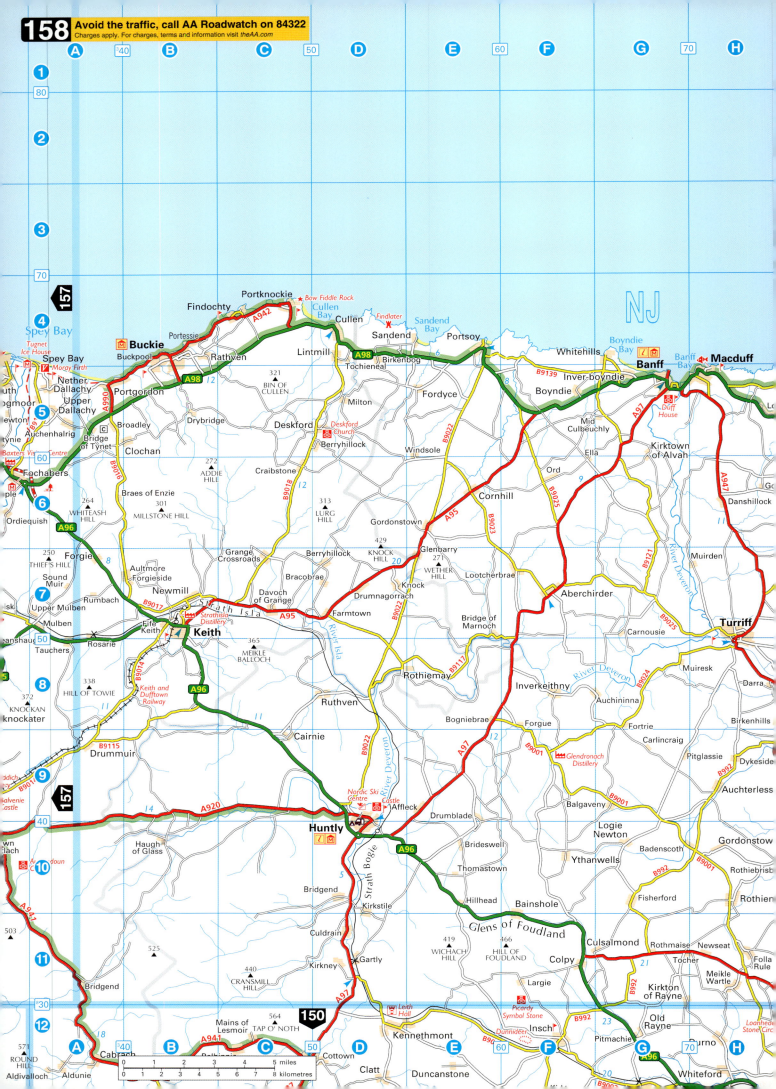

NB

164

Stoer
Bay of Clachtoll
B869
Rhicarn
Achmelvich Bay
Achmelvich
Baddidarrach
Soyea Island
Loch Inver
Inverkirkaig
Str
Rhu Coigach
Eilean Mòr
Enard Bay
Rubha Mòr
Reiff
Achnahaird
Altandhu
Eilean Mullagrach
Isle Ristol
Polbain
Loch Osgaig
St
Glas-leac Mòr
SUMMER ISLES
Achiltibuie
Tanera Beg
Badentarbat Bay
Polglass
Ben mor Coigach
Steornabhagh (Stornoway)
Tanera Mòr
Glas-leac Beag
Horse Island
Horse Sound
Achduart
Culnacraig
652
BEN MC COIGA
Eilean Dubh
Priest Island
Greenstone Point
Cailleach Head
Leac Dhonn
Isle Martin
Rudha Beag
Scoraig
Annat Bay
Mellon Udrigle
Stattic Point
Rhireavach
BEINN GHOBHLACH
635
GRUINARD ISLAND
Badluachrach
Little Loch Broom
Laide
Gruinard Bay
A832
Badrallach
Rudha Reidh
Foura
Cove
Mellon Charles
Ormiscaig
Gruinard
Badcaul
Ardessie
Camusnagaul
32
Aultbea
Little Gruinard River
Gruinard River
764
SAIL MHOR
296
AN CUAIDH
ISLE OF EWE
Dundonnell
NG
Melvaig
Loch Ewe
Lochan Gaineamhaich
Aultgrishin
347
CREAG-MHEAL BEAG
293
CNOC BREAC
Inverasdale
Strathnasheallag Forest
Naast
Loch Fada
1062
AN TEALLACH
Inverewe Garden
681
BEINN A' CHAISGEIN BEAG
Loch na Sealga
North Erradale
250
MEALL NA MEINE
13
Poolewe
Londubh
906
BEINN DEARG MHOR
Big Sand
Wester Ross
Fionn
Strath
A832
Smithstown
Longa Island
Lonemore
153
Auchtercairn
Heritage
Dubh Loch
154
Gairloch
Loch Gairloch
791
BEINN AIRIDH CHARR
Charlestown
Eilean Horrisdale
421
MEALL AN DOIREIN
Loch
Port Henderson
974
SGÙRRBÀN
1019
Badachro
B8056
Opinan
859
NN LÀIR
MULLACH COIRE MHIC FHEARCHAIR
nan Fada
South Erradale
Loch Bad an Sgalaig
Loch Maree Hotel
Letterewe
Loch Garbhaig

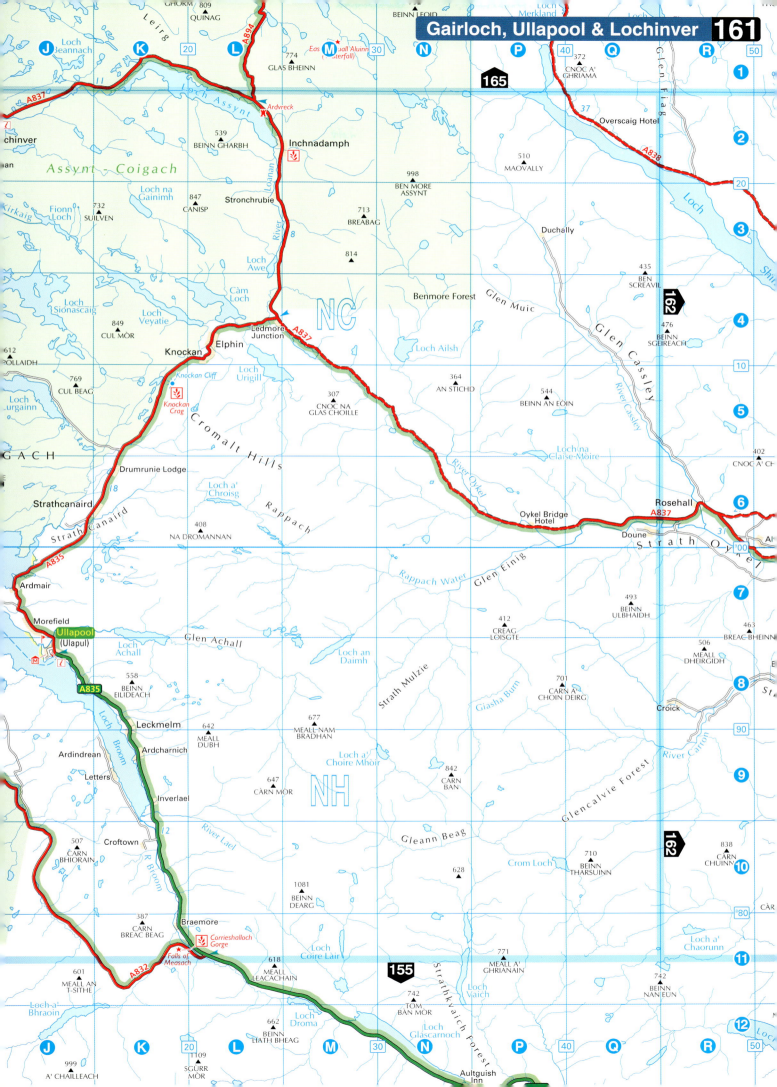

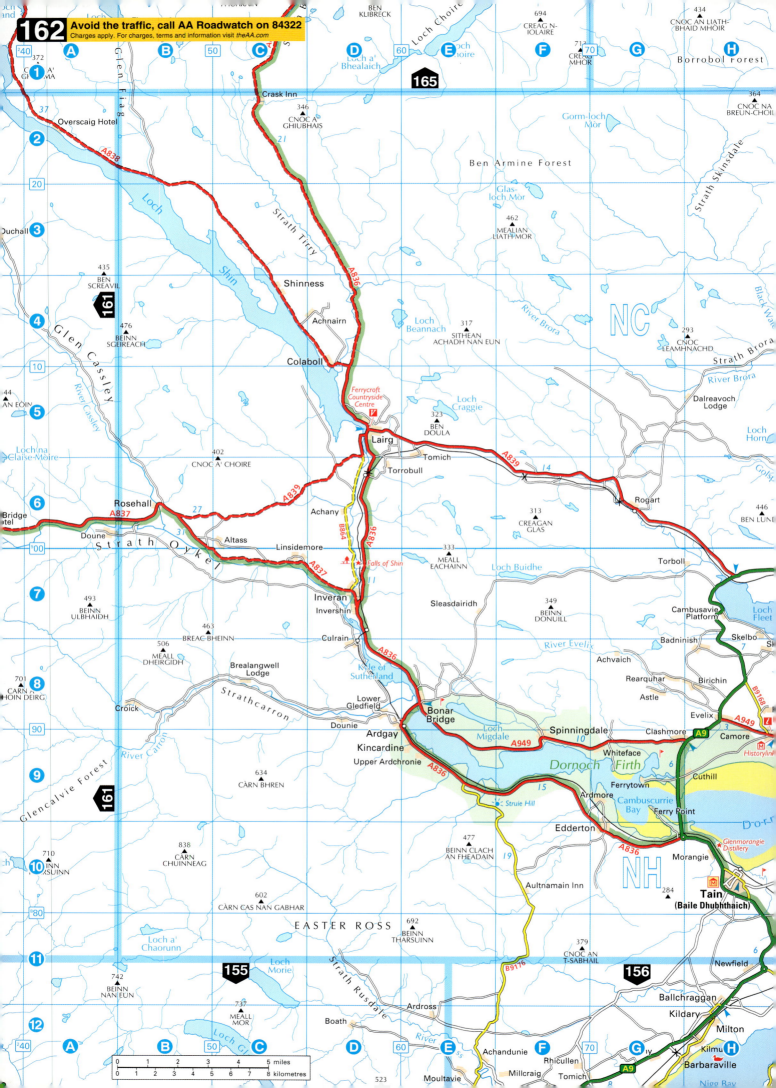

J
K
90
L
M
00
N
P
10
Q
R
20

166

167

1

202
CNOC DAIL-CHAIRN

Strath Free

Loch Ascaig

705
MORVEN

518
CNOC AN EIREANNACH

626
SCARABEN

Langwell Forest

Borgue

20

388
CREAG NAM FIADH

Learable Hill Cairns, Stone Row & Stone Circles

Strath of Kildonan

Kildonan Lodge

554
CREAG SCALABSDALE

Newport

Langwell House

Berriedale

2

20

Kildonan
416
BEINN DUBHAIN

401
CNOC NA MAOILE

A9

337
CNOC NA H-INNSE MOIRE

A897

Torrish

River Helmsdale

404
CREAG THORARAIDH

Ord of Caithness

3

20

421
CNOC NAN CRÙBAG MÒR

624
BEINN DHORAIN

591
BEINN NA MÈILICH

Timespan
West Helmsdale
East Helmsdale
Helmsdale

Navidale House Hotel

ND

4

Balnacoil Lodge

539
COL-BHEINN

Glen Loth

Gartymore

Portgower

10

Loch Brora

Lothmore

Lothbeg

21

5

520
BEN HORN

Dalchalm

Brora

6

378
CAGAR FEOSAIG

Doll

Backies

Carn Liath

A9

383
BEN BHRAGGIE

Rhives

Dunrobin Castle

Golspie

00

7

o Street
Fourpenny

Embo

8

Embo Street
rudy

Dornoch

90

ch Firth

Tarbat Ness

9

Innis Mhor

Brucefield

Wilkhaven

NJ

Portmahomack

10

Inver

B9165

Rockfield

Arboll

Toulvaddie

80

Lochslin

Loch Eye

Rhynie

Hill of Fearn

Balmuchy

Hilton of Cadboll Chapel (ruin)

11

9165

Fearn

B9166

Tullich

Hilton

Arabella

Balintore

Shandwick

Ankerville

Shandwick Bay

9175

12

Pitca

B9040

Nigg

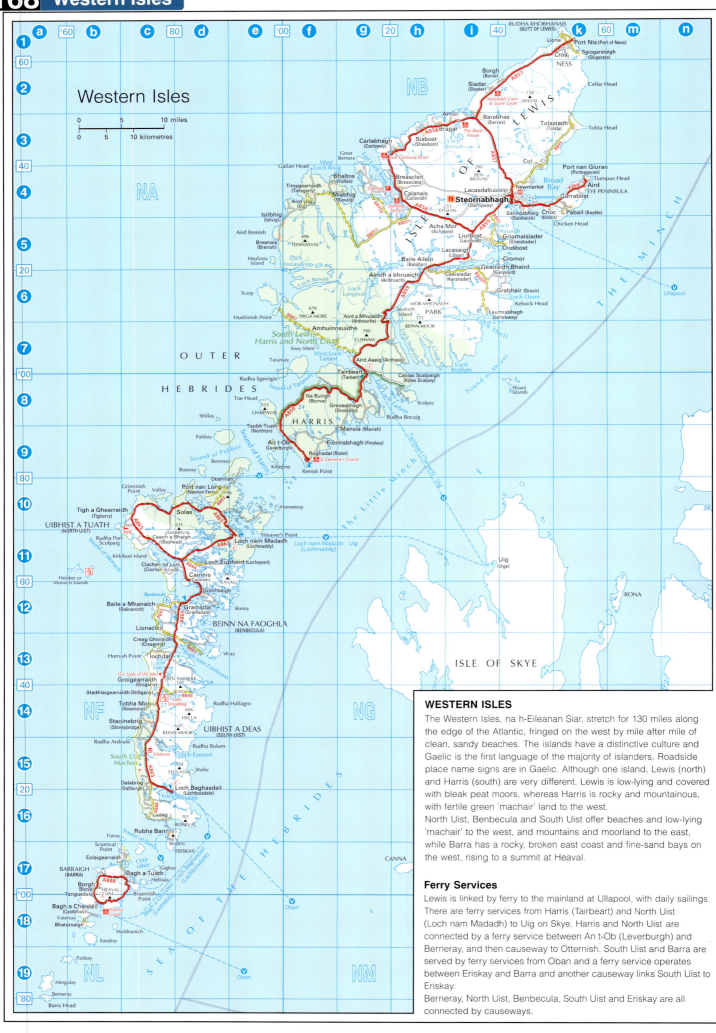

WESTERN ISLES

The Western Isles, na h-Eileanan Siar, stretch for 130 miles along the edge of the Atlantic, fringed on the west by mile after mile of clean, sandy beaches. The islands have a distinctive culture and Gaelic is the first language of the majority of islanders. Roadside place name signs are in Gaelic. Although one island, Lewis (north) and Harris (south) are very different. Lewis is low-lying and covered with bleak peat moors, whereas Harris is rocky and mountainous, with fertile green 'machair' land to the west.

North Uist, Benbecula and South Uist offer beaches and low-lying 'machair' to the west, and mountains and moorland to the east, while Barra has a rocky, broken east coast and fine-sand bays on the west, rising to a summit at Heaval.

Ferry Services

Lewis is linked by ferry to the mainland at Ullapool, with daily sailings. There are ferry services from Harris (Tairbeart) and North Uist (Loch nam Madadh) to Uig on Skye. Harris and North Uist are connected by a ferry service between An t-Ob (Leverburgh) and Berneray, and then causeway to Otternish. South Uist and Barra are served by ferry services from Oban and a ferry service operates between Eriskay and Barra and another causeway links South Uist to Eriskay.

Berneray, North Uist, Benbecula, South Uist and Eriskay are all connected by causeways.

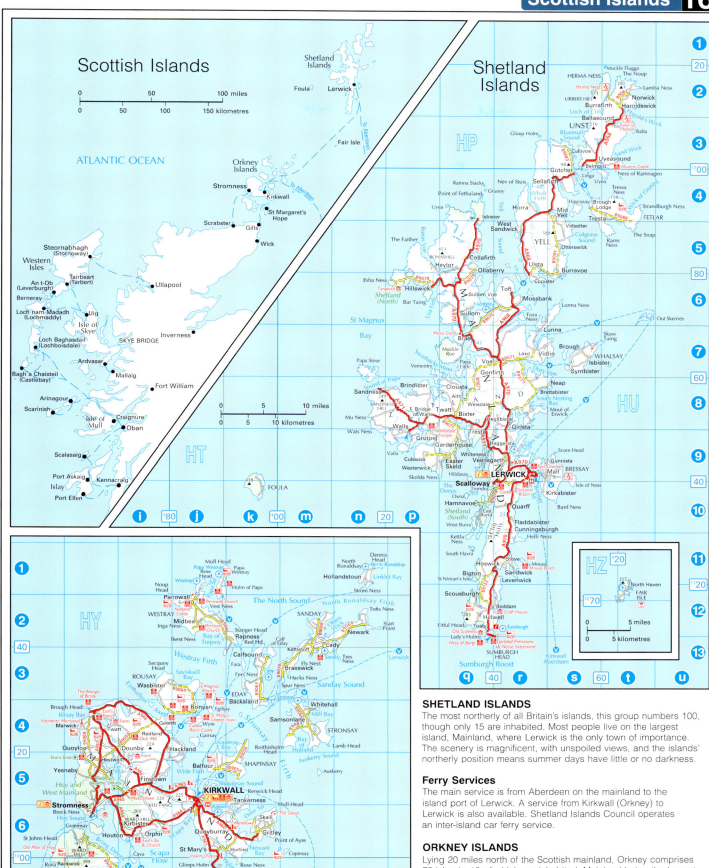

Scottish Islands

ATLANTIC OCEAN

Shetland Islands

Orkney Islands

SHETLAND ISLANDS

The most northerly of all Britain's islands, this group numbers 100, though only 15 are inhabited. Most people live on the largest island, Mainland, where Lerwick is the only town of importance. The scenery is magnificent, with unspoiled views, and the islands' northerly position means summer days have little or no darkness.

Ferry Services

The main service is from Aberdeen on the mainland to the island port of Lerwick. A service from Kirkwall (Orkney) to Lerwick is also available. Shetland Islands Council operates an inter-island car ferry service.

ORKNEY ISLANDS

Lying 20 miles north of the Scottish mainland, Orkney comprises 70 islands, 18 of which are inhabited, Mainland being the largest. Apart from Hoy, Orkney is generally green and flat, with few trees. The islands abound with prehistoric antiquities and rare birds. The climate is one of even temperatures and 'twilight' summer nights, but with violent winds at times.

Ferry Services

The main service is from Scrabster on the Caithness coast to Stromness and there is a further service from Gills (Caithness) to St Margaret's Hope on South Ronaldsay. A service from Aberdeen to Kirkwall provides a link to Shetland at Lerwick. Inter-island car ferry services are also operated (advance reservations recommended).

Legend / Key

M1	Toll-free motorway
M1 Toll	Toll motorway and booth
3	Motorway junctions with and without number
3 ●	Restricted motorway junctions
▪▪▪	Motorway under construction
N7	National primary route (Republic of Ireland)
N81	National secondary route (Republic of Ireland)
R116	Regional road (Republic of Ireland)
▸ 7	Distance in kilometres between symbols (Republic of Ireland)
A2	Primary route (Northern Ireland)
A42	A road (Northern Ireland)
B176	B road (Northern Ireland)
▸ 7	Distance in miles between symbols (Northern Ireland)
—	Minor road
▪▪▪	Road under construction
━━	Scenic route
━━	International boundary
Roscoff	Vehicle ferry
Troon	Fast vehicle ferry or catamaran
	National Park
	Gaeltacht (Irish language area)

To reflect the distances shown on road signs, distances are shown in miles in Northern Ireland and kilometres in the Republic of Ireland.

16 kilometres = 10 miles.

For key to touring information see page 1.

Ireland index

C12 Abbeydorney
D12 Abbeyfeale
G11 Abbeyleix
H12 Adamstown
D12 Adare
C14 Adrigole
H4 Aghadowey
E9 Ahascragh
J4 Aghoghill
B15 Allihies
B13 Anascaul
E4 An Bun Beag
E5 An Charraig
E4 An Clochán Liath
B14 An Coireán
C9 An Fhairche
J7 Annalong
G13 Annestown
G13 An Rinn
D9 An Spidéal
J5 Antrim
D12 Ardagh
E5 Ardara
H8 Ardee
C12 Ardfert
F12 Ardfinnan
K6 Ardglass
B14 Ardgroom
F8 Ardmore
J11 Arklow
H11 Arless
H6 Armagh
J3 Armoy
H13 Arthurstown
G7 Arvagh
J9 Ashbourne
J10 Ashford
H8 Athboy
D12 Athea
E9 Athenry
G7 Athleague
F9 Athlone
H10 Athy
G6 Augher
H6 Aughnacloy
J11 Aughrim
J11 Avoca

H11 Bagenalstown
D14 Baile Mhic Íre
H7 Bailieborough
J8 Balbriggan
D8 Balla
E7 Ballaghaderreen
D7 Ballina
E11 Ballina
E7 Ballinafad
G7 Ballinagh
E11 Ballinakill
F8 Ballinalee
G6 Ballinamallard
F7 Ballinamore
D14 Ballinascarty
E9 Ballinasloe
D8 Ballindine
D14 Ballineen
D12 Ballingarry
G12 Ballingarry
D14 Ballingeary
E14 Ballinhassig
D8 Ballinlough
D8 Ballinrobe
E15 Ballinspittle
E8 Ballintober
F5 Ballintra
H9 Ballivor
H11 Ballon
D9 Ballybaun
H7 Ballybay
F5 Ballybofey
C12 Ballybunion
J11 Ballycanew
K5 Ballycarry
J3 Ballycastle
C6 Ballycastle
J5 Ballyclare
G11 Ballycolla
B9 Ballyconneely
G7 Ballyconnell
F14 Ballycotton
F9 Ballycumber
C15 Ballydehob
D13 Ballydesmond
C12 Ballyduff
F13 Ballyduff
E7 Ballyfarnan
J4 Ballygalley
E9 Ballygar
E6 Ballygawley
H6 Ballygawley
K5 Ballygowan
H13 Ballyhack
G7 Ballyhaise
G12 Ballyhale
E8 Ballyhaunis
C12 Ballyheige
G8 Ballyjamesduff
F9 Ballykeeran
E12 Ballylanders
C14 Ballylickey
G3 Ballyliffin
C12 Ballylongford
F12 Ballylooby
H10 Ballylynan
F13 Ballymacarbry
F8 Ballymahon
D14 Ballymakeery
J4 Ballymena
E8 Ballymoe
H4 Ballymoney
F9 Ballymore
H10 Ballymore Eustace
E7 Ballymote
J6 Ballynahinch
J5 Ballynure

F13 Ballyporeen
G11 Ballyragget
G10 Ballyronan
H5 Ballyronan
E6 Ballysadare
F5 Ballyshannon
D10 Ballyvaughan
K5 Ballywalter
J8 Balrothery
C15 Baltimore
H10 Baltinglass
F10 Banagher
E14 Banbridge
K5 Bangor
C7 Bangor Erris
F12 Bansha
C14 Bantry
B6 Barna
B6 Béal an Mhuirthead
D14 Béal Átha an Ghaorthaidh
D9 Bearna
C13 Beaufort
F6 Belcoo
J5 Belfast
E14 Belgooly
H4 Bellagh
F6 Belleek
B6 Belmullet
G7 Belturbet
H6 Benburb
G12 Bennettsbridge
G5 Beragh
J8 Bettystown
F10 Birr
F6 Blacklion
J9 Blackrock
J12 Blackwater
E14 Blarney
H10 Blessington
D13 Boherbue
E8 Borris
F10 Borris in Ossory
F10 Borrisokane
F11 Borrisoleigh
E7 Boyle
G10 Bracknagh
J10 Bray
H13 Bridgetown
J9 Brittas
E11 Broadford
D12 Broadford
J4 Broughshane
E12 Bruff
E12 Bruree
E4 Bunbeg
H11 Bunclody
G3 Buncrana
E6 Bundoran
G13 Bunmahon
C6 Bun na hAbhna
C6 Bunnahowen
D7 Bunnyconnellan
D11 Bunratty
E13 Burnfort
H3 Bushmills
E13 Buttevant

F10 Cadamstown
E12 Caherconlish
B14 Caherdaniel
B14 Cahersiveen
F12 Cahir
H6 Caledon
G12 Callan
E9 Caltra
B13 Camp
H13 Campile
F12 Cappagh White
E11 Cappamore
F13 Cappoquin
H8 Carlanstown
J7 Carlingford
H11 Carlow
C9 Carna
G3 Carndonagh
J11 Carnew
J4 Carnlough
E7 Carracastle
F3 Carraig Airt
E5 Carrick
K5 Carrickart
H7 Carrickfergus
H7 Carrickmacross
G5 Carrickmore or Termon Rock
F7 Carrick-on-Shannon
G12 Carrick-on-Suir
F10 Carrigahorig
E4 Carrigaline
F7 Carrigallen
D14 Carriganimmy
G4 Carrigans
E14 Carrigtohill
J5 Carryduff
C9 Cashel
F12 Cashel
D8 Castlebar
J7 Castlebellingham
H7 Castleblaney
J12 Castlebridge
G11 Castlecomer
E11 Castleconnell
G5 Castlederg
H11 Castledermot
G4 Castlegregory
C13 Castleisland
C13 Castlemaine
F14 Castlemartyr
E8 Castleplunket
G8 Castlepollard
E8 Castlerea
H6 Castlerock
H6 Castleshane
G10 Castletown

B15 Castletown Bearhaven
E13 Castletownroche
D15 Castletownshend
J6 Castlewellan
B14 Cathair Dónall
C12 Causeway
G7 Cavan
H9 Celbridge
D7 Charlestown
E12 Charleville
H13 Cheekpoint
C9 Cill Charthaigh
C9 Cill Chiaráin
G5 Clady
H9 Clane
G9 Clara
D11 Clarecastle
D10 Claremorris
D10 Clarinbridge
F13 Clashmore
G4 Claudy
B9 Clifden
E6 Cliffony
G11 Clogh
F10 Cloghan
F13 Clogheen
G6 Clogher
H11 Clohamon
D15 Clonakilty
H9 Clonard
G10 Clonaslee
G9 Clonbulloge
C9 Clonbur
J9 Clondalkin
G7 Clones
E11 Clonlara
G3 Clonmany
F12 Clonmel
H8 Clonmellon
F11 Clonmore
F10 Clonony
F12 Clonoulty
H12 Clonroche
E8 Cloondara
K6 Clough
F10 Cloughjordan
F14 Cloyne
H5 Coagh
H5 Coalisland
E14 Cobh
H3 Coleraine
G8 Collinstown
H8 Collon
E6 Collooney
K5 Comber
F13 Conna
D9 Coole
H5 Cookstown
G8 Coole
C11 Cooraclare
G7 Cootehill
E14 Cork
C9 Cornamona
C9 Corr na Móna
D10 Corofin
E15 Courtmacsherry
J11 Courtown
J6 Craigavon
E10 Craughwell
K5 Crawfordsburn
E8 Creeslough
F4 Creeslough
D12 Croagh
E4 Croithlí
E4 Crolly
G8 Crookedwood
C15 Crookhaven
D10 Crookstown
E12 Croom
H8 Crossakeel
E14 Cross Barry
E14 Crosshaven
H7 Crossmaglen

D7 Crossmolina
J5 Crumlin
G3 Culdaff
G11 Cullybackey
J12 Curracloe
F9 Curraghbony
J4 Curry
J4 Cushendall
J3 Cushendun

G9 Daingean
J10 Delgany
G8 Delvin
J4 Derry
F6 Derrygonnelly
H3 Derrylin
H3 Dervock
B13 Dingle
J5 Doagh
K5 Donaghadee
G11 Donaghmore
H10 Donard
F5 Donegal
E13 Doneraile
C10 Doolin
E12 Doon
C11 Doonbeg
F9 Doon Cross Roads
E14 Douglas
H5 Downpatrick
F6 Dowra
B13 Draperstown
E14 Drimoleague
E6 Dromahair
J2 Dromcolliher
J6 Dromore
G5 Dromore
D6 Dromore West
E6 Drumcliff
H8 Drumcondra
F7 Drumkeeran
F8 Drumlish
F8 Drumod
F8 Drumquin
J5 Drumshanbo
F7 Drumsna
C12 Duagh
J9 Dublin
J8 Duleek
H13 Dunboyne
H13 Duncormick
J7 Dundalk
K5 Dunderrow
K5 Dundonald
K6 Dundrum
F12 Dundrum
F3 Dunfanaghy
H5 Dungannon
H12 Dungarvan
H12 Dungarvan
H4 Dungiven
E9 Dunglow
F14 Dungourney
E5 Dunkineely
J9 Dún Laoghaire
H10 Dunlavin
J8 Dunleer
J4 Dunloy
E8 Dunmanway
E8 Dunmore
H13 Dunmore East
J5 Dunmurry
H9 Dunshaughlin
G11 Durrow
C15 Durrus
J5 Dysart

D6 Easky
H9 Edenderry
E8 Edgeworthstown
G4 Eglinton
F8 Elphin
H6 Emyvale
H9 Enfield
D11 Ennis
H12 Enniscorthy
D11 Enniskean
F6 Enniskillen
D10 Ennistymon
F10 Eyrecourt

G4 Fahan
C13 Farranfore
E10 Feakle
F7 Fenagh
F9 Ferbane
E13 Fermoy
J12 Ferns
F12 Fethard
H13 Fethard
G8 Finnea
G6 Fintona
H10 Fivemiletown
H10 Fontstown
H12 Foulksmill
D7 Foxford
D11 Foynes
D13 Freemount
E8 Frenchpark
G11 Freshford
E8 Fuerty

E12 Galbally
D9 Galway
F6 Garrison
J8 Garristown
F14 Garryvoe
H4 Garvagh
G10 Geashill
J6 Gilford
D15 Glandore
E14 Glanmire
E13 Glanworth
H6 Glaslough
F9 Glassan
E5 Gleann Cholm Cille
J5 Glenarm
J5 Glenavy
B13 Glenbeigh
G8 Glencolumbkille
J10 Glenealy
C14 Glengarriff
H12 Glenmore
E8 Glennamaddy
E5 Glenties
D12 Glin
C9 Glinsk
C9 Glinsk
F12 Golden
C15 Goleen
H11 Goresbridge
J11 Gorey
D10 Gort
G5 Gortin
H11 Gowran
H12 Graiguenamanagh
E8 Granard
E6 Grange
J7 Greencastle
K5 Greyabbey
J10 Greystones
H4 Gulladuff

H11 Hacketstown
D9 Headford
H12 Herbertstown
J6 Hillsborough
J6 Hilltown
F11 Holycross
K5 Holywood
G9 Horseleap
E12 Hospital
J9 Howth

B13 Inch
D14 Inchigeelagh
E14 Inishannon
D6 Inishcrone
H12 Inistioge
F6 Irvinestown

G11 Johnstown

D13 Kanturk
F7 Keadew
H6 Keady
B7 Keel
F8 Keenagh
J4 Kells
H8 Kells
C14 Kenmare
F5 Kesh
G9 Kilbeggan
H8 Kilberry
E14 Kilbrittain
E8 Kilcar
H9 Kilcock
D10 Kilcolgan
E9 Kilconnell
J10 Kilcoole
F10 Kilcormac
H10 Kilcullen
J11 Kilcurry
H10 Kildare
H11 Kildavin
E13 Kildorrery
D10 Kilfenora
C14 Kilgarvan
C11 Kilkee
J7 Kilkeel
G11 Kilkenny
C9 Kilkieran
C12 Kilkinlea Lower
H9 Kill
G13 Kill
D11 Killadysert
D6 Killala
C13 Killarney
G7 Killashandra
F14 Killeagh
G10 Killeigh
F12 Killenaule
C11 Killimer
C11 Killimor
J9 Killiney
J13 Killinick
C13 Killorglin
K6 Killough
G9 Killucan
E5 Killybegs
K6 Killyleagh
J10 Kilmacanoge
F4 Kilmacrenan
C15 Kilmacthomas
G12 Kilmaganny
D8 Kilmaine
E12 Kilmallock
G11 Kilmanagh
G13 Kilmeadan
H9 Kilmeage
C15 Kilmeedy
D14 Kilmichael
H13 Kilmore Quay
J12 Kilmuckridge
G8 Kilnaleck
H4 Kilrea
C11 Kilrush
G12 Kilsheelan
D8 Kiltamagh
H12 Kiltealy
H11 Kiltegan
F9 Kiltoom
H7 Kingscourt
E6 Kinlough
G9 Kinnegad
F10 Kinnitty
E14 Kinsale
D10 Kinvarra
K5 Kircubbin

D8 Knock
F8 Knockcroghery
F12 Knocklofty
G12 Knocktopher

C10 Lahinch
F8 Lanesborough
J10 Laragh
K4 Larne
C14 Laragh
E11 Laurencetown
D15 Leap
C8 Leenane
H11 Leighlinbridge
F7 Leitrim
F9 Leixlip
G13 Lemybrien
B8 Letterfrack
F4 Letterkenny
G4 Lifford
H4 Limavady
E11 Limerick
H5 Lisbellaw
F9 Lisburn
C10 Liscannor
D13 Liscarroll
D10 Lisdoonvarna
F13 Lismore
G6 Lisnaskea
H3 Lisryan
C12 Listowel
D12 Loghill
G4 Londonderry
F8 Longford
J6 Loughbrickland
H6 Loughgall

E8 Loughglinn
E10 Loughrea
C8 Louisburgh
J9 Lucan
J6 Lurgan
J5 Lusk

F3 Machair Loiscthe
D14 Macroom
J6 Maghera
H4 Maghera
H5 Maghera
E6 Magherafelt
G6 Maguiresbridge
J9 Malahide
E5 Málainn Mhóir
G3 Malin
E5 Malin More
H4 Mallow
H6 Manorhamilton
H6 Markethill
J4 Martinstown
H9 Maynooth
J5 Mazetown
H6 Middletown
F14 Midleton
F4 Milford
D13 Millstreet
D13 Milltown
C11 Milltown Malbay
E13 Mitchelstown
F9 Moate
F7 Mohill
H6 Monaghan
G10 Monasterevin
F11 Moneygall
H5 Moneymore

170

E9	Monivea	G7	Newbliss	G5	Omagh	J9	Portraine	G4	Ray
G13	Mooncoin	H10	Newbridge	J7	Omeath	E11	Portroe	C9	Recess
J4	Moorfields	J6	Newcastle	H3	Portrush	B8	Renvyle
E9	Mountbellew	D12	Newcastle West	H3	Portstewart	E14	Ringaskiddy
	Bridge	F12	Newinn	D9	Portumna	G13	Ringville
F5	Mountcharles	D13	Newmarket	E14	Ovens	H7	Rockcorry
G10	Mountmellick	D11	Newmarket-on-			F8	Roosky
G10	Mountrath		Fergus	E12	Pallas Grean New	H12	Rosbercon
E10	Mountshannon	C7	Newport	B14	Parknasilla	J9	Shankill
G3	Moville	E11	Newport	D8	Partry	D11	Shannon
H6	Moy	H12	New Ross	H13	Passage East	F9	Shannonbridge
H8	Moynalty	J6	Newry	E12	Passage West	H7	Shercock
F9	Moyvore	G11	Newtown	E12	Patrickswell	H11	Shillelagh
C13	Muckross	K5	Newtownabbey	H11	Paulstown	F10	Shinrone
G4	Muff	G7	Newtownbutler	F5	Pettigo	D9	Shrule
E6	Mullaghmore	F8	Newtown Forbes	G5	Plumbridge	E11	Silvermines
G12	Mullinavat	H6	Newtownhamilton	H6	Pomeroy	G5	Sion Mills
G9	Mullingar	J10	Newtown Mount	H6	Portadown	D11	Sixmilebridge
C7	Mulrany		Kennedy	K6	Portaferry	J8	Skerries
H11	Myshall	G5	Newtownstewart	G10	Portarlington	D15	Skibbereen
		H8	Nobber	K6	Portavogie	H8	Slane
H10	Naas			H3	Portballintrae	E6	Sligo
J8	Naul	E11	Ogonnelloe	H4	Portglenone	G6	Smithborough
H8	Navan	H12	Oilgate	G10	Portlaoise	B14	Sneem
D8	Neale	G8	Oldcastle	J9	Portmarnock	C11	Spanish Point
E11	Nenagh			E4	Portnoo	D9	Spiddal
G4	Ray	E11	Scarriff	C9	Sraith Salach	F12	Tipperary
C9	Recess	C13	Scartaglin	H5	Stewartstown	E7	Tobercurry
B8	Renvyle	J6	Scarva	J9	Stillorgan	H4	Tobermore
E14	Ringaskiddy	C15	Schull	G12	Stonyford	F11	Toomyvara
G13	Ringville	F8	Scramoge	G4	Strabane	C15	Toormore
H7	Rockcorry	G5	Seskinore	G4	Stradbally	C13	Tralee
F8	Roosky	F14	Shanagarry	G7	Stradone	G13	Tramore
H12	Rosbercon	D12	Shanagolden	H9	Straffan	H8	Trim
J9	Shankill	J9		G8	Strandhill	D9	Tuam
D11	Shannon	D11	Shannon	K6	Strangford	E11	Tuamgraney
F9	Shannonbridge	F9	Shannonbridge	F5	Stranorlar	D11	Tulla
H7	Shercock	H7	Shercock	F8	Strokestown	G9	Tullamore
H11	Shillelagh	H11	Shillelagh	H9	Summerhill	H11	Tullow
F10	Shinrone	F10	Shinrone	F6	Swanlinbar	E8	Tulsk
D9	Shrule	D9	Shrule	H4	Swatragh	D7	Turlough
E11	Silvermines	E11	Silvermines	D7	Swinford	G9	Tyrrellspass
G5	Sion Mills	G5	Sion Mills	J9	Swords
D11	Sixmilebridge	D11	Sixmilebridge			G11	Urlingford
J8	Skerries	J8	Skerries	H12	Taghmon
D15	Skibbereen	D15	Skibbereen	C14	Tahilla	G8	Virginia
H8	Slane	H8	Slane	J9	Tallaght
E6	Sligo	E6	Sligo	F13	Tallow	H12	Warrenpoint
G6	Smithborough	G6	Smithborough	F13	Tallowbridge	G13	Waterford
B14	Sneem	B14	Sneem	J6	Tandragee	E13	Watergrasshill
C11	Spanish Point	C11	Spanish Point	F9	Tang	B14	Waterville
D9	Spiddal	D9	Spiddal	C12	Tarbert	C8	Westport
				F11	Templemore	J12	Wexford
				F11	Templetouhy	E14	Whitegate
				J8	Termonfeckin	K5	Whitehead
				G12	Thomastown	J10	Wicklow
				F11	Thurles	E11	Woodenbridge
				G10	Timahoe	E10	Woodford
				D15	Timoleague
				J11	Tinahely	F14	Youghal

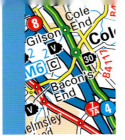

Restricted junctions

Motorway and Primary Route junctions which have access or exit restrictions are shown on the map pages thus:

M1 London - Leeds

Northbound
Access only from A1
(northbound)

Southbound
Exit only to A1
(southbound)

Northbound
Access only from A41
(northbound)

Southbound
Exit only to A41
(southbound)

Northbound
Access only from M25
(no link from A405)

Southbound
Exit only to M25 (no link from A405)

Northbound
Access only from A414

Southbound
Exit only to A414

Northbound
Exit only to M45

Southbound
Access only from M45

Northbound
Exit only to M6
(northbound)

Southbound
Access only from M6

Northbound
Exit only, no access

Southbound
Access only, no exit

Northbound
Access only from A42

Southbound
No restriction

Northbound
No exit, access only

Southbound
Exit only, no access

Northbound
Exit only, no access

Southbound
Access only, no exit

Northbound
Exit only to M621

Southbound
Access only from M621

Northbound
Exit only to A1(M)
(northbound)

Southbound
Access only from A1(M)
(southbound)

M2 Rochester - Faversham

Westbound
No exit to A2
(eastbound)

Eastbound
No access from A2
(westbound)

M3 Sunbury - Southampton

Northeastbound
Access only from A303,
no exit

Southwestbound
Exit only to A303,
no access

Northbound
Exit only, no access

Southbound
Access only, no exit

Northeastbound
Access from M27 only.
No exit

Southwestbound
No access to M27
(westbound)

M4 London - South Wales

Westbound
Access only from A4
(westbound)

Eastbound
Exit only to A4
(eastbound)

Westbound
No exit to A4 (westbound)

Eastbound
No restriction

Westbound
Exit only to M48

Eastbound
Access only from M48

Westbound
Access only from M48

Eastbound
Exit only to M48

Westbound
Exit only, no access

Eastbound
Access only, no exit

Westbound
Exit only, no access

Eastbound
Access only, no exit

Westbound
Exit only to A48(M)

Eastbound
Access only from A48(M)

Westbound
Exit only, no access

Eastbound
No restriction

Westbound
Access only, no exit

Eastbound
No access or exit

M5 Birmingham - Exeter

Northeastbound
Access only, no exit

Southwestbound
Exit only, no access

Northeastbound
Access only from A417
(westbound)

Southwestbound
Exit only to A417
(eastbound)

Northeastbound
No access, exit only

Southwestbound
No exit, access only

Northeastbound
Exit only to M49

Southwestbound
Access only from M49

Northeastbound
No restriction

Southwestbound
Access only from A30
(westbound)

M6 Toll Motorway

See M6 Toll Motorway map on page 179

M6 Rugby - Carlisle

Northbound
Exit only to M6 Toll

Southbound
Access only from M6 Toll

Northbound
Access only from M42
(southbound)

Southbound
Exit only to M42

Northbound
Exit only, no access

Southbound
Access only, no exit

Northbound
Exit only to M54

Southbound
Access only from M54

Northbound
Access only from M6 Toll

Southbound
Exit only to M6 Toll

Northbound
No restriction

Southbound
Access only from M56
(eastbound)

Northbound
Access only, no exit

Southbound
No restriction

Northbound
Access only, no exit

Southbound
Exit only, no access

Northbound
Exit only, no access

Southbound
Access only, no exit

Northbound
No direct access, use adjacent slip road to jct 29A

Southbound
No direct exit, use adjacent slip road from jct 29A

Northbound
Acces only, no exit

Southbound
Exit only, no access

Northbound
Access only from M61

Southbound
Exit only to M61

Northbound
Exit only, no access

Southbound
Access only, no exit

Northbound
Exit only, no access

Southbound
Access only, no exit

M8 Edinburgh - Bishopton

See Glasgow District map on pages 254-255

M9 Edinburgh - Dunblane

Northwestbound
Exit only to M9 spur

Southeastbound
Access only from M9 spur

Northwestbound
Access only, no exit

Southeastbound
Exit only, no access

Northwestbound
Exit only, no access

Southeastbound
Access only, no exit

Northwestbound
Access only, no exit

Southeastbound
Exit only to A905

Northwestbound
Exit only to M876 (southwestbound)

Southeastbound
Access only from M876 (northeastbound)

M11 London - Cambridge

Northbound
Access only from A406 (eastbound)

Southbound
Exit only to A406

Northbound
Exit only, no access

Southbound
Access only, no exit

Northbound
Exit only to A11

Southbound
Access only from A11

Northbound
Exit only, no access

Southbound
Access only, no exit

Northbound
Exit only, no access

Southbound
Access only, no exit

M20 Swanley - Folkestone

Northwestbound
Staggered junction; follow signs - access only

Southeastbound
Staggered junction; follow signs - exit only

Northwestbound
Exit only to M26 (westbound)

Southeastbound
Access only from M26 (eastbound)

Northwestbound
Access only from A20

Southeastbound
For access follow signs - exit only to A20

Northwestbound
No restriction

Southeastbound
For exit follow signs

Northwestbound
Access only, no exit

Southeastbound
Exit only, no access

M23 Hooley - Crawley

Northbound
Exit only to A23 (northbound)

Southbound
Access only from A23 (southbound)

Northbound
Access only, no exit

Southbound
Exit only, no access

M25 London Orbital Motorway

See M25 London Orbital Motorway map on page 178

M26 Sevenoaks - Wrotham

Westbound
Exit only to clockwise M25 (westbound)

Eastbound
Access only from anti-clockwise M25 (eastbound)

Westbound
Access only from M20 (northwestbound)

Eastbound
Exit only to M20 (southeastbound)

M27 Cadnam - Portsmouth

Westbound
Staggered junction; follow signs - access only from M3 (southbound). Exit only to M3 (northbound)

Eastbound
Staggered junction; follow signs - access only from M3 (southbound). Exit only to M3 (northbound)

Westbound
Exit only, no access

Eastbound
Access only, no exit

Westbound
Staggered junction; follow signs - exit only to M275 (southbound)

Eastbound
Staggered junction; follow signs - access only from M275 (northbound)

M40 London - Birmingham

Northwestbound
Exit only, no access

Southeastbound
Access only, no exit

Northwestbound
Exit only, no access

Southeastbound
Access only, no exit

Northwestbound
Exit only to M40/A40

Southeastbound
Access only from M40/A40

Northwestbound
Exit only, no access

Southeastbound
Access only, no exit

Northwestbound
Access only, no exit

Southeastbound
Exit only, no access

Northwestbound
Access only, no exit

Southeastbound
Exit only, no access

M42 Bromsgrove - Measham

See Birmingham District map on pages 252-253

M45 Coventry - M1

Westbound
Access only from A45 (northbound)

Eastbound
Exit only, no access

Westbound
Access only from M1 (northbound)

Eastbound
Exit only to M1 (southbound)

M53 Mersey Tunnel - Chester

Northbound
Access only from M56 (westbound). Exit only to M56 (eastbound)

Southbound
Access only from M56 (westbound). Exit only to M56 (eastbound)

M54 Telford

Westbound
Access only from M6 (northbound)

Eastbound
Exit only to M6 (southbound)

M56 North Cheshire

For junctions 1,2,3,4 & 7 see Manchester District map on pages 256-257

Westbound
Access only, no exit

Eastbound
No access or exit

Westbound
Exit only to M53

Eastbound
Access only from M53

M57 Liverpool Outer Ring Road

Northwestbound
Access only, no exit

Southeastbound
Exit only, no access

Northwestbound
Access only from A580 (westbound)

Southeastbound
Exit only, no access

M58 Liverpool - Wigan

Westbound
Exit only, no access

Eastbound
Access only, no exit

M60 Manchester Orbital

See Manchester District map on pages 256-257

M61 Manchester - Preston

Northwestbound
No access or exit

Southeastbound
Exit only, no access

Northwestbound
Exit only to M6 (northbound)

Southeastbound
Access only from M6 (southbound)

M62 Liverpool - Kingston upon Hull

Westbound
Access only, no exit

Eastbound
Exit only, no access

Westbound
No access to A1(M) (southbound)

Eastbound
No restriction

M65 Preston - Colne

Northeastbound
Exit only, no access

Southwestbound
Access only, no exit

Northeastbound
Access only, no exit

Southwestbound
Exit only, no access

M66 Bury

Northbound
Exit only to A56 (northbound)

Southbound
Access only from A56 (southbound)

Northbound
Exit only, no access

Southbound
Access only, no exit

M67 Hyde Bypass

Westbound
Access only, no exit

Eastbound
Exit only, no access

Westbound
Exit only, no access

Eastbound
Access only, no exit

Westbound
Exit only, no access

Eastbound
No restriction

M69 Coventry - Leicester

Northbound
Access only, no exit

Southbound
Exit only, no access

M73 East of Glasgow

Northbound
No access from or exit to A89. No access from M8 (eastbound)

Southbound
No access from or exit to A89. No exit to M8 (westbound)

M74 and A74(M) Glasgow - Gretna

Northbound
Exit only, no access

Southbound
Access only, no exit

Northbound
Access only, no exit

Southbound
Exit only, no access

Northbound
Access only, no exit

Southbound
Exit only, no access

Northbound
No access or exit

Southbound
Exit only, no access

Northbound
No restriction

Southbound
Access only, no exit

Northbound
Access only, no exit

Southbound
Exit only, no access

Northbound
Exit only, no access

Southbound
Access only, no exit

Northbound
Exit only, no access

Southbound
Access only, no exit

M77 South of Glasgow

Northbound
No exit to M8 (westbound)

Southbound
No access from M8 (eastbound)

Northbound
Access only, no exit

Southbound
Exit only, no access

Northbound
Access only, no exit

Southbound
Exit only, no access

Northbound
Access only, no exit

Southbound
No restriction

M80 Glasgow - Stirling

Northbound
Exit only, no access

Southbound
Access only, no exit

Northbound
Access only, no exit

Southbound
Exit only, no access

Northbound
Exit only to M876 (northeastbound)

Southbound
Access only from M876 (southwestbound)

M90 Forth Road Bridge - Perth

Northbound
Exit only to A92 (eastbound)

Southbound
Access only from A92 (westbound)

Northbound
Access only, no exit

Southbound
Exit only, no access

Northbound
Exit only, no access

Southbound
Access only, no exit

Northbound
No access from A912
No exit to A912 (southbound)

Southbound
No access from A912 (northbound).
No exit to A912

M180 Doncaster - Grimsby

Westbound
Access only, no exit

Eastbound
Exit only, no access

M606 Bradford Spur

Northbound
Exit only, no access

Southbound
No restriction

M621 Leeds - M1

Clockwise
Access only, no exit

Anticlockwise
Exit only, no access

Clockwise
No exit or access

Anticlockwise
No restriction

Clockwise
Access only, no exit

Anticlockwise
Exit only, no access

Clockwise
Exit only, no access

Anticlockwise
Access only, no exit

Clockwise
Exit only to M1
(southbound)

Anticlockwise
Access only from M1
(northbound)

M876 Bonnybridge - Kincardine Bridge

Northeastbound
Access only from M80
(northbound)

Southwestbound
Exit only to M80
(southbound)

Northeastbound
Exit only to M9
(eastbound)

Southwestbound
Access only from M9
(westbound)

A1(M) South Mimms - Baldock

Northbound
Exit only, no access

Southbound
Access only, no exit

Northbound
No restriction

Southbound
Exit only, no access

Northbound
Access only, no exit

Southbound
No access or exit

A1(M) East of Leeds

Northbound
No access to M62
(eastbound)

Southbound
No restriction

Northbound
Access only from M1
(northbound)

Southbound
Exit only to M1
(southbound)

A1(M) Scotch Corner - Newcastle upon Tyne

Northbound
Exit only to A66(M)
(eastbound)

Southbound
Access only from A66(M)
(westbound)

Northbound
No access. Exit only to
A194(M) & A1
(northbound)

Southbound
No exit. Access only from
A194(M) & A1
(southbound)

A3(M) Horndean - Havant

Northbound
Access only from A3

Southbound
Exit only to A3

Northbound
Exit only, no access

Southbound
Access only, no exit

A48(M) Cardiff Spur

Westbound
Access only from M4
(westbound)

Eastbound
Exit only to M4
(eastbound)

Westbound
Exit only to A48
(westbound)

Eastbound
Access only from A48
(eastbound)

A66(M) Darlington Spur

Westbound
Exit only to A1(M)
(southbound)

Eastbound
Access only from A1(M)
(northbound)

A194(M) Newcastle upon Tyne

Northbound
Access only from A1(M)
(northbound)

Southbound
Exit only to A1(M)
(southbound)

A12 M25 - Ipswich

Northeastbound
Access only, no exit

Southwestbound
No restriction

Northeastbound
Exit only, no access

Southwestbound
Access only, no exit

Northeastbound
Exit only, no access

Southwestbound
Access only, no exit

Northeastbound
Access only, no exit

Southwestbound
Exit only, no access

Northeastbound
No restriction

Southwestbound
Access only, no exit

Northeastbound
Exit only, no access

Southwestbound
Access only, no exit

Northeastbound
Access only, no exit

Southwestbound
Access only, no exit

Northeastbound
Exit only, no access

Southwestbound
Access only, no exit

With A120
Northeastbound
Exit only, no access

Southwestbound
Access only, no exit

Northeastbound
Access only, no exit

Southwestbound
Exit only, no access

Northeastbound
Exit only (for Stratford
St Mary and Dedham)

Southwestbound
Access only

A14 M1 Felixstowe

Westbound
Exit only to M6 & M1
(northbound)

Eastbound
Access only from M6 &
M1 (southbound)

Westbound
Exit only, no access

Eastbound
Access only, no exit

Westbound
Access only from A1307

Eastbound
Exit only to A1307

Westbound
Access only, no exit

Eastbound
Exit only, no access

Westbound
Exit only to A11

Eastbound
Access only from A11

Westbound
Access only from A11

Eastbound
Exit only to A11

Westbound
Exit only, no access

Eastbound
Access only, no exit

Westbound
Access only, no exit

Eastbound
Exit only, no access

A55 Holyhead - Chester

Westbound
Exit only, no access

Eastbound
Access only, no exit

Westbound
Access only, no exit

Eastbound
Exit only, no access

Westbound
Exit only, no access

Eastbound
No access or exit.

Westbound
Exit only, no access

Eastbound
No access or exit

Westbound
Exit only, no access

Eastbound
Access only, no exit

Westbound
Exit only to A5104

Eastbound
Access only from A5104

M25 London Orbital motorway

Refer also to atlas pages 36-37 and 50-51

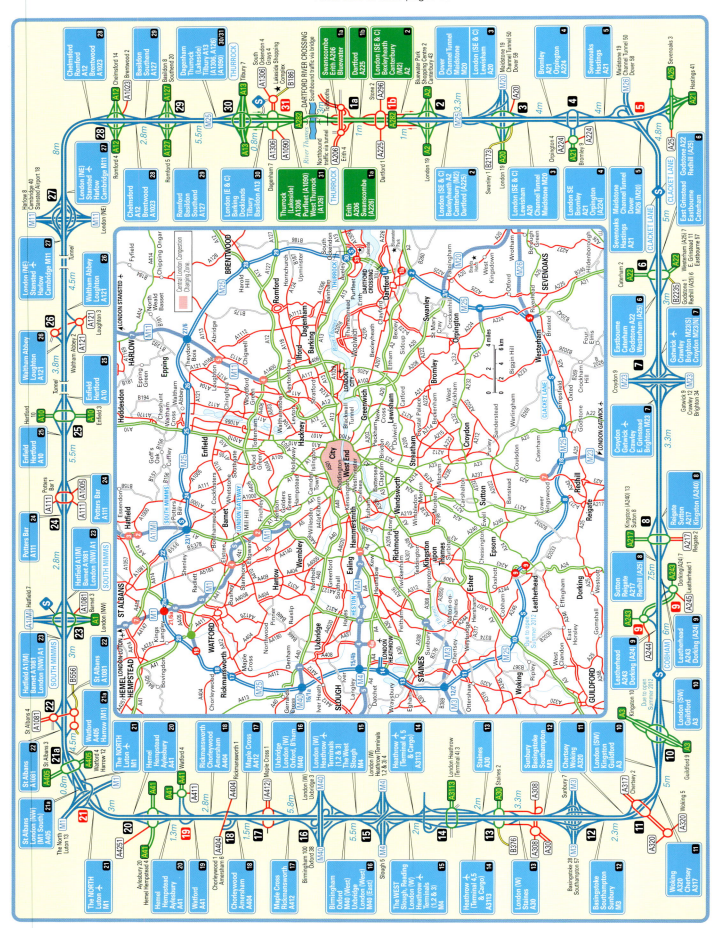

M6 Toll motorway

Refer also to atlas pages 58-59

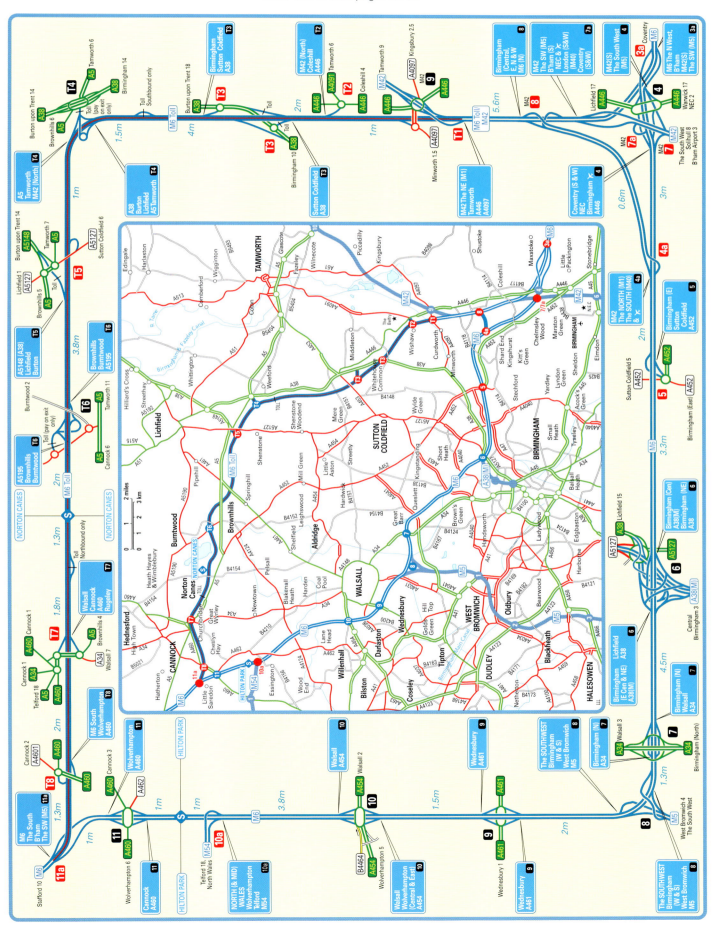

Street map symbols

District, town, port and airport plans

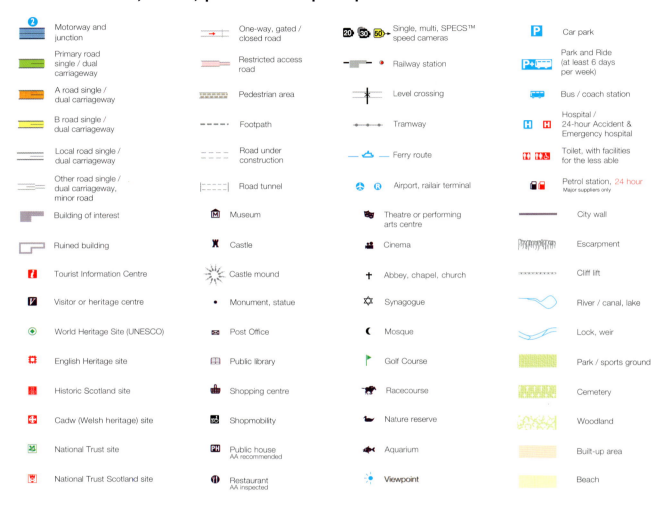

Motorway and junction	One-way, gated / closed road	Single, multi, SPECS™ speed cameras	Car park
Primary road single / dual carriageway	Restricted access road	Railway station	Park and Ride (at least 6 days per week)
A road single / dual carriageway	Pedestrian area	Level crossing	Bus / coach station
B road single / dual carriageway	Footpath	Tramway	Hospital / 24-hour Accident & Emergency hospital
Local road single / dual carriageway	Road under construction	Ferry route	Toilet, with facilities for the less able
Other road single / dual carriageway, minor road	Road tunnel	Airport, railair terminal	Petrol station, 24 hour Major suppliers only
Building of interest	Museum	Theatre or performing arts centre	City wall
Ruined building	Castle	Cinema	Escarpment
Tourist Information Centre	Castle mound	Abbey, chapel, church	Cliff lift
Visitor or heritage centre	Monument, statue	Synagogue	River / canal, lake
World Heritage Site (UNESCO)	Post Office	Mosque	Lock, weir
English Heritage site	Public library	Golf Course	Park / sports ground
Historic Scotland site	Shopping centre	Racecourse	Cemetery
Cadw (Welsh heritage) site	Shopmobility	Nature reserve	Woodland
National Trust site	Public house AA recommended	Aquarium	Built-up area
National Trust Scotland site	Restaurant AA inspected	Viewpoint	Beach

Central London street map (see pages 232 - 241)

Speed camera site (fixed location) with speed limit in mph	London Underground station	Docklands Light Railway (DLR) station
Section of road with two or more fixed camera sites; speed limit in mph	London Overground station	Light rapid transit system station
Average speed (SPECS™) camera system with speed limit in mph	Rail interchange	Central London Congestion Charging Zone

Royal Parks (opening and closing times for traffic)

Green Park	Constitution Hill: closed Sundays, 8 am-dusk
Hyde Park	Open 5 am-midnight
Regent's Park	Open 5 am-midnight
St James's Park	The Mall: closed Sundays, 8 am-dusk

Traffic regulations in the City of London include security checkpoints and restrict the number of entry and exit points.

Note: Oxford Street is closed to through-traffic (except buses & taxis) 7 am-7 pm Monday-Saturday. Restricted parts of Frith Street/Old Compton Street are closed to vehicles 12 noon-1 am daily.

Central London Congestion Charging Zone

The daily charge for driving or parking a vehicle on public roads in the Congestion Charging Zone (CCZ), during operating hours, is £10 per vehicle per day in advance or on the day of travel. Drivers can also pay the next charging day after travelling in the zone but this will cost £12. Payment permits entry, travel within and exit from the CCZ by the vehicle as often as required on that day.

The CCZ operates between 7am and 6pm, Mon–Fri only. There is no charge at weekends, public holidays or betwen 25th Dec and 1st Jan inclusive.

For up to date information on the CCZ, exemptions, discounts or ways to pay, telephone 0845 900 1234, visit www.cclondon.com or write to Congestion Charging, P.O. Box 4782, Worthing BN11 9PS. Textphone users can call 0207 649 9123.

Towns, ports & airports

Page 182..........Aberdeen
182..........Basingstoke
183..........Bath
184..........Birmingham
183..........Blackpool
185..........Bournemouth
185..........Bradford
186..........Brighton
186..........Bristol
187..........Cambridge
188..........Canterbury
188..........Cardiff
189..........Carlisle
189..........Cheltenham
190..........Chester
190..........Colchester
191..........Coventry
191..........Darlington
192..........Derby
192..........Doncaster
193..........Dover
193..........Dundee
194..........Durham
194..........Eastbourne
195..........Edinburgh
196..........Exeter
197..........Glasgow
196..........Gloucester

Page 198..........Great Yarmouth
198..........Guildford
199..........Harrogate
199..........Huddersfield
200..........Inverness
200..........Ipswich
201..........Kingston upon Hull
201..........Lancaster
202..........Leeds
203..........Leicester
203..........Lincoln
204..........Liverpool
79..........Llandudno
232–241..........LONDON
205..........Luton
205..........Maidstone
206..........Manchester
39..........Margate
208..........Middlesbrough
207..........Milton Keynes
209..........Newcastle upon Tyne
208..........Newport
4..........Newquay
210..........Northampton
210..........Norwich
211..........Nottingham
211..........Oldham
212..........Oxford

Page 213..........Perth
213..........Peterborough
214..........Plymouth
216..........Poole
215..........Portsmouth
216..........Preston
39..........Ramsgate
217..........Reading
217..........Salisbury
218..........Sheffield
218..........Shrewsbury
219..........Southampton
220..........Southend-on-Sea
220..........Stirling
221..........Stockton-on-Tees
221..........Stoke-on-Trent (Hanley)
222..........Stratford-upon-Avon
223..........Sunderland
222..........Swansea
224..........Swindon
224..........Taunton
225..........Torquay
225..........Tunbridge Wells
226..........Warwick
226..........Watford
227..........Winchester
227..........Wolverhampton
228..........Worcester
228..........York

Central London

Ferry Ports
Page 151..........Aberdeen Harbour
11..........Calais
11..........Dover, Port of
13..........Fishguard Harbour
53..........Harwich International Port
13..........Heysham Harbour
13..........Holyhead Harbour
13..........Liverpool Docks
11..........Newhaven Harbour
13..........Pembroke Dock
10..........Plymouth, Port of
10..........Poole, Port of
113..........Port of Tyne
11..........Portsmouth Harbour
13..........Stranraer Ferry Port
13..........Swansea, Port of
10..........Weymouth Harbour

Airports
229..........London Heathrow
229..........London Gatwick
229..........London Stansted
229..........London Luton
230..........London City
230..........Birmingham International
230..........Manchester
230..........East Midlands
231..........Leeds Bradford International
231..........Aberdeen
231..........Edinburgh
231..........Glasgow

Channel Tunnel
27..........Folkestone Terminal
27..........Calais / Coquelles Terminal

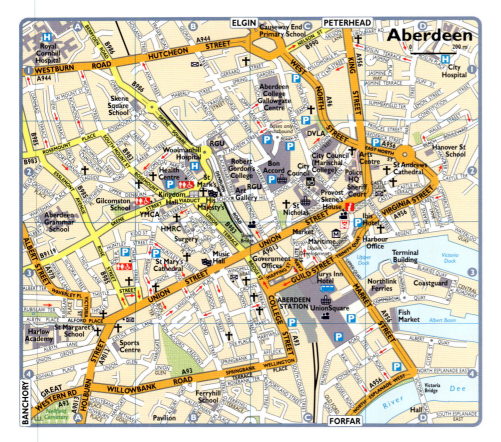

Aberdeen

Aberdeen is found on atlas page **151 N6**

C4 Affleck Street	B1 Maberly Street
A3 Albert Street	D2 Marischal Street
B4 Albury Road	C3 Market Street
A3 Alford Place	C1 Nelson Street
B1 Ann Street	C4 Palmerston Road
D2 Beach Boulevard	D1 Park Street
A2 Belgrave Terrace	C4 Portland Street
A1 Berryden Road	C4 Poynernook Road
B2 Blackfriars Street	D3 Regent Quay
B4 Bon Accord Crescent	A2 Richmond Street
B3 Bon Accord Street	A3 Rose Place
C3 Bridge Street	A3 Rose Street
B4 Caledonian Place	A2 Rosemount Place
C3 Carmelite Street	A2 Rosemount Viaduct
A3 Chapel Street	B2 St Andrew Street
B1 Charlotte Street	C1 St Clair Street
C3 College Street	C2 School Hill
D1 Constitution Street	B2 Skene Square
B3 Crimon Place	A3 Skene Street
C3 Crown Street	B2 Skene Terrace
B3 Dee Street	C4 South College Street
B2 Denburn Road	D4 South Esplanade East
B3 Diamond Street	A2 South Mount Street
D2 East North Street	B2 Spa Street
A2 Esslemont Avenue	B4 Springbank Street
C1 Gallowgate	B4 Springbank Terrace
B1 George Street	B3 Summer Street
B2 Gilcomston Park	D1 Summerfield Terrace
B3 Golden Square	A3 Thistle Lane
B3 Gordon Street	A3 Thistle Place
A4 Great Western Road	A3 Thistle Street
C3 Guild Street	C3 Trinity Quay
C3 Hadden Street	B3 Union Bridge
D2 Hanover Street	A4 Union Grove
A4 Hardgate	B3 Union Street
B4 Hardgate	B2 Union Terrace
C2 Harriet Street	A2 Upper Denburn
A4 Holburn Street	D4 Victoria Road
A3 Huntley Street	A3 Victoria Street
B1 Hutcheon Street	A1 View Terrace
D1 Jasmine Terrace	D2 Virginia Street
B2 John Street	C3 Wapping Street
A4 Justice Mill Lane	A3 Waverley Place
C1 King Street	C4 Wellington Place
B3 Langstane Place	C1 West North Street
A2 Leadside Road	A1 Westburn Road
A1 Loanhead Terrace	A2 Whitehall Place
C1 Loch Street	A4 Willowbank Road

Basingstoke

Basingstoke is found on atlas page **22 H4**

C1 Alencon Link	D3 London Road
D2 Allnutt Avenue	D3 London Street
C1 Basing View	A2 Lower Brook Street
C4 Beaconsfield Road	D3 Lytton Road
A4 Bounty Rise	B3 Market Place
A4 Bounty Road	C3 May Place
A3 Bramblys Close	C4 Montague Place
A3 Bramblys Drive	A2 Mortimer Lane
A3 Budd's Close	B3 New Road
C4 Castle Road	C2 New Road
B1 Chapel Hill	B3 New Street
B1 Chapel Hill	C1 Old Reading Road
C2 Chequers Road	A3 Penrith Road
A4 Chester Place	A2 Rayleigh Road
B2 Churchill Way	C3 Red Lion Lane
D1 Churchill Way East	A2 Rochford Road
A2 Churchill Way West	C2 St Mary's Court
B2 Church Square	A3 Sarum Hill
B2 Church Street	C2 Seal Road
B3 Church Street	A3 Solby's Road
C4 Cliddesden Road	A2 Southend Road
C1 Clifton Terrace	B4 Southern Road
A4 Cordale Road	A3 Stukeley Road
B4 Council Road	B4 Sylvia Close
D3 Crossborough Hill	B2 Timberlake Road
B3 Cross Street	B3 Victoria Street
A4 Devonshire Place	A1 Victory Roundabout
D2 Eastfield Avenue	B1 Vyne Road
D3 Eastfield Avenue	A3 Winchcombe Road
D2 Eastrop Lane	A4 Winchester Road
C1 Eastrop Roundabout	B3 Winchester Street
D2 Eastrop Way	A1 Winterthur Way
A2 Essex Road	A3 Worting Road
B4 Fairfields Road	C3 Wote Street
C2 Festival Way	
A2 Flaxfield Court	
A3 Flaxfield Road	
B3 Flaxfield Road	
A4 Frances Road	
A4 Frescade Crescent	
C2 Goat Lane	
C4 Hackwood Road	
A4 Hamelyn Road	
A4 Hardy Lane	
A4 Hawkfield Lane	
C3 Haymarket Yard	
B3 Joices Yard	
B4 Jubilee Road	

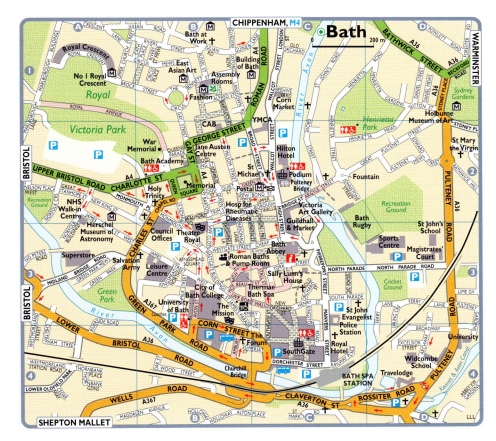

Bath

Bath is found on atlas page **20 D2**

D4	Archway Street	B3	Lower Borough Walls
C2	Argyle Street	A3	Lower Bristol Road
B3	Avon Street	A4	Lower Oldfield Park
B1	Bartlett Street	C3	Manvers Street
B2	Barton Street	A3	Midland Bridge Road
D1	Bathwick Street	B2	Milsom Street
B2	Beauford Square	A2	Monmouth Place
B3	Beau Street	B2	Monmouth Street
D1	Beckford Road	B2	New Bond Street
B1	Bennett Street	A2	New King Street
C2	Bridge Street	C3	New Orchard Street
C2	Broad Street	A3	Norfolk Buildings
D4	Broadway	C3	North Parade
A1	Brock Street	D3	North Parade Road
B2	Chapel Road	B2	Old King Street
A3	Charles Street	B1	Oxford Row
A2	Charlotte Street	C3	Pierrepont Street
C3	Cheap Street	B2	Princes Street
A4	Cheltenham Street	D2	Pulteney Road
B1	Circus Mews	B2	Queen Square
C4	Claverton Street	B2	Queen Street
B4	Corn Street	C4	Railway Place
D1	Daniel Street	B1	Rivers Street
C4	Dorchester Street	C1	Roman Road
D2	Edward Street	C4	Rossiter Road
B1	Gay Street	A1	Royal Avenue
B2	George Street	A1	Royal Crescent
C2	Great Pulteney Street	B3	St James's Parade
A2	Great Stanhope Street	C1	St John's Road
A3	Green Park Road	B3	Saw Close
B2	Green Street	C4	Southgate Street
C2	Grove Street	C3	South Parade
B1	Guinea Lane	C3	Stall Street
D1	Henrietta Gardens	D1	Sutton Street
C2	Henrietta Mews	D1	Sydney Place
C1	Henrietta Road	B1	The Circus
C2	Henrietta Street	A4	Thornbank Place
C3	Henry Street	B2	Union Street
C2	High Street	C2	Upper Borough Walls
B3	Hot Bath Street	A2	Upper Bristol Road
B3	James Street West	A1	Upper Church Street
B2	John Street	C2	Walcot Street
A1	Julian Road	A4	Wells Road
B1	Julian Road	B3	Westgate Buildings
B3	Kingsmead North	B3	Westgate Street
C3	Kingston Road	A4	Westmoreland Station Road
B1	Lansdown Road		
C1	London Street	C3	York Street

Blackpool

Blackpool is found on atlas page **88 C3**

B1	Abingdon Street	B3	Hornby Road
B3	Adelaide Street	D3	Hornby Road
B3	Albert Road	B3	Hull Road
C3	Albert Road	C4	Kay Street
C2	Alfred Street	C4	Kent Road
D4	Ashton Road	C2	King Street
B2	Bank Hey Street	C1	Larkhill Street
B1	Banks Street	D2	Leamington Road
C4	Belmont Avenue	D2	Leicester Road
D3	Bennett Avenue	C2	Leopold Grove
C4	Bethesda Road	D2	Lincoln Road
B2	Birley Street	C3	Livingstone Road
D4	Blenheim Avenue	B1	Lord Street
B4	Bonny Street	C4	Louise Street
C1	Buchanan Street	C1	Milbourne Street
C1	Butler Street	B3	New Bonny Street
D1	Caunce Street	C4	Palatine Road
C2	Cedar Square	D3	Palatine Road
C4	Central Drive	D2	Park Road
B4	Chapel Street	D4	Park Road
C1	Charles Street	D2	Peter Street
C3	Charnley Road	B4	Pier Street
B2	Cheapside	B1	Princess Parade
B2	Church Street	B1	Promenade
C2	Church Street	B1	Queen Street
D2	Church Street	D2	Raikes Parade
B2	Clifton Street	C3	Reads Avenue
D4	Clinton Avenue	D3	Reads Avenue
C2	Cookson Street	C2	Regent Road
B4	Coop Street	C4	Ribble Road
C3	Coronation Street	D3	Ripon Road
B2	Corporation Street	B4	Seasiders Way
B4	Dale Street	C1	Seed Street
B2	Deansgate	D1	Selbourne Road
B1	Dickson Road	C2	South King Street
C2	Edward Street	B1	Springfield Road
D1	Elizabeth Street	C3	Stanley Road
C1	Fisher Street	C1	Swainson Street
B4	Foxhall Road	B2	Talbot Road
D4	Freckleton Street	C1	Talbot Road
B1	General Street	C2	Topping Street
D1	George Street	B2	Tower Street
D1	Gorton Street	B3	Vance Road
D2	Granville Road	B2	Victoria Street
C1	Grosvenor Street	D1	Victory Road
D4	Harrison Street	B2	West Street
C4	Havelock Street	D3	Woolman Road
C1	High Street	B4	York Street

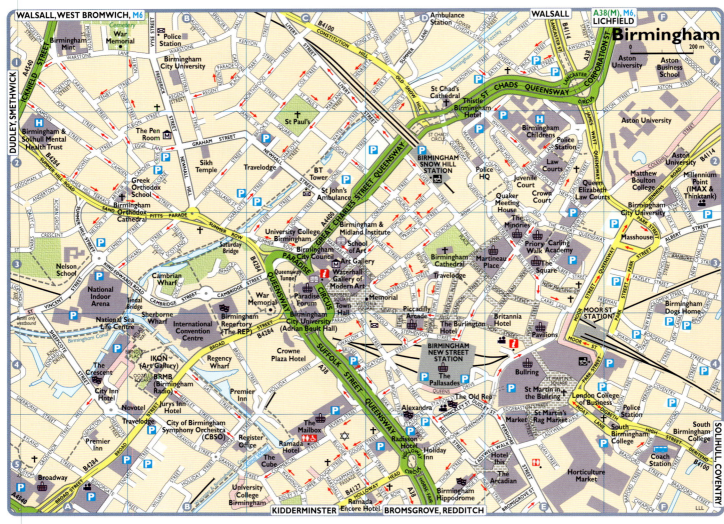

Birmingham

Birmingham is found on atlas page **58 G7**

A2 Acorn Grove	B1 Caroline Street	F2 Etna Street	D4 John Bright Street	E3 Old Square	D5 Smallbrook Queensway
E3 Albert Street	E3 Carrs Lane	D5 Exeter Street	B1 Kenyon Street	B4 Oozells Square	D2 Snow Hill Queensway
F3 Albert Street	A1 Carver Street	F3 Fazeley Street	A4 King Edward's Drive	F5 Oxford Street	B1 Spencer Street
B2 Albion Street	C3 Chamberlain Square	C3 Fleet Street	A3 King Edwards Road	C3 Paradise Circus	E1 Staniforth Street
F4 Allison Street	C5 Chapmans Passage	F3 Fox Street	D5 Ladywell Walk	Queensway	D5 Station Street
A2 Anderton Street	B3 Charlotte Street	B1 Frederick Street	E1 Lancaster Circus	C4 Paradise Street	E2 Steelhouse Lane
A2 Arthur Place	F5 Cheapside	E3 Freeman Street	E1 Lancaster Street	E4 Park Street	D4 Stephenson Street
F1 Aston Street	D3 Cherry Street	B4 Gas Street	B2 Legge Lane	A1 Pemberton Street	C4 Suffolk Street Queensway
B4 Atlas Way	D2 Church Street	E5 Gloucester Street	A3 Lighthouse Avenue	E5 Pershore Street	A2 Summer Hill Road
F3 Banbury Street	B3 Civic Close	A2 Goddman Street	C3 Lionel Street	D4 Pinfold Street	A2 Summer Hill Street
F5 Barford Street	A3 Clement Street	C5 Gough Street	C1 Livery Street	A1 Pope Street	A2 Summer Hill Terrace
F3 Bartholomew Street	D1 Cliveland Street	B2 Graham Street	B3 Louisa Street	A2 Powell Street	D1 Summer Lane
D3 Barwick Street	F2 Coleshill Street	B5 Granville Street	E1 Loveday Street	E1 Price Street	B3 Summer Row
E1 Bath Street	E2 Colmore Circus	C3 Great Charles Street	D1 Lower Loveday Street	E1 Princip Street	C4 Swallow Street
D4 Beak Street	Queensway	Queensway	C2 Ludgate Hill	F5 Printing House Street	D3 Temple Row
F4 Benacre Drive	D3 Colmore Row	F2 Grosvenor Street	D4 Lwr St Temple	D4 Queens Drive	D3 Temple Row West
D3 Bennetts Hill	C5 Commercial Street	A5 Grosvenor Street West	C5 Margaret Street	C3 Queensway Tunnel	D3 Temple Street
B4 Berkley Street	C1 Constitution Hill	B1 Hall Street	C5 Marshall Street	F5 Rea Street	A1 Tenby Street
A5 Bishopgate Street	D3 Cornwall Street	D1 Hampton Street	E3 Martineau Way	B1 Regent Parade	A1 Tenby Street North
C5 Blucher Street	E1 Corporation Street	B3 Helena Street	C1 Mary Ann Street	B1 Regent Place	A5 Tennant Street
C1 Bond Street	E3 Corporation Street	C1 Henrietta Street	F5 Mary Street	B1 Regent Street	E3 The Priory Queensway
F4 Bordesley Street	F4 Coventry Street	E4 High Street	F4 Meriden Street	C5 Ridley Street	D5 Thorp Street
D5 Bow Street	C1 Cox Street	F5 High Street Deritend	F5 Mill Lane	A5 Ruston Street	B3 Tindal Bridge
F5 Bradford Street	E3 Dale End	C4 Hill Street	E4 Moat Lane	A5 Ryland Street	F4 Trent Street
B4 Bridge Street	A3 Daley Close	D4 Hinckley Street	E4 Moor Street	E1 St Chads Queensway	E3 Union Street
B3 Brindley Drive	E2 Dalton Street	A1 Hingeston Street	E4 Moor Street Queensway	D5 St Jude's Pass	C5 Upper Gough Street
B4 Brindley Place	E5 Dean Street	B2 Holland Street	A1 Moreton Street	A3 St Marks Crescent	E1 Vesey Street
A5 Broad Street	E4 Digbeth	B5 Holliday Street	C4 Navigation Street	E4 St Martin's Square	C3 Victoria Square
E5 Bromsgrove St	D4 Dudley Street	B5 Holloway Circus	A3 Nelson Street	C1 St Paul's Square	B1 Vittoria Street
C2 Brook Street	C3 Eden Place	C5 Holloway Head	F4 New Bartholomew Street	D3 St Philip's Place	B1 Vyse Street
C4 Brunel Street	E4 Edgbaston Street	F1 Holt Street	F4 New Canal Street	A3 St Vincent Street	A1 Warstone Lane
E3 Bull Street	D3 Edmund Street	D5 Horse Fair	B2 Newhall Hill	A2 Sand Pitts Parade	C5 Washington Street
B3 Cambridge Street	B3 Edward Street	D1 Hospital St	C2 Newhall Street	B3 Saturday Bridge	D3 Waterloo Street
B2 Camden Drive	D5 Ellis Street	E5 Hurst Street	E3 New Meeting Street	B3 Scotland Street	C2 Water Street
A2 Camden Street	A5 Essington Street	A1 Icknield Street	D3 New Street	C5 Severn Street	D2 Weaman Street
D3 Cannon Street	D4 Ethel Street	D5 Inge Street	E2 Newton Street	D1 Shadwell Street	E2 Whittall Street
		B2 James Street	C1 Northwood Street	F4 Shaw's Passage	B5 William Street
		E2 James Watt Queensway	D1 Old Snow Hill	B2 Sheepcote Street	F1 Woodcock Street
		F2 Jennens Road		A4 Sherborne Street	
				B2 Sloane Street	

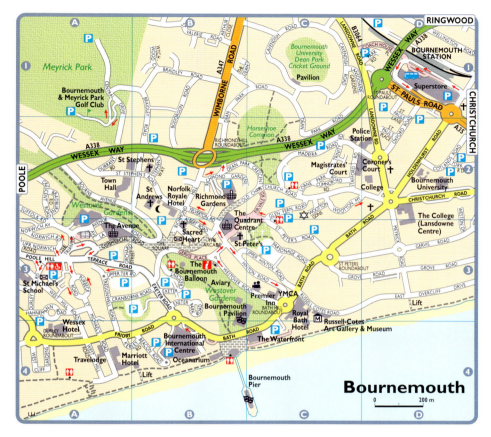

Bournemouth

Bournemouth is found on atlas page **13 J6**

B3	Albert Road	A3	Poole Hill
B1	Arthur Close	A4	Priory Road
A3	Avenue Lane	A3	Purbeck Road
A3	Avenue Road	B2	Richmond Gardens
B4	Bath Road	B3	Richmond Hill
B4	Beacon Road	C3	Russell Cotes Road
B2	Bodorgon Road	A3	St Michael's Road
A2	Bourne Avenue	D1	St Pauls Lane
A2	Bradburne Road	D2	St Paul's Place
B1	Braidley Road	D1	St Pauls Road
C1	Cavendish Road	C3	St Peter's Road
A1	Central Drive	A2	St Stephen's Road
D2	Christchurch Road	B1	St Valerie Road
D1	Coach House Place	C2	Stafford Road
A3	Commercial Road	B2	Stephen's Way
D2	Cotlands Road	A2	Suffolk Road
A3	Cranborne Road	A3	Terrace Road
A2	Crescent Road	B3	The Arcade
C2	Cumnor Road	B1	The Deans
B2	Dean Park Crescent	B3	The Square
B2	Dean Park Road	A3	The Triangle
A3	Durley Road	A3	Tregonwell Road
A2	Durrant Road	C2	Trinity Road
D3	East Overcliff Drive	C3	Upper Hinton Road
B3	Exeter Crescent	A3	Upper Norwich Road
B3	Exeter Park Road	A3	Upper Terrace Road
B3	Exeter Road	D1	Wellington Road
C2	Fir Vale Road	A2	Wessex Way
B3	Gervis Place	A3	West Hill Road
D3	Gervis Road	D2	Weston Drive
C2	Glen Fern Road	B3	Westover Road
C3	Grove Road	B1	Wimborne Road
A3	Hahnemann Road	C2	Wootton Gardens
B3	Hinton Road	C2	Wootton Mount
D2	Holdenhurst Road	B1	Wychwood Close
A4	Kerley Road	B2	Yelverton Road
C1	Lansdowne Gardens	D2	York Road
C1	Lansdowne Road		
C2	Lorne Park Road		
C2	Madeira Road		
D3	Meyrick Road		
A3	Norwich Avenue		
A3	Norwich Road		
C2	Old Christchurch Road		
A3	Orchard Street		
D2	Oxford Road		
D1	Park Road		
C3	Parsonage Road		

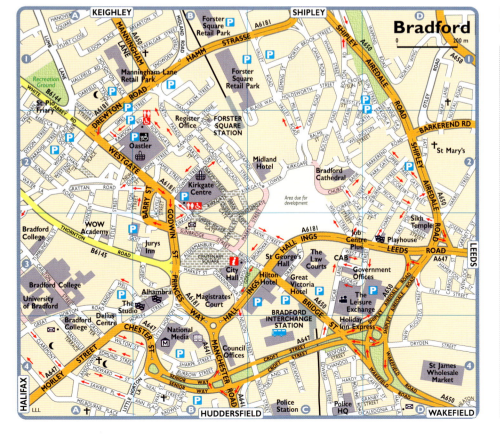

Bradford

Bradford is found on atlas page **90 F4**

B3	Aldermanbury	A2	Longcroft Link
B2	Bank Street	C2	Lower Kirkgate
D2	Barkerend Road	A1	Lumb Lane
B2	Barry Street	B4	Manchester Road
C4	Bolling Road	A1	Manningham Lane
C2	Bolton Road	B1	Manor Row
C3	Bridge Street	B3	Market Street
C3	Broadway	B1	Midland Road
D2	Burnett Street	A4	Morley Street
C1	Canal Road	B4	Nelson Street
A3	Carlton Street	C1	North Brook Street
B3	Centenary Square	B2	Northgate
C4	Chandos Street	B1	North Parade
B3	Channing Way	C2	North Street
D3	Chapel Street	D1	North Wing
B2	Cheapside	D1	Otley Road
A4	Chester Street	A2	Paradise Street
C2	Church Bank	D2	Peckover Street
A4	Claremont	B2	Piccadilly
C4	Croft Street	C2	Pine Street
A1	Darfield Street	B3	Princes Way
B2	Darley Street	A3	Randall Well Street
A2	Drewton Road	A2	Rawson Road
D4	Dryden Street	B2	Rawson Square
B2	Duke Street	A2	Rebecca Street
D3	East Parade	A4	Sawrey Place
A4	Edmund Street	B4	Senior Way
C4	Edward Street	C1	Shipley Airedale Road
A1	Eldon Place	C2	Stott Hill
D3	Filey Street	A2	Sunbridge Road
C3	George Street	B3	Sunbridge Street
B2	Godwin Street	A3	Tetley Street
A2	Grattan Road	A3	Thornton Road
A4	Great Horton Road	B1	Trafalgar Street
A4	Grove Terrace	B3	Tyrell Street
A1	Hallfield Road	D2	Upper Park Gate
B4	Hall Ings	B2	Upper Piccadilly
B1	Hamm Strasse	C1	Valley Road
C1	Holdsworth Street	C3	Vicar Lane
A1	Houghton Place	D4	Wakefield Road
A4	Howard Street	D1	Wapping Road
B3	Hustlergate	A2	Water Lane
A1	Infirmary Street	C2	Wellington Street
B2	John Street	A2	Westgate
A4	Lansdowne Place	C1	Wharf Street
D3	Leeds Road	A1	White Abbey Road
A4	Little Horton	A2	Wigan Street
B4	Little Horton Lane	A4	Wilton Street

Brighton

Brighton is found on atlas page **24 H10**

D3	Ardingley Street		D4	Madeira Place
D1	Ashton Rise		C4	Manchester Street
B3	Bartholomew Square		D4	Margaret Street
B3	Black Lion Street		D4	Marine Parade
D3	Blaker Street		B3	Market Street
B2	Bond Street		C2	Marlborough Place
A3	Boyces Street		B3	Meeting House Lane
B3	Brighton Place		B3	Middle Street
D4	Broad Street		D1	Morley Street
A1	Buckingham Road		B1	New Dorset Street
D4	Camelford Street		B2	New Road
A3	Cannon Place		D4	New Steine
D2	Carlton Hill		B3	Nile Street
A1	Centurion Road		B1	North Gardens
D3	Chapel Street		C2	North Place
C4	Charles Street		B1	North Road
C1	Cheltenham Place		B2	North Street
A1	Church Street		C3	Old Steine
B2	Church Street		B2	Portland Street
C2	Circus Street		A1	Powis Grove
A1	Clifton Hill		B3	Prince Albert Street
A1	Clifton Terrace		C3	Prince's Street
D3	Devonshire Place		B1	Queen's Gardens
B3	Dukes Lane		A2	Queen Square
B2	Duke Street		B2	Queen's Road
C3	East Street		A2	Regency Road
C2	Edward Street		A2	Regent Hill
D1	Elmore Street		C2	Regent Street
B1	Foundry Street		C1	Robert Street
B1	Frederick Street		D3	St James's Street
B2	Gardner Street		A1	St Nicholas Road
D3	George Street		B3	Ship Street Gardens
C1	Gloucester Place		B1	Spring Gardens
B1	Gloucester Road		C4	Steine Street
C1	Gloucester Street		D2	Sussex Street
B4	Grand Junction Road		C1	Sydney Street
C2	Grand Parade		B2	Tichborne Street
D3	High Street		C1	Tidy Street
D1	Ivory Place		B1	Upper Gardner Street
D2	John Street		A1	Upper Gloucester Road
C2	Jubilee Street		A2	Upper North Street
C1	Kensington Gardens		C1	Vine Street
C1	Kensington Street		D4	Wentworth Street
B1	Kew Street		A2	Western Road
A3	King's Road		A3	West Street
C2	Kingswood Street		D3	White Street
A1	Leopold Road		D2	William Street
B4	Little East Street		B2	Windsor Street

Bristol

Bristol is found on atlas page **31 Q10**

A3	Anchor Road		C2	Passage Street
D3	Avon Street		C1	Pembroke Street
B2	Baldwin Street		C1	Penn Street
D4	Bath Bridge		B3	Pero's Bridge
C1	Bond Street		A2	Perry Road
D2	Bond Street		C2	Philadelphia Street
C1	Broadmead		C4	Portwall Lane
D2	Broad Plain		C4	Prewett Street
B3	Broad Quay		B3	Prince Street
B2	Broad Street		B3	Queen Charlotte Street
C2	Broad Weir		B3	Queen Square
A3	Canons Way		C4	Redcliffe Hill
C3	Canynge Street		B4	Redcliffe Parade West
C2	Castle Street		C4	Redcliffe Way
A3	College Green		C4	Redcliff Mead Lane
B2	Colston Avenue		C3	Redcliff Street
B2	Colston Street		A1	Royal Fort Road
B4	Commercial Road		B2	Rupert Street
B2	Corn Street		B3	St Augustine's Parade
C3	Counterslip		A3	St George's Road
A4	Cumberland Road		D1	St Matthias Park
A3	Deanery Road		A1	St Michael's Hill
A3	Denmark Street		B2	St Stephen's Street
A3	Explore Lane		C3	St Thomas Street
C2	Fairfax Street		B2	Small Street
C3	Ferry Street		C4	Somerset Street
D3	Friary		A1	Southwell Street
A2	Frogmore Street		A1	Tankards Close
A3	Great George Street		B3	Tel Avenue
D1	Great George Street		C3	Temple Back
B4	Guinea Street		D3	Temple Back East
C1	Haymarket		D4	Temple Gate
A2	Hill Street		C3	Temple Street
B1	Horfield Road		D3	Temple Way
D1	Houlton Street		B4	The Grove
D2	Jacob Street		C1	The Horsefair
B3	King Street		C2	The Pithay
B2	Lewins Mead		D2	Tower Hill
A2	Lodge Street		A2	Trenchard Street
D2	Lower Castle Street		A1	Tyndall Avenue
A2	Lower Church Lane		C1	Union Street
B1	Lower Maudlin Street		B1	Upper Maudlin Street
B1	Marlborough Hill		C2	Victoria Street
B1	Marlborough Street		B4	Wapping Road
B3	Marsh Street		B3	Welsh Back
C2	Newgate		B1	Whitson Street
D2	Old Market Street		C2	Wine Street
A2	Park Street		A1	Woodland Road

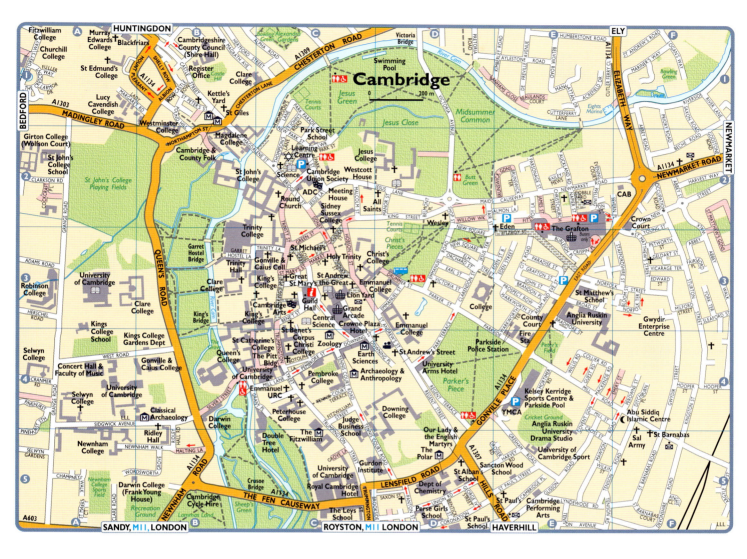

Cambridge

Cambridge is found on atlas page **62 G9**

F1	Abbey Road	E4	Collier Road	F2	Godstone Road	E5	Mawson Road	F5	St Barnabas Road	
F2	Abbey Street	D5	Coronation Street	D4	Gonville Place	F3	Milford Street	C3	St Mary's Street	
F3	Abbey Walk	E4	Covent Garden	E3	Grafton Street	C4	Mill Lane	F2	St Matthew's Gardens	
E1	Acrefield Drive	E4	Crispin Place	A3	Grange Road	E4	Mill Road	F3	St Matthew's Street	
E3	Adam And Eve Street	E4	Cross Street	A4	Grange Road	E4	Mill Street	E5	St Paul's Street	
B1	Albion Row	B5	Crusoe Bridge	B4	Grant Place	E4	Mortimer Road	B1	St Peter's Street	
C1	Alpha Road	E1	Cutler Ferry Close	C3	Green Street	B1	Mount Pleasant	E2	Salmon Lane	
E2	Auckland Road	E1	Cutterferry Lane	E5	Gresham Road	E2	Napier Street	F1	Saxon Road	
E1	Aylestone Road	E1	De Freville Avenue	E4	Guest Road	E2	Newmarket Road	D5	Saxon Street	
E2	Bailey Mews	F5	Devonshire Road	F4	Gwydir Street	B5	Newnham Road	F2	Severn Place	
D1	Banhams Close	F4	Ditchburn Place	F2	Harvest Way	A5	Newnham Walk	B1	Shelly Row	
E1	Beaulands Court	C4	Downing Place	E5	Harvey Road	C2	New Park Street	D2	Shop Street	
F2	Beche Road	C4	Downing Street	B1	Hertford Street	D3	New Square	A4	Sidgwick Avenue	
D2	Belmont Place	D5	Drosier Road	D5	Hills Road	F2	New Street	C2	Sidney Street	
E1	Belvoir Road	D3	Drummer Street	C3	Hobson Street	E3	Norfolk Street	B4	Silver Street	
C3	Bene't Street	D3	Earl Street	E1	Humberstone Road	F3	Norfolk Terrace	F3	Staffordshire Street	
D5	Bentick Street	E3	East Road	E2	James Street	B2	Northampton Street	F3	Sturton Street	
F3	Bloom Street	E3	Eden Street	C2	Jesus Lane	F2	Occupation Road	C3	Sussex Street	
E3	Bradmore Street	E3	Eden Street Back	D3	Jesus Terrace	D3	Orchard Street	E5	Tenison Avenue	
E3	Brandon Place	F3	Edward Street	E3	John Street	D5	Panton St	E5	Tenison Road	
C2	Bridge Street	F1	Elizabeth Way	E1	Kimberley Road	E3	Paradise Street	C4	Tennis Court Road	
E3	Broad Street	D3	Elm Street	B3	King's Bridge	D3	Parker Street	C4	Tennis Court Terrace	
D5	Brookside	F4	Emery Street	C3	King's Parade	C1	Park Parade	B5	The Fen Causeway	
E2	Brunswick Gardens	D3	Emmanuel Road	F4	Kingston Street	D3	Parkside	C2	Thompson's Lane	
E2	Brunswick Terrace	D3	Emmanuel Street	D2	King Street	C2	Park Street	C3	Trinity Lane	
E3	Burleigh Place	E2	Evening Court	A1	Lady Margaret Road	D4	Park Terrace	C3	Trinity Street	
E5	Cambridge Place	F3	Fairsford Place	D5	Lensfield Road	E2	Parsonage Street	C4	Trumpington Street	
B1	Castle Row	D2	Fair Street	F1	Logan's Way	C3	Peas Hill	D5	Union Road	
B1	Castle Street	E2	Fitzroy Lane	C2	Lwr Park Street	C4	Pembroke Street	F3	Vicarage Terrace	
A5	Champneys Walk	E3	Fitzroy Street	E5	Lyndewode Road	F4	Perowne Street	D1	Victoria Avenue	
B1	Chesterton Lane	C4	Fitzwilliam Street	E4	Mackenzie Road	F3	Petworth Street	D1	Victoria Bridge	
C1	Chesterton Road	B3	Garret Hostel Bridge	A1	Madingley Road	B1	Pound Hill	D3	Victoria Street	
E2	Christchurch Street	B3	Garret Hostel Lane	B1	Magdalene Street	F1	Priory Road	E3	Warkworth Street	
E3	City Road	F3	Geldart Street	B1	Magrath Avenue	E3	Prospect Row	E4	Warkworth Terrace	
D5	Clarendon Street	D5	George IV Street	D2	Maids Causeway	B3	Queen's Road	E2	Wellington Street	
E2	Cobble Yard	E5	Glisson Road	C2	Malcolm Street	D4	Regent Street	A4	West Road	
				B5	Malting Lane	D4	Regent Terrace	E5	Wilkin Street	
				D1	Manhattan Drive	F1	River Lane	E4	Willis Road	
				D2	Manor Street	F1	Riverside	D2	Willow Walk	
				F1	Mariner's Way	F1	St Andrew's Road	A5	Wordsworth Grove	
				C3	Market Street	D3	St Andrew's Street	F3	Young Street	

University Colleges

C3	Christ's College
A3	Clare College
B1	Clare College
B3	Clare College
C4	Corpus Christi College
B4	Darwin College
D4	Downing College
C3	Emmanuel College
D3	Emmanuel College
A1	Fitzwilliam College
A2	Girton College (Wolfson Court)
B3	Gonville & Caius College
B4	Gonville & Caius College
C2	Jesus College
B3	King's College
A1	Lucy Cavendish College
B2	Magdalene College
A1	Murray Edwards College
A5	Newnham College
C4	Pembroke College
C4	Peterhouse College
B4	Queen's College
A3	Robinson College
B4	St Catherine's College
A1	St Edmund's College
B2	St John's College
A4	Selwyn College
C2	Sidney Sussex College
B3	Trinity College
B1	Westminster College

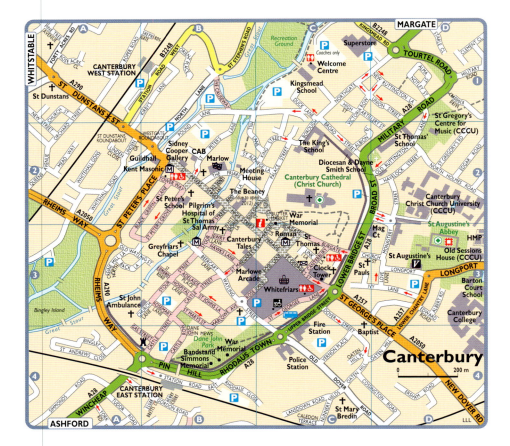

Canterbury

Canterbury is found on atlas page **39 K10**

B3	Adelaide Place		D1	Notley Street
D3	Albert Road		C4	Nunnery Fields
C2	Albion Place		C4	Oaten Hill
D1	Alma Street		C4	Old Dover Road
C1	Artillery Street		D2	Old Ruttington Lane
B3	Beercart Lane		A2	Orchard Street
B2	Best Lane		C2	Palace Street
A3	Black Griffin Lane		C3	Parade
C2	Borough		B4	Pin Hill
D2	Broad Street		B2	Pound Lane
C3	Burgate		A2	Queens Avenue
C2	Butter Market		A3	Rheims Way
C3	Canterbury Lane		B4	Rhodaus Town
B4	Castle Row		B3	Rose Lane
B3	Castle Street		B3	Rosemary Lane
C4	Cossington Road		B2	St Alphege Lane
C3	Dover Street		A1	St Dunstans Street
C1	Duck Lane		B3	St Edmunds Road
D2	Edgar Road		C3	St George's Lane
D3	Edward Road		C3	St George's Place
D4	Ersham Road		C3	St George's Street
A4	Gas Street		D2	St Gregory's Road
B4	Gordon Road		B3	St Johns Lane
B2	Guildhall Street		B3	St Margaret's Street
D2	Havelock Street		B3	St Marys Street
B3	Hawks Lane		B3	St Peter's Grove
B2	High Street		B2	St Peter's Lane
B3	Hospital Lane		A3	St Peter's Place
C3	Ivy Lane		B2	St Peters Street
B3	Jewry Lane		B4	Station Road East
C2	King Street		A1	Station Road West
B1	Kirby's Lane		B3	Stour Street
C4	Lansdown Road		D1	Sturry Road
A2	Linden Grove		C2	Sun Street
D3	Longport		B1	The Causeway
D3	Love Lane		B2	The Friars
C3	Lower Bridge Street		D1	Tourtel Road
D4	Lower Chantry Lane		B2	Tower Way
B3	Marlowe Avenue		A4	Tudor Road
A2	Mead Way		D1	Union Street
C3	Mercery Lane		C4	Upper Bridge Street
D2	Military Road		C4	Vernon Place
B1	Mill Lane		C1	Victoria Row
D3	Monastery Street		B3	Watling Street
D4	New Dover Road		A2	Whitehall Gardens
D1	New Ruttington Lane		A2	Whitehall Road
B1	North Lane		A4	Wincheap
C1	Northgate		A4	York Road

Cardiff

Cardiff is found on atlas page **30 G9**

D3	Adam Street		B1	Museum Avenue
D2	Adams Court		B1	Museum Place
D3	Adamscroft Place		D2	Newport Road Lane
D4	Atlantic Way		D2	North Luton Place
B2	Boulevard De Nantes		A1	North Road
C3	Bridge Street		D1	Oxford Lane
D4	Brigantine Place		D1	Oxford Street
C4	Bute Street		B1	Park Grove
C3	Bute Terrace		B1	Park Lane
B4	Callaghan Square		B1	Park Place
B3	Caroline Street		A3	Park Street
D1	Castle Lane		C3	Pellett Street
A2	Castle Street		A4	Pendyris Street
D3	Central Link		A3	Quay Street
B2	Charles Street		B2	Queen Street
C2	Churchill Way		C1	Richmond Crescent
A1	City Hall Road		C1	Richmond Road
D1	City Road		B1	St Andrew's Crescent
B2	Crockherbtown Lane		C1	St Andrew's Lane
B4	Custom House Street		B1	St Andrew's Place
C3	David Street		B2	St John Street
D3	Davis Street		B3	St Mary Street
C2	Dumfries Place		C1	St Peter's Street
D3	East Bay Close		C1	Salisbury Road
D1	East Grove		C3	Sandon Street
D4	Ellen Street		B4	Saunders Road
C2	Fford Churchill		D4	Schooner Way
D2	Fitzalan Place		C1	Senghennydd Road
D2	Fitzalan Road		B1	Stuttgarter Strasse
A4	Fitzhamon Embankment		B2	The Friary
D1	Glossop Road		B3	The Hayes
B2	Greyfriars Road		D1	The Parade
C3	Guildford Street		C1	The Walk
A3	Guildhall Place		B3	Trinity Street
A4	Havelock Street		A4	Tudor Street
B3	Hayes Bridge Road		D4	Tyndall Street
B2	Heol Siarl		D1	Vere Street
C4	Herbert Street		C2	Wesley Lane
B3	High Street		B4	West Canal Wharf
B2	High Street Arcade		C1	West Grove
B3	Hills Street		A3	Westgate Street
A1	King Edward VII Avenue		B3	Wharton Street
D2	Knox Road		C2	Windsor Lane
C4	Lloyd George Avenue		C1	Windsor Place
C3	Mary Ann Street		D3	Windsor Road
B4	Mill Lane		A3	Womanby Street
D2	Moira Place		A4	Wood Street
D2	Moira Terrace		B3	Working Street

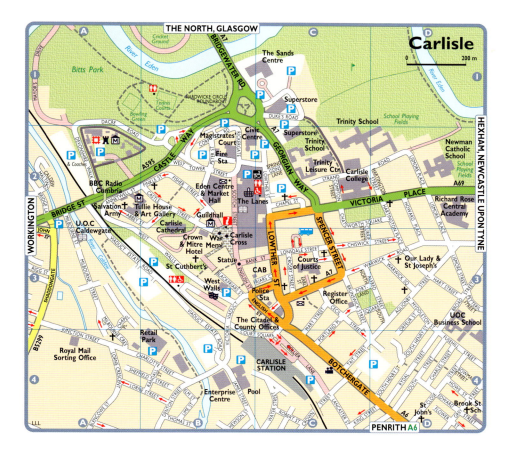

Carlisle

Carlisle is found on atlas page **110 G9**

A2	Abbey Street	D2	Howard Place
D3	Aglionby Street	D4	Howe Street
A2	Annetwell Street	B4	James Street
B3	Bank Street	A3	John Street
B3	Blackfriars Street	A4	Junction Street
A4	Blencowe Street	C4	King Street
C4	Botchergate	C4	Lancaster Street
A2	Bridge Lane	B4	Lime Street
A2	Bridge Street	D2	Lismore Place
B1	Bridgewater Road	D3	Lismore Street
D3	Broad Street	C3	Lonsdale Street
C3	Brunswick Street	A4	Lorne Crescent
A2	Caldew Maltings	A4	Lorne Street
B2	Castle Street	C2	Lowther Street
B2	Castle Way	C3	Mary Street
C3	Cecil Street	A1	Mayor's Drive
A3	Chapel Place	A3	Milbourne Crescent
C2	Chapel Street	A3	Milbourne Street
D4	Charles Street	D3	Myddleton Street
A4	Charlotte Street	D3	North Alfred Street
C2	Chatsworth Square	D3	Orfeur Street
C3	Chiswick Street	D3	Petteril Street
D4	Close Street	B2	Peter Street
C4	Collier Lane	C4	Portland Place
C2	Compton Street	C3	Port-Land Square
B2	Corp Road	B4	Randall Street
B4	Court Square	B2	Rickergate
C3	Crosby Street	A3	Rigg Street
C4	Crown Street	C4	Robert Street
C3	Currie Street	D4	Rydal Street
A1	Dacre Road	B2	Scotch Street
B4	Denton Street	A3	Shaddongate
A2	Devonshire Walk	A4	Sheffield Street
C1	Duke's Road	D3	South Alfred Street
D4	Edward Street	D4	South Henry Street
B4	Elm Street	C2	Spencer Street
B3	English Street	C2	Spring Gardens Lane
B2	Finkle Street	C2	Strand Road
B2	Fisher Street	C4	Tait Street
D4	Flower Street	B4	Thomas Street
C3	Friars Court	A3	Viaduct Estate Road
D4	Fusehill Street	C2	Victoria Place
C2	Georgian Way	B4	Victoria Viaduct
D4	Grey Street	D3	Warwick Road
D2	Hartington Place	D3	Warwick Square
D2	Hartington Street	C4	Water Street
D3	Hart Street	B2	West Tower Street
B4	Hewson Street	B3	West Walls

Cheltenham

Cheltenham is found on atlas page **46 H10**

C2	Albion Street	B4	Montpellier Parade
D2	All Saints' Road	B4	Montpellier Spa Road
B1	Ambrose Street	A4	Montpellier Street
D4	Argyll Road	A4	Montpellier Terrace
A4	Back Montpellier Terrace	A4	Montpellier Walk
B4	Bath Road	A1	New Street
C3	Bath Street	B2	North Street
B1	Baynham Way	D4	Old Bath Road
A3	Bayshill Road	B3	Oriel Road
A3	Bayshill Villas Lane	A3	Parabola Lane
B1	Bennington Street	A3	Parabola Road
C3	Berkeley Street	A1	Park Street
A1	Burton Street	D1	Pittville
D3	Carlton Street	D1	Pittville Circus
B2	Church Street	B2	Pittville Street
B2	Clarence Parade	C1	Portland Street
C1	Clarence Road	C1	Prestbury Road
B2	Clarence Street	D3	Priory Street
C4	College Road	B3	Promenade
B2	Crescent Terrace	A3	Queens Parade
A1	Devonshire Street	B2	Regent Street
D3	Duke Street	B3	Rodney Road
B1	Dunalley Street	B2	Royal Well
C1	Evesham Road	A2	Royal Well Lane
C2	Fairview Road	D2	St Anne's Road
D2	Fairview Street	D2	St Anne's Terrace
A3	Fauconberg Road	B2	St George's Place
D1	Glenfall Street	A2	St George's Road
C3	Grosvenor Street	B1	St George's Street
A1	Grove Street	A2	St James' Square
B1	Henrietta Street	C3	St James Street
D3	Hewlett Road	C2	St Johns Avenue
A1	High Street	B1	St Margaret's Road
C2	High Street	B1	St Paul's Street South
B3	Imperial Lane	C3	Sandford Street
B3	Imperial Square	D1	Selkirk Street
A2	Jessop Avenue	C2	Sherborne Street
D4	Keynsham Road	A1	Station Street
A1	King Street	B4	Suffolk Parade
A1	Knapp Road	B1	Swindon Road
A4	Lansdown Road	D3	Sydenham Villas Road
D2	Leighton Road	B4	Trafalgar Street
D3	London Road	D2	Union Street
D1	Malden Road	C3	Wellington Street
A1	Market Street	C3	Winchcombe Street
A1	Milsom Street	D2	Winstonian Road
B1	Monson Avenue	C3	Witcombe Place
B4	Montpellier Grove	D1	York Street

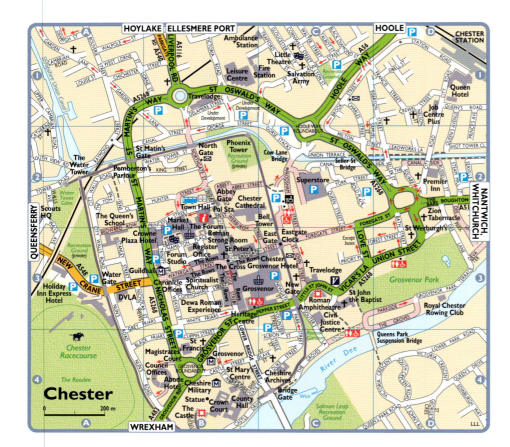

Chester

Chester is found on atlas page **81 N11**

C4	Albion Street	B3	Nicholas Street
D2	Bath Street	B2	Northgate Street
C1	Black Diamond Street	A3	Nun's Road
D2	Boughton	B1	Parkgate Road
A1	Bouverie Street	C3	Park Street
B3	Bridge Street	C3	Pepper Street
C1	Brook Street	B2	Princess Street
C2	Canal Side	C3	Priory Place
B4	Castle Street	C4	Queen's Park Road
C1	Charles Street	D1	Queen's Road
A1	Chichester Street	C2	Queen Street
D2	City Road	A2	Raymond Street
A2	City Walls Road	D2	Russell Street
B3	Commonhall Street	C1	St Anne Street
C1	Cornwall Street	D4	St John's Road
D1	Crewel Street	C3	St John Street
B4	Cuppin Street	A2	St Martin's Way
D2	Dee Hills Park	B4	St Mary's Hill
D2	Dee Lane	C4	St Olave Street
B1	Delamere Street	B1	St Oswald's Way
C4	Duke Street	B2	St Werburgh Street
B3	Eastgate Street	C2	Samuel Street
C1	Egerton Street	D2	Seller Street
C2	Foregate Street	B4	Shipgate Street
C3	Forest Street	C3	Souter's Lane
D1	Francis Street	A2	South View Road
C2	Frodsham Street	A3	Stanley Street
A1	Garden Lane	D1	Station Road
B2	George Street	D2	Steam Mill Street
C1	Gloucester Street	C4	Steele Street
C2	Gorse Stacks	C1	Talbot Street
D3	Grosvenor Park Terrace	A2	Tower Road
B4	Grosvenor Road	C1	Trafford Street
B4	Grosvenor Street	B3	Trinity Street
B3	Hamilton Place	D3	Union Street
C1	Hoole Way	C2	Union Terrace
B2	Hunter Street	A1	Upper Cambrian Road
B2	King Street	C3	Vicar's Lane
D2	Leadworks Lane	D4	Victoria Crescent
C3	Little St John Street	B1	Victoria Road
B1	Liverpool Road	C3	Volunteer Street
A1	Lorne Street	A1	Walpole Street
C3	Love Street	C1	Walter Street
B4	Lower Bridge Street	B3	Watergate Street
D4	Lower Park Road	B2	Water Tower Street
C2	Milton Street	B3	Weaver Street
A3	New Crane Street	B3	White Friars
C3	Newgate Street	C2	York Street

Colchester

Colchester is found on atlas page **52 G6**

C3	Abbey Gates	D4	Mill Street
A3	Alexandra Road	C4	Napier Road
A3	Balkerne Hill	D3	Nicholsons Green
A4	Beaconsfield Avenue	B1	North Bridge
A3	Burlington Road	B1	Northgate Street
A4	Butt Road	B1	North Hill
D1	Castle Road	B1	North Station Road
B3	Cedar Street	B1	Nunn's Road
B3	Chapel Street North	C3	Osborne Street
B3	Chapel Street South	A3	Papillon Road
B3	Church Street	A2	Pope's Lane
B3	Church Walk	C4	Portland Road
C4	Circular Road East	D3	Priory Street
B4	Circular Road North	C3	Queen Street
A4	Creffield Road	A2	Rawstorn Road
C4	Cromwell Road	D1	Roman Road
A3	Crouch Street	A2	St Alban's Road
B3	Crouch Street	D2	St Augustine Mews
A2	Crowhurst Road	C3	St Botolph's Street
C2	Culver Street East	C2	St Helen's Lane
B2	Culver Street West	B3	St John's Avenue
D2	East Hill	B3	St John's Street
B3	Essex Street	D3	St Julian Road
C4	Fairfax Road	A2	St Mary's Fields
C4	Flagstaff Road	B1	St Peter's Street
A4	Garland Road	A4	Salisbury Avenue
C2	George Street	A1	Sheepen Place
D4	Golden Noble Hill	A1	Sheepen Road
A3	Gray Road	C3	Short Wyre Street
B3	Headgate	B3	Sir Isaac's Walk
B2	Head Street	B4	South Street
A2	Henry Laver Court	B3	Southway
B2	High Street	C3	Stanwell Street
A4	Hospital Road	B2	Trinity Street
A3	Hospital Lane	B3	Walsingham Road
D4	Kendall Road	A4	Wellesley Road
D2	Land Lane	B3	Wellington Street
A3	Lexden Road	B1	West Stockwell Street
D1	Lincoln Way	B4	West Street
C2	Long Wyre Street	A1	Westway
C4	Lucas Road	C3	Whitewell Road
D3	Magdalen Street	A4	Wickham Road
C1	Maidenburgh Street	C2	William's Walk
A4	Maldon Road	D4	Winnock Road
A3	Manor Road		
C4	Mersea Road		
B1	Middle- Borough		
D4	Military Road		

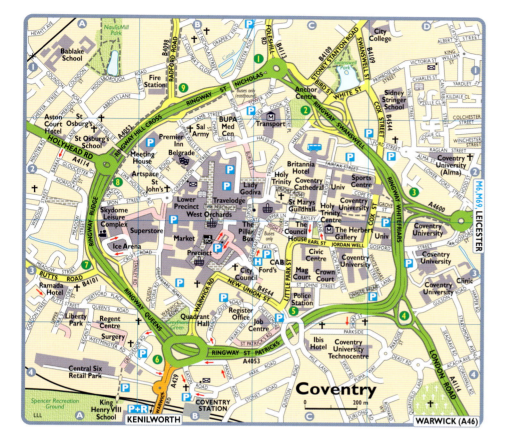

Coventry

Coventry is found on atlas page **59 M9**

A1	Abbotts Lane	A1	Mill Street
D4	Acacia Avenue	C3	Much Park Street
D2	Alma Street	B3	New Union Street
A2	Barras Lane	A2	Norfolk Street
C2	Bayley Lane	D4	Paradise Street
C1	Bird Street	B4	Park Road
B1	Bishop Street	C4	Parkside
B2	Broadgate	D1	Primrose Hill Street
B2	Burge Street	C2	Priory Row
A3	Butts Road	C2	Priory Street
A3	Butts Street	C4	Puma Way
D1	Canterbury Street	D4	Quaryfield Lane
A2	Chester Street	A3	Queen's Road
C3	Cheylesmore	B3	Queen Victoria Road
D4	Cornwall Road	C4	Quinton Road
B2	Corporation Street	B1	Radford Road
A1	Coundon Road	D2	Raglan Street
D1	Cox Street	A4	Regent Street
D2	Cox Street	A2	Ringway Hill Cross
A3	Croft Road	A3	Ringway Queens
C3	Earl Street	A3	Ringway Rudge
B4	Eaton Road	B1	Ringway St Nicholas
C2	Fairfax Street	B4	Ringway St Patricks
C1	Foleshill Road	C1	Ringway Swanswell
A2	Gloucester Street	D2	Ringway Whitefriars
D3	Gosford Street	C3	St Johns Street
B3	Greyfriars Lane	B1	St Nicholas Street
B3	Greyfriars Road	C3	Salt Lane
A4	Grosvenor Road	D4	Seagrave Road
D3	Gulson Road	A2	Spon Street
C2	Hales Street	A3	Stanley Road
A3	Hertford Place	B4	Stoney Road
C3	High Street	C1	Stoney Stanton Road
B2	Hill Street	D3	Strathmore Avenue
A2	Holyhead Road	C1	Swanswell Street
C3	Jordan Well	B1	Tower Street
B2	Lamb Street	C2	Trinity Street
B1	Leicester Row	B2	Upper Hill Street
C3	Little Park Street	A4	Upper Wells Street
D4	London Road	D1	Victoria Street
D2	Lower Ford Street	D1	Vine Street
A2	Lower Holyhead Road	B3	Warwick Road
B4	Manor House Road	B4	Warwick Road
B4	Manor Road	A4	Westminster Road
A3	Meadow Street	D3	White Friars Street
A1	Meriden Street	C1	White Street
A1	Middleborough Road	A3	Windsor Street
C4	Mile Lane	D1	Yardley Street

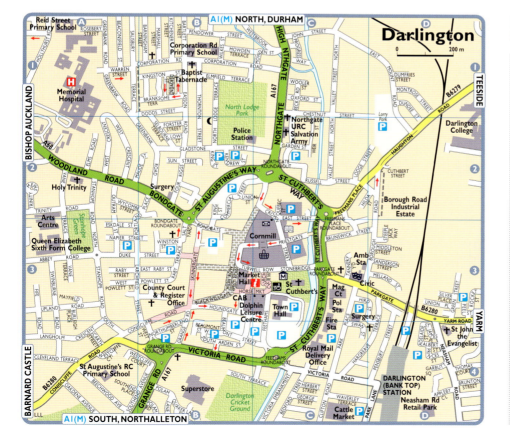

Darlington

Darlington is found on atlas page **103 Q8**

A3	Abbey Road	D4	Neasham Road
B1	Barningham Street	C2	Northgate
B1	Bartlett Street	B2	North Lodge Terrace
B3	Beaumont Street	B4	Northumberland Street
C4	Bedford Street	A4	Oakdene Avenue
A4	Beechwood Avenue	A2	Outram Street
B3	Blackwellgate	D3	Parkgate
B3	Bondgate	D4	Park Lane
D3	Borough Road	C4	Park Place
C3	Brunswick Street	B1	Pendower Street
D4	Brunton Street	D4	Pensbury Street
C1	Chestnut Street	B4	Polam Lane
A4	Cleveland Terrace	A3	Portland Place
C4	Clifton Road	B3	Powlett Street
B2	Commercial Street	C3	Priestgate
A4	Coniscliffe Road	B3	Raby Terrace
B1	Corporation Road	C2	Russell Street
B1	Corporation Road	B2	St Augustine's Way
C2	Crown Street	C2	St Cuthbert's Way
B1	Dodds Street	C3	St Cuthbert's Way
A3	Duke Street	C4	St Cuthbert's Way
B1	Easson Road	D4	St James Place
D1	East Mount Road	A1	Salisbury Terrace
B3	East Raby Street	B3	Salt Yard
C3	East Street	A4	Scarth Street
A2	Elms Road	B3	Skinnergate
C4	Feethams	B4	South Arden Street
A3	Fife Road	A4	Southend Avenue
B2	Four Riggs	A2	Stanhope Road North
C2	Freemans Place	A3	Stanhope Road South
B2	Gladstone Street	C3	Stonebridge
B4	Grange Road	B2	Sun Street
A1	Greenbank Road	C4	Swan Street
B2	Greenbank Road	A3	Swinburne Road
D3	Green Street	A2	Trinity Road
C4	Hargreave Terrace	B3	Tubwell Row
D2	Haughton Road	A3	Uplands Road
C1	High Northgate	C2	Valley Street North
B3	High Row	A2	Vane Terrace
A1	Hollyhurst Road	C4	Victoria Embankment
B3	Houndgate	B4	Victoria Road
D3	Jack Way Steeple	C4	Victoria Road
C1	John Street	A2	West Crescent
B2	Kendrew Street	A3	West Powlett Street
B1	Kingston Street	B3	West Row
A4	Langholm Crescent	B4	West Street
A3	Larchfield Street	A2	Woodland Road
A2	Maude Street	D3	Yarm Road

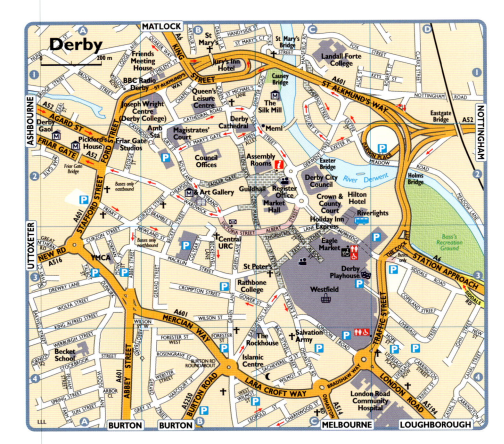

Derby

Derby is found on atlas page **72 B3**

A4	Abbey Street	A4	King Alfred Street
A1	Agard Street	B1	King Street
C3	Albert Street	B4	Lara Croft Way
B4	Babington Lane	B4	Leopold Street
C4	Back Sitwell Street	D4	Liversage Row
B3	Becket Street	D3	Liversage Street
B2	Bold Lane	A1	Lodge Lane
C4	Bradshaw Way	C3	London Road
B2	Bramble Street	B3	Macklin Street
A1	Bridge Street	C1	Mansfield Road
A1	Brook Street	D2	Meadow Lane
B4	Burton Road	D2	Meadow Road
D4	Canal Street	B3	Mercian Way
D4	Carrington Street	C3	Morledge
B1	Cathedral Road	A3	Newland Street
A2	Cavendish Court	A3	New Road
B1	Chapel Street	D4	New Street
D1	Clarke Street	D1	Nottingham Road
D3	Copeland Street	C4	Osmaston Road
B2	Corn Market	C1	Phoenix Street
B3	Crompton Street	B1	Queen Street
A2	Curzon Street	D1	Robert Street
A3	Curzon Street	B4	Rosengrave Street
C2	Darwin Place	C4	Sacheverel Street
C2	Derwent Street	B2	Sadler Gate
A3	Drewry Lane	C1	St Alkmund's Way
C1	Duke Street	B1	St Helen's Street
A3	Dunkirk	B2	St Mary's Gate
C3	East Street	C3	St Peter's Street
C3	Exchange Street	D3	Siddals Road
C2	Exeter Place	C1	Sowter Road
C2	Exeter Street	A4	Spring Street
A2	Ford Street	A3	Stafford Street
B4	Forester Street West	D3	Station Approach
A3	Forman Street	A4	Stockbrook Street
C1	Fox Street	B2	Strand
A2	Friary Street	C1	Stuart Street
B1	Full Street	A4	Sun Street
B3	Gerard Street	D3	The Cock Pitt
B3	Gower Street	C3	Thorntree Lane
B3	Green Lane	D4	Traffic Street
A4	Grey Street	D4	Trinity Street
B1	Handyside Street	B2	Victoria Street
B4	Harcourt Street	B2	Wardwick
B2	Iron Gate	A4	Werburgh Street
D4	John Street	C4	Wilmot Street
B2	Jury Street	A3	Wolfa Street
D1	Keys Street	A4	Woods Lane

Doncaster

Doncaster is found on atlas page **91 P10**

D3	Alderson Drive	B1	Montague Street
B3	Apley Road	B4	Nelson Street
A4	Balby Road Bridge	B1	Nether Hall Road
B3	Beechfield Road	A1	North Bridge Road
C1	Broxholme Lane	C4	North Street
C4	Carr House Road	D1	Osborne Road
B4	Carr Lane	C4	Palmer Street
C4	Chequer Avenue	B2	Park Road
C3	Chequer Road	B2	Park Terrace
C4	Childers Street	B2	Prince's Street
B1	Christ Church Road	A2	Priory Place
A1	Church View	B4	Prospect Place
B1	Church Way	C1	Queen's Road
C4	Clark Avenue	C4	Rainton Road
A4	Cleveland Street	C3	Ravensworth Road
B3	College Road	C1	Rectory Gardens
C4	Cooper Street	C2	Regent Square
B2	Coopers Terrace	D3	Roman Road
B1	Copley Road	C1	Royal Avenue
B3	Cunningham Road	B4	St James Street
D3	Danum Road	C1	St Mary's Road
B1	Dockin Hill Road	A2	St Sepulchre Gate
A2	Duke Street	A3	St Sepulchre Gate West
B2	East Laith Gate	C1	St Vincent Avenue
C3	Elmfield Road	C1	St Vincent Road
A4	Exchange Street	B2	Scot Lane
D3	Firbeck Road	B2	Silver Street
B2	Frances Street	B3	Somerset Road
B2	Georges Gate	C2	South Parade
C2	Glyn Avenue	C4	South Street
A4	Green Dyke Lane	A2	Spring Gardens
A1	Grey Friars' Road	A4	Stirling Street
C2	Hall Cross Hill	C4	Stockil Road
B2	Hall Gate	D4	Theobald Avenue
D4	Hamilton Road	C1	Thorne Road
B1	Hannington Street	C2	Thorne Road
A2	High Street	C2	Town Fields
C1	Highfield Road	D1	Town Moor Avenue
B4	Jarratt Street	A2	Trafford Way
C1	King's Road	C1	Vaughan Avenue
C2	Lawn Avenue	B3	Waterdale
C2	Lawn Road	D3	Welbeck Road
D4	Lime Tree Avenue	A2	West Laith Gate
D3	Manor Drive	A3	West Street
A2	Market Place	C3	Whitburn Road
B1	Market Road	B4	White Way
B1	Milbanke Street	D1	Windsor Road
B4	Milton Walk	B2	Wood Street

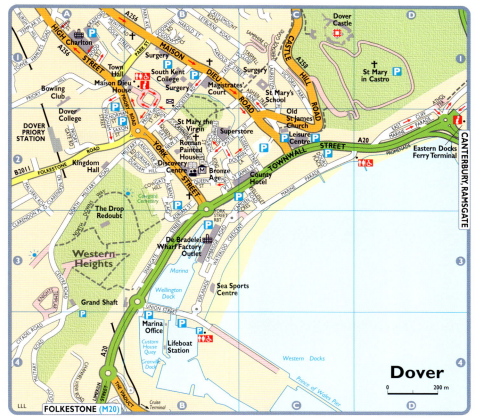

Dover

Dover is found on atlas page **27 P3**

B3	Adrian Street		B2	New Street
B2	Albany Place		A2	Norman Street
C1	Ashen Tree Lane		A3	North Downs Way
D1	Athol Terrace		A3	North Military Road
B2	Biggin Street		B1	Park Avenue
A1	Burgh Hill		B1	Park Street
B3	Cambridge Road		B2	Pencester Road
C2	Camden Crescent		A1	Peter Street
B2	Cannon Street		A2	Priory Gate Road
C1	Castle Hill Road		A1	Priory Hill
B1	Castlemount Road		A1	Priory Road
B2	Castle Street		B2	Priory Street
A3	Centre Road		D2	Promenade
A4	Channel View Road		B2	Queen's Gate
B2	Church Street		B2	Queen Street
A4	Citadel Road		B2	Russell Street
A3	Clarendon Place		B2	St James Street
A2	Clarendon Road		C1	Samphire Close
B2	Cowgate Hill		A2	Saxon Street
A1	Crafford Street		B3	Snargate Street
C2	Douro Place		A4	South Military Road
A1	Dolphin Lane		B2	Stembrook
A1	Dour Street		C1	Taswell Close
B2	Durham Close		B1	Taswell Street
B2	Durham Hill		A1	Templar Street
D2	East Cliff		A4	The Viaduct
A2	Effingham Street		A1	Tower Hamlets Road
B3	Esplanade		C2	Townwall Street
A2	Folkestone Road		B3	Union Street
B1	Godwyne Close		C1	Victoria Park
B1	Godwyne Road		B3	Waterloo Crescent
B1	Harold Street		C2	Wellesley Road
B1	Harold Street		A1	Wood Street
C1	Heritage Gardens		B2	York Street
A1	Hewitt Road		B3	York Street Roundabout
A1	High Street			
B2	King Street			
A3	Knights Templar			
B2	Lancaster Road			
C1	Laureston Place			
B1	Leyburne Road			
A4	Limekiln Street			
B1	Maison Dieu Road			
A2	Malvern Road			
C2	Marine Parade			
D2	Marine Parade			
B2	Military Road			
B2	Mill Lane			

Dundee

Dundee is found on atlas page **142 G11**

B2	Albert Square		B1	Laurel Bank
B2	Bank Street		A1	Lochee Road
A1	Barrack Road		D1	Marketgait
B2	Barrack Road		C1	Marketgait East
B2	Bell Street		D2	McDonald Street
D1	Blackscroft		B2	Meadowside
A1	Blinshall Street		A2	Miln Street
A2	Blinshall Street		C2	Murraygate
C1	Bonnybank Road		A4	Nethergate
A2	Brown Street		C2	New Inn Entry
C2	Candle Lane		B2	Nicoll Street
C2	Castle Street		B2	North Lindsay Street
C3	City Square		B1	North Marketgait
C2	Commercial Street		C1	North Victoria Road
D1	Constable Street		A3	Old Hawkhill
A1	Constitution Crescent		B2	Panmure Street
A1	Constitution Road		A3	Park Place
A2	Constitution Road		A4	Perth Road
A2	Court House Square		D1	Princes Street
C1	Cowgate		B1	Prospect Place
D1	Cowgate		C1	Queen Street
C3	Crighton Street		B2	Rattray Street
D1	Dens Street		B2	Reform Street
C3	Dock Street		B4	Riverside Drive
A2	Douglas Street		A4	Roseangle
B1	Dudhope Street		C1	St Andrews Street
C3	Earl Grey Place		A1	Scrimgeour Place
D2	East Dock Street		A4	Seabraes Lane
D1	East Whale Lane		C2	Seagate
B2	Euclid Crescent		A2	Session Street
B2	Euclid Street		C3	Shore Terrace
C1	Forebank Road		C3	South Marketgait
B2	Forester Street		B3	South Tay Street
D1	Foundry Lane		C3	South Victoria Dock Road
C2	Gellatly Street		B2	South Ward Road
B4	Greenmarket		C1	Sugarhouse Wynd
A2	Guthrie Street		D3	Tay Road Bridge
A3	Hawkhill		C2	Trades Lane
C3	High Street		B3	Union Street
B1	Hilltown		B1	Union Terrace
B1	Hilltown Terrace		B2	Ward Road
A3	Hunter Street		D1	Weavers Yard
A1	Infirmary Brae		A2	West Bell Street
B2	Johnston Street		A2	West Marketgait
C1	King Street		A3	West Port
C1	Kirk Lane		D2	West Victoria Dock Road
A1	Laburn Street		C3	Whitehall Place
C1	Ladywell Avenue		C3	Whitehall Street

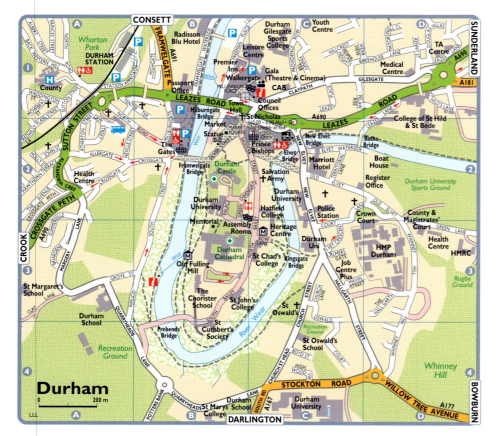

Durham

Durham is found on atlas page **103 Q2**

A1	Albert Street	D1	Mayorswell Close
A2	Alexandria Crescent	B1	Milburngate Bridge
A2	Allergate	B2	Millburngate
A2	Atherton Street	B1	Millennium Place
A1	Back Western Hill	A1	Mowbray Street
C1	Bakehouse Lane	A2	Neville Street
C2	Baths Bridge	C2	New Elvet
C3	Bow Lane	C2	New Elvet Bridge
C4	Boyd Street	A2	New Street
A3	Briardene	C3	North Bailey
C3	Church Lane	A1	North Road
C4	Church Street	C2	Old Elvet
C4	Church Street Head	C3	Oswald Court
A3	Clay Lane	B2	Owengate
C1	Claypath	B2	Palace Green
C3	Court Lane	C3	Palmers Gate
A2	Crossgate	C1	Pelaw Rise
A3	Crossgate Peth	A3	Pimlico
D1	Douglas Villas	B4	Potters Bank
C2	Elvet Bridge	B4	Prebends' Bridge
C3	Elvet Crescent	A1	Princes' Street
C2	Elvet Waterside	C1	Providence Row
C1	Finney Terrace	A3	Quarryheads Lane
A2	Flass Street	A2	Redhills Lane
B1	Framwelgate	D1	Renny Street
B2	Framwelgate Bridge	B2	Saddler Street
B1	Framwelgate Waterside	D1	St Hild's Lane
B1	Freeman Place	B2	Silver Street
C1	Gilesgate	B3	South Bailey
D3	Green Lane	C4	South Road
A3	Grove Street	B3	South Street
C3	Hallgarth Street	A1	Station Approach
A2	Hawthorn Terrace	C4	Stockton Road
B1	Highgate	A3	Summerville
C4	High Road View	A2	Sutton Street
C2	High Street	A1	Tenter Terrace
C1	Hillcrest	C2	Territorial Lane
A2	Holly Street	A2	The Avenue
A2	John Street	D3	The Hall Garth
C1	Keiper Heights	A1	Waddington Street
C3	Kingsgate Bridge	C1	Wear View
D1	Leazes Lane	D3	Whinney Hill
D2	Leazes Lane	D4	Willow Tree Avenue
C1	Leazes Place		
B1	Leazes Road		
A3	Margery Lane		
B2	Market Square		
C3	Mavin Street		

Eastbourne

Eastbourne is found on atlas page **25 P11**

A2	Arlington Road	D1	Langney Road
B2	Ashford Road	C2	Langney Road
C1	Ashford Road	B4	Lascelles Terrace
B1	Ashford Square	D1	Latimer Road
A1	Avenue Lane	B1	Leaf Road
C1	Belmore Road	B2	Lismore Road
A4	Blackwater Road	C1	Longstone Road
B3	Bolton Road	B3	Lushington Road
C1	Bourne Street	D2	Marine Parade
B3	Burlington Place	D1	Marine Road
C3	Burlington Road	B2	Mark Lane
A3	Camden Road	A3	Meads Road
B1	Carew Road	C1	Melbourne Road
A4	Carlisle Road	A2	Old Orchard Road
B4	Carlisle Road	A4	Old Wish Road
C1	Cavendish Avenue	C2	Pevensey Road
C1	Cavendish Place	C3	Promenade
C2	Ceylon Place	D2	Queen's Gardens
B3	Chiswick Place	A2	Saffrons Road
B3	College Road	A1	St Anne's Road
D2	Colonnade Gardens	D1	St Aubyn's Road
B1	Commercial Road	B1	St Leonard's Road
B4	Compton Street	D1	Seaside
C3	Compton Street	C2	Seaside Road
B3	Cornfield Lane	A2	Southfields Road
B2	Cornfield Road	A3	South Street
B3	Cornfield Terrace	B3	South Street
B3	Devonshire Place	B3	Spencer Road
C1	Dursley Road	B2	Station Street
C3	Elms Road	C2	Susan's Road
A1	Enys Road	B2	Sutton Road
A1	Eversfield Road	C1	Sydney Road
A3	Furness Road	B2	Terminus Road
B2	Gildredge Road	C3	Terminus Road
C3	Grand Parade	A1	The Avenue
A3	Grange Road	C2	Tideswell Road
A3	Grassington Road	C3	Trinity Place
A3	Grove Road	B3	Trinity Trees
B3	Hardwick Road	B1	Upper Avenue
A1	Hartfield Lane	A1	Upperton Gardens
A1	Hartfield Road	A1	Upperton Lane
C3	Hartington Place	A1	Upperton Road
C4	Howard Square	A3	West Street
B2	Hyde Gardens	A2	West Terrace
A2	Hyde Road	D1	Willowfield Road
A2	Ivy Terrace	B4	Wilmington Square
A4	Jevington Gardens	B3	Wish Road
B2	Junction Road	A3	York Road

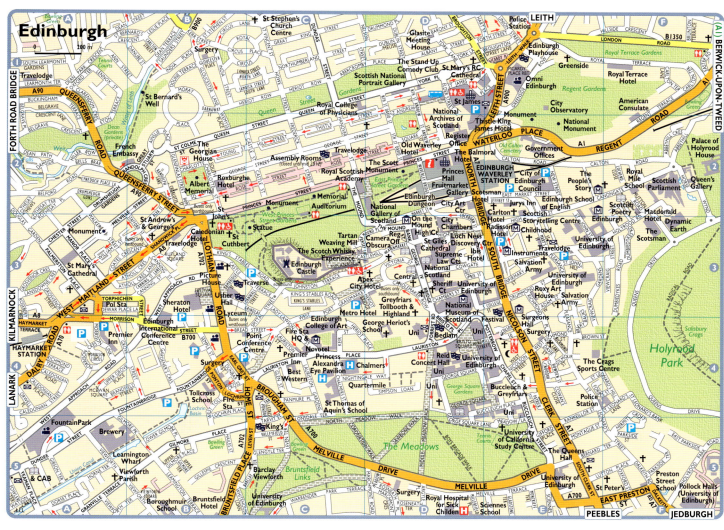

Edinburgh

Edinburgh is found on atlas page **127 P3**

F2 Abbeyhill
C1 Abercromby Place
E3 Adam Street
D1 Albany Street
A1 Ann Street
D5 Argyle Place
A3 Atholl Crescent Lane
D3 Bank Street
A2 Belford Road
A2 Belgrave Crescent
E5 Bernard Terrace
D5 Boys Brigade Walk
A4 Brandfield Street
B4 Bread Street
D4 Bristol Place
C4 Brougham Street
D1 Broughton Street
E1 Broughton Street Lane
F1 Brunton Terrace
B5 Bruntsfield Place
D4 Buccleuch Place
E4 Buccleuch Street
A4 Caledonian Place
A4 Caledonian Road
A4 Caledonian Street
E2 Calton Road
D3 Candlemaker Row
B3 Canning Street
E2 Canongate
F1 Carlton Terrace
C3 Castle Hill
C2 Castle Street
B3 Castle Terrace
C4 Chalmers Street
D3 Chambers Street
E4 Chapel Street

B2 Charlotte Square
A3 Chester Street Gardens
B1 Circus Lane
B1 Circus Place
A1 Clarendon Crescent
E4 Clerk Street
D2 Cockburn Street
E4 Cowan's Close
D3 Cowgate
F5 Dalkeith Road
A4 Dalry Road
B1 Danube Street
E4 Davie Street
A1 Dean Park Crescent
A1 Dean Street
A3 Dewar Place Lane
A3 Douglas Gardens
B1 Doune Terrace
E3 Drummond Street
D1 Dublin Street
F3 Dumbiedykes Road
B4 Dunbar Street
C1 Dundas Street
A5 Dundee Street
B4 Earl Grey Street
F1 Easter Road
E2 East Market Street
F5 East Parkside
F5 East Preston Street
D1 Elder Street
D4 Forrest Road
D1 Forth Street
A4 Fountainbridge
C2 Frederick Street
B4 Gardener's Crescent

D3 George IV Bridge
D4 George Square
D5 George Square Lane
B2 George Street
C2 George Street
E5 Gifford Place
B5 Gillespie Crescent
A5 Gilmore Park
B5 Gilmore Place
E4 Gilmour Street
B2 Glenfinlas Street
B1 Gloucester Lane
A5 Granville Terrace
C1 Great King Street
B2 Great Stuart Street
C3 Greenmarket
E1 Greenside Row
B3 Grindlay Street
A3 Grosvenor Street
A4 Grove Street
E4 Haddon's Court
C2 Hanover Street
A4 Haymarket Terrace
C1 Heriot Row
F5 Hermits Croft
D3 High Street
E3 High Street
E1 Hillside Crescent
C2 Hill Street
F5 Holyrood Park Road
E3 Holyrood Road
C4 Home Street
B2 Hope Street
F2 Horse Wynd
E4 Howden Street
C1 Howe Street
B1 India Place
B1 India Street
B1 Jamaica Street South Lane
D5 Jawbone Walk
C3 Johnston Terrace

C4 Keir Street
B1 Kerr Street
B3 King's Stables Road
C3 King's Stables Road
A3 Lady Lawson Street
C4 Lansdowne Crescent
C4 Lauriston Gardens
C4 Lauriston Place
C4 Lauriston Street
D3 Lawnmarket
B5 Leamington Terrace
E1 Leith Street
E1 Leith Walk
A1 Lennox Street
C5 Leven Place
B4 Lochrin Place
B4 Lochrin Street
E1 London Road
B3 Lothian Road
B5 Lower Gilmore Place
E5 Lutton Place
A2 Lynedoch Place Lane
A3 Manor Place
D5 Marchmont Crescent
D5 Marchmont Road
D2 Market Street
E5 Meadow Lane
C5 Melville Drive
A3 Melville Street
A3 Melville Terrace
D5 Middle Meadow Walk
D5 Millerfield Place
A2 Miller Row
E5 Moncrieff Terrace
E5 Montague Street
B1 Moray Place
A4 Morrison Link
A4 Morrison Street
D3 Mound Place
C1 Nelson Street
E2 New Street

E4 Nicolson Square
E4 Nicolson Street
C4 Nightingale Way
D2 North Bridge
C2 North Castle Street
C5 North Meadow Walk
D1 North St Andrew Street
D1 North St David Street
C1 Northumberland Street
F5 Oxford Street
A3 Palmerston Place
C4 Panmure Place
E3 Pleasance
B4 Ponton Street
E4 Potterrow
C2 Princes Street
F3 Queens Drive
A1 Queensferry Road
A2 Queensferry Street
B2 Queen Street
F3 Radical Road
C3 Ramsay Lane
B2 Randolph Crescent
B2 Randolph Lane
E5 Rankeillor Street
E2 Regent Road
E3 Richmond Place
B2 Rose Street
D5 Rosneath Place
A3 Rothesay Place
B1 Royal Circus
E1 Royal Terrace
D1 St Andrew Square
A1 St Bernard's Crescent
B2 St Colme Street
D1 St James Place
F4 St Leonard's Bank
E4 St Leonard's Hill
F4 St Leonard's Lane
F4 St Leonard's Street
E4 St Patrick Street

B1 St Stephen Street
C1 St Vincent Street
B1 Saunders Street
E5 Scienne Street
B4 Semple Street
B3 Shandwick Place
D4 Simpson Loan
E3 South Bridge
B2 South Charlotte Street
E5 South Clerk Street
A1 South Learmonth Gardens
D2 South St Andrew Street
D2 South St David Street
C4 Spittal Street
B3 Stafford Street
C5 Tarvit Street
C2 The Mound
C2 Thistle Street
A3 Torphichen Street
E1 Union Street
B5 Upper Gilmore Place
D3 Victoria Street
E4 Viewcraig Gardens
F3 Viewcraig Street
A5 Viewforth
A3 Walker Street
C5 Warrender Park Terrace
D2 Waterloo Place
D2 Waverley Bridge
A5 West Approach Road
A3 West Maitland Street
C4 West Nicolson Street
C4 West Port
E4 West Richmond Street
B4 West Toll Cross
A3 William Street
A5 Yeaman Place
D1 York Lane
D1 York Place
B2 Young Street

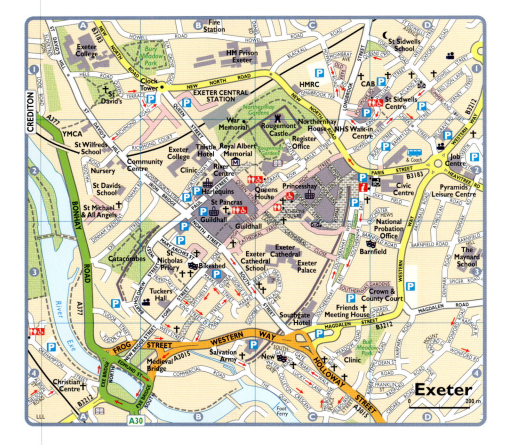

Exeter

Exeter is found on atlas page **9 M6**

D1	Acland Rd	D1	King William Street
D3	Archibald Road	C1	Longbrook Street
D3	Athelstan Road	B2	Lower North Street
C2	Bailey Street	D3	Magdalen Road
C2	Bampfylde Lane	C4	Magdalen Street
D2	Bampfylde Street	B3	Market Street
D3	Barnfield Road	C2	Martins Lane
B3	Bartholomew Street West	B3	Mary Arches Street
C3	Bear Street	C2	Musgrave Row
C2	Bedford Street	A4	New Bridge Street
D2	Belgrave Road	A1	New North Road
C1	Blackall Road	B2	Northernhay Street
A2	Bonhay Road	B3	North Street
D2	Bude Street	C1	Old Park Road
C4	Bull Meadow Road	D1	Oxford Road
C2	Castle Street	C3	Palace Gate
C3	Cathedral Close	D2	Paris Street
B3	Cathedral Yard	B2	Paul Street
D4	Cedars Road	B4	Preston Street
D1	Cheeke Street	C2	Princesshay
C3	Chichester Mews	C1	Queens Crescent
B4	Commercial Road	A1	Queen's Terrace
B3	Coombe Street	B1	Queen Street
C3	Deanery Place	D4	Radford Road
D4	Dean Street	D1	Red Lion Lane
D3	Denmark Road	B2	Richmond Court
A3	Dinham Crescent	A2	Richmond Road
A2	Dinham Road	C4	Roberts Road
D2	Dix's Field	C2	Roman Walk
C2	Eastgate	A1	St David's Hill
A4	Edmund Street	C2	Sidwell Street
B1	Elm Grove Road	D1	Sidwell Street
A3	Exe Street	B3	Smythen Street
D4	Fairpark Road	C3	Southernhay East
B3	Fore Street	C3	Southernhay Gardens
D4	Franklin Street	C3	Southernhay West
B3	Friern Hay Street	B3	South Street
A4	Frog Street	D3	Spicer Road
B3	George Street	D1	Summerland Street
B3	Guinea Street	D4	Temple Road
A2	Haldon Road	A4	Tudor Court
D2	Heavitree Road	A3	Tudor Street
A1	Hele Road	D1	Verney Street
C2	High Street	D1	Wells Street
C4	Holloway Street	B4	Western Way
B1	Howell Road	B4	West Street
B2	Iron Bridge	D4	Wonford Road
B3	King Street	D1	York Road

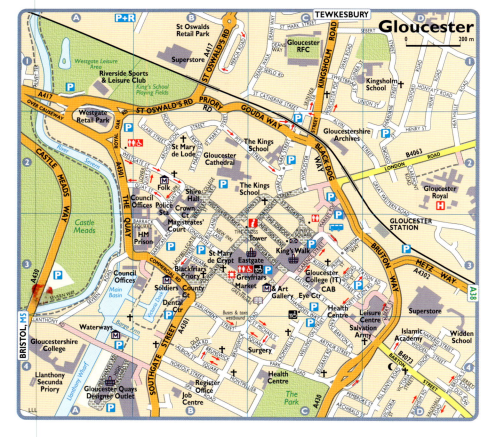

Gloucester

Gloucester is found on atlas page **46 F11**

D4	Albert Street	B4	Montpellier
B4	Albion Street	D4	Napier Street
D4	All Saints' Road	C3	Nettleton Road
C2	Alvin Street	B3	New Inn Lane
B2	Archdeacon Street	C3	New Inn Lane
C4	Archibald Street	B4	Norfolk Street
C2	Arthur Street	C3	Northgate Street
B3	Barbican Road	B4	Old Tram Road
B3	Barrack Square	A1	Over Causeway
D4	Barton Street	D1	Oxford Road
C3	Bedford Street	D2	Oxford Street
C4	Belgrave Road	C4	Park Road
B3	Berkeley Street	C2	Park Street
C2	Black Dog Way	B3	Parliament Street
D4	Blenheim Road	C4	Pembroke Street
B4	Brunswick Road	B2	Pitt Street
B4	Brunswick Square	B1	Priory Road
D3	Bruton Way	B2	Quay Street
B3	Bull Lane	A2	Royal Oak Road
A2	Castle Meads Way	C3	Russell Street
C3	Clarence Street	C2	St Aldate Street
B2	Clare Street	C1	St Catherine Street
C2	Commercial Road	B3	St John's Lane
C4	Cromwell Street	C1	St Mark Street
C1	Deans Walk	B2	St Mary's Square
C3	Eastgate Street	B2	St Mary's Street
B1	Gouda Way	C4	St Michael's Square
D2	Great Western Road	B1	St Oswald's Road
B3	Greyfriars	C1	Sebert Street
C3	Hampden Way	A3	Severn Road
C2	Hare Lane	D2	Sherborne Street
D2	Heathville Road	D4	Sinope Street
D1	Henry Road	B3	Southgate Street
D2	Henry Street	B4	Spa Road
A4	High Orchard Street	C3	Station Road
D1	Honyatt Road	D4	Swan Road
C4	King Barton Street	C1	Sweetbriar Street
C1	Kingsholm Road	B3	The Cross
C3	King's Square	C3	The Oxbode
B3	Ladybellegate Street	A2	The Quay
A4	Llanthony Road	C1	Union Street
D2	London Road	B2	Upper Quay Street
B3	Longsmith Street	D4	Vauxhall Road
C3	Market Parade	C4	Wellington Street
A4	Merchants' Road	A2	Westgate Street
B1	Mercia Road	D4	Widden Street
D3	Metz Way	C2	Worcester Parade
D4	Millbrook Street	C2	Worcester Street

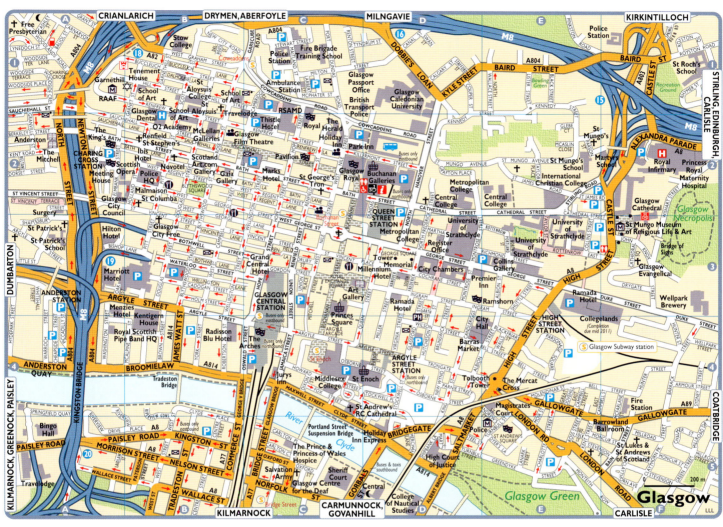

Glasgow

Glasgow is found on atlas page 125 P4

D5	Albert Bridge
D4	Albion Street
E3	Albion Street
F2	Alexandra Parade
A4	Anderston Quay
C4	Argyle Arcade
A3	Argyle Street
F4	Armour Street
A1	Ashley Street
F5	Bain Street
E1	Baird Street
A1	Baliol Street
F4	Barrack Street
B2	Bath Lane
A2	Bath Street
E4	Bell Street
A2	Berkeley Street
E4	Blackfriars Street
E1	Black Street
B2	Blythswood Square
B3	Blythswood Street
B3	Bothwell Lane
B3	Bothwell Street
D5	Bridgegate
F3	Bridge Of Sighs
C5	Bridge Street
B4	Broomielaw
B4	Brown Street
D4	Brunswick Street
B1	Buccleuch Lane
B1	Buccleuch Street
C4	Buchanan Street
B3	Cadogan Street
D1	Calgary Street
C1	Cambridge Street
D1	Canal Street

D4	Candleriggs
C5	Carlton Place
A1	Carnarvon Street
F1	Castle Street
F2	Castle Street
F3	Cathedral Square
D2	Cathedral Street
B5	Centre Street
F5	Chalmer Street
A1	Charing Cross
E5	Charlotte Street
A4	Cheapside Street
F5	Claythorn Avenue
F5	Claythorn Park
B4	Clyde Place
C4	Clyde Street
D3	Cochrane Street
E3	Collins Street
B5	Commerce Street
D1	Couper Street
C1	Cowcaddens Road
B1	Dalhousie Lane
A2	Dorset Street
B3	Douglas Street
C3	Drury Street
F3	Drygate
F3	Duke Street
D3	Dundas Street
D4	Dunlop Street
E5	Dyer's Lane
E4	East Campbell Street
A2	Elmbank Street
C4	Fox Street
E4	Gallowgate

B1	Garnethill Street
B2	Garnet Street
C1	Garscube Road
D3	Garth Street
D3	George Square
E3	George Street
B4	George V Bridge
C5	Glasgow Bridge
D4	Glassford Street
E2	Glebe Court
A2	Granville Street
E4	Great Dovehill
E5	Greendyke Street
F5	Green Street
D3	Hanover Street
E4	High Street
B1	Hill Street
B2	Holland Street
B3	Holm Street
C3	Hope Street
C4	Howard Street
F4	Hunter Street
D4	Hutcheson Street
A4	Hydepark Street
D3	Ingram Street
C4	Jamaica Street
B4	James Watt Street
F3	John Knox Street
D2	Kennedy Street
E1	Kennedy Street
A2	Kent Road
E5	Kent Street
C2	Killermont Street
A5	Kingston Bridge
B5	Kingston Street
D4	King Street
D1	Kyle Street
E5	Lanark Street

C1	Larbert Street
E1	Lister Street
E4	London Road
C1	Maitland Street
D3	Martha Street
D5	Mart Street
C4	Maxwell Street
B4	McAlpine Street
E2	McAslin Close
F4	McFarlane Street
C1	McPhater Street
D5	Merchant Lane
D4	Miller Street
F5	Millroad Drive
F5	Millroad Street
C1	Milton Street
C4	Mitchell Street
E5	Moir Street
E4	Molendinar Street
E5	Moncur Street
E5	Monteith Row
D3	Montrose Street
A5	Morrison Street
B5	Nelson Street
B1	New City Road
A2	Newton Street
D4	New Wynd
C5	Norfolk Street
D3	North Frederick Street
D3	North Hanover Street
E3	North Portland Street
A2	North Street
E1	North Wallace Street
C4	Osborne Street
C5	Oswald Street
C5	Oxford Street
A5	Paisley Road
D4	Parnie Street
E4	Parsonage Square
E2	Parson Street
B5	Paterson Street

E1	Pinkston Road
B2	Pitt Street
C1	Port Dundas Road
C5	Portland Street Suspension Bridge
C4	Queen Street
C3	Renfield Lane
C3	Renfield Street
C2	Renfrew Lane
B1	Renfrew Street
C1	Renton Street
F1	Rhymer Street
E3	Richmond Street
A4	Riverview Drive
B4	Robertson Street
B2	Rose Street
E5	Ross Street
E3	Rottenrow
E3	Rottenrow East
C3	Royal Exchange Square
F1	Royston Road
F1	Royston Square
E5	St Andrew's Square
E4	St Andrew's Street
E2	St James Road
D2	St Mungo Avenue
B3	St Vincent Lane
C3	St Vincent Place
A2	St Vincent Street
A2	St Vincent Terrace
D5	Saltmarket
A2	Sauchiehall Lane
B2	Sauchiehall Street
A1	Sauchiehall Street
B1	Scott Street
A3	Shaftesbury Street
D5	Shipbank Lane
E3	Shuttle Street
D3	South Frederick Street
F1	Springburn Road
A4	Springfield Quay

D1	Stafford Street
D5	Steel Street
F5	Stevenson Street
C1	Stewart Street
E2	Stirling Road
D4	Stockwell Place
D4	Stockwell Street
E5	Suffolk Street
F4	Sydney Street
E2	Taylor Place
E2	Taylor Street
B4	Tradeston Bridge
B5	Tradeston Street
D4	Trongate
D5	Turnbull Street
C1	Tyndrum Street
C3	Union Street
A5	Virginia Street
E4	Wallace Street
A4	Walls Street
A4	Warroch Street
A4	Washington Street
B3	Waterloo Street
B3	Wellington Lane
B3	Wellington Street
F4	Wellpark Street
B3	West Campbell Street
B2	West George Lane
B2	West George Street
B1	West Graham Street
C3	West Nile Street
C2	West Regent Lane
B2	West Regent Street
B5	West Street
D4	Wilson Street
F3	Wishart Street
A1	Woodlands Road
A1	Woodside Crescent
A1	Woodside Terrace
A1	Woodside Terrace Lane
B4	York Street

Great Yarmouth

Great Yarmouth is found on atlas page **77 Q10**

A1	Acle New Road	C1	North Denes Road
C2	Albemarle Road	D1	North Drive
C3	Albion Road	C2	North Market Road
B1	Alderson Road	A2	North Quay
B3	Alexandra Road	B1	Northgate Street
A4	Anson Road	B4	Nottingham Way
C3	Apsley Road	B1	Ormond Road
B1	Belvidere Road	C2	Paget Road
C4	Blackfriars Road	B1	Palgrave Road
A2	Brewery Street	A4	Pasteur Road
A3	Breydon Road	C2	Prince's Road
A1	Bridge Road	B2	Priory Plain
A3	Bridge Road	B4	Queen Street
A4	Bunn's Lane	B1	Rampart Road
B2	Church Plain	C3	Regent Road
A3	Critten's Road	C4	Rodney Road
C3	Crown Road	C3	Russell Road
B3	Dene Side	A3	St Francis Way
C4	Devonshire Road	C4	St George's Road
B1	East Road	B2	St Nicholas Road
C2	Euston Road	C4	St Peter's Plain
C2	Factory Road	C4	St Peter's Road
B1	Ferrier Road	C1	Sandown Road
A2	Fishers Quay	A3	Saw Mill Lane
B1	Frederick Road	A1	School Road
B2	Fullers Hill	A1	School Road Back
B1	Garrison Road	A1	Sidegate Road
A3	Gatacre Road	C3	South Market Road
A2	George Street	B3	South Quay
B3	Grey Friars Way	A4	Southtown Road
B1	Hammond Road	A4	Station Road
A3	High Mill Road	A3	Steam Mill Lane
B2	Howard Street North	C1	Stephenson Close
B3	Howard Street South	B3	Stonecutters Way
B3	King Street	A4	Tamworth Lane
B1	Kitchener Road	B2	Temple Road
A3	Ladyhaven Road	A2	The Conge
C4	Lancaster Road	B3	The Rows
A4	Lichfield Road	B4	Tolhouse Street
A2	Limekiln Walk	B1	Town Wall Road
C2	Manby Road	C3	Trafalgar Road
D3	Marine Parade	C3	Union Road
B1	Maygrove Road	C4	Victoria Road
C2	Middle Market Road	C2	Wellesley Road
B4	Middlegate	B1	West Road
B1	Moat Road	A4	Wolseley Road
C3	Nelson Road Central	B4	Yarmouth Way
C1	Nelson Road North	C4	York Road

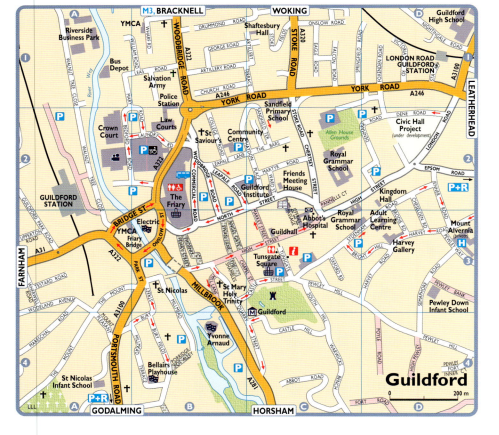

Guildford

Guildford is found on atlas page **23 Q5**

C4	Abbot Road	B4	Millmead Terrace
B3	Angel Gate	A4	Mount Pleasant
B1	Artillery Road	D1	Nightingale Road
C1	Artillery Terrace	B3	North Street
A2	Bedford Road	C1	Onslow Road
A3	Bridge Street	B3	Onslow Street
C3	Bright Hill	C3	Oxford Road
D3	Brodie Road	C2	Pannells Court
B4	Bury Fields	B3	Park Street
B4	Bury Street	D3	Pewley Bank
C4	Castle Hill	D4	Pewley Fort Inner Court
C3	Castle Street	C3	Pewley Hill
B3	Chapel Street	D3	Pewley Way
C2	Chertsey Street	B3	Phoenix Court
D2	Cheselden Road	B4	Porridge Pot Alley
B1	Church Road	A4	Portsmouth Road
B2	College Road	D4	Poyle Road
B2	Commercial Road	B3	Quarry Street
D2	Dene Road	C2	Sandfield Terrace
D2	Denmark Road	D3	Semaphore Road
B1	Drummond Road	C3	South Hill
C1	Eagle Road	C1	Springfield Road
D2	Epsom Road	D1	Station Approach
B1	Falcon Road	C1	Stoke Fields
C4	Fort Road	C1	Stoke Road
D1	Foxenden Road	B3	Swan Lane
A3	Friary Bridge	C3	Sydenham Road
B3	Friary Street	A3	Testard Road
B1	George Road	C2	The Bars
A2	Guildford Park Road	A4	The Mount
D3	Harvey Road	B3	The Shambles
C2	Haydon Place	C3	Tunsgate
D4	High Pewley	A3	Upperton Road
B3	High Street	D1	Victoria Road
C2	Jeffries Passage	A1	Walnut Tree Close
D2	Jenner Road	C2	Ward Street
B2	Laundry Road	C4	Warwicks Bench
B2	Leapale Lane	B1	Wharf Road
B2	Leapale Road	A3	Wherwell Road
B1	Leas Road	B1	William Road
D2	London Road	A3	Wodeland Avenue
A4	Mareschal Road	B1	Woodbridge Road
C3	Market Street	B1	York Road
C2	Martyr Road		
A1	Mary Road		
B3	Millbrook		
B3	Mill Lane		
B3	Millmead		

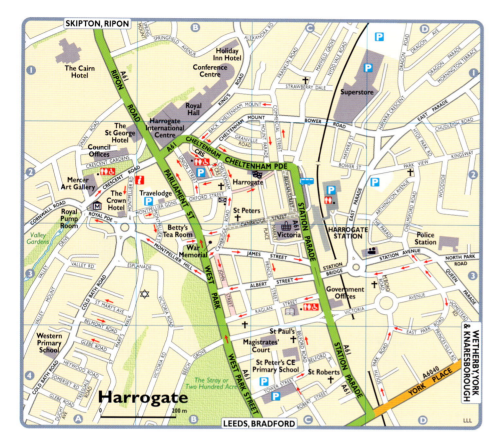

Harrogate

Harrogate is found on atlas page **97 M10**

C3	Albert Street	B2	Montpellier Street
B1	Alexandra Road	D1	Mornington Terrace
D2	Arthington Avenue	C2	Mount Parade
B2	Back Cheltenham Mount	D3	North Park Road
B4	Beech Grove	C1	Nydd Vale Road
C4	Belford Place	B2	Oxford Street
C4	Belford Road	D2	Park View
A3	Belmont Road	B2	Parliament Street
C2	Beulah Street	C3	Princes Street
C1	Bower Road	D4	Princes Villa Road
C2	Bower Street	D3	Queen Parade
B3	Cambridge Road	C3	Raglan Street
C2	Cambridge Street	A1	Ripon Road
D3	Chelmsford Road	C4	Robert Street
B2	Cheltenham Crescent	A2	Royal Parade
B2	Cheltenham Mount	A3	St Mary's Avenue
B2	Cheltenham Parade	A4	St Mary's Walk
D2	Chudleigh Road	A4	Somerset Road
A3	Cold Bath Road	D4	South Park Road
C1	Commercial Street	B1	Springfield Avenue
A2	Cornwall Road	B1	Spring Mount
A2	Crescent Gardens	D3	Station Avenue
A2	Crescent Road	C3	Station Bridge
D1	Dragon Avenue	C2	Station Parade
D1	Dragon Parade	C1	Strawberry Dale
D1	Dragon Road	A2	Swan Road
A4	Duchy Avenue	D2	The Parade
C2	East Parade	C4	Tower Street
D4	East Park Road	A4	Treesdale Road
A3	Esplanade	B2	Union Street
C1	Franklin Road	A3	Valley Drive
A4	Glebe Road	A3	Valley Mount
B2	Granville Road	A3	Valley Road
C2	Haywra Street	C3	Victoria Avenue
A4	Heywood Road	B3	Victoria Road
D3	Homestead Road	B3	West Park
D2	Hyde Park Road	B4	West Park Street
D2	Hywra Crescent	D2	Woodside
B3	James Street	D4	York Place
B3	John Street		
B1	King's Road		
D2	Kingsway		
C3	Market Place		
D3	Marlborough Road		
C1	Mayfield Grove		
B2	Montpellier Gardens		
B3	Montpellier Hill		
A2	Montpellier Road		

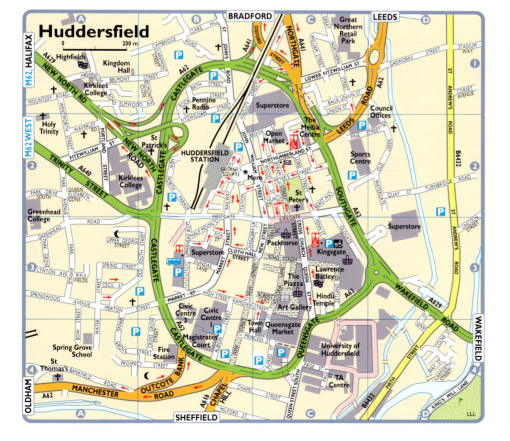

Huddersfield

Huddersfield is found on atlas page **90 E7**

B4	Albion Street	A2	New North Road
C4	Alfred Street	B4	New Street
C1	Back Union Street	C1	Northgate
A4	Bankfield Road	C2	Northumberland Street
B1	Bath Street	D2	Old Leeds Road
A1	Belmont Street	B3	Old South Street
C2	Brook Street	B4	Outcote Bank
C2	Byram Street	C1	Oxford Street
B1	Cambridge Road	A2	Park Avenue
D4	Carforth Street	A2	Park Drive South
B1	Castlegate	C4	Peel Street
B3	Chancery Lane	C2	Pine Street
B4	Chapel Hill	A2	Portland Street
B4	Chapel Hill	B4	Princess Street
C2	Church Street	A4	Prospect Street
B1	Clare Hill	D2	Quay Street
B1	Claremont Street	C3	Queen Street
B3	Cloth Hall Street	C4	Queen Street South
C3	Cross Church Street	C4	Queensgate
B3	Dundas Lane	B2	Railway Street
A2	Elizabeth Queen Gardens	B3	Ramsden Street
A1	Elmwood Avenue	B1	Rook Street
D4	Firth Street	D2	St Andrew's Road
A2	Fitzwilliam Street	B2	St George's Square
B2	Fitzwilliam Street	B1	St John's Road
D1	Gasworks Street	C2	St Peter's Street
C1	Great Northern Street	C2	Southgate
A3	Greenhead Road	A4	Spring Grove Street
B3	Half Moon Street	A3	Spring Street
B3	High Street	A3	Springwood Avenue
A1	Highfields Road	D1	Stadium Way
B2	John William Street	B2	Station Street
C3	King Street	A2	Trinity Street
D4	King's Mill Lane	D2	Turnbridge Road
C3	Kirkgate	C1	Union Street
C2	Leeds Road	A3	Upper George Street
D3	Lincoln Street	B3	Upperhead Row
C2	Lord Street	B2	Viaduct Street
C1	Lower Fitzwilliam Street	C3	Victoria Lane
A3	Lynton Avenue	D3	Wakefield Road
A4	Manchester Road	A3	Water Street
C3	Market Place	D2	Watergate
B3	Market Street	A2	Waverley Road
A3	Merton Street	A2	Wentworth Street
B4	Milford Street	B3	Westgate
A1	Mountjoy Road	C1	William Street
B2	New North Parade	C2	Wood Street
A1	New North Road	C3	Zetland Street

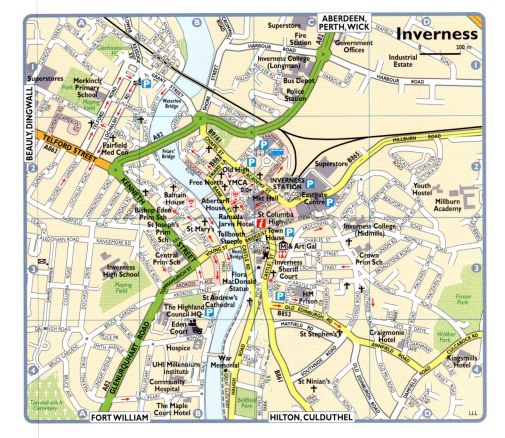

Inverness

Inverness is found on atlas page **156 B8**

D2	Abertaff Road		A1	Glendoe Terrace
B2	Academy Street		A4	Glenurquhart Road
B1	Anderson Street		C3	Gordon Terrace
D4	Annfield Road		B1	Grant Street
C3	Ardconnel Terrace		B4	Great Glen Way
B3	Ardross Street		C1	Harbour Road
C3	Argyle Street		D4	Harris Road
C3	Argyle Terrace		A2	Harrowden Road
A4	Ballifeary Lane		B4	Haugh Road
B4	Ballifeary Road		C3	High Street
B2	Bank Street		C4	Hill Park
C4	Bellfield Terrace		C3	Hill Street
A1	Benula Road		B2	Huntly Street
B1	Bernett Road		B1	Innes Street
A1	Birnie Terrace		D4	Islay Road
B4	Bishops Road		A2	Kenneth Street
B3	Bridge Street		B3	King Street
D3	Broadstone Road		D3	Kingsmills Road
A4	Bruce Avenue		A3	Laurel Avenue
A4	Bruce Gardens		A4	Lindsay Avenue
A4	Bruce Park		A2	Lochalsh Road
C1	Burnett Road		D3	Lovat Road
A3	Caledonian Road		A1	Lower Kessock Street
A2	Cameron Road		A4	Maxwell Drive
A2	Cameron Square		C4	Mayfield Road
A1	Carse Road		D3	Midmills Road
B3	Castle Road		D2	Millburn Road
C3	Castle Street		C3	Mitchell's Lane
B2	Chapel Street		C4	Muirfield Road
C3	Charles Street		C3	Old Edinburgh Road
A3	Columba Road		A4	Park Road
C2	Crown Circus		B3	Planefield Road
D2	Crown Drive		C3	Porterfield Road
C2	Crown Road		D4	Raasay Road
C3	Crown Street		A3	Rangemore Road
D4	Culcabock Road		A2	Ross Avenue
A4	Dalneigh Road		D1	Seafield Road
D4	Damfield Road		B1	Shore Street
D4	Darnaway Road		A4	Smith Avenue
C3	Denny Street		C3	Southside Place
A3	Dochfour Drive		C4	Southside Road
A1	Dunabran Road		A2	Telford Gardens
A2	Dunain Road		A2	Telford Road
B3	Duncraig Street		A2	Telford Street
D4	Erisky Road		B3	Tomnahurich Street
A3	Fairfield Road		D3	Union Road
C2	Falcon Square		C1	Walker Road
B2	Friars' Lane		B3	Young Street

Ipswich

Ipswich is found on atlas page **53 L3**

A3	Alderman Road		A2	London Road
B1	Anglesea Road		C3	Lower Brook Street
A1	Barrack Street		C3	Lower Orwell Street
B4	Belstead Road		B2	Museum Street
B1	Berners Street		C1	Neale Street
B2	Black Horse Lane		D3	Neptune Quay
D2	Blanche Street		B3	New Cardinal Street
C1	Bolton Lane		A1	Newson Street
D3	Bond Street		C2	Northgate Street
A1	Bramford Road		A1	Norwich Road
C4	Bridge Street		C2	Old Foundry Road
A2	Burlington Road		D2	Orchard Street
B4	Burrell Road		A1	Orford Street
A1	Cardigan Street		C3	Orwell Place
C2	Carr Street		D4	Orwell Quay
B3	Cavern Street		A3	Portman Road
B1	Cecil Road		A3	Princes Street
D1	Cemetery Road		B3	Princes Street
B1	Charles Street		A3	Quadling Street
D1	Christchurch Street		B3	Quadling Street
B2	Civic Drive		B3	Queen Street
A1	Clarkson Street		A4	Ranelagh Road
C2	Cobbold Street		A1	Redan Street
C3	College Street		A3	Russell Road
A4	Commercial Road		B1	St George's Street
A3	Constantine Road		D2	St Helen's Street
B4	Crafton Way		C2	St Margaret's Street
B2	Crown Street		B2	St Matthews Street
A1	Cumberland Street		B3	St Nicholas Street
A2	Dalton Road		B3	St Peter's Street
C4	Dock Street		B3	Silent Street
D4	Duke Street		A3	Sir Alf Ramsey Way
C3	Eagle Street		C2	Soane Street
B2	Elm Street		A1	South Street
B3	Falcon Street		C3	Star Lane
B1	Fonnereau Road		D1	Stoke Quay
C3	Foundation Street		D1	Suffolk Road
B3	Franciscan Way		C3	Tacket Street
A1	Geneva Road		B2	Tower Ramparts
A2	Great Gripping Street		D1	Tuddenham Avenue
C4	Great Whip Street		C3	Turret Lane
B3	Grey Friars Road		C4	Upper Orwell Street
D3	Grimwade Street		C4	Vernon Street
A2	Handford Road		A3	West End Road
D1	Hervey Road		B2	Westgate Street
B1	High Street		B4	Willoughby Road
C3	Key Street		B3	Wolsey Street
B2	King Street		D2	Woodbridge Road

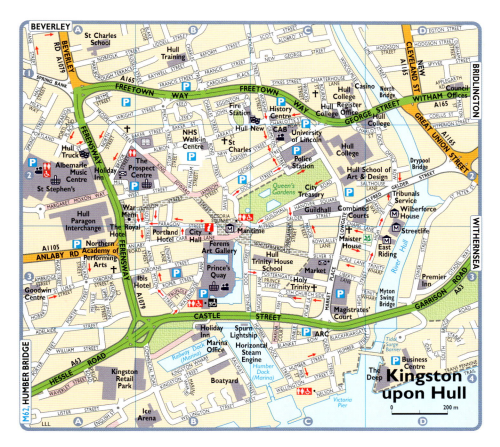

Kingston upon Hull

Kingston upon Hull is found on atlas page **93 J5**

A4	Adelaide Street	C3	Market Place
B2	Albion Street	A2	Mill Street
C2	Alfred Gelder Street	B3	Myton Street
A3	Anlaby Road	D1	New Cleveland Street
B2	Baker Street	B2	New Garden Street
A1	Beverley Road	C1	New George Street
C4	Blackfriargate	A1	Norfolk Street
C4	Blanket Row	B3	Osborne Street
B2	Bond Street	A3	Osborne Street
A2	Brook Street	B2	Paragon Street
B1	Caroline Street	A3	Pease Street
B3	Carr Lane	B1	Percy Street
B3	Castle Street	A3	Porter Street
C2	Chapel Lane	A2	Portland Place
B1	Charles Street	A2	Portland Street
C1	Charterhouse Lane	C3	Postergate
D3	Citadel Way	B3	Princes Dock Street
B4	Commercial Road	A1	Prospect Street
C3	Dagger Lane	C4	Queen Street
D2	Dock Office Row	B4	Railway Street
B2	Dock Street	B1	Raywell Street
D1	Durham Street	B1	Reform Street
B1	Egginton Street	A1	Russell Street
A2	Ferensway	A3	St Luke's Street
A1	Freetown Way	D2	St Peter Street
D2	Gandhi Way	B2	Saville Street
D3	Garrison Road	C3	Scale Lane
B2	George Street	C1	Scott Street
D1	George Street	C3	Silver Street
D1	Great Union Street	D4	South Bridge Road
C2	Grimston Street	C3	South Church Side
C2	Guildhall Road	B2	South Street
C2	Hanover Square	A1	Spring Bank
A4	Hessle Road	D1	Spyvee Street
C3	High Street	C1	Sykes Street
D1	Hodgson Street	D3	Tower Street
C4	Humber Dock Street	A3	Upper Union Street
C4	Humber Street	B2	Victoria Square
D1	Hyperion Street	B3	Waterhouse Lane
B2	Jameson Street	C4	Wellington Street
B2	Jarratt Street	B4	Wellington Street West
B2	King Edward Street	A2	West Street
B4	Kingston Street	C3	Whitefriargate
B1	Liddell Street	A4	William Street
C1	Lime Street	C1	Wincolmlee
A4	Lister Street	D1	Witham
C3	Lowgate	C1	Worship Street
A2	Margaret Moxon Way	A1	Wright Street

Lancaster

Lancaster is found on atlas page **95 K8**

D4	Aberdeen Road	A3	Lincoln Road
B4	Aldcliffe Road	B4	Lindow Street
C2	Alfred Street	C2	Lodge Street
D1	Ambleside Road	A2	Long Marsh Lane
D4	Balmoral Road	B1	Lune Street
D3	Bath Street	B3	Market Street
A3	Blades Street	A3	Meeting House Lane
D3	Bond Street	B3	Middle Street
D2	Borrowdale Road	D3	Moor Gate
C3	Brewery Lane	C3	Moor Lane
B2	Bridge Lane	B1	Morecambe Road
C3	Brock Street	C3	Nelson Street
D2	Bulk Road	C2	North Road
C3	Bulk Street	C1	Owen Road
B2	Cable Street	D3	Park Road
B3	Castle Hill	C2	Parliament Street
A3	Castle Park	D2	Patterdale Road
C2	Caton Road	B4	Penny Street
C3	Cheapside	B4	Portland Street
B3	China Street	D4	Primrose Street
B2	Church Street	D4	Prospect Street
B3	Common Garden Street	C4	Quarry Road
D4	Dale Street	B4	Queen Street
B3	Dallas Road	B4	Regent Street
D2	Dalton Road	D1	Ridge Lane
C3	Dalton Square	D1	Ridge Street
B2	Damside Street	C3	Robert Street
C1	Derby Road	C2	Rosemary Lane
C2	De Vitre Street	A1	St George's Quay
D4	Dumbarton Road	C2	St Leonard's Gate
D3	East Road	C4	St Peter's Road
C3	Edward Street	A3	Sibsey Street
A3	Fairfield Road	C4	South Road
B3	Fenton Street	A3	Station Road
C3	Gage Street	D4	Stirling Road
D2	Garnet Street	C3	Sulyard Street
C3	George Street	B3	Sun Street
D3	Grasmere Road	C4	Thurnham Street
D4	Gregson Road	D2	Troutbeck Road
B1	Greyhound Bridge Road	D3	Ulleswater Road
C3	Gt John Street	A3	West Road
B4	High Street	A3	Westbourne Road
A3	Kelsey Street	A3	Wheatfield Street
D2	Kentmere Road	D3	Williamson Road
B3	King Street	A3	Wingate-Saul Road
C1	Kingsway	D2	Wolseley Street
D4	Kirkes Road	D3	Woodville Street
D1	Langdale Road	D3	Wyresdale Road

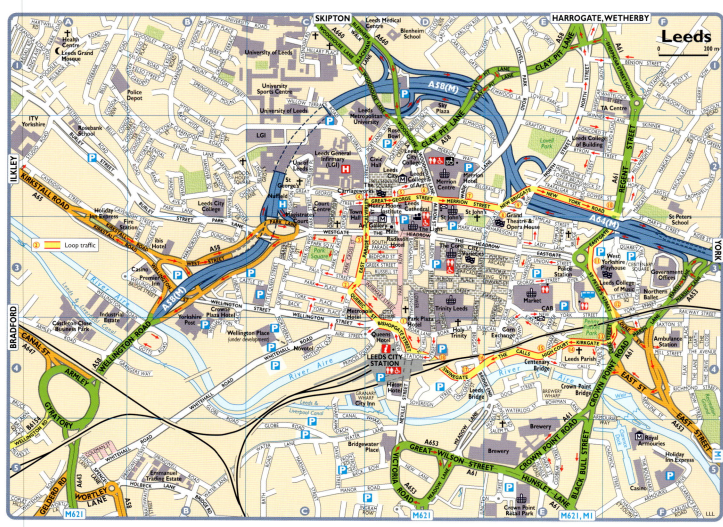

Leeds

Leeds is found on atlas page **90 H4**

B3	Abbey Street	C2	Calverley Street	D4	Duncan Street	E3	Kirkgate	E2	North Street	B5	Springwell Street
C4	Aire Street	A4	Canal Street	B3	Duncombe Street	A2	Kirkstall Road	C3	Oxford Place	A2	Studio Road
D3	Albion Place	C4	Canal Wharf	E3	Dyer Street	E3	Lady Lane	C3	Oxford Row	D4	Swinegate
D2	Albion Street	D1	Carlton Carr	C3	Eastgate	D3	Lands Lane	C3	Park Cross Street	E3	Templar Street
A1	Alexandra Road	D1	Carlton Hill	F4	East Parade	C2	Leighton Street	B2	Park Lane	F4	The Avenue
F2	Argyle Road	D1	Carlton Rise	F4	East Street	F2	Leyland Road	C3	Park Place	F5	The Boulevard
A4	Armley Gyratory	B3	Castle Street	A5	Gelderd Road	B1	Lifton Place	D3	Park Row	E4	The Calls
A4	Armley Road	C1	Cavendish Road	E3	George Street	F2	Lincoln Green Road	C3	Park Square East	D3	The Headrow
F5	Armouries Drive	A2	Cavendish Street	B4	Globe Road	B3	Lisbon Street	C3	Park Square North	C2	Thoresby Place
E4	Armouries Way	F3	Centenary Square	B4	Gotts Road	C3	Little Queen Street	C3	Park Square West	E2	Trafalgar Street
B2	Back Hyde Terrace	E3	Central Road	E2	Gower Street	E1	Lovell Park Hill	C3	Park Street	E3	Union Street
C5	Back Row	F5	Chadwick Street	E2	Grafton Street	E1	Lovell Park Road	F1	Pilot Street	D3	Upper Basinghall Street
C5	Bath Road	F1	Cherry Row	A4	Grangers Way	D3	Lower Basinghall Street	D2	Portland Crescent	E3	Vicar Lane
D3	Bedford Street	C2	Chorley Lane	C2	Great George Street	E2	Lower Brunswick Street	D2	Portland Way	D5	Victoria Road
D2	Belgrave Street	D3	City Square	D5	Great Wilson Street	B1	Lyddon Terrace	C4	Princes Square	B2	Victoria Street
A1	Belle Vue Road	B2	Claremont	D3	Greek Street	F2	Mabgate	F3	Quarry Hill	B2	Victoria Terrace
C2	Belmont Grove	F5	Clarence Road	B2	Hanover Avenue	F3	Macaulay Street	C3	Quebec Street	D2	Wade Lane
F1	Benson Street	B1	Clarendon Road	B2	Hanover Lane	C5	Manor Road	D2	Queen Square	B5	Water Lane
B3	Bingley Street	D2	Clay Pit Lane	B2	Hanover Square	D3	Mark Lane	D2	Queen Square Court	E4	Waterloo Street
D4	Bishopgate Street	B1	Cloberry Street	E3	Harewood Street	B3	Marlborough Street	C3	Queen Street	B3	Wellington Bridge Street
E5	Black Bull Street	D3	Commercial Street	E4	Harper Street	C5	Marshall Street	F3	Railway Street	A3	Wellington Road
C1	Blackman Lane	E2	Concord Street	E3	Harrison Street	F4	Marsh Lane	F2	Regent Street	A4	Wellington Road
C1	Blenheim Walk	B2	Consort Street	A1	Hartwell Road	E4	Maude Street	F4	Richmond Street	A5	Wellington Road
D4	Boar Lane	A1	Consort View	E4	High Court	D5	Meadow Lane	F3	Rider Street	B3	Wellington Street
E4	Bowman Lane	E3	County Arcade	B5	Holbeck Lane	E2	Melbourne Street	A1	Rosebank Road	A1	Westfield Road
F4	Bow Street	B1	Cromer Terrace	F2	Hope Road	D2	Merrion Street	F3	St Cecilia Street	C3	Westgate
B2	Brandon Road	F2	Cromwell Street	E4	Hunslet Road	D2	Merrion Way	A1	St John's Road	B3	West Street
D4	Bridge End	B1	Cross Kelso Road	E5	Hunslet Road	A1	Millbank Lane	F3	St Mary's Street	C4	Wharf Approach
B5	Bridge Road	F1	Cross Stamford Street	A1	Hyde Park Road	D2	Millennium Square	C3	St Paul's Street	E4	Wharf Street
E2	Bridge Street	E5	Crown Point Road	B2	Hyde Street	F4	Mill Street	F3	St Peter's Square	C4	Whitehall Quay
E3	Bridge Street	E5	Crown Street	B1	Hyde Terrace	F2	Millwright Street	F3	St Peter's Street	A5	Whitehall Road
D4	Briggate	E4	Cudbear Street	D3	Infirmary Street	B1	Mount Preston Street	E5	Salem Place	A5	Whitehall Road
A2	Burley Street	C5	David Street	D5	Junction Street	F1	Mushroom Street	F4	Saxton Lane	F1	Whitelock Street
D3	Butts Court	E4	Dock Street	B1	Kelso Road	F4	Neptune Street	E1	Sheepscar Grove	C1	Willow Terrace Road
E2	Byron Street	F4	Duke Street	B2	Kendal Lane	D4	Neville Street	F1	Sheepscar Street South	C1	Woodhouse Lane
E4	Call Lane	F4	Duke Street	E3	King Edward Street	E3	New Briggate	E1	Skinner Lane	B2	Woodhouse Square
				A1	King's Avenue	D4	New Lane	D3	South Parade	A1	Woodsley Road
				C3	King Street	D4	New Station Street	D4	Sovereign Street	A5	Wortley Lane
						E2	New York Road	A5	Spence Lane	A5	Wortley Lane
						E3	New York Street	B1	Springfield Mount	C3	York Place
						C4	Northern Street	B5	Springwell Road	F3	York Street

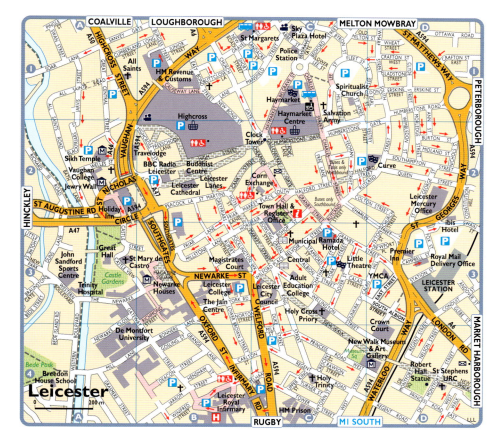

Leicester

Leicester is found on atlas page **72 F10**

C3	Albion Street	B4	Infirmary Road
A1	All Saints Road	B4	Jarrom Street
A2	Bath Lane	A1	Jarvis Street
C1	Bedford Street	C3	King Street
C1	Belgrave Gate	C1	Lee Street
C3	Belvoir Street	D3	London Road
C3	Bishop Street	B3	Lower Brown Street
B4	Bonners Lane	B3	Magazine Square
C3	Bowling Green Street	B1	Mansfield Street
B1	Burgess Street	B2	Market Place South
D2	Burton Street	C3	Market Street
C3	Calais Hill	A4	Mill Lane
D3	Campbell Street	D1	Morledge Street
B2	Cank Street	B3	Newarke Street
A3	Castle Street	C3	New Walk
C1	Charles Street	B3	Oxford Street
C3	Chatham Street	B2	Peacock Lane
C2	Cheapside	B3	Pocklington Walk
B1	Church Gate	D4	Princess Road East
D1	Clyde Street	C4	Princess Road West
C2	Colton Street	D2	Queen Street
D3	Conduit Street	C4	Regent Road
D1	Crafton Street West	D4	Regent Street
B4	Deacon Street	A2	Richard III Road
D4	De Montfort Street	C2	Rutland Street
C3	Dover Street	A2	St Augustine Road
C3	Duke Street	D2	St George Street
A3	Duns Lane	D2	St Georges Way
B1	East Bond Street Lane	C1	St James Street
D1	Erskine Street	D1	St Matthews Way
C1	Fleet Street	A2	St Nicholas Circle
B3	Friar Lane	A1	Sanvey Gate
C2	Gallowtree Gate	A1	Soar Lane
A3	Gateway Street	D3	South Albion Street
C2	Granby Street	D2	Southampton Street
A4	Grasmere Street	B3	Southgates
B1	Gravel Street	D3	Station Street
A1	Great Central Street	A3	The Newarke
B2	Greyfriars	C4	Tower Street
C2	Halford Street	A2	Vaughan Way
C2	Haymarket	D4	Waterloo Way
A1	Highcross Street	C3	Welford Road
B2	Highcross Street	A2	Welles Street
B2	High Street	C3	Wellington Street
C1	Hill Street	A4	Western Boulevard
B3	Horsefair Street	C4	West Street
C2	Humberstone Gate	D1	Wharf Street South
D1	Humberstone Road	C2	Yeoman Street

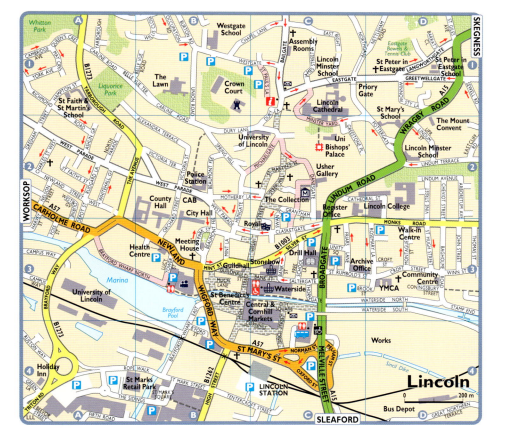

Lincoln

Lincoln is found on atlas page **86 C6**

B2	Alexandra Terrace	D3	Montague Street
D2	Arboretum Avenue	B2	Motherby Lane
D3	Bagholme Road	A2	Nelson Street
C1	Bailgate	B3	Newland
C3	Bank Street	A2	Newland Street West
B3	Beaumont Fee	C4	Norman Street
A1	Belle Vue Terrace	C1	Northgate
A3	Brayford Way	B3	Orchard Street
B4	Brayford Wharf East	C4	Oxford Street
A3	Brayford Wharf North	B3	Park Street
C3	Broadgate	C4	Pelham Street
B1	Burton Road	D2	Pottergate
A2	Carholme Road	A1	Queen's Crescent
A1	Carline Road	A1	Richmond Road
C2	Cathedral Street	A4	Rope Walk
B1	Chapel Lane	D3	Rosemary Lane
A2	Charles Street West	A2	Rudgard Lane
D2	Cheviot Street	D3	St Hugh Street
C3	City Square	B4	St Mark Street
C3	Clasketgate	C2	St Martin's Lane
B4	Cornhill	B4	St Mary's Street
D3	Croft Street	C3	St Rumbold's Street
C2	Danesgate	C3	Saltergate
A3	Depot Street	C3	Silver Street
B2	Dury Lane	C4	Sincil Street
C1	East Bight	B2	Spring Hill
C1	Eastgate	C2	Steer Hill
C3	Free School Lane	C3	Swan Street
C3	Friars Lane	B4	Tentercroft Street
C2	Grantham Street	A2	The Avenue
D1	Greetwellgate	C3	Thorngate
A2	Gresham Street	A4	Triton Road
B3	Guildhall Street	B1	Union Road
A1	Hampton Street	C3	Unity Square
B3	High Street	B2	Victoria Street
B3	Hungate	B2	Victoria Terrace
D3	John Street	D2	Vine Street
D1	Langworthgate	C3	Waterside North
C2	Lindum Road	C3	Waterside South
D2	Lindum Terrace	B1	Westgate
B3	Lucy Tower Street	A2	West Parade
A1	May Crescent	A2	Whitehall Grove
C4	Melville Street	B3	Wigford Way
C2	Michaelgate	D1	Winnow Sty Lane
C2	Minster Yard	D3	Winn Street
B3	Mint Lane	D2	Wragby Road
B3	Mint Street	A1	Yarborough Road
D3	Monks Road	A1	York Avenue

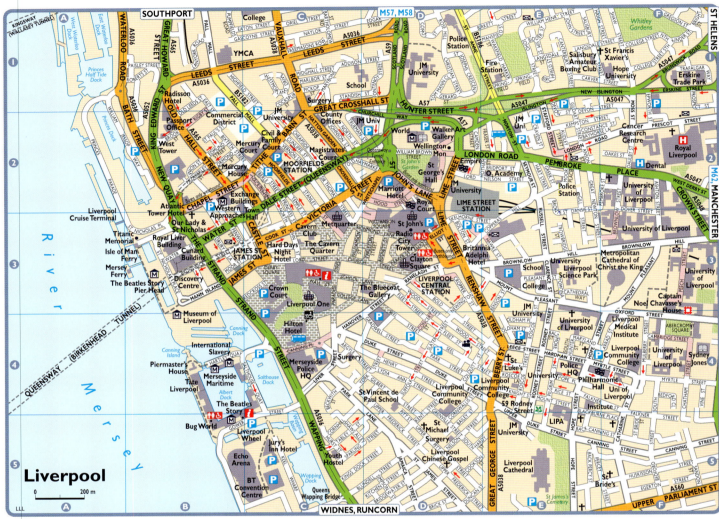

Liverpool

Liverpool is found on atlas page **81 L6**

C1 Addison Street	B2 Chapel Street	F1 Erskine Street	C5 Keel Wharf	B2 Ormond Street	E2 Seymour Street
E2 Anson Street	F4 Chatham Street	E4 Falkner Street	E2 Kempston Street	F4 Oxford Street	F1 Shaw Street
C4 Argyle Street	C2 Cheapside	B2 Fazakerley Street	D5 Kent Street	B1 Paisley Street	C2 Sir Thomas Street
F4 Arrad Street	D1 Christian Street	B3 Fenwick Street	F1 Kinder Street	B1 Pall Mall	D3 Skelhorne Street
F2 Ashton Street	D2 Churchill Way	D3 Fleet Street	B2 King Edward Street	C3 Paradise Street	D4 Slater Street
E2 Audley Street	C3 Church Street	D1 Fontenoy Street	A1 Kingsway (Wallasey Tunnel)	D3 Parker Street	E1 Soho Street
E5 Back Canning Street	E3 Clarence Street	E2 Fraser Street	D5 Kitchen Street	C4 Park Lane	C5 Sparling Street
E4 Baltimore Street	C1 Cockspur Street	B1 Gascoyne Street	E4 Knight Street	D4 Parr Street	E1 Springfield
B2 Bath Street	C3 College Lane	D1 Gerard Street	E1 Langsdale Street	F3 Peech Street	E2 Stafford Street
C4 Beckwith Street	F1 College Street North	D4 Gilbert Street	E4 Leece Street	E2 Pembroke Place	C2 Stanley Street
F5 Bedford Street South	F1 College Street South	D2 Gildart Street	B1 Leeds Street	F2 Pembroke Street	B3 Strand Street
E3 Benson Street	D4 Colquitt Street	E2 Gill Street	D2 Lime Street	E4 Percey Street	D4 Suffolk Street
E4 Berry Street	E2 Constance Street	C4 Liver Street	E4 Pilgrim Street	C5 Tabley Street
E1 Bidder Street	C3 Cook Street	D2 London Road	E3 Pleasant Street	D3 Tarleton Street
D1 Birkett Street	E3 Copperas Hill	E2 London Road	E3 Pomona Street	C2 Temple Street
B2 Bixteth Street	C5 Cornhill	D2 Lord Nelson Street	F2 Prescot Street	B3 The Strand
E5 Blackburne Place	D5 Cornwallis Street	C3 Lord Street	A2 Princes Parade	E3 Tithe Barn Street
C5 Blundell Street	E2 Craven Street	D4 Lydia Ann Street	F1 Prospect Street	F1 Trafalgar Way
D3 Bold Street	D3 Cropper Street	B3 Mann Island	A4 Queensway (Birkenhead Tunnel)	E3 Trowbridge Street
D3 Bosnett Street	C2 Crosshall Street	E1 Mansfield Street	C2 Trueman Street
D5 Bridgewater Street	F2 Crown Street	C1 Marybone	D3 Ranelagh Street	E5 Upper Duke Street
E2 Bridport Street	C2 Dale Street (Queensway)	E4 Maryland Street	C3 Redcross Street	D4 Upper Frederick Street
B2 Brook Street	E3 Dansie Street	C1 Midghall Street	D3 Renshaw Street	F5 Upper Parliament Street
E3 Brownlow Hill	F2 Daulby Street	C2 Moorfields	C3 Richmond Lane	D5 Upper Pitt Street
F3 Brownlow Street	C3 Derby Square	B3 Moor Street	B2 Rigby Street	C1 Vauxhall Road
F1 Brunswick Road	E2 Devon Street	F1 Moss Street	B2 Rodney Street	C2 Vernon Street
B3 Brunswick Street	F3 Dover Street	E3 Mount Pleasant	E4 Roscoe Street	C3 Victoria Street
F4 Cambridge Street	B3 Drury Lane	E4 Mount Street	D1 Rose Hill	E1 Wakefield Street
D2 Camden Street	D4 Duke Street	E4 Mulberry Street	E3 Russell Street	C3 Wall Street
C4 Canning Place	B1 East Street	C1 Naylor Street	D1 St Anne Street	C5 Wapping
E5 Canning Street	B1 Eaton Street	D5 Nelson Street	D5 St James Street	A1 Waterloo Road
E1 Canterbury Street	C2 Eberle Street	D4 Newington	D1 St Josephs Crescent	B3 Water Street
E1 Carver Street	B2 Edmund Street	E1 New Islington	B3 St Nicholas Place	F2 West Derby Street
C3 Castle Street	F5 Egerton Street	B2 New Quay	B2 St Paul's Street	C1 Westmorland Drive
F5 Catharine Street	D3 Elliot Street	C3 North John Street	C4 Salthouse Quay	D2 Whitechapel
E3 Cathedral Way	F1 Epworth Street	E2 Norton Street	F5 Sandon Street	E1 William Henry Street
		E4 Old Hall Street	C3 School Lane	A2 William Jessop Way
		E4 Oldham Street	D1 Scotland Road	D3 Williamson Square
		C2 Old Haymarket	D4 Seel Street	C3 Williamson Street
		B1 Old Leeds Street		D3 Wood Street
				C4 York Street

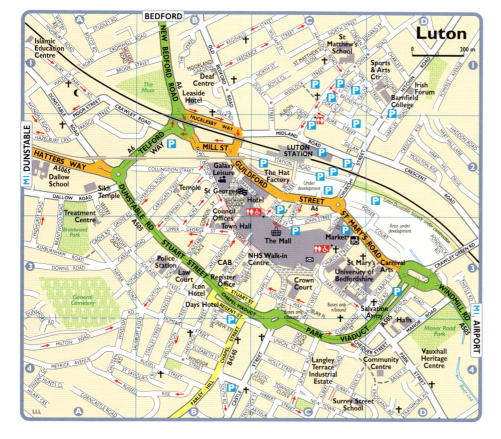

Luton

Luton is found on atlas page **50 C6**

B3	Adelaide Street	C4	Hibbert Street
C4	Albert Road	A1	Highbury Road
B2	Alma Street	C1	High Town Road
C4	Arthur Street	D1	Hitchin Road
A3	Ashburnham Road	C4	Holly Street
A1	Biscot Road	B2	Hucklesby Way
A3	Brantwood Road	B3	Inkerman Street
C1	Brunswick Street	C3	John Street
C2	Burr Street	B3	King Street
A1	Bury Park Road	C4	Latimer Road
B3	Buxton Road	B2	Liverpool Road
A3	Cardiff Road	D4	Manor Road
B2	Cardigan Street	A4	Meyrick Avenue
B4	Castle Street	C2	Midland Road
B4	Chapel Street	B2	Mill Street
B3	Chapel Viaduct	A4	Milton Road
D1	Charles Street	A1	Moor Street
C4	Chequer Street	A3	Napier Road
A4	Chiltern Road	B1	New Bedford Road
C2	Church Street	C4	New Town Street
C3	Church Street	B1	Old Bedford Road
C1	Cobden Street	C3	Park Street
B2	Collingdon Street	C3	Park Street West
D1	Concorde Street	C4	Park Viaduct
D3	Crawley Green Road	B3	Princess Street
A1	Crawley Road	B3	Regent Street
D2	Crescent Road	B1	Reginald Street
A1	Cromwell Road	A3	Rothesay Road
C4	Cumberland Street	A4	Russell Rise
A2	Dallow Road	B4	Russell Street
C1	Dudley Street	C3	St Mary's Road
B4	Dumfries Street	A4	Salisbury Road
A1	Dunstable Road	B4	Stanley Street
B4	Farley Hill	C2	Station Road
C3	Flowers Way	D4	Strathmore Ave
B1	Frederick Street	B3	Stuart Street
B3	George Street	C4	Surrey Street
B3	George Street West	B4	Tavistock Street
B3	Gordon Street	B2	Telford Way
A3	Grove Road	B3	Upper George Street
B2	Guildford Street	D3	Vicarage Street
D2	Hart Hill Drive	A1	Waldeck Road
D2	Hart Hill Lane	B4	Wellington Street
D2	Hartley Road	C1	Wenlock Street
B4	Hastings Street	D3	Windmill Road
A2	Hatters Way	B4	Windsor Street
C1	Havelock Road	A4	Winsdon Road
A2	Hazelbury Crescent	C1	York Street

Maidstone

Maidstone is found on atlas page **38 C10**

D1	Albany Street	B2	Market Buildings
D2	Albion Place	C2	Marsham Street
D1	Allen Street	D4	Meadow Walk
D3	Ashford Road	B3	Medway Street
B3	Bank Street	C4	Melville Road
B4	Barker Road	B3	Mill Street
A3	Bedford Place	D3	Mote Avenue
B3	Bishops Way	D3	Mote Road
C2	Brewer Street	D2	Old School Place
B3	Broadway	C4	Orchard Street
B3	Broadway	C3	Padsole Lane
C4	Brunswick Street	B3	Palace Avenue
A2	Buckland Hill	D1	Princes Street
A2	Buckland Road	C4	Priory Road
C1	Camden Street	B2	Pudding Lane
D3	Chancery Lane	D2	Queen Anne Road
A4	Charles Street	A4	Reginald Road
C2	Church Street	A3	Rocky Hill
B4	College Avenue	C3	Romney Place
C4	College Road	B2	Rose Yard
C1	County Road	A4	Rowland Close
D4	Crompton Gardens	A2	St Anne Court
D2	Cromwell Road	B2	St Faith's Street
A4	Douglas Road	D1	St Luke's Avenue
B2	Earl Street	D1	St Luke's Road
D4	Elm Grove	A2	St Peters Street
B1	Fairmeadow	B1	Sandling Road
A4	Florence Road	D2	Sittingbourne Road
D1	Foley Street	D3	Square Hill Road
C4	Foster Street	B1	Stacey Street
C3	Gabriel's Hill	B1	Station Road
C4	George Street	A3	Terrace Road
D4	Greenside	A4	Tonbridge Road
A4	Hart Street	C2	Tufton Street
D4	Hastings Road	C2	Union Street
C4	Hayle Road	C4	Upper Stone Street
D1	Heathorn Street	A3	Victoria Street
C1	Hedley Street	D2	Vinters Road
B3	High Street	C3	Wat Tyler Way
D1	Holland Road	B1	Week Street
C1	James Street	C1	Well Road
C1	Jeffrey Street	A4	Westree Road
C3	King Street	C1	Wheeler Street
D4	Kingsley Road	C1	Woollett Street
C4	Knightrider Street	C2	Wyatt Street
A1	Lesley Place		
A3	London Road		
C3	Lower Stone Street		

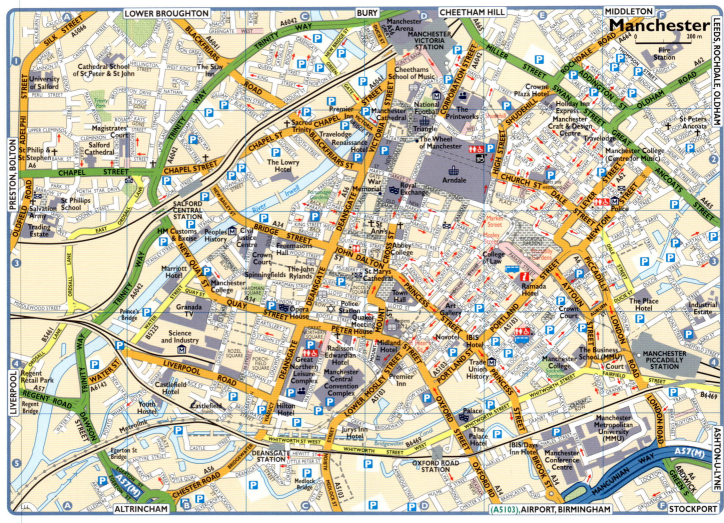

Manchester

Manchester is found on atlas page **82 H5**

E4	Abingdon Street	B2	Browning Street	A5	Dawson Street	E2	John Street	B2	New Bailey Street	C2	St Anns Square
E1	Addington Street	D3	Brown Street	C4	Deansgate	E2	Joiner Street	C1	New Bridge Street	C3	St Ann Street
A2	Adelphi Street	B1	Bury Street	D4	Dickinson Street	F3	Jutland Street	D2	New Cathedral Street	C3	St James Square
C5	Albion Street	B4	Byrom Street	B4	Duke Street	D3	Kennedy Street	A4	New Elm Road	D4	St James Street
E1	Angel Street	E1	Cable Street	F3	Dulcie Street	C1	King Street	E2	New George Street	C3	St Mary's Parsonage
F5	Ardwick Green South	D5	Cambridge Street	A3	East Ordsall Lane	C3	King Street	B3	New Quay Street	D4	St Peter's Square
C4	Artillery Street	C4	Camp Street	A5	Egerton Street	C3	King Street West	E3	Newton Street	B2	St Stephen Street
B4	Atherton Street	E4	Canal Street	F4	Fairfield Street	B2	Lamb Lane	E3	New York Street	F3	Store Street
C3	Atkinson Street	A1	Cannon Street	D4	Faulkner Street	F3	Laystall Street	D3	Nicholas Street	E1	Sharp Street
E4	Auburn Street	B1	Canon Green Drive	D1	Fennel Street	B3	Left Bank	A1	North George Street	E2	Shudehill
E3	Aytoun Street	B5	Castle Street	A2	Ford Street	F3	Lena Street	A1	North Hill Street	A1	Silk Street
E3	Back Piccadilly	D2	Cathedral Street	D3	Fountain Street	E2	Lever Street	A2	North Star Drive	E1	Simpson Street
A2	Bank Street	E5	Charles Street	B2	Frederick Street	C5	Little Lever Street	C1	Norton Street	C3	South King Street
F4	Baring Street	E5	Charlotte Street	B1	Garden Lane	C5	Little Peter Street	A3	Oldfield Road	E3	Spear Street
C4	Barton Street	E3	Chatham Street	B3	Gartside Street	B4	Liverpool Road	F1	Oldham Road	D3	Spring Gardens
F4	Berry Street	D3	Cheapside	F2	George Leigh Street	C3	Lloyd Street	E2	Oldham Street	F3	Station Approach
B1	Blackfriars Road	B5	Chester Road	D4	George Street	F4	London Road	A4	Ordsall Lane	E1	Swan Street
C2	Blackfriars Street	E3	China Lane	B2	Gore Street	D1	Long Millgate	D5	Oxford Road	F3	Tariff Street
B5	Blantyre Street	E4	Chorlton Street	E5	Granby Row	C4	Longworth Street	D4	Oxford Street	E2	Thomas Street
B2	Bloom Street	E2	Church Street	C1	Gravel Lane	B4	Lower Byrom Street	D3	Pall Mall	F1	Thompson Street
E4	Bloom Street	C5	City Road East	F2	Great Ancoats Street	C4	Lower Mosley Street	E3	Parker Street	D3	Tib Lane
F2	Blossom Street	A2	Cleminson Street	B3	Great Bridgewater Street	D5	Lower Ormond Street	A1	Peru Street	E2	Tib Street
F4	Boad Street	C1	College Land	D1	Great Ducie Street	E1	Ludgate Street	C4	Peter Street	D1	Todd Street
C1	Boond Street	C1	Collier Street	A2	Great George Street	E4	Major Street	E3	Piccadilly	C4	Tonman Street
D3	Booth Street	C5	Commercial Street	B5	Great Jackson Street	A5	Mancunian Way	E3	Piccadilly Gardens	F4	Travis Street
C4	Bootle Street	E2	Copperas Street	B4	Great John Street	D3	Marble Street	D4	Portland Street	A4	Trinity Way
E5	Brancaster Road	F2	Cornell Street	C1	Greengate	D2	Market Street	F3	Port Street	E2	Turner Street
C3	Brazenose Street	F2	Cotton Street	B1	Greengate West	D3	Marsden Street	A5	Potato Wharf	A2	Upper Cleminson Street
F3	Brewer Street	D2	Corporation Street	B1	Gun Street	E1	Marshall Street	D3	Princess Street	E2	Victoria Bridge Street
C3	Bridge Street	F2	Crosskeys Street	D1	Hanover Street	E1	Mason Street	B3	Quay Street	D2	Victoria Street
E2	Bridgewater Place	F1	Cross Street	C3	Hardman Street	A1	Mayan Avenue	C1	Queen Street	E2	Warwick Street
B4	Bridgewater Street	C2	Cross Street	C5	Hewitt Street	C5	Medlock Street	C3	Queen Street	C3	Watson Street
B5	Bridgewater Viaduct	D3	Cross Street	E2	High Street	A3	Middlewood Street	F2	Redhill Street	D2	Well Street
E5	Brook Street	E1	Dale Street	F2	Hood Street	E1	Miller Street	A4	Regent Road	B1	West King Street
A1	Brotherton Drive	E1	Dantzic Street	E3	Hope Street	E3	Minshull Street	D4	Reyner Street	D3	West Mosley Street
B2	Browncross Street			F2	Houndsworth Street	C1	Mirabel Street	B4	Rice Street	D5	Whitworth Street
				D5	Hulme Street	D3	Mosley Street	E4	Richmond Street	C5	Whitworth Street West
				A3	James Street	B1	Mount Street	E1	Rochdale Road	C4	Windmill Street
				F2	Jersey Street	D4	Mount Street	A3	Rodney Street	D2	Withy Grove
				C3	John Dalton Street	C4	Museum Street	A2	Rosamond Drive	C3	Wood Street
				B1	John Street	B1	Nathan Drive	E4	Sackville Street	D3	York Street

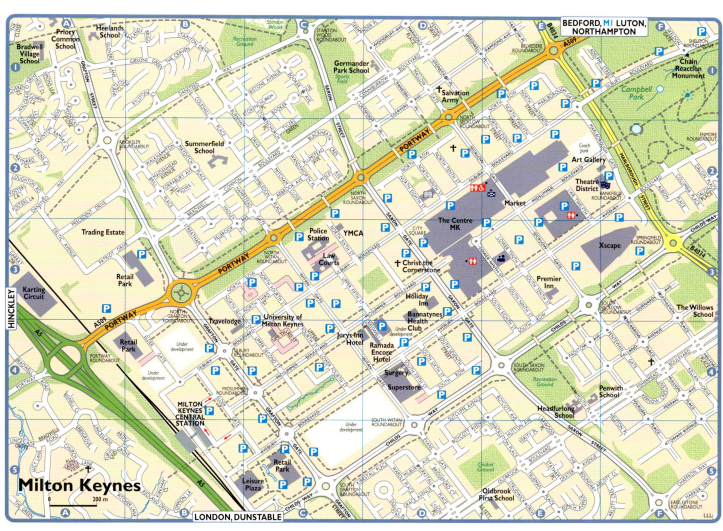

Milton Keynes

Milton Keynes is found on atlas page **49 N7**

E1	Adelphi Street	A2	Coppin Lane	A1	Holy Close	D1	North Secklow	C5	South Grafton Roundabout
F2	Albion Place	A1	Craddocks Close	E5	Hutton Avenue		Roundabout	E3	South Ninth Street
A5	All Saints View	D1	Cranesbill Place	C1	Ibistone Avenue	B3	North Second Street	D4	South Row
C2	Arbrook Avenue	D3	Cresswell Lane	F4	Kellan Drive	C3	North Sixth Street	E4	South Saxon Roundabout
A5	Ardys Court	F2	Dalgin Place	F4	Kernow Crescent	D2	North Tenth Street	F3	South Secklow
E5	Arlott Close	A2	Dansteed Way	B5	Kirkham Close	C3	North Third Street		Roundabout
F5	Arlott Crescent	A3	Deltic Avenue	C5	Kirkstall Place	E1	North Thirteenth Street	D4	South Seventh Street
A2	Atkins Close	E5	Dexter Avenue	E5	Larwood Place	E1	North Twelfth Street	D4	South Sixth Street
A2	Audley Mews	D5	Douglas Place	B2	Leasowe Place	C3	North Witan Roundabout	E3	South Tenth Street
C5	Avebury Boulevard	F5	Eaglestone Roundabout	A5	Linceslade Grove	E5	Oldbrook Boulevard	D5	South Witan Roundabout
E2	Bankfield Roundabout	A5	Ebbsgrove	A2	Loughton Road	A1	Overend Close	D1	Speedwell Place
E1	Belvedere Roundabout	E5	Edrich Avenue	C4	Lower Fourth Street	E4	Padstow Avenue	F3	Springfield Roundabout
A4	Bignell Close	B3	Eelbrook Avenue	E3	Lower Ninth Street	A3	Patriot Drive	B1	Stainton Drive
C2	Blackheath Crescent	B4	Elder Gate	E3	Lower Tenth Street	F3	Pencarrow Place	C1	Stanton Wood Roundabout
C1	Booker Avenue	F2	Enmore Roundabout	E2	Lower Twelfth Street	F4	Pentewan Gate	E5	Statham Place
D5	Boycott Avenue	D5	Evans Gate	A5	Lucy Lane	F4	Perran Avenue	C1	Stokenchurch Place
E4	Boycott Avenue	E4	Falmouth Place	B2	Maidenhead Avenue	A5	Pitcher Lane	D1	Stonecrop Place
B2	Bradwell Common	D1	Fennel Drive	D1	Mallow Gate	C2	Plumstead Avenue	B3	Streatham Place
	Boulevard	F4	Fishermead Boulevard	D1	Marigold Place	F4	Polruan Place	E5	Strudwick Drive
A4	Bradwell Road	B2	Forrabury Avenue	E1	Marlborough Gate	F3	Porthleven Place	D4	Sutcliffe Avenue
A5	Bradwell Road	A2	Fosters Lane	E2	Marlborough Gate	A4	Portway	F4	Talland Avenue
D5	Bridgeford Court	A3	Garrat Drive	F2	Marlborough Street	A4	Portway Roundabout	E5	The Boundary
B2	Brill Place	C1	Germander Place	B2	Mayditch Place	A3	Precedent Drive	A1	The Close
B1	Burnham Drive	B1	Gibsons Green	A2	Maynard Close	A2	Quinton Drive	B1	The Craven
F5	Chaffron Way	A1	Glovers Lane	C4	Midsummer Boulevard	A2	Ramsay Close	A5	The Green
C5	Childs Way	D5	Grace Avenue	E2	Midsummer Boulevard	E1	Ramsons Avenue	F5	Towan Avenue
F3	Childs Way	B4	Grafton Gate	B4	Midsummer Roundabout	B5	Redland Drive	B1	Tranlands Brigg
A5	Church Lane	A1	Grafton Street	D5	Milburn Avenue	A2	Rooksley Roundabout	E5	Trueman Place
D3	City Square	C5	Grafton Street	C2	Mitcham Close	B1	Rylstone Close	A5	Turvil End
D1	Cleavers Avenue	F3	Gurnards Avenue	F4	Mullion Place	D2	Saxon Gate	C2	Tylers Green
B1	Coleshill Place	B2	Hadley Place	D2	North Eighth Street	C1	Saxon Street	D5	Tyson Place
C1	Coltsfoot Place	B2	Hampstead Gate	E1	North Eleventh Street	D2	Secklow Gate	D5	Ulyett Place
F2	Columbia Place	F5	Harrier Drive	C3	North Fourth Street	E5	Shackleton Place	C3	Upper Fifth Street
B5	Common Lane	F4	Helford Place	B3	North Grafton	F1	Sheldon Roundabout	C4	Upper Fourth Street
C1	Conniburrow Boulevard	F4	Helston Place		Roundabout	B4	Silbury Boulevard	C4	Upper Second Street
				D2	North Ninth Street	B4	Silbury Roundabout	C4	Upper Third Street
				B3	North Row	A1	Simons Lea	E5	Verity Place
				D2	North Row	F1	Skeldon Place	A1	Walgrave Drive
				C2	North Saxon	E3	South Eighth Street	B2	Walkhampton Avenue
					Roundabout	D4	South Fifth Street	C2	Wandsworth Place
								D5	Wardle Place
								A1	Whetstone Close
								C2	Wimbledon Place
								C2	Wisely Avenue
								C3	Witan Gate
								D1	Woodruff Avenue
								E1	Yarrow Place

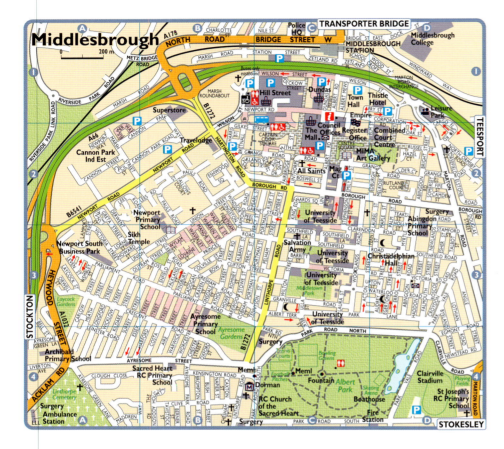

Middlesbrough

Middlesbrough is found on atlas page **104 E7**

A4	Acklam Road	A3	Heywood Street
C3	Acton Street	B4	Kensington Road
B4	Aire Street	A4	Kildare Street
B3	Albany Street	D3	Laurel Street
C2	Albert Road	A2	Lees Road
C2	Amber Street	B4	Linthorpe Road
B3	Athol Street	A4	Longford Street
D3	Audrey Street	A3	Lorne Street
B4	Ayresome Park Road	D3	Lothian Road
A4	Ayresome Street	A2	Marsh Street
C2	Borough Road	D2	Marton Road
B2	Bretnall Street	D2	Melrose Street
C1	Bridge Street East	A1	Metz Bridge Road
C1	Bridge Street West	D3	Myrtle Street
B4	Bush Street	D3	Newlands Road
D2	Camden Street	A2	Newport Road
A2	Cannon Park Road	D3	Palm Street
A2	Cannon Park Way	C3	Park Lane
A2	Cannon Street	C4	Park Road North
A3	Carlow Street	C4	Park Road South
C2	Centre Square	D4	Park Vale Road
D4	Clairville Road	A3	Parliament Road
C3	Clarendon Road	C2	Pearl Street
B3	Clifton Street	C3	Pelham Street
D1	Corporation Road	B3	Portman Street
B4	Costa Street	B3	Princes Road
B3	Craven Street	A1	Riverside Park Road
A3	Crescent Road	C2	Ruby Street
D3	Croydon Road	D2	Russel Street
A2	Derwent Street	B2	St Pauls Road
B3	Diamond Road	C3	Southfield Road
D4	Egmont Road	C1	Station Street
C2	Emily Street	B3	Stowe Street
D3	Errol Street	B4	Tavistock Street
A4	Essex Street	B3	Tennyson Street
C2	Fairbridge Street	A3	Union Street
D3	Falmouth Street	C3	Victoria Road
B3	Finsbury Street	A3	Victoria Street
B2	Fleetham Street	B2	Warren Street
B2	Garnet Street	D3	Waterloo Road
B3	Glebe Road	B3	Waverley Street
B2	Grange Road	A3	Wembley Street
D2	Grange Road	B2	Wilson Street
C3	Granville Road	C3	Wilton Street
B3	Gresham Road	B2	Windsor Street
B3	Harewood Street	C3	Woodlands Road
B4	Harford Street	B4	Worcester Street
B2	Hartington Road	C1	Zetland Road

Newport

Newport is found on atlas page **31 K7**

B3	Albert Terrace	B3	Jones Street
A2	Allt-Yr-Yn Avenue	C4	Keynsham Avenue
B3	Bailey Street	C4	King Street
D2	Bedford Road	C2	Kingsway
B3	Blewitt Street	C4	Kingsway
C1	Bond Street	A3	Llanthewy Road
B2	Bridge Street	B1	Locke Street
A3	Bryngwyn Road	C4	Lower Dock Street
A4	Brynhyfryd Avenue	B1	Lucas Street
A4	Brynhyfryd Road	B2	Market Street
A4	Caerau Crescent	C4	Mellon Street
A3	Caerau Road	B2	Mill Street
B2	Cambrian Road	B3	North Street
D3	Caroline Street	A3	Oakfield Road
D2	Cedar Road	C4	Park Square
C3	Charles Street	C1	Pugsley Street
D1	Chepstow Road	B1	Queen's Hill
C1	Clarence Place	A1	Queen's Hill Crescent
B4	Clifton Place	C4	Queen Street
B4	Clifton Road	B2	Queensway
A3	Clyffard Crescent	A4	Risca Road
A2	Clytha Park Road	C2	Rodney Road
C4	Clytha Square	D1	Rudry Street
A1	Colts Foot Close	C4	Ruperra Lane
C4	Commercial Street	D4	Ruperra Street
D1	Corelli Street	B3	St Edward Street
C2	Corn Street	B4	St Julian Street
D2	Corporation Road	A2	St Mark's Crescent
B2	Devon Place	B3	St Mary Street
B4	Dewsland Park Road	C2	St Vincent Road
D4	Dumfries Place	B3	St Woolos Road
B3	East Street	C3	School Lane
C1	East Usk Road	A2	Serpentine Road
B1	Factory Road	C2	Skinner Street
A2	Fields Road	A1	Sorrel Drive
B4	Friars Field	A3	Spencer Road
B4	Friars Road	B3	Stow Hill
C3	Friar Street	B4	Stow Hill
D4	George Street	A4	Stow Park Avenue
A2	Godfrey Road	C3	Talbot Lane
A2	Gold Tops	D1	Tregare Street
C2	Grafton Road	A3	Tunnel Terrace
D4	Granville Lane	C2	Upper Dock Street
D4	Granville Street	C3	Upper Dock Street
B2	High Street	D3	Usk Way
C3	Hill Street	B3	Victoria Crescent
C3	John Frost Square	B3	West Street
D4	John Street	A4	York Place

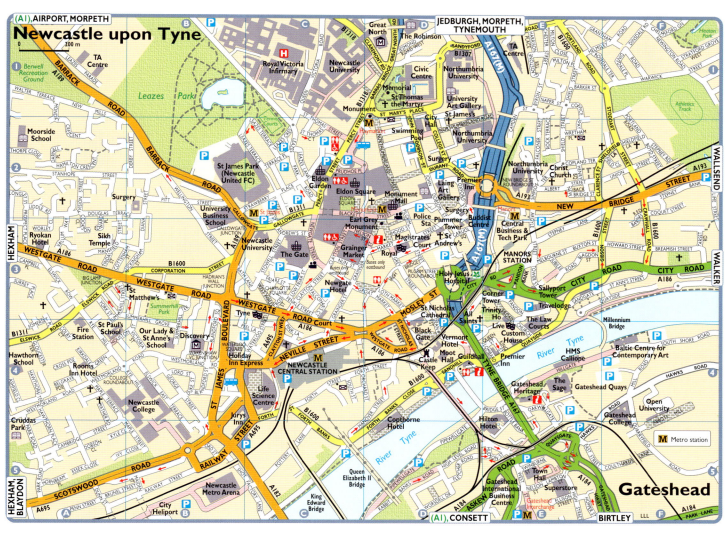

Newcastle upon Tyne

Newcastle upon Tyne is found on atlas page **113 K8**

F4	Abbots Hill	C4	Clayton Street West	F2	Field Close	E4	King Street	D2	Oxford Street	F2	Shieldfield Lane
E2	Albert Street	A4	Colby Court	D5	Fletcher Road	A4	Kirkdale Green	E3	Pandon	E2	Shield Street
E2	Argyle Street	A4	College Roundabout	C4	Forth Banks	A5	Kyle Close	E3	Pandon Bank	B5	Shot Factory Lane
D5	Askew Road	D2	College Street	D5	Forth Banks Close	E5	Lambton Street	F5	Park Lane	E2	Simpson Terrace
A2	Avision Street	A3	Cookson Close	C4	Forth Street	C2	Leazes Crescent	A5	Park Road	A4	Somerset Place
E2	Back New Bridge Street	E2	Copland Terrace	C3	Friars Street	C2	Leazes Lane	B4	Peel Lane	F4	South Shore Road
E1	Barker Street	E1	Coppice Way	B2	Gallowgate	C2	Leazes Park Road	A5	Penn Street	C4	South Street
A1	Barrack Road	F2	Coquet Street	B3	Gallowgate Junction	C2	Leazes Terrace	C2	Percy Street	A2	Stanhope Street
D1	Barras Bridge	B3	Corporation Street	E5	Gateshead Highway	A2	Liddle Road	D2	Pilgrim Street	F2	Stepney Bank
B3	Bath Lane	A3	Cottenham Street	B4	George Street	F2	Lime Street	C4	Pink Lane	E2	Stepney Lane
A4	Belgrave Parade	F5	Coulthards Lane	F3	Gibson Street	E4	Lombard Street	D5	Pipewellgate	F2	Stepney Road
A3	Big Lamp Junction	F2	Crawhall Road	E1	Gladstone Terrace	A2	Longley Street	B2	Pitt Street	F1	Stoddart Street
C2	Blackett Street	A4	Cross Parade	C3	Gloucester Terrace	B4	Lord Street	E1	Portland Road	C3	Stowell Street
E3	Blagdon Street	C3	Cross Street	E1	Grantham Road	D3	Loth Market	F1	Portland Road	F1	Stratford Grove West
B4	Blandford Square	A2	Darnell Place	D1	Great North Road	C3	Low Friar Street	C5	Pottery Lane	C2	Strawberry Place
B4	Blandford Street	D3	Dean Street	D3	Grey Street	B5	Maiden Street	A2	Prospect Place	B3	Summerhill Grove
E4	Bottle Bank	B2	Derby Street	C3	Groat Market	A3	Mansfield Street	C2	Prudhoe Place	A3	Summerhill Street
F2	Boyd Street	B3	Diana Street	A2	Hamilton Crescent	B5	Maple Street	F5	Quarryfield Road	B4	Summerhill Terrace
F3	Breamish Street	F1	Dinsdale Place	C5	Hanover Street	D3	Maple Terrace	E5	Quaysgate	E5	Swinburne Street
E4	Bridge Street	F1	Dinsdale Road	E1	Harrison Place	A4	Mather Road	F3	Quayside	F3	Tarset Road
E3	Broad Church	A5	Dobson Close	E5	Hawks Road	E3	Melbourne Street	E4	Quayside	C2	Terrace Place
A5	Brunel Street	A2	Douglas Terrace	A4	Hawthorn Place	F4	Mill Road	E4	Queen Street	A2	Thorpe Close
B3	Buckingham Street	B4	Duke Street	A4	Hawthorn Terrace	E1	Milton Close	C1	Queen Victoria Road	A3	Tindal Street
E3	Buxton Street	A5	Dunn Street	E1	Helmsley Road	E1	Milton Place	D5	Rabbit Banks Road	E3	Tower Street
E1	Byron Street	D2	Durant Road	E2	Henry Square	A1	Monday Crescent	B5	Railway Street	E4	Tyne Bridge
A5	Cambridge Street	E5	East Street	D3	High Bridge	D3	Mosley Street	F2	Red Barnes	F2	Union Street
E2	Camden Street	A3	Edward Place	D5	High Level Road	E1	Naper Street	B1	Richardson Road	A3	Vallum Way
A3	Campbell Place	C2	Eldon Square	E5	High Street	C3	Nelson Street	E2	Rock Terrace	B4	Victoria Street
D3	Caruol Square	E5	Ellison Street	E4	Hillgate	E5	Nelson Street	E1	Rosedale Terrace	A1	Walter Terrace
C3	Charlotte Square	B4	Elswick East Terrace	D3	Hood Street	C3	Neville Street	A4	Rye Hill	F1	Warwick Street
F1	Chelmsford Green	A3	Elswick Road	E5	Hopper Street	E2	New Bridge Street	C3	St Andrew's Street	B4	Waterloo Square
E1	Chester Street	A3	Elswick Row	A5	Hornbeam Place	C3	Newgate Street	F3	St Ann's Street	C4	Waterloo Street
E3	City Road	A5	Essex Close	A4	Houston Street	D1	Newington Road	B4	St James Boulevard	B2	Wellington Street
D1	Claremont Road	C3	Falconer's Court	F3	Howard Street	A1	New Mills	D1	St Mary's Place	A3	Westgate Road
E2	Clarence Street	E2	Falconer Street	E5	Hudson Street	D2	Northumberland Road	D4	St Nicholas Street	A4	Westmorland Road
C3	Clayton Street	C3	Fenkle Street	A5	Ivy Close	D2	Northumberland Street	C2	St Thomas' Court	E5	West Street
				D1	Jesmond Road West	C3	Nun Street	C1	St Thomas' Street	C3	West Walls
				D2	John Dobson Street	E4	Oakwellgate	E3	Sandgate	A3	Worley Close
				E3	Jubilee Road	C4	Orchard Street	D4	Sandhill	D5	Worsdell Drive
				C5	King Edward Bridge	B5	Ord Street	D1	Sandyford Road	E2	Wretham Place
								A5	Scotswood Road	A3	York Street

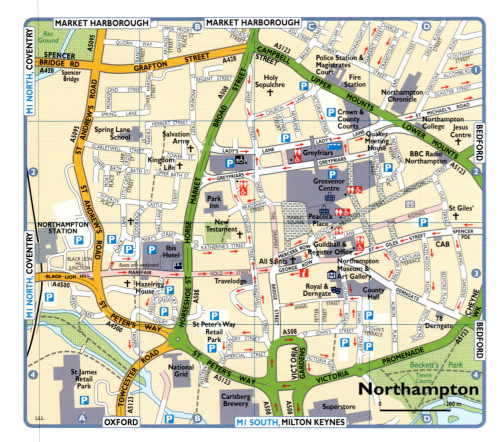

Northampton

Northampton is found on atlas page **60 G8**

C2	Abington Street	A2	Lower Bath Street
D2	Albert Place	A2	Lower Cross Street
D3	Albion Place	B1	Lower Harding Street
C3	Angel Street	D2	Lower Mounts
B1	Arundel Street	A3	Marefair
C1	Ash Street	C1	Margaret Street
C1	Bailiff Street	C2	Market Square
A3	Black Lion Hill	C3	Mercers Row
B2	Bradshaw Street	A2	Moat Place
C3	Bridge Street	A1	Monkspond Street
B1	Broad Street	C1	Newland
C1	Campbell Street	D2	Notredame Mews
D3	Castilian Street	D1	Overstone Road
B2	Castle Street	B3	Pike Lane
A3	Chalk Lane	A1	Quorn Way
D3	Cheyne Walk	B1	Regent Street
C1	Church Lane	C1	Robert Street
B2	College Street	A2	St Andrew's Road
B4	Commercial Street	B1	St Andrew's Street
C1	Connaught Street	D3	St Giles Street
B3	Court Road	D2	St Giles' Terrace
D1	Cranstoun Street	C4	St John's Street
B2	Crispin Street	B3	St Katherine's Street
D3	Derngate	A3	St Mary's Street
A3	Doddridge Street	D1	St Michael's Road
D1	Dunster Street	B4	St Peter's Way
C3	Dychurch Lane	A2	Scarletwell Street
D1	Earl Street	D4	Scholars Close
C3	Fetter Street	B1	Sheep Street
A2	Fitzroy Place	C2	Sheep Street
B4	Foundry Street	A1	Spencer Bridge Road
A1	Francis Street	D3	Spencer Parade
B3	Freeschool Lane	D3	Spring Gardens
C3	George Row	A1	Spring Lane
B3	Gold Street	C3	Swan Street
A1	Grafton Street	A4	Tanner Street
D1	Great Russel Street	C2	The Drapery
A3	Green Street	D2	The Ridings
B3	Gregory Street	A4	Towcester Road
B2	Greyfriars	B2	Tower Street
C3	Guildhall Road	B2	Upper Bath Street
D3	Hazelwood Road	C1	Upper Mounts
B2	Herbert Street	B1	Upper Priory Street
B3	Horse Market	C4	Victoria Gardens
B3	Horseshoe Street	C4	Victoria Promenade
C3	Kingswell Street	C1	Victoria Street
B2	Lady's Lane	D2	Wellington Street
A2	Little Cross Street	B4	Western Wharf

Norwich

Norwich is found on atlas page **77 J10**

B4	All Saints Green	C1	Palace Street
C2	Bank Plain	A2	Pottergate
A1	Barn Road	C2	Prince of Wales Road
C1	Bedding Lane	C2	Princes Street
B2	Bedford Street	C1	Quay Side
C4	Ber Street	B4	Queens Road
A3	Bethel Street	C2	Queen Street
D1	Bishopgate	B3	Rampant Horse Street
B3	Brigg Street	D2	Recorder Road
B1	Calvert Street	B3	Red Lion Street
C3	Castle Meadow	D3	Riverside Road
D2	Cathedral Street	D1	Riverside Walk
C3	Cattle Market Street	C3	Rose Lane
B3	Chantry Road	C3	Rouen Road
A3	Chapelfield East	A4	Rupert Street
A3	Chapelfield North	B2	St Andrews Street
A3	Chapelfield Road	A2	St Benedicts Street
A3	Cleveland Road	D2	St Faiths Lane
B1	Colegate	B1	St Georges Street
B2	Coslany Street	A2	St Giles Street
A2	Cow Hill	C4	St Julian Street
B3	Davey Place	B1	St Marys Plain
B2	Dove Street	B3	St Peters Street
B1	Duke Street	B4	St Stephens Road
A3	Earlham Road	A4	St Stephens Square
C2	Elm Hill	B4	St Stephens Street
B2	Exchange Street	A2	St Swithins Street
C3	Farmers Avenue	D2	St Verdast Street
D2	Ferry Lane	B4	Surrey Street
C1	Fishergate	A2	Ten Bell Lane
B1	Friars Quay	B3	Theatre Street
B3	Gentlemans Walk	C4	Thorn Lane
C3	Goldenball Street	C2	Tombland
A2	Grapes Hill	A1	Unicorn Yard
B3	Haymarket	A4	Union Street
A1	Heigham Street	B2	Upper Goat Lane
C2	King Street	C2	Upper King Street
B2	London Street	A2	Upper St Giles Street
B2	Lower Goat Lane	A3	Vauxhall Street
C1	Magdalen Street	A3	Walpole Street
C3	Market Avenue	C1	Wensum Street
A1	Mills Yard	A4	Wessex Street
D3	Mountergate	B3	Westlegate
D4	Music House Lane	A1	Westwick Street
B1	Muspole Street	D4	Wherry Road
A4	Norfolk Street	C1	Whitefriars
A1	Oak Street	B3	White Lion Street
B3	Orford Place	A2	Willow Lane

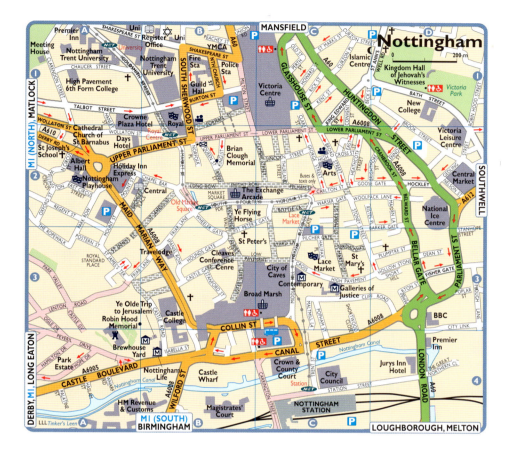

Nottingham

Nottingham is found on atlas page **72 F3**

B3	Albert Street
D2	Barker Gate
D1	Bath Street
D3	Bellar Gate
D2	Belward Street
C2	Broad Street
C3	Broadway
A2	Bromley Place
D1	Brook Street
B1	Burton Street
C4	Canal Street
C2	Carlton Street
C4	Carrington Street
A4	Castle Boulevard
B3	Castle Gate
B3	Castle Road
B2	Chapel Bar
A1	Chaucer Street
A1	Clarendon Street
C3	Cliff Road
B4	Collin Street
D2	Cranbrook Street
C2	Cumber Street
C1	Curzon Place
A2	Derby Road
B2	Exchange Walk
D3	Fisher Gate
C3	Fletcher Gate
B1	Forman Street
A3	Friar Lane
D2	Gedling Street
C2	George Street
C1	Glasshouse Street
A1	Goldsmith Street
C2	Goose Gate
C3	Halifax Place
C2	Heathcote Street
C2	High Cross Street
C3	High Pavement
D2	Hockley
D3	Hollow Stone
A4	Hope Drive
B3	Hounds Gate
C1	Howard Street
C1	Huntingdon Street
C1	Kent Street
C1	King Edward Street
B2	King Street
A3	Lenton Road
C2	Lincoln Street
B3	Lister Gate
D4	London Road
B2	Long Row
C2	Lower Parliament Street
B3	Low Pavement
A2	Maid Marian Way
B2	Market Street
C3	Middle Hill
B1	Milton Street
A3	Mount Street
B2	Norfolk Place
A2	North Circus Street
A3	Park Row
D3	Parliament Street
C2	Pelham Street
A4	Peveril Drive
C3	Pilcher Gate
C3	Popham Street
B2	Poultry
B2	Queen Street
A2	Regent Street
D1	St Ann's Well Road
A3	St James's Street
C3	St Marks Gate
C1	St Marks Street
C3	St Mary's Gate
B3	St Peter's Gate
A1	Shakespeare Street
B2	Smithy Row
B2	South Parade
B1	South Sherwood Street
B3	Spaniel Row
C4	Station Street
C2	Stoney Street
A1	Talbot Street
C2	Thurland Street
C4	Trent Street
A2	Upper Parliament Street
C2	Victoria Street
C2	Warser Gate
C3	Weekday Cross
A2	Wellington Circus
B2	Wheeler Gate
B4	Wilford Street
A1	Wollaton Street
C2	Woolpack Lane

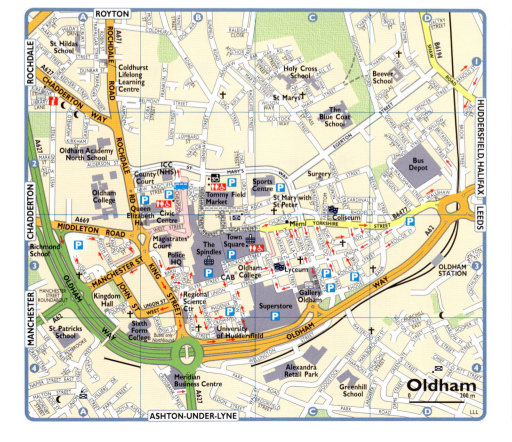

Oldham

Oldham is found on atlas page **83 K4**

B3	Ascroft Street
B1	Bar Gap Road
D4	Barlow Street
B3	Barn Street
D2	Beever Street
D2	Bell Street
B1	Belmont Street
A3	Booth Street
C3	Bow Street
D2	Brook Street
B3	Brunswick Street
C2	Cardinal Street
A1	Chadderton Way
B3	Chaucer Street
C3	Clegg Street
B1	Coldhurst Road
B4	Cromwell Street
B4	Crossbank Street
B2	Curzon Street
A1	Dunbar Street
B2	Eden Street
C2	Egerton Street
C3	Firth Street
B2	Fountain Street
B1	Franklin Street
D2	Gower Street
A2	Grange Street
C3	Greaves Street
D4	Greengate Street
D3	Hamilton Street
D4	Hardy Street
C4	Harmony Street
B2	Henshaw Street
C1	Higginshaw Road
A2	Highfield Street
B3	High Street
B3	Hobson Street
D4	Hooper Street
C1	Horsedge Street
A3	John Street
B3	King Street
D2	Lemnos Street
C1	Malby Street
A4	Malton Street
A3	Manchester Street
B3	Market Place
C4	Marlborough Street
A3	Middleton Road
D1	Mortimer Street
A4	Napier Street East
A2	New Radcliffe Street
A3	Oldham Way
B4	Park Road
A4	Park Street
B3	Peter Street
C3	Queen Street
B1	Radcliffe Street
B1	Raleigh Close
A1	Ramsden Street
D2	Regent Street
C3	Rhodes Bank
C2	Rhodes Street
B1	Rifle Street
A1	Rochdale Road
B2	Rock Street
C3	Roscoe Street
A1	Ruskin Street
A1	St Hilda's Drive
B1	St Marys Street
B2	St Mary's Way
D1	Shaw Road
C1	Shaw Street
C1	Siddall Street
B3	Silver Street
C3	Southgate Street
D4	South Hill Street
D3	Southlink
D2	Spencer Street
B1	Sunfield Road
D1	Thames Street
A1	Trafalgar Street
B1	Trinity Street
A1	Tulbury Street
B3	Union Street
A4	Union Street West
B3	Union Street West
D2	Wallshaw Street
B4	Wall Street
A1	Ward Street
C3	Waterloo Street
B4	Wellington Street
A2	West End Street
B3	West Street
D2	Willow Street
C4	Woodstock Street
C3	Yorkshire Street

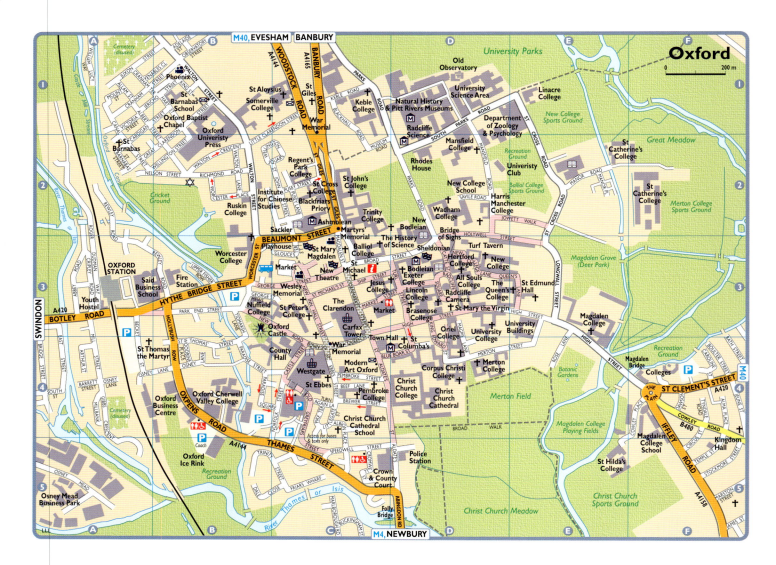

Oxford

Oxford is found on atlas page **34 F3**

A3	Abbey Road	C5	Cromwell Street	F5	Marston Street
D5	Abingdon Road	B5	Dale Close	D4	Merton Street
B1	Adelaide Street	F4	Dawson Street	A4	Millbank
A1	Albert Street	A4	East Street	A4	Mill Street
C4	Albion Place	C5	Folly Bridge	A1	Mount Street
A1	Allam Street	C5	Friars Wharf	C2	Museum Road
F4	Alma Place	B3	George Street	A2	Nelson Street
A4	Arthur Street	B3	George Street Mews	D3	New College Lane
C1	Banbury Road	A4	Gibbs Crescent	C3	New Inn Hall Street
A4	Barrett Street	C3	Gloucester Street	B3	New Road
F4	Bath Street	A2	Great Clarendon Street	C4	Norfolk Street
C3	Beaumont Street	B1	Hart Street	B1	Observatory Street
A3	Becket Street	D3	High Street	C4	Old Greyfriars Street
C4	Beef Lane	E4	High Street	A4	Osney Lane
C4	Blackhall Road	B3	Hollybush Row	B4	Osney Lane
C4	Blue Boar Street	D2	Holywell Street	A5	Osney Mead
C4	Bonn Square	B3	Hythe Bridge Street	B4	Oxpens Road
A3	Botley Road	F4	Iffley Road	B4	Paradise Square
F4	Boulter Street	F5	James Street	B4	Paradise Street
C4	Brewer Street	A1	Jericho Street	B3	Park End Street
A4	Bridge Street	D2	Jowett Walk	C1	Parks Road
C3	Broad Street	A1	Juxon Street	D2	Parks Road
D4	Broad Walk	C1	Keble Road	C4	Pembroke Street
C5	Buckingham Street	D3	King Edward Street	C4	Pike Terrace
A1	Canal Street	B1	King Street	C2	Pusey Lane
A2	Cardigan Street	B2	Little Clarendon Street	C2	Pusey Street
F4	Caroline Street	C4	Littlegate Street	D3	Queen's Lane
C4	Castle Street	E3	Longwall Street	C4	Queen Street
D3	Catte Street	E4	Magdalen Bridge	D3	Radcliffe Square
F5	Circus Street	C3	Magdalen Street	A2	Rewley Road
C3	Cornmarket Street	D3	Magpie Lane	B3	Rewley Road
F4	Cowley Place	E2	Manor Place	B2	Richmond Road
F4	Cowley Road	E2	Manor Road	A3	Roger Dudman Way
A1	Cranham Street	D2	Mansfield Road	E4	Rose Lane
A1	Cranham Terrace	C3	Market Street	C4	St Aldate's
A3	Cripley Road	C5	Marlborough Road	D5	St Aldate's

A2	St Barnabas Street		
F4	St Clement's Street		
E1	St Cross Road		
E2	St Cross Road		
C4	St Ebbes Street		
C2	St Giles		
C2	St John Street		
C3	St Michael's Street		
B4	St Thomas' Street		
D2	Savile Road		
C3	Ship Street		
D2	South Parks Road		
A4	South Street		
C5	Speedwell Street		
F5	Stockmore Street		
F5	Temple Street		
C5	Thames Street		
F4	The Plain		
B3	Tidmarsh Lane		
B5	Trinity Street		
D3	Turl Street		
C4	Turn Again Lane		
F4	Tyndale Road		
B3	Upper Fisher Row		
A1	Venables Close		
A1	Victoria Street		
B2	Walton Crescent		
B2	Walton Lane		
B1	Walton Street		
B2	Wellington Square		
B2	Wellington Street		
A1	William Lucy Way		
B4	Woodbine Place		
C1	Woodstock Road		
B2	Worcester Place		
B3	Worcester Street		

University Colleges

D3	All Souls College
C3	Balliol College
D3	Brasenose College
D4	Christ Church College
D4	Corpus Christi College
D3	Exeter College
D2	Harris Manchester College
D3	Hertford College
C3	Jesus College
C1	Keble College
E1	Linacre College
D3	Lincoln College
E3	Magdalen College
D2	Mansfield College
D4	Merton College
D3	New College
B3	Nuffield College
D3	Oriel College
C4	Pembroke College
B2	Ruskin College
F2	St Catherine's College
C2	St Cross College
E5	St Hilda's College
C2	St John's College
C3	St Peter's College
B1	Somerville College
D3	The Queen's College
C2	Trinity College
D3	University College
D2	Wadham College
B3	Worcester College

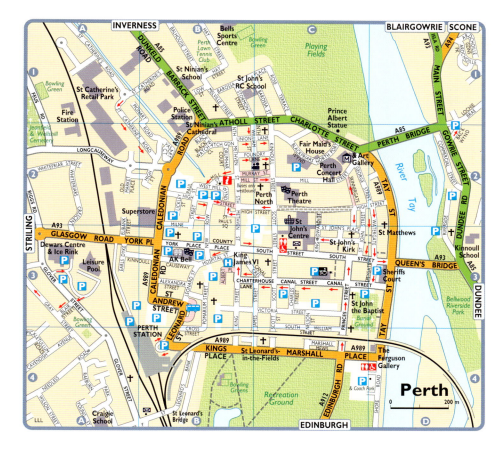

Perth

Perth is found on atlas page **134 E3**

B3	Albert Place	B1	Melville Street
B3	Alexandra Street	B2	Mill Street
D1	Ardchoille Park	C2	Mill Street
B1	Atholl Street	B2	Milne Street
D2	Back Wynd	A1	Monart Road
B1	Balhousie Street	B2	Murray Street
B1	Barossa Place	A4	Needless Road
B1	Barrack Street	B3	New Row
C2	Blackfriars Wynd	B2	North Methven Street
B2	Black Watch Garden	C2	North Port
B2	Caledonian Road	B2	North William Street
B3	Caledonian Road	A2	Old Market Place
C3	Canal Street	B2	Paul Street
A4	Cavendish Avenue	D2	Perth Bridge
C3	Charles Street	A4	Pickletullum Road
C2	Charlotte Street	B3	Pomarium Street
B3	Charterhouse Lane	C3	Princes Street
D2	Commercial Street	D3	Queen's Bridge
B3	County Place	A4	Raeburn Park
B4	Cross Street	A2	Riggs Road
D3	Dundee Road	D3	Riverside
B1	Dunkeld Road	C1	Rose Terrace
A3	Earls Dyke	B3	St Andrew Street
C4	Edinburgh Road	A1	St Catherine's Road
A1	Feus Road	C3	St John's Place
B2	Foundry Lane	C3	St John Street
C2	George Street	B4	St Leonard's Bank
A3	Glasgow Road	B2	St Paul's Square
A3	Glover Street	C2	Scott Street
A4	Glover Street	C3	Scott Street
D2	Gowrie Street	D4	Shore Road
A3	Gray Street	C2	Skinnergate
B1	Hay Street	B2	South Methven Street
B2	High Street	C3	South Street
C2	High Street	C4	South William Street
B3	Hospital Street	D3	Speygate
D1	Isla Road	B1	Stormont Street
C3	James Street	D2	Tay Street
C3	King Edward Street	D4	Tay Street
B4	Kings Place	B2	Union Lane
B3	King Street	C3	Victoria Street
A3	Kinnoull Causeway	D2	Watergate
C2	Kinnoull Street	B2	West Mill Wynd
B3	Leonard Street	A2	Whitefriars Crescent
D1	Lochie Brae	A2	Whitefriar Street
A2	Longcauseway	A4	Wilson Street
D1	Main Street	A3	York Place
C4	Marshall Place	B3	York Place

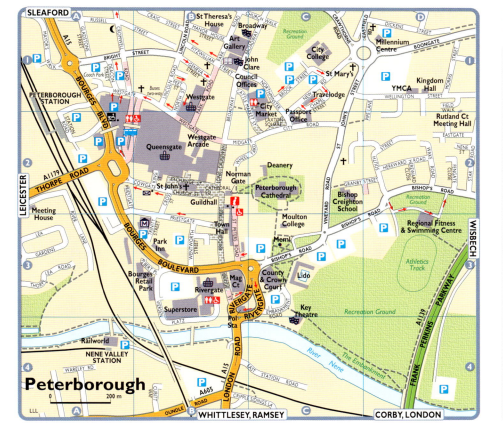

Peterborough

Peterborough is found on atlas page **74 C11**

B3	Albert Place	D2	Nene Street
C3	Bishop's Road	C1	New Road
D2	Bishop's Road	C1	Northminster
D1	Boongate	B1	North Street
A1	Bourges Boulevard	B4	Oundle Road
B3	Bridge Street	B1	Park Road
A1	Bright Street	B1	Peet Street
B2	Broadway	D2	Pipe Lane
C1	Brook Street	A2	Priestgate
B2	Cathedral Square	B3	Rivergate
B1	Cattle Market Street	A2	River Lane
C1	Chapel Street	A1	Russell Street
B2	Church Street	C2	St John's Street
C1	Church Walk	B3	St Peters Road
C2	City Road	D2	South Street
B2	Cowgate	D2	Star Road
B1	Craig Street	A2	Station Road
C1	Crawthorne Road	A3	Thorpe Lea Road
B4	Cripple Sidings Lane	A2	Thorpe Road
A1	Cromwell Road	B3	Trinity Street
B2	Cross Street	B3	Viersen Platz
B4	Cubitt Way	C3	Vineyard Road
A1	Deacon Street	D2	Wake Road
D1	Dickens Street	A4	Wareley Road
D1	Eastfield Road	D1	Wellington Street
D2	Eastgate	B3	Wentworth Street
C4	East Station Road	A1	Westgate
C3	Embankment Road	B2	Westgate
B2	Exchange Street		
D2	Fengate Close		
D1	Field Walk		
B1	Fitzwilliam Street		
D4	Frank Perkins Parkway		
B1	Geneva Street		
A1	Gladstone Street		
C2	Granby Street		
D1	Hereward Close		
D2	Hereward Road		
B2	King Street		
C2	Laxton Square		
A3	Lea Gardens		
B1	Lincoln Road		
B4	London Road		
B2	Long Causeway		
B1	Manor House Street		
A1	Mayor's Walk		
B2	Midgate		
D1	Morris Street		

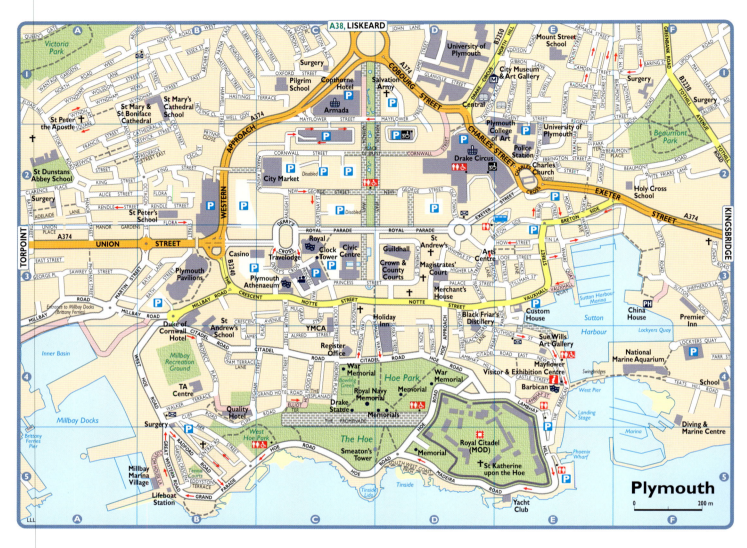

Plymouth

Plymouth is found on atlas page **6 D8**

E1	Addison Road
A2	Adelaide Lane
C4	Alfred Street
A2	Alice Street
A2	Anstis Street
B1	Archer Terrace
E1	Armada Street
C2	Armada Way
C4	Armada Way
A1	Arundel Crescent
C3	Athenaeum Street
F1	Baring Street
B3	Bath Lane
B3	Bath Street
E3	Batter Street
A2	Battery Street
F1	Beaumont Avenue
E2	Beaumont Place
F2	Beaumont Road
E2	Bilbury Street
D4	Blackfriars Lane
C1	Boon's Place
D3	Breton Side
D3	Buckwell Street
E1	Camden Street
E4	Castle Street
A2	Cathedral Street
D3	Catherine Street
B1	Cecil Street
B5	Central Road
E1	Chapel Street
E2	Charles Cross
D2	Charles Street
B4	Citadel Road
C4	Citadel Road
D4	Citadel Road East

C1	Claremont Street
A2	Clarence Place
B4	Cliff Road
D1	Cobourg Street
C2	Cornwall Street
C3	Courtenay Street
B3	Crescent Avenue
B5	Custom House Lane
C3	Derry's Cross
E1	Devonshire Street
D1	Drake Circus
A3	East Street
E2	Ebrington Street
B5	Eddystone Terrace
A1	Eldad Hill
C4	Elliot Street
C4	Elliot Terrace
B1	Essex Street
C1	Eton Avenue
C1	Eton Place
D2	Exeter Street
B2	Flora Court
B2	Flora Street
A2	Francis Street
B2	Frederick Street East
D4	Friar's Parade
B5	Garden Crescent
E2	Gasking Street
A3	George Place
E1	Gibbon Lane
E1	Gibbons Street
E1	Gilwell Street
D1	Glanville Street
C4	Grand Hotel Road
B5	Grand Parade
B5	Great Western Road

F1	Greenbank Road
E2	Hampton Street
B1	Harwell Street
B1	Hastings Street
B1	Hastings Terrace
E2	Hawkers Avenue
B1	Hetling Close
E3	Hicks Lane
D3	Higher Lane
E2	Hill Street
D4	Hoe Approach
D3	Hoegate Street
C5	Hoe Road
D3	Hoe Street
C4	Holyrood Place
E3	How Street
B1	Ilbert Street
D1	James Street
D1	John Lane
A2	King Street
F1	Ladywell Place
D4	Lambhay Hill
E4	Lambhay Street
B4	Leigham Street
B4	Leigham Terrace Lane
F1	Lipson Road
F4	Lockyers Quay
C3	Lockyer Street
E3	Looe Street
D5	Madeira Road
A3	Manor Gardens
A2	Manor Street
C2	Market Avenue
A3	Martin Street
C1	Mayflower Street
D1	Mayflower Street
F1	May Terrace
A3	Millbay Road
E2	Moon Street
E1	Mount Street

C3	Mulgrave Street
A2	Neswick Street
C2	New George Street
E4	New Street
E1	North Hill
A1	North Road West
E2	North Street
C3	Notte Street
B2	Octagon Street
D2	Old Town Street
C4	Osborne Place
C1	Oxford Street
D3	Palace Street
E2	Park Terrace
F4	Parr Street
B1	Patna Place
D3	Peacock Lane
B1	Penrose Street
A3	Phoenix Street
B5	Pier Street
C2	Place De Brest
F1	Plym Street
C3	Princess Street
C3	Princess Way
B4	Prospect Place
B2	Prynne Close
A1	Queen's Gate
B5	Radford Road
E1	Radnor Place
E1	Radnor Street
C2	Raleigh Street
E1	Regent Street
A2	Rendle Street
C3	Royal Parade
B4	St James Place
F3	St John's Bridge Road
F3	St John's Road
F1	Salisbury Road
A3	Sawrey Street
F3	Shepherd's Lane

D4	Southside Street
D5	South West Coast Path
E3	Stillman Street
A2	Stoke Road
D3	Sussex Street
F3	Sutton Road
B1	Sydney Street
D1	Tavistock Place
F4	Teats Hill Road
E4	The Barbican
B3	The Crescent
C4	The Esplanade
C4	The Promenade
E3	Tin Lane
F1	Tothill Avenue
F2	Tothill Road
E2	Trafalgar Street
A3	Union Place
A3	Union Street
E3	Vauxhall Quay
E3	Vauxhall Street
B4	Walker Terrace
A1	Wantage Gardens
B1	Well Garden
B2	Western Approach
A4	West Hoe Road
E3	Wharf Quay
D3	Whimple Street
F2	White Friars Lane
C3	Windsor Place
A1	Wolsdon Street
A1	Wyndham Lane
A1	Wyndham Mews
A1	Wyndham Square
A1	Wyndham Street East
D4	Zion Street

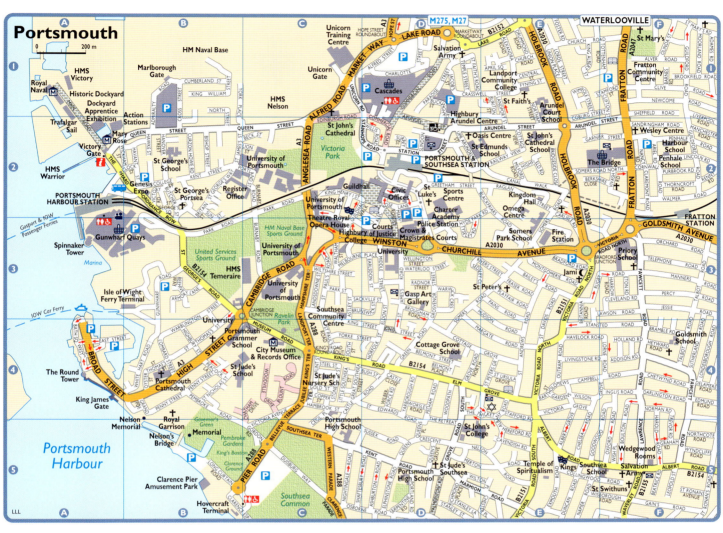

Portsmouth

Portsmouth is found on atlas page **14 H7**

F4 Addison Road
B2 Admiralty Road
E5 Albany Road
E5 Albert Grove
E5 Albert Road
D3 Alec Rose Lane
E1 Alexandra Road
C1 Alfred Road
D1 Alfred Street
F1 Alver Road
C2 Anglesea Road
F2 Ariel Road
B3 Armory Lane
D2 Arundel Street
E2 Arundel Street
D5 Ashburton Road
E3 Bailey's Road
A4 Bath Square
C5 Bellevue Terrace
D4 Belmont Place
B2 Bishop Street
E2 Blackfriars Road
C4 Blount Road
F5 Boulton Road
F4 Bramble Road
E2 Bridgeside Close
B2 Britain Street
A4 Broad Street
F1 Brookfield Road
C3 Brunswick Street
D1 Buckingham Street
C3 Cambridge Road
E4 Campbell Road
E2 Canal Walk
E2 Carlisle Road
C4 Castle Road

E5 Cavendish Road
E1 Central Street
D1 Charlotte Street
E5 Chelsea Road
E5 Chester Place
F4 Chetwynd Road
E1 Church Road
F2 Claremont Road
C5 Clarence Parade
F3 Cleveland Road
F1 Clive Road
B2 Clock Street
B2 College Street
E5 Collingwood Road
D1 Commercial Road
F2 Cornwall Road
D4 Cottage Grove
E2 Cottage View
D1 Crasswell Street
B2 Cross Street
B1 Cumberland Street
B2 Curzon Howe Road
F4 Darlington Road
E1 Drummond Road
C5 Duisburg Way
E5 Duncan Road
D3 Earlsdon Street
A4 East Street
C2 Edinburgh Road
D4 Eldon Street
E5 Elm Grove
D5 Elphinstone Road
E5 Exmouth Road
F3 Fawcett Road
F4 Fawcett Road
C4 Flint Street

E1 Foster Road
F2 Fratton Road
F5 Gain's Road
E2 Garnier Street
F3 Goldsmith Avenue
C4 Gold Street
E5 Goodwood Road
C5 Gordon Road
C4 Great Southsea Street
D4 Green Road
D2 Greetham Street
D3 Grosvenor Street
D4 Grove Road North
D5 Grove Road South
F1 Guildford Road
C2 Guildhall Walk
B3 Gunwharf Road
C4 Hambrook Street
C3 Hampshire Terrace
F5 Harold Road
B2 Havant Street
E4 Havelock Road
B2 Hawke Street
E5 Hereford Road
B4 Highbury Street
B4 High Street
E1 Holbrook Road
F4 Holland Road
E3 Hudson Road
D3 Hyde Park Road
F4 Inglis Road
F3 Jessie Road
C4 Jubilee Terrace
D5 Kent Road
B2 Kent Street
E1 King Albert Road
C2 King Henry I Street
C4 King's Road
C4 King's Terrace
C4 King Street
B1 King William Street

D1 Lake Road
E1 Landport Street
C3 Landport Terrace
C3 Landsdowne Street
F5 Lawrence Road
F3 Lawson Road
F5 Leopold Street
F2 Lincoln Road
C4 Little Southsea Street
E4 Livingstone Road
B4 Lombard Street
F4 Londesborough Road
E1 Lords Street
F4 Lorne Road
A1 Main Road
F3 Manners Road
D4 Margate Road
C1 Market Way
D5 Marmion Road
D2 Mary Rose Street
C3 Melbourne Place
D5 Merton Road
D3 Middle Street
E2 Milford Road
E3 Montgomerie Road
F1 Moorland Road
C4 Museum Road
E5 Napier Road
D5 Nelson Road
F1 Newcome Road
C5 Nightingale Road
F4 Norfolk Street
F4 Norman Road
F1 Olinda Street
F3 Orchard Road
B2 Ordnance Row
C5 Osborne Road
E4 Outram Road
F5 Oxford Road
B4 Oyster Street
E3 Pains Road

D5 Palmerston Road
D1 Paradise Street
B3 Park Road
D4 Pelham Road
B4 Pembroke Road
F2 Penhale Road
B4 Penny Street
F3 Percy Road
C5 Pier Road
E3 Playfair Road
D5 Portland Road
F2 Purbrook Road
D5 Queens Crescent
B2 Queen Street
E2 Raglan Street
E2 Railway View
D5 Richmond Place
D3 Rivers Street
E3 Rugby Road
C3 Sackville Street
E4 St Andrews Road
E4 St Bartholomews Gardens
E4 St Davids Road
D4 St Edwards Road
D1 St Faith's Road
B3 St George's Road
B2 St George's Square
B2 St George's Way
D3 St James's Road
B2 St James's Street
B4 St Nicholas Street
C3 St Paul's Road
E4 St Peters Grove
B4 St Thomas's Street
F2 Sandringham Road
C5 Shaftesbury Road
D4 Somers Road
E3 Somers Road
E2 Somers Road North
C5 Southsea Terrace
E3 Stafford Road

E1 Stamford Street
D2 Stanhope Road
E4 Stansted Road
D2 Station Street
C4 Steel Street
C4 Stone Street
D5 Sussex Road
F4 Sutherland Road
F4 Talbot Road
F3 Telephone Road
D1 Temple Street
A2 The Hard
D5 The Retreat
D4 The Thicket
F2 Thorncroft Road
F1 Tottenham Road
F4 Trevor Road
C1 Unicorn Road
D2 Upper Arundel Street
C5 Victoria Avenue
E4 Victoria Grove
E4 Victoria Road North
F3 Victoria Road North
E5 Victoria Road South
F2 Vivash Road
F2 Walmer Road
B4 Warblington Street
D3 Warwick Crescent
D3 Waterloo Road
F5 Waverley Road
C5 Western Parade
A4 West Street
B4 White Hart Road
E4 Wilson Grove
C3 Wiltshire Street
D3 Winston Churchill Avenue
E5 Wisborough Road
D4 Woodpath
C4 Woodville Drive
D4 Yarborough Road
C4 Yorke Street

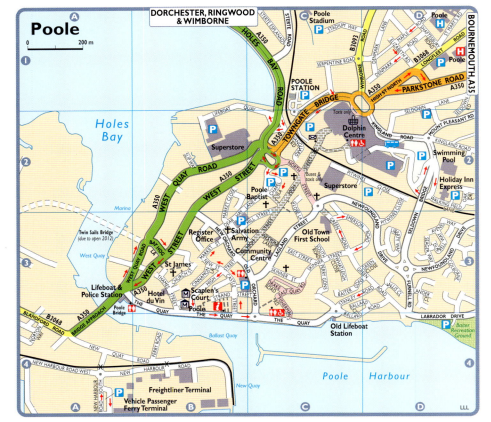

Poole

Poole is found on atlas page 12 H6

D3	Avenel Way	B3	New Street
C3	Baiter Gardens	C2	North Street
C3	Ballard Close	A4	Norton Way
C4	Ballard Road	D2	Oak Drive
B3	Bay Hog Lane	B3	Old Orchard
A3	Blandford Road	D1	Parkstone Road
A4	Bridge Approach	C3	Perry Gardens
B3	Castle Street	C2	Pitwines Close
C2	Chapel Lane	A3	Poole Bridge
B3	Church Street	D1	St Mary's Road
B3	Cinnamon Lane	D3	Seager Way
D3	Colborne	D3	Seldown Bridge
B3	Dear Hay Lane	D2	Seldown Lane
D1	Denmark Lane	D2	Seldown Road
D1	Denmark Road	C1	Serpentine Road
C3	Drake Road	D1	Shaftesbury Road
D3	Durrell Way	C3	Skinner Street
C3	East Quay Road	B2	Slip Way
C3	East Street	C3	South Road
D1	Elizabeth Road	C1	Stadium Way
C3	Emerson Road	C3	Stanley Road
B4	Ferry Road	C1	Sterte Esplanade
C3	Fisherman's Road	C1	Sterte Road
D3	Furnell Road	B3	Strand Street
C2	Globe Lane	B3	Thames Street
D3	Green Close	B3	The Quay
C3	Green Road	C2	Towngate Bridge
B3	High Street	A3	Twin Sails Bridge
D1	High Street North	D3	Vallis Close
C3	Hill Street	C2	Vanguard Road
C1	Holes Bay Road	D2	Walking Field Lane
D2	Kingland Road	C3	Westons Lane
D4	Labrador Drive	B3	West Quay Road
C3	Lagland Street	B3	West Street
D3	Lander Close	C3	Whatleigh Close
D3	Liberty Way	D1	Wimborne Road
B2	Lifeboat Quay		
D1	Longfleet Road		
D1	Maple Road		
B2	Market Close		
B3	Market Street		
D2	Mount Pleasant Road		
C2	Newfoundland Drive		
A4	New Harbour Road		
A4	New Harbour Road South		
A4	New Harbour Road West		
B3	New Orchard		
A4	New Quay Road		

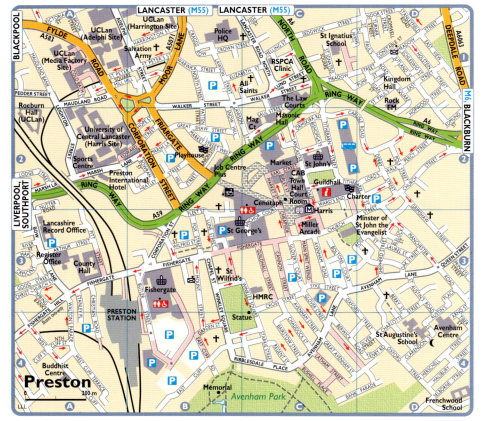

Preston

Preston is found on atlas page 88 G5

A1	Adelphi Street	C2	Lancaster Road
A3	Arthur Street	C1	Lancaster Road North
C4	Avenham Lane	C4	Latham Street
C3	Avenham Road	B1	Lawson Street
C3	Avenham Street	A2	Leighton Street
C4	Berwick Road	C1	Lund Street
C2	Birley Street	B3	Lune Street
C3	Boltons Court	D3	Manchester Road
A3	Bow Lane	C2	Market Street
B3	Butler Street	B2	Market Street West
C2	Carlisle Road	A2	Marsh Lane
C4	Chaddock Street	A1	Maudland Bank
B3	Chapel Street	A1	Maudland Road
D4	Charlotte Street	C1	Meadow Street
C3	Cheapside	B1	Moor Lane
A3	Christ Church Street	B3	Mount Street
C3	Church Street	C1	North Road
D4	Clarendon Street	D3	Oak Street
B2	Corporation Street	C2	Ormskirk Road
B3	Corporation Street	C3	Oxford Street
B1	Craggs Row	A1	Pedder Street
C3	Cross Street	D2	Percy Street
B1	Crown Street	A3	Pitt Street
D1	Deepdale Road	D2	Pole Street
D2	Derby Street	D1	Pump Street
C2	Earl Street	D3	Queen Street
B4	East Cliff	B4	Ribblesdale Place
D1	East Street	B2	Ring Way
D2	Edmund Street	C1	Ring Way
A2	Edward Street	D3	Rose Street
B1	Elizabeth Street	D3	St Austin's Road
B3	Fishergate	D1	St Paul's Road
A4	Fishergate Hill	D1	St Paul's Square
B3	Fleet Street	B1	St Peter's Street
B3	Fox Street	C1	Sedgwick Street
B2	Friargate	D3	Shepherd Street
A1	Fylde Road	B2	Snow Hill
C3	Glover Street	D1	Stanleyfield Road
C4	Great Avenham Street	C4	Starkie Street
B2	Great Shaw Street	C3	Syke Street
D2	Grimshaw Street	C2	Tithebarn Street
C3	Guildhall Street	B1	Walker Street
B1	Harrington Street	A3	Walton's Parade
B2	Heatley Street	C2	Ward's End
D4	Herschell Street	B1	Warwick Street
D1	Holstein Street	A4	West Cliff
D2	Hopwood Street	A4	West Cliff Terrace
D1	Jutland Street	B3	Winkley Square

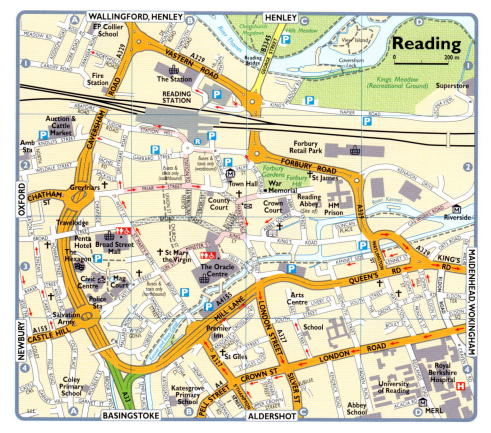

Reading

Reading is found on atlas page **35 K10**

C3	Abbey Square	D3	King's Road
C2	Abbey Street	B3	King Street
A1	Addison Road	A2	Knollys Street
A3	Anstey Road	C3	Livery Close
A3	Baker Street	C4	London Road
B2	Blagrave Street	C3	London Street
D4	Boult Street	A4	Mallard Row
B3	Bridge Street	B2	Market Place
A3	Broad Street	B4	Mill Lane
A4	Brook Street West	B3	Minster Street
B3	Buttermarket	C1	Napier Road
A1	Cardiff Road	C4	Newark Street
A3	Carey Street	A1	Northfield Road
A4	Castle Hill	B4	Parthia Close
A3	Castle Street	B4	Pell Street
A2	Caversham Road	D3	Prince's Street
A2	Chatham Street	C3	Queen's Road
A2	Cheapside	B2	Queen Victoria Street
B3	Church Street	D4	Redlands Road
B4	Church Street	A1	Ross Road
A4	Coley Place	A2	Sackville Street
D4	Craven Road	B4	St Giles Close
B4	Crossland Road	D3	St John's Road
B2	Cross Street	B3	St Mary's Butts
C4	Crown Street	C3	Sidmouth Street
B4	Deansgate Road	C4	Silver Street
C3	Duke Street	B3	Simmonds Street
C3	Duncan Place	B4	Southampton Street
C3	East Street	C3	South Street
D3	Eldon Road	B2	Station Hill
A4	Field Road	B2	Station Road
B4	Fobney Street	B3	Swan Place
C2	Forbury Road	A1	Swansea Road
B2	Friar Street	C2	The Forbury
A4	Garnet Street	A2	Tudor Road
B2	Garrard Street	B2	Union Street
D3	Gas Works Road	C4	Upper Crown Street
C1	George Street	A2	Vachel Road
A2	Greyfriars Road	B2	Valpy Street
B3	Gun Street	B1	Vastern Road
B4	Henry Street	B4	Waterside Gardens
A3	Howard Street	D3	Watlington Street
B4	Katesgrove Lane	A2	Weldale Street
D2	Kenavon Drive	A2	West Street
C4	Kendrick Road	A4	Wolseley Street
C3	Kennet Side	B3	Yield Hall Place
D3	Kennet Street	A1	York Road
C1	King's Meadow Road	A3	Zinzan Street

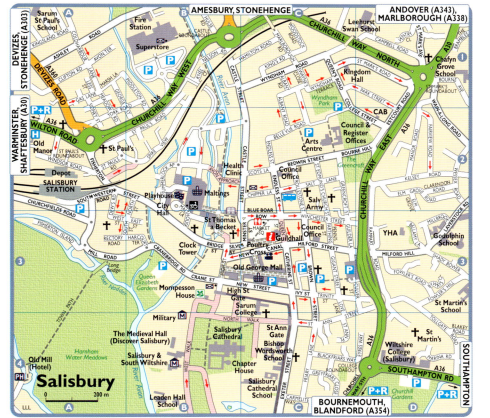

Salisbury

Salisbury is found on atlas page **21 M9**

C1	Albany Road	A1	Kingsland Road
A1	Ashley Road	C1	King's Road
B2	Avon Approach	D3	Laverstock Road
C2	Bedwin Street	B3	Malthouse Lane
C2	Belle Vue Road	D2	Manor Road
C4	Blackfriars Way	C1	Marlborough Road
C3	Blue Boar Row	A1	Meadow Road
D1	Bourne Avenue	A1	Middleton Road
C2	Bourne Hill	D3	Milford Hill
B3	Bridge Street	C3	Milford Street
C3	Brown Street	A3	Mill Road
D1	Campbell Road	C3	Minster Street
B1	Castle Street	B1	Nelson Road
C3	Catherine Street	B3	New Canal
C2	Chipper Lane	B3	New Street
A2	Churchfields Road	B3	North Street
D3	Churchill Way East	D1	Park Street
C1	Churchill Way North	C3	Pennyfarthing Street
C4	Churchill Way South	C1	Queen's Road
B2	Churchill Way West	C3	Queen Street
D2	Clarendon Road	D3	Rampart Road
A1	Clifton Road	A3	Rectory Road
A1	Coldharbour Lane	C2	Rollestone Street
C1	College Street	C4	St Ann Street
B3	Cranebridge Road	C2	St Edmund's Church Street
B3	Crane Street	D1	St Mark's Avenue
A1	Devizes Road	D1	St Mark's Road
A3	Dew's Road	B2	St Paul's Road
B3	East Street	C2	Salt Lane
D2	Elm Grove	C2	Scots Lane
D2	Elm Grove Road	A1	Sidney Street
C2	Endless Street	B3	Silver Street
D2	Estcourt Road	D4	Southampton Road
C4	Exeter Street	A3	South Street
D4	Eyres Way	A2	South Western Road
D2	Fairview Road	B2	Spire View
A2	Fisherton Street	D4	Summerlock Approach
D3	Fowler's Road	D4	Tollgate Road
C4	Friary Lane	C3	Trinity Street
A1	Gas Lane	D1	Wain-A-Long Road
A1	George Street	D2	Wessex Road
C3	Gigant Street	A3	West Street
C2	Greencroft Street	A2	Wilton Road
C3	Guilder Lane	C3	Winchester Street
C1	Hamilton Road	A2	Windsor Road
B3	High Street	C1	Woodstock Road
C3	Ivy Street	C1	Wyndham Road
D2	Kelsey Road	A2	York Road

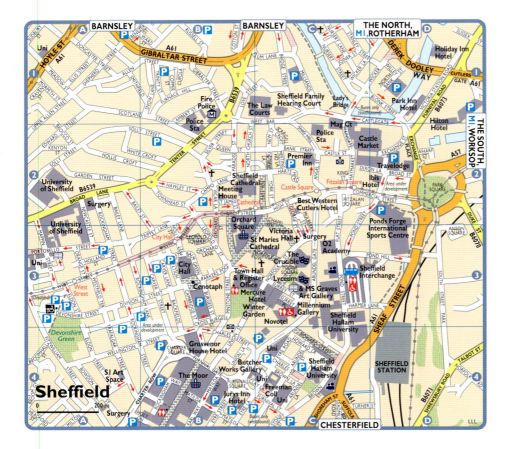

Sheffield

Sheffield is found on atlas page **84 E3**

C2	Angel Street	C4	Howard Street
C3	Arundel Gate	A1	Hoyle Street
C4	Arundel Street	C2	King Street
B3	Backfields	B1	Lambert Street
A2	Bailey Street	B3	Leopold Street
B3	Balm Green	A3	Mappin Street
C2	Bank Street	B4	Matilda Street
B3	Barkers Pool	C2	Meetinghouse Lane
A4	Bowdon Street	C2	Mulberry Street
A2	Broad Lane	A2	Newcastle Street
D2	Broad Street	C2	New Street
C4	Brown Street	C3	Norfolk Street
B3	Cambridge Street	B2	North Church Street
B2	Campo Lane	A3	Orange Street
B3	Carver Street	B3	Orchard Street
C1	Castlegate	B2	Paradise Street
C2	Castle Street	B3	Pinstone Street
B4	Charles Street	C3	Pond Hill
A4	Charter Row	C3	Pond Street
B2	Church Street	A3	Portobello Street
C2	Commercial Street	B2	Queen Street
B3	Cross Burgess Street	A2	Rockingham Street
D1	Cutlers Gate	B2	St James Street
D1	Derek Dooley Way	C2	Scargill Croft
A3	Devonshire Street	A1	Scotland Street
A3	Division Street	D4	Sheaf Street
C2	Dixon Lane	C4	Shoreham Street
D2	Duke Street	D4	Shrewsbury Road
D2	Exchange Street	B2	Silver Street
B4	Eyre Street	A1	Smithfield
C2	Fig Tree Lane	C2	Snig Hill
A4	Fitzwilliam Street	A2	Solly Street
C3	Flat Street	C4	Suffolk Road
B1	Furnace Hill	C3	Surrey Street
B4	Furnival Gate	D4	Talbot Street
D1	Furnival Road	B2	Tenter Street
C4	Furnival Street	B2	Townhead Street
A2	Garden Street	A4	Trafalgar Street
C2	George Street	B3	Trippet Lane
B1	Gibralter Street	B4	Union Street
C3	Harmer Lane	B2	Vicar Lane
C2	Harts Head	D1	Victoria Station Road
B2	Hawley Street	C2	Waingate
C2	Haymarket	A4	Wellington Street
C2	High Street	B2	West Bar
A3	Holland Street	A3	West Street
A2	Hollis Croft	A2	White Croft
B3	Holly Street	C2	York Street

Shrewsbury

Shrewsbury is found on atlas page **56 H2**

D3	Abbey Foregate	B1	Longner Street
D1	Albert Street	B4	Luciefelde Road
B1	Alma Street	B2	Mardol
C4	Back Lime Street	B3	Market Street
B2	Barker Street	C3	Milk Street
C3	Beeches Lane	D4	Moreton Crescent
C4	Belle Vue Gardens	B1	Mount Street
D4	Belle Vue Road	B3	Murivance
B3	Belmont	B1	Nettles Lane
C3	Belmont Bank	D1	Newpark Road
D1	Benyon Street	A2	New Street
D4	Betton Street	D1	North Street
B2	Bridge Street	D3	Old Coleham
D1	Burton Street	D3	Old Potts Way
C2	Butcher Row	A2	Park Avenue
A4	Canonbury	C4	Pengrove
C1	Castle Foregate	D4	Pound Close
C2	Castle Gates	C2	Pride Hill
C2	Castle Street	B3	Princess Street
C1	Chester Street	A2	Priory Road
B3	Claremont Bank	B3	Quarry Place
B3	Claremont Hill	A2	Quarry View
B3	Claremont Street	C4	Raby Crescent
D3	Coleham Head	B2	Raven Meadows
B3	College Hill	B2	Roushill
A2	Copthorne Road	B3	St Chad's Terrace
C1	Coton Hill	A1	St George's Street
B4	Crescent Lane	B3	St Johns Hill
B3	Cross Hill	C3	St Julians Friars
A1	Darwin Gardens	C2	St Mary's Place
A1	Darwin Street	C2	St Mary's Street
C3	Dogpole	C2	St Mary's Water Lane
A1	Drinkwater Street	D4	Salters Lane
C3	Fish Street	D1	Severn Bank
A2	Frankwell	D1	Severn Street
B2	Frankwell Quay	B3	Shop Latch
A2	Greenhill Avenue	B2	Smithfield Road
C4	Greyfriars Road	B3	Swan Hill
C3	High Street	D1	The Dana
B2	Hill's Lane	A1	The Mount
C1	Howard Street	B3	The Square
B1	Hunter Street	B3	Town Walls
B4	Kingsland Road	A2	Victoria Avenue
C4	Lime Street	D1	Victoria Street
C4	Longden Coleham	A2	Water Lane
C4	Longden Gardens	D1	Water Street
C4	Longden Road	D1	West Street
		C3	Wyle Cop

Southampton

Southampton is found on atlas page **14 D4**

C1	Above Bar Street	E5	Channel Way	E1	Hartington Road	E1	Northumberland Road	C2	South Front
E4	Albert Road North	D3	Chapel Road	B1	Havelock Road	D5	Ocean Way	C3	Strand
E5	Albert Road South	C1	Charlotte Place	B4	Herbert Walker Avenue	C2	Ogle Road	C2	Sussex Road
E5	Alcantara Crescent	B2	Civic Centre Road	C4	High Street	C5	Orchard Place	E4	Ted Bates Road
A1	Alexandra Road	D1	Clovelly Road	A1	Hill Lane	D1	Orchard Road	D5	Terminus Terrace
E4	Anderson's Road	D3	Coleman Street	D3	Houndwell Place	D4	Oxford Avenue	D3	The Compass
F5	Andes Close	D4	College Street	F1	Howell Close	E4	Oxford Street	B1	The Polygon
E4	Anglesea Terrace	A1	Commercial Road	F4	Itchen Bridge	C2	Paget Street	D4	Threefield Lane
D1	Argyle Road	D3	Cook Street	D3	James Street	C2	Palmerston Road	B5	Town Quay
E5	Asturias Way	D2	Cossack Green	D2	Johnson Street	C2	Park Walk	D1	Trinity Road
E1	Augustine Road	D2	Craven Street	D5	John Street	E1	Peel Street	C4	Upper Bugle Street
C4	Back Of The Walls	E4	Crosshouse Road	F1	Kent Street	B3	Pirelli Street	E2	Victoria Street
C3	Bargate Street	B1	Cumberland Place	D4	King Street	C5	Platform Road	C3	Vincent's Walk
C1	Bedford Place	D5	Cunard Road	D2	Kingsway	C5	Porter's Lane	B1	Water Lane
D4	Bell Street	E1	Derby Road	D5	Latimer Street	C3	Portland Street	A2	Western Esplanade
E2	Belvidere Road	B1	Devonshire Road	D4	Lime Street	B2	Portland Terrace	B4	Western Esplanade
F1	Belvidere Terrace	D4	Duke Street	C1	London Road	C3	Pound Tree Road	C2	West Marlands Road
C4	Bernard Street	C4	Eastgate Street	C5	Lower Canal Walk	D5	Queens Terrace	B2	West Park Road
B2	Blechynden Terrace	C1	East Park Terrace	E1	Lumpy Lane	C4	Queen's Way	A2	West Quay Road
F1	Bond Street	C3	East Street	A1	Mandela Way	E1	Radcliffe Road	C4	West Street
D1	Brinton's Road	E4	Elm Terrace	E3	Marine Parade	D4	Richmond Street	D4	White Star Place
E1	Britannia Road	E4	Endle Street	D4	Marsh Lane	A1	Roberts Road	F1	William Street
C5	Briton Street	D3	Evans Street	D3	Maryfield	E2	Rochester Street	E1	Wilson Street
D2	Broad Green	D1	Exmoor Road	B4	Mayflower Roundabout	E5	Royal Crescent Road	C5	Winkle Street
C1	Brunswick Place	E4	Floating Bridge Road	E3	Melbourne Street	D4	Russell Street	D2	Winton Street
C4	Brunswick Square	C4	Forest View	F1	Millbank Street	E4	Ryde Terrace	E1	Wolverton Road
C5	Bugle Street	E4	French Street	A1	Millbrook Road East	E1	St Alban's Road	A1	Wyndham Place
E1	Cable Street	E4	Glebe Road	B1	Morris Road	D1	St Andrews Road		
C4	Canal Walk	D2	Golden Grove	A2	Mountbatten Way	D1	St Marks Road		
D5	Canute Road	E3	Granville Road	E4	Nelson Street	D3	St Mary's Place		
D4	Captains Place	B1	Grosvenor Square	D5	Neptune Way	D1	St Mary's Road		
D4	Carpathia Drive	C4	Hamtun Street	C2	New Road	D2	St Mary Street		
C3	Castle Way	B1	Handel Road	D1	Nichols Road	C4	St Michael Street		
D4	Central Bridge	B1	Handel Terrace	D2	Northam Road	A1	Shirley Road		
D5	Central Road	C3	Hanover Buildings	D1	Northbrook Road	A3	Solent Road		
D4	Challis Court	B2	Harbour Parade	C2	North Front	A2	Southbrook Road		
								A2	Southern Road

Southend-on-Sea

Southend-on-Sea is found on atlas page **38 E4**

C3	Albert Road		D4	Kursaal Way
A3	Alexandra Road		C2	Lancaster Gardens
A3	Alexandra Street		D2	Leamington Road
D2	Ambleside Drive		A2	London Road
A2	Ashburnham Road		C4	Lucy Road
B3	Baltic Avenue		A2	Luker Road
A1	Baxter Avenue		C4	Marine Parade
D4	Beach Road		B1	Milton Street
D4	Beresford Road		A2	Napier Avenue
C1	Boscombe Road		A3	Nelson Street
D1	Bournemouth Park Road		D1	Oban Road
A3	Cambridge Road		D3	Old Southend Road
A3	Capel Terrace		D3	Outing Close
B3	Chancellor Road		B2	Pitmans Close
D2	Cheltenham Road		C3	Pleasant Road
B1	Chichester Road		B3	Portland Avenue
D1	Christchurch Road		A2	Princes Street
B3	Church Road		A3	Prittlewell Square
A3	Clarence Road		B2	Quebec Avenue
B3	Clarence Street		A2	Queen's Road
A4	Clifftown Parade		A1	Queensway
B3	Clifftown Road		B4	Royal Terrace
B1	Coleman Street		A3	Runwell Terrace
C2	Cromer Road		B1	St Ann's Road
A4	Devereux Road		C3	St Leonard's Road
D4	Eastern Esplanade		A3	Scratton Road
A2	Elmer Approach		B1	Short Street
A2	Elmer Avenue		D2	Southchurch Avenue
B1	Essex Street		B2	Southchurch Road
D1	Ferndown Close		D2	Stanier Close
D2	Fowler Close		C3	Stanley Road
A2	Gordon Place		C1	Sutton Road
A2	Gordon Road		C1	Swanage Road
C2	Grange Gardens		C2	Toledo Road
B3	Grover Street		B3	Tylers Avenue
B1	Guildford Road		C2	Tyrel Drive
A3	Hamlet Road		A1	Victoria Avenue
C4	Hartington Place		B2	Warrior Square East
C3	Hartington Road		B2	Warrior Square North
C2	Hastings Road		B2	Warrior Square
D4	Hawtree Close		C3	Wesley Road
C3	Herbert Grove		A4	Western Esplanade
B3	Heygate Avenue		B3	Weston Road
B2	High Street		B2	Whitegate Road
C2	Hillcrest Road		C1	Wimborne Road
D2	Honiton Road		D2	Windermere Road
C3	Horace Road		D3	Woodgrange Drive
C2	Kilworth Avenue		B3	York Road

Stirling

Stirling is found on atlas page **133 M9**

D2	Abbey Road		C3	King Street
D1	Abbotsford Place		C1	Lovers Walk
B4	Abercromby Place		B1	Lower Bridge Street
B3	Academy Road		B2	Lower Castlehill
A3	Albert Place		B2	Mar Place
D1	Alexandra Place		C3	Maxwell Place
B4	Allan Park		D4	Meadowforth Road
D2	Argyll Avenue		D1	Millar Place
A1	Back O' Hill Road		B3	Morris Terrace
B3	Baker Street		C3	Murray Place
A1	Ballengeich Road		C4	Ninians Road
A3	Balmoral Place		C2	Park Lane
B3	Bank Street		B4	Park Terrace
B2	Barn Road		C4	Pitt Terrace
C2	Barnton Street		D4	Players Road
B1	Bayne Street		C4	Port Street
B3	Bow Street		B3	Princes Street
B3	Broad Street		D1	Queenshaugh Drive
B1	Bruce Street		A4	Queens Road
C1	Burghmuir Road		B2	Queen Street
B2	Castle Court		A2	Raploch Road
B4	Clarendon Place		C2	Ronald Place
B3	Clarendon Road		C2	Rosebery Place
B3	Corn Exchange Road		C2	Rosebery Terrace
B1	Cowane Street		A3	Royal Gardens
C4	Craigs Roundabout		B3	St John Street
B2	Crofthead Court		B2	St Mary's Wynd
C1	Customs Roundabout		C3	Seaforth Place
D1	Dean Crescent		D1	Shiphaugh Place
C2	Douglas Street		C2	Shore Road
A1	Duff Crescent		B3	Spittal Street
B4	Dumbarton Road		D2	Sutherland Avenue
D1	Edward Avenue		B2	Tannery Lane
C1	Edward Road		B1	Union Street
D2	Forrest Road		B2	Upper Bridge Street
C2	Forth Crescent		A2	Upper Castlehill
C1	Forth Street		C4	Upper Craigs
C1	Forth View		A4	Victoria Place
B4	Glebe Avenue		B3	Victoria Road
B4	Glebe Crescent		A4	Victoria Square
A1	Glendevon Drive		C2	Viewfield Street
C2	Goosecroft Road		C2	Wallace Street
A1	Gowanhill Gardens		D1	Waverley Crescent
A3	Greenwood Avenue		C4	Wellgreen Lane
B1	Harvey Wynd		C4	Wellgreen Road
B2	Irvine Place		B2	Whinwell Road
C2	James Street		B4	Windsor Place
B4	Kings Park Road			

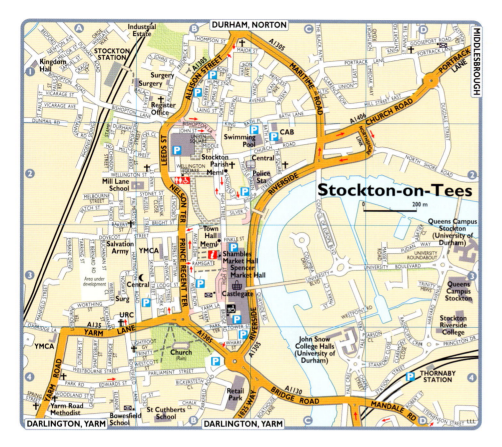

Stockton-on-Tees

Stockton-on-Tees is found on atlas page **104 D7**

B4	1825 Way	D3	Massey Road
B1	Allison Street	A2	Melbourne Street
B1	Alma Street	B2	Middle Street
C1	Bath Lane	A2	Mill Street West
A1	Bedford Street	B2	Nelson Terrace
B2	Bishop Street	D2	North Shore Road
A1	Bishopton Lane	D1	Northport Road
A1	Bishopton Road	C2	Northshore Link
A4	Bowesfield Lane	B1	Norton Road
B3	Bridge Road	A2	Palmerston Street
C4	Bridge Road	A4	Park Road
B2	Bright Street	C3	Park Terrace
A1	Britannia Road	B4	Parkfield Road
B3	Brunswick Street	B4	Parliament Street
A2	Bute Street	D1	Portrack Lane
D1	Church Road	B3	Prince Regent Terrace
C1	Clarence Row	C1	Princess Avenue
A2	Corportion Street	D4	Princeton Drive
C2	Council of Europe	C3	Quayside Road
	Boulevard	D3	Raddcliffe Crescent
B1	Cromwell Avenue	B3	Ramsgate
A2	Dixon Street	C4	Riverside
A3	Dovecot Street	B2	Russell Street
D1	Dugdale Street	A1	St Paul's Street
A1	Durham Road	B2	Silver Street
A2	Durham Street	B3	Skinner Street
A4	Edwards Street	D4	Station Street
B1	Farrer Street	B2	Sydney Street
C3	Finkle Street	D2	The Square
B1	Frederick Street	C2	Thistle Green
D3	Fudan Way	B1	Thomas Street
D1	Gooseport Road	B1	Thompson Street
A3	Hartington Road	B4	Tower Street
D3	Harvard Avenue	C1	Union Street East
B2	High Street	C3	University Boulevard
D1	Hill Street East	B2	Vane Street
B1	Hume Street	A1	Vicarage Street
A2	Hutchinson Street	A2	Wellington Street
B2	John Street	B3	West Row
B2	King Street	A4	Westbourne Street
D1	Knightport Road	C3	Westpoint Road
C2	Knowles Street	B4	Wharf Street
B1	Laing Street	B3	William Street
B2	Leeds Street	A4	Woodland Street
B2	Lobdon Street	A3	Worthing Street
B3	Lodge Street	C4	Yale Crescent
D4	Mandale Road	A4	Yarm Lane
C1	Maritime Road	A4	Yarm Road

Stoke-on-Trent (Hanley)

Stoke-on-Trent (Hanley) is found on atlas page **70 F5**

B3	Albion Street	C3	Lichfield Street
B3	Bagnall Street	D2	Linfield Road
D3	Balfour Street	D1	Lower Mayer Street
D1	Baskerville Road	A1	Lowther Street
B4	Bathesda Street	D3	Ludlow Street
C4	Bernard Street	B1	Malam Street
B3	Bethesda Street	B2	Marsh Street North
C3	Birch Terrace	B2	Marsh Street
C3	Botteslow Street	B3	Marsh Street South
B3	Broad Street	C1	Mayer Street
C1	Broom Street	B3	Mersey Street
B3	Brunswick Street	A4	Milton Street
B1	Bryan Street	A4	Mount Pleasant
C2	Bucknall New Road	D1	Mynors Street
D2	Bucknall Old Road	B2	New Hall Street
B4	Cardiff Grove	C4	Ogden Road
A1	Century Street	C3	Old Hall Street
C3	Charles Street	C1	Old Town Road
B3	Cheapside	B3	Pall Mall
A1	Chelwood Street	C2	Percy Street
A3	Clough Street	B3	Piccadilly
A4	Clyde Street	A1	Portland Street
D3	Commercial Road	B1	Potteries Way
A1	Denbigh Street	B2	Quadrant Road
C4	Derby Street	C4	Regent Road
D2	Dyke Street	A1	Rutland Street
C4	Eastwood Road	D1	St John Street
D2	Eaton Street	D3	St Luke Street
A2	Etruria Road	B1	Sampson Street
C1	Festing Street	A4	Sheaf Street
B2	Foundry Street	A4	Slippery Lane
C2	Garth Street	A4	Snow Hill
C3	Gilman Street	B2	Stafford Street
C2	Goodson Street	A4	Sun Street
C1	Grafton Street	C3	Tontine Street
B1	Hanover Street	B1	Town Road
C4	Harley Street	B1	Trafalgar Street
C2	Hillchurch	B2	Trinity Street
C2	Hillcrest Street	B1	Union Street
B4	Hinde Street	C2	Upper Hillchurch Street
B1	Hope Street	C2	Upper Huntbach Street
C3	Hordley Street	B3	Warner Street
C2	Huntbach Street	D3	Waterloo Street
C4	Jasper Street	D3	Well Street
D1	Jervis Street	D3	Wellington Road
D1	John Bright Street	D3	Wellington Street
B3	John Street	A4	Yates Street
D1	Keelings Road	B1	York Street

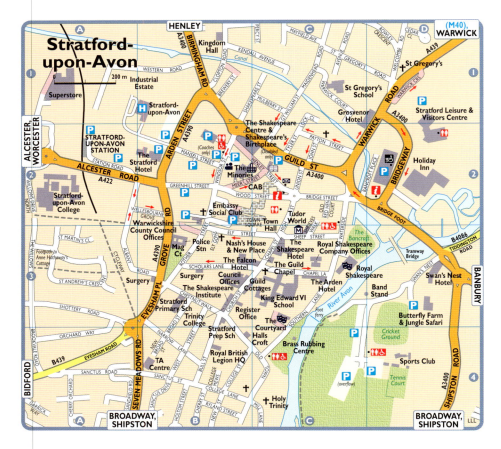

Stratford-upon-Avon

Stratford-upon-Avon is found on atlas page **47 P3**

A3	Albany Road	C2	Old Red Hen Court
A2	Alcester Road	C4	Old Town
B2	Arden Street	A4	Orchard Way
C1	Avenue Road	C2	Payton Street
C2	Bancroft Place	C1	Percy Street
B1	Birmingham Road	B3	Rother Street
B1	Brewery Street	D1	Rowley Crescent
D2	Bridge Foot	B4	Ryland Street
C2	Bridge Street	A3	St Andrew's Crescent
D2	Bridgeway	C1	St Gregory's Road
B4	Broad Street	A3	St Martin's Close
A4	Brookvale Road	B4	Sanctus Drive
B4	Bull Street	A4	Sanctus Road
D1	Cedar Close	B4	Sanctus Street
C3	Chapel Lane	A4	Sandfield Road
C3	Chapel Street	B3	Scholars Lane
A4	Cherry Orchard	A4	Seven Meadows Road
B4	Cherry Street	B1	Shakespeare Street
B3	Chestnut Walk	C3	Sheep Street
B3	Church Street	D4	Shipston Road
B1	Clopton Road	A3	Shottery Road
B4	College Lane	C3	Shrieves Walk
B4	College Mews	A2	Southern Lane
B4	College Street	A2	Station Road
B3	Ely Gardens	D3	Swan's Nest
B3	Ely Street	A3	The Willows
B3	Evesham Place	D3	Tiddington Road
A4	Evesham Road	B2	Town Square
A4	Garrick Way	D3	Tramway Bridge
C1	Great William Street	C2	Tyler Street
B2	Greenhill Street	C2	Union Street
B3	Grove Road	C1	Warwick Court
C2	Guild Street	D1	Warwick Crescent
B2	Henley Street	C2	Warwick Road
C3	High Street	C3	Waterside
B4	Holtom Street	D1	Welcombe Road
C2	John Street	B2	Wellesbourne Grove
B1	Kendall Avenue	B1	Western Road
C2	Lock Close	B4	West Street
C1	Maidenhead Road	A2	Willows Drive North
B2	Mansell Street	B2	Windsor Street
C1	Mayfield Avenue	B2	Wood Street
B2	Meer Street		
C4	Mill Lane		
C1	Mulberry Street		
B4	Narrow Lane		
B4	New Broad Street		
B4	New Street		

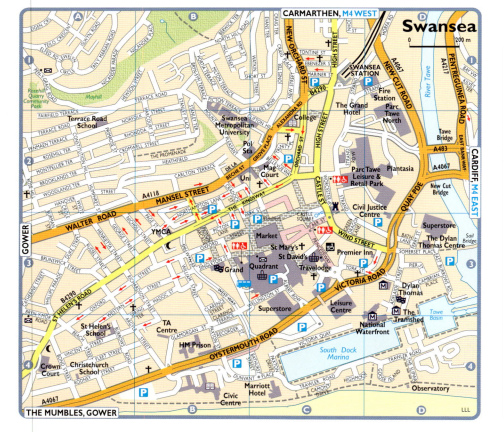

Swansea

Swansea is found on atlas page **29 J6**

D3	Adelaide Street	C1	New Orchard Street
C2	Alexandra Road	C1	New Street
A4	Argyle Street	A1	Nicander Parade
D3	Bath Lane	A3	Nicholl Street
A4	Beach Street	A2	Norfolk Street
A4	Bond Street	B1	North Hill Road
A3	Brunswick Street	B2	Northampton Lane
A4	Burrows Road	C2	Orchard Street
C3	Caer Street	A3	Oxford Street
B2	Carlton Terrace	B4	Oystermouth Road
C2	Castle Street	B3	Page Street
A3	Catherine Street	B3	Park Street
B3	Clarence Street	B4	Paxton Street
C2	Clifton Hill	D1	Pentreguinea Road
A2	Constituion Hill	A1	Pen-Y-Graig Road
B2	Cradock Street	B3	Picton Lane
C1	Craig Place	D3	Pier Street
A2	Cromwell Street	A2	Primrose Street
B2	De La Beche Street	C3	Princess Way
B3	Dillwyn Street	D2	Quay Parade
A3	Duke Street	B4	Recorder Street
B4	Dunvant Place	A2	Rhondda Street
D2	East Bank Way	A3	Richardson Street
D3	East Burrows Road	A4	Rodney Street
C1	Ebenezer Street	A2	Rose Hill
A1	Elfed Road	A3	Russel Street
D3	Ferry Street	A3	St Helen's Road
B1	Firm Street	B1	Short Street
A4	Fleet Street	B3	Singleton Street
A3	George Street	D3	Somerset Place
B4	Glamorgan Street	C1	Strand
C3	Green Lane Dragon	A1	Tan Y Marian Road
C2	Grove Place	A1	Teilo Crescent
A2	Hanover Street	B2	Terrace Road
B2	Harcourt Street	B2	The Kingsway
B2	Heathfield	C1	Tontine Street
A3	Henrietta Street	C4	Trawler Road
A1	Hewson Street	C4	Victoria Quay
C2	High Street	C3	Victoria Road
B1	Hill Street	A4	Vincent Street
A2	Humphrey Street	A3	Walter Road
A1	Islwyn Road	C1	Watkin Street
A1	Llewelyn Circle	C3	Wellington Street
B3	Madoc Street	B3	West Way
B2	Mansel Street	A4	Western Street
C1	Mariner Street	B3	William Street
B2	Mount Pleasant	C3	Wind Street
D1	New Cut Road	C3	York Street

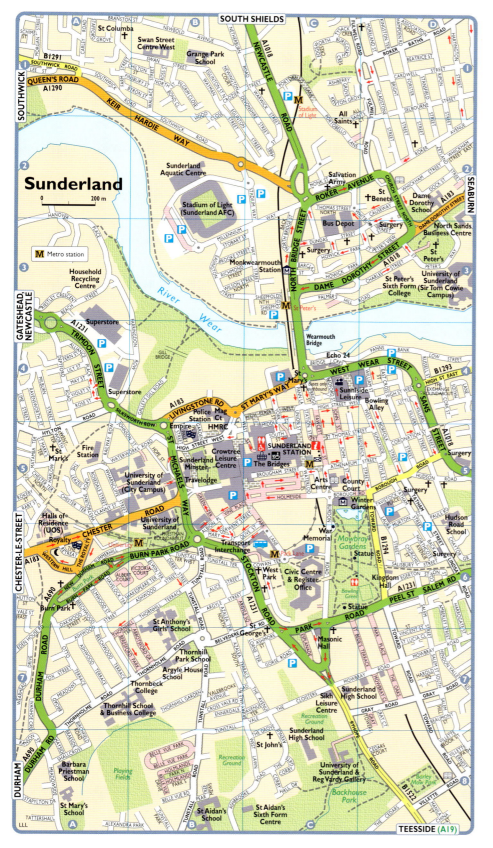

Sunderland

Sunderland is found on atlas page **113 N9**

B7	Abbotsford Green	A8	Meadowside
C2	Abbs Street	C5	Middle Street
B6	Albion Place	A4	Milburn Street
B6	Alice Street	B3	Millennium Way
A4	Alliance Place	C2	Monk Street
D6	Amberley Street	D1	Moreland Street
B6	Argyle Square	A1	Morgan Street
B6	Argyle Street	D7	Mowbray Road
B8	Ashbrooke Road	B1	Netherburn Road
C7	Ashmore Street	B1	Newbold Avenue
A7	Ashwood Street	C1	Newcastle Road
A7	Ashwood Terrace	A6	New Durham Road
D1	Association Road	D4	Nile Street
C5	Athenaeum Street	D5	Norfolk Street
B6	Azalea Terrace North	C3	North Bridge Street
B7	Azalea Terrace South	D6	Northcote Avenue
C3	Back North Bridge Street	B1	North Street
A3	Beach Street	A6	Oakwood Street
D7	Beaumont Street	B6	Olive Street
C4	Bedford Street	A7	Otto Terrace
A6	Beechwood Street	C3	Palmer's Hill Road
A7	Beechwood Terrace	D4	Panns Bank
B7	Belvedere Road	C5	Park Lane
A7	Beresford Park	D6	Park Place
A7	Birchfield Road	C6	Park Road
D5	Borough Road	D5	Pauls Road
C4	Bridge Crescent	D6	Peel Street
C4	Bridge Street	C1	Portobello Lane
C7	Briery Vale Road	A1	Queen's Road
D1	Bright Street	A5	Railway Row
B3	Brooke Street	A4	Ravensworth Street
C5	Brougham Street	B3	Richmond Street
C5	Burdon Road	D1	Ripon Street
B6	Burn Park Road	C2	Roker Avenue
D1	Cardwell Street	D1	Roker Baths Road
A1	Carley Road	A5	Rosedale Street
D3	Charles Street	B1	Ross Street
A6	Chester Road	D4	Russell Street
D6	Churchill Street	C7	Ryhope Road
D2	Church Street North	D7	St Bede's Terrace
A5	Clanny Street	C3	St Mary's Way
D4	Cork Street	B5	St Michaels Way
D5	Coronation Street	D3	St Peter's View
C6	Cowan Terrace	C5	St Thomas' Street
B7	Cross Vale Road	D6	Salem Road
B1	Crozier Street	D6	Salem Street
C3	Dame Dorothy Street	D7	Salem Street South
A4	Deptford Road	D6	Salisbury Street
B6	Derby Street	D4	Sans Street
B6	Derwent Street	D1	Selbourne Street
B1	Devonshire Street	A6	Shakespeare Terrace
D2	Dock Street	A8	Shallcross
C3	Dundas Street	C3	Sheepfolds Road
A7	Durham Road	A4	Silksworth Row
B3	Easington Street	C5	South Street
D4	East Cross Street	A1	Southwick Road
A7	Eden House Road	C2	Stadium Way
D6	Egerton Street	D1	Stansfield Street
B1	Eglinton Street	C4	Station Street
B1	Eglinton Street North	B3	Stobart Street
A6	Elmwood Street	C6	Stockton Road
B7	Ennerdale	B1	Swan Street
A1	Farm Street	D5	Tatham Street
B4	Farringdon Row	D5	Tatham Street Back
C4	Fawcett Street	C7	The Avenue
D1	Forster Street	C7	The Cloisters
A7	Fox Street	A6	The Royalty
D5	Foyle Street	C2	Thomas Street North
D5	Frederick Street	B6	Thornhill Terrace
C1	Fulwell Road	A7	Thornholme Road
B4	Galley's Gill Road	D5	Toward Road
D1	Gladstone Street	A4	Trimdon Street
C7	Gorse Road	B7	Tunstall Road
D7	Gray Road	B6	Tunstall Terrace
B5	Green Terrace	B6	Tunstall Terrace West
D1	Hampden Road	B8	Tunstall Vale
A2	Hanover Place	C4	Union Street
A5	Harlow Street	B7	Valebrooke Avenue
D6	Harrogate Street	D8	Villette Road
D1	Hartington Street	D4	Villiers Street
A6	Havelock Terrace	B5	Vine Place
C3	Hay Street	B1	Wallace Street
D7	Hendon Valley Road	C1	Warwick Street
D4	High Street East	C5	Waterloo Place
B5	High Street West	A5	Waterworks Road
C5	Holmeside	B1	Wayman Street
B5	Hope Street	A7	Wearhead Drive
C3	Howick Park	A5	Westbourne Road
D5	Hudson Road	A6	Western Hill
A5	Hylton Road	C8	West Lawn
A5	Johnson Street	C5	West Street
C4	John Street	D4	West Sunniside
A1	Keir Hardie Way	C4	West Wear Street
D5	Laura Street	A5	Wharncliffe Street
A4	Lime Street	D2	Whickham Street
D6	Lindsay Road	D2	Whickham Street East
D4	Little Villiers Street	D3	Whitburn Street
B4	Livingstone Road	D4	William Street
D4	Low Street	B3	Wilson Street North
B6	Mary Street	C4	York Street
D4	Mauds Lane	D2	Zetland Street

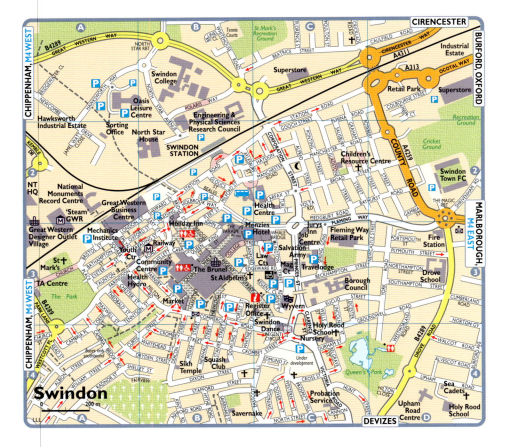

Swindon

Swindon is found on atlas page **33 M8**

A4	Albion Street	C3	Islington Street
C2	Alfred Street	B3	John Street
B4	Ashford Road	B3	King Street
B2	Aylesbury Street	A3	London Street
C2	Bathurst Road	C2	Manchester Road
C3	Beckhampton Street	B3	Market Street
B2	Bridge Street	A3	Maxwell Street
A3	Bristol Street	C2	Medgbury Road
C2	Broad Street	B2	Milford Street
A4	Cambria Bridge Road	B3	Milton Road
B3	Canal Walk	B3	Morley Street
C2	Carfax Street	B4	Morse Street
B3	Carr Street	D3	Newcastle Street
A3	Chester Street	A1	Newcombe Drive
A3	Church Place	B4	Newhall Street
D1	Cirencester Way	D3	Northampton Street
C3	Clarence Street	B1	North Star Avenue
B3	College Street	D1	Ocotal Way
B3	Commercial Road	A3	Park Lane
C2	Corporation Street	D3	Plymouth Street
D2	County Road	B1	Polaris Way
B4	Crombey Street	C2	Ponting Street
A4	Curtis Street	D3	Portsmouth Street
B4	Deacon Street	C3	Princes Street
B4	Dixon Street	C4	Prospect Hill
C4	Dover Street	B3	Queen Street
B4	Dowling Street	A4	Radnor Street
D4	Drove Road	C3	Regent Place
A4	Dryden Street	B3	Regent Street
C4	Eastcott Hill	C2	Rosebery Street
B2	East Street	C2	Salisbury Street
B3	Edgeware Road	B3	Sanford Street
C1	Elmina Road	B2	Sheppard Street
A3	Emlyn Square	D3	Southampton Street
C3	Euclid Street	C4	Stafford Street
A3	Faringdon Road	B4	Stanier Street
B3	Farnsby Street	B2	Station Road
B2	Fleet Street	C4	Swindon Road
C3	Fleming Way	A3	Tennyson Street
C2	Gladstone Street	A3	Theobald Street
C2	Gooch Street	C4	Victoria Road
C2	Graham Street	B3	Villett Street
A1	Great Western Way	A4	Westcott Place
C3	Groundwell Road	C4	Western Street
B3	Havelock Street	B4	Whitehead Street
A1	Hawksworth Way	B4	Whitney Street
C2	Haydon Street	A4	William Street
B2	Holbrook Way	D3	York Road

Taunton

Taunton is found on atlas page **18 H10**

B2	Albemarle Road	A3	Northfield Road
D3	Alfred Street	B3	North Street
C4	Alma Street	C1	Obridge Road
B2	Belvedere Road	D2	Obridge Viaduct
C4	Billetfield	B4	Old Pig Market
C4	Billet Street	A4	Parkfield Road
B2	Bridge Street	A4	Park Street
B2	Canal Road	B4	Paul Street
A4	Cann Street	C1	Plais Street
C3	Canon Street	A3	Portland Street
A4	Castle Street	B1	Priorswood Road
B1	Cheddon Road	C3	Priory Avenue
A1	Chip Lane	C2	Priory Bridge Road
D4	Church Street	D4	Queen Street
A3	Clarence Street	B1	Railway Street
A3	Cleveland Street	C3	Ranmer Road
A4	Compass Hill	A1	Raymond Street
D2	Critchard Way	A1	Rupert Street
A1	Cyril Street	B1	St Andrew's Road
B2	Deller's Wharf	C3	St Augustine Street
C3	Duke Street	B3	St James Street
C3	Eastbourne Road	A4	St John's Road
D4	Eastleigh Road	A1	Samuels Court
D3	East Reach	C4	South Road
C4	East Street	D4	South Street
B4	Fore Street	A2	Staplegrove Road
A1	Fowler Street	B2	Station Road
A2	French Weir Avenue	C3	Stephen Street
C3	Gloucester Road	C3	Stephen Way
D3	Grays Street	C3	Tancred Street
A1	Greenway Avenue	A2	The Avenue
C3	Gyffarde Street	B3	The Bridge
B4	Hammet Street	B4	The Crescent
C3	Haydon Road	C1	The Triangle
B1	Herbert Street	B1	Thomas Street
B4	High Street	D2	Toneway
C3	Hugo Street	B4	Tower Street
C4	Hurdle Way	D4	Trinity Road
C3	Laburnam Street	D4	Trinity Street
D2	Lambrook Road	B4	Upper High Street
C1	Lansdowne Road	D3	Victoria Gate
A1	Leslie Avenue	D3	Victoria Street
A2	Linden Grove	D4	Viney Street
B3	Lower Middle Street	A4	Wellington Road
B3	Magdalene Street	C3	Wilfred Road
B4	Mary Street	B1	William Street
A1	Maxwell Street	C2	Winchester Street
B3	Middle Street	B3	Wood Street

Torquay

Torquay is found on atlas page **7 N6**

B1	Abbey Road	D1	Middle Warbury Road
C1	Alexandra Road	A1	Mill Lane
C2	Alpine Road	D3	Montpellier Road
C1	Ash Hill Road	B1	Morgan Avenue
A1	Avenue Road	D3	Museum Road
A2	Bampfylde Road	B1	Palm Road
D4	Beacon Hill	D4	Parkhill Road
A1	Belgrave Road	C1	Pembroke Road
D3	Braddons Hill Road East	D1	Pennsylvania Road
C2	Braddons Hill Road West	C2	Pimlico
D2	Braddons Street	C1	Potters Hill
A1	Bridge Road	C1	Princes Road
D1	Camden Road	C2	Queen Street
C3	Cary Parade	A2	Rathmore Road
C3	Cary Road	C2	Rock Road
C1	Castle Lane	D1	Rosehill Road
C1	Castle Road	A1	St Efride's Road
D1	Cavern Road	B2	St Luke's Road
A2	Chestnut Avenue	C1	St Marychurch Road
A1	Church Lane	B2	Scarborough Road
A1	Church Street	A4	Seaway Lane
A1	Cleveland Road	B3	Shedden Hill Road
B2	Croft Hill	A3	Solbro Road
B2	Croft Road	D3	South Hill Road
A1	East Street	A1	South Street
C1	Ellacombe Road	C2	Stentiford Hill Road
A2	Falkland Road	D3	Strand
C3	Fleet Street	D1	Sutherland Road
D2	Grafton Road	C2	Temperance Street
A4	Hennapyn Road	D3	The Terrace
B1	Higher Union Lane	A4	Torbay Road
D2	Hillesdon Road	A1	Tor Church Road
D1	Hoxton Road	B1	Tor Hill Road
D3	Hunsdon Road	D3	Torwood Street
A3	King's Drive	B1	Trematon Ave
A1	Laburnum Street	D3	Trinity Hill
A2	Lime Avenue	B1	Union Street
D1	Lower Ellacombe Church Road	D2	Upper Braddons Hill
		D4	Vanehill Road
C2	Lower Union Lane	A1	Vansittart Road
D2	Lower Warbury Road	C3	Vaughan Parade
A1	Lucius Street	D4	Victoria Parade
B1	Lymington Road	C1	Victoria Road
B1	Magdalene Road	A1	Vine Road
C2	Market Street	A2	Walnut Road
D4	Meadfoot Lane	C1	Warberry Road West
C2	Melville Lane	B2	Warren Road
C2	Melville Street	C1	Wellington Road

Tunbridge Wells

Tunbridge Wells is found on atlas page **25 N3**

C1	Albert Street	B4	High Street
C4	Arundel Road	C2	Lansdowne Road
D2	Bayhall Road	B1	Lime Hill Road
C1	Belgrave Road	A4	Linden Park Road
B4	Berkeley Road	B4	Little Mount Sion
A1	Boyne Park	A2	London Road
C4	Buckingham Road	B2	Lonsdale Gardens
C3	Calverley Gardens	B4	Madeira Park
C2	Calverley Park	A4	Major York's Road
D2	Calverley Park Gardens	B1	Meadow Road
C2	Calverley Road	A1	Molyneux Park Road
C1	Calverley Street	C2	Monson Road
D4	Cambridge Gardens	B2	Monson Way
D3	Cambridge Street	A3	Mount Edgcumbe Road
D3	Camden Hill	A2	Mount Ephraim
D3	Camden Park	B1	Mount Ephraim Road
C1	Camden Road	C3	Mountfield Gardens
D2	Carlton Road	C3	Mountfield Road
A2	Castle Road	B2	Mount Pleasant Avenue
B3	Castle Street	B2	Mount Pleasant Road
B4	Chapel Place	B4	Mount Sion
B3	Christchurch Avenue	B4	Nevill Street
A2	Church Road	B1	Newton Road
B2	Civic Way	C4	Norfolk Road
C4	Claremont Gardens	D2	North Street
C4	Claremont Road	D3	Oakfield Court Road
B2	Clarence Road	D3	Park Street
B2	Crescent Road	D2	Pembury Road
B1	Culverden Street	C4	Poona Road
C1	Dale Street	D3	Prince's Street
B1	Dudley Road	D3	Prospect Road
B4	Eden Road	B1	Rock Villa Road
A4	Eridge Road	A1	Royal Chase
C4	Farmcombe Lane	D1	St James' Road
C4	Farmcombe Road	D1	Sandrock Road
D1	Ferndale	A1	Somerville Gardens
A4	Frant Road	B3	South Green
B4	Frog Lane	B3	Station Approach
C1	Garden Road	D1	Stone Street
C1	Garden Street	C3	Sutherland Road
D3	George Street	C1	Tunnel Road
B1	Goods Station Road	B1	Upper Grosvenor Road
C4	Grecian Road	B3	Vale Avenue
B1	Grosvenor Road	B3	Vale Road
C3	Grove Hill Gardens	C1	Victoria Road
C3	Grove Hill Road	B4	Warwick Park
C3	Guildford Road	C1	Wood Street
B1	Hanover Road	B2	York Road

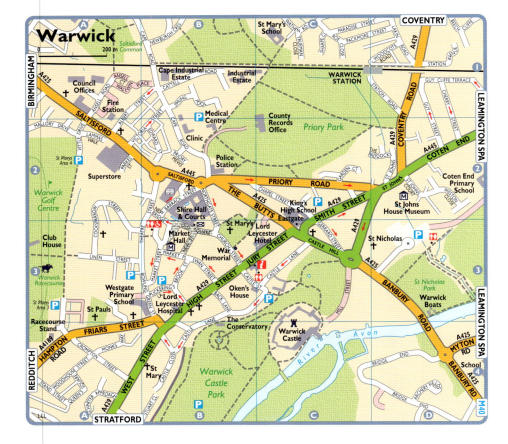

Warwick

Warwick is found on atlas page **59 L11**

A2	Albert Street	C1	Packmore Street
A1	Ansell Court	C1	Paradise Street
A1	Ansell Road	A2	Parkes Street
D4	Archery Fields	B2	Priory Mews
B3	Back Lane	C2	Priory Road
D3	Banbury Road	B3	Puckering's Lane
B2	Barrack Street	A4	Queen's Square
D1	Beech Cliffe	C1	Roe Close
B3	Bowling Green Street	D2	St Johns
D4	Bridge End	D2	St Johns Court
B3	Brook Street	A1	Saltisford
B1	Cape Road	C1	Sharpe Close
B4	Castle Close	C2	Smith Street
C3	Castle Hill	B1	Spring Pool
B4	Castle Lane	A4	Stand Street
B3	Castle Street	D1	Station Avenue
B1	Cattell Road	D1	Station Road
C2	Chapel Street	B4	Stuart Close
A4	Charter Approach	B3	Swan Street
D1	Cherry Street	B3	Theatre Street
B3	Church Street	B2	The Butts
A3	Cocksparrow Street	D2	The Paddocks
D2	Coten End	C1	Trueman Close
D2	Coventry Road	A2	Victoria Street
A4	Crompton Street	A2	Vittle Drive
B2	Edward Street	A1	Wallwin Place
A4	Friars Street	C1	Wathen Road
C2	Garden Court	D2	Weston Close
C3	Gerrard Street	A4	West Street
D1	Guy Cliffe Terrace	D1	Woodcote Road
D1	Guy Street	A4	Woodhouse Street
A4	Hampton Road		
B3	High Street		
B3	Jury Street		
D1	Lakin Road		
A2	Lammas Walk		
A3	Linen Street		
A2	Mallory Drive		
B3	Market Place		
B3	Market Street		
C3	Mill Street		
A4	Monks Way		
D4	Myton Road		
B2	New Bridge		
B1	Newburgh Crescent		
B3	New Street		
B2	Northgate Street		
B3	Old Square		

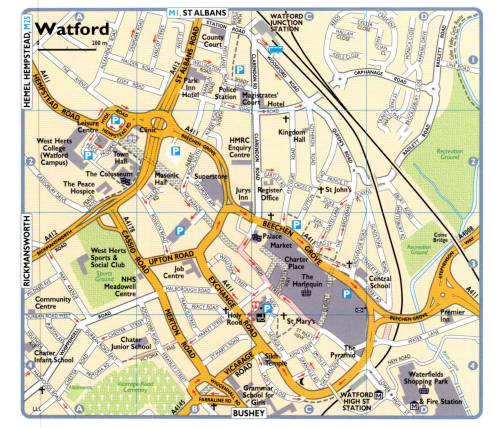

Watford

Watford is found on atlas page **50 D11**

B3	Addiscombe Road	A1	Malden Road
B2	Albert Road North	B4	Market Street
B2	Albert Road South	B3	Merton Road
A1	Alexandra Road	A3	Mildred Avenue
D1	Anglian Close	D1	Monica Close
C3	Beechen Grove	B1	Nascot Street
D2	Brocklesbury Close	D4	New Road
A4	Burton Avenue	C3	New Street
A2	Cassiobury Drive	C1	Orphanage Road
A3	Cassio Road	A3	Park Avenue
C3	Charter Way	A2	Peace Prospect
A4	Chester Road	B3	Percy Road
A4	Chester Street	A4	Pretoria Road
C1	Clarendon Road	C2	Prince Street
C2	Cross Street	C2	Queen's Road
A1	Denmark Road	C3	Queen Street
C3	Derby Road	D2	Radlett Road
C2	Duke Street	D1	Raphael Drive
A4	Durban Road East	C1	Reeds Crescent
A4	Durban Road West	A3	Rickmansworth Road
C3	Earl Street	B3	Rosslyn Road
D2	Ebury Road	B1	St Albans Road
A1	Essex Road	B1	St John's Road
C2	Estcourt Road	B4	St Mary's Road
B3	Exchange Road	D1	St Pauls Way
B4	Farraline Road	B1	Shady Lane
B4	Fernaly Street	D2	Shaftesbury Road
B3	Francis Street	C4	Smith Street
B1	Franklin Road	C2	Sotheron Road
C2	Gartlet Road	A4	Southsea Avenue
B2	Gaumont Approach	C3	Stanley Road
C4	George Street	B1	Station Road
D3	Gladstone Road	D3	Stephenson Way
C4	Granville Road	C2	Sutton Road
C3	Grosvenor Road	A1	The Avenue
B2	Halsey Road	C3	The Broadway
A4	Harwoods Road	C4	The Crescent
A1	Hempstead Road	B2	The Parade
C3	High Street	B3	Upton Road
A2	Hyde Road	B4	Vicarage Road
C1	Keele Close	D4	Water Lane
C4	King Street	B1	Wellington Road
C4	Lady's Close	B3	Wellstone Street
D1	Link Road	B1	Westland Road
C3	Loates Lane	B1	West Street
C3	Lord Street	A4	Whippendell Road
D4	Lower High Street	B4	Wiggenhall Road
B3	Malborough Road	C1	Woodford Road

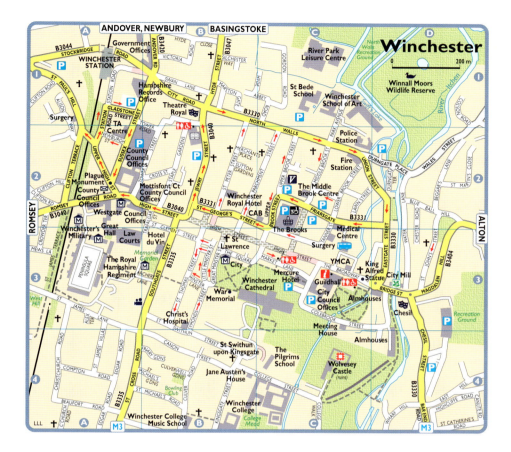

Winchester

Winchester is found on atlas page **22 E9**

A3	Alex Terrace	C3	Market Lane
A1	Alison Way	B1	Marston Gate
B1	Andover Road	B2	Merchants Place
A3	Archery Lane	A3	Mews Lane
D4	Bar End Road	C2	Middle Brook Street
A4	Beaufort Road	B3	Minster Lane
D2	Beggar's Lane	A2	Newburgh Street
D2	Blue Ball Hill	B1	North Walls
D3	Bridge Street	B2	Parchment Street
B4	Canon Street	C2	Park Avenue
D4	Canute Road	A2	Romsey Road
D3	Chesil Street	D4	St Catherine's Road
D2	Chester Road	B2	St Clement Street
A4	Christchurch Road	A4	St Cross Road
B1	City Road	B2	St George's Street
A2	Clifton Hill	A3	St James' Lane
A1	Clifton Road	A3	St James Terrace
A2	Clifton Terrace	A4	St James' Villas
C3	Colebrook Street	D3	St John's Street
B4	College Street	D2	St Martin's Close
C4	College Walk	B4	St Michael's Gardens
D1	Colson Road	B4	St Michael's Road
A4	Compton Road	A1	St Paul's Hill
B2	Cross Street	B2	St Peter Street
A3	Crowder Terrace	B3	St Swithun Street
B4	Culver Road	B3	St Thomas Street
B4	Culverwell Gardens	B1	Silchester Way
D2	Durngate Place	B3	Southgate Street
D2	Durngate Terrace	B2	Staple Gardens
D3	Eastgate Street	A1	Station Road
D4	East Hill	A1	Stockbridge Road
A4	Edgar Road	A2	Sussex Street
C2	Friarsgate	B2	Sutton Gardens
B4	Friary Gardens	B1	Swan Lane
A1	Gladstone Street	B3	Symonds Street
C1	Gordon Road	C3	Tanner Street
B3	Great Minster Street	C3	The Broadway
D4	Highcliffe Road	B3	The Square
B2	High Street	A1	Tower Road
B1	Hyde Abbey Road	A2	Tower Street
B1	Hyde Close	B3	Trafalgar Street
B1	Hyde Street	C2	Union Street
B2	Jewry Street	C2	Upper Brook Street
B4	Kingsgate Street	A2	Upper High Street
C2	Lawn Street	B1	Victoria Road
B3	Little Minster Street	D2	Wales Street
C2	Lower Brook Street	D3	Water Lane
D3	Magdalen Hill	D4	Wharf Hill

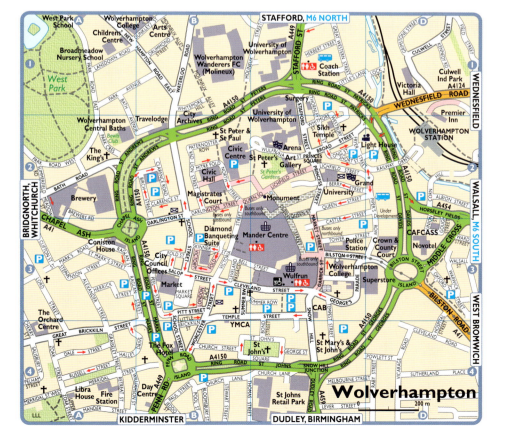

Wolverhampton

Wolverhampton is found on atlas page **58 D5**

A3	Alexander Street	B1	Park Road East
A1	Bath Avenue	A2	Park Road West
A2	Bath Road	B3	Peel Street
B3	Bell Street	B4	Penn Road
D3	Bilston Road	D2	Piper's Row
C3	Bilston Street	B3	Pitt Street
B2	Birch Street	D4	Powlett Street
C2	Broad Street	C2	Princess Street
C3	Castle Street	B2	Queen Square
A3	Chapel Ash	C2	Queen Street
B4	Church Lane	D4	Raby Street
B4	Church Street	A3	Raglan Street
B2	Clarence Road	D2	Railway Drive
B2	Clarence Street	B2	Red Lion Street
D4	Cleveland Road	A4	Retreat Street
B3	Cleveland Street	A2	Ring Road St Andrews
D2	Corn Hill	D2	Ring Road St Davids
D1	Culwell Street	C4	Ring Road St Georges
A4	Dale Street	B4	Ring Road St Johns
B3	Darlington Street	B3	Ring Road St Marks
C4	Dudley Road	C1	Ring Road St Patricks
C2	Dudley Street	B2	Ring Road St Peters
B3	Fold Street	A4	Russell Street
C2	Fryer Street	C4	St John's Square
C3	Garrick Street	A3	St Mark's Road
C3	George's Parade	A3	St Mark's Street
A4	Graiseley Street	B3	Salop Street
A4	Great Brickkiln Street	B3	School Street
C1	Great Western Street	B3	Skinner Street
D1	Grimstone Street	C3	Snow Hill
A3	Herrick Street	C1	Stafford Street
D2	Horseley Fields	A3	Stephenson Street
D4	Hospital Street	B4	Stewart Street
A1	Lansdown Road	B3	Summer Row
C4	Lever Street	D4	Sutherland Place
C2	Lichfield Street	B3	Temple Street
C1	Little's Lane	B4	Thomas Street
C2	Long Street	C3	Tower Street
A3	Lord Street	D4	Vicarage Road
A4	Mander Street	B3	Victoria Street
C3	Market Street	B1	Waterloo Road
A4	Merridal Street	D1	Wednesfield Road
D3	Middle Cross	C2	Westbury Street
B2	Mitre Fold	B1	Whitmore Hill
B1	Molineux Street	C2	Whitmore Street
A1	New Hampton Road East	B4	Worcester Street
B2	North Street	C2	Wulfruna Street
A1	Park Avenue	A4	Zoar Street

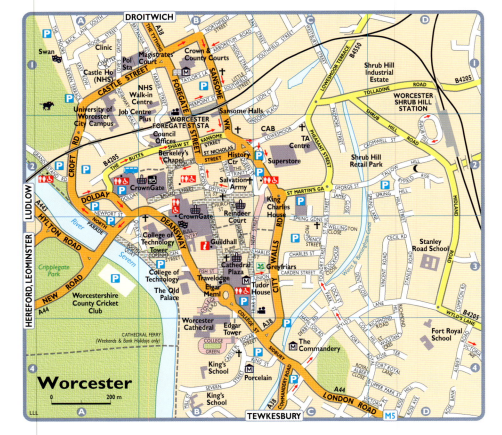

Worcester

Worcester is found on atlas page **46 G4**

D4	Albert Road	B1	Middle Street
B2	Angel Street	D2	Midland Road
B1	Arboretum Road	B4	Mill Street
A1	Back Lane South	A1	Moor Street
C3	Blockhouse Close	A2	Newport Street
A1	Britannia Road	A3	New Road
B2	Broad Street	C3	New Street
D2	Byfield Rise	B1	Northfield Street
C3	Carden Street	A3	North Parade
A1	Castle Street	C1	Padmore Street
A4	Cathedral Ferry	C3	Park Street
D3	Cecil Road	C2	Pheasant Street
C3	Charles Street	B1	Pierpoint Street
A1	Charter Place	C3	Providence Street
B2	Church Street	B3	Pump Street
C3	City Walls Road	A3	Quay Street
C4	Cole Hill	B2	Queen Street
B3	College Street	D4	Richmond Road
C4	Commandery Road	D4	Rose Hill
D3	Compton Road	D4	Rose Terrace
B3	Copenhagen Street	C2	St Martin's Gate
A2	Croft Road	B2	St Nicholas Street
D2	Cromwell Street	C3	St Paul's Street
B3	Deansway	B2	St Swithin Street
C3	Dent Close	B1	Sansome Walk
C4	Derby Road	B4	Severn Street
A2	Dolday	A1	Severn Terrace
B1	East Street	B2	Shaw Street
B4	Edgar Street	D2	Shrub Hill Road
B1	Farrier Street	C4	Sidbury
B3	Fish Street	C1	Southfield Street
B1	Foregate Street	D2	Spring Hill
C4	Fort Royal Hill	D3	Stanley Road
C3	Foundry Street	D2	Tallow Hill
C3	Friar Street	B1	Taylor's Lane
C2	George Street	A2	The Butts
A2	Grandstand Road	B2	The Cross
C3	Hamilton Road	A1	The Moors
B3	High Street	B2	The Shambles
D2	Hill Street	B1	The Tything
A3	Hylton Road	C1	Tolladine Road
B4	King Street	B2	Trinity Street
B1	Little Southfield Street	C3	Union Street
C3	Lock Street	D4	Upper Park Street
C4	London Road	D3	Vincent Road
A1	Love's Grove	C3	Wellington Close
C2	Lowesmoor	C1	Westbury Street
C1	Lowesmoor Terrace	C4	Wyld's Lane

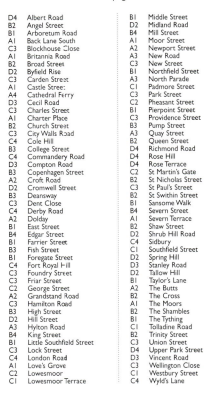

York

York is found on atlas page **98 C10**

C2	Aldwark	C3	Lower Ousegate
D4	Barbican Road	B3	Lower Priory Street
B4	Bishopgate Street	C2	Low Petergate
B3	Bishophill Senior	D3	Margaret Street
D2	Black Horse Lane	C2	Market Street
B2	Blake Street	A3	Micklegate
A4	Blossom Street	B1	Minster Yard
B1	Bootham	C1	Monkgate
B3	Bridge Street	B2	Museum Street
B3	Buckingham Street	D3	Navigation Road
D4	Cemetery Road	B2	New Street
C2	Church Street	B2	North Street
C3	Clifford Street	A3	Nunnery Lane
C1	College Street	C1	Ogleforth
C2	Colliergate	D2	Palmer Lane
B2	Coney Street	D2	Palmer Street
C3	Coppergate	D4	Paragon Street
B4	Cromwell Road	C2	Parliament Street
B2	Davygate	C2	Pavement
C1	Deangate	D2	Peasholme Green
B4	Dove Street	D3	Percy's Lane
B2	Duncombe Place	C3	Piccadilly
D2	Dundas Street	B4	Price's Lane
B3	Fairfax Street	C3	Priory Street
D4	Fawcett Street	A3	Queen Street
C2	Feasegate	B2	Rougier Street
B3	Fetter Lane	C2	St Andrewgate
C2	Finkle Street	D3	St Denys' Road
C4	Fishergate	B1	St Leonard's Place
D1	Foss Bank	B3	St Martins Lane
C3	Fossgate	C1	St Maurice's Road
D2	Foss Islands Road	C2	St Saviourgate
D3	George Street	C2	St Saviours Place
B1	Gillygate	A4	Scarcroft Road
C2	Goodramgate	C2	Shambles
B4	Hampden Street	C2	Skeldergate
C3	High Ousegate	B2	Spen Lane
B1	High Petergate	A3	Spurriergate
A4	Holgate Road	A3	Station Road
D4	Hope Street	B2	Stonegate
D2	Hungate	C2	Swinegate
D1	Jewbury	C2	The Stonebow
D4	Kent Street	A3	Toft Green
C3	King Street	C3	Tower Street
B4	Kyme Street	B3	Trinity Lane
B2	Lendal	B4	Victor Street
D4	Long Close Lane	D3	Walmgate
C1	Lord Mayor's Walk	B2	Wellington Road

Major airports

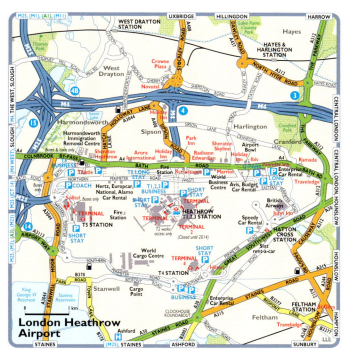

London Heathrow Airport – 16 miles west of London

Telephone: 0844 335 1801 or visit *www.heathrowairport.com*
Parking: short-stay, long-stay and business parking is available.
For booking and charges tel: 0844 335 1000
Public Transport: coach, bus, rail and London Underground.
There are several 4-star and 3-star hotels within easy reach of the airport.
Car hire facilities are available.

London Gatwick Airport – 35 miles south of London

Telephone: 0844 335 1802 or visit *www.gatwickairport.com*
Parking: short and long-stay parking is available at both the North and South terminals.
For booking and charges tel: 0844 811 8311 or visit *parking.gatwickairport.com*
Public Transport: coach, bus and rail.
There are several 4-star and 3-star hotels within easy reach of the airport.
Car hire facilities are available.

London Stansted Airport – 36 miles north east of London

Telephone: 0844 335 1803 or visit *www.stanstedairport.com*
Parking: short, mid and long-stay open-air parking is available.
For booking and charges tel: 0844 335 1000
Public Transport: coach, bus and direct rail link to London on the Stansted Express.
There are several hotels within easy reach of the airport.
Car hire facilities are available.

London Luton Airport – 33 miles north of London

Telephone: 01582 405100 or visit *www.london-luton.co.uk*
Parking: short-term, mid-term and long-stay parking is available.
For booking and charges tel: 01582 405 100
Public Transport: coach, bus and rail.
There are several hotels within easy reach of the airport.
Car hire facilities are available.

Major airports

London City Airport – 7 miles east of London

Telephone: 020 7646 0088 or visit *www.londoncityairport.com*
Parking: short and long-stay open-air parking is available.
For booking and charges tel: 0871 360 1390
Public Transport: easy access to the rail network, Docklands Light Railway and the London Underground.
There are 5-star, 4-star and 3-star hotels within easy reach of the airport.
Car hire facilities are available.

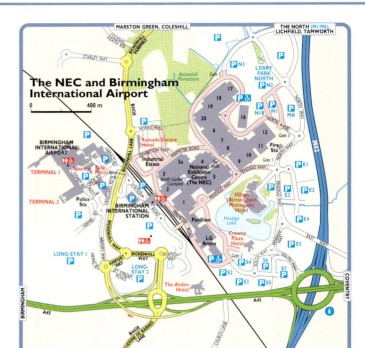

Birmingham International Airport – 8 miles east of Birmingham

Telephone: 0844 576 6000 or visit *www.birminghamairport.co.uk*
Parking: short, mid-term and long-stay parking is available.
For booking and charges tel: 0844 576 6000
Public Transport: Air-Rail Link service operates every 2 minutes to and from Birmingham International Railway Station & Interchange.
There is one 3-star hotel adjacent to the airport and several 4 and 3-star hotels within easy reach of the airport. Car hire facilities are available.

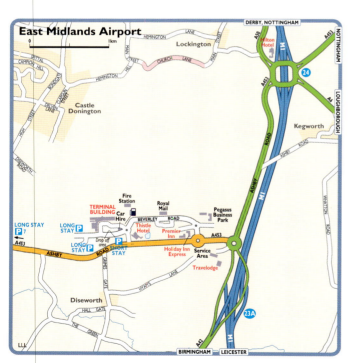

East Midlands Airport – 15 miles south west of Nottingham, next to the M1 at junctions 23A and 24

Telephone: 0871 919 9000 or visit *www.eastmidlandsairport.com*
Parking: short and long-stay parking is available.
For booking and charges tel: 0871 310 3300
Public Transport: bus and coach services to major towns and cities in the East Midlands.
Call 0870 608 2608 for information.
There are several 3-star hotels within easy reach of the airport.
Car hire facilities are available.

Manchester Airport – 10 miles south of Manchester

Telephone: 0871 271 0711 or visit *www.manchesterairport.co.uk*
Parking: short and long-stay parking is available.
For booking and charges tel: 0871 310 2200
Public Transport: bus, coach and rail.
There are several 4-star and 3-star hotels within easy reach of the airport.
Car hire facilities are available.

Major airports

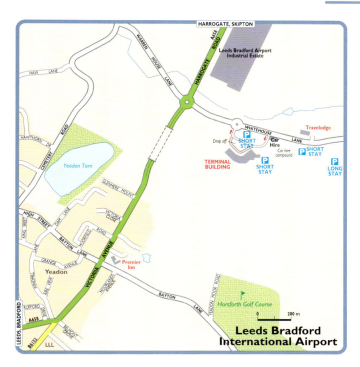

Leeds Bradford International Airport – 7 miles north east of Bradford and 9 miles north west of Leeds

Telephone: 0113 250 9696 or visit www.leedsbradfordairport.co.uk
Parking: short, mid-term and long-stay parking is available.
For booking and charges tel: 0113 250 9696
Public Transport: bus service operates every 30 minutes from Bradford, Leeds and Otley.
There are several 4-star and 3-star hotels within easy reach of the airport.
Car hire facilities are available.

Aberdeen Airport – 7 miles north west of Aberdeen

Telephone: 0844 481 6666 or visit www.aberdeenairport.com
Parking: short and long-stay parking is available.
For booking and charges tel: 0844 335 1000
Public Transport: regular bus service to central Aberdeen.
There are several 4-star and 3-star hotels within easy reach of the airport.
Car hire facilities are available.

Edinburgh Airport – 7 miles west of Edinburgh

Telephone: 0844 481 8989 or visit www.edinburghairport.com
Parking: short and long-stay parking is available.
For booking and charges tel: 0844 335 1000
Public Transport: regular bus services to central Edinburgh.
There are several 4-star and 3-star hotels within easy reach of the airport.
Car hire facilities are available.

Glasgow Airport – 8 miles west of Glasgow

Telephone: 0844 481 5555 or visit www.glasgowairport.com
Parking: short and long-stay parking is available.
For booking and charges tel: 0844 335 1000
Public Transport: regular coach services operate direct to central Glasgow and Edinburgh.
There are several 3-star hotels within easy reach of the airport.
Car hire facilities are available.

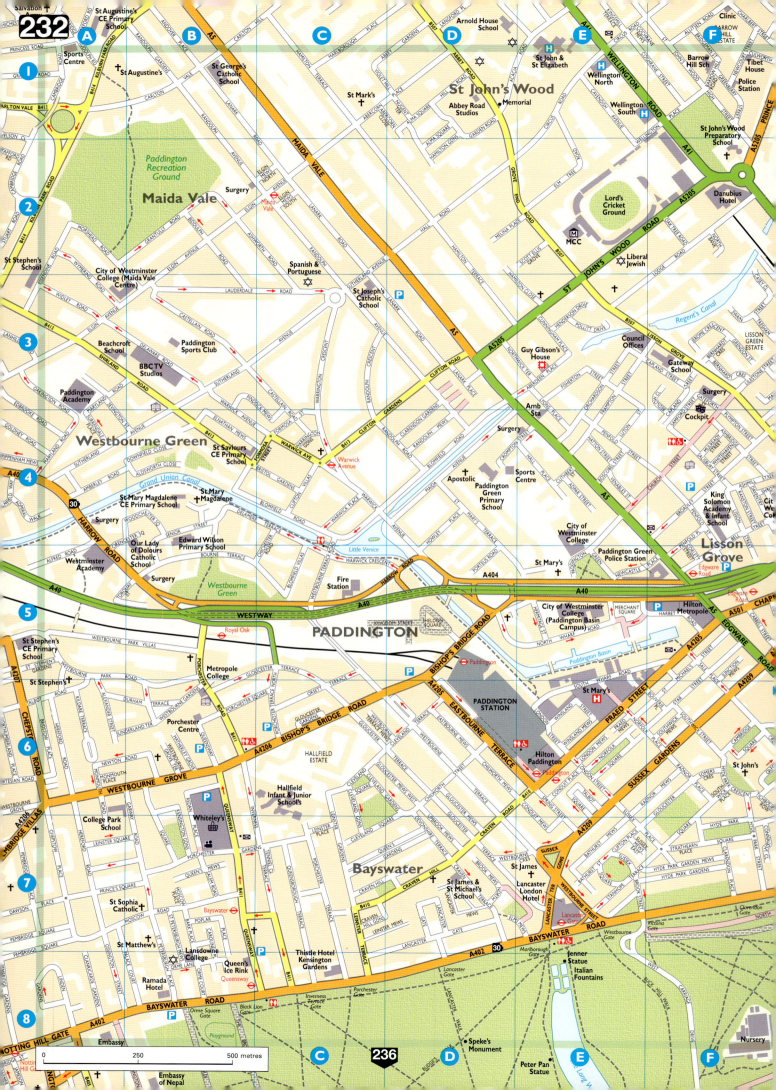

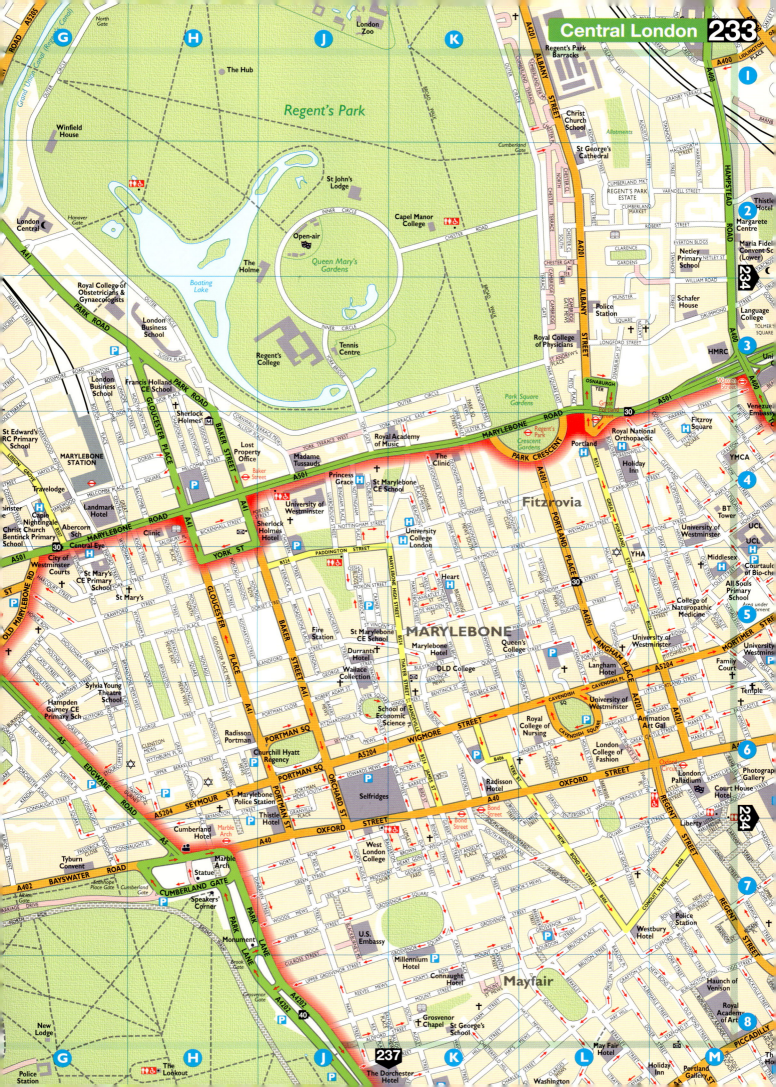

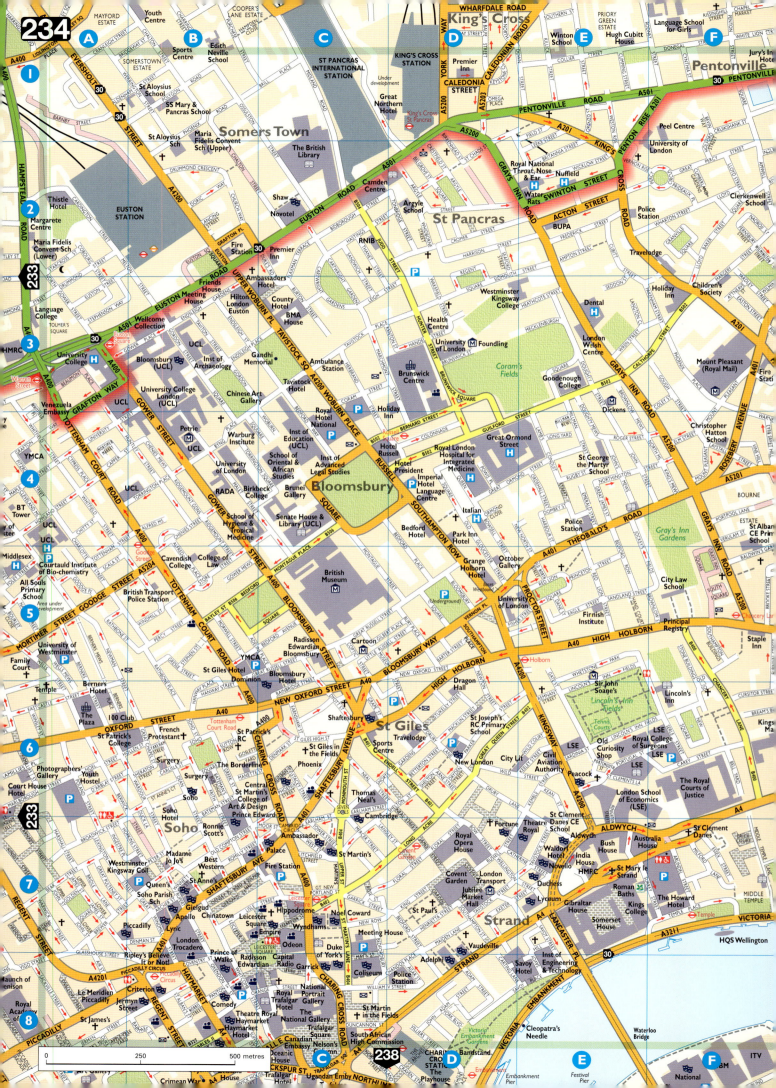

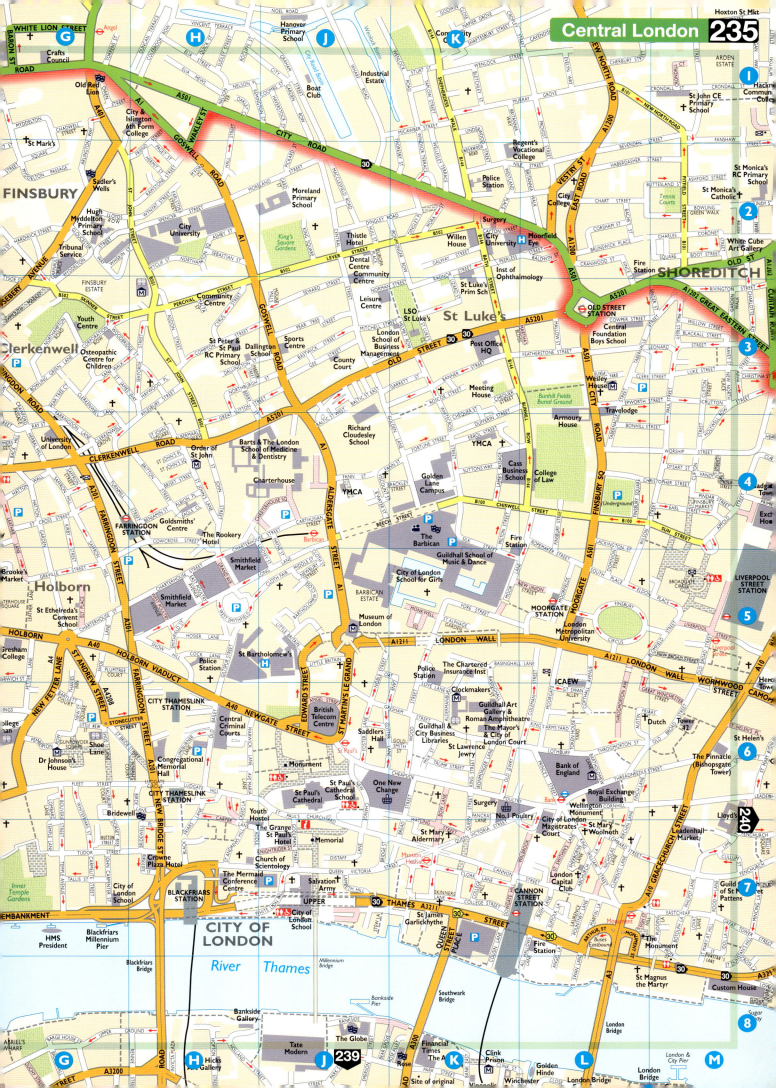

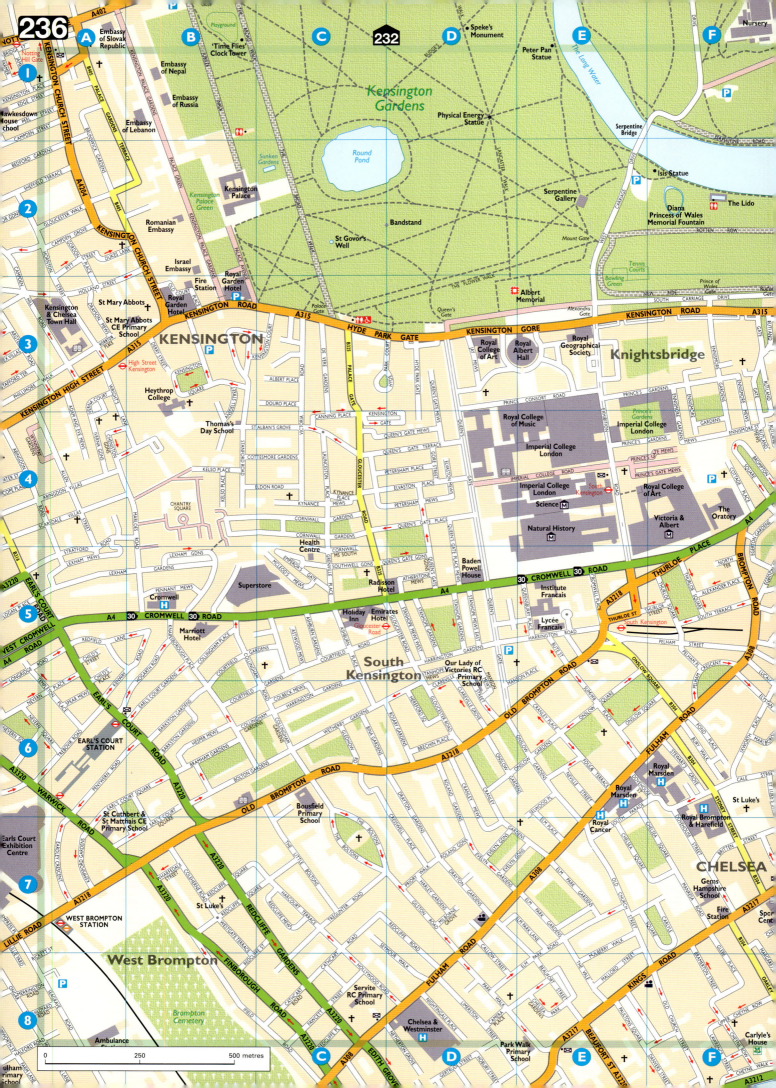

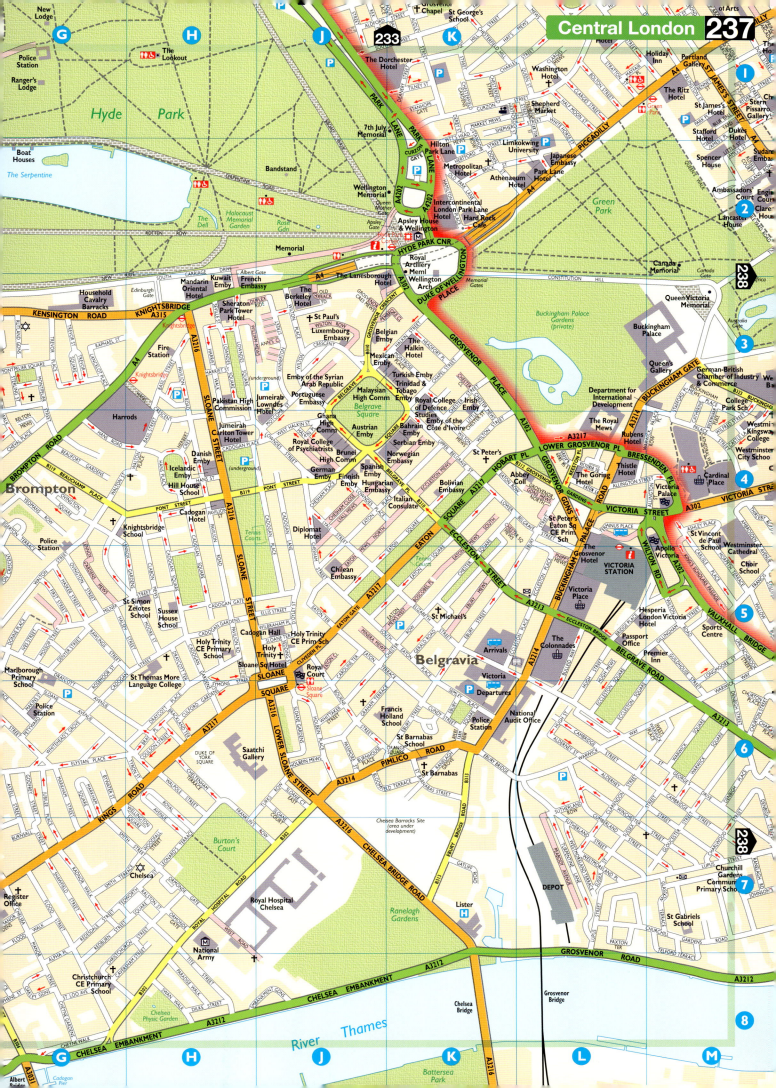

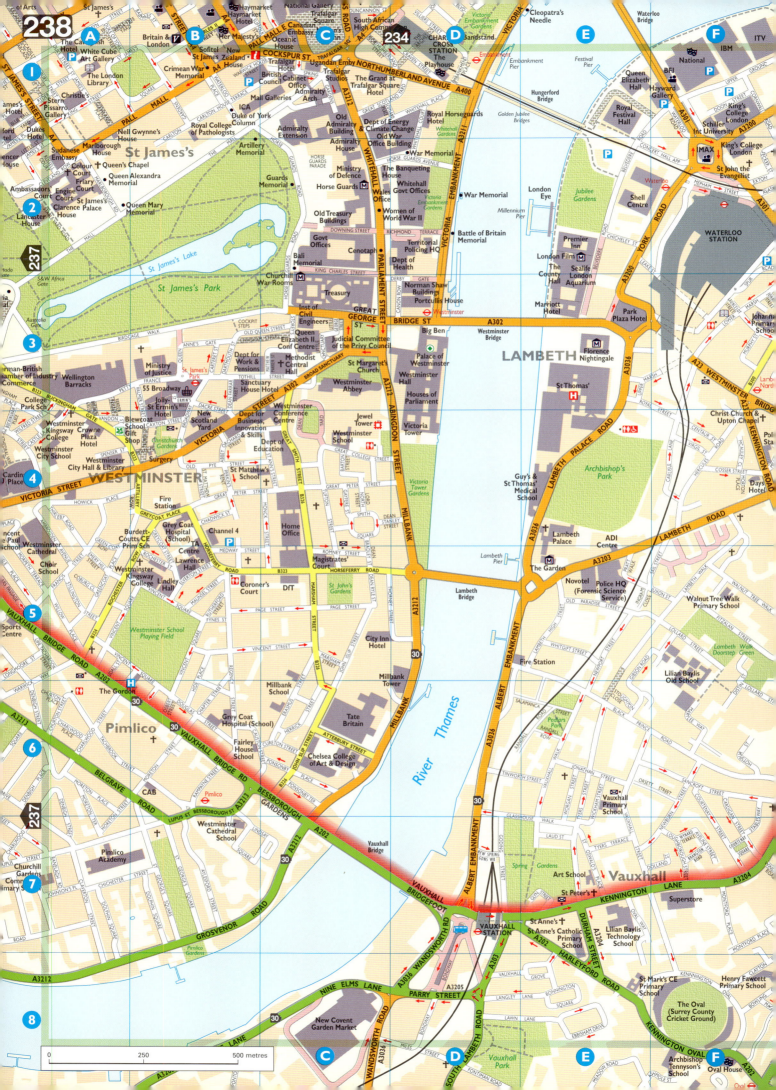

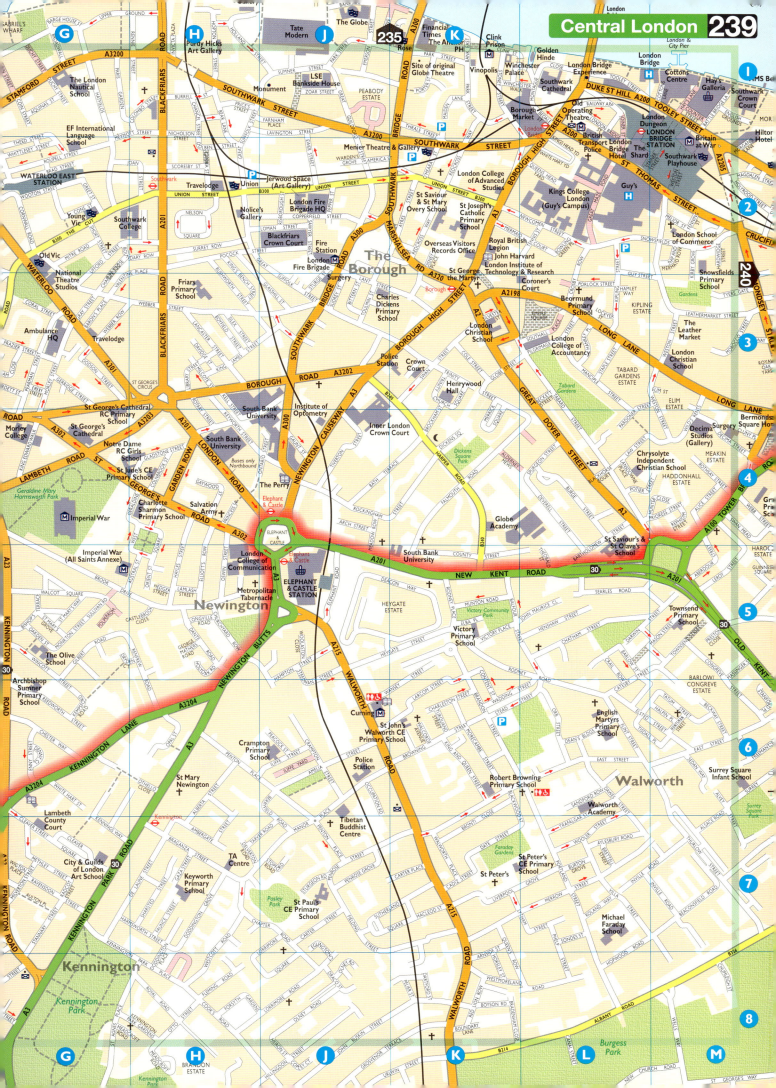

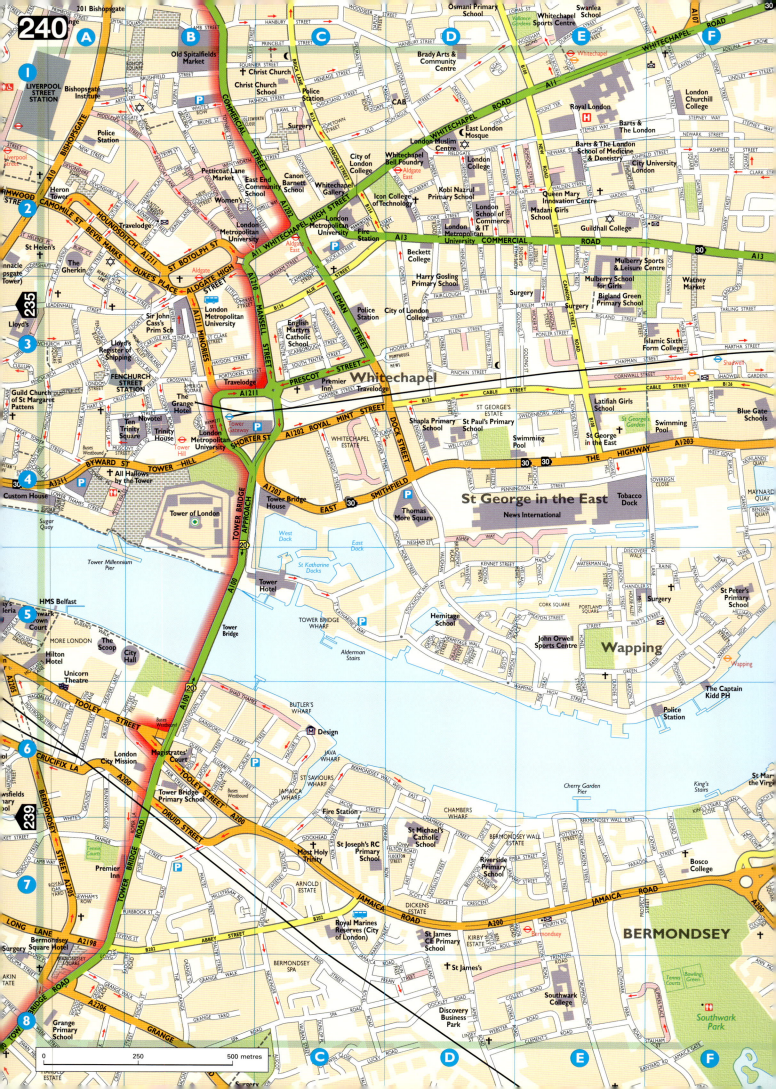

Central London street index

In this index, street and station names are listed in alphabetical order and written in full, but may be abbreviated on the map. Each entry is followed by its Postcode District and each street name is preceded by the page number and the grid reference to the square in which the name is found. Names are asterisked (*) in the index where there is insufficient space to show them on the map.

A

232 C1 **Abbey Gardens** NW8
238 B4 **Abbey Orchard Street** SW1P
232 D1 **Abbey Road** NW8
240 B7 **Abbey Street** SE1
235 L7 **Abchurch Lane** EC4N
232 C1 **Abercorn Close** NW8
232 C1 **Abercorn Place** NW8
232 E3 **Aberdeen Place** NW8
239 M5 **Aberdour Street** SE1
236 A4 **Abingdon Road** W8
238 C3 **Abingdon Street** SW1P
236 A4 **Abingdon Villas** W8
232 D1 **Acacia Road** NW8
241 L1 **Ackroyd Drive** E3
241 K5 **Acorn Walk** SE16
234 E2 **Acton Street** WC1X
236 A3 **Adam and Eve Mews** W8
233 K8 **Adam's Row** W1K
234 D8 **Adam Street** WC2N
235 H7 **Addle** EC4V
240 F1 **Adelina Grove** E1
234 B5 **Adeline Place** WC1B
240 D2 **Adler Street** E1
241 K5 **Admiral Place** SE16
232 A4 **Admiral Walk** W9
232 E4 **Adpar Street** W2
234 D8 **Agar Street** WC2N
235 H3 **Agdon Street** EC1V
241 L2 **Agnes Street** E14
241 G6 **Ainsty Street** SE16
234 A8 **Air Street** W1B
238 F2 **Alaska Street** SE1
239 L8 **Albany Road** SE5
233 L1 **Albany Street** NW1
233 L8 **Albemarle Street** W1S
235 H4 **Albermarle Way** EC1V
239 H6 **Alberta Street** SE17
237 G8 **Albert Bridge** SW3
238 D7 **Albert Embankment** SE1
241 H3 **Albert Gardens** E1
237 H2 **Albert Gate** SW1X
236 C3 **Albert Place** W8
233 G7 **Albion Gate** W2
235 H4 **Albion Place** EC1M
241 G7 **Albion Street** SE16
233 G7 **Albion Street** W2
234 A1 **Aldenham Street** NW1
235 K6 **Aldermanbury** EC2V
239 K4 **Alderney Mews** SE1
237 L6 **Alderney Street** SW1V
235 J4 **Aldersgate Street** EC1A
233 J8 **Aldford Street** W1K
240 B3 **Aldgate** EC3M
240 B2 **Aldgate** ⊖ EC3N
240 D2 **Aldgate East** ⊖ E1
240 B3 **Aldgate High Street** EC3N
232 B4 **Aldsworth Close** W9
234 E7 **Aldwych** WC2E
236 F5 **Alexander Place** SW7
232 A6 **Alexander Street** W2
236 E3 **Alexandra Gate** SW7
234 B4 **Alfred Mews** WC1E
234 B4 **Alfred Place** WC1E
232 A5 **Alfred Road** W2
239 M4 **Alice Street** SE1
240 C3 **Alie Street** E1
236 A4 **Allen Street** W8
235 L8 **All Hallows Lane** EC4R
237 L4 **Allington Street** SW1E
232 F1 **Allitsen Road** NW8
233 H4 **Allsop Place** NW1
232 D1 **Alma Square** NW8
237 G8 **Alpha Place** SW3
239 M7 **Alsace Road** SE17
240 C8 **Alscot Road** SE1
239 M6 **Alvey Street** SE17
239 H7 **Ambergate Street** SE17
232 A4 **Amberley Road** W9
238 A4 **Ambrosden Avenue** SW1P
239 J6 **Amelia Street** SE17
240 B3 **America Square** EC3N
239 J2 **America Street** SE1
234 E2 **Ampton Street** WC1X
234 F2 **Amwell Street** EC1R
241 M6 **Anchorage Point** E14
232 B1 **Andover Place** NW6
235 G1 **Angel** ⊖ N1
235 L8 **Angel Lane** EC4R
235 J6 **Angel Street** EC1A
240 F8 **Ann Moss Way** SE16
237 J3 **Ann's Close** SW1X
236 B4 **Ansdell Street** W8
241 H2 **Antill Terrace** E1
240 B2 **Antizan Street** E1
234 A8 **Apple Tree Yard** SW1Y
235 M4 **Appold Street** EC2A
237 J2 **Apsley Gate** W1J
239 G1 **Aquinas Street** SE1
241 H2 **Arbour Square** E1
241 J7 **Archangels** SE16
234 B7 **Archer Street** W1B
239 J4 **Arch Street** SE1
235 M1 **Arden Estate** N1
234 D2 **Argyle Square** WC1H
234 D2 **Argyle Street** WC1H
236 A3 **Argyll Road** W8
233 M6 **Argyll Street** W1F
237 M1 **Arlington Street** SW1A
235 G2 **Arlington Way** EC1R
234 D6 **Arne Street** WC2H
241 M8 **Arnhem Place** E14
240 C7 **Arnold Estate** SE1
239 K8 **Arnside Street** SE17
232 A6 **Artesian Road** W11
235 L7 **Arthur Street** EC4V
240 E4 **Artichoke Hill** E1W
240 A1 **Artillery Lane** E1
238 B4 **Artillery Row** SW1P
234 F7 **Arundel Street** WC2R
232 F4 **Ashbridge Street** NW8
236 C5 **Ashburn Gardens** SW7
236 C5 **Ashburn Place** SW7
235 H2 **Ashby Street** EC1V
240 D4 **Asher Way** E1W
240 E2 **Ashfield Street** E1
235 M2 **Ashford Street** N1
237 M4 **Ashley Place** SW1P
232 F4 **Ashmill Street** NW1
238 F8 **Ashmole Street** SW8
232 B2 **Ashworth Road** W9
240 C2 **Assam Street** E1
241 G1 **Assembly Place** E1
237 G6 **Astell Street** SW3
241 K1 **Aston Street** E14
236 C5 **Astwood Mews** SW7
236 D5 **Atherstone Mews** SW7
238 C6 **Atterbury Street** SW1P
234 F3 **Attneave Street** WC1X
233 L1 **Augustus Street** NW1
239 G7 **Aulton Place** SE11
235 L6 **Austin Friars** EC2N
237 M3 **Australia Gate** SW1A
239 H5 **Austral Street** SE11
238 F7 **Aveline Street** SE11
235 H6 **Ave Maria Lane** EC1A
241 J6 **Avenue Dock Hill** SE16
237 K6 **Avery Farm Row** SW1W
233 L7 **Avery Row** W1K
233 J5 **Aybrook Street** W1U
239 L7 **Aylesbury Road** SE17
235 H4 **Aylesbury Street** EC1R
238 B7 **Aylesford Street** SW1V
241 G2 **Aylward Street** E1
239 K2 **Ayres Street** SE1

B

234 B8 **Babmaes Street** SW1Y
235 L2 **Bache's Street** N1
240 D3 **Back Church Lane** E1
235 G4 **Back Hill** EC1R
240 B8 **Bacon Grove** SE1
234 C6 **Bainbridge Street** WC2H
233 J6 **Bakers Mews** W1U
235 G4 **Baker's Row** EC1R
233 H4 **Baker Street** NW1
233 J5 **Baker Street** W1U
233 H4 **Baker Street** ⊖ NW1
233 G3 **Balcombe Street** NW1
233 J7 **Balderton Street** W1K
234 F5 **Baldwin's Gardens** EC1N
235 L2 **Baldwin Street** EC1V
241 J1 **Bale Road** E1
234 D1 **Balfe Street** N1
233 K8 **Balfour Mews** W1K
233 J8 **Balfour Place** W1K
239 K5 **Balfour Street** SE17
235 J3 **Baltic Street East** EC1V
235 J4 **Baltic Street West** EC1Y
235 L6 **Bank** ⊖ ⊖ EC2R
239 K1 **Bank East** SE1
239 J1 **Bankside** SE1
235 K3 **Banner Street** EC1Y
240 E8 **Banyard Road** SE16
235 J4 **Barbican** ⊖ EC1A
235 J5 **Barbican Estate** EC2Y
239 G1 **Barge House Street** SE1
232 B7 **Bark Place** W2
236 B6 **Barkston Gardens** SW5
241 L4 **Barley Corn Way** E14
239 M5 **Barlow/Congreve Estate** SE17
233 L7 **Barlow Place** W1J
239 L5 **Barlow Street** SE17
241 H3 **Barnardo Street** E1
234 A1 **Barnby Street** NW1
241 J2 **Barnes Street** E14
240 A6 **Barnham Street** SE1
239 G3 **Baron's Place** SE1
235 G1 **Baron Street** N1
233 K6 **Barrett Street** W1U
232 F1 **Barrow Hill Estate** NW8
232 F1 **Barrow Hill Road** NW8
234 D5 **Barter Street** WC1A
235 J5 **Bartholomew Close** EC1A
235 L6 **Bartholomew Lane** EC2R
239 L5 **Bartholomew Street** SE1
235 G6 **Bartlett Court** EC4A
238 C4 **Barton Street** SW1P
237 H4 **Basil Street** SW3
241 K3 **Basin Approach** E14
235 K5 **Basinghall Lane** EC2V
235 K5 **Basinghall Street** EC2V
235 J3 **Bastwick Street** EC1V
234 B6 **Bateman's Buildings** W1D
234 B6 **Bateman Street** W1D
235 K2 **Bath Street** EC1V
239 J4 **Bath Terrace** SE1
232 E7 **Bathurst Mews** W2
232 E7 **Bathurst Street** W2
239 M1 **Battle Bridge Lane** SE1
240 D2 **Batty Street** E1
234 B5 **Bayley Street** WC1B
238 F3 **Baylis Road** SE1
232 B7 **Bayswater** ⊖ W2
232 D7 **Bayswater Road** W2
241 L1 **Baythorne Street** E3
239 M7 **Beaconsfield Road** SE17
234 A7 **Beak Street** W1F
239 J1 **Bear Grove** SE1
239 H1 **Bear Lane** SE1
237 G4 **Beauchamp Place** SW3
237 G4 **Beaufort Gardens** SW3
236 E8 **Beaufort Street** SW3
234 A3 **Beaumont Place** W1T
233 K4 **Beaumont Street** W1G
241 M3 **Beccles Street** E14
239 L3 **Beckett Street** SE1
239 M6 **Beckway Street** SE17
239 L1 **Bedale Street** SE1
234 C5 **Bedford Avenue** WC1B
234 C7 **Bedfordbury** WC2N
236 A2 **Bedford Gardens** W8
234 D4 **Bedford Place** WC1N
234 E4 **Bedford Row** WC1R
234 B5 **Bedford Square** WC1B
234 D7 **Bedford Street** WC2E
234 C3 **Bedford Way** WC1H
232 F3 **Bedlow Close** NW8
235 J4 **Beech Street** EC2Y
237 L4 **Beeston Place** SW1W
237 J3 **Belgrave Mews North** * SW1X
237 K4 **Belgrave Mews South** * SW1X
237 J4 **Belgrave Place** SW1X
237 L5 **Belgrave Road** SW1V
238 A6 **Belgrave Road** SW1V
237 J3 **Belgrave Square** SW1X
241 J2 **Belgrave Street** E1
234 D2 **Belgrove Street** WC1H
240 B1 **Bell Lane** E1
232 F4 **Bell Street** NW1
234 F6 **Bell Yard** WC2A
238 E2 **Belvedere Road** SE1
235 H4 **Benjamin Street** EC1M
241 J1 **Ben Jonson Road** E1
237 M1 **Bennett Street** SW1A
240 D7 **Ben Smith Way** SE16
240 F4 **Benson Quay** E1W
233 K6 **Bentinck Mews** W1U
233 K6 **Bentinck Street** W1U
241 H3 **Bere Street** E1W
241 K8 **Bergen Square** SE16
233 H6 **Berkeley Mews** W1H
233 L8 **Berkeley Square** W1J
233 L8 **Berkeley Street** W1J
240 E7 **Bermondsey** ⊖ ⊖ SE16
240 C8 **Bermondsey Spa** SE16
240 A8 **Bermondsey Square** SE1
240 A6 **Bermondsey Street** SE1
240 E7 **Bermondsey Wall East** SE16
240 D7 **Bermondsey Wall Estate** SE16
240 C6 **Bermondsey Wall West** SE16
234 D4 **Bernard Street** WC1N
234 A5 **Berners Mews** W1T
234 A6 **Berners Place** W1F
234 A5 **Berners Street** W1T
232 F3 **Bernhardt Crescent** NW8
239 J6 **Berryfield Road** SE17
235 H3 **Berry Street** EC1V
234 A6 **Berwick Street** W1F
238 B6 **Bessborough Gardens** SW1V
238 B6 **Bessborough Street** SW1V
234 D6 **Betterton Street** WC2H
235 L2 **Bevenden Street** N1
241 J5 **Bevin Close** SE16
240 D7 **Bevington Street** SE16
234 F1 **Bevin Way** WC1X
240 A2 **Bevis Marks** EC3A
240 F3 **Bewley Street** E1
233 H4 **Bickenhall Street** W1U
234 C2 **Bidborough Street** WC1H
232 B2 **Biddulph Road** W9
240 E3 **Bigland Street** E1
240 A3 **Billiter Square** EC3M
240 A3 **Billiter Street** EC3M
236 C6 **Bina Gardens** SW5
233 J4 **Bingham Place** W1U
233 K7 **Binney Street** W1K
241 M3 **Birchfield Street** E14
235 L7 **Birchin Lane** EC3V
238 A3 **Birdcage Walk** W1H
235 H6 **Birde Lane** EC4Y
233 K6 **Bird Street** W1C
234 D1 **Birkenhead Street** N1
232 C6 **Bishop's Bridge Road** W2
240 A2 **Bishopsgate** EC2M
240 B1 **Bishops Square** E1
239 G5 **Bishop's Terrace** SE11
239 J3 **Bittern Street** SE1
235 M3 **Blackall Street** EC2A
233 J7 **Blackburne's Mews** W1K
235 H7 **Blackfriars** ⇌ EC4V
235 H8 **Blackfriars Bridge** SE1
235 H7 **Black Friars Lane** EC4V
239 H3 **Blackfriars Road** SE1
239 L4 **Blackhorse Court** SE1
232 B8 **Black Lion Gate** W2
238 E6 **Black Prince Road** SE11
239 K6 **Blackwood Street** SE17
233 H5 **Blandford Street** W1U
233 L7 **Blenheim Street** W1S
235 K1 **Bletchley Street** N1
232 C4 **Blomfield Road** W9
235 M5 **Blomfield Street** EC2M
232 C5 **Blomfield Villas** W2
237 J6 **Bloomfield Terrace** SW1W
234 D5 **Bloomsbury Square** WC1A
234 C5 **Bloomsbury Street** WC1B
234 C5 **Bloomsbury Way** WC1A
241 K2 **Blount Street** E14
237 M1 **Blue Ball Yard** SW1A
241 J1 **Bohn Road** E1
233 L4 **Bolsover Street** W1W
236 B6 **Bolton Gardens** SW5
237 L1 **Bolton Street** W1J
233 K6 **Bond Street** ⊖ W1C
238 D8 **Bondway** SW8
235 L4 **Bonhill Street** EC2A
238 E8 **Bonnington Square** SW8
235 M2 **Boot Street** N1
239 K3 **Borough** ⊖ SE1
239 K3 **Borough High Street** SE1
239 H3 **Borough Road** SE1
237 K5 **Boscobel Place** SW1W
232 E4 **Boscobel Street** NW8
240 B6 **Boss Street** SE1
233 G3 **Boston Place** NW1
235 M7 **Botolph Lane** EC3R
239 K8 **Boundary Lane** SE17
239 G2 **Boundary Row** SE1
233 L7 **Bourdon Street** W1K
233 M5 **Bourlet Close** W1W
234 F4 **Bourne Estate** EC1N
237 J6 **Bourne Street** SW1W
232 B5 **Bourne Terrace** W2
232 F6 **Bouverie Place** W2
235 G6 **Bouverie Street** EC4Y
237 J3 **Bowland Yard** * SW1X
235 K6 **Bow Lane** EC4M
235 G3 **Bowling Green Lane** EC1R
239 L2 **Bowling Green Place** SE1
238 F8 **Bowling Green Street** SE11
235 M2 **Bowling Green Walk** N1
234 D4 **Bowsell Street** WC1N
234 D7 **Bow Street** WC2E
240 D3 **Boyd Street** E1
239 H3 **Boyfield Street** SE1
233 M7 **Boyle Street** W1S
239 K8 **Boyson Road** SE17
237 H6 **Brackland Terrace** SW3
235 J4 **Brackley Street** EC1Y
239 K8 **Bradenham Close** SE17
239 G2 **Brad Street** SE1
239 H7 **Braganza Street** SE17
240 C3 **Braham Street** E1
236 F7 **Bramerton Street** SW3
236 B6 **Bramham Gardens** SW5
241 J3 **Branch Road** E14
239 H8 **Brandon Estate** SE17
239 K6 **Brandon Street** SE17
238 F7 **Brangton Road** SE11
241 H6 **Bray Crescent** SE16
237 H6 **Bray Place** SW3
235 K7 **Bread Street** EC4M
234 F6 **Bream's Buildings** EC4A
236 D6 **Brechin Place** SW7
240 D4 **Breezer's Hill** E1W
233 G5 **Brendon Street** W1H
237 L4 **Bressenden Place** SW1W
239 L7 **Brettell Street** SE17
238 A3 **Brewers Green** W1H
234 A7 **Brewer Street** W1F
240 F6 **Brewhouse Lane** E1W
241 J5 **Brewhouse Walk** SE16
234 F7 **Brick Court** WC2R
240 C1 **Brick Lane** E1
237 K2 **Brick Street** W1J
235 H7 **Bridewell Place** EC4V
232 F1 **Bridgeman Street** NW8
237 L5 **Bridge Place** SW1V
240 D4 **Bridgeport Place** E1W
235 J7 **Bridge Street** EC4V
238 D3 **Bridge Street** SW1A
235 J4 **Bridgewater Street** EC2Y
234 A1 **Bridgeway Street** NW1
234 A7 **Bridle Lane** W1F
232 A6 **Bridstow Place** W2
241 L4 **Brightlingsea Place** E14
234 C1 **Brill Place** NW1
235 H4 **Briset Street** EC1M
232 B4 **Bristol Gardens** W9
234 E2 **Britannia Street** WC1X
235 L2 **Britannia Walk** N1
235 K1 **Britannia Way** N1
236 F7 **Britten Street** SW3
235 H4 **Britton Street** EC1M
233 L7 **Broadbent Street** W1K
235 M5 **Broadgate Circle** EC2M
232 F4 **Broadley Street** NW8
232 F4 **Broadley Terrace** NW1
233 J5 **Broadstone Place** W1U
233 K1 **Broad Walk** NW1
233 H7 **Broad Walk** W2
239 G1 **Broadwall** SE1
238 B4 **Broadway** W1H
234 A7 **Broadwick Street** W1F
239 K4 **Brockham Street** SE1
241 H3 **Brodlove Lane** E1W
241 J2 **Bromley Street** E1
237 G4 **Brompton Road** SW3
236 F5 **Brompton Road** SW7
236 F4 **Brompton Square** SW3
239 K7 **Bronti Close** SE17
239 G5 **Brook Drive** SE11
234 F5 **Brooke Street** EC1N
233 H8 **Brook Gate** W2
232 D7 **Brook Mews North** W2
233 K7 **Brook's Mews** W1K
233 K7 **Brook Street** W1K
232 E7 **Brook Street** W2
233 K7 **Brown Heart Gardens** W1K
233 K5 **Browning Mews** W1G
239 K6 **Browning Street** SE17
234 E3 **Brownlow Mews** WC1N
234 E5 **Brownlow Street** WC1V
233 G6 **Brown Street** W1H
241 G6 **Brunel Road** SE16
240 B1 **Brune Street** E1
240 A6 **Brunswick Close** SE1
236 A1 **Brunswick Gardens** W8
235 L2 **Brunswick Place** N1
241 J8 **Brunswick Quay** SE16
234 D3 **Brunswick Square** WC1N
234 D3 **Brunswick Street** WC1N
241 K3 **Brunton Place** E14
240 B1 **Brushfield Street** E1
233 L8 **Bruton Lane** W1J
233 L7 **Bruton Place** W1J
233 L8 **Bruton Street** W1J
241 K6 **Bryan Road** SE16
233 G5 **Bryanstone Mews West** W1H
233 H5 **Bryanston Mews East** W1H
233 G5 **Bryanston Place** W1H
233 H5 **Bryanston Square** W1H
233 H7 **Bryanston Street** W1C
232 E8 **Buck Hill Walk** W2
237 L3 **Buckingham Gate** SW1E
237 M3 **Buckingham Mews** SW1E
237 L5 **Buckingham Palace Road** SW1W
237 M4 **Buckingham Place** SW1E
235 L1 **Buckland Street** N1
240 C2 **Buckle Street** E1
241 J5 **Buckters Rents** SE16
236 D2 **Budge's Walk** W2
237 L5 **Bulleid Way** SW1V
233 K5 **Bulstrode Street** W1U
235 L3 **Bunhill Row** EC1Y
241 M1 **Burdett Estate** E14
241 L2 **Burdett Road** E14
238 F3 **Burdett Street** SE1
241 M1 **Burgess Street** E14
239 L4 **Burge Street** SE1
233 M8 **Burlington Arcade** W1J
233 M8 **Burlington Gardens** W1S
237 J6 **Burnhouse Place** SW1W
237 G7 **Burnsall Street** SW3
241 J5 **Burnside Close** SE16
239 H1 **Burrell Street** SE1
240 D3 **Burslem Street** E1
239 L7 **Burton Grove** SE17
234 C3 **Burton Street** WC1H
233 G6 **Burwood Place** W2
241 H5 **Bury Close** SE16
240 A2 **Bury Court** EC3A
234 D5 **Bury Place** WC1A
240 A2 **Bury Street** EC3A
238 A1 **Bury Street** SW1Y
236 F6 **Bury Walk** SW3
240 D5 **Bushell Street** E1W
235 L7 **Bush Lane** EC4V
241 J3 **Butcher Row** E14
236 E5 **Bute Street** SW7
238 B4 **Butler Place** W1H
240 C6 **Butler's Wharf** SE1
235 L2 **Buttesland Street** N1
241 K6 **Byefield Close** SE16
241 J5 **Bylands Close** SE16
234 B4 **Byng Place** WC1E
241 M6 **Byng Street** E14
240 A4 **Byward Street** EC3R
241 K5 **Bywater Place** SE16
237 G6 **Bywater Street** SW3

C

232 F5 **Cabbell Street** NW1
240 F3 **Cable Street** E1
239 K7 **Cadiz Street** SE17
237 H5 **Cadogan Gardens** SW3
237 H5 **Cadogan Gate** SW1X
237 J4 **Cadogan Lane** SW1X
237 J4 **Cadogan Place** SW1X
237 H5 **Cadogan Square** SW1X
237 G6 **Cadogan Street** SW3
234 D1 **Caledonian Road** N1
234 D1 **Caledonia Street** N1
236 F6 **Cale Street** SW3
236 D7 **Callow Street** SW3
234 E1 **Calshot Street** N1
234 E3 **Calthorpe Street** WC1X
234 C7 **Cambridge Circus** WC2H
232 A1 **Cambridge Gardens** NW6
233 L3 **Cambridge Gate** NW1
232 A1 **Cambridge Road** NW6
232 A2 **Cambridge Road** NW6
232 F6 **Cambridge Square** W2
237 L6 **Cambridge Street** SW1V
233 L2 **Cambridge Terrace** NW1
233 L3 **Cambridge Terrace Mews** NW1
241 K2 **Camdenhurst Street** E14
236 D8 **Camera Place** SW10
240 A2 **Camomile Street** EC3A
236 A2 **Campden Grove** W8
236 A2 **Campden Hill Road** W8
236 A1 **Campden Street** W8
240 C3 **Camperdown Street** E1
241 G7 **Canada Estate** SE16
237 M3 **Canada Gate** SW1A
241 H7 **Canada Street** SE16
241 G7 **Canada Water** ⊖ ⊖ SE16
241 L5 **Canada Wharf** SE16
239 L8 **Canal Street** SE5
241 L4 **Canary Riverside** E14
241 K1 **Candle Street** E1
236 C4 **Canning Place** W8
241 M4 **Cannon Drive** E14
235 K7 **Cannon Street** EC4N
235 K7 **Cannon Street** ⇌ ⊖ EC4R
240 E3 **Cannon Street Road** E1
241 G6 **Canon Beck Road** SE16
238 D3 **Canon Row** SW1A
241 M3 **Canton Street** E14
237 J3 **Capeners Close** * SW1X
232 E3 **Capland Street** NW8
234 A4 **Capper Street** WC1E
241 K5 **Capstan Way** SE16
241 L2 **Carbis Road** E14
233 L4 **Carburton Street** W1W
238 F6 **Cardigan Street** SE11
234 A2 **Cardington Street** NW1

234 F6 Carey Street WC2A
240 B3 Carlisle Avenue EC3N
238 F4 Carlisle Lane SE1
237 M5 Carlisle Place SW1P
234 B6 Carlisle Street W1D
233 K7 Carlos Place W1K
238 B2 Carlton Gardens SW1Y
232 B1 Carlton Hill NW6
238 B1 Carlton House Terrace SW1Y
232 A1 Carlton Vale NW6
232 B1 Carlton Vale NW6
236 F7 Carlyle Square SW3
235 G7 Carmelite Street EC4Y
233 M7 Carnaby Street W1F
232 B7 Caroline Place W2
241 H3 Caroline Street E1
237 J5 Caroline Terrace SW1W
233 K7 Carpenter Street W1K
237 L1 Carrington Street W1J
241 K1 Carr Street E14
238 B3 Carteret Street W1H
235 H7 Carter Lane EC4V
239 K7 Carter Place SE17
239 J7 Carter Street SE17
235 J4 Carthusian Street EC1M
234 D8 Carting Lane WC2R
234 C2 Cartwright Gardens WC1H
240 C4 Cartwright Street E1
232 F3 Casey Close NW8
240 C1 Casson Street E1
232 B3 Castellain Road W9
239 G5 Castlebrook Close SE11
237 M4 Castle Lane SW1E
239 L6 Catesby Street SE17
240 F7 Cathay Street SE16
236 C8 Cathcart Road SW10
237 M4 Cathedral Walk SW1E
237 M4 Catherine Place SW1E
234 D7 Catherine Street WC2E
233 G5 Cato Street W1H
238 B6 Causton Street SW1P
240 F1 Cavell Street E1
232 E1 Cavendish Avenue NW8
233 L6 Cavendish Place W1G
233 L6 Cavendish Square W1G
235 L1 Cavendish Street N1
237 G8 Caversham Street SW3
238 B4 Caxton Street W1H
235 K2 Cayton Street EC1V
238 F4 Centaur Street SE1
235 J2 Central Street EC1V
235 G1 Chadwell Street EC1R
238 B4 Chadwick Street SW1P
233 H4 Chagford Street NW1
234 B1 Chalton Street NW1
240 D7 Chambers Street SE16
240 C3 Chamber Street E1
240 D6 Chambers Wharf SE16
239 H1 Chancel Street SE1
234 F5 Chancery Lane WC2A
234 F5 Chancery Lane ⊖ WC1V
234 C8 Chandos Place WC2N
233 L5 Chandos Street W1G
236 B4 Chantry Square W8
234 F1 Chapel Market N1
232 F5 Chapel Street NW1
237 K3 Chapel Street SW1X
239 G3 Chaplin Close SE1
240 E3 Chapman Street E1
239 H7 Chapter Road SE17
238 B6 Chapter Street SW1P
241 H6 Chargrove Close SE16
238 D1 Charing Cross ⇌ ⊖ WC2N
234 B6 Charing Cross Road WC2H
234 C8 Charing Cross Road WC2N
232 F1 Charlbert Street NW8
234 B8 Charles II Street SW1Y
235 M2 Charles Square N1
237 K1 Charles Street W1J
239 K6 Charleston Street SE17
235 M3 Charlotte Road EC2A
234 A4 Charlotte Street W1T
238 A6 Charlwood Place SW1V
237 M7 Charlwood Street SW1V
238 A6 Charlwood Street SW1V
234 B1 Charrington Street NW1
235 H4 Charterhouse Square EC1M
235 G5 Charterhouse Street EC1M
235 L2 Chart Street N1
241 J2 Chaseley Street E14
239 L5 Chatham Street SE17
235 K6 Cheapside EC2V
237 K8 Chelsea Bridge SW1W
237 J7 Chelsea Bridge Road SW1W
237 G8 Chelsea Embankment SW3
236 F7 Chelsea Manor Gardens SW3
237 G7 Chelsea Manor Street SW3
236 E8 Chelsea Park Gardens SW3
236 E7 Chelsea Square SW3
237 H6 Cheltenham Terrace SW3
234 B4 Chenies Mews WC1E
234 B4 Chenies Street WC1E
236 A4 Cheniston Gardens W8
232 A7 Chepstow Place W2
232 A6 Chepstow Road W2
235 K3 Chequer Street EC1Y
235 L1 Cherbury Street N1
240 E7 Cherry Garden Street SE16
237 J4 Chesham Close SW1X
237 J4 Chesham Place SW1X
237 J4 Chesham Street SW1X
237 K3 Chester Close SW1X
233 L2 Chester Close North NW1
233 L2 Chester Close South NW1
237 K1 Chesterfield Gardens W1J
233 K8 Chesterfield Hill W1J
237 K1 Chesterfield Street W1J
233 L2 Chester Gate NW1
237 K3 Chester Mews SW1X
233 L1 Chester Place NW1
233 K2 Chester Road NW1
237 K5 Chester Row SW1W
237 K5 Chester Square SW1W
237 K4 Chester Square Mews SW1W
237 K4 Chester Street SW1X
233 L2 Chester Terrace NW1
239 G6 Chester Way SE11
237 G4 Cheval Place SW7
237 G8 Cheyne Gardens SW3
236 F8 Cheyne Row SW3
236 F8 Cheyne Walk SW3
238 E2 Chicheley Street SE1
232 A1 Chichester Road NW6
232 C5 Chichester Road W2
238 A7 Chichester Street SW1V
240 C1 Chicksand Street E1
240 E4 Chigwell Hill E1W
236 A5 Child's Place SW5
236 A5 Child's Street SW5
233 J4 Chiltern Street W1U
232 D6 Chilworth Mews W2
232 D6 Chilworth Street W2
241 G8 China Hall Mews SE16
232 A4 Chippenham Mews W9
235 J3 Chiswell Street EC1Y
234 A4 Chitty Street W1T
237 G8 Christchurch Street SW3
240 D3 Christian Street E1
235 M3 Christina Street EC2A
241 H6 Christopher Close SE16
235 L4 Christopher Street EC2A
241 H2 Chudleigh Street E1
239 M8 Chumleigh Street SE5
237 L7 Churchill Gardens Road SW1V
232 F4 Church Street NW8
234 B2 Church Way NW1
239 J2 Churchyard Row SE1
238 A6 Churton Place SW1V
238 A6 Churton Street SW1V
232 E1 Circus Road NW8
232 A5 Cirencester Square W2
235 J1 City Garden Row N1
235 J1 City Road EC1V
235 L3 City Road EC1Y
235 H6 City Thameslink ⇌ EC4M
237 H5 Clabon Mews SW1X
241 G7 Clack Street SE16
232 A8 Clanricarde Gardens W2
234 F1 Claremont Square N1
233 L2 Clarence Gardens NW1
241 G6 Clarence Mews SE16
232 D4 Clarendon Gardens W9
232 F7 Clarendon Gate W2
232 F7 Clarendon Place W2
237 L6 Clarendon Street SW1V
236 D6 Clareville Grove SW7
236 D6 Clareville Street SW7
237 L1 Clarges Mews W1J
237 L1 Clarges Street W1J
240 F2 Clark Street E1
238 A7 Claverton Street SW1V
240 F5 Clave Street E1W
233 H5 Clay Street W1U
238 F8 Clayton Street SE11
239 G7 Cleaver Square SE11
239 G7 Cleaver Street SE11
240 F5 Clegg Street E1W
241 L2 Clemence Street E14
235 L7 Clements Lane EC4N
240 E8 Clement's Road SE16
233 H6 Clenston Mews W1H
235 L3 Clere Street EC2A
235 G4 Clerkenwell Grove EC1R
235 G3 Clerkenwell Lane EC1R
235 G4 Clerkenwell Road EC1M
232 C6 Cleveland Gardens W2
233 M4 Cleveland Mews W1T
238 A1 Cleveland Place SW1Y
238 A2 Cleveland Row SW1A
232 C6 Cleveland Square W2
233 M4 Cleveland Street W1T
232 D6 Cleveland Terrace W2
233 M7 Clifford Street W1S
232 C4 Clifton Gardens W9
241 G6 Clifton Place SE16
232 E7 Clifton Place W2
232 D3 Clifton Road W9
235 M3 Clifton Street EC2A
232 C4 Clifton Villas W9
239 K1 Clink Street SE1
241 H6 Clipper Close SE16
233 M4 Clipstone Mews W1W
233 L4 Clipstone Street W1W
237 J5 Cliveden Place SW1W
235 K7 Cloak Lane EC4R
235 J5 Cloth Fair EC1A
235 J5 Cloth Street EC1A
239 K2 Cluny Place SE1
240 B2 Cobb Street E1
234 A2 Cobourg Street NW1
237 H5 Coburg Close SW1P
232 E1 Cochrane Mews NW8
232 E1 Cochrane Street NW8
235 H5 Cock Lane EC1A
238 C1 Cockspur Street SW1Y
240 D5 Codling Close * E1W
239 G1 Coin Street SE1
240 D2 Coke Street E1
236 C5 Colbeck Mews SW7
235 H1 Colebrook Row N1
236 B7 Coleherne Road SW10
235 L6 Coleman Street EC2R
235 K6 Cole Street SE1
234 F3 Coley Street WC1X
235 K7 College Hill EC4R
235 K7 College Street EC4R
240 D8 Collett Road SE16
234 E1 Collier Street N1
236 B6 Collingham Gardens SW5
236 B5 Collingham Place SW5
236 B5 Collingham Road SW5
239 H4 Colnbrook Street SE1
239 H1 Colombo Street SE1
234 D4 Colonnade WC1N
241 K2 Coltman Street E14
240 D2 Commercial Road E1
241 K3 Commercial Road E14
240 B1 Commercial Street E1
235 H3 Compton Street EC1V
238 E2 Concert Hall Approach SE1
241 K2 Conder Street E14
232 E6 Conduit Mews W2
232 E6 Conduit Place W2
233 L7 Conduit Street W1S
239 M5 Congreve Street SE17
232 F7 Connaught Close W2
233 G7 Connaught Place W2
233 G6 Connaught Square W2
233 G6 Connaught Street W2
239 G2 Cons Street SE1
237 L3 Constitution Hill SW1A
239 K5 Content Street SE17
233 M4 Conway Street W1T
241 H6 Cookham Crescent SE16
239 H8 Cook's Road SE17
235 J1 Coombs Street N1
234 B1 Cooper's Lane Estate NW1
240 B3 Cooper's Road EC3N
241 L2 Copenhagen Place E14
236 A4 Cope Place W8
239 J8 Copley Court SE17
241 H2 Copley Street E1
241 K1 Copperfield Road E3
239 J2 Copperfield Street SE1
235 L6 Copthall Avenue EC2R
234 C5 Coptic Street WC1A
239 G3 Coral Street SE1
234 C4 Coram Street WC1H
240 E5 Cork Square E1W
233 M8 Cork Street W1S
232 F4 Corlett Street NW1
235 L6 Cornhill EC3V
236 C4 Cornwall Gardens SW7
236 C5 Cornwall Mews South SW7
238 F1 Cornwall Road SE1
239 G2 Cornwall Road SE1
240 E3 Cornwall Street E1
233 H4 Cornwall Terrace Mews NW1
241 G2 Cornwood Drive E1
235 M2 Coronet Street N1
235 G3 Corporation Row EC1R
235 L2 Corsham Street N1
238 F4 Cosser Street SE1
233 G4 Cosway Street NW1
238 F6 Cottage Place SW3
236 B4 Cottesmore Gardens W8
239 M1 Cottons Lane SE1
237 H6 Coulson Street SW3
239 M1 Counter Street SE1
239 K5 County Street SE1
238 F7 Courtenay Square SE11
238 F6 Courtenay Street SE11
236 B5 Courtfield Gardens SW5
236 C5 Courtfield Road SW7
240 E1 Court Street E1
235 K8 Cousin Lane SE1
234 D7 Covent Garden WC2E
234 D7 Covent Garden ⊖ WC2E
234 B8 Coventry Street W1D
235 H4 Cowcross Street EC1M
235 L3 Cowper Street EC2A
239 L5 Crail Row SE17
233 J5 Cramer Street W1U
239 J6 Crampton Street SE17
234 C7 Cranbourn Street WC2H
234 A1 Cranleigh Street NW1
236 D6 Cranley Gardens SW7
236 D6 Cranley Mews SW7
236 E6 Cranley Place SW7
235 L1 Cranston Estate N1
235 L2 Cranwood Street EC1V
232 C7 Craven Hill W2
232 D7 Craven Hill W2
232 C7 Craven Hill Gardens W2
232 D7 Craven Road W2
238 D1 Craven Street WC2N
232 D7 Craven Terrace W2
235 G3 Crawford Passage EC1R
233 G5 Crawford Place W1H
233 G5 Crawford Street W1H
240 A3 Creechurch Lane EC3A
235 H7 Creed Lane EC4V
240 B4 Crescent EC3N
236 D6 Cresswell Place SW10
241 G1 Cressy Place E1
234 D2 Crestfield Street WC1H
240 A8 Crimscott Street SE1
240 B1 Crispin Street E1
234 D2 Cromer Street WC1H
232 D4 Crompton Street W2
236 E5 Cromwell Place SW7
236 B5 Cromwell Road SW5
236 E5 Cromwell Road SW7
235 M1 Crondall Court N1
235 L1 Crondall Street N1
235 K1 Cropley Street N1
239 L3 Crosby Row SE1
240 A4 Cross Lane EC3R
240 B3 Crosswall EC3N
240 E3 Crowder Street E1
240 A6 Crucifix Lane SE1
234 F1 Cruikshank Street WC1X
240 A3 Crutched Friars EC3N
241 M6 Cuba Street E14
234 E2 Cubitt Street WC1X
237 H6 Culford Gardens SW3
240 F7 Culling Road SE16
235 M7 Cullum Street EC3M
233 J8 Culross Street W1K
232 F1 Culworth Street NW8
234 F2 Cumberland Gardens WC1X
233 G7 Cumberland Gate W2
233 L2 Cumberland Market NW1
237 L6 Cumberland Street SW1V
233 K1 Cumberland Terrace NW1
233 L1 Cumberland
Terrace Mews NW1
241 G6 Cumberland Wharf SE16
234 E1 Cumming Street N1
237 K6 Cundy Street SW1W
232 E3 Cunningham Place NW8
238 C6 Cureton Street SW1P
240 B6 Curlew Street SE1
234 F6 Cursitor Street EC4A
235 M3 Curtain Road EC2A
235 M4 Curtain Road EC2A
237 K2 Curzon Gate W2
237 K1 Curzon Street W1J
232 E4 Cuthbert Street W2
240 A2 Cutler Street E1
234 F1 Cynthia Street N1
234 A4 Cypress Place W1T
235 H3 Cyrus Street EC1V

D

238 B3 Dacre Street W1H
241 J1 Dakin Place E1
235 H3 Dallington Street EC1V
240 F2 Damien Street E1
234 E5 Dane Street WC1R
234 B7 Dansey Place W1D
239 H5 Dante Road SE11
236 F8 Danvers Street SW3
234 A6 D'arblay Street W1F
239 K8 Dartford Street SE17
238 B3 Dartmouth Street W1H
239 L5 Darwin Street SE17
239 K7 Date Street SE17
240 D1 Davenant Street E1
232 F4 Daventry Street NW1
239 H3 Davidge Street SE1
233 K7 Davies Mews W1K
233 K7 Davies Street W1K
239 L6 Dawes Street SE17
232 A7 Dawson Place W2
239 J5 Deacon Way SE17
241 G8 Deal Porters Way SE16
240 D1 Deal Street E1
238 C5 Dean Bradley Street SW1P
241 H6 Dean Close SE16
240 F3 Deancross Street E1
237 K1 Deanery Street W1K
238 B3 Dean Farrar Street W1H
238 C5 Dean Ryle Street SW1P
239 L6 Dean's Buildings SE17
238 C4 Dean Stanley Street SW1P
234 B6 Dean Street W1D
238 C4 Dean Yard SW1P
239 M4 Decima Street SE1
241 J6 Deck Close SE16
241 K7 Defoe Close SE16
232 B4 Delamere Terrace W2
239 H7 De Laune Street SE17
232 B3 Delaware Road W9
240 F3 Dellow Street E1
239 H7 Delverton Road SE17
237 M6 Denbigh Place SW1V
234 B7 Denman Street W1D
234 C6 Denmark Street WC2H
239 G6 Denny Close SE11
237 G5 Denyer Street SW3
238 D3 Derby Gate SW1A
237 K1 Derby Street W1J
233 L6 Dering Street W1S
236 B3 Derry Street W8
236 C3 De Vere Gardens W8
239 L4 Deverell Street SE1
241 G3 Devonport Street E1
233 K4 Devonshire Close W1G
233 K4 Devonshire
Mews South W1G
233 K4 Devonshire
Mews West W1G
233 K4 Devonshire Place W1G
233 K4 Devonshire
Place Mews W1G
240 A2 Devonshire Row EC2M
240 A2 Devonshire Square EC2M
233 K4 Devonshire Street W1G
232 D7 Devonshire Terrace W2
233 K5 De Walden Street W1G
240 D7 Dickens Estate SE16
239 K4 Dickens Square SE1
237 H8 Dilke Street SW3
235 L2 Dingley Place EC1V
235 J2 Dingley Road EC1V
240 E5 Discovery Walk E1W
239 K2 Disney Place SE1
235 J7 Distaff Lane EC4V
238 F6 Distin Street SE11
240 C7 Dockhead SE1
240 D8 Dockley Road SE16
240 D4 Dock Street E1
239 H7 Doddington Grove SE17
239 H8 Doddington Place SE17
239 G3 Dodson Street SE1
241 M2 Dod Street E14
239 H2 Dolben Street SE1
238 E7 Dolland Street SE11
238 A7 Dolphin Square SW1V
238 B7 Dolphin Square SW1V
234 E4 Dombey Street WC1N
235 L5 Dominion Street EC2A
234 F1 Donegal Street N1
241 J1 Dongola Road E1
237 G5 Donne Place SW3
238 F1 Doon Street SE1
241 L2 Dora Street E14
234 B2 Doric Way NW1
235 G7 Dorset Rise EC4Y
233 H4 Dorset Square NW1
233 H5 Dorset Street W1U
234 E3 Doughty Mews WC1N
234 E3 Doughty Street WC1N
238 B6 Douglas Street SW1P
236 C3 Douro Place W8
240 D5 Douthwaite Square * E1W
236 E6 Dovehouse Street SW3
237 L1 Dover Street W1J
233 L8 Dover Street W1S
235 K7 Dowgate Hill EC4R
232 B4 Downfield Close W9
238 C2 Downing Street SW1A
237 K2 Down Street W1J
241 K6 Downtown Road SE16
237 J5 D'Oyley Street SW1X
239 J8 Draco Street SE17
241 H6 Drake Close SE16
237 G5 Draycott Avenue SW3
237 H6 Draycott Place SW3
237 H5 Draycott Terrace SW3
236 A3 Drayson Mews W8
236 D6 Drayton Gardens SW10
240 A6 Druid Street SE1
240 B6 Druid Street SE1
234 B2 Drummond Crescent NW1
240 E8 Drummond Road SE16
234 A3 Drummond Street NW1
234 D6 Drury Lane WC2B
239 G5 Dryden Court SE11
234 D6 Dryden Street WC2B
233 L5 Duchess Mews W1G
233 L5 Duchess Street W1B
239 G1 Duchy Street SE1
241 J1 Duckett Street E1
234 B6 Duck Lane W1F
235 K4 Dufferin Street EC1Y
237 K3 Duke of Wellington
Place SW1W
237 H6 Duke of York Square SW3
234 A8 Duke of York Street SW1Y
241 K4 Duke Shore Wharf E14
236 A2 Dukes Lane W8
240 B2 Duke's Place EC3A
234 C2 Duke's Road WC1H
233 K7 Duke Street W1K
233 J6 Duke Street W1U
239 L1 Duke Street Hill SE1
238 A1 Duke Street St James's SW1Y
241 L4 Dunbar Wharf E14
234 C8 Duncannon Street WC2N
235 H1 Duncan Terrace N1
240 E5 Dundee Street E1W
241 L4 Dundee Wharf E14
241 H2 Dunelm Street E1
240 C8 Dunlop Place SE16
233 H7 Dunraven Street W1K
240 A3 Dunster Court EC3R
237 H3 Duplex Ride SW1X
241 L6 Durand's Wharf SE16
241 J1 Durham Row E1
238 E7 Durham Street SE11
232 A6 Durham Terrace W2
234 C6 Dyott Street WC2H
235 M4 Dysart Street EC2A

E

235 H4 Eagle Close EC1M
234 E5 Eagle Street WC1R
236 A7 Eardley Crescent SW5
234 C7 Earlham Street WC2H
236 A6 Earl's Court ⇌ ⊖ SW5
236 B6 Earl's Court Gardens SW5
236 A6 Earl's Court Road SW5
236 A6 Earl's Court Square SW5
235 H2 Earlstoke Street EC1V
235 M4 Earl Street EC2A
234 C6 Earnshaw Street WC2H
241 H2 East Arbour Street E1
232 D6 Eastbourne Mews W2
232 D6 Eastbourne Terrace W2
234 A6 Eastcastle Street W1W
235 M7 Eastcheap EC3M
241 K1 Eastfield Street E14
241 M3 East India Dock
Road E14
240 D6 East Lane SE16
234 F3 Easton Street WC1X
235 H5 East Poultry
Avenue EC1A
235 L2 East Road N1
240 C4 East Smithfield E1W
239 L6 East Street SE17
237 J5 Eaton Close SW1W
237 J5 Eaton Gate SW1W
237 L4 Eaton Lane SW1W
237 J5 Eaton Mews
North SW1W
237 K5 Eaton Mews
South SW1W
237 K5 Eaton Mews
West SW1W
237 J4 Eaton Place SW1X
237 K4 Eaton Row SW1W
237 K5 Eaton Square SW1W
237 J5 Eaton Terrace SW1W
238 E8 Ebbisham Drive SW8
237 K6 Ebury Bridge SW1W
237 K7 Ebury Bridge
Road SW1W
237 K5 Ebury Mews SW1W
237 K6 Ebury Square SW1W
237 K5 Ebury Street SW1W
237 L5 Eccleston Bridge SW1W
237 K4 Eccleston Mews SW1X
237 L5 Eccleston Place SW1W
237 L6 Eccleston Square SW1V
237 K4 Eccleston Street SW1X
232 A3 Edbrooke Road W9
236 A1 Edge Street W8
232 F5 Edgware Road W2
232 F5 Edgware Road ⊖ NW1
237 H3 Edinburgh Gate SW1X
236 C8 Edith Grove SW10
233 J6 Edwards Mews W1H
235 J6 Edward Street EC1A
236 F5 Egerton Crescent SW3
236 F5 Egerton Gardens SW3
237 G4 Egerton Terrace SW3
239 J7 Eglington Court SE17
239 K5 Elba Place SE17
235 L5 Eldon Place EC2M
236 B4 Eldon Road W8
241 H6 Eleanor Close SE16
239 J4 Elephant & Castle SE1
239 J5 Elephant & Castle ⇌ ⊖ SE1
240 F6 Elephant Lane SE16
239 J5 Elephant Road SE17
241 G3 Elf Row E1W
241 K7 Elgar Street SE16
232 B2 Elgin Avenue W9
232 C2 Elgin Mews North W9
232 C2 Elgin Mews South W9
235 H1 Elia Mews N1
235 H1 Elia Street N1
239 M3 Elim Estate SE1
239 M3 Elim Street SE1
237 K5 Elizabeth Street SW1W
240 D3 Ellen Street E1
239 H5 Elliott's Row SE11
237 J5 Ellis Street SW1X
232 A4 Elmfield Way W9
236 E7 Elm Park Gardens SW10
236 E7 Elm Park Lane SW3
236 E8 Elm Park Road SW3
236 E7 Elm Place SW7
232 D7 Elms Mews W2
234 F4 Elm Street WC1X
232 E2 Elm Tree Road NW8
232 B4 Elnathan Mews W9
241 J1 Elsa Street E1
239 L6 Elsted Street SE17
236 D4 Elvaston Mews SW7
236 D4 Elvaston Place SW7
238 B5 Elverton Street SW1P
235 G5 Ely Place EC1N
237 G6 Elystan Place SW3
236 F6 Elystan Street SW3
238 D1 Embankment ⊖ WC2N
237 H8 Embankment
Gardens SW3
238 D1 Embankment
Place WC2N
240 D7 Emba Street SE16
234 E4 Emerald Street WC1N
239 J1 Emerson Street SE1
238 A5 Emery Hill Street SW1P
239 G3 Emery Street SE1
236 C5 Emperor's Gate SW7
239 L3 Empire Square SE1
236 A7 Empress Place SW6
234 C6 Endell Street WC2H
234 B3 Endsleigh Gardens WC1H
234 B3 Endsleigh Place WC1H
234 B3 Endsleigh Street WC1H
233 G5 Enford Street W1H
239 M1 English Grounds SE1
240 C8 Enid Street SE16
236 F3 Ennismore Gardens SW7
236 F3 Ennismore
Gardens Mews SW7
236 F3 Ennismore Mews SW7
236 F4 Ennismore Street SW7
239 G6 Enny Street SE11
240 D4 Ensign Street E1
235 L3 Epworth Street EC2A
238 C6 Erasmus Street SW1P
235 K4 Errol Street EC1Y
232 A3 Essendine Road W9
234 F7 Essex Street WC2R
236 A3 Essex Villas W8
235 J2 Europa Place EC1V
234 B2 Euston ⇌ ⊖ ⊖ NW1
234 B3 Euston Road NW1
234 B2 Euston Square NW1
234 A3 Euston Square ⊖ NW1
234 A3 Euston Street NW1
236 D7 Evelyn Gardens SW7
235 L1 Evelyn Way N1
234 A1 Eversholt Street NW1
233 M2 Everton Buildings NW1
239 J2 Ewer Street SE1
241 G1 Ewhurst Close E1
234 D7 Exeter Street WC2E
236 E3 Exhibition Road SW7
235 G3 Exmouth Market EC1R
239 M6 Exon Street SE17
238 F2 Exton Street SE1
234 F4 Eyre Street Hill EC1R

F

240 D3 Fairclough Street E1
240 B6 Fair Street SE1
239 K4 Falmouth Road SE1
235 J4 Fann Street EC1M
235 M1 Fanshaw Street N1
234 B6 Fareham Street W1D
236 A1 Farmer Street W8
236 A8 Farm Lane SW6
233 K8 Farm Street W1K
239 J1 Farnham Place SE1
241 M3 Farrance Street E14
235 G4 Farringdon ⇌ ⊖ EC1M
235 G4 Farringdon Lane EC1R
234 F3 Farringdon Road EC1R
235 H5 Farringdon Street EC1M
241 J5 Farrins Rents SE16
241 K7 Farrow Place SE16
240 F5 Farthing Fields * E1W
240 B1 Fashion Street E1
239 H7 Faunce Street SE17
236 C8 Fawcett Street SW10
235 L3 Featherstone Street EC1Y
240 A3 Fenchurch Avenue EC3M
240 A3 Fenchurch Buildings EC3M
240 A3 Fenchurch Place EC3M
240 A3 Fenchurch Street EC3M
240 A3 Fenchurch Street ⇌ EC3M
240 B8 Fendall Street SE1
239 M2 Fenning Street SE1
234 F2 Fernsbury Street WC1X
235 G6 Fetter Lane EC4A
240 D2 Fieldgate Street E1
239 J7 Fielding Street SE17
234 E1 Field Street WC1X
236 B8 Finborough Road SW10
235 L6 Finch Lane EC3V
241 K8 Finland Street SE16
235 L5 Finsbury Circus EC2M
235 G3 Finsbury Estate EC1R
235 M4 Finsbury Market EC2A
235 L4 Finsbury Square EC2A
235 L4 Finsbury Street EC2Y
237 G5 First Street SW3
241 J6 Fishermans Drive SE16
234 D5 Fisher Street WC1R
232 E3 Fisherton Street NW8
235 L7 Fish Street Hill EC3R
238 F5 Fitzalan Street SE11
233 J6 Fitzhardinge Street W1H
233 M4 Fitzroy Square W1T
233 M4 Fitzroy Street W1T
241 J3 Flamborough Street E14
240 C4 Flank Street E1
234 C3 Flaxman Terrace WC1H
235 G6 Fleet Street EC4A
239 H8 Fleming Road SE17
240 D3 Fletcher Street E1
239 L6 Flint Street SE17
234 C6 Flitcroft Street WC2H
240 D7 Flockton Street SE16
237 G7 Flood Street SW3
237 G7 Flood Walk SW3
234 D7 Floral Street WC2E
233 M5 Foley Street W1W
238 D8 Fontiman Road SW8
240 D3 Forbes Street E1
240 D2 Fordham Street E1
240 F2 Ford Square E1
235 K5 Fore Street EC2Y
232 C4 Formosa Street W9
233 G6 Forset Street W1H
239 H8 Forsyth Gardens SE17
240 B1 Fort Street E1
235 K4 Fortune Street EC1Y
235 J6 Foster Lane EC2V
236 E6 Foulis Terrace SW7
241 J5 Foundry Close SE16
240 B1 Fournier Street E1
240 E5 Fowey Close E1W
232 E4 Frampton Street NW8
238 A5 Francis Street SW1P
240 F8 Frankland Close SE16
237 H6 Franklin's Row SW3
239 G3 Frazier Street SE1
240 C8 Frean Street SE16
233 G7 Frederick Close W2
234 E2 Frederick Street WC1X
237 J3 Frederic Mews * SW1X
239 M6 Freemantle Street SE17
235 H2 Friend Street EC1V
234 B6 Frith Street W1D
240 E1 Fulbourne Street E1
240 F7 Fulford Street SE16
236 D8 Fulham Road SW10
236 F6 Fulham Road SW3
234 F5 Furnival Street EC4A
238 B5 Fynes Street SW1P

G

239 G1 Gabriel's Wharf SE1
240 B6 Gainsford Street SE1
241 G6 Galleon Close SE16
241 K2 Galsworthy Avenue E14
235 K2 Galway Street EC1V
239 H2 Gambia Street SE1
232 D1 Garden Road NW8
239 H4 Garden Row SE1
241 H1 Garden Street E1
235 M3 Garden Walk EC2A
235 J2 Gard Street EC1V
241 M4 Garford Street E14
235 G3 Garnault Place EC1R
240 F4 Garnet Street E1W
235 K3 Garrett Street EC1Y
234 C7 Garrick Street WC2E
241 H7 Garterway SE16
232 B6 Garway Road W2
240 E8 Gataker Street * SE16
236 F3 Gate Mews SW7
232 F3 Gateforth Street NW8
233 L3 Gate Mews NW1
235 M3 Gatesborough Street * EC2A
235 G4 Gate Street WC2A
237 K7 Gatliff Road SW1W
239 J4 Gaunt Street SE1
238 C4 Gayfere Street SW1P
239 H4 Gaywood Street SE1
239 H7 Gaza Street SE17
240 C7 Gedling Place SE1
235 J3 Gee Street EC1V
239 H5 George Mathers Road SE11
240 C7 George Row SE16
233 H6 George Street W1H
233 K7 George Yard W1K
239 H4 Geraldine SE1
237 K5 Gerald Road SW1W
234 B7 Gerrard Street W1D
239 G3 Gerridge Street SE1
236 D8 Gertrude Street SW10
238 E5 Gibson Road SE11
234 C5 Gilbert Place WC1A
239 G5 Gilbert Road SE11
233 K7 Gilbert Street W1K
233 L5 Gildea Street W1W
237 M5 Gillingham Street SW1V
241 L3 Gill Street E14
236 D7 Gilston Road SW10
235 H5 Giltspur Street EC1A
239 H4 Gladstone Street SE1
241 G4 Glamis Place E1W
241 G4 Glamis Road E1W
237 M7 Glasgow Terrace SW1V
239 J3 Glasshill Street SE1
234 A8 Glasshouse Street W1B
238 D7 Glasshouse Walk SE11
236 F7 Glebe Place SW3
236 C6 Gledhow Road SW5
233 H4 Glentworth Street NW1
241 J5 Globe Pond Road SE16
239 K3 Globe Street SE1
240 A4 Gloucester Court * EC3R
232 C6 Gloucester Gardens W2
232 D6 Gloucester Mews W2
232 C6 Gloucester Mews West W2
233 H3 Gloucester Place NW1
233 H5 Gloucester Place W1U
233 H5 Gloucester Place Mews W1U
236 C4 Gloucester Road SW7
236 D6 Gloucester Road SW7
236 C5 Gloucester Road ⊖ SW7
232 F6 Gloucester Square W2
237 M7 Gloucester Street SW1V
232 B5 Gloucester Terrace W2
232 D6 Gloucester Terrace W2
236 A2 Gloucester Walk W8
235 G2 Gloucester Way EC1R
238 E7 Glyn Street SE11
237 G6 Godfrey Street SW3
238 D7 Goding Street SE11
235 J7 Godliman Street EC4V
235 K1 Godwin Close N1
238 D1 Golden Jubilee Bridge WC2N
235 J4 Golden Lane EC1Y
234 A7 Golden Square W1F
240 E3 Golding Street E1
232 A4 Goldney Road W9
235 K6 Goldsmith Street EC2V
241 G8 Gomm Road SE16
234 A5 Goodge Place W1T
234 A5 Goodge Street W1T
234 B5 Goodge Street ⊖ W1E
240 C8 Goodwin Close SE16
236 A2 Gordon Place W8
234 B3 Gordon Square WC1H
234 B3 Gordon Street WC1H
236 D4 Gore Street SW7
240 A2 Goring Street * EC3A
233 L5 Gosfield Street W1W
234 B6 Goslett Yard WC2H
235 H1 Goswell Road EC1V
234 F3 Gough Street WC1X
240 B2 Goulston Street E1
234 B5 Gower Mews WC1E
234 A3 Gower Place NW1
234 B3 Gower Street WC1E
240 D2 Gower's Walk E1
235 M7 Gracechurch Street EC3V
234 B2 Grafton Place NW1
233 L8 Grafton Street W1S
234 A4 Grafton Way W1T
235 J1 Graham Street N1
237 J6 Graham Terrace SW1W
233 M1 Granby Terrace NW1
235 H5 Grand Avenue EC1A
240 B8 Grange Road SE1
240 A8 Grange Walk SE1
240 B8 Grange Yard SE1
232 B2 Grantully Road W9
233 J6 Granville Place W1H
232 A1 Granville Road NW6
234 F2 Granville Square WC1X
234 C6 Grape Street WC2H
240 B2 Gravel Lane E1
234 D2 Grays Inn Road WC1X
234 F5 Grays Inn Square WC1R
239 G3 Gray Street SE1
233 L6 Great Castle Street W1G
233 G4 Great Central Street NW1
234 B6 Great Chapel Street W1D
238 C4 Great College Street SW1P
233 H6 Great Cumberland Place W1H
239 K3 Great Dover Street SE1
235 M3 Great Eastern Street EC2A
238 C3 Great George Street SW1P
239 J1 Great Guildford Street SE1
234 E4 Great James Street WC1N
233 M7 Great Marlborough Street W1F
239 L2 Great Maze Pond SE1
234 C7 Great New Portland Street WC2H
240 D1 Greatorex Street E1
234 D4 Great Ormond Street WC1N
234 F2 Great Percy Street WC1X
238 B4 Great Peter Street SW1P
233 L4 Great Portland Street W1W
233 L4 Great Portland Street ⊖ W1W
234 A7 Great Pulteney Street W1F
234 D6 Great Queen Street WC2B
234 C5 Great Russell Street WC1B
238 C1 Great Scotland Yard SW1A
238 C4 Great Smith Street SW1P
239 H2 Great Suffolk Street SE1
235 H4 Great Sutton Street EC1V
235 L6 Great Swan Alley EC2R
233 M4 Great Titchfield Street W1W
235 M7 Great Tower Street EC3M
240 A4 Great Tower Street EC3R
235 L6 Great Winchester Street EC2N
234 B7 Great Windmill Street W1D
234 B6 Greek Street W1D
241 J6 Greenacre Square SE16
240 E5 Green Bank E1W
232 F1 Greenberry Street NW8
238 A5 Greencoat Place SW1P
238 A4 Green Coat Row SW1P
240 D2 Greenfield Road E1
238 F3 Greenham Close SE1
237 M1 Green Park ⊖ W1J
233 J7 Green Street W1K
233 L4 Greenwell Street W1W
239 G2 Greet Street SE1
241 L4 Grenade Street E14
232 F3 Grendon Street NW8
236 C5 Grenville Place SW7
235 J6 Gresham Street EC2V
234 B5 Gresse Street W1D
235 G5 Greville Street EC1N
238 B4 Greycoat Place SW1P
238 B4 Greycoat Street SW1P
240 A8 Grigg's Place SE1
237 L8 Grosvenor Bridge SW8
237 J3 Grosvenor Crescent SW1X
237 J3 Grosvenor Crescent Mews SW1X
237 L4 Grosvenor Gardens SW1W
237 L4 Grosvenor Gardens Mews East SW1W
237 L4 Grosvenor Gardens Mews North SW1W
237 L4 Grosvenor Gardens Mews South * SW1W
233 H8 Grosvenor Gate W2
233 L7 Grosvenor Hill W1K
237 K3 Grosvenor Place SW1X
237 L8 Grosvenor Road SW1V
233 J7 Grosvenor Square W1K
233 K7 Grosvenor Street W1K
239 J8 Grosvenor Terrace SE5
232 D2 Grove End Road NW8
237 M5 Guildhouse Street SW1V
234 D4 Guilford Street WC1N
239 M5 Guinness Square SE1
241 K8 Gulliver Street SE16
235 G6 Gunpowder Square EC4A
240 B1 Gun Street E1
240 C2 Gunthorpe Street E1
235 J6 Gutter Lane EC2V
239 L3 Guy Street SE1

H

235 L2 Haberdasher Street N1
239 M4 Haddonhall Estate SE1
240 F3 Hainton Close E1
240 F2 Halcrow Street * E1
237 L1 Half Moon Street W1J
236 A8 Halford Road SW6
237 J4 Halkin Place SW1X
237 K3 Halkin Street SW1X
233 L5 Hallam Street W1W
241 K1 Halley Street E14
232 C6 Hallfield Estate W2
232 E4 Hall Place W2
232 D2 Hall Road NW8
235 H2 Hall Street EC1V
239 M6 Halpin Place SE17
237 G5 Halsey Street SW3
232 D2 Hamilton Close NW8
241 K7 Hamilton Close SE16
232 D2 Hamilton Gardens NW8
237 K2 Hamilton Place W1J
232 C1 Hamilton Terrace NW8
239 L3 Hamlet Way SE1
240 B4 Hammett Street EC3N
234 B1 Hampden Close NW1
233 H6 Hampden Gurney Street W2
233 M2 Hampstead Road NW1
239 J6 Hampton Street SE17
240 C1 Hanbury Street E1
234 E5 Hand Court WC1V
234 D3 Handel Street WC1N
239 G3 Hankey Place SE1
241 G1 Hannibal Road E1
233 L6 Hanover Square W1S
233 L7 Hanover Street W1S
237 H3 Hans Crescent SW3
233 M4 Hanson Street W1W
237 H4 Hans Place SW1X
237 G4 Hans Road SW3
237 H4 Hans Street SW1X
234 B6 Hanway Place W1T
234 B6 Hanway Street W1T
232 F5 Harbet Road W2
234 E4 Harbour Street WC1N
233 G5 Harcourt Street W1H
236 C7 Harcourt Terrace SW10
241 G3 Hardinge Street E1W
235 G2 Hardwick Street EC1R
239 M2 Hardwidge Street SE1
241 H6 Hardy Close SE16
233 L6 Harewood Place W1G
233 G4 Harewood Row NW1
233 G4 Harewoood Avenue NW1
241 J1 Harford Street E1
238 E8 Harleyford Road SE11
236 D7 Harley Gardens SW10
233 K4 Harley Street W1G
239 G7 Harmsworth Street SE17
240 A8 Harold Estate SE1
239 K4 Harper Road SE1
237 H3 Harriet Street SW1X
237 H3 Harriet Walk SW1X
236 C6 Harrington Gardens SW7
236 E5 Harrington Road SW7
233 M1 Harrington Square NW1
233 M2 Harrington Street NW1
234 D2 Harrison Street WC1H
233 G6 Harrowby Street W1H
240 B2 Harrow Place E1
232 A4 Harrow Road W2
240 A3 Hart Street EC3R
237 G5 Hasker Street SW3
234 C2 Hastings Street WC1H
239 G1 Hatfields SE1
232 B6 Hatherley Grove W2
241 G6 Hatteraick Road SE16
235 G4 Hatton Garden EC1N
232 E4 Hatton Street W2
235 G4 Hatton Wall EC1N
241 H3 Havering Street E1
235 J1 Haverstock Street N1
241 H6 Hawke Place * SE16
240 B3 Haydon Street EC3N
233 G4 Hayes Place NW1
233 L8 Hay Hill W1J
239 H5 Hayles Street SE11
234 B8 Haymarket SW1Y
235 J4 Hayne Street EC1A
239 M1 Hay's Lane SE1
233 L8 Hay's Mews W1J
235 H3 Haywood Place EC1R
237 K3 Headfort Place SW1X
241 H2 Head Street E1
241 K2 Hearnshaw Street E14
235 M4 Hearn Street EC2A
234 E3 Heathcote Street WC1N
233 M7 Heddon Street W1B
234 A7 Heddon Street W1S
239 H5 Hedger Street SE11
239 J8 Heiron Street SE17
240 D5 Hellings Street E1W
235 K3 Helmet Row EC1V
241 L8 Helsinki Square SE16
232 E3 Henderson Drive NW8
240 A3 Heneage Lane EC3A
240 C1 Heneage Street E1
233 L6 Henrietta Place W1G
234 D7 Henrietta Street WC2E
240 D2 Henriques Street E1
239 L5 Henshaw Street SE17
235 G4 Herbal Hill EC1R
237 H4 Herbert Crescent SW1X
234 C3 Herbrand Street WC1H
238 F4 Hercules Road SE1
232 A6 Hereford Road W2
236 D6 Hereford Square SW7
232 E5 Hermitage Street W2
240 D5 Hermitage Wall E1W
235 H2 Hermit Street EC1V
241 K5 Heron Place SE16
241 M5 Heron Quay E14
238 C6 Herrick Street SW1P
237 K2 Hertford Street W1J
241 M4 Hertsmere Road E14
236 B6 Hesper Mews SW5
240 E3 Hessel Street E1
235 M3 Hewett Street EC2A
239 J5 Heygate Estate SE17
239 J5 Heygate Street SE17
238 B6 Hide Place SW1P
234 E5 High Holborn WC1V
236 A3 High Street Kensington ⊖ W8
236 A8 Hildyard Road SW6
240 F5 Hilliards Court E1W
239 J8 Hillingdon Street SE17
232 D1 Hill Road NW8
233 M6 Hills Place W1F
233 K8 Hill Street W1J
233 K6 Hinde Street W1U
241 M3 Hind Grove E14
241 M3 Hindgrove Area E14
241 G8 Hithe Grove SE16
237 K4 Hobart Place SW1W
236 D8 Hobury Street SW10
236 B6 Hogarth Road SW5
237 J6 Holbein Mews SW1W
237 J6 Holbein Place SW1W
235 G5 Holborn EC1N
234 E5 Holborn ⊖ WC2B
235 G5 Holborn Viaduct EC1N
234 F2 Holford Street WC1X
239 H1 Holland Street SE1
236 A3 Holland Street W8
234 A6 Hollen Street W1F
233 L6 Holles Street W1C
236 C8 Hollywood Road SW10
239 H5 Holyoak Road SE11
239 M2 Holyrood Street SE1
240 A6 Holyrood Street SE1
235 M4 Holywell Row EC2A
235 M1 Homefield Street * N1
233 G5 Homer Row W1H
233 G5 Homer Street W1H
240 D3 Hooper Street E1
240 C1 Hopetown Street E1
234 A7 Hopkins Street W1F
239 H1 Hopton Street SE1
239 L8 Hopwood Road SE17
236 A3 Hornton Place W8
236 A2 Hornton Street W8
234 B7 Horse & Dolphin Yard W1D
241 J3 Horseferry Road E14
238 B4 Horseferry Road SW1P
238 C2 Horse Guards Avenue SW1A
238 C2 Horse Guards Parade SW1A
238 C2 Horse Guards Road SW1A
240 B6 Horselydown Lane SE1
239 K8 Horsley Street SE17
235 H5 Hosier Lane EC1A
241 G8 Hothfield Place SE16
238 F8 Hotspur Street SE11
234 E6 Houghton Street WC2A
240 A2 Houndsditch EC3A
238 A4 Howick Place SW1E
234 A4 Howland Street W1T
241 K7 Howland Way SE16
232 D4 Howley Place W2
235 M2 Hoxton Square N1
235 M1 Hoxton Street N1
237 L6 Hugh Mews SW1V
237 L6 Hugh Street SW1V
237 L6 Hugh Street SW1V
241 J6 Hull Close SE16
235 J2 Hull Street EC1V
238 E1 Hungerford Bridge SE1
239 M4 Hunter Close SE1
234 D3 Hunter Street WC1N
234 A4 Huntley Street WC1E
239 M6 Huntsman Street SE17
233 H3 Huntsworth Mews NW1
241 H6 Hurley Crescent SE16
241 M7 Hutching's Street E14
235 G7 Hutton Street EC4Y
237 K2 Hyde Park Corner W1J
237 K2 Hyde Park Corner ⊖ W1J
236 D3 Hyde Park Court SW7
232 F6 Hyde Park Crescent W2
232 F7 Hyde Park Garden Mews W2
232 F7 Hyde Park Gardens W2
236 C3 Hyde Park Gate SW7
236 D3 Hyde Park Gate SW7
232 F7 Hyde Park Square W2
232 F7 Hyde Park Street W2

I

235 M7 Idol Lane EC3R
236 B8 Ifield Road SW10
239 J6 Iliffe Street SE17
239 J6 Iliffe Yard SE17
236 D4 Imperial College Road SW7
240 B3 India Street EC3N
234 A7 Ingestre Place W1F
234 F2 Inglebert Street EC1R
238 E5 Ingram Close SE11
233 J2 Inner Circle NW1
232 B6 Inverness Terrace W2
232 C8 Inverness Terrace Gate W2
239 H1 Invicta Plaza SE1
239 L7 Inville Road SE17
235 K6 Ironmonger Lane EC2V
235 K2 Ironmonger Row EC1V
234 C8 Irving Street WC2N
241 G6 Isambard Place SE16
241 K3 Island Row E14
236 A4 Iverna Court W8
236 A4 Iverna Gardens W8
237 G5 Ives Street SW3
233 G4 Ivor Place NW1
236 F6 Ixworth Place SW3

J

240 C6 Jacob Street SE1
240 F8 Jamaica Gate SE16
240 C7 Jamaica Road SE1
240 E7 Jamaica Road SE16
241 G2 Jamaica Street E1
240 C6 Jamaica Wharf SE1
233 K6 James Street W1U
234 D7 James Street WC2E
236 A1 Jameson Street W8
241 K1 Jamuna Close E14
240 D7 Janeway Street SE16
241 J4 Jardine Road E1W
240 C6 Java Wharf SE1
236 D3 Jay Mews SW7
234 A8 Jermyn Street SW1Y
232 F3 Jerome Crescent NW8
240 B3 Jewery Street EC3N
239 G2 Joan Street SE1
234 E4 Jockey's Fields WC1R
238 F3 Johanna Street SE1
234 D8 John Adam Street WC2N
235 G7 John Carpenter Street EC4Y
240 D7 John Felton Road SE16
240 C4 John Fisher Street E1
238 C5 John Islip Street SW1P
233 L6 John Prince's Street W1G
240 D7 John Roll Way SE16
239 J8 John Ruskin Street SE5
238 C6 John Slip Street SW1P
234 E4 John's Mews WC1N
238 A7 Johnson's Place SW1V
241 G3 Johnson Street E1
234 E4 John Street WC1N
239 L1 Joiner Street SE1
238 E6 Jonathan Street SE11
237 G6 Jubilee Place SW3
241 G2 Jubilee Street E1
236 B1 Jubilee Walk W8
234 C2 Judd Street WC1H
232 F5 Junction Mews W2
238 E5 Juxon Street SE11

K

241 H5 Katherine Close SE16
234 E6 Kean Street WC2B
241 J6 Keel Close SE16
234 E6 Keeley Street WC2B
240 E7 Keeton's Road SE16
239 H3 Kell Street SE1
236 B4 Kelso Place W8
234 E6 Kemble Street WC2B
236 A7 Kempsford Gardens SW5
239 G6 Kempsford Road SE11
233 J5 Kendall Place W1U
233 G6 Kendal Street W2
240 D5 Kennet Street E1W
241 G6 Kenning Street SE16
239 G7 Kennings Way SE11
239 H7 Kennington ⊖ SE11
238 E7 Kennington Lane SE11
238 E8 Kennington Oval SE11
239 G8 Kennington Park Gardens SE11
239 G7 Kennington Park Place SE11
239 G7 Kennington Park Road SE11
238 F4 Kennington Road SE1
239 G5 Kennington Road SE11
238 F8 Kennnington Oval SE11
233 J5 Kenrick Place W1U
236 A1 Kensington Church Street W8
236 B3 Kensington Court W8
232 B6 Kensington Gardens Square W2
236 C4 Kensington Gate W8
236 D3 Kensington Gore SW7
236 A4 Kensington High Street W8
236 B1 Kensington Palace Gardens W8
236 B2 Kensington Palace Gardens W8
236 A1 Kensington Place W8
237 G3 Kensington Road SW7
236 B3 Kensington Road W8
236 B3 Kensington Square W8
234 C3 Kenton Street WC1H
236 A6 Kenway Road SW5
234 D1 Keystone Close N1
239 H4 Keyworth Street SE1
232 A2 Kilburn Park Road NW6
232 A6 Kildare Terrace W2
234 E1 Killick Street N1
241 H6 Kinburn Street SE16
240 E2 Kinder Street E1
241 H5 King & Queen Wharf SE16
239 K6 King and Queen Street SE17
238 C2 King Charles Street SW1A
232 C5 Kingdom Street W2
239 G4 King Edward Walk SE1
239 H3 King James Street SE1
233 M7 Kingly Street W1F
235 L6 King's Arms Yard EC2R
239 H2 King's Bench Street SE1
235 H7 Kingscote Street EC4V
234 D1 King's Cross ⇌ N1C
234 E2 King's Cross Road WC1X
234 D1 King's Cross St Pancras ⊖ N1C
239 L1 Kings Head Yard SE1
234 F4 King's Mews WC1N
232 E1 Kingsmill Terrace NW8
235 J2 King Square EC1V
236 E8 Kings Road SW3
237 M5 King's Scholars Passage SW1P
240 F6 King's Stairs Close SE16
234 D7 King Street EC2V
238 A1 King Street SW1Y
235 K6 King Street WC2E
234 E6 Kingsway WC2B
235 L7 King William Street EC4N
237 J3 Kinnerton Place North * SW1X
237 J3 Kinnerton Place South * SW1X
237 J3 Kinnerton Street SW1X
237 J3 Kinnerton Yard * SW1X
239 L3 Kipling Estate SE1
239 L3 Kipling Street SE1
240 D7 Kirby Estate SE16
239 M3 Kirby Grove SE1
235 G4 Kirby Street EC1N
236 B5 Knaresborough Place SW5

235 H7 Knightrider Street EC4V
237 H3 Knightsbridge SW1X
237 H3 Knightsbridge ⊖ SW3
233 H4 Knox Street NW1
236 C4 Kynance Mews SW7
236 C4 Kynance Place SW7

L

235 L4 Lackington Street EC2A
240 B6 Lafone Street SE1
241 H5 Lagado Mews SE16
238 D5 Lambeth Bridge SW1P
238 E5 Lambeth High Street SE1
235 J7 Lambeth Hill EC4V
238 F3 Lambeth North ⊖ SE1
238 E4 Lambeth Palace Road SE1
238 F4 Lambeth Road SE1
238 F5 Lambeth Walk SE11
234 E4 Lamb's Conduit Street WC1N
235 K4 Lamb's Passage EC1Y
240 B1 Lamb Street E1
240 A7 Lamb Way SE1
239 H5 Lamlash Street SE11
232 D3 Lanark Place W9
232 B1 Lanark Road W9
232 D7 Lancaster Gate W2
232 D8 Lancaster Gate W2
232 E7 Lancaster Gate ⊖ W2
232 D7 Lancaster Mews W2
234 E7 Lancaster Place WC2E
239 H3 Lancaster Street SE1
232 E7 Lancaster Terrace W2
232 D8 Lancaster Walk W2
237 G3 Lancelot Place SW7
234 B2 Lancing Street NW1
237 J3 Lanesborough Place * SW1X
240 E3 Langdale Street E1
232 D1 Langford Place NW8
233 L5 Langham Place W1B
233 L5 Langham Street W1W
233 M5 Langham Street W1W
238 D8 Langley Lane SW8
234 C7 Langley Street WC2H
234 E3 Langton Close WC1X
232 A3 Lanhill Road W9
239 L4 Lansdowne Place SE1
239 J3 Lant Street SE1
239 K6 Larcom Street SE17
232 B3 Lauderdale Road W9
238 E7 Laud Street SE11
238 F3 Launcelot Street SE1
236 C4 Launceston Place W8
235 L7 Laurence Pountney Lane EC4V
241 K5 Lavender Road SE16
241 K4 Lavender Wharf SE16
239 J1 Lavington Street SE1
238 D8 Lawn Lane SW8
236 F8 Lawrence Street SW3
241 L6 Lawrence Wharf SE16
239 L4 Law Street SE1
233 L3 Laxton Place NW1
234 F4 Laystall Street EC1R
240 A3 Leadenhall Street EC3A
235 M6 Leadenhall Street EC3V
238 E2 Leake Street SE1
235 G4 Leather Lane EC1N
239 M3 Leathermarket Street SE1
234 E2 Leeke Street WC1X
233 J7 Lees Place W1K
234 B7 Leicester Square WC2H
234 C7 Leicester Square ⊖ WC2H
234 B7 Leicester Street WC2H
234 C3 Leigh Street WC1H
232 C6 Leinster Gardens W2
232 C7 Leinster Mews W2
232 C7 Leinster Place W2
232 A7 Leinster Square W2
232 C7 Leinster Terrace W2
240 C3 Leman Street E1
237 G4 Lennox Gardens SW1X
237 G5 Lennox Gardens Mews SW1X
235 L3 Leonard Street EC2A
241 M1 Leopold Estate E3
241 L1 Leopold Street E3
239 M5 Leroy Street SE1
235 J2 Lever Street EC1V
238 B3 Lewisham Street W1H
236 A5 Lexham Gardens W8
236 A5 Lexham Mews W8
234 A7 Lexington Street W1F
240 B2 Leyden Street E1
241 H5 Leydon Close SE16
239 H3 Library Street SE1
234 A1 Lidlington Place NW1
232 F3 Lilestone Street NW8
240 D5 Lilley Close E1W
236 A7 Lillie Road SW6
236 A7 Lillie Yard SW6
235 H6 Limeburner Lane EC4M
240 D5 Lime Close E1W
241 L4 Limehouse Causeway E14
241 L3 Limehouse Link E14
241 J3 Limehouse ⇌ ⊖ E14
236 D8 Limerston Street SW10
235 M7 Lime Street EC3M
234 E6 Lincoln's Inn Fields WC2A
232 A8 Linden Gardens W2
240 F1 Lindley Street E1
238 B7 Lindsay Square SW1V
235 H4 Lindsey Street EC1A
233 G3 Linhope Street NW1
240 D8 Linsey Street SE16
234 B7 Lisle Street WC2H
232 F3 Lisson Green Estate NW8
233 G4 Lisson Grove NW1
232 F3 Lisson Grove NW8
232 F4 Lisson Street NW1
234 C7 Litchfield Street WC2H
233 M6 Little Argyll Street W1F
235 J5 Little Britain EC1A
237 K4 Little Chester Street SW1X
238 C3 Little George Street SW1P
234 A7 Little Marlborough Street W1F
235 G6 Little New Street EC4A
233 L6 Little Portland Street W1G
234 C5 Little Russell Street WC1A
237 M2 Little St James's Street SW1A
238 C3 Little Sanctuary SW1A
240 B3 Little Somerset Street E1
233 M5 Little Titchfield Street W1W
239 K7 Liverpool Grove SE17
235 M5 Liverpool Street EC2M
235 M5 Liverpool Street ⇌ ⊖ EC2M
235 K3 Lizard Street EC1V
240 D7 Llewellyn Street SE16
234 F2 Lloyd Baker Street WC1X
240 B3 Lloyd's Avenue EC3N
234 F2 Lloyd Square WC1X
235 G2 Lloyds Row EC1R
234 F2 Lloyd Street WC1X
241 L2 Locksley Estate E14
241 L1 Locksley Street E14
239 L3 Lockyer Street SE1
232 F3 Lodge Road NW8
240 D7 Loftie Street SE16
236 A5 Logan Place W8
240 B1 Lolesworth Close E1
238 F5 Lollard Street SE11
238 F6 Lollard Street SE11
239 J2 Loman Street SE1
240 D1 Lomas Street E1
235 G6 Lombard Lane EC4Y
235 L7 Lombard Street EC3V
235 L8 London Bridge EC4R
239 L1 London Bridge ⇌ ⊖ SE1
239 L1 London Bridge Street SE1
232 E6 London Mews W2
239 H4 London Road SE1
240 A3 London Street EC3R
232 E6 London Street W2
235 K5 London Wall EC2M
234 D7 Long Acre WC2E
233 L3 Longford Street NW1
235 J5 Long Lane EC1A
239 L3 Long Lane SE1
237 M5 Longmoore Street SW1V
236 A5 Longridge Road SW5
239 H5 Longville Road SE11
240 A8 Long Walk SE1
234 E4 Long Yard WC1N
238 C4 Lord North Street SW1P
234 E1 Lorenzo Street WC1X
239 J8 Lorrimore Road SE17
239 H8 Lorrimore Square SE17
235 L6 Lothbury EC2R
238 F7 Loughborough Street SE11
235 M7 Lovat Lane EC3R
235 K6 Love Lane EC2V
241 K7 Lovell Place SE16
241 K2 Lowell Street E14
237 K4 Lower Belgrave Street SW1W
237 L4 Lower Grosvenor Place SW1W
234 A7 Lower James Street W1F
234 A7 Lower John Street W1F
238 F3 Lower Marsh SE1
241 G7 Lower Road SE16
237 J6 Lower Sloane Street SW1W
240 A4 Lower Thames Street EC3R
237 J4 Lowndes Close * SW1X
237 J4 Lowndes Place SW1X
237 H3 Lowndes Square SW1X
237 J4 Lowndes Street SW1X
236 F5 Lucan Place SW3
240 C8 Lucey Road SE16
235 H6 Ludgate Circus EC4M
235 H6 Ludgate Hill EC4M
235 M3 Luke Street EC2A
241 G3 Lukin Street E1
233 K7 Lumley Street W1K
237 L7 Lupus Street SW1V
238 B7 Lupus Street SW1V
232 E4 Luton Street W2
233 J4 Luxborough Street W1U
237 J4 Lyall Mews SW1X
237 J4 Lyall Street SW1X
232 E3 Lyons Place NW8
239 K7 Lytham Street SE17

M

235 J2 Macclesfield Road EC1V
234 B7 Macclesfield Street * W1D
240 E5 Mace Close E1W
234 D6 Macklin Street WC2B
233 M2 Mackworth Street NW1
239 K7 Macleod Street SE17
233 M7 Maddox Street W1S
239 M2 Magdalen Street SE1
238 F8 Magee Street SE11
240 C6 Maguire Street SE1
232 D4 Maida Avenue W9
232 C2 Maida Vale W9
232 C2 Maida Vale ⊖ W9
239 K1 Maiden Lane SE1
234 D7 Maiden Lane WC2E
240 D7 Major Road SE16
237 G6 Makins Street SW3
234 B4 Malet Street WC1E
236 E8 Mallord Street SW3
232 F3 Mallory Street NW8
235 L3 Mallow Street EC1Y
235 H3 Malta Street EC1V
240 B7 Maltby Street SE1
233 J6 Manchester Square W1U
233 J5 Manchester Street W1U
239 L3 Manciple Street SE1
233 K6 Mandeville Place W1U
234 B6 Manette Street W1D
241 M6 Manilla Street E14
235 H2 Manningford Close EC1V
239 J7 Manor Place SE17
236 F7 Manresa Road SW3
240 C3 Mansell Street E1
233 K5 Mansfield Mews W1G
233 L5 Mansfield Street W1G
235 K7 Mansion House ⊖ EC4V
236 D5 Manson Mews SW7
236 D6 Manson Place SW7
241 J6 Mapleleaf Square SE16
240 F1 Maples Place E1
233 M4 Maple Street W1T
233 H7 Marble Arch ⊖ W1C
234 C3 Marchmont Street WC1H
233 L6 Margaret Street W1W
236 F7 Margaretta Terrace SW3
234 F3 Margery Street WC1X
240 E7 Marigold Street SE16
240 C7 Marine Street SE16
237 K1 Market Mews W1J
233 M6 Market Place W1W
237 G6 Markham Square SW3
237 G6 Markham Street SW3
240 A4 Mark Lane EC3R
232 E7 Marlborough Gate W2
232 C1 Marlborough Place NW8
238 A2 Marlborough Road SW1A
236 F6 Marlborough Street SW3
236 B4 Marloes Road W8
241 H6 Marlow Way SE16
241 K2 Maroon Street E14
234 A7 Marshall Street W1F
239 J2 Marshalsea Road SE1
238 C5 Marsham Street SW1P
241 M5 Marsh Wall E14
235 K3 Martha's Buildings EC1V
240 F3 Martha Street E1
235 L7 Martin Lane EC4V
232 A4 Maryland Road W9
232 A4 Marylands Road W9
233 G4 Marylebone ⇌ ⊖ NW1
233 K5 Marylebone High Street W1U
233 K6 Marylebone Lane W1U
233 G4 Marylebone Road NW1
233 K5 Marylebone Street W1G
238 F6 Marylee Way SE11
241 M2 Masjid Lane E14
239 M5 Mason Street SE17
239 M6 Massinger Street SE17
241 J1 Masters Street E1
241 J2 Matlock Street E14
238 C3 Matthew Parker Street W1H
238 B5 Maunsel Street SW1P
237 L1 Mayfair Place W1J
240 F7 Mayflower Street SE16
234 A1 Mayford Estate NW1
240 F4 Maynards Quay E1W
234 C8 May's Street WC2N
238 F4 Mcauley Close SE1
236 C5 Mcleod's Mews SW7
239 G8 Meadcroft Road SE11
239 H8 Meadcroft Road SE11
238 E8 Meadow Road SW8
239 J5 Meadow Row SE1
238 F4 Mead Row SE1
239 M4 Meakin Estate SE1
234 E3 Mecklenburgh Square WC1N
238 B5 Medway Street SW1P
240 E5 Meeting House Alley E1W
233 G4 Melcombe Place NW1
233 H4 Melcombe Street W1U
232 D2 Melina Place NW8
239 M2 Melior Street SE1
234 A2 Melton Street NW1
237 K3 Memorial Gates SW1W
238 F2 Mepham Street SE1
234 C7 Mercer Street WC2H
232 E5 Merchant Square W2
234 F2 Merlin Street EC1R
239 K2 Mermaid Court SE1
239 K4 Merrick Square SE1
236 A8 Merrington Road SW6
239 L7 Merrow Street SE17
239 G7 Methley Street SE11
239 G2 Meymott Street SE1
235 K1 Micawber Street N1
236 A8 Micklethwaite Lane SW6
240 A1 Middlesex Street E1
240 B2 Middlesex Street E1
235 J5 Middle Street EC1A
234 F7 Middle Temple WC2R
234 F7 Middle Temple Lane EC4Y
241 H6 Middleton Drive SE16
234 C1 Midland Road NW1
241 H6 Midship Close SE16
236 D7 Milborne Grove SW10
239 H3 Milcote Street SE1
238 D8 Miles Street SW8
234 F7 Milford Lane WC2R
235 K6 Milk Street EC2V
241 G4 Milk Yard E1W
238 D4 Millbank SW1P
235 J8 Millennium Bridge SE1
241 M6 Millennium Harbour E14
241 L4 Milligan Street E14
234 E4 Millman Mews WC1N
234 E4 Millman Street WC1N
241 K3 Mill Place E14
240 B7 Millstream Road SE1
240 C6 Mill Street SE1
233 L7 Mill Street W1S
237 G5 Milner Street SW3
235 K4 Milton Street EC2Y
239 G7 Milverton Street SE11
240 A4 Mincing Lane EC3M
237 J5 Minera Mews SW1W
240 B3 Minories EC3N
235 J3 Mitchell Street EC1V
239 G2 Mitre Road SE1
240 A3 Mitre Street EC3A
233 G5 Molyneux Street W1H
238 C4 Monck Street SW1P
239 G5 Monkton Street SE11
235 K5 Monkwell Square EC2Y
232 A6 Monmouth Place W2
232 A6 Monmouth Road W2
234 C6 Monmouth Street WC2H
239 L1 Montague Close SE1
234 C5 Montague Place EC3R
234 C5 Montague Street WC1B
233 H5 Montagu Mansions W1U
233 H5 Montagu Mews North W1H
233 H6 Montagu Mews West W1H
233 H5 Montagu Place W1H
233 H5 Montagu Row W1U
233 H5 Montagu Square W1H
233 H6 Montagu Street W1H
238 F7 Montford Place SE11
240 C1 Monthorpe Road E1
237 G3 Montpelier Square SW7
237 G3 Montpelier Street SW7
236 G3 Montpelier Walk SW7
237 K3 Montrose Place SW1X
235 L7 Monument ⊖ WC1B
235 L7 Monument Street EC3R
235 M7 Monument Street EC3R
241 G4 Monza Street E1W
241 G7 Moodkee Street SE16
237 H5 Moore Street SW3
235 L5 Moorfields EC2Y
235 L6 Moorgate EC2R
235 L5 Moorgate ⇌ ⊖ EC2Y
235 K5 Moor Lane EC2Y
234 C7 Moor Street W1D
235 K2 Mora Street EC1V
239 K6 Morecambe Street SE17
235 H2 Moreland Street EC1V
240 A5 More London SE1
238 A6 Moreton Place SW1V
238 B6 Moreton Street SW1V
238 A6 Moreton Terrace SW1V
239 M2 Morgan's Lane SE1
240 A5 Morgan's Lane SE1
239 G3 Morley Street SE1
233 M1 Mornington Crescent NW1
233 L1 Mornington Place NW1
233 L1 Mornington Terrace NW1
240 A7 Morocco Street SE1
237 M5 Morpeth Terrace SW1P
240 F3 Morris Street E1
232 A2 Morshead Road W9
234 A4 Mortimer Market WC1E
234 A5 Mortimer Street W1T
233 M5 Mortimer Street W1W
238 F4 Morton Place SE1
234 B5 Morwell Street WC1B
232 B7 Moscow Place W2
232 B7 Moscow Road W2
237 G5 Mossop Street SW3
237 J4 Motcomb Street SW1X
236 E2 Mount Gate W2
235 J3 Mount Mills EC1V
234 F4 Mount Pleasant WC1X
233 K8 Mount Row W1K
233 K8 Mount Street W1K
233 K8 Mount Street Mews W1K
240 E1 Mount Terrace E1
233 J5 Moxon Street W1U
240 D2 Mulberry Street E1
236 E8 Mulberry Walk SW3
232 F4 Mulready Street NW8
235 M2 Mundy Street N1
233 L3 Munster Square NW1
239 K5 Munton Road SE17
238 F3 Murphy Street SE1
235 K1 Murray Grove N1
241 G2 Musbury Street E1
240 A4 Muscovy Street EC3N
234 C5 Museum Street WC1A
235 G2 Myddelton Passage EC1R
235 G1 Myddelton Square EC1R
235 G3 Myddelton Street EC1R
240 D2 Myrdle Street E1

N

234 F2 Naoroji Street WC1X
235 K1 Napier Grove N1
241 K4 Narrow Street E14
233 L2 Nash Street NW1
233 M5 Nassau Street W1W
240 C2 Nathaniel Close * E1
234 C6 Neal Street WC2H
240 C8 Neckinger SE1
241 H7 Needleman Street SE16
232 A1 Nelson Close NW6
235 H1 Nelson Place N1
239 H2 Nelson Square SE1
240 E2 Nelson Street E1
235 H1 Nelson Terrace N1
241 G7 Neptune Street SE16
240 D4 Nesham Street E1W
236 D8 Netherton Grove SW10
233 M2 Netley Street NW1
236 A6 Nevern Place SW5
236 A6 Nevern Square SW5
236 E6 Neville Street SW7
240 E2 Newark Street E1
241 M8 New Atlas Wharf E14
233 L7 New Bond Street W1S
233 L8 New Bond Street W1S
235 H6 New Bridge Street EC4V
235 M5 New Broad Street EC2M
233 M7 New Burlington Street W1S
238 F7 Newburn Street SE11
235 J5 Newbury Street EC1A
232 E5 Newcastle Place W2
233 K5 New Cavendish Street W1G
235 J6 New Change EC4M
239 L8 New Church Road SE5
239 K2 Newcomen Street SE1
232 F1 Newcourt Street NW8
241 L3 Newell Street E14
235 G6 New Fetter Lane EC4A
235 H6 Newgate Street WC1A
240 B2 New Goulston Street E1
240 A7 Newham's Row SE1
239 H6 Newington Butts SE1
239 J4 Newington Causeway SE1
239 K5 New Kent Road SE1
240 F4 Newlands Quay E1W
234 A5 Newman Street W1T
235 M3 New North Place EC2A
235 L1 New North Road N1
234 D4 New North Street WC1N
234 C6 New Oxford Street WC1A
238 E5 Newport Street SE11
233 H6 New Quebec Street W1H
236 E3 New Ride SW7
240 E2 New Road E1
234 C7 New Row WC2N
238 D7 New Spring Gardens Walk SE1
234 F6 New Square WC2A
240 A2 New Street EC2M
235 G6 New Street Square EC4A
232 A6 Newton Road W2
234 D5 Newton Street WC2B
235 K5 New Union Street EC2Y
235 L7 Nicholas Lane EC3V
239 H1 Nicholson Street SE1
236 D8 Nightingale Place SW10
235 K2 Nile Street N1
238 C8 Nine Elms Lane SW8
235 J6 Noble Street EC2V
235 J1 Noel Road N1
234 A6 Noel Street W1F
241 L2 Norbiton Road E14
233 G6 Norfolk Crescent W2
232 E6 Norfolk Place W2
232 E6 Norfolk Square W2
235 J3 Norman Street EC1V
234 B8 Norris Street SW1Y
235 G3 Northampton Road EC1R
235 H2 Northampton Square EC1V
233 J7 North Audley Street W1K
232 F2 North Bank NW8
235 H3 Northburgh Street EC1V
232 F7 North Carriage Drive W2
234 D1 Northdown Street N1
241 K4 Northey Street E14
234 A2 North Gower Street NW1
234 E4 Northington Street WC1N
234 E4 North Mews WC1N
233 G7 North Ride W2
233 J7 North Row W1K
240 C3 North Tenter Street E1
236 F5 North Terrace SW3
240 B3 Northumberland Alley EC3N
238 C1 Northumberland Avenue WC2N
232 A6 Northumberland Place W2
238 C1 Northumberland Street WC2N
232 E5 North Wharf Road W2
232 D3 Northwick Terrace NW8
241 K7 Norway Gate SE16
241 L3 Norway Place E14
234 F5 Norwich Street EC4A
233 J4 Nottingham Place W1U
233 J4 Nottingham Street W1U
232 A8 Notting Hill Gate W11
236 A1 Notting Hill Gate ⊖ W11
232 D1 Nugent Terrace NW8
233 G6 Nutford Place W1H

O

239 G5 Oakden Street SE11
232 A3 Oakington Road W9
241 L3 Oak Lane E14
235 H1 Oakley Close N1
237 G8 Oakley Gardens SW3
234 A1 Oakley Square NW1
236 F8 Oakley Street SW3
232 F2 Oak Tree Road NW8
235 J5 Oat Lane EC1A
239 J6 Occupation Road SE17
241 J1 Ocean Square E1
241 L7 Odessa Street SE16
233 M5 Ogle Street W1W
235 H6 Old Bailey EC4M
237 J3 Old Barrack Yard SW1X
233 M8 Old Bond Street W1S
235 M6 Old Broad Street EC2N
236 B6 Old Brompton Road SW5
236 D6 Old Brompton Road SW7
233 M7 Old Burlington Street W1S
233 J4 Oldbury Place W1U
240 B2 Old Castle Street E1
233 L6 Old Cavendish Street W1G
241 H2 Old Church Road E1
236 E7 Old Church Street SW3
234 B7 Old Compton Street W1D
236 B3 Old Court Place W8
234 D4 Old Gloucester Street WC1N
240 C7 Old Jamaica Road SE16
235 K6 Old Jewry EC2R
239 M5 Old Kent Road SE1
233 G5 Old Marylebone Road NW1
240 C1 Old Montague Street E1
234 E5 Old North Street WC1X
238 E5 Old Paradise Street SE11
237 K2 Old Park Lane W1J
238 B4 Old Pye Street SW1P
238 B3 Old Queen Street W1H
234 F6 Old Square WC2A
235 J3 Old Street EC1V
235 L3 Old Street ⇌ ⊖ EC1Y
235 L3 Oliver's Yard EC1Y
239 J8 Olney Road SE17
239 K2 O'meara Street SE1
234 D1 Omega Place N1
241 J8 Onega Gate SE16
236 A8 Ongar Road SW6
236 D6 Onslow Gardens SW7
236 E5 Onslow Square SW7
236 E6 Onslow Square SW7
239 J4 Ontario Street SE1
241 M4 Ontario Way E14
239 H6 Opal Street SE1
241 G8 Orange Place SE16
237 K6 Orange Square SW1W
240 D5 Orange Street E1W
234 B8 Orange Street WC2H
239 L6 Orb Street SE17
232 E4 Orchardson Street NW8
233 J6 Orchard Street W1H
234 E4 Ordehall Street WC1N
239 H5 Orient Street SE11
232 B8 Orme Court W2
232 B8 Orme Lane W2
232 B8 Orme Square Gate W2
234 D4 Ormond Close WC1N
237 H7 Ormonde Gate SW3
234 A8 Ormond Yard SW1Y
238 E6 Orsett Street SE11
232 C6 Orsett Terrace W2
240 D5 Orton Street E1W
238 B6 Osbert Street SW1V
240 C2 Osborn Street E1
241 K7 Oslo Square SE16
233 L3 Osnaburgh Street NW1
233 L3 Osnaburgh Terrace NW1
233 J5 Ossington Buildings W1U
232 A7 Ossington Street W2
234 B1 Ossulston Street NW1
239 H5 Oswin Street SE11
239 H6 Othello Close SE1
239 H8 Otto Street SE17
233 H3 Outer Circle NW1
233 K1 Outer Circle NW1
238 F8 Oval ⊖ SE11
238 E7 Oval Way SE11
237 G4 Ovington Square SW3
237 G5 Ovington Street SW3
235 G1 Owen Street EC1V
234 B8 Oxendon Street SW1Y
233 M6 Oxford Circus ⊖ W1B
232 A1 Oxford Road NW6
232 F6 Oxford Square W2
233 L6 Oxford Street W1C
234 A6 Oxford Street WC1A

P

240 E3 Pace Place E1
241 H5 Pacific Wharf SE16
232 D6 Paddington ⇌ ⊖ W2
232 E5 Paddington Green W2
233 J5 Paddington Street W1U
241 K5 Pageant Crescent SE16
238 B5 Page Street SW1P
235 H2 Paget Street EC1V
234 E3 Pakenham Street WC1X
236 B2 Palace Avenue W8
232 A7 Palace Court W2
236 A1 Palace Gardens Terrace W8
236 C3 Palace Gate W8
236 B2 Palace Green W8
237 M4 Palace Place SW1E
237 M4 Palace Street SW1E
238 A1 Pall Mall SW1Y
238 B1 Pall Mall East SW1Y
238 B3 Palmer Street W1H
235 K6 Pancras Lane EC4N
234 B8 Panton Street SW1Y
240 E7 Paradise Street SE16
237 H8 Paradise Walk SW3
239 L4 Pardoner Street SE1
235 H3 Pardon Street EC1V
240 D2 Parfett Street E1
239 G1 Paris Garden SE1
233 K4 Park Crescent W1B
240 C7 Parker's Row SE1

234 D6 Parker Street WC2B
233 H7 Park Lane W1K
237 J1 Park Lane W2
237 M1 Park Place SW1A
233 H3 Park Road NW1
233 L3 Park Square East NW1
233 K3 Park Square Mews NW1
233 K3 Park Square West NW1
239 K1 Park Street SE1
233 J7 Park Street W1K
233 L1 Park Village East NW1
236 D8 Park Walk SW10
233 G6 Park West Place W2
238 C2 Parliament Street SW1A
238 B2 Parry Street SW8
237 J6 Passmore Street SW1W
234 A4 Pater Street W8
241 K5 Pattina Walk SE16
235 M3 Paul Street EC2A
236 E8 Paultons Square SW3
233 G3 Paveley Street NW1
237 H3 Pavilion Road SW1X
237 H4 Pavilion Street SW1X
237 L7 Paxton Terrace SW1V
237 L7 Peabody Avenue SW1V
239 J1 Peabody Estate SE1
239 J6 Peacock Street SE17
240 F5 Pearl Street E1W
239 G3 Pearman Street SE1
235 G3 Pear Tree Court EC1R
241 G4 Peartree Lane E1W
235 J3 Pear Tree Street EC1V
236 A1 Peel Street W8
235 K2 Peerless Street EC1V
236 F6 Pelham Crescent SW7
236 F5 Pelham Place SW7
236 F5 Pelham Street SW7
239 K8 Pelier Street SE17
235 G6 Pemberton Row EC4A
232 A8 Pembridge Gardens W2
232 A7 Pembridge Place W2
232 A7 Pembridge Square W2
232 A7 Pembridge Villas W11
237 J3 Pembroke Close SW1X
240 F5 Penang Street E1W
232 F5 Penfold Place NW8
232 E4 Penfold Street NW8
232 A5 Pennant Mews W8
240 D4 Pennington Street E1W
241 M4 Pennyfields E14
239 J7 Penrose Grove SE17
239 J7 Penrose Street SE17
240 F7 Penryn Road SE16
239 H6 Penton Place SE17
234 E2 Penton Rise WC1X
234 F1 Penton Street N1
234 E1 Pentonville Road N1
236 A6 Penywern Road SW5
239 J2 Pepper Street SE1
240 A4 Pepys Street EC3N
235 H3 Percival Street EC1V
234 F2 Percy Circus WC1X
234 B5 Percy Street W1T
238 B4 Perkin's Rent SW1P
236 D4 Petersham Mews SW7
236 C4 Petersham Place SW7
234 B7 Peter Street W1F
233 L3 Peto Place NW1
240 B2 Petticoat Lane E1
238 A3 Petty France W1H
240 A4 Petty Wales EC3R
237 G6 Petyward SW3
239 L7 Phelp Street SE17
237 G8 Phene Street SW3
236 A3 Phillimore Walk W8
235 M7 Philpot Lane EC3M
240 E2 Philpot Street E1
237 L5 Phipp's Mews SW1W
235 M3 Phipp Street EC2A
234 F3 Phoenix Place WC1X
234 B1 Phoenix Road NW1
234 C6 Phoenix Street WC2H
234 A8 Piccadilly W1J
237 L2 Piccadilly W1J
237 M1 Piccadilly Arcade SW1Y
234 A8 Piccadilly Circus W1B
234 B8 Piccadilly Circus ⊖ W1J
235 J2 Pickard Street EC1V
233 K6 Picton Place W1U
240 E6 Pier Head E1W
241 M3 Pigott Street E14
239 L3 Pilgrimage Street SE1
238 B6 Pimlico ⊖ SW1V
237 J6 Pimlico Road SW1W
240 D3 Pinchin Street E1
235 M4 Pindar Street EC2A
232 B3 Pindock Mews W9
234 F3 Pine Street EC1R
235 M1 Pitfield Street N1
241 H3 Pitsea Street E1
237 K2 Pitt's Head Mews W1J
236 A2 Pitt Street W8
241 L2 Pixley Street E14
235 L3 Platina Street * EC2A
241 L3 Plover Way SE16
240 D2 Plumbers Row E1
235 G5 Plumtree Court EC4A
232 F4 Plympton Street NW8
239 H2 Pocock Street SE1
234 A6 Poland Street W1F
233 L7 Pollen Street W1S
232 E3 Pollitt Drive NW8
239 G5 Polperrom SE11
234 B1 Polygon Road NW1
236 F6 Pond Place SW3
240 E3 Ponler Street E1
238 C6 Ponsonby Place SW1P
238 C6 Ponsonby Terrace SW1P
238 B8 Ponton Road SW1V
237 H4 Pont Street SW1X
241 H6 Poolmans Street SE16
240 B7 Pope Street SE1
232 B7 Poplar Place W2
235 H6 Poppin's Court EC4A
232 B7 Porchester Gardens W2
232 C8 Porchester Gate W2
232 G6 Porchester Place W2
232 B5 Porchester Road W2
232 B6 Porchester Square W2
232 C7 Porchester Terrace W2
232 C6 Porchester Terrace North W2
239 L1 Porlock Street SE1
233 H4 Porter Street NW1
232 D5 Porteus Road W2
233 L4 Portland Place W1B
233 L5 Portland Place W1B
240 E5 Portland Square E1W
239 L7 Portland Street SE17
233 J6 Portman Close W1H
233 J6 Portman Mews South W1H
233 J6 Portman Square W1H
233 J6 Portman Street W1H
234 F4 Portpool Lane EC1N
233 G6 Portsea Place W2
234 E6 Portsmouth Street WC2A
240 B3 Portsoken Street E1
234 E6 Portugal Street WC2A
239 L4 Potier Street SE1
240 B6 Potters Fields SE1
240 E7 Pottery Street SE16
235 K6 Poultry EC2V
234 D4 Powis Place WC1N
232 E6 Praed Mews W2
232 E6 Praed Street W2
238 E5 Pratt Walk SE1
241 M4 Premier Place E14
240 C3 Prescot Street E1
239 M5 Preston Close SE1
239 H1 Price's Street SE1
234 F2 Prideaux Place WC1X
240 A1 Primrose Street EC2A
232 F1 Prince Albert Road NW8
236 D3 Prince Consort Road SW7
240 C1 Princelet Street E1
236 F3 Prince of Wales Gate SW7
233 M8 Princes Arcade SW1Y
234 A8 Princes Arcade SW1Y
236 E3 Prince's Gardens SW7
236 E4 Prince's Gate Mews SW7
241 H5 Princes Riverside Road SE16
232 A7 Prince's Square W2
232 A1 Princess Road NW6
239 H4 Princess Street SE1
233 L6 Princes Street W1B
235 L6 Prince's Street EC2R
234 E5 Princeton Street WC1R
239 L4 Prioress Street SE1
234 E1 Priory Green Estate N1
236 D7 Priory Walk SW10
234 E5 Proctor Street WC1V
241 G5 Prospect Place E1W
240 E7 Prospect Street SE16
233 J7 Provident Court W1K
235 L1 Provost Street N1
240 F5 Prusom Street E1W
235 M7 Pudding Lane EC3R
240 D3 Pumphouse Mews E1
240 A7 Purbrook Street SE1
235 M1 Purcell Street N1
234 B1 Purchese Street NW1

Q

241 J7 Quebec Way SE16
238 B3 Queen Anne's Gate W1H
233 K5 Queen Ann Street W1G
240 B6 Queen Elizabeth Street SE1
237 J2 Queen Mother Gate W2
232 C7 Queensborough Terrace W2
236 E5 Queensburry Place SW7
232 C7 Queen's Gardens W2
236 D3 Queen's Gate SW7
236 D4 Queen's Gate SW7
236 D5 Queen's Gate Gardens SW7
236 D4 Queen's Gate Mews SW7
236 D4 Queen's Gate Place SW7
236 D4 Queen's Gate
Place Mews SW7
236 C4 Queen's Gate Terrace SW7
239 L2 Queens Head Yard SE1
232 B7 Queen's Mews W2
234 D4 Queen Square WC1N
239 K7 Queen's Row SE17
235 K7 Queen Street EC4N
237 L1 Queen Street W1J
235 K7 Queen Street Place EC4N
240 A5 Queen's Walk SE1
237 M2 Queen's Walk SW1A
232 B6 Queensway W2
232 B8 Queensway ⊖ W2
235 J7 Queen Victoria Street EC4V
235 H1 Quick Street N1

R

241 K2 Raby Street E14
240 B8 Radcliffe Road SE1
239 G7 Radcot Street SE11
232 E6 Radnor Mews W2
232 F6 Radnor Place W2
235 K3 Radnor Street EC1V
237 G7 Radnor Walk SW3
239 L1 Railway Approach SE1
241 G6 Railway Avenue SE16
234 D1 Railway Street N1
240 F5 Raine Street E1W
237 H7 Ralston Street SW3
233 M6 Ramillies Place W1F
233 M6 Ramillies Street W1F
240 E2 Rampart Street E1
238 B6 Rampayne Street SW1V
238 D6 Randall Road SE11
238 E6 Randall Row SE11
232 B1 Randolph Avenue W9
232 C3 Randolph Crescent W9
232 B1 Randolph Gardens NW6
232 D4 Randolph Mews W9
232 C4 Randolph Road W9
237 K6 Ranelagh Grove SW1W
237 K8 Ranelagh Road SW1V
240 B3 Rangoon Street * EC3N
232 F4 Ranston Street NW8
237 G3 Raphael Street SW7
241 J3 Ratcliffe Cross Street E1W
241 J3 Ratcliffe Lane E14
234 B5 Rathbone Place W1T
234 A5 Rathbone Street W1T
240 F1 Raven Row E1
239 G7 Ravensdon Street SE11
235 M3 Ravey Street EC2A
237 G5 Rawlings Street SW3
235 H2 Rawstone Street EC1V
235 G4 Ray Street EC1R
240 E5 Reardon Place E1W
240 E5 Reardon Street E1W
241 H1 Rectory Square E1
232 B6 Redan Place W2
237 G7 Redburn Street SW3
241 G4 Redcastle Close E1W
237 B7 Redcliffe Gardens SW10
236 C7 Redcliffe Mews SW10
236 C8 Redcliffe Place SW10
236 D7 Redcliffe Road SW10
236 B7 Redcliffe Square SW10
236 B8 Redcliffe Street SW10
239 K2 Redcross Way SE1
237 G7 Redesdale Street SW3
236 A5 Redfield Lane SW5
233 L1 Redhill Street NW1
239 K8 Red Lion Row SE5
234 E5 Red Lion Square WC1R
234 E5 Red Lion Street WC2B
241 G1 Redman's Road E1
233 J7 Red Place W1K
241 J8 Redriff Road SE16
239 G6 Reedworth Street SE11
233 J8 Reeves Mews W1K
240 D1 Regal Close E1
234 B1 Regan Way N1
238 B5 Regency Street SW1P
234 A7 Regent Place W1B
233 L4 Regent's Park ⊖ W1B
233 L2 Regent's Park Estate NW1
234 D2 Regent Square WC1H
234 B8 Regent Street SW1Y
233 M7 Regent Street W1S
237 G4 Relton Mews SW7
239 H4 Remington Street N1
234 E6 Remnant Street WC2A
241 G7 Renforth Street SE16
239 H5 Renfrew Road SE11
239 H1 Rennie Street SE1
239 M4 Rephidim Street SE1
241 K2 Repton Street E14
241 K7 Reveley Square SE16
233 J8 Rex Place W1K
241 L2 Rhodeswell Road E14
241 M3 Rich Street E14
236 A8 Rickett Street SW6
234 B4 Ridgemount Street WC1E
234 B4 Ridgemount Gardens WC1E
233 M5 Riding House Street W1W
240 B7 Riley Road SE1
239 J2 Risborough Street SE1
241 G7 Risdon Street SE16
234 F1 Rissinghill Street N1
234 F2 River Street EC1R
235 M3 Rivington Street EC2A
233 J6 Robert Adam Street W1U
241 J7 Roberts Close SE16
233 L2 Robert Street NW1
238 A5 Rochester Row SW1P
238 B5 Rochester Street SW1P
239 J4 Rockingham Street SE1
235 H1 Rocliffe Street N1
240 D5 Roding Mews E1W
233 H5 Rodmarton Street W1U
239 K5 Rodney Place SE17
239 K5 Rodney Road SE17
234 E1 Rodney Street N1
234 E4 Roger Street WC1N
236 D6 Roland Gardens SW7
239 L7 Roland Way SE17
240 E2 Romford Street E1
234 B7 Romilly Street W1D
238 C5 Romney Street SW1P
235 M7 Rood Lane EC3M
241 K7 Ropemaker Road SE16
235 L4 Ropemaker Street EC2Y
240 B7 Roper Lane SE1
241 K8 Rope Street SE16
241 G2 Rope Walk Gardens E1
236 D6 Rosary Gardens SW7
235 K3 Roscoe Street EC1Y
235 K8 Rose Alley SE1
234 F3 Rosebery Avenue EC1R
237 G6 Rosemoor Street SW3
234 C7 Rose Street WC2E
233 G3 Rossmore Road NW1
239 K8 Rotary Street SE1
241 G6 Rotherhithe ⊖ SE16
241 G6 Rotherhithe Street SE16
241 J4 Rotherhithe Street SE16
241 H5 Rotherhithe Tunnel SE16
239 M4 Rothsay Street SE1
236 F2 Rotten Row W2
240 C8 Rouel Road SE16
239 G2 Roupell Street SE1
237 H6 Royal Avenue SW3
237 H7 Royal Hospital Road SW3
240 C4 Royal Mint Street E1
232 B5 Royal Oak ⊖ W2
240 A7 Royal Oak Yard SE1
239 H8 Royal Road SE17
238 E3 Royal Street SE1
232 A1 Rudolph Road NW6
234 E4 Rugby Street WC1N
240 E4 Rum Close E1W
240 F7 Rupack Street SE16
234 B7 Rupert Street W1D
239 H2 Rushworth Street SE1
238 A2 Russell Court SW1A
234 C4 Russell Square WC1B
234 D7 Russell Street WC2E
241 K6 Russia Dock Road SE16
238 B5 Rutherford Street SW1P
237 G3 Rutland Gardens SW7
236 F3 Rutland Gate SW7
236 F4 Rutland Mews SW7
236 F4 Rutland Street SW7
238 A1 Ryder Street SW1Y

S

234 A8 Sackville Street W1S
235 G4 Saffron Hill EC1N
235 G4 Saffron Street EC1N
238 F5 Sail Street SE11
239 G8 St Agnes Place SE11
236 B4 St Alban's Grove W8
234 B8 St Alban's Street SW1Y
235 K5 St Alphage Garden EC2Y
235 H7 St Andrews Hill EC4V
233 L3 St Andrew's Place NW1
235 G5 St Andrew Street EC4A
234 B6 St Anne's Court W1F
238 C4 St Ann's Street SW1P
233 K7 St Anselm's Place W1K
237 K6 St Barnabas Street SW1W
240 B2 St Botolph Street EC3N
235 G6 St Bride Street EC4A
234 D2 St Chads Street WC1H
240 B3 St Clare Street EC3N
234 E6 St Clements Lane WC2A
235 G4 St Cross Street EC1N
235 M8 St Dunstan's Hill EC3R
235 M7 St Dunstan's Lane EC3R
241 J7 St Elmos Road SE16
238 B3 St Ermin's Hill W1H
239 H3 St George's Circus SE1
237 M6 St George's Drive SW1V
240 D3 St George's Estate E1
235 M7 St George's Lane * EC3R
239 G4 St George's Road SE1
238 B7 St George's Square SW1V
233 L7 St George Street W1S
234 C6 St Giles High Street WC2H
235 M6 St Helen's Place EC3A
234 B8 St James Market * SW1Y
238 B3 St James's Park ⊖ W1H
237 M2 St James's Place SW1A
240 D8 St James's Road SE16
238 A1 St James's Square SW1Y
237 M1 St James's Street SW1A
235 G3 St James Way EC1R
235 H4 St John's Lane EC1M
235 H4 St John's Place EC1M
235 H4 St John's Square EC1V
235 H2 St John Street EC1V
232 F1 St John's Wood
High Street NW8
232 E3 St John's Wood Road NW8
240 C5 St Katharine's Way E1W
237 H7 St Leonard's Terrace SW3
237 G8 St Loo Avenue SW3
235 K3 St Luke's Close EC1V
236 F6 St Luke's Street SW3
240 C2 St Manningtree E1
240 C3 St Mark Street E1
234 C7 St Martin's Lane WC2N
235 J6 St Martin's le Grand EC1A
235 M8 St Mary at Hill EC3R
240 A3 St Mary Avenue EC3A
240 F7 St Mary Church Street SE16
239 G5 St Mary's Grove SE11
232 D4 St Mary's Terrace W2
239 G5 St Mary's Way SE11
238 B4 St Matthew Street SW1P
232 F6 St Michael's Street W2
240 F7 St Olav's Square SE16
238 E7 St Oswald's Place SE11
234 C1 St Pancras
International ⇌ NW1
235 J6 St Paul's ⊖ EC1A
241 J5 St Paul's Avenue SE16
235 J6 St Paul's Churchyard EC4M
241 L1 St Paul's Way E3
232 B7 St Petersburgh Mews W2
232 B7 St Petersburgh Place W2
240 C6 St Saviours Wharf SE1
232 A5 St Stephen's Gardens W2
235 L7 St Swithin's Lane EC4N
239 L2 St Thomas Street SE1
233 J5 St Vincent Street W1U
238 D6 Salamanca Street SE1
232 B7 Salem Road W2
232 F5 Sale Place W2
235 G6 Salisbury Court EC4Y
233 H4 Salisbury Place W1H
232 F4 Salisbury Street NW8
241 J2 Salmon Lane E14
241 J5 Salter Road SE16
241 M4 Salter Street E14
232 F4 Samford Street NW8
240 D5 Sampson Street E1W
238 F6 Sancroft Street SE11
239 L6 Sandford Row SE17
234 E5 Sandland Street WC1R
241 L6 Sandpiper Close SE16
234 C2 Sandwich Street WC1H
240 B1 Sandy's Row E1
235 G3 Sans Walk EC1R
234 E6 Sardinia Street WC2A
240 B3 Savage Gardens EC3N
233 M7 Savile Row W1S
234 E8 Savoy Hill WC2R
234 D8 Savoy Place WC2R
234 E7 Savoy Street WC2E
239 J2 Sawyer Street SE1
234 A5 Scala Street W1T
240 E5 Scandrett Street E1W
240 C3 Scarborough Street E1
236 A4 Scarsdale Villas W8
241 H6 Schooner Close * SE16
239 H2 Scoresby Street SE1
237 H3 Scotch House Junction SW1X
238 C1 Scotland Place SW1A
232 E2 Scott Ellis Grove NW8
240 D7 Scott Lidgett Crescent SE16
235 M3 Scrutton Street EC2A
234 D2 Seaford Street WC1H
236 A8 Seagrave Road SW6
239 L5 Searles Road SE1
235 H2 Sebastian Street EC1V
238 F2 Secker Street SE1
239 M6 Sedan Way SE17
237 J5 Sedding Street SW1X
234 E3 Seddon Street WC1X
240 A4 Seething Lane EC3N
235 H3 Sekforde Street EC1R
241 M1 Selsey Street E14
236 E6 Selwood Place SW7
237 K6 Semley Place SW1W
232 B4 Senior Street W2
241 H2 Senrab Street E1
234 F6 Serle Street WC2A
236 E1 Serpentine Bridge W2
236 F2 Serpentine Road W2
241 G7 Seth Street SE16
240 D2 Settles Street E1
234 C6 Seven Dials WC2H
237 H3 Seville Street SW1X
232 A3 Sevington Street W9
235 J3 Seward Street EC1V
233 J6 Seymour Mews W1H
233 G5 Seymour Place W1H
233 H6 Seymour Street W1H
233 G7 Seymour Street W2
236 C7 Seymour Walk SW10
240 B6 Shad Thames SE1
240 C6 Shad Thames SE1
240 F3 Shadwell ⊖ ⊖ E1
240 F3 Shadwell Gardens E1
234 B7 Shaftesbury Avenue W1D
234 C6 Shaftesbury Avenue WC2H
235 K1 Shaftesbury Street N1
240 A6 Shand Street SE1
239 H7 Sharsted Street SE17
241 K2 Shaw Crescent E14
237 G7 Shawfield Street SW3
236 A2 Sheffield Terrace W8
232 D5 Sheldon Square W2
241 M1 Shelmerdine Close E3
234 D6 Shelton Street WC2H
235 K1 Shepherdess Walk N1
237 K1 Shepherd Street W1J
234 B6 Sheraton Street W1F
235 L7 Sherborne Lane EC4N
239 M2 Ship and Mermaid Row SE1
241 K7 Shipwright Road SE16
232 A3 Shirland Road W9
235 G5 Shoe Lane EC4A
240 B4 Shorter Street EC3N
234 C6 Shorts Gardens WC2H
239 G2 Short Street SE1
241 K4 Shoulder of Mutton Alley E14
233 G5 Shouldham Street W1H
232 F4 Shroton Street NW1
233 H4 Siddons Lane W1H
234 D3 Sidmouth Street WC1N
240 F2 Sidney Square E1
240 F1 Sidney Street E1
239 H3 Silex Street SE1
235 K4 Silk Street EC2Y
241 K5 Silver Walk SE16
239 K3 Silvester Street SE1
235 L3 Singer Street EC2A
237 J6 Skinner Place * SW1W
235 K7 Skinners Lane EC4V
235 G3 Skinner Street EC1R
240 F8 Slippers Place SE16
237 G6 Sloane Avenue SW3
237 J6 Sloane Court SW3
237 J6 Sloane Court East SW3
237 J6 Sloane Gardens SW1W
237 J5 Sloane Square SW1W
237 J6 Sloane Square ⊖ SW1W
237 H3 Sloane Street SW1X
237 J5 Sloane Terrace SW1X
240 E5 Smeaton Street E1W
235 H5 Smithfield Street EC1A
238 C4 Smith Square SW1P
237 G7 Smith Street SW3
237 G7 Smith Terrace SW3
241 G1 Smithy Street E1
235 M4 Snowden Street EC2A
235 H5 Snow Hill EC1A
239 L2 Snowsfields SE1
234 B6 Soho Square W1D
234 B6 Soho Street W1D
241 K7 Somerford Way SE16
232 F6 Somers Crescent W2
234 A1 Somerstown Estate NW1
239 L7 Sondes Street SE17
238 A3 South & West Africa
Gate SW1A
239 L3 Southall Place SE1
234 F5 Southampton
Buildings WC2A
234 D5 Southampton Place WC1A
234 D4 Southampton Row WC1B
234 D7 Southampton Street WC2E
233 K8 South Audley Street W1K
237 H3 South Carriage Drive SW1X
236 F3 South Carriage Drive SW7
237 J5 South Eaton Place SW1W
234 E1 Southern Street N1
236 E4 South Kensington ⊖ SW7
236 E5 South Kensington ⊖ SW7
238 D8 South Lambeth Road SW8
233 K7 South Molton Lane W1K
233 K7 South Molton Street W1K
236 E7 South Parade SW3
235 L5 South Place EC2M
241 L8 South Sea Street SE16
234 F5 South Square WC1R
237 J1 South Street W1K
240 C3 South Tenter Street E1
236 F5 South Terrace SW7
239 H2 Southwark ⊖ SE1
235 K8 Southwark Bridge SE1
239 J3 Southwark Bridge Road SE1
240 E8 Southwark Park Road SE16
239 H1 Southwark Street SE1
236 C5 Southwell Gardens SW7
232 E6 South Wharf Road W2
232 F6 Southwick Mews W2
232 F6 Southwick Place W2
232 F6 Southwick Street W2
240 F4 Sovereign Close E1W
241 J4 Sovereign Crescent SE16
233 J5 Spanish Place W1U
240 C8 Spa Road SE16
236 A6 Spear Mews SW5
240 C1 Spelman Street E1
241 K7 Spence Close SE16
235 H2 Spencer Street EC1V
238 A4 Spenser Street SW1E
241 J4 Spert Street E14
240 A1 Spital Square E1
238 C1 Spring Gardens SW1A
232 E6 Spring Street W2
239 L4 Spurgeon Street SE1
238 F3 Spur Road SE1
238 F7 Stables Way SE11
238 A2 Stable Yard Road SW1A
234 C6 Stacey Street WC2H
237 M3 Stafford Place SW1E
232 A2 Stafford Road NW6
233 M8 Stafford Street W1S
236 A3 Stafford Terrace W8
239 L2 Stainer Street SE1
241 M2 Stainsby Road E14
240 F8 Stalham Street SE16
239 G1 Stamford Street SE1
239 M6 Stanford Place SE1
236 B4 Stanford Road W8
241 H6 Stanhope Close * SE16
236 D5 Stanhope Gardens SW7
237 K1 Stanhope Gate W1K
236 D5 Stanhope Mews SW7
236 D5 Stanhope Mews East SW7
236 D5 Stanhope Mews West SW7
233 G7 Stanhope Place W2
233 G7 Stanhope Place Gate W2
237 K1 Stanhope Row W1J
233 M1 Stanhope Street NW1
232 E7 Stanhope Terrace W2
239 G7 Stannary Street SE11
241 J5 Staples Close SE16
239 L3 Staple Street SE1
234 A2 Starcross Street NW1
232 F6 Star Street W2
241 J5 Stave Yard Road SE16
239 K6 Stead Street SE17
239 J5 Steedman Street SE17
233 J3 Steel's Lane E1
241 K7 Steeres Way SE16
234 A3 Stephenson Way NW1
234 B5 Stephen Street W1T
241 H1 Stepney Green E1
241 J1 Stepney High Street E1
240 E1 Stepney Way E1
237 G3 Sterling Street SW7
240 E5 Stevedore Street E1W
240 A7 Stevens Street SE1
240 B1 Steward Street * E1
236 F6 Stewart's Grove SW3
235 J7 Stew Lane EC4V
238 A5 Stillington Street SW1P
240 D5 Stockholm Way E1W
241 M3 Stocks Place E14
234 F5 Stone Buildings WC2A
235 G6 Stonecutter Street EC4A
240 B2 Stoney Lane E1
239 K1 Stoney Street SE1
239 J7 Stopford Road SE17
234 B5 Store Street WC1E
238 C3 Storey's W1H

240 D8 Storks Road SE16
238 E6 Stoughton Close SE11
233 G6 Stourcliffe Street W1H
241 M6 Strafford Street E14
234 D8 Strand WC2R
233 K6 Stratford Place W1C
236 A5 Stratford Road W8
232 F7 Strathearn Place W2
237 L1 Stratton Street W1J
240 B2 Strype Street E1
232 A2 Stuart Road NW6
234 D6 Stukeley Street WC2B
239 J7 Sturgeon Road SE17
239 J3 Sturge Street SE1
235 K1 Sturt Street N1
240 D3 Stutfield Street E1
235 H1 Sudley Street N1
239 J3 Sudrey Street SE1
235 L7 Suffolk Lane EC4V
234 B8 Suffolk Street SW1Y
240 A4 Sugar Quay Walk EC3R
239 G5 Sullivan Road SE11
241 G2 Summercourt Road E1
236 E6 Summer Place SW7
234 F4 Summers Street EC1R
239 J1 Sumner Street SE1
232 A6 Sunderland Terrace W2
240 D8 Sun Passage SE16
235 M4 Sun Street EC2M
232 A4 Surrendale Place W9
241 H7 Surrey Quays Road SE16
239 H2 Surrey Row SE1
239 M6 Surrey Square SE17
234 E7 Surrey Street WC2E
241 H6 Surrey Water Road SE16
232 E6 Sussex Gardens W2
232 E7 Sussex Mews East W2
233 H3 Sussex Place NW1
232 E6 Sussex Place W2
232 E7 Sussex Square W2
237 L7 Sussex Street SW1V
232 A4 Sutherland Avenue W9
237 L6 Sutherland Row SW1V
239 J7 Sutherland Square SE17
237 L7 Sutherland Street SW1V
234 B8 Sutton Row W1D
241 G3 Sutton Street E1
235 K4 Suttons Way EC1Y
232 F3 Swain Street NW8
233 L6 Swallow Place W1B
234 A8 Swallow Street W1B
235 L8 Swan Lane EC4R
239 M4 Swan Mead SE1
241 G6 Swan Road SE16
239 K3 Swan Street SE1
237 H8 Swan Walk SW3
240 E4 Swedenborg Gardens E1
240 C7 Sweeney Crescent SE1
234 E2 Swinton Street WC1X
236 F6 Sydney Street SW3
237 H6 Symons Street SW3

T

239 L3 Tabard Gardens Estate SE1
239 L3 Tabard Street SE1
235 L3 Tabernacle Street EC2A
238 B6 Tachbrook Street SW1V
232 A6 Talbot Road W2
232 E6 Talbot Square W2
235 G7 Tallis Street EC4Y
236 A8 Tamworth Street SW6
240 A7 Tanner Street SE1
235 K1 Taplow Street N1
240 F3 Tarling Street E1
239 H7 Tarver Road SE17
239 M6 Tatum Street SE17
233 G3 Taunton Place NW1
234 C3 Tavistock Place WC1H
234 C3 Tavistock Square WC1H
234 D7 Tavistock Street WC2E
234 B3 Taviton Street WC1H
241 K6 Teak Close SE16
237 G7 Tedworth Square SW3
237 M7 Telford Terrace SW1V
241 G6 Temeraire Street SE16
234 F7 Temple ⊖ WC2R
235 G7 Temple Avenue EC4Y
235 G7 Temple Lane EC4Y
234 F7 Temple Place WC2R
236 A5 Templeton Place SW5
240 E5 Tench Street E1W
232 C7 Tenniel Close W2
239 L2 Tennis Street SE1
233 L6 Tenterden Street W1S
240 B1 Tenterground E1
241 J8 Teredo Street SE16
237 L4 Terminus Place SW1V
241 H6 Thame Road SE16
234 C2 Thanet Street WC1H
235 G6 Thavies Inn EC4A
233 K5 Thayer Street W1U
234 D8 The Arches WC2N
236 C7 The Boltons SW10
232 B8 The Broad Walk W2
236 C2 The Broad Walk W8
239 G2 The Cut SE1
239 G2 Theed Street SE1
236 D3 The Flower Walk W2
240 B8 The Grange SE1
240 E4 The Highway E1W
236 C7 The Little Boltons SW10
238 B2 The Mall SW1A
241 L3 The Mitre E14
234 E4 Theobald's Road WC1X
239 L5 Theobald Street SE1
236 E8 The Vale SW3
238 A4 Thirleby Road SW1P
240 D4 Thomas More Street E1W
241 M2 Thomas Road E14
235 K1 Thoresby Street N1
238 C5 Thorney Street SW1P
233 H4 Thornton Place W1H
239 K1 Thrale Street SE1
240 C1 Thrawl Street E1
235 L6 Threadneedle Street EC2R
241 L3 Three Colt Street E14
240 B6 Three Oak Lane SE1
235 L6 Throgmorton Avenue EC2N
235 L6 Throgmorton Street EC2N
240 D8 Thurland Road SE16
236 F5 Thurloe Place SW7
236 F5 Thurloe Square SW7
236 E5 Thurloe Street SW7
239 M7 Thurlow Street SE17
232 F6 Tichbourne Row W2
241 M8 Tiller Road E14
240 E3 Tillman Street E1
237 K1 Tilney Street W1J
241 J6 Timber Pond Road SE16
241 G1 Tinsley Road E1
238 D6 Tinworth Street SE11
239 L6 Tisdall Place SE17
237 H8 Tite Street SW3
239 J4 Tiverton Street SE1
235 L6 Token House Yard EC2R
234 A3 Tolmer's Square NW1
241 K2 Tomlin's Terrace E14
234 D2 Tonbridge Street WC1H
239 L1 Tooley Street SE1
240 B6 Tooley Street SE1
236 A2 Tor Gardens W8
232 A5 Torquay Street W2
235 G1 Torrens Street EC1V
240 D5 Torrington Place E1W
234 B4 Torrington Place WC1E
234 B4 Torrington Square WC1E
238 B3 Tothill Street W1H
234 A4 Tottenham Court Road W1T
234 B6 Tottenham Court Road ⊖ W1D
234 A5 Tottenham Street W1T
239 J3 Toulmin Street SE1
240 B5 Tower Bridge EC3N
240 B5 Tower Bridge Approach EC3N
240 A7 Tower Bridge Road SE1
240 C5 Tower Bridge Wharf E1W
240 B4 Tower Gateway ⊖ EC3N
240 B4 Tower Hill EC3N
240 B4 Tower Hill ⊖ EC3N
240 A4 Tower Place EC3R
234 C7 Tower Street WC2H
239 M5 Townsend Street SE17
240 B1 Toynbee Street E1
241 H1 Trafalgar Gardens E1
238 C1 Trafalgar Square WC2N
239 L7 Trafalgar Street SE17
232 F5 Transept Street NW1
237 L1 Trebeck Street W1J
236 A6 Trebovir Road SW5
236 C7 Tregunter Road SW10
240 E8 Trenton Road SE16
232 F5 Tresham Crescent NW8
237 G3 Trevor Place SW7
237 G3 Trevor Square SW7
237 G3 Trevor Street SW7
241 M4 Trinidad Street E14
239 K3 Trinity Church Square SE1
240 B4 Trinity Square EC3N
239 K3 Trinity Street SE1
235 K6 Trump Street EC2V
235 G7 Tudor Street EC4Y
238 C4 Tufton Street SW1P
241 G6 Tunnel Road SE16
237 J6 Turks Row SW3
241 L2 Turner's Road E3
240 E2 Turner Street E1
235 G4 Turnmill Street EC1N
237 L7 Turpentine Lane SW1V
239 K6 Turquand Street SE17
239 M3 Tyers Gate SE1
238 F7 Tyers Street SE11
238 E7 Tyers Terrace SE11
237 H6 Tyron Street SW3
235 G3 Tysoe Street EC1R

U

238 A5 Udall Street SW1P
239 G3 Ufford Street SE1
233 K6 Ulster Place W1G
240 E2 Umberston Street E1
240 A2 Undershaft EC3A
235 K2 Underwood Road N1
235 K1 Underwood Street N1
239 H2 Union Street SE1
234 A4 University Street WC1E
232 D6 Upbrook Mews W2
237 K4 Upper Belgrave Street SW1X
233 H6 Upper Berkeley Street W1H
233 J7 Upper Brook Street W1K
236 F8 Upper Cheyne Row SW3
233 J8 Upper Grosvenor Street W1K
238 F1 Upper Ground SE1
233 K3 Upper Harley Street NW1
234 A7 Upper James Street W1F
234 A7 Upper John Street W1F
238 E3 Upper Marsh SE1
233 H5 Upper Montagu Street W1H
234 C7 Upper St Martin's WC2H
238 A5 Upper Tachbrook Street SW1V
235 J7 Upper Thames Street EC4V
233 K4 Upper Wimpole Street W1G
234 B2 Upper Woburn Place WC1H
239 J8 Urlwin Street SE5
236 A1 Uxbridge Street W8

V

239 G3 Valentine Place SE1
238 A3 Vandon Passage W1H
238 A4 Vandon Street W1H
235 M4 Vandy Street EC2A
240 E2 Varden Street E1
233 M2 Varndell Street NW1
240 C8 Vauban Street SE16
241 L7 Vaughan Street SE16
240 D5 Vaughan Way E1W
238 D7 Vauxhall ⇌ ⊖ SE11
238 C7 Vauxhall Bridge SW1V
238 D7 Vauxhall Bridgefoot SE1
237 M5 Vauxhall Bridge Road SW1V
238 D8 Vauxhall Grove SW8
238 E6 Vauxhall Street SE11
238 E6 Vauxhall Walk SE11
232 E4 Venables Street W2
233 K6 Vere Street W1G
234 D5 Vernon Place WC1A
234 E2 Vernon Rise WC1X
234 F4 Verulam Street WC1X
235 L2 Vestry Street N1
237 L5 Victoria ⇌ ⊖ SW1V
238 D2 Victoria Embankment SW1A
234 F7 Victoria Embankment WC2R
232 F7 Victoria Gate W2
236 C4 Victoria Road W8
237 L4 Victoria Square SW1W
237 L4 Victoria Street SW1E
239 K5 Victory Place SE17
241 K7 Victory Way SE16
233 M8 Vigo Street W1S
239 L7 Villa Street SE17
234 D8 Villiers Street WC2N
241 K7 Vincent Close SE16
238 B5 Vincent Square SW1P
238 B5 Vincent Street SW1P
235 H1 Vincent Terrace N1
235 L2 Vince Street EC1V
240 D1 Vine Court E1
240 E5 Vinegar Street E1W
234 F4 Vine Hill EC1R
240 A6 Vine Lane SE1
240 B3 Vine Street EC3N
232 C1 Violet Hill NW8
238 F4 Virgil Street SE1
240 D4 Virginia Street E1W
235 J4 Viscount Street EC2Y

W

239 K6 Wadding Street SE17
234 D3 Wakefield Street WC1H
241 J3 Wakeling Street E14
235 H2 Wakley Street EC1V
235 L7 Walbrook EC4N
239 K6 Walcorde Avenue SE17
239 G5 Walcot Square SE11
240 E2 Walden Street E1
241 M1 Wallwood Street E14
238 F5 Walnut Tree Walk SE11
237 H6 Walpole Street SW3
241 H2 Walter Terrace E1
237 H4 Walton Place SW3
237 G4 Walton Street SW3
239 K7 Walworth Place SE17
239 J5 Walworth Road SE17
238 C8 Wandsworth Road SW8
239 J6 Wansey Street SE17
240 F5 Wapping ⊖ E1W
240 E6 Wapping High Street E1W
240 F4 Wapping Lane E1W
241 G5 Wapping Wall E1W
239 J2 Warden's Grove SE1
234 B6 Wardour Street W1F
234 F4 Warner Street EC1R
233 M4 Warren Street W1T
233 M3 Warren Street ⊖ NW1
232 C3 Warrington Crescent W9
232 C4 Warrington Gardens W9
232 B3 Warwick Avenue W9
232 C4 Warwick Avenue ⊖ W9
232 C5 Warwick Crescent W2
238 B1 Warwick House Street SW1Y
235 H6 Warwick Lane EC4M
232 C4 Warwick Place W9
236 A6 Warwick Road SW5
237 L4 Warwick Row SW1E
237 M6 Warwick Square SW1V
234 A7 Warwick Street W1B
237 L6 Warwick Way SW1V
234 F5 Waterhouse Square EC1N
238 F2 Waterloo ⇌ ⊖ SE1
238 E1 Waterloo Bridge SE1
234 E8 Waterloo Bridge WC2R
239 G2 Waterloo East ⇌ SE1
238 B1 Waterloo Place SW1Y
238 F1 Waterloo Road SE1
239 G2 Waterloo Road SE1
240 E5 Waterman Way E1W
240 D7 Waterside Close SE16
235 K7 Watling Street EC4N
240 F3 Watney Street E1
240 E5 Watts Street E1W
240 D5 Waveney Close E1W
233 K8 Waverton Street W1J
240 A6 Weavers Lane SE1
239 G3 Webber Row SE1
239 H3 Webber Street SE1
240 A8 Webb Street SE1
240 D8 Webster Road SE16
233 K7 Weigh House Street W1K
233 K5 Welbeck Street W1G
233 K6 Welbeck Way W1G
240 E5 Welland Mews E1W
240 D4 Wellclose Square E1
241 H2 Wellesley Street E1
235 K2 Wellesley Terrace N1
237 H6 Wellington Square SW3
232 E2 Wellington Place NW8
232 E1 Wellington Road NW8
234 D7 Wellington Street WC2E
234 A5 Wells Mews W1T
234 A5 Wells Street W1T
239 M8 Wells Way SE5
235 K1 Wenlock Road N1
235 K1 Wenlock Street N1
240 B2 Wentworth Street E1
234 A1 Werrington Street NW1
233 K5 Wesley Street W1G
241 G2 West Arbour Street E1
232 D7 Westbourne Crescent W2
232 B6 Westbourne Gardens W2
232 E7 Westbourne Gate W2
232 A6 Westbourne Grove W2
232 B6 Westbourne Grove Terrace W2
232 A5 Westbourne Park Road W2
232 A5 Westbourne Park Villas W2
232 E7 Westbourne Street W2
232 D6 Westbourne Terrace W2
232 C6 Westbourne Terrace Mews W2
232 C5 Westbourne Terrace Road W2
236 A7 West Brompton ⇌ ⊖ ⊖ SW5
236 E2 West Carriage Drive W2
239 H8 Westcott Road SE17
236 A5 West Cromwell Road SW5
241 G6 Western Place SE16
241 M4 Westferry ⊖ E14
241 M5 Westferry Circus E14
241 M5 Westferry Road E14
240 F4 West Gardens E1W
236 B7 Westgate Terrace SW10
237 J4 West Halkin Street SW1X
241 M5 West India Avenue E14
241 M3 West India Dock Road E14
235 K2 Westland Place N1
240 E7 West Lane SE16
238 D3 Westminster ⊖ SW1P
238 D3 Westminster Bridge SE1
238 F3 Westminster Bridge Road SE1
237 L7 Westmoreland Place SW1V
239 K8 Westmoreland Road SE17
233 K5 Westmoreland Street W1G
237 L7 Westmoreland Terrace SW1V
234 E1 Weston Rise WC1X
239 M2 Weston Street SE1
239 M3 Weston Street SE1
241 H2 Westport Street E1
235 H5 West Poultry Avenue EC1A
237 H7 West Road SW3
235 H5 West Smithfield EC1A
239 H4 West Square SE11
234 C7 West Street WC2H
240 C3 West Tenter Street E1
237 M6 West Warwick Place SW1V
232 B5 Westway W2
236 C6 Wetherby Gardens SW5
240 D2 Weyhill Road E1
233 L5 Weymouth Mews W1G
233 K5 Weymouth Street W1G
234 D1 Wharfdale Road N1
236 B7 Wharfedale Street SW10
235 J1 Wharf Road N1
234 F2 Wharton Street WC1X
233 K5 Wheatley Street W1G
234 E5 Whetstone Park WC2A
234 D2 Whidborne Street WC1H
235 G2 Whiskin Street EC1R
234 B8 Whitcomb Street WC2H
240 E1 Whitechapel ⊖ ⊖ E1
240 C4 Whitechapel Estate E1
240 C2 Whitechapel High Street E1
240 D1 Whitechapel Road E1
235 K3 Whitecross Street EC1Y
235 G6 Whitefriars Street EC4Y
238 C2 Whitehall SW1A
238 D2 Whitehall Court SW1A
238 D1 Whitehall Place SW1A
239 G6 White Hart Street SE11
239 L2 White Hart Yard SE1
232 F4 Whitehaven Street NW8
237 G6 Whitehead's Grove SW3
241 H1 White Horse Lane E1
241 J1 Whitehorse Road E1
241 J3 Whitehorse Road E1
237 L1 White Horse Street W1J
240 B2 White Kennett Street E1
235 H7 White Lion Hill EC4V
234 F1 White Lion Street N1
240 A7 White's Grounds SE1
240 B1 White's Row E1
241 J1 White Tower Way E1
234 A4 Whitfield Place W1T
234 A4 Whitfield Street W1T
238 E5 Whitgift Street SE11
237 J6 Whittaker Street SW1W
239 G2 Whittlesey Street SE1
240 E3 Wicker Street E1
241 G1 Wickham Close E1
238 E7 Wickham Street SE11
234 E2 Wicklow Street WC1X
240 A1 Widegate Street E1
232 A3 Widley Road W9
233 K5 Wigmore Place W1G
233 K6 Wigmore Street W1U
239 G7 Wigton Place SE11
237 J5 Wilbraham Place SW1X
234 E6 Wild Court WC2B
239 M4 Wild's Rents SE1
234 D6 Wild Street WC2B
237 M4 Wilfred Street SW1E
240 B1 Wilkes Street E1
234 C8 William IV Street WC2N
237 H3 William Mews SW1X
233 M3 William Road NW1
238 A5 Willow Place SW1P
235 M3 Willow Street EC2A
234 F3 Wilmington Square WC1X
234 F2 Wilmington Street WC1X
240 E7 Wilson Grove SE16
235 L4 Wilson Street EC2A
237 J3 Wilton Crescent SW1X
237 K4 Wilton Mews SW1X
237 J3 Wilton Place SW1X
237 L4 Wilton Road SW1V
237 J3 Wilton Row SW1X
237 K4 Wilton Street SW1X
233 K5 Wimpole Mews W1G
233 K5 Wimpole Street W1G
237 L6 Winchester Street SW1V
239 K1 Winchester Walk SE1
239 G5 Wincott Street SE11
238 F7 Windmill Road SE11
234 B5 Windmill Street W1T
241 H6 Windrose Close SE16
235 K1 Windsor Terrace N1
240 F5 Wine Close E1W
234 B7 Winnett Street W1D
232 E6 Winsland Mews W2
232 E6 Winsland Street W2
234 A6 Winsley Street W1W
240 E1 Winthrop Street E1
234 C3 Woburn Place WC1H
234 C4 Woburn Squuare WC1H
240 E1 Wodeham Gardens E1
241 H7 Wolfe Crescent SE16
240 C6 Wolseley Street SE1
235 G3 Woodbridge Street EC1R
232 A4 Woodchester Square W9
237 H7 Woodfall Street SW3
241 H7 Woodland Crescent SE16
240 C1 Woodseer Street E1
233 J7 Woods Mews W1K
240 A8 Woods Place SE1
233 K6 Woodstock Street W1C
235 K6 Wood Street EC2V
239 J5 Woolaston Close SE1
239 L7 Wooler Street SE17
239 G2 Wooton Street SE1
238 E6 Worgan Street SE11
241 H8 Worgan Street SE16
235 M5 Wormwood Street EC2M
235 M4 Worship Street EC2A
234 E3 Wren Street WC1X
236 A3 Wright's Lane W8
241 L7 Wyatt Close SE16
235 H2 Wyclif Street EC1V
232 A2 Wymering Road W9
238 F7 Wynard Terrace SE11
233 H5 Wyndham Place W1H
233 G4 Wyndham Street W1H
236 A4 Wynnstay Gardens W8
235 H2 Wynyat Street EC1V
233 H6 Wythburn Place W1H

Y

240 C8 Yalding Road SE16
234 F2 Yardley Street WC1X
237 G4 Yeomans Row SW3
234 D8 York Boulevard WC2N
233 J3 York Bridge NW1
233 J4 York Gate NW1
238 E2 York Road SE1
241 K3 Yorkshire Road E14
241 J2 York Square E14
233 G5 York Street W1H
233 J4 York Terrace East NW1
233 J4 York Terrace West NW1
234 D1 York Way N1

Z

239 J1 Zoar Street SE1

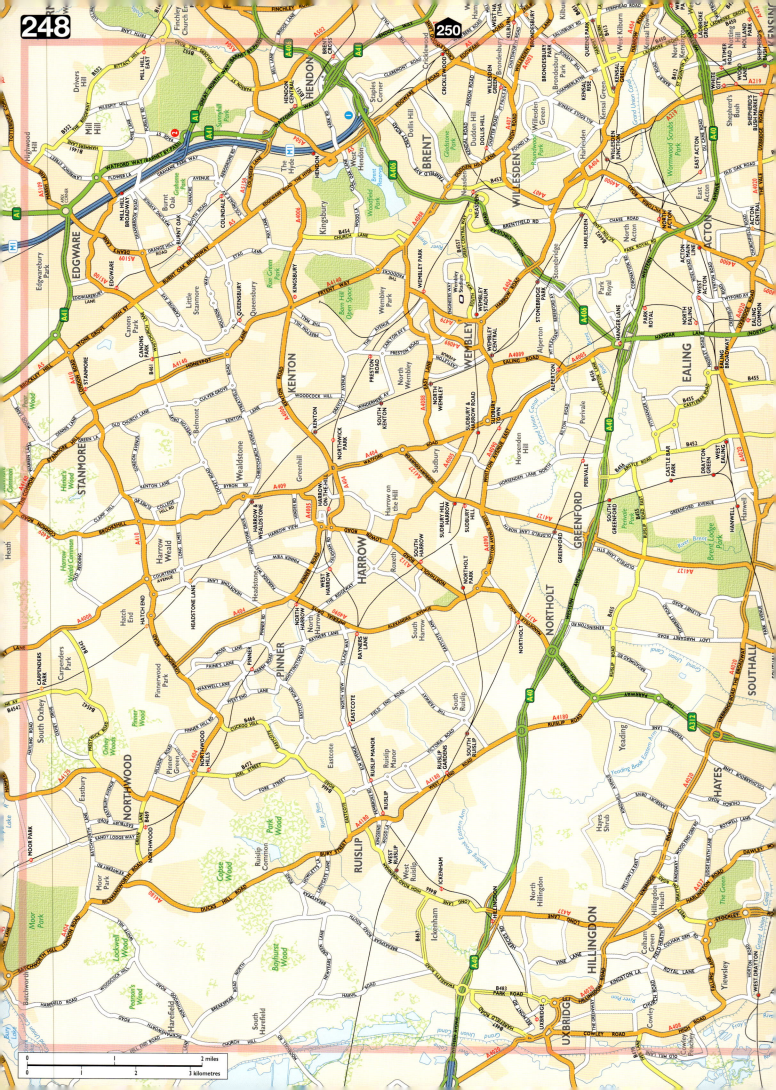

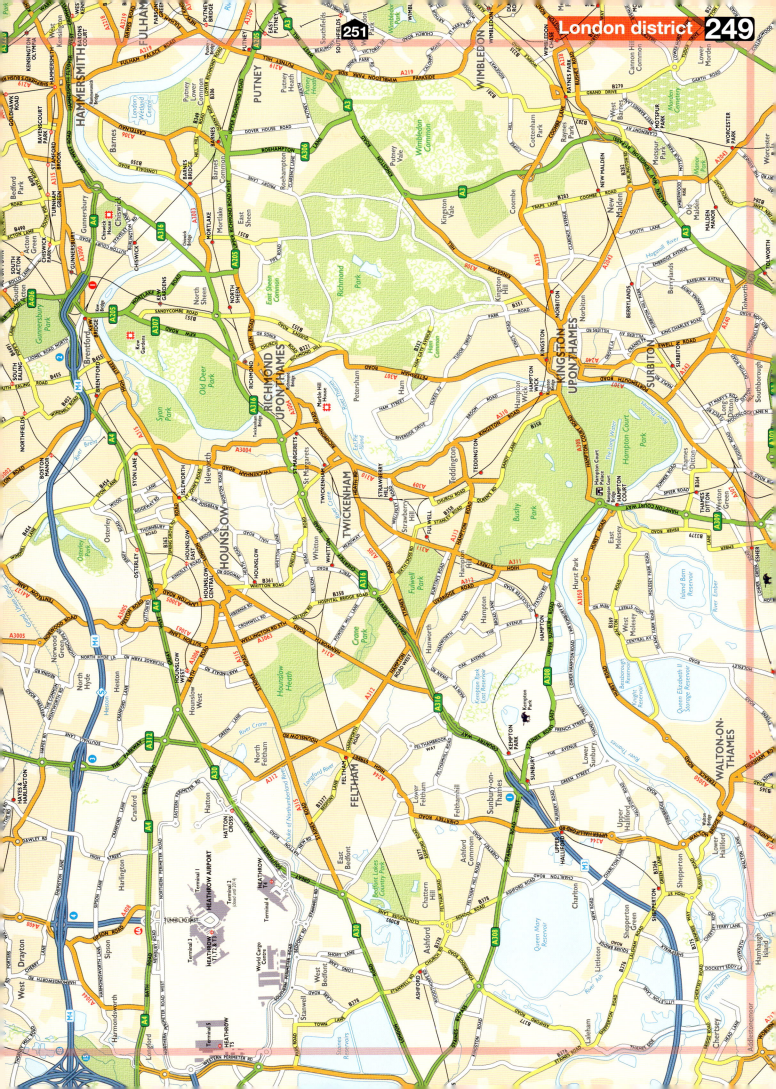

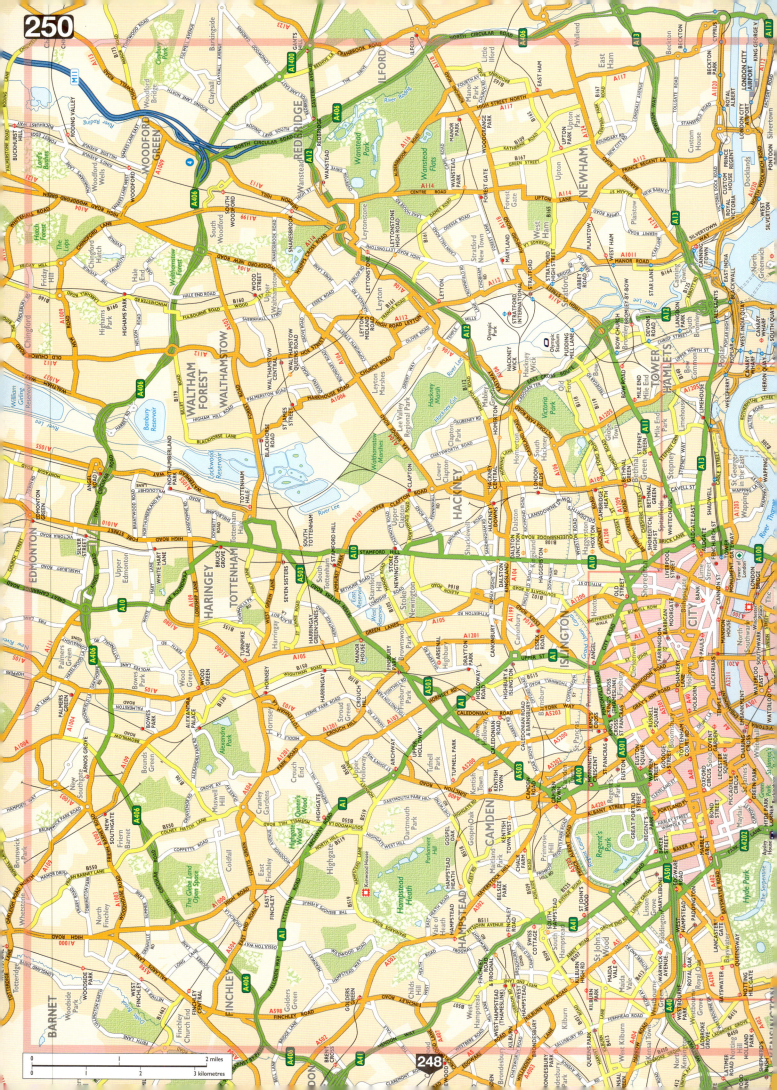

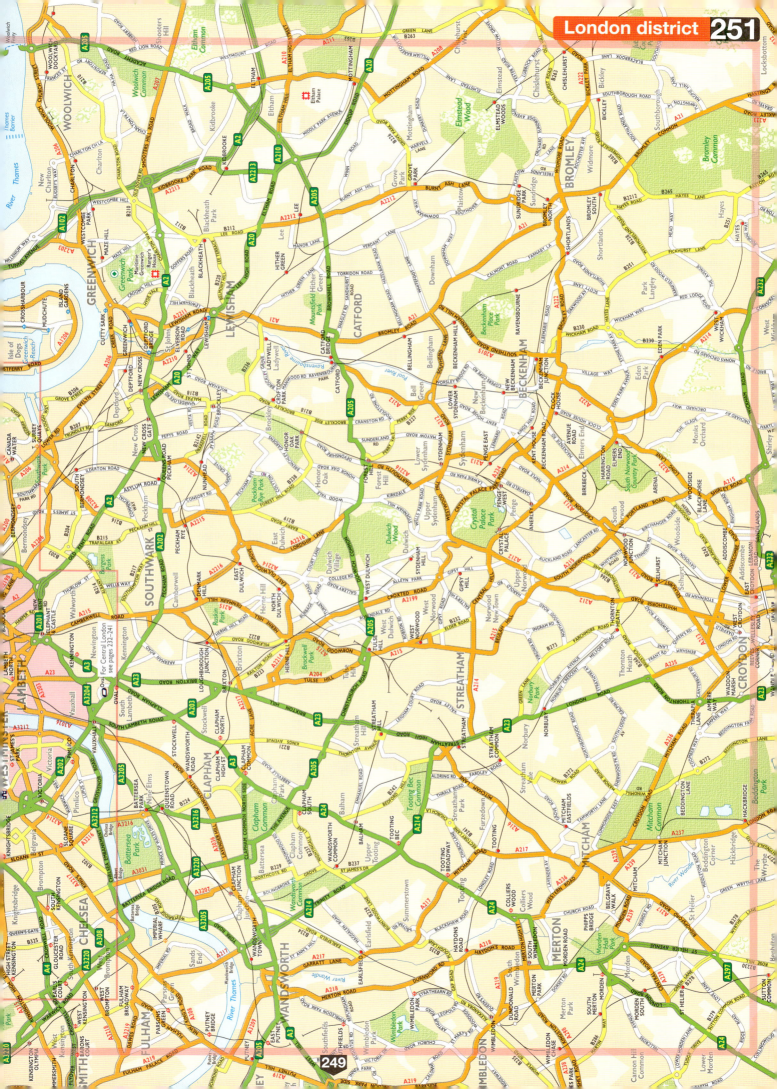

For Central London see pages 232–241

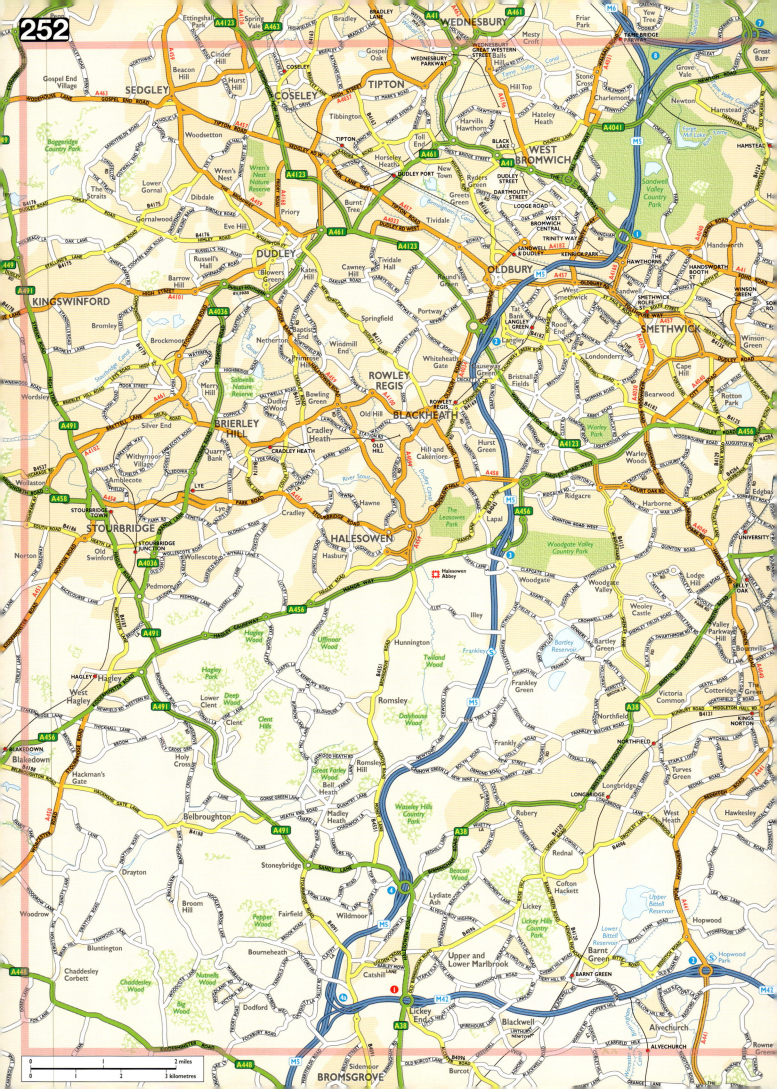

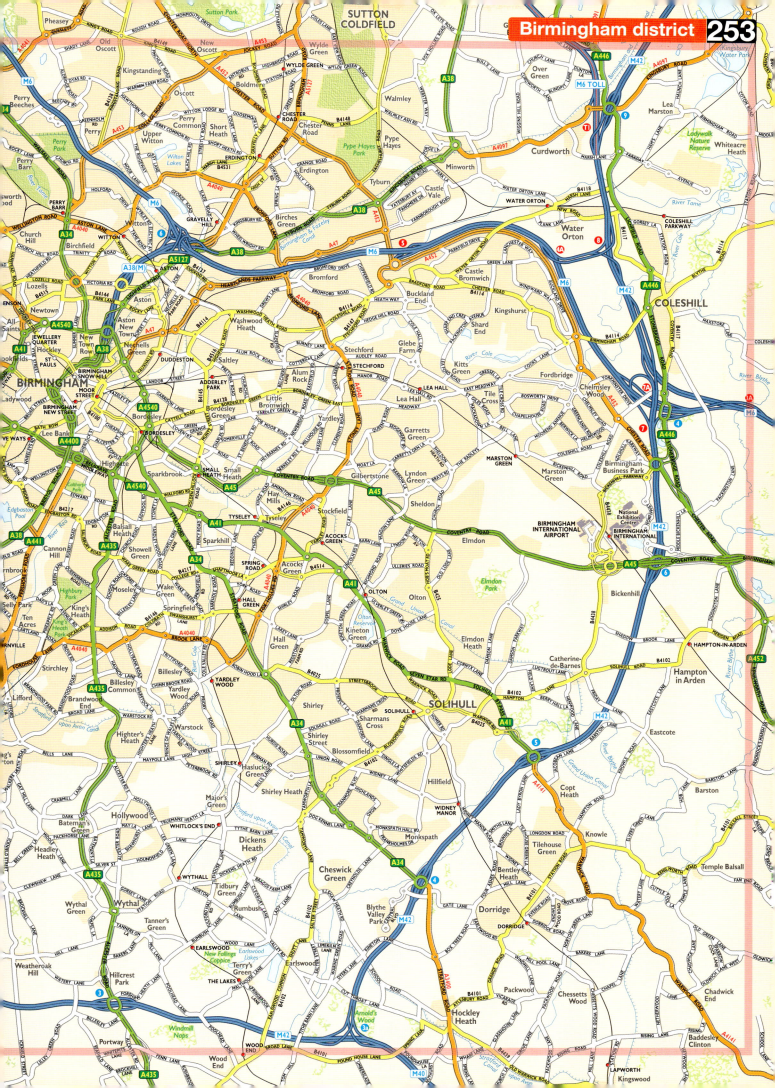

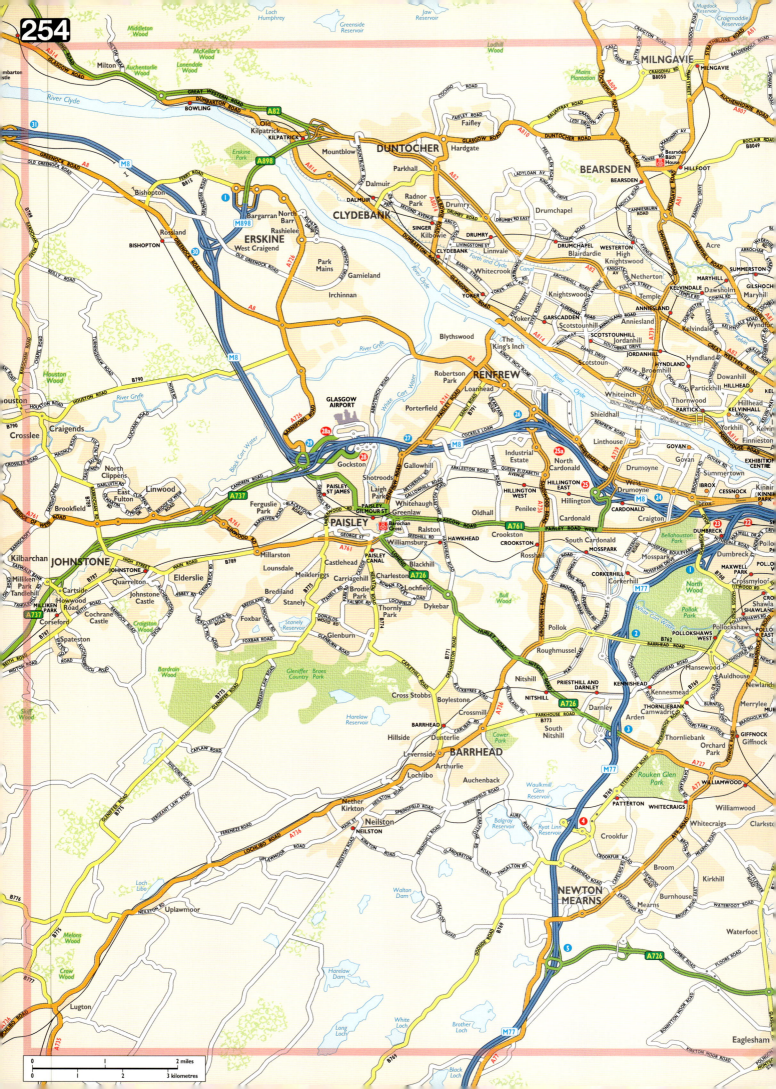

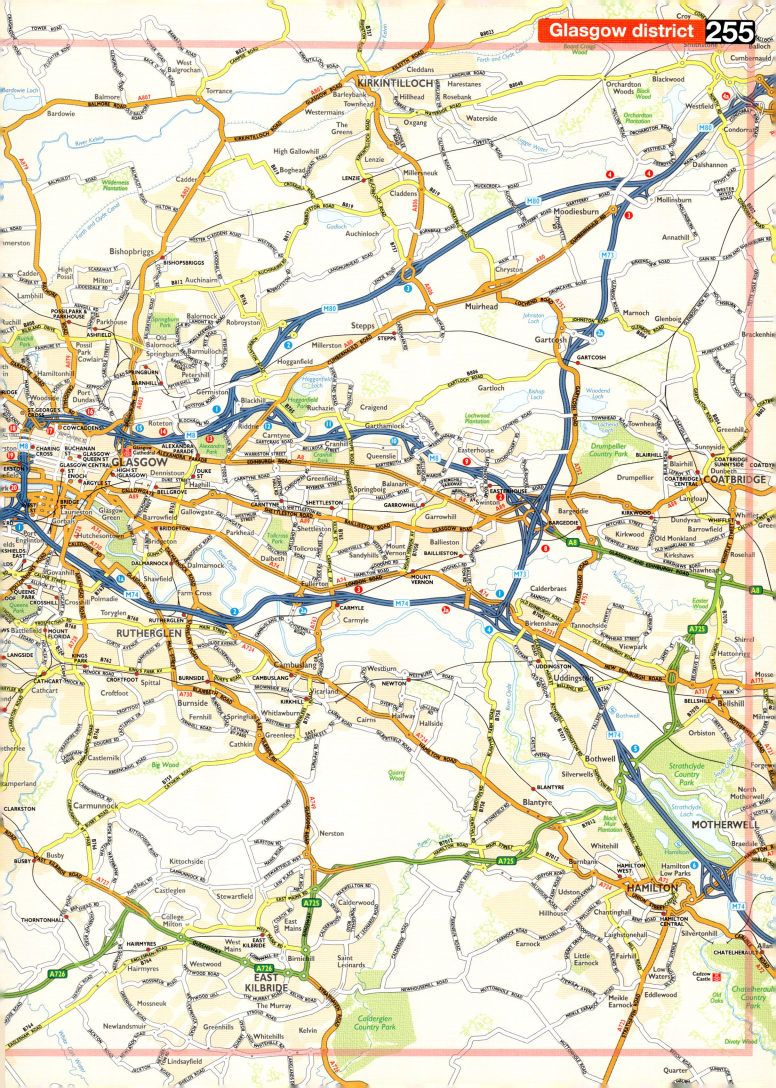

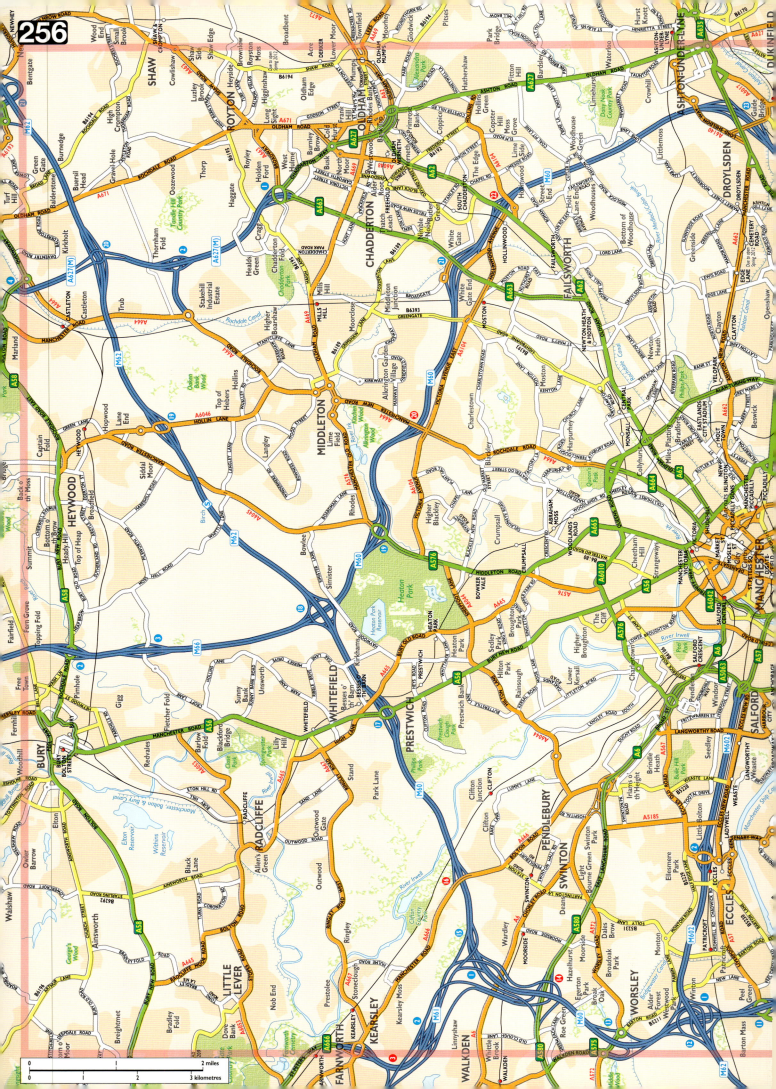

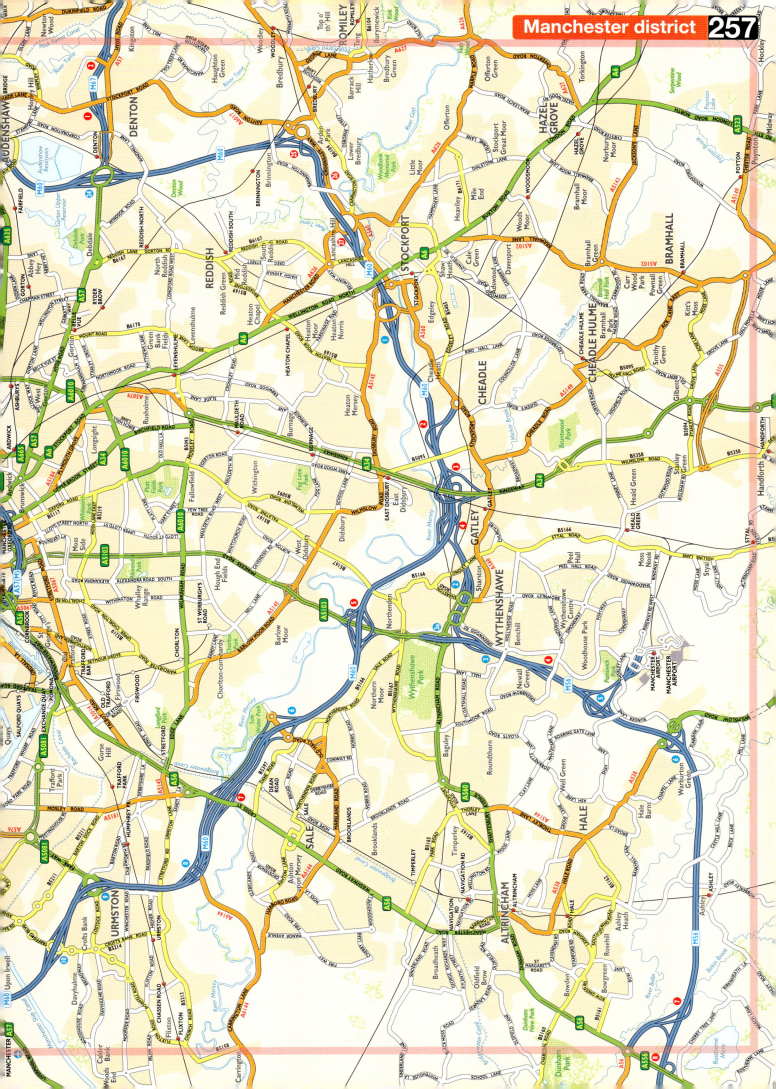

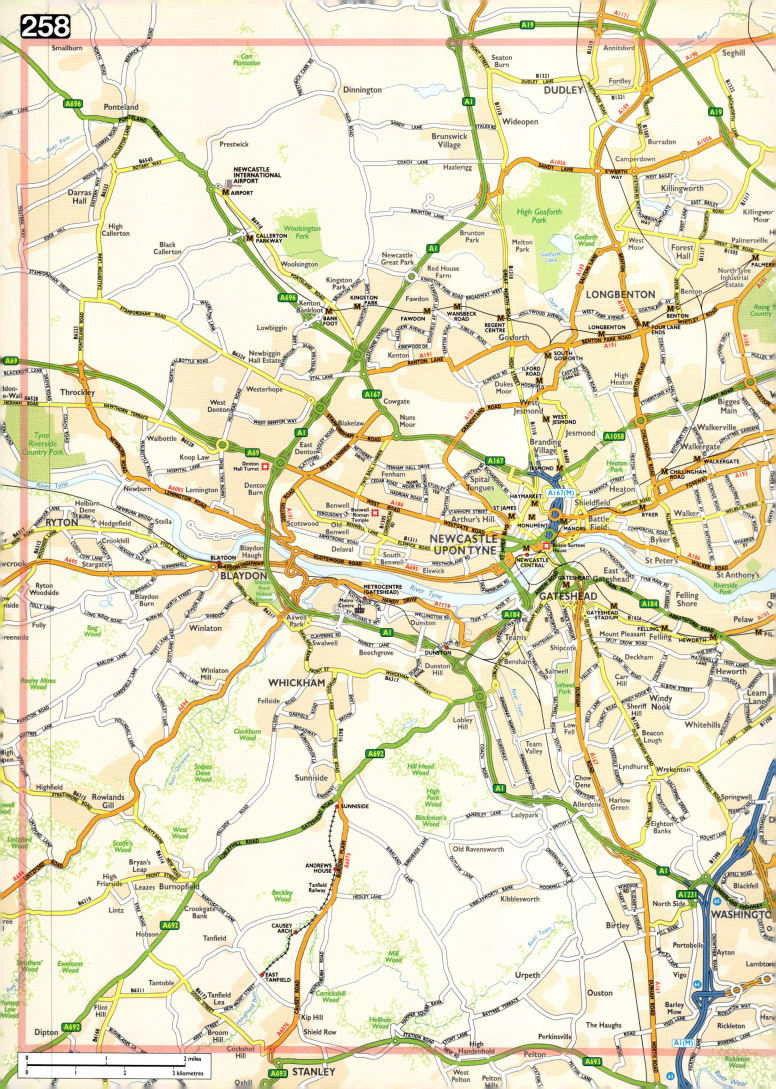

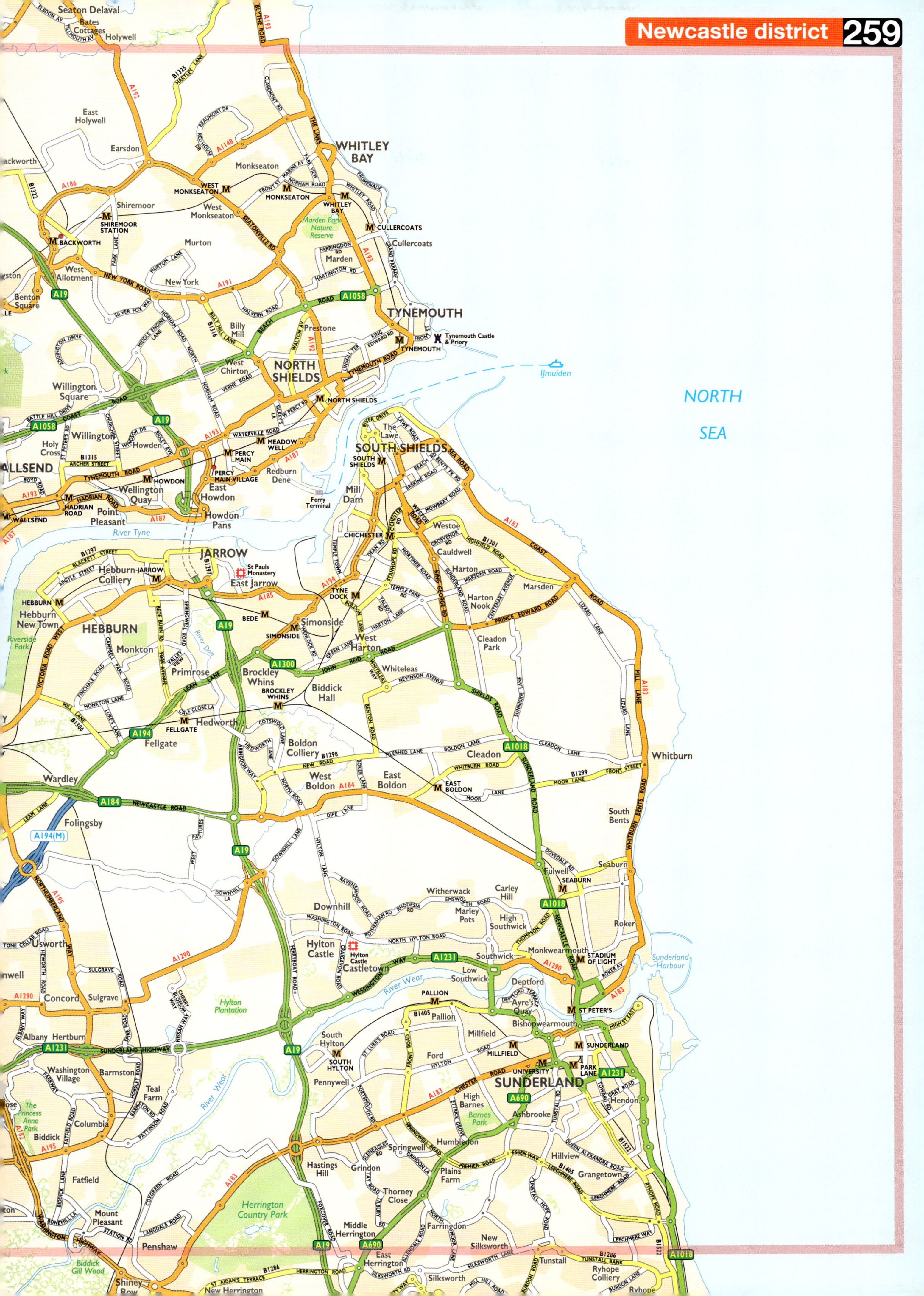
NORTH SEA
Seaton Delaval
Bates Cottages
Holywell
East Holywell
Earsdon
Backworth
WHITLEY BAY
Monkseaton
WEST MONKSEATON
MONKSEATON
WHITLEY BAY
West Monkseaton
Shiremoor
SHIREMOOR STATION
BACKWORTH
Marden Park Nature Reserve
CULLERCOATS
Cullercoats
Murton
Marden
West Allotment
New York
Benton Square
TYNEMOUTH
Prestone
Tynemouth Castle & Priory
Billy Mill
TYNEMOUTH
IJmuiden
West Chirton
NORTH SHIELDS
Willington Square
NORTH SHIELDS
The Lawe
SOUTH SHIELDS
SOUTH SHIELDS
Willington
Holy Cross
Howden
MEADOW WELL
PERCY MAIN
WALLSEND
HOWDON
PERCY MAIN VILLAGE
Redburn Dene
Wellington Quay
East Howdon
Mill Dam
Ferry Terminal
HADRIAN ROAD
Point Pleasant
WALLSEND
Howdon Pans
River Tyne
Westoe
CHICHESTER
Cauldwell
JARROW
St Pauls Monastery
Hebburn-Jarrow Colliery
East Jarrow
Harton
Marsden
HEBBURN
Hebburn New Town
TYNE DOCK
Harton Nook
BEDE
Simonside
SIMONSIDE
Cleadon Park
Riverside Park
HEBBURN
Monkton
West Harton
River Don
Primrose
Brockley Whins
Whiteleas
BROCKLEY WHINS
Biddick Hall
Hedworth
FELLGATE
Fellgate
Boldon Colliery
Cleadon
Whitburn
West Boldon
East Boldon
EAST BOLDON
Wardley
South Bents
Folingsby
Seaburn
Fulwell
SEABURN
Witherwack
Carley Hill
Downhill
Marley Pots
High Southwick
Roker
Usworth
Hylton Castle
Hylton Castle
Castletown
Monkwearmouth
STADIUM OF LIGHT
Sunderland Harbour
Southwick
Low Southwick
Deptford
River Wear
PALLION
Pallion
Ayre's Quay
Concord
Sulgrave
Hylton Plantation
ST PETER'S
Bishopwearmouth
Albany
Hertburn
South Hylton
Millfield
SUNDERLAND
MILLFIELD
SOUTH HYLTON
Ford
Washington Village
Barmston
UNIVERSITY
PARK LANE
SUNDERLAND
Pennywell
Teal Farm
High Barnes
Hendon
The Princess Anne Park
Columbia
Barnes Park
Ashbrooke
Biddick
Humbledon
Springwell
Hillview
Hastings Hill
Grindon
Plains Farm
Grangetown
Fatfield
Thorney Close
Herrington Country Park
Mount Pleasant
Middle Herrington
Farringdon
Penshaw
New Silksworth
East Herrington
Tunstall
Ryhope Colliery
Biddick Gill Wood
Silksworth
Shiney Row
New Herrington
Ryhope
A19
A1058
A193
A187
A185
A194
A1300
A184
A194(M)
A195
A1290
A1231
A1018
A183
A690
A186
A191
A192
A1148
B1322
B1325
B1297
B1315
B1316
B1298
B1299
B1301
B1306
B1405
B1286
B1522

Index to place names

This index lists places appearing in the main-map section of the atlas in alphabetical order. The reference before each name gives the atlas page number and grid reference of the square in which the place appears. The map shows counties, unitary authorities and administrative areas, together with a list of the abbreviated name forms used in the index.

The top 100 places of tourist interest are indexed in **red** (or **green** if a World Heritage site), motorway service areas in **blue** and airports in **blue** *italic*.

Scotland

Abers	**Aberdeenshire**
Ag & B	**Argyll and Bute**
Angus	**Angus**
Border	**Scottish Borders**
C Aber	**City of Aberdeen**
C Dund	**City of Dundee**
C Edin	**City of Edinburgh**
C Glas	**City of Glasgow**
Clacks	**Clackmannanshire (1)**
D & G	**Dumfries & Galloway**
E Ayrs	**East Ayrshire**
E Duns	**East Dunbartonshire (2)**
E Loth	**East Lothian**
E Rens	**East Renfrewshire (3)**
Falk	**Falkirk**
Fife	**Fife**
Highld	**Highland**
Inver	**Inverclyde (4)**
Mdloth	**Midlothian (5)**
Moray	**Moray**
N Ayrs	**North Ayrshire**
N Lans	**North Lanarkshire (6)**
Ork	**Orkney Islands**
P & K	**Perth & Kinross**
Rens	**Renfrewshire (7)**
S Ayrs	**South Ayrshire**
Shet	**Shetland Islands**
S Lans	**South Lanarkshire**
Stirlg	**Stirling**
W Duns	**West Dunbartonshire (8)**
W Isls	**Western Isles (Na h-Eileanan an Iar)**
W Loth	**West Lothian**

Wales

Blae G	**Blaenau Gwent (9)**
Brdgnd	**Bridgend (10)**
Caerph	**Caerphilly (11)**
Cardif	**Cardiff**
Carmth	**Carmarthenshire**
Cerdgn	**Ceredigion**
Conwy	**Conwy**
Denbgs	**Denbighshire**
Flints	**Flintshire**
Gwynd	**Gwynedd**
IoA	**Isle of Anglesey**
Mons	**Monmouthshire**
Myr Td	**Merthyr Tydfil (12)**
Neath	**Neath Port Talbot (13)**
Newpt	**Newport (14)**
Pembks	**Pembrokeshire**
Powys	**Powys**
Rhondd	**Rhondda Cynon Taff (15)**
Swans	**Swansea**
Torfn	**Torfaen (16)**
V Clam	**Vale of Glamorgan (17)**
Wrexhm	**Wrexham**

Channel Islands & Isle of Man

Guern	**Guernsey**
Jersey	**Jersey**
IoM	**Isle of Man**

England

BaNES	**Bath & N E Somerset (18)**
Barns	**Barnsley (19)**
Bed	**Bedford**
Birm	**Birmingham**
Bl w D	**Blackburn with Darwen (20)**
Bmouth	**Bournemouth**
Bolton	**Bolton (21)**
Bpool	**Blackpool**
Br & H	**Brighton & Hove (22)**
Br For	**Bracknell Forest (23)**
Bristl	**City of Bristol**
Bucks	**Buckinghamshire**
Bury	**Bury (24)**
C Beds	**Central Bedfordshire**
C Brad	**City of Bradford**
C Derb	**City of Derby**
C KuH	**City of Kingston upon Hull**
C Leic	**City of Leicester**
C Nott	**City of Nottingham**
C Pete	**City of Peterborough**
C Plym	**City of Plymouth**
C Port	**City of Portsmouth**
C Sotn	**City of Southampton**
C Stke	**City of Stoke-on-Trent**
C York	**City of York**
Calder	**Calderdale (25)**
Cambs	**Cambridgeshire**
Ches E	**Cheshire East**
Ches W	**Cheshire West and Chester**
Cnwll	**Cornwall**
Covtry	**Coventry**
Cumb	**Cumbria**
Darltn	**Darlington (26)**
Derbys	**Derbyshire**
Devon	**Devon**
Donc	**Doncaster (27)**
Dorset	**Dorset**
Dudley	**Dudley (28)**
Dur	**Durham**
E R Yk	**East Riding of Yorkshire**

E Susx	**East Sussex**
Essex	**Essex**
Gatesd	**Gateshead (29)**
Gloucs	**Gloucestershire**
Gt Lon	**Greater London**
Halton	**Halton (30)**
Hants	**Hampshire**
Hartpl	**Hartlepool (31)**
Herefs	**Herefordshire**
Herts	**Hertfordshire**
IoS	**Isles of Scilly**
IoW	**Isle of Wight**
Kent	**Kent**
Kirk	**Kirklees (32)**
Knows	**Knowsley (33)**
Lancs	**Lancashire**
Leeds	**Leeds**
Leics	**Leicestershire**
Lincs	**Lincolnshire**
Lpool	**Liverpool**
Luton	**Luton**
M Keyn	**Milton Keynes**
Manch	**Manchester**
Medway	**Medway**
Middsb	**Middlesbrough**
NE Lin	**North East Lincolnshire**
N Linc	**North Lincolnshire**
N Som	**North Somerset (34)**
N Tyne	**North Tyneside (35)**
N u Ty	**Newcastle upon Tyne**
N York	**North Yorkshire**
Nhants	**Northamptonshire**
Norfk	**Norfolk**
Notts	**Nottinghamshire**
Nthumb	**Northumberland**
Oldham	**Oldham (36)**
Oxon	**Oxfordshire**
Poole	**Poole**
R & Cl	**Redcar & Cleveland**
Readg	**Reading**
Rochdl	**Rochdale (37)**
Rothm	**Rotherham (38)**
Rutlnd	**Rutland**
S Glos	**South Gloucestershire (39)**
S on T	**Stockton-on-Tees (40)**
S Tyne	**South Tyneside (41)**
Salfd	**Salford (42)**
Sandw	**Sandwell (43)**
Sefton	**Sefton (44)**
Sheff	**Sheffield**
Shrops	**Shropshire**
Slough	**Slough (45)**
Solhll	**Solihull (46)**
Somset	**Somerset**
St Hel	**St Helens (47)**
Staffs	**Staffordshire**
Sthend	**Southend-on-Sea**
Stockp	**Stockport (48)**
Suffk	**Suffolk**
Sundld	**Sunderland**
Surrey	**Surrey**
Swindn	**Swindon**
Tamesd	**Tameside (49)**
Thurr	**Thurrock (50)**
Torbay	**Torbay**
Traffd	**Trafford (51)**
W & M	**Windsor and Maidenhead (52)**
W Berk	**West Berkshire**
W Susx	**West Sussex**
Wakefd	**Wakefield (53)**
Warrtn	**Warrington (54)**
Warwks	**Warwickshire**
Wigan	**Wigan (55)**
Wilts	**Wiltshire**
Wirral	**Wirral (56)**
Wokham	**Wokingham (57)**
Wolves	**Wolverhampton (58)**
Worcs	**Worcestershire**
Wrekin	**Telford & Wrekin (59)**
Wsall	**Walsall (60)**

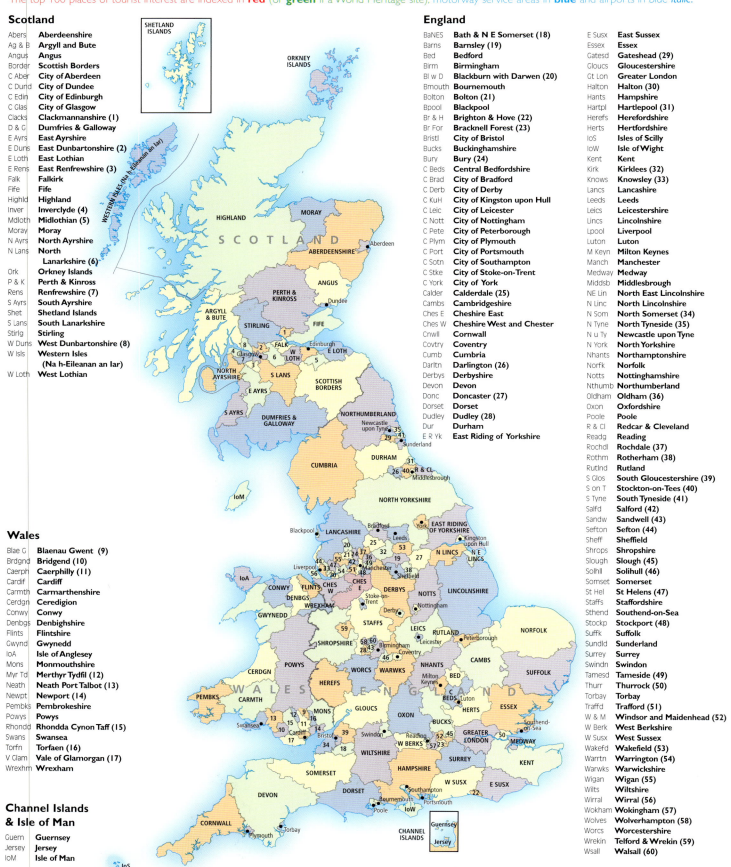

A

20 D10 Abbas Combe Somset
57 P11 Abberley Worcs
57 N11 Abberley Common Worcs
52 H8 Abberton Essex
47 J4 Abberton Worcs
119 M8 Abberwick Nthumb
51 N8 Abbess Roding Essex
10 C2 Abbey Devon
55 P10 Abbeycwmhir Powys
84 D4 Abbeydale Sheff
45 M8 Abbey Dore Herefs
70 H3 Abbey Green Staffs
19 J11 Abbey Hill Somset
129 K7 Abbey St Bathans Border
95 M10 Abbeystead Lancs
110 C10 Abbey Town Cumb
89 J6 Abbey Village Lancs
37 L5 Abbey Wood Gt Lon
118 B8 Abbotrule Border
16 F9 Abbots Bickington Devon
71 K10 Abbots Bromley Staffs
11 M7 Abbotsbury Dorset
83 M6 Abbot's Chair Derbys
134 E5 Abbots Deuglie P & K
16 G6 Abbotsham Devon
7 M5 Abbotskerswell Devon
50 C10 Abbots Langley Herts
7 L9 Abbotsleigh Devon
31 P10 Abbots Leigh N Som
62 B9 Abbotsley Cambs
47 K3 Abbots Morton Worcs
62 B5 Abbots Ripton Cambs
47 L4 Abbot's Salford Warwks
22 G8 Abbotstone Hants
22 C10 Abbotswood Hants
22 E8 Abbots Worthy Hants
22 B6 Abbotts Ann Hants
12 G4 Abbott Street Dorset
56 F9 Abcott Shrops
57 K7 Abdon Shrops
46 C11 Abenhall Gloucs
43 J2 Aberaeron Cerdgn
30 D4 Aberaman Rhondd
55 J2 Aberangell Gwynd
42 F6 Aber-arad Carmth
147 Q2 Aberarder Highld
134 F4 Aberargie P & K
43 J2 Aberarth Cerdgn
29 K7 Aberavon Neath
42 G6 Aber-banc Cerdgn
30 G4 Aberbargoed Caerph
30 H4 Aberbeeg Blae G
30 E4 Abercanaid Myr Td
30 H6 Abercarn Caerph
40 G4 Abercastle Pembks
55 J4 Abercegir Powys
147 J7 Aberchalder Lodge Highld
158 F7 Aberchirder Abers
44 G10 Aber Clydach Powys
29 M2 Abercraf Powys
29 M5 Abercregan Neath
30 D5 Abercwmboi Rhondd
41 P2 Abercych Pembks
30 E6 Abercynon Rhondd
134 D3 Aberdalgie P & K
30 D4 Aberdare Rhondd
66 B9 Aberdaron Gwynd
151 N6 Aberdeen C Aber
151 M5 Aberdeen Airport C Aber
66 G4 Aberdesach Gwynd
134 F10 Aberdour Fife
29 L5 Aberdulais Neath
54 E5 Aberdyfi Gwynd
44 F5 Aberedw Powys
40 E4 Abereiddy Pembks
66 F7 Abererch Gwynd
30 E4 Aberfan Myr Td
141 L8 Aberfeldy P & K
78 F11 Aberffraw IoA
54 F9 Aberffrwd Cerdgn
91 L3 Aberford Leeds
132 G7 Aberfoyle Stirlg
29 P8 Abergarw Brdgnd
29 M4 Abergarwed Neath
31 J2 Abergavenny Mons
80 C9 Abergele Conwy
43 K6 Aber-giar Carmth
43 L8 Abergorlech Carmth
44 B4 Abergwesyn Powys
42 H10 Abergwili Carmth
54 H4 Abergwydol Powys
29 N5 Abergwynfi Neath
79 M10 Abergwyngregyn Gwynd
54 F3 Abergynolwyn Gwynd
55 P6 Aberhafesp Powys
55 J5 Aberhosan Powys
29 N8 Aberkenfig Brdgnd
128 D4 Aberlady E Loth
143 J6 Aberlemno Angus
54 H3 Aberllefenni Gwynd
44 H7 Aberllynfi Powys
157 P9 Aberlour Moray
54 F10 Aber-Magwr Cerdgn
43 L3 Aber-meurig Cerdgn
69 K3 Abermorddu Flints
56 B6 Abermule Powys
42 F10 Abernant Carmth
30 D4 Aber-nant Rhondd
134 F4 Abernethy P & K
142 D11 Abernyte P & K
42 E4 Aberporth Cerdgn
66 E9 Abersoch Gwynd
31 J4 Abersychan Torfn
30 D10 Aberthin V Glam
30 H4 Abertillery Blae G
30 F7 Abertridwr Caerph
68 D11 Abertridwr Powys
30 F3 Abertysswg Caerph
134 B4 Aberuthven P & K
44 D9 Aberyscir Powys
54 D8 Aberystwyth Cerdgn
54 E8 Aberystwyth Crematorium Cerdgn
34 E5 Abingdon Oxon
36 D11 Abinger Common Surrey
36 C11 Abinger Hammer Surrey
60 G8 Abington Nhants
116 C6 Abington S Lans
50 H2 Abington Pigotts Cambs
116 C6 Abington Services S Lans
24 D7 Abingworth W Susx
73 J6 Ab Kettleby Leics
47 K4 Ab Lench Worcs
33 M3 Ablington Gloucs
21 N5 Ablington Wilts
83 Q8 Abney Derbys
71 J4 Above Church Staffs
150 E8 Aboyne Abers
82 D4 Abram Wigan
155 Q10 Abriachan Highld
51 L11 Abridge Essex
126 D2 Abronhill N Lans
32 D10 Abson S Glos
48 H5 Abthorpe Nhants
87 M5 Aby Lincs
98 B11 Acaster Malbis C York
91 P2 Acaster Selby N York
89 M5 Accrington Lancs
89 M5 Accrington Crematorium Lancs
136 F5 Acha Ag & B
123 N4 Achahoish Ag & B
141 R8 Achalader P & K
138 G11 Achaleven Ag & B
168 i5 Acha Mor W Isls
155 J5 Achanalt Highld
156 A3 Achandunie Highld
162 D6 Achany Highld
138 B4 Acharacle Highld
138 C7 Acharn Highld
141 J9 Acharn P & K
167 L8 Achavanich Highld
160 G6 Achduart Highld
164 G9 Achfary Highld
144 C6 A'Chill Highld
160 G5 Achiltibuie Highld
166 B4 Achina Highld
120 E8 Achinhoan Ag & B
154 B9 Achintee Highld
153 Q10 Achintraid Highld
160 H2 Achmelvich Highld
153 R11 Achmore Highld
168 i5 Achmore W Isls
164 B10 Achnacarnin Highld
146 F10 Achnacarry Highld
145 J6 Achnacloich Highld
147 L4 Achnaconeran Highld
138 F9 Achnacraig Ag & B
137 M5 Achnadrish House Ag & B
141 L10 Achnafauld P & K
156 B3 Achnagarron Highld
137 M2 Achnaha Highld
160 G4 Achnahaird Highld
162 D4 Achnairn Highld
138 F5 Achnalea Highld
130 F10 Achnamara Ag & B
154 G6 Achnasheen Highld
154 D8 Achnashellach Lodge Highld
157 P11 Achnastank Moray
137 L2 Achosnich Highld
138 C8 Achranich Highld
166 H3 Achreamie Highld
139 L4 Achriabhach Highld
164 G6 Achriesgill Highld
165 Q4 Achtoty Highld
61 M4 Achurch Nhants
162 G8 Achvaich Highld
166 G4 Achvarasdal Highld
167 Q6 Ackergill Highld
104 E7 Acklam Middsb
98 F8 Acklam N York
57 P5 Ackleton Shrops
119 P10 Acklington Nthumb
91 L6 Ackton Wakefd
91 L7 Ackworth Moor Top Wakefd
77 N9 Acle Norfk
58 H8 Acock's Green Birm
39 P8 Acol Kent
98 B10 Acomb C York
112 D7 Acomb Nthumb
10 D2 Acombe Somset
45 Q8 Aconbury Herefs
89 M6 Acre Lancs
69 J6 Acrefair Wrexhm
70 A4 Acton Ches E
12 G9 Acton Dorset
36 F4 Acton Gt Lon
56 E8 Acton Shrops
70 E6 Acton Staffs
52 E2 Acton Suffk
58 B11 Acton Worcs
46 C4 Acton Beauchamp Herefs
82 C9 Acton Bridge Ches W
57 J4 Acton Burnell Shrops
46 C4 Acton Green Herefs
69 K4 Acton Park Wrexhm
57 J4 Acton Pigott Shrops
57 L5 Acton Round Shrops
56 H7 Acton Scott Shrops
70 G11 Acton Trussell Staffs
32 F8 Acton Turville S Glos
70 D9 Adbaston Staffs
19 Q10 Adber Dorset
72 F3 Adbolton Notts
48 E7 Adderbury Oxon
70 B7 Adderley Shrops
119 M4 Adderstone Nthumb
126 H5 Addiewell W Loth
96 G11 Addingham C Brad
49 K9 Addington Bucks
37 J8 Addington Gt Lon
37 Q9 Addington Kent
36 H7 Addiscombe Gt Lon
36 C8 Addlestone Surrey
36 C7 Addlestonemoor Surrey
87 P7 Addlethorpe Lincs
70 B11 Adeney Wrekin
50 C9 Adeyfield Herts
55 P4 Adfa Powys
56 G10 Adforton Herefs
39 M11 Adisham Kent
47 P9 Adlestrop Gloucs
92 D6 Adlingfleet E R Yk
83 K8 Adlington Ches E
89 J8 Adlington Lancs
71 J10 Admaston Staffs
57 L2 Admaston Wrekin
47 P5 Admington Warwks
42 F6 Adpar Cerdgn
19 J9 Adsborough Somset
18 G7 Adscombe Somset
49 K9 Adstock Bucks
48 G4 Adstone Nhants
83 J7 Adswood Stockp
24 C6 Adversane W Susx
157 L11 Advie Highld
90 G5 Adwalton Leeds
35 J5 Adwell Oxon
91 N9 Adwick Le Street Donc
91 M10 Adwick upon Dearne Donc
109 L3 Ae D & G
109 M3 Ae Bridgend D & G
29 N5 Afan Forest Park Neath
89 M8 Affetside Bury
158 E9 Affleck Abers
12 D6 Affpuddle Dorset
146 F3 Affric Lodge Highld
80 G10 Afon-wen Flints
7 L6 Afton Devon
13 P7 Afton IoW
82 H4 Agecroft Crematorium Salfd
96 G3 Agglethorpe N York
81 M7 Aigburth Lpool
99 L11 Aike E R Yk
111 J11 Aiketgate Cumb
110 D11 Aikhead Cumb
110 E10 Aikton Cumb
87 M5 Ailby Lincs
45 L5 Ailey Herefs
74 B11 Ailsworth C Pete
97 M4 Ainderby Quernhow N York
97 M2 Ainderby Steeple N York
53 K7 Aingers Green Essex
88 C8 Ainsdale Sefton
88 B8 Ainsdale-on-Sea Sefton
111 K11 Ainstable Cumb
89 M8 Ainsworth Bury
105 K9 Ainthorpe N York
81 M5 Aintree Sefton
127 L5 Ainville W Loth
130 F7 Aird Ag & B
106 E5 Aird D & G
168 k4 Aird W Isls
168 g6 Aird a Mhulaidh W Isls
168 g7 Aird Asaig W Isls
153 N9 Aird Dhubh Highld
131 K2 Airdeny Ag & B
137 N10 Aird of Kinloch Ag & B
145 J7 Aird of Sleat Highld
126 D4 Airdrie N Lans
126 D4 Airdriehill N Lans
108 E6 Airds of Kells D & G
168 f4 Aird Uig W Isls
168 h6 Airidh a bhruaich W Isls
108 G9 Airieland D & G
142 E7 Airlie Angus
92 B6 Airmyn E R Yk
141 Q10 Airntully P & K
145 M6 Airor Highld
133 Q10 Airth Falk
96 D9 Airton N York
73 Q3 Aisby Lincs
85 Q2 Aisby Lincs
102 E11 Aisgill Cumb
6 H6 Aish Devon
7 L7 Aish Devon
18 G7 Aisholt Somset
97 L3 Aiskew N York
98 F3 Aislaby N York
105 N9 Aislaby N York
104 D8 Aislaby S on T
86 B4 Aisthorpe Lincs
169 q8 Aith Shet
119 J5 Akeld Nthumb
49 K7 Akeley Bucks
53 K2 Akenham Suffk
5 Q7 Albaston Cnwll
56 F2 Alberbury Shrops
24 G7 Albourne W Susx
24 G7 Albourne Green W Susx
57 Q4 Albrighton Shrops
69 N11 Albrighton Shrops
65 K4 Alburgh Norfk
51 K6 Albury Herts
35 J3 Albury Oxon
36 B11 Albury Surrey
51 K6 Albury End Herts
36 C11 Albury Heath Surrey
76 H5 Alby Hill Norfk
155 Q6 Alcaig Highld
56 H7 Alcaston Shrops
47 L3 Alcester Warwks
58 G8 Alcester Lane End Birm
25 M9 Alciston E Susx
18 C5 Alcombe Somset
32 F11 Alcombe Wilts
61 Q5 Alconbury Cambs
61 Q5 Alconbury Weston Cambs
97 P7 Aldborough N York
76 H5 Aldborough Norfk
33 Q9 Aldbourne Wilts
93 M3 Aldbrough E R Yk
103 P8 Aldbrough St John N York
35 Q2 Aldbury Herts
95 K8 Aldcliffe Lancs
141 L5 Aldclune P & K
65 P10 Aldeburgh Suffk
65 N3 Aldeby Norfk
50 D11 Aldenham Herts
21 N9 Alderbury Wilts
84 F11 Aldercar Derbys
76 G8 Alderford Norfk
13 K2 Alderholt Dorset
32 E6 Alderley Gloucs
82 H9 Alderley Edge Ches E
59 N8 Aldermans Green Covtry
34 G11 Aldermaston W Berk
47 P5 Alderminster Warwks
71 N9 Alder Moor Staffs
69 N3 Aldersey Green Ches W
23 N4 Aldershot Hants
47 K8 Alderton Gloucs
49 K5 Alderton Nhants
69 N10 Alderton Shrops
53 P3 Alderton Suffk
32 F8 Alderton Wilts
71 Q4 Alderwasley Derbys
97 L7 Aldfield N York
69 M3 Aldford Ches W
73 P10 Aldgate Rutlnd
52 F6 Aldham Essex
52 J2 Aldham Suffk
15 P5 Aldingbourne W Susx
94 F6 Aldingham Cumb
27 J4 Aldington Kent
47 L6 Aldington Worcs
27 J4 Aldington Corner Kent
150 B2 Aldivalloch Moray
132 D9 Aldochlay Ag & B
56 G9 Aldon Shrops
109 P11 Aldoth Cumb
62 F6 Aldreth Cambs
58 G4 Aldridge Wsall
65 N9 Aldringham Suffk
98 G8 Aldro N York
33 N3 Aldsworth Gloucs
15 L5 Aldsworth W Susx
150 B2 Aldunie Moray
84 B9 Aldwark Derbys
97 Q8 Aldwark N York
15 P7 Aldwick W Susx
61 M4 Aldwincle Nhants
34 G9 Aldworth W Berk
125 K2 Alexandria W Duns
18 G7 Aley Somset
16 D9 Alfardisworthy Devon
10 C5 Alfington Devon
24 B4 Alfold Surrey
24 B4 Alfold Bars W Susx
24 B3 Alfold Crossways Surrey
150 F4 Alford Abers
87 N5 Alford Lincs
20 B8 Alford Somset
87 M5 Alford Crematorium Lincs
84 F9 Alfreton Derbys
46 D4 Alfrick Worcs
46 D4 Alfrick Pound Worcs
25 M10 Alfriston E Susx
74 E3 Algarkirk Lincs
20 B8 Alhampton Somset
92 E6 Alkborough N Linc
32 E3 Alkerton Gloucs
48 C6 Alkerton Oxon
27 N3 Alkham Kent
69 P7 Alkington Shrops
71 M7 Alkmonton Derbys
7 L8 Allaleigh Devon
149 L9 Allanaquoich Abers
126 E6 Allanbank N Lans
129 M9 Allanton Border
126 E6 Allanton N Lans
126 C7 Allanton S Lans
32 B4 Allaston Gloucs
22 E10 Allbrook Hants
21 L2 All Cannings Wilts
112 B9 Allendale Nthumb
59 J5 Allen End Warwks
112 C11 Allenheads Nthumb
112 G10 Allensford Dur
51 L7 Allen's Green Herts
45 P7 Allensmore Herefs
72 B4 Allenton C Derb
17 P6 Aller Devon
19 M9 Aller Somset
100 E3 Allerby Cumb
9 P6 Allercombe Devon
18 B5 Allerford Somset
98 H4 Allerston N York
98 F11 Allerthorpe E R Yk
90 E4 Allerton C Brad
156 D4 Allerton Highld
81 M7 Allerton Lpool
91 L5 Allerton Bywater Leeds
97 P9 Allerton Mauleverer N York
59 M8 Allesley Covtry
72 A3 Allestree C Derb
3 K4 Allet Common Cnwll
73 L10 Allexton Leics
83 L11 Allgreave Ches E
38 D6 Allhallows Medway
38 D6 Allhallows-on-Sea Medway
153 Q6 Alligin Shuas Highld
70 F11 Allimore Green Staffs
11 K6 Allington Dorset
38 C10 Allington Kent
73 M2 Allington Lincs
21 L2 Allington Wilts
21 P7 Allington Wilts
32 G9 Allington Wilts
94 H5 Allithwaite Cumb
133 P9 Alloa Clacks
100 E2 Allonby Cumb
82 F10 Allostock Ches W
114 F4 Alloway S Ayrs
10 H2 Allowenshay Somset
65 L5 All Saints South Elmham Suffk
57 N5 Allscott Shrops
57 L2 Allscott Wrekin
56 H5 All Stretton Shrops
81 K11 Alltami Flints
139 M7 Alltchaorunn Highld
44 F5 Alltmawr Powys
42 H8 Alltwalis Carmth
29 K4 Alltwen Neath
43 K5 Alltyblaca Cerdgn
11 P2 Allweston Dorset
64 E7 Allwood Green Suffk
45 L4 Almeley Herefs
45 L4 Almeley Wooton Herefs
12 F5 Almer Dorset
91 P9 Almholme Donc
70 C8 Almington Staffs
15 M7 Almodington W Susx
134 D2 Almondbank P & K
90 F8 Almondbury Kirk
32 B8 Almondsbury S Glos
97 Q7 Alne N York
156 B4 Alness Highld
119 J8 Alnham Nthumb
119 P8 Alnmouth Nthumb
119 N8 Alnwick Nthumb
36 E4 Alperton Gt Lon
52 E4 Alphamstone Essex
64 B11 Alpheton Suffk
9 M6 Alphington Devon
77 K11 Alpington Norfk
84 B8 Alport Derbys
69 Q3 Alpraham Ches E
53 J7 Alresford Essex
59 J2 Alrewas Staffs
70 D3 Alsager Ches E
70 D5 Alsagers Bank Staffs
71 M4 Alsop en le Dale Derbys
111 P11 Alston Cumb
10 G4 Alston Devon
47 J8 Alstone Gloucs
19 K5 Alstone Somset
71 L3 Alstonefield Staffs
19 M4 Alston Sutton Somset
17 N7 Alswear Devon
83 K4 Alt Oldham
160 F4 Altandhu Highld
5 L5 Altarnun Cnwll
162 C6 Altass Highld
138 B10 Altcreich Ag & B
124 C3 Altgaltraig Ag & B
89 M4 Altham Lancs
38 F2 Althorne Essex
92 D9 Althorpe N Linc
166 H7 Altnabreac Station Highld
165 N9 Altnaharra Highld
91 K6 Altofts Wakefd
84 E8 Alton Derbys
23 K7 Alton Hants
71 K6 Alton Staffs
21 N5 Alton Wilts
21 M2 Alton Barnes Wilts
11 Q4 Alton Pancras Dorset
21 M2 Alton Priors Wilts
71 K6 Alton Towers Staffs
82 G7 Altrincham Traffd
82 F7 Altrincham Crematorium Traffd
132 F7 Altskeith Hotel Stirlg
133 P8 Alva Clacks
81 P10 Alvanley Ches W
72 B4 Alvaston C Derb
58 F10 Alvechurch Worcs
59 K4 Alvecote Warwks
21 J10 Alvediston Wilts
57 P8 Alveley Shrops
17 J6 Alverdiscott Devon
14 H7 Alverstoke Hants
14 G9 Alverstone IoW
91 J6 Alverthorpe Wakefd
73 K2 Alverton Notts
157 L5 Alves Moray
33 Q4 Alvescot Oxon
32 B7 Alveston S Glos
47 P3 Alveston Warwks
87 L2 Alvingham Lincs
32 B4 Alvington Gloucs
74 B11 Alwalton C Pete
118 H9 Alwinton Nthumb
90 H2 Alwoodley Leeds
91 J2 Alwoodley Gates Leeds
142 C8 Alyth P & K
84 D10 Ambergate Derbys
86 H11 Amber Hill Lincs
32 G4 Amberley Gloucs
24 B8 Amberley W Susx
84 E9 Amber Row Derbys
25 N8 Amberstone E Susx
119 Q10 Amble Nthumb
58 C7 Amblecote Dudley
90 D5 Ambler Thorn C Brad
101 L10 Ambleside Cumb
41 K5 Ambleston Pembks
48 H11 Ambrosden Oxon
92 E8 Amcotts N Linc
62 F5 America Cambs
35 Q5 Amersham Bucks
35 Q5 Amersham Common Bucks
35 Q5 Amersham Old Town Bucks
35 Q5 Amersham on the Hill Bucks
70 H9 Amerton Staffs
21 N6 Amesbury Wilts
168 f7 Amhuinnsuidhe W Isls
59 K4 Amington Staffs
109 M4 Amisfield Town D & G
78 G6 Amlwch IoA
28 H2 Ammanford Carmth
98 E6 Amotherby N York
22 D10 Ampfield Hants
98 B5 Ampleforth N York
33 L4 Ampney Crucis Gloucs
33 L4 Ampney St Mary Gloucs
33 L4 Ampney St Peter Gloucs
22 B6 Amport Hants
50 B3 Ampthill C Beds
64 B7 Ampton Suffk
41 N9 Amroth Pembks
141 L10 Amulree P & K
50 E8 Amwell Herts
138 E5 Anaheilt Highld
73 P2 Ancaster Lincs
56 B7 Anchor Shrops
129 P11 Ancroft Nthumb
118 B6 Ancrum Border
15 Q6 Ancton W Susx
87 P5 Anderby Lincs
19 K8 Andersea Somset
18 H8 Andersfield Somset
12 E5 Anderson Dorset
82 D9 Anderton Ches W
6 C8 Anderton Cnwll
22 C5 Andover Hants
47 K11 Andoversford Gloucs
80 f2 Andreas IoM
66 B9 Anelog Gwynd
36 H7 Anerley Gt Lon
81 M6 Anfield Lpool
81 M6 Anfield Crematorium Lpool
2 F6 Angarrack Cnwll
3 K6 Angarrick Cnwll
57 K9 Angelbank Shrops
18 G11 Angersleigh Somset
110 D9 Angerton Cumb
40 G10 Angle Pembks
78 G8 Anglesey IoA
24 C10 Angmering W Susx
97 R11 Angram N York
102 G11 Angram N York
2 H10 Angrouse Cnwll
112 D7 Anick Nthumb
156 E3 Ankerville Highld
73 K7 Ankle Hill Leics
92 H5 Anlaby E R Yk
75 P5 Anmer Norfk
15 J4 Anmore Hants
110 C7 Annan D & G
109 P2 Annandale Water Services D & G
94 B3 Annaside Cumb
154 A7 Annat Highld
126 C3 Annathill N Lans
22 C6 Anna Valley Hants
114 H3 Annbank S Ayrs
47 N4 Anne Hathaway's Cottage Warwks
84 H10 Annesley Notts
84 G10 Annesley Woodhouse Notts
113 J10 Annfield Plain Dur
125 N4 Anniesland C Glas
113 L6 Annitsford N Tyne
56 H3 Annscroft Shrops
88 C5 Ansdell Lancs
20 B8 Ansford Somset
59 M6 Ansley Warwks
71 N9 Anslow Staffs
71 M10 Anslow Gate Staffs
71 N10 Anslow Lees Staffs
23 P8 Ansteadbrook Surrey
23 K6 Anstey Hants
51 K4 Anstey Herts
72 F9 Anstey Leics

135 P7 Anstruther Fife
24 G6 Ansty W Susx
59 P8 Ansty Warwks
21 J9 Ansty Wilts
12 C4 Ansty Cross Dorset
14 H4 Anthill Common Hants
36 B8 Anthonys Surrey
110 C9 Anthorn Cumb
77 K5 Antingham Norfk
168 f9 An t-Ob W Isls
87 K11 Anton's Gowt Lincs
5 Q11 Antony Cnwll
82 D9 Antrobus Ches W
16 F11 Anvil Corner Devon
27 K2 Anvil Green Kent
86 F10 Anwick Lincs
108 C9 Anwoth D & G
37 K9 Aperfield Gt Lon
58 E10 Apes Dale Worcs
73 Q11 Apethorpe Nhants
70 F11 Apeton Staffs
86 F5 Apley Lincs
84 E5 Apperknowle Derbys
46 G9 Apperley Gloucs
90 F3 Apperley Bridge C Brad
112 G9 Apperley Dene Nthumb
96 C2 Appersett N York
138 G8 Appin Ag & B
92 G8 Appleby N Linc
102 C6 Appleby-in-Westmorland Cumb
59 M3 Appleby Magna Leics
59 M3 Appleby Parva Leics
50 H10 Appleby Street Herts
153 N9 Applecross Highld
9 Q2 Appledore Devon
16 H5 Appledore Devon
26 G6 Appledore Kent
26 G5 Appledore Heath Kent
34 F6 Appleford Oxon
109 P4 Applegarth Town D & G
91 K8 Applehaigh Wakefd
22 B5 Appleshaw Hants
101 J5 Applethwaite Cumb
81 Q7 Appleton Halton
34 D4 Appleton Oxon
82 D8 Appleton Warrtn
98 E3 Appleton-le-Moors N York
98 E6 Appleton-le-Street N York
91 P2 Appleton Roebuck N York
82 D8 Appleton Thorn Warrtn
104 C10 Appleton Wiske N York
117 Q7 Appletreehall Border
96 G8 Appletreewick N York
18 E10 Appley Somset
88 G9 Appley Bridge Lancs
14 G10 Apse Heath IoW
50 D4 Apsley End C Beds
15 M6 Apuldram W Susx
156 E2 Arabella Highld
143 L9 Arbirlot Angus
163 K10 Arboll Highld
35 L11 Arborfield Wokham
35 L11 Arborfield Cross Wokham
84 E3 Arbourthorne Sheff
143 L9 Arbroath Angus
143 P2 Arbuthnott Abers
26 E4 Arcadia Kent
28 D4 Archddu Carmth
103 Q7 Archdeacon Newton Darltn
132 E11 Archencarroch W Duns
157 N9 Archiestown Moray
11 c1 Archirondel Jersey
70 D2 Arclid Green Ches E
159 P10 Ardallie Abers
131 M3 Ardanaiseig Hotel Ag & B
153 Q10 Ardaneaskan Highld
153 Q10 Ardarroch Highld
122 F10 Ardbeg Ag & B
124 D4 Ardbeg Ag & B
131 P11 Ardbeg Ag & B
161 K9 Ardcharnich Highld
137 K12 Ardchiavaig Ag & B
131 K5 Ardchonnel Ag & B
132 H5 Ardchullarie More Stirlg
131 Q9 Arddarroch Ag & B
69 J11 Arddleen Powys
146 E9 Ardechive Highld
124 H9 Ardeer N Ayrs
50 H5 Ardeley Herts
145 Q2 Ardelve Highld
132 D11 Arden Ag & B
47 M4 Ardens Grafton Warwks
130 G3 Ardentallen Ag & B
131 P10 Ardentinny Ag & B
124 C3 Ardentraive Ag & B
140 G10 Ardeonaig Stirlg
156 D7 Ardersier Highld
160 H9 Ardessie Highld
130 G7 Ardfern Ag & B
123 J5 Ardfernal Ag & B
162 D8 Ardgay Highld
139 J5 Ardgour Highld
124 G3 Ardgowan Inver
124 F3 Ardhallow Ag & B
168 g7 Ardhasig W Isls
153 P6 Ardheslaig Highld
161 K9 Ardindrean Highld
24 H5 Ardingly W Susx
34 D7 Ardington Oxon
34 D7 Ardington Wick Oxon
124 B4 Ardlamont Ag & B
53 J6 Ardleigh Essex
52 H5 Ardleigh Heath Essex
142 D9 Ardler P & K
48 F9 Ardley Oxon
51 M8 Ardley End Essex
132 C4 Ardlui Ag & B
130 C10 Ardlussa Ag & B
161 J7 Ardmair Highld
124 D4 Ardmaleish Ag & B
133 K10 Ardminish Ag & B
138 C3 Ardmolich Highld
125 J2 Ardmore Ag & B
162 G9 Ardmore Highld
131 P11 Ardnadam Ag & B
155 P8 Ardnagrask Highld
154 A10 Ardnarff Highld
138 E5 Ardnastang Highld
123 N8 Ardpatrick Ag & B
130 H10 Ardrishaig Ag & B
155 R3 Ardross Highld
124 G9 Ardrossan N Ayrs
91 K9 Ardsley Barns
91 J5 Ardsley East Leeds
137 P3 Ardslignish Highld
122 G9 Ardtalla Ag & B
138 A3 Ardtoe Highld
130 F5 Arduaine Ag & B
155 Q5 Ardullie Highld
145 K7 Ardvasar Highld
133 J3 Ardvorlich P & K
168 g6 Ardvourlie W Isls
106 F8 Ardwell D & G
83 J5 Ardwick Manch
57 P10 Areley Kings Worcs
138 B4 Arevegaig Highld
23 M7 Arford Hants
30 G5 Argoed Caerph
69 K10 Argoed Shrops
44 D2 Argoed Mill Powys
25 N5 Argos Hill E Susx
131 Q7 Argyll Forest Park Ag & B
168 h6 Aribruach W Isls
137 J11 Aridhglas Ag & B
136 F6 Arileod Ag & B
136 G4 Arinagour Ag & B
130 H2 Ariogan Ag & B
145 L10 Arisaig Highld
145 L11 Arisaig House Highld
97 N8 Arkendale N York
51 L4 Arkesden Essex
95 M6 Arkholme Lancs
100 F3 Arkleby Cumb
110 G2 Arkleton D & G
103 K10 Arkle Town N York
50 F11 Arkley Gt Lon
91 P9 Arksey Donc
84 F6 Arkwright Town Derbys
46 H10 Arle Gloucs
100 D7 Arlecdon Cumb
48 C5 Arlescote Warwks
50 E3 Arlesey C Beds
57 M2 Arleston Wrekin
82 E8 Arley Ches E
59 L6 Arley Warwks
32 D2 Arlingham Gloucs
17 L3 Arlington Devon
25 M9 Arlington E Susx
33 M3 Arlington Gloucs
17 L3 Arlington Beccott Devon
145 K7 Armadale Highld
166 C4 Armadale Highld
126 G4 Armadale W Loth
100 G5 Armaside Cumb
111 K11 Armathwaite Cumb
77 K11 Arminghall Norfk
71 K11 Armitage Staffs
90 E8 Armitage Bridge Kirk
90 H4 Armley Leeds
47 P6 Armscote Warwks
70 G5 Armshead Staffs
61 N3 Armston Nhants
91 Q10 Armthorpe Donc
136 G3 Arnabost Ag & B
94 D4 Arnaby Cumb
96 D6 Arncliffe N York
96 D6 Arncliffe Cote N York
135 N6 Arncroach Fife
157 P8 Arndilly House Moray
12 G7 Arne Dorset
60 D2 Arnesby Leics
134 E5 Arngask P & K
145 P5 Arnisdale Highld
153 K8 Arnish Highld
127 Q5 Arniston Mdloth
168 i3 Arnol W Isls
93 K2 Arnold E R Yk
85 J11 Arnold Notts
133 J9 Arnprior Stirlg
95 K5 Arnside Cumb
137 P6 Aros Ag & B
69 N7 Arowry Wrexhm
94 G4 Arrad Foot Cumb
92 H2 Arram E R Yk
120 H4 Arran N Ayrs
97 K2 Arrathorne N York
14 F9 Arreton IoW
153 N6 Arrina Highld
62 D10 Arrington Cambs
132 B7 Arrochar Ag & B
47 L3 Arrow Warwks
58 F10 Arrowfield Top Worcs
56 G3 Arscott Shrops
156 A8 Artafallie Highld
90 H2 Arthington Leeds
60 G4 Arthingworth Nhants
54 E2 Arthog Gwynd
159 N10 Arthrath Abers
91 K3 Arthursdale Leeds
159 P11 Artrochie Abers
24 B9 Arundel W Susx
100 E6 Asby Cumb
124 E5 Ascog Ag & B
35 P11 Ascot W & M
48 B8 Ascott Warwks
48 B11 Ascott Earl Oxon
48 B11 Ascott-under-Wychwood Oxon
97 N5 Asenby N York
73 J7 Asfordby Leics
73 J7 Asfordby Hill Leics
86 F11 Asgarby Lincs
87 K7 Asgarby Lincs
7 L9 Ash Devon
17 J10 Ash Devon
12 E2 Ash Dorset
37 P8 Ash Kent
39 N10 Ash Kent
19 J10 Ash Somset
19 N10 Ash Somset
23 P4 Ash Surrey
34 G9 Ashampstead W Berk
34 G9 Ashampstead Green W Berk
64 H11 Ashbocking Suffk
71 M5 Ashbourne Derbys
18 E10 Ashbrittle Somset
25 Q8 Ashburnham Place E Susx
7 K4 Ashburton Devon
8 D5 Ashbury Devon
33 Q7 Ashbury Oxon
92 E9 Ashby N Linc
87 M7 Ashby by Partney Lincs
93 N10 Ashby cum Fenby NE Lin
86 E9 Ashby de la Launde Lincs
72 B7 Ashby-de-la-Zouch Leics
73 J8 Ashby Folville Leics
60 C2 Ashby Magna Leics
60 B3 Ashby Parva Leics
87 K6 Ashby Puerorum Lincs
60 C7 Ashby St Ledgers Nhants
77 L11 Ashby St Mary Norfk
46 H8 Ashchurch Gloucs
9 M9 Ashcombe Devon
19 K2 Ashcombe N Som
19 M7 Ashcott Somset
51 N2 Ashdon Essex
22 F4 Ashe Hants
52 G11 Asheldham Essex
52 B3 Ashen Essex
35 K2 Ashendon Bucks
35 P4 Asheridge Bucks
22 C11 Ashfield Hants
46 A10 Ashfield Herefs
133 M7 Ashfield Stirlg
65 J9 Ashfield cum Thorpe Suffk
63 N9 Ashfield Green Suffk
65 K7 Ashfield Green Suffk
24 F5 Ashfold Crossways W Susx
6 H9 Ashford Devon
17 J4 Ashford Devon
26 H3 Ashford Kent
36 C6 Ashford Surrey
57 J10 Ashford Bowdler Shrops
57 J10 Ashford Carbonell Shrops
22 G2 Ashford Hill Hants
83 Q11 Ashford in the Water Derbys
126 D7 Ashgill S Lans
23 P5 Ash Green Surrey
59 M8 Ash Green Warwks
10 B2 Ashill Devon
76 B11 Ashill Norfk
19 K11 Ashill Somset
38 E3 Ashingdon Essex
113 L3 Ashington Nthumb
12 H5 Ashington Poole
19 Q10 Ashington Somset
24 D7 Ashington W Susx
117 P6 Ashkirk Border
14 E6 Ashlett Hants
46 F9 Ashleworth Gloucs
46 F9 Ashleworth Quay Gloucs
63 L8 Ashley Cambs
82 G8 Ashley Ches E
17 M9 Ashley Devon
13 K4 Ashley Dorset
32 H6 Ashley Gloucs
13 N5 Ashley Hants
22 C8 Ashley Hants
27 P2 Ashley Kent
60 G2 Ashley Nhants
70 D7 Ashley Staffs
32 F11 Ashley Wilts
35 Q3 Ashley Green Bucks
71 P4 Ashleyhay Derbys
13 K4 Ashley Heath Dorset
56 H11 Ashley Moor Herefs
69 Q7 Ash Magna Shrops
22 D3 Ashmansworth Hants
16 E8 Ashmansworthy Devon
32 E5 Ashmead Green Gloucs
5 P2 Ashmill Devon
17 P7 Ash Mill Devon
20 H11 Ashmore Dorset
34 F11 Ashmore Green W Berk
48 B3 Ashorne Warwks
84 D8 Ashover Derbys
84 D8 Ashover Hay Derbys
59 M10 Ashow Warwks
69 Q7 Ash Parva Shrops
46 B6 Ashperton Herefs
7 L7 Ashprington Devon
18 G9 Ash Priors Somset
17 L9 Ashreigney Devon
52 H2 Ash Street Suffk
36 E9 Ashtead Surrey
9 P2 Ash Thomas Devon
74 B9 Ashton C Pete
81 Q11 Ashton Ches W
2 G8 Ashton Cnwll
9 L8 Ashton Devon
22 F11 Ashton Hants
45 Q2 Ashton Herefs
124 G2 Ashton Inver
49 L5 Ashton Nhants
61 N3 Ashton Nhants
19 M5 Ashton Somset
20 G3 Ashton Common Wilts
20 H3 Ashton Hill Wilts
82 C5 Ashton-in-Makerfield Wigan
33 K6 Ashton Keynes Wilts
47 J7 Ashton under Hill Worcs
83 K5 Ashton-under-Lyne Tamesd
82 G6 Ashton upon Mersey Traffd
13 P2 Ashurst Hants
25 M3 Ashurst Kent
88 F9 Ashurst Lancs
24 E7 Ashurst W Susx
25 K3 Ashurstwood W Susx
23 N4 Ash Vale Surrey
5 P2 Ashwater Devon
50 G3 Ashwell Herts
73 M8 Ashwell Rutlnd
19 L11 Ashwell Somset
50 G2 Ashwell End Herts
64 G2 Ashwellthorpe Norfk
20 B5 Ashwick Somset
75 P7 Ashwicken Norfk
58 C7 Ashwood Staffs
94 E5 Askam in Furness Cumb
91 P8 Askern Donc
11 L6 Askerswell Dorset
35 M3 Askett Bucks
101 P6 Askham Cumb
85 M6 Askham Notts
98 B11 Askham Bryan C York
98 A11 Askham Richard C York
131 J9 Asknish Ag & B
96 D2 Askrigg N York
97 J11 Askwith N York
74 A4 Aslackby Lincs
64 H3 Aslacton Norfk
73 J3 Aslockton Notts
19 N7 Asney Somset
64 H9 Aspall Suffk
100 F2 Aspatria Cumb
51 J5 Aspenden Herts
83 M7 Aspenshaw Derbys
74 E3 Asperton Lincs
70 E8 Aspley Staffs
49 P7 Aspley Guise C Beds
49 P8 Aspley Heath C Beds
58 G10 Aspley Heath Warwks
89 J9 Aspull Wigan
82 D5 Aspull Common Wigan
92 B5 Asselby E R Yk
87 N5 Asserby Lincs
87 N5 Asserby Turn Lincs
52 F4 Assington Suffk
63 N10 Assington Green Suffk
70 E2 Astbury Ches E
49 J4 Astcote Nhants
87 J5 Asterby Lincs
56 F3 Asterley Shrops
56 F6 Asterton Shrops
33 Q2 Asthall Oxon
34 B2 Asthall Leigh Oxon
162 G8 Astle Highld
69 P11 Astley Shrops
59 M7 Astley Warwks
82 F4 Astley Wigan
57 P11 Astley Worcs
57 N5 Astley Abbots Shrops
89 L8 Astley Bridge Bolton
57 Q11 Astley Cross Worcs
82 F5 Astley Green Wigan
58 G7 Aston Birm
69 R5 Aston Ches E
82 C9 Aston Ches W
83 Q8 Aston Derbys
81 L11 Aston Flints
45 P2 Aston Herefs
50 G6 Aston Herts
34 B4 Aston Oxon
84 G3 Aston Rothm
57 Q6 Aston Shrops
69 P9 Aston Shrops
70 D6 Aston Staffs
70 F10 Aston Staffs
70 G8 Aston Staffs
35 L8 Aston Wokham
57 L3 Aston Wrekin
49 M10 Aston Abbotts Bucks
57 L8 Aston Botterell Shrops
47 M2 Aston Cantlow Warwks
35 N2 Aston Clinton Bucks
46 C10 Aston Crews Herefs
46 H8 Aston Cross Gloucs
50 G6 Aston End Herts
57 M6 Aston-Eyre Shrops
58 E11 Aston Fields Worcs
59 Q6 Aston Flamville Leics
82 C9 Aston Heath Ches W
46 C10 Aston Ingham Herefs
70 A3 Aston juxta Mondrum Ches E
48 E4 Aston le Walls Nhants
47 N7 Aston Magna Gloucs
57 J7 Aston Munslow Shrops
56 F8 Aston on Clun Shrops
56 E3 Aston Pigott Shrops
56 E3 Aston Rogers Shrops
35 K5 Aston Rowant Oxon
35 L3 Aston Sandford Bucks
47 K7 Aston Somerville Worcs
47 M6 Aston-sub-Edge Gloucs
34 G7 Aston Tirrold Oxon
72 C5 Aston-upon-Trent Derbys
34 G7 Aston Upthorpe Oxon
48 F7 Astrop Nhants
35 N2 Astrope Herts
50 F3 Astwick C Beds
84 F8 Astwith Derbys
49 Q5 Astwood M Keyn
58 D11 Astwood Worcs
47 K2 Astwood Bank Worcs
46 G3 Astwood Crematorium Worcs
73 R3 Aswarby Lincs
87 L6 Aswardby Lincs
57 J3 Atcham Shrops
47 K4 Atch Lench Worcs
12 C6 Athelhampton Dorset
65 J7 Athelington Suffk
19 K9 Athelney Somset
128 E4 Athelstaneford E Loth
14 E11 Atherfield Green IoW
17 K7 Atherington Devon
24 B10 Atherington W Susx
19 L11 Atherstone Somset
59 M5 Atherstone Warwks
47 P4 Atherstone on Stour Warwks
82 E4 Atherton Wigan
103 Q10 Atley Hill N York
71 N5 Atlow Derbys
154 B10 Attadale Highld
72 E4 Attenborough Notts
86 C2 Atterby Lincs
84 E3 Attercliffe Sheff
57 L5 Atterley Shrops
72 B11 Atterton Leics
64 E2 Attleborough Norfk
59 N6 Attleborough Warwks
76 G8 Attlebridge Norfk
63 M10 Attleton Green Suffk
99 P10 Atwick E R Yk
32 G11 Atworth Wilts
45 P5 Auberrow Herefs
86 B8 Aubourn Lincs
149 N2 Auchbreck Moray
159 L11 Auchedly Abers
143 N2 Auchenblae Abers
133 M10 Auchenbowie Stirlg
108 G10 Auchencairn D & G
109 L4 Auchencairn D & G
121 K6 Auchencairn N Ayrs
129 M7 Auchencrow Border
127 P5 Auchendinny Mdloth
126 H7 Auchengray S Lans
157 R5 Auchenhalrig Moray
126 E9 Auchenheath S Lans
115 R8 Auchenhessnane D & G
124 B3 Auchenlochan Ag & B
125 K8 Auchenmade N Ayrs
106 H7 Auchenmalg D & G
125 K8 Auchentiber N Ayrs
131 L7 Auchindrain Ag & B
161 K10 Auchindrean Highld
158 G8 Auchininna Abers
115 L3 Auchinleck E Ayrs
126 B3 Auchinloch N Lans
126 C2 Auchinstarry N Lans
139 K3 Auchintore Highld
159 Q10 Auchiries Abers
148 F8 Auchlean Highld
151 M8 Auchlee Abers
150 G3 Auchleven Abers
126 E10 Auchlochan S Lans
150 F7 Auchlossan Abers
132 G2 Auchlyne Stirlg
115 K2 Auchmillan E Ayrs
143 M9 Auchmithie Angus
134 G7 Auchmuirbridge Fife
142 H5 Auchnacree Angus
159 M9 Auchnagatt Abers
149 N3 Auchnarrow Moray
106 C5 Auchnotteroch D & G
157 Q7 Auchroisk Moray
133 Q5 Auchterarder P & K
147 K6 Auchteraw Highld
148 G3 Auchterblair Highld
153 Q2 Auchtercairn Highld
134 G8 Auchterderran Fife
142 E10 Auchterhouse Angus
158 H9 Auchterless Abers
134 G5 Auchtermuchty Fife
155 N6 Auchterneed Highld
134 G9 Auchtertool Fife
145 P2 Auchtertyre Highld
132 H3 Auchtubh Stirlg
167 Q3 Auckengill Highld
91 Q10 Auckley Donc
83 K5 Audenshaw Tamesd
70 B6 Audlem Ches E
70 D4 Audley Staffs
51 M3 Audley End Essex
52 D4 Audley End Essex
64 B11 Audley End Suffk
51 M3 Audley End House Essex
70 E10 Audmore Staffs
58 C7 Audnam Dudley
101 J3 Aughertree Cumb
92 B3 Aughton E R Yk
88 D9 Aughton Lancs
95 M7 Aughton Lancs
84 G3 Aughton Rothm
21 P3 Aughton Wilts
88 E9 Aughton Park Lancs
156 G6 Auldearn Highld
45 P4 Aulden Herefs
109 K3 Auldgirth D & G
125 Q7 Auldhouse S Lans
146 A3 Ault a' chruinn Highld
160 D9 Aultbea Highld
160 A9 Aultgrishin Highld
155 L3 Aultguish Inn Highld
84 G7 Ault Hucknall Derbys
158 B7 Aultmore Moray
147 N3 Aultnagoire Highld
162 F10 Aultnamain Inn Highld
73 Q8 Aunby Lincs
9 P4 Aunk Devon
73 Q3 Aunsby Lincs
31 Q7 Aust S Glos
74 E6 Austendike Lincs
85 L2 Austerfield Donc
90 B9 Austerlands Oldham
91 K4 Austhorpe Leeds
90 E9 Austonley Kirk
59 L3 Austrey Warwks
95 R7 Austwick N York
87 L4 Authorpe Lincs
87 P6 Authorpe Row Lincs
33 M11 Avebury Wilts
33 L11 Avebury Trusloe Wilts
37 N4 Aveley Thurr
32 G5 Avening Gloucs
85 N10 Averham Notts
6 H9 Aveton Gifford Devon
148 F5 Aviemore Highld
34 C11 Avington W Berk
156 C6 Avoch Highld
13 K5 Avon Hants
126 G3 Avonbridge Falk
48 D4 Avon Dassett Warwks
31 P9 Avonmouth Bristl
7 J7 Avonwick Devon
22 B10 Awbridge Hants
31 Q7 Awkley S Glos
10 C4 Awliscombe Devon
32 D3 Awre Gloucs
72 D2 Awsworth Notts
58 C9 Axborough Worcs
19 M4 Axbridge Somset
22 H6 Axford Hants
33 P10 Axford Wilts
10 F5 Axminster Devon
10 F6 Axmouth Devon
80 G8 Axton Flints
103 Q6 Aycliffe Dur
112 F7 Aydon Nthumb
32 B4 Aylburton Gloucs
111 P11 Ayle Nthumb
9 P6 Aylesbeare Devon
35 M2 Aylesbury Bucks
93 M9 Aylesby NE Lin
38 B10 Aylesford Kent
39 M11 Aylesham Kent
72 F10 Aylestone C Leic
72 F10 Aylestone Park C Leic
76 H4 Aylmerton Norfk
76 H6 Aylsham Norfk
46 C7 Aylton Herefs
47 M10 Aylworth Gloucs
56 G11 Aymestrey Herefs
48 F8 Aynho Nhants
50 F8 Ayot Green Herts
50 E7 Ayot St Lawrence Herts
50 F7 Ayot St Peter Herts
114 F3 Ayr S Ayrs
96 F3 Aysgarth N York
18 D11 Ayshford Devon
94 H4 Ayside Cumb
73 M10 Ayston Rutlnd
51 N7 Aythorpe Roding Essex
129 N7 Ayton Border
97 L6 Azerley N York

B

7 N5 Babbacombe Torbay
72 D2 Babbington Notts
69 K9 Babbinswood Shrops
51 J7 Babbs Green Herts
19 Q9 Babcary Somset
44 A7 Babel Carmth
63 M11 Babel Green Suffk
80 H10 Babell Flints
8 G9 Babeny Devon
34 D4 Bablock Hythe Oxon
62 H10 Babraham Cambs
85 L4 Babworth Notts
78 G8 Bachau IoA
56 H8 Bache Shrops
56 C6 Bacheldre Powys
26 D9 Bachelor's Bump E Susx
169 e3 Backaland Ork
94 H4 Backbarrow Cumb
41 Q7 Backe Carmth
159 P7 Backfolds Abers
81 M10 Backford Ches W
81 M10 Backford Cross Ches W
163 J6 Backies Highld
145 L10 Back of Keppoch Highld

71 K4 **Back o' th' Brook** Staffs
63 M9 **Back Street** Suffk
31 N11 **Backwell** N Som
113 M6 **Backworth** N Tyne
59 J7 **Bacon's End** Solhll
76 G4 **Baconsthorpe** Norfk
45 M8 **Bacton** Herefs
77 L5 **Bacton** Norfk
64 F8 **Bacton** Suffk
64 E8 **Bacton Green** Suffk
89 P6 **Bacup** Lancs
153 P3 **Badachro** Highld
33 N8 **Badbury** Swindn
60 C9 **Badby** Nhants
164 E8 **Badcall** Highld
164 F5 **Badcall** Highld
160 G8 **Badcaul** Highld
70 G4 **Baddeley Edge** C Stke
70 G4 **Baddeley Green** C Stke
59 K10 **Baddesley Clinton** Warwks
59 L5 **Baddesley Ensor** Warwks
160 H2 **Baddidarrach** Highld
127 L7 **Baddinsgill** Border
158 G10 **Badenscoth** Abers
149 Q4 **Badenyon** Abers
5 L4 **Badgall** Cnwll
74 H11 **Badgeney** Cambs
57 P5 **Badger** Shrops
2 D7 **Badger's Cross** Cnwll
37 L8 **Badgers Mount** Kent
46 H11 **Badgeworth** Gloucs
19 L4 **Badgworth** Somset
5 M4 **Badharlick** Cnwll
145 N2 **Badicaul** Highld
65 L8 **Badingham** Suffk
38 H11 **Badlesmere** Kent
116 F7 **Badlieu** Border
167 M7 **Badlipster** Highld
160 F8 **Badluachrach** Highld
162 H8 **Badninish** Highld
160 H8 **Badrallach** Highld
47 L6 **Badsey** Worcs
23 N5 **Badshot Lea** Surrey
91 M8 **Badsworth** Wakefd
64 D8 **Badwell Ash** Suffk
64 E8 **Badwell Green** Suffk
12 C2 **Bagber** Dorset
97 Q4 **Bagby** N York
87 L6 **Bag Enderby** Lincs
33 K3 **Bagendon** Gloucs
57 M8 **Bagginswood** Shrops
100 G2 **Baggrow** Cumb
168 b18 **Bagh a Chaisteil** W Isls
39 J11 **Bagham** Kent
168 c17 **Bagh a Tuath** W Isls
81 J9 **Bagillt** Flints
59 M10 **Baginton** Warwks
29 K6 **Baglan** Neath
90 G3 **Bagley** Leeds
69 M9 **Bagley** Shrops
19 N5 **Bagley** Somset
23 J6 **Bagmore** Hants
70 G4 **Bagnall** Staffs
34 E11 **Bagnor** W Berk
57 K10 **Bagot** Shrops
23 P2 **Bagshot** Surrey
34 B11 **Bagshot** Wilts
32 C7 **Bagstone** S Glos
84 G10 **Bagthorpe** Notts
72 C9 **Bagworth** Leics
45 N9 **Bagwy Llydiart** Herefs
90 F3 **Baildon** C Brad
90 E3 **Baildon Green** C Brad
168 b15 **Baile Ailein** W Isls
168 c12 **Baile a Mhanaich** W Isls
136 H11 **Baile Mor** Ag & B
23 J9 **Bailey Green** Hants
111 K5 **Baileyhead** Cumb
90 E5 **Bailiff Bridge** Calder
126 B5 **Baillieston** C Glas
95 K9 **Bailrigg** Lancs
96 D2 **Bainbridge** N York
158 F10 **Bainshole** Abers
74 A9 **Bainton** C Pete
99 K10 **Bainton** E R Yk
48 G9 **Bainton** Oxon
135 L5 **Baintown** Fife
118 C7 **Bairnkine** Border
51 J7 **Baker's End** Herts
37 P4 **Baker Street** Thurr
83 M5 **Bakewell** Derbys
68 B7 **Bala** Gwynd
168 h5 **Balallan** W Isls
155 M11 **Balbeg** Highld
134 F2 **Balbeggie** P & K
155 P8 **Balblair** Highld
156 C4 **Balblair** Highld
91 P10 **Balby** Donc
108 H11 **Balcary** D & G
155 P9 **Balchraggan** Highld
164 E4 **Balchreick** Highld
24 H4 **Balcombe** W Susx
24 H4 **Balcombe Lane** W Susx
135 Q6 **Balcomie Links** Fife
97 N5 **Baldersby** N York
97 N5 **Baldersby St James** N York
89 J4 **Balderstone** Lancs
89 Q8 **Balderstone** Rochdl
85 P10 **Balderton** Notts
3 K5 **Baldhu** Cnwll
135 L5 **Baldinnie** Fife
134 C4 **Baldinnies** P & K
50 F4 **Baldock** Herts
50 F3 **Baldock Services** Herts
142 H11 **Baldovie** C Dund
80 f5 **Baldrine** IoM
26 D9 **Baldslow** E Susx
80 e5 **Baldwin** IoM
110 F10 **Baldwinholme** Cumb
70 D7 **Baldwin's Gate** Staffs
25 J3 **Baldwin's Hill** W Susx
76 E4 **Bale** Norfk
142 D11 **Baledgarno** P & K
136 B7 **Balemartine** Ag & B
127 M4 **Balerno** C Edin
134 H7 **Balfarg** Fife
143 J4 **Balfield** Angus
169 d5 **Balfour** Ork
132 G10 **Balfron** Stirlg
158 G9 **Balgaveny** Abers
135 L2 **Balgonar** Fife
106 F9 **Balgowan** D & G
147 Q9 **Balgowan** Highld
152 F4 **Balgown** Highld
106 C5 **Balgracie** D & G
116 B6 **Balgray** S Lans
36 G6 **Balham** Gt Lon
142 D8 **Balhary** P & K
142 A10 **Balholmie** P & K
166 E3 **Baligill** Highld
142 D6 **Balintore** Angus
156 F2 **Balintore** Highld
156 C3 **Balintraid** Highld
168 c12 **Balivanich** W Isls
97 Q4 **Balk** N York
142 E9 **Balkeerie** Angus
92 C5 **Balkholme** E R Yk
80 c7 **Ballabeg** IoM
139 K6 **Ballachulish** Highld
80 b7 **Ballafesson** IoM
80 g3 **Ballajora** IoM
80 b7 **Ballakilpheric** IoM
80 c7 **Ballamodha** IoM
124 C5 **Ballanlay** Ag & B
114 A11 **Ballantrae** S Ayrs
38 F3 **Ballards Gore** Essex
59 L6 **Ballards Green** Warwks
80 c7 **Ballasalla** IoM
150 B8 **Ballater** Abers
80 d3 **Ballaugh** IoM
156 D2 **Ballchraggan** Highld
128 D4 **Ballencrieff** E Loth
136 B6 **Ballevullin** Ag & B
70 F4 **Ball Green** C Stke
70 H3 **Ball Haye Green** Staffs
22 D2 **Ball Hill** Hants
71 N4 **Ballidon** Derbys
120 G4 **Balliekine** N Ayrs
131 N8 **Balliemore** Ag & B
114 D9 **Balligmorrie** S Ayrs
132 G4 **Ballimore** Stirlg
157 M10 **Ballindalloch** Moray
134 H2 **Ballindean** P & K
52 E3 **Ballingdon** Suffk
35 P4 **Ballinger Common** Bucks
46 A8 **Ballingham** Herefs
134 F8 **Ballingry** Fife
141 N7 **Ballinluig** P & K
142 G7 **Ballinshoe** Angus
141 R6 **Ballintuim** P & K
156 C8 **Balloch** Highld
126 C3 **Balloch** N Lans
133 N4 **Balloch** P & K
114 F8 **Balloch** S Ayrs
132 D11 **Balloch** W Duns
23 Q9 **Balls Cross** W Susx
25 L3 **Balls Green** E Susx
32 G5 **Ball's Green** Gloucs
137 L7 **Ballygown** Ag & B
122 E6 **Ballygrant** Ag & B
136 F4 **Ballyhaugh** Ag & B
145 P2 **Balmacara** Highld
108 E5 **Balmaclellan** D & G
108 E12 **Balmae** D & G
132 E9 **Balmaha** Stirlg
135 J6 **Balmalcolm** Fife
108 D11 **Balmangan** D & G
151 P4 **Balmedie** Abers
69 M8 **Balmer Heath** Shrops
135 K3 **Balmerino** Fife
13 P4 **Balmerlawn** Hants
120 H5 **Balmichael** N Ayrs
149 P9 **Balmoral Castle Grounds** Abers
125 P3 **Balmore** E Duns
163 K11 **Balmuchy** Highld
134 G10 **Balmule** Fife
135 L3 **Balmullo** Fife
163 J4 **Balnacoil Lodge** Highld
154 C8 **Balnacra** Highld
149 P9 **Balnacroft** Abers
156 B10 **Balnafoich** Highld
141 M7 **Balnaguard** P & K
136 C2 **Balnahard** Ag & B
137 M9 **Balnahard** Ag & B
155 M11 **Balnain** Highld
165 J3 **Balnakeil** Highld
91 P7 **Balne** N York
141 P10 **Balquharn** P & K
132 G3 **Balquhidder** Stirlg
59 K9 **Balsall Common** Solhll
58 G8 **Balsall Heath** Birm
59 K9 **Balsall Street** Solhll
48 C6 **Balscote** Oxon
63 J10 **Balsham** Cambs
169 t3 **Baltasound** Shet
70 D4 **Balterley** Staffs
70 D4 **Balterley Green** Staffs
70 C4 **Balterley Heath** Staffs
107 M4 **Baltersan** D & G
19 P8 **Baltonsborough** Somset
130 F4 **Balvicar** Ag & B
145 P4 **Balvraid** Highld
156 E11 **Balvraid** Highld
2 F7 **Balwest** Cnwll
88 H5 **Bamber Bridge** Lancs
51 N6 **Bamber's Green** Essex
119 N4 **Bamburgh** Nthumb
119 N3 **Bamburgh Castle** Nthumb
84 B4 **Bamford** Derbys
89 P8 **Bamford** Rochdl
101 P7 **Bampton** Cumb
18 C10 **Bampton** Devon
34 B4 **Bampton** Oxon
101 P7 **Bampton Grange** Cumb
139 L2 **Banavie** Highld
48 E6 **Banbury** Oxon
48 E6 **Banbury Crematorium** Oxon
28 E2 **Bancffosfelen** Carmth
150 H8 **Banchory** Abers
151 N7 **Banchory-Devenick** Abers
28 D2 **Bancycapel** Carmth
42 F11 **Bancyfelin** Carmth
42 H7 **Banc-y-ffordd** Carmth
142 C11 **Bandirran** P & K
94 G3 **Bandrake Head** Cumb
158 G5 **Banff** Abers
79 K10 **Bangor** Gwynd
79 K10 **Bangor Crematorium** Gwynd
69 L5 **Bangor-is-y-coed** Wrexhm
5 L2 **Bangors** Cnwll
88 D9 **Bangor's Green** Lancs
64 C7 **Bangrove** Suffk
64 F4 **Banham** Norfk
13 N3 **Bank** Hants
109 M7 **Bankend** D & G
141 Q10 **Bankfoot** P & K
115 L5 **Bankglen** E Ayrs
101 K11 **Bank Ground** Cumb
151 N6 **Bankhead** C Aber
116 D2 **Bankhead** S Lans
96 D10 **Bank Newton** N York
126 D2 **Banknock** Falk
111 L8 **Banks** Cumb
88 D6 **Banks** Lancs
58 E11 **Banks Green** Worcs
110 C4 **Bankshill** D & G
46 B2 **Bank Street** Worcs
90 E6 **Bank Top** Calder
88 G9 **Bank Top** Lancs
77 J6 **Banningham** Norfk
51 Q6 **Bannister Green** Essex
133 N9 **Bannockburn** Stirlg
36 G9 **Banstead** Surrey
6 H10 **Bantham** Devon
126 C2 **Banton** N Lans
19 L3 **Banwell** N Som
38 F9 **Bapchild** Kent
21 J7 **Bapton** Wilts
168 i3 **Barabhas** W Isls
125 J11 **Barassie** S Ayrs
156 C3 **Barbaraville** Highld
83 P8 **Barber Booth** Derbys
94 H4 **Barber Green** Cumb
114 H4 **Barbieston** S Ayrs
95 N4 **Barbon** Cumb
69 R3 **Barbridge** Ches E
17 N2 **Barbrook** Devon
60 B6 **Barby** Nhants
138 H9 **Barcaldine** Ag & B
47 Q7 **Barcheston** Warwks
110 H8 **Barclose** Cumb
25 K8 **Barcombe** E Susx
25 K7 **Barcombe Cross** E Susx
90 C3 **Barcroft** C Brad
96 H2 **Barden** N York
37 N11 **Barden Park** Kent
51 P4 **Bardfield End Green** Essex
51 Q5 **Bardfield Saling** Essex
86 F7 **Bardney** Lincs
72 C8 **Bardon** Leics
111 Q8 **Bardon Mill** Nthumb
125 P3 **Bardowie** E Duns
25 Q5 **Bardown** E Susx
125 J3 **Bardrainney** Inver
94 G6 **Bardsea** Cumb
91 K2 **Bardsey** Leeds
66 A10 **Bardsey Island** Gwynd
83 K4 **Bardsley** Oldham
64 C7 **Bardwell** Suffk
95 K8 **Bare** Lancs
3 K8 **Bareppa** Cnwll
107 K4 **Barfad** D & G
76 G10 **Barford** Norfk
47 Q2 **Barford** Warwks
48 D8 **Barford St John** Oxon
21 L8 **Barford St Martin** Wilts
48 D8 **Barford St Michael** Oxon
39 N11 **Barfrestone** Kent
84 E11 **Bargate** Derbys
126 B5 **Bargeddie** N Lans
30 G5 **Bargoed** Caerph
107 L2 **Bargrennan** D & G
61 P5 **Barham** Cambs
39 M11 **Barham** Kent
64 G11 **Barham** Suffk
27 M2 **Barham Crematorium** Kent
62 E8 **Bar Hill** Cambs
74 A8 **Barholm** Lincs
72 G9 **Barkby** Leics
72 G9 **Barkby Thorpe** Leics
69 P9 **Barkers Green** Shrops
73 K4 **Barkestone-le-Vale** Leics
35 L11 **Barkham** Wokham
37 K4 **Barking** Gt Lon
64 F11 **Barking** Suffk
37 K3 **Barkingside** Gt Lon
64 F11 **Barking Tye** Suffk
90 D7 **Barkisland** Calder
3 J3 **Barkla Shop** Cnwll
73 N2 **Barkston** Lincs
91 M3 **Barkston Ash** N York
51 J3 **Barkway** Herts
126 B5 **Barlanark** C Glas
70 F7 **Barlaston** Staffs
23 Q11 **Barlavington** W Susx
84 G5 **Barlborough** Derbys
91 Q4 **Barlby** N York
72 C9 **Barlestone** Leics
51 K3 **Barley** Herts
89 N2 **Barley** Lancs
51 K3 **Barleycroft End** Herts
91 K11 **Barley Hole** Rothm
73 L9 **Barleythorpe** Rutlnd
38 F4 **Barling** Essex
86 E6 **Barlings** Lincs
108 H9 **Barlochan** D & G
84 D6 **Barlow** Derbys
113 J8 **Barlow** Gatesd
91 Q5 **Barlow** N York
98 F11 **Barmby Moor** E R Yk
92 A5 **Barmby on the Marsh** E R Yk
75 R4 **Barmer** Norfk
38 B10 **Barming Heath** Kent
120 F3 **Barmollack** Ag & B
67 L11 **Barmouth** Gwynd
104 B7 **Barmpton** Darltn
99 P9 **Barmston** E R Yk
65 P5 **Barnaby Green** Suffk
131 L9 **Barnacarry** Ag & B
74 A9 **Barnack** C Pete
59 N8 **Barnacle** Warwks
103 L7 **Barnard Castle** Dur
34 D2 **Barnard Gate** Oxon
63 M11 **Barnardiston** Suffk
108 H9 **Barnbarroch** D & G
91 M10 **Barnburgh** Donc
65 P4 **Barnby** Suffk
91 Q9 **Barnby Dun** Donc
85 Q10 **Barnby in the Willows** Notts
85 L4 **Barnby Moor** Notts
106 E10 **Barncorkrie** D & G
37 L5 **Barnehurst** Gt Lon
36 F5 **Barnes** Gt Lon
37 P11 **Barnes Street** Kent
50 F11 **Barnet** Gt Lon
93 J9 **Barnetby le Wold** N Linc
50 F11 **Barnet Gate** Gt Lon
76 D5 **Barney** Norfk
64 B6 **Barnham** Suffk
15 Q6 **Barnham** W Susx
76 F10 **Barnham Broom** Norfk
143 M6 **Barnhead** Angus
142 H11 **Barnhill** C Dund
69 N4 **Barnhill** Ches W
157 L6 **Barnhill** Moray
106 C3 **Barnhills** D & G
103 L8 **Barningham** Dur
64 D6 **Barningham** Suffk
93 M10 **Barnoldby le Beck** NE Lin
96 C11 **Barnoldswick** Lancs
91 N8 **Barnsdale Bar** Donc
24 D5 **Barns Green** W Susx
91 J9 **Barnsley** Barns
33 L4 **Barnsley** Gloucs
91 K9 **Barnsley Crematorium** Barns
39 N10 **Barnsole** Kent
17 K5 **Barnstaple** Devon
51 P7 **Barnston** Essex
81 K8 **Barnston** Wirral
73 J3 **Barnstone** Notts
58 F10 **Barnt Green** Worcs
127 M3 **Barnton** C Edin
82 D10 **Barnton** Ches W
61 M4 **Barnwell All Saints** Nhants
61 N4 **Barnwell St Andrew** Nhants
46 G11 **Barnwood** Gloucs
45 P3 **Baron's Cross** Herefs
101 P2 **Baronwood** Cumb
114 E9 **Barr** S Ayrs
168 b17 **Barra** W Isls
168 c17 *Barra Airport* W Isls
107 L8 **Barrachan** D & G
168 b17 **Barraigh** W Isls
136 A7 **Barrapoll** Ag & B
102 F8 **Barras** Cumb
112 D6 **Barrasford** Nthumb
80 d4 **Barregarrow** IoM
69 Q3 **Barrets Green** Ches E
125 M6 **Barrhead** E Rens
114 D11 **Barrhill** S Ayrs
62 E11 **Barrington** Cambs
19 L11 **Barrington** Somset
2 G6 **Barripper** Cnwll
125 K7 **Barrmill** N Ayrs
167 N2 **Barrock** Highld
46 G10 **Barrow** Gloucs
89 L3 **Barrow** Lancs
73 M7 **Barrow** Rutlnd
57 M4 **Barrow** Shrops
20 D8 **Barrow** Somset
63 N8 **Barrow** Suffk
75 L10 **Barroway Drove** Norfk
89 K8 **Barrow Bridge** Bolton
118 G8 **Barrow Burn** Nthumb
73 M3 **Barrowby** Lincs
73 N10 **Barrowden** Rutlnd
89 P3 **Barrowford** Lancs
31 P11 **Barrow Gurney** N Som
93 J6 **Barrow Haven** N Linc
84 F5 **Barrow Hill** Derbys
94 E7 **Barrow-in-Furness** Cumb
94 D7 **Barrow Island** Cumb
81 N4 **Barrow Nook** Lancs
70 B3 **Barrow's Green** Ches E
20 F8 **Barrow Street** Wilts
93 J6 **Barrow-upon-Humber** N Linc
72 F7 **Barrow upon Soar** Leics
72 B5 **Barrow upon Trent** Derbys
20 B2 **Barrow Vale** BaNES
143 J11 **Barry** Angus
30 F11 **Barry** V Glam
30 F11 **Barry Island** V Glam
72 H8 **Barsby** Leics
65 M4 **Barsham** Suffk
59 K9 **Barston** Solhll
45 R6 **Bartestree** Herefs
159 K11 **Barthol Chapel** Abers
52 B7 **Bartholomew Green** Essex
70 D4 **Barthomley** Ches E
13 P2 **Bartley** Hants
58 F8 **Bartley Green** Birm
63 J11 **Bartlow** Cambs
62 F9 **Barton** Cambs
69 M4 **Barton** Ches W
47 L9 **Barton** Gloucs
45 K3 **Barton** Herefs
88 D9 **Barton** Lancs
88 G3 **Barton** Lancs
103 P9 **Barton** N York
34 G3 **Barton** Oxon
7 N5 **Barton** Torbay
47 M4 **Barton** Warwks
75 P9 **Barton Bendish** Norfk
32 F5 **Barton End** Gloucs
71 M11 **Barton Green** Staffs
48 H8 **Barton Hartshorn** Bucks
98 E8 **Barton Hill** N York
72 E4 **Barton in Fabis** Notts
72 B9 **Barton in the Beans** Leics
50 C4 **Barton-le-Clay** C Beds
98 E6 **Barton-le-Street** N York
98 E8 **Barton-le-Willows** N York
63 M6 **Barton Mills** Suffk
13 M6 **Barton-on-Sea** Hants
47 Q8 **Barton-on-the-Heath** Warwks
19 P8 **Barton St David** Somset
61 J5 **Barton Seagrave** Nhants
22 D6 **Barton Stacey** Hants
17 M3 **Barton Town** Devon
77 M7 **Barton Turf** Norfk
71 M11 **Barton-under-Needwood** Staffs
92 H6 **Barton-upon-Humber** N Linc
82 G5 **Barton upon Irwell** Salfd
92 H6 **Barton Waterside** N Linc
91 J9 **Barugh** Barns
91 J9 **Barugh Green** Barns
168 i3 **Barvas** W Isls
63 J5 **Barway** Cambs
72 C11 **Barwell** Leics
17 K10 **Barwick** Devon
51 J7 **Barwick** Herts
11 M2 **Barwick** Somset
91 L3 **Barwick in Elmet** Leeds
69 M10 **Baschurch** Shrops
48 D2 **Bascote** Warwks
48 C2 **Bascote Heath** Warwks
64 E9 **Base Green** Suffk
70 H4 **Basford Green** Staffs
89 K2 **Bashall Eaves** Lancs
89 L2 **Bashall Town** Lancs
13 M5 **Bashley** Hants
38 B4 **Basildon** Essex
38 C4 **Basildon & District Crematorium** Essex
22 H4 **Basingstoke** Hants
22 G5 **Basingstoke Crematorium** Hants
84 C6 **Baslow** Derbys
19 K5 **Bason Bridge** Somset
31 J7 **Bassaleg** Newpt
128 G10 **Bassendean** Border
100 H4 **Bassenthwaite** Cumb
22 D11 **Bassett** C Sotn
50 H2 **Bassingbourn** Cambs
72 G3 **Bassingfield** Notts
86 B9 **Bassingham** Lincs
73 P5 **Bassingthorpe** Lincs
50 H5 **Bassus Green** Herts
37 P9 **Basted** Kent
74 B8 **Baston** Lincs
77 N8 **Bastwick** Norfk
19 K3 **Batch** Somset
36 C2 **Batchworth** Herts
36 C2 **Batchworth Heath** Herts
11 N4 **Batcombe** Dorset
20 C7 **Batcombe** Somset
82 E9 **Bate Heath** Ches E
50 D7 **Batford** Herts
20 D2 **Bath** BaNES
32 E11 **Bathampton** BaNES
18 E10 **Bathealton** Somset
32 E11 **Batheaston** BaNES
32 E11 **Bathford** BaNES
126 H4 **Bathgate** W Loth
85 N9 **Bathley** Notts
5 M7 **Bathpool** Cnwll
19 J9 **Bathpool** Somset
53 N5 **Bath Side** Essex
126 G4 **Bathville** W Loth
19 Q4 **Bathway** Somset
90 G6 **Batley** Kirk
47 N8 **Batsford** Gloucs
7 J11 **Batson** Devon
104 G9 **Battersby** N York
36 G5 **Battersea** Gt Lon
6 F9 **Battisborough Cross** Devon
64 F11 **Battisford** Suffk
64 E11 **Battisford Tye** Suffk
26 C8 **Battle** E Susx
44 E8 **Battle** Powys
19 K4 **Battleborough** Somset
47 J10 **Battledown** Gloucs
142 H6 **Battledykes** Angus
69 P11 **Battlefield** Shrops
86 H9 **Battle of Britain Memorial Flight** Lincs
38 C3 **Battlesbridge** Essex
49 Q9 **Battlesden** C Beds
18 B9 **Battleton** Somset
64 C9 **Battlies Green** Suffk
13 P5 **Battramsley Cross** Hants
23 M6 **Batt's Corner** Hants
46 G6 **Baughton** Worcs
22 G2 **Baughurst** Hants
150 G9 **Baulds** Abers
34 B6 **Baulking** Oxon
86 H6 **Baumber** Lincs
33 K4 **Baunton** Gloucs
57 M9 **Baveney Wood** Shrops
21 K8 **Baverstock** Wilts
76 H10 **Bawburgh** Norfk
76 E7 **Bawdeswell** Norfk
19 K7 **Bawdrip** Somset
53 P3 **Bawdsey** Suffk
75 N6 **Bawsey** Norfk
85 K2 **Bawtry** Donc
89 M5 **Baxenden** Lancs
59 L5 **Baxterley** Warwks
64 E9 **Baxter's Green** Suffk
152 D7 **Bay** Highld
168 k4 **Bayble** W Isls
22 F10 **Baybridge** Hants
112 E10 **Baybridge** Nthumb
94 F6 **Baycliff** Cumb
33 Q9 **Baydon** Wilts
50 H9 **Bayford** Herts
20 D9 **Bayford** Somset
168 c11 **Bayhead** W Isls
95 K10 **Bay Horse** Lancs
37 M10 **Bayley's Hill** Kent
64 G11 **Baylham** Suffk
48 F9 **Baynard's Green** Oxon
104 H9 **Baysdale Abbey** N York
45 R9 **Baysham** Herefs
56 H3 **Bayston Hill** Shrops
52 B3 **Baythorne End** Essex
57 M10 **Bayton** Worcs
57 N10 **Bayton Common** Worcs
34 E4 **Bayworth** Oxon
32 D10 **Beach** S Glos
49 L7 **Beachampton** Bucks
75 Q9 **Beachamwell** Norfk
31 Q6 **Beachley** Gloucs
25 N11 **Beachy Head** E Susx
10 D3 **Beacon** Devon
52 G7 **Beacon End** Essex
25 M4 **Beacon Hill** E Susx
26 D5 **Beacon Hill** Kent
85 P10 **Beacon Hill** Notts
23 N7 **Beacon Hill** Surrey
64 G11 **Beacon Hill Services** Suffk
35 L5 **Beacon's Bottom** Bucks
35 P6 **Beaconsfield** Bucks
35 Q7 **Beaconsfield Services** Bucks
98 D4 **Beadlam** N York
50 D3 **Beadlow** C Beds
119 P5 **Beadnell** Nthumb
17 K8 **Beaford** Devon
91 N5 **Beal** N York
119 L2 **Beal** Nthumb
5 P8 **Bealbury** Cnwll
5 P6 **Bealsmill** Cnwll
71 N9 **Beam Hill** Staffs
71 K7 **Beamhurst** Staffs
11 K4 **Beaminster** Dorset
113 K10 **Beamish** Dur
96 G10 **Beamsley** N York
37 N6 **Bean** Kent
32 H11 **Beanacre** Wilts
119 L7 **Beanley** Nthumb
8 D8 **Beardon** Devon
89 K5 **Beardwood** Bl w D
9 N4 **Beare** Devon
24 E2 **Beare Green** Surrey
47 N2 **Bearley** Warwks
47 N2 **Bearley Cross** Warwks
103 P2 **Bearpark** Dur
125 N3 **Bearsden** E Duns
38 D10 **Bearsted** Kent
70 C7 **Bearstone** Shrops
58 F7 **Bearwood** Birm
45 M3 **Bearwood** Herefs
12 H5 **Bearwood** Poole
116 F10 **Beattock** D & G

51 N9 Beauchamp Roding Essex
84 D4 Beauchief Sheff
59 J11 Beaudesert Warwks
30 G2 Beaufort Blae G
14 C6 Beaulieu Hants
14 C6 Beaulieu House Hants
13 P3 Beaulieu Road Station Hants
155 P8 Beauly Highld
79 L9 Beaumaris IoA
110 F9 Beaumont Cumb
53 L7 Beaumont Essex
11 b2 Beaumont Jersey
103 Q7 Beaumont Hill Darltn
59 K10 Beausale Warwks
22 G9 Beauworth Hants
8 C5 Beaworthy Devon
52 B6 Beazley End Essex
81 L8 Bebington Wirral
113 L4 Bebside Nthumb
65 N4 Beccles Suffk
88 F6 Becconsall Lancs
57 P4 Beckbury Shrops
37 J7 Beckenham Gt Lon
37 J7 Beckenham Crematorium Gt Lon
100 D9 Beckermet Cumb
75 Q11 Beckett End Norfk
94 D3 Beckfoot Cumb
100 G10 Beckfoot Cumb
102 B11 Beck Foot Cumb
109 N11 Beckfoot Cumb
47 J7 Beckford Worcs
33 L11 Beckhampton Wilts
105 M10 Beck Hole N York
85 Q10 Beckingham Lincs
85 N3 Beckingham Notts
20 F4 Beckington Somset
56 F9 Beckjay Shrops
26 E7 Beckley E Susx
13 M5 Beckley Hants
34 G2 Beckley Oxon
63 L5 Beck Row Suffk
96 F11 Becks C Brad
94 E4 Beck Side Cumb
94 H4 Beck Side Cumb
37 K4 Beckton Gt Lon
97 L10 Beckwithshaw N York
37 L3 Becontree Gt Lon
11 b1 Becquet Vincent Jersey
97 L3 Bedale N York
103 L4 Bedburn Dur
20 G11 Bedchester Dorset
30 E7 Beddau Rhondd
67 K5 Beddgelert Gwynd
25 K9 Beddingham E Susx
36 H7 Beddington Gt Lon
36 G7 Beddington Corner Gt Lon
65 J8 Bedfield Suffk
65 J8 Bedfield Little Green Suffk
61 M11 Bedford Bed
61 N10 Bedford Crematorium Bed
26 B5 Bedgebury Cross Kent
24 B6 Bedham W Susx
15 K5 Bedhampton Hants
64 H8 Bedingfield Suffk
64 H8 Bedingfield Green Suffk
97 L8 Bedlam N York
113 L4 Bedlington Nthumb
30 E4 Bedlinog Myr Td
31 Q10 Bedminster Bristl
31 Q10 Bedminster Down Bristl
50 C8 Bedmond Herts
70 H11 Bednall Staffs
118 B7 Bedrule Border
56 F9 Bedstone Shrops
30 G7 Bedwas Caerph
30 G4 Bedwellty Caerph
59 N7 Bedworth Warwks
59 M7 Bedworth Woodlands Warwks
72 H9 Beeby Leics
23 J7 Beech Hants
70 F7 Beech Staffs
23 J2 Beech Hill W Berk
21 L3 Beechingstoke Wilts
34 E9 Beedon W Berk
34 E9 Beedon Hill W Berk
99 N10 Beeford E R Yk
84 C7 Beeley Derbys
93 M10 Beelsby NE Lin
34 G11 Beenham W Berk
35 M9 Beenham's Heath W & M
5 J3 Beeny Cnwll
10 E7 Beer Devon
19 M8 Beer Somset
19 K10 Beercrocombe Somset
11 N2 Beer Hackett Dorset
7 L10 Beesands Devon
87 N4 Beesby Lincs
7 L10 Beeson Devon
61 Q11 Beeston C Beds
69 P3 Beeston Ches W
90 H4 Beeston Leeds
76 C8 Beeston Norfk
72 E3 Beeston Notts
76 H3 Beeston Regis Norfk
109 J7 Beeswing D & G
95 K5 Beetham Cumb
10 F2 Beetham Somset
76 D8 Beetley Norfk
30 H8 Began Cardif
34 E2 Begbroke Oxon
75 J9 Begdale Cambs
41 M9 Begelly Pembks
90 H6 Beggarington Hill Leeds
45 K2 Beggar's Bush Powys
56 B9 Beguildy Powys
77 M10 Beighton Norfk
84 F4 Beighton Sheff
168 d12 Beinn Na Faoghla W Isls
125 K7 Beith N Ayrs
39 L10 Bekesbourne Kent
39 L10 Bekesbourne Hill Kent
77 K8 Belaugh Norfk
58 D9 Belbroughton Worcs
12 C3 Belchalwell Dorset
12 C3 Belchalwell Street Dorset
52 D3 Belchamp Otten Essex
52 C3 Belchamp St Paul Essex
52 D3 Belchamp Walter Essex
87 J5 Belchford Lincs
119 M4 Belford Nthumb
72 F9 Belgrave C Leic
128 H4 Belhaven E Loth
151 N4 Belhelvie Abers
150 D2 Belhinnie Abers
150 B5 Bellabeg Abers
45 M6 Bellamore Herefs
130 F9 Bellanoch Ag & B
92 D5 Bellasize E R Yk
142 C6 Bellaty Angus
50 G9 Bell Bar Herts
96 D9 Bell Busk N York
87 M5 Belleau Lincs
58 D9 Bell End Worcs
96 H2 Bellerby N York
8 G9 Bellever Devon
110 G9 Belle Vue Cumb
91 J7 Belle Vue Wakefd
116 D6 Bellfield S Lans
126 E11 Bellfield S Lans
58 D9 Bell Heath Worcs
23 K10 Bell Hill Hants
35 P3 Bellingdon Bucks
112 B4 Bellingham Nthumb
120 C4 Belloch Ag & B
120 C5 Bellochantuy Ag & B
69 P5 Bell o' th' Hill Ches W
13 J2 Bellows Cross Dorset
64 H11 Bells Cross Suffk
126 C5 Bellshill N Lans
119 M4 Bellshill Nthumb
126 E6 Bellside N Lans
127 J4 Bellsquarry W Loth
25 P3 Bells Yew Green E Susx
20 B2 Belluton BaNES
156 A6 Belmaduthy Highld
73 Q8 Belmesthorpe Rutlnd
89 K7 Belmont Bl w D
36 G8 Belmont Gt Lon
114 F4 Belmont S Ayrs
169 s3 Belmont Shet
150 B4 Belnacraig Abers
4 F9 Belowda Cnwll
84 D11 Belper Derbys
84 D11 Belper Lane End Derbys
84 H5 Belph Derbys
112 G5 Belsay Nthumb
117 R5 Belses Border
7 K7 Belsford Devon
50 B10 Belsize Herts
53 K3 Belstead Suffk
8 F6 Belstone Devon
89 L6 Belthorn Lancs
39 L8 Beltinge Kent
111 Q8 Beltingham Nthumb
92 D9 Beltoft N Linc
72 C6 Belton Leics
73 N3 Belton Lincs
92 C9 Belton N Linc
77 P11 Belton Norfk
73 L10 Belton Rutlnd
37 Q11 Beltring Kent
37 L5 Belvedere Gt Lon
73 L4 Belvoir Leics
73 L4 Belvoir Castle Leics
14 H9 Bembridge IoW
21 M8 Bemerton Wilts
99 P6 Bempton E R Yk
65 Q5 Benacre Suffk
168 d12 Benbecula W Isls
168 c12 Benbecula Airport W Isls
115 P8 Benbuie D & G
138 G10 Benderloch Ag & B
26 D5 Benenden Kent
112 G10 Benfieldside Dur
77 L6 Bengates Norfk
50 H8 Bengeo Herts
47 K6 Bengeworth Worcs
65 M9 Benhall Green Suffk
65 M9 Benhall Street Suffk
143 Q4 Benholm Abers
98 A9 Beningbrough N York
50 G6 Benington Herts
87 L11 Benington Lincs
87 M11 Benington Sea End Lincs
79 J8 Benllech IoA
131 N10 Benmore Ag & B
5 M3 Bennacott Cnwll
121 J7 Bennan N Ayrs
101 M6 Bennet Head Cumb
92 D5 Bennetland E R Yk
35 L5 Bennett End Bucks
139 M3 Ben Nevis Highld
86 H4 Benniworth Lincs
26 B2 Benover Kent
96 H11 Ben Rhydding C Brad
125 J9 Benslie N Ayrs
34 H6 Benson Oxon
51 M5 Bentfield Green Essex
57 M4 Benthall Shrops
46 H11 Bentham Gloucs
151 L7 Benthoul C Aber
56 E4 Bentlawn Shrops
91 P9 Bentley Donc
92 H3 Bentley E R Yk
23 L6 Bentley Hants
53 K4 Bentley Suffk
59 L5 Bentley Warwks
50 G11 Bentley Heath Herts
59 J9 Bentley Heath Solhll
17 M4 Benton Devon
110 F2 Bentpath D & G
17 N5 Bentwichen Devon
23 J6 Bentworth Hants
142 E11 Benvie Angus
11 L4 Benville Dorset
62 D2 Benwick Cambs
58 G11 Beoley Worcs
145 L9 Beoraidbeg Highld
23 N11 Bepton W Susx
51 L5 Berden Essex
40 E4 Berea Pembks
6 C5 Bere Alston Devon
6 D6 Bere Ferrers Devon
2 H9 Berepper Cnwll
12 D6 Bere Regis Dorset
77 L11 Bergh Apton Norfk
19 M7 Berhill Somset
34 G5 Berinsfield Oxon
32 C5 Berkeley Gloucs
32 C5 Berkeley Heath Gloucs
32 D4 Berkeley Road Gloucs
35 Q3 Berkhamsted Herts
20 F5 Berkley Somset
59 K9 Berkswell Solhll
36 H5 Bermondsey Gt Lon
59 N7 Bermuda Warwks
145 P3 Bernera Highld
152 G7 Bernisdale Highld
34 H6 Berrick Prior Oxon
34 H6 Berrick Salome Oxon
163 Q2 Berriedale Highld
101 L5 Berrier Cumb
56 B4 Berriew Powys
119 K2 Berrington Nthumb
57 J3 Berrington Shrops
57 K11 Berrington Worcs
57 K11 Berrington Green Worcs
19 J4 Berrow Somset
46 E8 Berrow Worcs
46 D3 Berrow Green Worcs
90 E8 Berry Brow Kirk
16 H9 Berry Cross Devon
17 K3 Berry Down Cross Devon
31 Q2 Berry Hill Gloucs
41 L2 Berry Hill Pembks
158 D5 Berryhillock Moray
158 D7 Berryhillock Moray
17 K2 Berrynarbor Devon
7 L6 Berry Pomeroy Devon
37 K9 Berry's Green Gt Lon
69 K5 Bersham Wrexhm
80 G9 Berthengam Flints
25 M9 Berwick E Susx
33 L10 Berwick Bassett Wilts
113 J5 Berwick Hill Nthumb
21 L7 Berwick St James Wilts
20 H10 Berwick St John Wilts
20 H8 Berwick St Leonard Wilts
129 P9 Berwick-upon-Tweed Nthumb
73 L5 Bescaby Leics
88 D8 Bescar Lancs
69 Q9 Besford Shrops
46 H6 Besford Worcs
91 Q10 Bessacarr Donc
34 E4 Bessels Leigh Oxon
89 N9 Besses o' th' Barn Bury
99 P7 Bessingby E R Yk
76 H4 Bessingham Norfk
25 P4 Bestbeech Hill E Susx
64 F2 Besthorpe Norfk
85 P8 Besthorpe Notts
85 J11 Bestwood Village Notts
99 L11 Beswick E R Yk
56 G5 Betchcott Shrops
36 F10 Betchworth Surrey
43 L2 Bethania Cerdgn
67 N6 Bethania Gwynd
53 J7 Beth Chatto Garden Essex
68 C7 Bethel Gwynd
79 J11 Bethel Gwynd
78 F10 Bethel IoA
68 F10 Bethel Powys
26 F3 Bethersden Kent
79 L11 Bethesda Gwynd
41 L7 Bethesda Pembks
43 N9 Bethlehem Carmth
36 H4 Bethnal Green Gt Lon
70 D5 Betley Staffs
37 P6 Betsham Kent
39 P11 Betteshanger Kent
10 H4 Bettiscombe Dorset
69 N7 Bettisfield Wrexhm
70 B7 Betton Shrops
57 J3 Betton Strange Shrops
31 J6 Bettws Newpt
43 L4 Bettws Bledrws Cerdgn
55 Q5 Bettws Cedewain Powys
42 F5 Bettws Evan Cerdgn
31 L3 Bettws-Newydd Mons
166 B4 Bettyhill Highld
29 P7 Betws Brdgnd
28 H2 Betws Carmth
67 J3 Betws Garmon Gwynd
68 D5 Betws Gwerfil Goch Denbgs
67 P3 Betws-y-Coed Conwy
80 C10 Betws-yn-Rhos Conwy
42 E5 Beulah Cerdgn
44 C4 Beulah Powys
24 H9 Bevendean Br & H
85 L6 Bevercotes Notts
92 H3 Beverley E R Yk
32 G6 Beverston Gloucs
32 C5 Bevington Gloucs
100 H4 Bewaldeth Cumb
111 L6 Bewcastle Cumb
57 P9 Bewdley Worcs
97 J7 Bewerley N York
99 P11 Bewholme E R Yk
25 Q4 Bewlbridge Kent
26 B10 Bexhill E Susx
37 L6 Bexley Gt Lon
37 L5 Bexleyheath Gt Lon
23 P9 Bexleyhill W Susx
38 E10 Bexon Kent
75 M10 Bexwell Norfk
64 C9 Beyton Suffk
64 C9 Beyton Green Suffk
168 f4 Bhaltos W Isls
168 b18 Bhatarsaigh W Isls
32 C6 Bibstone S Glos
33 M3 Bibury Gloucs
48 G10 Bicester Oxon
59 J8 Bickenhill Solhll
74 D3 Bicker Lincs
74 D3 Bicker Bar Lincs
74 D3 Bicker Gauntlet Lincs
82 D4 Bickershaw Wigan
81 N4 Bickerstaffe Lancs
69 P4 Bickerton Ches E
7 L11 Bickerton Devon
97 Q10 Bickerton N York
119 J10 Bickerton Nthumb
58 C2 Bickford Staffs
7 L4 Bickington Devon
17 J5 Bickington Devon
6 E6 Bickleigh Devon
9 M3 Bickleigh Devon
17 J5 Bickleton Devon
69 P5 Bickley Ches W
37 K7 Bickley Gt Lon
99 J2 Bickley N York
57 L10 Bickley Worcs
69 P5 Bickley Moss Ches W
52 C11 Bicknacre Essex
18 F7 Bicknoller Somset
38 E10 Bicknor Kent
13 K2 Bickton Hants
45 P2 Bicton Herefs
56 D8 Bicton Shrops
69 M11 Bicton Shrops
25 N2 Bidborough Kent
23 K5 Bidden Hants
26 E4 Biddenden Kent
26 E3 Biddenden Green Kent
61 M10 Biddenham Bed
32 G10 Biddestone Wilts
19 L4 Biddisham Somset
48 H7 Biddlesden Bucks
119 J9 Biddlestone Nthumb
70 F3 Biddulph Staffs
70 G3 Biddulph Moor Staffs
16 H6 Bideford Devon
47 M4 Bidford-on-Avon Warwks
81 K6 Bidston Wirral
92 C2 Bielby E R Yk
151 M7 Bieldside C Aber
14 F11 Bierley IoW
49 M11 Bierton Bucks
107 L9 Big Balcraig D & G
6 H9 Bigbury Devon
6 H10 Bigbury-on-Sea Devon
93 J9 Bigby Lincs
115 N8 Big Carlae D & G
94 D7 Biggar Cumb
116 E3 Biggar S Lans
71 M3 Biggin Derbys
71 P5 Biggin Derbys
91 N4 Biggin N York
37 K9 Biggin Hill Gt Lon
37 K8 Biggin Hill Airport Gt Lon
50 E2 Biggleswade C Beds
110 F4 Bigholms D & G
166 E4 Bighouse Highld
22 H8 Bighton Hants
110 E10 Biglands Cumb
15 Q4 Bignor W Susx
30 H3 Big Pit Blaenavon Torfn
100 D8 Bigrigg Cumb
160 B11 Big Sand Highld
169 q11 Bigton Shet
72 E2 Bilborough C Nott
18 D6 Bilbrook Somset
58 C4 Bilbrook Staffs
98 A11 Bilbrough N York
167 N6 Bilbster Highld
103 P6 Bildershaw Dur
52 G2 Bildeston Suffk
5 M3 Billacott Cnwll
37 Q2 Billericay Essex
73 J10 Billesdon Leics
47 M3 Billesley Warwks
74 B4 Billingborough Lincs
82 B4 Billinge St Hel
64 H6 Billingford Norfk
76 E7 Billingford Norfk
104 E6 Billingham S on T
86 G10 Billinghay Lincs
91 L10 Billingley Barns
24 C5 Billingshurst W Susx
57 N8 Billingsley Shrops
49 P10 Billington C Beds
89 L3 Billington Lancs
70 F10 Billington Staffs
77 N9 Billockby Norfk
103 N3 Billy Row Dur
88 G3 Bilsborrow Lancs
87 N5 Bilsby Lincs
15 Q6 Bilsham W Susx
26 H5 Bilsington Kent
85 K8 Bilsthorpe Notts
85 L8 Bilsthorpe Moor Notts
127 P5 Bilston Mdloth
58 E5 Bilston Wolves
72 B9 Bilstone Leics
27 J2 Bilting Kent
93 L4 Bilton E R Yk
97 M9 Bilton N York
97 Q11 Bilton N York
119 P8 Bilton Nthumb
59 Q10 Bilton Warwks
119 P8 Bilton Banks Nthumb
86 H2 Binbrook Lincs
103 P4 Binchester Blocks Dur
11 P8 Bincombe Dorset
20 B5 Binegar Somset
24 E7 Bines Green W Susx
35 M10 Binfield Br For
35 K9 Binfield Heath Oxon
112 E6 Bingfield Nthumb
73 J3 Bingham Notts
12 C4 Bingham's Melcombe Dorset
90 E3 Bingley C Brad
69 P11 Bings Shrops
76 D4 Binham Norfk
59 N9 Binley Covtry
22 D4 Binley Hants
59 N9 Binley Woods Warwks
12 E7 Binnegar Dorset
126 F3 Binniehill Falk
23 Q5 Binscombe Surrey
34 E3 Binsey Oxon
14 G8 Binstead IoW
23 L6 Binsted Hants
15 Q5 Binsted W Susx
47 M4 Binton Warwks
76 E7 Bintree Norfk
56 E4 Binweston Shrops
52 F8 Birch Essex
89 P9 Birch Rochdl
75 Q4 Bircham Newton Norfk
75 Q4 Bircham Tofts Norfk
51 M6 Birchanger Essex
51 M6 Birchanger Green Services Essex
71 L8 Birch Cross Staffs
90 E7 Birchencliffe Kirk
56 H11 Bircher Herefs
58 G6 Birchfield Birm
52 F8 Birch Green Essex
50 G8 Birch Green Herts
46 G5 Birch Green Worcs
30 G9 Birchgrove Cardif
29 K5 Birchgrove Swans
25 K5 Birchgrove W Susx
69 P2 Birch Heath Ches W
81 Q10 Birch Hill Ches W
39 P8 Birchington Kent
59 L6 Birchley Heath Warwks
59 L4 Birchmoor Warwks
49 Q8 Birchmoor Green C Beds
84 B8 Birchover Derbys
89 N9 Birch Services Rochdl
83 M7 Birch Vale Derbys
10 E2 Birch Wood Somset
82 E6 Birchwood Warrtn
85 K2 Bircotes Notts
52 B3 Birdbrook Essex
97 Q5 Birdforth N York
15 M6 Birdham W Susx
59 P11 Birdingbury Warwks
32 H2 Birdlip Gloucs
111 M7 Birdoswald Cumb
98 G7 Birdsall N York
90 G9 Birds Edge Kirk
51 N9 Birds Green Essex
57 P7 Birdsgreen Shrops
10 H4 Birdsmoorgate Dorset
64 E11 Bird Street Suffk
91 J10 Birdwell Barns
46 D11 Birdwood Gloucs
118 E3 Birgham Border
162 H8 Birichin Highld
88 H8 Birkacre Lancs
104 B10 Birkby N York
88 C8 Birkdale Sefton
158 D4 Birkenbog Abers
81 L7 Birkenhead Wirral
158 H8 Birkenhills Abers
90 G5 Birkenshaw Kirk
149 Q9 Birkhall Abers
142 F11 Birkhill Angus
117 J7 Birkhill D & G
73 P6 Birkholme Lincs
91 N5 Birkin N York
90 H5 Birks Leeds
111 Q7 Birkshaw Nthumb
45 P4 Birley Herefs
84 D2 Birley Carr Sheff
37 Q8 Birling Kent
119 P9 Birling Nthumb
25 N11 Birling Gap E Susx
46 H6 Birlingham Worcs
58 G7 Birmingham Birm
59 J8 Birmingham Airport Solhll
141 P9 Birnam P & K
159 N11 Birness Abers
150 F8 Birse Abers
150 E8 Birsemore Abers
90 G5 Birstall Kirk
72 F9 Birstall Leics
97 K9 Birstwith N York
74 B4 Birthorpe Lincs
113 L9 Birtley Gatesd
56 F11 Birtley Herefs
112 C5 Birtley Nthumb
113 L9 Birtley Crematorium Gatesd
46 E7 Birts Street Worcs
73 M11 Bisbrooke Rutlnd
86 H4 Biscathorpe Lincs
3 R3 Biscovey Cnwll
35 M7 Bisham W & M
47 J4 Bishampton Worcs
17 N6 Bish Mill Devon
103 P5 Bishop Auckland Dur
86 D2 Bishopbridge Lincs
125 Q3 Bishopbriggs E Duns
92 G3 Bishop Burton E R Yk
104 B4 Bishop Middleham Dur
157 N5 Bishopmill Moray
97 M7 Bishop Monkton N York
86 C2 Bishop Norton Lincs
39 L11 Bishopsbourne Kent
21 K2 Bishops Cannings Wilts
56 E7 Bishop's Castle Shrops
11 P2 Bishop's Caundle Dorset
47 J9 Bishop's Cleeve Gloucs
46 C5 Bishop's Frome Herefs
35 Q10 Bishops Gate Surrey
51 P7 Bishop's Green Essex
22 F2 Bishop's Green Hants
18 H10 Bishops Hull Somset
48 C3 Bishop's Itchington Warwks
18 G9 Bishops Lydeard Somset
46 F10 Bishop's Norton Gloucs
17 P7 Bishop's Nympton Devon
70 D9 Bishop's Offley Staffs
51 L6 Bishop's Stortford Herts
22 H8 Bishop's Sutton Hants
48 B2 Bishop's Tachbrook Warwks
17 K6 Bishop's Tawton Devon
7 N4 Bishopsteignton Devon
22 E11 Bishopstoke Hants
28 G7 Bishopston Swans
35 M2 Bishopstone Bucks
25 L10 Bishopstone E Susx
45 N6 Bishopstone Herefs
39 M8 Bishopstone Kent
33 P8 Bishopstone Swindn
21 L9 Bishopstone Wilts
20 G6 Bishopstrow Wilts
19 Q3 Bishop Sutton BaNES
22 G11 Bishop's Waltham Hants
10 F2 Bishopswood Somset
58 B3 Bishop's Wood Staffs
31 Q11 Bishopsworth Bristl
97 L8 Bishop Thornton N York
98 B11 Bishopthorpe C York
104 C6 Bishopton Darltn
125 L3 Bishopton Rens
47 N3 Bishopton Warwks
98 F9 Bishop Wilton E R Yk
31 L7 Bishton Newpt
71 J10 Bishton Staffs
32 H3 Bisley Gloucs
23 Q3 Bisley Surrey
23 P3 Bisley Camp Surrey
88 C2 Bispham Bpool
88 F8 Bispham Green Lancs
3 K5 Bissoe Cnwll
13 K4 Bisterne Hants
37 N10 Bitchet Green Kent
73 P5 Bitchfield Lincs
17 J3 Bittadon Devon
6 H7 Bittaford Devon
76 C8 Bittering Norfk
57 K9 Bitterley Shrops
14 E4 Bitterne C Sotn
60 B3 Bitteswell Leics
32 C11 Bitton S Glos
35 K8 Bix Oxon
169 q8 Bixter Shet
72 F11 Blaby Leics
129 L9 Blackadder Border
7 L8 Blackawton Devon
100 D9 Blackbeck Cumb
10 B3 Blackborough Devon
75 N7 Blackborough End Norfk
33 Q4 Black Bourton Oxon
25 M6 Blackboys E Susx
84 D11 Blackbrook Derbys
82 B5 Blackbrook St Hel
70 D7 Blackbrook Staffs
36 E11 Blackbrook Surrey
151 L5 Blackburn Abers
89 K5 Blackburn Bl w D
84 E2 Blackburn Rothm
126 H4 Blackburn W Loth
89 K6 Blackburn with Darwen Services Bl w D
113 J7 Black Callerton N u Ty
64 F2 Black Car Norfk
24 G3 Black Corner W Susx
115 M6 Blackcraig E Ayrs
138 G11 Black Crofts Ag & B
4 E9 Black Cross Cnwll
82 G10 Blackden Heath Ches E

151 P5 Blackdog Abers
9 K3 Black Dog Devon
8 D9 Blackdown Devon
10 H4 Blackdown Dorset
109 P10 Blackdyke Cumb
91 J9 Blacker Barns
91 K10 Blacker Hill Barns
37 L6 Blackfen Gt Lon
14 D6 Blackfield Hants
110 G8 Blackford Cumb
133 P6 Blackford P & K
19 M5 Blackford Somset
20 C9 Blackford Somset
72 A7 Blackfordby Leics
14 E11 Blackgang IoW
127 M2 Blackhall C Edin
104 E3 Blackhall Dur
104 E3 Blackhall Colliery Dur
112 H9 Blackhall Mill Gatesd
117 N3 Blackhaugh Border
52 H7 Blackheath Essex
37 J5 Blackheath Gt Lon
58 E7 Blackheath Sandw
65 N7 Blackheath Suffk
36 B11 Blackheath Surrey
112 G5 Black Heddon Nthumb
159 Q6 Blackhill Abers
159 Q9 Blackhill Abers
112 G10 Blackhill Dur
159 M8 Blackhill of Clackriach Abers
9 N6 Blackhorse Devon
74 E3 Blackjack Lincs
33 K11 Blackland Wilts
89 Q2 Black Lane Ends Lancs
116 E9 Blacklaw D & G
83 J4 Blackley Manch
82 H4 Blackley Crematorium Manch
142 A5 Blacklunans P & K
45 Q7 Blackmarstone Herefs
29 P7 Blackmill Brdgnd
23 L8 Blackmoor Hants
90 H3 Black Moor Leeds
19 N2 Blackmoor N Som
90 D8 Blackmoorfoot Kirk
51 P10 Blackmore Essex
52 B5 Blackmore End Essex
50 E7 Blackmore End Herts
127 K2 Blackness Falk
23 L6 Blacknest Hants
35 Q11 Blacknest W & M
52 C7 Black Notley Essex
89 P2 Blacko Lancs
28 H6 Black Pill Swans
88 C3 Blackpool Bpool
7 L4 Blackpool Devon
7 M9 Blackpool Devon
88 C4 Blackpool Airport Lancs
111 K5 Blackpool Gate Cumb
126 F4 Blackridge W Loth
41 J2 Blackrock Cnwll
30 H2 Blackrock Mons
89 J8 Blackrod Bolton
157 M10 Blacksboat Moray
109 M7 Blackshaw D & G
90 B5 Blackshaw Head Calder
64 G8 Blacksmith's Green Suffk
89 L6 Blacksnape Bl w D
24 F7 Blackstone W Susx
65 Q4 Black Street Suffk
41 J9 Black Tar Pembks
48 H11 Blackthorn Oxon
64 C9 Blackthorpe Suffk
92 D6 Blacktoft E R Yk
151 M7 Blacktop C Aber
8 C3 Black Torrington Devon
71 P5 Blackwall Derbys
3 J4 Blackwater Cnwll
23 M3 Blackwater Hants
14 F9 Blackwater IoW
19 J11 Blackwater Somset
120 H6 Blackwaterfoot N Ayrs
110 H10 Blackwell Cumb
103 Q8 Blackwell Darltn
83 P10 Blackwell Derbys
84 F9 Blackwell Derbys
47 P6 Blackwell Warwks
58 E10 Blackwell Worcs
46 E9 Blackwellsend Green Gloucs
30 G5 Blackwood Caerph
109 K3 Blackwood D & G
126 D9 Blackwood S Lans
70 G3 Blackwood Hill Staffs
81 M11 Blacon Ches W
12 C3 Bladbean Kent
107 M7 Bladnoch D & G
34 E2 Bladon Oxon
19 M10 Bladon Somset
42 D5 Blaenannerch Cerdgn
67 N5 Blaenau Ffestiniog Gwynd
31 J3 Blaenavon Torfn
44 C7 Blaen Dyryn Powys
43 N3 Blaenffos Pembks
29 P6 Blaengarw Brdgnd
54 E8 Blaengeuffordd Cerdgn
29 N3 Blaengwrach Neath
29 N5 Blaengwynfi Neath
30 D5 Blaenllechau Rhondd
43 M2 Blaenpennal Cerdgn
54 D9 Blaenplwyf Cerdgn
42 E5 Blaenporth Cerdgn
29 P5 Blaenrhondda Rhondd
41 P5 Blaenwaun Carmth
42 F9 Blaen-y-Coed Carmth
30 F2 Blaen-y-cwm Blae G
55 J9 Blaenycwm Cerdgn
29 P5 Blaen-y-cwm Rhondd
19 P3 Blagdon N Som
18 H11 Blagdon Somset
7 M6 Blagdon Torbay
18 H11 Blagdon Hill Somset
111 P11 Blagill Cumb
88 F9 Blaguegate Lancs
139 J2 Blaich Highld
138 B4 Blain Highld
30 H3 Blaina Blae G
141 L4 Blair Atholl P & K
133 L8 Blair Drummond Stirlg
142 B8 Blairgowrie P & K
134 B10 Blairhall Fife
134 B8 Blairingone P & K
133 N8 Blairlogie Stirlg
131 P11 Blairmore Ag & B
164 E5 Blairmore Highld
124 B4 Blair's Ferry Ag & B
46 D11 Blaisdon Gloucs
57 Q9 Blakebrook Worcs
58 C9 Blakedown Worcs
52 B7 Blake End Essex
70 H5 Blakeley Lane Staffs
82 C10 Blakemere Ches W
45 M6 Blakemere Herefs
7 K6 Blakemore Devon
58 F4 Blakenall Heath Wsall
32 C3 Blakeney Gloucs
76 E3 Blakeney Norfk
70 C5 Blakenhall Ches E
58 D5 Blakenhall Wolves
58 B8 Blakeshall Worcs
48 H4 Blakesley Nhants
112 E10 Blanchland Nthumb
12 F3 Blandford Camp Dorset
12 E3 Blandford Forum Dorset
12 E3 Blandford St Mary Dorset
97 K10 Bland Hill N York
125 N2 Blanefield Stirlg
86 E8 Blankney Lincs
126 B6 Blantyre S Lans
139 L4 Blar a' Chaorainn Highld
147 Q9 Blargie Highld
139 K4 Blarmachfoldach Highld
13 L3 Blashford Hants
73 L11 Blaston Leics
73 P11 Blatherwycke Nhants
94 F3 Blawith Cumb
108 D4 Blawquhairn D & G
65 M10 Blaxhall Suffk
91 R10 Blaxton Donc
113 J8 Blaydon Gatesd
19 N5 Bleadney Somset
19 K3 Bleadon N Som
20 E8 Bleak Street Somset
39 K9 Blean Kent
86 F4 Bleasby Lincs
85 M11 Bleasby Notts
95 M11 Bleasdale Lancs
102 D8 Bleatarn Cumb
57 K10 Bleathwood Herefs
135 L4 Blebocraigs Fife
56 C11 Bleddfa Powys
47 P10 Bledington Gloucs
35 L4 Bledlow Bucks
35 L5 Bledlow Ridge Bucks
20 G3 Bleet Wilts
128 D7 Blegbie E Loth
102 B4 Blencarn Cumb
110 C11 Blencogo Cumb
15 K4 Blendworth Hants
100 G2 Blennerhasset Cumb
48 F11 Bletchingdon Oxon
36 H10 Bletchingley Surrey
49 N8 Bletchley M Keyn
69 R8 Bletchley Shrops
41 L6 Bletherston Pembks
61 M9 Bletsoe Bed
34 F7 Blewbury Oxon
76 H6 Blickling Norfk
85 J9 Blidworth Notts
85 J10 Blidworth Bottoms Notts
118 F8 Blindburn Nthumb
100 F4 Blindcrake Cumb
37 J11 Blindley Heath Surrey
5 J7 Blisland Cnwll
13 L2 Blissford Hants
57 N10 Bliss Gate Worcs
49 K4 Blisworth Nhants
71 K11 Blithbury Staffs
109 P10 Blitterlees Cumb
47 N8 Blockley Gloucs
77 L10 Blofield Norfk
77 L9 Blofield Heath Norfk
64 E6 Blo Norton Norfk
118 A6 Bloomfield Border
70 C8 Blore Staffs
71 L5 Blore Staffs
23 K5 Blounce Hants
71 K8 Blounts Green Staffs
88 D7 Blowick Sefton
48 D7 Bloxham Oxon
86 E10 Bloxholm Lincs
58 E4 Bloxwich Wsall
12 E6 Bloxworth Dorset
97 J9 Blubberhouses N York
4 E10 Blue Anchor Cnwll
18 D6 Blue Anchor Somset
38 B9 Blue Bell Hill Kent
83 P8 Blue John Cavern Derbys
81 L5 Blundellsands Sefton
65 Q2 Blundeston Suffk
61 Q10 Blunham C Beds
33 M7 Blunsdon St Andrew Swindn
58 D10 Bluntington Worcs
62 E6 Bluntisham Cambs
5 N9 Blunts Cnwll
58 H11 Blunts Green Warwks
70 F6 Blurton C Stke
86 B2 Blyborough Lincs
65 N6 Blyford Suffk
57 Q2 Blymhill Staffs
57 Q2 Blymhill Lawn Staffs
85 K3 Blyth Notts
113 M4 Blyth Nthumb
127 L8 Blyth Bridge Border
65 N6 Blythburgh Suffk
113 M4 Blyth Crematorium Nthumb
128 F10 Blythe Border
70 H6 Blythe Bridge Staffs
59 K6 Blythe End Warwks
70 H6 Blythe Marsh Staffs
85 K3 Blyth Services Notts
85 Q2 Blyton Lincs
135 P5 Boarhills Fife
14 H5 Boarhunt Hants
38 C10 Boarley Kent
89 N6 Boarsgreave Lancs
25 M4 Boarshead E Susx
88 H9 Boar's Head Wigan
34 E4 Boars Hill Oxon
34 H2 Boarstall Bucks
8 D6 Boasley Cross Devon
155 Q3 Boath Highld
148 G4 Boat of Garten Highld
38 E8 Bobbing Kent
57 Q6 Bobbington Staffs
51 M9 Bobbingworth Essex
5 K10 Bocaddon Cnwll
52 C7 Bocking Essex
52 C6 Bocking Churchstreet Essex
46 A2 Bockleton Worcs
5 J9 Boconnoc Cnwll
159 R9 Boddam Abers
169 q12 Boddam Shet
46 G9 Boddington Gloucs
78 E8 Bodedern IoA
80 E9 Bodelwyddan Denbgs
45 Q4 Bodenham Herefs
21 N9 Bodenham Wilts
45 Q4 Bodenham Moor Herefs
78 G6 Bodewryd IoA
80 F10 Bodfari Denbgs
78 G9 Bodffordd IoA
66 E7 Bodfuan Gwynd
76 G3 Bodham Norfk
26 C6 Bodiam E Susx
26 C6 Bodiam Castle E Susx
48 E7 Bodicote Oxon
4 F7 Bodieve Cnwll
5 J11 Bodinnick Cnwll
25 Q8 Bodle Street Green E Susx
4 H8 Bodmin Cnwll
5 K6 Bodmin Moor Cnwll
79 Q10 Bodnant Garden Conwy
64 A2 Bodney Norfk
78 F11 Bodorgan IoA
27 K2 Bodsham Kent
4 G9 Bodwen Cnwll
59 J5 Bodymoor Heath Warwks
156 A7 Bogallan Highld
159 P10 Bogbrae Abers
125 L11 Bogend S Ayrs
128 C5 Boggs Holdings E Loth
127 N4 Boghall Mdloth
126 H4 Boghall W Loth
126 D9 Boghead S Lans
157 R5 Bogmoor Moray
143 L3 Bogmuir Abers
158 E8 Bogniebrae Abers
15 P7 Bognor Regis W Susx
148 G3 Bogroy Highld
108 D4 Bogue D & G
5 Q8 Bohetherick Cnwll
3 M7 Bohortha Cnwll
146 H11 Bohuntine Highld
2 B7 Bojewyan Cnwll
4 H9 Bokiddick Cnwll
103 N6 Bolam Dur
112 H4 Bolam Nthumb
6 H11 Bolberry Devon
82 B7 Bold Heath St Hel
58 H6 Boldmere Birm
113 M8 Boldon Colliery S Tyne
13 P5 Boldre Hants
103 K8 Boldron Dur
85 N3 Bole Notts
84 C9 Bolehill Derbys
84 D6 Bole Hill Derbys
2 H6 Bolenowe Cnwll
18 C11 Bolham Devon
10 D2 Bolham Water Devon
3 K3 Bolingey Cnwll
83 K9 Bollington Ches E
83 K9 Bollington Cross Ches E
32 D2 Bollow Gloucs
24 G6 Bolney W Susx
61 N9 Bolnhurst Bed
143 L7 Bolshan Angus
84 G6 Bolsover Derbys
90 D7 Bolster Moor Kirk
90 H11 Bolsterstone Sheff
97 Q3 Boltby N York
150 C5 Boltenstone Abers
35 L6 Bolter End Bucks
89 L9 Bolton Bolton
102 B6 Bolton Cumb
128 E6 Bolton E Loth
98 F10 Bolton E R Yk
119 M8 Bolton Nthumb
96 G10 Bolton Abbey N York
96 G10 Bolton Bridge N York
96 A11 Bolton by Bowland Lancs
111 J7 Boltonfellend Cumb
100 H2 Boltongate Cumb
95 K7 Bolton le Sands Lancs
100 H2 Bolton Low Houses Cumb
100 H2 Bolton New Houses Cumb
103 Q11 Bolton-on-Swale N York
91 N2 Bolton Percy N York
95 K7 Bolton Town End Lancs
91 M10 Bolton Upon Dearne Barns
89 J8 Bolton West Services Lancs
5 K6 Bolventor Cnwll
113 L4 Bomarsund Nthumb
69 N11 Bomere Heath Shrops
162 E8 Bonar Bridge Highld
139 J11 Bonawe Ag & B
92 H7 Bonby N Linc
41 P3 Boncath Pembks
118 A8 Bonchester Bridge Border
14 G11 Bonchurch IoW
8 G4 Bondleigh Devon
88 F2 Bonds Lancs
8 H9 Bonehill Devon
59 J4 Bonehill Staffs
134 C11 Bo'ness Falk
58 F2 Boney Hay Staffs
125 K2 Bonhill W Duns
57 Q4 Boningale Shrops
118 C6 Bonjedward Border
126 E6 Bonkle N Lans
143 K10 Bonnington Angus
27 J4 Bonnington Kent
135 K7 Bonnybank Fife
126 E2 Bonnybridge Falk
159 L7 Bonnykelly Abers
127 Q4 Bonnyrigg Mdloth
142 E10 Bonnyton Angus
84 C9 Bonsall Derbys
110 D6 Bonshaw Tower D & G
45 M11 Bont Mons
67 M11 Bontddu Gwynd
55 K4 Bont-Dolgadfan Powys
54 F7 Bont-goch or Elerch Cerdgn
87 N6 Bonthorpe Lincs
54 E11 Bontnewydd Cerdgn
66 H3 Bontnewydd Gwynd
68 E3 Bontuchel Denbgs
30 E10 Bonvilston V Glam
68 F6 Bonwm Denbgs
29 J5 Bon-y-maen Swans
17 J4 Boode Devon
35 M6 Booker Bucks
69 Q9 Booley Shrops
128 F10 Boon Border
70 E4 Boon Hill Staffs
14 F4 Boorley Green Hants
105 J7 Boosbeck R & Cl
52 D5 Boose's Green Essex
100 G10 Boot Cumb
90 C5 Booth Calder
86 C9 Boothby Graffoe Lincs
73 P4 Boothby Pagnell Lincs
92 B5 Boothferry E R Yk
83 K8 Booth Green Ches E
82 F4 Boothstown Salfd
90 D5 Booth Town Calder
60 G8 Boothville Nhants
94 C3 Bootle Cumb
81 L5 Bootle Sefton
82 G10 Boots Green Ches W
53 M2 Boot Street Suffk
103 K10 Booze N York
57 L11 Boraston Shrops
10 c1 Bordeaux Guern
38 E9 Borden Kent
23 M10 Borden W Susx
110 C10 Border Cumb
111 M4 Border Forest Park
96 D7 Bordley N York
23 L7 Bordon Camp Hants
52 C10 Boreham Essex
20 G6 Boreham Wilts
25 Q8 Boreham Street E Susx
50 E11 Borehamwood Herts
110 C2 Boreland D & G
152 B7 Boreraig Highld
57 J3 Boreton Shrops
168 b17 Borgh W Isls
168 j2 Borgh W Isls
165 Q5 Borgie Highld
108 D11 Borgue D & G
167 K11 Borgue Highld
52 D3 Borley Essex
52 D3 Borley Green Essex
64 D9 Borley Green Suffk
152 F3 Borneskitaig Highld
108 D11 Borness D & G
97 N7 Boroughbridge N York
37 P9 Borough Green Kent
69 L4 Borras Head Wrexhm
72 C4 Borrowash Derbys
97 P3 Borrowby N York
105 L7 Borrowby N York
101 J8 Borrowdale Cumb
134 B11 Borrowstoun Falk
38 B8 Borstal Medway
54 E8 Borth Cerdgn
117 N8 Borthwickbrae Border
117 N8 Borthwickshiels Border
67 K7 Borth-y-Gest Gwynd
152 G8 Borve Highld
168 b17 Borve W Isls
168 f8 Borve W Isls
168 j2 Borve W Isls
95 L6 Borwick Lancs
101 K11 Borwick Lodge Cumb
94 D5 Borwick Rails Cumb
2 B7 Bosavern Cnwll
46 C6 Bosbury Herefs
4 G8 Boscarne Cnwll
4 H3 Boscastle Cnwll
13 K6 Boscombe Bmouth
21 P7 Boscombe Wilts
3 Q3 Boscoppa Cnwll
15 M6 Bosham W Susx
15 M6 Bosham Hoe W Susx
41 J12 Bosherston Pembks
2 C7 Boskednan Cnwll
2 C9 Boskenna Cnwll
83 K11 Bosley Ches E
4 D9 Bosoughan Cnwll
98 E8 Bossall N York
4 H4 Bossiney Cnwll
27 L2 Bossingham Kent
18 A5 Bossington Somset
82 E11 Bostock Green Ches W
74 F2 Boston Lincs
87 K11 Boston Crematorium Lincs
97 P11 Boston Spa Leeds
2 C7 Boswarthan Cnwll
3 P5 Boswinger Cnwll
2 B7 Botallack Cnwll
50 G11 Botany Bay Gt Lon
72 D10 Botcheston Leics
64 E6 Botesdale Suffk
113 K3 Bothal Nthumb
34 F9 Bothampstead W Berk
85 L6 Bothamsall Notts
100 G3 Bothel Cumb
11 K6 Bothenhampton Dorset
126 C6 Bothwell S Lans
126 C6 Bothwell Services S Lans
35 Q4 Botley Bucks
14 F4 Botley Hants
34 E3 Botley Oxon
49 K10 Botolph Claydon Bucks
24 E9 Botolphs W Susx
27 K5 Botolph's Bridge Kent
73 L3 Bottesford Leics
92 E9 Bottesford N Linc
62 H8 Bottisham Cambs
135 K3 Bottomcraig Fife
88 F5 Bottom of Hutton Lancs
89 K8 Bottom o' th' Moor Bolton
89 Q6 Bottoms Calder
2 B9 Bottoms Cnwll
59 K6 Botts Green Warwks
5 Q9 Botusfleming Cnwll
66 D8 Botwnnog Gwynd
37 L11 Bough Beech Kent
44 G7 Boughrood Powys
31 Q5 Boughspring Gloucs
60 G7 Boughton Nhants
75 P10 Boughton Norfk
85 L7 Boughton Notts
26 H2 Boughton Aluph Kent
49 Q7 Boughton End C Beds
38 C11 Boughton Green Kent
26 E2 Boughton Malherbe Kent
38 C11 Boughton Monchelsea Kent
39 J10 Boughton Street Kent
105 L7 Boulby R & Cl
90 C6 Boulder Clough Calder
14 C9 Bouldnor IoW
57 J7 Bouldon Shrops
119 Q8 Boulmer Nthumb
41 J8 Boulston Pembks
86 C7 Boultham Lincs
62 D9 Bourn Cambs
74 A6 Bourne Lincs
37 M9 Bournebridge Essex
58 F8 Bournebrook Birm
61 M8 Bourne End Bed
35 N7 Bourne End Bucks
49 Q6 Bourne End C Beds
50 B9 Bourne End Herts
13 J6 Bournemouth Bmouth
13 K5 Bournemouth Airport Dorset
13 K6 Bournemouth Crematorium Bmouth
32 H4 Bournes Green Gloucs
38 F4 Bournes Green Sthend
58 E10 Bournheath Worcs
113 M10 Bournmoor Dur
32 D6 Bournstream Gloucs
58 F8 Bournville Birm
20 E8 Bourton Dorset
19 L2 Bourton N Som
33 P7 Bourton Oxon
57 K5 Bourton Shrops
21 K2 Bourton Wilts
59 P10 Bourton on Dunsmore Warwks
47 N8 Bourton-on-the-Hill Gloucs
47 N10 Bourton-on-the-Water Gloucs
136 H3 Bousd Ag & B
110 E9 Boustead Hill Cumb
94 G3 Bouth Cumb
96 H6 Bouthwaite N York
47 K3 Bouts Worcs
35 P9 Boveney Bucks
13 J2 Boveridge Dorset
9 K9 Bovey Tracey Devon
50 B10 Bovingdon Herts
35 M7 Bovingdon Green Bucks
51 M9 Bovinger Essex
12 D7 Bovington Dorset
12 D7 Bovington Camp Dorset
12 D7 Bovington Tank Museum Dorset
110 F9 Bow Cumb
7 L7 Bow Devon
8 H4 Bow Devon
37 J4 Bow Gt Lon
169 c7 Bow Ork
102 H6 Bowbank Dur
49 P8 Bow Brickhill M Keyn
32 G3 Bowbridge Gloucs
104 B3 Bowburn Dur
14 E9 Bowcombe IoW
10 C6 Bowd Devon
117 R4 Bowden Border
7 L9 Bowden Devon
32 H11 Bowden Hill Wilts
82 G7 Bowdon Traffd
167 M4 Bower Highld
31 Q10 Bower Ashton Bristl
21 K10 Bowerchalke Wilts
20 H2 Bowerhill Wilts
19 N11 Bower Hinton Somset
52 G3 Bower House Tye Suffk
167 M4 Bowermadden Highld
70 E7 Bowers Staffs
38 C4 Bowers Gifford Essex
134 D9 Bowershall Fife
91 L5 Bower's Row Leeds
103 J8 Bowes Dur
88 F2 Bowgreave Lancs
109 M7 Bowhouse D & G
5 K5 Bowithick Cnwll
81 N4 Bowker's Green Lancs
117 P2 Bowland Border
95 J3 Bowland Bridge Cumb
45 Q4 Bowley Herefs
45 Q4 Bowley Town Herefs
23 P7 Bowlhead Green Surrey
90 F4 Bowling C Brad
125 L3 Bowling W Duns
69 L5 Bowling Bank Wrexhm
46 F4 Bowling Green Worcs
101 K11 Bowmanstead Cumb
122 D8 Bowmore Ag & B
110 D8 Bowness-on-Solway Cumb
101 M11 Bowness-on-Windermere Cumb
135 J5 Bow of Fife Fife
143 J8 Bowriefauld Angus
101 L4 Bowscale Cumb
119 J2 Bowsden Nthumb
101 N11 Bowston Cumb
54 E7 Bow Street Cerdgn
64 E2 Bow Street Norfk
76 H10 Bowthorpe Norfk
32 G4 Box Gloucs
32 F11 Box Wilts
32 D2 Boxbush Gloucs
46 C10 Boxbush Gloucs
61 M11 Box End Bed
52 G3 Boxford Suffk
34 D10 Boxford W Berk
15 P5 Boxgrove W Susx
36 E10 Box Hill Surrey
38 C10 Boxley Kent
50 B9 Boxmoor Herts
16 C11 Box's Shop Cnwll
52 G5 Boxted Essex
52 H5 Boxted Essex
64 A11 Boxted Suffk
52 H5 Boxted Cross Essex
32 F6 Boxwell Gloucs
62 D8 Boxworth Cambs
62 E7 Boxworth End Cambs
63 M9 Boyden End Suffk
39 M8 Boyden Gate Kent
71 M7 Boylestone Derbys
158 F5 Boyndie Abers
159 M5 Boyndlie Abers
99 N7 Boynton E R Yk
143 L8 Boysack Angus
11 P2 Boys Hill Dorset
84 E7 Boythorpe Derbys
5 N3 Boyton Cnwll
53 Q2 Boyton Suffk
21 J7 Boyton Wilts
51 P9 Boyton Cross Essex
52 B3 Boyton End Suffk
61 K9 Bozeat Nhants
80 d6 Braaid IoM
65 K9 Brabling Green Suffk
27 K3 Brabourne Kent
27 J3 Brabourne Lees Kent
167 P3 Brabstermire Highld
152 F10 Bracadale Highld
74 A8 Braceborough Lincs
86 C7 Bracebridge Heath Lincs
86 C7 Bracebridge Low Fields Lincs
73 Q3 Braceby Lincs

96 C11 Bracewell Lancs
84 E9 Brackenfield Derbys
126 C4 Brackenhirst N Lans
110 E11 Brackenthwaite Cumb
97 L10 Brackenthwaite N York
15 M7 Bracklesham W Susx
146 F11 Brackletter Highld
48 G7 Brackley Nhants
48 H6 Brackley Hatch Nhants
35 N11 Bracknell Br For
133 N6 Braco P & K
158 D7 Bracobrae Moray
64 H2 Bracon Ash Norfk
145 M9 Bracora Highld
145 M9 Bracorina Highld
5 P3 Bradaford Devon
71 N4 Bradbourne Derbys
104 B5 Bradbury Dur
48 H5 Bradden Nhants
5 K9 Braddock Cnwll
70 F4 Bradeley C Stke
35 M5 Bradenham Bucks
33 K9 Bradenstoke Wilts
9 Q3 Bradfield Devon
53 K5 Bradfield Essex
77 K5 Bradfield Norfk
84 C2 Bradfield Sheff
34 H10 Bradfield W Berk
64 B10 Bradfield Combust Suffk
70 B3 Bradfield Green Ches E
53 K5 Bradfield Heath Essex
64 C10 Bradfield St Clare Suffk
64 C10 Bradfield St George Suffk
90 F4 Bradford C Brad
5 J6 Bradford Cnwll
16 G10 Bradford Devon
112 G5 Bradford Nthumb
119 N4 Bradford Nthumb
11 M2 Bradford Abbas Dorset
20 F2 Bradford Leigh Wilts
20 F2 Bradford-on-Avon Wilts
18 G10 Bradford-on-Tone Somset
11 P6 Bradford Peverell Dorset
17 K5 Bradiford Devon
14 H9 Brading IoW
71 N5 Bradley Derbys
22 H6 Bradley Hants
90 F6 Bradley Kirk
96 F4 Bradley N York
93 M9 Bradley NE Lin
70 F11 Bradley Staffs
58 E5 Bradley Wolves
47 J2 Bradley Worcs
69 K4 Bradley Wrexhm
69 P5 Bradley Common Ches W
19 J7 Bradley Green Somset
59 L4 Bradley Green Warwks
47 J2 Bradley Green Worcs
71 K6 Bradley in the Moors Staffs
32 B8 Bradley Stoke S Glos
72 F4 Bradmore Notts
19 K7 Bradney Somset
9 N4 Bradninch Devon
17 L5 Bradninch Devon
71 J3 Bradnop Staffs
45 K3 Bradnor Green Herefs
11 K6 Bradpole Dorset
89 L8 Bradshaw Bolton
90 D5 Bradshaw Calder
90 D8 Bradshaw Kirk
5 P5 Bradstone Devon
70 D2 Bradwall Green Ches E
83 Q8 Bradwell Derbys
17 J3 Bradwell Devon
52 D7 Bradwell Essex
49 M6 Bradwell M Keyn
77 Q11 Bradwell Norfk
70 F5 Bradwell Crematorium Staffs
52 H10 Bradwell-on-Sea Essex
52 G10 Bradwell Waterside Essex
16 E9 Bradworthy Devon
156 B5 Brae Highld
169 q7 Brae Shet
133 M11 Braeface Falk
143 M7 Braehead Angus
107 M7 Braehead D & G
126 H7 Braehead S Lans
149 M9 Braemar Abers
161 K11 Braemore Highld
167 J11 Braemore Highld
147 J9 Brae Roy Lodge Highld
124 G3 Braeside Inver
142 D6 Braes of Coul Angus
158 A6 Braes of Enzie Moray
169 f3 Braeswick Ork
131 K6 Braevallich Ag & B
103 Q6 Brafferton Darltn
97 P6 Brafferton N York
60 H9 Brafield-on-the-Green Nhants
168 h3 Bragar W Isls
50 G6 Bragbury End Herts
126 E8 Braidwood S Lans
71 P6 Brailsford Derbys
71 P6 Brailsford Green Derbys
32 C3 Brain's Green Gloucs
52 C7 Braintree Essex
64 G7 Braiseworth Suffk
22 C9 Braishfield Hants
90 C2 Braithwaite C Brad
100 H6 Braithwaite Cumb
84 H2 Braithwell Donc
91 L7 Braken Hill Wakefd
24 E8 Bramber W Susx
22 E10 Brambridge Hants
72 E3 Bramcote Notts
59 P7 Bramcote Warwks
72 E3 Bramcote Crematorium Notts
22 H9 Bramdean Hants
77 K11 Bramerton Norfk
50 G7 Bramfield Herts
65 M7 Bramfield Suffk
53 K2 Bramford Suffk
83 J8 Bramhall Stockp
91 L2 Bramham Leeds
90 H2 Bramhope Leeds
23 J3 Bramley Hants
90 G3 Bramley Leeds
84 G2 Bramley Rothm
24 B2 Bramley Surrey
22 H3 Bramley Corner Hants
23 J3 Bramley Green Hants
96 H9 Bramley Head N York
39 M10 Bramling Kent
9 M5 Brampford Speke Devon
62 B6 Brampton Cambs
102 C6 Brampton Cumb
111 K8 Brampton Cumb
85 P5 Brampton Lincs
77 J7 Brampton Norfk
91 L10 Brampton Rothm
65 N5 Brampton Suffk
46 B9 Brampton Abbotts Herefs
60 G3 Brampton Ash Nhants
56 F10 Brampton Bryan Herefs
84 G3 Brampton-en-le-Morthen Rothm
71 K8 Bramshall Staffs
21 Q11 Bramshaw Hants
23 K2 Bramshill Hants
23 M8 Bramshott Hants
19 M9 Bramwell Somset
137 N2 Branault Highld
75 Q2 Brancaster Norfk
75 Q2 Brancaster Staithe Norfk
103 P3 Brancepeth Dur
157 K7 Branchill Moray
87 L11 Brand End Lincs
157 N3 Branderburgh Moray
99 N11 Brandesburton E R Yk
65 J9 Brandeston Suffk
46 D9 Brand Green Gloucs
16 G11 Brandis Corner Devon
76 G7 Brandiston Norfk
103 P2 Brandon Dur
86 B11 Brandon Lincs
119 K7 Brandon Nthumb
63 N3 Brandon Suffk
59 P9 Brandon Warwks
63 K3 Brandon Bank Norfk
63 K2 Brandon Creek Norfk
76 F10 Brandon Parva Norfk
98 B6 Brandsby N York
92 H11 Brandy Wharf Lincs
2 C8 Brane Cnwll
51 Q5 Bran End Essex
12 H6 Branksome Poole
13 J6 Branksome Park Poole
22 D6 Bransbury Hants
85 Q5 Bransby Lincs
10 D7 Branscombe Devon
46 E4 Bransford Worcs
13 L5 Bransgore Hants
93 K4 Bransholme C KuH
57 M9 Bransley Shrops
58 G10 Branson's Cross Worcs
73 L5 Branston Leics
86 D7 Branston Lincs
71 N10 Branston Staffs
86 E7 Branston Booths Lincs
14 G10 Branstone IoW
86 B10 Brant Broughton Lincs
53 K5 Brantham Suffk
100 E6 Branthwaite Cumb
101 J3 Branthwaite Cumb
92 F5 Brantingham E R Yk
91 Q10 Branton Donc
119 K7 Branton Nthumb
97 P8 Branton Green N York
118 G3 Branxton Nthumb
69 P2 Brassey Green Ches W
71 N4 Brassington Derbys
37 L9 Brasted Kent
37 L10 Brasted Chart Kent
150 H8 Brathens Abers
87 N8 Bratoft Lincs
86 B4 Brattleby Lincs
18 B5 Bratton Somset
20 H4 Bratton Wilts
57 L2 Bratton Wrekin
8 C6 Bratton Clovelly Devon
17 L4 Bratton Fleming Devon
20 C9 Bratton Seymour Somset
51 J5 Braughing Herts
51 K6 Braughing Friars Herts
60 B7 Braunston Nhants
73 L9 Braunston Rutlnd
72 F10 Braunstone Leics
16 H4 Braunton Devon
98 E5 Brawby N York
166 D3 Brawl Highld
104 F9 Braworth N York
35 P9 Bray W & M
60 G4 Braybrooke Nhants
33 K7 Braydon Wilts
33 J6 Braydon Brook Wilts
33 K7 Braydon Side Wilts
17 M5 Brayford Devon
25 Q8 Bray's Hill E Susx
5 N7 Bray Shop Cnwll
100 D9 Braystones Cumb
97 K11 Braythorn N York
91 Q4 Brayton N York
35 N9 Braywick W & M
35 N9 Braywoodside W & M
5 M3 Brazacott Cnwll
27 L2 Breach Kent
38 D8 Breach Kent
50 E6 Breachwood Green Herts
69 M7 Breaden Heath Shrops
72 B3 Breadsall Derbys
32 D4 Breadstone Gloucs
45 K4 Breadward Herefs
2 G9 Breage Cnwll
155 N9 Breakachy Highld
36 C3 Breakspear Crematorium Gt Lon
162 C8 Brealangwell Lodge Highld
32 B3 Bream Gloucs
21 N11 Breamore Hants
19 J3 Brean Somset
168 e5 Breanais W Isls
90 C5 Brearley Calder
97 M8 Brearton N York
168 h4 Breascleit W Isls
168 h4 Breasclete W Isls
72 D4 Breaston Derbys
43 K8 Brechfa Carmth
143 L5 Brechin Angus
64 D3 Breckles Norfk
44 E9 Brecon Powys
44 E10 Brecon Beacons National Park
83 K6 Bredbury Stockp
26 D8 Brede E Susx
46 B3 Bredenbury Herefs
65 K11 Bredfield Suffk
38 E9 Bredgar Kent
38 C9 Bredhurst Kent
46 H7 Bredon Worcs
46 H7 Bredon's Hardwick Worcs
46 H7 Bredon's Norton Worcs
45 L6 Bredwardine Herefs
72 C6 Breedon on the Hill Leics
126 H5 Breich W Loth
89 L9 Breightmet Bolton
92 B4 Breighton E R Yk
45 P7 Breinton Herefs
33 J10 Bremhill Wilts
17 M6 Bremridge Devon
25 Q2 Brenchley Kent
16 F10 Brendon Devon
17 P2 Brendon Devon
18 D8 Brendon Hill Somset
123 P3 Brenfield Ag & B
168 e5 Brenish W Isls
113 K5 Brenkley N u Ty
52 F2 Brent Eleigh Suffk
36 E5 Brentford Gt Lon
73 K7 Brentingby Leics
19 K4 Brent Knoll Somset
6 H7 Brent Mill Devon
51 K4 Brent Pelham Herts
37 N2 Brentwood Essex
26 H6 Brenzett Kent
26 H6 Brenzett Green Kent
71 K11 Brereton Staffs
70 D2 Brereton Green Ches E
82 H11 Brereton Heath Ches E
71 K11 Brereton Hill Staffs
169 s9 Bressay Shet
64 F5 Bressingham Norfk
64 F5 Bressingham Common Norfk
71 P10 Bretby Derbys
71 P10 Bretby Crematorium Derbys
59 P9 Bretford Warwks
47 L6 Bretforton Worcs
88 F6 Bretherton Lancs
169 r8 Brettabister Shet
64 C5 Brettenham Norfk
64 D11 Brettenham Suffk
84 B5 Bretton Derbys
69 L2 Bretton Flints
51 N6 Brewers End Essex
36 H10 Brewer Street Surrey
58 C3 Brewood Staffs
12 D6 Briantspuddle Dorset
51 N5 Brick End Essex
50 H9 Brickendon Herts
50 D10 Bricket Wood Herts
84 D4 Brick Houses Sheff
52 B5 Brickkiln Green Essex
47 J6 Bricklehampton Worcs
80 f1 Bride IoM
100 F4 Bridekirk Cumb
41 N2 Bridell Pembks
8 D7 Bridestowe Devon
158 E10 Brideswell Abers
9 K7 Bridford Devon
39 L11 Bridge Kent
94 D4 Bridge End Cumb
110 G11 Bridge End Cumb
6 H9 Bridge End Devon
103 K3 Bridge End Dur
51 Q4 Bridge End Essex
74 B3 Bridge End Lincs
100 E5 Bridgefoot Cumb
51 L3 Bridge Green Essex
19 Q10 Bridgehampton Somset
97 M6 Bridge Hewick N York
112 G10 Bridgehill Dur
97 J7 Bridgehouse Gate N York
14 G6 Bridgemary Hants
70 C5 Bridgemere Ches E
158 D10 Bridgend Abers
122 D7 Bridgend Ag & B
143 J4 Bridgend Angus
29 P9 Bridgend Brdgnd
42 C5 Bridgend Cerdgn
101 M8 Bridgend Cumb
116 F9 Bridgend D & G
6 F9 Bridgend Devon
135 K5 Bridgend Fife
158 A11 Bridgend Moray
134 E3 Bridgend P & K
127 J2 Bridgend W Loth
142 D7 Bridgend of Lintrathen Angus
150 F4 Bridge of Alford Abers
133 M8 Bridge of Allan Stirlg
149 M3 Bridge of Avon Moray
157 M10 Bridge of Avon Moray
140 E8 Bridge of Balgie P & K
142 B5 Bridge of Brewlands Angus
149 L3 Bridge of Brown Highld
142 A7 Bridge of Cally P & K
150 H8 Bridge of Canny Abers
142 D7 Bridge of Craigisla Angus
108 F9 Bridge of Dee D & G
151 N6 Bridge of Don C Aber
156 G9 Bridge of Dulsie Highld
150 H10 Bridge of Dye Abers
134 E4 Bridge of Earn P & K
140 D6 Bridge of Ericht P & K
151 J9 Bridge of Feugh Abers
166 H3 Bridge of Forss Highld
150 B8 Bridge of Gairn Abers
140 D6 Bridge of Gaur P & K
158 E7 Bridge of Marnoch Abers
139 P10 Bridge of Orchy Ag & B
141 L4 Bridge of Tilt P & K
158 A5 Bridge of Tynet Moray
169 p8 Bridge of Walls Shet
125 K4 Bridge of Weir Rens
17 M9 Bridge Reeve Devon
16 D11 Bridgerule Devon
56 F5 Bridges Shrops
45 N6 Bridge Sollers Herefs
52 E2 Bridge Street Suffk
5 N4 Bridgetown Cnwll
18 B8 Bridgetown Somset
81 P10 Bridge Trafford Ches W
32 C10 Bridge Yate S Glos
64 D4 Bridgham Norfk
57 N6 Bridgnorth Shrops
19 J7 Bridgwater Somset
19 K8 Bridgwater Services Somset
99 P7 Bridlington E R Yk
11 K6 Bridport Dorset
46 A10 Bridstow Herefs
89 N3 Brierfield Lancs
91 L8 Brierley Barns
46 B11 Brierley Gloucs
45 P3 Brierley Herefs
58 D7 Brierley Hill Dudley
104 E4 Brierton Hartpl
101 J6 Briery Cumb
92 H9 Brigg N Linc
77 L6 Briggate Norfk
105 N9 Briggswath N York
100 E4 Brigham Cumb
101 J6 Brigham Cumb
99 M10 Brigham E R Yk
90 E6 Brighouse Calder
14 D10 Brighstone IoW
84 C9 Brightgate Derbys
34 C4 Brighthampton Oxon
90 H11 Brightholmlee Sheff
8 F5 Brightley Devon
25 Q6 Brightling E Susx
53 J8 Brightlingsea Essex
24 H10 Brighton Br & H
3 N3 Brighton Cnwll
81 L5 Brighton le Sands Sefton
126 G2 Brightons Falk
34 D9 Brightwalton W Berk
34 D9 Brightwalton Green W Berk
34 D9 Brightwalton Holt W Berk
53 N3 Brightwell Suffk
35 J5 Brightwell Baldwin Oxon
34 G6 Brightwell-cum-Sotwell Oxon
35 J6 Brightwell Upperton Oxon
103 L8 Brignall Dur
132 G6 Brig o'Turk Stirlg
93 N10 Brigsley NE Lin
95 K3 Brigsteer Cumb
61 K3 Brigstock Nhants
35 J2 Brill Bucks
3 J8 Brill Cnwll
45 K5 Brilley Herefs
57 J11 Brimfield Herefs
57 J11 Brimfield Cross Herefs
84 F6 Brimington Derbys
9 K9 Brimley Devon
32 H2 Brimpsfield Gloucs
22 G2 Brimpton W Berk
22 G2 Brimpton Common W Berk
32 G4 Brimscombe Gloucs
81 L8 Brimstage Wirral
84 D4 Brincliffe Sheff
92 B4 Brind E R Yk
19 P7 Brindham Somset
169 p8 Brindister Shet
88 H6 Brindle Lancs
57 Q2 Brineton Staffs
60 H2 Bringhurst Leics
46 D3 Bringsty Common Herefs
61 N5 Brington Cambs
76 E5 Brinningham Norfk
85 M10 Brinkely Notts
87 L6 Brinkhill Lincs
63 K10 Brinkley Cambs
59 P9 Brinklow Warwks
33 K8 Brinkworth Wilts
89 J6 Brinscall Lancs
19 M4 Brinscombe Somset
19 M2 Brinsea N Som
84 G11 Brinsley Notts
45 N6 Brinsop Herefs
84 F3 Brinsworth Rothm
76 E4 Brinton Norfk
169 d4 Brinyan Ork
110 H10 Brisco Cumb
76 C7 Brisley Norfk
32 B10 Brislington Bristl
26 F4 Brissenden Green Kent
31 Q10 Bristol Bristl
31 P11 Bristol Airport N Som
31 Q10 Bristol Zoo Bristl
76 F5 Briston Norfk
6 F5 Brisworthy Devon
89 P6 Britannia Lancs
21 N9 Britford Wilts
30 F4 Brithdir Caerph
67 P11 Brithdir Gwynd
38 B10 British Legion Village Kent
29 K6 Briton Ferry Neath
35 J6 Britwell Salome Oxon
7 N7 Brixham Torbay
6 F8 Brixton Devon
36 H5 Brixton Gt Lon
20 G7 Brixton Deverill Wilts
60 F6 Brixworth Nhants
33 Q3 Brize Norton Oxon
33 Q3 Brize Norton Airport Oxon
58 C11 Broad Alley Worcs
33 M6 Broad Blunsdon Swindn
83 L6 Broadbottom Tamesd
15 M5 Broadbridge W Susx
24 D4 Broadbridge Heath W Susx
47 N7 Broad Campden Gloucs
90 D7 Broad Carr Calder
21 K9 Broad Chalke Wilts
89 P6 Broad Clough Lancs
9 N5 Broadclyst Devon
125 J3 Broadfield Inver
41 M10 Broadfield Pembks
145 K3 Broadford Highld
26 B4 Broad Ford Kent
24 C6 Broadford Bridge W Susx
117 J8 Broadgairhill Border
64 D9 Broadgrass Green Suffk
63 L8 Broad Green Cambs
52 E7 Broad Green Essex
46 E3 Broad Green Worcs
58 E10 Broad Green Worcs
129 M9 Broadhaugh Border
40 G8 Broad Haven Pembks
82 G7 Broadheath Traffd
57 M11 Broadheath Worcs
10 C4 Broadhembury Devon
7 L5 Broadhempston Devon
63 J5 Broad Hill Cambs
33 M9 Broad Hinton Wilts
85 Q6 Broadholme Lincs
26 D8 Broadland Row E Susx
28 C3 Broadlay Carmth
22 D2 Broad Layings Hants
51 K9 Broadley Essex
89 P7 Broadley Lancs
158 A5 Broadley Moray
51 K9 Broadley Common Essex
47 M5 Broad Marston Worcs
12 B7 Broadmayne Dorset
70 E5 Broad Meadow Staffs
22 H5 Broadmere Hants
46 B11 Broadmoor Gloucs
41 L9 Broadmoor Pembks
8 H4 Broadnymett Devon
94 C2 Broad Oak Cumb
11 J5 Broadoak Dorset
25 P6 Broad Oak E Susx
26 D8 Broad Oak E Susx
32 C2 Broadoak Gloucs
23 L4 Broad Oak Hants
45 P10 Broad Oak Herefs
39 L9 Broad Oak Kent
82 B5 Broad Oak St Hel
69 L3 Broadoak Wrexhm
65 K6 Broad Road Suffk
51 Q8 Broad's Green Essex
39 Q8 Broadstairs Kent
31 P4 Broadstone Mons
12 H5 Broadstone Poole
57 J7 Broadstone Shrops
26 E8 Broad Street E Susx
51 N7 Broad Street Essex
27 K3 Broad Street Kent
38 D10 Broad Street Kent
38 C7 Broad Street Medway
21 M3 Broad Street Wilts
52 E10 Broad Street Green Essex
33 L9 Broad Town Wilts
46 E3 Broadwas Worcs
50 F6 Broadwater Herts
24 D10 Broadwater W Susx
58 B9 Broadwaters Worcs
28 C3 Broadway Carmth
41 Q8 Broadway Carmth
40 G8 Broadway Pembks
19 K11 Broadway Somset
65 M6 Broadway Suffk
47 L7 Broadway Worcs
31 Q2 Broadwell Gloucs
47 P9 Broadwell Gloucs
33 Q4 Broadwell Oxon
59 Q11 Broadwell Warwks
11 P8 Broadwey Dorset
11 J4 Broadwindsor Dorset
8 F3 Broadwood Kelly Devon
5 Q4 Broadwoodwidger Devon
45 L6 Brobury Herefs
153 K8 Brochel Highld
139 J11 Brochroy Ag & B
88 G2 Brock Lancs
46 E4 Brockamin Worcs
22 H11 Brockbridge Hants
65 J6 Brockdish Norfk
58 C10 Brockencote Worcs
13 P4 Brockenhurst Hants
126 E10 Brocketsbrae S Lans
64 G8 Brockford Green Suffk
64 G8 Brockford Street Suffk
60 D8 Brockhall Nhants
36 E11 Brockham Surrey
46 H9 Brockhampton Gloucs
47 K10 Brockhampton Gloucs
15 K5 Brockhampton Hants
46 A8 Brockhampton Herefs
46 C3 Brockhampton Estate Herefs
11 Q3 Brockhampton Green Dorset
90 F8 Brockholes Kirk
84 D8 Brockhurst Derbys
59 Q8 Brockhurst Warwks
101 K2 Brocklebank Cumb
93 K8 Brocklesby Lincs
31 N11 Brockley N Som
64 A7 Brockley Suffk
63 M11 Brockley Green Suffk
64 A11 Brockley Green Suffk
101 N3 Brockleymoor Cumb
58 D7 Brockmoor Dudley
8 C5 Brockscombe Devon
22 F2 Brock's Green Hants
56 E4 Brockton Shrops
56 E7 Brockton Shrops
57 K6 Brockton Shrops
57 N4 Brockton Shrops
70 E8 Brockton Staffs
31 P4 Brockweir Gloucs
22 H9 Brockwood Park Hants
46 G11 Brockworth Gloucs
4 G8 Brocton Cnwll
70 H11 Brocton Staffs
121 K4 Brodick N Ayrs
156 H6 Brodie Moray
91 N9 Brodsworth Donc
152 H4 Brogaig Highld
49 Q7 Brogborough C Beds
32 H7 Brokenborough Wilts
83 J10 Broken Cross Ches E
82 E10 Broken Cross Ches W
20 F4 Brokerswood Wilts
81 M8 Bromborough Wirral
64 G6 Brome Suffk
64 H6 Brome Street Suffk
65 L11 Bromeswell Suffk
110 C11 Bromfield Cumb
56 H9 Bromfield Shrops
61 M10 Bromham Bed
33 J11 Bromham Wilts
91 J11 Bromley Barns
58 D7 Bromley Dudley
37 K7 Bromley Gt Lon
57 N5 Bromley Shrops
37 K7 Bromley Common Gt Lon
53 J6 Bromley Cross Essex
26 G4 Bromley Green Kent
56 E4 Bromlow Shrops
38 C8 Brompton Medway
104 C11 Brompton N York
99 J4 Brompton-by-Sawdon N York
103 P11 Brompton-on-Swale N York
18 E8 Brompton Ralph Somset
18 C8 Brompton Regis Somset
46 C10 Bromsash Herefs
46 D8 Bromsberrow Gloucs
46 D8 Bromsberrow Heath Gloucs
58 E10 Bromsgrove Worcs
70 D11 Bromstead Heath Staffs
46 C4 Bromyard Herefs
46 C3 Bromyard Downs Herefs
67 N8 Bronaber Gwynd
54 E11 Bronant Cerdgn
57 J7 Broncroft Shrops
42 F5 Brongest Cerdgn
69 N7 Bronington Wrexhm
44 G8 Bronllys Powys
42 H10 Bronwydd Carmth
45 J5 Bronydd Powys
69 J7 Bronygarth Shrops
79 Q9 Bron-y-Nant Crematorium Conwy
41 Q9 Brook Carmth

13	N2	**Brook** Hants	
22	B9	**Brook** Hants	
14	C10	**Brook** IoW	
27	J3	**Brook** Kent	
23	P7	**Brook** Surrey	
36	C11	**Brook** Surrey	
65	K2	**Brooke** Norfk	
73	L9	**Brooke** Rutlnd	
93	M11	**Brookenby** Lincs	
61	N8	**Brook End** Bed	
61	Q11	**Brook End** C Beds	
61	N6	**Brook End** Cambs	
49	P6	**Brook End** M Keyn	
125	L5	**Brookfield** Rens	
34	H5	**Brookhampton** Oxon	
20	B9	**Brookhampton** Somset	
13	N2	**Brook Hill** Hants	
80	F11	**Brook House** Denbgs	
95	L8	**Brookhouse** Lancs	
84	H3	**Brookhouse** Rothm	
70	E2	**Brookhouse Green** Ches E	
83	M7	**Brookhouses** Derbys	
26	G6	**Brookland** Kent	
82	G6	**Brooklands** Traffd	
50	F10	**Brookmans Park** Herts	
55	Q5	**Brooks** Powys	
72	H7	**Brooksby** Leics	
39	N8	**Brooks End** Kent	
24	D6	**Brooks Green** W Susx	
37	N2	**Brook Street** Essex	
26	F5	**Brook Street** Kent	
52	D2	**Brook Street** Suffk	
24	H5	**Brook Street** W Susx	
32	F2	**Brookthorpe** Gloucs	
75	P11	**Brookville** Norfk	
23	Q3	**Brookwood** Surrey	
50	E2	**Broom** C Beds	
84	F2	**Broom** Rothm	
47	L4	**Broom** Warwks	
65	M3	**Broome** Norfk	
56	G8	**Broome** Shrops	
58	D9	**Broome** Worcs	
82	F7	**Broomedge** Warrtn	
119	M8	**Broome Park** Nthumb	
24	D6	**Broomer's Corner** W Susx	
24	C7	**Broomershill** W Susx	
52	B9	**Broomfield** Essex	
38	D11	**Broomfield** Kent	
39	L8	**Broomfield** Kent	
18	H8	**Broomfield** Somset	
69	M11	**Broomfields** Shrops	
92	E5	**Broomfleet** E R Yk	
76	D7	**Broom Green** Norfk	
35	Q11	**Broomhall** W & M	
112	F8	**Broomhaugh** Nthumb	
91	L10	**Broom Hill** Barns	
12	H4	**Broom Hill** Dorset	
84	H11	**Broom Hill** Notts	
119	P10	**Broomhill** Nthumb	
58	D9	**Broom Hill** Worcs	
70	A5	**Broomhill Green** Ches E	
112	F8	**Bromley** Dur	
103	P2	**Broompark** Dur	
46	D8	**Broom's Green** Gloucs	
76	A6	**Broomsthorpe** Norfk	
38	H9	**Broom Street** Kent	
163	L6	**Brora** Highld	
57	M4	**Broseley** Shrops	
74	E8	**Brotherhouse Bar** Lincs	
102	H3	**Brotherlee** Dur	
87	J11	**Brothertoft** Lincs	
91	M5	**Brotherton** N York	
105	J7	**Brotton** R & Cl	
166	H5	**Broubster** Highld	
102	E8	**Brough** Cumb	
83	Q8	**Brough** Derbys	
92	F5	**Brough** E R Yk	
167	M2	**Brough** Highld	
85	P9	**Brough** Notts	
169	s7	**Brough** Shet	
69	Q6	**Broughall** Shrops	
169	s4	**Brough Lodge** Shet	
102	E8	**Brough Sowerby** Cumb	
116	Q3	**Broughton** Border	
35	M2	**Broughton** Bucks	
62	C5	**Broughton** Cambs	
69	K2	**Broughton** Flints	
22	B8	**Broughton** Hants	
88	G4	**Broughton** Lancs	
49	N7	**Broughton** M Keyn	
92	G9	**Broughton** N Linc	
96	D10	**Broughton** N York	
98	F6	**Broughton** N York	
60	H5	**Broughton** Nhants	
48	D7	**Broughton** Oxon	
82	H4	**Broughton** Salfd	
70	D8	**Broughton** Staffs	
29	P10	**Broughton** V Glam	
60	B2	**Broughton Astley** Leics	
94	F4	**Broughton Beck** Cumb	
20	G2	**Broughton Gifford** Wilts	
47	J2	**Broughton Green** Worcs	
46	H4	**Broughton Hackett** Worcs	
94	E3	**Broughton-in-Furness** Cumb	
107	N8	**Broughton Mains** D & G	
94	E2	**Broughton Mills** Cumb	
100	E4	**Broughton Moor** Cumb	
33	P4	**Broughton Poggs** Oxon	
94	E3	**Broughton Tower** Cumb	
142	H11	**Broughty Ferry** C Dund	
94	F6	**Brow End** Cumb	
102	D9	**Brownber** Cumb	
22	G7	**Brown Candover** Hants	
88	D8	**Brown Edge** Lancs	
70	G4	**Brown Edge** Staffs	
69	N2	**Brown Heath** Ches W	
69	N9	**Brownheath** Shrops	
159	L9	**Brownhill** Abers	
135	N4	**Brownhills** Fife	
58	F3	**Brownhills** Wsall	
119	N6	**Brownieside** Nthumb	
22	G3	**Browninghill Green** Hants	
70	F3	**Brown Lees** Staffs	
70	E2	**Brownlow Heath** Ches E	
100	D6	**Brownrigg** Cumb	
110	C10	**Brownrigg** Cumb	
12	H7	**Brownsea Island** Dorset	
58	G6	**Brown's Green** Birm	
16	D6	**Brownsham** Devon	
32	G4	**Browns Hill** Gloucs	
60	B5	**Brownsover** Warwks	
6	H8	**Brownston** Devon	
64	F9	**Brown Street** Suffk	
75	N7	**Brow-of-the-Hill** Norfk	
77	P11	**Browston Green** Norfk	
99	J2	**Broxa** N York	

51	J9	**Broxbourne** Herts	
128	H4	**Broxburn** E Loth	
127	K3	**Broxburn** W Loth	
119	P7	**Broxfield** Nthumb	
51	N5	**Broxted** Essex	
69	N4	**Broxton** Ches W	
25	L8	**Broyle Side** E Susx	
167	P9	**Bruan** Highld	
141	K4	**Bruar** P & K	
163	L9	**Brucefield** Highld	
124	E6	**Bruchag** Ag & B	
69	M2	**Bruera** Ches W	
47	Q10	**Bruern Abbey** Oxon	
122	C7	**Bruichladdich** Ag & B	
65	L8	**Bruisyard** Suffk	
65	L8	**Bruisyard Street** Suffk	
92	E9	**Brumby** N Linc	
71	L2	**Brund** Staffs	
77	L10	**Brundall** Norfk	
65	K8	**Brundish** Suffk	
65	K7	**Brundish Street** Suffk	
138	C3	**Brunery** Highld	
2	E6	**Brunnion** Cnwll	
56	F8	**Brunslow** Shrops	
113	K6	**Brunswick Village** N u Ty	
90	H5	**Bruntcliffe** Leeds	
96	C11	**Brunthwaite** C Brad	
60	D3	**Bruntingthorpe** Leics	
135	J3	**Brunton** Fife	
119	P6	**Brunton** Nthumb	
21	P3	**Brunton** Wilts	
17	M10	**Brushford** Devon	
18	B9	**Brushford** Somset	
20	C7	**Bruton** Somset	
58	C11	**Bryan's Green** Worcs	
12	E3	**Bryanston** Dorset	
35	N5	**Bryant's Bottom** Bucks	
110	C6	**Brydekirk** D & G	
2	b2	**Bryher** IoS	
69	J4	**Brymbo** Wrexhm	
19	P11	**Brympton** Somset	
28	F4	**Bryn** Carmth	
82	D10	**Bryn** Ches W	
29	M6	**Bryn** Neath	
56	D7	**Bryn** Shrops	
82	C4	**Bryn** Wigan	
29	K2	**Brynamman** Carmth	
41	M3	**Brynberian** Pembks	
29	L6	**Brynbryddan** Neath	
67	L7	**Bryn-bwbach** Gwynd	
30	C8	**Bryncae** Rhondd	
29	P8	**Bryncethin** Brdgnd	
66	H6	**Bryncir** Gwynd	
29	K5	**Bryn-coch** Neath	
66	C8	**Bryncroes** Gwynd	
54	E4	**Bryncrug** Gwynd	
78	E10	**Bryn Du** IoA	
67	N9	**Bryn-Eden** Gwynd	
68	F5	**Bryneglwys** Denbgs	
69	K6	**Brynfields** Wrexhm	
80	H10	**Brynford** Flints	
82	C4	**Bryn Gates** Wigan	
30	D7	**Bryn Golau** Rhondd	
78	F9	**Bryngwran** IoA	
31	L3	**Bryngwyn** Mons	
44	H3	**Bryngwyn** Powys	
41	K3	**Bryn-Henllan** Pembks	
42	F4	**Brynhoffnant** Cerdgn	
88	E5	**Bryning** Lancs	
30	H4	**Brynithel** Blae G	
30	G2	**Brynmawr** Blae G	
66	C8	**Bryn-mawr** Gwynd	
29	P8	**Brynmenyn** Brdgnd	
28	H6	**Brynmill** Swans	
30	C8	**Brynna** Rhondd	
55	Q4	**Bryn-penarth** Powys	
67	K2	**Brynrefail** Gwynd	
78	H7	**Brynrefail** IoA	
30	D8	**Brynsadler** Rhondd	
68	E4	**Bryn Saith Marchog** Denbgs	
78	H11	**Brynsiencyn** IoA	
78	H8	**Brynteg** IoA	
69	J2	**Bryn-y-bal** Flints	
79	Q9	**Bryn-y-Maen** Conwy	
69	J6	**Bryn-yr-Eos** Wrexhm	
144	F3	**Bualintur** Highld	
80	H9	**Buarth-draw** Flints	
59	N10	**Bubbenhall** Warwks	
92	B3	**Bubwith** E R Yk	
117	L8	**Buccleuch** Border	
132	F10	**Buchanan Smithy** Stirlg	
159	R8	**Buchanhaven** Abers	
133	Q2	**Buchanty** P & K	
133	L7	**Buchany** Stirlg	
132	H9	**Buchlyvie** Stirlg	
110	G11	**Buckabank** Cumb	
61	Q7	**Buckden** Cambs	
96	D5	**Buckden** N York	
77	M10	**Buckenham** Norfk	
10	C4	**Buckerell** Devon	
7	J5	**Buckfast** Devon	
7	J5	**Buckfastleigh** Devon	
135	K8	**Buckhaven** Fife	
45	Q11	**Buckholt** Mons	
5	P2	**Buckhorn** Devon	
20	E10	**Buckhorn Weston** Dorset	
37	K2	**Buckhurst Hill** Essex	
158	B4	**Buckie** Moray	
49	J8	**Buckingham** Bucks	
35	N2	**Buckland** Bucks	
6	H10	**Buckland** Devon	
47	L7	**Buckland** Gloucs	
13	P5	**Buckland** Hants	
51	J4	**Buckland** Herts	
27	P3	**Buckland** Kent	
34	B5	**Buckland** Oxon	
36	F10	**Buckland** Surrey	
16	G7	**Buckland Brewer** Devon	
35	P3	**Buckland Common** Bucks	
20	E4	**Buckland Dinham** Somset	
16	H10	**Buckland Filleigh** Devon	
7	J4	**Buckland in the Moor** Devon	
6	D5	**Buckland Monachorum** Devon	
11	P3	**Buckland Newton** Dorset	
11	P8	**Buckland Ripers** Dorset	
10	F2	**Buckland St Mary** Somset	
7	K9	**Buckland-Tout-Saints** Devon	
34	G10	**Bucklebury** W Berk	
14	D6	**Bucklers Hard** Hants	
53	M3	**Bucklesham** Suffk	
69	J2	**Buckley** Flints	
59	J11	**Buckley Green** Warwks	
82	F8	**Bucklow Hill** Ches E	

73	M6	**Buckminster** Leics	
70	G5	**Bucknall** C Stke	
86	G7	**Bucknall** Lincs	
48	G9	**Bucknell** Oxon	
56	F10	**Bucknell** Shrops	
158	B4	**Buckpool** Moray	
151	M6	**Bucksburn** C Aber	
16	F7	**Buck's Cross** Devon	
24	C4	**Bucks Green** W Susx	
88	H6	**Buckshaw Village** Lancs	
50	C10	**Bucks Hill** Herts	
23	M6	**Bucks Horn Oak** Hants	
16	F7	**Buck's Mills** Devon	
99	P6	**Buckton** E R Yk	
56	F10	**Buckton** Herefs	
119	L3	**Buckton** Nthumb	
61	P5	**Buckworth** Cambs	
85	K7	**Budby** Notts	
70	C5	**Buddileigh** Staffs	
16	C10	**Bude** Cnwll	
9	N4	**Budge's Shop** Cnwll	
119	N3	**Budle** Nthumb	
9	Q8	**Budleigh Salterton** Devon	
25	L6	**Budlett's Common** E Susx	
3	K7	**Budock Water** Cnwll	
70	B6	**Buerton** Ches E	
60	E9	**Bugbrooke** Nhants	
7	L8	**Bugford** Devon	
70	F2	**Buglawton** Ches E	
4	G10	**Bugle** Cnwll	
20	E10	**Bugley** Dorset	
98	F9	**Bugthorpe** E R Yk	
57	L4	**Buildwas** Shrops	
44	E4	**Builth Road** Powys	
44	E4	**Builth Wells** Powys	
35	P2	**Bulbourne** Herts	
21	L8	**Bulbridge** Wilts	
73	R5	**Bulby** Lincs	
21	N6	**Bulford** Wilts	
21	N6	**Bulford Camp** Wilts	
69	P4	**Bulkeley** Ches E	
59	N7	**Bulkington** Warwks	
20	H3	**Bulkington** Wilts	
16	F9	**Bulkworthy** Devon	
97	N2	**Bullamoor** N York	
78	G6	**Bull Bay** IoA	
84	E10	**Bullbridge** Derbys	
35	N11	**Bullbrook** Br For	
50	F9	**Bullen's Green** Herts	
46	E11	**Bulley** Gloucs	
100	E3	**Bullgill** Cumb	
45	Q7	**Bullinghope** Herefs	
22	E6	**Bullington** Hants	
86	E5	**Bullington** Lincs	
39	L8	**Bullockstone** Kent	
50	G7	**Bull's Green** Herts	
65	N3	**Bull's Green** Norfk	
52	D3	**Bulmer** Essex	
98	D7	**Bulmer** N York	
52	D4	**Bulmer Tye** Essex	
37	P3	**Bulphan** Thurr	
10	D7	**Bulstone** Devon	
50	B10	**Bulstrode** Herts	
26	C10	**Bulverhythe** E Susx	
159	M8	**Bulwark** Abers	
72	E2	**Bulwell** C Nott	
61	L2	**Bulwick** Nhants	
51	K9	**Bumble's Green** Essex	
145	L10	**Bunacaimb** Highld	
146	F10	**Bunarkaig** Highld	
69	Q3	**Bunbury** Ches E	
69	Q3	**Bunbury Heath** Ches E	
155	R8	**Bunchrew** Highld	
24	D8	**Buncton** W Susx	
145	Q2	**Bundalloch** Highld	
137	K11	**Bunessan** Ag & B	
65	L4	**Bungay** Suffk	
87	J10	**Bunker's Hill** Lincs	
122	F5	**Bunnahabhain** Ag & B	
72	F5	**Bunny** Notts	
155	M11	**Buntait** Highld	
51	J5	**Buntingford** Herts	
64	G3	**Bunwell** Norfk	
64	G3	**Bunwell Hill** Norfk	
71	N7	**Bupton** Derbys	
83	M10	**Burbage** Derbys	
59	P4	**Burbage** Leics	
21	P2	**Burbage** Wilts	
45	L2	**Burcher** Herefs	
25	Q4	**Burchett's Green** E Susx	
35	M8	**Burchett's Green** W & M	
21	L8	**Burcombe** Wilts	
34	G5	**Burcot** Oxon	
58	E10	**Burcot** Worcs	
58	N5	**Burcote** Shrops	
49	N10	**Burcott** Bucks	
98	H8	**Burdale** N York	
52	F5	**Bures** Essex	
33	Q2	**Burford** Oxon	
57	K11	**Burford** Shrops	
137	K6	**Burg** Ag & B	
24	F6	**Burgate** Suffk	
23	L9	**Burgates** Hants	
50	D4	**Burge End** Herts	
24	H7	**Burgess Hill** W Susx	
65	J11	**Burgh** Suffk	
110	F9	**Burgh by Sands** Cumb	
77	P10	**Burgh Castle** Norfk	
22	E2	**Burghclere** Hants	
157	L4	**Burghead** Moray	
35	J11	**Burghfield** W Berk	
35	J11	**Burghfield Common** W Berk	
36	F9	**Burgh Heath** Surrey	
26	B6	**Burgh Hill** E Susx	
45	P6	**Burghill** Herefs	
6	G10	**Burgh Island** Devon	
87	P7	**Burgh le Marsh** Lincs	
77	J6	**Burgh next Aylsham** Norfk	
86	H3	**Burgh on Bain** Lincs	
77	N9	**Burgh St Margaret** Norfk	
65	P3	**Burgh St Peter** Norfk	
91	N7	**Burghwallis** Donc	
38	B9	**Burham** Kent	
13	P5	**Buriton** Hants	
69	R4	**Burland** Ches E	
4	F7	**Burlawn** Cnwll	
32	G4	**Burleigh** Gloucs	
18	E11	**Burlescombe** Devon	
12	C6	**Burleston** Dorset	
17	L11	**Burlestone** Devon	
13	M4	**Burley** Hants	
73	L9	**Burley** Rutlnd	
56	H8	**Burley** Shrops	
69	R6	**Burleydam** Ches E	

46	A5	**Burley Gate** Herefs	
97	J11	**Burley in Wharfedale** C Brad	
13	M4	**Burley Lawn** Hants	
13	M4	**Burley Street** Hants	
90	F2	**Burley Wood Head** C Brad	
77	M9	**Burlingham Green** Norfk	
45	K3	**Burlingjobb** Powys	
57	P2	**Burlington** Shrops	
69	N9	**Burlton** Shrops	
27	K5	**Burmarsh** Kent	
47	Q7	**Burmington** Warwks	
91	P5	**Burn** N York	
83	M7	**Burnage** Manch	
71	P8	**Burnaston** Derbys	
101	P7	**Burnbanks** Cumb	
126	F6	**Burnbrae** N Lans	
98	G11	**Burnby** E R Yk	
91	J11	**Burn Cross** Sheff	
15	Q6	**Burndell** W Susx	
89	L9	**Burneden** Bolton	
89	Q8	**Burnedge** Rochdl	
101	P11	**Burneside** Cumb	
97	M4	**Burneston** N York	
32	C11	**Burnett** BaNES	
117	N8	**Burnfoot** Border	
117	Q7	**Burnfoot** Border	
109	L2	**Burnfoot** D & G	
110	F3	**Burnfoot** D & G	
117	M11	**Burnfoot** D & G	
134	B7	**Burnfoot** P & K	
35	P8	**Burnham** Bucks	
93	J7	**Burnham** N Linc	
75	R2	**Burnham Deepdale** Norfk	
50	G7	**Burnham Green** Herts	
76	A3	**Burnham Market** Norfk	
76	A3	**Burnham Norton** Norfk	
38	F2	**Burnham-on-Crouch** Essex	
19	K5	**Burnham-on-Sea** Somset	
76	A3	**Burnham Overy** Norfk	
76	A3	**Burnham Overy Staithe** Norfk	
76	B3	**Burnham Thorpe** Norfk	
159	R9	**Burnhaven** Abers	
116	B11	**Burnhead** D & G	
151	J4	**Burnhervie** Abers	
57	P4	**Burnhill Green** Staffs	
113	J7	**Burnhope** Dur	
125	K7	**Burnhouse** N Ayrs	
99	L2	**Burniston** N York	
89	N4	**Burnley** Lancs	
89	N4	**Burnley Crematorium** Lancs	
129	P7	**Burnmouth** Border	
88	C2	**Burn Naze** Lancs	
133	L7	**Burn of Cambus** Stirlg	
113	J9	**Burnopfield** Dur	
111	J9	**Burnrigg** Cumb	
96	F8	**Burnsall** N York	
142	G6	**Burnside** Angus	
143	J7	**Burnside** Angus	
134	F6	**Burnside** Fife	
157	M4	**Burnside** Moray	
127	K2	**Burnside** W Loth	
142	G11	**Burnside of Duntrune** Angus	
36	B10	**Burntcommon** Surrey	
71	N8	**Burntheath** Derbys	
53	J6	**Burnt Heath** Essex	
34	G10	**Burnt Hill** W Berk	
3	K6	**Burnthouse** Cnwll	
103	M6	**Burnt Houses** Dur	
134	G10	**Burntisland** Fife	
25	M5	**Burnt Oak** E Susx	
58	G3	**Burntwood** Staffs	
58	G3	**Burntwood Green** Staffs	
97	L8	**Burnt Yates** N York	
18	G11	**Burnworthy** Somset	
36	B10	**Burpham** Surrey	
24	B9	**Burpham** W Susx	
113	L6	**Burradon** N Tyne	
119	J9	**Burradon** Nthumb	
169	t2	**Burrafirth** Shet	
2	H7	**Burras** Cnwll	
169	s5	**Burraton** Cnwll	
169	s5	**Burravoe** Shet	
102	C7	**Burrells** Cumb	
142	C10	**Burrelton** P & K	
10	G3	**Burridge** Devon	
17	K4	**Burridge** Devon	
14	F4	**Burridge** Hants	
97	K3	**Burrill** N York	
92	D9	**Burringham** N Linc	
17	L8	**Burrington** Devon	
56	G10	**Burrington** Herefs	
19	N3	**Burrington** N Som	
63	K9	**Burrough End** Cambs	
63	K9	**Burrough Green** Cambs	
73	K8	**Burrough on the Hill** Leics	
95	N6	**Burrow** Lancs	
18	B6	**Burrow** Somset	
19	L8	**Burrow Bridge** Somset	
23	Q2	**Burrowhill** Surrey	
36	C11	**Burrows Cross** Surrey	
28	E6	**Burry** Swans	
28	E6	**Burry Green** Swans	
28	D4	**Burry Port** Carmth	
88	E8	**Burscough** Lancs	
88	E8	**Burscough Bridge** Lancs	
92	D4	**Bursea** E R Yk	
99	M11	**Burshill** E R Yk	
14	E5	**Bursledon** Hants	
70	F5	**Burslem** C Stke	
53	J3	**Burstall** Suffk	
11	J4	**Burstock** Dorset	
64	G5	**Burston** Norfk	
70	G8	**Burston** Staffs	
24	H2	**Burstow** Surrey	
93	M5	**Burstwick** E R Yk	
96	C3	**Burtersett** N York	
111	K8	**Burtholme** Cumb	
63	N8	**Burthorpe Green** Suffk	
110	H11	**Burthwaite** Cumb	
4	E10	**Burthy** Cnwll	
19	L6	**Burtle Hill** Somset	
74	E3	**Burtoft** Lincs	
69	P2	**Burton** Ches W	
81	L10	**Burton** Ches W	
11	P6	**Burton** Dorset	
13	L6	**Burton** Dorset	
86	C6	**Burton** Lincs	
119	N4	**Burton** Nthumb	
41	J9	**Burton** Pembks	
11	L2	**Burton** Somset	
18	H7	**Burton** Somset	
20	F8	**Burton** Wilts	

32	F9	**Burton** Wilts	
99	N8	**Burton Agnes** E R Yk	
11	K7	**Burton Bradstock** Dorset	
73	P5	**Burton Coggles** Lincs	
93	L3	**Burton Constable Hall** E R Yk	
48	C4	**Burton Dassett** Warwks	
51	M6	**Burton End** Essex	
63	L11	**Burton End** Suffk	
99	M6	**Burton Fleming** E R Yk	
59	L9	**Burton Green** Warwks	
69	K3	**Burton Green** Wrexhm	
59	P7	**Burton Hastings** Warwks	
95	L5	**Burton-in-Kendal** Cumb	
95	L5	**Burton-in-Kendal Services** Cumb	
95	P6	**Burton in Lonsdale** N York	
72	G2	**Burton Joyce** Notts	
61	K6	**Burton Latimer** Nhants	
73	K7	**Burton Lazars** Leics	
97	M8	**Burton Leonard** N York	
72	F6	**Burton on the Wolds** Leics	
72	H11	**Burton Overy** Leics	
74	B2	**Burton Pedwardine** Lincs	
93	M4	**Burton Pidsea** E R Yk	
91	M5	**Burton Salmon** N York	
52	D6	**Burton's Green** Essex	
92	E7	**Burton upon Stather** N Linc	
71	N10	**Burton upon Trent** Staffs	
86	B6	**Burton Waters** Lincs	
82	C6	**Burtonwood** Warrtn	
82	C6	**Burtonwood Services** Warrtn	
69	P3	**Burwardsley** Ches W	
57	L7	**Burwarton** Shrops	
25	Q6	**Burwash** E Susx	
25	P6	**Burwash Common** E Susx	
25	Q6	**Burwash Weald** E Susx	
63	J7	**Burwell** Cambs	
87	L5	**Burwell** Lincs	
78	G6	**Burwen** IoA	
169	d8	**Burwick** Ork	
89	N8	**Bury** Bury	
62	C4	**Bury** Cambs	
18	B9	**Bury** Somset	
24	B8	**Bury** W Susx	
50	D8	**Bury End** C Beds	
51	L6	**Bury Green** Herts	
64	B9	**Bury St Edmunds** Suffk	
98	F8	**Burythorpe** N York	
125	P6	**Busby** E Rens	
97	N4	**Busby Stoop** N York	
33	P5	**Buscot** Oxon	
143	P4	**Bush** Abers	
16	C10	**Bush** Cnwll	
45	P4	**Bush Bank** Herefs	
58	D4	**Bushbury** Wolves	
58	D4	**Bushbury Crematorium** Wolves	
72	H10	**Bushby** Leics	
50	D11	**Bushey** Herts	
36	D2	**Bushey Heath** Herts	
65	J4	**Bush Green** Norfk	
64	C10	**Bush Green** Suffk	
50	H11	**Bush Hill Park** Gt Lon	
46	G8	**Bushley** Worcs	
46	G8	**Bushley Green** Worcs	
61	P8	**Bushmead** Bed	
56	G7	**Bushmoor** Shrops	
33	N8	**Bushton** Wilts	
102	B2	**Busk** Cumb	
86	E3	**Buslingthorpe** Lincs	
32	G4	**Bussage** Gloucs	
19	L7	**Bussex** Somset	
25	N5	**Butcher's Cross** E Susx	
19	P2	**Butcombe** N Som	
124	C4	**Bute** Ag & B	
19	P7	**Butleigh** Somset	
19	P7	**Butleigh Wootton** Somset	
35	M3	**Butler's Cross** Bucks	
84	H11	**Butler's Hill** Notts	
48	B4	**Butlers Marston** Warwks	
65	M11	**Butley** Suffk	
53	Q2	**Butley High Corner** Suffk	
98	E9	**Butterambe** N York	
129	K7	**Butterdean** Border	
103	M5	**Butterknowle** Dur	
9	N3	**Butterleigh** Devon	
84	F10	**Butterley** Derbys	
100	G7	**Buttermere** Cumb	
22	B2	**Buttermere** Wilts	
70	E6	**Butters Green** Staffs	
90	E5	**Buttershaw** C Brad	
141	Q8	**Butterstone** P & K	
70	E6	**Butterton** Staffs	
71	K3	**Butterton** Staffs	
104	C4	**Butterwick** Dur	
87	L11	**Butterwick** Lincs	
98	E5	**Butterwick** N York	
99	K6	**Butterwick** N York	
70	B4	**Butt Green** Ches E	
56	C3	**Buttington** Powys	
57	N9	**Buttonbridge** Shrops	
57	P9	**Buttonoak** Shrops	
14	D5	**Buttsash** Hants	
16	D11	**Buttsbear Cross** Cnwll	
52	C11	**Butt's Green** Essex	
64	E10	**Buxhall** Suffk	
64	E10	**Buxhall Fen Street** Suffk	
25	L6	**Buxted** E Susx	
83	N10	**Buxton** Derbys	
77	J7	**Buxton** Norfk	
76	H7	**Buxton Heath** Norfk	
44	H10	**Bwlch** Powys	
69	J4	**Bwlchgwyn** Wrexhm	
43	L3	**Bwlchllan** Cerdgn	
42	G10	**Bwlchnewydd** Carmth	
68	G11	**Bwlchtocyn** Gwynd	
68	G11	**Bwlch-y-cibau** Powys	
44	G7	**Bwlch-y-Ddar** Powys	
42	H5	**Bwlchyfadfa** Cerdgn	
55	P5	**Bwlch-y-ffridd** Powys	
41	P3	**Bwlch-y-groes** Pembks	
28	G5	**Bwlchymyrdd** Swans	
55	N10	**Bwlch-y-sarnau** Powys	
113	J9	**Byermoor** Gatesd	
103	P4	**Byers Green** Dur	
48	F4	**Byfield** Nhants	
36	C8	**Byfleet** Surrey	
45	M6	**Byford** Herefs	
50	G3	**Bygrave** Herts	
113	L8	**Byker** N u Ty	
68	C2	**Bylchau** Conwy	
82	F11	**Byley** Ches W	

28 F5 **Bynea** Carmth
118 E10 **Byrness** Nthumb
9 P8 **Bystock** Devon
61 N5 **Bythorn** Cambs
45 M2 **Byton** Herefs
112 F8 **Bywell** Nthumb
23 Q10 **Byworth** W Susx

C

16 G7 **Cabbacott** Devon
93 K10 **Cabourne** Lincs
122 G7 **Cabrach** Ag & B
150 B2 **Cabrach** Moray
95 K11 **Cabus** Lancs
25 L5 **Cackle Street** E Susx
25 Q7 **Cackle Street** E Susx
26 D8 **Cackle Street** E Susx
9 M3 **Cadbury** Devon
17 M8 **Cadbury Barton** Devon
125 Q3 **Cadder** E Duns
50 C7 **Caddington** C Beds
117 P3 **Caddonfoot** Border
91 N10 **Cadeby** Donc
72 C10 **Cadeby** Leics
9 M3 **Cadeleigh** Devon
25 P6 **Cade Street** E Susx
3 J11 **Cadgwith** Cnwll
134 H7 **Cadham** Fife
82 F6 **Cadishead** Salfd
28 H5 **Cadle** Swans
88 G4 **Cadley** Lancs
21 P4 **Cadley** Wilts
33 P11 **Cadley** Wilts
35 L6 **Cadmore End** Bucks
13 P2 **Cadnam** Hants
92 H10 **Cadney** N Linc
68 H2 **Cadole** Flints
30 F11 **Cadoxton** V Glam
29 L5 **Cadoxton Juxta-Neath** Neath
68 D7 **Cadwst** Denbgs
67 J2 **Caeathro** Gwynd
29 M2 **Caehopkin** Powys
86 C3 **Caenby** Lincs
43 N6 **Caeo** Carmth
29 N6 **Caerau** Brdgnd
30 F9 **Caerau** Cardif
29 M2 **Cae'r-bont** Powys
28 G2 **Cae'r bryn** Carmth
67 M11 **Caerdeon** Gwynd
40 E5 **Caer Farchell** Pembks
78 E9 **Caergeiliog** IoA
69 K3 **Caergwrle** Flints
79 P10 **Caerhun** Conwy
117 M10 **Caerlanrig** Border
31 K6 **Caerleon** Newpt
31 K6 **Caerleon Roman Amphitheatre** Newpt
66 H2 **Caernarfon** Gwynd
66 H2 **Caernarfon Castle** Gwynd
30 G7 **Caerphilly** Caerph
55 N6 **Caersws** Powys
42 G3 **Caerwedros** Cerdgn
31 N6 **Caerwent** Mons
80 G10 **Caerwys** Flints
67 P11 **Caerynwch** Gwynd
45 M11 **Caggle Street** Mons
79 L8 **Caim** IoA
168 d11 **Cairinis** W Isls
130 G9 **Cairnbaan** Ag & B
159 P4 **Cairnbulg** Abers
129 M7 **Cairncross** Border
125 J3 **Cairncurran** Inver
131 P5 **Cairndow** Ag & B
134 C10 **Cairneyhill** Fife
106 E8 **Cairngarroch** D & G
149 K7 **Cairngorms National Park**
158 C9 **Cairnie** Abers
159 L9 **Cairnorrie** Abers
106 E4 **Cairnryan** D & G
157 Q7 **Cairnty** Moray
77 Q9 **Caister-on-Sea** Norfk
93 K10 **Caistor** Lincs
77 J11 **Caistor St Edmund** Norfk
58 C10 **Cakebole** Worcs
64 F3 **Cake Street** Norfk
52 G4 **Calais Street** Suffk
168 h4 **Calanais** W Isls
14 D9 **Calbourne** IoW
87 L5 **Calceby** Lincs
80 H10 **Calcot** Flints
33 L2 **Calcot** Gloucs
35 J10 **Calcot** W Berk
35 J10 **Calcot Row** W Berk
157 P5 **Calcots** Moray
39 L9 **Calcott** Kent
56 G2 **Calcott** Shrops
97 M9 **Calcutt** N York
33 M6 **Calcutt** Wilts
101 K2 **Caldbeck** Cumb
96 G3 **Caldbergh** N York
61 P3 **Caldecote** Cambs
62 D9 **Caldecote** Cambs
50 F3 **Caldecote** Herts
49 J4 **Caldecote** Nhants
62 E9 **Caldecote Highfields** Cambs
61 L7 **Caldecott** Nhants
34 E5 **Caldecott** Oxon
61 J2 **Caldecott** Rutlnd
49 N7 **Caldecotte** M Keyn
100 D10 **Calder** Cumb
126 D5 **Calderbank** N Lans
100 D9 **Calder Bridge** Cumb
89 Q7 **Calderbrook** Rochdl
126 E4 **Caldercruix** N Lans
91 J7 **Calder Grove** Wakefd
126 B9 **Caldermill** S Lans
89 Q7 **Caldermore** Rochdl
95 L11 **Calder Vale** Lancs
126 B6 **Calderwood** S Lans
41 M11 **Caldey Island** Pembks
31 N7 **Caldicot** Mons
58 F5 **Caldmore** Wsall
103 N8 **Caldwell** N York
81 J7 **Caldy** Wirral
43 N9 **Caledfwlch** Carmth
3 L5 **Calenick** Cnwll
80 a8 **Calf of Man** IoM
63 M11 **Calford Green** Suffk
169 e3 **Calfsound** Ork
137 K5 **Calgary** Ag & B
157 K6 **Califer** Moray
126 G2 **California** Falk
77 Q8 **California** Norfk
7 J8 **California Cross** Devon
72 B6 **Calke** Derbys
153 M6 **Callakille** Highld
133 J6 **Callander** Stirlg
168 h4 **Callanish** W Isls
57 L5 **Callaughton** Shrops
3 K3 **Callestick** Cnwll
145 K7 **Calligarry** Highld
5 P8 **Callington** Cnwll
71 M10 **Callingwood** Staffs
45 P8 **Callow** Herefs
46 F4 **Callow End** Worcs
33 K8 **Callow Hill** Wilts
47 K2 **Callow Hill** Worcs
57 N10 **Callow Hill** Worcs
57 K11 **Callows Grave** Worcs
13 P2 **Calmore** Hants
33 K3 **Calmsden** Gloucs
33 J10 **Calne** Wilts
84 F6 **Calow** Derbys
14 E6 **Calshot** Hants
6 C5 **Calstock** Cnwll
33 K11 **Calstone Wellington** Wilts
76 H5 **Calthorpe** Norfk
77 N6 **Calthorpe Street** Norfk
101 N2 **Calthwaite** Cumb
96 D9 **Calton** N York
71 L5 **Calton** Staffs
69 Q3 **Calveley** Ches E
84 B6 **Calver** Derbys
69 R7 **Calverhall** Shrops
45 M5 **Calver Hill** Herefs
9 M2 **Calverleigh** Devon
90 G3 **Calverley** Leeds
84 B6 **Calver Sough** Derbys
49 J10 **Calvert** Bucks
49 L7 **Calverton** M Keyn
85 K11 **Calverton** Notts
141 K4 **Calvine** P & K
109 P10 **Calvo** Cumb
116 G3 **Calzeat** Border
32 E5 **Cam** Gloucs
138 D5 **Camasachoirce** Highld
138 D5 **Camasine** Highld
146 A2 **Camas Luinie** Highld
153 J10 **Camastianavaig** Highld
155 P9 **Camault Muir** Highld
26 G8 **Camber** E Susx
23 N2 **Camberley** Surrey
36 H5 **Camberwell** Gt Lon
91 Q5 **Camblesforth** N York
112 F3 **Cambo** Nthumb
113 M4 **Cambois** Nthumb
2 G5 **Camborne** Cnwll
62 D9 **Cambourne** Cambs
62 G9 **Cambridge** Cambs
32 D4 **Cambridge** Gloucs
62 G9 *Cambridge Airport* Cambs
62 E8 **Cambridge City Crematorium** Cambs
62 E7 **Cambridge Services** Cambs
2 H4 **Cambrose** Cnwll
133 P9 **Cambus** Clacks
162 H7 **Cambusavie Platform** Highld
133 M9 **Cambusbarron** Stirlg
133 N9 **Cambuskenneth** Stirlg
125 Q5 **Cambuslang** S Lans
150 C8 **Cambus o' May** Abers
116 E3 **Cambuswallace** S Lans
36 G4 **Camden Town** Gt Lon
20 B3 **Cameley** BaNES
5 J5 **Camelford** Cnwll
133 P11 **Camelon** Falk
157 J11 **Camerory** Highld
46 E7 **Camer's Green** Worcs
20 C3 **Camerton** BaNES
100 D4 **Camerton** Cumb
140 E6 **Camghouran** P & K
117 R4 **Camieston** Border
151 N8 **Cammachmore** Abers
86 B4 **Cammeringham** Lincs
162 H9 **Camore** Highld
120 D7 **Campbeltown** Ag & B
120 C7 *Campbeltown Airport* Ag & B
113 L6 **Camperdown** N Tyne
109 J2 **Cample** D & G
142 C10 **Campmuir** P & K
127 K4 **Camps** W Loth
91 N8 **Campsall** Donc
65 L10 **Campsea Ash** Suffk
51 P2 **Camps End** Cambs
50 D3 **Campton** C Beds
118 C8 **Camptown** Border
40 H6 **Camrose** Pembks
141 K8 **Camserney** P & K
139 K3 **Camusnagaul** Highld
160 H9 **Camusnagaul** Highld
153 N9 **Camusteel** Highld
153 N9 **Camusterrach** Highld
21 Q11 **Canada** Hants
94 G5 **Canal Foot** Cumb
41 L7 **Canaston Bridge** Pembks
149 Q8 **Candacraig** Abers
87 N7 **Candlesby** Lincs
64 E7 **Candle Street** Suffk
57 J3 **Candover Green** Shrops
116 F2 **Candy Mill** Border
35 J9 **Cane End** Oxon
38 F3 **Canewdon** Essex
12 H4 **Canford Bottom** Dorset
13 J7 **Canford Cliffs** Poole
31 Q9 **Canford Crematorium** Bristl
12 H6 **Canford Heath** Poole
12 H5 **Canford Magna** Poole
64 F8 **Canhams Green** Suffk
167 P2 **Canisbay** Highld
84 F2 **Canklow** Rothm
59 M9 **Canley** Covtry
59 M9 **Canley Crematorium** Covtry
20 G10 **Cann** Dorset
144 B6 **Canna** Highld
155 K11 **Cannich** Highld
19 J7 **Cannington** Somset
37 K4 **Canning Town** Gt Lon
58 E2 **Cannock** Staffs
70 H11 **Cannock Chase** Staffs
58 F2 **Cannock Wood** Staffs
45 N6 **Cannon Bridge** Herefs
110 G5 **Canonbie** D & G
46 B6 **Canon Frome** Herefs
45 P5 **Canon Pyon** Herefs
48 G4 **Canons Ashby** Nhants
2 E6 **Canonstown** Cnwll
39 K10 **Canterbury** Kent
39 L10 **Canterbury Cathedral** Kent
77 M11 **Cantley** Norfk
57 J3 **Cantlop** Shrops
30 G9 **Canton** Cardif
156 D8 **Cantraywood** Highld
95 N6 **Cantsfield** Lancs
38 C5 **Canvey Island** Essex
86 C7 **Canwick** Lincs
5 L3 **Canworthy Water** Cnwll
139 L2 **Caol** Highld
168 h8 **Caolas Scalpaigh** W Isls
136 D6 **Caoles** Ag & B
146 D9 **Caonich** Highld
25 P2 **Capel** Kent
24 E2 **Capel** Surrey
54 F8 **Capel Bangor** Cerdgn
43 M3 **Capel Betws Lleucu** Cerdgn
78 H8 **Capel Coch** IoA
67 N3 **Capel Curig** Conwy
42 G5 **Capel Cynon** Cerdgn
43 J10 **Capel Dewi** Carmth
43 J6 **Capel Dewi** Cerdgn
54 E8 **Capel-Dewi** Cerdgn
67 Q3 **Capel Garmon** Conwy
53 Q2 **Capel Green** Suffk
43 J10 **Capel Gwyn** Carmth
78 E9 **Capel Gwyn** IoA
43 P10 **Capel Gwynfe** Carmth
28 G2 **Capel Hendre** Carmth
43 L9 **Capel Isaac** Carmth
41 Q3 **Capel Iwan** Carmth
27 N4 **Capel le Ferne** Kent
10 c1 **Capelles** Guern
30 E9 **Capel Llanilltern** Cardif
78 G10 **Capel Mawr** IoA
78 G7 **Capel Parc** IoA
53 Q2 **Capel St Andrew** Suffk
53 J4 **Capel St Mary** Suffk
54 E9 **Capel Seion** Cerdgn
54 G9 **Capel Trisant** Cerdgn
66 G5 **Capeluchaf** Gwynd
79 N9 **Capelulo** Conwy
45 K8 **Capel-y-ffin** Powys
79 J11 **Capel-y-graig** Gwynd
81 M10 **Capenhurst** Ches W
95 L6 **Capernwray** Lancs
112 F4 **Capheaton** Nthumb
125 L6 **Caplaw** E Rens
65 K8 **Capon's Green** Suffk
117 J6 **Cappercleuch** Border
38 C8 **Capstone** Medway
7 L8 **Capton** Devon
18 E7 **Capton** Somset
141 Q9 **Caputh** P & K
5 M7 **Caradon Town** Cnwll
125 N2 **Carbeth Inn** Stirlg
4 G10 **Carbis** Cnwll
2 E6 **Carbis Bay** Cnwll
152 F11 **Carbost** Highld
152 G8 **Carbost** Highld
84 E3 **Carbrook** Sheff
76 C11 **Carbrooke** Norfk
85 K6 **Carburton** Notts
3 Q3 **Carclaze** Cnwll
73 J2 **Car Colston** Notts
91 N9 **Carcroft** Donc
134 G8 **Cardenden** Fife
56 F2 **Cardeston** Shrops
110 G10 **Cardewlees** Cumb
157 M9 **Cardhu** Moray
30 G9 **Cardiff** Cardif
30 E11 *Cardiff Airport* V Glam
30 H8 **Cardiff Gate Services** Cardif
30 E9 **Cardiff West Services** Cardif
42 C5 **Cardigan** Cerdgn
63 K11 **Cardinal's Green** Cambs
61 N11 **Cardington** Bed
57 J5 **Cardington** Shrops
5 J8 **Cardinham** Cnwll
106 F11 **Cardrain** D & G
117 L3 **Cardrona** Border
125 J2 **Cardross** Ag & B
106 F11 **Cardryne** D & G
110 C9 **Cardurnock** Cumb
73 Q7 **Careby** Lincs
143 J5 **Careston** Angus
41 K10 **Carew** Pembks
41 K10 **Carew Cheriton** Pembks
41 K10 **Carew Newton** Pembks
45 R8 **Carey** Herefs
126 D6 **Carfin** N Lans
128 E9 **Carfraemill** Border
77 M9 **Cargate Green** Norfk
109 L5 **Cargenbridge** D & G
142 B10 **Cargill** P & K
110 G9 **Cargo** Cumb
6 C6 **Cargreen** Cnwll
3 M6 **Cargurrel** Cnwll
118 E3 **Carham** Nthumb
18 D6 **Carhampton** Somset
3 J5 **Carharrack** Cnwll
140 F6 **Carie** P & K
168 d11 **Carinish** W Isls
14 E9 **Carisbrooke** IoW
94 H5 **Cark** Cumb
5 Q9 **Carkeel** Cnwll
168 h3 **Carlabhagh** W Isls
3 M3 **Carland Cross** Cnwll
103 P7 **Carlbury** Darltn
73 Q8 **Carlby** Lincs
118 F8 **Carlcroft** Nthumb
83 Q4 **Carlecotes** Barns
2 G7 **Carleen** Cnwll
97 K6 **Carlesmoor** N York
100 D9 **Carleton** Cumb
101 P5 **Carleton** Cumb
110 H10 **Carleton** Cumb
88 C3 **Carleton** Lancs
96 E11 **Carleton** N York
91 M6 **Carleton** Wakefd
88 C3 **Carleton Crematorium** Bpool
76 F10 **Carleton Forehoe** Norfk
64 G3 **Carleton Rode** Norfk
77 L11 **Carleton St Peter** Norfk
3 K8 **Carlidnack** Cnwll
158 G9 **Carlincraig** Abers
20 C3 **Carlingcott** BaNES
105 K7 **Carlin How** R & Cl
110 G9 **Carlisle** Cumb
111 J8 *Carlisle Airport* Cumb
110 G10 **Carlisle Crematorium** Cumb
4 D8 **Carloggas** Cnwll
127 M6 **Carlops** Border
168 h3 **Carloway** W Isls
91 K8 **Carlton** Barns
61 L9 **Carlton** Bed
63 K10 **Carlton** Cambs
91 J5 **Carlton** Leeds
72 B10 **Carlton** Leics
91 Q6 **Carlton** N York
96 G4 **Carlton** N York
98 C3 **Carlton** N York
72 G2 **Carlton** Notts
104 C6 **Carlton** S on T
65 M9 **Carlton** Suffk
65 Q4 **Carlton Colville** Suffk
72 H11 **Carlton Curlieu** Leics
63 K10 **Carlton Green** Cambs
97 Q5 **Carlton Husthwaite** N York
104 F10 **Carlton-in-Cleveland** N York
85 J4 **Carlton in Lindrick** Notts
86 B9 **Carlton-le-Moorland** Lincs
97 N4 **Carlton Miniott** N York
85 N8 **Carlton-on-Trent** Notts
86 B11 **Carlton Scroop** Lincs
126 E7 **Carluke** S Lans
3 R3 **Carlyon Bay** Cnwll
115 Q2 **Carmacoup** S Lans
42 H10 **Carmarthen** Carmth
43 L11 **Carmel** Carmth
80 H9 **Carmel** Flints
66 H4 **Carmel** Gwynd
116 C3 **Carmichael** S Lans
70 G5 **Carmountside Crematorium** C Stke
125 P6 **Carmunnock** C Glas
125 Q5 **Carmyle** C Glas
143 J9 **Carmyllie** Angus
99 N7 **Carnaby** E R Yk
135 N6 **Carnbee** Fife
134 D7 **Carnbo** P & K
2 H5 **Carn Brea** Cnwll
151 M2 **Carnbrogie** Abers
145 Q2 **Carndu** Highld
126 B8 **Carnduff** S Lans
3 K9 **Carne** Cnwll
3 N6 **Carne** Cnwll
4 F10 **Carne** Cnwll
125 M11 **Carnell** E Ayrs
4 D8 **Carnewas** Cnwll
95 K6 **Carnforth** Lancs
146 B3 **Carn-gorm** Highld
40 F5 **Carnhedryn** Pembks
2 G6 **Carnhell Green** Cnwll
151 L6 **Carnie** Abers
2 H5 **Carnkie** Cnwll
3 J7 **Carnkie** Cnwll
3 K3 **Carnkiet** Cnwll
55 M5 **Carno** Powys
134 C10 **Carnock** Fife
3 K5 **Carnon Downs** Cnwll
158 G7 **Carnousie** Abers
143 K11 **Carnoustie** Angus
4 G10 **Carnsmerry** Cnwll
126 H8 **Carnwath** S Lans
2 B7 **Carnyorth** Cnwll
59 L9 **Carol Green** Solhll
3 P3 **Carpalla** Cnwll
96 F3 **Carperby** N York
84 H2 **Carr** Rothm
120 F4 **Carradale** Ag & B
148 G3 **Carrbridge** Highld
83 L4 **Carrbrook** Tamesd
11 b1 **Carrefour** Jersey
78 F7 **Carreglefn** IoA
91 J6 **Carr Gate** Wakefd
92 C9 **Carrhouse** N Linc
131 J10 **Carrick** Ag & B
131 P9 **Carrick Castle** Ag & B
134 C11 **Carriden** Falk
87 K9 **Carrington** Lincs
127 Q5 **Carrington** Mdloth
82 F6 **Carrington** Traffd
67 P5 **Carrog** Conwy
68 F6 **Carrog** Denbgs
133 P11 **Carron** Falk
157 N9 **Carron** Moray
116 B11 **Carronbridge** D & G
133 L11 **Carron Bridge** Stirlg
133 P11 **Carronshore** Falk
31 M6 **Carrow Hill** Mons
112 B11 **Carr Shield** Nthumb
109 P6 **Carrutherstown** D & G
125 K2 **Carruth House** Inver
84 G7 **Carr Vale** Derbys
104 B2 **Carrville** Dur
137 N11 **Carsaig** Ag & B
107 K4 **Carseriggan** D & G
109 L9 **Carsethorn** D & G
36 G8 **Carshalton** Gt Lon
71 P4 **Carsington** Derbys
120 C10 **Carskey** Ag & B
107 N7 **Carsluith** D & G
115 L9 **Carsphairn** D & G
126 G8 **Carstairs** S Lans
126 H8 **Carstairs Junction** S Lans
34 B5 **Carswell Marsh** Oxon
22 B10 **Carter's Clay** Hants
51 M8 **Carters Green** Essex
33 Q3 **Carterton** Oxon
112 F10 **Carterway Heads** Nthumb
4 G10 **Carthew** Cnwll
97 M4 **Carthorpe** N York
119 K10 **Cartington** Nthumb
126 F8 **Cartland** S Lans
84 D5 **Cartledge** Derbys
94 H5 **Cartmel** Cumb
95 J3 **Cartmel Fell** Cumb
28 E3 **Carway** Carmth
110 H6 **Carwinley** Cumb
32 F3 **Cashe's Green** Gloucs
12 G2 **Cashmoor** Dorset
34 E2 **Cassington** Oxon
104 B3 **Cassop Colliery** Dur
2 D8 **Castallack** Cnwll
10 b2 **Castel** Guern
79 P11 **Castell** Conwy
31 J6 **Castell-y-bwch** Torfn
95 N5 **Casterton** Cumb
4 H10 **Castle** Cnwll
75 R7 **Castle Acre** Norfk
61 J9 **Castle Ashby** Nhants
168 b18 **Castlebay** W Isls
96 F2 **Castle Bolton** N York
58 H7 **Castle Bromwich** Solhll
73 P7 **Castle Bytham** Lincs
41 K5 **Castlebythe** Pembks
56 B3 **Castle Caereinion** Powys
51 P2 **Castle Camps** Cambs
111 K9 **Castle Carrock** Cumb
126 D2 **Castlecary** Falk
20 B8 **Castle Cary** Somset
32 F9 **Castle Combe** Wilts
72 C5 **Castle Donington** Leics
108 G8 **Castle Douglas** D & G
33 M5 **Castle Eaton** Swindn
104 D3 **Castle Eden** Dur
74 B9 **Castle End** C Pete
91 L5 **Castleford** Wakefd
46 C5 **Castle Frome** Herefs
2 D7 **Castle Gate** Cnwll
95 L2 **Castle Green** Cumb
23 Q2 **Castle Green** Surrey
71 P11 **Castle Gresley** Derbys
52 C4 **Castle Hedingham** Essex
117 J3 **Castlehill** Border
167 L3 **Castlehill** Highld
25 Q2 **Castle Hill** Kent
53 K2 **Castle Hill** Suffk
125 K2 **Castlehill** W Duns
106 F6 **Castle Kennedy** D & G
131 L8 **Castle Lachlan** Ag & B
40 H11 **Castlemartin** Pembks
125 P6 **Castlemilk** C Glas
40 H4 **Castle Morris** Pembks
46 E7 **Castlemorton** Worcs
46 E7 **Castlemorton Common** Worcs
110 D2 **Castle O'er** D & G
56 G4 **Castle Pulverbatch** Shrops
101 J6 **Castlerigg Stone Circle** Cumb
75 N6 **Castle Rising** Norfk
112 G11 **Castleside** Dur
156 C8 **Castle Stuart** Highld
49 M6 **Castlethorpe** M Keyn
92 G9 **Castlethorpe** N Linc
111 K3 **Castleton** Border
83 Q8 **Castleton** Derbys
105 J9 **Castleton** N York
31 J8 **Castleton** Newpt
89 P8 **Castleton** Rochdl
11 P10 **Castletown** Dorset
167 L3 **Castletown** Highld
80 c8 **Castletown** IoM
113 N9 **Castletown** Sundld
97 L11 **Castley** N York
64 D2 **Caston** Norfk
74 B11 **Castor** C Pete
28 G7 **Caswell Bay** Swans
123 R10 **Catacol** N Ayrs
83 M10 **Cat and Fiddle** Derbys
31 Q8 **Catbrain** S Glos
31 P4 **Catbrook** Mons
81 J10 **Catch** Flints
2 C8 **Catchall** Cnwll
59 L9 **Catchem's Corner** Solhll
113 J10 **Catchgate** Dur
84 F3 **Catcliffe** Rothm
33 K9 **Catcomb** Wilts
19 L7 **Catcott** Somset
19 M6 **Catcott Burtle** Somset
36 H9 **Caterham** Surrey
77 M7 **Catfield** Norfk
77 N7 **Catfield Common** Norfk
37 J6 **Catford** Gt Lon
88 F3 **Catforth** Lancs
125 P5 **Cathcart** C Glas
44 G9 **Cathedine** Powys
59 J8 **Catherine-de-Barnes** Solhll
90 D5 **Catherine Slack** C Brad
15 J4 **Catherington** Hants
10 H6 **Catherston Leweston** Dorset
57 M9 **Catherton** Shrops
14 G5 **Catisfield** Hants
46 C6 **Catley** Herefs
89 P7 **Catley Lane Head** Rochdl
147 Q9 **Catlodge** Highld
89 P3 **Catlow** Lancs
111 J5 **Catlowdy** Cumb
51 L3 **Catmere End** Essex
34 E8 **Catmore** W Berk
7 K4 **Caton** Devon
95 L8 **Caton** Lancs
95 M7 **Caton Green** Lancs
8 G9 **Cator Court** Devon
115 K2 **Catrine** E Ayrs
31 L6 **Cat's Ash** Newpt
26 B9 **Catsfield** E Susx
26 B9 **Catsfield Stream** E Susx
19 P9 **Catsgore** Somset
19 Q8 **Catsham** Somset
58 E10 **Catshill** Worcs
57 N5 **Catstree** Shrops
120 C9 **Cattadale** Ag & B
97 P10 **Cattal** N York
53 K5 **Cattawade** Suffk
88 F2 **Catterall** Lancs
69 Q6 **Catteralslane** Shrops
103 P11 **Catterick** N York
103 P11 **Catterick Bridge** N York
103 N11 **Catterick Garrison** N York
101 N4 **Catterlen** Cumb
143 R2 **Catterline** Abers
97 R11 **Catterton** N York
23 Q6 **Catteshall** Surrey
60 C5 **Catthorpe** Leics
64 B8 **Cattishall** Suffk
11 M5 **Cattistock** Dorset
97 N5 **Catton** N York
112 B9 **Catton** Nthumb
99 N11 **Catwick** E R Yk
61 N6 **Catworth** Cambs
32 H2 **Caudle Green** Gloucs
50 B2 **Caulcott** C Beds
48 F10 **Caulcott** Oxon
143 M8 **Cauldcots** Angus
133 J9 **Cauldhame** Stirlg
117 Q7 **Cauldmill** Border
71 K5 **Cauldon** Staffs
71 K5 **Cauldon Lowe** Staffs
71 P11 **Cauldwell** Derbys
109 K9 **Caulkerbush** D & G
110 H4 **Caulside** D & G
11 P2 **Caundle Marsh** Dorset
58 C8 **Caunsall** Worcs
85 M8 **Caunton** Notts
23 K10 **Causeway** Hants
95 K3 **Causeway End** Cumb
107 M6 **Causeway End** D & G
51 Q7 **Causeway End** Essex
116 E3 **Causewayend** S Lans
109 P10 **Causewayhead** Cumb
133 N8 **Causewayhead** Stirlg
151 N4 **Causeyend** Abers
113 J2 **Causey Park** Nthumb

113 J2 Causey Park Bridge Nthumb
63 P11 Cavendish Suffk
63 N6 Cavenham Suffk
48 G9 Caversfield Oxon
35 K10 Caversham Readg
70 H6 Caverswall Staffs
118 D5 Caverton Mill Border
92 C4 Cavil E R Yk
156 E7 Cawdor Highld
86 F5 Cawkwell Lincs
91 P3 Cawood N York
6 C8 Cawsand Cnwll
76 G7 Cawston Norfk
59 Q10 Cawston Warwks
98 F3 Cawthorn N York
90 H9 Cawthorne Barns
98 C5 Cawton N York
62 D9 Caxton Cambs
62 D9 Caxton End Cambs
62 C8 Caxton Gibbet Cambs
57 K10 Caynham Shrops
86 B11 Caythorpe Lincs
85 L11 Caythorpe Notts
99 M4 Cayton N York
168 c11 Ceann a Bhaigh W Isls
146 G5 Ceannacroc Lodge Highld
168 i5 Cearsiadar W Isls
31 P4 Ceciliford Mons
31 J7 Cefn Newpt
80 D11 Cefn Berain Conwy
68 B4 Cefn-brith Conwy
29 K2 Cefn-bryn-brain Carmth
29 M2 Cefn Byrle Powys
68 H8 Cefn Canel Powys
68 F9 Cefn Coch Powys
30 D3 Cefn-coed-y-cymmer Myr Td
29 N8 Cefn Cribwr Brdgnd
29 N8 Cefn Cross Brdgnd
68 C7 Cefn-ddwysarn Gwynd
56 D7 Cefn-Einion Shrops
28 G2 Cefneithin Carmth
44 C5 Cefngorwydd Powys
69 J6 Cefn-mawr Wrexhm
30 D4 Cefnpennar Rhondd
69 K3 Cefn-y-bedd Flints
41 N5 Cefn-y-pant Carmth
78 H9 Ceint IoA
43 M5 Cellan Cerdgn
135 P7 Cellardyke Fife
70 H5 Cellarhead Staffs
101 N5 Celleron Cumb
30 H5 Celynen Caerph
78 F6 Cemaes IoA
55 J3 Cemmaes Powys
55 J4 Cemmaes Road Powys
41 Q2 Cenarth Cerdgn
40 F5 Cerbyd Pembks
135 L5 Ceres Fife
11 P4 Cerne Abbas Dorset
33 L5 Cerney Wick Gloucs
78 G10 Cerrigceinwen IoA
68 C5 Cerrigydrudion Conwy
77 N8 Cess Norfk
67 J2 Ceunant Gwynd
46 G8 Chaceley Gloucs
3 K5 Chacewater Cnwll
49 J7 Chackmore Bucks
48 E6 Chacombe Nhants
47 K5 Chadbury Worcs
89 Q9 Chadderton Oldham
89 Q9 Chadderton Fold Oldham
72 B3 Chaddesden C Derb
58 C10 Chaddesley Corbett Worcs
8 C9 Chaddlehanger Devon
34 D9 Chaddleworth W Berk
48 B10 Chadlington Oxon
48 B4 Chadshunt Warwks
73 K6 Chadwell Leics
57 P2 Chadwell Shrops
61 N7 Chadwell End Bed
37 L3 Chadwell Heath Gt Lon
37 P5 Chadwell St Mary Thurr
58 B11 Chadwick Worcs
59 K10 Chadwick End Solhll
82 B5 Chadwick Green St Hel
10 H2 Chaffcombe Somset
37 P5 Chafford Hundred Thurr
8 H7 Chagford Devon
25 J7 Chailey E Susx
74 H10 Chainbridge Cambs
26 B2 Chainhurst Kent
12 H3 Chalbury Dorset
12 H3 Chalbury Common Dorset
36 H9 Chaldon Surrey
14 E11 Chale IoW
14 E11 Chale Green IoW
36 B2 Chalfont Common Bucks
35 Q6 Chalfont St Giles Bucks
36 B2 Chalfont St Peter Bucks
32 G4 Chalford Gloucs
35 K4 Chalford Oxon
20 G4 Chalford Wilts
50 B5 Chalgrave C Beds
34 H5 Chalgrove Oxon
37 Q6 Chalk Kent
51 P8 Chalk End Essex
35 K9 Chalkhouse Green Oxon
10 H3 Chalkway Somset
38 E9 Chalkwell Kent
6 H10 Challaborough Devon
17 M3 Challacombe Devon
107 L4 Challoch D & G
38 H11 Challock Kent
11 M4 Chalmington Dorset
50 B5 Chalton C Beds
61 P10 Chalton C Beds
23 K11 Chalton Hants
35 Q9 Chalvey Slough
25 M9 Chalvington E Susx
26 F3 Chambers Green Kent
50 C11 Chandler's Cross Herts
46 E7 Chandlers Cross Worcs
22 D11 Chandler's Ford Hants
61 P9 Channel's End Bed
93 J4 Chanterlands Crematorium C KuH
20 D5 Chantry Somset
53 K3 Chantry Suffk
100 H4 Chapel Cumb
134 H9 Chapel Fife
91 J3 Chapel Allerton Leeds
19 M4 Chapel Allerton Somset
4 F6 Chapel Amble Cnwll
60 F7 Chapel Brampton Nhants
62 C2 Chapelbridge Cambs
70 E7 Chapel Chorlton Staffs
25 P6 Chapel Cross E Susx
61 P9 Chapel End Bed
50 C2 Chapel End C Beds
61 P4 Chapel End Cambs
59 M6 Chapel End Warwks
52 B4 Chapelend Way Essex
83 N8 Chapel-en-le-Frith Derbys
89 M9 Chapel Field Bury
74 H6 Chapelgate Lincs
48 E2 Chapel Green Warwks
59 L7 Chapel Green Warwks
91 P5 Chapel Haddlesey N York
126 D5 Chapelhall N Lans
159 Q10 Chapel Hill Abers
86 H10 Chapel Hill Lincs
31 P5 Chapel Hill Mons
97 M11 Chapel Hill N York
117 J7 Chapelhope Border
110 F6 Chapelknowe D & G
56 E9 Chapel Lawn Shrops
95 Q5 Chapel le Dale N York
18 F9 Chapel Leigh Somset
83 N8 Chapel Milton Derbys
151 J3 Chapel of Garioch Abers
106 F9 Chapel Rossan D & G
25 P8 Chapel Row E Susx
52 C11 Chapel Row Essex
34 G11 Chapel Row W Berk
94 E4 Chapels Cumb
87 Q6 Chapel St Leonards Lincs
101 K9 Chapel Stile Cumb
143 L8 Chapelton Angus
17 K6 Chapelton Devon
126 B8 Chapelton S Lans
89 L7 Chapeltown Bl w D
4 D10 Chapel Town Cnwll
149 N3 Chapeltown Moray
91 K11 Chapeltown Sheff
20 F5 Chapmanslade Wilts
5 P3 Chapmans Well Devon
50 H7 Chapmore End Herts
52 E6 Chappel Essex
5 N8 Charaton Cnwll
10 G3 Chard Somset
10 G4 Chard Junction Somset
10 G2 Chardleigh Green Somset
10 G4 Chardstock Devon
32 D6 Charfield S Glos
46 H11 Chargrove Gloucs
26 G2 Charing Kent
26 G2 Charing Crematorium Kent
26 F2 Charing Heath Kent
38 G11 Charing Hill Kent
47 N7 Charingworth Gloucs
48 C11 Charlbury Oxon
32 D11 Charlcombe BaNES
33 J9 Charlcutt Wilts
47 Q3 Charlecote Warwks
58 F6 Charlemont Sandw
17 M5 Charles Devon
23 N6 Charleshill Surrey
142 F8 Charleston Angus
151 N7 Charlestown C Aber
90 F3 Charlestown C Brad
90 B5 Charlestown Calder
3 Q3 Charlestown Cnwll
83 M6 Charlestown Derbys
11 P9 Charlestown Dorset
134 D11 Charlestown Fife
153 Q3 Charlestown Highld
156 A8 Charlestown Highld
82 H4 Charlestown Salfd
64 E11 Charles Tye Suffk
83 M6 Charlesworth Derbys
18 H7 Charlinch Somset
134 H5 Charlottetown Fife
37 K5 Charlton Gt Lon
22 C5 Charlton Hants
50 E5 Charlton Herts
48 F7 Charlton Nhants
112 B4 Charlton Nthumb
34 D7 Charlton Oxon
19 J9 Charlton Somset
20 B6 Charlton Somset
20 C4 Charlton Somset
36 C7 Charlton Surrey
15 N4 Charlton W Susx
20 H10 Charlton Wilts
33 J7 Charlton Wilts
47 K5 Charlton Worcs
58 B10 Charlton Worcs
57 K2 Charlton Wrekin
47 K10 Charlton Abbots Gloucs
19 P9 Charlton Adam Somset
21 N10 Charlton-All-Saints Wilts
11 P5 Charlton Down Dorset
57 K3 Charlton Hill Shrops
20 C10 Charlton Horethorne Somset
47 J10 Charlton Kings Gloucs
19 P9 Charlton Mackrell Somset
12 F4 Charlton Marshall Dorset
20 D9 Charlton Musgrove Somset
48 G11 Charlton-on-Otmoor Oxon
12 E4 Charlton on the Hill Dorset
21 M3 Charlton St Peter Wilts
23 J8 Charlwood Hants
24 F2 Charlwood Surrey
11 P6 Charminster Dorset
10 H6 Charmouth Dorset
49 J10 Charndon Bucks
34 C6 Charney Bassett Oxon
88 H7 Charnock Green Lancs
88 H7 Charnock Richard Lancs
88 H7 Charnock Richard Crematorium Lancs
88 G7 Charnock Richard Services Lancs
65 K10 Charsfield Suffk
38 C11 Chart Corner Kent
22 G3 Charter Alley Hants
129 K10 Charterhall Border
19 N3 Charterhouse Somset
133 M9 Chartershall Stirlg
34 B2 Charterville Allotments Oxon
39 K11 Chartham Kent
39 K11 Chartham Hatch Kent
26 C2 Chart Hill Kent
35 P4 Chartridge Bucks
26 D2 Chart Sutton Kent
38 D11 Chartway Street Kent
35 L9 Charvil Wokham
60 B9 Charwelton Nhants
58 F3 Chase Terrace Staffs
58 F3 Chasetown Staffs
47 P9 Chastleton Oxon
16 E11 Chasty Devon
89 M2 Chatburn Lancs
70 D8 Chatcull Staffs
30 H7 Chatham Caerph
38 C8 Chatham Medway
52 B8 Chatham Green Essex
119 N5 Chathill Nthumb
46 G2 Chatley Worcs
84 C6 Chatsworth House Derbys
38 C7 Chattenden Medway
51 Q5 Chatter End Essex
62 E3 Chatteris Cambs
89 M7 Chatterton Lancs
53 J3 Chattisham Suffk
118 E7 Chatto Border
119 L5 Chatton Nthumb
50 C6 Chaul End C Beds
17 N9 Chawleigh Devon
34 E4 Chawley Oxon
61 Q9 Chawston Bed
23 K7 Chawton Hants
32 D2 Chaxhill Gloucs
35 J9 Chazey Heath Oxon
71 J6 Cheadle Staffs
83 J7 Cheadle Stockp
83 J7 Cheadle Heath Stockp
83 J7 Cheadle Hulme Stockp
36 F8 Cheam Gt Lon
35 P11 Cheapside W & M
35 K2 Chearsley Bucks
70 F9 Chebsey Staffs
35 J8 Checkendon Oxon
70 C5 Checkley Ches E
46 A7 Checkley Herefs
71 J7 Checkley Staffs
70 C5 Checkley Green Ches E
63 N9 Chedburgh Suffk
19 N4 Cheddar Somset
49 P11 Cheddington Bucks
70 H4 Cheddleton Staffs
70 H4 Cheddleton Heath Staffs
18 H9 Cheddon Fitzpaine Somset
32 H6 Chedglow Wilts
65 M2 Chedgrave Norfk
11 K3 Chedington Dorset
65 M6 Chediston Suffk
65 M6 Chediston Green Suffk
33 L2 Chedworth Gloucs
19 K7 Chedzoy Somset
26 H4 Cheeseman's Green Kent
82 H4 Cheetham Hill Manch
8 H2 Cheldon Devon
82 H10 Chelford Ches E
72 B4 Chellaston C Derb
61 L9 Chellington Bed
57 N7 Chelmarsh Shrops
56 H6 Chelmick Shrops
53 M4 Chelmondiston Suffk
83 P11 Chelmorton Derbys
52 B10 Chelmsford Essex
51 Q9 Chelmsford Crematorium Essex
59 J7 Chelmsley Wood Solhll
36 G5 Chelsea Gt Lon
37 L8 Chelsfield Gt Lon
37 J9 Chelsham Surrey
18 G10 Chelston Somset
52 G3 Chelsworth Suffk
46 H10 Cheltenham Gloucs
47 J10 Cheltenham Crematorium Gloucs
61 L7 Chelveston Nhants
31 N11 Chelvey N Som
20 B2 Chelwood BaNES
25 K5 Chelwood Common E Susx
25 K4 Chelwood Gate E Susx
33 J6 Chelworth Wilts
33 L6 Chelworth Lower Green Wilts
33 L6 Chelworth Upper Green Wilts
56 G8 Cheney Longville Shrops
50 B11 Chenies Bucks
31 P6 Chepstow Mons
89 K9 Chequerbent Bolton
75 J9 Chequers Corner Norfk
33 K10 Cherhill Wilts
32 H5 Cherington Gloucs
47 Q7 Cherington Warwks
17 N2 Cheriton Devon
22 G9 Cheriton Hants
27 M4 Cheriton Kent
28 E6 Cheriton Swans
9 J6 Cheriton Bishop Devon
9 L3 Cheriton Fitzpaine Devon
41 J11 Cheriton or Stackpole Elidor Pembks
70 B11 Cherrington Wrekin
92 G2 Cherry Burton E R Yk
62 G9 Cherry Hinton Cambs
46 G4 Cherry Orchard Worcs
86 D6 Cherry Willingham Lincs
36 B7 Chertsey Surrey
48 F9 Cherwell Valley Services Oxon
12 C5 Cheselbourne Dorset
35 Q4 Chesham Bucks
89 N8 Chesham Bury
35 Q5 Chesham Bois Bucks
51 J10 Cheshunt Herts
11 N9 Chesil Beach Dorset
38 E9 Chesley Kent
58 E3 Cheslyn Hay Staffs
59 J10 Chessetts Wood Warwks
36 E8 Chessington Gt Lon
36 E8 Chessington World of Adventures Gt Lon
81 N11 Chester Ches W
20 C6 Chesterblade Somset
81 N11 Chester Cathedral Ches W
81 M11 Chester Crematorium Ches W
84 E6 Chesterfield Derbys
58 G3 Chesterfield Staffs
84 E6 Chesterfield Crematorium Derbys
84 F8 Chesterfield Services Derbys
128 B7 Chesterhill Mdloth
113 L10 Chester-le-Street Dur
113 L11 Chester Moor Dur
118 B6 Chesters Border
118 B8 Chesters Border
81 P10 Chester Services Ches W
62 G8 Chesterton Cambs
74 B11 Chesterton Cambs
33 K4 Chesterton Gloucs
48 G10 Chesterton Oxon
57 P5 Chesterton Shrops
70 E5 Chesterton Staffs
48 C3 Chesterton Green Warwks
112 B7 Chesterwood Nthumb
81 N10 Chester Zoo Ches W
39 K8 Chestfield Kent
38 E9 Chestnut Street Kent
6 H7 Cheston Devon
70 C8 Cheswardine Shrops
129 Q10 Cheswick Nthumb
58 H9 Cheswick Green Solhll
11 N3 Chetnole Dorset
9 N2 Chettiscombe Devon
62 H4 Chettisham Cambs
12 G2 Chettle Dorset
57 M6 Chetton Shrops
48 H9 Chetwode Bucks
70 C10 Chetwynd Wrekin
70 D11 Chetwynd Aston Wrekin
63 L8 Cheveley Cambs
37 L9 Chevening Kent
14 E10 Cheverton IoW
63 N9 Chevington Suffk
118 E9 Cheviot Hills
18 C10 Chevithorne Devon
19 Q2 Chew Magna BaNES
89 K9 Chew Moor Bolton
19 Q2 Chew Stoke BaNES
32 C11 Chewton Keynsham BaNES
19 Q4 Chewton Mendip Somset
8 F5 Chichacott Devon
49 P5 Chicheley M Keyn
15 N6 Chichester W Susx
15 N5 Chichester Crematorium W Susx
11 N8 Chickerell Dorset
65 J6 Chickering Suffk
20 H8 Chicklade Wilts
45 K4 Chickward Herefs
23 J11 Chidden Hants
23 Q7 Chiddingfold Surrey
25 M8 Chiddingly E Susx
37 M12 Chiddingstone Kent
37 M11 Chiddingstone Causeway Kent
11 J6 Chideock Dorset
15 L6 Chidham W Susx
90 H6 Chidswell Kirk
34 E10 Chieveley W Berk
34 E10 Chieveley Services W Berk
51 Q8 Chignall St James Essex
51 Q8 Chignall Smealy Essex
37 K2 Chigwell Essex
37 L2 Chigwell Row Essex
22 C6 Chilbolton Hants
22 F9 Chilcomb Hants
11 L6 Chilcombe Dorset
20 B4 Chilcompton Somset
59 L2 Chilcote Leics
81 M9 Childer Thornton Ches W
12 D2 Child Okeford Dorset
34 C7 Childrey Oxon
70 B9 Child's Ercall Shrops
47 L7 Childswickham Worcs
81 N7 Childwall Lpool
50 D8 Childwick Bury Herts
50 D8 Childwick Green Herts
11 M5 Chilfrome Dorset
15 M4 Chilgrove W Susx
39 J11 Chilham Kent
8 B4 Chilla Devon
8 B8 Chillaton Devon
39 N11 Chillenden Kent
14 E10 Chillerton IoW
65 M11 Chillesford Suffk
119 L5 Chillingham Nthumb
7 K10 Chillington Devon
10 H2 Chillington Somset
21 J8 Chilmark Wilts
26 G3 Chilmington Green Kent
48 B11 Chilson Oxon
5 Q7 Chilsworthy Cnwll
16 E10 Chilsworthy Devon
50 D7 Chiltern Green C Beds
35 L5 Chiltern Hills
35 P5 Chilterns Crematorium Bucks
19 P11 Chilthorne Domer Somset
35 J2 Chilton Bucks
9 L4 Chilton Devon
103 Q5 Chilton Dur
27 N3 Chilton Kent
34 E7 Chilton Oxon
52 E3 Chilton Suffk
22 G6 Chilton Candover Hants
19 Q10 Chilton Cantelo Somset
34 B10 Chilton Foliat Wilts
19 L6 Chilton Polden Somset
63 N11 Chilton Street Suffk
19 J7 Chilton Trinity Somset
72 E3 Chilwell Notts
22 D11 Chilworth Hants
36 B11 Chilworth Surrey
34 C4 Chimney Oxon
23 J3 Chineham Hants
37 J2 Chingford Gt Lon
83 M8 Chinley Derbys
35 L4 Chinnor Oxon
112 C5 Chipchase Castle Nthumb
70 C8 Chipnall Shrops
63 L7 Chippenham Cambs
32 H10 Chippenham Wilts
50 B10 Chipperfield Herts
51 J4 Chipping Herts
89 J2 Chipping Lancs
47 N7 Chipping Campden Gloucs
52 D8 Chipping Hill Essex
48 B9 Chipping Norton Oxon
51 N10 Chipping Ongar Essex
32 D8 Chipping Sodbury S Glos
48 E5 Chipping Warden Nhants
18 D9 Chipstable Somset
37 M9 Chipstead Kent
36 G9 Chipstead Surrey
56 D5 Chirbury Shrops
69 J7 Chirk Wrexhm
129 M8 Chirnside Border
129 M8 Chirnsidebridge Border
21 L3 Chirton Wilts
33 Q11 Chisbury Wilts
11 K2 Chiselborough Somset
33 N8 Chiseldon Swindn
34 G5 Chiselhampton Oxon
117 N8 Chisholme Border
37 K6 Chislehurst Gt Lon
39 M9 Chislet Kent
90 C5 Chisley Calder
50 D10 Chiswell Green Herts
36 F5 Chiswick Gt Lon
62 E11 Chiswick End Cambs
83 L6 Chisworth Derbys
26 D7 Chitcombe E Susx
23 M10 Chithurst W Susx
62 G7 Chittering Cambs
21 J6 Chitterne Wilts
17 M7 Chittlehamholt Devon
17 L6 Chittlehampton Devon
33 J11 Chittoe Wilts
7 K11 Chivelstone Devon
17 J5 Chivenor Devon
106 F5 Chlenry D & G
23 Q2 Chobham Surrey
21 P6 Cholderton Wilts
35 P3 Cholesbury Bucks
112 D6 Chollerford Nthumb
112 D6 Chollerton Nthumb
70 A3 Cholmondeston Ches E
34 G7 Cholsey Oxon
45 P3 Cholstrey Herefs
104 G11 Chop Gate N York
113 L4 Choppington Nthumb
112 H9 Chopwell Gatesd
69 Q4 Chorley Ches E
88 H7 Chorley Lancs
57 M8 Chorley Shrops
58 G2 Chorley Staffs
50 B11 Chorleywood Herts
50 B11 Chorleywood West Herts
70 C4 Chorlton Ches E
82 H6 Chorlton-cum-Hardy Manch
69 N5 Chorlton Lane Ches W
56 F7 Choulton Shrops
69 N3 Chowley Ches W
51 K3 Chrishall Essex
124 G3 Chrisswell Inver
75 J11 Christchurch Cambs
13 L6 Christchurch Dorset
31 Q2 Christchurch Gloucs
31 K7 Christchurch Newpt
33 J9 Christian Malford Wilts
81 N11 Christleton Ches W
35 K6 Christmas Common Oxon
19 L3 Christon N Som
119 P6 Christon Bank Nthumb
9 K7 Christow Devon
24 D5 Christ's Hospital W Susx
25 L4 Chuck Hatch E Susx
9 L9 Chudleigh Devon
9 K9 Chudleigh Knighton Devon
17 M9 Chulmleigh Devon
83 M6 Chunal Derbys
89 L5 Church Lancs
46 E11 Churcham Gloucs
70 C11 Church Aston Wrekin
60 F7 Church Brampton Nhants
102 E8 Church Brough Cumb
71 N8 Church Broughton Derbys
3 J11 Church Cove Cnwll
23 M4 Church Crookham Hants
46 G11 Churchdown Gloucs
70 E11 Church Eaton Staffs
61 N9 Church End Bed
61 P9 Church End Bed
35 K3 Church End Bucks
49 Q10 Church End C Beds
49 Q8 Church End C Beds
50 B4 Church End C Beds
50 B7 Church End C Beds
50 E3 Church End C Beds
61 Q10 Church End C Beds
61 N6 Church End Cambs
62 B4 Church End Cambs
62 D5 Church End Cambs
62 G9 Church End Cambs
38 H3 Churchend Essex
51 P6 Church End Essex
52 B6 Church End Essex
52 B8 Church End Essex
46 G7 Church End Gloucs
36 F2 Church End Gt Lon
23 J3 Church End Hants
50 D8 Church End Herts
50 G4 Church End Herts
51 K6 Church End Herts
74 D4 Church End Lincs
93 R11 Church End Lincs
59 K6 Church End Warwks
59 L6 Church End Warwks
48 C9 Church Enstone Oxon
91 N3 Church Fenton N York
58 F6 Churchfield Sandw
50 H10 Churchgate Herts
51 L8 Churchgate Street Essex
10 D5 Church Green Devon
71 P11 Church Gresley Derbys
34 D2 Church Hanborough Oxon
58 F2 Church Hill Staffs
105 J11 Church Houses N York
10 F4 Churchill Devon
17 K3 Churchill Devon
19 M3 Churchill N Som
47 Q10 Churchill Oxon
46 H4 Churchill Worcs
58 C9 Churchill Worcs
10 E2 Churchinford Somset
12 F8 Church Knowle Dorset
85 P5 Church Laneham Notts
60 F2 Church Langton Leics
59 Q9 Church Lawford Warwks
70 E3 Church Lawton Ches E
71 J7 Church Leigh Staffs
47 K4 Church Lench Worcs
71 M6 Church Mayfield Staffs
70 B2 Church Minshull Ches E
15 N7 Church Norton W Susx
60 B4 Churchover Warwks
57 J5 Church Preen Shrops
56 G4 Church Pulverbatch Shrops
10 D2 Churchstanton Somset
56 D6 Churchstoke Powys

7 J9 Churchstow Devon
60 D9 Church Stowe Nhants
52 C3 Church Street Essex
38 B7 Church Street Kent
65 P5 Church Street Suffk
56 H6 Church Stretton Shrops
93 P11 Churchthorpe Lincs
88 C2 Churchtown Bpool
4 H6 Churchtown Cnwll
84 C8 Churchtown Derbys
17 M3 Churchtown Devon
80 f3 Churchtown IoM
88 F2 Churchtown Lancs
92 C9 Church Town N Linc
88 D7 Churchtown Sefton
30 E7 Church Village Rhondd
85 J7 Church Warsop Notts
72 C4 Church Wilne Derbys
111 N5 Churnsike Lodge Nthumb
7 N7 Churston Ferrers Torbay
23 N7 Churt Surrey
69 M3 Churton Ches W
90 H5 Churwell Leeds
66 G7 Chwilog Gwynd
2 D7 Chyandour Cnwll
2 H9 Chyanvounder Cnwll
3 K5 Chyeowling Cnwll
2 D7 Chysauster Cnwll
2 H9 Chyvarloe Cnwll
56 B4 Cil Powys
80 H11 Cilcain Flints
43 K2 Cilcennin Cerdgn
56 C4 Cilcewydd Powys
29 L4 Cilfrew Neath
30 E6 Cilfynydd Rhondd
41 N2 Cilgerran Pembks
43 P9 Cilgwyn Carmth
66 H4 Cilgwyn Gwynd
43 K3 Ciliau-Aeron Cerdgn
29 K3 Cilmaengwyn Neath
44 E4 Cilmery Powys
41 Q4 Cilrhedyn Pembks
43 L10 Cilsan Carmth
68 A6 Ciltalgarth Gwynd
43 Q7 Cilycwm Carmth
29 L5 Cimla Neath
32 C2 Cinderford Gloucs
58 D6 Cinder Hill Wolves
35 Q8 Cippenham Slough
33 K4 Cirencester Gloucs
103 P11 Citadilla N York
36 H4 City Gt Lon
30 C9 City V Glam
37 K4 City Airport Gt Lon
78 H7 City Dulas IoA
37 K3 City of London Crematorium Gt Lon
136 F4 Clabhach Ag & B
131 N11 Clachaig Ag & B
123 N8 Clachan Ag & B
130 F4 Clachan Ag & B
138 F9 Clachan Ag & B
153 J10 Clachan Highld
168 d11 Clachan-a-Luib W Isls
136 B6 Clachan Mor Ag & B
168 d11 Clachan na Luib W Isls
125 Q2 Clachan of Campsie E Duns
130 F4 Clachan-Seil Ag & B
156 A8 Clachnaharry Highld
164 B11 Clachtoll Highld
142 A5 Clackavoid P & K
37 K10 Clacket Lane Services Surrey
133 Q9 Clackmannan Clacks
157 N6 Clackmarras Moray
53 L8 Clacton-on-Sea Essex
131 M3 Cladich Ag & B
47 L3 Cladswell Worcs
138 C8 Claggan Highld
152 C7 Claigan Highld
20 C3 Clandown BaNES
23 J11 Clanfield Hants
33 Q4 Clanfield Oxon
8 H4 Clannaborough Devon
22 B5 Clanville Hants
20 B8 Clanville Somset
123 Q8 Claonaig Ag & B
12 H4 Clapgate Dorset
51 K6 Clapgate Herts
61 M10 Clapham Bed
9 L7 Clapham Devon
36 G5 Clapham Gt Lon
95 Q7 Clapham N York
24 C9 Clapham W Susx
61 M10 Clapham Green Bed
27 J4 Clap Hill Kent
101 L10 Clappersgate Cumb
11 J3 Clapton Somset
20 B4 Clapton Somset
31 N10 Clapton-in-Gordano N Som
47 N11 Clapton-on-the-Hill Gloucs
17 M7 Clapworthy Devon
54 E8 Clarach Cerdgn
112 H8 Claravale Gatesd
41 L6 Clarbeston Pembks
41 K6 Clarbeston Road Pembks
85 M4 Clarborough Notts
63 N11 Clare Suffk
108 G7 Clarebrand D & G
109 N7 Clarencefield D & G
112 F7 Clarewood Nthumb
117 Q7 Clarilaw Border
22 G4 Clarken Green Hants
24 E3 Clark's Green Surrey
125 P6 Clarkston E Rens
162 G9 Clashmore Highld
164 B10 Clashmore Highld
164 C10 Clashnessie Highld
149 N3 Clashnoir Moray
134 B3 Clathy P & K
134 C3 Clathymore P & K
150 E2 Clatt Abers
55 M6 Clatter Powys
51 P8 Clatterford End Essex
18 E8 Clatworthy Somset
88 G3 Claughton Lancs
95 M7 Claughton Lancs
81 L7 Claughton Wirral
19 J8 Clavelshay Somset
59 J11 Claverdon Warwks
31 N11 Claverham N Som
51 L4 Clavering Essex
57 P6 Claverley Shrops
20 E2 Claverton BaNES
20 E2 Claverton Down BaNES
30 E9 Clawdd-coch V Glam
68 E4 Clawdd-newydd Denbgs
95 L5 Clawthorpe Cumb
5 P2 Clawton Devon
86 F2 Claxby Lincs
87 N6 Claxby Lincs
98 D9 Claxton N York
77 L11 Claxton Norfk
59 Q7 Claybrooke Magna Leics
65 P5 Clay Common Suffk
60 C5 Clay Coton Nhants
84 E8 Clay Cross Derbys
48 E5 Claydon Oxon
53 K2 Claydon Suffk
26 B3 Clay End Herts
110 G5 Claygate D & G
26 B3 Claygate Kent
36 E8 Claygate Surrey
37 P9 Claygate Cross Kent
37 K2 Clayhall Gt Lon
18 D10 Clayhanger Devon
58 F4 Clayhanger Wsall
18 G11 Clayhidon Devon
26 D7 Clayhill E Susx
13 P3 Clayhill Hants
62 H8 Clayhithe Cambs
167 L5 Clayock Highld
62 E10 Claypit Hill Cambs
32 E3 Claypits Gloucs
85 P11 Claypole Lincs
87 M5 Claythorpe Lincs
90 E4 Clayton C Brad
91 M9 Clayton Donc
24 G8 Clayton W Susx
88 H5 Clayton Green Lancs
89 M4 Clayton-le-Moors Lancs
88 H6 Clayton-le-Woods Lancs
90 H8 Clayton West Kirk
85 M3 Clayworth Notts
144 G10 Cleadale Highld
113 N8 Cleadon S Tyne
6 E5 Clearbrook Devon
31 Q3 Clearwell Gloucs
31 Q3 Clearwell Meend Gloucs
103 Q8 Cleasby N York
169 d8 Cleat Ork
103 M7 Cleatlam Dur
100 D8 Cleator Cumb
100 D7 Cleator Moor Cumb
90 F5 Cleckheaton Kirk
57 K8 Cleedownton Shrops
57 K9 Cleehill Shrops
126 D6 Cleekhimin N Lans
57 K8 Clee St Margaret Shrops
57 K9 Cleestanton Shrops
93 P9 Cleethorpes NE Lin
57 L9 Cleeton St Mary Shrops
31 N11 Cleeve N Som
34 H8 Cleeve Oxon
47 J9 Cleeve Hill Gloucs
47 L5 Cleeve Prior Worcs
128 F3 Cleghornie E Loth
45 N7 Clehonger Herefs
134 D8 Cleish P & K
126 D6 Cleland N Lans
50 B8 Clement's End C Beds
37 M6 Clement Street Kent
131 J2 Clenamacrie Ag & B
33 N11 Clench Common Wilts
75 L6 Clenchwarton Norfk
159 J5 Clenerty Abers
58 D9 Clent Worcs
57 M9 Cleobury Mortimer Shrops
57 L7 Cleobury North Shrops
120 C5 Cleongart Ag & B
156 F7 Clephanton Highld
117 K11 Clerkhill D & G
115 R7 Cleuch-head D & G
33 L9 Clevancy Wilts
31 M10 Clevedon N Som
48 C10 Cleveley Oxon
88 C2 Cleveleys Lancs
33 J7 Cleverton Wilts
19 M4 Clewer Somset
76 E3 Cley next the Sea Norfk
101 Q6 Cliburn Cumb
23 J4 Cliddesden Hants
59 K5 Cliff Warwks
89 L4 Cliffe Lancs
38 B6 Cliffe Medway
91 R4 Cliffe N York
103 P7 Cliffe N York
26 E9 Cliff End E Susx
38 B7 Cliffe Woods Medway
45 L4 Clifford Herefs
91 L2 Clifford Leeds
47 N4 Clifford Chambers Warwks
46 D10 Clifford's Mesne Gloucs
39 P9 Cliffsend Kent
31 Q10 Clifton Bristl
50 E3 Clifton C Beds
72 E4 Clifton C Nott
98 B10 Clifton C York
90 F6 Clifton Calder
101 P5 Clifton Cumb
71 M6 Clifton Derbys
17 L3 Clifton Devon
91 N11 Clifton Donc
88 F4 Clifton Lancs
97 J11 Clifton N York
113 K4 Clifton Nthumb
48 E8 Clifton Oxon
82 G4 Clifton Salfd
46 F5 Clifton Worcs
59 L2 Clifton Campville Staffs
34 F5 Clifton Hampden Oxon
49 P4 Clifton Reynes M Keyn
60 B5 Clifton upon Dunsmore Warwks
46 D2 Clifton upon Teme Worcs
39 Q7 Cliftonville Kent
15 Q6 Climping W Susx
20 E5 Clink Somset
97 L9 Clint N York
151 L5 Clinterty C Aber
76 E9 Clint Green Norfk
118 B4 Clintmains Border
55 J2 Clipiau Gwynd
77 N9 Clippesby Norfk
73 P7 Clipsham Rutlnd
60 F4 Clipston Nhants
72 G4 Clipston Notts
49 P9 Clipstone C Beds
85 J8 Clipstone Notts
89 L2 Clitheroe Lancs
69 P10 Clive Shrops
93 J10 Clixby Lincs
33 J6 Cloatley Wilts
68 E4 Clocaenog Denbgs
158 B5 Clochan Moray
82 B6 Clock Face St Hel
56 C3 Cloddiau Powys
45 L9 Clodock Herefs
20 D6 Cloford Somset
159 P9 Clola Abers
50 C3 Clophill C Beds
61 N4 Clopton Nhants
65 J11 Clopton Suffk
65 J11 Clopton Corner Suffk
63 N10 Clopton Green Suffk
64 D10 Clopton Green Suffk
10 c1 Clos du Valle Guern
109 J2 Closeburn D & G
109 K2 Closeburnmill D & G
80 c6 Closeclark IoM
11 M2 Closworth Somset
50 G4 Clothall Herts
69 P2 Clotton Ches W
59 Q7 Cloudesley Bush Warwks
46 A7 Clouds Herefs
89 Q9 Clough Oldham
89 Q6 Clough Foot Calder
90 D7 Clough Head Calder
99 L2 Cloughton N York
105 R11 Cloughton Newlands N York
169 q8 Clousta Shet
142 E3 Clova Angus
16 E7 Clovelly Devon
117 P3 Clovenfords Border
139 J5 Clovulin Highld
89 N5 Clow Bridge Lancs
84 G5 Clowne Derbys
57 N10 Clows Top Worcs
69 L6 Cloy Wrexhm
146 D5 Cluanie Inn Highld
146 D5 Cluanie Lodge Highld
5 M3 Clubworthy Cnwll
107 L6 Clugston D & G
56 E8 Clun Shrops
156 F8 Clunas Highld
56 F8 Clunbury Shrops
41 M7 Clunderwen Carmth
148 D2 Clune Highld
146 F10 Clunes Highld
56 F9 Clungunford Shrops
141 R9 Clunie P & K
56 E8 Clunton Shrops
134 G8 Cluny Fife
20 B3 Clutton BaNES
69 N4 Clutton Ches W
20 B3 Clutton Hill BaNES
67 K2 Clwt-y-bont Gwynd
30 H2 Clydach Mons
29 J4 Clydach Swans
30 C6 Clydach Vale Rhondd
125 M3 Clydebank W Duns
41 Q3 Clydey Pembks
33 L9 Clyffe Pypard Wilts
131 Q11 Clynder Ag & B
29 M4 Clyne Neath
66 G5 Clynnog-fawr Gwynd
45 J6 Clyro Powys
9 N6 Clyst Honiton Devon
9 P4 Clyst Hydon Devon
9 N7 Clyst St George Devon
9 P4 Clyst St Lawrence Devon
9 N6 Clyst St Mary Devon
168 j4 Cnoc W Isls
54 F10 Cnwch Coch Cerdgn
5 M6 Coad's Green Cnwll
84 E5 Coal Aston Derbys
30 G3 Coalbrookvale Blae G
126 E11 Coalburn S Lans
112 H8 Coalburns Gatesd
32 E4 Coaley Gloucs
38 C2 Coalhill Essex
57 M3 Coalmoor Wrekin
32 C8 Coalpit Heath S Glos
58 F5 Coal Pool Wsall
57 M4 Coalport Wrekin
133 Q8 Coalsnaughton Clacks
65 J7 Coal Street Suffk
134 H8 Coaltown of Balgonie Fife
135 J8 Coaltown of Wemyss Fife
72 C8 Coalville Leics
111 N9 Coanwood Nthumb
19 N10 Coat Somset
126 C4 Coatbridge N Lans
126 C4 Coatdyke N Lans
33 N8 Coate Swindn
21 K2 Coate Wilts
74 F11 Coates Cambs
33 J4 Coates Gloucs
86 B4 Coates Lincs
85 P4 Coates Notts
23 Q11 Coates W Susx
104 G5 Coatham R & Cl
103 Q6 Coatham Mundeville Darltn
17 L6 Cobbaton Devon
47 J11 Coberley Gloucs
45 P7 Cobhall Common Herefs
37 Q7 Cobham Kent
36 D8 Cobham Surrey
36 D9 Cobham Services Surrey
51 Q7 Coblers Green Essex
21 K10 Cobley Dorset
45 P2 Cobnash Herefs
10 b1 Cobo Guern
70 F5 Cobridge C Stke
159 M5 Coburby Abers
84 F6 Cock Alley Derbys
104 H11 Cockayne N York
62 C11 Cockayne Hatley C Beds
69 L5 Cock Bank Wrexhm
47 L4 Cock Bevington Warwks
149 P6 Cock Bridge Abers
129 K5 Cockburnspath Border
52 D11 Cock Clarks Essex
63 M10 Cock & End Suffk
128 C4 Cockenzie and Port Seton E Loth
88 G6 Cocker Bar Lancs
89 L5 Cocker Brook Lancs
95 K10 Cockerham Lancs
100 F4 Cockermouth Cumb
50 D6 Cockernhoe Herts
90 G5 Cockersdale Leeds
28 H6 Cockett Swans
103 M6 Cockfield Dur
64 C11 Cockfield Suffk
50 G11 Cockfosters Gt Lon
51 Q7 Cock Green Essex
23 N11 Cocking W Susx
23 N11 Cocking Causeway W Susx
7 M6 Cockington Torbay
19 M5 Cocklake Somset
100 H10 Cockley Beck Cumb
75 Q10 Cockley Cley Norfk
26 E8 Cock Marling E Susx
35 L8 Cockpole Green Wokham
3 K3 Cocks Cnwll
57 K7 Cockshutford Shrops
69 M9 Cockshutt Shrops
38 C11 Cock Street Kent
76 D3 Cockthorpe Norfk
2 E7 Cockwells Cnwll
9 N8 Cockwood Devon
18 H6 Cockwood Somset
83 M9 Cockyard Derbys
45 N8 Cockyard Herefs
64 G11 Coddenham Suffk
69 N3 Coddington Ches W
46 D6 Coddington Herefs
85 P10 Coddington Notts
21 J7 Codford St Mary Wilts
21 J7 Codford St Peter Wilts
50 F7 Codicote Herts
24 C6 Codmore Hill W Susx
84 F11 Codnor Derbys
32 D9 Codrington S Glos
58 C4 Codsall Staffs
58 B4 Codsall Wood Staffs
30 D7 Coedely Rhondd
31 J8 Coedkernew Newpt
31 L2 Coed Morgan Mons
69 J4 Coedpoeth Wrexhm
69 J3 Coed Talon Flints
69 K11 Coedway Powys
42 G5 Coed-y-Bryn Cerdgn
31 L6 Coed-y-caerau Newpt
31 K5 Coed-y-paen Mons
44 H10 Coed-yr-ynys Powys
67 K10 Coed Ystumgwern Gwynd
29 N2 Coelbren Powys
7 M5 Coffinswell Devon
61 M9 Coffle End Bed
9 N8 Cofton Devon
58 F9 Cofton Hackett Worcs
30 G10 Cogan V Glam
60 H8 Cogenhoe Nhants
34 C3 Cogges Oxon
52 E7 Coggeshall Essex
25 N5 Coggin's Mill E Susx
148 C4 Coignafearn Highld
149 Q8 Coilacriech Abers
132 H6 Coilantogle Stirlg
152 F10 Coillore Highld
29 P8 Coity Brdgnd
168 j4 Col W Isls
162 D4 Colaboll Highld
4 D9 Colan Cnwll
10 B7 Colaton Raleigh Devon
152 C8 Colbost Highld
103 N11 Colburn N York
102 C6 Colby Cumb
80 b7 Colby IoM
77 J5 Colby Norfk
52 G6 Colchester Essex
52 G7 Colchester Crematorium Essex
34 F11 Cold Ash W Berk
60 E5 Cold Ashby Nhants
32 E10 Cold Ashton S Glos
47 M11 Cold Aston Gloucs
165 P4 Coldbackie Highld
102 D10 Coldbeck Cumb
41 M8 Cold Blow Pembks
49 P4 Cold Brayfield M Keyn
95 Q6 Cold Cotes N York
24 H9 Coldean Br & H
7 L4 Coldeast Devon
90 B5 Colden Calder
22 E10 Colden Common Hants
65 N9 Coldfair Green Suffk
74 H10 Coldham Cambs
86 D4 Cold Hanworth Lincs
3 K4 Coldharbour Cnwll
9 Q2 Coldharbour Devon
31 Q4 Coldharbour Gloucs
50 D7 Cold Harbour Herts
34 H9 Cold Harbour Oxon
24 D2 Coldharbour Surrey
20 G5 Cold Harbour Wilts
70 A10 Cold Hatton Wrekin
70 A10 Cold Hatton Heath Wrekin
113 P11 Cold Hesledon Dur
91 K8 Cold Hiendley Wakefd
49 J4 Cold Higham Nhants
129 N6 Coldingham Border
98 A4 Cold Kirby N York
70 F8 Coldmeece Staffs
73 J9 Cold Newton Leics
5 L4 Cold Northcott Cnwll
52 E11 Cold Norton Essex
73 L8 Cold Overton Leics
27 N2 Coldred Kent
17 M10 Coldridge Devon
118 F3 Coldstream Border
24 B7 Coldwaltham W Susx
45 N7 Coldwell Herefs
159 N10 Coldwells Abers
57 K8 Cold Weston Shrops
20 C8 Cole Somset
56 E7 Colebatch Shrops
6 E7 Colebrook C Plym
9 P3 Colebrook Devon
9 J5 Colebrooke Devon
86 C8 Coleby Lincs
92 E7 Coleby N Linc
59 K7 Cole End Warwks
9 J4 Coleford Devon
31 Q2 Coleford Gloucs
20 C5 Coleford Somset
18 F8 Coleford Water Somset
64 H4 Colegate End Norfk
50 G8 Cole Green Herts
51 K4 Cole Green Herts
22 E4 Cole Henley Hants
12 H4 Colehill Dorset
50 E8 Coleman Green Herts
25 K4 Coleman's Hatch E Susx
69 M8 Colemere Shrops
23 K8 Colemore Hants
57 N5 Colemore Green Shrops
134 E2 Colenden P & K
72 C7 Coleorton Leics
32 F10 Colerne Wilts
33 K2 Colesbourne Gloucs
7 K9 Cole's Cross Devon
10 H4 Coles Cross Dorset
61 P9 Colesden Bed
53 K3 Coles Green Suffk
35 P5 Coleshill Bucks
33 P6 Coleshill Oxon
59 K7 Coleshill Warwks
10 B4 Colestocks Devon
19 Q3 Coley BaNES
24 F4 Colgate W Susx
135 M7 Colinsburgh Fife
127 N4 Colinton C Edin
124 C3 Colintraive Ag & B
76 C6 Colkirk Norfk
136 G4 Coll Ag & B
142 C11 Collace P & K
169 q5 Collafirth Shet
136 F4 Coll Airport Ag & B
7 J11 Collaton Devon
7 M6 Collaton St Mary Torbay
157 L4 College of Roseisle Moray
23 N2 College Town Br For
134 H5 Collessie Fife
17 M8 Colleton Mills Devon
37 M2 Collier Row Gt Lon
51 J6 Collier's End Herts
26 C7 Collier's Green E Susx
26 C4 Colliers Green Kent
26 B2 Collier Street Kent
113 M11 Colliery Row Sundld
151 Q2 Collieston Abers
109 M5 Collin D & G
21 P4 Collingbourne Ducis Wilts
21 P3 Collingbourne Kingston Wilts
97 N11 Collingham Leeds
85 P8 Collingham Notts
46 B2 Collington Herefs
60 G9 Collingtree Nhants
82 C6 Collins Green Warrtn
46 D3 Collins Green Worcs
143 L8 Colliston Angus
10 B4 Colliton Devon
73 P10 Collyweston Nhants
114 B10 Colmonell S Ayrs
61 P9 Colmworth Bed
36 B5 Colnbrook Slough
62 E5 Colne Cambs
89 P3 Colne Lancs
90 F6 Colne Bridge Kirk
89 P2 Colne Edge Lancs
52 D5 Colne Engaine Essex
76 H10 Colney Norfk
50 F9 Colney Heath Herts
50 E10 Colney Street Herts
33 L3 Coln Rogers Gloucs
33 M3 Coln St Aldwyns Gloucs
33 L2 Coln St Dennis Gloucs
136 b2 Colonsay Ag & B
136 b3 Colonsay Airport Ag & B
158 F11 Colpy Abers
117 L2 Colquhar Border
4 H7 Colquite Cnwll
16 F9 Colscott Devon
96 H4 Colsterdale N York
73 N6 Colsterworth Lincs
73 J4 Colston Bassett Notts
157 L5 Coltfield Moray
23 L4 Colt Hill Hants
77 K8 Coltishall Norfk
94 G3 Colton Cumb
91 K4 Colton Leeds
91 N2 Colton N York
76 G10 Colton Norfk
71 J10 Colton Staffs
25 P2 Colt's Hill Kent
9 N5 Columbjohn Devon
44 H4 Colva Powys
109 J10 Colvend D & G
46 E6 Colwall Herefs
112 E5 Colwell Nthumb
71 J10 Colwich Staffs
72 G2 Colwick Notts
29 P9 Colwinston V Glam
15 P6 Colworth W Susx
80 B9 Colwyn Bay Conwy
10 F6 Colyford Devon
10 E6 Colyton Devon
7 J11 Combe Devon
45 L2 Combe Herefs
48 D11 Combe Oxon
22 C2 Combe W Berk
12 G5 Combe Almer Dorset
23 P7 Combe Common Surrey
20 E2 Combe Down BaNES
7 L5 Combe Fishacre Devon
18 G8 Combe Florey Somset
20 D3 Combe Hay BaNES
7 N4 Combeinteignhead Devon
17 K2 Combe Martin Devon
10 D4 Combe Raleigh Devon
82 D9 Comberbach Ches W
59 J3 Comberford Staffs
62 E9 Comberton Cambs
56 H11 Comberton Herefs
10 G2 Combe St Nicholas Somset
10 F6 Combpyne Devon
71 K7 Combridge Staffs
48 B4 Combrook Warwks
83 M9 Combs Derbys
64 E10 Combs Suffk
64 E10 Combs Ford Suffk
19 J6 Combwich Somset
150 H6 Comers Abers
58 B11 Comhampton Worcs
63 J8 Commercial End Cambs
55 J4 Commins Coch Powys
105 J8 Commondale N York
88 C4 Common Edge Bpool
100 D6 Common End Cumb
5 L8 Common Moor Cnwll
33 M7 Common Platt Wilts
82 B10 Commonside Ches W
71 N6 Commonside Derbys
84 D5 Common Side Derbys
69 N9 Commonwood Shrops
69 L4 Commonwood Wrexhm
19 J8 Compass Somset
83 L6 Compstall Stockp
108 E10 Compstonend D & G
7 M6 Compton Devon
22 B9 Compton Hants
22 E9 Compton Hants
57 Q8 Compton Staffs
23 Q5 Compton Surrey
34 F8 Compton W Berk
15 L4 Compton W Susx
21 M4 Compton Wilts
20 G11 Compton Abbas Dorset
47 L11 Compton Abdale Gloucs

33 K10 Compton Bassett Wilts
33 Q7 Compton Beauchamp Oxon
19 L3 Compton Bishop Somset
21 K9 Compton Chamberlayne Wilts
20 B2 Compton Dando BaNES
19 N8 Compton Dundon Somset
19 M11 Compton Durville Somset
31 Q8 Compton Greenfield S Glos
19 P3 Compton Martin BaNES
20 B9 Compton Pauncefoot Somset
11 M6 Compton Valence Dorset
48 B4 Compton Verney Warwks
134 C10 Comrie Fife
133 M3 Comrie P & K
139 J4 Conaglen House Highld
145 Q2 Conchra Highld
141 Q9 Concraigie P & K
95 K9 Conder Green Lancs
47 J7 Conderton Worcs
47 N9 Condicote Gloucs
126 C3 Condorrat N Lans
56 H3 Condover Shrops
46 G11 Coney Hill Gloucs
24 D6 Coneyhurst Common W Susx
98 E6 Coneysthorpe N York
97 N9 Coneythorpe N York
64 D6 Coney Weston Suffk
23 M8 Conford Hants
5 M6 Congdon's Shop Cnwll
72 B9 Congerstone Leics
75 P6 Congham Norfk
70 F2 Congleton Ches E
67 N6 Congl-y-wal Gwynd
19 M2 Congresbury N Som
58 D2 Congreve Staffs
109 L7 Conheath D & G
156 H7 Conicavel Moray
86 H9 Coningsby Lincs
61 Q3 Conington Cambs
62 D7 Conington Cambs
91 N11 Conisbrough Donc
93 R11 Conisholme Lincs
101 K11 Coniston Cumb
93 L3 Coniston E R Yk
96 D10 Coniston Cold N York
96 E7 Conistone N York
81 K11 Connah's Quay Flints
138 G11 Connel Ag & B
115 M5 Connel Park E Ayrs
2 F6 Connor Downs Cnwll
155 P6 Conon Bridge Highld
96 E11 Cononley N York
70 H5 Consall Staffs
112 H10 Consett Dur
97 J2 Constable Burton N York
89 N6 Constable Lee Lancs
3 J8 Constantine Cnwll
4 D7 Constantine Bay Cnwll
155 N6 Contin Highld
79 P9 Conwy Conwy
38 G9 Conyer Kent
64 B8 Conyer's Green Suffk
26 B10 Cooden E Susx
16 G10 Cookbury Devon
16 F10 Cookbury Wick Devon
35 N7 Cookham W & M
35 N7 Cookham Dean W & M
35 N7 Cookham Rise W & M
47 L3 Cookhill Worcs
65 L6 Cookley Suffk
58 B8 Cookley Worcs
35 J6 Cookley Green Oxon
151 M9 Cookney Abers
25 K8 Cooksbridge E Susx
58 D11 Cooksey Green Worcs
53 L8 Cook's Green Essex
64 D11 Cooks Green Suffk
70 G6 Cookshill Staffs
4 H8 Cooksland Cnwll
51 P9 Cooksmill Green Essex
82 C10 Cookson Green Ches W
24 D6 Coolham W Susx
38 C6 Cooling Medway
38 B7 Cooling Street Medway
2 G5 Coombe Cnwll
3 L5 Coombe Cnwll
3 N3 Coombe Cnwll
7 N4 Coombe Devon
9 K8 Coombe Devon
10 C6 Coombe Devon
32 E6 Coombe Gloucs
23 J10 Coombe Hants
21 M4 Coombe Wilts
21 M9 Coombe Bissett Wilts
7 N4 Coombe Cellars Devon
23 J10 Coombe Cross Hants
46 G9 Coombe Hill Gloucs
12 D8 Coombe Keynes Dorset
7 N5 Coombe Pafford Torbay
24 E9 Coombes W Susx
45 M2 Coombes-Moor Herefs
20 E8 Coombe Street Somset
58 E7 Coombeswood Dudley
51 L10 Coopersale Common Essex
51 L10 Coopersale Street Essex
37 L11 Cooper's Corner Kent
25 L6 Coopers Green E Susx
50 E9 Coopers Green Herts
39 P9 Cooper Street Kent
89 J9 Cooper Turning Bolton
24 C8 Cootham W Susx
53 K3 Copdock Suffk
52 F7 Copford Green Essex
97 M8 Copgrove N York
169 r6 Copister Shet
61 P11 Cople Bed
90 D6 Copley Calder
103 L5 Copley Dur
83 L5 Copley Tamesd
83 Q9 Coplow Dale Derbys
98 B11 Copmanthorpe C York
70 E9 Copmere End Staffs
88 E3 Copp Lancs
16 C11 Coppathorne Cnwll
70 G11 Coppenhall Staffs
70 C3 Coppenhall Moss Ches E
2 F6 Copperhouse Cnwll
57 N8 Coppicegate Shrops
61 Q5 Coppingford Cambs
26 F2 Coppins Corner Kent
9 J4 Copplestone Devon
88 H8 Coppull Lancs
88 H8 Coppull Moor Lancs
24 E6 Copsale W Susx
89 K4 Copster Green Lancs
59 Q7 Copston Magna Warwks
39 N9 Cop Street Kent
51 K10 Copthall Green Essex
59 J9 Copt Heath Solhll
97 M6 Copt Hewick N York
5 M3 Copthorne Cnwll
24 H3 Copthorne W Susx
72 D8 Copt Oak Leics
76 C4 Copy's Green Norfk
13 P2 Copythorne Hants
52 H3 Coram Street Suffk
37 N3 Corbets Tey Gt Lon
11 a2 Corbiere Jersey
112 E8 Corbridge Nthumb
61 J3 Corby Nhants
73 Q6 Corby Glen Lincs
111 J9 Corby Hill Cumb
121 K5 Cordon N Ayrs
84 D5 Cordwell Derbys
57 L10 Coreley Shrops
35 P7 Cores End Bucks
18 H11 Corfe Somset
12 G8 Corfe Castle Dorset
12 G5 Corfe Mullen Dorset
56 H7 Corfton Shrops
149 P6 Corgarff Abers
22 H10 Corhampton Hants
25 Q2 Corks Pond Kent
59 M7 Corley Warwks
59 L7 Corley Ash Warwks
59 L8 Corley Moor Warwks
59 M7 Corley Services Warwks
142 E4 Cormuir Angus
52 E3 Cornard Tye Suffk
8 G7 Corndon Devon
88 E4 Corner Row Lancs
94 C2 Corney Cumb
104 B4 Cornforth Dur
158 E6 Cornhill Abers
118 G3 Cornhill-on-Tweed Nthumb
89 Q5 Cornholme Calder
51 Q3 Cornish Hall End Essex
136 B6 Cornoigmore Ag & B
102 F2 Cornriggs Dur
103 M2 Cornsay Dur
103 N2 Cornsay Colliery Dur
155 Q6 Corntown Highld
29 P9 Corntown V Glam
47 Q9 Cornwell Oxon
6 G7 Cornwood Devon
7 L7 Cornworthy Devon
139 L2 Corpach Highld
76 G6 Corpusty Norfk
150 D7 Corrachree Abers
139 J5 Corran Highld
145 P6 Corran Highld
80 g4 Corrany IoM
110 D3 Corrie D & G
121 K3 Corrie N Ayrs
120 H7 Corriecravie N Ayrs
121 K4 Corriegills N Ayrs
146 H9 Corriegour Lodge Hotel Highld
155 L5 Corriemoille Highld
155 L11 Corrimony Highld
85 Q2 Corringham Lincs
38 B5 Corringham Thurr
54 H3 Corris Gwynd
54 G3 Corris Uchaf Gwynd
131 P7 Corrow Ag & B
145 K3 Corry Highld
8 F5 Corscombe Devon
11 L3 Corscombe Dorset
46 E9 Corse Gloucs
46 F8 Corse Lawn Gloucs
32 G10 Corsham Wilts
150 H6 Corsindae Abers
20 F5 Corsley Wilts
20 F5 Corsley Heath Wilts
108 G5 Corsock D & G
32 C11 Corston BaNES
32 H8 Corston Wilts
127 M3 Corstorphine C Edin
67 L10 Cors-y-Gedol Gwynd
142 F6 Cortachy Angus
65 Q2 Corton Suffk
20 H6 Corton Wilts
20 B10 Corton Denham Somset
139 K4 Coruanan Highld
68 E6 Corwen Denbgs
11 N7 Coryates Dorset
8 C8 Coryton Devon
38 B5 Coryton Thurr
72 E11 Cosby Leics
58 D6 Coseley Dudley
57 Q3 Cosford Shrops
49 L6 Cosgrove Nhants
15 J5 Cosham C Port
41 K10 Cosheston Pembks
141 J8 Coshieville P & K
72 D2 Cossall Notts
72 D2 Cossall Marsh Notts
72 G8 Cossington Leics
19 L6 Cossington Somset
76 H9 Costessey Norfk
72 F5 Costock Notts
73 L6 Coston Leics
76 F10 Coston Norfk
34 C4 Cote Oxon
19 K6 Cote Somset
82 C11 Cotebrook Ches W
111 J10 Cotehill Cumb
95 K3 Cotes Cumb
72 F6 Cotes Leics
70 E8 Cotes Staffs
60 B4 Cotesbach Leics
70 E8 Cotes Heath Staffs
18 G9 Cotford St Luke Somset
72 G3 Cotgrave Notts
151 M4 Cothal Abers
85 N11 Cotham Notts
18 G8 Cothelstone Somset
103 K7 Cotherstone Dur
34 E5 Cothill Oxon
10 E4 Cotleigh Devon
72 D2 Cotmanhay Derbys
62 F9 Coton Cambs
60 E6 Coton Nhants
69 P8 Coton Shrops
59 J4 Coton Staffs
70 E10 Coton Staffs
70 H8 Coton Staffs
70 F10 Coton Clanford Staffs
70 H8 Coton Hayes Staffs
56 H2 Coton Hill Shrops
71 M9 Coton in the Clay Staffs
71 N11 Coton in the Elms Derbys
71 P11 Coton Park Derbys
33 J3 Cotswolds
7 K6 Cott Devon
22 D6 Cottage End Hants
88 G4 Cottam Lancs
85 P5 Cottam Notts
62 F7 Cottenham Cambs
96 B2 Cotterdale N York
50 H5 Cottered Herts
58 F8 Cotteridge Birm
61 M2 Cotterstock Nhants
60 F6 Cottesbrooke Nhants
73 N8 Cottesmore Rutlnd
92 H4 Cottingham E R Yk
60 H2 Cottingham Nhants
90 E3 Cottingley C Brad
90 H4 Cottingley Hall Crematorium Leeds
48 G8 Cottisford Oxon
64 F8 Cotton Suffk
61 N11 Cotton End Bed
89 Q3 Cotton Tree Lancs
150 E2 Cottown Abers
151 K4 Cottown Abers
159 K9 Cottown of Gight Abers
6 C5 Cotts Devon
69 R11 Cotwall Wrekin
70 G8 Cotwalton Staffs
5 J10 Couch's Mill Cnwll
46 A10 Coughton Herefs
47 L2 Coughton Warwks
123 M6 Coulaghailtro Ag & B
154 C9 Coulags Highld
100 C9 Coulderton Cumb
150 E7 Coull Abers
131 Q10 Coulport Ag & B
36 G9 Coulsdon Gt Lon
21 J4 Coulston Wilts
116 E4 Coulter S Lans
23 Q11 Coultershaw Bridge W Susx
18 H6 Coultings Somset
98 C6 Coulton N York
135 K3 Coultra Fife
57 K3 Cound Shrops
57 K4 Coundlane Shrops
103 P5 Coundon Dur
103 P5 Coundon Grange Dur
96 D3 Countersett N York
21 N6 Countess Wilts
52 E5 Countess Cross Essex
9 M7 Countess Wear Devon
72 F11 Countesthorpe Leics
17 N2 Countisbury Devon
142 C10 Coupar Angus P & K
88 H5 Coup Green Lancs
102 D7 Coupland Cumb
118 H4 Coupland Nthumb
123 P10 Cour Ag & B
27 J4 Court-at-Street Kent
145 L8 Courteachan Highld
49 L4 Courteenhall Nhants
43 L10 Court Henry Carmth
38 H3 Courtsend Essex
18 H8 Courtway Somset
128 B6 Cousland Mdloth
25 Q4 Cousley Wood E Susx
131 Q11 Cove Ag & B
129 K5 Cove Border
18 C11 Cove Devon
23 N3 Cove Hants
160 C8 Cove Highld
151 P7 Cove Bay C Aber
65 P6 Cove Bottom Suffk
65 Q5 Covehithe Suffk
58 D3 Coven Staffs
62 G4 Coveney Cambs
87 K2 Covenham St Bartholomew Lincs
87 K2 Covenham St Mary Lincs
58 D3 Coven Heath Staffs
59 M9 Coventry Covtry
59 N10 *Coventry Airport* Warwks
3 K10 Coverack Cnwll
2 H7 Coverack Bridges Cnwll
96 H3 Coverham N York
61 N6 Covington Cambs
116 D3 Covington S Lans
95 N5 Cowan Bridge Lancs
25 P8 Cowbeech E Susx
74 E7 Cowbit Lincs
30 C10 Cowbridge V Glam
83 N10 Cowdale Derbys
25 L2 Cowden Kent
134 F9 Cowdenbeath Fife
25 L2 Cowden Pound Kent
25 L2 Cowden Station Kent
71 Q5 Cowers Lane Derbys
14 E7 Cowes IoW
97 Q3 Cowesby N York
21 Q10 Cowesfield Green Wilts
24 F6 Cowfold W Susx
95 R3 Cowgill Cumb
64 F8 Cow Green Suffk
32 B6 Cowhill S Glos
133 N10 Cowie Stirlg
99 K7 Cowlam E R Yk
9 M5 Cowley Devon
33 J2 Cowley Gloucs
36 C4 Cowley Gt Lon
34 F4 Cowley Oxon
88 H7 Cowling Lancs
90 B2 Cowling N York
97 K3 Cowling N York
63 M10 Cowlinge Suffk
90 F7 Cowmes Kirk
89 N6 Cowpe Lancs
113 L4 Cowpen Nthumb
104 E6 Cowpen Bewley S on T
15 J4 Cowplain Hants
102 G2 Cowshill Dur
19 N2 Cowslip Green N Som
97 P10 Cowthorpe N York
56 F10 Coxall Herefs
70 B6 Coxbank Ches E
72 B2 Coxbench Derbys
19 P7 Coxbridge Somset
65 N5 Cox Common Suffk
5 K2 Coxford Cnwll
76 B6 Coxford Norfk
57 Q7 Coxgreen Staffs
38 B11 Coxheath Kent
104 B3 Coxhoe Dur
19 P6 Coxley Somset
90 H7 Coxley Wakefd
19 P6 Coxley Wick Somset
5 Q7 Coxpark Cnwll
51 N11 Coxtie Green Essex
98 A5 Coxwold N York
29 P9 Coychurch Brdgnd
29 P8 Coychurch Crematorium Brdgnd
114 H4 Coylton S Ayrs
148 G5 Coylumbridge Highld
29 N7 Coytrahen Brdgnd
58 F11 Crabbs Cross Worcs
13 J3 Crab Orchard Dorset
24 F5 Crabtree W Susx
69 K6 Crabtree Green Wrexhm
102 C6 Crackenthorpe Cumb
5 J2 Crackington Haven Cnwll
70 E4 Crackley Staffs
59 L10 Crackley Warwks
57 P2 Crackleybank Shrops
103 J11 Crackpot N York
96 E8 Cracoe N York
10 B2 Craddock Devon
51 L6 Cradle End Herts
58 D7 Cradley Dudley
46 D5 Cradley Herefs
58 D7 Cradley Heath Sandw
44 E8 Cradoc Powys
5 P11 Crafthole Cnwll
49 N11 Crafton Bucks
95 K6 Crag Foot Lancs
149 J2 Craggan Highld
90 G3 Cragg Hill Leeds
113 K10 Craghead Dur
44 B10 Crai Powys
158 C6 Craibstone Moray
143 J8 Craichie Angus
143 M6 Craig Angus
154 D8 Craig Highld
115 L5 Craigbank E Ayrs
127 N7 Craigburn Border
29 J4 Craigcefnparc Swans
110 F3 Craigcleuch D & G
159 K11 Craigdam Abers
130 G6 Craigdhu Ag & B
151 J5 Craigearn Abers
157 P9 Craigellachie Moray
134 E3 Craigend P & K
125 M3 Craigend Rens
132 C11 Craigendoran Ag & B
125 L4 Craigends Rens
107 K5 Craighlaw D & G
122 H6 Craighouse Ag & B
141 R9 Craigie P & K
125 L11 Craigie S Ayrs
159 M4 Craigiefield Abers
108 G9 Craigley D & G
29 K4 Craig Llangiwg Neath
127 N3 Craiglockhart C Edin
127 Q3 Craigmillar C Edin
69 J7 Craignant Shrops
115 Q10 Craigneston D & G
126 D4 Craigneuk N Lans
126 D6 Craigneuk N Lans
138 C10 Craignure Ag & B
143 M5 Craigo Angus
30 C9 Craig Penllyn V Glam
135 K5 Craigrothie Fife
132 F3 Craigruie Stirlg
52 B4 Craig's End Essex
143 J10 Craigton Angus
151 L7 Craigton C Aber
125 M7 Craigton E Rens
142 E7 Craigton of Airlie Angus
29 K4 Craig-y-Duke Neath
44 A11 Craig-y-nos Powys
135 Q6 Crail Fife
118 C6 Crailing Border
92 C11 Craiselound N Linc
97 K3 Crakehall N York
97 P6 Crakehill N York
71 K7 Crakemarsh Staffs
98 E8 Crambe N York
113 L5 Cramlington Nthumb
127 M2 Cramond C Edin
127 M2 Cramond Bridge C Edin
22 C10 Crampmoor Hants
82 G11 Cranage Ches E
70 E7 Cranberry Staffs
13 J2 Cranborne Dorset
35 P10 Cranbourne Br For
26 C4 Cranbrook Kent
26 C4 Cranbrook Common Kent
91 J10 Crane Moor Barns
76 C9 Crane's Corner Norfk
49 Q6 Cranfield C Beds
16 E7 Cranford Devon
36 D5 Cranford Gt Lon
61 K5 Cranford St Andrew Nhants
61 K5 Cranford St John Nhants
32 G2 Cranham Gloucs
37 N3 Cranham Gt Lon
47 M4 Cranhill Warwks
81 Q5 Crank St Hel
24 C3 Cranleigh Surrey
64 E7 Cranmer Green Suffk
14 C8 Cranmore IoW
20 C6 Cranmore Somset
73 K11 Cranoe Leics
65 L9 Cransford Suffk
128 H7 Cranshaws Border
80 g1 Cranstal IoM
99 L10 Cranswick E R Yk
4 B9 Crantock Cnwll
86 D11 Cranwell Lincs
63 N2 Cranwich Norfk
76 D11 Cranworth Norfk
130 F6 Craobh Haven Ag & B
6 E5 Crapstone Devon
131 K8 Crarae Ag & B
162 C2 Crask Inn Highld
155 N9 Crask of Aigas Highld
119 Q7 Craster Nthumb
45 K7 Craswall Herefs
58 D3 Crateford Staffs
65 L6 Cratfield Suffk
151 K8 Crathes Abers
151 J8 Crathes Castle Abers
149 P8 Crathie Abers
147 P9 Crathie Highld
104 D9 Crathorne N York
56 G8 Craven Arms Shrops
112 H8 Crawcrook Gatesd
81 P4 Crawford Lancs
116 D6 Crawford S Lans
116 B6 Crawfordjohn S Lans
22 D8 Crawley Hants
34 B2 Crawley Oxon
24 G3 Crawley W Susx
24 H3 Crawley Down W Susx
103 J2 Crawleyside Dur
89 N5 Crawshawbooth Lancs
143 R2 Crawton Abers
52 F8 Craxe's Green Essex
96 D5 Cray N York
37 M5 Crayford Gt Lon
98 B6 Crayke N York
76 F5 Craymere Beck Norfk
38 B3 Crays Hill Essex
34 H8 Cray's Pond Oxon
71 N9 Craythorne Staffs
9 N2 Craze Lowman Devon
35 L8 Crazies Hill Wokham
17 Q8 Creacombe Devon
138 H9 Creagan Inn Ag & B
168 c13 Creag Ghoraidh W Isls
168 c13 Creagorry W Isls
139 Q4 Creaguaineach Lodge Highld
69 P8 Creamore Bank Shrops
60 F6 Creaton Nhants
110 D6 Creca D & G
45 P6 Credenhill Herefs
9 K4 Crediton Devon
107 K2 Creebank D & G
107 M4 Creebridge D & G
12 F8 Creech Dorset
19 J9 Creech Heathfield Somset
19 J9 Creech St Michael Somset
3 N4 Creed Cnwll
37 L4 Creekmouth Gt Lon
38 F2 Creeksea Essex
64 F10 Creeting St Mary Suffk
73 Q6 Creeton Lincs
107 N6 Creetown D & G
80 a8 Cregneash IoM
80 e5 Cregny Baa IoM
44 G4 Cregrina Powys
135 J3 Creich Fife
30 E8 Creigiau Cardif
6 D8 Cremyll Cnwll
57 K4 Cressage Shrops
83 Q10 Cressbrook Derbys
41 L9 Cresselly Pembks
35 M6 Cressex Bucks
52 C7 Cressing Essex
113 L2 Cresswell Nthumb
41 L9 Cresswell Pembks
70 H7 Cresswell Staffs
84 H6 Creswell Derbys
58 G2 Creswell Green Staffs
65 J9 Cretingham Suffk
123 M6 Cretshengan Ag & B
70 C3 Crewe Ches E
69 M4 Crewe Ches W
70 C3 Crewe Crematorium Ches E
70 C3 Crewe Green Ches E
69 K11 Crew Green Powys
11 J3 Crewkerne Somset
50 H10 Crews Hill Station Gt Lon
72 B4 Crewton C Derb
132 D2 Crianlarich Stirlg
43 K4 Cribyn Cerdgn
66 H7 Criccieth Gwynd
84 D10 Crich Derbys
84 D10 Crich Carr Derbys
128 B7 Crichton Mdloth
31 N6 Crick Mons
60 C6 Crick Nhants
44 F6 Crickadarn Powys
10 H3 Cricket St Thomas Somset
69 J10 Crickheath Shrops
45 J11 Crickhowell Powys
33 L6 Cricklade Wilts
36 F3 Cricklewood Gt Lon
91 N6 Cridling Stubbs N York
133 P3 Crieff P & K
4 G9 Criggan Cnwll
69 J11 Criggion Powys
91 J7 Crigglestone Wakefd
89 P8 Crimble Rochdl
159 Q6 Crimond Abers
75 N10 Crimplesham Norfk
47 P5 Crimscote Warwks
155 M9 Crinaglack Highld
130 F9 Crinan Ag & B
126 E6 Crindledyke N Lans
76 H10 Cringleford Norfk
96 F11 Cringles C Brad
41 M8 Crinow Pembks
2 E6 Cripplesease Cnwll
13 J2 Cripplestyle Dorset
26 C7 Cripp's Corner E Susx
148 B2 Croachy Highld
4 G7 Croanford Cnwll
37 M7 Crockenhill Kent
35 K7 Crocker End Oxon
15 P5 Crockerhill W Susx
9 J6 Crockernwell Devon
45 Q11 Crocker's Ash Herefs
20 G6 Crockerton Wilts
108 H6 Crocketford D & G
98 C11 Crockey Hill C York
37 K10 Crockham Hill Kent
37 P11 Crockhurst Street Kent
52 H6 Crockleford Heath Essex
10 G2 Crock Street Somset
29 N5 Croeserw Neath
40 F4 Croes-goch Pembks
42 G6 Croes-lan Cerdgn
67 L6 Croesor Gwynd
42 H11 Croesyceiliog Carmth
31 K5 Croesyceiliog Torfn
31 K6 Croes-y-mwyalch Torfn
31 K4 Croes-y-pant Mons
72 E11 Croft Leics
87 P8 Croft Lincs
82 D6 Croft Warrtn
132 F10 Croftamie Stirlg
2 H6 Croft Mitchell Cnwll
110 F10 Crofton Cumb
91 K7 Crofton Wakefd
21 Q2 Crofton Wilts
103 Q9 Croft-on-Tees N York
161 K10 Croftown Highld
157 P7 Crofts Moray
82 G5 Crofts Bank Traffd
157 Q6 Crofts of Dipple Moray
159 P5 Crofts of Savoch Abers
28 F6 Crofty Swans
68 D7 Crogen Gwynd
130 E2 Croggan Ag & B
111 L11 Croglin Cumb
162 B8 Croick Highld
156 D4 Cromarty Highld
134 D11 Crombie Fife
149 K2 Cromdale Highld
50 G5 Cromer Herts
77 J3 Cromer Norfk

84 C9 Cromford Derbys
32 C6 Cromhall S Glos
32 C7 Cromhall Common S Glos
168 j5 Cromor W Isls
89 Q9 Crompton Fold Oldham
85 N8 Cromwell Notts
115 M3 Cronberry E Ayrs
23 L5 Crondall Hants
80 e6 Cronkbourne IoM
80 d4 Cronk-y-Voddy IoM
81 P7 Cronton Knows
101 N11 Crook Cumb
103 N3 Crook Dur
100 G2 Crookdake Cumb
88 H9 Crooke Wigan
46 B11 Crooked End Gloucs
125 M10 Crookedholm E Ayrs
34 B10 Crooked Soley Wilts
84 D3 Crookes Sheff
112 H10 Crookhall Dur
118 H3 Crookham Nthumb
22 F2 Crookham W Berk
23 L4 Crookham Village Hants
116 G5 Crook Inn Border
95 L4 Crooklands Cumb
134 C7 Crook of Devon P & K
71 N7 Cropper Derbys
48 E5 Cropredy Oxon
72 F8 Cropston Leics
47 J5 Cropthorne Worcs
98 F3 Cropton N York
72 H3 Cropwell Bishop Notts
72 H3 Cropwell Butler Notts
168 k1 Cros W Isls
168 i5 Crosbost W Isls
100 E3 Crosby Cumb
80 d6 Crosby IoM
92 E8 Crosby N Linc
81 L5 Crosby Sefton
102 D9 Crosby Garret Cumb
102 B8 Crosby Ravensworth Cumb
100 E3 Crosby Villa Cumb
19 Q6 Croscombe Somset
69 M9 Crosemere Shrops
90 E8 Crosland Edge Kirk
90 E8 Crosland Hill Kirk
19 M4 Cross Somset
123 P9 Crossaig Ag & B
136 B7 Crossapoll Ag & B
45 N11 Cross Ash Mons
26 C2 Cross-at-Hand Kent
24 B9 Crossbush W Susx
100 E3 Crosscanonby Cumb
3 J3 Cross Coombe Cnwll
77 J4 Crossdale Street Norfk
61 N9 Cross End Bed
52 E5 Cross End Essex
88 D6 Crossens Sefton
90 E2 Cross Flatts C Brad
134 D10 Crossford Fife
126 E8 Crossford S Lans
5 N4 Crossgate Cnwll
74 D5 Crossgate Lincs
70 G7 Crossgate Staffs
128 B6 Crossgatehall E Loth
125 K9 Crossgates E Ayrs
134 E10 Crossgates Fife
91 K4 Cross Gates Leeds
99 L4 Crossgates N York
44 F2 Crossgates Powys
95 M8 Crossgill Lancs
5 P4 Cross Green Devon
91 J4 Cross Green Leeds
58 D3 Cross Green Staffs
64 A11 Cross Green Suffk
64 B10 Cross Green Suffk
64 D11 Cross Green Suffk
28 G2 Cross Hands Carmth
41 N6 Crosshands Carmth
125 M11 Crosshands E Ayrs
41 L8 Cross Hands Pembks
84 F11 Cross Hill Derbys
134 F8 Crosshill Fife
114 F6 Crosshill S Ayrs
96 F11 Cross Hills N York
125 K10 Crosshouse E Ayrs
57 J3 Cross Houses Shrops
57 M6 Cross Houses Shrops
25 N6 Cross in Hand E Susx
42 G3 Cross Inn Cerdgn
43 K2 Cross Inn Cerdgn
41 M9 Cross Inn Pembks
30 E8 Cross Inn Rhondd
132 C10 Cross Keys Ag & B
30 H6 Crosskeys Caerph
32 G10 Cross Keys Wilts
166 H3 Crosskirk Highld
94 G3 Crosslands Cumb
14 F9 Cross Lane IoW
57 N5 Cross Lane Head Shrops
2 H9 Cross Lanes Cnwll
3 K5 Cross Lanes Cnwll
98 A8 Cross Lanes N York
69 K11 Crosslanes Shrops
69 L5 Cross Lanes Wrexhm
125 L4 Crosslee Rens
90 G6 Crossley Kirk
108 F7 Crossmichael D & G
44 G10 Cross Oak Powys
158 H11 Cross of Jackston Abers
71 P5 Cross o' th' hands Derbys
24 G6 Crosspost W Susx
150 F6 Crossroads Abers
151 K9 Crossroads Abers
64 H6 Cross Street Suffk
143 J6 Crosston Angus
82 G9 Cross Town Ches E
45 N11 Crossway Mons
44 F3 Crossway Powys
31 P6 Crossway Green Mons
58 B11 Crossway Green Worcs
12 C7 Crossways Dorset
41 M3 Crosswell Pembks
95 J2 Crosthwaite Cumb
88 F7 Croston Lancs
77 K8 Crostwick Norfk
77 L6 Crostwight Norfk
37 P9 Crouch Kent
39 J10 Crouch Kent
36 H3 Crouch End Gt Lon
21 L9 Croucheston Wilts
11 Q2 Crouch Hill Dorset
37 K11 Crough House Green Kent
48 F8 Croughton Nhants
159 K4 Crovie Abers
13 L4 Crow Hants
2 G7 Crowan Cnwll
25 M4 Crowborough E Susx
25 M4 Crowborough Town E Susx
18 F7 Crowcombe Somset
83 P11 Crowdecote Derbys
83 N5 Crowden Derbys
8 C5 Crowden Devon
22 E10 Crowdhill Hants
37 N9 Crowdleham Kent
83 Q4 Crow Edge Barns
35 K5 Crowell Oxon
62 D9 Crow End Cambs
48 H6 Crowfield Nhants
64 G10 Crowfield Suffk
64 G10 Crowfield Green Suffk
77 L7 Crowgate Street Norfk
51 N11 Crow Green Essex
129 J5 Crowhill E Loth
46 B9 Crow Hill Herefs
84 D5 Crowhole Derbys
26 C9 Crowhurst E Susx
37 J11 Crowhurst Surrey
37 J11 Crowhurst Lane End Surrey
74 D8 Crowland Lincs
64 E7 Crowland Suffk
2 E7 Crowlas Cnwll
92 C8 Crowle N Linc
46 H3 Crowle Worcs
46 H3 Crowle Green Worcs
34 H7 Crowmarsh Gifford Oxon
65 K7 Crown Corner Suffk
6 D7 Crownhill C Plym
49 M7 Crownhill Crematorium M Keyn
23 Q6 Crownpits Surrey
76 F11 Crownthorpe Norfk
2 G7 Crowntown Cnwll
2 B8 Crows-an-Wra Cnwll
51 Q5 Crow's Green Essex
76 D10 Crowshill Norfk
5 M8 Crow's Nest Cnwll
56 F4 Crowsnest Shrops
23 M2 Crowthorne Wokham
82 C10 Crowton Ches W
59 J2 Croxall Staffs
93 L11 Croxby Lincs
103 Q3 Croxdale Dur
71 K7 Croxden Staffs
50 C11 Croxley Green Herts
81 N5 Croxteth Lpool
62 B8 Croxton Cambs
93 J8 Croxton N Linc
64 B4 Croxton Norfk
76 D5 Croxton Norfk
70 D8 Croxton Staffs
70 D8 Croxtonbank Staffs
69 Q4 Croxton Green Ches E
73 L5 Croxton Kerrial Leics
156 D8 Croy Highld
126 C2 Croy N Lans
16 G4 Croyde Devon
16 G4 Croyde Bay Devon
62 D11 Croydon Cambs
36 H7 Croydon Gt Lon
36 H7 Croydon Crematorium Gt Lon
148 B9 Crubenmore Highld
56 G3 Cruckmeole Shrops
56 G2 Cruckton Shrops
159 Q10 Cruden Bay Abers
70 A11 Crudgington Wrekin
33 J6 Crudwell Wilts
8 D5 Cruft Devon
56 B10 Crug Powys
4 E6 Crugmeer Cnwll
43 N7 Crugybar Carmth
56 B8 Crug-y-byddar Powys
30 H5 Crumlin Caerph
5 L11 Crumplehorn Cnwll
82 H4 Crumpsall Manch
27 J2 Crundale Kent
41 J7 Crundale Pembks
41 N8 Crunwear Pembks
9 L2 Cruwys Morchard Devon
22 D3 Crux Easton Hants
11 N5 Cruxton Dorset
28 E2 Crwbin Carmth
35 N5 Cryers Hill Bucks
41 N4 Crymmych Pembks
29 L4 Crynant Neath
36 H6 Crystal Palace Gt Lon
153 N6 Cuaig Highld
130 F5 Cuan Ag & B
59 M11 Cubbington Warwks
4 B10 Cubert Cnwll
90 G10 Cubley Barns
49 M10 Cublington Bucks
45 N7 Cublington Herefs
24 H5 Cuckfield W Susx
20 E9 Cucklington Somset
85 J6 Cuckney Notts
74 D6 Cuckoo Bridge Lincs
23 K6 Cuckoo's Corner Hants
69 L2 Cuckoo's Nest Ches W
34 G4 Cuddesdon Oxon
35 K2 Cuddington Bucks
82 C10 Cuddington Ches W
69 N5 Cuddington Heath Ches W
88 F3 Cuddy Hill Lancs
37 K9 Cudham Gt Lon
8 D9 Cudliptown Devon
13 J5 Cudnell Bmouth
91 K9 Cudworth Barns
10 H2 Cudworth Somset
82 B7 Cuerdley Cross Warrtn
23 J3 Cufaude Hants
50 H10 Cuffley Herts
138 H6 Cuil Highld
155 R6 Culbokie Highld
17 Q2 Culbone Somset
155 N9 Culburnie Highld
156 B9 Culcabock Highld
156 F7 Culcharry Highld
82 E6 Culcheth Warrtn
158 D11 Culdrain Abers
153 N9 Culduie Highld
64 A7 Culford Suffk
102 B5 Culgaith Cumb
34 F6 Culham Oxon
164 B10 Culkein Highld
164 D10 Culkein Drumbeg Highld
32 H5 Culkerton Gloucs
158 D4 Cullen Moray
113 N6 Cullercoats N Tyne
151 K7 Cullerlie Abers
156 A5 Cullicudden Highld
90 D3 Cullingworth C Brad
144 G3 Cuillin Hills Highld
130 E5 Cullipool Ag & B
169 s3 Cullivoe Shet
156 C8 Culloden Highld
9 P3 Cullompton Devon
9 P3 Cullompton Services Devon
18 F11 Culm Davy Devon
56 H8 Culmington Shrops
10 C2 Culmstock Devon
160 H6 Culnacraig Highld
108 G10 Culnaightrie D & G
153 J5 Culnaknock Highld
53 M2 Culpho Suffk
162 D8 Culrain Highld
134 B10 Culross Fife
114 F5 Culroy S Ayrs
158 G11 Culsalmond Abers
107 N8 Culscadden D & G
107 K7 Culshabbin D & G
169 p9 Culswick Shet
151 N3 Cultercullen Abers
151 M7 Cults C Aber
37 P8 Culverstone Green Kent
73 Q2 Culverthorpe Lincs
48 F5 Culworth Nhants
114 D5 Culzean Castle & Country Park S Ayrs
126 D3 Cumbernauld N Lans
126 D2 Cumbernauld Village N Lans
87 P6 Cumberworth Lincs
110 F11 Cumdivock Cumb
159 K7 Cuminestown Abers
129 K8 Cumledge Border
110 G10 Cummersdale Cumb
109 P7 Cummertrees D & G
157 L4 Cummingston Moray
115 L3 Cumnock E Ayrs
34 E4 Cumnor Oxon
111 L10 Cumrew Cumb
109 N3 Cumrue D & G
111 J10 Cumwhinton Cumb
111 K10 Cumwhitton Cumb
97 P6 Cundall N York
125 K9 Cunninghamhead N Ayrs
169 r10 Cunningsburgh Shet
135 K5 Cupar Fife
135 K5 Cupar Muir Fife
84 C6 Curbar Derbys
14 F4 Curbridge Hants
34 B3 Curbridge Oxon
14 F4 Curdridge Hants
59 J6 Curdworth Warwks
19 J11 Curland Somset
34 E10 Curridge W Berk
127 M4 Currie C Edin
19 K10 Curry Mallet Somset
19 L9 Curry Rivel Somset
26 E4 Curteis Corner Kent
26 B3 Curtisden Green Kent
7 J8 Curtisknowle Devon
2 H9 Cury Cnwll
150 E5 Cushnie Abers
18 G8 Cushuish Somset
45 J6 Cusop Herefs
107 N11 Cutcloy D & G
18 B7 Cutcombe Somset
89 P8 Cutgate Rochdl
162 H9 Cuthill Highld
67 L11 Cutiau Gwynd
51 N4 Cutler's Green Essex
4 H9 Cutmadoc Cnwll
5 N9 Cutmere Cnwll
58 C11 Cutnall Green Worcs
47 L8 Cutsdean Gloucs
91 L6 Cutsyke Wakefd
84 D6 Cutthorpe Derbys
5 P9 Cuttivett Cnwll
35 J5 Cuxham Oxon
38 B8 Cuxton Medway
93 L10 Cuxwold Lincs
30 G3 Cwm Blae G
80 F9 Cwm Denbgs
29 L6 Cwmafan Neath
30 D5 Cwmaman Rhondd
43 L5 Cwmann Carmth
31 J3 Cwmavon Torfn
28 E4 Cwm-bach Carmth
41 Q5 Cwmbach Carmth
44 H7 Cwmbach Powys
30 D4 Cwmbach Rhondd
44 E4 Cwmbach Llechrhyd Powys
55 L8 Cwmbelan Powys
31 J6 Cwmbran Torfn
54 G8 Cwmbrwyno Cerdgn
28 E4 Cwm Capel Carmth
30 H6 Cwmcarn Caerph
31 N3 Cwmcarvan Mons
30 H3 Cwm-celyn Blae G
55 K2 Cwm-Cewydd Gwynd
41 Q2 Cwm-cou Cerdgn
44 G11 Cwm Crawnon Powys
30 C4 Cwmdare Rhondd
43 M8 Cwmdu Carmth
44 H10 Cwmdu Powys
28 H6 Cwmdu Swans
42 G8 Cwmduad Carmth
28 H4 Cwm Dulais Swans
43 P8 Cwmdwr Carmth
29 N7 Cwmfelin Brdgnd
30 E4 Cwmfelin Myr Td
41 N7 Cwmfelin Boeth Carmth
30 G6 Cwmfelinfach Caerph
41 P6 Cwmfelin Mynach Carmth
42 H11 Cwmffrwd Carmth
29 L2 Cwmgiedd Powys
29 K2 Cwmgorse Carmth
28 G2 Cwmgwili Carmth
29 N4 Cwmgwrach Neath
42 F7 Cwmhiraeth Carmth
43 N9 Cwm-Ifor Carmth
44 B5 Cwm Irfon Powys
43 J11 Cwmisfael Carmth
55 J3 Cwm Llinau Powys
29 K2 Cwmllynfell Neath
29 F2 Cwmmawr Carmth
41 Q4 Cwm Morgan Carmth
29 P5 Cwmparc Rhondd
42 G7 Cwmpengraig Carmth
67 P5 Cwm Penmachno Conwy
30 D4 Cwmpennar Rhondd
44 H10 Cwmrhos Powys
29 J5 Cwmrhydyceirw Swans
43 J3 Cwmsychbant Cerdgn
30 H3 Cwmtillery Blae G
29 L2 Cwm-twrch Isaf Powys
29 L2 Cwm-twrch Uchaf Powys
28 G2 Cwm-y-glo Carmth
67 K2 Cwm-y-glo Gwynd
45 K10 Cwmyoy Mons
54 H10 Cwmystwyth Cerdgn
54 F5 Cwrt Gwynd
43 J5 Cwrt-newydd Cerdgn
45 J11 Cwrt-y-gollen Powys
55 Q3 Cyfronydd Powys
29 K4 Cylibebyll Neath
29 N5 Cymer Neath
30 D6 Cymmer Rhondd
43 R6 Cynghordy Carmth
28 E3 Cynheidre Carmth
29 M5 Cynonville Neath
68 E6 Cynwyd Denbgs
42 G9 Cynwyl Elfed Carmth

D

7 N5 Daccombe Devon
101 N5 Dacre Cumb
97 J8 Dacre N York
97 J8 Dacre Banks N York
102 G3 Daddry Shield Dur
49 J7 Dadford Bucks
72 C11 Dadlington Leics
28 F4 Dafen Carmth
76 D10 Daffy Green Norfk
37 M4 Dagenham Gt Lon
33 J3 Daglingworth Gloucs
49 Q11 Dagnall Bucks
64 E9 Dagworth Suffk
114 E7 Dailly S Ayrs
7 M5 Dainton Devon
135 L4 Dairsie Fife
82 E4 Daisy Hill Bolton
90 H5 Daisy Hill Leeds
168 c15 Dalabrog W Isls
131 K5 Dalavich Ag & B
108 H8 Dalbeattie D & G
71 P8 Dalbury Derbys
80 b6 Dalby IoM
87 M7 Dalby Lincs
98 C6 Dalby N York
141 N7 Dalcapon P & K
163 L5 Dalchalm Highld
146 H5 Dalchreichart Highld
133 L4 Dalchruin P & K
134 C2 Dalcrue P & K
87 J7 Dalderby Lincs
9 P8 Dalditch Devon
101 P2 Dale Cumb
72 C3 Dale Derbys
40 F9 Dale Pembks
101 J6 Dale Bottom Cumb
84 B8 Dale End Derbys
96 E11 Dale End N York
26 B5 Dale Hill E Susx
105 L7 Dalehouse N York
138 C4 Dalelia Highld
124 H8 Dalgarven N Ayrs
134 F11 Dalgety Bay Fife
115 L5 Dalgig E Ayrs
133 M3 Dalginross P & K
141 N8 Dalguise P & K
166 E6 Dalhalvaig Highld
63 M8 Dalham Suffk
168 c15 Daliburgh W Isls
127 Q4 Dalkeith Mdloth
157 L7 Dallas Moray
65 K10 Dallinghoo Suffk
25 Q7 Dallington E Susx
60 F8 Dallington Nhants
97 J6 Dallow N York
131 P2 Dalmally Ag & B
132 G8 Dalmary Stirlg
115 J6 Dalmellington E Ayrs
127 L2 Dalmeny C Edin
156 B4 Dalmore Highld
125 M3 Dalmuir W Duns
138 C4 Dalnabreck Highld
140 H3 Dalnacardoch P & K
148 F4 Dalnahaitnach Highld
140 F3 Dalnaspidal P & K
166 H8 Dalnawillan Lodge Highld
141 J6 Daloist P & K
134 D7 Dalqueich P & K
114 F8 Dalquhairn S Ayrs
162 H5 Dalreavoch Lodge Highld
124 H8 Dalry N Ayrs
114 G5 Dalrymple E Ayrs
126 D7 Dalserf S Lans
120 B9 Dalsmeran Ag & B
110 G10 Dalston Cumb
36 H4 Dalston Gt Lon
109 K3 Dalswinton D & G
95 L5 Dalton Cumb
109 P6 Dalton D & G
88 F9 Dalton Lancs
97 P5 Dalton N York
103 M9 Dalton N York
112 H6 Dalton Nthumb
84 G2 Dalton Rothm
94 E6 Dalton-in-Furness Cumb
113 P11 Dalton-le-Dale Dur
84 G2 Dalton Magna Rothm
103 Q9 Dalton-on-Tees N York
84 G2 Dalton Parva Rothm
104 E4 Dalton Piercy Hartpl
133 J3 Dalveich Stirlg
147 Q11 Dalwhinnie Highld
10 E4 Dalwood Devon
50 G5 Damask Green Herts
21 M11 Damerham Hants
77 N10 Damgate Norfk
64 E4 Dam Green Norfk
38 E9 Danaway Kent
52 C10 Danbury Essex
105 K9 Danby N York
105 J10 Danby Bottom N York
104 B11 Danby Wiske N York
157 P8 Dandaleith Moray
127 Q4 Danderhall Mdloth
83 L11 Danebridge Ches E
50 H6 Dane End Herts
25 N4 Danegate E Susx
25 K5 Danehill E Susx
72 F10 Dane Hills C Leic
76 F10 Danemoor Green Norfk
57 N6 Danesford Shrops
84 F8 Danesmoor Derbys
39 J11 Dane Street Kent
26 G3 Daniel's Water Kent
158 H6 Danshillock Abers
128 F6 Danskine E Loth
93 N4 Danthorpe E R Yk
58 H11 Danzey Green Warwks
71 J9 Dapple Heath Staffs
23 M2 Darby Green Hants
89 L9 Darcy Lever Bolton
45 J11 Dardy Powys
30 H2 Daren-felen Mons
37 N6 Darenth Kent
82 C8 Daresbury Halton
91 L10 Darfield Barns
85 J5 Darfoulds Notts
39 J9 Dargate Kent
5 M8 Darite Cnwll
38 C8 Darland Medway
69 L3 Darland Wrexhm
58 E5 Darlaston Wsall
58 E5 Darlaston Green Wsall
97 K9 Darley N York
72 B3 Darley Abbey C Derb
84 C8 Darley Bridge Derbys
84 C8 Darley Dale Derbys
59 J10 Darley Green Solhll
50 D6 Darleyhall Herts
97 J9 Darley Head N York
47 P6 Darlingscott Warwks
103 Q8 Darlington Darltn
103 Q8 Darlington Crematorium Darltn
69 Q8 Darliston Shrops
85 N6 Darlton Notts
58 H3 Darnford Staffs
117 Q4 Darnick Border
55 J4 Darowen Powys
158 H8 Darra Abers
16 C8 Darracott Devon
16 H4 Darracott Devon
113 J6 Darras Hall Nthumb
91 M7 Darrington Wakefd
65 N8 Darsham Suffk
20 B6 Darshill Somset
37 M6 Dartford Kent
7 K6 Dartington Devon
6 H4 Dartmeet Devon
8 G9 Dartmoor National Park Devon
7 M8 Dartmouth Devon
91 J8 Darton Barns
125 P10 Darvel E Ayrs
25 Q7 Darwell Hole E Susx
89 K6 Darwen Bl w D
35 Q9 Datchet W & M
50 G7 Datchworth Herts
50 G7 Datchworth Green Herts
89 L9 Daubhill Bolton
157 N9 Daugh of Kinermony Moray
33 J8 Dauntsey Wilts
157 J10 Dava Highld
82 E10 Davenham Ches W
83 K7 Davenport Stockp
82 H9 Davenport Green Ches E
82 H7 Davenport Green Traffd
60 C8 Daventry Nhants
127 N2 Davidson's Mains C Edin
5 K4 Davidstow Cnwll
37 P8 David Street Kent
117 J10 Davington D & G
38 H9 Davington Hill Kent
151 J2 Daviot Abers
156 C10 Daviot Highld
156 C9 Daviot House Highld
25 M7 Davis's Town E Susx
158 C7 Davoch of Grange Moray
82 G5 Davyhulme Traffd
58 F4 Daw End Wsall
36 F11 Dawesgreen Surrey
57 M3 Dawley Wrekin
9 N9 Dawlish Devon
9 N9 Dawlish Warren Devon
80 B10 Dawn Conwy
18 G10 Daws Green Somset
38 D4 Daws Heath Essex
5 N5 Daw's House Cnwll
74 H4 Dawsmere Lincs
85 J11 Daybrook Notts
70 D3 Day Green Ches E
70 H8 Dayhills Staffs
58 E9 Dayhouse Bank Worcs
47 P9 Daylesford Gloucs
80 G10 Ddol Flints
68 D11 Ddol-Cownwy Powys
39 Q11 Deal Kent
100 E5 Dean Cumb
7 J6 Dean Devon
17 L2 Dean Devon
17 N2 Dean Devon
21 J11 Dean Dorset
22 D8 Dean Hants
22 G11 Dean Hants
89 P5 Dean Lancs
48 B10 Dean Oxon
20 C6 Dean Somset
37 N7 Dean Bottom Kent
117 M8 Deanburnhaugh Border
7 J6 Deancombe Devon
34 E3 Dean Court Oxon
89 K9 Deane Bolton
22 F4 Deane Hants
21 J11 Dean End Dorset
90 H10 Dean Head Barns
90 C7 Deanhead Kirk
21 J11 Deanland Dorset
15 K4 Deanlane End W Susx
7 J6 Dean Prior Devon
112 B8 Deanraw Nthumb
83 J8 Dean Row Ches E
127 J4 Deans W Loth
100 E5 Deanscales Cumb
49 L7 Deanshanger Nhants
157 R7 Deanshaugh Moray
133 L7 Deanston Stirlg
38 B11 Dean Street Kent
100 E3 Dearham Cumb
89 Q7 Dearnley Rochdl
65 J11 Debach Suffk
51 K11 Debden Essex
51 N4 Debden Essex
51 N4 Debden Green Essex
64 H9 Debenham Suffk
46 F5 Deblin's Green Worcs
127 J3 Dechmont W Loth
127 J4 Dechmont Road W Loth
48 E8 Deddington Oxon
53 J5 Dedham Essex
53 J5 Dedham Heath Essex
35 P9 Dedworth W & M
61 K2 Deene Nhants
61 L2 Deenethorpe Nhants
90 H11 Deepcar Sheff
23 P3 Deepcut Surrey
95 Q4 Deepdale Cumb
96 C5 Deepdale N York
74 B9 Deeping Gate C Pete
74 C9 Deeping St James Lincs

74 D7 Deeping St Nicholas Lincs
46 G8 Deerhurst Gloucs
46 G9 Deerhurst Walton Gloucs
38 G9 Deerton Street Kent
46 H6 Defford Worcs
44 C9 Defynnog Powys
79 P9 Deganwy Conwy
130 F5 Degnish Ag & B
91 Q2 Deighton C York
104 C10 Deighton N York
67 K2 Deiniolen Gwynd
4 H5 Delabole Cnwll
82 C11 Delamere Ches W
151 P3 Delfrigs Abers
17 J7 Delley Devon
157 K11 Delliefure Highld
15 M6 Dell Quay W Susx
34 C2 Delly End Oxon
149 M4 Delnabo Moray
157 M10 Delnashaugh Inn Moray
156 C3 Delny Highld
90 B9 Delph Oldham
112 H11 Delves Dur
52 C4 Delvin End Essex
73 Q3 Dembleby Lincs
4 F9 Demelza Cnwll
91 M11 Denaby Donc
91 M11 Denaby Main Donc
36 D10 Denbies Surrey
80 F11 Denbigh Denbgs
135 K4 Denbrae Fife
7 L5 Denbury Devon
84 E11 Denby Derbys
84 E11 Denby Bottles Derbys
90 G9 Denby Dale Kirk
34 C6 Denchworth Oxon
94 E6 Dendron Cumb
50 B3 Denel End C Beds
134 B4 Denfield P & K
61 L5 Denford Nhants
52 G11 Dengie Essex
36 B3 Denham Bucks
63 N8 Denham Suffk
64 H7 Denham Suffk
63 N8 Denham End Suffk
36 B3 Denham Green Bucks
64 H7 Denham Green Suffk
159 N7 Denhead Abers
135 M5 Denhead Fife
142 F11 Denhead of Gray C Dund
117 R7 Denholm Border
90 D4 Denholme C Brad
90 D4 Denholme Clough C Brad
66 F7 Denio Gwynd
15 J4 Denmead Hants
151 N5 Denmore C Aber
24 E5 Denne Park W Susx
65 K8 Dennington Suffk
133 N11 Denny Falk
133 N11 Dennyloanhead Falk
134 H4 Den of Lindores Fife
90 B8 Denshaw Oldham
151 L8 Denside Abers
27 M3 Densole Kent
63 N10 Denston Suffk
71 K6 Denstone Staffs
39 K9 Denstroude Kent
95 Q3 Dent Cumb
61 Q3 Denton Cambs
103 P7 Denton Darltn
25 L10 Denton E Susx
27 M2 Denton Kent
37 Q6 Denton Kent
73 M4 Denton Lincs
96 H11 Denton N York
60 H9 Denton Nhants
65 K4 Denton Norfk
34 G4 Denton Oxon
83 K5 Denton Tamesd
75 M10 Denver Norfk
119 P8 Denwick Nthumb
76 E11 Deopham Norfk
64 E2 Deopham Green Norfk
63 N9 Depden Suffk
63 N9 Depden Green Suffk
37 J5 Deptford Gt Lon
21 K7 Deptford Wilts
72 B3 Derby C Derb
15 K5 Derby Devon
80 c8 Derbyhaven IoM
71 P9 Derby Services Derbys
72 C5 Derby South Services Derbys
141 L7 Derculich P & K
76 D9 Dereham Norfk
30 F4 Deri Caerph
16 E11 Derril Devon
27 M2 Derringstone Kent
70 F10 Derrington Staffs
16 E11 Derriton Devon
33 J10 Derry Hill Wilts
92 D9 Derrythorpe N Linc
75 N4 Dersingham Norfk
137 L5 Dervaig Ag & B
68 E4 Derwen Denbgs
43 L10 Derwen Fawr Carmth
54 G5 Derwenlas Powys
101 J6 Derwent Water Cumb
43 M11 Derwydd Carmth
60 H4 Desborough Nhants
72 D10 Desford Leics
158 D5 Deskford Moray
119 L3 Detchant Nthumb
38 C10 Detling Kent
57 M7 Deuxhill Shrops
31 N5 Devauden Mons
54 G9 Devil's Bridge Cerdgn
59 L6 Devitts Green Warwks
21 K2 Devizes Wilts
6 D8 Devonport C Plym
133 Q8 Devonside Clacks
3 K6 Devoran Cnwll
128 B7 Dewarton Mdloth
12 C5 Dewlish Dorset
90 G6 Dewsbury Kirk
90 G6 Dewsbury Moor Kirk
90 G6 Dewsbury Moor Crematorium Kirk
68 H11 Deytheur Powys
31 P11 Dial N Som
23 P9 Dial Green W Susx
24 E7 Dial Post W Susx
11 K4 Dibberford Dorset
14 D5 Dibden Hants
14 D5 Dibden Purlieu Hants
58 H9 Dickens Heath Solhll
64 H5 Dickleburgh Norfk
47 L8 Didbrook Gloucs
34 F6 Didcot Oxon
34 F6 Didcot Railway Centre Oxon
61 Q7 Diddington Cambs
57 J7 Diddlebury Shrops
45 P8 Didley Herefs
23 M11 Didling W Susx
32 F7 Didmarton Gloucs
82 H6 Didsbury Manch
6 H6 Didworthy Devon
86 E10 Digby Lincs
152 H4 Digg Highld
90 C9 Diggle Oldham
88 F9 Digmoor Lancs
50 F7 Digswell Herts
50 G8 Digswell Water Herts
43 J3 Dihewyd Cerdgn
77 L6 Dilham Norfk
70 H6 Dilhorne Staffs
89 M5 Dill Hall Lancs
61 P7 Dillington Cambs
112 E8 Dilston Nthumb
20 G5 Dilton Wilts
20 F5 Dilton Marsh Wilts
45 N4 Dilwyn Herefs
89 L7 Dimple Bolton
84 C8 Dimple Derbys
41 Q4 Dinas Carmth
4 E7 Dinas Cnwll
66 D7 Dinas Gwynd
41 K3 Dinas Pembks
30 D6 Dinas Rhondd
66 G3 Dinas Dinlle Gwynd
67 R11 Dinas-Mawddwy Gwynd
30 G10 Dinas Powys V Glam
19 Q6 Dinder Somset
45 Q7 Dinedor Herefs
31 N2 Dingestow Mons
81 M7 Dingle Lpool
26 D5 Dingleden Kent
60 G3 Dingley Nhants
155 P6 Dingwall Highld
68 D6 Dinmael Conwy
150 D8 Dinnet Abers
113 K6 Dinnington N u Ty
84 H3 Dinnington Rothm
11 J2 Dinnington Somset
67 K2 Dinorwic Gwynd
35 L2 Dinton Bucks
21 K8 Dinton Wilts
109 P2 Dinwoodie D & G
16 E8 Dinworthy Devon
18 H10 Dipford Somset
23 K3 Dipley Hants
120 F4 Dippen Ag & B
121 K7 Dippen N Ayrs
23 M5 Dippenhall Surrey
8 B3 Dippermill Devon
8 B8 Dippertown Devon
157 Q6 Dipple Moray
114 D7 Dipple S Ayrs
7 J7 Diptford Devon
113 J10 Dipton Dur
112 D8 Diptonmill Nthumb
128 E3 Dirleton E Loth
112 C11 Dirt Pot Nthumb
45 K2 Discoed Powys
72 D6 Diseworth Leics
97 N6 Dishforth N York
83 L8 Disley Ches E
64 G5 Diss Norfk
44 E3 Disserth Powys
100 D6 Distington Cumb
100 D6 Distington Hall Crematorium Cumb
21 L8 Ditchampton Wilts
20 B7 Ditcheat Somset
65 L3 Ditchingham Norfk
24 H7 Ditchling E Susx
57 J2 Ditherington Shrops
32 F11 Ditteridge Wilts
7 M7 Dittisham Devon
38 B10 Ditton Kent
63 L9 Ditton Green Cambs
57 L7 Ditton Priors Shrops
47 J8 Dixton Gloucs
31 P2 Dixton Mons
5 K2 Dizzard Cnwll
90 B9 Dobcross Oldham
5 L8 Dobwalls Cnwll
9 J7 Doccombe Devon
155 R9 Dochgarroch Highld
23 M6 Dockenfield Surrey
95 M6 Docker Lancs
75 Q3 Docking Norfk
45 R3 Docklow Herefs
101 L6 Dockray Cumb
110 E11 Dockray Cumb
7 J10 Dodbrooke Devon
51 N11 Doddinghurst Essex
62 F2 Doddington Cambs
38 F10 Doddington Kent
85 Q6 Doddington Lincs
119 J4 Doddington Nthumb
57 L9 Doddington Shrops
9 L7 Doddiscombsleigh Devon
69 R6 Dodd's Green Ches E
75 N4 Doddshill Norfk
5 N9 Doddy Cross Cnwll
60 D8 Dodford Nhants
58 D10 Dodford Worcs
32 E8 Dodington S Glos
18 G6 Dodington Somset
69 L2 Dodleston Ches W
17 J8 Dodscott Devon
125 N7 Dodside E Rens
71 J8 Dod's Leigh Staffs
91 J9 Dodworth Barns
91 J10 Dodworth Bottom Barns
91 J10 Dodworth Green Barns
58 H5 Doe Bank Birm
84 G7 Doe Lea Derbys
86 H9 Dogdyke Lincs
90 F8 Dogley Lane Kirk
23 L4 Dogmersfield Hants
33 L7 Dogridge Wilts
74 C10 Dogsthorpe C Pete
9 N5 Dog Village Devon
55 P2 Dolanog Powys
55 J11 Dolau Powys
43 N6 Dolaucothi Carmth
67 J6 Dolbenmaen Gwynd
70 C9 Doley Staffs
55 L4 Dolfach Powys
55 J3 Dol-for Powys
55 Q7 Dolfor Powys
79 P11 Dolgarrog Conwy
67 N11 Dolgellau Gwynd
54 F4 Dolgoch Gwynd
42 H8 Dol-gran Carmth
163 K6 Doll Highld
134 B8 Dollar Clacks
134 B8 Dollarfield Clacks
56 D11 Dolley Green Powys
54 F8 Dollwen Cerdgn
80 H10 Dolphin Flints
95 L10 Dolphinholme Lancs
127 L8 Dolphinton S Lans
17 K9 Dolton Devon
80 B10 Dolwen Conwy
67 N4 Dolwyddelan Conwy
54 E7 Dolybont Cerdgn
45 J3 Dolyhir Powys
69 J11 Domgay Powys
118 G2 Donaldson's Lodge Nthumb
91 P10 Doncaster Donc
91 P10 Doncaster Carr Donc
91 R8 Doncaster North Services Donc
20 H10 Donhead St Andrew Wilts
20 H10 Donhead St Mary Wilts
134 F10 Donibristle Fife
18 E6 Doniford Somset
74 D3 Donington Lincs
86 H4 Donington on Bain Lincs
72 D5 Donington Park Services Leics
74 D4 Donington Southing Lincs
59 M2 Donisthorpe Leics
27 K5 Donkey Street Kent
23 P2 Donkey Town Surrey
47 N9 Donnington Gloucs
46 D8 Donnington Herefs
57 K3 Donnington Shrops
34 E11 Donnington W Berk
15 N6 Donnington W Susx
57 N2 Donnington Wrekin
57 N2 Donnington Wood Wrekin
10 G2 Donyatt Somset
24 E5 Doomsday Green W Susx
114 F4 Doonfoot S Ayrs
114 F4 Doonholm S Ayrs
149 K4 Dorback Lodge Highld
11 P6 Dorchester Dorset
34 G6 Dorchester Oxon
59 L4 Dordon Warwks
84 D4 Dore Sheff
155 Q11 Dores Highld
36 E11 Dorking Surrey
52 F4 Dorking Tye Suffk
25 K2 Dormans Land Surrey
25 J2 Dormans Park Surrey
46 A6 Dormington Herefs
47 J3 Dormston Worcs
47 P8 Dorn Gloucs
35 P9 Dorney Bucks
145 Q2 Dornie Highld
162 H9 Dornoch Highld
110 D7 Dornock D & G
167 J6 Dorrery Highld
59 J10 Dorridge Solhll
86 E10 Dorrington Lincs
56 H4 Dorrington Shrops
70 C6 Dorrington Shrops
47 M5 Dorsington Warwks
45 L6 Dorstone Herefs
35 J2 Dorton Bucks
59 K5 Dosthill Staffs
78 F10 Dothan IoA
11 K5 Dottery Dorset
5 K9 Doublebois Cnwll
32 G6 Doughton Gloucs
80 e6 Douglas IoM
116 A4 Douglas S Lans
142 G11 Douglas and Angus C Dund
80 e6 Douglas Borough Crematorium IoM
131 P8 Douglas Pier Ag & B
142 G8 Douglastown Angus
116 B3 Douglas Water S Lans
126 E11 Douglas West S Lans
20 B6 Doulting Somset
169 b4 Dounby Ork
161 Q6 Doune Highld
133 L7 Doune Stirlg
114 C8 Dounepark S Ayrs
162 D8 Dounie Highld
6 E5 Dousland Devon
69 L10 Dovaston Shrops
84 G10 Dove Green Notts
83 N9 Dove Holes Derbys
100 E4 Dovenby Cumb
27 P3 Dover Kent
82 D4 Dover Wigan
27 P3 Dover Castle Kent
53 M5 Dovercourt Essex
58 C11 Doverdale Worcs
71 L8 Doveridge Derbys
36 G11 Doversgreen Surrey
141 P8 Dowally P & K
88 E4 Dowbridge Lancs
47 K11 Dowdeswell Gloucs
30 E3 Dowlais Myr Td
17 K9 Dowland Devon
10 H2 Dowlish Ford Somset
10 H2 Dowlish Wake Somset
33 L5 Down Ampney Gloucs
5 N11 Downderry Cnwll
37 K8 Downe Gt Lon
32 F5 Downend Gloucs
14 F9 Downend IoW
32 C9 Downend S Glos
34 E9 Downend W Berk
142 F11 Downfield C Dund
5 M7 Downgate Cnwll
5 P7 Downgate Cnwll
38 B2 Downham Essex
37 J6 Downham Gt Lon
89 M2 Downham Lancs
75 M10 Downham Market Norfk
46 G10 Down Hatherley Gloucs
19 Q9 Downhead Somset
20 C5 Downhead Somset
4 D8 Downhill Cnwll
134 D2 Downhill P & K
88 D9 Downholland Cross Lancs
103 M11 Downholme N York
5 P3 Downicarey Devon
151 N9 Downies Abers
80 H9 Downing Flints
35 M5 Downley Bucks
8 H4 Down St Mary Devon
24 H9 Downs Crematorium Br & H
20 B4 Downside Somset
20 B6 Downside Somset
36 D9 Downside Surrey
6 E8 Down Thomas Devon
13 N6 Downton Hants
21 N10 Downton Wilts
74 B5 Dowsby Lincs
74 E8 Dowsdale Lincs
70 F10 Doxey Staffs
119 N6 Doxford Nthumb
32 D10 Doynton S Glos
30 H7 Draethen Caerph
126 D8 Draffan S Lans
92 F8 Dragonby N Linc
24 D6 Dragons Green W Susx
85 M2 Drakeholes Notts
57 Q8 Drakelow Worcs
124 H7 Drakemyre N Ayrs
46 H5 Drakes Broughton Worcs
6 C4 Drakewalls Cnwll
96 F10 Draughton N York
60 G5 Draughton Nhants
92 A5 Drax N York
91 R5 Drax Hales N York
59 P10 Draycote Warwks
33 N9 Draycot Foliat Swindn
72 C4 Draycott Derbys
47 N7 Draycott Gloucs
57 Q6 Draycott Shrops
19 N4 Draycott Somset
19 Q10 Draycott Somset
46 G5 Draycott Worcs
71 M9 Draycott in the Clay Staffs
70 H6 Draycott in the Moors Staffs
9 J2 Drayford Devon
15 J5 Drayton C Port
60 H2 Drayton Leics
74 D3 Drayton Lincs
76 H9 Drayton Norfk
34 E6 Drayton Oxon
48 D6 Drayton Oxon
19 M10 Drayton Somset
58 D9 Drayton Worcs
59 J4 Drayton Bassett Staffs
35 P2 Drayton Beauchamp Bucks
59 J4 Drayton Manor Park Staffs
49 M9 Drayton Parslow Bucks
34 G5 Drayton St Leonard Oxon
96 G9 Drebley N York
80 g3 Dreemskerry IoM
40 H8 Dreen Hill Pembks
28 F2 Drefach Carmth
42 G7 Drefach Carmth
43 J5 Drefach Cerdgn
42 G7 Drefelin Carmth
125 K10 Dreghorn N Ayrs
27 M3 Drellingore Kent
128 E4 Drem E Loth
70 G6 Dresden C Stke
8 H6 Drewsteignton Devon
87 L6 Driby Lincs
99 L9 Driffield E R Yk
33 L5 Driffield Gloucs
33 L5 Driffield Cross Roads Gloucs
2 C8 Drift Cnwll
100 E11 Drigg Cumb
90 G5 Drighlington Leeds
137 P5 Drimnin Highld
11 J4 Drimpton Dorset
138 H2 Drimsallie Highld
98 B11 Dringhouses C York
64 D9 Drinkstone Suffk
64 D9 Drinkstone Green Suffk
11 M3 Drive End Dorset
50 F6 Driver's End Herts
71 J9 Drointon Staffs
46 G2 Droitwich Worcs
134 E4 Dron P & K
84 E5 Dronfield Derbys
84 D5 Dronfield Woodhouse Derbys
114 H4 Drongan E Ayrs
142 E10 Dronley Angus
12 C3 Droop Dorset
84 E2 Dropping Well Rothm
22 H11 Droxford Hants
83 K5 Droylsden Tamesd
68 D6 Druid Denbgs
40 G7 Druidston Pembks
139 K3 Druimarbin Highld
139 J8 Druimavuic Ag & B
123 M5 Druimdrishaig Ag & B
145 L11 Druimindarroch Highld
124 A2 Drum Ag & B
134 C7 Drum P & K
116 C3 Drumalbin S Lans
164 D10 Drumbeg Highld
158 E9 Drumblade Abers
106 E9 Drumbreddon D & G
153 P11 Drumbuie Highld
110 E9 Drumburgh Cumb
109 J10 Drumburn D & G
125 N3 Drumchapel C Glas
140 G6 Drumchastle P & K
125 Q10 Drumclog S Lans
135 L7 Drumeldrie Fife
116 G4 Drumelzier Border
145 L4 Drumfearn Highld
151 J8 Drumfrennie Abers
142 G7 Drumgley Angus
148 D7 Drumguish Highld
157 M11 Drumin Moray
115 K8 Drumjohn D & G
107 J2 Drumlamford S Ayrs
150 G6 Drumlasie Abers
110 E10 Drumleaning Cumb
120 C8 Drumlemble Ag & B
151 K11 Drumlithie Abers
107 L8 Drummoddie D & G
106 F10 Drummore D & G
158 A9 Drummuir Moray
155 P11 Drumnadrochit Highld
106 F10 Drumnaglaur D & G
158 D7 Drumnagorrach Moray
109 J5 Drumpark D & G
161 K6 Drumrunie Lodge Highld
114 E5 Drumshang S Ayrs
152 H8 Drumuie Highld
148 G3 Drumuillie Highld
133 K7 Drumvaich Stirlg
134 E6 Drunzie P & K
119 Q11 Druridge Nthumb
69 J2 Drury Flints
102 C7 Drybeck Cumb
158 B5 Drybridge Moray
125 K10 Drybridge N Ayrs
46 B11 Drybrook Gloucs
118 A4 Dryburgh Border
85 Q11 Dry Doddington Lincs
62 E8 Dry Drayton Cambs
132 F10 Drymen Stirlg
159 M8 Drymuir Abers
152 G11 Drynoch Highld
34 E4 Dry Sandford Oxon
43 L10 Dryslwyn Carmth
37 Q3 Dry Street Essex
57 K3 Dryton Shrops
159 J5 Dubford Abers
64 H8 Dublin Suffk
161 P3 Duchally Highld
50 C2 Duck End Bed
62 B8 Duck End Cambs
51 Q4 Duck End Essex
51 Q5 Duck End Essex
52 B7 Duckend Green Essex
69 N4 Duckington Ches W
34 C3 Ducklington Oxon
61 P9 Duck's Cross Bed
51 L3 Duddenhoe End Essex
127 P3 Duddingston C Edin
73 P10 Duddington Nhants
18 H10 Duddlestone Somset
25 L5 Duddleswell E Susx
57 M8 Duddlewick Shrops
118 H2 Duddo Nthumb
69 P2 Duddon Ches W
94 D3 Duddon Bridge Cumb
81 Q11 Duddon Common Ches W
69 K7 Dudleston Shrops
69 L7 Dudleston Heath Shrops
58 D6 Dudley Dudley
113 L6 Dudley N Tyne
90 F4 Dudley Hill C Brad
58 E6 Dudley Port Sandw
57 L10 Dudnill Shrops
13 J5 Dudsbury Dorset
35 Q3 Dudswell Herts
72 A2 Duffield Derbys
29 M5 Duffryn Neath
157 Q9 Dufftown Moray
157 M4 Duffus Moray
102 C5 Dufton Cumb
98 H7 Duggleby N York
153 P11 Duirinish Highld
145 M5 Duisdalemore Highld
139 J2 Duisky Highld
30 F2 Dukestown Blae G
53 J3 Duke Street Suffk
83 K5 Dukinfield Tamesd
83 K5 Dukinfield Crematorium Tamesd
78 H7 Dulas IoA
19 Q6 Dulcote Somset
9 Q3 Dulford Devon
141 K8 Dull P & K
126 C2 Dullatur N Lans
63 K9 Dullingham Cambs
63 K9 Dullingham Ley Cambs
148 H3 Dulnain Bridge Highld
61 Q8 Duloe Bed
5 L10 Duloe Cnwll
18 B9 Dulverton Somset
36 H6 Dulwich Gt Lon
125 K2 Dumbarton W Duns
47 K7 Dumbleton Gloucs
109 L5 Dumfries D & G
132 G11 Dumgoyne Stirlg
22 G5 Dummer Hants
39 Q8 Dumpton Kent
143 M6 Dun Angus
140 H6 Dunalastair P & K
124 F3 Dunan Ag & B
145 J2 Dunan Highld
140 C6 Dunan P & K
120 C10 Dunaverty Ag & B
19 K6 Dunball Somset
128 H4 Dunbar E Loth
167 L11 Dunbeath Highld
138 F11 Dunbeg Ag & B
133 M7 Dunblane Stirlg
134 H4 Dunbog Fife
22 B9 Dunbridge Hants
155 Q6 Duncanston Highld
150 F2 Duncanstone Abers
9 L7 Dunchideock Devon
59 Q10 Dunchurch Warwks
49 J4 Duncote Nhants
109 L4 Duncow D & G
134 E6 Duncrievie P & K
23 Q11 Duncton W Susx
142 G11 Dundee C Dund
135 K2 Dundee Airport C Dund
142 F11 Dundee Crematorium C Dund
19 N8 Dundon Somset
125 K11 Dundonald S Ayrs
160 H9 Dundonnell Highld
110 D11 Dundraw Cumb
147 J5 Dundreggan Highld
108 F11 Dundrennan D & G
31 Q11 Dundry N Som
151 K6 Dunecht Abers
134 D10 Dunfermline Fife
134 E10 Dunfermline Crematorium Fife
33 M5 Dunfield Gloucs
83 Q4 Dunford Bridge Barns
38 F10 Dungate Kent
126 B10 Dungavel S Lans
20 G4 Dunge Wilts
27 J8 Dungeness Kent
84 C3 Dungworth Sheff
85 P6 Dunham Notts
81 P10 Dunham-on-the-Hill Ches W
46 H2 Dunhampstead Worcs
58 B11 Dunhampton Worcs
82 F7 Dunham Town Traffd
82 F7 Dunham Woodhouses Traffd
86 D5 Dunholme Lincs
135 N5 Dunino Fife
133 N11 Dunipace Falk
141 P9 Dunkeld P & K
20 D3 Dunkerton BaNES
10 C3 Dunkeswell Devon
97 M11 Dunkeswick N York
81 M10 Dunkirk Ches W
39 J10 Dunkirk Kent
32 E7 Dunkirk S Glos
21 J2 Dunkirk Wilts
37 P10 Dunk's Green Kent
143 K4 Dunlappie Angus

22 E4 Dunley Hants
57 P11 Dunley Worcs
125 L8 Dunlop E Ayrs
147 P3 Dunmaglass Highld
4 G8 Dunmere Cnwll
133 P10 Dunmore Falk
167 M2 Dunnet Highld
143 J8 Dunnichen Angus
134 C5 Dunning P & K
98 D10 Dunnington C York
99 P10 Dunnington E R Yk
47 L4 Dunnington Warwks
89 N5 Dunnockshaw Lancs
38 C9 Dunn Street Kent
124 F2 Dunoon Ag & B
157 J8 Dunphail Moray
106 G6 Dunragit D & G
129 K9 Duns Border
84 B6 Dunsa Derbys
74 B5 Dunsby Lincs
89 L8 Dunscar Bolton
109 J4 Dunscore D & G
91 Q9 Dunscroft Donc
104 H7 Dunsdale R & Cl
35 K9 Dunsden Green Oxon
16 E10 Dunsdon Devon
24 B3 Dunsfold Surrey
9 K7 Dunsford Devon
134 G5 Dunshalt Fife
159 N8 Dunshillock Abers
84 G8 Dunsill Notts
105 N8 Dunsley N York
58 C8 Dunsley Staffs
35 N3 Dunsmore Bucks
95 P11 Dunsop Bridge Lancs
50 B6 Dunstable C Beds
71 M10 Dunstall Staffs
46 G6 Dunstall Common Worcs
63 M8 Dunstall Green Suffk
119 P7 Dunstan Nthumb
119 P6 Dunstan Steads Nthumb
18 C6 Dunster Somset
48 E9 Duns Tew Oxon
113 K8 Dunston Gatesd
86 E8 Dunston Lincs
77 J11 Dunston Norfk
70 G11 Dunston Staffs
6 F8 Dunstone Devon
8 H9 Dunstone Devon
70 G11 Dunston Heath Staffs
91 Q9 Dunsville Donc
93 J3 Dunswell E R Yk
127 K8 Dunsyre S Lans
5 P6 Dunterton Devon
48 C9 Dunthrop Oxon
33 J3 Duntisbourne Abbots Gloucs
33 J3 Duntisbourne Leer Gloucs
33 J3 Duntisbourne Rouse Gloucs
11 P3 Duntish Dorset
125 M3 Duntocher W Duns
49 M10 Dunton Bucks
50 F2 Dunton C Beds
76 B5 Dunton Norfk
60 B2 Dunton Bassett Leics
37 M9 Dunton Green Kent
37 Q2 Dunton Wayletts Essex
152 G3 Duntulm Highld
114 E4 Dunure S Ayrs
28 G6 Dunvant Swans
152 D8 Dunvegan Highld
65 P7 Dunwich Suffk
70 G3 Dunwood Staffs
110 H10 Durdar Cumb
3 K8 Durgan Cnwll
103 Q2 Durham Dur
103 Q2 Durham Cathedral Dur
103 Q2 Durham Crematorium Dur
104 B3 Durham Services Dur
104 C8 Durham Tees Valley Airport S on T
116 B10 Durisdeer D & G
116 B10 Durisdeermill D & G
91 J7 Durkar Wakefd
19 J7 Durleigh Somset
22 F11 Durley Hants
21 P2 Durley Wilts
22 F11 Durley Street Hants
39 N10 Durlock Kent
39 P9 Durlock Kent
46 B7 Durlow Common Herefs
89 Q7 Durn Rochdl
165 K3 Durness Highld
151 J2 Durno Abers
138 H6 Duror Highld
131 K6 Durran Ag & B
24 D9 Durrington W Susx
21 N6 Durrington Wilts
151 K8 Durris Abers
32 E5 Dursley Gloucs
46 C10 Dursley Cross Gloucs
19 J9 Durston Somset
12 E3 Durweston Dorset
60 F8 Duston Nhants
148 G3 Duthil Highld
56 C9 Dutlas Powys
51 P5 Duton Hill Essex
5 N4 Dutson Cnwll
82 C9 Dutton Ches W
62 G11 Duxford Cambs
34 C5 Duxford Oxon
62 G11 Duxford Aircraft Museum Cambs
79 N9 Dwygyfylchi Conwy
78 G11 Dwyran IoA
151 M5 Dyce C Aber
52 B4 Dyer's End Essex
28 E4 Dyfatty Carmth
54 F2 Dyffrydan Gwynd
29 N6 Dyffryn Brdgnd
30 E4 Dyffryn Myr Td
30 E10 Dyffryn V Glam
67 K10 Dyffryn Ardudwy Gwynd
54 H8 Dyffryn Castell Cerdgn
29 N2 Dyffryn Cellwen Neath
74 B6 Dyke Lincs
156 H6 Dyke Moray
142 C7 Dykehead Angus
142 F6 Dykehead Angus
126 F6 Dykehead N Lans
132 H8 Dykehead Stirlg
143 N4 Dykelands Abers
142 D6 Dykends Angus
158 H9 Dykeside Abers
55 K6 Dylife Powys
27 K6 Dymchurch Kent
46 D8 Dymock Gloucs
32 D9 Dyrham S Glos
135 J9 Dysart Fife
80 F9 Dyserth Denbgs

E

58 E9 Eachway Worcs
112 H6 Eachwick Nthumb
95 J11 Eagland Hill Lancs
85 Q7 Eagle Lincs
85 Q7 Eagle Barnsdale Lincs
85 Q7 Eagle Moor Lincs
104 D7 Eaglescliffe S on T
100 E5 Eaglesfield Cumb
110 D6 Eaglesfield D & G
125 P7 Eaglesham E Rens
89 L8 Eagley Bolton
80 c6 Eairy IoM
85 L8 Eakring Notts
92 C8 Ealand N Linc
36 E4 Ealing Gt Lon
111 N9 Eals Nthumb
101 P5 Eamont Bridge Cumb
96 D11 Earby Lancs
89 K6 Earcroft Bl w D
57 N6 Eardington Shrops
45 N3 Eardisland Herefs
45 L5 Eardisley Herefs
69 L9 Eardiston Shrops
57 M11 Eardiston Worcs
62 E5 Earith Cambs
119 J5 Earle Nthumb
82 C5 Earlestown St Hel
35 K10 Earley Wokham
76 H10 Earlham Norfk
77 J10 Earlham Crematorium Norfk
152 F5 Earlish Highld
61 J8 Earls Barton Nhants
52 E6 Earls Colne Essex
47 J3 Earls Common Worcs
46 G6 Earl's Croome Worcs
57 L9 Earlsditton Shrops
59 M9 Earlsdon Covtry
25 P7 Earl's Down E Susx
135 M7 Earlsferry Fife
36 G6 Earlsfield Gt Lon
159 K11 Earlsford Abers
64 E8 Earl's Green Suffk
90 H6 Earlsheaton Kirk
72 D11 Earl Shilton Leics
65 J9 Earl Soham Suffk
83 N11 Earl Sterndale Derbys
117 R3 Earlston Border
125 L10 Earlston E Ayrs
64 G10 Earl Stonham Suffk
36 G11 Earlswood Surrey
58 H10 Earlswood Warwks
31 N6 Earlswood Common Mons
15 M7 Earnley W Susx
88 G6 Earnshaw Bridge Lancs
113 M6 Earsdon N Tyne
113 J2 Earsdon Nthumb
65 L4 Earsham Norfk
98 C9 Earswick C York
15 P5 Eartham W Susx
32 C7 Earthcott S Glos
104 G9 Easby N York
130 E4 Easdale Ag & B
23 P10 Easebourne W Susx
59 Q9 Easenhall Warwks
23 P6 Eashing Surrey
35 J2 Easington Bucks
104 D2 Easington Dur
93 Q7 Easington E R Yk
119 M4 Easington Nthumb
35 J5 Easington Oxon
105 K7 Easington R & Cl
104 D2 Easington Colliery Dur
113 N11 Easington Lane Sundld
98 A7 Easingwold N York
39 N11 Easole Street Kent
142 E9 Eassie and Nevay Angus
30 D11 East Aberthaw V Glam
7 K9 East Allington Devon
17 R6 East Anstey Devon
22 C5 East Anton Hants
103 P11 East Appleton N York
14 G9 East Ashey IoW
15 M5 East Ashling W Susx
22 D5 East Aston Hants
99 K3 East Ayton N York
5 M2 East Balsdon Cnwll
30 H3 East Bank Blae G
86 G4 East Barkwith Lincs
38 B11 East Barming Kent
105 M8 East Barnby N York
50 G11 East Barnet Gt Lon
129 J4 East Barns E Loth
76 C5 East Barsham Norfk
76 H4 East Beckham Norfk
36 C6 East Bedfont Gt Lon
53 J5 East Bergholt Suffk
90 F5 East Bierley Kirk
76 D8 East Bilney Norfk
25 L10 East Blatchington E Susx
12 E6 East Bloxworth Dorset
113 N8 East Boldon S Tyne
14 C6 East Boldre Hants
119 M7 East Bolton Nthumb
104 B8 Eastbourne Darltn
25 P11 Eastbourne E Susx
25 P10 Eastbourne Crematorium E Susx
19 K7 East Bower Somset
76 C10 East Bradenham Norfk
19 K4 East Brent Somset
65 P8 Eastbridge Suffk
72 H2 East Bridgford Notts
103 J7 East Briscoe Dur
30 G10 Eastbrook V Glam
17 M5 East Buckland Devon
9 Q8 East Budleigh Devon
90 C2 Eastburn C Brad
99 K9 Eastburn E R Yk
35 Q8 East Burnham Bucks
12 D7 East Burton Dorset
36 D2 Eastbury Herts
34 B9 Eastbury W Berk
112 H11 East Butsfield Dur
92 D9 East Butterwick N Linc
96 F10 Eastby N York
127 K4 East Calder W Loth
76 H11 East Carleton Norfk
90 G2 East Carlton Leeds
60 H3 East Carlton Nhants
12 C8 East Chaldon (Chaldon Herring) Dorset
34 C7 East Challow Oxon
7 K10 East Charleton Devon
11 M3 East Chelborough Dorset
25 J7 East Chiltington E Susx
11 K2 East Chinnock Somset
21 M4 East Chisenbury Wilts
21 Q5 East Cholderton Hants
38 G7 Eastchurch Kent
36 C10 East Clandon Surrey
49 K9 East Claydon Bucks
31 M10 East Clevedon N Som
11 L2 East Coker Somset
32 G4 Eastcombe Gloucs
18 G8 East Combe Somset
20 B6 East Compton Somset
7 L7 East Cornworthy Devon
109 P9 East Cote Cumb
36 D3 Eastcote Gt Lon
49 J4 Eastcote Nhants
59 J9 Eastcote Solhll
16 D8 Eastcott Cnwll
21 K3 Eastcott Wilts
92 B2 East Cottingwith E R Yk
21 P2 Eastcourt Wilts
33 J6 Eastcourt Wilts
14 F7 East Cowes IoW
91 R6 East Cowick E R Yk
104 B10 East Cowton N York
113 L5 East Cramlington Nthumb
20 C6 East Cranmore Somset
12 F8 East Creech Dorset
110 F11 East Curthwaite Cumb
25 N11 East Dean E Susx
46 C10 East Dean Gloucs
21 Q9 East Dean Hants
15 P4 East Dean W Susx
7 L9 Eastdown Devon
17 L3 East Down Devon
85 N5 East Drayton Notts
36 H5 East Dulwich Gt Lon
31 Q11 East Dundry N Som
93 J5 East Ella C KuH
61 P9 East End Bed
49 Q6 East End C Beds
93 L4 East End E R Yk
93 N5 East End E R Yk
38 F3 Eastend Essex
51 K8 East End Essex
14 C7 East End Hants
22 D2 East End Hants
51 L5 East End Herts
26 D4 East End Kent
38 G7 East End Kent
49 P6 East End M Keyn
31 N10 East End N Som
48 C11 East End Oxon
20 C5 East End Somset
53 K4 East End Suffk
149 P9 Easter Balmoral Abers
31 Q8 Easter Compton S Glos
156 D7 Easter Dalziel Highld
15 P5 Eastergate W Susx
126 B4 Easterhouse C Glas
127 N5 Easter Howgate Mdloth
155 Q6 Easter Kinkell Highld
155 Q9 Easter Moniack Highld
59 L9 Eastern Green Covtry
151 L7 Easter Ord Abers
135 P6 Easter Pitkierie Fife
169 q9 Easter Skeld Shet
118 E4 Easter Softlaw Border
21 K4 Easterton Wilts
19 K4 Eastertown Somset
21 P4 East Everleigh Wilts
38 B11 East Farleigh Kent
60 F4 East Farndon Nhants
92 D11 East Ferry Lincs
126 F5 Eastfield N Lans
99 L4 Eastfield N York
86 D3 East Firsby Lincs
128 E4 East Fortune E Loth
91 L4 East Garforth Leeds
34 C9 East Garston W Berk
103 J3 Eastgate Dur
74 B7 Eastgate Lincs
76 G7 Eastgate Norfk
34 D7 East Ginge Oxon
72 G8 East Goscote Leics
21 Q2 East Grafton Wilts
65 N8 East Green Suffk
21 P9 East Grimstead Wilts
25 J3 East Grinstead W Susx
26 F7 East Guldeford E Susx
60 E7 East Haddon Nhants
34 F7 East Hagbourne Oxon
93 K7 East Halton N Linc
37 K4 East Ham Gt Lon
81 M8 Eastham Wirral
81 M8 Eastham Ferry Wirral
35 M11 Easthampstead Park Crematorium Br For
45 N2 Easthampton Herefs
34 D6 East Hanney Oxon
52 C11 East Hanningfield Essex
91 M7 East Hardwick Wakefd
64 D4 East Harling Norfk
104 D11 East Harlsey N York
21 M9 East Harnham Wilts
19 Q3 East Harptree BaNES
104 D7 East Hartburn S on T
113 L5 East Hartford Nthumb
23 L11 East Harting W Susx
20 H9 East Hatch Wilts
62 C10 East Hatley Cambs
97 J2 East Hauxwell N York
143 K10 East Haven Angus
35 L11 Eastheath Wokham
74 C2 East Heckington Lincs
103 N2 East Hedleyhope Dur
163 N3 East Helmsdale Highld
34 E7 East Hendred Oxon
99 J5 East Heslerton N York
19 M2 East Hewish N Som
25 M7 East Hoathly E Susx
12 E7 East Holme Dorset
57 K5 Easthope Shrops
52 F7 Easthorpe Essex
85 M10 Easthorpe Notts
19 Q5 East Horrington Somset
36 C10 East Horsley Surrey
119 K4 East Horton Nthumb
13 J5 East Howe Bmouth
98 C9 East Huntington C York
19 K5 East Huntspill Somset
50 D7 East Hyde C Beds
17 N2 East Ilkerton Devon
34 E8 East Ilsley W Berk
8 H3 Eastington Devon
32 E3 Eastington Gloucs
33 M2 Eastington Gloucs
87 L8 East Keal Lincs
33 M11 East Kennett Wilts
91 K2 East Keswick Leeds
125 Q7 East Kilbride S Lans
8 C5 East Kimber Devon
87 K8 East Kirkby Lincs
12 D7 East Knighton Dorset
17 Q7 East Knowstone Devon
20 G8 East Knoyle Wilts
19 M11 East Lambrook Somset
89 M9 East Lancashire Crematorium Bury
108 H6 Eastlands D & G
27 P2 East Langdon Kent
60 F2 East Langton Leics
15 N5 East Lavant W Susx
23 P11 East Lavington W Susx
103 N9 East Layton N York
33 P4 Eastleach Martin Gloucs
33 N3 Eastleach Turville Gloucs
72 F5 East Leake Notts
118 G3 East Learmouth Nthumb
6 H8 East Leigh Devon
7 K7 East Leigh Devon
8 G3 East Leigh Devon
16 H6 Eastleigh Devon
22 E11 Eastleigh Hants
76 B8 East Lexham Norfk
38 G10 Eastling Kent
128 F4 East Linton E Loth
23 L9 East Liss Hants
34 D7 East Lockinge Oxon
37 J4 East London Crematorium Gt Lon
92 C11 East Lound N Linc
12 E8 East Lulworth Dorset
99 J7 East Lutton N York
18 G9 East Lydeard Somset
19 Q8 East Lydford Somset
38 B10 East Malling Kent
37 Q9 East Malling Heath Kent
15 M4 East Marden W Susx
85 M6 East Markham Notts
21 L11 East Martin Hants
96 D10 East Marton N York
23 J10 East Meon Hants
18 C11 East Mere Devon
52 H9 East Mersea Essex
72 D5 East Midlands Airport Leics
36 D7 East Molesey Surrey
75 P10 Eastmoor Norfk
12 F6 East Morden Dorset
90 D2 East Morton C Brad
116 B10 East Morton D & G
98 D5 East Ness N York
93 N3 East Newton E R Yk
15 J7 Eastney C Port
46 D7 Eastnor Herefs
73 K10 East Norton Leics
92 D7 Eastoft N Linc
7 L4 East Ogwell Devon
61 P6 Easton Cambs
110 E9 Easton Cumb
8 H7 Easton Devon
11 P10 Easton Dorset
22 F8 Easton Hants
73 N5 Easton Lincs
76 G9 Easton Norfk
19 P5 Easton Somset
65 K10 Easton Suffk
34 D10 Easton W Berk
32 G10 Easton Wilts
32 G7 Easton Grey Wilts
31 P9 Easton-in-Gordano N Som
61 J9 Easton Maudit Nhants
73 Q10 Easton on the Hill Nhants
21 P2 Easton Royal Wilts
20 F11 East Orchard Dorset
129 P9 East Ord Nthumb
5 P3 East Panson Devon
13 J5 East Parley Dorset
37 Q11 East Peckham Kent
41 J10 East Pennar Pembks
19 Q7 East Pennard Somset
61 Q7 East Perry Cambs
7 K11 East Portlemouth Devon
7 K11 East Prawle Devon
24 C10 East Preston W Susx
11 Q3 East Pulham Dorset
16 F8 East Putford Devon
18 F6 East Quantoxhead Somset
38 D8 East Rainham Medway
113 M11 East Rainton Sundld
93 M11 East Ravendale NE Lin
76 B6 East Raynham Norfk
74 E11 Eastrea Cambs
99 L7 East Riding Crematorium E R Yk
110 D7 Eastriggs D & G
91 K2 East Rigton Leeds
92 C5 Eastrington E R Yk
19 L2 East Rolstone N Som
33 P6 Eastrop Swindn
104 D10 East Rounton N York
76 A6 East Rudham Norfk
76 H3 East Runton Norfk
77 L6 East Ruston Norfk
39 P11 Eastry Kent
128 D6 East Saltoun E Loth
23 N10 Eastshaw W Susx
36 F6 East Sheen Gt Lon
34 C10 East Shefford W Berk
113 L4 East Sleekburn Nthumb
77 P8 East Somerton Norfk
85 N2 East Stockwith Lincs
12 E7 East Stoke Dorset
85 N11 East Stoke Notts
20 F10 East Stour Dorset
39 N9 East Stourmouth Kent
17 L6 East Stowford Devon
22 F6 East Stratton Hants
27 P2 East Studdal Kent
26 D2 East Sutton Kent
5 K9 East Taphouse Cnwll
16 H6 East-the-Water Devon
119 N10 East Thirston Nthumb
37 Q5 East Tilbury Thurr
23 K8 East Tisted Hants
86 F4 East Torrington Lincs
76 F9 East Tuddenham Norfk
21 Q9 East Tytherley Hants
33 J10 East Tytherton Wilts
9 K3 East Village Devon
32 B10 Eastville Bristl
87 M9 Eastville Lincs
57 J6 East Wall Shrops
75 P7 East Walton Norfk
19 P4 East Water Somset
8 G6 East Week Devon
73 K5 Eastwell Leics
22 B10 East Wellow Hants
135 J8 East Wemyss Fife
126 H4 East Whitburn W Loth
51 K8 Eastwick Herts
37 L5 East Wickham Gt Lon
41 L10 East Williamston Pembks
75 N7 East Winch Norfk
21 P8 East Winterslow Wilts
15 L7 East Wittering W Susx
96 H3 East Witton N York
84 G11 Eastwood Notts
38 D4 Eastwood Sthend
112 D3 East Woodburn Nthumb
62 F2 Eastwood End Cambs
22 D2 East Woodhay Hants
20 E6 East Woodlands Somset
23 L7 East Worldham Hants
64 C3 East Wretham Norfk
16 D8 East Youlstone Devon
59 N11 Eathorpe Warwks
83 J11 Eaton Ches E
69 Q2 Eaton Ches W
73 K5 Eaton Leics
77 J10 Eaton Norfk
85 M5 Eaton Notts
34 D4 Eaton Oxon
56 F7 Eaton Shrops
57 J7 Eaton Shrops
45 N7 Eaton Bishop Herefs
49 Q10 Eaton Bray C Beds
57 K3 Eaton Constantine Shrops
61 Q9 Eaton Ford Cambs
49 Q10 Eaton Green C Beds
33 Q5 Eaton Hastings Oxon
57 J3 Eaton Mascott Shrops
61 Q9 Eaton Socon Cambs
70 B10 Eaton upon Tern Shrops
82 D6 Eaves Brow Warrtn
59 L8 Eaves Green Solhll
98 H4 Ebberston N York
21 J10 Ebbesborne Wake Wilts
30 G3 Ebbw Vale Blae G
112 H9 Ebchester Dur
19 L2 Ebdon N Som
9 N7 Ebford Devon
32 F3 Ebley Gloucs
69 N5 Ebnal Ches W
45 P3 Ebnall Herefs
47 N6 Ebrington Gloucs
8 D6 Ebsworthy Devon
22 E3 Ecchinswell Hants
129 K6 Ecclaw Border
110 C6 Ecclefechan D & G
118 E2 Eccles Border
38 B9 Eccles Kent
82 G5 Eccles Salfd
84 D4 Ecclesall Sheff
82 F5 Eccles Crematorium Salfd
84 E2 Ecclesfield Sheff
45 M5 Eccles Green Herefs
70 E9 Eccleshall Staffs
90 F3 Eccleshill C Brad
127 K3 Ecclesmachan W Loth
77 N6 Eccles on Sea Norfk
64 E4 Eccles Road Norfk
69 M2 Eccleston Ches W
88 G7 Eccleston Lancs
81 P5 Eccleston St Hel
88 G7 Eccleston Green Lancs
151 J6 Echt Abers
118 D5 Eckford Border
84 F5 Eckington Derbys
46 H6 Eckington Worcs
60 H8 Ecton Nhants
71 K3 Ecton Staffs
83 P7 Edale Derbys
169 e3 Eday Ork
169 e3 Eday Airport Ork
24 F8 Edburton W Susx
109 P11 Edderside Cumb
162 G10 Edderton Highld
39 L8 Eddington Kent
127 N8 Eddleston Border
126 C7 Eddlewood S Lans
37 K11 Edenbridge Kent
89 N7 Edenfield Lancs
101 Q4 Edenhall Cumb
73 R6 Edenham Lincs
95 J5 Eden Mount Cumb
37 J7 Eden Park Gt Lon
3 Q3 Eden Project Cnwll
84 B7 Edensor Derbys
132 C9 Edentaggart Ag & B
91 Q9 Edenthorpe Donc
66 D7 Edern Gwynd
19 P7 Edgarley Somset
58 G8 Edgbaston Birm
3 J7 Edgcombe Cnwll
49 J10 Edgcott Bucks
17 Q4 Edgcott Somset
32 F3 Edge Gloucs
56 F3 Edge Shrops
69 Q10 Edgebolton Shrops
31 Q2 Edge End Gloucs
76 F5 Edgefield Norfk
76 F5 Edgefield Green Norfk
89 L9 Edgefold Bolton
69 N4 Edge Green Ches W
48 C5 Edgehill Warwks
69 L11 Edgerley Shrops
90 E7 Edgerton Kirk
89 N6 Edgeside Lancs
32 H3 Edgeworth Gloucs
9 K2 Edgeworthy Devon
7 M5 Edginswell Torbay
47 K2 Edgiock Worcs
70 C11 Edgmond Wrekin
70 C10 Edgmond Marsh Wrekin
56 F7 Edgton Shrops
36 E2 Edgware Gt Lon
89 L7 Edgworth Bl w D
152 E7 Edinbane Highld
127 P3 Edinburgh C Edin
127 L3 Edinburgh Airport C Edin
127 P3 Edinburgh Castle C Edin
127 N2 Edinburgh Royal Botanic Gardens C Edin
127 N3 Edinburgh Zoo C Edin
59 K2 Edingale Staffs
108 H8 Edingham D & G
85 L9 Edingley Notts
77 L5 Edingthorpe Norfk

77 L5 **Edingthorpe Green** Norfk
129 M9 **Edington** Border
113 J4 **Edington** Nthumb
19 L7 **Edington** Somset
20 H4 **Edington** Wilts
19 L6 **Edington Burtle** Somset
19 L4 **Edingworth** Somset
16 D7 **Edistone** Devon
19 K5 **Edithmead** Somset
73 N9 **Edith Weston** Rutlnd
49 Q11 **Edlesborough** Bucks
119 M9 **Edlingham** Nthumb
86 H6 **Edlington** Lincs
111 J9 **Edmond Castle** Cumb
13 J2 **Edmondsham** Dorset
113 K11 **Edmondsley** Dur
73 M7 **Edmondthorpe** Leics
4 F7 **Edmonton** Cnwll
36 H2 **Edmonton** Gt Lon
112 F10 **Edmundbyers** Dur
118 D3 **Ednam** Border
71 N6 **Ednaston** Derbys
141 L7 **Edradynate** P & K
129 L8 **Edrom** Border
58 P8 **Edstaston** Shrops
47 N2 **Edstone** Warwks
46 C3 **Edvin Loach** Herefs
72 F3 **Edwalton** Notts
52 F3 **Edwardstone** Suffk
30 E5 **Edwardsville** Myr Td
43 M8 **Edwinsford** Carmth
85 K7 **Edwinstowe** Notts
50 F2 **Edworth** C Beds
46 B3 **Edwyn Ralph** Herefs
143 L4 **Edzell** Angus
143 L4 **Edzell Woods** Abers
29 L5 **Efail-fach** Neath
30 E8 **Efail Isaf** Rhondd
66 F7 **Efailnewydd** Gwynd
68 G9 **Efail-Rhyd** Powys
41 M5 **Efailwen** Carmth
68 F3 **Efenechtyd** Denbgs
110 F2 **Effgill** D & G
36 D10 **Effingham** Surrey
71 M11 **Efflinch** Staffs
9 L4 **Efford** Devon
6 E7 **Efford Crematorium** C Plym
22 D4 **Egbury** Hants
23 Q10 **Egdean** W Susx
89 L8 **Egerton** Bolton
26 F2 **Egerton** Kent
26 E2 **Egerton Forstal** Kent
52 P6 **Eggborough** N York
6 E7 **Eggbuckland** C Plym
17 M9 **Eggesford** Devon
49 Q9 **Eggington** C Beds
71 P9 **Egginton** Derbys
104 D8 **Egglescliffe** S on T
103 J6 **Eggleston** Dur
36 B6 **Egham** Surrey
35 Q10 **Egham Wick** Surrey
73 M9 **Egleton** Rutlnd
119 M7 **Eglingham** Nthumb
4 G7 **Egloshayle** Cnwll
5 M4 **Egloskerry** Cnwll
79 Q10 **Eglwysbach** Conwy
30 D11 **Eglwys-Brewis** V Glam
69 N6 **Eglwys Cross** Wrexhm
54 F5 **Eglwys Fach** Cerdgn
41 M3 **Eglwyswrw** Pembks
85 M7 **Egmanton** Notts
100 D8 **Egremont** Cumb
81 L6 **Egremont** Wirral
105 M9 **Egton** N York
105 M10 **Egton Bridge** N York
35 Q7 **Egypt** Bucks
22 E6 **Egypt** Hants
144 G10 **Eigg** Highld
52 F6 **Eight Ash Green** Essex
145 P4 **Eilanreach** Highld
54 H8 **Eisteddfa Gurig** Cerdgn
44 B2 **Elan Valley** Powys
44 C2 **Elan Village** Powys
32 F4 **Elberton** S Glos
15 P6 **Elbridge** W Susx
6 E8 **Elburton** C Plym
33 M8 **Elcombe** Swindn
34 C11 **Elcot** W Berk
74 F11 **Eldernell** Cambs
46 E8 **Eldersfield** Worcs
125 L5 **Elderslie** Rens
51 N4 **Elder Street** Essex
103 P5 **Eldon** Dur
90 E2 **Eldwick** C Brad
151 L10 **Elfhill** Abers
119 N4 **Elford** Nthumb
59 J2 **Elford** Staffs
157 N5 **Elgin** Moray
144 H5 **Elgol** Highld
27 L3 **Elham** Kent
135 M7 **Elie** Fife
119 J9 **Elilaw** Nthumb
78 F8 **Elim** IoA
14 C4 **Eling** Hants
85 L5 **Elkesley** Notts
33 J2 **Elkstone** Gloucs
158 F6 **Ella** Abers
7 N6 **Ellacombe** Torbay
90 E6 **Elland** Calder
90 E6 **Elland Lower Edge** Calder
123 M4 **Ellary** Ag & B
71 L6 **Ellastone** Staffs
95 K9 **Ellel** Lancs
129 J7 **Ellemford** Border
130 E4 **Ellenabeich** Ag & B
100 D3 **Ellenborough** Cumb
82 F4 **Ellenbrook** Salfd
70 E9 **Ellenhall** Staffs
24 C3 **Ellen's Green** Surrey
104 D11 **Ellerbeck** N York
105 L8 **Ellerby** N York
69 R10 **Ellerdine Heath** Wrekin
9 N4 **Ellerhayes** Devon
139 J8 **Elleric** Ag & B
92 F5 **Ellerker** E R Yk
90 C2 **Ellers** N York
92 B3 **Ellerton** E R Yk
103 Q11 **Ellerton** N York
70 C9 **Ellerton** Shrops
35 M3 **Ellesborough** Bucks
69 L8 **Ellesmere** Shrops
81 N9 **Ellesmere Port** Ches W
13 K3 **Ellingham** Hants
65 M3 **Ellingham** Norfk
119 N5 **Ellingham** Nthumb
97 J4 **Ellingstring** N York
61 Q6 **Ellington** Cambs
113 L2 **Ellington** Nthumb
61 Q6 **Ellington Thorpe** Cambs
20 E5 **Elliots Green** Somset
22 H5 **Ellisfield** Hants
153 J4 **Ellishader** Highld
72 C8 **Ellistown** Leics
159 N11 **Ellon** Abers
101 M3 **Ellonby** Cumb
65 N4 **Ellough** Suffk
92 F5 **Elloughton** E R Yk
31 Q3 **Ellwood** Gloucs
75 J9 **Elm** Cambs
58 D11 **Elmbridge** Worcs
51 L3 **Elmdon** Essex
59 J8 **Elmdon** Solhll
59 J8 **Elmdon Heath** Solhll
15 Q6 **Elmer** W Susx
37 J7 **Elmers End** Gt Lon
88 G9 **Elmer's Green** Lancs
72 D11 **Elmesthorpe** Leics
52 C10 **Elm Green** Essex
58 H2 **Elmhurst** Staffs
47 J6 **Elmley Castle** Worcs
58 C11 **Elmley Lovett** Worcs
46 E11 **Elmore** Gloucs
46 E11 **Elmore Back** Gloucs
37 M3 **Elm Park** Gt Lon
16 C7 **Elmscott** Devon
53 J2 **Elmsett** Suffk
57 N11 **Elms Green** Worcs
53 J7 **Elmstead Heath** Essex
53 J7 **Elmstead Market** Essex
53 J7 **Elmstead Row** Essex
27 K3 **Elmsted** Kent
39 N9 **Elmstone** Kent
46 H9 **Elmstone Hardwicke** Gloucs
99 K9 **Elmswell** E R Yk
64 D9 **Elmswell** Suffk
84 H6 **Elmton** Derbys
161 L4 **Elphin** Highld
128 B6 **Elphinstone** E Loth
151 L6 **Elrick** Abers
107 K8 **Elrig** D & G
112 C8 **Elrington** Nthumb
112 D2 **Elsdon** Nthumb
91 K11 **Elsecar** Barns
51 M5 **Elsenham** Essex
34 F2 **Elsfield** Oxon
92 H8 **Elsham** N Linc
76 F8 **Elsing** Norfk
96 D11 **Elslack** N York
14 H6 **Elson** Hants
69 L7 **Elson** Shrops
116 F2 **Elsrickle** S Lans
23 P6 **Elstead** Surrey
23 M11 **Elsted** W Susx
73 R6 **Elsthorpe** Lincs
104 B6 **Elstob** Dur
88 H4 **Elston** Lancs
85 N11 **Elston** Notts
21 L6 **Elston** Wilts
17 M8 **Elstone** Devon
61 N11 **Elstow** Bed
50 E11 **Elstree** Herts
93 M4 **Elstronwick** E R Yk
88 E3 **Elswick** Lancs
113 K8 **Elswick** N u Ty
62 D8 **Elsworth** Cambs
101 K10 **Elterwater** Cumb
37 K6 **Eltham** Gt Lon
37 K6 **Eltham Crematorium** Gt Lon
62 C9 **Eltisley** Cambs
89 M8 **Elton** Bury
61 N2 **Elton** Cambs
81 P9 **Elton** Ches W
84 B8 **Elton** Derbys
32 D2 **Elton** Gloucs
56 H10 **Elton** Herefs
73 K3 **Elton** Notts
104 D7 **Elton** S on T
81 P10 **Elton Green** Ches W
112 G8 **Eltringham** Nthumb
116 D7 **Elvanfoot** S Lans
72 C4 **Elvaston** Derbys
63 P4 **Elveden** Suffk
23 M3 **Elvetham Heath** Hants
128 D5 **Elvingston** E Loth
98 E11 **Elvington** C York
39 N11 **Elvington** Kent
17 M5 **Elwell** Devon
104 E4 **Elwick** Hartpl
119 M3 **Elwick** Nthumb
70 C2 **Elworth** Ches E
18 E8 **Elworthy** Somset
62 H4 **Ely** Cambs
30 F9 **Ely** Cardif
49 N5 **Emberton** M Keyn
100 G4 **Embleton** Cumb
104 D5 **Embleton** Dur
119 P6 **Embleton** Nthumb
163 J8 **Embo** Highld
20 B4 **Emborough** Somset
163 J8 **Embo Street** Highld
96 F10 **Embsay** N York
13 N3 **Emery Down** Hants
90 G8 **Emley** Kirk
90 G8 **Emley Moor** Kirk
35 M11 **Emmbrook** Wokham
35 K9 **Emmer Green** Readg
84 G5 **Emmett Carr** Derbys
35 K4 **Emmington** Oxon
75 J9 **Emneth** Norfk
75 K9 **Emneth Hungate** Norfk
73 N9 **Empingham** Rutlnd
23 L8 **Empshott** Hants
23 K8 **Empshott Green** Hants
57 J2 **Emstrey Crematorium** Shrops
15 K5 **Emsworth** Hants
34 D11 **Enborne** W Berk
22 D2 **Enborne Row** W Berk
57 J5 **Enchmarsh** Shrops
72 E11 **Enderby** Leics
95 L4 **Endmoor** Cumb
70 G4 **Endon** Staffs
70 G4 **Endon Bank** Staffs
51 J11 **Enfield** Gt Lon
50 H11 **Enfield Crematorium** Gt Lon
51 J11 **Enfield Lock** Gt Lon
51 J11 **Enfield Wash** Gt Lon
21 M4 **Enford** Wilts
32 C8 **Engine Common** S Glos
45 Q4 **England's Gate** Herefs
34 H10 **Englefield** W Berk
35 Q10 **Englefield Green** Surrey
70 D4 **Engleseabrook** Ches E
46 A11 **English Bicknor** Gloucs
20 D2 **Englishcombe** BaNES
69 N9 **English Frankton** Shrops
4 D7 **Engollan** Cnwll
22 C5 **Enham-Alamein** Hants
18 H7 **Enmore** Somset
20 G10 **Enmore Green** Dorset
100 E7 **Ennerdale Bridge** Cumb
4 F10 **Enniscaven** Cnwll
141 Q5 **Enochdhu** P & K
137 K6 **Ensay** Ag & B
13 J5 **Ensbury** Bmouth
69 M11 **Ensdon** Shrops
17 K6 **Ensis** Devon
70 G9 **Enson** Staffs
48 C10 **Enstone** Oxon
116 B10 **Enterkinfoot** D & G
104 E9 **Enterpen** N York
58 B7 **Enville** Staffs
168 c17 **Eolaigearraidh** W Isls
32 E2 **Epney** Gloucs
85 L11 **Epperstone** Notts
51 L10 **Epping** Essex
51 K9 **Epping Green** Essex
50 G9 **Epping Green** Herts
51 K10 **Epping Upland** Essex
103 N8 **Eppleby** N York
92 H4 **Eppleworth** E R Yk
36 F8 **Epsom** Surrey
48 C6 **Epwell** Oxon
92 C10 **Epworth** N Linc
92 C10 **Epworth Turbary** N Linc
69 L6 **Erbistock** Wrexhm
58 H6 **Erdington** Birm
25 N3 **Eridge Green** E Susx
25 M4 **Eridge Station** E Susx
123 Q4 **Erines** Ag & B
138 G9 **Eriska** Ag & B
168 c17 **Eriskay** W Isls
63 M5 **Eriswell** Suffk
37 M5 **Erith** Gt Lon
21 J4 **Erlestoke** Wilts
6 G8 **Ermington** Devon
76 H5 **Erpingham** Norfk
38 F10 **Erriottwood** Kent
147 P3 **Errogie** Highld
134 G3 **Errol** P & K
125 M3 **Erskine** Rens
106 D4 **Ervie** D & G
53 M5 **Erwarton** Suffk
44 F6 **Erwood** Powys
104 B9 **Eryholme** N York
68 H3 **Eryrys** Denbgs
2 B8 **Escalls** Cnwll
103 N4 **Escomb** Dur
18 F7 **Escott** Somset
91 Q2 **Escrick** N York
42 G9 **Esgair** Carmth
54 D11 **Esgair** Cerdgn
54 H3 **Esgairgeiliog** Powys
43 M6 **Esgerdawe** Carmth
79 Q9 **Esgyryn** Conwy
103 N2 **Esh** Dur
36 D8 **Esher** Surrey
90 F2 **Esholt** C Brad
119 P11 **Eshott** Nthumb
96 D9 **Eshton** N York
103 N2 **Esh Winning** Dur
155 N9 **Eskadale** Highld
127 Q4 **Eskbank** Mdloth
100 F10 **Eskdale Green** Cumb
117 K11 **Eskdalemuir** D & G
93 Q11 **Eskham** Lincs
91 Q7 **Eskholme** Donc
103 M6 **Esperley Lane Ends** Dur
88 E3 **Esprick** Lancs
73 Q8 **Essendine** Rutlnd
50 G9 **Essendon** Herts
156 A10 **Essich** Highld
58 E4 **Essington** Staffs
151 N2 **Esslemont** Abers
104 F7 **Eston** R & Cl
118 H3 **Etal** Nthumb
21 K2 **Etchilhampton** Wilts
26 B6 **Etchingham** E Susx
27 L4 **Etchinghill** Kent
71 J11 **Etchinghill** Staffs
25 M6 **Etchingwood** E Susx
76 E9 **Etling Green** Norfk
32 C3 **Etloe** Gloucs
35 Q9 **Eton** W & M
35 P9 **Eton Wick** W & M
70 F5 **Etruria** C Stke
148 B9 **Etteridge** Highld
102 G5 **Ettersgill** Dur
70 C2 **Ettiley Heath** Ches E
58 D5 **Ettingshall** Wolves
47 Q5 **Ettington** Warwks
74 B9 **Etton** C Pete
92 G2 **Etton** E R Yk
117 K8 **Ettrick** Border
117 M6 **Ettrickbridge** Border
117 K8 **Ettrickhill** Border
71 P8 **Etwall** Derbys
57 M7 **Eudon George** Shrops
64 B6 **Euston** Suffk
75 J11 **Euximoor Drove** Cambs
88 H7 **Euxton** Lancs
45 K2 **Evancoyd** Powys
155 R4 **Evanton** Highld
86 E11 **Evedon** Lincs
57 N3 **Evelith** Shrops
162 H8 **Evelix** Highld
45 K2 **Evenjobb** Powys
48 G8 **Evenley** Nhants
47 P9 **Evenlode** Gloucs
103 N6 **Evenwood** Dur
103 N6 **Evenwood Gate** Dur
20 B7 **Evercreech** Somset
92 D2 **Everingham** E R Yk
21 P4 **Everleigh** Wilts
99 K3 **Everley** N York
49 Q8 **Eversholt** C Beds
11 M4 **Evershot** Dorset
23 L2 **Eversley** Hants
23 L2 **Eversley Cross** Hants
92 F4 **Everthorpe** E R Yk
62 B10 **Everton** C Beds
13 N6 **Everton** Hants
81 L6 **Everton** Lpool
85 L2 **Everton** Notts
110 G5 **Evertown** D & G
46 C5 **Evesbatch** Herefs
47 K6 **Evesham** Worcs
72 G10 **Evington** C Leic
90 H11 **Ewden Village** Sheff
36 F8 **Ewell** Surrey
27 N3 **Ewell Minnis** Kent
34 H6 **Ewelme** Oxon
33 K5 **Ewen** Gloucs
29 P9 **Ewenny** V Glam
86 F11 **Ewerby** Lincs
86 F11 **Ewerby Thorpe** Lincs
24 C2 **Ewhurst** Surrey
26 C7 **Ewhurst Green** E Susx
24 C3 **Ewhurst Green** Surrey
81 L11 **Ewloe** Flints
81 K11 **Ewloe Green** Flints
89 K5 **Ewood** Bl w D
89 M6 **Ewood Bridge** Lancs
8 B5 **Eworthy** Devon
23 M5 **Ewshot** Hants
45 M9 **Ewyas Harold** Herefs
8 F4 **Exbourne** Devon
18 B10 **Exbridge** Somset
14 D6 **Exbury** Hants
25 M11 **Exceat** E Susx
97 L3 **Exelby** N York
9 M6 **Exeter** Devon
9 N6 *Exeter Airport* Devon
9 M6 **Exeter & Devon Crematorium** Devon
9 N6 **Exeter Services** Devon
17 R4 **Exford** Somset
56 H3 **Exfordsgreen** Shrops
47 M3 **Exhall** Warwks
59 N7 **Exhall** Warwks
35 J8 **Exlade Street** Oxon
90 C2 **Exley Head** C Brad
9 M7 **Exminster** Devon
17 R4 **Exmoor National Park**
9 P8 **Exmouth** Devon
63 K7 **Exning** Suffk
27 L3 **Exted** Kent
9 N7 **Exton** Devon
22 H10 **Exton** Hants
73 N8 **Exton** Rutlnd
18 B8 **Exton** Somset
9 M6 **Exwick** Devon
84 B5 **Eyam** Derbys
48 F5 **Eydon** Nhants
74 D10 **Eye** C Pete
45 P2 **Eye** Herefs
64 G7 **Eye** Suffk
74 D10 **Eye Green** C Pete
73 J7 **Eye Kettleby** Leics
129 N7 **Eyemouth** Border
62 C11 **Eyeworth** C Beds
38 D11 **Eyhorne Street** Kent
65 L11 **Eyke** Suffk
61 Q9 **Eynesbury** Cambs
37 M7 **Eynsford** Kent
34 D3 **Eynsham** Oxon
11 J6 **Eype** Dorset
152 G7 **Eyre** Highld
27 N2 **Eythorne** Kent
45 P2 **Eyton** Herefs
56 F8 **Eyton** Shrops
56 F7 **Eyton** Shrops
69 M10 **Eyton** Shrops
69 L6 **Eyton** Wrexhm
57 K3 **Eyton on Severn** Shrops
57 M2 **Eyton upon the Weald Moors** Wrekin

F

22 C3 **Faccombe** Hants
104 E10 **Faceby** N York
68 D11 **Fachwen** Powys
89 P7 **Facit** Lancs
84 G8 **Fackley** Notts
69 Q4 **Faddiley** Ches E
98 D3 **Fadmoor** N York
29 J4 **Faerdre** Swans
29 J4 **Fagwyr** Swans
125 M3 **Faifley** W Duns
31 P10 **Failand** N Som
115 J2 **Failford** S Ayrs
83 J4 **Failsworth** Oldham
54 E2 **Fairbourne** Gwynd
91 M5 **Fairburn** N York
83 N10 **Fairfield** Derbys
26 G6 **Fairfield** Kent
58 D9 **Fairfield** Worcs
33 N4 **Fairford** Gloucs
33 N4 **Fairford Park** Gloucs
109 J9 **Fairgirth** D & G
75 N7 **Fair Green** Norfk
88 C5 **Fairhaven** Lancs
169 t12 **Fair Isle** Shet
23 Q4 **Fairlands** Surrey
124 G7 **Fairlie** N Ayrs
26 E9 **Fairlight** E Susx
10 B5 **Fairmile** Devon
36 D8 **Fairmile** Surrey
117 P4 **Fairnilee** Border
22 E11 **Fair Oak** Hants
70 D8 **Fairoak** Staffs
23 J2 **Fair Oak Green** Hants
37 P8 **Fairseat** Kent
52 C8 **Fairstead** Essex
75 M6 **Fairstead** Norfk
77 K7 **Fairstead** Norfk
25 L5 **Fairwarp** E Susx
30 F9 **Fairwater** Cardif
16 G7 **Fairy Cross** Devon
76 C6 **Fakenham** Norfk
64 C6 **Fakenham Magna** Suffk
128 C7 **Fala** Mdloth
128 C7 **Fala Dam** Mdloth
48 G6 **Falcut** Nhants
86 E4 **Faldingworth** Lincs
11 c2 **Faldouet** Jersey
32 C6 **Falfield** S Glos
53 N4 **Falkenham** Suffk
133 P11 **Falkirk** Falk
134 H6 **Falkland** Fife
116 D3 **Fallburn** S Lans
84 E8 **Fallgate** Derbys
133 N9 **Fallin** Stirlg
119 N6 **Fallodon** Nthumb
83 J6 **Fallowfield** Manch
112 D7 **Fallowfield** Nthumb
131 K5 **Falls of Blarghour** Ag & B
25 J9 **Falmer** E Susx
3 L7 **Falmouth** Cnwll
117 M9 **Falnash** Border
99 L3 **Falsgrave** N York
111 P3 **Falstone** Nthumb
164 E7 **Fanagmore** Highld
50 B5 **Fancott** C Beds
155 N9 **Fanellan** Highld
98 B2 **Fangdale Beck** N York
98 F10 **Fangfoss** E R Yk
137 L7 **Fanmore** Ag & B
154 H4 **Fannich Lodge** Highld
118 B2 **Fans** Border
49 N8 **Far Bletchley** M Keyn
62 B2 **Farcet** Cambs
60 G9 **Far Cotton** Nhants
57 K9 **Farden** Shrops
14 G5 **Fareham** Hants
101 K11 **Far End** Cumb
58 G2 **Farewell** Staffs
57 N9 **Far Forest** Worcs
87 K5 **Farforth** Lincs
32 E4 **Far Green** Gloucs
33 Q5 **Faringdon** Oxon
88 G5 **Farington** Lancs
111 L9 **Farlam** Cumb
31 P11 **Farleigh** N Som
37 J8 **Farleigh** Surrey
20 F3 **Farleigh Hungerford** Somset
22 H5 **Farleigh Wallop** Hants
87 N6 **Farlesthorpe** Lincs
95 L4 **Farleton** Cumb
95 M7 **Farleton** Lancs
84 C8 **Farley** Derbys
71 K6 **Farley** Staffs
21 P9 **Farley** Wilts
63 M10 **Farley Green** Suffk
36 C11 **Farley Green** Surrey
23 K2 **Farley Hill** Wokham
32 E2 **Farleys End** Gloucs
15 J5 **Farlington** C Port
98 C7 **Farlington** N York
57 L8 **Farlow** Shrops
20 C2 **Farmborough** BaNES
51 P8 **Farmbridge End** Essex
47 L9 **Farmcote** Gloucs
57 P6 **Farmcote** Shrops
43 M6 **Farmers** Carmth
47 M11 **Farmington** Gloucs
34 E3 **Farmoor** Oxon
82 B4 **Far Moor** Wigan
2 H7 **Farms Common** Cnwll
72 B7 **Farm Town** Leics
158 D7 **Farmtown** Moray
84 D11 **Farnah Green** Derbys
37 K8 **Farnborough** Gt Lon
23 N4 **Farnborough** Hants
34 D8 **Farnborough** W Berk
48 D5 **Farnborough** Warwks
23 N3 **Farnborough Park** Hants
23 N3 **Farnborough Street** Hants
23 Q6 **Farncombe** Surrey
61 K8 **Farndish** Bed
69 M4 **Farndon** Ches W
85 N10 **Farndon** Notts
119 Q3 **Farne Islands** Nthumb
143 L6 **Farnell** Angus
21 J11 **Farnham** Dorset
51 L6 **Farnham** Essex
97 M8 **Farnham** N York
65 M9 **Farnham** Suffk
23 M5 **Farnham** Surrey
35 Q7 **Farnham Common** Bucks
51 L5 **Farnham Green** Essex
35 Q8 **Farnham Royal** Bucks
37 M7 **Farningham** Kent
90 H4 **Farnley** Leeds
97 K11 **Farnley** N York
90 F8 **Farnley Tyas** Kirk
85 K9 **Farnsfield** Notts
89 L9 **Farnworth** Bolton
81 Q7 **Farnworth** Halton
32 H4 **Far Oakridge** Gloucs
148 E7 **Farr** Highld
156 B11 **Farr** Highld
166 B4 **Farr** Highld
147 P3 **Farraline** Highld
9 P6 **Farringdon** Devon
20 B3 **Farrington Gurney** BaNES
101 L11 **Far Sawrey** Cumb
90 G3 **Farsley** Leeds
52 D11 **Farther Howegreen** Essex
26 D2 **Farthing Green** Kent
48 F7 **Farthinghoe** Nhants
27 N3 **Farthingloe** Kent
48 H4 **Farthingstone** Nhants
37 K8 **Farthing Street** Gt Lon
90 F7 **Fartown** Kirk
90 G4 **Fartown** Leeds
10 D5 **Farway** Devon
139 J8 **Fasnacloich** Ag & B
147 J2 **Fasnakyle** Highld
139 J2 **Fassfern** Highld
113 L10 **Fatfield** Sundld
111 K10 **Faugh** Cumb
71 M9 **Fauld** Staffs
126 G5 **Fauldhouse** W Loth
52 C8 **Faulkbourne** Essex
20 D4 **Faulkland** Somset
69 Q8 **Fauls** Shrops
38 H9 **Faversham** Kent
97 P6 **Fawdington** N York
113 K7 **Fawdon** N u Ty
119 K7 **Fawdon** Nthumb
71 K2 **Fawfieldhead** Staffs
37 N7 **Fawkham Green** Kent
48 C11 **Fawler** Oxon
35 L7 **Fawley** Bucks
14 E6 **Fawley** Hants
34 C8 **Fawley** W Berk
46 A9 **Fawley Chapel** Herefs
81 J11 **Fawnog** Flints
60 C9 **Fawsley** Nhants
92 E6 **Faxfleet** E R Yk
24 F4 **Faygate** W Susx
81 M5 **Fazakerley** Lpool
59 K4 **Fazeley** Staffs
97 J4 **Fearby** N York
156 E2 **Fearn** Highld
140 H9 **Fearnan** P & K
153 N6 **Fearnbeg** Highld
82 D6 **Fearnhead** Warrtn
153 N5 **Fearnmore** Highld
124 A2 **Fearnoch** Ag & B
58 D3 **Featherstone** Staffs
91 L6 **Featherstone** Wakefd
47 K2 **Feckenham** Worcs
52 E7 **Feering** Essex
103 J11 **Feetham** N York
96 A7 **Feizor** N York
25 J3 **Felbridge** Surrey
77 J4 **Felbrigg** Norfk
25 J2 **Felcourt** Surrey
50 B10 **Felden** Herts
42 G7 **Felindre** Carmth
43 L10 **Felindre** Carmth
43 P9 **Felindre** Carmth
43 L3 **Felindre** Cerdgn
44 H10 **Felindre** Powys
56 B8 **Felindre** Powys

28 H4 Felindre Swans
41 M3 Felindre Farchog Pembks
43 K3 Felin Fach Cerdgn
44 F8 Felinfach Powys
28 F4 Felinfoel Carmth
43 K10 Felingwm Isaf Carmth
43 K10 Felingwm Uchaf Carmth
44 G7 Felin-newydd Powys
97 Q4 Felixkirk N York
53 P5 Felixstowe Suffk
53 P4 Felixstowe Ferry Suffk
118 H2 Felkington Nthumb
91 K8 Felkirk Wakefd
113 L8 Felling Gatesd
90 C2 Fell Lane C Brad
101 K3 Fell Side Cumb
61 L9 Felmersham Bed
77 K6 Felmingham Norfk
15 P7 Felpham W Susx
64 C10 Felsham Suffk
51 Q6 Felsted Essex
36 D6 Feltham Gt Lon
36 C6 Felthamhill Surrey
76 H8 Felthorpe Norfk
46 A5 Felton Herefs
31 P11 Felton N Som
119 N10 Felton Nthumb
69 L11 Felton Butler Shrops
63 M2 Feltwell Norfk
90 F7 Fenay Bridge Kirk
89 N3 Fence Lancs
84 F3 Fence Rothm
113 M11 Fence Houses Sundld
48 G11 Fencott Oxon
87 N8 Fendike Corner Lincs
62 G8 Fen Ditton Cambs
62 D7 Fen Drayton Cambs
74 D6 Fen End Lincs
59 K10 Fen End Solhll
119 L2 Fenham Nthumb
89 K5 Feniscliffe Bl w D
89 J5 Feniscowles Bl w D
10 C5 Feniton Devon
62 F2 Fenland Crematorium Cambs
57 P8 Fenn Green Shrops
38 C6 Fenn Street Medway
71 M5 Fenny Bentley Derbys
10 C5 Fenny Bridges Devon
48 D4 Fenny Compton Warwks
72 B11 Fenny Drayton Leics
49 N8 Fenny Stratford M Keyn
113 J2 Fenrother Nthumb
62 D7 Fenstanton Cambs
63 P10 Fenstead End Suffk
64 D2 Fen Street Norfk
64 H9 Fen Street Suffk
70 F6 Fenton C Stke
62 D5 Fenton Cambs
111 K9 Fenton Cumb
85 P5 Fenton Lincs
85 Q10 Fenton Lincs
85 N4 Fenton Notts
119 J4 Fenton Nthumb
128 E3 Fenton Barns E Loth
91 P7 Fenwick Donc
125 M9 Fenwick E Ayrs
112 G6 Fenwick Nthumb
119 L2 Fenwick Nthumb
3 L6 Feock Cnwll
122 F6 Feolin Ferry Ag & B
125 J9 Fergushill N Ayrs
152 B7 Feriniquarrie Highld
10 c2 Fermain Bay Guern
142 H5 Fern Angus
30 C5 Ferndale Rhondd
13 J4 Ferndown Dorset
156 H8 Ferness Highld
33 Q6 Fernham Oxon
46 G3 Fernhill Heath Worcs
23 N9 Fernhurst W Susx
135 J4 Fernie Fife
126 C7 Ferniegair S Lans
152 F11 Fernilea Highld
83 M9 Fernilee Derbys
85 P10 Fernwood Notts
97 N8 Ferrensby N York
92 G6 Ferriby Sluice N Linc
145 L6 Ferrindonald Highld
24 C10 Ferring W Susx
91 M6 Ferrybridge Wakefd
91 M6 Ferrybridge Services Wakefd
143 N6 Ferryden Angus
103 Q4 Ferryhill Dur
162 G9 Ferry Point Highld
28 C2 Ferryside Carmth
162 G9 Ferrytown Highld
64 F5 Fersfield Norfk
139 R2 Fersit Highld
148 F7 Feshiebridge Highld
36 D9 Fetcham Surrey
169 t4 Fetlar Shet
159 N7 Fetterangus Abers
143 M3 Fettercairn Abers
48 F9 Fewcott Oxon
97 J10 Fewston N York
43 M10 Ffairfach Carmth
54 G11 Ffair Rhos Cerdgn
43 M6 Ffald-y-Brenin Carmth
45 J11 Ffawyddog Powys
67 N6 Ffestiniog Gwynd
67 M6 Ffestiniog Railway Gwynd
68 F2 Ffordd-las Denbgs
28 G4 Fforest Carmth
45 K10 Fforest Mons
28 H5 Fforest Fach Swans
29 K4 Fforest Goch Neath
42 G5 Ffostrasol Cerdgn
69 J3 Ffrith Flints
42 G4 Ffynnonddewi Cerdgn
80 G8 Ffynnongroyw Flints
43 K4 Ffynnon-Oer Cerdgn
165 L11 Fiag Lodge Highld
37 J8 Fickleshole Surrey
46 H8 Fiddington Gloucs
18 H6 Fiddington Somset
12 D2 Fiddleford Dorset
4 C10 Fiddlers Green Cnwll
51 L10 Fiddlers Hamlet Essex
71 J8 Field Staffs
94 H4 Field Broughton Cumb
76 E4 Field Dalling Norfk
101 N3 Fieldhead Cumb
72 D9 Field Head Leics
20 E10 Fifehead Magdalen Dorset
12 C2 Fifehead Neville Dorset
12 C2 Fifehead St Quintin Dorset
158 B7 Fife Keith Moray
47 P11 Fifield Oxon
35 P9 Fifield W & M
21 M4 Fifield Wilts
21 N5 Figheldean Wilts
32 H7 Filands Wilts
77 P9 Filby Norfk
99 N4 Filey N York
49 N5 Filgrave M Keyn
33 P4 Filkins Oxon
8 H2 Filleigh Devon
17 M6 Filleigh Devon
86 B3 Fillingham Lincs
59 L7 Fillongley Warwks
23 J9 Filmore Hill Hants
32 B9 Filton S Glos
98 H8 Fimber E R Yk
142 H6 Finavon Angus
75 N9 Fincham Norfk
23 L2 Finchampstead Wokham
131 J7 Fincharn Ag & B
15 K4 Finchdean Hants
51 Q4 Finchingfield Essex
36 G2 Finchley Gt Lon
71 Q8 Findern Derbys
157 J5 Findhorn Moray
148 E2 Findhorn Bridge Highld
158 C4 Findochty Moray
134 C4 Findo Gask P & K
151 N8 Findon Abers
24 D9 Findon W Susx
155 R5 Findon Mains Highld
150 G7 Findrack House Abers
61 K6 Finedon Nhants
73 P11 Fineshade Nhants
65 J8 Fingal Street Suffk
134 F4 Fingask P & K
35 L6 Fingest Bucks
97 J3 Finghall N York
110 E9 Fingland Cumb
115 Q4 Fingland D & G
39 P11 Finglesham Kent
52 H7 Fingringhoe Essex
52 B3 Finkle Green Essex
91 J11 Finkle Street Barns
140 E11 Finlarig Stirlg
48 H8 Finmere Oxon
140 D6 Finnart P & K
64 F8 Finningham Suffk
91 R11 Finningley Donc
168 f9 Finsbay W Isls
58 E10 Finstall Worcs
94 H3 Finsthwaite Cumb
48 C11 Finstock Oxon
169 c5 Finstown Ork
159 J7 Fintry Abers
133 J10 Fintry Stirlg
150 G9 Finzean Abers
137 J11 Fionnphort Ag & B
168 f9 Fionnsbhagh W Isls
95 N2 Firbank Cumb
85 J3 Firbeck Rothm
97 L3 Firby N York
98 E7 Firby N York
89 Q8 Firgrove Rochdl
25 L9 Firle E Susx
87 N8 Firsby Lincs
21 P8 Firsdown Wilts
103 M4 Fir Tree Dur
14 G8 Fishbourne IoW
15 M6 Fishbourne W Susx
15 M5 Fishbourne Roman Palace W Susx
104 C4 Fishburn Dur
133 P8 Fishcross Clacks
15 N6 Fisher W Susx
158 G10 Fisherford Abers
127 Q3 Fisherrow E Loth
22 E10 Fisher's Pond Hants
95 J11 Fisher's Row Lancs
23 P8 Fisherstreet W Susx
156 C7 Fisherton Highld
114 E4 Fisherton S Ayrs
21 K7 Fisherton de la Mere Wilts
59 J3 Fisherwick Staffs
35 N8 Fishery Estate W & M
41 J3 Fishguard Pembks
91 R8 Fishlake Donc
8 D3 Fishleigh Devon
74 E3 Fishmere End Lincs
138 B9 Fishnish Pier Ag & B
10 H5 Fishpond Bottom Dorset
32 B9 Fishponds Bristl
74 G2 Fishtoft Lincs
87 K11 Fishtoft Drove Lincs
88 H5 Fishwick Lancs
152 E11 Fiskavaig Highld
86 D6 Fiskerton Lincs
85 M10 Fiskerton Notts
93 N4 Fitling E R Yk
21 M5 Fittleton Wilts
24 B7 Fittleworth W Susx
74 H8 Fitton End Cambs
69 M11 Fitz Shrops
18 F9 Fitzhead Somset
18 G9 Fitzroy Somset
91 L7 Fitzwilliam Wakefd
25 L6 Five Ash Down E Susx
25 N5 Five Ashes E Susx
18 E6 Five Bells Somset
46 B5 Five Bridges Herefs
82 B9 Fivecrosses Ches W
19 L10 Fivehead Somset
5 L5 Fivelanes Cnwll
31 M6 Five Lanes Mons
37 P11 Five Oak Green Kent
11 c2 Five Oaks Jersey
24 C5 Five Oaks W Susx
28 E3 Five Roads Carmth
38 D11 Five Wents Kent
52 G9 Flack's Green Essex
35 N7 Flackwell Heath Bucks
47 J5 Fladbury Worcs
169 r10 Fladdabister Shet
83 P11 Flagg Derbys
99 Q6 Flamborough E R Yk
99 R6 Flamborough Head E R Yk
98 F5 Flamingo Land Theme Park N York
50 C8 Flamstead Herts
15 Q6 Flansham W Susx
91 J6 Flanshaw Wakefd
90 D3 Flappit Spring C Brad
96 D9 Flasby N York
83 M11 Flash Staffs
152 E7 Flashader Highld
50 B10 Flaunden Herts
73 K2 Flawborough Notts
97 Q7 Flawith N York
31 P11 Flax Bourton N Som
97 N9 Flaxby N York
46 C11 Flaxley Gloucs
82 C10 Flaxmere Ches W
18 F7 Flaxpool Somset
98 D8 Flaxton N York
60 D2 Fleckney Leics
60 B8 Flecknoe Warwks
85 P6 Fledborough Notts
11 N8 Fleet Dorset
15 K6 Fleet Hants
23 M4 Fleet Hants
74 G6 Fleet Lincs
14 F5 Fleetend Hants
74 G6 Fleet Hargate Lincs
23 L3 Fleet Services Hants
94 G11 Fleetwood Lancs
30 D11 Flemingston V Glam
126 B6 Flemington S Lans
63 P7 Flempton Suffk
37 M11 Fletcher Green Kent
5 J8 Fletchersbridge Cnwll
100 H2 Fletchertown Cumb
25 K6 Fletching E Susx
30 G5 Fleur-de-lis Caerph
16 C10 Flexbury Cnwll
23 P4 Flexford Surrey
100 D4 Flimby Cumb
26 B5 Flimwell E Susx
81 J10 Flint Flints
85 M11 Flintham Notts
81 J10 Flint Mountain Flints
93 M3 Flinton E R Yk
59 L8 Flint's Green Solhll
26 C4 Flishinghurst Kent
75 P5 Flitcham Norfk
50 C3 Flitton C Beds
50 B4 Flitwick C Beds
92 E8 Flixborough N Linc
92 E8 Flixborough Stather N Linc
99 L5 Flixton N York
65 L4 Flixton Suffk
82 F6 Flixton Traffd
90 G8 Flockton Kirk
90 H7 Flockton Green Kirk
118 H3 Flodden Nthumb
152 H3 Flodigarry Highld
94 H5 Flookburgh Cumb
64 H2 Flordon Norfk
60 D8 Flore Nhants
119 J10 Flotterton Nthumb
25 P8 Flowers Green E Susx
53 J2 Flowton Suffk
90 H6 Flushdyke Wakefd
3 L7 Flushing Cnwll
10 B6 Fluxton Devon
47 J3 Flyford Flavell Worcs
38 B5 Fobbing Thurr
157 Q6 Fochabers Moray
30 F3 Fochriw Caerph
92 E7 Fockerby N Linc
19 Q9 Foddington Somset
55 M2 Foel Powys
28 F2 Foelgastell Carmth
29 N6 Foel y Dyffryn Brdgnd
92 C3 Foggathorpe E R Yk
129 K10 Fogo Border
157 N6 Fogwatt Moray
164 E7 Foindle Highld
142 B5 Folda Angus
71 J7 Fole Staffs
59 N8 Foleshill Covtry
11 P2 Folke Dorset
27 M4 Folkestone Kent
73 R4 Folkingham Lincs
13 N10 Folkington E Susx
61 P3 Folksworth Cambs
99 M5 Folkton N York
158 H11 Folla Rule Abers
97 M10 Follifoot N York
8 E5 Folly Gate Devon
23 M5 Folly Hill Surrey
30 D11 Fonmon V Glam
20 H8 Fonthill Bishop Wilts
20 H8 Fonthill Gifford Wilts
20 G11 Fontmell Magna Dorset
12 D2 Fontmell Parva Dorset
15 P5 Fontwell W Susx
30 E11 Font-y-gary V Glam
83 Q9 Foolow Derbys
37 L6 Foots Cray Gt Lon
150 B5 Forbestown Abers
103 N8 Forcett N York
130 H7 Ford Ag & B
35 L3 Ford Bucks
84 F4 Ford Derbys
6 G8 Ford Devon
7 K10 Ford Devon
16 G7 Ford Devon
47 L9 Ford Gloucs
118 H3 Ford Nthumb
56 G2 Ford Shrops
18 E9 Ford Somset
19 Q4 Ford Somset
71 K4 Ford Staffs
15 Q6 Ford W Susx
21 N8 Ford Wilts
32 F9 Ford Wilts
8 D6 Forda Devon
25 M2 Fordcombe Kent
134 F10 Fordell Fife
56 C4 Forden Powys
51 Q7 Ford End Essex
7 K5 Forder Green Devon
95 K11 Ford Green Lancs
63 K6 Fordham Cambs
52 F6 Fordham Essex
75 M11 Fordham Norfk
52 F6 Fordham Heath Essex
56 G2 Ford Heath Shrops
13 K2 Fordingbridge Hants
99 L5 Fordon E R Yk
143 N2 Fordoun Abers
64 F8 Ford's Green Suffk
52 F6 Fordstreet Essex
18 G11 Ford Street Somset
9 K5 Fordton Devon
34 B2 Fordwells Oxon
39 L10 Fordwich Kent
158 E5 Fordyce Abers
70 G10 Forebridge Staffs
72 A5 Foremark Derbys
10 b2 Forest Guern
103 Q10 Forest N York
96 A10 Forest Becks Lancs
119 L11 Forestburn Gate Nthumb
83 L10 Forest Chapel Ches E
37 K5 Forest Gate Gt Lon
24 D2 Forest Green Surrey
113 L7 Forest Hall N Tyne
111 L9 Forest Head Cumb
37 J6 Forest Hill Gt Lon
34 G3 Forest Hill Oxon
102 G4 Forest-in-Teesdale Dur
97 M9 Forest Lane Head N York
134 B9 Forest Mill Clacks
32 B2 Forest of Dean Gloucs
37 L2 Forest Park Crematorium Gt Lon
25 K4 Forest Row E Susx
14 E9 Forest Side IoW
15 L4 Forestside W Susx
85 J8 Forest Town Notts
142 H7 Forfar Angus
134 D4 Forgandenny P & K
54 H5 Forge Powys
31 J5 Forge Hammer Torfn
30 H3 Forge Side Torfn
158 A7 Forgie Moray
158 B7 Forgieside Moray
158 F8 Forgue Abers
58 G9 Forhill Worcs
88 C9 Formby Sefton
64 G3 Forncett End Norfk
64 H3 Forncett St Mary Norfk
64 H3 Forncett St Peter Norfk
64 A8 Fornham All Saints Suffk
64 B8 Fornham St Martin Suffk
156 G7 Fornighty Highld
157 J6 Forres Moray
70 H6 Forsbrook Staffs
167 M10 Forse Highld
58 G10 Forshaw Heath Warwks
166 E8 Forsinard Highld
11 P5 Forston Dorset
147 K6 Fort Augustus Highld
134 D4 Forteviot P & K
126 G7 Forth S Lans
46 G8 Forthampton Gloucs
10 b1 Fort Hommet Guern
140 H8 Fortingall P & K
10 c1 Fort le Marchant Guern
22 D6 Forton Hants
95 K10 Forton Lancs
69 M11 Forton Shrops
10 G3 Forton Somset
70 D10 Forton Staffs
158 G8 Fortrie Abers
156 C6 Fortrose Highld
11 P10 Fortuneswell Dorset
139 L3 Fort William Highld
35 P6 Forty Green Bucks
50 H11 Forty Hill Gt Lon
64 G10 Forward Green Suffk
22 B3 Fosbury Wilts
47 P10 Foscot Oxon
49 J5 Foscote Nhants
74 F4 Fosdyke Lincs
74 F4 Fosdyke Bridge Lincs
141 J6 Foss P & K
33 L2 Fossebridge Gloucs
42 H2 Foss-y-ffin Cerdgn
91 R8 Fosterhouses Donc
51 L9 Foster Street Essex
71 M8 Foston Derbys
60 D2 Foston Leics
73 M2 Foston Lincs
98 D7 Foston N York
99 N9 Foston on the Wolds E R Yk
87 K2 Fotherby Lincs
100 D4 Fothergill Cumb
61 N2 Fotheringhay Nhants
169 k10 Foula Shet
110 H11 Foulbridge Cumb
91 K7 Foulby Wakefd
129 N8 Foulden Border
75 Q11 Foulden Norfk
59 K6 Foul End Warwks
25 P7 Foul Mile E Susx
38 G3 Foulness Island Essex
10 b2 Foulon Vale Crematorium Guern
89 P2 Foulridge Lancs
76 E7 Foulsham Norfk
128 C10 Fountainhall Border
59 J9 Four Ashes Solhll
57 Q7 Four Ashes Staffs
58 D3 Four Ashes Staffs
64 E7 Four Ashes Suffk
10 b2 Four Cabots Guern
69 J11 Four Crosses Powys
58 E3 Four Crosses Staffs
37 L11 Four Elms Kent
19 Q8 Four Foot Somset
18 H7 Four Forks Somset
89 J9 Four Gates Bolton
75 J7 Four Gotes Cambs
90 H10 Four Lane End Barns
69 Q2 Four Lane Ends Ches W
2 H6 Four Lanes Cnwll
70 E3 Fourlanes End Ches E
23 J7 Four Marks Hants
78 D9 Four Mile Bridge IoA
58 H5 Four Oaks Birm
26 E7 Four Oaks E Susx
46 C9 Four Oaks Gloucs
59 K8 Four Oaks Solhll
163 J8 Fourpenny Highld
34 G9 Four Points W Berk
28 D3 Four Roads Carmth
47 P8 Four Shire Stone Warwks
112 C7 Fourstones Nthumb
26 C6 Four Throws Kent
37 P10 Four Wents Kent
62 H11 Fourwentways Services Cambs
21 K9 Fovant Wilts
151 P3 Foveran Abers
5 J11 Fowey Cnwll
82 E5 Fowley Common Warrtn
97 Q11 Fowlhall Kent
142 E11 Fowlis Angus
133 Q3 Fowlis Wester P & K
62 F11 Fowlmere Cambs
46 A8 Fownhope Herefs
125 M5 Foxbar Rens
8 C7 Foxcombe Devon
23 Q4 Fox Corner Surrey
47 K11 Foxcote Gloucs
20 D3 Foxcote Somset
80 c6 Foxdale IoM
52 D3 Foxearth Essex
37 P7 Foxendown Kent
94 E3 Foxfield Cumb
33 J9 Foxham Wilts
51 N11 Fox Hatch Essex
13 P2 Foxhills Hants
3 P3 Foxhole Cnwll
99 L6 Foxholes N York
25 M7 Foxhunt Green E Susx
48 H4 Foxley Nhants
76 E7 Foxley Norfk
32 G7 Foxley Wilts
58 F11 Foxlydiate Worcs
52 H6 Fox Street Essex
71 J5 Foxt Staffs
62 F11 Foxton Cambs
104 C6 Foxton Dur
60 F3 Foxton Leics
104 D11 Foxton N York
96 C5 Foxup N York
82 D11 Foxwist Green Ches W
57 L9 Foxwood Shrops
46 A9 Foy Herefs
147 M3 Foyers Highld
156 F7 Foynesfield Highld
2 F7 Fraddam Cnwll
4 E10 Fraddon Cnwll
59 J2 Fradley Staffs
70 H8 Fradswell Staffs
99 P8 Fraisthorpe E R Yk
25 L6 Framfield E Susx
77 K11 Framingham Earl Norfk
77 K11 Framingham Pigot Norfk
65 K9 Framlingham Suffk
11 N5 Frampton Dorset
74 F3 Frampton Lincs
32 C8 Frampton Cotterell S Glos
32 H4 Frampton Mansell Gloucs
32 D3 Frampton on Severn Gloucs
74 F2 Frampton West End Lincs
64 H10 Framsden Suffk
103 Q2 Framwellgate Moor Dur
57 Q9 Franche Worcs
82 D9 Frandley Ches W
5 P3 Frankaborough Devon
81 J7 Frankby Wirral
77 L7 Frankfort Norfk
45 Q5 Franklands Gate Herefs
58 E8 Frankley Worcs
58 E8 Frankley Services Worcs
44 G3 Franksbridge Powys
59 P10 Frankton Warwks
25 N3 Frant E Susx
159 N4 Fraserburgh Abers
53 J7 Frating Essex
53 J7 Frating Green Essex
15 J6 Fratton C Port
5 P11 Freathy Cnwll
63 L6 Freckenham Suffk
88 E5 Freckleton Lancs
84 D6 Freebirch Derbys
73 L6 Freeby Leics
22 E5 Freefolk Hants
71 J6 Freehay Staffs
34 D2 Freeland Oxon
77 N10 Freethorpe Norfk
77 N11 Freethorpe Common Norfk
74 G2 Freiston Lincs
17 J5 Fremington Devon
103 K11 Fremington N York
32 B9 Frenchay S Glos
8 G7 Frenchbeer Devon
37 L10 French Street Kent
141 K6 Frenich P & K
23 M6 Frensham Surrey
88 B9 Freshfield Sefton
20 E2 Freshford Wilts
13 P7 Freshwater IoW
13 P7 Freshwater Bay IoW
41 K11 Freshwater East Pembks
65 K6 Fressingfield Suffk
53 L4 Freston Suffk
167 Q3 Freswick Highld
32 D2 Fretherne Gloucs
77 J8 Frettenham Norfk
134 H6 Freuchie Fife
41 J8 Freystrop Pembks
58 F6 Friar Park Sandw
25 L4 Friar's Gate E Susx
98 E3 Friars' Hill N York
11 N7 Friar Waddon Dorset
75 J10 Friday Bridge Cambs
65 J10 Friday Street Suffk
65 L11 Friday Street Suffk
65 M9 Friday Street Suffk
36 D11 Friday Street Surrey
98 H9 Fridaythorpe E R Yk
71 M2 Friden Derbys
90 D6 Friendly Calder
36 G2 Friern Barnet Gt Lon
86 E4 Friesthorpe Lincs
86 B11 Frieston Lincs
35 L6 Frieth Bucks
84 G10 Friezeland Notts
34 D5 Frilford Oxon
34 F10 Frilsham W Berk
23 N3 Frimley Surrey
23 N3 Frimley Green Surrey
38 B8 Frindsbury Medway
75 P4 Fring Norfk
48 H9 Fringford Oxon
38 E10 Frinsted Kent
53 M7 Frinton-on-Sea Essex
143 K8 Friockheim Angus
54 E2 Friog Gwynd
72 H7 Frisby on the Wreake Leics
87 N9 Friskney Lincs
87 N9 Friskney Eaudike Lincs
25 N11 Friston E Susx
65 N9 Friston Suffk
84 E10 Fritchley Derbys
13 M2 Fritham Hants
87 K11 Frith Bank Lincs
57 M11 Frith Common Worcs
16 H8 Frithelstock Devon
16 H8 Frithelstock Stone Devon
23 M7 Frithend Hants
50 B9 Frithsden Herts
87 K10 Frithville Lincs
26 D3 Frittenden Kent
7 L10 Frittiscombe Devon
65 J3 Fritton Norfk
77 P11 Fritton Norfk
48 F9 Fritwell Oxon
90 E3 Frizinghall C Brad
100 D7 Frizington Cumb
32 E4 Frocester Gloucs
57 J4 Frodesley Shrops

81 Q9 **Frodsham** Ches W
118 E5 **Frogden** Border
62 E11 **Frog End** Cambs
62 H9 **Frog End** Cambs
84 B5 **Froggatt** Derbys
71 J5 **Froghall** Staffs
13 L2 **Frogham** Hants
39 N11 **Frogham** Kent
7 K10 **Frogmore** Devon
74 C8 **Frognall** Lincs
3 K5 **Frogpool** Cnwll
57 Q11 **Frog Pool** Worcs
5 N8 **Frogwell** Cnwll
60 B2 **Frolesworth** Leics
20 E5 **Frome** Somset
11 M4 **Frome St Quintin** Dorset
46 C5 **Fromes Hill** Herefs
80 F11 **Fron** Denbgs
66 F7 **Fron** Gwynd
67 J4 **Fron** Gwynd
56 B5 **Fron** Powys
56 C4 **Fron** Powys
69 J6 **Froncysyllte** Denbgs
68 B7 **Fron-goch** Gwynd
69 J6 **Fron Isaf** Wrexhm
45 P5 **Frostenden** Suffk
103 K3 **Frosterley** Dur
49 Q8 **Froxfield** C Beds
33 Q11 **Froxfield** Wilts
23 K9 **Froxfield Green** Hants
22 D10 **Fryern Hill** Hants
51 P10 **Fryerning** Essex
98 D6 **Fryton** N York
137 Q6 **Fuinary** Highld
86 B10 **Fulbeck** Lincs
62 H9 **Fulbourn** Cambs
33 Q2 **Fulbrook** Oxon
22 E8 **Fulflood** Hants
98 C11 **Fulford** C York
18 H9 **Fulford** Somset
70 H7 **Fulford** Staffs
36 G5 **Fulham** Gt Lon
24 F8 **Fulking** W Susx
17 M4 **Fullaford** Devon
125 J10 **Fullarton** N Ayrs
51 M5 **Fuller's End** Essex
69 N4 **Fuller's Moor** Ches W
52 B8 **Fuller Street** Essex
37 N9 **Fuller Street** Kent
22 C7 **Fullerton** Hants
87 J6 **Fulletby** Lincs
47 Q5 **Fullready** Warwks
98 E9 **Full Sutton** E R Yk
125 L7 **Fullwood** E Ayrs
35 Q7 **Fulmer** Bucks
76 D5 **Fulmodeston** Norfk
86 E5 **Fulnetby** Lincs
74 E6 **Fulney** Lincs
90 F9 **Fulstone** Kirk
93 P11 **Fulstow** Lincs
48 C10 **Fulwell** Oxon
113 N9 **Fulwell** Sundld
88 G4 **Fulwood** Lancs
84 G9 **Fulwood** Notts
84 D3 **Fulwood** Sheff
18 H10 **Fulwood** Somset
64 H2 **Fundenhall** Norfk
15 M5 **Funtington** W Susx
14 G5 **Funtley** Hants
133 M2 **Funtullich** P & K
10 F4 **Furley** Devon
131 L7 **Furnace** Ag & B
28 F4 **Furnace** Carmth
54 F5 **Furnace** Cerdgn
59 K6 **Furnace End** Warwks
25 K5 **Furner's Green** E Susx
83 M8 **Furness Vale** Derbys
51 K5 **Furneux Pelham** Herts
26 E4 **Further Quarter** Kent
49 L6 **Furtho** Nhants
17 N2 **Furzehill** Devon
12 H4 **Furzehill** Dorset
87 J6 **Furzehills** Lincs
15 J4 **Furzeley Corner** Hants
35 N8 **Furze Platt** W & M
21 Q11 **Furzley** Hants
10 E2 **Fyfett** Somset
51 N9 **Fyfield** Essex
21 Q5 **Fyfield** Hants
34 D5 **Fyfield** Oxon
21 N2 **Fyfield** Wilts
33 M11 **Fyfield** Wilts
21 K9 **Fyfield Bavant** Wilts
105 P10 **Fylingthorpe** N York
23 M10 **Fyning** W Susx
159 J10 **Fyvie** Abers

G

125 M7 **Gabroc Hill** E Ayrs
72 H8 **Gaddesby** Leics
50 C8 **Gaddesden Row** Herts
78 H7 **Gadfa** IoA
114 H3 **Gadgirth** S Ayrs
69 L7 **Gadlas** Shrops
44 H10 **Gaer** Powys
31 M5 **Gaer-llwyd** Mons
78 H10 **Gaerwen** IoA
48 D9 **Gagingwell** Oxon
125 J10 **Gailes** N Ayrs
58 D2 **Gailey** Staffs
103 N7 **Gainford** Dur
85 P3 **Gainsborough** Lincs
52 B4 **Gainsford End** Essex
153 Q2 **Gairloch** Highld
146 F11 **Gairlochy** Highld
134 E8 **Gairneybridge** P & K
102 B9 **Gaisgill** Cumb
110 G11 **Gaitsgill** Cumb
117 P3 **Galashiels** Border
95 K9 **Galgate** Lancs
20 B9 **Galhampton** Somset
130 G2 **Gallanachbeg** Ag & B
130 G2 **Gallanachmore** Ag & B
69 P4 **Gallantry Bank** Ches E
134 H9 **Gallatown** Fife
59 M6 **Galley Common** Warwks
52 B11 **Galleywood** Essex
147 P10 **Gallovie** Highld
114 H10 **Galloway Forest Park**
142 G9 **Gallowfauld** Angus
142 B10 **Gallowhill** P & K
52 F6 **Gallows Green** Essex
46 H2 **Gallows Green** Worcs
35 J8 **Gallowstree Common** Oxon
145 P3 **Galltair** Highld
67 K2 **Gallt-y-foel** Gwynd
23 M4 **Gally Hill** Hants
25 L3 **Gallypot Street** E Susx
6 H10 **Galmpton** Devon
7 M7 **Galmpton** Torbay
97 L6 **Galphay** N York
125 N10 **Galston** E Ayrs
83 M11 **Gamballs Green** Staffs
102 B3 **Gamblesby** Cumb
52 C9 **Gambles Green** Essex
110 E10 **Gamelsby** Cumb
83 M6 **Gamesley** Derbys
62 B10 **Gamlingay** Cambs
62 B10 **Gamlingay Cinques** Cambs
62 B10 **Gamlingay Great Heath** Cambs
96 G4 **Gammersgill** N York
159 J5 **Gamrie** Abers
72 F3 **Gamston** Notts
85 M5 **Gamston** Notts
45 Q11 **Ganarew** Herefs
138 F11 **Ganavan Bay** Ag & B
5 N8 **Gang** Cnwll
67 N10 **Ganllwyd** Gwynd
143 K3 **Gannachy** Angus
93 K4 **Ganstead** E R Yk
98 D6 **Ganthorpe** N York
99 K5 **Ganton** N York
50 G11 **Ganwick Corner** Herts
9 J9 **Gappah** Devon
157 Q7 **Garbity** Moray
64 E5 **Garboldisham** Norfk
148 D3 **Garbole** Highld
149 Q5 **Garchory** Abers
81 L11 **Garden City** Flints
35 M11 **Gardeners Green** Wokham
159 K5 **Gardenstown** Abers
90 H11 **Garden Village** Sheff
169 q9 **Garderhouse** Shet
92 G2 **Gardham** E R Yk
20 E6 **Gare Hill** Somset
131 Q9 **Garelochhead** Ag & B
34 D5 **Garford** Oxon
91 L4 **Garforth** Leeds
96 D10 **Gargrave** N York
133 L9 **Gargunnock** Stirlg
79 M9 **Garizim** Conwy
65 J5 **Garlic Street** Norfk
107 N8 **Garlieston** D & G
39 P8 **Garlinge** Kent
39 K11 **Garlinge Green** Kent
151 K6 **Garlogie** Abers
159 K7 **Garmond** Abers
157 Q5 **Garmouth** Moray
57 L3 **Garmston** Shrops
29 J2 **Garnant** Carmth
66 H6 **Garn-Dolbenmaen** Gwynd
101 P11 **Garnett Bridge** Cumb
66 D8 **Garnfadryn** Gwynd
126 B4 **Garnkirk** N Lans
28 H3 **Garnswllt** Swans
30 H3 **Garn-yr-erw** Torfn
168 k4 **Garrabost** W Isls
115 K4 **Garrallan** E Ayrs
3 J9 **Garras** Cnwll
67 L6 **Garreg** Gwynd
102 D2 **Garrigill** Cumb
97 J2 **Garriston** N York
108 C4 **Garroch** D & G
106 F10 **Garrochtrie** D & G
124 D7 **Garrochty** Ag & B
152 H5 **Garros** Highld
95 Q3 **Garsdale** Cumb
96 A2 **Garsdale Head** Cumb
33 J7 **Garsdon** Wilts
70 H8 **Garshall Green** Staffs
34 G4 **Garsington** Oxon
95 K11 **Garstang** Lancs
50 D10 **Garston** Herts
81 N8 **Garston** Lpool
122 D7 **Gartachossan** Ag & B
126 B4 **Gartcosh** N Lans
29 N6 **Garth** Brdgnd
31 K6 **Garth** Mons
44 D5 **Garth** Powys
56 D10 **Garth** Powys
69 J6 **Garth** Wrexhm
126 B4 **Garthamlock** C Glas
44 E8 **Garthbrengy** Powys
43 L3 **Gartheli** Cerdgn
56 B5 **Garthmyl** Powys
73 L6 **Garthorpe** Leics
92 D7 **Garthorpe** N Linc
54 E8 **Garth Penrhyncoch** Cerdgn
101 P11 **Garth Row** Cumb
95 L3 **Garths** Cumb
158 D11 **Gartly** Abers
132 G8 **Gartmore** Stirlg
126 D5 **Gartness** N Lans
132 G10 **Gartness** Stirlg
132 E10 **Gartocharn** W Duns
93 N3 **Garton** E R Yk
99 K9 **Garton-on-the-Wolds** E R Yk
163 N4 **Gartymore** Highld
128 F5 **Garvald** E Loth
138 H2 **Garvan** Highld
136 b3 **Garvard** Ag & B
155 L5 **Garve** Highld
130 D5 **Garvellachs** Ag & B
76 E10 **Garvestone** Norfk
124 H3 **Garvock** Inver
45 P10 **Garway** Herefs
45 P10 **Garway Common** Herefs
45 N9 **Garway Hill** Herefs
168 i6 **Garyvard** W Isls
20 E8 **Gasper** Wilts
32 G11 **Gastard** Wilts
64 D5 **Gasthorpe** Norfk
51 L7 **Gaston Green** Essex
14 E9 **Gatcombe** IoW
95 L3 **Gatebeck** Cumb
85 P4 **Gate Burton** Lincs
85 J4 **Gateford** Notts
91 P5 **Gateforth** N York
125 K10 **Gatehead** E Ayrs
98 D9 **Gate Helmsley** N York
111 Q3 **Gatehouse** Nthumb
108 C9 **Gatehouse of Fleet** D & G
76 D7 **Gateley** Norfk
97 M3 **Gatenby** N York
100 G7 **Gatesgarth** Cumb
118 E6 **Gateshaw** Border
113 L8 **Gateshead** Gatesd
69 N2 **Gates Heath** Ches W
142 G9 **Gateside** Angus
125 M6 **Gateside** E Rens
134 F6 **Gateside** Fife
125 K7 **Gateside** N Ayrs
116 B10 **Gateslack** D & G
88 G9 **Gathurst** Wigan
82 H7 **Gatley** Stockp
36 G10 **Gatton** Surrey
117 Q3 **Gattonside** Border
24 G2 *Gatwick Airport* W Susx
55 M11 **Gaufron** Powys
72 H10 **Gaulby** Leics
135 K3 **Gauldry** Fife
142 C7 **Gauldswell** P & K
89 M5 **Gaulkthorn** Lancs
75 J9 **Gaultree** Norfk
69 Q5 **Gaunton's Bank** Ches E
12 H3 **Gaunt's Common** Dorset
51 N5 **Gaunt's End** Essex
86 G6 **Gautby** Lincs
129 K9 **Gavinton** Border
91 J9 **Gawber** Barns
49 J8 **Gawcott** Bucks
83 J11 **Gawsworth** Ches E
90 H6 **Gawthorpe** Wakefd
95 P3 **Gawthrop** Cumb
94 F4 **Gawthwaite** Cumb
52 C11 **Gay Bowers** Essex
48 C4 **Gaydon** Warwks
49 M5 **Gayhurst** M Keyn
96 C3 **Gayle** N York
103 M9 **Gayles** N York
24 C6 **Gay Street** W Susx
49 K4 **Gayton** Nhants
75 P7 **Gayton** Norfk
70 H9 **Gayton** Staffs
81 K8 **Gayton** Wirral
87 M4 **Gayton le Marsh** Lincs
75 P7 **Gayton Thorpe** Norfk
75 M6 **Gaywood** Norfk
63 M8 **Gazeley** Suffk
3 J9 **Gear** Cnwll
168 i6 **Gearraidh Bhaird** W Isls
152 D5 **Geary** Highld
64 C10 **Gedding** Suffk
61 J4 **Geddington** Nhants
72 G2 **Gedling** Notts
74 H6 **Gedney** Lincs
74 H6 **Gedney Broadgate** Lincs
75 J5 **Gedney Drove End** Lincs
74 H5 **Gedney Dyke** Lincs
74 F8 **Gedney Hill** Lincs
83 L6 **Gee Cross** Tamesd
73 P10 **Geeston** Rutlnd
65 M3 **Geldeston** Norfk
30 C6 **Gelli** Rhondd
31 J6 **Gelli** Torfn
68 F2 **Gellifor** Denbgs
30 F5 **Gelligaer** Caerph
30 G6 **Gelligroes** Caerph
29 K4 **Gelligron** Neath
67 M7 **Gellilydan** Gwynd
29 K4 **Gellinudd** Neath
41 L7 **Gelly** Pembks
141 Q10 **Gellyburn** P & K
41 Q6 **Gellywen** Carmth
108 G9 **Gelston** D & G
86 B11 **Gelston** Lincs
99 N9 **Gembling** E R Yk
58 G2 **Gentleshaw** Staffs
110 E2 **Georgefield** D & G
35 Q8 **George Green** Bucks
16 H4 **Georgeham** Devon
167 L5 **Georgemas Junction Station** Highld
17 N7 **George Nympton** Devon
30 G3 **Georgetown** Blae G
2 D6 **Georgia** Cnwll
169 c4 **Georth** Ork
79 L11 **Gerlan** Gwynd
8 B6 **Germansweek** Devon
2 F8 **Germoe** Cnwll
3 M6 **Gerrans** Cnwll
36 B3 **Gerrards Cross** Bucks
105 K8 **Gerrick** R & Cl
52 D4 **Gestingthorpe** Essex
56 C2 **Geuffordd** Powys
82 D9 **Gib Hill** Ches W
87 Q9 **Gibraltar** Lincs
85 M11 **Gibsmere** Notts
32 G10 **Giddeahall** Wilts
12 D7 **Giddy Green** Dorset
37 M2 **Gidea Park** Gt Lon
8 G7 **Gidleigh** Devon
125 P6 **Giffnock** E Rens
128 E6 **Gifford** E Loth
134 H5 **Giffordtown** Fife
96 B8 **Giggleswick** N York
123 K10 **Gigha** Ag & B
92 D5 **Gilberdyke** E R Yk
46 F6 **Gilbert's End** Worcs
22 H8 **Gilbert Street** Hants
128 D6 **Gilchriston** E Loth
100 F3 **Gilcrux** Cumb
90 G5 **Gildersome** Leeds
85 J3 **Gildingwells** Rothm
103 Q2 **Gilesgate Moor** Dur
30 D11 **Gileston** V Glam
30 G5 **Gilfach** Caerph
30 C6 **Gilfach Goch** Brdgnd
42 H3 **Gilfachrheda** Cerdgn
100 D6 **Gilgarran** Cumb
101 M5 **Gill** Cumb
98 D3 **Gillamoor** N York
3 K8 **Gillan** Cnwll
152 D6 **Gillen** Highld
110 C2 **Gillesbie** D & G
98 C5 **Gilling East** N York
20 F9 **Gillingham** Dorset
38 C8 **Gillingham** Medway
65 N3 **Gillingham** Norfk
103 N9 **Gilling West** N York
167 M5 **Gillock** Highld
70 F3 **Gillow Heath** Staffs
167 P2 **Gills** Highld
26 C5 **Gill's Green** Kent
117 L6 **Gilmanscleuch** Border
127 P4 **Gilmerton** C Edin
133 P3 **Gilmerton** P & K
103 J8 **Gilmonby** Dur
60 C3 **Gilmorton** Leics
72 F9 **Gilroes Crematorium** C Leic
111 M7 **Gilsland** Nthumb
59 J7 **Gilson** Warwks
90 E3 **Gilstead** C Brad
128 C8 **Gilston** Border
51 K8 **Gilston** Herts
51 K8 **Gilston Park** Herts
84 G11 **Giltbrook** Notts
30 H2 **Gilwern** Mons
77 K4 **Gimingham** Norfk
83 L9 **Ginclough** Ches E
25 P8 **Gingers Green** E Susx
64 F9 **Gipping** Suffk
87 J11 **Gipsey Bridge** Lincs
125 J9 **Girdle Toll** N Ayrs
90 E4 **Girlington** C Brad
169 r8 **Girlsta** Shet
104 C9 **Girsby** N York
61 Q11 **Girtford** C Beds
108 D10 **Girthon** D & G
62 F8 **Girton** Cambs
85 P7 **Girton** Notts
114 C8 **Girvan** S Ayrs
96 B11 **Gisburn** Lancs
65 Q4 **Gisleham** Suffk
64 F7 **Gislingham** Suffk
64 G4 **Gissing** Norfk
10 C5 **Gittisham** Devon
45 J3 **Gladestry** Powys
128 D5 **Gladsmuir** E Loth
29 K4 **Glais** Swans
105 L9 **Glaisdale** N York
142 F8 **Glamis** Angus
67 L4 **Glanaber** Gwynd
41 J7 **Glanafon** Pembks
29 J2 **Glanaman** Carmth
76 E3 **Glandford** Norfk
43 K6 **Glan-Duar** Carmth
41 N5 **Glandwr** Pembks
66 H6 **Glan-Dwyfach** Gwynd
54 F5 **Glandyfi** Cerdgn
45 J11 **Glangrwyney** Powys
29 N6 **Glanllynfi** Brdgnd
56 B6 **Glanmule** Powys
41 M2 **Glanrhyd** Pembks
29 L3 **Glan-rhyd** Powys
119 L8 **Glanton** Nthumb
119 L8 **Glanton Pike** Nthumb
11 P3 **Glanvilles Wootton** Dorset
80 H9 **Glan-y-don** Flints
30 F8 **Glan-y-llyn** Rhondd
55 L8 **Glan-y-nant** Powys
68 B6 **Glan-yr-afon** Gwynd
68 D6 **Glan-yr-afon** Gwynd
79 L8 **Glan-yr-afon** IoA
28 H3 **Glan-yr-afon** Swans
61 M2 **Glapthorn** Nhants
84 G7 **Glapwell** Derbys
44 H7 **Glasbury** Powys
80 D10 **Glascoed** Denbgs
31 K4 **Glascoed** Mons
59 K4 **Glascote** Staffs
44 H4 **Glascwm** Powys
68 B4 **Glasfryn** Conwy
125 P4 **Glasgow** C Glas
125 M4 *Glasgow Airport* Rens
125 P4 **Glasgow Science Centre** C Glas
79 K11 **Glasinfryn** Gwynd
145 L8 **Glasnacardoch Bay** Highld
144 H5 **Glasnakille** Highld
54 G5 **Glaspwll** Powys
26 C4 **Glassenbury** Kent
126 C8 **Glassford** S Lans
91 L6 **Glass Houghton** Wakefd
46 D10 **Glasshouse** Gloucs
46 D10 **Glasshouse Hill** Gloucs
97 J8 **Glasshouses** N York
110 E8 **Glasson** Cumb
95 J9 **Glasson** Lancs
101 Q3 **Glassonby** Cumb
143 K7 **Glasterlaw** Angus
73 M10 **Glaston** Rutlnd
19 P7 **Glastonbury** Somset
61 Q3 **Glatton** Cambs
82 E6 **Glazebrook** Warrtn
82 E5 **Glazebury** Warrtn
57 N7 **Glazeley** Shrops
84 E4 **Gleadless** Sheff
82 H11 **Gleadsmoss** Ches E
94 F6 **Gleaston** Cumb
147 N4 **Glebe** Highld
91 J3 **Gledhow** Leeds
108 D10 **Gledpark** D & G
69 K7 **Gledrid** Shrops
52 D2 **Glemsford** Suffk
157 P9 **Glenallachie** Moray
145 L9 **Glenancross** Highld
137 P7 **Glenaros House** Ag & B
80 f3 **Glen Auldyn** IoM
120 C4 **Glenbarr** Ag & B
158 E7 **Glenbarry** Abers
137 P3 **Glenbeg** Highld
151 K11 **Glenbervie** Abers
126 C4 **Glenboig** N Lans
137 Q3 **Glenborrodale** Highld
131 N8 **Glenbranter** Ag & B
116 F6 **Glenbreck** Border
144 F3 **Glenbrittle House** Highld
115 P2 **Glenbuck** E Ayrs
142 F5 **Glencally** Angus
109 L7 **Glencaple** D & G
154 E7 **Glencarron Lodge** Highld
134 F3 **Glencarse** P & K
149 L11 **Glen Clunie Lodge** Abers
139 L6 **Glencoe** Highld
116 F5 **Glencothe** Border
134 F9 **Glencraig** Fife
115 Q10 **Glencrosh** D & G
152 B8 **Glendale** Highld
131 K11 **Glendaruel** Ag & B
134 B7 **Glendevon** P & K
147 L6 **Glendoe Lodge** Highld
134 G3 **Glendoick** P & K
134 H4 **Glenduckie** Fife
133 Q5 **Gleneagles** P & K
122 D9 **Glenegedale** Ag & B
145 P4 **Glenelg** Highld
157 J8 **Glenerney** Moray
134 E5 **Glenfarg** P & K
72 E9 **Glenfield** Leics
145 R11 **Glenfinnan** Highld
146 G10 **Glenfintaig Lodge** Highld
134 F4 **Glenfoot** P & K
131 Q4 **Glenfyne Lodge** Ag & B
125 J7 **Glengarnock** N Ayrs
167 K3 **Glengolly** Highld
137 L4 **Glengorm Castle** Ag & B
152 G9 **Glengrasco** Highld
116 G4 **Glenholm** Border
115 M10 **Glenhoul** D & G
142 C5 **Glenisla** Angus
131 N11 **Glenkin** Ag & B
150 C5 **Glenkindie** Abers
149 M2 **Glenlivet** Moray
108 F8 **Glenlochar** D & G
134 F7 **Glenlomond** P & K
106 G6 **Glenluce** D & G
131 N10 **Glenmassen** Ag & B
126 D4 **Glenmavis** N Lans
80 b6 **Glen Maye** IoM
80 g4 **Glen Mona** IoM
152 G9 **Glenmore** Highld
148 H6 **Glenmore Lodge** Highld
139 L3 **Glen Nevis House** Highld
133 P8 **Glenochil** Clacks
72 F11 **Glen Parva** Leics
142 G5 **Glenquiech** Angus
123 Q6 **Glenralloch** Ag & B
101 L7 **Glenridding** Cumb
134 H7 **Glenrothes** Fife
147 P9 **Glenshero Lodge** Highld
124 D2 **Glenstriven** Ag & B
86 D2 **Glentham** Lincs
114 H11 **Glen Trool Lodge** D & G
107 L2 **Glentrool Village** D & G
148 B9 **Glentruim House** Highld
86 B3 **Glentworth** Lincs
138 B2 **Glenuig** Highld
152 H10 **Glenvarragill** Highld
80 d6 **Glen Vine** IoM
106 G3 **Glenwhilly** D & G
115 R2 **Glespin** S Lans
45 R10 **Glewstone** Herefs
74 C9 **Glinton** C Pete
73 K11 **Glooston** Leics
83 M6 **Glossop** Derbys
119 Q10 **Gloster Hill** Nthumb
46 F11 **Gloucester** Gloucs
46 G11 **Gloucester Crematorium** Gloucs
46 G10 *Gloucestershire Airport* Gloucs
96 F11 **Glusburn** N York
166 H9 **Glutt Lodge** Highld
4 E9 **Gluvian** Cnwll
48 D10 **Glympton** Oxon
42 F5 **Glynarthen** Cerdgn
68 H7 **Glyn Ceiriog** Wrexhm
29 N5 **Glyncorrwg** Neath
25 L9 **Glynde** E Susx
25 L8 **Glyndebourne** E Susx
68 F6 **Glyndyfrdwy** Denbgs
29 N3 **Glynneath** Neath
4 H8 **Glynn Valley Crematorium** Cnwll
30 E7 **Glyntaff** Rhondd
30 E7 **Glyntaff Crematorium** Rhondd
44 A11 **Glyntawe** Powys
42 G7 **Glynteg** Carmth
70 E10 **Gnosall** Staffs
70 E10 **Gnosall Heath** Staffs
73 K11 **Goadby** Leics
73 K5 **Goadby Marwood** Leics
33 K9 **Goatacre** Wilts
26 D7 **Goatham Green** E Susx
20 C11 **Goathill** Dorset
105 M10 **Goathland** N York
19 J8 **Goathurst** Somset
37 L10 **Goathurst Common** Kent
26 H2 **Goat Lees** Kent
69 K8 **Gobowen** Shrops
23 Q6 **Godalming** Surrey
65 K8 **Goddard's Corner** Suffk
26 D5 **Goddard's Green** Kent
10 C4 **Godford Cross** Devon
48 H9 **Godington** Oxon
83 L5 **Godley** Tamesd
62 B6 **Godmanchester** Cambs
11 P5 **Godmanstone** Dorset
39 J11 **Godmersham** Kent
19 N6 **Godney** Somset
2 G7 **Godolphin Cross** Cnwll
29 L3 **Godre'r-graig** Neath
21 N11 **Godshill** Hants
14 F10 **Godshill** IoW
71 J8 **Godstone** Staffs
37 J10 **Godstone** Surrey
8 D9 **Godsworthy** Devon
13 L5 **Godwinscroft** Hants
31 K3 **Goetre** Mons
50 H10 **Goff's Oak** Herts
31 J2 **Gofilon** Mons
127 M3 **Gogar** C Edin
54 F8 **Goginan** Cerdgn
67 J6 **Golan** Gwynd
5 J11 **Golant** Cnwll
5 N7 **Golberdon** Cnwll
82 D5 **Golborne** Wigan
90 D7 **Golcar** Kirk
31 L8 **Goldcliff** Newpt
25 M8 **Golden Cross** E Susx
37 P11 **Golden Green** Kent
43 L11 **Golden Grove** Carmth
70 F4 **Goldenhill** C Stke
41 J10 **Golden Hill** Pembks
23 K6 **Golden Pot** Hants
84 F10 **Golden Valley** Derbys
36 F3 **Golders Green** Gt Lon
36 G3 **Golders Green Crematorium** Gt Lon
22 F2 **Goldfinch Bottom** W Berk
52 F10 **Goldhanger** Essex
62 H2 **Gold Hill** Cambs
12 D2 **Gold Hill** Dorset
57 J4 **Golding** Shrops
61 N10 **Goldington** Bed
97 N9 **Goldsborough** N York
105 M8 **Goldsborough** N York
58 E6 **Golds Green** Sandw
2 E7 **Goldsithney** Cnwll
39 N9 **Goldstone** Kent
70 C9 **Goldstone** Shrops
23 Q3 **Goldsworth Park** Surrey
91 M10 **Goldthorpe** Barns
16 F7 **Goldworthy** Devon
26 C4 **Golford** Kent
26 C4 **Golford Green** Kent
156 E7 **Gollanfield** Highld
96 H4 **Gollinglith Foot** N York
69 K3 **Golly** Wrexhm
18 D7 **Golsoncott** Somset
163 J6 **Golspie** Highld
21 N7 **Gomeldon** Wilts
90 G5 **Gomersal** Kirk
36 C11 **Gomshall** Surrey
85 L11 **Gonalston** Notts
73 N3 **Gonerby Hill Foot** Lincs
169 q7 **Gonfirth** Shet
6 E6 **Goodameavy** Devon
51 P8 **Good Easter** Essex
75 Q10 **Gooderstone** Norfk
17 L5 **Goodleigh** Devon
92 E2 **Goodmanham** E R Yk
37 L3 **Goodmayes** Gt Lon
38 H9 **Goodnestone** Kent

39 N11 Goodnestone Kent
45 R11 Goodrich Herefs
46 A11 Goodrich Castle Herefs
7 M7 Goodrington Torbay
89 N5 Goodshaw Lancs
89 N5 Goodshaw Fold Lancs
7 K4 Goodstone Devon
40 H3 Goodwick Pembks
22 C6 Goodworth Clatford Hants
59 M7 Goodyers End Warwks
92 B6 Goole E R Yk
92 C6 Goole Fields E R Yk
47 K4 Goom's Hill Worcs
3 J4 Goonbell Cnwll
3 K3 Goonhavern Cnwll
3 J4 Goonvrea Cnwll
151 K11 Goosecruives Abers
8 G6 Gooseford Devon
53 K6 Goose Green Essex
26 D4 Goose Green Kent
37 P10 Goose Green Kent
32 C10 Goose Green S Glos
24 D7 Goose Green W Susx
82 C4 Goose Green Wigan
16 C8 Gooseham Cnwll
46 H2 Goosehill Green Worcs
45 P7 Goose Pool Herefs
34 C6 Goosey Oxon
88 H3 Goosnargh Lancs
82 G10 Goostrey Ches E
31 P9 Gordano Services N Som
79 M10 Gorddinog Conwy
118 B2 Gordon Border
117 L5 Gordon Arms Hotel Border
158 E6 Gordonstown Abers
158 H10 Gordonstown Abers
45 K3 Gore Powys
127 Q5 Gorebridge Mdloth
74 H8 Gorefield Cambs
52 E8 Gore Pit Essex
21 M3 Gores Wilts
39 N8 Gore Street Kent
11 c2 Gorey Jersey
34 H8 Goring Oxon
24 D10 Goring-by-Sea W Susx
35 J9 Goring Heath Oxon
77 Q11 Gorleston on Sea Norfk
58 D6 Gornal Wood Crematorium Dudley
158 H6 Gorrachie Abers
3 P5 Gorran Churchtown Cnwll
3 Q5 Gorran Haven Cnwll
3 P5 Gorran High Lanes Cnwll
42 H6 Gorrig Cerdgn
54 E9 Gors Cerdgn
80 H9 Gorsedd Flints
33 N7 Gorse Hill Swindn
28 G5 Gorseinon Swans
71 P4 Gorseybank Derbys
43 J4 Gorsgoch Cerdgn
28 G2 Gorslas Carmth
46 C9 Gorsley Gloucs
46 C9 Gorsley Common Herefs
82 D10 Gorstage Ches W
155 L5 Gorstan Highld
69 L2 Gorstella Ches W
57 N10 Gorst Hill Worcs
71 L9 Gorsty Hill Staffs
138 C11 Gorten Ag & B
147 N3 Gorthleck Highld
83 J5 Gorton Manch
64 H10 Gosbeck Suffk
74 D4 Gosberton Lincs
74 C5 Gosberton Clough Lincs
52 C6 Gosfield Essex
10 C5 Gosford Devon
100 E10 Gosforth Cumb
113 K7 Gosforth N u Ty
19 P8 Gosling Street Somset
50 E5 Gosmore Herts
58 C6 Gospel End Staffs
23 P8 Gospel Green W Susx
14 H7 Gosport Hants
49 Q6 Gossard's Green C Beds
32 D4 Gossington Gloucs
119 L2 Goswick Nthumb
72 E4 Gotham Notts
47 J9 Gotherington Gloucs
18 H9 Gotton Somset
26 B4 Goudhurst Kent
87 J5 Goulceby Lincs
159 J9 Gourdas Abers
142 F11 Gourdie C Dund
143 Q3 Gourdon Abers
124 G2 Gourock Inver
125 N4 Govan C Glas
7 K9 Goveton Devon
91 Q6 Gowdall E R Yk
155 P6 Gower Highld
28 F6 Gower Swans
28 G5 Gowerton Swans
134 D10 Gowkhall Fife
98 F10 Gowthorpe E R Yk
93 L2 Goxhill E R Yk
93 K6 Goxhill N Linc
168 i6 Grabhair W Isls
74 A5 Graby Lincs
3 J11 Grade Cnwll
69 Q4 Gradeley Green Ches E
23 P11 Graffham W Susx
61 Q7 Grafham Cambs
24 B2 Grafham Surrey
45 P7 Grafton Herefs
97 P8 Grafton N York
33 Q4 Grafton Oxon
69 M11 Grafton Shrops
46 A2 Grafton Worcs
47 J7 Grafton Worcs
47 J3 Grafton Flyford Worcs
49 L5 Grafton Regis Nhants
61 K4 Grafton Underwood Nhants
26 E2 Grafty Green Kent
68 H3 Graianrhyd Denbgs
79 Q10 Graig Conwy
80 F10 Graig Denbgs
68 F4 Graig-fechan Denbgs
38 E6 Grain Medway
90 B9 Grains Bar Oldham
93 N11 Grainsby Lincs
93 Q11 Grainthorpe Lincs
3 N4 Grampound Cnwll
3 N3 Grampound Road Cnwll
168 d12 Gramsdal W Isls
168 d12 Gramsdale W Isls
49 L9 Granborough Bucks
73 K3 Granby Notts
59 Q11 Grandborough Warwks
11 c2 Grand Chemins Jersey
10 b1 Grandes Rocques Guern
72 C5 Grand Prix Collection Donington Leics
141 M7 Grandtully P & K
101 J7 Grange Cumb
38 C8 Grange Medway
134 H2 Grange P & K
81 J7 Grange Wirral
158 C7 Grange Crossroads Moray
157 K5 Grange Hall Moray
116 D2 Grangehall S Lans
37 K2 Grange Hill Essex
84 B9 Grangemill Derbys
90 G7 Grange Moor Kirk
133 Q11 Grangemouth Falk
134 H4 Grange of Lindores Fife
95 J5 Grange-over-Sands Cumb
134 C11 Grangepans Falk
104 F6 Grangetown R & Cl
113 P10 Grangetown Sundld
113 K10 Grange Villa Dur
99 N9 Gransmoor E R Yk
51 Q6 Gransmore Green Essex
40 G4 Granston Pembks
62 F9 Grantchester Cambs
73 N3 Grantham Lincs
73 N3 Grantham Crematorium Lincs
73 M3 Grantham North Services Lincs
127 N2 Granton C Edin
149 J2 Grantown-on-Spey Highld
45 Q2 Grantsfield Herefs
129 L6 Grantshouse Border
82 D7 Grappenhall Warrtn
93 J10 Grasby Lincs
101 K9 Grasmere Cumb
83 L4 Grasscroft Oldham
81 M7 Grassendale Lpool
101 K2 Grassgarth Cumb
52 B4 Grass Green Essex
96 F8 Grassington N York
84 F7 Grassmoor Derbys
85 N7 Grassthorpe Notts
21 Q6 Grateley Hants
71 J8 Gratwich Staffs
62 C8 Graveley Cambs
50 F5 Graveley Herts
58 H6 Gravelly Hill Birm
56 E4 Gravelsbank Shrops
39 J9 Graveney Kent
37 Q6 Gravesend Kent
168 i6 Gravir W Isls
92 F11 Grayingham Lincs
101 Q11 Grayrigg Cumb
37 P5 Grays Thurr
23 N7 Grayshott Hants
100 C5 Grayson Green Cumb
23 P8 Grayswood Surrey
104 F5 Graythorpe Hartpl
35 J11 Grazeley Wokham
91 L11 Greasbrough Rothm
81 K7 Greasby Wirral
84 G11 Greasley Notts
62 H11 Great Abington Cambs
61 L5 Great Addington Nhants
47 M3 Great Alne Warwks
88 C9 Great Altcar Lancs
51 J8 Great Amwell Herts
102 C8 Great Asby Cumb
64 D8 Great Ashfield Suffk
104 G8 Great Ayton N York
52 B11 Great Baddow Essex
32 F8 Great Badminton S Glos
51 Q4 Great Bardfield Essex
61 P10 Great Barford Bed
58 F5 Great Barr Sandw
33 P2 Great Barrington Gloucs
81 P11 Great Barrow Ches W
64 B8 Great Barton Suffk
98 E5 Great Barugh N York
112 E4 Great Bavington Nthumb
53 M2 Great Bealings Suffk
21 Q2 Great Bedwyn Wilts
53 K7 Great Bentley Essex
60 H8 Great Billing Nhants
75 Q4 Great Bircham Norfk
64 G11 Great Blakenham Suffk
101 N4 Great Blencow Cumb
70 A10 Great Bolas Wrekin
36 D10 Great Bookham Surrey
2 C7 Great Bosullow Cnwll
48 E5 Great Bourton Oxon
60 F3 Great Bowden Leics
63 L10 Great Bradley Suffk
52 E9 Great Braxted Essex
64 E11 Great Bricett Suffk
49 P8 Great Brickhill Bucks
70 F9 Great Bridgeford Staffs
60 E7 Great Brington Nhants
53 J6 Great Bromley Essex
100 E4 Great Broughton Cumb
104 F9 Great Broughton N York
82 E9 Great Budworth Ches W
104 B7 Great Burdon Darltn
37 Q2 Great Burstead Essex
104 F9 Great Busby N York
51 N7 Great Canfield Essex
87 M3 Great Carlton Lincs
73 Q9 Great Casterton Rutlnd
20 G2 Great Chalfield Wilts
26 G3 Great Chart Kent
57 P2 Great Chatwell Staffs
70 F4 Great Chell C Stke
51 M2 Great Chesterford Essex
21 J4 Great Cheverell Wilts
51 K3 Great Chishill Cambs
53 L8 Great Clacton Essex
91 J7 Great Cliffe Wakefd
100 D5 Great Clifton Cumb
93 M9 Great Coates NE Lin
47 J6 Great Comberton Worcs
37 P9 Great Comp Kent
111 J10 Great Corby Cumb
52 E3 Great Cornard Suffk
93 M2 Great Cowden E R Yk
33 Q6 Great Coxwell Oxon
60 H5 Great Cransley Nhants
76 B11 Great Cressingham Norfk
101 J6 Great Crosthwaite Cumb
71 M7 Great Cubley Derbys
124 F6 Great Cumbrae Island N Ayrs
73 J8 Great Dalby Leics
61 J8 Great Doddington Nhants
45 Q11 Great Doward Herefs
76 B9 Great Dunham Norfk
51 P6 Great Dunmow Essex
21 M7 Great Durnford Wilts
51 P5 Great Easton Essex
60 H2 Great Easton Leics
88 E2 Great Eccleston Lancs
98 E4 Great Edstone N York
64 E2 Great Ellingham Norfk
20 D5 Great Elm Somset
60 C9 Great Everdon Nhants
62 E10 Great Eversden Cambs
97 L2 Great Fencote N York
64 E10 Great Finborough Suffk
74 A8 Greatford Lincs
76 B9 Great Fransham Norfk
50 B8 Great Gaddesden Herts
71 K7 Greatgate Staffs
61 P4 Great Gidding Cambs
98 G10 Great Givendale E R Yk
65 L9 Great Glemham Suffk
72 H11 Great Glen Leics
73 M3 Great Gonerby Lincs
62 C9 Great Gransden Cambs
50 G2 Great Green Cambs
65 K4 Great Green Norfk
64 C10 Great Green Suffk
64 C8 Great Green Suffk
98 F5 Great Habton N York
74 B2 Great Hale Lincs
51 M7 Great Hallingbury Essex
23 L8 Greatham Hants
104 E5 Greatham Hartpl
24 B7 Greatham W Susx
35 M4 Great Hampden Bucks
61 J6 Great Harrowden Nhants
89 L4 Great Harwood Lancs
34 H4 Great Haseley Oxon
93 L2 Great Hatfield E R Yk
70 H10 Great Haywood Staffs
91 P6 Great Heck N York
52 E4 Great Henny Essex
20 H3 Great Hinton Wilts
64 D3 Great Hockham Norfk
53 M8 Great Holland Essex
35 N11 Great Hollands Br For
52 G5 Great Horkesley Essex
51 K5 Great Hormead Herts
90 E4 Great Horton C Brad
49 L8 Great Horwood Bucks
91 L9 Great Houghton Barns
60 G9 Great Houghton Nhants
83 Q9 Great Hucklow Derbys
99 N9 Great Kelk E R Yk
35 M3 Great Kimble Bucks
35 N5 Great Kingshill Bucks
101 J9 Great Langdale Cumb
103 Q11 Great Langton N York
52 B8 Great Leighs Essex
93 K9 Great Limber Lincs
49 N6 Great Linford M Keyn
64 B7 Great Livermere Suffk
84 B6 Great Longstone Derbys
113 L11 Great Lumley Dur
56 H3 Great Lyth Shrops
46 E5 Great Malvern Worcs
52 D5 Great Maplestead Essex
88 C3 Great Marton Bpool
75 Q6 Great Massingham Norfk
76 G10 Great Melton Norfk
81 J6 Great Meols Wirral
34 H4 Great Milton Oxon
35 N4 Great Missenden Bucks
89 L3 Great Mitton Lancs
39 Q11 Great Mongeham Kent
64 H3 Great Moulton Norfk
51 J6 Great Munden Herts
102 E8 Great Musgrave Cumb
69 L11 Great Ness Shrops
52 B7 Great Notley Essex
31 L2 Great Oak Mons
53 L6 Great Oakley Essex
61 J3 Great Oakley Nhants
50 D5 Great Offley Herts
102 D7 Great Ormside Cumb
110 F10 Great Orton Cumb
97 P8 Great Ouseburn N York
60 F4 Great Oxendon Nhants
51 Q9 Great Oxney Green Essex
76 A9 Great Palgrave Norfk
26 B3 Great Pattenden Kent
62 B8 Great Paxton Cambs
88 D4 Great Plumpton Lancs
77 L9 Great Plumstead Norfk
73 N4 Great Ponton Lincs
17 J9 Great Potheridge Devon
91 L5 Great Preston Leeds
48 F7 Great Purston Nhants
62 C4 Great Raveley Cambs
47 N11 Great Rissington Gloucs
48 B8 Great Rollright Oxon
41 J6 Great Rudbaxton Pembks
76 D6 Great Ryburgh Norfk
119 K8 Great Ryle Nthumb
56 H4 Great Ryton Shrops
51 Q5 Great Saling Essex
101 Q3 Great Salkeld Cumb
51 P3 Great Sampford Essex
58 E3 Great Saredon Staffs
81 M11 Great Saughall Ches W
63 N8 Great Saxham Suffk
34 C9 Great Shefford W Berk
62 G10 Great Shelford Cambs
104 B10 Great Smeaton N York
76 C5 Great Snoring Norfk
33 J8 Great Somerford Wilts
70 C9 Great Soudley Shrops
104 B6 Great Stainton Darltn
38 E3 Great Stambridge Essex
61 P8 Great Staughton Cambs
87 M8 Great Steeping Lincs
32 B8 Great Stoke S Glos
39 P10 Great Stonar Kent
27 J7 Greatstone-on-Sea Kent
101 Q6 Great Strickland Cumb
62 B6 Great Stukeley Cambs
86 H5 Great Sturton Lincs
81 M9 Great Sutton Ches W
57 J8 Great Sutton Shrops
112 D5 Great Swinburne Nthumb
48 D9 Great Tew Oxon
52 E6 Great Tey Essex
63 L10 Great Thurlow Suffk
16 H8 Great Torrington Devon
119 K10 Great Tosson Nthumb
52 E9 Great Totham Essex
52 E9 Great Totham Essex
86 H2 Great Tows Lincs
94 F6 Great Urswick Cumb
38 F4 Great Wakering Essex
52 F3 Great Waldingfield Suffk
76 C4 Great Walsingham Norfk
51 Q8 Great Waltham Essex
82 H9 Great Warford Ches E
37 N2 Great Warley Essex
47 J8 Great Washbourne Gloucs
8 H7 Great Weeke Devon
61 K3 Great Weldon Nhants
64 B10 Great Welnetham Suffk
53 J4 Great Wenham Suffk
112 F6 Great Whittington Nthumb
52 G8 Great Wigborough Essex
63 J9 Great Wilbraham Cambs
21 L7 Great Wishford Wilts
76 G7 Great Witchingham Norfk
32 H2 Great Witcombe Gloucs
57 P11 Great Witley Worcs
47 Q8 Great Wolford Warwks
48 G6 Greatworth Nhants
63 L11 Great Wratting Suffk
50 F5 Great Wymondley Herts
58 E3 Great Wyrley Staffs
69 Q11 Great Wytheford Shrops
77 Q10 Great Yarmouth Norfk
77 Q11 Great Yarmouth Crematorium Norfk
52 C4 Great Yeldham Essex
87 M7 Grebby Lincs
80 d5 Greeba IoM
80 F11 Green Denbgs
94 H4 Green Bank Cumb
126 G5 Greenburn W Loth
113 J11 Greencroft Hall Dur
23 N7 Green Cross Surrey
19 Q4 Green Down Somset
61 M11 Green End Bed
61 N8 Green End Bed
61 P10 Green End Bed
61 P8 Green End Bed
61 Q4 Green End Cambs
62 B6 Green End Cambs
62 E9 Green End Cambs
62 G7 Green End Cambs
62 G8 Green End Cambs
50 G4 Green End Herts
50 H4 Green End Herts
50 H6 Green End Herts
48 B10 Greenend Oxon
59 L7 Green End Warwks
131 Q9 Greenfield Ag & B
50 C4 Greenfield C Beds
80 H9 Greenfield Flints
146 G7 Greenfield Highld
83 L4 Greenfield Oldham
35 K6 Greenfield Oxon
36 D4 Greenford Gt Lon
126 D3 Greengairs N Lans
90 F3 Greengates C Brad
100 F3 Greengill Cumb
88 E3 Greenhalgh Lancs
18 E10 Greenham Somset
34 E11 Greenham W Berk
97 Q9 Green Hammerton N York
111 Q3 Greenhaugh Nthumb
110 G11 Green Head Cumb
111 N7 Greenhead Nthumb
58 E2 Green Heath Staffs
82 F4 Greenheys Salfd
109 P5 Greenhill D & G
126 E2 Greenhill Falk
46 D5 Greenhill Herefs
39 L8 Greenhill Kent
116 C4 Greenhill S Lans
33 L7 Green Hill Wilts
84 F11 Greenhillocks Derbys
37 N5 Greenhithe Kent
125 N10 Greenholm E Ayrs
101 Q9 Greenholme Cumb
117 R6 Greenhouse Border
96 H8 Greenhow Hill N York
167 M3 Greenland Highld
84 E3 Greenland Sheff
35 L7 Greenlands Bucks
9 J9 Green Lane Devon
47 L2 Green Lane Worcs
129 J10 Greenlaw Border
109 M5 Greenlea D & G
133 N6 Greenloaning P & K
90 H11 Green Moor Barns
89 M8 Greenmount Bury
92 D5 Green Oak E R Yk
124 H2 Greenock Inver
94 G4 Greenodd Cumb
19 Q4 Green Ore Somset
101 N10 Green Quarter Cumb
76 G8 Greensgate Norfk
116 E2 Greenshields S Lans
112 H8 Greenside Gatesd
90 F7 Greenside Kirk
49 J5 Greens Norton Nhants
52 H6 Greenstead Essex
52 D6 Greenstead Green Essex
51 M10 Greensted Essex
26 C9 Green Street E Susx
46 G11 Green Street Gloucs
50 E11 Green Street Herts
51 L6 Green Street Herts
46 G5 Green Street Worcs
37 L8 Green Street Green Gt Lon
37 N6 Green Street Green Kent
52 H2 Greenstreet Green Suffk
51 K7 Green Tye Herts
46 D8 Greenway Gloucs
19 K10 Greenway Somset
30 E10 Greenway V Glam
57 N10 Greenway Worcs
37 J5 Greenwich Gt Lon
47 K8 Greet Gloucs
57 K10 Greete Shrops
87 K6 Greetham Lincs
73 N8 Greetham Rutlnd
90 D6 Greetland Calder
88 H5 Gregson Lane Lancs
19 M7 Greinton Somset
80 c7 Grenaby IoM
61 J8 Grendon Nhants
59 L5 Grendon Warwks
46 A3 Grendon Green Herefs
49 J10 Grendon Underwood Bucks
6 D4 Grenofen Devon
84 D2 Grenoside Sheff
84 D2 Grenoside Crematorium Sheff
168 g8 Greosabhagh W Isls
69 K4 Gresford Wrexhm
76 H4 Gresham Norfk
152 E7 Greshornish House Hotel Highld
76 D8 Gressenhall Norfk
76 D8 Gressenhall Green Norfk
95 M7 Gressingham Lancs
70 C4 Gresty Green Ches E
103 L8 Greta Bridge Dur
110 F7 Gretna D & G
110 F7 Gretna Green D & G
110 F7 Gretna Services D & G
47 K8 Gretton Gloucs
61 J2 Gretton Nhants
57 J5 Gretton Shrops
97 K5 Grewelthorpe N York
65 P7 Grey Friars Suffk
97 J6 Greygarth N York
92 C9 Grey Green N Linc
19 L8 Greylake Somset
109 N3 Greyrigg D & G
35 K8 Greys Green Oxon
100 E5 Greysouthen Cumb
101 M4 Greystoke Cumb
143 J9 Greystone Angus
23 K4 Greywell Hants
10 H4 Gribb Dorset
92 C3 Gribthorpe E R Yk
59 N7 Griff Warwks
31 J5 Griffithstown Torfn
72 C7 Griffydam Leics
23 M8 Griggs Green Hants
89 J8 Grimeford Village Lancs
84 E3 Grimesthorpe Sheff
91 L9 Grimethorpe Barns
46 F2 Grimley Worcs
114 F5 Grimmet S Ayrs
87 L3 Grimoldby Lincs
69 L9 Grimpo Shrops
88 H4 Grimsargh Lancs
93 N8 Grimsby NE Lin
93 N9 Grimsby Crematorium NE Lin
49 J4 Grimscote Nhants
16 D10 Grimscott Cnwll
168 j5 Grimshader W Isls
89 L6 Grimshaw Bl w D
88 F8 Grimshaw Green Lancs
73 Q6 Grimsthorpe Lincs
93 N3 Grimston E R Yk
72 H6 Grimston Leics
75 P6 Grimston Norfk
11 N6 Grimstone Dorset
64 C8 Grimstone End Suffk
5 Q3 Grinacombe Moor Devon
99 N6 Grindale E R Yk
57 P4 Grindle Shrops
84 B5 Grindleford Derbys
95 R11 Grindleton Lancs
69 P6 Grindley Brook Shrops
83 Q9 Grindlow Derbys
118 H2 Grindon Nthumb
104 C5 Grindon S on T
71 K4 Grindon Staffs
112 B7 Grindon Hill Nthumb
118 H2 Grindonrigg Nthumb
85 M2 Gringley on the Hill Notts
110 G9 Grinsdale Cumb
69 P10 Grinshill Shrops
103 K11 Grinton N York
168 j5 Griomaisiader W Isls
168 d12 Griomsaigh W Isls
136 F4 Grishipoll Ag & B
25 K6 Grisling Common E Susx
99 M4 Gristhorpe N York
64 C2 Griston Norfk
169 e6 Gritley Ork
33 K8 Grittenham Wilts
32 G8 Grittleton Wilts
94 E4 Grizebeck Cumb
94 G2 Grizedale Cumb
72 E9 Groby Leics
68 D2 Groes Conwy
30 E8 Groes-faen Rhondd
66 D7 Groesffordd Gwynd
80 E10 Groesffordd Marli Denbgs
56 C2 Groesllwyd Powys
66 H3 Groeslon Gwynd
67 J2 Groeslon Gwynd
30 F7 Groes-Wen Caerph
168 c14 Grogarry W Isls
120 F3 Grogport Ag & B
168 c14 Groigearraidh W Isls
65 M10 Gromford Suffk
80 F8 Gronant Flints
25 M3 Groombridge E Susx
168 g8 Grosebay W Isls
45 N10 Grosmont Mons
105 M9 Grosmont N York
52 G3 Groton Suffk
83 L4 Grotton Oldham
11 c2 Grouville Jersey
49 P10 Grove Bucks
11 P10 Grove Dorset
39 M9 Grove Kent
85 M5 Grove Notts
34 D6 Grove Oxon
41 J10 Grove Pembks
38 C10 Grove Green Kent
26 B3 Grovenhurst Kent
37 K6 Grove Park Gt Lon
32 C7 Grovesend S Glos
28 G4 Grovesend Swans
37 N7 Grubb Street Kent
160 E9 Gruinard Highld
122 C6 Gruinart Ag & B
144 E2 Grula Highld
137 N7 Gruline Ag & B
2 C8 Grumbla Cnwll
65 J11 Grundisburgh Suffk
169 p9 Gruting Shet
139 L8 Gualachulain Highld
74 G8 Guanockgate Lincs
135 M4 Guardbridge Fife
46 F5 Guarlford Worcs
141 P8 Guay P & K
10 b2 Guernsey Airport Guern
26 E9 Guestling Green E Susx
26 E8 Guestling Thorn E Susx
76 F6 Guestwick Norfk
83 K5 Guide Bridge Tamesd
113 L3 Guide Post Nthumb
50 G2 Guilden Morden Cambs
81 N11 Guilden Sutton Ches W

23 Q5 Guildford Surrey
23 Q5 Guildford Crematorium Surrey
38 D9 Guildstead Kent
142 A11 Guildtown P & K
60 E6 Guilsborough Nhants
56 C2 Guilsfield Powys
39 N10 Guilton Kent
114 G5 Guiltreehill S Ayrs
17 K4 Guineaford Devon
104 H7 Guisborough R & Cl
90 F2 Guiseley Leeds
76 E6 Guist Norfk
47 L10 Guiting Power Gloucs
128 D3 Gullane E Loth
64 A10 Gulling Green Suffk
2 D7 Gulval Cnwll
6 D4 Gulworthy Devon
41 M10 Gumfreston Pembks
60 E3 Gumley Leics
4 D10 Gummow's Shop Cnwll
92 B3 Gunby E R Yk
73 N6 Gunby Lincs
87 N7 Gunby Lincs
22 H8 Gundleton Hants
26 C5 Gun Green Kent
25 N8 Gun Hill E Susx
59 L7 Gun Hill Warwks
17 L5 Gunn Devon
103 J11 Gunnerside N York
112 D6 Gunnerton Nthumb
92 D8 Gunness N Linc
6 C4 Gunnislake Cnwll
169 s9 Gunnista Shet
74 C10 Gunthorpe C Pete
92 D11 Gunthorpe N Linc
76 E5 Gunthorpe Norfk
72 H2 Gunthorpe Notts
65 Q2 Gunton Suffk
2 H9 Gunwalloe Cnwll
18 C8 Gupworthy Somset
14 E7 Gurnard IoW
83 K10 Gurnett Ches E
20 B5 Gurney Slade Somset
29 L3 Gurnos Powys
38 H10 Gushmere Kent
12 H2 Gussage All Saints Dorset
12 G2 Gussage St Andrew Dorset
12 G2 Gussage St Michael Dorset
27 P3 Guston Kent
169 s4 Gutcher Shet
143 K7 Guthrie Angus
74 H10 Guyhirn Cambs
74 G10 Guyhirn Gull Cambs
20 F10 Guy's Marsh Dorset
119 P10 Guyzance Nthumb
80 F8 Gwaenysgor Flints
78 F9 Gwalchmai IoA
67 L3 Gwastadnant Gwynd
29 J2 Gwaun-Cae-Gurwen Carmth
42 C5 Gwbert on Sea Cerdgn
2 G5 Gwealavellan Cnwll
3 J8 Gweek Cnwll
31 L4 Gwehelog Mons
44 F6 Gwenddwr Powys
3 J5 Gwennap Cnwll
31 K5 Gwent Crematorium Mons
3 J10 Gwenter Cnwll
81 J11 Gwernaffield Flints
31 M4 Gwernesney Mons
43 K8 Gwernogle Carmth
68 H2 Gwernymynydd Flints
69 K4 Gwersyllt Wrexhm
80 G8 Gwespyr Flints
3 P3 Gwindra Cnwll
2 F6 Gwinear Cnwll
2 F5 Gwithian Cnwll
78 G7 Gwredog IoA
30 G5 Gwrhay Caerph
68 E5 Gwyddelwern Denbgs
43 J7 Gwyddgrug Carmth
69 J4 Gwynfryn Wrexhm
55 P11 Gwystre Powys
68 A2 Gwytherin Conwy
69 K5 Gyfelia Wrexhm
66 G5 Gyrn-goch Gwynd

H

56 F4 Habberley Shrops
57 Q9 Habberley Worcs
89 N4 Habergham Lancs
87 P7 Habertoft Lincs
23 M10 Habin W Susx
93 K8 Habrough NE Lin
74 B5 Hacconby Lincs
73 Q3 Haceby Lincs
65 L10 Hacheston Suffk
36 G7 Hackbridge Gt Lon
84 F4 Hackenthorpe Sheff
76 F11 Hackford Norfk
97 K2 Hackforth N York
70 A5 Hack Green Ches E
169 c4 Hackland Ork
60 H9 Hackleton Nhants
39 P11 Hacklinge Kent
58 C9 Hackman's Gate Worcs
99 K2 Hackness N York
19 K5 Hackness Somset
36 H4 Hackney Gt Lon
86 C4 Hackthorn Lincs
101 P6 Hackthorpe Cumb
37 N3 Hacton Gt Lon
118 E3 Hadden Border
35 K3 Haddenham Bucks
62 G5 Haddenham Cambs
128 E5 Haddington E Loth
86 B8 Haddington Lincs
65 N2 Haddiscoe Norfk
159 K10 Haddo Abers
61 P2 Haddon Cambs
83 P4 Hade Edge Kirk
83 M5 Hadfield Derbys
51 K7 Hadham Cross Herts
51 K6 Hadham Ford Herts
38 D4 Hadleigh Essex
52 H3 Hadleigh Suffk
52 G3 Hadleigh Heath Suffk
46 G2 Hadley Worcs
57 M2 Hadley Wrekin
71 L10 Hadley End Staffs
50 G11 Hadley Wood Gt Lon
37 P10 Hadlow Kent
25 M6 Hadlow Down E Susx
69 P10 Hadnall Shrops
112 E7 Hadrian's Wall Nthumb
51 N2 Hadstock Essex
46 H2 Hadzor Worcs
26 E3 Haffenden Quarter Kent
80 B11 Hafodunos Conwy
69 K5 Hafod-y-bwch Wrexhm
30 H4 Hafod-y-coed Blae G
30 H5 Hafodyrynys Caerph
89 P3 Haggate Lancs
111 J6 Haggbeck Cumb
169 q9 Haggersta Shet
119 K2 Haggerston Nthumb
17 K2 Haggington Hill Devon
126 D2 Haggs Falk
45 R6 Hagley Herefs
58 D8 Hagley Worcs
52 G4 Hagmore Green Suffk
87 K8 Hagnaby Lincs
87 N5 Hagnaby Lincs
87 K7 Hagworthingham Lincs
89 J9 Haigh Wigan
88 H4 Haighton Green Lancs
100 D9 Haile Cumb
47 K8 Hailes Gloucs
51 J8 Hailey Herts
34 C2 Hailey Oxon
34 H7 Hailey Oxon
25 N9 Hailsham E Susx
61 Q8 Hail Weston Cambs
37 L2 Hainault Gt Lon
39 Q8 Haine Kent
77 J8 Hainford Norfk
86 G4 Hainton Lincs
90 D3 Hainworth C Brad
99 N8 Haisthorpe E R Yk
40 G9 Hakin Pembks
85 L10 Halam Notts
134 E10 Halbeath Fife
9 P2 Halberton Devon
167 M4 Halcro Highld
95 L5 Hale Cumb
81 P8 Hale Halton
21 N11 Hale Hants
20 D9 Hale Somset
23 M5 Hale Surrey
82 G7 Hale Traffd
81 P8 Hale Bank Halton
82 G7 Halebarns Traffd
25 N8 Hale Green E Susx
88 D2 Hale Nook Lancs
65 M2 Hales Norfk
70 C8 Hales Staffs
74 F5 Halesgate Lincs
71 M6 Hales Green Derbys
58 E8 Halesowen Dudley
39 K10 Hales Place Kent
37 Q11 Hale Street Kent
38 F3 Halesville Essex
65 M6 Halesworth Suffk
81 P7 Halewood Knows
7 L4 Halford Devon
56 G8 Halford Shrops
47 Q5 Halford Warwks
95 L3 Halfpenny Cumb
58 B6 Halfpenny Green Staffs
97 K4 Halfpenny Houses N York
43 M8 Halfway Carmth
44 A8 Halfway Carmth
84 F4 Halfway Sheff
34 D11 Halfway W Berk
23 P10 Halfway Bridge W Susx
56 E2 Halfway House Shrops
38 F7 Halfway Houses Kent
90 D5 Halifax Calder
125 L7 Halket E Ayrs
167 K5 Halkirk Highld
81 J10 Halkyn Flints
125 L7 Hall E Rens
72 D3 Hallam Fields Derbys
25 L7 Halland E Susx
73 K11 Hallaton Leics
20 B3 Hallatrow BaNES
111 L9 Hallbankgate Cumb
95 N3 Hallbeck Cumb
90 H7 Hall Cliffe Wakefd
88 E4 Hall Cross Lancs
100 H11 Hall Dunnerdale Cumb
31 Q8 Hallen S Glos
61 M11 Hall End Bed
50 C3 Hall End C Beds
84 E9 Hallfield Gate Derbys
104 B2 Hallgarth Dur
126 F2 Hall Glen Falk
58 H8 Hall Green Birm
152 D6 Hallin Highld
38 B9 Halling Medway
87 K3 Hallington Lincs
112 E5 Hallington Nthumb
89 K8 Halliwell Bolton
85 L10 Halloughton Notts
46 F3 Hallow Worcs
46 F3 Hallow Heath Worcs
7 L11 Hallsands Devon
51 K9 Hall's Green Essex
50 G5 Hall's Green Herts
94 D3 Hallthwaites Cumb
5 K4 Hallworthy Cnwll
116 H2 Hallyne Border
70 D5 Halmer End Staffs
46 C5 Halmond's Frome Herefs
32 D4 Halmore Gloucs
15 P5 Halnaker W Susx
88 D8 Halsall Lancs
48 G6 Halse Nhants
18 F9 Halse Somset
2 E6 Halsetown Cnwll
93 N5 Halsham E R Yk
17 J4 Halsinger Devon
52 D5 Halstead Essex
37 L8 Halstead Kent
73 K9 Halstead Leics
11 L3 Halstock Dorset
18 F7 Halsway Somset
101 L3 Haltcliff Bridge Cumb
92 H4 Haltemprice Crematorium E R Yk
86 H8 Haltham Lincs
87 L11 Haltoft End Lincs
35 N3 Halton Bucks
82 B8 Halton Halton
95 L8 Halton Lancs
91 K4 Halton Leeds
112 E7 Halton Nthumb
69 K7 Halton Wrexhm
96 F10 Halton East N York
87 M8 Halton Fenside Lincs
96 C5 Halton Gill N York
95 L7 Halton Green Lancs
87 M7 Halton Holegate Lincs
111 M9 Halton Lea Gate Nthumb
5 Q8 Halton Quay Cnwll
112 F7 Halton Shields Nthumb
96 B10 Halton West N York
111 P8 Haltwhistle Nthumb
77 N10 Halvergate Norfk
7 K8 Halwell Devon
8 B5 Halwill Devon
8 B4 Halwill Junction Devon
10 E4 Ham Devon
32 C5 Ham Gloucs
47 J10 Ham Gloucs
36 E6 Ham Gt Lon
39 P11 Ham Kent
19 J9 Ham Somset
20 C5 Ham Somset
22 B2 Ham Wilts
35 L7 Hambleden Bucks
14 H4 Hambledon Hants
23 Q7 Hambledon Surrey
14 E5 Hamble-le-Rice Hants
88 D2 Hambleton Lancs
91 P4 Hambleton N York
88 D2 Hambleton Moss Side Lancs
19 L10 Hambridge Somset
32 B9 Hambrook S Glos
15 L5 Hambrook W Susx
20 F9 Ham Common Dorset
87 K7 Hameringham Lincs
61 P5 Hamerton Cambs
46 E6 Ham Green Herefs
26 E6 Ham Green Kent
38 D8 Ham Green Kent
31 P9 Ham Green N Som
47 K2 Ham Green Worcs
37 Q8 Ham Hill Kent
126 C6 Hamilton S Lans
126 C6 Hamilton Services S Lans
11 M3 Hamlet Dorset
25 N9 Hamlins E Susx
24 C9 Hammerpot W Susx
36 F5 Hammersmith Gt Lon
58 G3 Hammerwich Staffs
25 K3 Hammerwood E Susx
50 H10 Hammond Street Herts
12 D2 Hammoon Dorset
169 q10 Hamnavoe Shet
25 P10 Hampden Park E Susx
51 N4 Hamperden End Essex
47 L11 Hampnett Gloucs
91 N8 Hampole Donc
13 J5 Hampreston Dorset
95 J4 Hampsfield Cumb
95 K10 Hampson Green Lancs
36 G3 Hampstead Gt Lon
34 F9 Hampstead Norreys W Berk
97 L9 Hampsthwaite N York
61 Q2 Hampton C Pete
10 F5 Hampton Devon
36 D7 Hampton Gt Lon
39 L8 Hampton Kent
57 N7 Hampton Shrops
33 N6 Hampton Swindn
47 K6 Hampton Worcs
45 R7 Hampton Bishop Herefs
36 E7 Hampton Court Palace & Gardens Gt Lon
32 G5 Hampton Fields Gloucs
69 P5 Hampton Green Ches W
69 P5 Hampton Heath Ches W
59 K8 Hampton in Arden Solhll
57 N7 Hampton Loade Shrops
58 C11 Hampton Lovett Worcs
47 Q3 Hampton Lucy Warwks
59 L11 Hampton Magna Warwks
47 Q2 Hampton on the Hill Warwks
48 F11 Hampton Poyle Oxon
36 E7 Hampton Wick Gt Lon
21 P11 Hamptworth Wilts
76 C7 Hamrow Norfk
25 K8 Hamsey E Susx
37 J9 Hamsey Green Surrey
71 L11 Hamstall Ridware Staffs
58 G6 Hamstead Birm
14 D8 Hamstead IoW
34 D11 Hamstead Marshall W Berk
103 M4 Hamsterley Dur
112 H9 Hamsterley Dur
26 H5 Hamstreet Kent
19 Q8 Ham Street Somset
19 L3 Hamwood N Som
12 G6 Hamworthy Poole
71 M9 Hanbury Staffs
47 J2 Hanbury Worcs
73 Q4 Hanby Lincs
63 K11 Hanchet End Suffk
70 E6 Hanchurch Staffs
164 D7 Handa Island Highld
105 K7 Handale R & Cl
9 P5 Hand and Pen Devon
81 N11 Handbridge Ches W
24 G5 Handcross W Susx
83 J8 Handforth Ches E
69 P2 Hand Green Ches W
69 N3 Handley Ches W
84 E8 Handley Derbys
51 Q10 Handley Green Essex
71 K11 Handsacre Staffs
58 F7 Handsworth Birm
84 F3 Handsworth Sheff
35 N6 Handy Cross Bucks
70 F6 Hanford C Stke
12 D2 Hanford Dorset
90 H6 Hanging Heaton Kirk
60 G6 Hanging Houghton Nhants
21 K7 Hanging Langford Wilts
24 G9 Hangleton Br & H
24 C10 Hangleton W Susx
32 B10 Hanham S Glos
70 B5 Hankelow Ches E
33 J6 Hankerton Wilts
25 P9 Hankham E Susx
70 F5 Hanley C Stke
46 F6 Hanley Castle Worcs
57 M11 Hanley Child Worcs
46 F6 Hanley Swan Worcs
57 M11 Hanley William Worcs
96 C8 Hanlith N York
69 N7 Hanmer Wrexhm
17 L6 Hannaford Devon
87 N5 Hannah Lincs
22 F3 Hannington Hants
60 H6 Hannington Nhants
33 N6 Hannington Swindn
33 N5 Hannington Wick Swindn
50 D4 Hanscombe End C Beds
49 M5 Hanslope M Keyn
74 A6 Hanthorpe Lincs
36 E5 Hanwell Gt Lon
48 D6 Hanwell Oxon
56 G3 Hanwood Shrops
36 D6 Hanworth Gt Lon
76 H4 Hanworth Norfk
116 B4 Happendon S Lans
116 B4 Happendon Services S Lans
77 M5 Happisburgh Norfk
77 M6 Happisburgh Common Norfk
81 P10 Hapsford Ches W
89 M4 Hapton Lancs
64 H2 Hapton Norfk
7 K7 Harberton Devon
7 K7 Harbertonford Devon
39 K10 Harbledown Kent
58 F8 Harborne Birm
59 Q9 Harborough Magna Warwks
118 H10 Harbottle Nthumb
7 J6 Harbourneford Devon
58 E11 Harbours Hill Worcs
13 K2 Harbridge Hants
13 K2 Harbridge Green Hants
48 C3 Harbury Warwks
73 J4 Harby Leics
85 Q6 Harby Notts
9 L8 Harcombe Devon
10 D6 Harcombe Devon
10 G5 Harcombe Bottom Devon
90 D3 Harden C Brad
58 F4 Harden Wsall
32 H10 Hardenhuish Wilts
151 K7 Hardgate Abers
108 H7 Hardgate D & G
97 L8 Hardgate N York
125 N3 Hardgate W Duns
24 B7 Hardham W Susx
88 D3 Hardhorn Lancs
76 E11 Hardingham Norfk
60 G9 Hardingstone Nhants
20 D4 Hardington Somset
11 L2 Hardington Mandeville Somset
11 L3 Hardington Marsh Somset
11 L2 Hardington Moor Somset
16 C7 Hardisworthy Devon
14 D5 Hardley Hants
77 M11 Hardley Street Norfk
49 P5 Hardmead M Keyn
96 C2 Hardraw N York
89 M6 Hardsough Lancs
84 F8 Hardstoft Derbys
14 H6 Hardway Hants
20 D8 Hardway Somset
49 M11 Hardwick Bucks
62 E9 Hardwick Cambs
60 H7 Hardwick Nhants
65 J4 Hardwick Norfk
34 C3 Hardwick Oxon
48 G9 Hardwick Oxon
84 G3 Hardwick Rothm
58 G5 Hardwick Wsall
32 E2 Hardwicke Gloucs
46 H9 Hardwicke Gloucs
52 F7 Hardy's Green Essex
25 N8 Harebeating E Susx
87 K7 Hareby Lincs
90 D3 Hare Croft C Brad
36 C2 Harefield Gt Lon
53 K6 Hare Green Essex
35 M9 Hare Hatch Wokham
71 M7 Harehill Derbys
91 J4 Harehills Leeds
119 L6 Harehope Nthumb
117 Q6 Harelaw Border
110 H5 Harelaw D & G
113 J10 Harelaw Dur
26 D4 Hareplain Kent
102 B2 Harescough Cumb
32 F2 Harescombe Gloucs
32 F2 Haresfield Gloucs
22 E8 Harestock Hants
51 K9 Hare Street Essex
51 M10 Hare Street Essex
51 J5 Hare Street Herts
97 M11 Harewood Leeds
45 Q9 Harewood End Herefs
6 G7 Harford Devon
64 G3 Hargate Norfk
83 P9 Hargatewall Derbys
69 N2 Hargrave Ches W
61 M6 Hargrave Nhants
63 N9 Hargrave Suffk
110 G8 Harker Cumb
53 L5 Harkstead Suffk
59 K2 Harlaston Staffs
73 M4 Harlaxton Lincs
67 K8 Harlech Gwynd
69 N11 Harlescott Shrops
36 F4 Harlesden Gt Lon
84 G5 Harlesthorpe Derbys
7 K9 Harleston Devon
65 J5 Harleston Norfk
64 E9 Harleston Suffk
60 F8 Harlestone Nhants
89 P3 Harle Syke Lancs
91 K11 Harley Rothm
57 K4 Harley Shrops
50 B4 Harlington C Beds
91 M10 Harlington Donc
36 C5 Harlington Gt Lon
152 D9 Harlosh Highld
51 K8 Harlow Essex
112 G7 Harlow Hill Nthumb
92 B3 Harlthorpe E R Yk
62 E10 Harlton Cambs
4 D6 Harlyn Cnwll
12 G8 Harman's Cross Dorset
96 H3 Harmby N York
50 G7 Harmer Green Herts
69 N10 Harmer Hill Shrops
36 C5 Harmondsworth Gt Lon
86 C8 Harmston Lincs
57 K4 Harnage Shrops
112 G4 Harnham Nthumb
33 L4 Harnhill Gloucs
37 M2 Harold Hill Gt Lon
40 G7 Haroldston West Pembks
169 t2 Haroldswick Shet
37 N2 Harold Wood Gt Lon
98 C4 Harome N York
50 D8 Harpenden Herts
10 B6 Harpford Devon
99 M8 Harpham E R Yk
75 Q5 Harpley Norfk
46 C2 Harpley Worcs
60 E8 Harpole Nhants
167 K5 Harpsdale Highld
35 L8 Harpsden Oxon
86 B3 Harpswell Lincs
83 J4 Harpurhey Manch
83 N10 Harpur Hill Derbys
110 H10 Harraby Cumb
17 K6 Harracott Devon
145 L3 Harrapool Highld
134 B2 Harrietfield P & K
38 E11 Harrietsham Kent
36 H3 Harringay Gt Lon
100 C5 Harrington Cumb
87 L6 Harrington Lincs
60 G4 Harrington Nhants
73 N11 Harringworth Nhants
168 f8 Harris W Isls
70 F3 Harriseahead Staffs
100 G2 Harriston Cumb
97 M10 Harrogate N York
97 M10 Harrogate Crematorium N York
61 K9 Harrold Bed
90 C9 Harrop Dale Oldham
36 E3 Harrow Gt Lon
5 Q7 Harrowbarrow Cnwll
61 N11 Harrowden Bed
103 Q7 Harrowgate Village Darltn
64 B11 Harrow Green Suffk
36 E3 Harrow on the Hill Gt Lon
36 E2 Harrow Weald Gt Lon
62 F10 Harston Cambs
73 L4 Harston Leics
92 D2 Harswell E R Yk
104 E4 Hart Hartpl
112 G3 Hartburn Nthumb
64 A11 Hartest Suffk
25 L3 Hartfield E Susx
62 C6 Hartford Cambs
82 D10 Hartford Ches W
18 C9 Hartford Somset
23 L3 Hartfordbridge Hants
51 Q7 Hartford End Essex
103 N9 Hartforth N York
20 F11 Hartgrove Dorset
69 N3 Harthill Ches W
126 G5 Harthill N Lans
84 G4 Harthill Rothm
71 L2 Hartington Derbys
112 F3 Hartington Nthumb
16 D7 Hartland Devon
16 C7 Hartland Quay Devon
58 B10 Hartlebury Worcs
104 F4 Hartlepool Hartpl
104 F4 Hartlepool Crematorium Hartpl
102 E9 Hartley Cumb
26 C5 Hartley Kent
37 P7 Hartley Kent
113 M5 Hartley Nthumb
37 P7 Hartley Green Kent
70 H9 Hartley Green Staffs
23 J3 Hartley Wespall Hants
23 L3 Hartley Wintney Hants
38 D9 Hartlip Kent
98 E2 Hartoft End N York
98 E8 Harton N York
113 N7 Harton S Tyne
56 H7 Harton Shrops
46 E10 Hartpury Gloucs
90 F6 Hartshead Kirk
90 F6 Hartshead Moor Services Calder
70 F5 Hartshill C Stke
59 M6 Hartshill Warwks
71 Q10 Hartshorne Derbys
119 J7 Hartside Nthumb
101 M8 Hartsop Cumb
104 E3 Hart Station Hartpl
18 E9 Hartswell Somset
49 L4 Hartwell Nhants
97 K8 Hartwith N York
126 E6 Hartwood N Lans
117 N6 Hartwoodmyres Border
37 Q8 Harvel Kent
47 L5 Harvington Worcs
58 C10 Harvington Worcs
85 L2 Harwell Notts
34 E7 Harwell Oxon
53 N5 Harwich Essex
89 L8 Harwood Bolton
102 F4 Harwood Dur
105 Q11 Harwood Dale N York
89 L8 Harwood Lee Bolton
50 G6 Harwood Park Crematorium Herts
85 K2 Harworth Notts
58 E8 Hasbury Dudley
24 B3 Hascombe Surrey
60 F5 Haselbech Nhants
11 K2 Haselbury Plucknett Somset
59 K11 Haseley Warwks
59 K11 Haseley Green Warwks
59 K10 Haseley Knob Warwks
47 M3 Haselor Warwks
46 F9 Hasfield Gloucs
40 G9 Hasguard Pembks
88 D9 Haskayne Lancs
65 J11 Hasketon Suffk
84 E7 Hasland Derbys
23 P8 Haslemere Surrey
89 M6 Haslingden Lancs
62 F10 Haslingfield Cambs
70 C3 Haslington Ches E
70 D3 Hassall Ches E
70 D3 Hassall Green Ches E
27 J2 Hassell Street Kent
77 M10 Hassingham Norfk
100 G7 Hassness Cumb
24 H7 Hassocks W Susx
84 B6 Hassop Derbys
23 P8 Haste Hill Surrey
167 P6 Haster Highld
87 N7 Hasthorpe Lincs
27 J2 Hastingleigh Kent
26 D10 Hastings E Susx
19 K11 Hastings Somset
26 D9 Hastings Borough Crematorium E Susx
51 L9 Hastingwood Essex
35 P3 Hastoe Herts
104 C2 Haswell Dur
104 C2 Haswell Plough Dur
61 Q11 Hatch C Beds

19 K10 Hatch Beauchamp Somset
61 N8 Hatch End Bed
36 D2 Hatch End Gt Lon
14 C6 Hatchet Gate Hants
50 D8 Hatching Green Herts
82 C10 Hatchmere Ches W
93 M10 Hatcliffe NE Lin
91 R9 Hatfield Donc
46 A3 Hatfield Herefs
50 F9 Hatfield Herts
46 G4 Hatfield Worcs
51 M7 Hatfield Broad Oak Essex
51 M7 Hatfield Heath Essex
52 C9 Hatfield Peverel Essex
92 A9 Hatfield Woodhouse Donc
34 B6 Hatford Oxon
22 B4 Hatherden Hants
8 D4 Hatherleigh Devon
72 E6 Hathern Leics
33 N3 Hatherop Gloucs
84 B4 Hathersage Derbys
84 B4 Hathersage Booths Derbys
70 B5 Hatherton Ches E
58 E2 Hatherton Staffs
62 C10 Hatley St George Cambs
5 Q9 Hatt Cnwll
83 L6 Hattersley Tamesd
22 H7 Hattingley Hants
159 Q10 Hatton Abers
142 H9 Hatton Angus
71 N8 Hatton Derbys
36 C5 Hatton Gt Lon
86 G5 Hatton Lincs
56 H6 Hatton Shrops
82 C8 Hatton Warrtn
59 K11 Hatton Warwks
69 N2 Hatton Heath Ches W
151 L4 Hatton of Fintray Abers
115 J2 Haugh E Ayrs
87 M5 Haugh Lincs
89 Q8 Haugh Rochdl
87 K4 Haugham Lincs
125 Q2 Haughhead E Duns
119 K5 Haugh Head Nthumb
64 E9 Haughley Suffk
64 E9 Haughley Green Suffk
158 B10 Haugh of Glass Moray
108 H7 Haugh of Urr D & G
143 L6 Haughs of Kinnaird Angus
85 L6 Haughton Notts
69 K11 Haughton Powys
57 M5 Haughton Shrops
57 N3 Haughton Shrops
69 L9 Haughton Shrops
69 Q11 Haughton Shrops
70 F10 Haughton Staffs
83 K6 Haughton Green Tamesd
104 B7 Haughton le Skerne Darltn
69 Q3 Haughton Moss Ches E
50 H6 Haultwick Herts
59 K2 Haunton Staffs
11 b1 Hautes Croix Jersey
62 F10 Hauxton Cambs
70 F2 Havannah Ches E
15 K5 Havant Hants
45 N4 Haven Herefs
86 H10 Haven Bank Lincs
93 L5 Haven Side E R Yk
14 G8 Havenstreet IoW
91 K8 Havercroft Wakefd
41 J7 Haverfordwest Pembks
63 L11 Haverhill Suffk
94 D5 Haverigg Cumb
37 M2 Havering-atte-Bower Gt Lon
49 M6 Haversham M Keyn
94 G4 Haverthwaite Cumb
104 E6 Haverton Hill S on T
19 N2 Havyat N Som
19 P7 Havyatt Somset
81 L11 Hawarden Flints
46 H5 Hawbridge Worcs
52 C7 Hawbush Green Essex
94 E6 Hawcoat Cumb
42 F5 Hawen Cerdgn
96 C3 Hawes N York
65 J2 Hawe's Green Norfk
46 F2 Hawford Worcs
117 Q8 Hawick Border
10 G4 Hawkchurch Devon
63 N10 Hawkedon Suffk
26 D2 Hawkenbury Kent
20 G4 Hawkeridge Wilts
9 Q7 Hawkerland Devon
32 E7 Hawkesbury S Glos
59 N8 Hawkesbury Warwks
32 E7 Hawkesbury Upton S Glos
59 L8 Hawkes End Covtry
83 L7 Hawk Green Stockp
119 P8 Hawkhill Nthumb
26 C5 Hawkhurst Kent
25 M7 Hawkhurst Common E Susx
27 M4 Hawkinge Kent
27 M3 Hawkinge Crematorium Kent
23 K9 Hawkley Hants
82 C4 Hawkley Wigan
17 R5 Hawkridge Somset
110 G11 Hawksdale Cumb
89 M7 Hawkshaw Bury
101 L11 Hawkshead Cumb
101 K11 Hawkshead Hill Cumb
116 A3 Hawksland S Lans
51 Q4 Hawkspur Green Essex
69 Q8 Hawkstone Shrops
96 E6 Hawkswick N York
90 F2 Hawksworth Leeds
85 N11 Hawksworth Notts
38 E3 Hawkwell Essex
112 G6 Hawkwell Nthumb
23 N3 Hawley Hants
37 M6 Hawley Kent
47 L10 Hawling Gloucs
98 A3 Hawnby N York
90 C3 Haworth C Brad
35 P3 Hawridge Bucks
64 B10 Hawstead Suffk
64 B10 Hawstead Green Suffk
113 P11 Hawthorn Dur
23 J8 Hawthorn Hants
30 E7 Hawthorn Rhondd
35 N10 Hawthorn Hill Br For
86 H9 Hawthorn Hill Lincs
73 Q5 Hawthorpe Lincs
85 N10 Hawton Notts
98 C9 Haxby C York
98 C9 Haxby Gates C York
92 C11 Haxey N Linc
92 C10 Haxey Carr N Linc
37 K11 Haxted Surrey
21 M5 Haxton Wilts
3 P3 Hay Cnwll
4 F7 Hay Cnwll
20 D2 Haycombe Crematorium BaNES
82 C5 Haydock St Hel
20 C4 Haydon BaNES
20 C11 Haydon Dorset
19 J10 Haydon Somset
112 B8 Haydon Bridge Nthumb
33 M7 Haydon Wick Swindn
5 P7 Haye Cnwll
36 C4 Hayes Gt Lon
37 K7 Hayes Gt Lon
36 C4 Hayes End Gt Lon
131 M3 Hayfield Ag & B
83 M7 Hayfield Derbys
57 L2 Haygate Wrekin
75 K7 Hay Green Norfk
143 J9 Hayhillock Angus
2 F6 Hayle Cnwll
58 E8 Hayley Green Dudley
15 K6 Hayling Island Hants
70 B4 Haymoor Green Ches E
9 J7 Hayne Devon
18 C11 Hayne Devon
50 C2 Haynes (Church End) C Beds
50 C2 Haynes (Northwood End) C Beds
50 D2 Haynes (Silver End) C Beds
50 C2 Haynes (West End) C Beds
45 J6 Hay-on-Wye Powys
40 G5 Hayscastle Pembks
40 H5 Hayscastle Cross Pembks
37 N11 Haysden Kent
51 J5 Hay Street Herts
100 F2 Hayton Cumb
111 K9 Hayton Cumb
98 G11 Hayton E R Yk
85 M4 Hayton Notts
57 J8 Hayton's Bent Shrops
9 J9 Haytor Vale Devon
16 F9 Haytown Devon
24 H6 Haywards Heath W Susx
91 P8 Haywood Donc
45 P8 Haywood Herefs
85 K9 Haywood Oaks Notts
25 Q8 Hazards Green E Susx
126 E8 Hazelbank S Lans
12 B3 Hazelbury Bryan Dorset
52 D11 Hazeleigh Essex
23 K3 Hazeley Hants
85 M11 Hazelford Notts
83 K7 Hazel Grove Stockp
83 L4 Hazelhurst Tamesd
58 F2 Hazelslade Staffs
25 Q3 Hazel Street Kent
51 Q2 Hazel Stub Suffk
135 J3 Hazelton Walls Fife
84 D11 Hazelwood Derbys
35 N5 Hazlemere Bucks
113 K6 Hazlerigg N u Ty
71 J5 Hazles Staffs
47 L11 Hazleton Gloucs
75 N3 Heacham Norfk
22 E8 Headbourne Worthy Hants
45 K3 Headbrook Herefs
26 D3 Headcorn Kent
90 H3 Headingley Leeds
34 F3 Headington Oxon
103 N7 Headlam Dur
126 G6 Headlesscross N Lans
58 F11 Headless Cross Worcs
22 F2 Headley Hants
23 M7 Headley Hants
36 F10 Headley Surrey
23 M7 Headley Down Hants
58 G9 Headley Heath Worcs
16 F11 Headon Devon
85 M5 Headon Notts
111 K10 Heads Nook Cumb
84 E10 Heage Derbys
97 R11 Healaugh N York
103 K11 Healaugh N York
82 H7 Heald Green Stockp
17 L2 Heale Devon
18 H10 Heale Somset
19 L9 Heale Somset
97 J4 Healey N York
112 F9 Healey Nthumb
89 P7 Healey Rochdl
90 H7 Healey Wakefd
112 G11 Healeyfield Dur
93 M8 Healing NE Lin
2 D7 Heamoor Cnwll
84 F11 Heanor Derbys
17 J4 Heanton Punchardon Devon
85 Q3 Heapham Lincs
23 M7 Hearn Hants
59 N6 Heart of England Crematorium Warwks
126 G5 Heart of Scotland Services N Lans
38 E9 Hearts Delight Kent
17 N5 Heasley Mill Devon
145 K4 Heast Highld
84 G7 Heath Derbys
91 K6 Heath Wakefd
49 P9 Heath and Reach C Beds
24 C7 Heath Common W Susx
71 L2 Heathcote Derbys
70 B9 Heathcote Shrops
35 N5 Heath End Bucks
22 D2 Heath End Hants
72 B6 Heath End Leics
47 P2 Heath End Warwks
72 B8 Heather Leics
9 K9 Heathfield Devon
25 N6 Heathfield E Susx
96 H7 Heathfield N York
18 G9 Heathfield Somset
48 F11 Heathfield Village Oxon
58 G10 Heath Green Worcs
109 L5 Heath Hall D & G
58 F2 Heath Hayes & Wimblebury Staffs
57 P2 Heath Hill Shrops
19 M5 Heath House Somset
36 C5 Heathrow Airport Gt Lon
10 E4 Heathstock Devon
57 Q6 Heathton Shrops
58 D5 Heath Town Wolves
104 E10 Heathwaite N York
71 K9 Heatley Staffs
82 F7 Heatley Warrtn
89 K9 Heaton Bolton
90 E3 Heaton C Brad
95 J8 Heaton Lancs
113 L7 Heaton N u Ty
70 H2 Heaton Staffs
83 J6 Heaton Chapel Stockp
83 J6 Heaton Mersey Stockp
83 J6 Heaton Norris Stockp
88 E8 Heaton's Bridge Lancs
37 N9 Heaverham Kent
83 K7 Heaviley Stockp
9 M6 Heavitree Devon
113 M8 Hebburn S Tyne
96 F8 Hebden N York
90 B5 Hebden Bridge Calder
82 D11 Hebden Green Ches W
50 H6 Hebing End Herts
41 N5 Hebron Carmth
78 H8 Hebron IoA
113 J3 Hebron Nthumb
23 K2 Heckfield Hants
64 H6 Heckfield Green Suffk
52 F7 Heckfordbridge Essex
74 B2 Heckington Lincs
90 G6 Heckmondwike Kirk
33 J11 Heddington Wilts
112 H7 Heddon-on-the-Wall Nthumb
65 L3 Hedenham Norfk
14 E4 Hedge End Hants
35 Q7 Hedgerley Bucks
35 Q7 Hedgerley Green Bucks
19 K9 Hedging Somset
112 G9 Hedley on the Hill Nthumb
58 E2 Hednesford Staffs
93 L5 Hedon E R Yk
35 P7 Hedsor Bucks
46 A4 Hegdon Hill Herefs
169 q8 Heglibister Shet
103 P6 Heighington Darltn
86 D7 Heighington Lincs
57 P10 Heightington Worcs
118 D4 Heiton Border
7 J4 Hele Devon
9 N4 Hele Devon
17 J2 Hele Devon
18 G10 Hele Somset
16 C11 Helebridge Cnwll
9 J2 Hele Lane Devon
132 B11 Helensburgh Ag & B
125 K11 Helenton S Ayrs
3 K8 Helford Cnwll
3 K8 Helford Passage Cnwll
76 B6 Helhoughton Norfk
51 Q2 Helions Bumpstead Essex
84 H2 Hellaby Rothm
4 H7 Helland Cnwll
4 H7 Hellandbridge Cnwll
22 C2 Hell Corner W Berk
5 M4 Hellescott Cnwll
77 J9 Hellesdon Norfk
2 E5 Hellesveor Cnwll
60 B9 Hellidon Nhants
96 C9 Hellifield N York
25 N8 Hellingly E Susx
77 L11 Hellington Norfk
119 N11 Helm Nthumb
48 G6 Helmdon Nhants
90 D8 Helme Kirk
64 H10 Helmingham Suffk
103 N3 Helmington Row Dur
163 N3 Helmsdale Highld
89 M6 Helmshore Lancs
98 C4 Helmsley N York
97 P7 Helperby N York
99 K6 Helperthorpe N York
74 B2 Helpringham Lincs
74 B9 Helpston C Pete
81 P9 Helsby Ches W
87 P6 Helsey Lincs
2 H8 Helston Cnwll
4 H5 Helstone Cnwll
101 P6 Helton Cumb
103 L10 Helwith N York
96 B7 Helwith Bridge N York
77 L9 Hemblington Norfk
19 Q7 Hembridge Somset
50 C9 Hemel Hempstead Herts
6 F7 Hemerdon Devon
91 R4 Hemingbrough N York
86 H6 Hemingby Lincs
91 K10 Hemingfield Barns
62 C6 Hemingford Abbots Cambs
62 C6 Hemingford Grey Cambs
64 G11 Hemingstone Suffk
72 D5 Hemington Leics
61 N3 Hemington Nhants
20 D4 Hemington Somset
53 N3 Hemley Suffk
104 F8 Hemlington Middsb
99 M10 Hempholme E R Yk
65 J3 Hempnall Norfk
65 J3 Hempnall Green Norfk
157 L5 Hempriggs Moray
51 P3 Hempstead Essex
38 C9 Hempstead Medway
76 G4 Hempstead Norfk
77 N6 Hempstead Norfk
46 F11 Hempsted Gloucs
76 C6 Hempton Norfk
48 D8 Hempton Oxon
77 P8 Hemsby Norfk
86 B2 Hemswell Lincs
86 B3 Hemswell Cliff Lincs
91 L8 Hemsworth Wakefd
10 C2 Hemyock Devon
31 Q9 Henbury Bristl
83 J10 Henbury Ches E
7 J8 Hendham Devon
56 C5 Hendomen Powys
36 F3 Hendon Gt Lon
113 P9 Hendon Sundld
36 F2 Hendon Crematorium Gt Lon
3 J6 Hendra Cnwll
4 G6 Hendra Cnwll
29 P8 Hendre Brdgnd
80 H11 Hendre Flints
31 N2 Hendre Mons
28 G4 Hendy Carmth
78 G9 Heneglwys IoA
24 F7 Henfield W Susx
5 P3 Henford Devon
26 G4 Henghurst Kent
30 G6 Hengoed Caerph
45 J4 Hengoed Powys
69 J8 Hengoed Shrops
63 P7 Hengrave Suffk
51 M5 Henham Essex
55 Q3 Heniarth Powys
19 J10 Henlade Somset
11 P4 Henley Dorset
46 H11 Henley Gloucs
56 H7 Henley Shrops
57 J9 Henley Shrops
19 M8 Henley Somset
64 H11 Henley Suffk
23 N9 Henley W Susx
59 N9 Henley Green Covtry
59 J11 Henley-in-Arden Warwks
35 L8 Henley-on-Thames Oxon
23 P4 Henley Park Surrey
26 B9 Henley's Down E Susx
37 Q7 Henley Street Kent
42 G6 Henllan Cerdgn
80 E11 Henllan Denbgs
41 N7 Henllan Amgoed Carmth
31 J6 Henllys Torfn
50 E3 Henlow C Beds
9 K8 Hennock Devon
52 E4 Henny Street Essex
79 P10 Henryd Conwy
41 K5 Henry's Moat (Castell Hendre) Pembks
91 P6 Hensall N York
111 Q8 Henshaw Nthumb
100 C7 Hensingham Cumb
65 P4 Henstead Suffk
22 E10 Hensting Hants
20 D11 Henstridge Somset
20 D10 Henstridge Ash Somset
20 D10 Henstridge Marsh Somset
35 L4 Henton Oxon
19 N5 Henton Somset
46 F3 Henwick Worcs
5 M7 Henwood Cnwll
34 E4 Henwood Oxon
29 J5 Heol-las Swans
44 C10 Heol Senni Powys
29 P8 Heol-y-Cyw Brdgnd
119 L6 Hepburn Nthumb
119 J10 Hepple Nthumb
113 K4 Hepscott Nthumb
90 B5 Heptonstall Calder
90 F9 Hepworth Kirk
64 D7 Hepworth Suffk
40 G9 Herbrandston Pembks
45 Q7 Hereford Herefs
45 P6 Hereford Crematorium Herefs
39 Q8 Hereson Kent
152 F3 Heribusta Highld
128 C9 Heriot Border
127 M3 Hermiston C Edin
117 Q11 Hermitage Border
11 P3 Hermitage Dorset
34 F10 Hermitage W Berk
15 L5 Hermitage W Susx
91 J10 Hermit Hill Barns
42 G8 Hermon Carmth
78 F11 Hermon IoA
41 P4 Hermon Pembks
39 L8 Herne Kent
39 L8 Herne Bay Kent
39 L8 Herne Common Kent
36 H6 Herne Hill Gt Lon
37 Q10 Herne Pound Kent
17 K6 Herner Devon
39 J9 Hernhill Kent
5 L9 Herodsfoot Cnwll
39 N11 Heronden Kent
37 P2 Herongate Essex
114 B11 Heronsford S Ayrs
36 B2 Heronsgate Herts
23 J5 Herriard Hants
65 P2 Herringfleet Suffk
50 C2 Herring's Green Bed
63 M6 Herringswell Suffk
84 F2 Herringthorpe Rothm
113 N10 Herrington Sundld
39 M9 Hersden Kent
16 D10 Hersham Cnwll
36 D8 Hersham Surrey
25 P8 Herstmonceux E Susx
12 H9 Herston Dorset
169 d7 Herston Ork
50 H8 Hertford Herts
51 J8 Hertford Heath Herts
50 H8 Hertingfordbury Herts
88 E6 Hesketh Bank Lancs
89 J2 Hesketh Lane Lancs
101 K3 Hesket Newmarket Cumb
88 G7 Heskin Green Lancs
104 D3 Hesleden Dur
96 C6 Hesleden N York
85 K2 Hesley Donc
112 B4 Hesleyside Nthumb
98 C10 Heslington C York
97 R10 Hessay C York
5 N10 Hessenford Cnwll
64 C9 Hessett Suffk
92 H5 Hessle E R Yk
91 L7 Hessle Wakefd
95 K7 Hest Bank Lancs
64 H8 Hestley Green Suffk
36 D5 Heston Gt Lon
36 D5 Heston Services Gt Lon
169 b5 Hestwall Ork
81 K8 Heswall Wirral
48 G9 Hethe Oxon
76 G11 Hethersett Norfk
111 J7 Hethersgill Cumb
110 H7 Hetherside Cumb
69 P4 Hetherson Green Ches W
118 G5 Hethpool Nthumb
103 Q3 Hett Dur
96 E9 Hetton N York
113 N11 Hetton-le-Hole Sundld
119 K3 Hetton Steads Nthumb
112 G6 Heugh Nthumb
150 B5 Heughhead Abers
129 M7 Heugh Head Border
65 L7 Heveningham Suffk
37 L11 Hever Kent
95 K4 Heversham Cumb
76 H7 Hevingham Norfk
3 P4 Hewas Water Cnwll
31 Q4 Hewelsfield Gloucs
90 D3 Hewenden C Brad
19 M2 Hewish N Som
11 J3 Hewish Somset
10 H4 Hewood Dorset
112 D8 Hexham Nthumb
37 M6 Hextable Kent
91 P10 Hexthorpe Donc
50 D4 Hexton Herts
5 P5 Hexworthy Cnwll
6 H4 Hexworthy Devon
89 P2 Hey Lancs
51 P11 Heybridge Essex
52 E10 Heybridge Essex
52 E10 Heybridge Basin Essex
6 D9 Heybrook Bay Devon
51 K3 Heydon Cambs
76 G6 Heydon Norfk
73 Q3 Heydour Lincs
82 H7 Hey Head Manch
88 C5 Hey Houses Lancs
136 B7 Heylipoll Ag & B
169 p5 Heylor Shet
83 L5 Heyrod Tamesd
95 J8 Heysham Lancs
97 J8 Heyshaw N York
23 N11 Heyshott W Susx
89 Q9 Heyside Oldham
20 H6 Heytesbury Wilts
48 C9 Heythrop Oxon
89 P8 Heywood Rochdl
20 G4 Heywood Wilts
92 G10 Hibaldstow N Linc
91 M9 Hickleton Donc
77 N7 Hickling Norfk
72 H5 Hickling Notts
77 N7 Hickling Green Norfk
77 N7 Hickling Heath Norfk
39 J10 Hickmans Green Kent
39 L9 Hicks Forstal Kent
24 G6 Hickstead W Susx
47 N6 Hidcote Bartrim Gloucs
47 N6 Hidcote Boyce Gloucs
91 L7 High Ackworth Wakefd
91 J9 Higham Barns
84 E9 Higham Derbys
37 P11 Higham Kent
38 B7 Higham Kent
89 N3 Higham Lancs
52 H4 Higham Suffk
63 M7 Higham Suffk
112 H5 Higham Dykes Nthumb
61 L7 Higham Ferrers Nhants
50 D4 Higham Gobion C Beds
37 J2 Higham Hill Gt Lon
72 B11 Higham on the Hill Leics
8 C4 Highampton Devon
37 J2 Highams Park Gt Lon
112 G3 High Angerton Nthumb
106 E8 High Ardwell D & G
109 K3 High Auldgirth D & G
101 Q2 High Bankhill Cumb
51 K11 High Beach Essex
95 P7 High Bentham N York
100 H4 High Bewaldeth Cumb
17 L7 High Bickington Devon
96 B5 High Bickwith N York
95 N5 High Biggins Cumb
126 B6 High Blantyre S Lans
126 E2 High Bonnybridge Falk
101 M10 High Borrans Cumb
96 F11 High Bradley N York
17 M5 High Bray Devon
22 E10 Highbridge Hants
19 K5 Highbridge Somset
25 J4 Highbrook W Susx
25 N2 High Brooms Kent
17 J7 High Bullen Devon
90 F8 Highburton Kirk
36 H3 Highbury Gt Lon
20 C5 Highbury Somset
119 P9 High Buston Nthumb
113 J6 High Callerton Nthumb
95 N5 High Casterton Cumb
98 E10 High Catton E R Yk
22 D3 Highclere Hants
13 M6 Highcliffe Dorset
103 N7 High Close Dur
34 C3 High Cogges Oxon
76 D10 High Common Norfk
103 P7 High Coniscliffe Darltn
111 J9 High Crosby Cumb
3 J8 High Cross Cnwll
125 L8 High Cross E Ayrs
23 K9 High Cross Hants
51 J7 High Cross Herts
88 C3 Highcross Lancs
24 F7 High Cross W Susx
59 K11 High Cross Warwks
106 F10 High Drummore D & G
113 M11 High Dubmire Sundld
51 P8 High Easter Essex
91 P6 High Eggborough N York
97 J4 High Ellington N York
20 C6 Higher Alham Somset
12 C4 Higher Ansty Dorset
88 D4 Higher Ballam Lancs
88 G4 Higher Bartle Lancs
49 Q8 Higher Berry End C Beds
12 B6 Higher Bockhampton Dorset
7 N8 Higher Brixham Torbay
9 P5 Higher Burrowton Devon
69 P3 Higher Burwardsley Ches W
69 Q11 High Ercall Wrekin
10 H2 Higher Chillington Somset
16 E7 Higher Clovelly Devon
18 B8 Highercombe Somset
11 L6 Higher Coombe Dorset
83 L8 Higher Disley Ches E
82 E4 Higher Folds Wigan
89 P2 Higherford Lancs
7 N5 Higher Gabwell Devon
11 L3 Higher Halstock Leigh Dorset
89 N3 Higher Harpers Lancs
95 J8 Higher Heysham Lancs
83 K10 Higher Hurdsfield Ches E
82 F5 Higher Irlam Salfd
11 L5 Higher Kingcombe Dorset
69 K2 Higher Kinnerton Flints
82 E9 Higher Marston Ches W
17 K4 Higher Muddiford Devon
20 D10 Higher Nyland Dorset
90 B8 Higher Ogden Rochdl
2 H8 Higher Pentire Cnwll
88 G5 Higher Penwortham Lancs

5 P2 Higher Prestacott Devon
96 B6 Higher Studfold N York
3 L5 Higher Town Cnwll
4 G9 Higher Town Cnwll
2 c1 Higher Town IoS
5 Q11 Higher Tregantle Cnwll
88 H5 Higher Walton Lancs
82 C7 Higher Walton Warrtn
10 F3 Higher Wambrook Somset
11 Q5 Higher Waterston Dorset
12 D4 Higher Whatcombe Dorset
89 J6 Higher Wheelton Lancs
82 D8 Higher Whitley Ches W
82 E9 Higher Wincham Ches W
11 M4 Higher Wraxhall Dorset
69 N6 Higher Wych Ches W
103 N5 High Etherley Dur
87 L11 High Ferry Lincs
92 B3 Highfield E R Yk
112 H9 Highfield Gatesd
125 J7 Highfield N Ayrs
91 N9 Highfields Donc
90 G9 High Flats Kirk
52 C6 High Garrett Essex
25 K4 Highgate E Susx
36 G3 Highgate Gt Lon
26 C5 Highgate Kent
103 N4 High Grange Dur
97 K7 High Grantley N York
101 M10 High Green Cumb
90 G8 High Green Kirk
64 H4 High Green Norfk
76 G10 High Green Norfk
91 J11 High Green Sheff
57 N8 High Green Shrops
64 B9 High Green Suffk
46 G5 High Green Worcs
112 B2 Highgreen Manor Nthumb
26 L4 High Halden Kent
38 C6 High Halstow Medway
19 M8 High Ham Somset
100 D5 High Harrington Cumb
97 M9 High Harrogate N York
104 C2 High Haswell Dur
69 R10 High Hatton Shrops
119 Q10 High Hauxley Nthumb
105 P9 High Hawsker N York
101 N2 High Hesket Cumb
90 H9 High Hoyland Barns
92 G3 High Hunsley E R Yk
25 L5 High Hurstwood E Susx
98 F7 High Hutton N York
100 H3 High Ireby Cumb
76 G5 High Kelling Norfk
97 R5 High Kilburn N York
99 M4 High Killerby N York
101 P7 High Knipe Cumb
103 M5 High Lands Dur
148 E7 Highland Wildlife Park Highld
83 J11 Highlane Ches E
84 F4 Highlane Derbys
83 L7 High Lane Stockp
2 F6 High Lanes Cnwll
51 M9 High Laver Essex
109 P11 Highlaws Cumb
46 E10 Highleadon Gloucs
82 F8 High Legh Ches E
15 M7 Highleigh W Susx
104 E8 High Leven S on T
57 N8 Highley Shrops
20 B3 High Littleton BaNES
100 G5 High Lorton Cumb
98 G5 High Marishes N York
85 P6 High Marnham Notts
91 N10 High Melton Donc
112 G8 High Mickley Nthumb
110 E11 Highmoor Cumb
35 K8 Highmoor Oxon
35 K8 Highmoor Cross Oxon
31 N7 Highmoor Hill Mons
113 M11 High Moorsley Sundld
46 E11 Highnam Gloucs
46 E10 Highnam Green Gloucs
113 N10 High Newport Sundld
95 J4 High Newton Cumb
94 F3 High Nibthwaite Cumb
70 D9 High Offley Staffs
51 N10 High Ongar Essex
70 E11 High Onn Staffs
52 H7 High Park Corner Essex
115 J6 High Pennyvenie E Ayrs
21 N7 High Post Wilts
31 Q11 Highridge N Som
51 P7 High Roding Essex
101 L3 High Row Cumb
101 L6 High Row Cumb
95 N8 High Salter Lancs
24 D9 High Salvington W Susx
110 C11 High Scales Cumb
100 D4 High Seaton Cumb
96 C2 High Shaw N York
100 H4 High Side Cumb
112 H9 High Spen Gatesd
39 M8 Highstead Kent
38 F9 Highsted Kent
103 M2 High Stoop Dur
3 P3 High Street Cnwll
26 B5 High Street Kent
39 J9 Highstreet Kent
65 N10 High Street Suffk
65 N7 High Street Suffk
52 C5 Highstreet Green Essex
23 Q7 Highstreet Green Surrey
109 N5 Hightae D & G
58 G9 Highter's Heath Birm
104 E4 High Throston Hartpl
70 F2 Hightown Ches E
13 L4 Hightown Hants
81 L4 Hightown Sefton
58 E2 High Town Staffs
64 D10 Hightown Green Suffk
87 J7 High Toynton Lincs
119 K9 High Trewhitt Nthumb
113 K10 High Urpeth Dur
134 C10 High Valleyfield Fife
112 D7 High Warden Nthumb
45 P5 Highway Herefs
33 K10 Highway Wilts
7 L4 Highweek Devon
112 H9 High Westwood Dur
71 K8 Highwood Staffs
36 F2 Highwood Hill Gt Lon
31 Q5 High Woolaston Gloucs
104 C9 High Worsall N York
33 P6 Highworth Swindn
101 L11 High Wray Cumb
51 L8 High Wych Herts
35 N6 High Wycombe Bucks
75 R10 Hilborough Norfk
84 G9 Hilcote Derbys
21 M3 Hilcott Wilts
37 N11 Hildenborough Kent
37 N11 Hilden Park Kent
62 H11 Hildersham Cambs
70 H8 Hilderstone Staffs
99 P7 Hilderthorpe E R Yk
11 N3 Hilfield Dorset
75 M11 Hilgay Norfk
32 B5 Hill S Glos
59 Q11 Hill Warwks
91 N5 Hillam N York
102 E7 Hillbeck Cumb
39 M8 Hillborough Kent
23 L9 Hill Brow Hants
12 G4 Hillbutts Dorset
70 D7 Hill Chorlton Staffs
71 P5 Hillclifflane Derbys
77 N7 Hill Common Norfk
18 F9 Hill Common Somset
20 G6 Hill Deverill Wilts
87 K11 Hilldyke Lincs
103 K3 Hill End Dur
134 C8 Hill End Fife
134 E11 Hillend Fife
46 H7 Hill End Gloucs
127 P4 Hillend Mdloth
126 E4 Hillend N Lans
28 D6 Hillend Swans
31 Q2 Hillersland Gloucs
8 H5 Hillerton Devon
49 J9 Hillesden Bucks
32 E7 Hillesley Gloucs
18 G10 Hillfarrance Somset
38 D9 Hill Green Kent
23 P9 Hillgrove W Susx
46 A5 Hillhampton Herefs
158 E10 Hillhead Abers
7 N8 Hillhead Devon
14 F6 Hill Head Hants
116 D2 Hillhead S Lans
159 Q9 Hillhead of Cocklaw Abers
59 J2 Hilliard's Cross Staffs
167 L4 Hilliclay Highld
36 C4 Hillingdon Gt Lon
125 N5 Hillington C Glas
75 P5 Hillington Norfk
14 E8 Hillis Corner IoW
60 B6 Hillmorton Warwks
89 M5 Hillock Vale Lancs
134 F9 Hill of Beath Fife
163 J11 Hill of Fearn Highld
108 G8 Hillowton D & G
58 C9 Hillpool Worcs
22 G11 Hillpound Hants
71 K11 Hill Ridware Staffs
151 N8 Hillside Abers
143 N5 Hillside Angus
7 J6 Hillside Devon
90 F7 Hill Side Kirk
46 E2 Hill Side Worcs
84 G7 Hills Town Derbys
22 B11 Hillstreet Hants
169 p6 Hillswick Shet
103 J6 Hill Top Dur
14 D6 Hill Top Hants
90 D8 Hill Top Kirk
84 E2 Hill Top Rothm
58 E6 Hill Top Sandw
91 J7 Hill Top Wakefd
169 q12 Hillwell Shet
33 K9 Hilmarton Wilts
20 G3 Hilperton Wilts
20 G3 Hilperton Marsh Wilts
15 J6 Hilsea C Port
93 N4 Hilston E R Yk
22 D10 Hiltingbury Hants
129 M9 Hilton Border
62 C7 Hilton Cambs
102 D6 Hilton Cumb
71 N8 Hilton Derbys
12 C4 Hilton Dorset
103 N6 Hilton Dur
156 F2 Hilton Highld
104 E8 Hilton S on T
57 P5 Hilton Shrops
58 E4 Hilton Park Services Staffs
46 H3 Himbleton Worcs
58 C6 Himley Staffs
95 L4 Hincaster Cumb
36 E7 Hinchley Wood Surrey
59 P6 Hinckley Leics
64 E6 Hinderclay Suffk
105 L7 Hinderwell N York
69 K8 Hindford Shrops
23 N7 Hindhead Surrey
89 L4 Hindle Fold Lancs
112 F9 Hindley Nthumb
82 D4 Hindley Wigan
82 D4 Hindley Green Wigan
46 G3 Hindlip Worcs
76 E6 Hindolveston Norfk
20 H8 Hindon Wilts
76 D4 Hindringham Norfk
76 E11 Hingham Norfk
58 C7 Hinksford Staffs
70 B9 Hinstock Shrops
53 J3 Hintlesham Suffk
32 C4 Hinton Gloucs
13 M5 Hinton Hants
45 L7 Hinton Herefs
32 D9 Hinton S Glos
56 G3 Hinton Shrops
57 M8 Hinton Shrops
13 M5 Hinton Admiral Hants
22 H9 Hinton Ampner Hants
19 Q3 Hinton Blewett BaNES
20 E3 Hinton Charterhouse BaNES
47 K6 Hinton Green Worcs
48 G7 Hinton-in-the-Hedges Nhants
22 G9 Hinton Marsh Hants
12 H3 Hinton Martell Dorset
47 K6 Hinton on the Green Worcs
33 P8 Hinton Parva Swindn
11 J2 Hinton St George Somset
20 E11 Hinton St Mary Dorset
34 C5 Hinton Waldrist Oxon
57 L10 Hints Shrops
59 J4 Hints Staffs
61 K8 Hinwick Bed
26 H3 Hinxhill Kent
62 G11 Hinxton Cambs
50 F2 Hinxworth Herts
90 E5 Hipperholme Calder
119 P8 Hipsburn Nthumb
103 N11 Hipswell N York
151 J7 Hirn Abers
68 D10 Hirnant Powys
113 L3 Hirst Nthumb
91 Q6 Hirst Courtney N York
68 F2 Hirwaen Denbgs
30 C3 Hirwaun Rhondd
17 J6 Hiscott Devon
62 F8 Histon Cambs
64 D11 Hitcham Suffk
64 D11 Hitcham Causeway Suffk
64 D11 Hitcham Street Suffk
50 E5 Hitchin Herts
37 J6 Hither Green Gt Lon
8 H5 Hittisleigh Devon
92 D4 Hive E R Yk
71 J9 Hixon Staffs
39 N10 Hoaden Kent
71 L10 Hoar Cross Staffs
45 Q9 Hoarwithy Herefs
39 M9 Hoath Kent
25 Q3 Hoathly Kent
56 E9 Hobarris Shrops
63 M10 Hobbles Green Suffk
51 L11 Hobbs Cross Essex
51 L8 Hobbs Cross Essex
118 A8 Hobkirk Border
77 Q11 Hobland Hall Norfk
84 G11 Hobsick Notts
113 J9 Hobson Dur
72 H7 Hoby Leics
18 F9 Hoccombe Somset
76 F9 Hockering Norfk
85 M9 Hockerton Notts
83 K8 Hockley Ches E
59 L9 Hockley Covtry
38 D3 Hockley Essex
59 K4 Hockley Staffs
59 J10 Hockley Heath Solhll
49 Q9 Hockliffe C Beds
63 M3 Hockwold cum Wilton Norfk
18 D11 Hockworthy Devon
50 H9 Hoddesdon Herts
89 L6 Hoddlesden Bl w D
110 C6 Hoddom Cross D & G
110 C6 Hoddom Mains D & G
82 H11 Hodgehill Ches E
41 K11 Hodgeston Pembks
69 R9 Hodnet Shrops
85 K3 Hodsock Notts
37 P8 Hodsoll Street Kent
33 N8 Hodson Swindn
84 H5 Hodthorpe Derbys
22 G11 Hoe Hants
76 D8 Hoe Norfk
14 H4 Hoe Gate Hants
102 C7 Hoff Cumb
38 H10 Hogben's Hill Kent
64 B10 Hoggards Green Suffk
49 M10 Hoggeston Bucks
59 K6 Hoggrill's End Warwks
26 E8 Hog Hill E Susx
89 J5 Hoghton Lancs
89 J5 Hoghton Bottoms Lancs
71 N4 Hognaston Derbys
87 P6 Hogsthorpe Lincs
74 G6 Holbeach Lincs
74 G5 Holbeach Bank Lincs
74 G5 Holbeach Clough Lincs
74 F8 Holbeach Drove Lincs
74 G5 Holbeach Hurn Lincs
74 G7 Holbeach St Johns Lincs
74 G4 Holbeach St Mark's Lincs
74 H4 Holbeach St Matthew Lincs
84 H6 Holbeck Notts
84 H6 Holbeck Woodhouse Notts
47 K3 Holberrow Green Worcs
6 G8 Holbeton Devon
36 H4 Holborn Gt Lon
38 B9 Holborough Kent
72 B2 Holbrook Derbys
84 F4 Holbrook Sheff
53 L4 Holbrook Suffk
84 E11 Holbrook Moor Derbys
59 M8 Holbrooks Covtry
119 K3 Holburn Nthumb
14 D6 Holbury Hants
7 P4 Holcombe Devon
20 C5 Holcombe Somset
18 E11 Holcombe Rogus Devon
60 G7 Holcot Nhants
96 A11 Holden Lancs
60 E7 Holdenby Nhants
89 P6 Holden Gate Calder
51 P5 Holder's Green Essex
57 K7 Holdgate Shrops
86 E11 Holdingham Lincs
10 G4 Holditch Dorset
90 D5 Holdsworth Calder
83 M6 Holehouse Derbys
46 B9 Hole-in-the-Wall Herefs
16 G10 Holemoor Devon
24 D8 Hole Street W Susx
18 G6 Holford Somset
98 B10 Holgate C York
94 H5 Holker Cumb
76 B3 Holkham Norfk
76 B3 Holkham Hall Norfk
16 F11 Hollacombe Devon
86 H11 Holland Fen Lincs
88 G9 Holland Lees Lancs
53 L8 Holland-on-Sea Essex
169 g1 Hollandstoun Ork
110 E7 Hollee D & G
53 Q3 Hollesley Suffk
7 M6 Hollicombe Torbay
38 D10 Hollingbourne Kent
24 H9 Hollingbury Br & H
49 N9 Hollingdon Bucks
91 K4 Hollingthorpe Leeds
71 N7 Hollington Derbys
71 K7 Hollington Staffs
83 M5 Hollingworth Tamesd
82 H8 Hollinlane Ches E
89 N9 Hollins Bury
84 D6 Hollins Derbys
70 H5 Hollins Staffs
83 N11 Hollinsclough Staffs
84 E4 Hollins End Sheff
82 E6 Hollins Green Warrtn
95 K10 Hollins Lane Lancs
57 N3 Hollinswood Wrekin
69 P7 Hollinwood Shrops
83 K4 Hollinwood Crematorium Oldham
25 Q6 Hollingrove E Susx
17 L9 Hollocombe Devon
84 D9 Holloway Derbys
36 H3 Holloway Gt Lon
20 G8 Holloway Wilts
60 E6 Hollowell Nhants
81 P11 Hollowmoor Heath Ches W
110 G5 Hollows D & G
30 G4 Hollybush Caerph
114 G4 Hollybush E Ayrs
46 E7 Hollybush Herefs
75 J9 Holly End Norfk
46 G6 Holly Green Worcs
69 Q6 Hollyhurst Ches E
93 P5 Hollym E R Yk
58 G9 Hollywood Worcs
90 E9 Holmbridge Kirk
24 D2 Holmbury St Mary Surrey
3 Q3 Holmbush Cnwll
70 G10 Holmcroft Staffs
61 Q3 Holme Cambs
95 L5 Holme Cumb
90 E9 Holme Kirk
92 F9 Holme N Linc
97 N4 Holme N York
85 P9 Holme Notts
89 P5 Holme Chapel Lancs
91 P2 Holme Green N York
76 B10 Holme Hale Norfk
45 R7 Holme Lacy Herefs
45 L4 Holme Marsh Herefs
75 P2 Holme next the Sea Norfk
99 K11 Holme on the Wolds E R Yk
72 G3 Holme Pierrepont Notts
45 Q6 Holmer Herefs
35 P5 Holmer Green Bucks
109 P11 Holme St Cuthbert Cumb
82 G11 Holmes Chapel Ches E
84 D5 Holmesfield Derbys
25 M8 Holmes Hill E Susx
88 E7 Holmeswood Lancs
36 G10 Holmethorpe Surrey
92 D3 Holme upon Spalding Moor E R Yk
84 F7 Holmewood Derbys
90 D5 Holmfield Calder
90 E9 Holmfirth Kirk
115 L3 Holmhead E Ayrs
93 Q6 Holmpton E R Yk
100 E11 Holmrook Cumb
125 K10 Holmsford Bridge Crematorium N Ayrs
25 P5 Holmshurst E Susx
113 K11 Holmside Dur
111 K11 Holmwrangle Cumb
7 J5 Holne Devon
11 P3 Holnest Dorset
18 B5 Holnicote Somset
16 E11 Holsworthy Devon
16 F10 Holsworthy Beacon Devon
12 H4 Holt Dorset
76 F4 Holt Norfk
20 G2 Holt Wilts
46 F2 Holt Worcs
69 M4 Holt Wrexhm
98 D10 Holtby C York
58 G11 Holt End Worcs
46 F2 Holt Fleet Worcs
88 D9 Holt Green Lancs
13 J4 Holt Heath Dorset
46 F2 Holt Heath Worcs
34 H3 Holton Oxon
20 C9 Holton Somset
65 N6 Holton Suffk
86 F4 Holton cum Beckering Lincs
12 F6 Holton Heath Dorset
25 Q5 Holton Hill E Susx
93 N10 Holton le Clay Lincs
93 J11 Holton le Moor Lincs
53 J4 Holton St Mary Suffk
39 N11 Holt Street Kent
25 L3 Holtye E Susx
80 H9 Holway Flints
11 P2 Holwell Dorset
50 E4 Holwell Herts
73 J6 Holwell Leics
33 P3 Holwell Oxon
102 H5 Holwick Dur
12 C8 Holworth Dorset
23 K6 Holybourne Hants
58 D9 Holy Cross Worcs
51 J10 Holyfield Essex
78 C8 Holyhead IoA
78 D8 Holy Island IoA
119 M2 Holy Island Nthumb
119 M2 Holy Island Nthumb
84 D7 Holymoorside Derbys
35 N9 Holyport W & M
119 J10 Holystone Nthumb
126 D5 Holytown N Lans
50 B7 Holywell C Beds
62 D6 Holywell Cambs
4 B10 Holywell Cnwll
11 M4 Holywell Dorset
80 H9 Holywell Flints
113 M6 Holywell Nthumb
59 K11 Holywell Warwks
90 D7 Holywell Green Calder
18 F10 Holywell Lake Somset
63 M5 Holywell Row Suffk
109 K4 Holywood D & G
109 L5 Holywood Village D & G
57 L4 Homer Shrops
81 L4 Homer Green Sefton
65 K4 Homersfield Suffk
95 M3 Homescales Cumb
46 A10 Hom Green Herefs
21 M9 Homington Wilts
40 H9 Honeyborough Pembks
47 M6 Honeybourne Worcs
8 F4 Honeychurch Devon
39 K9 Honey Hill Kent
21 M2 Honeystreet Wilts
52 G4 Honey Tye Suffk
59 K10 Honiley Warwks
77 L6 Honing Norfk
76 G9 Honingham Norfk
73 N2 Honington Lincs
64 C7 Honington Suffk
47 Q6 Honington Warwks
10 D4 Honiton Devon
90 E8 Honley Kirk
70 C11 Honnington Wrekin
37 J6 Honor Oak Crematorium Gt Lon
39 N9 Hoo Kent
58 B10 Hoobrook Worcs
91 J10 Hood Green Barns
91 K11 Hood Hill Rothm
6 E8 Hooe C Plym
25 Q8 Hooe E Susx
50 E6 Hoo End Herts
82 F8 Hoo Green Ches E
88 C3 Hoohill Bpool
62 F2 Hook Cambs
10 G3 Hook Devon
92 C5 Hook E R Yk
36 E8 Hook Gt Lon
14 F5 Hook Hants
23 K4 Hook Hants
41 J8 Hook Pembks
33 L8 Hook Wilts
56 H3 Hookagate Shrops
46 F6 Hook Bank Worcs
11 L4 Hooke Dorset
51 N10 Hook End Essex
70 C7 Hookgate Staffs
25 Q3 Hook Green Kent
37 P6 Hook Green Kent
48 C8 Hook Norton Oxon
32 C5 Hook Street Gloucs
33 L8 Hook Street Wilts
9 L5 Hookway Devon
24 G2 Hookwood Surrey
36 G9 Hooley Surrey
89 P8 Hooley Bridge Rochdl
6 E5 Hoo Meavy Devon
38 C7 Hoo St Werburgh Medway
81 M9 Hooton Ches W
84 H2 Hooton Levitt Rothm
91 M9 Hooton Pagnell Donc
91 M11 Hooton Roberts Rothm
48 E9 Hopcrofts Holt Oxon
83 Q8 Hope Derbys
6 H10 Hope Devon
69 K3 Hope Flints
56 D3 Hope Powys
56 E4 Hope Shrops
57 K10 Hope Shrops
71 L4 Hope Staffs
56 H6 Hope Bowdler Shrops
51 N6 Hope End Green Essex
117 K7 Hopehouse Border
157 L4 Hopeman Moray
46 B11 Hope Mansell Herefs
56 F8 Hopesay Shrops
91 K6 Hopetown Wakefd
45 Q4 Hope under Dinmore Herefs
98 C10 Hopgrove C York
97 P9 Hopperton N York
74 C8 Hop Pole Lincs
59 P8 Hopsford Warwks
57 P6 Hopstone Shrops
71 P4 Hopton Derbys
69 L10 Hopton Shrops
70 G9 Hopton Staffs
64 D6 Hopton Suffk
57 J8 Hopton Cangeford Shrops
56 F9 Hopton Castle Shrops
56 F9 Hoptonheath Shrops
65 Q2 Hopton on Sea Norfk
57 L9 Hopton Wafers Shrops
59 J4 Hopwas Staffs
89 P9 Hopwood Rochdl
58 F9 Hopwood Worcs
58 F10 Hopwood Park Services Worcs
25 N7 Horam E Susx
74 B3 Horbling Lincs
90 H7 Horbury Wakefd
33 N4 Horcott Gloucs
104 D2 Horden Dur
56 G7 Horderley Shrops
13 N5 Hordle Hants
69 L8 Hordley Shrops
28 E3 Horeb Carmth
42 G6 Horeb Cerdgn
31 Q9 Horfield Bristl
65 J7 Horham Suffk
52 G6 Horkesley Heath Essex
92 G7 Horkstow N Linc
48 D6 Horley Oxon
24 G2 Horley Surrey
19 Q8 Hornblotton Green Somset
95 M7 Hornby Lancs
97 K2 Hornby N York
104 C9 Hornby N York
87 J7 Horncastle Lincs
37 M3 Hornchurch Gt Lon
129 N10 Horncliffe Nthumb
129 N10 Horndean Border
15 K4 Horndean Hants
8 D8 Horndon Devon
37 Q4 Horndon on the Hill Thurr
24 H2 Horne Surrey
18 B5 Horner Somset
52 C11 Horne Row Essex
52 G3 Horners Green Suffk
25 L5 Horney Common E Susx
36 B2 Horn Hill Bucks
77 L8 Horning Norfk
73 L11 Horninghold Leics
71 N9 Horninglow Staffs
62 G8 Horningsea Cambs
20 F6 Horningsham Wilts
76 C7 Horningtoft Norfk
5 M9 Horningtops Cnwll
10 G2 Hornsbury Somset
111 K10 Hornsby Cumb
111 K10 Hornsbygate Cumb
16 F7 Horns Cross Devon
26 D7 Horns Cross E Susx
99 P11 Hornsea E R Yk
36 H3 Hornsey Gt Lon
37 L9 Horn's Green Gt Lon
27 L4 Horn Street Kent
48 C5 Hornton Oxon
33 P8 Horpit Swindn
169 r4 Horra Shet
6 E5 Horrabridge Devon
64 A9 Horringer Suffk
14 F9 Horringford IoW
89 L8 Horrocks Fold Bolton
89 M2 Horrocksford Lancs
17 J5 Horsacott Devon
5 Q6 Horsebridge Devon
25 N8 Horsebridge E Susx
22 B8 Horsebridge Hants

56 F3 Horsebridge Shrops
70 H4 Horsebridge Staffs
58 C2 Horsebrook Staffs
31 M11 Horsecastle N Som
2 G7 Horsedown Cnwll
74 C8 Horsegate Lincs
57 M3 Horsehay Wrekin
63 K11 Horseheath Cambs
96 F4 Horsehouse N York
23 Q3 Horsell Surrey
69 M6 Horseman's Green Wrexhm
35 L4 Horsenden Bucks
77 P7 Horsey Norfk
19 K7 Horsey Somset
77 P7 Horsey Corner Norfk
76 H8 Horsford Norfk
90 G3 Horsforth Leeds
24 E4 Horsham W Susx
46 D3 Horsham Worcs
77 J8 Horsham St Faith Norfk
86 G7 Horsington Lincs
20 D10 Horsington Somset
72 B2 Horsley Derbys
32 F5 Horsley Gloucs
112 G7 Horsley Nthumb
118 F11 Horsley Nthumb
53 K6 Horsley Cross Essex
53 K6 Horsleycross Street Essex
84 D5 Horsley-Gate Derbys
117 Q7 Horsleyhill Border
35 L6 Horsley's Green Bucks
72 B2 Horsley Woodhouse Derbys
26 B3 Horsmonden Kent
34 G3 Horspath Oxon
77 K8 Horstead Norfk
25 J5 Horsted Keynes W Susx
49 P11 Horton Bucks
12 H3 Horton Dorset
96 C10 Horton Lancs
49 M4 Horton Nhants
32 E8 Horton S Glos
69 N9 Horton Shrops
10 G2 Horton Somset
70 G3 Horton Staffs
36 E8 Horton Surrey
28 E7 Horton Swans
36 B5 Horton W & M
21 K2 Horton Wilts
57 M2 Horton Wrekin
19 K11 Horton Cross Somset
34 G2 Horton-cum-Studley Oxon
69 N5 Horton Green Ches W
22 E11 Horton Heath Hants
96 B6 Horton in Ribblesdale N York
37 N7 Horton Kirby Kent
89 J8 Horwich Bolton
83 M8 Horwich End Derbys
17 J6 Horwood Devon
88 F8 Hoscar Lancs
117 M8 Hoscote Border
73 J5 Hose Leics
37 L10 Hosey Hill Kent
133 P3 Hosh P & K
169 r11 Hoswick Shet
92 E4 Hotham E R Yk
26 G3 Hothfield Kent
72 F6 Hoton Leics
111 Q3 Hott Nthumb
70 C4 Hough Ches E
83 J9 Hough Ches E
73 M2 Hougham Lincs
90 G4 Hough End Leeds
81 P7 Hough Green Halton
86 B11 Hough-on-the-Hill Lincs
62 C6 Houghton Cambs
110 H9 Houghton Cumb
22 B8 Houghton Hants
112 H7 Houghton Nthumb
41 J9 Houghton Pembks
24 B8 Houghton W Susx
50 B2 Houghton Conquest C Beds
113 M10 Houghton Gate Dur
26 F7 Houghton Green E Susx
82 D6 Houghton Green Warrtn
103 P6 Houghton le Side Darltn
113 M11 Houghton-le-Spring Sundld
72 H10 Houghton on the Hill Leics
50 B6 Houghton Regis C Beds
76 C4 Houghton St Giles Norfk
23 K3 Hound Green Hants
128 G10 Houndslow Border
18 F9 Houndsmoor Somset
129 L7 Houndwood Border
36 D5 Hounslow Gt Lon
156 F6 Househill Highld
90 F7 Houses Hill Kirk
151 M2 Housieside Abers
125 L4 Houston Rens
167 L10 Houstry Highld
169 c6 Houton Ork
24 G10 Hove Br & H
90 E6 Hove Edge Calder
85 L11 Hoveringham Notts
77 L8 Hoveton Norfk
98 D5 Hovingham N York
91 J11 Howbrook Barns
46 B8 How Caple Herefs
92 B5 Howden E R Yk
103 N4 Howden-le-Wear Dur
167 P4 Howe Highld
80 a8 Howe IoM
97 N4 Howe N York
65 K2 Howe Norfk
82 E4 Howe Bridge Wigan
82 E4 Howe Bridge Crematorium Wigan
52 B11 Howe Green Essex
52 D11 Howegreen Essex
86 F11 Howell Lincs
50 B2 How End C Beds
159 J8 Howe of Teuchar Abers
110 C7 Howes D & G
51 Q4 Howe Street Essex
51 Q8 Howe Street Essex
44 F3 Howey Powys
100 C6 Howgate Cumb
127 N6 Howgate Mdloth
96 B11 Howgill Lancs
119 Q7 Howick Nthumb
70 B10 Howle Wrekin
46 B10 Howle Hill Herefs
51 N4 Howlett End Essex
10 F3 Howley Somset
111 K9 How Mill Cumb
168 c14 Howmore W Isls
118 E7 Hownam Border
110 F11 Howrigg Cumb
92 H10 Howsham N Linc
98 E8 Howsham N York
118 G4 Howtel Nthumb
38 E8 Howt Green Kent
45 N9 Howton Herefs
101 M7 Howtown Cumb
125 K5 Howwood Rens
64 H6 Hoxne Suffk
169 b7 Hoy Ork
81 J7 Hoylake Wirral
91 K10 Hoyland Common Barns
91 K10 Hoyland Nether Barns
90 H10 Hoyland Swaine Barns
23 P11 Hoyle W Susx
91 K9 Hoyle Mill Barns
96 D5 Hubberholme N York
40 G9 Hubberston Pembks
74 E2 Hubbert's Bridge Lincs
97 L11 Huby N York
98 B7 Huby N York
6 H4 Huccaby Devon
46 G11 Hucclecote Gloucs
38 D10 Hucking Kent
84 H11 Hucknall Notts
90 E7 Huddersfield Kirk
90 E6 Huddersfield Crematorium Kirk
46 H3 Huddington Worcs
50 B8 Hudnall Herts
103 M10 Hudswell N York
98 H9 Huggate E R Yk
72 C8 Hugglescote Leics
35 N5 Hughenden Valley Bucks
57 K5 Hughley Shrops
2 c2 Hugh Town IoS
17 J9 Huish Devon
21 M2 Huish Wilts
18 E9 Huish Champflower Somset
19 M9 Huish Episcopi Somset
49 P7 Hulcote C Beds
49 N11 Hulcott Bucks
9 P8 Hulham Devon
71 N5 Hulland Derbys
71 P5 Hulland Ward Derbys
32 G8 Hullavington Wilts
38 D2 Hullbridge Essex
82 H5 Hulme Manch
70 G5 Hulme Staffs
82 D6 Hulme Warrtn
71 L3 Hulme End Staffs
82 H11 Hulme Walfield Ches E
82 F8 Hulse Heath Ches E
89 K9 Hulton Lane Ends Bolton
14 C10 Hulverstone IoW
76 C9 Hulver Street Norfk
65 P4 Hulver Street Suffk
9 L9 Humber Devon
45 Q3 Humber Herefs
93 J8 Humberside Airport N Linc
93 P9 Humberston NE Lin
72 G9 Humberstone C Leic
97 P7 Humberton N York
128 D7 Humbie E Loth
93 M4 Humbleton E R Yk
119 J5 Humbleton Nthumb
73 Q4 Humby Lincs
118 D2 Hume Border
112 D6 Humshaugh Nthumb
167 Q2 Huna Highld
89 M4 Huncoat Lancs
72 E11 Huncote Leics
118 B7 Hundalee Border
84 E5 Hundall Derbys
103 J6 Hunderthwaite Dur
87 L7 Hundleby Lincs
86 H10 Hundle Houses Lincs
41 J10 Hundleton Pembks
63 M11 Hundon Suffk
88 E6 Hundred End Lancs
44 G4 Hundred House Powys
72 H9 Hungarton Leics
13 L2 Hungerford Hants
18 D6 Hungerford Somset
34 B11 Hungerford W Berk
34 C10 Hungerford Newtown W Berk
89 K9 Hunger Hill Bolton
88 G8 Hunger Hill Lancs
45 N7 Hungerstone Herefs
73 M5 Hungerton Lincs
70 B9 Hungryhatton Shrops
99 M5 Hunmanby N York
59 N11 Hunningham Warwks
58 E8 Hunnington Worcs
60 F9 Hunsbury Hill Nhants
51 K8 Hunsdon Herts
97 P10 Hunsingore N York
91 J4 Hunslet Leeds
101 Q3 Hunsonby Cumb
75 N2 Hunstanton Norfk
112 D11 Hunstanworth Dur
70 B5 Hunsterson Ches E
64 D8 Hunston Suffk
15 N6 Hunston W Susx
64 D8 Hunston Green Suffk
20 B2 Hunstrete BaNES
90 F5 Hunsworth Kirk
47 K2 Hunt End Worcs
17 M2 Hunter's Inn Devon
124 F2 Hunter's Quay Ag & B
19 K9 Huntham Somset
142 H3 Hunthill Lodge Angus
62 B6 Huntingdon Cambs
65 L7 Huntingfield Suffk
20 F9 Huntingford Dorset
98 C9 Huntington C York
69 M2 Huntington Ches W
128 D5 Huntington E Loth
45 K4 Huntington Herefs
45 P6 Huntington Herefs
58 E2 Huntington Staffs
46 D11 Huntley Gloucs
158 D10 Huntly Abers
22 E6 Hunton Hants
26 B2 Hunton Kent
97 J2 Hunton N York
50 C10 Hunton Bridge Herts
64 F4 Hunt's Corner Norfk
18 B6 Huntscott Somset
81 N7 Hunt's Cross Lpool
35 N4 Hunts Green Bucks
59 J5 Hunts Green Warwks
18 D10 Huntsham Devon
17 J7 Huntshaw Devon
17 J7 Huntshaw Cross Devon
19 K5 Huntspill Somset
19 J8 Huntstile Somset
19 K8 Huntworth Somset
103 N4 Hunwick Dur
76 F4 Hunworth Norfk
19 L11 Hurcott Somset
21 N8 Hurdcott Wilts
83 K10 Hurdsfield Ches E
35 M8 Hurley W & M
59 K5 Hurley Warwks
35 M8 Hurley Bottom W & M
59 K5 Hurley Common Warwks
125 M10 Hurlford E Ayrs
88 D8 Hurlston Green Lancs
13 K5 Hurn Dorset
87 M11 Hurn's End Lincs
22 D9 Hursley Hants
12 C6 Hurst Dorset
103 K10 Hurst N York
19 N11 Hurst Somset
35 L10 Hurst Wokham
22 D5 Hurstbourne Priors Hants
22 C4 Hurstbourne Tarrant Hants
26 B6 Hurst Green E Susx
53 J8 Hurst Green Essex
89 K3 Hurst Green Lancs
37 J10 Hurst Green Surrey
58 D6 Hurst Hill Dudley
45 M5 Hurstley Herefs
24 G7 Hurstpierpoint W Susx
24 G7 Hurst Wickham W Susx
89 P4 Hurstwood Lancs
169 e6 Hurtiso Ork
23 P5 Hurtmore Surrey
104 D4 Hurworth Burn Dur
104 B9 Hurworth-on-Tees Darltn
103 Q9 Hurworth Place Darltn
103 J7 Hury Dur
60 D4 Husbands Bosworth Leics
49 Q7 Husborne Crawley C Beds
97 R6 Husthwaite N York
7 K8 Hutcherleigh Devon
84 D4 Hutcliffe Wood Crematorium Sheff
91 P6 Hut Green N York
84 G9 Huthwaite Notts
87 P5 Huttoft Lincs
129 N9 Hutton Border
101 M5 Hutton Cumb
99 L10 Hutton E R Yk
51 P11 Hutton Essex
88 F5 Hutton Lancs
19 L3 Hutton N Som
104 B10 Hutton Bonville N York
99 K4 Hutton Buscel N York
97 M6 Hutton Conyers N York
99 L10 Hutton Cranswick E R Yk
101 N3 Hutton End Cumb
97 J3 Hutton Hang N York
104 D3 Hutton Henry Dur
98 E2 Hutton-le-Hole N York
104 G8 Hutton Lowcross R & Cl
103 M8 Hutton Magna Dur
105 M9 Hutton Mulgrave N York
95 M5 Hutton Roof Cumb
101 L4 Hutton Roof Cumb
104 E9 Hutton Rudby N York
97 Q5 Hutton Sessay N York
97 R10 Hutton Wandesley N York
9 M5 Huxham Devon
19 Q7 Huxham Green Somset
69 P2 Huxley Ches W
81 N6 Huyton Knows
94 B3 Hycemoor Cumb
32 G4 Hyde Gloucs
13 L2 Hyde Hants
83 K6 Hyde Tamesd
35 K11 Hyde End Wokham
35 P4 Hyde Heath Bucks
70 G11 Hyde Lea Staffs
23 Q6 Hydestile Surrey
86 B7 Hykeham Moor Lincs
116 C2 Hyndford Bridge S Lans
136 B8 Hynish Ag & B
56 E6 Hyssington Powys
32 C5 Hystfield Gloucs
14 D5 Hythe Hants
27 L5 Hythe Kent
19 M4 Hythe Somset
36 B6 Hythe End W & M
94 B3 Hyton Cumb

I

12 C3 Ibberton Dorset
84 B9 Ible Derbys
13 L3 Ibsley Hants
72 C9 Ibstock Leics
35 L6 Ibstone Bucks
22 C4 Ibthorpe Hants
105 N9 Iburndale N York
22 G4 Ibworth Hants
31 L11 Icelton N Som
139 J11 Ichrachan Ag & B
75 R11 Ickburgh Norfk
36 C3 Ickenham Gt Lon
34 H3 Ickford Bucks
39 M10 Ickham Kent
50 E4 Ickleford Herts
26 E8 Icklesham E Susx
51 L2 Ickleton Cambs
63 N6 Icklingham Suffk
90 B2 Ickornshaw N York
61 Q11 Ickwell Green C Beds
63 P8 Ickworth Suffk
47 P10 Icomb Gloucs
47 P11 Idbury Oxon
17 K10 Iddesleigh Devon
9 L6 Ide Devon
9 L9 Ideford Devon
37 L10 Ide Hill Kent
26 F7 Iden E Susx
26 B4 Iden Green Kent
26 D5 Iden Green Kent
90 F3 Idle C Brad
3 L4 Idless Cnwll
47 Q6 Idlicote Warwks
21 N7 Idmiston Wilts
42 H11 Idole Carmth
71 P5 Idridgehay Derbys
152 F5 Idrigill Highld
33 Q8 Idstone Oxon
34 F4 Iffley Oxon
24 G3 Ifield W Susx
24 B4 Ifold W Susx
13 K6 Iford Bmouth
25 K9 Iford E Susx
31 N7 Ifton Mons
69 K7 Ifton Heath Shrops
69 Q7 Ightfield Shrops
37 N9 Ightham Kent
65 N10 Iken Suffk
71 L4 Ilam Staffs
19 P10 Ilchester Somset
119 K6 Ilderton Nthumb
37 K3 Ilford Gt Lon
19 L11 Ilford Somset
17 J2 Ilfracombe Devon
72 D2 Ilkeston Derbys
65 M4 Ilketshall St Andrew Suffk
65 M4 Ilketshall St John Suffk
65 M5 Ilketshall St Lawrence Suffk
65 L4 Ilketshall St Margaret Suffk
96 H11 Ilkley C Brad
5 M6 Illand Cnwll
58 E8 Illey Dudley
70 D2 Illidge Green Ches E
90 D5 Illingworth Calder
2 H5 Illogan Cnwll
73 J11 Illston on the Hill Leics
35 L3 Ilmer Bucks
47 P6 Ilmington Warwks
10 H2 Ilminster Somset
9 J9 Ilsington Devon
12 C6 Ilsington Dorset
28 G6 Ilston Swans
97 J5 Ilton N York
19 L11 Ilton Somset
120 G3 Imachar N Ayrs
93 L8 Immingham NE Lin
93 L7 Immingham Dock NE Lin
62 F8 Impington Cambs
81 P9 Ince Ches W
81 L4 Ince Blundell Sefton
82 C4 Ince-in-Makerfield Wigan
155 M4 Inchbae Lodge Hotel Highld
143 L4 Inchbare Angus
157 Q6 Inchberry Moray
154 D5 Incheril Highld
125 M4 Inchinnan Rens
146 F7 Inchlaggan Highld
134 G2 Inchmichael P & K
147 K5 Inchnacardoch Hotel Highld
161 M2 Inchnadamph Highld
134 H2 Inchture P & K
154 H10 Inchvuilt Highld
134 F3 Inchyra P & K
4 E10 Indian Queens Cnwll
65 N4 Ingate Place Suffk
51 P11 Ingatestone Essex
90 G9 Ingbirchworth Barns
97 L7 Ingerthorpe N York
70 H10 Ingestre Staffs
86 B4 Ingham Lincs
77 M6 Ingham Norfk
64 B7 Ingham Suffk
77 M6 Ingham Corner Norfk
75 J7 Ingleborough Norfk
72 A5 Ingleby Derbys
104 D10 Ingleby Arncliffe N York
104 D8 Ingleby Barwick S on T
104 E10 Ingleby Cross N York
104 G9 Ingleby Greenhow N York
8 F3 Ingleigh Green Devon
20 D2 Inglesbatch BaNES
33 P5 Inglesham Swindn
109 L7 Ingleston D & G
103 N6 Ingleton Dur
95 P6 Ingleton N York
88 G3 Inglewhite Lancs
112 F6 Ingoe Nthumb
88 G4 Ingol Lancs
75 N4 Ingoldisthorpe Norfk
87 Q7 Ingoldmells Lincs
73 Q5 Ingoldsby Lincs
119 K7 Ingram Nthumb
37 P2 Ingrave Essex
90 D3 Ingrow C Brad
101 M11 Ings Cumb
31 Q7 Ingst S Glos
73 P9 Ingthorpe Rutlnd
76 H6 Ingworth Norfk
47 K3 Inkberrow Worcs
103 M3 Inkerman Dur
159 M10 Inkhorn Abers
22 C2 Inkpen W Berk
167 N2 Inkstack Highld
20 H2 Inmarsh Wilts
124 F3 Innellan Ag & B
117 L3 Innerleithen Border
135 K7 Innerleven Fife
106 E5 Innermessan D & G
129 J5 Innerwick E Loth
157 P5 Innesmill Moray
150 G2 Insch Abers
148 E7 Insh Highld
88 F3 Inskip Lancs
88 F3 Inskip Moss Side Lancs
16 H5 Instow Devon
6 C8 Insworke Cnwll
84 E4 Intake Sheff
149 N9 Inver Abers
163 K10 Inver Highld
141 P9 Inver P & K
145 N11 Inverailort Highld
153 Q6 Inveralligin Highld
159 P4 Inverallochy Abers
162 D7 Inveran Highld
131 M6 Inveraray Ag & B
153 K10 Inverarish Highld
142 H9 Inverarity Angus
132 C4 Inverarnan Stirlg
160 C10 Inverasdale Highld
132 C8 Inverbeg Ag & B
143 Q3 Inverbervie Abers
158 G5 Inver-boyndie Abers
139 J8 Invercreran House Hotel Ag & B
148 F5 Inverdruie Highld
127 Q3 Inveresk E Loth
138 H10 Inveresragan Ag & B
160 D10 Inverewe Garden Highld
149 K10 Inverey Abers
147 N3 Inverfarigaig Highld
138 H9 Inverfolla Ag & B
147 J7 Invergarry Highld
133 L2 Invergeldie P & K
146 G10 Invergloy Highld
156 C4 Invergordon Highld
142 E11 Invergowrie P & K
145 M6 Inverguseran Highld
140 G6 Inverhadden P & K
132 D2 Inverherive Hotel Stirlg
145 N7 Inverie Highld
131 K4 Inverinan Ag & B
145 R3 Inverinate Highld
143 M8 Inverkeilor Angus
134 E11 Inverkeithing Fife
158 F8 Inverkeithny Abers
124 G3 Inverkip Inver
160 H3 Inverkirkaig Highld
161 K9 Inverlael Highld
139 Q2 Inverlair Highld
130 H6 Inverliever Lodge Ag & B
131 P2 Inverlochy Ag & B
150 C11 Invermark Angus
147 L4 Invermoriston Highld
166 B4 Invernaver Highld
156 B8 Inverness Highld
156 A9 Inverness Crematorium Highld
156 D7 Inverness Dalcross Airport Highld
131 N8 Invernoaden Ag & B
139 P9 Inveroran Hotel Ag & B
142 G6 Inverquharity Angus
159 P8 Inverquhomery Abers
146 H11 Inverroy Highld
138 G6 Inversanda Highld
146 A4 Invershiel Highld
162 D7 Invershin Highld
167 M9 Invershore Highld
132 C6 Inversnaid Hotel Stirlg
159 Q8 Inverugie Abers
132 C6 Inveruglas Ag & B
148 E7 Inveruglass Highld
151 K3 Inverurie Abers
8 E5 Inwardleigh Devon
52 E8 Inworth Essex
168 c13 Iochdar W Isls
136 H10 Iona Ag & B
23 N10 Iping W Susx
7 L5 Ipplepen Devon
34 H7 Ipsden Oxon
71 J5 Ipstones Staffs
53 L3 Ipswich Suffk
53 L2 Ipswich Crematorium Suffk
81 K8 Irby Wirral
87 N8 Irby in the Marsh Lincs
93 L10 Irby upon Humber NE Lin
61 K7 Irchester Nhants
100 H3 Ireby Cumb
95 P5 Ireby Lancs
50 D2 Ireland C Beds
94 E5 Ireleth Cumb
102 G3 Ireshopeburn Dur
71 P5 Ireton Wood Derbys
82 F6 Irlam Salfd
73 Q5 Irnham Lincs
32 C8 Iron Acton S Glos
75 J11 Iron Bridge Cambs
57 M4 Ironbridge Wrekin
57 M4 Ironbridge Gorge Shrops
47 L4 Iron Cross Warwks
108 E5 Ironmacannie D & G
36 F11 Irons Bottom Surrey
84 F10 Ironville Derbys
77 M7 Irstead Norfk
111 J8 Irthington Cumb
61 K6 Irthlingborough Nhants
99 L4 Irton N York
125 J10 Irvine N Ayrs
125 J10 Irvine Maritime Centre N Ayrs
166 G3 Isauld Highld
169 q4 Isbister Shet
169 s7 Isbister Shet
25 K7 Isfield E Susx
61 J6 Isham Nhants
23 L6 Isington Hants
58 C8 Islandpool Worcs
122 E4 Islay Ag & B
122 D9 Islay Airport Ag & B
19 L10 Isle Abbotts Somset
19 L10 Isle Brewers Somset
63 K6 Isleham Cambs
37 J5 Isle of Dogs Gt Lon
38 E6 Isle of Grain Medway
168 i4 Isle of Lewis W Isls
80 e4 Isle of Man IoM
80 c8 Isle of Man Ronaldsway Airport IoM
137 Q8 Isle of Mull Ag & B
12 H8 Isle of Purbeck Dorset
38 G8 Isle of Sheppey Kent
152 G10 Isle of Skye Highld
39 P8 Isle of Thanet Kent
94 D7 Isle of Walney Cumb
107 N10 Isle of Whithorn D & G
14 F9 Isle of Wight IoW
14 F8 Isle of Wight Crematorium IoW
145 M5 Isleornsay Highld
2 c2 Isles of Scilly St Mary's Airport IoS
109 L6 Islesteps D & G
10 c1 Islet Village Guern
36 E5 Isleworth Gt Lon
72 C6 Isley Walton Leics
168 f5 Islibhig W Isls
36 H4 Islington Gt Lon
36 G2 Islington Crematorium Gt Lon
61 L5 Islip Nhants
34 F2 Islip Oxon
168 f5 Islivig W Isls
57 L2 Isombridge Wrekin
37 P6 Istead Rise Kent
22 F8 Itchen Abbas Hants
22 G8 Itchen Stoke Hants
24 D5 Itchingfield W Susx
32 C7 Itchington S Glos
76 G5 Itteringham Norfk
8 G5 Itton Devon
31 N5 Itton Mons
31 N5 Itton Common Mons
101 M2 Ivegill Cumb
102 H11 Ivelet N York
36 B4 Iver Bucks
36 B4 Iver Heath Bucks
112 H10 Iveston Dur
49 P11 Ivinghoe Bucks
49 Q11 Ivinghoe Aston Bucks

45 P3 Ivington Herefs
45 P3 Ivington Green Herefs
6 G7 Ivybridge Devon
26 H6 Ivychurch Kent
20 G10 Ivy Cross Dorset
37 N10 Ivy Hatch Kent
76 B10 Ivy Todd Norfk
38 F8 Iwade Kent
12 E2 Iwerne Courtney or Shroton Dorset
12 E2 Iwerne Minster Dorset
64 C7 Ixworth Suffk
64 C7 Ixworth Thorpe Suffk

J

88 H5 Jack Green Lancs
97 J10 Jack Hill N York
9 P5 Jack-in-the-Green Devon
21 Q7 Jack's Bush Hants
84 F10 Jacksdale Notts
90 F9 Jackson Bridge Kirk
125 P7 Jackton S Lans
5 K2 Jacobstow Cnwll
8 E4 Jacobstowe Devon
36 B10 Jacobs Well Surrey
41 L11 Jameston Pembks
155 N6 Jamestown Highld
132 D11 Jamestown W Duns
167 L10 Janetstown Highld
167 Q6 Janets-town Highld
109 P3 Jardine Hall D & G
113 M8 Jarrow S Tyne
25 M5 Jarvis Brook E Susx
52 B6 Jasper's Green Essex
126 E2 Jawcraig Falk
53 L9 Jaywick Essex
35 N10 Jealott's Hill Br For
97 P2 Jeater Houses N York
118 B6 Jedburgh Border
41 L9 Jeffreyston Pembks
156 C4 Jemimaville Highld
10 c2 Jerbourg Guern
11 a2 Jersey Airport Jersey
11 b2 Jersey Crematorium Jersey
29 K6 Jersey Marine Neath
86 B6 Jerusalem Lincs
113 L7 Jesmond N u Ty
25 N10 Jevington E Susx
31 N2 Jingle Street Mons
50 B8 Jockey End Herts
82 G10 Jodrell Bank Ches E
101 M4 Johnby Cumb
81 N8 John Lennon Airport Lpool
167 Q2 John o' Groats Highld
26 B7 John's Cross E Susx
143 P4 Johnshaven Abers
77 M8 Johnson's Street Norfk
40 H8 Johnston Pembks
117 J10 Johnstone D & G
125 L5 Johnstone Rens
109 P2 Johnstonebridge D & G
42 G11 Johnstown Carmth
69 K5 Johnstown Wrexhm
127 Q3 Joppa C Edin
54 D11 Joppa Cerdgn
114 H4 Joppa S Ayrs
35 Q6 Jordans Bucks
40 H4 Jordanston Pembks
84 E4 Jordanthorpe Sheff
37 M6 Joyden's Wood Kent
26 D2 Jubilee Corner Kent
91 K10 Jump Barns
25 L4 Jumper's Town E Susx
112 D9 Juniper Nthumb
127 M4 Juniper Green C Edin
131 L2 Jura Ag & B
80 e2 Jurby IoM
8 G8 Jurston Devon

K

102 E8 Kaber Cumb
126 H8 Kaimend S Lans
124 B3 Kames Ag & B
115 N2 Kames E Ayrs
3 L5 Kea Cnwll
92 D8 Keadby N Linc
87 L8 Keal Cotes Lincs
97 M11 Kearby Town End N York
82 G4 Kearsley Bolton
112 F5 Kearsley Nthumb
27 N3 Kearsney Kent
95 N5 Kearstwick Cumb
103 J11 Kearton N York
95 Q7 Keasden N York
6 G8 Keaton Devon
82 C8 Keckwick Halton
87 K3 Keddington Lincs
87 L3 Keddington Corner Lincs
63 M11 Kedington Suffk
71 Q6 Kedleston Derbys
93 L8 Keelby Lincs
70 E5 Keele Staffs
70 E6 Keele Services Staffs
70 E5 Keele University Staffs
61 M11 Keeley Green Bed
90 D4 Keelham C Brad
40 H7 Keeston Pembks
20 H3 Keevil Wilts
72 D5 Kegworth Leics
2 G5 Kehelland Cnwll
150 G4 Keig Abers
90 D2 Keighley C Brad
90 C3 Keighley Crematorium C Brad
133 P9 Keilarsbrae Clacks
134 B2 Keillour P & K
149 M9 Keiloch Abers
122 H6 Keils Ag & B
19 P8 Keinton Mandeville Somset
109 J2 Keir Mill D & G
111 Q10 Keirsleywell Row Nthumb
73 Q5 Keisby Lincs
102 D6 Keisley Cumb
167 P4 Keiss Highld
158 B7 Keith Moray
142 C10 Keithick P & K
143 L5 Keithock Angus
155 P6 Keithtown Highld
89 Q2 Kelbrook Lancs
73 Q2 Kelby Lincs
101 Q8 Keld Cumb
102 G10 Keld N York
98 F4 Keld Head N York
98 E3 Keldholme N York
92 D10 Kelfield N Linc
91 P3 Kelfield N York
85 N9 Kelham Notts
109 P7 Kelhead D & G
5 Q4 Kellacott Devon
88 E5 Kellamergh Lancs
142 H10 Kellas Angus
157 M7 Kellas Moray
7 L11 Kellaton Devon
102 C9 Kelleth Cumb
76 F3 Kelling Norfk
91 P6 Kellington N York
104 B3 Kelloe Dur
115 P5 Kelloholm D & G
100 C7 Kells Cumb
5 P5 Kelly Devon
5 P7 Kelly Bray Cnwll
60 F5 Kelmarsh Nhants
33 P5 Kelmscott Oxon
65 M8 Kelsale Suffk
81 Q11 Kelsall Ches W
50 H3 Kelshall Herts
110 C10 Kelsick Cumb
118 D4 Kelso Border
84 D8 Kelstedge Derbys
86 H3 Kelstern Lincs
81 K10 Kelsterton Flints
32 D11 Kelston BaNES
141 J8 Keltneyburn P & K
109 L6 Kelton D & G
134 E9 Kelty Fife
52 E8 Kelvedon Essex
51 N11 Kelvedon Hatch Essex
2 B8 Kelynack Cnwll
17 M2 Kemacott Devon
135 L5 Kemback Fife
57 N4 Kemberton Shrops
33 J5 Kemble Gloucs
33 J5 Kemble Wick Gloucs
47 J7 Kemerton Worcs
31 K4 Kemeys Commander Mons
151 J4 Kemnay Abers
26 H2 Kempe's Corner Kent
46 C9 Kempley Gloucs
46 C9 Kempley Green Gloucs
46 G5 Kempsey Worcs
33 N5 Kempsford Gloucs
58 H10 Kemps Green Warwks
22 H4 Kempshott Hants
61 M11 Kempston Bed
50 B2 Kempston Hardwick Bed
56 F8 Kempton Shrops
24 H10 Kemp Town Br & H
37 N9 Kemsing Kent
38 F8 Kemsley Kent
38 D9 Kemsley Street Kent
26 G5 Kenardington Kent
45 N6 Kenchester Herefs
33 Q4 Kencot Oxon
95 L2 Kendal Cumb
45 N9 Kenderchurch Herefs
32 C9 Kendleshire S Glos
29 M8 Kenfig Brdgnd
29 M8 Kenfig Hill Brdgnd
59 L10 Kenilworth Warwks
36 H8 Kenley Gt Lon
57 K4 Kenley Shrops
153 P6 Kenmore Highld
141 J8 Kenmore P & K
9 M7 Kenn Devon
31 M11 Kenn N Som
123 P7 Kennacraig Ag & B
5 M5 Kennards House Cnwll
2 F8 Kenneggy Cnwll
9 K3 Kennerleigh Devon
81 M4 Kennessee Green Sefton
133 Q9 Kennet Clacks
150 E2 Kennethmont Abers
63 L7 Kennett Cambs
9 M7 Kennford Devon
64 E4 Kenninghall Norfk
26 H2 Kennington Kent
34 F4 Kennington Oxon
135 K7 Kennoway Fife
19 K11 Kenny Somset
63 L5 Kennyhill Suffk
98 F7 Kennythorpe N York
136 B6 Kenovay Ag & B
152 G7 Kensaleyre Highld
36 G5 Kensington Gt Lon
50 B7 Kensworth Common C Beds
139 J6 Kentallen Highld
25 N3 Kent and Sussex Crematorium Kent
45 N9 Kentchurch Herefs
63 M7 Kentford Suffk
70 E3 Kent Green Ches E
39 P8 Kent International Airport Kent
9 Q3 Kentisbeare Devon
17 L3 Kentisbury Devon
17 L3 Kentisbury Ford Devon
36 G4 Kentish Town Gt Lon
101 N10 Kentmere Cumb
9 N8 Kenton Devon
36 E3 Kenton Gt Lon
113 K7 Kenton N u Ty
64 H8 Kenton Suffk
113 K7 Kenton Bankfoot N u Ty
138 B4 Kentra Highld
94 H5 Kents Bank Cumb
46 D10 Kent's Green Gloucs
22 B10 Kent's Oak Hants
26 C8 Kent Street E Susx
37 Q10 Kent Street Kent
69 M8 Kenwick Shrops
3 L4 Kenwyn Cnwll
82 D5 Kenyon Warrtn
165 J3 Keoldale Highld
145 Q3 Keppoch Highld
97 Q2 Kepwick N York
59 M8 Keresley Covtry
82 H11 Kermincham Ches E
7 K10 Kernborough Devon
46 A11 Kerne Bridge Herefs
130 G2 Kerrera Ag & B
83 K9 Kerridge Ches E
83 K9 Kerridge-end Ches E
2 C8 Kerris Cnwll
55 Q6 Kerry Powys
124 E5 Kerrycroy Ag & B
85 M8 Kersall Notts
9 Q8 Kersbrook Devon
17 L6 Kerscott Devon
52 H3 Kersey Suffk
52 G3 Kersey Tye Suffk
52 G3 Kersey Upland Suffk
168 i5 Kershader W Isls
111 J4 Kershopefoot Cumb
47 J6 Kersoe Worcs
10 B3 Kerswell Devon
46 G5 Kerswell Green Worcs
2 F7 Kerthen Wood Cnwll
53 M2 Kesgrave Suffk
65 Q4 Kessingland Suffk
65 Q4 Kessingland Beach Suffk
3 P4 Kestle Cnwll
4 C10 Kestle Mill Cnwll
37 K8 Keston Gt Lon
101 J6 Keswick Cumb
77 J11 Keswick Norfk
87 L5 Ketsby Lincs
61 J5 Kettering Nhants
61 J5 Kettering Crematorium Nhants
76 H11 Ketteringham Norfk
142 C10 Kettins P & K
64 D11 Kettlebaston Suffk
135 J6 Kettlebridge Fife
59 K4 Kettlebrook Staffs
65 K9 Kettleburgh Suffk
51 K7 Kettle Green Herts
109 P5 Kettleholm D & G
105 M7 Kettleness N York
83 L9 Kettleshulme Ches E
97 K9 Kettlesing N York
97 K9 Kettlesing Bottom N York
76 D5 Kettlestone Norfk
85 P5 Kettlethorpe Lincs
169 f3 Kettletoft Ork
96 E6 Kettlewell N York
73 P10 Ketton Rutlnd
36 E5 Kew Gt Lon
19 K2 Kewstoke N Som
91 J9 Kexbrough Barns
98 E10 Kexby C York
85 Q3 Kexby Lincs
70 F2 Key Green Ches E
105 M10 Key Green N York
72 H9 Keyham Leics
13 P6 Keyhaven Hants
93 M5 Keyingham E R Yk
24 H7 Keymer W Susx
32 C11 Keynsham BaNES
61 N8 Keysoe Bed
61 N8 Keysoe Row Bed
61 M5 Keyston Cambs
38 E9 Key Street Kent
72 G4 Keyworth Notts
18 H10 Kibbear Somset
113 K9 Kibblesworth Gatesd
60 E2 Kibworth Beauchamp Leics
60 E2 Kibworth Harcourt Leics
37 K6 Kidbrooke Gt Lon
100 E6 Kidburngill Cumb
58 C3 Kiddemore Green Staffs
58 B9 Kidderminster Worcs
48 D10 Kiddington Oxon
76 G11 Kidd's Moor Norfk
34 E2 Kidlington Oxon
35 J9 Kidmore End Oxon
107 M10 Kidsdale D & G
70 E4 Kidsgrove Staffs
96 E4 Kidstones N York
28 D3 Kidwelly Carmth
138 G10 Kiel Crofts Ag & B
111 M2 Kielder Nthumb
122 F6 Kiells Ag & B
125 L5 Kilbarchan Rens
145 L6 Kilbeg Highld
123 M7 Kilberry Ag & B
125 J7 Kilbirnie N Ayrs
123 M4 Kilbride Ag & B
124 C4 Kilbride Ag & B
157 K5 Kilbuiack Moray
84 E11 Kilburn Derbys
36 F4 Kilburn Gt Lon
97 R5 Kilburn N York
72 G11 Kilby Leics
123 P7 Kilchamaig Ag & B
124 E7 Kilchattan Ag & B
136 b2 Kilchattan Ag & B
138 E10 Kilcheran Ag & B
137 M3 Kilchoan Highld
122 B7 Kilchoman Ag & B
131 L3 Kilchrenan Ag & B
135 M7 Kilconquhar Fife
46 C9 Kilcot Gloucs
155 Q7 Kilcoy Highld
131 Q11 Kilcreggan Ag & B
104 H9 Kildale N York
120 E8 Kildalloig Ag & B
156 D3 Kildary Highld
124 B4 Kildavaig Ag & B
124 C4 Kildavanan Ag & B
163 L2 Kildonan Highld
121 K7 Kildonan N Ayrs
163 L2 Kildonan Lodge Highld
144 G10 Kildonnan Highld
106 E6 Kildrochet House D & G
150 D4 Kildrummy Abers
96 F11 Kildwick N York
124 A2 Kilfinan Ag & B
146 H8 Kilfinnan Highld
80 F11 Kilford Denbgs
41 M9 Kilgetty Pembks
114 E7 Kilgrammie S Ayrs
31 N5 Kilgwrrwg Common Mons
99 M8 Kilham E R Yk
118 G4 Kilham Nthumb
136 A7 Kilkenneth Ag & B
120 C7 Kilkenzie Ag & B
120 D8 Kilkerran Ag & B
16 D9 Kilkhampton Cnwll
84 G4 Killamarsh Derbys
28 H6 Killay Swans
132 G10 Killearn Stirlg
156 B6 Killen Highld
103 N7 Killerby Darltn
9 N4 Killerton Devon
140 D6 Killichonan P & K
146 G11 Killiechonate Highld
137 N7 Killiechronan Ag & B
141 M5 Killiecrankie P & K
154 B11 Killilan Highld
167 P5 Killimster Highld
140 E11 Killin Stirlg
97 L9 Killinghall N York
95 N3 Killington Cumb
17 M2 Killington Devon
95 M2 Killington Lake Services Cumb
113 L6 Killingworth N Tyne
3 L5 Killiow Cnwll
128 D10 Killochyett Border
125 K3 Kilmacolm Inver
133 J6 Kilmahog Stirlg
130 F9 Kilmahumaig Ag & B
152 G3 Kilmaluag Highld
135 K3 Kilmany Fife
125 L10 Kilmarnock E Ayrs
130 G8 Kilmartin Ag & B
125 L9 Kilmaurs E Ayrs
130 H5 Kilmelford Ag & B
20 C4 Kilmersdon Somset
22 G9 Kilmeston Hants
120 C7 Kilmichael Ag & B
130 H9 Kilmichael Glassary Ag & B
130 F10 Kilmichael of Inverlussa Ag & B
10 F5 Kilmington Devon
20 E7 Kilmington Wilts
20 E7 Kilmington Common Wilts
20 E7 Kilmington Street Wilts
155 N9 Kilmorack Highld
130 H2 Kilmore Ag & B
145 L6 Kilmore Highld
123 M5 Kilmory Ag & B
137 N1 Kilmory Highld
121 J7 Kilmory N Ayrs
152 D8 Kilmuir Highld
152 F3 Kilmuir Highld
156 B8 Kilmuir Highld
156 D3 Kilmuir Highld
131 P11 Kilmun Ag & B
122 C5 Kilnave Ag & B
126 F8 Kilncadzow S Lans
26 B4 Kilndown Kent
35 M9 Kiln Green Wokham
100 H4 Kilnhill Cumb
82 D11 Kilnhouses Ches W
91 M11 Kilnhurst Rothm
130 G3 Kilninver Ag & B
112 F9 Kiln Pit Hill Nthumb
93 R7 Kilnsea E R Yk
96 E7 Kilnsey N York
99 K11 Kilnwick E R Yk
98 G11 Kilnwick Percy E R Yk
136 b2 Kiloran Ag & B
120 H6 Kilpatrick N Ayrs
45 N8 Kilpeck Herefs
92 C5 Kilpin E R Yk
92 C5 Kilpin Pike E R Yk
135 P7 Kilrenny Fife
60 C6 Kilsby Nhants
134 G2 Kilspindie P & K
106 F10 Kilstay D & G
126 C2 Kilsyth N Lans
155 P9 Kiltarlity Highld
105 K7 Kilton R & Cl
105 J7 Kilton Thorpe R & Cl
152 F4 Kilvaxter Highld
18 F6 Kilve Somset
73 L2 Kilvington Notts
125 J9 Kilwinning N Ayrs
76 F11 Kimberley Norfk
72 D2 Kimberley Notts
84 F2 Kimberworth Rothm
113 L11 Kimblesworth Dur
35 M3 Kimble Wick Bucks
61 P7 Kimbolton Cambs
45 Q2 Kimbolton Herefs
60 C3 Kimcote Leics
12 F9 Kimmeridge Dorset
119 J3 Kimmerston Nthumb
21 Q5 Kimpton Hants
50 E7 Kimpton Herts
16 E9 Kimworthy Devon
166 E10 Kinbrace Highld
133 M6 Kinbuck Stirlg
135 M4 Kincaple Fife
133 Q10 Kincardine Fife
162 E9 Kincardine Highld
150 F8 Kincardine O'Neil Abers
142 B10 Kinclaven P & K
151 N7 Kincorth C Aber
157 J5 Kincorth House Moray
148 E6 Kincraig Highld
141 N8 Kincraigie P & K
141 N8 Kindallachan P & K
123 L9 Kinerarach Ag & B
47 L9 Kineton Gloucs
48 B4 Kineton Warwks
134 F3 Kinfauns P & K
124 D6 Kingarth Ag & B
54 H3 King Arthur's Labyrinth Gwynd
151 M8 Kingcausie Abers
31 M3 Kingcoed Mons
86 E2 Kingerby Lincs
16 D10 Kingford Devon
47 Q10 Kingham Oxon
109 L6 Kingholm Quay D & G
134 H10 Kinghorn Fife
134 G8 Kinglassie Fife
142 E6 Kingoldrum Angus
135 J2 Kingoodie P & K
45 P6 King's Acre Herefs
6 C8 Kingsand Cnwll
35 N3 Kingsash Bucks
135 P5 Kingsbarns Fife
7 J10 Kingsbridge Devon
18 C7 Kingsbridge Somset
28 G5 Kings Bridge Swans
71 L11 King's Bromley Staffs
152 F6 Kingsburgh Highld
36 E3 Kingsbury Gt Lon
59 K5 Kingsbury Warwks
19 M10 Kingsbury Episcopi Somset
45 R9 King's Caple Herefs
22 F3 Kingsclere Hants
73 Q11 King's Cliffe Nhants
32 F5 Kingscote Gloucs
17 J8 Kingscott Devon
47 L3 King's Coughton Warwks
121 K6 Kingscross N Ayrs
19 P9 Kingsdon Somset
27 Q2 Kingsdown Kent
33 N7 Kingsdown Swindn
32 F11 Kingsdown Wilts
33 N7 Kingsdown Crematorium Swindn
134 F9 Kingseat Fife
35 K3 Kingsey Bucks
24 E3 Kingsfold W Susx
151 M6 Kingsford C Aber
125 L8 Kingsford E Ayrs
57 Q8 Kingsford Worcs
39 Q7 Kingsgate Kent
46 E8 Kings Green Gloucs
64 C9 Kingshall Street Suffk
17 K4 Kingsheanton Devon
58 G8 King's Heath Birm
37 Q9 Kings Hill Kent
58 E5 King's Hill Wsall
139 P7 Kings House Hotel Highld
132 H3 Kingshouse Hotel Stirlg
59 J7 Kingshurst Solhll
110 C10 Kingside Hill Cumb
7 M5 Kingskerswell Devon
135 J6 Kingskettle Fife
11 K5 Kingsland Dorset
45 N2 Kingsland Herefs
78 D8 Kingsland IoA
50 C10 Kings Langley Herts
82 C10 Kingsley Ches W
23 L7 Kingsley Hants
71 J5 Kingsley Staffs
23 N8 Kingsley Green W Susx
60 G8 Kingsley Park Nhants
57 P5 Kingslow Shrops
75 M6 King's Lynn Norfk
102 B6 Kings Meaburn Cumb
14 G4 Kingsmead Hants
10 b2 King's Mills Guern
81 Q4 King's Moss St Hel
142 H8 Kingsmuir Angus
117 K3 Kings Muir Border
135 N6 Kingsmuir Fife
59 Q9 Kings Newnham Warwks
72 B5 King's Newton Derbys
26 H4 Kingsnorth Kent
58 G9 King's Norton Birm
72 H10 King's Norton Leics
17 M8 Kings Nympton Devon
45 N4 King's Pyon Herefs
62 C5 Kings Ripton Cambs
22 C8 King's Somborne Hants
11 Q2 King's Stag Dorset
32 F4 King's Stanley Gloucs
48 E7 King's Sutton Nhants
58 G6 Kingstanding Birm
7 M4 Kingsteignton Devon
83 N10 King Sterndale Derbys
45 P8 Kingsthorne Herefs
60 G8 Kingsthorpe Nhants
62 D9 Kingston Cambs
5 P6 Kingston Cnwll
6 G9 Kingston Devon
9 Q7 Kingston Devon
12 C3 Kingston Dorset
12 G9 Kingston Dorset
128 E3 Kingston E Loth
13 K4 Kingston Hants
14 E10 Kingston IoW
39 L11 Kingston Kent
24 C10 Kingston W Susx
34 D5 Kingston Bagpuize Oxon
35 K5 Kingston Blount Oxon
20 F7 Kingston Deverill Wilts
45 N7 Kingstone Herefs
10 H2 Kingstone Somset
71 K9 Kingstone Staffs
33 Q7 Kingstone Winslow Oxon
34 B7 Kingston Lisle Oxon
25 J9 Kingston near Lewes E Susx
72 E5 Kingston on Soar Notts
157 Q4 Kingston on Spey Moray
11 M6 Kingston Russell Dorset
18 H9 Kingston St Mary Somset
31 M11 Kingston Seymour N Som
35 K4 Kingston Stert Oxon
93 J5 Kingston upon Hull C KuH
36 E7 Kingston upon Thames Gt Lon
36 E7 Kingston upon Thames Crematorium Gt Lon
110 G9 Kingstown Cumb
50 E6 King's Walden Herts
7 M8 Kingswear Devon
151 M6 Kingswells C Aber
31 P9 Kings Weston Bristl
58 C7 Kingswinford Dudley
49 J11 Kingswood Bucks
32 D6 Kingswood Gloucs
38 D11 Kingswood Kent
56 C4 Kingswood Powys
32 B10 Kingswood S Glos
18 F7 Kingswood Somset
36 F9 Kingswood Surrey
59 J10 Kingswood Warwks
59 J10 Kingswood Brook Warwks
45 K4 Kingswood Common Herefs
58 B4 Kingswood Common Staffs
22 E8 Kings Worthy Hants
86 F5 Kingthorpe Lincs
45 K3 Kington Herefs
32 B6 Kington S Glos
47 J3 Kington Worcs
32 H9 Kington Langley Wilts
20 E10 Kington Magna Dorset
32 H9 Kington St Michael Wilts
148 D7 Kingussie Highld
19 P8 Kingweston Somset
159 M11 Kinharrachie Abers
109 K7 Kinharvie D & G
133 Q4 Kinkell Bridge P & K
159 P9 Kinknockie Abers
127 M4 Kinleith C Edin
57 N8 Kinlet Shrops
144 F8 Kinloch Highld
164 H10 Kinloch Highld
165 N6 Kinloch Highld
142 A9 Kinloch P & K
132 F7 Kinlochard Stirlg
164 F5 Kinlochbervie Highld
138 H2 Kinlocheil Highld
154 D5 Kinlochewe Highld
146 B6 Kinloch Hourn Highld
147 N10 Kinlochlaggan Highld
139 M5 Kinlochleven Highld
138 C3 Kinlochmoidart Highld
145 M11 Kinlochnanuagh Highld
140 G6 Kinloch Rannoch P & K
157 K5 Kinloss Moray
80 D8 Kinmel Bay Conwy
151 L4 Kinmuck Abers
151 M4 Kinmundy Abers
122 C11 Kinnabus Ag & B
159 N9 Kinnadie Abers
141 N6 Kinnaird P & K

143 Q2 Kinneff Abers
116 E10 Kinnelhead D & G
143 L7 Kinnell Angus
69 K10 Kinnerley Shrops
45 L5 Kinnersley Herefs
46 G6 Kinnersley Worcs
45 J2 Kinnerton Powys
56 F5 Kinnerton Shrops
69 K2 Kinnerton Green Flints
134 F7 Kinnesswood P & K
103 L6 Kinninvie Dur
142 F6 Kinnordy Angus
72 H4 Kinoulton Notts
134 E7 Kinross P & K
142 B11 Kinrossie P & K
134 E7 Kinross Services P & K
50 D7 Kinsbourne Green Herts
70 B6 Kinsey Heath Ches E
56 F11 Kinsham Herefs
46 H7 Kinsham Worcs
91 L8 Kinsley Wakefd
13 J5 Kinson Bmouth
146 B4 Kintail Highld
34 C11 Kintbury W Berk
157 J5 Kintessack Moray
134 E4 Kintillo P & K
56 G10 Kinton Herefs
69 L11 Kinton Shrops
151 K4 Kintore Abers
122 G9 Kintour Ag & B
122 D10 Kintra Ag & B
137 J10 Kintra Ag & B
130 G7 Kintraw Ag & B
120 D4 Kintyre Ag & B
148 G4 Kinveachy Highld
58 B8 Kinver Staffs
103 Q11 Kiplin N York
91 L4 Kippax Leeds
133 J9 Kippen Stirlg
108 H10 Kippford or Scaur D & G
25 P2 Kipping's Cross Kent
169 c6 Kirbister Ork
77 K10 Kirby Bedon Norfk
73 J7 Kirby Bellars Leics
65 M3 Kirby Cane Norfk
59 L9 Kirby Corner Covtry
53 M7 Kirby Cross Essex
72 E10 Kirby Fields Leics
99 J7 Kirby Grindalythe N York
97 N7 Kirby Hill N York
103 M9 Kirby Hill N York
97 Q3 Kirby Knowle N York
53 M7 Kirby le Soken Essex
98 F5 Kirby Misperton N York
72 E10 Kirby Muxloe Leics
97 P2 Kirby Sigston N York
98 G9 Kirby Underdale E R Yk
97 N4 Kirby Wiske N York
24 B5 Kirdford W Susx
167 N5 Kirk Highld
169 r10 Kirkabister Shet
108 D11 Kirkandrews D & G
110 G9 Kirkandrews upon Eden Cumb
110 F9 Kirkbampton Cumb
109 L9 Kirkbean D & G
91 Q8 Kirk Bramwith Donc
110 D9 Kirkbride Cumb
97 L2 Kirkbridge N York
143 J9 Kirkbuddo Angus
117 K3 Kirkburn Border
99 K9 Kirkburn E R Yk
90 F8 Kirkburton Kirk
81 N5 Kirkby Knows
86 E2 Kirkby Lincs
104 F9 Kirkby N York
97 L2 Kirkby Fleetham N York
86 E9 Kirkby Green Lincs
84 G9 Kirkby in Ashfield Notts
94 E4 Kirkby-in-Furness Cumb
86 E11 Kirkby la Thorpe Lincs
95 N5 Kirkby Lonsdale Cumb
96 C8 Kirkby Malham N York
72 D10 Kirkby Mallory Leics
97 K6 Kirkby Malzeard N York
98 E3 Kirkby Mills N York
98 D3 Kirkbymoorside N York
86 H8 Kirkby on Bain Lincs
97 M11 Kirkby Overblow N York
102 E9 Kirkby Stephen Cumb
102 B5 Kirkby Thore Cumb
73 R5 Kirkby Underwood Lincs
91 N2 Kirkby Wharf N York
84 G10 Kirkby Woodhouse Notts
134 H9 Kirkcaldy Fife
134 H9 Kirkcaldy Crematorium Fife
111 K7 Kirkcambeck Cumb
108 E10 Kirkchrist D & G
106 D4 Kirkcolm D & G
115 P5 Kirkconnel D & G
109 L7 Kirkconnell D & G
107 K5 Kirkcowan D & G
108 E10 Kirkcudbright D & G
81 L6 Kirkdale Lpool
97 N10 Kirk Deighton N York
92 H5 Kirk Ella E R Yk
116 B2 Kirkfieldbank S Lans
109 J7 Kirkgunzeon D & G
72 D2 Kirk Hallam Derbys
88 E4 Kirkham Lancs
98 E7 Kirkham N York
90 H6 Kirkhamgate Wakefd
97 Q9 Kirk Hammerton N York
112 F4 Kirkharle Nthumb
111 N11 Kirkhaugh Nthumb
90 F7 Kirkheaton Kirk
112 F5 Kirkheaton Nthumb
155 Q8 Kirkhill Highld
116 D9 Kirkhope S Lans
111 L9 Kirkhouse Cumb
91 Q8 Kirkhouse Green Donc
145 J4 Kirkibost Highld
142 E9 Kirkinch P & K
107 M7 Kirkinner D & G
126 B3 Kirkintilloch E Duns
71 P4 Kirk Ireton Derbys
100 E7 Kirkland Cumb
102 B4 Kirkland Cumb
109 M3 Kirkland D & G
115 P5 Kirkland D & G
115 R9 Kirkland D & G
100 G2 Kirkland Guards Cumb
71 P7 Kirk Langley Derbys
104 G6 Kirkleatham R & Cl
104 D9 Kirklevington S on T
65 Q3 Kirkley Suffk
97 M4 Kirklington N York
85 L9 Kirklington Notts
110 H7 Kirklinton Cumb
127 L3 Kirkliston C Edin
107 N6 Kirkmabreck D & G
106 F10 Kirkmaiden D & G
103 Q4 Kirk Merrington Dur
80 d3 Kirk Michael IoM
141 Q6 Kirkmichael P & K
114 F6 Kirkmichael S Ayrs
126 D9 Kirkmuirhill S Lans
118 H4 Kirknewton Nthumb
127 L4 Kirknewton W Loth
158 D11 Kirkney Abers
126 E5 Kirk of Shotts N Lans
101 Q2 Kirkoswald Cumb
114 D6 Kirkoswald S Ayrs
109 K2 Kirkpatrick D & G
108 G6 Kirkpatrick Durham D & G
110 E6 Kirkpatrick-Fleming D & G
91 Q9 Kirk Sandall Donc
94 C4 Kirksanton Cumb
91 N7 Kirk Smeaton N York
90 H3 Kirkstall Leeds
86 G8 Kirkstead Lincs
158 D10 Kirkstile Abers
110 G2 Kirkstile D & G
101 M9 Kirkstone Pass Inn Cumb
167 P2 Kirkstyle Highld
91 K6 Kirkthorpe Wakefd
150 G2 Kirkton Abers
109 L4 Kirkton D & G
135 K2 Kirkton Fife
145 P2 Kirkton Highld
154 B9 Kirkton Highld
134 B4 Kirkton P & K
117 J3 Kirkton Manor Border
142 E7 Kirkton of Airlie Angus
142 E10 Kirkton of Auchterhouse Angus
156 E8 Kirkton of Barevan Highld
142 B11 Kirkton of Collace P & K
150 B4 Kirkton of Glenbuchat Abers
151 P2 Kirkton of Logie Buchan Abers
143 J5 Kirkton of Menmuir Angus
143 J10 Kirkton of Monikie Angus
158 G11 Kirkton of Rayne Abers
151 K6 Kirkton of Skene Abers
142 F10 Kirkton of Strathmartine Angus
142 G10 Kirkton of Tealing Angus
150 G5 Kirkton of Tough Abers
159 N4 Kirktown Abers
159 Q7 Kirktown Abers
158 G5 Kirktown of Alvah Abers
151 L2 Kirktown of Bourtie Abers
151 M10 Kirktown of Fetteresso Abers
157 Q10 Kirktown of Mortlach Moray
151 Q2 Kirktown of Slains Abers
116 G2 Kirkurd Border
169 d5 Kirkwall Ork
169 d6 Kirkwall Airport Ork
112 E4 Kirkwhelpington Nthumb
118 F5 Kirk Yetholm Border
93 K8 Kirmington N Linc
86 G2 Kirmond le Mire Lincs
124 F2 Kirn Ag & B
142 F7 Kirriemuir Angus
65 K2 Kirstead Green Norfk
110 D6 Kirtlebridge D & G
63 L9 Kirtling Cambs
63 L9 Kirtling Green Cambs
48 E11 Kirtlington Oxon
166 B4 Kirtomy Highld
74 F3 Kirton Lincs
85 L7 Kirton Notts
53 N3 Kirton Suffk
74 E2 Kirton End Lincs
125 K2 Kirtonhill W Duns
74 E2 Kirton Holme Lincs
92 F11 Kirton in Lindsey N Linc
107 M7 Kirwaugh D & G
153 Q10 Kishorn Highld
60 E9 Kislingbury Nhants
47 P8 Kitebrook Warwks
59 J11 Kite Green Warwks
59 Q11 Kites Hardwick Warwks
5 L2 Kitleigh Cnwll
88 G9 Kitt Green Wigan
18 E10 Kittisford Somset
28 G7 Kittle Swans
59 J7 Kitt's Green Birm
151 N6 Kittybrewster C Aber
23 J8 Kitwood Hants
45 P8 Kivernoll Herefs
84 G4 Kiveton Park Rothm
85 P4 Knaith Lincs
85 P3 Knaith Park Lincs
20 F10 Knap Corner Dorset
23 Q3 Knaphill Surrey
19 K9 Knapp Somset
22 D10 Knapp Hill Hants
85 M9 Knapthorpe Notts
98 B10 Knapton C York
98 H5 Knapton N York
77 L5 Knapton Norfk
45 N4 Knapton Green Herefs
62 D8 Knapwell Cambs
97 N9 Knaresborough N York
111 N10 Knarsdale Nthumb
159 L9 Knaven Abers
97 P3 Knayton N York
50 G6 Knebworth Herts
92 B5 Knedlington E R Yk
85 M8 Kneesall Notts
50 H2 Kneesworth Cambs
85 M11 Kneeton Notts
28 E7 Knelston Swans
70 G7 Knenhall Staffs
64 D5 Knettishall Suffk
17 M4 Knightacott Devon
48 D4 Knightcote Warwks
70 E9 Knightley Staffs
70 E10 Knightley Dale Staffs
72 G10 Knighton C Leic
6 E9 Knighton Devon
11 N2 Knighton Dorset
12 H5 Knighton Poole
56 D10 Knighton Powys
18 G6 Knighton Somset
70 C6 Knighton Staffs
70 D9 Knighton Staffs
33 Q10 Knighton Wilts
57 L11 Knighton on Teme Worcs
46 G9 Knightsbridge Gloucs
4 H5 Knightsmill Cnwll
46 D3 Knightwick Worcs
45 K2 Knill Herefs
73 L4 Knipton Leics
112 H11 Knitsley Dur
71 N4 Kniveton Derbys
102 C5 Knock Cumb
145 L6 Knock Highld
158 D7 Knock Moray
168 j4 Knock W Isls
167 K11 Knockally Highld
161 L4 Knockan Highld
157 M9 Knockando Moray
155 Q9 Knockbain Highld
156 A6 Knockbain Highld
124 F5 Knock Castle N Ayrs
167 L4 Knockdee Highld
124 E3 Knockdow Ag & B
32 F7 Knockdown Wilts
114 F8 Knockeen S Ayrs
121 K6 Knockenkelly N Ayrs
125 L10 Knockentiber E Ayrs
37 N6 Knockhall Kent
37 L9 Knockholt Kent
37 L9 Knockholt Pound Kent
69 K10 Knockin Shrops
125 L10 Knockinlaw E Ayrs
37 N8 Knockmill Kent
106 C5 Knocknain D & G
123 J5 Knockrome Ag & B
80 c4 Knocksharry IoM
108 C4 Knocksheen D & G
108 G6 Knockvennie Smithy D & G
65 N9 Knodishall Suffk
65 N9 Knodishall Common Suffk
19 N9 Knole Somset
31 Q8 Knole Park S Glos
82 H9 Knolls Green Ches E
69 L7 Knolton Wrexhm
20 H6 Knook Wilts
73 L9 Knossington Leics
94 H11 Knott End-on-Sea Lancs
61 M8 Knotting Bed
61 M8 Knotting Green Bed
91 N6 Knottingley Wakefd
81 N6 Knotty Ash Lpool
35 P6 Knotty Green Bucks
57 K9 Knowbury Shrops
107 K3 Knowe D & G
115 M9 Knowehead D & G
114 E5 Knoweside S Ayrs
32 B10 Knowle Bristl
9 J4 Knowle Devon
9 P3 Knowle Devon
9 Q8 Knowle Devon
16 H4 Knowle Devon
57 K10 Knowle Shrops
59 J9 Knowle Solhll
18 C6 Knowle Somset
9 P5 Knowle Cross Devon
110 H9 Knowlefield Cumb
89 J3 Knowle Green Lancs
35 Q11 Knowle Hill Surrey
10 G2 Knowle St Giles Somset
14 G5 Knowle Village Hants
89 Q6 Knowle Wood Calder
52 C3 Knowl Green Essex
35 M9 Knowl Hill W & M
12 H3 Knowlton Dorset
39 N11 Knowlton Kent
81 N5 Knowsley Knows
81 P6 Knowsley Safari Park Knows
17 Q7 Knowstone Devon
97 L9 Knox N York
26 C3 Knox Bridge Kent
56 D10 Knucklas Powys
61 K7 Knuston Nhants
82 G9 Knutsford Ches E
82 F9 Knutsford Services Ches E
70 E5 Knutton Staffs
90 D7 Krumlin Calder
3 J10 Kuggar Cnwll
145 N2 Kyleakin Highld
145 N2 Kyle of Lochalsh Highld
145 N3 Kylerhea Highld
164 F10 Kylesku Highld
145 P9 Kylesmorar Highld
168 h8 Kyles Scalpay W Isls
164 F10 Kylestrome Highld
46 B7 Kynaston Herefs
69 L10 Kynaston Shrops
70 B11 Kynnersley Wrekin
46 B2 Kyre Green Worcs
46 B2 Kyre Park Worcs
57 K11 Kyrewood Worcs
18 E10 Kyrle Somset

L

10 b2 La Bellieuse Guern
168 i5 Lacasaigh W Isls
168 j4 Lacasdal W Isls
93 M9 Laceby NE Lin
35 M4 Lacey Green Bucks
82 F10 Lach Dennis Ches W
104 G7 Lackenby R & Cl
63 N6 Lackford Suffk
63 N6 Lackford Green Suffk
32 H11 Lacock Wilts
48 D3 Ladbroke Warwks
70 H4 Ladderedge Staffs
37 Q11 Laddingford Kent
87 L10 Lade Bank Lincs
3 M3 Ladock Cnwll
169 f2 Lady Ork
135 J6 Ladybank Fife
5 N4 Ladycross Cnwll
116 C5 Ladygill S Lans
94 D3 Lady Hall Cumb
129 M10 Ladykirk Border
46 A8 Ladyridge Herefs
63 N9 Lady's Green Suffk
58 G7 Ladywood Birm
46 G2 Ladywood Worcs
10 c1 La Fontenelle Guern
10 b2 La Fosse Guern
109 J3 Lag D & G
138 A5 Laga Highld
122 F10 Lagavulin Ag & B
121 J7 Lagg N Ayrs
146 H8 Laggan Highld
147 Q9 Laggan Highld
148 F7 Lagganlia Highld
10 c1 La Greve Guern
11 a1 La Greve de Lecq Jersey
11 c2 La Hougue Bie Jersey
10 b2 La Houguette Guern
165 K5 Laid Highld
160 E8 Laide Highld
144 G10 Laig Highld
125 M8 Laigh Clunch E Ayrs
125 M9 Laigh Fenwick E Ayrs
115 M3 Laigh Glenmuir E Ayrs
126 C7 Laighstonehall S Lans
37 Q3 Laindon Essex
162 D5 Lairg Highld
90 F4 Laisterdyke C Brad
101 N4 Laithes Cumb
8 D7 Lake Devon
17 K5 Lake Devon
14 G10 Lake IoW
12 G6 Lake Poole
21 M7 Lake Wilts
100 H9 Lake District National Park Cumb
63 M4 Lakenheath Suffk
24 B3 Laker's Green Surrey
75 K11 Lakesend Norfk
94 H3 Lakeside Cumb
36 C7 Laleham Surrey
29 N9 Laleston Brdgnd
3 K7 Lamanva Cnwll
52 E4 Lamarsh Essex
77 J7 Lamas Norfk
118 D2 Lambden Border
25 Q3 Lamberhurst Kent
25 Q3 Lamberhurst Down Kent
129 P8 Lamberton Border
36 H5 Lambeth Gt Lon
36 G6 Lambeth Crematorium Gt Lon
63 M10 Lambfair Green Suffk
85 K11 Lambley Notts
111 N9 Lambley Nthumb
34 B9 Lambourn W Berk
37 L2 Lambourne End Essex
34 B9 Lambourn Woodlands W Berk
89 L3 Lamb Roe Lancs
24 F3 Lambs Green W Susx
40 H7 Lambston Pembks
5 L9 Lamellion Cnwll
8 C9 Lamerton Devon
113 L9 Lamesley Gatesd
116 D4 Lamington S Lans
121 K5 Lamlash N Ayrs
101 M3 Lamonby Cumb
4 G9 Lamorick Cnwll
2 C9 Lamorna Cnwll
3 M5 Lamorran Cnwll
5 K8 Lampen Cnwll
43 L5 Lampeter Cerdgn
41 N8 Lampeter Velfrey Pembks
41 K10 Lamphey Pembks
100 E6 Lamplugh Cumb
60 G6 Lamport Nhants
20 C7 Lamyatt Somset
5 N2 Lana Devon
16 E10 Lana Devon
116 B2 Lanark S Lans
95 K8 Lancaster Lancs
95 K8 Lancaster & Morecambe Crematorium Lancs
95 L10 Lancaster Services (Forton) Lancs
31 P5 Lancaut Gloucs
113 J11 Lanchester Dur
24 E10 Lancing W Susx
10 c1 L'Ancresse Guern
62 G7 Landbeach Cambs
16 H7 Landcross Devon
151 J7 Landerberry Abers
21 Q11 Landford Wilts
167 L10 Land-hallow Highld
81 K7 Landican Crematorium Wirral
28 E6 Landimore Swans
17 K5 Landkey Devon
29 J5 Landore Swans
5 P9 Landrake Cnwll
7 K5 Landscove Devon
2 A8 Land's End Cnwll
2 A8 Land's End Cnwll
2 B8 Land's End Airport Cnwll
41 K8 Landshipping Pembks
5 P6 Landue Cnwll
6 C6 Landulph Cnwll
63 K7 Landwade Suffk
4 C9 Lane Cnwll
5 L5 Laneast Cnwll
89 P3 Lane Bottom Lancs
35 M6 Lane End Bucks
4 G8 Lane End Cnwll
22 G9 Lane End Hants
37 N6 Lane End Kent
96 C11 Lane End Lancs
82 E6 Lane End Warrtn
20 F5 Lane End Wilts
71 N8 Lane Ends Derbys
89 M4 Lane Ends Lancs
90 B2 Lane Ends N York
58 C4 Lane Green Staffs
85 P5 Laneham Notts
102 F2 Lanehead Dur
103 M8 Lane Head Dur
111 Q3 Lanehead Nthumb
82 D5 Lane Head Wigan
58 E4 Lane Head Wsall
88 E3 Lane Heads Lancs
89 Q2 Laneshaw Bridge Lancs
89 M6 Lane Side Lancs
5 Q2 Langaford Devon
19 J9 Langaller Somset
73 J4 Langar Notts
125 K3 Langbank Rens
96 G10 Langbar N York
104 G8 Langbaurgh N York
96 B8 Langcliffe N York
99 J2 Langdale End N York
5 N4 Langdon Cnwll
102 G4 Langdon Beck Dur
14 D5 Langdown Hants
135 J7 Langdyke Fife
52 H8 Langenhoe Essex
50 E2 Langford C Beds
9 P4 Langford Devon
52 D10 Langford Essex
19 N2 Langford N Som
85 P9 Langford Notts
33 P4 Langford Oxon
18 F10 Langford Budville Somset
20 E9 Langham Dorset
52 H5 Langham Essex
76 E3 Langham Norfk
73 L8 Langham Rutlnd
64 D8 Langham Suffk
89 L4 Langho Lancs
110 G4 Langholm D & G
28 H7 Langland Swans
117 Q3 Langlee Border
83 K10 Langley Ches E
84 F11 Langley Derbys
47 K9 Langley Gloucs
14 D6 Langley Hants
50 F6 Langley Herts
38 D11 Langley Kent
112 B8 Langley Nthumb
47 Q11 Langley Oxon
89 P9 Langley Rochdl
36 B5 Langley Slough
18 E9 Langley Somset
23 M9 Langley W Susx
47 N2 Langley Warwks
32 H9 Langley Burrell Wilts
50 C10 Langleybury Herts
112 B8 Langley Castle Nthumb
71 P7 Langley Common Derbys
71 P7 Langley Green Derbys
52 E7 Langley Green Essex
47 N2 Langley Green Warwks
51 K4 Langley Lower Green Essex
18 E9 Langley Marsh Somset
84 F11 Langley Mill Derbys
103 Q2 Langley Moor Dur
113 K11 Langley Park Dur
77 M11 Langley Street Norfk
51 K4 Langley Upper Green Essex
25 P10 Langney E Susx
85 J3 Langold Notts
5 M4 Langore Cnwll
19 M9 Langport Somset
87 J11 Langrick Lincs
32 D11 Langridge BaNES
17 K7 Langridgeford Devon
110 C11 Langrigg Cumb
23 K10 Langrish Hants
90 G10 Langsett Barns
133 M5 Langside P & K
15 K6 Langstone Hants
31 L7 Langstone Newpt
97 K2 Langthorne N York
97 N7 Langthorpe N York
103 K10 Langthwaite N York
99 L7 Langtoft E R Yk
74 B8 Langtoft Lincs
103 N7 Langton Dur
86 H7 Langton Lincs
87 L6 Langton Lincs
98 F7 Langton N York
86 F5 Langton by Wragby Lincs
25 M3 Langton Green Kent
64 G7 Langton Green Suffk
11 N8 Langton Herring Dorset
12 F3 Langton Long Blandford Dorset
12 H9 Langton Matravers Dorset
16 H8 Langtree Devon
16 H8 Langtree Week Devon
101 Q4 Langwathby Cumb
163 Q2 Langwell House Highld
84 H7 Langwith Derbys
84 H7 Langwith Junction Derbys
86 E5 Langworth Lincs
4 H9 Lanhydrock House & Gardens Cnwll
4 G9 Lanivet Cnwll
3 P3 Lanjeth Cnwll
4 H6 Lank Cnwll
4 H10 Lanlivery Cnwll
3 J6 Lanner Cnwll
5 M6 Lanoy Cnwll
5 K10 Lanreath Cnwll
5 K11 Lansallos Cnwll
4 H5 Lanteglos Cnwll
5 J11 Lanteglos Highway Cnwll
118 B6 Lanton Border
118 H4 Lanton Nthumb
10 b1 La Passee Guern
8 H3 Lapford Devon
122 E10 Laphroaig Ag & B
58 C2 Lapley Staffs
11 a2 La Pulente Jersey
59 J10 Lapworth Warwks
138 B8 Larachbeg Highld
133 P11 Larbert Falk
88 E2 Larbreck Lancs
158 F11 Largie Abers
131 J10 Largiemore Ag & B
135 M6 Largoward Fife
124 G6 Largs N Ayrs
121 K7 Largybeg N Ayrs
121 K7 Largymore N Ayrs
9 Q5 Larkbeare Devon
124 G2 Larkfield Inver
38 B10 Larkfield Kent
126 D7 Larkhall S Lans
21 M6 Larkhill Wilts
64 D4 Larling Norfk
11 c2 La Rocque Jersey
10 b1 La Rousaillerie Guern
103 K7 Lartington Dur
32 F6 Lasborough Gloucs
23 J6 Lasham Hants
8 B3 Lashbrook Devon
16 G10 Lashbrook Devon
26 D3 Lashenden Kent
70 G3 Lask Edge Staffs
127 Q4 Lasswade Mdloth
98 E2 Lastingham N York
19 M5 Latcham Somset
51 J6 Latchford Herts
35 J4 Latchford Oxon
52 E11 Latchingdon Essex
5 Q7 Latchley Cnwll
82 E5 Lately Common Warrtn
49 N6 Lathbury M Keyn
167 M10 Latheron Highld
167 L10 Latheronwheel Highld
135 M6 Lathones Fife
50 B11 Latimer Bucks
32 C8 Latteridge S Glos
20 C9 Lattiford Somset
33 L5 Latton Wilts
128 E10 Lauder Border

28 B2 **Laugharne** Carmth
85 P5 **Laughterton** Lincs
25 L8 **Laughton** E Susx
60 E3 **Laughton** Leics
74 A4 **Laughton** Lincs
92 D11 **Laughton** Lincs
84 H3 **Laughton-en-le-Morthen** Rothm
16 C10 **Launcells** Cnwll
16 D10 **Launcells Cross** Cnwll
5 N5 **Launceston** Cnwll
48 H10 **Launton** Oxon
143 N3 **Laurencekirk** Abers
108 E8 **Laurieston** D & G
126 G2 **Laurieston** Falk
49 P4 **Lavendon** M Keyn
52 F2 **Lavenham** Suffk
30 G11 **Lavernock** V Glam
111 J8 **Laversdale** Cumb
21 N8 **Laverstock** Wilts
22 E5 **Laverstoke** Hants
47 L7 **Laverton** Gloucs
97 K6 **Laverton** N York
20 E4 **Laverton** Somset
10 b2 **La Villette** Guern
69 L3 **Lavister** Wrexhm
126 E7 **Law** S Lans
140 G10 **Lawers** P & K
53 J5 **Lawford** Essex
18 F7 **Lawford** Somset
126 F7 **Law Hill** S Lans
5 P5 **Lawhitton** Cnwll
97 P5 **Lawkland** N York
96 A7 **Lawkland Green** N York
57 M3 **Lawley** Wrekin
70 E9 **Lawnhead** Staffs
90 H3 **Lawns Wood Crematorium** Leeds
41 K9 **Lawrenny** Pembks
64 B11 **Lawshall** Suffk
64 B11 **Lawshall Green** Suffk
45 N3 **Lawton** Herefs
168 i5 **Laxay** W Isls
168 j4 **Laxdale** W Isls
80 f5 **Laxey** IoM
65 K7 **Laxfield** Suffk
164 F7 **Laxford Bridge** Highld
169 r7 **Laxo** Shet
92 C5 **Laxton** E R Yk
73 P11 **Laxton** Nhants
85 M7 **Laxton** Notts
90 C2 **Laycock** C Brad
52 F8 **Layer Breton** Essex
52 G7 **Layer-de-la-Haye** Essex
52 F8 **Layer Marney** Essex
52 H3 **Layham** Suffk
34 C11 **Layland's Green** W Berk
10 H4 **Laymore** Dorset
35 Q6 **Layter's Green** Bucks
92 B3 **Laytham** E R Yk
110 D9 **Laythes** Cumb
104 G7 **Lazenby** R & Cl
101 P3 **Lazonby** Cumb
84 D9 **Lea** Derbys
46 C10 **Lea** Herefs
85 P3 **Lea** Lincs
56 F7 **Lea** Shrops
56 G3 **Lea** Shrops
33 J7 **Lea** Wilts
156 A9 **Leachkin** Highld
127 N6 **Leadburn** Border
86 B10 **Leadenham** Lincs
51 N8 **Leaden Roding** Essex
112 H10 **Leadgate** Dur
112 H9 **Leadgate** Nthumb
116 B7 **Leadhills** S Lans
38 E11 **Leadingcross Green** Kent
84 B4 **Leadmill** Derbys
48 B11 **Leafield** Oxon
50 C6 **Leagrave** Luton
70 B2 **Leahead** Ches W
71 J9 **Lea Heath** Staffs
97 P2 **Leake** N York
87 L10 **Leake Common Side** Lincs
105 L9 **Lealholm** N York
105 L9 **Lealholm Side** N York
153 J5 **Lealt** Highld
84 B5 **Leam** Derbys
59 K6 **Lea Marston** Warwks
59 P11 **Leamington Hastings** Warwks
59 M11 **Leamington Spa** Warwks
113 M11 **Leamside** Dur
25 N8 **Leap Cross** E Susx
95 K4 **Leasgill** Cumb
86 E11 **Leasingham** Lincs
103 Q4 **Leasingthorne** Dur
36 E9 **Leatherhead** Surrey
97 K11 **Leathley** N York
69 N11 **Leaton** Shrops
57 L2 **Leaton** Wrekin
88 F4 **Lea Town** Lancs
38 H11 **Leaveland** Kent
52 G4 **Leavenheath** Suffk
98 F8 **Leavening** N York
37 K8 **Leaves Green** Gt Lon
95 R3 **Lea Yeat** Cumb
99 M4 **Lebberston** N York
10 b2 **Le Bigard** Guern
10 b2 **Le Bourg** Guern
11 c2 **Le Bourg** Jersey
33 P5 **Lechlade on Thames** Gloucs
122 C6 **Lecht Gruinart** Ag & B
95 N5 **Leck** Lancs
140 H9 **Leckbuie** P & K
22 C7 **Leckford** Hants
49 K7 **Leckhampstead** Bucks
34 D9 **Leckhampstead** W Berk
34 D9 **Leckhampstead Thicket** W Berk
46 H11 **Leckhampton** Gloucs
161 K9 **Leckmelm** Highld
30 G10 **Leckwith** V Glam
92 H2 **Leconfield** E R Yk
138 G10 **Ledaig** Ag & B
49 P10 **Ledburn** Bucks
46 D7 **Ledbury** Herefs
46 C8 **Leddington** Gloucs
45 N4 **Ledgemoor** Herefs
45 N2 **Ledicot** Herefs
161 L4 **Ledmore Junction** Highld
81 M10 **Ledsham** Ches W
91 M5 **Ledsham** Leeds
91 L5 **Ledston** Leeds
7 J9 **Ledstone** Devon
91 L4 **Ledston Luck** Leeds
48 D9 **Ledwell** Oxon
16 H2 **Lee** Devon
37 J5 **Lee** Gt Lon
22 C11 **Lee** Hants
69 M8 **Lee** Shrops
56 H5 **Leebotwood** Shrops
69 P9 **Lee Brockhurst** Shrops
94 E7 **Leece** Cumb
37 Q3 **Lee Chapel** Essex
35 P4 **Lee Clump** Bucks
35 P4 **Lee Common** Bucks
38 D11 **Leeds** Kent
90 H4 **Leeds** Leeds
90 G2 *Leeds Bradford Airport* Leeds
38 D11 **Leeds Castle** Kent
2 G7 **Leedstown** Cnwll
70 B2 **Lee Green** Ches E
70 H3 **Leek** Staffs
59 L11 **Leek Wootton** Warwks
6 F7 **Lee Mill** Devon
90 C4 **Leeming** C Brad
97 L3 **Leeming** N York
97 L3 **Leeming Bar** N York
6 F6 **Lee Moor** Devon
14 G6 **Lee-on-the-Solent** Hants
90 C3 **Lees** C Brad
71 P7 **Lees** Derbys
83 L4 **Lees** Oldham
71 P7 **Lees Green** Derbys
73 K8 **Leesthorpe** Leics
24 G2 **Lee Street** Surrey
69 J2 **Leeswood** Flints
134 G3 **Leetown** P & K
82 E10 **Leftwich** Ches W
45 J11 **Legar** Powys
87 L4 **Legbourne** Lincs
101 K7 **Legburthwaite** Cumb
118 A2 **Legerwood** Border
35 P10 **Legoland** W & M
10 b2 **Le Gron** Guern
86 F3 **Legsby** Lincs
11 c2 **Le Haguais** Jersey
11 c2 **Le Hocq** Jersey
72 F10 **Leicester** C Leic
72 E10 **Leicester Forest East** Leics
72 E10 **Leicester Forest East Services** Leics
72 D8 **Leicester (Markfield) Services** Leics
17 N9 **Leigh** Devon
11 N3 **Leigh** Dorset
46 G9 **Leigh** Gloucs
37 M11 **Leigh** Kent
56 E4 **Leigh** Shrops
36 F11 **Leigh** Surrey
82 E5 **Leigh** Wigan
33 L6 **Leigh** Wilts
46 E4 **Leigh** Worcs
38 D5 **Leigh Beck** Essex
32 G9 **Leigh Delamere** Wilts
32 G9 **Leigh Delamere Services** Wilts
26 F5 **Leigh Green** Kent
125 Q7 **Leigh Knoweglass** S Lans
18 D7 **Leighland Chapel** Somset
38 D4 **Leigh-on-Sea** Sthend
12 H5 **Leigh Park** Dorset
46 E3 **Leigh Sinton** Worcs
58 G4 **Leighswood** Wsall
32 F6 **Leighterton** Gloucs
97 J5 **Leighton** N York
56 C3 **Leighton** Powys
57 L3 **Leighton** Shrops
20 D6 **Leighton** Somset
61 P5 **Leighton Bromswold** Cambs
49 P9 **Leighton Buzzard** C Beds
20 C5 **Leigh upon Mendip** Somset
31 Q10 **Leigh Woods** N Som
56 G11 **Leinthall Earls** Herefs
56 G11 **Leinthall Starkes** Herefs
56 G10 **Leintwardine** Herefs
60 B3 **Leire** Leics
65 N9 **Leiston** Suffk
127 P2 **Leith** C Edin
118 E2 **Leitholm** Border
2 E6 **Lelant** Cnwll
93 M4 **Lelley** E R Yk
57 N9 **Lem Hill** Worcs
118 E4 **Lempitlaw** Border
168 i6 **Lemreway** W Isls
50 F8 **Lemsford** Herts
47 K5 **Lenchwick** Worcs
114 B9 **Lendalfoot** S Ayrs
132 H6 **Lendrick** Stirlg
159 R9 **Lendrum Terrace** Abers
38 E11 **Lenham** Kent
26 F2 **Lenham Heath** Kent
147 N2 **Lenie** Highld
118 G2 **Lennel** Border
108 D10 **Lennox Plunton** D & G
125 Q2 **Lennoxtown** E Duns
35 P8 **Lent** Bucks
72 F3 **Lenton** C Nott
73 Q4 **Lenton** Lincs
76 F8 **Lenwade** Norfk
126 B3 **Lenzie** E Duns
150 E5 **Leochel-Cushnie** Abers
58 H3 **Leomansley** Staffs
45 P3 **Leominster** Herefs
32 F4 **Leonard Stanley** Gloucs
11 a1 **Leoville** Jersey
14 D7 **Lepe** Hants
152 B8 **Lephin** Highld
98 F8 **Leppington** N York
90 G7 **Lepton** Kirk
130 H2 **Lerags** Ag & B
10 a2 **L'Eree** Guern
5 J10 **Lerryn** Cnwll
169 r9 **Lerwick** Shet
10 b2 **Les Arquets** Guern
119 P8 **Lesbury** Nthumb
10 c2 **Les Hubits** Guern
150 F3 **Leslie** Abers
134 H7 **Leslie** Fife
10 b2 **Les Lohiers** Guern
126 E10 **Lesmahagow** S Lans
10 b2 **Les Murchez** Guern
5 J3 **Lesnewth** Cnwll
10 b2 **Les Nicolles** Guern
10 c1 **Les Quartiers** Guern
11 a2 **Les Quennevais** Jersey
10 b2 **Les Sages** Guern
77 M6 **Lessingham** Norfk
110 D10 **Lessonhall** Cumb
3 K9 **Lestowder** Cnwll
10 b2 **Les Villets** Guern
106 D5 **Leswalt** D & G
11 a1 **L'Etacq** Jersey
50 E11 **Letchmore Heath** Herts
50 F4 **Letchworth Garden City** Herts
34 C8 **Letcombe Bassett** Oxon
34 C7 **Letcombe Regis** Oxon
143 J8 **Letham** Angus
118 C9 **Letham** Border
133 P10 **Letham** Falk
135 J5 **Letham** Fife
143 L8 **Letham Grange** Angus
142 A9 **Lethendy** P & K
150 F3 **Lethenty** Abers
159 K9 **Lethenty** Abers
65 K10 **Letheringham** Suffk
76 F4 **Letheringsett** Norfk
8 H8 **Lettaford** Devon
154 C3 **Letterewe** Highld
145 Q3 **Letterfearn** Highld
146 H9 **Letterfinlay Lodge Hotel** Highld
145 M10 **Lettermorar** Highld
161 K9 **Letters** Highld
116 B6 **Lettershaw** S Lans
40 H5 **Letterston** Pembks
149 J4 **Lettoch** Highld
157 L11 **Lettoch** Highld
45 L5 **Letton** Herefs
56 F10 **Letton** Herefs
37 L9 **Lett's Green** Kent
50 G8 **Letty Green** Herts
85 J3 **Letwell** Rothm
135 M3 **Leuchars** Fife
168 i6 **Leumrabhagh** W Isls
168 i5 **Leurbost** W Isls
3 Q4 **Levalsa Meor** Cnwll
70 F11 **Levedale** Staffs
51 L6 **Level's Green** Essex
99 N11 **Leven** E R Yk
135 K7 **Leven** Fife
95 K3 **Levens** Cumb
51 J6 **Levens Green** Herts
83 J6 **Levenshulme** Manch
169 r11 **Levenwick** Shet
168 f9 **Leverburgh** W Isls
74 H8 **Leverington** Cambs
50 C9 **Leverstock Green** Herts
87 M11 **Leverton** Lincs
10 b1 **Le Villocq** Guern
53 M4 **Levington** Suffk
98 G2 **Levisham** N York
34 B3 **Lew** Oxon
5 M5 **Lewannick** Cnwll
8 C7 **Lewdown** Devon
25 K8 **Lewes** E Susx
40 H6 **Leweston** Pembks
37 J6 **Lewisham** Gt Lon
37 J6 **Lewisham Crematorium** Gt Lon
147 N2 **Lewiston** Highld
29 P7 **Lewistown** Brdgnd
45 L3 **Lewis Wych** Herefs
35 K5 **Lewknor** Oxon
16 E11 **Leworthy** Devon
17 M4 **Leworthy** Devon
38 G9 **Lewson Street** Kent
88 F3 **Lewth** Lancs
8 C7 **Lewtrenchard** Devon
52 G6 **Lexden** Essex
19 J7 **Lexworthy** Somset
5 K8 **Ley** Cnwll
37 Q9 **Leybourne** Kent
96 H2 **Leyburn** N York
70 D5 **Leycett** Staffs
50 E6 **Leygreen** Herts
35 Q4 **Ley Hill** Bucks
88 G6 **Leyland** Lancs
82 C4 **Leyland Green** St Hel
151 K5 **Leylodge** Abers
159 P7 **Leys** Abers
142 D10 **Leys** P & K
38 H7 **Leysdown-on-Sea** Kent
143 L8 **Leysmill** Angus
142 F8 **Leys of Cossans** Angus
45 R2 **Leysters** Herefs
37 J3 **Leyton** Gt Lon
37 J3 **Leytonstone** Gt Lon
5 N6 **Lezant** Cnwll
2 H7 **Lezerea** Cnwll
157 P5 **Lhanbryde** Moray
44 D9 **Libanus** Powys
116 D2 **Libberton** S Lans
127 P4 **Liberton** C Edin
58 H3 **Lichfield** Staffs
58 E9 **Lickey** Worcs
58 E10 **Lickey End** Worcs
58 E10 **Lickey Rock** Worcs
23 P9 **Lickfold** W Susx
8 C8 **Liddaton Green** Devon
138 D6 **Liddesdale** Highld
33 P8 **Liddington** Swindn
84 D5 **Lidgate** Derbys
63 M9 **Lidgate** Suffk
91 R10 **Lidget** Donc
85 K7 **Lidgett** Notts
26 D8 **Lidham Hill** E Susx
49 Q7 **Lidlington** C Beds
38 C9 **Lidsing** Kent
142 E11 **Liff** Angus
58 G8 **Lifford** Birm
5 P4 **Lifton** Devon
5 P4 **Liftondown** Devon
48 B3 **Lighthorne** Warwks
48 C3 **Lighthorne Heath** Warwks
23 P2 **Lightwater** Surrey
70 G6 **Lightwood** C Stke
70 A6 **Lightwood Green** Ches E
69 L6 **Lightwood Green** Wrexhm
60 C5 **Lilbourne** Nhants
119 K6 **Lilburn Tower** Nthumb
70 C11 **Lilleshall** Wrekin
50 D5 **Lilley** Herts
34 D9 **Lilley** W Berk
117 Q5 **Lilliesleaf** Border
49 K7 **Lillingstone Dayrell** Bucks
49 K6 **Lillingstone Lovell** Bucks
11 N2 **Lillington** Dorset
12 H7 **Lilliput** Poole
18 G5 **Lilstock** Somset
57 N2 **Lilyhurst** Shrops
89 J7 **Limbrick** Lancs
50 C6 **Limbury** Luton
56 F11 **Limebrook** Herefs
89 N8 **Limefield** Bury
126 C7 **Limekilnburn** S Lans
134 D11 **Limekilns** Fife
126 F3 **Limerigg** Falk
14 D10 **Limerstone** IoW
111 Q11 **Limestone Brae** Nthumb
46 F8 **Lime Street** Worcs
19 P10 **Limington** Somset
115 M2 **Limmerhaugh** E Ayrs
77 M11 **Limpenhoe** Norfk
20 E2 **Limpley Stoke** Wilts
37 K10 **Limpsfield** Surrey
37 K10 **Limpsfield Chart** Surrey
84 H10 **Linby** Notts
23 N8 **Linchmere** W Susx
109 L5 **Lincluden** D & G
86 C6 **Lincoln** Lincs
86 C6 **Lincoln Crematorium** Lincs
57 Q11 **Lincomb** Worcs
7 J10 **Lincombe** Devon
16 H2 **Lincombe** Devon
95 J4 **Lindale** Cumb
94 E5 **Lindal in Furness** Cumb
24 H5 **Lindfield** W Susx
23 M7 **Lindford** Hants
90 E7 **Lindley** Kirk
97 K11 **Lindley** N York
82 H9 **Lindow End** Ches E
57 M11 **Lindridge** Worcs
51 P5 **Lindsell** Essex
52 G2 **Lindsey** Suffk
52 G2 **Lindsey Tye** Suffk
19 L7 **Liney** Somset
13 L3 **Linford** Hants
37 Q5 **Linford** Thurr
90 D3 **Lingbob** C Brad
105 J7 **Lingdale** R & Cl
56 F11 **Lingen** Herefs
25 J2 **Lingfield** Surrey
77 M10 **Lingwood** Norfk
152 F4 **Linicro** Highld
46 F8 **Linkend** Worcs
22 C3 **Linkenholt** Hants
26 D6 **Linkhill** Kent
5 N7 **Linkinhorne** Cnwll
134 H9 **Linktown** Fife
157 N5 **Linkwood** Moray
56 F6 **Linley** Shrops
46 C4 **Linley Green** Herefs
57 M5 **Linleygreen** Shrops
126 H2 **Linlithgow** W Loth
118 G9 **Linshiels** Nthumb
162 C7 **Linsidemore** Highld
49 P9 **Linslade** C Beds
65 L6 **Linstead Parva** Suffk
110 H9 **Linstock** Cumb
58 E10 **Linthurst** Worcs
90 E8 **Linthwaite** Kirk
129 L8 **Lintlaw** Border
158 D4 **Lintmill** Moray
118 E5 **Linton** Border
63 J11 **Linton** Cambs
71 P11 **Linton** Derbys
46 C9 **Linton** Herefs
38 C11 **Linton** Kent
97 N11 **Linton** Leeds
96 E8 **Linton** N York
113 L2 **Linton** Nthumb
71 P11 **Linton Heath** Derbys
46 C10 **Linton Hill** Herefs
97 Q8 **Linton-on-Ouse** N York
13 L3 **Linwood** Hants
86 F3 **Linwood** Lincs
125 L5 **Linwood** Rens
168 c13 **Lionacleit** W Isls
168 k1 **Lional** W Isls
25 N7 **Lions Green** E Susx
23 M8 **Liphook** Hants
70 C8 **Lipley** Shrops
81 K6 **Liscard** Wirral
18 A8 **Liscombe** Somset
5 M9 **Liskeard** Cnwll
138 E9 **Lismore** Ag & B
23 L9 **Liss** Hants
99 N9 **Lissett** E R Yk
23 L9 **Liss Forest** Hants
86 F4 **Lissington** Lincs
52 E3 **Liston** Essex
30 G8 **Lisvane** Cardif
31 K7 **Liswerry** Newpt
76 B8 **Litcham** Norfk
29 P8 **Litchard** Brdgnd
48 H4 **Litchborough** Nhants
22 E4 **Litchfield** Hants
81 L5 **Litherland** Sefton
50 H2 **Litlington** Cambs
25 M10 **Litlington** E Susx
62 H11 **Little Abington** Cambs
61 L6 **Little Addington** Nhants
107 M8 **Little Airies** D & G
50 F5 **Little Almshoe** Herts
47 M2 **Little Alne** Warwks
88 C9 **Little Altcar** Sefton
51 J8 **Little Amwell** Herts
102 C9 **Little Asby** Cumb
58 G5 **Little Aston** Staffs
14 E11 **Little Atherfield** IoW
104 G8 **Little Ayton** N York
52 C10 **Little Baddow** Essex
32 F8 **Little Badminton** S Glos
110 E9 **Little Bampton** Cumb
51 Q4 **Little Bardfield** Essex
61 Q9 **Little Barford** Bed
76 G5 **Little Barningham** Norfk
33 P2 **Little Barrington** Gloucs
81 P11 **Little Barrow** Ches W
98 F5 **Little Barugh** N York
112 E5 **Little Bavington** Nthumb
53 M2 **Little Bealings** Suffk
105 N10 **Littlebeck** N York
33 Q11 **Little Bedwyn** Wilts
53 K6 **Little Bentley** Essex
50 G9 **Little Berkhamsted** Herts
60 H8 **Little Billing** Nhants
49 P10 **Little Billington** C Beds
45 Q8 **Little Birch** Herefs
88 C2 **Little Bispham** Bpool
53 K2 **Little Blakenham** Suffk
101 N4 **Little Blencow** Cumb
58 F4 **Little Bloxwich** Wsall
24 B6 **Little Bognor** W Susx
71 P4 **Little Bolehill** Derbys
82 F7 **Little Bollington** Ches E
36 D10 **Little Bookham** Surrey
9 K2 **Littleborough** Devon
85 P4 **Littleborough** Notts
89 Q7 **Littleborough** Rochdl
39 M10 **Littlebourne** Kent
48 E6 **Little Bourton** Oxon
60 F3 **Little Bowden** Leics
63 L10 **Little Bradley** Suffk
45 L2 **Little Brampton** Herefs
56 F8 **Little Brampton** Shrops
52 D9 **Little Braxted** Essex
143 K5 **Little Brechin** Angus
11 M7 **Littlebredy** Dorset
49 P8 **Little Brickhill** M Keyn
70 F9 **Little Bridgeford** Staffs
60 E8 **Little Brington** Nhants
53 J6 **Little Bromley** Essex
100 E4 **Little Broughton** Cumb
82 C11 **Little Budworth** Ches W
156 A7 **Littleburn** Highld
37 Q2 **Little Burstead** Essex
51 M3 **Littlebury** Essex
51 L3 **Littlebury Green** Essex
73 Q7 **Little Bytham** Lincs
51 N6 **Little Canfield** Essex
87 L3 **Little Carlton** Lincs
85 N9 **Little Carlton** Notts
73 Q9 **Little Casterton** Rutlnd
93 K2 **Little Catwick** E R Yk
61 P6 **Little Catworth** Cambs
87 L4 **Little Cawthorpe** Lincs
35 Q5 **Little Chalfont** Bucks
26 F2 **Little Chart** Kent
51 M2 **Little Chesterford** Essex
26 B3 **Little Cheveney** Kent
21 J4 **Little Cheverell** Wilts
51 K3 **Little Chishill** Cambs
53 L8 **Little Clacton** Essex
33 Q4 **Little Clanfield** Oxon
100 E5 **Little Clifton** Cumb
93 M9 **Little Coates** NE Lin
47 J6 **Little Comberton** Worcs
26 B10 **Little Common** E Susx
37 P9 **Little Comp** Kent
47 Q8 **Little Compton** Warwks
111 J9 **Little Corby** Cumb
52 F4 **Little Cornard** Suffk
21 M4 **Littlecott** Wilts
46 B4 **Little Cowarne** Herefs
33 Q6 **Little Coxwell** Oxon
97 K2 **Little Crakehall** N York
60 H5 **Little Cransley** Nhants
76 B11 **Little Cressingham** Norfk
81 L4 **Little Crosby** Sefton
100 H5 **Little Crosthwaite** Cumb
71 M7 **Little Cubley** Derbys
73 K8 **Little Dalby** Leics
32 C2 **Littledean** Gloucs
45 Q8 **Little Dewchurch** Herefs
63 L9 **Little Ditton** Cambs
45 Q11 **Little Doward** Herefs
22 B3 **Littledown** Hants
62 H4 **Little Downham** Cambs
99 L9 **Little Driffield** E R Yk
76 B9 **Little Dunham** Norfk
141 P9 **Little Dunkeld** P & K
51 Q6 **Little Dunmow** Essex
21 M8 **Little Durnford** Wilts
51 P6 **Little Easton** Essex
72 B2 **Little Eaton** Derbys
64 E2 **Little Ellingham** Norfk
20 D5 **Little Elm** Somset
60 C9 **Little Everdon** Nhants
62 E10 **Little Eversden** Cambs
33 P4 **Little Faringdon** Oxon
97 L2 **Little Fencote** N York
91 N3 **Little Fenton** N York
76 C9 **Little Fransham** Norfk
35 Q2 **Little Gaddesden** Herts
45 N10 **Little Garway** Herefs
61 P4 **Little Gidding** Cambs
65 L10 **Little Glemham** Suffk
46 C10 **Little Gorsley** Herefs
62 C9 **Little Gransden** Cambs
73 J2 **Little Green** Notts
20 D5 **Little Green** Somset
87 K2 **Little Grimsby** Lincs
85 M4 **Little Gringley** Notts
98 E5 **Little Habton** N York
51 K6 **Little Hadham** Herts
74 B2 **Little Hale** Lincs
72 D2 **Little Hallam** Derbys
51 M7 **Little Hallingbury** Essex
9 P8 **Littleham** Devon
16 G7 **Littleham** Devon
35 N4 **Little Hampden** Bucks
24 B10 **Littlehampton** W Susx
12 D2 **Little Hanford** Dorset
61 J6 **Little Harrowden** Nhants
34 H4 **Little Haseley** Oxon
93 L2 **Little Hatfield** E R Yk
77 K7 **Little Hautbois** Norfk
40 G8 **Little Haven** Pembks
24 E4 **Littlehaven** W Susx
58 H4 **Little Hay** Staffs
83 M7 **Little Hayfield** Derbys
71 J10 **Little Haywood** Staffs
70 F11 **Little Heath** Staffs
35 J10 **Little Heath** W Berk
7 L6 **Littlehempston** Devon
57 K11 **Little Hereford** Herefs
52 G5 **Little Horkesley** Essex
51 K5 **Little Hormead** Herts
25 L7 **Little Horsted** E Susx
90 F4 **Little Horton** C Brad
21 K2 **Little Horton** Wilts
49 L8 **Little Horwood** Bucks
91 L9 **Little Houghton** Barns
60 H9 **Little Houghton** Nhants
119 P7 **Littlehoughton** Nthumb
83 Q9 **Little Hucklow** Derbys
82 F4 **Little Hulton** Salfd
34 F10 **Little Hungerford** W Berk
97 Q5 **Little Hutton** N York
61 K7 **Little Irchester** Nhants
99 M9 **Little Kelk** E R Yk
20 E5 **Little Keyford** Somset
35 M3 **Little Kimble** Bucks
48 B4 **Little Kineton** Warwks
35 N5 **Little Kingshill** Bucks
108 H8 **Little Knox** D & G
101 K10 **Little Langdale** Cumb
21 K7 **Little Langford** Wilts
51 M9 **Little Laver** Essex
82 D9 **Little Leigh** Ches W
52 B8 **Little Leighs** Essex
89 M9 **Little Lever** Bolton
49 M6 **Little Linford** M Keyn
19 N10 **Little Load** Somset
34 H2 **Little London** Bucks
74 H11 **Little London** Cambs
25 N6 **Little London** E Susx
51 L5 **Little London** Essex
51 Q3 **Little London** Essex
46 D11 **Little London** Gloucs
22 C5 **Little London** Hants
22 H3 **Little London** Hants
90 G3 **Little London** Leeds
74 D6 **Little London** Lincs
74 H6 **Little London** Lincs
87 K6 **Little London** Lincs

75 L6 Little London Norfk
55 N7 Little London Powys
83 Q10 Little Longstone Derbys
70 D5 Little Madeley Staffs
46 E6 Little Malvern Worcs
81 L11 Little Mancot Flints
52 D5 Little Maplestead Essex
46 C7 Little Marcle Herefs
17 J9 Little Marland Devon
35 N7 Little Marlow Bucks
75 Q6 Little Massingham Norfk
76 H10 Little Melton Norfk
149 Q8 Littlemill Abers
156 G7 Littlemill Highld
31 K4 Little Mill Mons
34 H4 Little Milton Oxon
35 P5 Little Missenden Bucks
39 P11 Little Mongeham Kent
84 E8 Littlemoor Derbys
19 K8 Little Moor Somset
34 F4 Littlemore Oxon
102 E8 Little Musgrave Cumb
69 M11 Little Ness Shrops
81 K9 Little Neston Ches W
41 J5 Little Newcastle Pembks
103 M7 Little Newsham Dur
19 N11 Little Norton Somset
53 M6 Little Oakley Essex
61 J3 Little Oakley Nhants
61 L9 Little Odell Bed
50 D5 Little Offley Herts
102 D7 Little Ormside Cumb
110 G9 Little Orton Cumb
63 K3 Little Ouse Cambs
97 P8 Little Ouseburn N York
72 A4 Littleover C Derb
60 F4 Little Oxendon Nhants
59 K8 Little Packington Warwks
26 B2 Little Pattenden Kent
61 P8 Little Paxton Cambs
4 E7 Little Petherick Cnwll
88 D4 Little Plumpton Lancs
77 L9 Little Plumstead Norfk
73 N4 Little Ponton Lincs
63 J3 Littleport Cambs
63 J3 Littleport Bridge Cambs
14 F6 Little Posbrook Hants
17 J9 Little Potheridge Devon
91 K4 Little Preston Leeds
48 G4 Little Preston Nhants
82 D11 Littler Ches W
62 C5 Little Raveley Cambs
92 D6 Little Reedness E R Yk
97 N10 Little Ribston N York
47 N11 Little Rissington Gloucs
47 Q8 Little Rollright Oxon
84 C7 Little Rowsley Derbys
76 D6 Little Ryburgh Norfk
119 K8 Little Ryle Nthumb
56 H4 Little Ryton Shrops
101 Q3 Little Salkeld Cumb
51 Q4 Little Sampford Essex
23 M2 Little Sandhurst Br For
58 D3 Little Saredon Staffs
81 M11 Little Saughall Ches W
63 P8 Little Saxham Suffk
155 L6 Little Scatwell Highld
62 G10 Little Shelford Cambs
59 K11 Little Shrewley Warwks
9 M3 Little Silver Devon
88 D3 Little Singleton Lancs
91 R3 Little Skipwith N York
91 N7 Little Smeaton N York
76 D5 Little Snoring Norfk
32 E8 Little Sodbury S Glos
32 D8 Little Sodbury End S Glos
22 C8 Little Somborne Hants
33 J8 Little Somerford Wilts
70 C9 Little Soudley Shrops
96 B7 Little Stainforth N York
104 B6 Little Stainton Darltn
81 N10 Little Stanney Ches W
61 P8 Little Staughton Bed
87 M8 Little Steeping Lincs
70 G8 Little Stoke Staffs
27 J7 Littlestone-on-Sea Kent
64 G9 Little Stonham Suffk
72 H10 Little Stretton Leics
56 G6 Little Stretton Shrops
101 Q7 Little Strickland Cumb
62 B5 Little Stukeley Cambs
70 E8 Little Sugnall Staffs
81 M9 Little Sutton Ches W
57 J8 Little Sutton Shrops
112 D5 Little Swinburne Nthumb
108 F10 Little Sypland D & G
48 C9 Little Tew Oxon
52 E7 Little Tey Essex
62 H5 Little Thetford Cambs
97 Q5 Little Thirkleby N York
76 F4 Little Thornage Norfk
88 D2 Little Thornton Lancs
104 D2 Little Thorpe Dur
72 E11 Littlethorpe Leics
97 M7 Littlethorpe N York
63 L10 Little Thurlow Suffk
63 L10 Little Thurlow Green Suffk
37 P5 Little Thurrock Thurr
142 E7 Littleton Angus
19 Q2 Littleton BaNES
81 N11 Littleton Ches W
108 D9 Littleton D & G
12 E4 Littleton Dorset
22 E8 Littleton Hants
19 N8 Littleton Somset
23 Q5 Littleton Surrey
36 C7 Littleton Surrey
32 F8 Littleton Drew Wilts
31 Q7 Littleton-on-Severn S Glos
21 K4 Littleton Pannell Wilts
16 H8 Little Torrington Devon
52 E9 Little Totham Essex
100 H7 Little Town Cumb
104 B2 Littletown Dur
89 K3 Little Town Lancs
82 D6 Little Town Warrtn
72 A9 Little Twycross Leics
94 F6 Little Urswick Cumb
38 F4 Little Wakering Essex
51 M2 Little Walden Essex
52 F2 Little Waldingfield Suffk
76 C4 Little Walsingham Norfk
52 B9 Little Waltham Essex
37 P2 Little Warley Essex
47 J8 Little Washbourne Gloucs
92 G4 Little Weighton E R Yk
61 K3 Little Weldon Nhants
64 B10 Little Welnetham Suffk
87 K3 Little Welton Lincs
53 J4 Little Wenham Suffk
57 L3 Little Wenlock Wrekin
20 B9 Little Weston Somset
14 G9 Little Whitefield IoW
65 K6 Little Whittingham Green Suffk
112 E7 Little Whittington Nthumb
35 M9 Littlewick Green W & M
62 H9 Little Wilbraham Cambs
11 J4 Littlewindsor Dorset
46 H11 Little Witcombe Gloucs
46 E2 Little Witley Worcs
34 G6 Little Wittenham Oxon
47 Q7 Little Wolford Warwks
58 E3 Littlewood Staffs
36 G8 Little Woodcote Gt Lon
49 N10 Littleworth Bucks
34 B5 Littleworth Oxon
58 F2 Littleworth Staffs
70 G10 Littleworth Staffs
24 E6 Littleworth W Susx
46 G4 Littleworth Worcs
47 J2 Littleworth Worcs
35 P7 Littleworth Common Bucks
63 L11 Little Wratting Suffk
61 L8 Little Wymington Bed
50 F5 Little Wymondley Herts
58 F3 Little Wyrley Staffs
69 Q11 Little Wytheford Shrops
52 C4 Little Yeldham Essex
51 Q7 Littley Green Essex
83 Q9 Litton Derbys
96 D6 Litton N York
19 Q4 Litton Somset
11 L6 Litton Cheney Dorset
168 i5 Liurbost W Isls
81 L6 Liverpool Lpool
90 F6 Liversedge Kirk
9 K9 Liverton Devon
105 K7 Liverton R & Cl
105 K7 Liverton Mines R & Cl
38 E11 Liverton Street Kent
127 K4 Livingston W Loth
127 J4 Livingston Village W Loth
80 H10 Lixwm Flints
3 J11 Lizard Cnwll
78 C8 Llaingoch IoA
55 P8 Llaithddu Powys
55 K4 Llan Powys
67 L11 Llanaber Gwynd
66 F6 Llanaelhaearn Gwynd
54 F10 Llanafan Cerdgn
44 D3 Llanafan-Fawr Powys
44 D4 Llanafan-fechan Powys
79 J7 Llanallgo IoA
66 G7 Llanarmon Gwynd
68 G8 Llanarmon Dyffryn Ceiriog Wrexhm
68 G3 Llanarmon-yn-Ial Denbgs
42 H3 Llanarth Cerdgn
31 L2 Llanarth Mons
43 K11 Llanarthne Carmth
80 G8 Llanasa Flints
78 F7 Llanbabo IoA
54 E8 Llanbadarn Fawr Cerdgn
55 P9 Llanbadarn Fynydd Powys
44 G5 Llanbadarn-y-garreg Powys
31 L5 Llanbadoc Mons
78 F6 Llanbadrig IoA
31 L6 Llanbeder Newpt
67 K9 Llanbedr Gwynd
44 G5 Llanbedr Powys
45 J10 Llanbedr Powys
68 F3 Llanbedr-Dyffryn-Clwyd Denbgs
79 J8 Llanbedrgoch IoA
66 E8 Llanbedrog Gwynd
79 P11 Llanbedr-y-Cennin Conwy
67 K2 Llanberis Gwynd
30 D11 Llanbethery V Glam
55 Q10 Llanbister Powys
30 C10 Llanblethian V Glam
41 P6 Llanboidy Carmth
30 F6 Llanbradach Caerph
55 K4 Llanbrynmair Powys
30 D11 Llancadle V Glam
30 D10 Llancarfan V Glam
31 L4 Llancayo Mons
45 P10 Llancloudy Herefs
54 E6 Llancynfelyn Cerdgn
30 G9 Llandaff Cardif
67 K9 Llandanwg Gwynd
29 K5 Llandarcy Neath
41 Q8 Llandawke Carmth
78 H10 Llanddaniel Fab IoA
43 K11 Llanddarog Carmth
54 D10 Llanddeiniol Cerdgn
79 J11 Llanddeiniolen Gwynd
68 C7 Llandderfel Gwynd
43 Q10 Llanddeusant Carmth
78 E7 Llanddeusant IoA
44 F8 Llanddew Powys
28 E7 Llanddewi Swans
43 N3 Llanddewi Brefi Cerdgn
44 E5 Llanddewi'r Cwm Powys
31 L2 Llanddewi Rhydderch Mons
41 M7 Llanddewi Velfrey Pembks
55 Q11 Llanddewi Ystradenni Powys
67 Q2 Llanddoget Conwy
79 K9 Llanddona IoA
41 Q8 Llanddowror Carmth
80 C9 Llanddulas Conwy
67 K10 Llanddwywe Gwynd
79 J9 Llanddyfnan IoA
67 L7 Llandecwyn Gwynd
44 E8 Llandefaelog Powys
44 G9 Llandefaelog-Tre'r-Graig Powys
44 G7 Llandefalle Powys
79 K10 Llandegfan IoA
68 G4 Llandegla Denbgs
44 G2 Llandegley Powys
31 K5 Llandegveth Mons
66 D9 Llandegwning Gwynd
43 M10 Llandeilo Carmth
44 F6 Llandeilo Graban Powys
44 B8 Llandeilo'r Fan Powys
40 G5 Llandeloy Pembks
31 M4 Llandenny Mons
31 M6 Llandevaud Newpt
31 M7 Llandevenny Mons
45 Q9 Llandinabo Herefs
55 N7 Llandinam Powys
41 M6 Llandissilio Pembks
31 P4 Llandogo Mons
30 C10 Llandough V Glam
30 G10 Llandough V Glam
43 Q8 Llandovery Carmth
29 P10 Llandow V Glam
43 N6 Llandre Carmth
54 E7 Llandre Cerdgn
41 M5 Llandre Isaf Pembks
68 D7 Llandrillo Denbgs
79 Q8 Llandrillo-yn-Rhos Conwy
44 F2 Llandrindod Wells Powys
69 J11 Llandrinio Powys
79 P8 Llandudno Conwy
79 P9 Llandudno Junction Conwy
44 B6 Llandulas Powys
66 H3 Llandwrog Gwynd
43 M11 Llandybie Carmth
28 D2 Llandyfaelog Carmth
43 M11 Llandyfan Carmth
42 F6 Llandyfriog Cerdgn
78 G7 Llandyfrydog IoA
79 K10 Llandygai Gwynd
41 P2 Llandygwydd Cerdgn
68 G5 Llandynan Denbgs
80 G11 Llandyrnog Denbgs
56 B5 Llandyssil Powys
42 H6 Llandysul Cerdgn
30 H8 Llanedeyrn Cardif
28 G3 Llanedi Carmth
44 F7 Llaneglwys Powys
54 E3 Llanegryn Gwynd
43 K10 Llanegwad Carmth
78 H6 Llaneilian IoA
80 B9 Llanelian-yn-Rhôs Conwy
68 F4 Llanelidan Denbgs
44 H8 Llanelieu Powys
31 K2 Llanellen Mons
28 F4 Llanelli Carmth
28 F4 Llanelli Crematorium Carmth
67 N11 Llanelltyd Gwynd
30 H2 Llanelly Mons
44 E4 Llanelwedd Powys
67 K10 Llanenddwyn Gwynd
66 D9 Llanengan Gwynd
68 A11 Llanerch Gwynd
56 E6 Llanerch Powys
78 G8 Llanerchymedd IoA
55 N3 Llanerfyl Powys
78 E8 Llanfachraeth IoA
67 P10 Llanfachreth Gwynd
78 E10 Llanfaelog IoA
66 C9 Llanfaelrhys Gwynd
45 N11 Llanfaenor Mons
79 L9 Llanfaes IoA
44 E9 Llanfaes Powys
78 E7 Llanfaethlu IoA
67 K9 Llanfair Gwynd
55 Q3 Llanfair Caereinion Powys
43 M4 Llanfair Clydogau Cerdgn
68 F3 Llanfair Dyffryn Clwyd Denbgs
79 M10 Llanfairfechan Conwy
31 L3 Llanfair Kilgeddin Mons
41 N3 Llanfair-Nant-Gwyn Pembks
79 J10 Llanfair P G IoA
80 C10 Llanfair Talhaiarn Conwy
56 C9 Llanfair Waterdine Shrops
78 E6 Llanfairynghornwy IoA
78 E9 Llanfair-yn-Neubwll IoA
41 N6 Llanfallteg Carmth
41 M7 Llanfallteg West Carmth
54 D9 Llanfarian Cerdgn
68 G10 Llanfechain Powys
78 F6 Llanfechell IoA
68 G2 Llanferres Denbgs
78 F7 Llanfflewyn IoA
78 E8 Llanfigael IoA
43 J7 Llanfihangel-ar-arth Carmth
68 C5 Llanfihangel Glyn Myfyr Conwy
44 C8 Llanfihangel Nant Bran Powys
44 H3 Llanfihangel-nant-Melan Powys
56 B11 Llanfihangel Rhydithon Powys
31 N7 Llanfihangel Rogiet Mons
44 G9 Llanfihangel Tal-y-llyn Powys
43 J10 Llanfihangel-uwch-Gwili Carmth
54 F9 Llanfihangel-y-Creuddyn Cerdgn
68 E11 Llanfihangel-yng-Ngwynfa Powys
78 E9 Llanfihangel yn Nhowyn IoA
54 F3 Llanfihangel-y-pennant Gwynd
67 J6 Llanfihangel-y-pennant Gwynd
67 K8 Llanfihangel-y-traethau Gwynd
44 G8 Llanfilo Powys
31 J2 Llanfoist Mons
68 B7 Llanfor Gwynd
31 K6 Llanfrechfa Torfn
67 L6 Llanfrothen Gwynd
44 F9 Llanfrynach Powys
68 F3 Llanfwrog Denbgs
78 E8 Llanfwrog IoA
68 F11 Llanfyllin Powys
43 L9 Llanfynydd Carmth
69 J3 Llanfynydd Flints
41 P4 Llanfyrnach Pembks
55 N2 Llangadfan Powys
28 D3 Llangadog Carmth
43 P9 Llangadog Carmth
78 F11 Llangadwaladr IoA
68 G8 Llangadwaladr Powys
78 G11 Llangaffo IoA
42 G11 Llangain Carmth
44 C5 Llangammarch Wells Powys
30 C9 Llangan V Glam
45 Q10 Llangarron Herefs
44 G9 Llangasty-Talyllyn Powys
43 L10 Llangathen Carmth
45 J11 Llangattock Powys
45 M10 Llangattock Lingoed Mons
45 P11 Llangattock-Vibon-Avel Mons
68 G10 Llangedwyn Powys
78 H9 Llangefni IoA
29 P7 Llangeinor Brdgnd
43 M3 Llangeitho Cerdgn
42 G7 Llangeler Carmth
54 D3 Llangelynin Gwynd
28 E2 Llangendeirne Carmth
28 G4 Llangennech Carmth
28 D6 Llangennith Swans
45 J11 Llangenny Powys
80 B11 Llangernyw Conwy
66 D9 Llangian Gwynd
29 K3 Llangiwg Neath
40 H4 Llangloffan Pembks
41 N5 Llanglydwen Carmth
79 L9 Llangoed IoA
42 D5 Llangoedmor Cerdgn
68 H6 Llangollen Denbgs
41 M5 Llangolman Pembks
44 G9 Llangors Powys
31 N3 Llangovan Mons
68 B8 Llangower Gwynd
42 F4 Llangranog Cerdgn
78 G10 Llangristiolus IoA
45 Q11 Llangrove Herefs
45 M9 Llangua Mons
56 C10 Llangunllo Powys
42 H10 Llangunnor Carmth
55 L9 Llangurig Powys
68 C6 Llangwm Conwy
31 M5 Llangwm Mons
41 J9 Llangwm Pembks
66 C8 Llangwnnadl Gwynd
80 G11 Llangwyfan Denbgs
78 G9 Llangwyllog IoA
54 D10 Llangwyryfon Cerdgn
43 M4 Llangybi Cerdgn
66 G6 Llangybi Gwynd
31 L5 Llangybi Mons
28 H5 Llangyfelach Swans
68 F2 Llangynhafal Denbgs
44 H11 Llangynidr Powys
41 Q7 Llangynin Carmth
42 G6 Llangynllo Cerdgn
28 B2 Llangynog Carmth
68 E9 Llangynog Powys
29 N7 Llangynwyd Brdgnd
44 F9 Llanhamlach Powys
30 D8 Llanharan Rhondd
30 D8 Llanharry Rhondd
31 L6 Llanhennock Mons
30 H4 Llanhilleth Blae G
78 H11 Llanidan IoA
55 M8 Llanidloes Powys
66 D8 Llaniestyn Gwynd
45 J7 Llanigon Powys
54 E9 Llanilar Cerdgn
30 C8 Llanilid Rhondd
42 H3 Llanina Cerdgn
43 M3 Llanio Cerdgn
30 G8 Llanishen Cardif
31 N4 Llanishen Mons
79 L11 Llanllechid Gwynd
44 C4 Llanlleonfel Powys
31 L5 Llanllowell Mons
55 P4 Llanllugan Powys
42 G11 Llanllwch Carmth
55 Q6 Llanllwchaiarn Powys
43 J7 Llanllwni Carmth
66 H4 Llanllyfni Gwynd
28 D6 Llanmadoc Swans
30 C11 Llanmaes V Glam
31 L7 Llanmartin Newpt
56 B6 Llanmerewig Powys
30 C10 Llanmihangel V Glam
41 P9 Llanmiloe Carmth
28 F6 Llanmorlais Swans
80 D10 Llannefydd Conwy
28 F3 Llannon Carmth
66 F7 Llannor Gwynd
54 C11 Llanon Cerdgn
31 K3 Llanover Mons
42 H9 Llanpumsaint Carmth
68 F9 Llanrhaeadr-ym-Mochnant Powys
40 F4 Llanrhian Pembks
28 E6 Llanrhidian Swans
79 P8 Llanrhos Conwy
67 P2 Llanrhychwyn Conwy
78 E7 Llanrhyddlad IoA
54 C11 Llanrhystud Cerdgn
45 P11 Llanrothal Herefs
67 J2 Llanrug Gwynd
30 H8 Llanrumney Cardif
67 Q2 Llanrwst Conwy
41 Q8 Llansadurnen Carmth
43 N8 Llansadwrn Carmth
79 K9 Llansadwrn IoA
28 C3 Llansaint Carmth
29 J5 Llansamlet Swans
79 Q9 Llansanffraid Glan Conwy Conwy
80 C11 Llansannan Conwy
30 C9 Llansannor V Glam
44 G10 Llansantffraed Powys
55 M11 Llansantffraed-Cwmdeuddwr Powys
44 F4 Llansantffraed-in-Elvel Powys
54 C11 Llansantffraid Cerdgn
68 H10 Llansantffraid-ym-Mechain Powys
43 M7 Llansawel Carmth
68 H9 Llansilin Powys
31 M4 Llansoy Mons
44 E9 Llanspyddid Powys
40 H10 Llanstadwell Pembks
28 C2 Llansteffan Carmth
44 G6 Llanstephan Powys
31 K6 Llantarnam Torfn
41 N8 Llanteg Pembks
45 L11 Llanthewy Skirrid Mons
45 K9 Llanthony Mons
31 L2 Llantilio-Crossenny Mons
45 L11 Llantilio Pertholey Mons
78 F8 Llantrisant IoA
31 L5 Llantrisant Mons
30 D8 Llantrisant Rhondd
30 D10 Llantrithyd V Glam
30 E7 Llantwit Fardre Rhondd
30 C11 Llantwit Major V Glam
68 G6 Llantysilio Denbgs
68 A8 Llanuwchllyn Gwynd
31 M6 Llanvaches Newpt
31 M6 Llanvair Discoed Mons
31 L2 Llanvapley Mons
45 M11 Llanvetherine Mons
45 L8 Llanveynoe Herefs
45 L10 Llanvihangel Crucorney Mons
31 K3 Llanvihangel Gobion Mons
31 M2 Llanvihangel-Ystern-Llewern Mons
45 Q9 Llanwarne Herefs
68 D11 Llanwddyn Powys
31 J2 Llanwenarth Mons
43 J5 Llanwenog Cerdgn
31 L7 Llanwern Newpt
41 Q5 Llanwinio Carmth
66 H3 Llanwnda Gwynd
40 H3 Llanwnda Pembks
43 K5 Llanwnnen Cerdgn
55 N6 Llanwnog Powys
30 D5 Llanwonno Rhondd
43 P8 Llanwrda Carmth
54 H4 Llanwrin Powys
44 D2 Llanwrthwl Powys
44 B5 Llanwrtyd Powys
44 B5 Llanwrtyd Wells Powys
55 P4 Llanwyddelan Powys
68 H10 Llanyblodwel Shrops
28 B2 Llanybri Carmth
43 K6 Llanybydder Carmth
41 L6 Llanycefn Pembks
41 J3 Llanychaer Bridge Pembks
43 M5 Llanycrwys Carmth
68 B11 Llanymawddwy Gwynd
69 J10 Llanymynech Powys
78 E8 Llanynghenedl IoA
68 F2 Llanynys Denbgs
69 L4 Llan-y-pwll Wrexhm
44 E2 Llanyre Powys
66 H7 Llanystumdwy Gwynd
44 G9 Llanywern Powys
41 L7 Llawhaden Pembks
68 H8 Llawnt Shrops
55 L6 Llawryglyn Powys
69 K3 Llay Wrexhm
78 F8 Llechcynfarwy IoA
44 F9 Llechfaen Powys
30 F3 Llechrhyd Caerph
41 P2 Llechryd Cerdgn
78 E9 Llechylched IoA
54 E10 Lledrod Cerdgn
66 E7 Lleyn Peninsula Gwynd
68 A7 Llidiardau Gwynd
43 K7 Llidiartnenog Carmth
68 F6 Llidiart-y-parc Denbgs
66 F6 Llithfaen Gwynd
80 G9 Lloc Flints
44 H6 Llowes Powys
30 C4 Llwydcoed Rhondd
30 C3 Llwydcoed Crematorium Rhondd
68 D11 Llwydiarth Powys
68 E2 Llwyn Denbgs
42 H3 Llwyncelyn Cerdgn
42 G3 Llwyndafydd Cerdgn
56 C4 Llwynderw Powys
41 Q4 Llwyn-drain Pembks
45 K11 Llwyn-du Mons
66 F6 Llwyndyrys Gwynd
54 D3 Llwyngwril Gwynd
28 F5 Llwynhendy Carmth
68 H7 Llwynmawr Wrexhm
30 D2 Llwyn-on Myr Td
41 N8 Llwyn-y-brain Carmth
43 L3 Llwyn-y-groes Cerdgn
30 C6 Llwynypia Rhondd
69 J10 Llynclys Shrops
78 G9 Llynfaes IoA
81 J11 Llyn-y-pandy Flints
80 B9 Llysfaen Conwy
43 J2 Llyswen Cerdgn
44 G7 Llyswen Powys
30 C10 Llysworney V Glam
41 K6 Llys-y-frân Pembks
44 B8 Llywel Powys
84 C3 Load Brook Sheff
126 H2 Loan Falk
129 N9 Loanend Nthumb
127 P4 Loanhead Mdloth
109 L9 Loaningfoot D & G
125 J11 Loans S Ayrs
16 H4 Lobb Devon
8 C7 Lobhillcross Devon
145 N11 Lochailort Highld
138 B9 Lochaline Highld
106 E6 Lochans D & G
109 L4 Locharbriggs D & G
131 J4 Lochavich Ag & B
131 N2 Lochawe Ag & B
168 c16 Loch Baghasdail W Isls
168 c16 Lochboisdale W Isls
137 Q10 Lochbuie Ag & B
154 A10 Lochcarron Highld
138 C11 Lochdon Ag & B
138 C11 Lochdonhead Ag & B
123 N4 Lochead Ag & B
132 H3 Lochearnhead Stirlg
142 F11 Lochee C Dund
138 H2 Locheilside Station Highld
155 Q10 Lochend Highld
168 d11 Locheport W Isls
168 d11 Loch Euphoirt W Isls
109 J6 Lochfoot D & G
131 J9 Lochgair Ag & B
134 F9 Lochgelly Fife
130 H10 Lochgilphead Ag & B
131 Q7 Lochgoilhead Ag & B
134 H5 Lochieheads Fife
157 P5 Lochill Moray
156 H10 Lochindorb Lodge Highld
160 H2 Lochinver Highld
132 E5 Loch Lomond and The Trossachs National Park
155 K5 Lochluichart Highld
109 N4 Lochmaben D & G
168 e11 Lochmaddy W Isls
154 B3 Loch Maree Hotel Highld
168 e11 Loch nam Madadh W Isls
147 N2 Loch Ness Highld
134 F8 Lochore Fife
124 A7 Lochranza N Ayrs
143 N5 Lochside Abers
109 L5 Lochside D & G
156 E7 Lochside Highld
163 J10 Lochslin Highld
107 J2 Lochton S Ayrs
143 J5 Lochty Angus

135 N6 Lochty Fife
138 D6 Lochuisge Highld
125 K6 Lochwinnoch Rens
116 F11 Lochwood D & G
4 G9 Lockengate Cnwll
109 P4 Lockerbie D & G
33 M11 Lockeridge Wilts
22 B9 Lockerley Hants
19 L3 Locking N Som
82 D6 Locking Stumps Warrtn
99 K11 Lockington E R Yk
72 D5 Lockington Leics
70 B9 Lockleywood Shrops
37 K7 Locksbottom Gt Lon
14 D8 Locksgreen IoW
14 F5 Locks Heath Hants
98 G3 Lockton N York
73 K10 Loddington Leics
60 H5 Loddington Nhants
7 J9 Loddiswell Devon
65 M2 Loddon Norfk
62 H8 Lode Cambs
59 J8 Lode Heath Solhll
11 K6 Loders Dorset
58 F8 Lodge Hill Crematorium Birm
23 P10 Lodsworth W Susx
91 J5 Lofthouse Leeds
96 H6 Lofthouse N York
91 J6 Lofthouse Gate Wakefd
105 K7 Loftus R & Cl
115 L3 Logan E Ayrs
94 D2 Loganbeck Cumb
126 H5 Loganlea W Loth
70 C7 Loggerheads Staffs
143 M5 Logie Angus
135 L3 Logie Fife
157 J7 Logie Moray
150 C7 Logie Coldstone Abers
158 G10 Logie Newton Abers
143 M5 Logie Pert Angus
141 N7 Logierait P & K
151 N2 Logierieve Abers
41 N6 Login Carmth
62 E8 Lolworth Cambs
153 M7 Lonbain Highld
98 H11 Londesborough E R Yk
36 G5 London Gt Lon
3 Q4 London Apprentice Cnwll
26 E4 London Beach Kent
50 E10 London Colney Herts
97 M3 Londonderry N York
61 K7 London End Nhants
36 E2 London Gateway Services Gt Lon
73 P3 Londonthorpe Lincs
160 D10 Londubh Highld
153 P2 Lonemore Highld
31 P10 Long Ashton N Som
57 P10 Long Bank Worcs
73 L2 Long Bennington Lincs
113 L7 Longbenton N Tyne
47 N9 Longborough Gloucs
11 M6 Long Bredy Dorset
58 F9 Longbridge Birm
47 Q2 Longbridge Warwks
20 G6 Longbridge Deverill Wilts
60 D7 Long Buckby Nhants
110 F9 Longburgh Cumb
11 N2 Longburton Dorset
7 K6 Long Cause Devon
73 J5 Long Clawson Leics
84 B9 Longcliffe Derbys
7 L7 Longcombe Devon
14 F4 Long Common Hants
70 F10 Long Compton Staffs
47 Q8 Long Compton Warwks
33 Q6 Longcot Oxon
35 J3 Long Crendon Bucks
12 G2 Long Crichel Dorset
110 D9 Longcroft Cumb
35 Q11 Longcross Surrey
56 G3 Longden Shrops
56 G3 Longden Common Shrops
36 E7 Long Ditton Surrey
58 G2 Longdon Staffs
46 F7 Longdon Worcs
58 G2 Longdon Green Staffs
46 F7 Longdon Heath Worcs
69 R11 Longdon upon Tern Wrekin
9 L6 Longdown Devon
3 J7 Longdowns Cnwll
92 A5 Long Drax N York
84 F6 Long Duckmanton Derbys
72 D4 Long Eaton Derbys
37 P7 Longfield Kent
59 N8 Longford Covtry
71 N7 Longford Derbys
46 F10 Longford Gloucs
36 C5 Longford Gt Lon
37 M9 Longford Kent
70 A8 Longford Shrops
70 C11 Longford Wrekin
134 H2 Longforgan P & K
128 H8 Longformacus Border
119 M10 Longframlington Nthumb
81 P10 Long Green Ches W
46 F8 Long Green Worcs
13 J5 Longham Dorset
76 C8 Longham Norfk
34 D2 Long Hanborough Oxon
159 R10 Longhaven Abers
87 L11 Long Hedges Lincs
113 K3 Longhirst Nthumb
46 C11 Longhope Gloucs
169 c7 Longhope Ork
112 H2 Longhorsley Nthumb
119 P7 Longhoughton Nthumb
59 P11 Long Itchington Warwks
101 J3 Longlands Cumb
71 N7 Longlane Derbys
59 Q9 Long Lawford Warwks
20 F6 Longleat Safari Park Wilts
46 G11 Longlevens Gloucs
90 D6 Longley Calder
90 E9 Longley Kirk
46 D4 Longley Green Worcs
142 D9 Longleys P & K
19 N10 Long Load Somset
158 H5 Longmanhill Abers
49 N11 Long Marston Herts
97 R10 Long Marston N York
47 N5 Long Marston Warwks
102 C6 Long Marton Cumb
56 G8 Long Meadowend Shrops
52 E2 Long Melford Suffk
23 L8 Longmoor Camp Hants
157 N6 Longmorn Moray
83 J10 Longmoss Ches E
32 H6 Long Newnton Gloucs
118 A5 Longnewton Border
128 E7 Long Newton E Loth
104 C7 Longnewton S on T
32 E2 Longney Gloucs
128 C4 Longniddry E Loth
56 H4 Longnor Shrops
71 K2 Longnor Staffs
22 D5 Longparish Hants
110 H8 Longpark Cumb
96 B9 Long Preston N York
89 J3 Longridge Lancs
70 G11 Longridge Staffs
126 G5 Longridge W Loth
126 E3 Longriggend N Lans
93 K2 Long Riston E R Yk
2 E7 Longrock Cnwll
70 H4 Longsdon Staffs
82 B4 Longshaw Wigan
159 P8 Longside Abers
89 Q9 Long Sight Oldham
70 B7 Longslow Shrops
62 E7 Longstanton Cambs
22 C7 Longstock Hants
41 M9 Longstone Pembks
62 D10 Longstowe Cambs
64 H3 Long Stratton Norfk
49 L5 Long Street M Keyn
21 M4 Longstreet Wilts
23 K5 Long Sutton Hants
74 H6 Long Sutton Lincs
19 N9 Long Sutton Somset
74 C11 Longthorpe C Pete
64 E8 Long Thurlow Suffk
101 M6 Longthwaite Cumb
70 G6 Longton C Stke
88 F5 Longton Lancs
110 G7 Longtown Cumb
45 L9 Longtown Herefs
11 c2 Longueville Jersey
57 J6 Longville in the Dale Shrops
69 R11 Long Waste Wrekin
72 D6 Long Whatton Leics
35 L3 Longwick Bucks
34 F6 Long Wittenham Oxon
112 G3 Longwitton Nthumb
108 F8 Longwood D & G
57 L3 Longwood Shrops
34 C5 Longworth Oxon
128 E7 Longyester E Loth
29 K5 Lon-las Swans
159 P6 Lonmay Abers
152 D8 Lonmore Highld
5 M11 Looe Cnwll
38 C11 Loose Kent
8 H3 Loosebeare Devon
74 F5 Loosegate Lincs
35 M4 Loosley Row Bucks
158 F7 Lootcherbrae Abers
21 Q7 Lopcombe Corner Wilts
11 J2 Lopen Somset
69 N9 Loppington Shrops
119 K9 Lorbottle Nthumb
15 L5 Lordington W Susx
75 L8 Lordsbridge Norfk
38 C9 Lords Wood Medway
142 B8 Lornty P & K
84 F11 Loscoe Derbys
11 K5 Loscombe Dorset
157 N3 Lossiemouth Moray
69 R8 Lostford Shrops
3 P4 Lost Gardens of Heligan Cnwll
82 E10 Lostock Gralam Ches W
82 E10 Lostock Green Ches W
88 G5 Lostock Hall Lancs
89 K9 Lostock Hall Fold Bolton
89 K9 Lostock Junction Bolton
5 J10 Lostwithiel Cnwll
163 L4 Lothbeg Highld
96 E11 Lothersdale N York
163 M4 Lothmore Highld
35 P6 Loudwater Bucks
72 E7 Loughborough Leics
72 E7 Loughborough Crematorium Leics
28 G5 Loughor Swans
51 K11 Loughton Essex
49 M7 Loughton M Keyn
57 L8 Loughton Shrops
73 R7 Lound Lincs
85 L3 Lound Notts
65 Q2 Lound Suffk
9 J9 Lounston Devon
72 B7 Lount Leics
87 K3 Louth Lincs
89 N5 Love Clough Lancs
15 J4 Lovedean Hants
21 P10 Lover Wilts
91 P11 Loversall Donc
51 P10 Loves Green Essex
104 C11 Lovesome Hill N York
41 L9 Loveston Pembks
19 Q8 Lovington Somset
91 M7 Low Ackworth Wakefd
112 G4 Low Angerton Nthumb
46 E8 Lowbands Gloucs
106 D4 Low Barbeth D & G
86 E6 Low Barlings Lincs
105 K11 Low Bell End N York
95 N7 Low Bentham N York
95 N5 Low Biggins Cumb
102 B10 Low Borrowbridge Cumb
84 C2 Low Bradfield Sheff
96 F11 Low Bradley N York
101 M2 Low Braithwaite Cumb
92 C10 Low Burnham N Linc
119 P9 Low Buston Nthumb
100 C6 Lowca Cumb
98 E10 Low Catton E R Yk
103 Q8 Low Coniscliffe Darltn
110 H9 Low Crosby Cumb
85 L11 Lowdham Notts
104 B8 Low Dinsdale Darltn
69 N8 Lowe Shrops
70 H3 Lowe Hill Staffs
97 K4 Low Ellington N York
18 H7 Lower Aisholt Somset
12 C4 Lower Ansty Dorset
46 G9 Lower Apperley Gloucs
48 H11 Lower Arncott Oxon
9 K8 Lower Ashton Devon
35 K8 Lower Assendon Oxon
88 D4 Lower Ballam Lancs
88 F4 Lower Bartle Lancs
34 H9 Lower Basildon W Berk
45 M3 Lower Bearwood Herefs
24 F5 Lower Beeding W Susx
61 L3 Lower Benefield Nhants
58 E11 Lower Bentley Worcs
57 P6 Lower Beobridge Shrops
84 F10 Lower Birchwood Derbys
48 E4 Lower Boddington Nhants
2 B7 Lower Boscaswell Cnwll
23 M6 Lower Bourne Surrey
48 B7 Lower Brailes Warwks
145 L3 Lower Breakish Highld
83 K6 Lower Bredbury Stockp
46 F3 Lower Broadheath Worcs
45 M4 Lower Broxwood Herefs
46 B8 Lower Buckenhill Herefs
45 Q7 Lower Bullingham Herefs
21 N11 Lower Burgate Hants
9 P5 Lower Burrowton Devon
45 N3 Lower Burton Herefs
61 Q11 Lower Caldecote C Beds
32 D4 Lower Cam Gloucs
19 L3 Lower Canada N Som
60 B9 Lower Catesby Nhants
44 E7 Lower Chapel Powys
21 J9 Lower Chicksgrove Wilts
22 B4 Lower Chute Wilts
36 H3 Lower Clapton Gt Lon
58 D9 Lower Clent Worcs
9 K4 Lower Creedy Devon
83 M8 Lower Crossings Derbys
90 G9 Lower Cumberworth Kirk
89 K5 Lower Darwen Bl w D
61 N7 Lower Dean Bed
90 G9 Lower Denby Kirk
153 P5 Lower Diabaig Highld
25 N8 Lower Dicker E Susx
56 H8 Lower Dinchope Shrops
56 E8 Lower Down Shrops
97 P8 Lower Dunsforth N York
46 B5 Lower Egleton Herefs
71 K3 Lower Elkstone Staffs
71 L6 Lower Ellastone Staffs
35 J3 Lower End Bucks
49 P7 Lower End M Keyn
60 H9 Lower End Nhants
61 J8 Lower End Nhants
21 N4 Lower Everleigh Wilts
14 D7 Lower Exbury Hants
27 N2 Lower Eythorne Kent
31 P10 Lower Failand N Som
23 K7 Lower Farringdon Hants
36 C6 Lower Feltham Gt Lon
24 B7 Lower Fittleworth W Susx
80 c6 Lower Foxdale IoM
69 L8 Lower Frankton Shrops
41 J8 Lower Freystrop Pembks
23 L6 Lower Froyle Hants
7 N5 Lower Gabwell Devon
162 D8 Lower Gledfield Highld
19 N6 Lower Godney Somset
58 D6 Lower Gornal Dudley
50 D3 Lower Gravenhurst C Beds
50 E4 Lower Green Herts
51 K4 Lower Green Herts
25 N2 Lower Green Kent
25 P2 Lower Green Kent
76 D4 Lower Green Norfk
58 D3 Lower Green Staffs
63 M7 Lower Green Suffk
65 L10 Lower Hacheston Suffk
36 C7 Lower Halliford Surrey
11 L3 Lower Halstock Leigh Dorset
38 E8 Lower Halstow Kent
12 G6 Lower Hamworthy Poole
39 L11 Lower Hardres Kent
45 K2 Lower Harpton Herefs
38 D9 Lower Hartlip Kent
84 E10 Lower Hartshay Derbys
35 L2 Lower Hartwell Bucks
70 E7 Lower Hatton Staffs
94 E3 Lower Hawthwaite Cumb
45 K3 Lower Hergest Herefs
48 E10 Lower Heyford Oxon
95 J8 Lower Heysham Lancs
38 B7 Lower Higham Kent
53 L4 Lower Holbrook Suffk
69 L9 Lower Hordley Shrops
24 B7 Lower Horncroft W Susx
89 N4 Lowerhouse Lancs
90 F7 Lower Houses Kirk
46 E5 Lower Howsell Worcs
82 F6 Lower Irlam Salfd
72 B2 Lower Kilburn Derbys
32 E7 Lower Kilcott Gloucs
122 C11 Lower Killeyan Ag & B
11 M5 Lower Kingcombe Dorset
36 F10 Lower Kingswood Surrey
69 K2 Lower Kinnerton Ches W
19 N2 Lower Langford N Som
135 L7 Lower Largo Fife
71 J7 Lower Leigh Staffs
47 P8 Lower Lemington Gloucs
55 M11 Lower Llanfadog Powys
17 J6 Lower Lovacott Devon
17 L4 Lower Loxhore Devon
46 A11 Lower Lydbrook Gloucs
56 G11 Lower Lye Herefs
30 H7 Lower Machen Newpt
45 L8 Lower Maes-coed Herefs
13 J4 Lower Mannington Dorset
20 E6 Lower Marston Somset
31 Q4 Lower Meend Gloucs
18 H8 Lower Merridge Somset
48 F6 Lower Middleton Cheney Nhants
19 P5 Lower Milton Somset
47 J5 Lower Moor Worcs
32 B6 Lower Morton S Glos
51 J9 Lower Nazeing Essex
47 P2 Lower Norton Warwks
20 E10 Lower Nyland Dorset
30 G11 Lower Penarth V Glam
58 C5 Lower Penn Staffs
13 P6 Lower Pennington Hants
88 G5 Lower Penwortham Lancs
82 F10 Lower Peover Ches E
89 Q8 Lower Place Rochdl
35 K2 Lower Pollicott Bucks
47 N5 Lower Quinton Warwks
38 D8 Lower Rainham Medway
52 H4 Lower Raydon Suffk
18 D7 Lower Roadwater Somset
95 N8 Lower Salter Lancs
33 J8 Lower Seagry Wilts
51 L8 Lower Sheering Essex
49 Q6 Lower Shelton C Beds
35 L9 Lower Shiplake Oxon
48 E2 Lower Shuckburgh Warwks
47 N10 Lower Slaughter Gloucs
90 H6 Lower Soothill Kirk
32 C3 Lower Soudley Gloucs
27 M3 Lower Standen Kent
32 H8 Lower Stanton St Quintin Wilts
38 D6 Lower Stoke Medway
32 C6 Lower Stone Gloucs
58 G4 Lower Stonnall Staffs
64 D3 Lower Stow Bedon Norfk
12 D5 Lower Street Dorset
26 B9 Lower Street E Susx
77 K4 Lower Street Norfk
63 N10 Lower Street Suffk
64 G11 Lower Street Suffk
82 D8 Lower Stretton Warrtn
11 K5 Lower Stroud Dorset
50 C5 Lower Sundon C Beds
14 E5 Lower Swanwick Hants
47 N9 Lower Swell Gloucs
48 D7 Lower Tadmarton Oxon
9 Q4 Lower Tale Devon
71 J7 Lower Tean Staffs
65 N2 Lower Thurlton Norfk
2 H8 Lower Town Cnwll
7 J4 Lower Town Devon
46 B6 Lower Town Herefs
41 J3 Lower Town Pembks
5 N6 Lower Trebullett Cnwll
3 K6 Lower Treluswell Cnwll
48 B5 Lower Tysoe Warwks
65 K11 Lower Ufford Suffk
9 L8 Lower Upcott Devon
22 F11 Lower Upham Hants
38 C7 Lower Upnor Medway
18 F7 Lower Vexford Somset
82 D7 Lower Walton Warrtn
12 B5 Lower Waterston Dorset
19 M4 Lower Weare Somset
60 D9 Lower Weedon Nhants
45 K4 Lower Welson Herefs
46 H7 Lower Westmancote Worcs
12 D4 Lower Whatcombe Dorset
20 D5 Lower Whatley Somset
82 D9 Lower Whitley Ches W
32 D5 Lower Wick Gloucs
46 F4 Lower Wick Worcs
22 H6 Lower Wield Hants
25 N10 Lower Willingdon E Susx
82 H11 Lower Withington Ches E
35 M7 Lower Woodend Bucks
21 M7 Lower Woodford Wilts
11 M4 Lower Wraxhall Dorset
46 E6 Lower Wyche Worcs
90 F5 Lower Wyke C Brad
73 J9 Lowesby Leics
65 Q3 Lowestoft Suffk
100 F6 Loweswater Cumb
113 L9 Low Fell Gatesd
24 G3 Lowfield Heath W Susx
132 F10 Low Gartachorrans Stirlg
112 D8 Low Gate Nthumb
111 K9 Low Gettbridge Cumb
102 B11 Lowgill Cumb
95 P8 Lowgill Lancs
97 K6 Low Grantley N York
97 K9 Low Green N York
57 Q9 Low Habberley Worcs
19 M4 Low Ham Somset
97 L9 Low Harrogate N York
105 P9 Low Hawsker N York
111 J11 Low Hesket Cumb
98 F7 Low Hutton N York
94 F3 Lowick Cumb
61 L4 Lowick Nhants
119 K3 Lowick Nthumb
94 F3 Lowick Bridge Cumb
94 F3 Lowick Green Cumb
101 P7 Low Knipe Cumb
97 J8 Low Laithe N York
103 M5 Lowlands Dur
31 J5 Lowlands Torfn
86 G5 Low Langton Lincs
83 M7 Low Leighton Derbys
100 G5 Low Lorton Cumb
98 G5 Low Marishes N York
85 P7 Low Marnham Notts
119 M3 Low Middleton Nthumb
105 J11 Low Mill N York
90 F5 Low Moor C Brad
113 M11 Low Moorsley Sundld
100 C6 Low Moresby Cumb
95 J4 Low Newton Cumb
100 G2 Low Row Cumb
101 L3 Low Row Cumb
111 L8 Low Row Cumb
103 J11 Low Row N York
106 D4 Low Salchrie D & G
92 F8 Low Santon N Linc
59 J11 Lowsonford Warwks
77 L7 Low Street Norfk
37 Q5 Low Street Thurr
64 H2 Low Tharston Norfk
101 P6 Lowther Cumb
101 P6 Lowther Castle Cumb
99 M8 Lowthorpe E R Yk
8 G4 Lowton Devon
18 G11 Lowton Somset
82 D5 Lowton Wigan
82 D5 Lowton Common Wigan
82 D5 Lowton St Mary's Wigan
134 C10 Low Torry Fife
87 J6 Low Toynton Lincs
91 L10 Low Valley Barns
94 G4 Low Wood Cumb
104 C9 Low Worsall N York
101 L10 Low Wray Cumb
18 B11 Loxbeare Devon
24 B3 Loxhill Surrey
17 L4 Loxhore Devon
17 L4 Loxhore Cott Devon
47 Q4 Loxley Warwks
71 K8 Loxley Green Staffs
46 D6 Loxter Herefs
19 L3 Loxton N Som
24 B4 Loxwood W Susx
165 P7 Loyal Lodge Highld
60 F3 Lubenham Leics
87 M11 Lucasgate Lincs
23 P2 Lucas Green Surrey
18 B6 Luccombe Somset
14 G11 Luccombe Village IoW
119 N4 Lucker Nthumb
5 P7 Luckett Cnwll
52 D5 Lucking Street Essex
32 F8 Luckington Wilts
135 L3 Lucklawhill Fife
32 F10 Lucknam Wilts
18 B7 Luckwell Bridge Somset
45 N2 Lucton Herefs
103 P8 Lucy Cross N York
168 c16 Ludag W Isls
93 N11 Ludborough Lincs
6 H8 Ludbrook Devon
41 M8 Ludchurch Pembks
90 C5 Luddenden Calder
90 C5 Luddenden Foot Calder
38 G9 Luddenham Court Kent
37 Q7 Luddesdown Kent
92 D7 Luddington N Linc
47 N4 Luddington Warwks
61 P4 Luddington in the Brook Nhants
86 G3 Ludford Lincs
57 J10 Ludford Shrops
49 J11 Ludgershall Bucks
21 Q4 Ludgershall Wilts
2 E7 Ludgvan Cnwll
77 M8 Ludham Norfk
57 J9 Ludlow Shrops
10 H2 Ludney Somset
20 H10 Ludwell Wilts
104 C2 Ludworth Dur
50 G5 Luffenhall Herts
5 N3 Luffincott Devon
128 D4 Luffness E Loth
115 L3 Lugar E Ayrs
128 F5 Luggate Burn E Loth
45 N2 Lugg Green Herefs
126 D3 Luggiebank N Lans
125 L7 Lugton E Ayrs
45 R6 Lugwardine Herefs
145 J2 Luib Highld
130 E5 Luing Ag & B
45 N6 Lulham Herefs
59 K2 Lullington Derbys
25 M10 Lullington E Susx
20 E4 Lullington Somset
31 P11 Lulsgate Bottom N Som
46 D3 Lulsley Worcs
12 D8 Lulworth Camp Dorset
90 C6 Lumb Calder
89 N6 Lumb Lancs
90 B6 Lumbutts Calder
91 M4 Lumby N York
125 Q3 Lumloch E Duns
150 F7 Lumphanan Abers
134 F9 Lumphinnans Fife
150 D3 Lumsden Abers
143 M7 Lunan Angus
142 H7 Lunanhead Angus
134 D2 Luncarty P & K
99 K11 Lund E R Yk
91 R4 Lund N York
142 D10 Lundie Angus
135 L7 Lundin Links Fife
135 L7 Lundin Mill Fife
16 A2 Lundy Devon
65 J3 Lundy Green Norfk
130 E6 Lunga Ag & B
169 r7 Lunna Shet
37 Q9 Lunsford Kent
26 B9 Lunsford's Cross E Susx
81 L4 Lunt Sefton
45 M3 Luntley Herefs
10 D3 Luppitt Devon
7 J8 Lupridge Devon
91 J7 Lupset Wakefd
95 M4 Lupton Cumb
23 P9 Lurgashall W Susx
18 B11 Lurley Devon
87 K7 Lusby Lincs
7 K7 Luscombe Devon
6 G8 Luson Devon
132 D9 Luss Ag & B
130 C10 Lussagiven Ag & B
152 D6 Lusta Highld
9 J8 Lustleigh Devon
45 P2 Luston Herefs
143 M4 Luthermuir Abers
135 J4 Luthrie Fife
58 D8 Lutley Dudley
9 M9 Luton Devon
10 B4 Luton Devon
50 C6 Luton Luton
38 C8 Luton Medway
50 D6 Luton Airport Luton
60 B4 Lutterworth Leics
6 F7 Lutton Devon
6 H6 Lutton Devon
74 H5 Lutton Lincs
61 P3 Lutton Nhants
18 C7 Luxborough Somset
4 H10 Luxulyan Cnwll
83 L4 Luzley Tamesd
167 M9 Lybster Highld
56 E7 Lydbury North Shrops
17 M4 Lydcott Devon
26 H7 Lydd Kent
27 J7 Lydd Airport Kent
27 N2 Lydden Kent
39 Q8 Lydden Kent
73 M11 Lyddington Rutlnd
18 F8 Lydeard St Lawrence Somset
23 K3 Lyde Green Hants
8 D7 Lydford Devon
19 Q8 Lydford on Fosse Somset
89 Q5 Lydgate Calder
90 B7 Lydgate Rochdl
56 E6 Lydham Shrops
33 L7 Lydiard Green Wilts
33 L7 Lydiard Millicent Wilts
33 M8 Lydiard Tregoze Swindn
81 M4 Lydiate Sefton
58 E9 Lydiate Ash Worcs
12 B2 Lydlinch Dorset
32 B4 Lydney Gloucs
41 L11 Lydstep Pembks
58 D8 Lye Dudley
19 N2 Lye Cross N Som
35 Q4 Lye Green Bucks

25 M4 Lye Green E Susx
59 J11 Lye Green Warwks
57 P10 Lye Head Worcs
20 F5 Lye's Green Wilts
34 C6 Lyford Oxon
27 K3 Lymbridge Green Kent
10 G6 Lyme Regis Dorset
27 L3 Lyminge Kent
13 P5 Lymington Hants
24 B10 Lyminster W Susx
82 E7 Lymm Warrtn
82 E8 Lymm Services Warrtn
27 K4 Lympne Kent
19 K4 Lympsham Somset
9 N8 Lympstone Devon
17 N2 Lynbridge Devon
148 D7 Lynchat Highld
76 H10 Lynch Green Norfk
13 P3 Lyndhurst Hants
73 N10 Lyndon Rutlnd
58 H7 Lyndon Green Birm
117 J2 Lyne Border
36 B7 Lyne Surrey
69 M8 Lyneal Shrops
46 B8 Lyne Down Herefs
9 L9 Lyneham Devon
47 Q10 Lyneham Oxon
33 K9 Lyneham Wilts
33 K9 *Lyneham Airport* Wilts
111 K6 Lyneholmford Cumb
113 L2 Lynemouth Nthumb
151 K5 Lyne of Skene Abers
103 L5 Lynesack Dur
169 c7 Lyness Ork
76 F8 Lyng Norfk
19 K9 Lyng Somset
17 N2 Lynmouth Devon
58 G4 Lynn Staffs
70 D11 Lynn Wrekin
38 F9 Lynsted Kent
16 C10 Lynstone Cnwll
17 N2 Lynton Devon
11 P3 Lyon's Gate Dorset
45 L3 Lyonshall Herefs
12 F5 Lytchett Matravers Dorset
12 G6 Lytchett Minster Dorset
167 N4 Lyth Highld
88 D5 Lytham Lancs
88 C5 Lytham St Anne's Lancs
56 H3 Lythbank Shrops
105 M8 Lythe N York
167 J3 Lythmore Highld

M

3 K7 Mabe Burnthouse Cnwll
87 P4 Mablethorpe Lincs
83 K10 Macclesfield Ches E
83 K10 Macclesfield Crematorium Ches E
158 H5 Macduff Abers
120 D10 Macharioch Ag & B
30 H7 Machen Caerph
120 G5 Machrie N Ayrs
120 B7 Machrihanish Ag & B
136 b3 Machrins Ag & B
54 G4 Machynlleth Powys
28 F5 Machynys Carmth
71 Q7 Mackworth Derbys
128 C5 Macmerry E Loth
8 D6 Maddaford Devon
134 B3 Madderty P & K
21 L6 Maddington Wilts
126 G2 Maddiston Falk
15 Q4 Madehurst W Susx
70 D6 Madeley Staffs
57 M4 Madeley Wrekin
70 D5 Madeley Heath Staffs
10 C2 Madford Devon
62 E8 Madingley Cambs
45 N7 Madley Herefs
46 F5 Madresfield Worcs
2 D7 Madron Cnwll
78 H8 Maenaddwyn IoA
79 P11 Maenan Conwy
41 L5 Maenclochog Pembks
30 D9 Maendy V Glam
3 K8 Maenporth Cnwll
67 M6 Maentwrog Gwynd
42 G3 Maen-y-groes Cerdgn
16 C10 Maer Cnwll
70 D7 Maer Staffs
43 N9 Maerdy Carmth
30 C5 Maerdy Rhondd
69 K10 Maesbrook Shrops
69 K9 Maesbury Shrops
69 K9 Maesbury Marsh Shrops
31 J7 Maes-glas Newpt
41 P6 Maesgwynne Carmth
68 H2 Maeshafn Denbgs
42 G6 Maesllyn Cerdgn
44 E5 Maesmynis Powys
44 E5 Maesmynis Powys
29 N6 Maesteg Brdgnd
43 L11 Maesybont Carmth
30 G6 Maesycwmmer Caerph
51 M9 Magdalen Laver Essex
157 Q8 Maggieknockater Moray
51 L5 Maggots End Essex
25 P8 Magham Down E Susx
81 M4 Maghull Sefton
60 B4 Magna Park Leics
31 M7 Magor Mons
31 M7 Magor Services Mons
24 G3 Maidenbower W Susx
20 F7 Maiden Bradley Wilts
7 N5 Maidencombe Torbay
10 F5 Maidenhayne Devon
31 Q11 Maiden Head N Som
35 N8 Maidenhead W & M
113 J11 Maiden Law Dur
11 M5 Maiden Newton Dorset
114 D6 Maidens S Ayrs
35 P10 Maiden's Green Br For
87 K5 Maidenwell Lincs
41 J11 Maiden Wells Pembks
48 H4 Maidford Nhants
49 K7 Maids Moreton Bucks
38 C10 Maidstone Kent
38 D10 Maidstone Services Kent
60 F5 Maidwell Nhants
169 r9 Mail Shet
31 K7 Maindee Newpt
169 d6 Mainland Ork
169 r8 Mainland Shet
104 B4 Mainsforth Dur
143 J5 Mains of Balhall Angus
143 L3 Mains of Balnakettle Abers
157 L11 Mains of Dalvey Highld
143 N3 Mains of Haulkerton Abers
150 D2 Mains of Lesmoir Abers
143 J6 Mains of Melgunds Angus
109 K9 Mainsriddle D & G
56 D7 Mainstone Shrops
46 F10 Maisemore Gloucs
58 H9 Major's Green Worcs
72 B2 Makeney Derbys
7 J11 Malborough Devon
83 N8 Malcoff Derbys
36 E8 Malden Rushett Gt Lon
52 E10 Maldon Essex
96 D8 Malham N York
152 H5 Maligar Highld
145 L8 Mallaig Highld
145 L8 Mallaigvaig Highld
127 M4 Malleny Mills C Edin
51 L5 Mallows Green Essex
78 G11 Malltraeth IoA
55 K2 Mallwyd Gwynd
32 H7 Malmesbury Wilts
17 P2 Malmsmead Devon
69 N5 Malpas Ches W
3 L5 Malpas Cnwll
31 K6 Malpas Newpt
46 D10 Malswick Gloucs
87 K4 Maltby Lincs
84 H2 Maltby Rothm
104 E8 Maltby S on T
87 N4 Maltby le Marsh Lincs
52 G7 Malting Green Essex
26 F3 Maltman's Hill Kent
98 F6 Malton N York
46 E6 Malvern Hills
46 E5 Malvern Link Worcs
46 E6 Malvern Wells Worcs
57 M10 Mamble Worcs
31 K4 Mamhilad Mons
3 K9 Manaccan Cnwll
55 Q4 Manafon Powys
168 g9 Manais W Isls
9 J8 Manaton Devon
87 L3 Manby Lincs
59 M5 Mancetter Warwks
82 H5 Manchester Manch
82 H8 *Manchester Airport* Manch
81 L11 Mancot Flints
146 H7 Mandally Highld
129 L9 Manderston House Border
62 G3 Manea Cambs
58 H5 Maney Birm
103 P8 Manfield N York
11 K5 Mangerton Dorset
32 C9 Mangotsfield S Glos
50 D6 Mangrove Green Herts
2 H7 Manhay Cnwll
168 g9 Manish W Isls
90 B6 Mankinholes Calder
81 Q10 Manley Ches W
30 G4 Manmoel Caerph
136 B7 Mannel Ag & B
21 M3 Manningford Bohune Wilts
21 M3 Manningford Bruce Wilts
90 E3 Manningham C Brad
24 F5 Manning's Heath W Susx
13 J3 Mannington Dorset
53 K5 Manningtree Essex
151 N7 Mannofield C Aber
41 L11 Manorbier Pembks
41 K10 Manorbier Newton Pembks
43 N9 Manordeilo Carmth
118 C4 Manorhill Border
40 H3 Manorowen Pembks
37 K3 Manor Park Gt Lon
37 K3 Manor Park Crematorium Gt Lon
45 M6 Mansell Gamage Herefs
45 N5 Mansell Lacy Herefs
95 N4 Mansergh Cumb
115 M5 Mansfield E Ayrs
84 H8 Mansfield Notts
84 H9 Mansfield & District Crematorium Notts
84 H8 Mansfield Woodhouse Notts
94 F4 Mansriggs Cumb
20 F11 Manston Dorset
39 P8 Manston Kent
91 K4 Manston Leeds
12 G3 Manswood Dorset
73 N3 Manthorpe Lincs
73 R7 Manthorpe Lincs
92 F10 Manton N Linc
85 K5 Manton Notts
73 M10 Manton Rutlnd
33 N11 Manton Wilts
51 L5 Manuden Essex
51 M8 Manwood Green Essex
20 C9 Maperton Somset
85 M8 Maplebeck Notts
36 B2 Maple Cross Herts
35 J9 Mapledurham Oxon
23 J4 Mapledurwell Hants
24 E6 Maplehurst W Susx
37 N8 Maplescombe Kent
71 M5 Mapleton Derbys
37 L11 Mapleton Kent
72 C2 Mapperley Derbys
72 F2 Mapperley Park C Nott
11 L5 Mapperton Dorset
58 G11 Mappleborough Green Warwks
93 M2 Mappleton E R Yk
91 J8 Mapplewell Barns
12 B3 Mappowder Dorset
3 K3 Marazanvose Cnwll
2 E7 Marazion Cnwll
69 Q5 Marbury Ches E
74 H11 March Cambs
116 D8 March S Lans
34 E5 Marcham Oxon
69 Q9 Marchamley Shrops
69 Q8 Marchamley Wood Shrops
71 L8 Marchington Staffs
71 L9 Marchington Woodlands Staffs
66 E9 Marchros Gwynd
69 L5 Marchwiel Wrexhm
14 C4 Marchwood Hants
29 P11 Marcross V Glam
45 Q5 Marden Herefs
26 B3 Marden Kent
21 L3 Marden Wilts
51 N10 Marden Ash Essex
26 B3 Marden Beech Kent
25 M4 Mardens Hill E Susx
26 C3 Marden Thorn Kent
50 G7 Mardlebury Herts
45 L11 Mardy Mons
73 J9 Marefield Leics
87 J8 Mareham le Fen Lincs
87 J7 Mareham on the Hill Lincs
84 E11 Marehay Derbys
24 C7 Marehill W Susx
25 L6 Maresfield E Susx
93 K5 Marfleet C KuH
69 L3 Marford Wrexhm
29 L7 Margam Neath
29 L7 Margam Crematorium Neath
20 F11 Margaret Marsh Dorset
51 N8 Margaret Roding Essex
51 Q10 Margaretting Essex
51 Q10 Margaretting Tye Essex
39 Q7 Margate Kent
121 K5 Margnaheglish N Ayrs
108 C10 Margrie D & G
105 J7 Margrove Park R & Cl
75 P9 Marham Norfk
16 C11 Marhamchurch Cnwll
74 B10 Marholm C Pete
79 J8 Marian-glas IoA
17 N7 Mariansleigh Devon
38 F7 Marine Town Kent
151 J6 Marionburgh Abers
152 H5 Marishader Highld
6 D6 Maristow Devon
109 N4 Marjoriebanks D & G
19 L5 Mark Somset
25 L2 Markbeech Kent
87 N5 Markby Lincs
19 L5 Mark Causeway Somset
25 N4 Mark Cross E Susx
72 A3 Markeaton C Derb
72 A3 Markeaton Crematorium C Derb
72 C10 Market Bosworth Leics
74 B8 Market Deeping Lincs
70 B8 Market Drayton Shrops
60 F3 Market Harborough Leics
21 K4 Market Lavington Wilts
73 M7 Market Overton Rutlnd
86 F3 Market Rasen Lincs
86 H5 Market Stainton Lincs
85 J7 Market Warsop Notts
92 E2 Market Weighton E R Yk
64 D6 Market Weston Suffk
72 D9 Markfield Leics
30 G4 Markham Caerph
85 M6 Markham Moor Notts
134 H7 Markinch Fife
97 L7 Markington N York
128 F4 Markle E Loth
19 Q2 Marksbury BaNES
14 E8 Mark's Corner IoW
52 F7 Marks Tey Essex
5 P10 Markwell Cnwll
50 C7 Markyate Herts
33 N11 Marlborough Wilts
45 Q4 Marlbrook Herefs
58 E10 Marlbrook Worcs
47 L4 Marlcliff Warwks
7 M6 Marldon Devon
25 N7 Marle Green E Susx
65 L10 Marlesford Suffk
39 L11 Marley Kent
39 P11 Marley Kent
69 Q5 Marley Green Ches E
113 K9 Marley Hill Gatesd
76 G10 Marlingford Norfk
40 E9 Marloes Pembks
35 M7 Marlow Bucks
56 G9 Marlow Herefs
35 M7 Marlow Bottom Bucks
37 K11 Marlpit Hill Kent
25 L5 Marlpits E Susx
26 B9 Marlpits E Susx
84 F11 Marlpool Derbys
20 E11 Marnhull Dorset
83 L7 Marple Stockp
83 L7 Marple Bridge Stockp
91 N9 Marr Donc
103 L11 Marrick N York
41 P9 Marros Carmth
90 C8 Marsden Kirk
113 N8 Marsden S Tyne
89 P3 Marsden Height Lancs
96 D3 Marsett N York
35 M3 Marsh Bucks
90 C3 Marsh C Brad
10 F2 Marsh Devon
50 E8 Marshall's Heath Herts
50 E9 Marshalswick Herts
76 H7 Marsham Norfk
34 G5 Marsh Baldon Oxon
34 D11 Marsh Benham W Berk
39 P10 Marshborough Kent
56 G7 Marshbrook Shrops
93 Q11 Marshchapel Lincs
50 C5 Marsh Farm Luton
31 J8 Marshfield Newpt
32 E10 Marshfield S Glos
5 K3 Marshgate Cnwll
48 H10 Marsh Gibbon Bucks
9 P6 Marsh Green Devon
25 K2 Marsh Green Kent
57 L2 Marsh Green Wrekin
75 K9 Marshland St James Norfk
84 F5 Marsh Lane Derbys
31 Q3 Marsh Lane Gloucs
88 D7 Marshside Sefton
18 C6 Marsh Street Somset
10 H5 Marshwood Dorset
103 M10 Marske N York
104 H6 Marske-by-the-Sea R & Cl
82 E5 Marsland Green Wigan
82 E9 Marston Ches W
45 M3 Marston Herefs
73 M2 Marston Lincs
34 F3 Marston Oxon
58 B2 Marston Staffs
70 G9 Marston Staffs
59 K6 Marston Warwks
21 J3 Marston Wilts
59 J7 Marston Green Solhll
59 N7 Marston Jabbet Warwks
19 Q10 Marston Magna Somset
33 M5 Marston Meysey Wilts
71 L7 Marston Montgomery Derbys
49 Q6 Marston Moretaine C Beds
71 N9 Marston on Dove Derbys
48 F6 Marston St Lawrence Nhants
45 R3 Marston Stannett Herefs
60 E3 Marston Trussell Nhants
45 R11 Marstow Herefs
35 P2 Marsworth Bucks
21 Q2 Marten Wilts
82 G9 Marthall Ches E
77 P8 Martham Norfk
21 L11 Martin Hants
27 P2 Martin Kent
86 F9 Martin Lincs
86 H7 Martin Lincs
101 M7 Martindale Cumb
86 G8 Martin Dales Lincs
21 L10 Martin Drove End Hants
17 M2 Martinhoe Devon
46 G2 Martin Hussingtree Worcs
82 E7 Martinscroft Warrtn
11 N7 Martinstown Dorset
53 M2 Martlesham Suffk
53 M2 Martlesham Heath Suffk
41 K8 Martletwy Pembks
46 E2 Martley Worcs
19 N11 Martock Somset
83 J11 Marton Ches E
82 D11 Marton Ches W
94 E5 Marton Cumb
93 L3 Marton E R Yk
99 Q7 Marton E R Yk
85 P4 Marton Lincs
104 F7 Marton Middsb
97 P8 Marton N York
98 E4 Marton N York
56 D4 Marton Shrops
59 P11 Marton Warwks
97 N6 Marton-le-Moor N York
36 C9 Martyr's Green Surrey
22 F8 Martyr Worthy Hants
169 b4 Marwick Ork
17 J4 Marwood Devon
155 N7 Marybank Highld
155 P6 Maryburgh Highld
151 M8 Maryculter Abers
129 L8 Marygold Border
125 P4 Maryhill C Glas
143 M4 Marykirk Abers
31 P3 Maryland Mons
36 G4 Marylebone Gt Lon
88 H9 Marylebone Wigan
157 M10 Marypark Moray
100 D3 Maryport Cumb
106 F11 Maryport D & G
8 B8 Marystow Devon
8 D9 Mary Tavy Devon
143 M6 Maryton Angus
150 F8 Marywell Abers
151 N8 Marywell Abers
143 M9 Marywell Angus
97 K4 Masham N York
51 Q8 Mashbury Essex
113 K6 Mason N u Ty
95 P5 Masongill N York
114 G3 Masonhill Crematorium S Ayrs
84 G5 Mastin Moor Derbys
51 M8 Matching Essex
51 M8 Matching Green Essex
51 M8 Matching Tye Essex
112 F6 Matfen Nthumb
25 Q2 Matfield Kent
31 P6 Mathern Mons
46 D5 Mathon Herefs
40 G4 Mathry Pembks
76 H5 Matlask Norfk
84 D9 Matlock Derbys
84 D8 Matlock Bank Derbys
84 C9 Matlock Bath Derbys
84 C9 Matlock Dale Derbys
46 G11 Matson Gloucs
101 L6 Matterdale End Cumb
85 L3 Mattersey Notts
85 L3 Mattersey Thorpe Notts
23 K3 Mattingley Hants
76 F9 Mattishall Norfk
76 F9 Mattishall Burgh Norfk
115 J2 Mauchline E Ayrs
159 M8 Maud Abers
11 c1 Maufant Jersey
47 P9 Maugersbury Gloucs
80 g3 Maughold IoM
155 M10 Mauld Highld
50 C3 Maulden C Beds
102 B7 Maulds Meaburn Cumb
97 N3 Maunby N York
45 R4 Maund Bryan Herefs
18 E9 Maundown Somset
77 P9 Mautby Norfk
71 K11 Mavesyn Ridware Staffs
87 L7 Mavis Enderby Lincs
109 N11 Mawbray Cumb
88 F8 Mawdesley Lancs
29 M8 Mawdlam Brdgnd
3 J8 Mawgan Cnwll
4 D8 Mawgan Porth Cnwll
70 C3 Maw Green Ches E
3 J4 Mawla Cnwll
3 K8 Mawnan Cnwll
3 K8 Mawnan Smith Cnwll
60 H5 Mawsley Nhants
87 N6 Mawthorpe Lincs
74 B9 Maxey C Pete
59 K7 Maxstoke Warwks
27 K3 Maxted Street Kent
118 B4 Maxton Border
27 P3 Maxton Kent
109 L5 Maxwell Town D & G
5 M3 Maxworthy Cnwll
28 H7 Mayals Swans
70 F5 May Bank Staffs
114 E6 Maybole S Ayrs
36 B9 Maybury Surrey
24 D3 Mayes Green Surrey
25 N5 Mayfield E Susx
128 B7 Mayfield Mdloth
71 M5 Mayfield Staffs
23 Q3 Mayford Surrey
46 D10 May Hill Gloucs
52 F11 Mayland Essex
52 F11 Maylandsea Essex
25 N7 Maynard's Green E Susx
58 G9 Maypole Birm
39 M9 Maypole Kent
45 P11 Maypole Mons
65 N2 Maypole Green Norfk
64 C10 Maypole Green Suffk
65 K8 Maypole Green Suffk
35 K8 May's Green Oxon
36 C9 May's Green Surrey
16 C8 Mead Devon
20 C3 Meadgate BaNES
35 M3 Meadle Bucks
103 P3 Meadowfield Dur
56 E4 Meadowtown Shrops
5 Q5 Meadwell Devon
70 F7 Meaford Staffs
101 P11 Meal Bank Cumb
109 P11 Mealrigg Cumb
100 H2 Mealsgate Cumb
90 H3 Meanwood Leeds
96 B8 Mearbeck N York
19 N6 Meare Somset
19 J10 Meare Green Somset
19 K9 Meare Green Somset
125 N6 Mearns E Rens
60 H7 Mears Ashby Nhants
72 A8 Measham Leics
95 J4 Meathop Cumb
93 J3 Meaux E R Yk
6 E5 Meavy Devon
60 H2 Medbourne Leics
16 D8 Meddon Devon
85 J7 Meden Vale Notts
87 K9 Medlam Lincs
88 E3 Medlar Lancs
35 M8 Medmenham Bucks
112 H10 Medomsley Dur
23 J7 Medstead Hants
38 B9 Medway Crematorium Kent
38 D9 Medway Services Medway
70 H2 Meerbrook Staffs
45 M4 Meer Common Herefs
51 K4 Meesden Herts
70 A10 Meeson Wrekin
17 J10 Meeth Devon
63 M9 Meeting Green Suffk
77 L6 Meeting House Hill Norfk
41 Q6 Meidrim Carmth
56 B2 Meifod Powys
142 D9 Meigle P & K
115 Q5 Meikle Carco D & G
126 C7 Meikle Earnock S Lans
124 D5 Meikle Kilmory Ag & B
141 P10 Meikle Obney P & K
142 B10 Meikleour P & K
158 H11 Meikle Wartle Abers
28 E2 Meinciau Carmth
70 G6 Meir C Stke
70 G6 Meir Heath Staffs
51 J2 Melbourn Cambs
72 B5 Melbourne Derbys
92 C2 Melbourne E R Yk
3 N3 Melbur Cnwll
16 F8 Melbury Devon
20 G10 Melbury Abbas Dorset
11 M3 Melbury Bubb Dorset
11 M3 Melbury Osmond Dorset
11 M3 Melbury Sampford Dorset
61 M7 Melchbourne Bed
12 C4 Melcombe Bingham Dorset
8 E6 Meldon Devon
112 H4 Meldon Nthumb
112 H3 Meldon Park Nthumb
62 E11 Meldreth Cambs
133 L8 Meldrum Stirlg
130 G5 Melfort Ag & B
80 F8 Meliden Denbgs
41 N8 Melinau Pembks
55 J5 Melin-byrhedyn Powys
29 M4 Melincourt Neath
67 Q2 Melin-y-coed Conwy
55 P3 Melin-y-ddol Powys
68 D5 Melin-y-wig Denbgs
101 Q5 Melkinthorpe Cumb
111 P8 Melkridge Nthumb
20 H2 Melksham Wilts
2 H8 Mellangoose Cnwll
34 E9 Mell Green W Berk
110 H11 Mellguards Cumb
95 M6 Melling Lancs
81 M4 Melling Sefton
81 N4 Melling Mount Sefton
64 F7 Mellis Suffk
160 C8 Mellon Charles Highld
160 D7 Mellon Udrigle Highld
89 K4 Mellor Lancs
83 L7 Mellor Stockp
89 J4 Mellor Brook Lancs
20 D5 Mells Somset
65 N6 Mells Suffk
102 B3 Melmerby Cumb
96 G3 Melmerby N York
97 M5 Melmerby N York
165 N4 Melness Highld
64 A10 Melon Green Suffk
11 K5 Melplash Dorset
117 Q4 Melrose Border
169 b8 Melsetter Ork
103 N9 Melsonby N York
90 E8 Meltham Kirk
90 E8 Meltham Mills Kirk
92 G5 Melton E R Yk
65 K11 Melton Suffk
98 F10 Meltonby E R Yk
76 E5 Melton Constable Norfk
73 K7 Melton Mowbray Leics
93 J8 Melton Ross N Linc
160 A9 Melvaig Highld
69 K11 Melverley Shrops
69 K11 Melverley Green Shrops
166 E4 Melvich Highld
10 F4 Membury Devon
34 B9 Membury Services W Berk
159 N5 Memsie Abers
142 G6 Memus Angus
4 H11 Menabilly Cnwll
3 J4 Menagissey Cnwll
79 K10 Menai Bridge IoA
65 K5 Mendham Suffk
19 P4 Mendip Hills
64 G8 Mendlesham Suffk
64 F9 Mendlesham Green Suffk
5 M9 Menheniot Cnwll
57 N11 Menithwood Worcs
115 R6 Mennock D & G
90 F2 Menston C Brad
133 P8 Menstrie Clacks

92 B4 Menthorpe N York
49 P11 Mentmore Bucks
145 N10 Meoble Highld
56 H2 Meole Brace Shrops
22 H11 Meonstoke Hants
37 P7 Meopham Kent
37 P7 Meopham Green Kent
37 P7 Meopham Station Kent
62 F4 Mepal Cambs
50 D3 Meppershall C Beds
45 L5 Merbach Herefs
82 F8 Mere Ches E
20 F8 Mere Wilts
88 E7 Mere Brow Lancs
89 P4 Mereclough Lancs
58 H5 Mere Green Birm
47 J2 Mere Green Worcs
82 E10 Mere Heath Ches W
38 D9 Meresborough Medway
37 Q10 Mereworth Kent
59 K8 Meriden Solhll
152 F11 Merkadale Highld
12 H5 Merley Poole
40 H8 Merlin's Bridge Pembks
69 N10 Merrington Shrops
40 H11 Merrion Pembks
11 J2 Merriott Somset
8 D9 Merrivale Devon
36 B10 Merrow Surrey
12 H4 Merry Field Hill Dorset
36 D2 Merry Hill Herts
58 C5 Merryhill Wolves
72 D9 Merry Lees Leics
5 M8 Merrymeet Cnwll
52 H8 Mersea Island Essex
27 J3 Mersham Kent
36 G10 Merstham Surrey
15 N6 Merston W Susx
14 F9 Merstone IoW
3 M5 Merther Cnwll
42 G10 Merthyr Carmth
44 D7 Merthyr Cynog Powys
30 F11 Merthyr Dyfan V Glam
29 N9 Merthyr Mawr Brdgnd
30 D3 Merthyr Tydfil Myr Td
30 E5 Merthyr Vale Myr Td
17 J9 Merton Devon
36 G6 Merton Gt Lon
64 C2 Merton Norfk
48 G11 Merton Oxon
17 P8 Meshaw Devon
52 E8 Messing Essex
92 E10 Messingham N Linc
65 K5 Metfield Suffk
5 Q8 Metherell Cnwll
86 E8 Metheringham Lincs
135 K8 Methil Fife
135 K7 Methilhill Fife
91 K5 Methley Leeds
91 K5 Methley Junction Leeds
159 L10 Methlick Abers
134 C2 Methven P & K
63 M2 Methwold Norfk
63 M2 Methwold Hythe Norfk
65 M4 Mettingham Suffk
76 J4 Metton Norfk
3 Q5 Mevagissey Cnwll
91 M10 Mexborough Donc
167 N2 Mey Highld
66 C8 Meyllteyrn Gwynd
33 M4 Meysey Hampton Gloucs
168 f4 Miabhig W Isls
168 f4 Miavaig W Isls
45 Q9 Michaelchurch Herefs
45 L8 Michaelchurch Escley Herefs
45 J4 Michaelchurch-on-Arrow Powys
30 H8 Michaelstone-y-Fedw Newpt
30 G10 Michaelston-le-Pit V Glam
4 H6 Michaelstow Cnwll
32 D5 Michaelwood Services Gloucs
6 H5 Michelcombe Devon
22 F7 Micheldever Hants
22 F6 Micheldever Station Hants
22 B9 Michelmersh Hants
64 G9 Mickfield Suffk
84 H2 Micklebring Donc
105 M8 Mickleby N York
91 L4 Micklefield Leeds
50 B11 Micklefield Green Herts
36 E10 Mickleham Surrey
71 Q8 Mickleover C Derb
90 E2 Micklethwaite C Brad
110 E10 Micklethwaite Cumb
103 J6 Mickleton Dur
47 N6 Mickleton Gloucs
91 L5 Mickletown Leeds
81 N11 Mickle Trafford Ches W
84 D5 Mickley Derbys
97 L5 Mickley N York
64 A10 Mickley Green Suffk
112 G8 Mickley Square Nthumb
159 M5 Mid Ardlaw Abers
169 d2 Midbea Ork
150 G7 Mid Beltie Abers
13 L5 Mid Bockhampton Dorset
127 K4 Mid Calder W Loth
167 N9 Mid Clyth Highld
158 G5 Mid Culbeuchly Abers
35 K7 Middle Assendon Oxon
48 E9 Middle Aston Oxon
48 D9 Middle Barton Oxon
110 D5 Middlebie D & G
141 L4 Middlebridge P & K
11 K2 Middle Chinnock Somset
49 K9 Middle Claydon Bucks
91 L9 Middlecliffe Barns
8 H7 Middlecott Devon
33 J3 Middle Duntisbourne Gloucs
96 H3 Middleham N York
84 F5 Middle Handley Derbys
64 D4 Middle Harling Norfk
5 M8 Middlehill Cnwll
32 F11 Middlehill Wilts
56 H7 Middlehope Shrops
131 J10 Middle Kames Ag & B
45 L5 Middle Littleton Worcs
70 D5 Middle Madeley Staffs
45 L8 Middle Maes-coed Herefs
11 P3 Middlemarsh Dorset
71 L6 Middle Mayfield Staffs
40 F5 Middle Mill Pembks
6 D4 Middlemore Devon
26 E4 Middle Quarter Kent
86 E3 Middle Rasen Lincs
7 N5 Middle Rocombe Devon
95 N8 Middle Salter Lancs
104 E7 Middlesbrough Middsb
101 M2 Middlesceugh Cumb
95 M3 Middleshaw Cumb
96 G6 Middlesmoor N York
18 G10 Middle Stoford Somset
38 D6 Middle Stoke Medway
103 Q4 Middlestone Dur
103 P4 Middlestone Moor Dur
19 M5 Middle Stoughton Somset
90 H7 Middlestown Wakefd
32 E4 Middle Street Gloucs
5 K9 Middle Taphouse Cnwll
118 C2 Middlethird Border
136 A7 Middleton Ag & B
95 N3 Middleton Cumb
71 M2 Middleton Derbys
84 C9 Middleton Derbys
52 E4 Middleton Essex
22 D6 Middleton Hants
57 J11 Middleton Herefs
95 J9 Middleton Lancs
91 J5 Middleton Leeds
96 H11 Middleton N York
98 F3 Middleton N York
60 H3 Middleton Nhants
75 N7 Middleton Norfk
112 G4 Middleton Nthumb
119 M3 Middleton Nthumb
134 E6 Middleton P & K
89 P9 Middleton Rochdl
57 J9 Middleton Shrops
69 K9 Middleton Shrops
65 N8 Middleton Suffk
28 D7 Middleton Swans
59 J5 Middleton Warwks
48 E6 Middleton Cheney Nhants
89 P9 Middleton Crematorium Rochdl
70 H7 Middleton Green Staffs
119 J5 Middleton Hall Nthumb
102 H5 Middleton-in-Teesdale Dur
65 N8 Middleton Moor Suffk
104 C8 Middleton One Row Darltn
104 E9 Middleton-on-Leven N York
15 Q6 Middleton-on-Sea W Susx
45 Q2 Middleton on the Hill Herefs
99 J11 Middleton on the Wolds E R Yk
151 N5 Middleton Park C Aber
57 L6 Middleton Priors Shrops
97 M5 Middleton Quernhow N York
104 B8 Middleton St George Darltn
57 M7 Middleton Scriven Shrops
48 F10 Middleton Stoney Oxon
103 P9 Middleton Tyas N York
100 C9 Middletown Cumb
2 b3 Middle Town IoS
31 N10 Middletown N Som
56 E2 Middletown Powys
48 B6 Middle Tysoe Warwks
21 Q7 Middle Wallop Hants
82 F11 Middlewich Ches E
21 P8 Middle Winterslow Wilts
5 M6 Middlewood Cnwll
45 K6 Middlewood Herefs
21 M7 Middle Woodford Wilts
64 F9 Middlewood Green Suffk
125 N11 Middleyard E Ayrs
32 F4 Middle Yard Gloucs
19 L8 Middlezoy Somset
103 P5 Middridge Dur
20 E2 Midford BaNES
88 G6 Midge Hall Lancs
111 M9 Midgeholme Cumb
34 G11 Midgham W Berk
90 C5 Midgley Calder
90 H8 Midgley Wakefd
36 E11 Mid Holmwood Surrey
90 G11 Midhopestones Sheff
23 N10 Midhurst W Susx
15 N5 Mid Lavant W Susx
117 Q5 Midlem Border
155 M10 Mid Mains Highld
19 N9 Midney Somset
124 C6 Midpark Ag & B
20 C4 Midsomer Norton BaNES
165 N4 Midtown Highld
87 L9 Midville Lincs
48 B3 Mid Warwickshire Crematorium Warwks
83 K8 Midway Ches E
169 s4 Mid Yell Shet
150 C6 Migvie Abers
20 C11 Milborne Port Somset
12 D5 Milborne St Andrew Dorset
20 C10 Milborne Wick Somset
112 H5 Milbourne Nthumb
33 J7 Milbourne Wilts
102 C5 Milburn Cumb
32 C6 Milbury Heath S Glos
97 P7 Milby N York
48 D8 Milcombe Oxon
52 G2 Milden Suffk
63 M6 Mildenhall Suffk
33 P11 Mildenhall Wilts
56 E10 Milebrook Powys
26 C2 Milebush Kent
33 J11 Mile Elm Wilts
52 G6 Mile End Essex
31 Q2 Mile End Gloucs
65 L4 Mile End Suffk
76 C8 Mileham Norfk
24 F9 Mile Oak Br & H
25 Q2 Mile Oak Kent
59 J4 Mile Oak Staffs
45 R2 Miles Hope Herefs
134 D10 Milesmark Fife
83 J5 Miles Platting Manch
38 F7 Mile Town Kent
118 H4 Milfield Nthumb
84 E11 Milford Derbys
16 C7 Milford Devon
55 P6 Milford Powys
70 H10 Milford Staffs
23 P6 Milford Surrey
40 H9 Milford Haven Pembks
13 N6 Milford on Sea Hants
31 Q3 Milkwall Gloucs
11 a1 Millais Jersey
23 M9 Milland W Susx
23 M9 Milland Marsh W Susx
90 C6 Mill Bank Calder
101 J5 Millbeck Cumb
159 P9 Millbreck Abers
23 M6 Millbridge Surrey
50 B3 Millbrook C Beds
14 C4 Millbrook C Sotn
6 C8 Millbrook Cnwll
11 b2 Millbrook Jersey
83 L5 Millbrook Tamesd
83 L7 Mill Brow Stockp
151 K6 Millbuie Abers
155 Q7 Millbuie Highld
7 L9 Millcombe Devon
77 L11 Mill Common Norfk
65 N5 Mill Common Suffk
26 D7 Millcorner E Susx
156 B3 Millcraig Highld
7 J6 Mill Cross Devon
71 L4 Milldale Staffs
35 L7 Mill End Bucks
62 D4 Mill End Cambs
32 D5 Millend Gloucs
50 H4 Mill End Herts
127 Q4 Millerhill Mdloth
83 P10 Miller's Dale Derbys
71 P4 Millers Green Derbys
51 N9 Miller's Green Essex
125 Q4 Millerston C Glas
89 P7 Millgate Lancs
63 K11 Mill Green Cambs
51 P10 Mill Green Essex
50 F8 Mill Green Herts
74 D6 Mill Green Lincs
64 G5 Mill Green Norfk
70 B9 Millgreen Shrops
58 G4 Mill Green Staffs
71 K10 Mill Green Staffs
52 G3 Mill Green Suffk
64 D10 Mill Green Suffk
64 G9 Mill Green Suffk
65 L9 Mill Green Suffk
45 K5 Millhalf Herefs
10 E4 Millhayes Devon
95 K6 Millhead Lancs
126 C7 Millheugh S Lans
25 P9 Mill Hill E Susx
36 F2 Mill Hill Gt Lon
124 B3 Millhouse Ag & B
101 L3 Millhouse Cumb
109 P3 Millhousebridge D & G
90 G10 Millhouse Green Barns
91 L10 Millhouses Barns
84 D4 Millhouses Sheff
125 L5 Milliken Park Rens
41 J8 Millin Cross Pembks
98 G10 Millington E R Yk
70 E8 Millmeece Staffs
95 L4 Millness Cumb
133 N4 Mill of Drummond P & K
132 D11 Mill of Haldane W Duns
94 D4 Millom Cumb
5 K2 Millook Cnwll
2 F7 Millpool Cnwll
5 J7 Millpool Cnwll
124 F7 Millport N Ayrs
95 J4 Mill Side Cumb
37 Q9 Mill Street Kent
76 F8 Mill Street Norfk
64 F7 Mill Street Suffk
84 D5 Millthorpe Derbys
95 P2 Millthrop Cumb
151 M7 Milltimber C Aber
149 P6 Milltown Abers
150 D4 Milltown Abers
5 J10 Milltown Cnwll
110 F5 Milltown D & G
84 E8 Milltown Derbys
17 K4 Milltown Devon
150 H7 Milltown of Campfield Abers
157 P9 Milltown of Edinvillie Moray
150 G7 Milltown of Learney Abers
134 E7 Milnathort P & K
125 P3 Milngavie E Duns
89 Q8 Milnrow Rochdl
95 K4 Milnthorpe Cumb
91 J7 Milnthorpe Wakefd
152 B8 Milovaig Highld
57 L10 Milson Shrops
38 F10 Milstead Kent
21 N5 Milston Wilts
74 B4 Milthorpe Lincs
48 G5 Milthorpe Nhants
70 G4 Milton C Stke
62 G8 Milton Cambs
111 L8 Milton Cumb
106 H7 Milton D & G
108 H6 Milton D & G
71 Q9 Milton Derbys
153 N9 Milton Highld
155 N11 Milton Highld
155 Q8 Milton Highld
156 D3 Milton Highld
167 P6 Milton Highld
125 K4 Milton Inver
37 Q6 Milton Kent
149 M4 Milton Moray
158 D5 Milton Moray
19 K2 Milton N Som
31 L7 Milton Newpt
85 M6 Milton Notts
34 E6 Milton Oxon
48 E7 Milton Oxon
141 Q5 Milton P & K
41 K10 Milton Pembks
19 N10 Milton Somset
132 G7 Milton Stirlg
125 L3 Milton W Duns
12 D4 Milton Abbas Dorset
5 Q6 Milton Abbot Devon
127 P5 Milton Bridge Mdloth
49 Q8 Milton Bryan C Beds
20 C7 Milton Clevedon Somset
6 D5 Milton Combe Devon
35 J4 Milton Common Oxon
16 F9 Milton Damerel Devon
32 D2 Milton End Gloucs
33 M4 Milton End Gloucs
61 M9 Milton Ernest Bed
69 N3 Milton Green Ches W
34 E6 Milton Hill Oxon
49 N7 Milton Keynes M Keyn
21 N2 Milton Lilbourne Wilts
60 F9 Milton Malsor Nhants
140 F10 Milton Morenish P & K
150 F7 Milton of Auchinhove Abers
135 J7 Milton of Balgonie Fife
132 E9 Milton of Buchanan Stirlg
126 B2 Milton of Campsie E Duns
156 B9 Milton of Leys Highld
151 M7 Milton of Murtle C Aber
150 B8 Milton of Tullich Abers
20 E9 Milton on Stour Dorset
38 F9 Milton Regis Kent
25 M10 Milton Street E Susx
47 Q11 Milton-under-Wychwood Oxon
18 F9 Milverton Somset
59 M11 Milverton Warwks
70 H8 Milwich Staffs
80 H10 Milwr Flints
131 K8 Minard Ag & B
12 G2 Minchington Dorset
32 G4 Minchinhampton Gloucs
118 F4 Mindrum Nthumb
18 C5 Minehead Somset
69 J4 Minera Wrexhm
33 K6 Minety Wilts
67 K7 Minffordd Gwynd
138 B4 Mingarrypark Highld
87 K8 Miningsby Lincs
5 M7 Minions Cnwll
114 F5 Minishant S Ayrs
55 K2 Minllyn Gwynd
107 M4 Minnigaff D & G
39 N8 Minnis Bay Kent
159 J5 Minnonie Abers
70 B2 Minshull Vernon Ches E
97 N8 Minskip N York
13 N2 Minstead Hants
23 N10 Minsted W Susx
38 G7 Minster Kent
39 P9 Minster Kent
56 F3 Minsterley Shrops
34 B2 Minster Lovell Oxon
46 E11 Minsterworth Gloucs
11 P4 Minterne Magna Dorset
11 P4 Minterne Parva Dorset
86 G6 Minting Lincs
159 N8 Mintlaw Abers
75 N7 Mintlyn Crematorium Norfk
117 R6 Minto Border
56 G7 Minton Shrops
41 K8 Minwear Pembks
59 J6 Minworth Birm
100 C7 Mirehouse Cumb
167 P4 Mireland Highld
90 G7 Mirfield Kirk
32 H3 Miserden Gloucs
30 D5 Miskin Rhondd
30 D8 Miskin Rhondd
85 L2 Misson Notts
60 C4 Misterton Leics
85 N2 Misterton Notts
11 K3 Misterton Somset
53 K5 Mistley Essex
53 K5 Mistley Heath Essex
36 G7 Mitcham Gt Lon
46 C11 Mitcheldean Gloucs
3 M3 Mitchell Cnwll
116 D11 Mitchellslacks D & G
31 N2 Mitchel Troy Mons
113 J3 Mitford Nthumb
3 J3 Mithian Cnwll
70 F11 Mitton Staffs
48 H8 Mixbury Oxon
90 D5 Mixenden Calder
64 E10 Moats Tye Suffk
82 G9 Mobberley Ches E
71 J6 Mobberley Staffs
45 M6 Moccas Herefs
79 Q9 Mochdre Conwy
55 P7 Mochdre Powys
107 K8 Mochrum D & G
13 L3 Mockbeggar Hants
26 B2 Mockbeggar Kent
100 E6 Mockerkin Cumb
6 H8 Modbury Devon
70 G7 Moddershall Staffs
79 J7 Moelfre IoA
68 G9 Moelfre Powys
67 J3 Moel Tryfan Gwynd
116 F9 Moffat D & G
61 P11 Moggerhanger C Beds
71 Q11 Moira Leics
38 H11 Molash Kent
144 G5 Mol-chlach Highld
68 H2 Mold Flints
90 F7 Moldgreen Kirk
51 N6 Molehill Green Essex
52 B7 Molehill Green Essex
92 H2 Molescroft E R Yk
112 H4 Molesden Nthumb
61 N5 Molesworth Cambs
17 Q6 Molland Devon
81 M10 Mollington Ches W
48 D5 Mollington Oxon
126 C3 Mollinsburn N Lans
43 K2 Monachty Cerdgn
143 P2 Mondynes Abers
65 J10 Monewden Suffk
134 D2 Moneydie P & K
35 N9 Moneyrow Green W & M
115 Q9 Moniaive D & G
142 H11 Monifieth Angus
142 H10 Monikie Angus
134 H5 Monimail Fife
41 M2 Monington Pembks
91 K9 Monk Bretton Barns
50 F11 Monken Hadley Gt Lon
91 N5 Monk Fryston N York
46 B6 Monkhide Herefs
110 F9 Monkhill Cumb
57 L6 Monkhopton Shrops
45 P3 Monkland Herefs
16 H7 Monkleigh Devon
29 P10 Monknash V Glam
8 E3 Monkokehampton Devon
113 M6 Monkseaton N Tyne
52 G2 Monks Eleigh Suffk
24 F5 Monk's Gate W Susx
82 H10 Monks Heath Ches E
22 H3 Monk Sherborne Hants
27 K3 Monks Horton Kent
18 E7 Monksilver Somset
59 Q8 Monks Kirby Warwks
65 J8 Monk Soham Suffk
58 H9 Monkspath Solhll
35 M4 Monks Risborough Bucks
87 M7 Monksthorpe Lincs
51 P5 Monk Street Essex
31 K4 Monkswood Mons
10 D4 Monkton Devon
39 N9 Monkton Kent
114 G2 Monkton S Ayrs
113 M8 Monkton S Tyne
29 P10 Monkton V Glam
20 E2 Monkton Combe BaNES
20 G7 Monkton Deverill Wilts
32 F11 Monkton Farleigh Wilts
19 J9 Monkton Heathfield Somset
12 H2 Monkton Up Wimborne Dorset
10 G5 Monkton Wyld Dorset
113 N9 Monkwearmouth Sundld
23 J8 Monkwood Hants
58 D5 Monmore Green Wolves
31 P2 Monmouth Mons
45 M6 Monnington on Wye Herefs
107 L9 Monreith D & G
19 N11 Montacute Somset
89 K8 Montcliffe Bolton
56 G2 Montford Shrops
69 M11 Montford Bridge Shrops
150 F4 Montgarrie Abers
56 C5 Montgomery Powys
82 G5 Monton Salfd
143 N6 Montrose Angus
10 b2 Mont Saint Guern
22 B6 Monxton Hants
83 Q11 Monyash Derbys
150 H4 Monymusk Abers
133 P2 Monzie P & K
126 B3 Moodiesburn N Lans
135 J4 Moonzie Fife
91 J3 Moor Allerton Leeds
11 J5 Moorbath Dorset
87 J8 Moorby Lincs
45 M3 Moorcot Herefs
12 G3 Moor Crichel Dorset
13 J6 Moordown Bmouth
82 C8 Moore Halton
49 Q10 Moor End C Beds
90 D5 Moor End Calder
17 M10 Moor End Devon
32 D4 Moorend Gloucs
88 D2 Moor End Lancs
91 Q3 Moor End N York
92 A7 Moorends Donc
22 E11 Moorgreen Hants
50 H5 Moor Green Herts
84 G11 Moorgreen Notts
84 D6 Moorhall Derbys
45 M5 Moorhampton Herefs
90 E3 Moorhead C Brad
90 G5 Moor Head Leeds
110 E10 Moorhouse Cumb
110 F9 Moorhouse Cumb
91 M8 Moorhouse Donc
85 N7 Moorhouse Notts
37 K10 Moorhouse Bank Surrey
19 K8 Moorland Somset
19 L7 Moorlinch Somset
97 R9 Moor Monkton N York
100 D8 Moor Row Cumb
110 D11 Moor Row Cumb
105 J8 Moorsholm R & Cl
20 E11 Moorside Dorset
88 E4 Moor Side Lancs
88 F3 Moor Side Lancs
90 G3 Moorside Leeds
87 J9 Moor Side Lincs
89 Q9 Moorside Oldham
27 K4 Moorstock Kent
58 E8 Moor Street Birm
38 D8 Moor Street Medway
5 L9 Moorswater Cnwll
91 M8 Moorthorpe Wakefd
6 E4 Moortown Devon
13 L4 Moortown Hants
14 D10 Moortown IoW
90 H3 Moortown Leeds
93 J11 Moortown Lincs
69 R11 Moortown Wrekin
162 H10 Morangie Highld
145 L9 Morar Highld
158 A5 Moray Crematorium Moray
61 P2 Morborne Cambs
9 J3 Morchard Bishop Devon
11 J6 Morcombelake Dorset
73 N10 Morcott Rutlnd
69 J9 Morda Shrops
12 F5 Morden Dorset
36 G7 Morden Gt Lon
45 R7 Mordiford Herefs
104 B5 Mordon Dur
56 E6 More Shrops
18 C9 Morebath Devon
118 E6 Morebattle Border
95 J8 Morecambe Lancs
33 M7 Moredon Swindn
161 J7 Morefield Highld
27 M4 Morehall Kent
7 K8 Moreleigh Devon
140 F10 Morenish P & K
100 C7 Moresby Parks Cumb
22 F9 Morestead Hants
12 D7 Moreton Dorset
51 M9 Moreton Essex
45 Q2 Moreton Herefs
35 J4 Moreton Oxon
70 D11 Moreton Staffs
71 L9 Moreton Staffs
81 K7 Moreton Wirral
69 Q10 Moreton Corbet Shrops
9 J7 Moretonhampstead Devon
47 P8 Moreton-in-Marsh Gloucs
46 B5 Moreton Jeffries Herefs
69 Q10 Moretonmill Shrops
48 B3 Moreton Morrell Warwks
45 Q5 Moreton on Lugg Herefs
48 B4 Moreton Paddox Warwks
48 G5 Moreton Pinkney Nhants
70 A8 Moreton Say Shrops
32 E3 Moreton Valence Gloucs
42 F4 Morfa Cerdgn
67 J7 Morfa Bychan Gwynd
66 G3 Morfa Dinlle Gwynd
29 N3 Morfa Glas Neath
66 D6 Morfa Nefyn Gwynd
30 F8 Morganstown Cardif
21 N10 Morgan's Vale Wilts
128 F5 Morham E Loth

54 E9 Moriah Cerdgn
102 B6 Morland Cumb
82 H8 Morley Ches E
72 B2 Morley Derbys
103 M5 Morley Dur
90 H5 Morley Leeds
82 H8 Morley Green Ches E
64 F2 Morley St Botolph Norfk
5 N7 Mornick Cnwll
127 N3 Morningside C Edin
126 E6 Morningside N Lans
65 J3 Morningthorpe Norfk
113 J3 Morpeth Nthumb
143 N5 Morphie Abers
71 L11 Morrey Staffs
71 J4 Morridge Side Staffs
29 J5 Morriston Swans
76 E3 Morston Norfk
16 H2 Mortehoe Devon
84 G3 Morthen Rothm
23 J2 Mortimer W Berk
35 J11 Mortimer Common W Berk
45 N2 Mortimer's Cross Herefs
22 H2 Mortimer West End Hants
36 F5 Mortlake Gt Lon
36 E5 Mortlake Crematorium Gt Lon
101 N3 Morton Cumb
110 G10 Morton Cumb
84 F8 Morton Derbys
14 H9 Morton IoW
74 A6 Morton Lincs
85 P2 Morton Lincs
85 M10 Morton Notts
69 J10 Morton Shrops
85 Q8 Morton Hall Lincs
127 P4 Mortonhall Crematorium C Edin
97 M2 Morton-on-Swale N York
76 G8 Morton on the Hill Norfk
103 N6 Morton Tinmouth Dur
2 C6 Morvah Cnwll
5 M10 Morval Cnwll
146 B3 Morvich Highld
57 M6 Morville Shrops
57 M6 Morville Heath Shrops
6 C5 Morwellham Quay Devon
16 C8 Morwenstow Cnwll
84 F4 Mosborough Sheff
125 M9 Moscow E Ayrs
57 P6 Mose Shrops
101 L4 Mosedale Cumb
58 G8 Moseley Birm
58 D5 Moseley Wolves
46 F3 Moseley Worcs
89 L9 Moses Gate Bolton
136 B7 Moss Ag & B
91 P8 Moss Donc
69 K4 Moss Wrexhm
150 D4 Mossat Abers
169 r6 Mossbank Shet
81 Q5 Moss Bank St Hel
100 C5 Mossbay Cumb
114 H3 Mossblown S Ayrs
82 F7 Mossbrow Traffd
118 C7 Mossburnford Border
108 E6 Mossdale D & G
115 J7 Mossdale E Ayrs
88 E2 Moss Edge Lancs
82 E9 Moss End Ches E
126 C5 Mossend N Lans
100 F5 Mosser Mains Cumb
70 F2 Mossley Ches E
83 L4 Mossley Tamesd
117 M11 Mosspaul Hotel Border
110 C10 Moss Side Cumb
156 F6 Moss-side Highld
88 D4 Moss Side Lancs
81 M4 Moss Side Sefton
157 Q6 Mosstodloch Moray
107 P7 Mossyard D & G
88 G8 Mossy Lea Lancs
11 K3 Mosterton Dorset
83 J4 Moston Manch
69 Q9 Moston Shrops
70 C2 Moston Green Ches E
80 H8 Mostyn Flints
20 G9 Motcombe Dorset
6 G9 Mothecombe Devon
101 M5 Motherby Cumb
126 C6 Motherwell N Lans
36 F7 Motspur Park Gt Lon
37 K6 Mottingham Gt Lon
22 B9 Mottisfont Hants
14 D10 Mottistone IoW
83 L5 Mottram in Longdendale Tamesd
83 J9 Mottram St Andrew Ches E
10 b2 Mouilpied Guern
81 Q10 Mouldsworth Ches W
141 M6 Moulin P & K
24 H9 Moulsecoomb Br & H
34 G8 Moulsford Oxon
49 P6 Moulsoe M Keyn
156 A3 Moultavie Highld
82 E11 Moulton Ches W
74 F6 Moulton Lincs
103 P10 Moulton N York
60 G7 Moulton Nhants
63 L8 Moulton Suffk
30 E11 Moulton V Glam
74 E7 Moulton Chapel Lincs
77 M10 Moulton St Mary Norfk
74 F5 Moulton Seas End Lincs
4 B10 Mount Cnwll
5 J8 Mount Cnwll
90 D7 Mount Kirk
30 D4 Mountain C Brad
30 D5 Mountain Ash Rhondd
127 M8 Mountain Cross Border
39 J11 Mountain Street Kent
4 C4 Mount Ambrose Cnwll
52 F5 Mount Bures Essex
26 B7 Mountfield E Susx
155 Q5 Mountgerald House Highld
3 J4 Mount Hawke Cnwll
2 H10 Mount Hermon Cnwll
4 D9 Mountjoy Cnwll
127 P6 Mount Lothian Mdloth
51 P11 Mountnessing Essex
31 P6 Mounton Mons
70 D3 Mount Pleasant Ches E
71 P11 Mount Pleasant Derbys
84 D11 Mount Pleasant Derbys
103 Q4 Mount Pleasant Dur
93 N3 Mount Pleasant E R Yk
25 K7 Mount Pleasant E Susx
64 D3 Mount Pleasant Norfk
63 M11 Mount Pleasant Suffk
47 K2 Mount Pleasant Worcs
113 J10 Mountsett Crematorium Dur
72 F8 Mountsorrel Leics
21 K10 Mount Sorrel Wilts
90 D5 Mount Tabor Calder
23 P6 Mousehill Surrey
2 D8 Mousehole Cnwll
109 N6 Mouswald D & G
70 F3 Mow Cop Ches E
118 F6 Mowhaugh Border
72 F9 Mowmacre Hill C Leic
60 D3 Mowsley Leics
147 L11 Moy Highld
156 D11 Moy Highld
145 Q4 Moyle Highld
41 M2 Moylegrove Pembks
120 C3 Muasdale Ag & B
151 N9 Muchalls Abers
45 Q8 Much Birch Herefs
46 B5 Much Cowarne Herefs
45 P8 Much Dewchurch Herefs
19 M10 Muchelney Somset
19 M10 Muchelney Ham Somset
51 K7 Much Hadham Herts
88 F6 Much Hoole Lancs
88 F6 Much Hoole Town Lancs
5 L10 Muchlarnick Cnwll
46 C8 Much Marcle Herefs
57 L5 Much Wenlock Shrops
144 F12 Muck Highld
37 Q4 Mucking Thurr
37 Q5 Muckingford Thurr
76 G3 Muckleburgh Collection Norfk
11 N6 Muckleford Dorset
70 C7 Mucklestone Staffs
57 L5 Muckley Shrops
87 L4 Muckton Lincs
17 K4 Muddiford Devon
25 M8 Muddles Green E Susx
13 L6 Mudeford Dorset
19 Q11 Mudford Somset
19 Q11 Mudford Sock Somset
19 N5 Mudgley Somset
38 H7 Mud Row Kent
125 P2 Mugdock Stirlg
152 G10 Mugeary Highld
71 P6 Mugginton Derbys
71 P6 Muggintonlane End Derbys
112 F11 Muggleswick Dur
158 H7 Muirden Abers
143 K10 Muirdrum Angus
158 G8 Muiresk Abers
142 E11 Muirhead Angus
134 H6 Muirhead Fife
126 B4 Muirhead N Lans
115 N2 Muirkirk E Ayrs
133 L11 Muirmill Stirlg
150 F5 Muir of Fowlis Abers
157 M6 Muir of Miltonduff Moray
155 P7 Muir of Ord Highld
146 E11 Muirshearlich Highld
159 N10 Muirtack Abers
133 Q5 Muirton P & K
155 N5 Muirton Mains Highld
142 B9 Muirton of Ardblair P & K
102 H11 Muker N York
76 H11 Mulbarton Norfk
157 R7 Mulben Moray
2 D7 Mulfra Cnwll
137 Q9 Mull Ag & B
17 J3 Mullacott Cross Devon
2 H10 Mullion Cnwll
2 H10 Mullion Cove Cnwll
87 P6 Mumby Lincs
46 B4 Munderfield Row Herefs
46 C4 Munderfield Stocks Herefs
77 L4 Mundesley Norfk
63 P2 Mundford Norfk
65 L2 Mundham Norfk
52 E11 Mundon Hill Essex
26 F2 Mundy Bois Kent
101 L4 Mungrisdale Cumb
156 A7 Munlochy Highld
124 H8 Munnoch N Ayrs
46 C6 Munsley Herefs
57 J7 Munslow Shrops
8 G7 Murchington Devon
47 L6 Murcot Worcs
48 G11 Murcott Oxon
33 J6 Murcott Wilts
167 L3 Murkle Highld
146 C9 Murlaggan Highld
23 K3 Murrell Green Hants
142 H10 Murroes Angus
74 G9 Murrow Cambs
49 M9 Mursley Bucks
38 F9 Murston Kent
142 H6 Murthill Angus
141 R10 Murthly P & K
98 C10 Murton C York
102 D6 Murton Cumb
113 N11 Murton Dur
113 M6 Murton N Tyne
129 P10 Murton Nthumb
10 F6 Musbury Devon
98 D5 Muscoates N York
127 Q3 Musselburgh E Loth
73 L3 Muston Leics
99 M5 Muston N York
58 C10 Mustow Green Worcs
36 G3 Muswell Hill Gt Lon
108 E11 Mutehill D & G
65 P4 Mutford Suffk
133 P4 Muthill P & K
9 P3 Mutterton Devon
57 N2 Muxton Wrekin
167 L6 Mybster Highld
43 Q8 Myddfai Carmth
69 N10 Myddle Shrops
43 J3 Mydroilyn Cerdgn
88 F3 Myerscough Lancs
3 L6 Mylor Cnwll
3 L6 Mylor Bridge Cnwll
41 M4 Mynachlog ddu Pembks
80 H10 Myndd-llan Flints
56 F7 Myndtown Shrops
31 N6 Mynydd-bach Mons
29 J5 Mynydd-Bach Swans
54 G9 Mynydd Buch Cerdgn
28 D3 Mynyddgarreg Carmth
69 J2 Mynydd Isa Flints
79 L11 Mynydd Llandygai Gwynd
66 E8 Mynytho Gwynd
151 J8 Myrebird Abers
118 A11 Myredykes Border
23 N3 Mytchett Surrey
90 B5 Mytholm Calder
90 C5 Mytholmroyd Calder
88 D4 Mythop Lancs
97 P7 Myton-on-Swale N York

N

160 C10 Naast Highld
89 J5 Nab's Head Lancs
168 f8 Na Buirgh W Isls
98 B11 Naburn C York
90 E3 Nab Wood Crematorium C Brad
27 J3 Naccolt Kent
39 L11 Nackington Kent
53 M3 Nacton Suffk
99 M9 Nafferton E R Yk
32 G5 Nag's Head Gloucs
46 B11 Nailbridge Gloucs
18 H9 Nailsbourne Somset
31 N10 Nailsea N Som
72 C9 Nailstone Leics
32 F5 Nailsworth Gloucs
156 F6 Nairn Highld
36 F11 Nalderswood Surrey
2 G7 Nancegollan Cnwll
2 D6 Nancledra Cnwll
66 D8 Nanhoron Gwynd
80 H11 Nannerch Flints
72 E7 Nanpantan Leics
4 F10 Nanpean Cnwll
2 B8 Nanquidno Cnwll
4 G8 Nanstallon Cnwll
30 D2 Nant-ddu Powys
42 G3 Nanternis Cerdgn
43 J10 Nantgaredig Carmth
30 F7 Nantgarw Rhondd
55 M11 Nant-glas Powys
68 D2 Nantglyn Denbgs
55 M9 Nantgwyn Powys
67 L4 Nant Gwynant Gwynd
67 J4 Nantlle Gwynd
69 J10 Nantmawr Shrops
55 N11 Nantmel Powys
67 L5 Nantmor Gwynd
67 L3 Nant Peris Gwynd
70 B4 Nantwich Ches E
30 F2 Nant-y-Bwch Blae G
43 J11 Nant-y-caws Carmth
31 K3 Nant-y-derry Mons
29 M6 Nantyffyllon Brdgnd
30 G2 Nantyglo Blae G
68 H9 Nant-y-gollen Shrops
29 P8 Nant-y-moel Brdgnd
79 M10 Nant-y-pandy Conwy
35 M5 Naphill Bucks
46 G5 Napleton Worcs
96 C10 Nappa N York
48 E2 Napton on the Hill Warwks
41 M8 Narberth Pembks
72 E11 Narborough Leics
75 P8 Narborough Norfk
5 N10 Narkurs Cnwll
66 H5 Nasareth Gwynd
60 E5 Naseby Nhants
49 L8 Nash Bucks
37 K8 Nash Gt Lon
45 L2 Nash Herefs
31 K8 Nash Newpt
57 L10 Nash Shrops
57 P8 Nash End Worcs
35 M3 Nash Lee Bucks
23 J5 Nash's Green Hants
37 P7 Nash Street Kent
73 R11 Nassington Nhants
32 E3 Nastend Gloucs
51 J6 Nasty Herts
102 E9 Nateby Cumb
88 F2 Nateby Lancs
59 J2 National Memorial Arboretum Staffs
72 F9 National Space Science Centre C Leic
95 L3 Natland Cumb
52 H2 Naughton Suffk
47 M10 Naunton Gloucs
46 G7 Naunton Worcs
47 J4 Naunton Beauchamp Worcs
86 C9 Navenby Lincs
51 M11 Navestock Essex
51 N11 Navestock Side Essex
163 N3 Navidale House Hotel Highld
156 D5 Navity Highld
98 D4 Nawton N York
52 G5 Nayland Suffk
51 K9 Nazeing Essex
51 K9 Nazeing Gate Essex
13 L5 Neacroft Hants
59 M8 Neal's Green Warwks
169 s8 Neap Shet
71 K5 Near Cotton Staffs
101 L11 Near Sawrey Cumb
36 F3 Neasden Gt Lon
104 B8 Neasham Darltn
29 L5 Neath Neath
23 K6 Neatham Hants
77 L7 Neatishead Norfk
54 C11 Nebo Cerdgn
67 Q3 Nebo Conwy
66 H4 Nebo Gwynd
78 H6 Nebo IoA
76 B10 Necton Norfk
164 D10 Nedd Highld
113 K4 Nedderton Nthumb
52 G2 Nedging Suffk
52 H2 Nedging Tye Suffk
65 J5 Needham Norfk
64 F10 Needham Market Suffk
63 M7 Needham Street Suffk
62 D6 Needingworth Cambs
57 M9 Neen Savage Shrops
57 M10 Neen Sollars Shrops
57 L7 Neenton Shrops
66 E6 Nefyn Gwynd
125 M6 Neilston E Rens
30 F5 Nelson Caerph
89 P3 Nelson Lancs
116 B2 Nemphlar S Lans
19 P2 Nempnett Thrubwell BaNES
111 Q11 Nenthall Cumb
102 E2 Nenthead Cumb
118 C3 Nenthorn Border
9 J5 Neopardy Devon
24 F7 Nep Town W Susx
68 H2 Nercwys Flints
122 B8 Nereabolls Ag & B
125 Q6 Nerston S Lans
119 J4 Nesbit Nthumb
96 G11 Nesfield N York
81 L9 Ness Ches W
81 L9 Ness Botanic Gardens Ches W
69 L11 Nesscliffe Shrops
81 K9 Neston Ches W
32 G11 Neston Wilts
57 L6 Netchwood Shrops
82 H9 Nether Alderley Ches E
21 M5 Netheravon Wilts
117 Q2 Nether Blainslie Border
159 J6 Netherbrae Abers
72 H5 Nether Broughton Leics
126 D8 Netherburn S Lans
11 K5 Netherbury Dorset
110 G6 Netherby Cumb
97 M11 Netherby N York
11 P5 Nether Cerne Dorset
109 P3 Nethercleuch D & G
19 Q11 Nether Compton Dorset
60 B8 Nethercote Warwks
5 P2 Nethercott Devon
16 H4 Nethercott Devon
151 L3 Nether Crimond Abers
157 R5 Nether Dallachy Moray
31 Q4 Netherend Gloucs
9 M4 Nether Exe Devon
26 B8 Netherfield E Susx
72 F7 Netherfield Leics
72 G2 Netherfield Notts
26 B8 Netherfield Road E Susx
116 C8 Nether Fingland S Lans
92 C11 Nethergate N Linc
76 F6 Nethergate Norfk
21 M9 Netherhampton Wilts
84 F5 Nether Handley Derbys
142 F9 Nether Handwick Angus
91 L11 Nether Haugh Rothm
11 J3 Netherhay Dorset
85 M5 Nether Headon Notts
84 E10 Nether Heage Derbys
60 E9 Nether Heyford Nhants
116 E8 Nether Howcleugh S Lans
95 L7 Nether Kellet Lancs
159 Q9 Nether Kinmundy Abers
71 L8 Netherland Green Staffs
84 H6 Nether Langwith Notts
108 F12 Netherlaw D & G
151 M9 Netherley Abers
109 M3 Nethermill D & G
159 M9 Nethermuir Abers
36 G9 Netherne-on-the-Hill Surrey
90 E7 Netheroyd Hill Kirk
84 B5 Nether Padley Derbys
125 N6 Netherplace E Rens
98 B10 Nether Poppleton C York
101 K3 Nether Row Cumb
59 L2 Netherseal Derbys
97 Q2 Nether Silton N York
56 D10 Nether Skyborry Shrops
18 G7 Nether Stowey Somset
51 N8 Nether Street Essex
21 J2 Netherstreet Wilts
90 E9 Netherthong Kirk
84 F6 Netherthorpe Derbys
143 J6 Netherton Angus
7 M4 Netherton Devon
58 D7 Netherton Dudley
22 C3 Netherton Hants
45 Q9 Netherton Herefs
90 E8 Netherton Kirk
126 D7 Netherton N Lans
119 J9 Netherton Nthumb
34 D5 Netherton Oxon
142 A7 Netherton P & K
57 N8 Netherton Shrops
125 P2 Netherton Stirlg
90 H7 Netherton Wakefd
47 J6 Netherton Worcs
100 C9 Nethertown Cumb
167 Q1 Nethertown Highld
89 L3 Nethertown Lancs
71 L11 Nethertown Staffs
116 G2 Netherurd Border
22 B7 Nether Wallop Hants
100 F10 Nether Wasdale Cumb
110 G11 Nether Welton Cumb
47 P10 Nether Westcote Gloucs
59 K6 Nether Whitacre Warwks
116 A7 Nether Whitecleuch S Lans
35 K2 Nether Winchendon Bucks
112 G2 Netherwitton Nthumb
149 J3 Nethy Bridge Highld
14 E5 Netley Hants
13 P2 Netley Marsh Hants
35 J7 Nettlebed Oxon
20 B5 Nettlebridge Somset
11 L5 Nettlecombe Dorset
14 F11 Nettlecombe IoW
50 B8 Nettleden Herts
86 D5 Nettleham Lincs
37 Q10 Nettlestead Kent
37 Q10 Nettlestead Green Kent
14 H8 Nettlestone IoW
113 L11 Nettlesworth Dur
93 K10 Nettleton Lincs
32 F9 Nettleton Wilts
32 F9 Nettleton Shrub Wilts
6 F9 Netton Devon
21 M7 Netton Wilts
43 P10 Neuadd Carmth
55 L9 Neuadd-ddu Powys
38 C3 Nevendon Essex
41 L2 Nevern Pembks
60 H2 Nevill Holt Leics
109 L7 New Abbey D & G
159 L5 New Aberdour Abers
37 J8 New Addington Gt Lon
97 J11 Newall Leeds
22 G8 New Alresford Hants
142 C8 New Alyth P & K
74 D10 Newark C Pete
169 g2 Newark Ork
85 N10 Newark-on-Trent Notts
92 H2 New Arram E R Yk
126 D6 Newarthill N Lans
37 P7 New Ash Green Kent
85 P10 New Balderton Notts
27 L3 Newbarn Kent
37 P7 New Barn Kent
50 G11 New Barnet Gt Lon
61 J8 New Barton Nhants
127 Q4 Newbattle Mdloth
119 L6 New Bewick Nthumb
110 C7 Newbie D & G
94 B2 Newbiggin Cumb
94 F7 Newbiggin Cumb
101 N5 Newbiggin Cumb
102 B5 Newbiggin Cumb
111 L11 Newbiggin Cumb
102 H5 Newbiggin Dur
112 H11 Newbiggin Dur
96 E2 Newbiggin N York
96 F3 Newbiggin N York
113 M3 Newbiggin-by-the-Sea Nthumb
142 D9 Newbigging Angus
142 G10 Newbigging Angus
142 H10 Newbigging Angus
127 J8 Newbigging S Lans
102 D10 Newbiggin-on-Lune Cumb
59 Q9 New Bilton Warwks
84 E6 Newbold Derbys
72 C7 Newbold Leics
59 Q9 Newbold on Avon Warwks
47 P5 Newbold on Stour Warwks
47 Q3 Newbold Pacey Warwks
59 Q8 Newbold Revel Warwks
72 C10 Newbold Verdon Leics
87 K9 New Bolingbroke Lincs
74 D9 Newborough C Pete
78 G11 Newborough IoA
71 L9 Newborough Staffs
48 F7 Newbottle Nhants
113 M10 Newbottle Sundld
86 C6 New Boultham Lincs
53 N3 Newbourne Suffk
49 M6 New Bradwell M Keyn
84 E6 New Brampton Derbys
103 P2 New Brancepeth Dur
127 L3 Newbridge C Edin
30 H5 Newbridge Caerph
43 K3 Newbridge Cerdgn
2 C7 Newbridge Cnwll
3 K5 Newbridge Cnwll
109 K5 Newbridge D & G
21 Q11 Newbridge Hants
14 D9 Newbridge IoW
98 G3 New Bridge N York
34 D4 Newbridge Oxon
69 J6 Newbridge Wrexhm
46 F7 Newbridge Green Worcs
31 L6 Newbridge-on-Usk Mons
44 E3 Newbridge on Wye Powys
81 K11 New Brighton Flints
81 L6 New Brighton Wirral
84 G10 New Brinsley Notts
105 J6 New Brotton R & Cl
112 C7 Newbrough Nthumb
69 K4 New Broughton Wrexhm
64 F3 New Buckenham Norfk
9 J4 Newbuildings Devon
151 P2 Newburgh Abers
159 N6 Newburgh Abers
134 G4 Newburgh Fife
88 F8 Newburgh Lancs
98 A5 Newburgh Priory N York
113 J7 Newburn N u Ty
82 F4 New Bury Bolton
20 C5 Newbury Somset
34 E11 Newbury W Berk
20 F6 Newbury Wilts
37 K3 Newbury Park Gt Lon
101 Q6 Newby Cumb
96 B11 Newby Lancs
95 Q7 Newby N York
99 L2 Newby N York
104 F8 Newby N York
94 H3 Newby Bridge Cumb
110 G10 Newby Cross Cumb
111 J9 Newby East Cumb
101 Q6 Newby Head Cumb
159 K7 New Byth Abers
110 G10 Newby West Cumb
97 N3 Newby Wiske N York
45 N11 Newcastle Mons
56 D8 Newcastle Shrops
113 J6 Newcastle Airport Nthumb
42 F6 Newcastle Emlyn Carmth
111 J3 Newcastleton Border
70 E5 Newcastle-under-Lyme Staffs
113 K8 Newcastle upon Tyne N u Ty
41 P3 Newchapel Pembks
70 F4 Newchapel Staffs
25 J2 Newchapel Surrey
30 G2 Newchurch Blae G
45 M4 Newchurch Herefs
14 G9 Newchurch IoW
27 J5 Newchurch Kent
31 N5 Newchurch Mons
45 J4 Newchurch Powys
71 L10 Newchurch Staffs
89 N3 Newchurch in Pendle Lancs
76 H9 New Costessey Norfk
109 P11 New Cowper Cumb
127 Q3 Newcraighall C Edin
91 K7 New Crofton Wakefd
54 E9 New Cross Cerdgn
37 J5 New Cross Gt Lon
19 M11 New Cross Somset
115 M5 New Cumnock E Ayrs
26 D8 New Cut E Susx
159 L8 New Deer Abers
113 L5 New Delaval Nthumb
90 B9 New Delph Oldham
36 B4 New Denham Bucks
24 E2 Newdigate Surrey
60 F8 New Duston Nhants
98 C9 New Earswick C York
84 G11 New Eastwood Notts
91 N11 New Edlington Donc
157 N5 New Elgin Moray
93 L3 New Ellerby E R Yk
35 N10 Newell Green Br For
37 K6 New Eltham Gt Lon
47 L2 New End Worcs
26 D6 Newenden Kent

74 C10 New England C Pete
52 B3 New England Essex
46 D9 Newent Gloucs
90 H4 New Farnley Leeds
81 L7 New Ferry Wirral
103 P4 Newfield Dur
113 K10 Newfield Dur
156 D2 Newfield Highld
74 C11 New Fletton C Pete
13 N3 New Forest National Park
22 G4 Newfound Hants
91 M5 New Fryston Wakefd
40 G6 Newgale Pembks
108 D5 New Galloway D & G
76 E3 Newgate Norfk
50 H9 Newgate Street Herts
135 L6 New Gilston Fife
2 b1 New Grimsby IoS
69 R5 Newhall Ches E
71 P10 Newhall Derbys
119 N5 Newham Nthumb
113 M5 New Hartley Nthumb
127 P2 Newhaven C Edin
71 M2 Newhaven Derbys
25 K10 Newhaven E Susx
36 C8 New Haw Surrey
41 M10 New Hedges Pembks
113 M10 New Herrington Sundld
89 Q8 Newhey Rochdl
76 B4 New Holkham Norfk
93 J6 New Holland N Linc
105 N8 Newholm N York
84 G7 New Houghton Derbys
75 Q5 New Houghton Norfk
126 D5 Newhouse N Lans
96 B6 New Houses N York
82 C4 New Houses Wigan
95 M2 New Hutton Cumb
38 B10 New Hythe Kent
25 K6 Newick E Susx
27 K4 Newingreen Kent
27 L4 Newington Kent
38 E9 Newington Kent
34 H5 Newington Oxon
56 G8 Newington Shrops
32 F6 Newington Bagpath Gloucs
43 J7 New Inn Carmth
31 K5 New Inn Torfn
56 D9 New Invention Shrops
77 J10 New Lakenham Norfk
116 B2 New Lanark S Lans
93 J4 Newland C KuH
94 G5 Newland Cumb
92 D5 Newland E R Yk
31 Q3 Newland Gloucs
92 A6 Newland N York
34 C3 Newland Oxon
17 Q4 Newland Somset
46 E5 Newland Worcs
128 B7 Newlandrig Mdloth
111 K2 Newlands Border
101 K3 Newlands Cumb
112 G9 Newlands Nthumb
157 P7 Newlands of Dundurcas Moray
88 E8 New Lane Lancs
82 D6 New Lane End Warrtn
110 G4 New Langholm D & G
87 M9 New Leake Lincs
159 N7 New Leeds Abers
91 K9 New Lodge Barns
88 G5 New Longton Lancs
106 G5 New Luce D & G
2 D8 Newlyn Cnwll
4 C10 Newlyn East Cnwll
151 M4 Newmachar Abers
126 E6 Newmains N Lans
36 F7 New Malden Gt Lon
51 M8 Newman's End Essex
52 E3 Newman's Green Suffk
63 K8 Newmarket Suffk
168 j4 Newmarket W Isls
104 H6 New Marske R & Cl
34 F3 New Marston Oxon
69 K8 New Marton Shrops
151 K11 New Mill Abers
117 P8 Newmill Border
2 D7 New Mill Cnwll
35 P2 New Mill Herts
90 F9 New Mill Kirk
158 B7 Newmill Moray
91 J7 Newmillerdam Wakefd
142 G5 Newmill of Inshewan Angus
127 M4 Newmills C Edin
3 M3 New Mills Cnwll
83 M7 New Mills Derbys
134 C10 Newmills Fife
31 P3 Newmills Mons
55 P4 New Mills Powys
142 A11 Newmiln P & K
125 N10 Newmilns E Ayrs
13 M5 New Milton Hants
53 K5 New Mistley Essex
41 L5 New Moat Pembks
69 L8 Newnes Shrops
51 Q9 Newney Green Essex
32 C2 Newnham Gloucs
23 K4 Newnham Hants
50 F3 Newnham Herts
38 G10 Newnham Kent
60 C9 Newnham Nhants
57 L11 Newnham Worcs
85 L7 New Ollerton Notts
58 G6 New Oscott Birm
159 L6 New Pitsligo Abers
4 E6 New Polzeath Cnwll
5 N4 Newport Cnwll
12 E5 Newport Dorset
92 E4 Newport E R Yk
51 M4 Newport Essex
32 D5 Newport Gloucs
163 Q2 Newport Highld
14 F9 Newport IoW
31 K7 Newport Newpt
77 Q8 Newport Norfk
41 L3 Newport Pembks
70 C11 Newport Wrekin
135 L2 Newport-on-Tay Fife
49 N6 Newport Pagnell M Keyn
49 N6 Newport Pagnell Services M Keyn
24 C5 Newpound Common W Susx
114 F3 New Prestwick S Ayrs
42 G3 New Quay Cerdgn
4 C9 Newquay Cnwll
52 H7 New Quay Essex
4 D9 Newquay Airport Cnwll
77 K9 New Rackheath Norfk
45 J2 New Radnor Powys
101 N3 New Rent Cumb
112 G9 New Ridley Nthumb
90 B2 New Road Side N York
27 J7 New Romney Kent
91 Q11 New Rossington Donc
54 G10 New Row Cerdgn
89 J3 New Row Lancs
133 P9 New Sauchie Clacks
82 H11 Newsbank Ches E
158 H11 Newseat Abers
88 G3 Newsham Lancs
97 N4 Newsham N York
103 M8 Newsham N York
113 M5 Newsham Nthumb
91 K7 New Sharlston Wakefd
92 B5 Newsholme E R Yk
96 B10 Newsholme Lancs
119 N4 New Shoreston Nthumb
113 N10 New Silksworth Sundld
105 J7 New Skelton R & Cl
90 F8 Newsome Kirk
73 N3 New Somerby Lincs
36 G2 New Southgate Crematorium Gt Lon
88 H9 New Springs Wigan
117 R4 Newstead Border
84 H10 Newstead Notts
119 N5 Newstead Nthumb
126 D6 New Stevenston N Lans
45 L3 New Street Herefs
72 C7 New Swannington Leics
91 M4 Newthorpe N York
84 G11 Newthorpe Notts
38 C4 New Thundersley Essex
24 G8 Newtimber W Susx
86 D3 Newtoft Lincs
131 L8 Newton Ag & B
118 B6 Newton Border
29 M9 Newton Brdgnd
50 F2 Newton C Beds
62 F11 Newton Cambs
74 H8 Newton Cambs
30 H9 Newton Cardif
69 P3 Newton Ches W
81 N11 Newton Ches W
82 B9 Newton Ches W
94 E6 Newton Cumb
84 F9 Newton Derbys
45 L8 Newton Herefs
45 Q4 Newton Herefs
56 F11 Newton Herefs
155 Q7 Newton Highld
156 C8 Newton Highld
156 D4 Newton Highld
167 P7 Newton Highld
88 C3 Newton Lancs
95 M6 Newton Lancs
95 P10 Newton Lancs
73 Q3 Newton Lincs
127 Q4 Newton Mdloth
157 M5 Newton Moray
157 Q5 Newton Moray
98 H6 Newton N York
61 J4 Newton Nhants
76 A8 Newton Norfk
72 H2 Newton Notts
112 F8 Newton Nthumb
118 H9 Newton Nthumb
116 C4 Newton S Lans
126 B5 Newton S Lans
58 F6 Newton Sandw
69 M8 Newton Shrops
18 F7 Newton Somset
71 J9 Newton Staffs
52 F3 Newton Suffk
127 K2 Newton W Loth
60 B5 Newton Warwks
21 P10 Newton Wilts
7 M4 Newton Abbot Devon
110 D9 Newton Arlosh Cumb
103 Q6 Newton Aycliffe Dur
104 E5 Newton Bewley Hartpl
49 P4 Newton Blossomville M Keyn
61 L7 Newton Bromswold Nhants
72 B9 Newton Burgoland Leics
119 P5 Newton-by-the-Sea Nthumb
86 D3 Newton by Toft Lincs
5 N8 Newton Ferrers Cnwll
6 F9 Newton Ferrers Devon
168 d10 Newton Ferry W Isls
65 J2 Newton Flotman Norfk
127 Q5 Newtongrange Mdloth
31 P6 Newton Green Mons
72 G11 Newton Harcourt Leics
83 J4 Newton Heath Manch
151 N9 Newtonhill Abers
91 J6 Newton Hill Wakefd
91 M2 Newton Kyme N York
97 K3 Newton-le-Willows N York
82 C5 Newton-le-Willows St Hel
127 Q5 Newtonloan Mdloth
49 M8 Newton Longville Bucks
125 N6 Newton Mearns E Rens
143 L5 Newtonmill Angus
148 C8 Newtonmore Highld
103 P9 Newton Morrell N York
41 J9 Newton Mountain Pembks
105 L7 Newton Mulgrave N York
134 F5 Newton of Balcanquhal P & K
135 N7 Newton of Balcormo Fife
97 R9 Newton on Ouse N York
98 G2 Newton-on-Rawcliffe N York
69 N10 Newton on the Hill Shrops
119 N9 Newton-on-the-Moor Nthumb
85 P6 Newton on Trent Lincs
10 B7 Newton Poppleford Devon
48 H8 Newton Purcell Oxon
59 L3 Newton Regis Warwks
101 N4 Newton Reigny Cumb
9 L5 Newton St Cyres Devon
77 J8 Newton St Faith Norfk
20 D2 Newton St Loe BaNES
16 G9 Newton St Petrock Devon
71 P9 Newton Solney Derbys
22 D6 Newton Stacey Hants
107 M4 Newton Stewart D & G
21 P6 Newton Tony Wilts
17 J6 Newton Tracey Devon
104 G8 Newton under Roseberry R & Cl
112 H3 Newton Underwood Nthumb
98 E11 Newton upon Derwent E R Yk
23 K8 Newton Valence Hants
109 P2 Newton Wamphray D & G
88 F4 Newton with Scales Lancs
30 G3 Newtown Blae G
82 B9 Newtown Ches W
2 F8 Newtown Cnwll
5 M6 Newtown Cnwll
101 P6 Newtown Cumb
109 P11 Newtown Cumb
110 G8 Newtown Cumb
111 K8 Newtown Cumb
115 Q5 Newtown D & G
83 L8 Newtown Derbys
9 Q5 Newtown Devon
17 P6 Newtown Devon
11 K4 Newtown Dorset
12 G3 New Town Dorset
21 J11 New Town Dorset
21 J11 New Town Dorset
25 L6 New Town E Susx
32 C4 Newtown Gloucs
13 N2 Newtown Hants
14 H4 Newtown Hants
22 E2 Newtown Hants
45 P3 Newtown Herefs
45 Q8 Newtown Herefs
46 B5 Newtown Herefs
46 D7 Newtown Herefs
147 K7 Newtown Highld
14 D8 Newtown IoW
88 G7 Newtown Lancs
61 L5 New Town Nhants
119 J4 Newtown Nthumb
119 K10 Newtown Nthumb
119 K5 Newtown Nthumb
12 H6 Newtown Poole
55 Q6 Newtown Powys
30 E5 Newtown Rhondd
69 M10 Newtown Shrops
69 N8 Newtown Shrops
10 F2 Newtown Somset
58 E4 Newtown Staffs
70 G2 Newtown Staffs
82 C4 Newtown Wigan
20 H9 Newtown Wilts
21 Q2 Newtown Wilts
33 Q10 New Town Wilts
46 G3 Newtown Worcs
58 D9 Newtown Worcs
3 J9 Newtown-in-St Martin Cnwll
72 E9 Newtown Linford Leics
125 K6 Newtown of Beltrees Rens
117 R4 Newtown St Boswells Border
72 D10 Newtown Unthank Leics
30 F4 New Tredegar Caerph
126 E10 New Trows S Lans
84 E7 New Tupton Derbys
142 D9 Newtyle Angus
75 J9 New Walsoken Cambs
93 N10 New Waltham NE Lin
84 E5 New Whittington Derbys
128 C5 New Winton E Loth
34 C2 New Yatt Oxon
36 C3 Newyears Green Gt Lon
131 K5 Newyork Ag & B
86 H9 New York Lincs
113 M6 New York N Tyne
97 J8 New York N York
45 L3 Nextend Herefs
41 J9 Neyland Pembks
80 b6 Niarbyl IoM
32 C3 Nibley Gloucs
32 C8 Nibley S Glos
32 D5 Nibley Green Gloucs
18 F11 Nicholashayne Devon
28 F7 Nicholaston Swans
111 K7 Nickies Hill Cumb
97 M8 Nidd N York
151 N7 Nigg C Aber
156 E3 Nigg Highld
156 D4 Nigg Ferry Highld
32 D10 Nimlet BaNES
111 Q10 Ninebanks Nthumb
33 M7 Nine Elms Swindn
40 E6 Nine Wells Pembks
26 B9 Ninfield E Susx
14 C9 Ningwood IoW
118 C5 Nisbet Border
129 K9 Nisbet Hill Border
14 F11 Niton IoW
125 N5 Nitshill C Glas
37 N9 Noah's Ark Kent
37 Q2 Noak Bridge Essex
37 M2 Noak Hill Gt Lon
90 H9 Noblethorpe Barns
56 H2 Nobold Shrops
60 E8 Nobottle Nhants
86 E8 Nocton Lincs
77 M11 Nogdam End Norfk
34 F2 Noke Oxon
40 G7 Nolton Pembks
40 G7 Nolton Haven Pembks
69 P5 No Man's Heath Ches W
59 L3 No Man's Heath Warwks
5 M10 No Man's Land Cnwll
9 K2 Nomansland Devon
21 Q11 Nomansland Wilts
69 N9 Noneley Shrops
39 N11 Nonington Kent
95 L4 Nook Cumb
111 J5 Nook Cumb
36 E7 Norbiton Gt Lon
88 C2 Norbreck Bpool
46 D6 Norbridge Herefs
69 Q5 Norbury Ches E
71 L6 Norbury Derbys
36 H7 Norbury Gt Lon
56 F6 Norbury Shrops
70 D10 Norbury Staffs
69 Q5 Norbury Common Ches E
70 D10 Norbury Junction Staffs
58 B11 Norchard Worcs
82 D8 Norcott Brook Ches W
88 C2 Norcross Lancs
75 L10 Nordelph Norfk
89 P8 Norden Rochdl
57 M5 Nordley Shrops
77 P10 Norfolk Broads Norfk
129 N10 Norham Nthumb
90 D6 Norland Town Calder
82 C10 Norley Ches W
14 C7 Norleywood Hants
25 K8 Norlington E Susx
86 C3 Normanby Lincs
92 E7 Normanby N Linc
98 E4 Normanby N York
104 F7 Normanby R & Cl
93 K11 Normanby le Wold Lincs
61 Q2 Norman Cross Cambs
23 P4 Normandy Surrey
25 Q9 Norman's Bay E Susx
9 Q4 Norman's Green Devon
72 A4 Normanton C Derb
73 L2 Normanton Leics
86 B11 Normanton Lincs
85 M10 Normanton Notts
73 N9 Normanton Rutlnd
91 K6 Normanton Wakefd
21 M6 Normanton Wilts
72 B8 Normanton le Heath Leics
72 E6 Normanton on Soar Notts
72 G4 Normanton on the Wolds Notts
85 N7 Normanton on Trent Notts
88 C3 Normoss Lancs
23 P6 Norney Surrey
20 G2 Norrington Common Wilts
5 Q8 Norris Green Cnwll
81 M6 Norris Green Lpool
72 A7 Norris Hill Leics
90 G6 Norristhorpe Kirk
64 D2 Northacre Norfk
49 Q10 Northall Bucks
97 N2 Northallerton N York
76 D9 Northall Green Norfk
14 D4 Northam C Sotn
16 H6 Northam Devon
60 G8 Northampton Nhants
58 B11 Northampton Worcs
84 H4 North Anston Rothm
35 P11 North Ascot Br For
48 E9 North Aston Oxon
50 G10 Northaw Herts
10 F2 Northay Somset
22 C10 North Baddesley Hants
139 K5 North Ballachulish Highld
20 B9 North Barrow Somset
76 C4 North Barsham Norfk
38 C4 North Benfleet Essex
15 P6 North Bersted W Susx
128 E3 North Berwick E Loth
103 N4 North Bitchburn Dur
113 M4 North Blyth Nthumb
14 H4 North Boarhunt Hants
13 L5 North Bockhampton Dorset
74 C9 Northborough C Pete
39 P11 Northbourne Kent
8 H8 North Bovey Devon
20 G3 North Bradley Wilts
8 C8 North Brentor Devon
20 D7 North Brewham Somset
23 Q7 North Bridge Surrey
26 B7 Northbridge Street E Susx
22 F7 Northbrook Hants
48 E10 Northbrook Oxon
50 G2 North Brook End Cambs
16 H3 North Buckland Devon
77 M10 North Burlingham Norfk
20 B9 North Cadbury Somset
86 B5 North Carlton Lincs
85 J4 North Carlton Notts
92 E4 North Cave E R Yk
33 K3 North Cerney Gloucs
25 J6 North Chailey E Susx
23 Q9 Northchapel W Susx
21 N11 North Charford Hants
119 N6 North Charlton Nthumb
36 F7 North Cheam Gt Lon
20 C9 North Cheriton Somset
11 J6 North Chideock Dorset
35 Q3 Northchurch Herts
92 E3 North Cliffe E R Yk
85 P6 North Clifton Notts
103 Q4 North Close Dur
87 L2 North Cockerington Lincs
138 G11 North Connel Ag & B
29 M8 North Cornelly Brdgnd
3 K10 North Corner Cnwll
93 P10 North Cotes Lincs
5 N3 Northcott Devon
10 B2 Northcott Devon
10 C3 Northcott Devon
2 H5 North Country Cnwll
34 E5 Northcourt Oxon
65 P4 North Cove Suffk
103 Q10 North Cowton N York
49 P6 North Crawley M Keyn
37 L6 North Cray Gt Lon
76 B4 North Creake Norfk
19 K9 North Curry Somset
99 J10 North Dalton E R Yk
97 N10 North Deighton N York
17 J5 North Devon Crematorium Devon
39 Q7 Northdown Kent
38 F10 North Downs
92 A3 North Duffield N York
152 G3 North Duntulm Highld
36 F7 North East Surrey Crematorium Gt Lon
84 E7 Northedge Derbys
27 L3 North Elham Kent
87 J2 North Elkington Lincs
76 D7 North Elmham Norfk
91 M8 North Elmsall Wakefd
35 K6 Northend Bucks
15 J6 North End C Port
110 F9 North End Cumb
20 F9 North End Dorset
93 L2 North End E R Yk
93 N4 North End E R Yk
51 Q7 North End Essex
21 M11 North End Hants
22 G9 North End Hants
72 F7 North End Leics
74 D2 North End Lincs
87 M3 North End Lincs
92 H11 North End Lincs
93 P10 North End Lincs
93 K6 North End N Linc
31 M11 North End N Som
61 L7 North End Nhants
64 D3 North End Norfk
119 M10 North End Nthumb
81 L4 North End Sefton
15 Q6 North End W Susx
24 D9 North End W Susx
48 C4 Northend Warwks
82 H7 Northenden Manch
35 P7 Northend Woods Bucks
160 A10 North Erradale Highld
72 G10 North Evington C Leic
38 E2 North Fambridge Essex
92 G5 North Ferriby E R Yk
58 F9 Northfield Birm
151 N6 Northfield C Aber
92 H5 Northfield E R Yk
73 Q9 Northfields Lincs
37 P6 Northfleet Kent
99 N10 North Frodingham E R Yk
13 L2 North Gorley Hants
65 J4 North Green Norfk
65 L9 North Green Suffk
65 M8 North Green Suffk
86 D6 North Greetwell Lincs
98 G7 North Grimston N York
38 B8 North Halling Medway
15 K6 North Hayling Hants
119 L4 North Hazelrigg Nthumb
17 N5 North Heasley Devon
24 C6 North Heath W Susx
18 D10 North Hele Devon
5 M6 North Hill Cnwll
36 C4 North Hillingdon Gt Lon
34 E3 North Hinksey Village Oxon
36 E11 North Holmwood Surrey
7 J7 North Huish Devon
86 B7 North Hykeham Lincs
26 D7 Northiam E Susx
61 P11 Northill C Beds
32 D3 Northington Gloucs
22 G7 Northington Hants
92 H10 North Kelsey Lincs
156 B8 North Kessock Highld
93 K7 North Killingholme N Linc
97 P3 North Kilvington N York
60 D4 North Kilworth Leics
13 L4 North Kingston Hants
86 G10 North Kyme Lincs
99 Q6 North Landing E R Yk
87 K10 Northlands Lincs
33 M2 Northleach Gloucs
35 M3 North Lee Bucks
97 L6 North Lees N York
10 D5 Northleigh Devon
17 L5 Northleigh Devon
27 K2 North Leigh Kent
34 C2 North Leigh Oxon
85 N4 North Leverton with Habblesthorpe Notts
8 D5 Northlew Devon
47 L5 North Littleton Worcs
19 N7 Northload Bridge Somset
64 E5 North Lopham Norfk
73 N10 North Luffenham Rutlnd
23 M11 North Marden W Susx
49 L10 North Marston Bucks
128 B8 North Middleton Mdloth
119 J6 North Middleton Nthumb
159 K9 North Millbrex Abers
106 E7 North Milmain D & G
17 N6 North Molton Devon
34 D4 Northmoor Oxon
34 G7 North Moreton Oxon
142 F7 Northmuir Angus
15 N6 North Mundham W Susx
85 N9 North Muskham Notts
92 F3 North Newbald E R Yk
48 D6 North Newington Oxon
21 M3 North Newnton Wilts
19 K8 North Newton Somset
15 K6 Northney Hants
32 D5 North Nibley Gloucs
22 F4 North Oakley Hants
37 N3 North Ockendon Gt Lon
36 D4 Northolt Gt Lon
81 J11 Northop Flints
81 K11 Northop Hall Flints
104 F7 North Ormesby Middsb
87 J2 North Ormsby Lincs
90 G6 Northorpe Kirk
74 A7 Northorpe Lincs
74 D3 Northorpe Lincs
92 E11 Northorpe Lincs
97 N3 North Otterington N York
19 N7 Northover Somset
19 P10 Northover Somset
86 E2 North Owersby Lincs
90 E5 Northowram Calder
11 K3 North Perrott Somset
19 J8 North Petherton Somset
5 M4 North Petherwin Cnwll
76 B10 North Pickenham Norfk
47 J4 North Piddle Worcs
11 L5 North Poorton Dorset
12 F7 Northport Dorset
13 L3 North Poulner Hants
134 E11 North Queensferry Fife
17 P5 North Radworthy Devon
86 D11 North Rauceby Lincs
77 J4 Northrepps Norfk
87 L4 North Reston Lincs
97 L11 North Rigton N York
13 L5 North Ripley Hants
83 J11 North Rode Ches E
169 g1 North Ronaldsay Ork
169 g1 North Ronaldsay Airport Ork
100 H4 North Row Cumb
75 M7 North Runcton Norfk
94 D7 North Scale Cumb
85 P7 North Scarle Lincs
113 L3 North Seaton Nthumb
113 L3 North Seaton Colliery Nthumb
138 G9 North Shian Ag & B
113 N7 North Shields N Tyne
38 F4 North Shoebury Sthend
88 C3 North Shore Bpool
74 E11 North Side C Pete
100 C5 North Side Cumb
105 J7 North Skelton R & Cl

93 R11 **North Somercotes** Lincs
97 L5 **North Stainley** N York
102 F8 **North Stainmore** Cumb
37 P4 **North Stifford** Thurr
32 D11 **North Stoke** BaNES
34 H7 **North Stoke** Oxon
24 B8 **North Stoke** W Susx
63 J7 **North Street** Cambs
21 N11 **North Street** Hants
22 H8 **North Street** Hants
38 H10 **North Street** Kent
38 D7 **North Street** Medway
34 H10 **North Street** W Berk
119 P4 **North Sunderland** Nthumb
5 N2 **North Tamerton** Cnwll
8 G4 **North Tawton** Devon
133 M10 **North Third** Stirlg
93 N11 **North Thoresby** Lincs
119 P10 **North Togston** Nthumb
168 e9 **Northton** W Isls
17 J10 **North Town** Devon
19 Q6 **North Town** Somset
35 N8 **North Town** W & M
76 E9 **North Tuddenham** Norfk
168 c10 **North Uist** W Isls
118 G10 **Northumberland National Park** Nthumb
113 J7 **North Walbottle** N u Ty
77 K5 **North Walsham** Norfk
22 G5 **North Waltham** Hants
23 K4 **North Warnborough** Hants
18 F9 **Northway** Somset
28 G7 **Northway** Swans
51 L10 **North Weald Bassett** Essex
85 N3 **North Wheatley** Notts
7 M5 **North Whilborough** Devon
82 E10 **Northwich** Ches W
31 Q11 **North Wick** BaNES
31 Q7 **Northwick** S Glos
19 L5 **Northwick** Somset
46 F3 **Northwick** Worcs
19 Q3 **North Widcombe** BaNES
86 G3 **North Willingham** Lincs
84 F7 **North Wingfield** Derbys
73 N6 **North Witham** Lincs
75 Q11 **Northwold** Norfk
70 F5 **Northwood** C Stke
84 C8 **Northwood** Derbys
36 C2 **Northwood** Gt Lon
14 E8 **Northwood** IoW
69 N8 **Northwood** Shrops
46 D11 **Northwood Green** Gloucs
11 P2 **North Wootton** Dorset
75 M6 **North Wootton** Norfk
19 Q6 **North Wootton** Somset
32 F9 **North Wraxall** Wilts
33 M8 **North Wroughton** Swindn
105 K10 **North York Moors National Park**
91 N7 **Norton** Donc
25 L10 **Norton** E Susx
46 G10 **Norton** Gloucs
82 C8 **Norton** Halton
50 F4 **Norton** Herts
13 P7 **Norton** IoW
45 N10 **Norton** Mons
19 K2 **Norton** N Som
98 F6 **Norton** N York
60 C8 **Norton** Nhants
85 J6 **Norton** Notts
56 E11 **Norton** Powys
104 D6 **Norton** S on T
84 E4 **Norton** Sheff
56 H8 **Norton** Shrops
57 K3 **Norton** Shrops
57 L8 **Norton** Shrops
57 N4 **Norton** Shrops
64 D8 **Norton** Suffk
28 H7 **Norton** Swans
15 P5 **Norton** W Susx
32 G8 **Norton** Wilts
46 G4 **Norton** Worcs
47 K5 **Norton** Worcs
20 H6 **Norton Bavant** Wilts
70 F8 **Norton Bridge** Staffs
58 F3 **Norton Canes** Staffs
58 F3 **Norton Canes Services** Staffs
45 M5 **Norton Canon** Herefs
76 F6 **Norton Corner** Norfk
85 Q9 **Norton Disney** Lincs
20 E7 **Norton Ferris** Wilts
18 G9 **Norton Fitzwarren** Somset
13 P7 **Norton Green** IoW
19 Q2 **Norton Hawkfield** BaNES
51 P10 **Norton Heath** Essex
70 C7 **Norton in Hales** Shrops
70 F4 **Norton in the Moors** C Stke
59 M3 **Norton-Juxta-Twycross** Leics
97 P6 **Norton-le-Clay** N York
47 P2 **Norton Lindsey** Warwks
64 D9 **Norton Little Green** Suffk
20 B2 **Norton Malreward** BaNES
51 N10 **Norton Mandeville** Essex
20 E3 **Norton St Philip** Somset
65 N2 **Norton Subcourse** Norfk
19 N11 **Norton sub Hamdon** Somset
45 M5 **Norton Wood** Herefs
85 N8 **Norwell** Notts
85 M8 **Norwell Woodhouse** Notts
77 J10 **Norwich** Norfk
77 J9 *Norwich Airport* Norfk
77 J10 **Norwich Cathedral** Norfk
77 J8 **Norwich (St Faith) Crematorium** Norfk
169 t2 **Norwick** Shet
133 P9 **Norwood** Clacks
84 G4 **Norwood** Derbys
27 J5 **Norwood** Kent
19 N3 **Norwood End** Essex
90 E5 **Norwood Green** Calder
36 D5 **Norwood Green** Gt Lon
24 F2 **Norwood Hill** Surrey
74 H11 **Norwoodside** Cambs
73 J11 **Noseley** Leics
6 F9 **Noss Mayo** Devon
97 L4 **Nosterfield** N York
51 P2 **Nosterfield End** Cambs
145 Q2 **Nostie** Highld
47 M10 **Notgrove** Gloucs
29 M9 **Nottage** Brdgnd
5 P9 **Notter** Cnwll
72 F3 **Nottingham** C Nott
11 P8 **Nottington** Dorset
91 J8 **Notton** Wakefd
32 H11 **Notton** Wilts
52 C9 **Nounsley** Essex
57 Q11 **Noutard's Green** Worcs
64 B9 **Nowton** Suffk
56 G2 **Nox** Shrops
35 J7 **Nuffield** Oxon
98 G11 **Nunburnholme** E R Yk
84 H10 **Nuncargate** Notts
111 J11 **Nunclose** Cumb
59 N6 **Nuneaton** Warwks
34 G5 **Nuneham Courtenay** Oxon
36 H5 **Nunhead** Gt Lon
99 N11 **Nunkeeling** E R Yk
97 R9 **Nun Monkton** N York
20 D5 **Nunney** Somset
20 D6 **Nunney Catch** Somset
45 R6 **Nunnington** Herefs
98 D5 **Nunnington** N York
93 N9 **Nunsthorpe** NE Lin
98 C10 **Nunthorpe** C York
104 F8 **Nunthorpe** Middsb
104 F8 **Nunthorpe Village** Middsb
21 N9 **Nunton** Wilts
97 M6 **Nunwick** N York
112 C6 **Nunwick** Nthumb
32 B5 **Nupdown** S Glos
49 N11 **Nup End** Bucks
32 E3 **Nupend** Gloucs
35 N10 **Nuptown** Br For
22 C11 **Nursling** Hants
23 L10 **Nursted** Hants
21 K2 **Nursteed** Wilts
58 B5 **Nurton** Staffs
15 L5 **Nutbourne** W Susx
24 C7 **Nutbourne** W Susx
36 H10 **Nutfield** Surrey
72 E2 **Nuthall** Notts
51 K4 **Nuthampstead** Herts
24 E5 **Nuthurst** W Susx
25 K5 **Nutley** E Susx
22 H6 **Nutley** Hants
89 M7 **Nuttall** Bury
91 Q10 **Nutwell** Donc
167 Q4 **Nybster** Highld
15 N7 **Nyetimber** W Susx
23 M10 **Nyewood** W Susx
17 N10 **Nymet Rowland** Devon
8 H4 **Nymet Tracey** Devon
32 F4 **Nympsfield** Gloucs
18 F10 **Nynehead** Somset
19 M8 **Nythe** Somset
15 P5 **Nyton** W Susx

O

72 G10 **Oadby** Leics
38 E9 **Oad Street** Kent
46 F2 **Oakall Green** Worcs
71 J6 **Oakamoor** Staffs
127 K4 **Oakbank** W Loth
8 D5 **Oak Cross** Devon
30 G5 **Oakdale** Caerph
18 G9 **Oake** Somset
58 C4 **Oaken** Staffs
95 L11 **Oakenclough** Lancs
57 N2 **Oakengates** Wrekin
81 K10 **Oakenholt** Flints
103 N3 **Oakenshaw** Dur
90 F5 **Oakenshaw** Kirk
84 E10 **Oakerthorpe** Derbys
43 J3 **Oakford** Cerdgn
18 B10 **Oakford** Devon
18 B10 **Oakfordbridge** Devon
83 K11 **Oakgrove** Ches E
73 M9 **Oakham** Rutlnd
70 D4 **Oakhanger** Ches E
23 L7 **Oakhanger** Hants
20 B5 **Oakhill** Somset
37 N10 **Oakhurst** Kent
62 F8 **Oakington** Cambs
44 E4 **Oaklands** Powys
46 E11 **Oakle Street** Gloucs
61 M10 **Oakley** Bed
34 H2 **Oakley** Bucks
134 C10 **Oakley** Fife
22 G4 **Oakley** Hants
35 L4 **Oakley** Oxon
12 H5 **Oakley** Poole
64 H6 **Oakley** Suffk
35 P9 **Oakley Green** W & M
55 M7 **Oakley Park** Powys
32 H4 **Oakridge** Gloucs
89 K4 **Oaks** Lancs
56 G4 **Oaks** Shrops
33 J6 **Oaksey** Wilts
71 M8 **Oaks Green** Derbys
111 K5 **Oakshaw Ford** Cumb
23 K9 **Oakshott** Hants
59 M2 **Oakthorpe** Leics
104 C8 **Oak Tree** Darltn
72 B3 **Oakwood** C Derb
112 D7 **Oakwood** Nthumb
90 C3 **Oakworth** C Brad
38 H9 **Oare** Kent
17 P2 **Oare** Somset
21 N2 **Oare** Wilts
73 Q3 **Oasby** Lincs
19 L9 **Oath** Somset
142 H6 **Oathlaw** Angus
36 C7 **Oatlands Park** Surrey
130 H2 **Oban** Ag & B
138 G10 *Oban Airport* Ag & B
56 E9 **Obley** Shrops
141 P10 **Obney** P & K
20 C11 **Oborne** Dorset
74 A8 **Obthorpe** Lincs
64 H7 **Occold** Suffk
167 N9 **Occumster** Highld
115 K3 **Ochiltree** E Ayrs
72 C3 **Ockbrook** Derbys
58 E6 **Ocker Hill** Sandw
46 E2 **Ockeridge** Worcs
36 C9 **Ockham** Surrey
137 P1 **Ockle** Highld
24 D2 **Ockley** Surrey
46 A5 **Ocle Pychard** Herefs
99 L7 **Octon** E R Yk
19 P11 **Odcombe** Somset
20 D2 **Odd Down** BaNES
46 H3 **Oddingley** Worcs
47 P9 **Oddington** Gloucs
48 G11 **Oddington** Oxon
61 L9 **Odell** Bed
8 C4 **Odham** Devon
23 K4 **Odiham** Hants
90 F5 **Odsal** C Brad
50 G3 **Odsey** Cambs
21 M9 **Odstock** Wilts
72 B9 **Odstone** Leics
59 N11 **Offchurch** Warwks
47 L5 **Offenham** Worcs
83 K7 **Offerton** Stockp
113 M9 **Offerton** Sundld
25 K8 **Offham** E Susx
37 Q9 **Offham** Kent
24 B9 **Offham** W Susx
70 D9 **Offleymarsh** Staffs
62 B7 **Offord Cluny** Cambs
62 B7 **Offord D'Arcy** Cambs
53 J2 **Offton** Suffk
10 D5 **Offwell** Devon
33 N10 **Ogbourne Maizey** Wilts
33 N10 **Ogbourne St Andrew** Wilts
33 P10 **Ogbourne St George** Wilts
90 D4 **Ogden** Calder
112 H5 **Ogle** Nthumb
81 N8 **Oglet** Lpool
29 N9 **Ogmore** V Glam
29 N9 **Ogmore-by-Sea** V Glam
29 P6 **Ogmore Vale** Brdgnd
79 L11 **Ogwen Bank** Gwynd
12 D2 **Okeford Fitzpaine** Dorset
8 E5 **Okehampton** Devon
84 C8 **Oker Side** Derbys
24 D3 **Okewood Hill** Surrey
9 L9 **Olchard** Devon
60 G6 **Old** Nhants
151 N6 **Old Aberdeen** C Aber
22 G8 **Old Alresford** Hants
164 C10 **Oldany** Highld
115 Q8 **Old Auchenbrack** D & G
72 F2 **Old Basford** C Nott
23 J4 **Old Basing** Hants
76 D8 **Old Beetley** Norfk
58 H11 **Oldberrow** Warwks
119 L6 **Old Bewick** Nthumb
87 L7 **Old Bolingbroke** Lincs
90 G2 **Old Bramhope** Leeds
84 D6 **Old Brampton** Derbys
108 G7 **Old Bridge of Urr** D & G
64 F3 **Old Buckenham** Norfk
22 E3 **Old Burghclere** Hants
37 N9 **Oldbury** Kent
58 E7 **Oldbury** Sandw
57 N6 **Oldbury** Shrops
59 M6 **Oldbury** Warwks
32 B6 **Oldbury Naite** S Glos
32 B6 **Oldbury-on-Severn** S Glos
32 F7 **Oldbury on the Hill** Gloucs
98 B3 **Old Byland** N York
91 Q10 **Old Cantley** Donc
104 B3 **Old Cassop** Dur
29 P9 **Old Castle** Brdgnd
45 L10 **Oldcastle** Mons
69 N5 **Oldcastle Heath** Ches W
77 J9 **Old Catton** Norfk
56 D6 **Old Churchstoke** Powys
93 N9 **Old Clee** NE Lin
18 D6 **Old Cleeve** Somset
85 K8 **Old Clipstone** Notts
80 B9 **Old Colwyn** Conwy
85 J3 **Oldcotes** Notts
114 D8 **Old Dailly** S Ayrs
72 H6 **Old Dalby** Leics
83 P9 **Old Dam** Derbys
159 N8 **Old Deer** Abers
19 P5 **Old Ditch** Somset
91 N11 **Old Edlington** Donc
103 P5 **Old Eldon** Dur
93 L3 **Old Ellerby** E R Yk
53 P4 **Old Felixstowe** Suffk
90 C3 **Oldfield** C Brad
46 F2 **Oldfield** Worcs
74 C11 **Old Fletton** C Pete
20 E4 **Oldford** Somset
45 R11 **Old Forge** Herefs
45 P10 **Old Furnace** Herefs
83 M6 **Old Glossop** Derbys
92 B6 **Old Goole** E R Yk
2 b1 **Old Grimsby** IoS
51 J6 **Old Hall Green** Herts
64 B10 **Oldhall Green** Suffk
77 L5 **Old Hall Street** Norfk
83 K4 **Oldham** Oldham
129 J5 **Oldhamstocks** E Loth
51 L8 **Old Harlow** Essex
52 H7 **Old Heath** Essex
75 N2 **Old Hunstanton** Norfk
62 D5 **Old Hurst** Cambs
95 M3 **Old Hutton** Cumb
3 L5 **Old Kea** Cnwll
125 M3 **Old Kilpatrick** W Duns
50 F6 **Old Knebworth** Herts
77 J10 **Old Lakenham** Norfk
32 C10 **Oldland** S Glos
89 L3 **Old Langho** Lancs
80 f5 **Old Laxey** IoM
87 M10 **Old Leake** Lincs
98 F6 **Old Malton** N York
151 L2 **Oldmeldrum** Abers
5 P7 **Oldmill** Cnwll
59 L11 **Old Milverton** Warwks
19 K3 **Oldmixon** N Som
64 F9 **Old Newton** Suffk
104 B3 **Old Quarrington** Dur
72 F2 **Old Radford** C Nott
45 K3 **Old Radnor** Powys
150 H2 **Old Rayne** Abers
26 H7 **Old Romney** Kent
24 F9 **Old Shoreham** W Susx
164 F5 **Oldshoremore** Highld
37 P10 **Old Soar** Kent
32 E8 **Old Sodbury** S Glos
73 P4 **Old Somerby** Lincs
98 A5 **Oldstead** N York
49 L6 **Old Stratford** Nhants
141 K4 **Old Struan** P & K
119 N10 **Old Swarland** Nthumb
58 D8 **Old Swinford** Dudley
102 B9 **Old Tebay** Cumb
97 P4 **Old Thirsk** N York
90 C5 **Old Town** Calder
95 M4 **Old Town** Cumb
101 N2 **Old Town** Cumb
25 N11 **Old Town** E Susx
2 c2 **Old Town** IoS
82 H5 **Old Trafford** Traffd
84 E7 **Old Tupton** Derbys
111 J8 **Oldwall** Cumb
28 E6 **Oldwalls** Swans
50 D2 **Old Warden** C Beds
17 R7 **Oldways End** Somset
61 N5 **Old Weston** Cambs
167 Q7 **Old Wick** Highld
35 Q10 **Old Windsor** W & M
39 J11 **Old Wives Lees** Kent
36 B9 **Old Woking** Surrey
49 M6 **Old Wolverton** M Keyn
86 H7 **Old Woodhall** Lincs
69 N10 **Old Woods** Shrops
167 J6 **Olgrinmore** Highld
71 L11 **Olive Green** Staffs
22 E9 **Oliver's Battery** Hants
169 q5 **Ollaberry** Shet
153 J10 **Ollach** Highld
82 G9 **Ollerton** Ches E
85 L7 **Ollerton** Notts
70 A9 **Ollerton** Shrops
43 M3 **Olmarch** Cerdgn
51 P2 **Olmstead Green** Cambs
49 N4 **Olney** M Keyn
167 L3 **Olrig House** Highld
58 H8 **Olton** Solhll
32 B7 **Olveston** S Glos
46 F2 **Ombersley** Worcs
85 L7 **Ompton** Notts
111 P7 **Once Brewed** Nthumb
80 e6 **Onchan** IoM
71 J3 **Onecote** Staffs
64 E10 **Onehouse** Suffk
31 M2 **Onen** Mons
56 F11 **Ongar Street** Herefs
56 H9 **Onibury** Shrops
139 J5 **Onich** Highld
29 M2 **Onllwyn** Neath
70 D6 **Onneley** Staffs
51 Q7 **Onslow Green** Essex
23 Q5 **Onslow Village** Surrey
82 C10 **Onston** Ches W
84 E11 **Openwoodgate** Derbys
153 N3 **Opinan** Highld
157 Q6 **Orbliston** Moray
152 D9 **Orbost** Highld
87 N7 **Orby** Lincs
18 H10 **Orchard Portman** Somset
21 L5 **Orcheston** Wilts
45 P9 **Orcop** Herefs
45 P9 **Orcop Hill** Herefs
158 F6 **Ord** Abers
150 H5 **Ordhead** Abers
150 D7 **Ordie** Abers
157 Q6 **Ordiequish** Moray
112 D9 **Ordley** Nthumb
85 M5 **Ordsall** Notts
26 D9 **Ore** E Susx
56 H11 **Oreleton Common** Herefs
57 M8 **Oreton** Shrops
65 N11 **Orford** Suffk
82 D6 **Orford** Warrtn
12 F6 **Organford** Dorset
71 L11 **Orgreave** Staffs
26 H5 **Orlestone** Kent
56 H11 **Orleton** Herefs
57 N11 **Orleton** Worcs
61 J6 **Orlingbury** Nhants
101 J5 **Ormathwaite** Cumb
104 F7 **Ormesby** R & Cl
77 P9 **Ormesby St Margaret** Norfk
77 P9 **Ormesby St Michael** Norfk
160 D8 **Ormiscaig** Highld
128 C6 **Ormiston** E Loth
137 M3 **Ormsaigmore** Highld
123 M5 **Ormsary** Ag & B
88 E9 **Ormskirk** Lancs
113 J11 **Ornsby Hill** Dur
136 b4 **Oronsay** Ag & B
169 c6 **Orphir** Ork
37 L7 **Orpington** Gt Lon
81 L5 **Orrell** Sefton
82 B4 **Orrell** Wigan
88 G9 **Orrell Post** Wigan
80 d3 **Orrisdale** IoM
108 G11 **Orroland** D & G
37 P4 **Orsett** Thurr
70 E11 **Orslow** Staffs
73 K2 **Orston** Notts
101 J4 **Orthwaite** Cumb
95 L10 **Ortner** Lancs
102 B9 **Orton** Cumb
60 H5 **Orton** Nhants
58 C5 **Orton** Staffs
74 C11 **Orton Longueville** C Pete
59 M4 **Orton-on-the-Hill** Leics
110 F10 **Orton Rigg** Cumb
74 C11 **Orton Waterville** C Pete
62 E10 **Orwell** Cambs
89 J4 **Osbaldeston** Lancs
89 J4 **Osbaldeston Green** Lancs
98 C10 **Osbaldwick** C York
72 C10 **Osbaston** Leics
69 K10 **Osbaston** Shrops
14 F8 **Osborne** IoW
14 F8 **Osborne House** IoW
73 R3 **Osbournby** Lincs
81 Q11 **Oscroft** Ches W
152 E9 **Ose** Highld
72 C7 **Osgathorpe** Leics
86 E2 **Osgodby** Lincs
91 Q4 **Osgodby** N York
99 M4 **Osgodby** N York
153 J10 **Oskaig** Highld
137 M7 **Oskamull** Ag & B
71 M6 **Osmaston** Derbys
11 Q8 **Osmington** Dorset
12 B8 **Osmington Mills** Dorset
91 J4 **Osmondthorpe** Leeds
104 E11 **Osmotherley** N York
34 E3 **Osney** Oxon
38 H9 **Ospringe** Kent
90 H6 **Ossett** Wakefd
85 N8 **Ossington** Notts
38 F2 **Ostend** Essex
36 E5 **Osterley** Gt Lon
98 C5 **Oswaldkirk** N York
89 L5 **Oswaldtwistle** Lancs
69 J9 **Oswestry** Shrops
37 M9 **Otford** Kent
38 C11 **Otham** Kent
38 D11 **Otham Hole** Kent
19 L8 **Othery** Somset
97 K11 **Otley** Leeds
65 J10 **Otley** Suffk
65 J10 **Otley Green** Suffk
22 E10 **Otterbourne** Hants
96 C9 **Otterburn** N York
112 C2 **Otterburn** Nthumb
131 J11 **Otter Ferry** Ag & B
5 K3 **Otterham** Cnwll
18 H6 **Otterhampton** Somset
38 D8 **Otterham Quay** Kent
5 K4 **Otterham Station** Cnwll
168 e10 **Otternish** W Isls
36 B8 **Ottershaw** Surrey
169 s5 **Otterswick** Shet
10 B7 **Otterton** Devon
14 D6 **Otterwood** Hants
10 C5 **Ottery St Mary** Devon
27 L3 **Ottinge** Kent
93 N6 **Ottringham** E R Yk
110 E9 **Oughterby** Cumb
96 C4 **Oughtershaw** N York
100 F2 **Oughterside** Cumb
84 D2 **Oughtibridge** Sheff
82 E7 **Oughtrington** Warrtn
98 A6 **Oulston** N York
110 D10 **Oulton** Cumb
91 K5 **Oulton** Leeds
76 G6 **Oulton** Norfk
70 D10 **Oulton** Staffs
70 G7 **Oulton** Staffs
65 Q3 **Oulton** Suffk
65 Q3 **Oulton Broad** Suffk
76 H6 **Oulton Street** Norfk
61 M3 **Oundle** Nhants
58 C6 **Ounsdale** Staffs
102 B4 **Ousby** Cumb
63 M9 **Ousden** Suffk
92 D6 **Ousefleet** E R Yk
113 L10 **Ouston** Dur
119 M4 **Outchester** Nthumb
39 M11 **Out Elmstead** Kent
101 L11 **Outgate** Cumb
102 E10 **Outhgill** Cumb
58 H11 **Outhill** Warwks
70 D8 **Outlands** Staffs
90 D7 **Outlane** Kirk
93 Q6 **Out Newton** E R Yk
88 E2 **Out Rawcliffe** Lancs
75 K10 **Outwell** Norfk
21 M11 **Outwick** Hants
36 H11 **Outwood** Surrey
91 J6 **Outwood** Wakefd
89 M9 **Outwood Gate** Bury
72 C7 **Outwoods** Leics
70 D11 **Outwoods** Staffs
91 J5 **Ouzlewell Green** Leeds
90 D5 **Ovenden** Calder
62 E6 **Over** Cambs
82 D11 **Over** Ches W
46 F11 **Over** Gloucs
31 Q8 **Over** S Glos
71 P7 **Over Burrows** Derbys
47 J7 **Overbury** Worcs
11 P8 **Overcombe** Dorset
19 Q11 **Over Compton** Dorset
89 K9 **Overdale Crematorium** Bolton
61 N2 **Over End** Cambs
84 D6 **Overgreen** Derbys
59 J6 **Over Green** Warwks
84 B7 **Over Haddon** Derbys
95 L7 **Over Kellet** Lancs
48 D10 **Over Kiddington** Oxon
19 N7 **Overleigh** Somset
71 M11 **Overley** Staffs
31 P2 **Over Monnow** Mons
48 B9 **Over Norton** Oxon
82 G10 **Over Peover** Ches E
81 M9 **Overpool** Ches W
161 Q2 **Overscaig Hotel** Highld
71 P11 **Overseal** Derbys
97 P2 **Over Silton** N York
39 J10 **Oversland** Kent
47 L3 **Oversley Green** Warwks
60 G7 **Overstone** Nhants
18 G7 **Over Stowey** Somset
77 J3 **Overstrand** Norfk
19 M11 **Over Stratton** Somset
21 L7 **Overstreet** Wilts
82 F9 **Over Tabley** Ches E
48 E6 **Overthorpe** Nhants
151 M5 **Overton** C Aber
81 Q9 **Overton** Ches W
22 F5 **Overton** Hants
95 J9 **Overton** Lancs
98 B9 **Overton** N York
57 J10 **Overton** Shrops
28 E7 **Overton** Swans
90 H7 **Overton** Wakefd
69 L6 **Overton** Wrexhm
69 L6 **Overton Bridge** Wrexhm
70 E2 **Overton Green** Ches E
95 N5 **Overtown** Lancs
126 E7 **Overtown** N Lans
33 N9 **Overtown** Swindn
91 K7 **Overtown** Wakefd
21 Q7 **Over Wallop** Hants
59 L6 **Over Whitacre** Warwks
84 G6 **Over Woodhouse** Derbys
48 D9 **Over Worton** Oxon
34 G6 **Overy** Oxon
49 L10 **Oving** Bucks
15 P6 **Oving** W Susx
25 J10 **Ovingdean** Br & H
112 G8 **Ovingham** Nthumb
103 M8 **Ovington** Dur
52 C3 **Ovington** Essex
22 G8 **Ovington** Hants
76 C11 **Ovington** Norfk
112 G8 **Ovington** Nthumb
14 E6 **Ower** Hants
22 B11 **Ower** Hants
12 C7 **Owermoigne** Dorset
56 E6 **Owlbury** Shrops
84 D3 **Owlerton** Sheff
32 E5 **Owlpen** Gloucs
65 K8 **Owl's Green** Suffk
23 M2 **Owlsmoor** Br For
35 L3 **Owlswick** Bucks
86 D3 **Owmby** Lincs
93 J10 **Owmby** Lincs
22 F10 **Owslebury** Hants
91 P8 **Owston** Donc
73 K9 **Owston** Leics
92 D10 **Owston Ferry** N Linc
93 N4 **Owstwick** E R Yk
93 P5 **Owthorne** E R Yk
72 H4 **Owthorpe** Notts
104 E5 **Owton Manor** Hartpl
75 P10 **Oxborough** Norfk
11 K5 **Oxbridge** Dorset

87 K5 Oxcombe Lincs
84 G6 Oxcroft Derbys
51 Q5 Oxen End Essex
95 L3 Oxenholme Cumb
90 C4 Oxenhope C Brad
94 G3 Oxen Park Cumb
19 M6 Oxenpill Somset
47 J8 Oxenton Gloucs
22 B3 Oxenwood Wilts
34 F3 Oxford Oxon
48 E11 Oxford Airport Oxon
34 G3 Oxford Crematorium Oxon
34 H4 Oxford Services Oxon
50 D11 Oxhey Herts
113 J10 Oxhill Dur
48 B5 Oxhill Warwks
58 D4 Oxley Wolves
52 F9 Oxley Green Essex
25 Q6 Oxley's Green E Susx
62 G3 Oxlode Cambs
118 C7 Oxnam Border
77 J7 Oxnead Norfk
36 D8 Oxshott Surrey
36 D8 Oxshott Heath Surrey
90 H10 Oxspring Barns
37 J10 Oxted Surrey
128 D9 Oxton Border
91 N2 Oxton N York
85 K10 Oxton Notts
28 E7 Oxwich Swans
28 E7 Oxwich Green Swans
76 C6 Oxwick Norfk
161 P6 Oykel Bridge Hotel Highld
150 H2 Oyne Abers
28 H7 Oystermouth Swans
32 E6 Ozleworth Gloucs

P

168 k4 Pabail W Isls
11 Q2 Packers Hill Dorset
72 B8 Packington Leics
70 F4 Packmoor C Stke
59 L11 Packmores Warwks
142 G7 Padanaram Angus
49 K8 Padbury Bucks
36 G4 Paddington Gt Lon
82 D7 Paddington Warrtn
27 L4 Paddlesworth Kent
37 Q8 Paddlesworth Kent
25 Q2 Paddock Wood Kent
69 P8 Paddolgreen Shrops
83 M5 Padfield Derbys
82 D7 Padgate Warrtn
51 P11 Padhams Green Essex
89 M4 Padiham Lancs
97 J9 Padside N York
4 E6 Padstow Cnwll
34 H11 Padworth W Berk
103 P3 Page Bank Dur
15 N7 Pagham W Susx
38 F3 Paglesham Essex
7 M6 Paignton Torbay
59 Q8 Pailton Warwks
25 P6 Paine's Cross E Susx
71 J8 Painleyhill Staffs
44 H5 Painscastle Powys
112 G8 Painshawfield Nthumb
98 G9 Painsthorpe E R Yk
32 G3 Painswick Gloucs
38 G10 Painter's Forstal Kent
125 M5 Paisley Rens
65 Q3 Pakefield Suffk
64 C8 Pakenham Suffk
68 C7 Pale Gwynd
51 Q2 Pale Green Essex
21 Q6 Palestine Hants
35 N9 Paley Street W & M
58 F5 Palfrey Wsall
64 G6 Palgrave Suffk
12 C6 Pallington Dorset
5 K6 Palmersbridge Cnwll
36 H2 Palmers Green Gt Lon
115 K4 Palmerston E Ayrs
30 F11 Palmerstown V Glam
108 H9 Palnackie D & G
107 N5 Palnure D & G
84 G7 Palterton Derbys
22 H3 Pamber End Hants
22 H3 Pamber Green Hants
22 H2 Pamber Heath Hants
46 H8 Pamington Gloucs
12 G4 Pamphill Dorset
62 G11 Pampisford Cambs
19 N5 Panborough Somset
143 K10 Panbride Angus
16 D10 Pancrasweek Devon
30 D11 Pancross V Glam
30 G7 Pandy Caerph
54 E4 Pandy Gwynd
68 A9 Pandy Gwynd
45 L10 Pandy Mons
55 L4 Pandy Powys
68 G7 Pandy Wrexhm
68 E4 Pandy'r Capel Denbgs
67 R2 Pandy Tudur Conwy
52 B6 Panfield Essex
34 H9 Pangbourne W Berk
24 G8 Pangdean W Susx
46 B5 Panks Bridge Herefs
97 M10 Pannal N York
97 L10 Pannal Ash N York
150 C8 Pannanich Wells Hotel Abers
69 J10 Pant Shrops
80 H9 Pantasaph Flints
40 H4 Panteg Pembks
5 K8 Pantersbridge Cnwll
29 P8 Pant-ffrwyth Brdgnd
66 H5 Pant Glas Gwynd
54 H5 Pantglas Powys
43 L9 Pant-Gwyn Carmth
29 J4 Pant-lasau Swans
58 J8 Pant Mawr Powys
86 G5 Panton Lincs
68 D2 Pant-pastynog Denbgs
54 G4 Pantperthog Gwynd
55 M10 Pant-y-dwr Powys
56 B4 Pant-y-ffridd Powys
28 H2 Pantyffynnon Carmth
31 J5 Pantygaseg Torfn
29 P6 Pant-y-gog Brdgnd
45 M5 Pantymenyn Carmth
68 G2 Pant-y-mwyn Flints
77 M9 Panxworth Norfk
169 d1 Papa Westray Airport Ork
100 F4 Papcastle Cumb
167 Q6 Papigoe Highld
128 F5 Papple E Loth
84 H10 Papplewick Notts
62 C8 Papworth Everard Cambs
62 C8 Papworth St Agnes Cambs
3 R3 Par Cnwll
39 N9 Paramour Street Kent
88 F8 Parbold Lancs
19 Q7 Parbrook Somset
24 C5 Parbrook W Susx
68 A8 Parc Gwynd
41 M8 Parc Gwyn Crematorium Pembks
42 D4 Parcllyn Cerdgn
31 M6 Parc Seymour Newpt
100 E6 Pardshaw Cumb
65 L9 Parham Suffk
109 K2 Park D & G
111 N8 Park Nthumb
2 H5 Park Bottom Cnwll
83 K4 Park Bridge Tamesd
25 M3 Park Corner E Susx
35 J7 Park Corner Oxon
35 N8 Park Corner W & M
88 D5 Park Crematorium Lancs
49 Q4 Park End Bed
32 B3 Parkend Gloucs
112 C5 Park End Nthumb
37 P11 Parkers Green Kent
53 M5 Parkeston Essex
53 M5 Parkeston Quay Essex
26 H4 Park Farm Kent
81 K9 Parkgate Ches W
110 D11 Parkgate Cumb
109 M3 Parkgate D & G
26 B9 Parkgate E Susx
51 Q5 Parkgate Essex
14 F5 Park Gate Hants
26 E5 Parkgate Kent
37 M8 Parkgate Kent
90 F2 Park Gate Leeds
24 F2 Parkgate Surrey
58 D10 Park Gate Worcs
51 L5 Park Green Essex
64 G9 Park Green Suffk
143 L8 Parkgrove Crematorium Angus
125 M3 Parkhall W Duns
16 F7 Parkham Devon
16 F7 Parkham Ash Devon
84 E10 Park Head Derbys
31 Q5 Park Hill Gloucs
31 P4 Parkhouse Mons
28 F7 Parkmill Swans
36 E4 Park Royal Gt Lon
113 P11 Parkside Dur
126 E6 Parkside N Lans
69 L3 Parkside Wrexhm
12 H6 Parkstone Poole
50 D10 Park Street Herts
24 D4 Park Street W Susx
90 E6 Park Wood Crematorium Calder
13 K5 Parley Green Dorset
35 L7 Parmoor Bucks
51 K9 Parndon Essex
51 K9 Parndon Wood Crematorium Essex
17 M2 Parracombe Devon
41 L3 Parrog Pembks
100 F3 Parsonby Cumb
84 D2 Parson Cross Sheff
74 G9 Parson Drove Cambs
52 H6 Parson's Heath Essex
71 P9 Parson's Hill Derbys
125 N4 Partick C Glas
82 F6 Partington Traffd
87 M7 Partney Lincs
100 C6 Parton Cumb
24 E7 Partridge Green W Susx
45 K10 Partrishow Powys
71 M4 Parwich Derbys
51 N10 Paslow Wood Common Essex
49 L7 Passenham Nhants
23 M8 Passfield Hants
51 M11 Passingford Bridge Essex
74 C10 Paston C Pete
77 L5 Paston Norfk
70 H10 Pasturefields Staffs
8 C5 Patchacott Devon
24 H9 Patcham Br & H
50 D11 Patchetts Green Herts
24 C9 Patching W Susx
17 L3 Patchole Devon
32 B8 Patchway S Glos
97 J7 Pateley Bridge N York
52 F8 Paternoster Heath Essex
19 L8 Pathe Somset
134 H9 Pathhead Fife
128 B7 Pathhead Mdloth
47 N3 Pathlow Warwks
134 D5 Path of Condie P & K
51 K5 Patmore Heath Herts
114 H5 Patna E Ayrs
21 L3 Patney Wilts
80 b5 Patrick IoM
97 K2 Patrick Brompton N York
82 G5 Patricroft Salfd
93 P6 Patrington E R Yk
93 P6 Patrington Haven E R Yk
39 L10 Patrixbourne Kent
101 L7 Patterdale Cumb
57 Q5 Pattingham Staffs
49 J4 Pattishall Nhants
52 D7 Pattiswick Green Essex
57 K5 Patton Shrops
2 D8 Paul Cnwll
49 K5 Paulerspury Nhants
93 L5 Paull E R Yk
21 M8 Paul's Dene Wilts
20 C3 Paulton BaNES
46 C4 Paunton Herefs
119 M11 Pauperhaugh Nthumb
70 D11 Pave Lane Wrekin
61 L9 Pavenham Bed
19 J6 Pawlett Somset
118 G4 Pawston Nthumb
47 N7 Paxford Gloucs
129 N9 Paxton Border
38 F11 Payden Street Kent
10 B4 Payhembury Devon
2 H5 Paynter's Lane End Cnwll
96 B10 Paythorne Lancs
56 G10 Paytoe Herefs
25 K10 Peacehaven E Susx
83 N9 Peak Dale Derbys
83 Q6 Peak District National Park
83 P9 Peak Forest Derbys
74 E7 Peak Hill Lincs
74 C9 Peakirk C Pete
25 Q2 Pearson's Green Kent
46 A8 Peartree Green Herefs
34 E2 Peartree Services Oxon
20 D3 Peasedown St John BaNES
84 F11 Peasehill Derbys
76 F8 Peaseland Green Norfk
34 E9 Peasemore W Berk
65 M8 Peasenhall Suffk
24 G4 Pease Pottage W Susx
24 G4 Pease Pottage Services W Susx
24 C2 Peaslake Surrey
81 Q6 Peasley Cross St Hel
26 E7 Peasmarsh E Susx
10 G3 Peasmarsh Somset
23 Q5 Peasmarsh Surrey
159 M4 Peathill Abers
135 M6 Peat Inn Fife
60 C2 Peatling Magna Leics
60 C3 Peatling Parva Leics
57 J7 Peaton Shrops
52 E5 Pebmarsh Essex
47 M5 Pebworth Worcs
90 B5 Pecket Well Calder
69 P3 Peckforton Ches E
36 H5 Peckham Gt Lon
72 D10 Peckleton Leics
68 F10 Pedairffordd Powys
27 K4 Pedlinge Kent
58 D8 Pedmore Dudley
19 M7 Pedwell Somset
117 K2 Peebles Border
80 b5 Peel IoM
88 D4 Peel Lancs
14 G6 Peel Common Hants
27 L4 Peene Kent
26 E6 Peening Quarter Kent
72 C7 Peggs Green Leics
50 D4 Pegsdon C Beds
113 K3 Pegswood Nthumb
39 Q9 Pegwell Kent
153 J11 Peinchorran Highld
152 G6 Peinlich Highld
40 H7 Pelcomb Pembks
40 H7 Pelcomb Bridge Pembks
40 H7 Pelcomb Cross Pembks
52 G8 Peldon Essex
25 P4 Pell Green E Susx
58 F4 Pelsall Wsall
58 F4 Pelsall Wood Wsall
113 L10 Pelton Dur
113 L10 Pelton Fell Dur
109 P11 Pelutho Cumb
5 L10 Pelynt Cnwll
28 F4 Pemberton Carmth
82 C4 Pemberton Wigan
26 E2 Pembles Cross Kent
28 D4 Pembrey Carmth
45 M3 Pembridge Herefs
41 J10 Pembroke Pembks
41 J10 Pembroke Dock Pembks
40 F6 Pembrokeshire Coast National Park Pembks
25 P2 Pembury Kent
45 R9 Pen-allt Herefs
31 P2 Penallt Mons
41 M11 Penally Pembks
3 P5 Penare Cnwll
30 G10 Penarth V Glam
41 M7 Penblewin Pembks
54 F8 Pen-bont Rhydybeddau Cerdgn
42 E4 Penbryn Cerdgn
42 H7 Pencader Carmth
66 G6 Pencaenewydd Gwynd
128 C6 Pencaitland E Loth
78 F10 Pencarnisiog IoA
43 K5 Pencarreg Carmth
5 J5 Pencarrow Cnwll
44 F9 Pencelli Powys
28 F5 Penclawdd Swans
30 C8 Pencoed Brdgnd
46 A4 Pencombe Herefs
45 Q9 Pencoyd Herefs
45 R10 Pencraig Herefs
68 D9 Pencraig Powys
2 B7 Pendeen Cnwll
29 P3 Penderyn Rhondd
41 P9 Pendine Carmth
82 G4 Pendlebury Salfd
89 M3 Pendleton Lancs
46 E8 Pendock Worcs
4 G6 Pendoggett Cnwll
11 L2 Pendomer Somset
30 E9 Pendoylan V Glam
29 P8 Pendre Brdgnd
54 H4 Penegoes Powys
3 L5 Penelewey Cnwll
41 L6 Pen-ffordd Pembks
30 G5 Pengam Caerph
30 H9 Pengam Cardif
37 J6 Penge Gt Lon
4 H5 Pengelly Cnwll
78 H6 Pengorffwysfa IoA
5 M8 Pengover Green Cnwll
31 K3 Pen-groes-oped Mons
80 E9 Pengwern Denbgs
2 H10 Penhale Cnwll
4 E10 Penhale Cnwll
4 H9 Penhale Cnwll
5 Q11 Penhale Cnwll
3 K3 Penhallow Cnwll
3 J6 Penhalurick Cnwll
3 J6 Penhalvean Cnwll
33 N7 Penhill Swindn
31 M6 Penhow Newpt
25 Q7 Penhurst E Susx
54 E3 Peniarth Gwynd
127 N6 Penicuik Mdloth
42 H10 Peniel Carmth
68 D2 Peniel Denbgs
152 H9 Penifiler Highld
120 F7 Peninver Ag & B
67 K2 Penisarwaun Gwynd
90 G10 Penistone Barns
3 K7 Penjerrick Cnwll
82 C7 Penketh Warrtn
114 D8 Penkill S Ayrs
58 D2 Penkridge Staffs
5 L2 Penlean Cnwll
20 G4 Penleigh Wilts
69 M6 Penley Wrexhm
28 H5 Penllergaer Swans
78 F8 Pen-llyn IoA
30 C9 Penllyn V Glam
78 G11 Pen-lon IoA
67 P4 Penmachno Conwy
30 G5 Penmaen Caerph
28 F7 Penmaen Swans
79 N9 Penmaenan Conwy
79 N9 Penmaenmawr Conwy
67 M11 Penmaenpool Gwynd
30 E11 Penmark V Glam
79 L8 Penmon IoA
67 J6 Penmorfa Gwynd
3 L4 Penmount Crematorium Cnwll
79 J10 Penmynydd IoA
35 P6 Penn Bucks
58 C5 Penn Wolves
54 F4 Pennal Gwynd
159 K4 Pennan Abers
43 K2 Pennant Cerdgn
68 D8 Pennant Denbgs
55 K5 Pennant Powys
68 D9 Pennant-Melangell Powys
28 G7 Pennard Swans
56 F5 Pennerley Shrops
9 L4 Pennicott Devon
90 B3 Pennines
94 F5 Pennington Cumb
13 P5 Pennington Hants
89 J9 Pennington Green Wigan
44 G9 Pennorth Powys
35 P5 Penn Street Bucks
32 D10 Pennsylvania S Glos
94 G4 Penny Bridge Cumb
137 N10 Pennycross Ag & B
77 L7 Pennygate Norfk
137 N10 Pennyghael Ag & B
114 E5 Pennyglen S Ayrs
84 H5 Penny Green Derbys
74 G5 Penny Hill Lincs
9 L2 Pennymoor Devon
113 N9 Pennywell Sundld
42 D5 Penparc Cerdgn
54 D8 Penparcau Cerdgn
30 F5 Penpedairheol Caerph
31 K4 Penpedairheol Mons
31 K4 Penperlleni Mons
4 H4 Penpethy Cnwll
4 H10 Penpillick Cnwll
3 L6 Penpol Cnwll
5 J11 Penpoll Cnwll
2 G6 Penponds Cnwll
4 H7 Penpont Cnwll
108 H2 Penpont D & G
44 D9 Penpont Powys
6 G8 Penquit Devon
5 N6 Penrest Cnwll
41 Q3 Penrherber Carmth
41 P2 Pen-rhiw Pembks
30 E5 Penrhiwceiber Rhondd
29 K2 Pen Rhiwfawr Neath
42 G6 Penrhiw-llan Cerdgn
42 F5 Penrhiw-pal Cerdgn
66 E8 Penrhos Gwynd
78 D8 Penrhos IoA
31 M2 Penrhos Mons
29 M2 Penrhos Powys
79 K10 Penrhos garnedd Gwynd
79 Q8 Penrhyn Bay Conwy
79 L10 Penrhyn Castle Gwynd
54 E8 Penrhyncoch Cerdgn
67 L7 Penrhyndeudraeth Gwynd
79 Q8 Penrhyn-side Conwy
28 E7 Penrice Swans
120 G3 Penrioch N Ayrs
101 P4 Penrith Cumb
4 D7 Penrose Cnwll
101 M5 Penruddock Cumb
3 K7 Penryn Cnwll
80 D9 Pensarn Conwy
57 N11 Pensax Worcs
81 K8 Pensby Wirral
20 E8 Penselwood Somset
20 B2 Pensford BaNES
46 H6 Pensham Worcs
113 M10 Penshaw Sundld
25 M2 Penshurst Kent
37 M11 Penshurst Station Kent
5 M7 Pensilva Cnwll
58 D7 Pensnett Dudley
9 J4 Penstone Devon
55 P6 Penstrowed Powys
3 Q4 Pentewan Cnwll
79 K11 Pentir Gwynd
4 B9 Pentire Cnwll
41 M9 Pentlepoir Pembks
63 P11 Pentlow Essex
63 P11 Pentlow Street Essex
75 P8 Pentney Norfk
110 H5 Pentonbridge Cumb
22 B5 Penton Grafton Hants
22 B5 Penton Mewsey Hants
79 J9 Pentraeth IoA
68 E2 Pentre Denbgs
81 L11 Pentre Flints
31 K3 Pentre Mons
31 M4 Pentre Mons
55 P7 Pentre Powys
56 B7 Pentre Powys
56 D6 Pentre Powys
30 C5 Pentre Rhondd
69 L11 Pentre Shrops
69 J6 Pentre Wrexhm
43 L5 Pentre bach Cerdgn
81 J9 Pentre Bach Flints
30 E4 Pentrebach Myr Td
44 C8 Pentre-bach Powys
56 B2 Pentrebeirdd Powys
78 H10 Pentre Berw IoA
67 N4 Pentre-bont Conwy
69 K5 Pentrebychan Crematorium Wrexhm
42 F6 Pentre-cagel Carmth
68 F4 Pentre-celyn Denbgs
55 K3 Pentre-celyn Powys
29 J6 Pentre-chwyth Swans
69 J8 Pentre-clawdd Shrops
42 G7 Pentre-cwrt Carmth
68 G5 Pentredwr Denbgs
67 J7 Pentrefelin Gwynd
78 G6 Pentrefelin IoA
81 K10 Pentre Ffwrndan Flints
67 R4 Pentrefoelas Conwy
41 N4 Pentregalar Pembks
42 G4 Pentregat Cerdgn
43 M11 Pentre-Gwenlais Carmth
67 K9 Pentre Gwynfryn Gwynd
81 J10 Pentre Halkyn Flints
56 E9 Pentre Hodrey Shrops
80 D10 Pentre Isaf Conwy
68 E2 Pentre Llanrhaeadr Denbgs
56 B5 Pentre Llifior Powys
44 D4 Pentre-llwyn-llwyd Powys
54 E9 Pentre-llyn Cerdgn
68 C4 Pentre-llyn-cymmer Conwy
55 K4 Pentre-Maw Powys
30 C9 Pentre Meyrick V Glam
31 J4 Pentre-piod Torfn
31 J7 Pentre-poeth Newpt
42 G4 Pentre'rbryn Cerdgn
43 M5 Pentre'r-felin Cerdgn
79 Q11 Pentre'r Felin Conwy
44 C8 Pentre'r-felin Powys
68 D2 Pentre Saron Denbgs
67 Q2 Pentre-tafarn-y-fedw Conwy
43 R7 Pentre ty gwyn Carmth
84 E10 Pentrich Derbys
21 K11 Pentridge Dorset
30 H4 Pen-twyn Caerph
31 P3 Pen-twyn Mons
31 J4 Pen-twyn Torfn
30 G5 Pentwynmaur Caerph
30 F8 Pentyrch Cardif
4 G10 Penwithick Cnwll
22 D2 Penwood Hants
44 B11 Penwyllt Powys
43 M10 Penybanc Carmth
44 G2 Penybont Powys
68 H10 Pen-y-bont Powys
68 E10 Pen-y-bont-fawr Powys
41 N2 Pen-y-bryn Pembks
29 M2 Pen-y-cae Powys
69 J5 Penycae Wrexhm
31 M5 Pen-y-cae-mawr Mons
66 B9 Penycaerau Gwynd
80 G9 Pen-y-cefn Flints
31 N3 Pen-y-clawdd Mons
30 E7 Pen-y-coedcae Rhondd
40 G6 Pen-y-cwn Pembks
29 N8 Pen-y-fai Brdgnd
80 H11 Pen-y-felin Flints
69 K2 Penyffordd Flints
67 J3 Penyffridd Gwynd
54 E7 Pen-y-garn Cerdgn
68 F10 Pen-y-Garnedd Powys
44 H9 Pen-y-genffordd Powys
66 C8 Pen-y-graig Gwynd
30 D6 Penygraig Rhondd
28 G2 Penygroes Carmth
66 H4 Penygroes Gwynd
67 M3 Pen-y-Gwryd Gwynd
30 C9 Pen-y-lan V Glam
28 E4 Pen-y-Mynydd Carmth
69 K2 Penymynydd Flints
67 L3 Pen-y-pass Gwynd
31 M2 Pen-yr-Heol Mons
30 D3 Pen-yr-Heolgerrig Myr Td
78 H6 Penysarn IoA
68 H4 Pen-y-stryt Denbgs
30 C4 Penywaun Rhondd
2 D7 Penzance Cnwll
2 D7 Penzance Heliport Cnwll
46 H4 Peopleton Worcs
82 G10 Peover Heath Ches E
23 P6 Peper Harow Surrey
70 A10 Peplow Shrops
51 P8 Pepper's Green Essex
50 C7 Pepperstock C Beds
125 K9 Perceton N Ayrs
159 N4 Percyhorner Abers
10 b2 Perelle Guern
21 Q5 Perham Down Wilts
18 C5 Periton Somset
36 E4 Perivale Gt Lon
9 P6 Perkins Village Devon
113 L10 Perkinsville Dur
85 K6 Perlethorpe Notts
3 K6 Perranarworthal Cnwll
3 K3 Perranporth Cnwll
2 E8 Perranuthnoe Cnwll
3 K3 Perranwell Cnwll
3 K6 Perranwell Cnwll
3 K6 Perran Wharf Cnwll
3 K3 Perranzabuloe Cnwll
33 K3 Perrott's Brook Gloucs
58 G6 Perry Birm
58 G6 Perry Barr Birm
58 G6 Perry Barr Crematorium Birm
52 D7 Perry Green Essex
51 K7 Perry Green Herts
33 J7 Perry Green Wilts
46 B9 Perrystone Hill Herefs
10 G3 Perry Street Somset
70 E9 Pershall Staffs
46 H5 Pershore Worcs
61 N7 Pertenhall Bed
134 E3 Perth P & K
134 D2 Perth Crematorium P & K
69 L8 Perthy Shrops
46 A6 Perton Herefs
58 C5 Perton Staffs
20 G7 Pertwood Wilts
74 C11 Peterborough C Pete
74 C10 Peterborough Crematorium C Pete
61 P2 Peterborough Services Cambs
45 L7 Peterchurch Herefs
151 L7 Peterculter C Aber
159 R8 Peterhead Abers
104 D2 Peterlee Dur
23 K10 Petersfield Hants
50 D7 Peter's Green Herts
36 E6 Petersham Gt Lon
16 H9 Peters Marland Devon
31 J9 Peterstone Wentlooge Newpt
30 E9 Peterston-super-Ely V Glam
45 R10 Peterstow Herefs
8 D9 Peter Tavy Devon
39 K11 Petham Kent
5 M4 Petherwin Gate Cnwll
17 J10 Petrockstow Devon
49 N5 Petsoe End M Keyn
27 J2 Pet Street Kent
26 E9 Pett E Susx
64 H10 Pettaugh Suffk
39 L11 Pett Bottom Kent
142 G9 Petterden Angus
116 D2 Pettinain S Lans
65 L10 Pettistree Suffk
18 D10 Petton Devon

69 M9 Petton Shrops
37 L7 Petts Wood Gt Lon
134 H10 Pettycur Fife
32 E7 Petty France S Glos
151 N3 Pettymuk Abers
23 Q10 Petworth W Susx
25 P9 Pevensey E Susx
25 Q10 Pevensey Bay E Susx
21 N2 Pewsey Wilts
35 L7 Pheasant's Hill Bucks
46 H3 Phepson Worcs
113 M10 Philadelphia Sundld
16 D7 Philham Devon
117 N5 Philiphaugh Border
2 F6 Phillack Cnwll
3 M6 Philleigh Cnwll
51 P7 Philpot End Essex
127 K2 Philpstoun W Loth
46 B9 Phocle Green Herefs
23 L3 Phoenix Green Hants
148 C9 Phones Highld
19 M9 Pibsbury Somset
100 D6 Pica Cumb
59 K5 Piccadilly Warwks
50 B9 Piccotts End Herts
91 N9 Pickburn Donc
98 F4 Pickering N York
22 C5 Picket Piece Hants
13 L3 Picket Post Hants
59 L8 Pickford Covtry
59 L8 Pickford Green Covtry
97 M4 Pickhill N York
56 G5 Picklescott Shrops
82 E9 Pickmere Ches E
18 G9 Pickney Somset
70 C10 Pickstock Wrekin
89 L6 Pickup Bank Bl w D
16 H3 Pickwell Devon
73 K8 Pickwell Leics
32 G10 Pickwick Wilts
73 Q4 Pickworth Lincs
73 P8 Pickworth Rutlnd
81 N10 Picton Ches W
80 G8 Picton Flints
104 D9 Picton N York
25 K10 Piddinghoe E Susx
35 M6 Piddington Bucks
49 M4 Piddington Nhants
48 H11 Piddington Oxon
11 Q5 Piddlehinton Dorset
11 Q5 Piddletrenthide Dorset
62 D5 Pidley Cambs
103 P7 Piercebridge Darltn
169 d2 Pierowall Ork
46 H9 Piff's Elm Gloucs
113 J3 Pigdon Nthumb
47 P2 Pigeon Green Warwks
12 H4 Pig Oak Dorset
45 M5 Pig Street Herefs
71 M3 Pikehall Derbys
12 H4 Pilford Dorset
51 N11 Pilgrims Hatch Essex
85 Q2 Pilham Lincs
31 P9 Pill N Som
5 P9 Pillaton Cnwll
5 P9 Pillatonmill Cnwll
47 Q5 Pillerton Hersey Warwks
47 Q5 Pillerton Priors Warwks
56 D11 Pilleth Powys
91 J10 Pilley Barns
13 P5 Pilley Hants
13 P5 Pilley Bailey Hants
31 K7 Pillgwenlly Newpt
16 H6 Pillhead Devon
95 J11 Pilling Lancs
94 H11 Pilling Lane Lancs
31 Q7 Pilning S Glos
27 J8 Pilot Inn Kent
71 L2 Pilsbury Derbys
11 J5 Pilsdon Dorset
73 R9 Pilsgate C Pete
84 B6 Pilsley Derbys
84 F8 Pilsley Derbys
77 M9 Pilson Green Norfk
25 K6 Piltdown E Susx
17 K5 Pilton Devon
61 M4 Pilton Nhants
73 N10 Pilton Rutlnd
19 Q6 Pilton Somset
28 D7 Pilton Green Swans
89 L2 Pimlico Lancs
48 H6 Pimlico Nhants
12 F3 Pimperne Dorset
74 D5 Pinchbeck Lincs
74 C5 Pinchbeck Bars Lincs
74 D6 Pinchbeck West Lincs
91 R7 Pincheon Green Donc
104 G8 Pinchinthorpe R & Cl
88 G7 Pincock Lancs
88 D8 Pinfold Lancs
64 A10 Pinford End Suffk
28 D4 Pinged Carmth
35 J11 Pingewood W Berk
50 G5 Pin Green Herts
9 N6 Pinhoe Devon
59 L8 Pinkett's Booth Covtry
32 G7 Pinkney Wilts
59 N9 Pinley Covtry
59 K11 Pinley Green Warwks
53 M4 Pin Mill Suffk
114 C9 Pinminnoch S Ayrs
114 D9 Pinmore S Ayrs
10 C7 Pinn Devon
36 D3 Pinner Gt Lon
36 D3 Pinner Green Gt Lon
69 Q5 Pinsley Green Ches E
47 J5 Pinvin Worcs
114 D10 Pinwherry S Ayrs
84 G10 Pinxton Derbys
45 Q6 Pipe and Lyde Herefs
56 H10 Pipe Aston Herefs
70 C6 Pipe Gate Shrops
58 G3 Pipehill Staffs
156 F7 Piperhill Highld
5 M5 Pipers Pool Cnwll
60 H3 Pipewell Nhants
17 J4 Pippacott Devon
88 H6 Pippin Street Lancs
44 H7 Pipton Powys
23 P3 Pirbright Surrey
23 P3 Pirbright Camp Surrey
118 C5 Pirnie Border
120 G3 Pirnmill N Ayrs
50 D4 Pirton Herts
46 G5 Pirton Worcs
54 F9 Pisgah Cerdgn
35 K7 Pishill Oxon
66 E6 Pistyll Gwynd
141 K4 Pitagowan P & K
159 N5 Pitblae Abers
134 D2 Pitcairngreen P & K
156 E3 Pitcalnie Highld
151 J2 Pitcaple Abers
142 E4 Pitcarity Angus
32 G3 Pitchcombe Gloucs
49 L10 Pitchcott Bucks
74 E4 Pitcher Row Lincs
57 J4 Pitchford Shrops
35 L4 Pitch Green Bucks
23 N7 Pitch Place Surrey
23 Q4 Pitch Place Surrey
157 M10 Pitchroy Moray
20 C8 Pitcombe Somset
29 N10 Pitcot V Glam
128 G5 Pitcox E Loth
150 H4 Pitfichie Abers
158 G9 Pitglassie Abers
162 H8 Pitgrudy Highld
135 J6 Pitlessie Fife
141 M6 Pitlochry P & K
150 H2 Pitmachie Abers
148 C7 Pitmain Highld
151 M2 Pitmedden Abers
151 M2 Pitmedden Garden Abers
18 H11 Pitminster Somset
143 K8 Pitmuies Angus
150 H5 Pitmunie Abers
19 N9 Pitney Somset
134 G2 Pitroddie P & K
135 L5 Pitscottie Fife
38 B4 Pitsea Essex
83 K4 Pitses Oldham
60 G7 Pitsford Nhants
49 P11 Pitstone Bucks
18 D11 Pitt Devon
22 E9 Pitt Hants
143 N3 Pittarrow Abers
32 D5 Pitt Court Gloucs
135 P7 Pittenweem Fife
134 H8 Pitteuchar Fife
104 B2 Pittington Dur
150 H3 Pittodrie House Hotel Abers
21 P8 Pitton Wilts
37 P11 Pitt's Wood Kent
159 N4 Pittulie Abers
4 F6 Pityme Cnwll
113 L11 Pity Me Dur
26 F2 Pivington Kent
65 J6 Pixey Green Suffk
36 E10 Pixham Surrey
126 D4 Plains N Lans
4 F6 Plain Street Cnwll
57 J5 Plaish Shrops
37 K4 Plaistow Gt Lon
24 B4 Plaistow W Susx
21 Q11 Plaitford Hants
82 D5 Plank Lane Wigan
78 D9 Plas Cymyran IoA
23 K10 Plastow Green Hants
37 P9 Platt Kent
82 D4 Platt Bridge Wigan
69 P7 Platt Lane Shrops
38 E11 Platts Heath Kent
113 L11 Plawsworth Dur
37 P10 Plaxtol Kent
26 F7 Playden E Susx
53 M2 Playford Suffk
35 K9 Play Hatch Oxon
3 L5 Playing Place Cnwll
46 E8 Playley Green Gloucs
56 G3 Plealey Shrops
133 N10 Plean Stirlg
134 G5 Pleasance Fife
89 J5 Pleasington Bl w D
89 J5 Pleasington Crematorium Bl w D
84 H8 Pleasley Derbys
84 H8 Pleasleyhill Notts
11 Q2 Pleck Dorset
51 N5 Pledgdon Green Essex
91 J7 Pledwick Wakefd
10 b1 Pleinheaume Guern
11 a1 Plemont Jersey
81 P10 Plemstall Ches W
111 P8 Plenmeller Nthumb
51 Q8 Pleshey Essex
153 Q11 Plockton Highld
56 F7 Plowden Shrops
56 F4 Plox Green Shrops
26 F2 Pluckley Kent
26 F3 Pluckley Station Kent
26 F3 Pluckley Thorne Kent
39 N9 Plucks Gutter Kent
100 G3 Plumbland Cumb
95 K2 Plumgarths Cumb
82 F10 Plumley Ches E
94 G5 Plumpton Cumb
101 N3 Plumpton Cumb
25 J8 Plumpton E Susx
48 G5 Plumpton Nhants
49 K6 Plumpton End Nhants
25 J7 Plumpton Green E Susx
101 P3 Plumpton Head Cumb
37 K5 Plumstead Gt Lon
76 G5 Plumstead Norfk
76 G4 Plumstead Green Norfk
72 G4 Plumtree Notts
26 D2 Plumtree Green Kent
73 K4 Plungar Leics
26 F4 Plurenden Kent
11 Q4 Plush Dorset
5 M5 Plusha Cnwll
5 N7 Plushabridge Cnwll
42 G4 Plwmp Cerdgn
6 D8 Plymouth C Plym
6 E6 Plymouth Airport C Plym
6 E7 Plympton C Plym
6 E8 Plymstock C Plym
9 Q4 Plymtree Devon
98 C3 Pockley N York
98 G11 Pocklington E R Yk
74 D6 Pode Hole Lincs
19 P10 Podimore Somset
61 K8 Podington Bed
70 D7 Podmore Staffs
53 K9 Point Clear Essex
74 B4 Pointon Lincs
13 K6 Pokesdown Bmouth
160 F4 Polbain Highld
5 N10 Polbathic Cnwll
127 J5 Polbeth W Loth
4 G8 Polbrock Cnwll
2 H7 Poldark Mine Cnwll
61 N3 Polebrook Nhants
46 F4 Pole Elm Worcs
25 N10 Polegate E Susx
90 D7 Pole Moor Kirk
59 L4 Polesworth Warwks
2 B9 Polgigga Cnwll
160 G5 Polglass Highld
3 P3 Polgooth Cnwll
115 P7 Polgown D & G
24 B10 Poling W Susx
24 B9 Poling Corner W Susx
4 H11 Polkerris Cnwll
77 L5 Pollard Street Norfk
91 Q7 Pollington E R Yk
138 D4 Polloch Highld
125 P5 Pollokshaws C Glas
125 P5 Pollokshields C Glas
3 P4 Polmassick Cnwll
4 H11 Polmear Cnwll
126 G2 Polmont Falk
145 N11 Polnish Highld
5 L11 Polperro Cnwll
5 J11 Polruan Cnwll
19 P6 Polsham Somset
52 G4 Polstead Suffk
52 G3 Polstead Heath Suffk
130 G8 Poltalloch Ag & B
3 J10 Poltescoe Cnwll
9 N5 Poltimore Devon
127 P5 Polton Mdloth
129 J9 Polwarth Border
5 M5 Polyphant Cnwll
4 E6 Polzeath Cnwll
127 N6 Pomathorn Mdloth
83 P11 Pomeroy Derbys
44 G7 Ponde Powys
62 C2 Pondersbridge Cambs
51 J11 Ponders End Gt Lon
3 K6 Ponsanooth Cnwll
100 E9 Ponsonby Cumb
3 K10 Ponsongath Cnwll
7 J4 Ponsworthy Devon
28 G3 Pont Abraham Services Carmth
11 c2 Pontac Jersey
28 H2 Pontamman Carmth
28 D2 Pontantwn Carmth
29 K4 Pontardawe Neath
28 G4 Pontarddulais Swans
43 K10 Pont-ar-gothi Carmth
44 B9 Pont-ar-Hydfer Powys
43 P10 Pont-ar-llechau Carmth
42 H9 Pontarsais Carmth
69 J2 Pontblyddyn Flints
67 N3 Pont Cyfyng Conwy
79 P11 Pont Dolgarrog Conwy
55 N6 Pontdolgoch Powys
31 J7 Pont-Ebbw Newpt
91 M6 Pontefract Wakefd
91 L6 Pontefract Crematorium Wakefd
113 J6 Ponteland Nthumb
54 G8 Ponterwyd Cerdgn
56 F3 Pontesbury Shrops
56 F3 Pontesbury Hill Shrops
56 G3 Pontesford Shrops
68 H7 Pontfadog Wrexhm
41 K4 Pontfaen Pembks
44 D8 Pont-faen Powys
42 F4 Pontgarreg Cerdgn
41 M2 Pontgarreg Pembks
28 E3 Ponthenry Carmth
31 K6 Ponthir Torfn
42 E5 Ponthirwaun Cerdgn
30 G5 Pontllanfraith Caerph
28 H5 Pontlliw Swans
30 F3 Pontlottyn Caerph
66 G4 Pontlyfni Gwynd
28 F3 Pont Morlais Carmth
29 P3 Pontneddfechan Neath
31 J5 Pontnewydd Torfn
31 J4 Pontnewynydd Torfn
67 M2 Pont Pen-y-benglog Gwynd
54 G11 Pontrhydfendigaid Cerdgn
67 R9 Pont Rhyd-sarn Gwynd
29 N7 Pont Rhyd-y-cyff Brdgnd
29 L6 Pont-rhyd-y-fen Neath
54 G10 Pontrhydygroes Cerdgn
31 J5 Pontrhydyrun Torfn
45 M9 Pontrilas Herefs
55 Q2 Pont Robert Powys
67 J2 Pont-rug Gwynd
25 Q7 Ponts Green E Susx
42 H5 Pontshaen Cerdgn
46 B10 Pontshill Herefs
30 E2 Pontsticill Myr Td
29 N3 Pont Walby Neath
42 H6 Pontwelly Carmth
28 E3 Pontyates Carmth
28 F2 Pontyberem Carmth
69 K7 Pont-y-blew Wrexhm
69 J3 Pontybodkin Flints
30 D8 Pontyclun Rhondd
29 P6 Pontycymer Brdgnd
41 M3 Pontyglasier Pembks
30 D6 Pontygwaith Rhondd
41 M3 Pontygynon Pembks
67 P4 Pont-y-pant Conwy
31 J4 Pontypool Torfn
31 K5 Pontypool Road Torfn
30 E7 Pontypridd Rhondd
40 H5 Pont-yr-hafod Pembks
29 P7 Pont-yr-Rhyl Brdgnd
30 H6 Pontywaun Caerph
2 H5 Pool Cnwll
2 b2 Pool IoS
97 K11 Pool Leeds
12 H6 Poole Poole
12 H5 Poole Crematorium Poole
33 J5 Poole Keynes Gloucs
160 D10 Poolewe Highld
101 N6 Pooley Bridge Cumb
64 F5 Pooley Street Norfk
70 F3 Poolfold Staffs
45 R4 Pool Head Herefs
46 D9 Poolhill Gloucs
134 C7 Pool of Muckhart Clacks
56 D2 Pool Quay Powys
52 C4 Pool Street Essex
37 L11 Pooting's Kent
22 G6 Popham Hants
37 J4 Poplar Gt Lon
65 N8 Poplar Street Suffk
14 D8 Porchfield IoW
77 K11 Poringland Norfk
2 H7 Porkellis Cnwll
18 A5 Porlock Somset
17 R2 Porlock Weir Somset
123 N8 Portachoillan Ag & B
153 P11 Port-an-Eorna Highld
138 G8 Port Appin Ag & B
122 F6 Port Askaig Ag & B
124 A4 Portavadie Ag & B
124 D4 Port Bannatyne Ag & B
31 P9 Portbury N Som
110 D8 Port Carlisle Cumb
122 C8 Port Charlotte Ag & B
14 H5 Portchester Hants
14 H5 Portchester Crematorium Hants
104 E6 Port Clarence S on T
124 B3 Port Driseach Ag & B
28 E7 Port Einon Swans
122 E10 Port Ellen Ag & B
151 K3 Port Elphinstone Abers
106 D3 Portencalzie D & G
124 F8 Portencross N Ayrs
80 a8 Port Erin IoM
11 N7 Portesham Dorset
158 B4 Portessie Moray
80 g3 Port e Vullen IoM
40 H7 Portfield Gate Pembks
5 Q4 Portgate Devon
4 G5 Port Gaverne Cnwll
125 J3 Port Glasgow Inver
158 A5 Portgordon Moray
163 N4 Portgower Highld
4 C9 Porth Cnwll
30 D6 Porth Rhondd
3 K9 Porthallow Cnwll
5 L11 Porthallow Cnwll
29 M9 Porthcawl Brdgnd
4 D7 Porthcothan Cnwll
2 B9 Porthcurno Cnwll
66 D6 Porth Dinllaen Gwynd
153 P3 Port Henderson Highld
40 F4 Porthgain Pembks
2 B9 Porthgwarra Cnwll
70 E5 Porthill Staffs
3 L5 Porthkea Cnwll
30 E11 Porthkerry V Glam
2 G8 Porthleven Cnwll
67 K7 Porthmadog Gwynd
2 C6 Porthmeor Cnwll
3 K8 Porth Navas Cnwll
3 P5 Portholland Cnwll
3 K10 Porthoustock Cnwll
3 Q3 Porthpean Cnwll
2 H4 Porthtowan Cnwll
69 L5 Porthwgan Wrexhm
43 K11 Porthyrhyd Carmth
69 J10 Porth-y-Waen Shrops
131 Q9 Portincaple Ag & B
11 a1 Portinfer Jersey
92 C4 Portington E R Yk
131 K5 Portinnisherrich Ag & B
101 J6 Portinscale Cumb
4 F5 Port Isaac Cnwll
31 N9 Portishead N Som
158 C4 Portknockie Moray
11 P10 Portland Dorset
151 N8 Portlethen Abers
109 J10 Portling D & G
3 N6 Portloe Cnwll
106 E9 Port Logan D & G
5 L11 Portlooe Cnwll
163 L10 Portmahomack Highld
67 K7 Portmeirion Gwynd
3 Q5 Portmellon Cnwll
144 F12 Port Mor Highld
13 P5 Portmore Hants
105 L7 Port Mulgrave N York
138 G8 Portnacroish Ag & B
168 k4 Portnaguran W Isls
122 A9 Portnahaven Ag & B
152 E11 Portnalong Highld
168 k4 Port nan Giuran W Isls
168 d10 Port nan Long W Isls
168 k1 Port Nis W Isls
127 Q3 Portobello C Edin
113 L9 Portobello Gatesd
58 E5 Portobello Wolves
132 H7 Port of Menteith Stirlg
168 k1 Port of Ness W Isls
21 N7 Porton Wilts
5 Q6 Portontown Devon
106 C7 Portpatrick D & G
4 F5 Port Quin Cnwll
138 F8 Port Ramsay Ag & B
2 H4 Portreath Cnwll
152 H9 Portree Highld
80 b8 Port St Mary IoM
3 M6 Portscatho Cnwll
14 H6 Portsea C Port
166 E3 Portskerra Highld
31 N7 Portskewett Mons
24 G9 Portslade Br & H
24 G9 Portslade-by-Sea Br & H
106 C6 Portslogan D & G
14 H7 Portsmouth C Port
89 Q5 Portsmouth Calder
80 d7 Port Soderick IoM
14 H5 Port Solent C Port
131 L3 Portsonachan Hotel Ag & B
158 E4 Portsoy Abers
81 L8 Port Sunlight Wirral
14 D4 Portswood C Sotn
29 L7 Port Talbot Neath
29 J6 Port Tennant Swans
137 L2 Portuairk Highld
45 P6 Portway Herefs
45 P7 Portway Herefs
58 E7 Portway Sandw
58 G10 Portway Worcs
122 A9 Port Wemyss Ag & B
107 K9 Port William D & G
5 P11 Portwrinkle Cnwll
107 N10 Portyerrock D & G
9 K5 Posbury Devon
57 M4 Posenhall Shrops
63 N11 Poslingford Suffk
117 J4 Posso Border
8 G9 Postbridge Devon
35 K4 Postcombe Oxon
12 G6 Post Green Dorset
27 K4 Postling Kent
77 K10 Postwick Norfk
150 G8 Potarch Abers
49 Q8 Potsgrove C Beds
50 B9 Potten End Herts
39 N8 Potten Street Kent
99 K5 Potter Brompton N York
64 H3 Pottergate Street Norfk
86 E7 Potterhanworth Lincs
86 E7 Potterhanworth Booths Lincs
77 N8 Potter Heigham Norfk
21 J3 Potterne Wilts
21 J3 Potterne Wick Wilts
35 P4 Potter Row Bucks
50 F10 Potters Bar Herts
95 K10 Potters Brook Lancs
58 B8 Potter's Cross Staffs
50 D9 Potters Crouch Herts
26 E2 Potter's Forstal Kent
59 N8 Potters Green Covtry
25 M6 Potter's Green E Susx
51 J6 Potter's Green Herts
50 F7 Pottersheath Herts
72 D11 Potters Marston Leics
71 L7 Potter Somersal Derbys
49 L6 Potterspury Nhants
151 N4 Potterton Abers
91 L3 Potterton Leeds
76 C7 Potthorpe Norfk
20 F6 Pottle Street Wilts
104 E10 Potto N York
62 B11 Potton C Beds
75 P6 Pott Row Norfk
52 F7 Pott's Green Essex
83 K9 Pott Shrigley Ches E
16 C10 Poughill Cnwll
9 L3 Poughill Devon
13 L3 Poulner Hants
21 J3 Poulshot Wilts
33 L4 Poulton Gloucs
81 L6 Poulton Wirral
88 C3 Poulton-le-Fylde Lancs
33 L5 Poulton Priory Gloucs
57 N10 Pound Bank Worcs
11 P6 Poundbury Dorset
28 G6 Poundffald Swans
25 L5 Poundgate E Susx
25 M6 Pound Green E Susx
63 M10 Pound Green Suffk
57 P9 Pound Green Worcs
24 G3 Pound Hill W Susx
48 H9 Poundon Bucks
25 M2 Poundsbridge Kent
7 J4 Poundsgate Devon
5 L2 Poundstock Cnwll
22 E2 Pound Street Hants
25 M6 Pounsley E Susx
107 N8 Pouton D & G
65 M7 Pouy Street Suffk
24 G2 Povey Cross Surrey
119 L7 Powburn Nthumb
9 N8 Powderham Devon
11 L5 Powerstock Dorset
109 P7 Powfoot D & G
46 D6 Pow Green Herefs
110 D9 Powhill Cumb
46 F4 Powick Worcs
134 C8 Powmill P & K
12 B8 Poxwell Dorset
36 B5 Poyle Slough
24 G8 Poynings W Susx
20 C10 Poyntington Dorset
83 K8 Poynton Ches E
69 Q11 Poynton Wrekin
69 Q11 Poynton Green Wrekin
41 J7 Poyston Cross Pembks
64 D10 Poystreet Green Suffk
2 F8 Praa Sands Cnwll
37 L8 Pratt's Bottom Gt Lon
2 G6 Praze-an-Beeble Cnwll
2 H10 Predannack Wollas Cnwll
69 Q8 Prees Shrops
94 H11 Preesall Lancs
69 Q8 Prees Green Shrops
69 J7 Preesgweene Shrops
69 Q7 Prees Heath Shrops
69 Q7 Prees Higher Heath Shrops
69 Q8 Prees Lower Heath Shrops
119 K8 Prendwick Nthumb
42 H6 Pren-gwyn Cerdgn
67 K6 Prenteg Gwynd
81 L7 Prenton Wirral
81 P6 Prescot Knows
10 B2 Prescott Devon
57 M8 Prescott Shrops
69 M10 Prescott Shrops
142 B4 Presnerb Angus
118 F3 Pressen Nthumb
80 F8 Prestatyn Denbgs
83 J9 Prestbury Ches E
47 J10 Prestbury Gloucs
45 L2 Presteigne Powys
20 B6 Prestleigh Somset
89 M9 Prestolee Bolton
129 K8 Preston Border
24 H9 Preston Br & H
7 M4 Preston Devon
11 Q8 Preston Dorset
93 L4 Preston E R Yk
33 K4 Preston Gloucs
50 E6 Preston Herts
38 H9 Preston Kent
39 M9 Preston Kent
88 G5 Preston Lancs
119 N5 Preston Nthumb
73 M10 Preston Rutlnd
57 J2 Preston Shrops
18 E7 Preston Somset
64 C11 Preston Suffk
7 M6 Preston Torbay
33 K9 Preston Wilts
33 Q10 Preston Wilts
59 J11 Preston Bagot Warwks
49 J9 Preston Bissett Bucks
18 F9 Preston Bowyer Somset
69 P10 Preston Brockhurst Shrops
82 C8 Preston Brook Halton
22 H6 Preston Candover Hants
48 G4 Preston Capes Nhants
88 H4 Preston Crematorium Lancs
34 H6 Preston Crowmarsh Oxon
60 G9 Preston Deanery Nhants
59 J11 Preston Green Warwks
69 N11 Preston Gubbals Shrops
56 G2 Preston Montford Shrops
47 P5 Preston on Stour Warwks
104 D7 Preston on Tees S on T
82 C8 Preston on the Hill Halton
45 M6 Preston on Wye Herefs
128 B5 Prestonpans E Loth
95 L4 Preston Patrick Cumb
19 P11 Preston Plucknett Somset
39 N9 Preston Street Kent
96 G2 Preston-under-Scar N York
70 B11 Preston upon the Weald Moors Wrekin
45 R5 Preston Wynne Herefs

82 H4 **Prestwich** Bury
113 J6 **Prestwick** Nthumb
114 G2 **Prestwick** S Ayrs
114 G2 **Prestwick Airport** S Ayrs
35 N4 **Prestwood** Bucks
58 C7 **Prestwood** Staffs
29 P6 **Price Town** Brdgnd
63 J4 **Prickwillow** Cambs
19 P4 **Priddy** Somset
8 B3 **Priestacott** Devon
83 P10 **Priestcliffe** Derbys
83 P10 **Priestcliffe Ditch** Derbys
95 L6 **Priest Hutton** Lancs
125 P10 **Priestland** E Ayrs
90 E5 **Priestley Green** Calder
56 D5 **Priest Weston** Shrops
37 Q8 **Priestwood Green** Kent
60 B2 **Primethorpe** Leics
76 F8 **Primrose Green** Norfk
129 K8 **Primrosehill** Border
62 E3 **Primrose Hill** Cambs
84 F9 **Primrose Hill** Derbys
58 D7 **Primrose Hill** Dudley
88 D9 **Primrose Hill** Lancs
118 F5 **Primsidemill** Border
41 M8 **Princes Gate** Pembks
35 M4 **Princes Risborough** Bucks
59 P10 **Princethorpe** Warwks
6 F4 **Princetown** Devon
15 L5 **Prinsted** W Susx
68 E2 **Prion** Denbgs
111 J7 **Prior Rigg** Cumb
56 H9 **Priors Halton** Shrops
48 E3 **Priors Hardwick** Warwks
57 N2 **Priorslee** Wrekin
48 E3 **Priors Marston** Warwks
46 G10 **Priors Norton** Gloucs
33 M7 **Priory Vale** Swindn
45 K5 **Priory Wood** Herefs
30 D9 **Prisk** V Glam
20 C2 **Priston** BaNES
64 G4 **Pristow Green** Norfk
38 E4 **Prittlewell** Sthend
23 J9 **Privett** Hants
17 K4 **Prixford** Devon
3 M4 **Probus** Cnwll
128 E4 **Prora** E Loth
100 F2 **Prospect** Cumb
2 G7 **Prospidnick** Cnwll
159 K5 **Protstonhill** Abers
112 G8 **Prudhoe** Nthumb
2 F8 **Prussia Cove** Cnwll
20 B2 **Publow** BaNES
51 J6 **Puckeridge** Herts
19 L11 **Puckington** Somset
32 C9 **Pucklechurch** S Glos
46 G7 **Puckrup** Gloucs
82 F11 **Puddinglake** Ches W
81 L10 **Puddington** Ches W
9 K2 **Puddington** Devon
64 F3 **Puddledock** Norfk
12 C6 **Puddletown** Dorset
45 R3 **Pudleston** Herefs
90 G4 **Pudsey** Leeds
24 B7 **Pulborough** W Susx
70 C10 **Puleston** Wrekin
69 L3 **Pulford** Ches W
11 Q3 **Pulham** Dorset
64 H4 **Pulham Market** Norfk
65 J4 **Pulham St Mary** Norfk
32 B6 **Pullens Green** S Glos
50 C4 **Pulloxhill** C Beds
127 K4 **Pumpherston** W Loth
43 N6 **Pumsaint** Carmth
41 K5 **Puncheston** Pembks
11 L7 **Puncknowle** Dorset
25 P6 **Punnett's Town** E Susx
15 J5 **Purbrook** Hants
37 N5 **Purfleet** Thurr
19 K5 **Puriton** Somset
52 D11 **Purleigh** Essex
36 H8 **Purley** Gt Lon
35 J9 **Purley** W Berk
56 D9 **Purlogue** Shrops
32 G11 **Purlpit** Wilts
62 G3 **Purls Bridge** Cambs
20 C11 **Purse Caundle** Dorset
58 C10 **Purshull Green** Worcs
56 F8 **Purslow** Shrops
91 L7 **Purston Jaglin** Wakefd
10 H3 **Purtington** Somset
32 C3 **Purton** Gloucs
32 C4 **Purton** Gloucs
33 L7 **Purton** Wilts
33 L6 **Purton Stoke** Wilts
49 K5 **Pury End** Nhants
34 C5 **Pusey** Oxon
46 B7 **Putley** Herefs
46 B7 **Putley Green** Herefs
32 E3 **Putloe** Gloucs
36 F6 **Putney** Gt Lon
36 F6 **Putney Vale Crematorium** Gt Lon
16 G3 **Putsborough** Devon
35 N2 **Puttenham** Herts
23 P5 **Puttenham** Surrey
52 D3 **Puttock End** Essex
11 N8 **Putton** Dorset
49 L6 **Puxley** Nhants
19 M2 **Puxton** N Som
28 E4 **Pwll** Carmth
40 H10 **Pwllcrochan** Pembks
30 H2 **Pwll-du** Mons
68 F4 **Pwll-glas** Denbgs
44 E8 **Pwllgloyw** Powys
66 F7 **Pwllheli** Gwynd
31 P6 **Pwllmeyric** Mons
41 Q7 **Pwll Trap** Carmth
29 L6 **Pwll-y-glaw** Neath
79 Q9 **Pydew** Conwy
84 F10 **Pye Bridge** Derbys
24 G8 **Pyecombe** W Susx
31 K7 **Pye Corner** Newpt
58 E2 **Pye Green** Staffs
29 M8 **Pyle** Brdgnd
18 F8 **Pyleigh** Somset
20 B7 **Pylle** Somset
62 G3 **Pymoor** Cambs
11 K6 **Pymore** Dorset
36 B9 **Pyrford** Surrey
35 J5 **Pyrton** Oxon
61 J6 **Pytchley** Nhants
16 E11 **Pyworthy** Devon

Q

56 C8 **Quabbs** Shrops
74 D4 **Quadring** Lincs
74 D4 **Quadring Eaudike** Lincs
49 K10 **Quainton** Bucks
30 E5 **Quaker's Yard** Myr Td
113 J10 **Quaking Houses** Dur
18 G7 **Quantock Hills** Somset
169 r10 **Quarff** Shet
21 Q6 **Quarley** Hants
72 A2 **Quarndon** Derbys
14 G8 **Quarr Hill** IoW
125 K4 **Quarrier's Village** Inver
73 R2 **Quarrington** Lincs
104 B3 **Quarrington Hill** Dur
82 C11 **Quarrybank** Ches W
58 D7 **Quarry Bank** Dudley
157 M5 **Quarrywood** Moray
124 F5 **Quarter** N Ayrs
126 C7 **Quarter** S Lans
57 N6 **Quatford** Shrops
57 P7 **Quatt** Shrops
103 N2 **Quebec** Dur
32 F2 **Quedgeley** Gloucs
63 J4 **Queen Adelaide** Cambs
38 F7 **Queenborough** Kent
19 Q10 **Queen Camel** Somset
32 B11 **Queen Charlton** BaNES
17 Q8 **Queen Dart** Devon
132 G7 **Queen Elizabeth Forest Park** Stirlg
46 G7 **Queenhill** Worcs
20 E8 **Queen Oak** Dorset
14 G10 **Queen's Bower** IoW
90 E4 **Queensbury** C Brad
81 L11 **Queensferry** Flints
69 K9 **Queen's Head** Shrops
126 B4 **Queenslie** C Glas
61 M11 **Queen's Park** Bed
60 G8 **Queen's Park** Nhants
37 Q11 **Queen Street** Kent
33 K7 **Queen Street** Wilts
126 B2 **Queenzieburn** N Lans
51 M4 **Quendon** Essex
72 G8 **Queniborough** Leics
33 M4 **Quenington** Gloucs
95 L8 **Quernmore** Lancs
58 G6 **Queslett** Birm
5 N9 **Quethiock** Cnwll
34 G9 **Quick's Green** W Berk
64 E4 **Quidenham** Norfk
22 F4 **Quidhampton** Hants
21 M8 **Quidhampton** Wilts
69 P8 **Quina Brook** Shrops
48 H4 **Quinbury End** Nhants
58 E8 **Quinton** Dudley
49 L4 **Quinton** Nhants
49 L4 **Quinton Green** Nhants
4 C9 **Quintrell Downs** Cnwll
71 L6 **Quixhall** Staffs
129 K7 **Quixwood** Border
5 Q2 **Quoditch** Devon
133 N3 **Quoig** P & K
72 F7 **Quorn** Leics
116 D3 **Quothquan** S Lans
169 e6 **Quoyburray** Ork
169 b4 **Quoyloo** Ork

R

153 K9 **Raasay** Highld
26 C2 **Rabbit's Cross** Kent
50 F7 **Rableyheath** Herts
110 C10 **Raby** Cumb
81 L9 **Raby** Wirral
116 G4 **Rachan Mill** Border
79 L11 **Rachub** Gwynd
17 R8 **Rackenford** Devon
24 B8 **Rackham** W Susx
77 K9 **Rackheath** Norfk
109 M6 **Racks** D & G
169 b7 **Rackwick** Ork
71 P7 **Radbourne** Derbys
89 M9 **Radcliffe** Bury
119 Q10 **Radcliffe** Nthumb
72 G3 **Radcliffe on Trent** Notts
49 J8 **Radclive** Bucks
33 Q5 **Radcot** Oxon
156 C6 **Raddery** Highld
18 D9 **Raddington** Somset
135 M6 **Radernie** Fife
59 M8 **Radford** Covtry
48 B2 **Radford Semele** Warwks
18 H7 **Radlet** Somset
50 E10 **Radlett** Herts
17 N7 **Radley** Devon
34 F5 **Radley** Oxon
51 P9 **Radley Green** Essex
69 Q3 **Radmore Green** Ches E
35 L5 **Radnage** Bucks
20 C4 **Radstock** BaNES
48 G6 **Radstone** Nhants
48 C5 **Radway** Warwks
61 M9 **Radwell** Bed
50 F3 **Radwell** Herts
51 P3 **Radwinter** Essex
51 P3 **Radwinter End** Essex
30 F8 **Radyr** Cardif
86 D11 **RAF College (Cranwell)** Lincs
157 K6 **Rafford** Moray
72 H7 **Ragdale** Leics
56 H6 **Ragdon** Shrops
2 D8 **Raginnis** Cnwll
31 M3 **Raglan** Mons
85 P6 **Ragnall** Notts
148 E2 **Raigbeg** Highld
46 G3 **Rainbow Hill** Worcs
81 P4 **Rainford** St Hel
37 M4 **Rainham** Gt Lon
38 D8 **Rainham** Medway
81 P6 **Rainhill** St Hel
81 Q6 **Rainhill Stoops** St Hel
83 K9 **Rainow** Ches E
82 H4 **Rainsough** Bury
97 N5 **Rainton** N York
85 J9 **Rainworth** Notts
102 B9 **Raisbeck** Cumb
111 P11 **Raise** Cumb
98 H8 **Raisthorpe** N York
134 G2 **Rait** P & K
87 K4 **Raithby** Lincs
87 L7 **Raithby** Lincs
105 N8 **Raithwaite** N York
23 M9 **Rake** Hants
89 Q8 **Rakewood** Rochdl
148 C8 **Ralia** Highld
43 L5 **Ram** Carmth
152 B9 **Ramasaig** Highld
3 J7 **Rame** Cnwll
6 C9 **Rame** Cnwll
32 C9 **Ram Hill** S Glos
26 G2 **Ram Lane** Kent
11 M4 **Rampisham** Dorset
94 E7 **Rampside** Cumb
62 F7 **Rampton** Cambs
85 P5 **Rampton** Notts
89 M7 **Ramsbottom** Bury
33 Q10 **Ramsbury** Wilts
167 K11 **Ramscraigs** Highld
23 K10 **Ramsdean** Hants
22 G3 **Ramsdell** Hants
48 C11 **Ramsden** Oxon
46 H5 **Ramsden** Worcs
38 B3 **Ramsden Bellhouse** Essex
38 B2 **Ramsden Heath** Essex
62 C3 **Ramsey** Cambs
53 M5 **Ramsey** Essex
80 g3 **Ramsey** IoM
62 D3 **Ramsey Forty Foot** Cambs
62 B4 **Ramsey Heights** Cambs
52 F10 **Ramsey Island** Essex
40 D6 **Ramsey Island** Pembks
62 C3 **Ramsey Mereside** Cambs
62 C3 **Ramsey St Mary's** Cambs
39 Q8 **Ramsgate** Kent
96 H6 **Ramsgill** N York
103 M5 **Ramshaw** Dur
112 E11 **Ramshaw** Dur
53 P3 **Ramsholt** Suffk
118 D10 **Ramshope** Nthumb
71 K5 **Ramshorn** Staffs
8 G6 **Ramsley** Devon
23 P8 **Ramsnest Common** Surrey
86 H5 **Ranby** Lincs
85 L4 **Ranby** Notts
86 F5 **Rand** Lincs
36 E9 **Randalls Park Crematorium** Surrey
32 F3 **Randwick** Gloucs
125 K4 **Ranfurly** Rens
71 M10 **Rangemore** Staffs
32 C7 **Rangeworthy** S Glos
115 J5 **Rankinston** E Ayrs
73 L8 **Ranksborough** Rutlnd
52 B8 **Rank's Green** Essex
140 B6 **Rannoch Station** P & K
18 B6 **Ranscombe** Somset
85 L3 **Ranskill** Notts
70 F10 **Ranton** Staffs
70 E10 **Ranton Green** Staffs
77 M9 **Ranworth** Norfk
133 M9 **Raploch** Stirlg
169 e2 **Rapness** Ork
19 K11 **Rapps** Somset
108 G11 **Rascarrel** D & G
131 N11 **Rashfield** Ag & B
58 D11 **Rashwood** Worcs
97 Q6 **Raskelf** N York
30 G2 **Rassau** Blae G
90 E6 **Rastrick** Calder
145 R4 **Ratagan** Highld
72 E9 **Ratby** Leics
72 A11 **Ratcliffe Culey** Leics
72 D5 **Ratcliffe on Soar** Notts
72 G8 **Ratcliffe on the Wreake** Leics
21 N6 **Ratfyn** Wilts
159 N5 **Rathen** Abers
135 K3 **Rathillet** Fife
96 B9 **Rathmell** N York
127 L3 **Ratho** C Edin
127 L3 **Ratho Station** C Edin
158 B4 **Rathven** Moray
22 D10 **Ratlake** Hants
48 C5 **Ratley** Warwks
39 M11 **Ratling** Kent
56 G5 **Ratlinghope** Shrops
75 K8 **Rattan Row** Norfk
167 N2 **Rattar** Highld
101 K2 **Ratten Row** Cumb
110 G11 **Ratten Row** Cumb
88 E2 **Ratten Row** Lancs
7 J6 **Rattery** Devon
64 D10 **Rattlesden** Suffk
25 N10 **Ratton Village** E Susx
142 B8 **Rattray** P & K
110 G11 **Raughton** Cumb
110 G11 **Raughton Head** Cumb
61 L6 **Raunds** Nhants
91 M11 **Ravenfield** Rothm
100 E11 **Ravenglass** Cumb
46 D4 **Ravenhills Green** Worcs
65 M2 **Raveningham** Norfk
105 Q10 **Ravenscar** N York
80 e3 **Ravensdale** IoM
61 N10 **Ravensden** Bed
102 G10 **Ravenseat** N York
85 J10 **Ravenshead** Notts
69 R4 **Ravensmoor** Ches E
90 G6 **Ravensthorpe** Kirk
60 E6 **Ravensthorpe** Nhants
72 C8 **Ravenstone** Leics
49 M4 **Ravenstone** M Keyn
102 D10 **Ravenstonedale** Cumb
126 G8 **Ravenstruther** S Lans
103 M9 **Ravensworth** N York
105 P9 **Raw** N York
98 B10 **Rawcliffe** C York
92 A6 **Rawcliffe** E R Yk
92 A6 **Rawcliffe Bridge** E R Yk
90 G3 **Rawdon** Leeds
90 G3 **Rawdon Crematorium** Leeds
38 F10 **Rawling Street** Kent
91 L11 **Rawmarsh** Rothm
58 F2 **Rawnsley** Staffs
38 C3 **Rawreth** Essex
10 E3 **Rawridge** Devon
89 N6 **Rawtenstall** Lancs
52 H4 **Raydon** Suffk
112 D2 **Raylees** Nthumb
38 D3 **Rayleigh** Essex
10 G5 **Raymond's Hill** Devon
52 B7 **Rayne** Essex
36 F7 **Raynes Park** Gt Lon
63 J7 **Reach** Cambs
89 M4 **Read** Lancs
35 K10 **Reading** Readg
35 K9 **Reading Crematorium** Readg
35 J11 **Reading Services** W Berk
26 F5 **Reading Street** Kent
39 Q8 **Reading Street** Kent
102 B7 **Reagill** Cumb
2 G6 **Realwa** Cnwll
162 G8 **Rearquhar** Highld
72 H8 **Rearsby** Leics
70 A4 **Rease Heath** Ches E
166 G4 **Reay** Highld
39 M8 **Reculver** Kent
18 E11 **Red Ball** Devon
41 L10 **Redberth** Pembks
50 D8 **Redbourn** Herts
92 G11 **Redbourne** N Linc
31 P3 **Redbrook** Gloucs
69 P6 **Redbrook** Wrexhm
26 F4 **Redbrook Street** Kent
156 G8 **Redburn** Highld
111 Q8 **Redburn** Nthumb
104 H6 **Redcar** R & Cl
108 H7 **Redcastle** D & G
155 Q8 **Redcastle** Highld
110 E11 **Red Dial** Cumb
126 G2 **Redding** Falk
126 G2 **Reddingmuirhead** Falk
83 J6 **Reddish** Stockp
58 F11 **Redditch** Worcs
58 F11 **Redditch Crematorium** Worcs
63 P9 **Rede** Suffk
65 K5 **Redenhall** Norfk
22 B5 **Redenham** Hants
112 C4 **Redesmouth** Nthumb
143 P3 **Redford** Abers
143 K9 **Redford** Angus
23 N9 **Redford** W Susx
117 M7 **Redfordgreen** Border
30 D7 **Redgate** Rhondd
134 D2 **Redgorton** P & K
64 E6 **Redgrave** Suffk
151 K7 **Redhill** Abers
13 J5 **Red Hill** Bmouth
50 H4 **Redhill** Herts
19 N2 **Redhill** N Som
36 G10 **Redhill** Surrey
47 M3 **Red Hill** Warwks
65 N5 **Redisham** Suffk
31 Q9 **Redland** Bristl
169 c4 **Redland** Ork
64 H7 **Redlingfield** Suffk
64 H7 **Redlingfield Green** Suffk
63 L6 **Red Lodge** Suffk
89 N7 **Red Lumb** Rochdl
20 D8 **Redlynch** Somset
21 P10 **Redlynch** Wilts
100 F4 **Redmain** Cumb
57 P11 **Redmarley** Worcs
46 E8 **Redmarley D'Abitot** Gloucs
104 C6 **Redmarshall** S on T
73 K3 **Redmile** Leics
96 F2 **Redmire** N York
143 P2 **Redmyre** Abers
58 F9 **Rednal** Birm
69 L9 **Rednal** Shrops
118 A3 **Redpath** Border
153 N4 **Redpoint** Highld
16 D10 **Red Post** Cnwll
88 H9 **Red Rock** Wigan
41 P8 **Red Roses** Carmth
119 Q11 **Red Row** Nthumb
2 H5 **Redruth** Cnwll
20 H2 **Redstocks** Wilts
142 B11 **Redstone** P & K
41 M7 **Redstone Cross** Pembks
70 E4 **Red Street** Staffs
89 N9 **Redvales** Bury
79 J8 **Red Wharf Bay** IoA
31 M8 **Redwick** Newpt
31 P7 **Redwick** S Glos
103 P6 **Redworth** Darltn
51 J3 **Reed** Herts
77 N11 **Reedham** Norfk
92 C6 **Reedness** E R Yk
86 H7 **Reeds Beck** Lincs
89 N6 **Reeds Holme** Lancs
86 D6 **Reepham** Lincs
76 G7 **Reepham** Norfk
103 K11 **Reeth** N York
59 L9 **Reeves Green** Solhll
80 f2 **Regaby** IoM
19 P2 **Regil** N Som
160 F4 **Reiff** Highld
36 G10 **Reigate** Surrey
99 N5 **Reighton** N York
151 M4 **Reisque** Abers
167 P6 **Reiss** Highld
4 B10 **Rejerrah** Cnwll
2 H7 **Releath** Cnwll
2 F7 **Relubbus** Cnwll
156 H8 **Relugas** Moray
35 L8 **Remenham** Wokham
35 L8 **Remenham Hill** Wokham
72 F6 **Rempstone** Notts
33 K3 **Rendcomb** Gloucs
65 L9 **Rendham** Suffk
65 L11 **Rendlesham** Suffk
125 N4 **Renfrew** Rens
61 N10 **Renhold** Bed
84 G5 **Renishaw** Derbys
119 P7 **Rennington** Nthumb
125 K2 **Renton** W Duns
101 Q2 **Renwick** Cumb
77 N8 **Repps** Norfk
71 Q9 **Repton** Derbys
156 C8 **Resaurie** Highld
3 P5 **Rescassa** Cnwll
3 P4 **Rescorla** Cnwll
138 C5 **Resipole** Highld
2 G5 **Reskadinnick** Cnwll
156 B4 **Resolis** Highld
29 M4 **Resolven** Neath
131 Q6 **Rest and be thankful** Ag & B
129 M7 **Reston** Border
3 L6 **Restronguet** Cnwll
143 J7 **Reswallie** Angus
4 E9 **Reterth** Cnwll
85 M4 **Retford** Notts
4 G9 **Retire** Cnwll
38 C2 **Rettendon** Essex
4 D10 **Retyn** Cnwll
87 J8 **Revesby** Lincs
7 J11 **Rew** Devon
7 K4 **Rew** Devon
9 M5 **Rewe** Devon
14 E8 **Rew Street** IoW
5 Q4 **Rexon** Devon
65 P6 **Reydon** Suffk
76 E10 **Reymerston** Norfk
41 L9 **Reynalton** Pembks
28 E7 **Reynoldston** Swans
5 P6 **Rezare** Cnwll
31 L4 **Rhadyr** Mons
43 Q6 **Rhandirmwyn** Carmth
55 M11 **Rhayader** Powys
155 P8 **Rheindown** Highld
80 H10 **Rhes-y-cae** Flints
68 F2 **Rhewl** Denbgs
68 G6 **Rhewl** Denbgs
80 G8 **Rhewl-fawr** Flints
80 H8 **Rhewl Mostyn** Flints
164 C11 **Rhicarn** Highld
164 G6 **Rhiconich** Highld
156 B3 **Rhicullen** Highld
29 P3 **Rhigos** Rhondd
160 G7 **Rhireavach** Highld
163 J6 **Rhives** Highld
30 G8 **Rhiwbina** Cardif
67 M5 **Rhiwbryfdir** Gwynd
31 J7 **Rhiwderyn** Newpt
67 K2 **Rhiwen** Gwynd
30 D7 **Rhiwinder** Rhondd
68 B7 **Rhiwlas** Gwynd
79 K11 **Rhiwlas** Gwynd
68 G8 **Rhiwlas** Powys
30 E8 **Rhiwsaeson** Rhondd
19 J8 **Rhode** Somset
37 Q11 **Rhoden Green** Kent
85 J5 **Rhodesia** Notts
27 L3 **Rhodes Minnis** Kent
40 E5 **Rhodiad-y-brenin** Pembks
108 F9 **Rhonehouse** D & G
30 E11 **Rhoose** V Glam
42 G7 **Rhos** Carmth
68 F2 **Rhos** Denbgs
29 K4 **Rhos** Neath
78 F6 **Rhosbeirio** IoA
79 J9 **Rhoscefnhir** IoA
78 D9 **Rhoscolyn** IoA
40 H10 **Rhoscrowther** Pembks
81 J11 **Rhosesmor** Flints
66 F7 **Rhos-fawr** Gwynd
67 J3 **Rhosgadfan** Gwynd
78 G7 **Rhosgoch** IoA
44 H5 **Rhosgoch** Powys
43 K2 **Rhos Haminiog** Cerdgn
41 N2 **Rhoshill** Pembks
66 C9 **Rhoshirwaun** Gwynd
66 H6 **Rhoslan** Gwynd
54 D3 **Rhoslefain** Gwynd
69 J5 **Rhosllanerchrugog** Wrexhm
78 H7 **Rhôs Lligwy** IoA
43 M10 **Rhosmaen** Carmth
78 H9 **Rhosmeirch** IoA
78 E10 **Rhosneigr** IoA
69 L4 **Rhosnesni** Wrexhm
79 Q8 **Rhôs-on-Sea** Conwy
69 K4 **Rhosrobin** Wrexhm
28 D7 **Rhossili** Swans
66 H3 **Rhostryfan** Gwynd
69 K5 **Rhostyllen** Wrexhm
78 G7 **Rhosybol** IoA
68 F10 **Rhos y-brithdir** Powys
69 K8 **Rhosygadfa** Shrops
54 E10 **Rhos-y-garth** Cerdgn
68 B8 **Rhos-y-gwaliau** Gwynd
66 C7 **Rhos-y-llan** Gwynd
69 J6 **Rhosymedre** Wrexhm
56 D11 **Rhos-y-meirch** Powys
132 B11 **Rhu** Ag & B
80 F9 **Rhuallt** Denbgs
124 C3 **Rhubodach** Ag & B
69 Q2 **Rhuddall Heath** Ches W
43 J6 **Rhuddlan** Cerdgn
80 E9 **Rhuddlan** Denbgs
44 G5 **Rhulen** Powys
123 M10 **Rhunahaorine** Ag & B
67 L6 **Rhyd** Gwynd
42 H9 **Rhydargaeau** Carmth
43 L7 **Rhydcymerau** Carmth
46 F5 **Rhydd** Worcs
67 K4 **Rhyd-Ddu** Gwynd
29 K5 **Rhydding** Neath
68 C2 **Rhydgaled** Conwy
67 Q4 **Rhydlanfair** Conwy
42 F5 **Rhydlewis** Cerdgn
66 B9 **Rhydlios** Gwynd
68 A4 **Rhyd-lydan** Conwy
42 H5 **Rhydowen** Cerdgn
54 D11 **Rhydrosser** Cerdgn
45 J5 **Rhydspence** Herefs
68 H4 **Rhydtalog** Flints
68 B7 **Rhyd-uchaf** Gwynd
66 E8 **Rhyd-y-clafdy** Gwynd
68 H8 **Rhydycroesau** Shrops
54 D9 **Rhydyfelin** Cerdgn
30 E7 **Rhydyfelin** Rhondd
80 C9 **Rhyd-y-foel** Conwy
29 K3 **Rhydyfro** Neath
79 K11 **Rhyd-y-groes** Gwynd
67 Q10 **Rhydymain** Gwynd
31 K3 **Rhyd-y-meirch** Mons
81 J11 **Rhydymwyn** Flints
54 E7 **Rhyd-y pennau** Cerdgn
54 E4 **Rhyd-yr-onnen** Gwynd
67 M6 **Rhyd-y-sarn** Gwynd
80 E8 **Rhyl** Denbgs
30 F3 **Rhymney** Caerph
134 F3 **Rhynd** P & K
150 D2 **Rhynie** Abers
163 J11 **Rhynie** Highld
57 P10 **Ribbesford** Worcs
88 H4 **Ribbleton** Lancs
88 E4 **Ribby** Lancs
89 K3 **Ribchester** Lancs
84 D9 **Riber** Derbys
93 L9 **Riby** Lincs
91 Q3 **Riccall** N York
111 K2 **Riccarton** Border
125 L10 **Riccarton** E Ayrs
56 H11 **Richards Castle** Herefs
36 B5 **Richings Park** Bucks
36 E6 **Richmond** Gt Lon
103 N10 **Richmond** N York
84 F3 **Richmond** Sheff
10 b2 **Richmond Fort** Guern
18 F8 **Rich's Holford** Somset
70 G10 **Rickerscote** Staffs
19 N3 **Rickford** N Som
7 K11 **Rickham** Devon
64 E6 **Rickinghall** Suffk
51 L4 **Rickling** Essex
51 M5 **Rickling Green** Essex
36 C2 **Rickmansworth** Herts
117 Q6 **Riddell** Border
84 F10 **Riddings** Derbys
17 L9 **Riddlecombe** Devon
90 D2 **Riddlesden** C Brad
19 Q3 **Ridge** BaNES
12 F7 **Ridge** Dorset
50 F10 **Ridge** Herts
21 J8 **Ridge** Wilts
44 F2 **Ridgebourne** Powys

36 H11 Ridge Green Surrey
59 L6 Ridge Lane Warwks
27 M3 Ridge Row Kent
84 F4 Ridgeway Derbys
47 K2 Ridgeway Worcs
46 D5 Ridgeway Cross Herefs
52 B3 Ridgewell Essex
25 L7 Ridgewood E Susx
49 Q7 Ridgmont C Beds
112 F8 Riding Mill Nthumb
37 P8 Ridley Kent
111 Q8 Ridley Nthumb
69 Q4 Ridley Green Ches E
77 L5 Ridlington Norfk
73 L10 Ridlington Rutlnd
77 L5 Ridlington Street Norfk
112 D4 Ridsdale Nthumb
98 B3 Rievaulx N York
98 B4 Rievaulx Abbey N York
110 E7 Rigg D & G
126 D3 Riggend N Lans
156 F7 Righoul Highld
95 N4 Rigmadon Park Cumb
87 M5 Rigsby Lincs
116 B3 Rigside S Lans
89 J5 Riley Green Lancs
58 H2 Rileyhill Staffs
5 M7 Rilla Mill Cnwll
5 M7 Rillaton Cnwll
98 H6 Rillington N York
96 B11 Rimington Lancs
20 B10 Rimpton Somset
93 P5 Rimswell E R Yk
41 J5 Rinaston Pembks
57 N5 Rindleford Shrops
108 E9 Ringford D & G
84 C4 Ringinglow Sheff
76 G9 Ringland Norfk
25 L6 Ringles Cross E Susx
38 E10 Ringlestone Kent
89 M9 Ringley Bolton
25 K8 Ringmer E Susx
6 H9 Ringmore Devon
7 N4 Ringmore Devon
88 F8 Ring o'Bells Lancs
157 P9 Ringorm Moray
74 G10 Ring's End Cambs
65 N4 Ringsfield Suffk
65 N4 Ringsfield Corner Suffk
35 Q2 Ringshall Herts
64 E11 Ringshall Suffk
64 F11 Ringshall Stocks Suffk
61 L5 Ringstead Nhants
75 P2 Ringstead Norfk
13 L3 Ringwood Hants
27 Q2 Ringwould Kent
2 F8 Rinsey Cnwll
2 G8 Rinsey Croft Cnwll
25 M8 Ripe E Susx
84 E10 Ripley Derbys
13 L5 Ripley Hants
97 L8 Ripley N York
36 C9 Ripley Surrey
92 G4 Riplingham E R Yk
23 J10 Riplington Hants
97 M6 Ripon N York
74 A5 Rippingale Lincs
39 Q11 Ripple Kent
46 G7 Ripple Worcs
90 C7 Ripponden Calder
122 D11 Risabus Ag & B
45 Q4 Risbury Herefs
92 F8 Risby N Linc
63 P7 Risby Suffk
30 H6 Risca Caerph
93 L2 Rise E R Yk
25 P4 Riseden E Susx
26 B4 Riseden Kent
74 D5 Risegate Lincs
86 C5 Riseholme Lincs
100 D4 Risehow Cumb
61 M8 Riseley Bed
23 K2 Riseley Wokham
64 H8 Rishangles Suffk
89 L4 Rishton Lancs
90 C7 Rishworth Calder
89 M5 Rising Bridge Lancs
72 D3 Risley Derbys
82 E6 Risley Warrtn
97 K7 Risplith N York
22 B2 Rivar Wilts
52 D8 Rivenhall End Essex
27 N3 River Kent
23 P10 River W Susx
62 H7 River Bank Cambs
155 P7 Riverford Highld
37 M9 Riverhead Kent
12 C2 Rivers Corner Dorset
89 J8 Rivington Lancs
17 R7 Roachill Devon
49 L4 Roade Nhants
65 K3 Road Green Norfk
111 K6 Roadhead Cumb
126 F8 Roadmeetings S Lans
115 L4 Roadside E Ayrs
167 L4 Roadside Highld
18 D7 Roadwater Somset
152 D9 Roag Highld
94 E7 Roa Island Cumb
114 E7 Roan of Craigoch S Ayrs
51 L4 Roast Green Essex
30 G9 Roath Cardif
117 N8 Roberton Border
116 C5 Roberton S Lans
26 B7 Robertsbridge E Susx
90 F6 Roberttown Kirk
41 L7 Robeston Wathen Pembks
110 D6 Robgill Tower D & G
70 G3 Robin Hill Staffs
88 G8 Robin Hood Lancs
91 J5 Robin Hood Leeds
58 H8 Robin Hood Crematorium Solhll
91 R11 *Robin Hood Doncaster Sheffield Airport* Donc
52 B4 Robinhood End Essex
105 Q9 Robin Hood's Bay N York
6 E6 Roborough Devon
17 K8 Roborough Devon
81 N6 Roby Knows
88 G9 Roby Mill Lancs
71 L7 Rocester Staffs
40 G6 Roch Pembks
89 P8 Rochdale Rochdl
89 P8 Rochdale Crematorium Rochdl
4 F9 Roche Cnwll
38 B8 Rochester Medway
118 F11 Rochester Nthumb
38 E3 Rochford Essex
57 L11 Rochford Worcs
40 G6 Roch Gate Pembks
4 E6 Rock Cnwll
29 L6 Rock Neath
119 P6 Rock Nthumb
24 D8 Rock W Susx
57 N10 Rock Worcs
9 P6 Rockbeare Devon
21 M11 Rockbourne Hants
110 G8 Rockcliffe Cumb
108 H10 Rockcliffe D & G
110 F8 Rockcliffe Cross Cumb
70 F3 Rock End Staffs
7 N6 Rockend Torbay
81 L7 Rock Ferry Wirral
163 L10 Rockfield Highld
31 N2 Rockfield Mons
17 P2 Rockford Devon
13 L3 Rockford Hants
57 J9 Rockgreen Shrops
32 C6 Rockhampton S Glos
4 H5 Rockhead Cnwll
56 D9 Rockhill Shrops
58 E11 Rock Hill Worcs
61 J2 Rockingham Nhants
64 D2 Rockland All Saints Norfk
77 L11 Rockland St Mary Norfk
64 D2 Rockland St Peter Norfk
85 M6 Rockley Notts
33 N10 Rockley Wilts
89 P6 Rockliffe Lancs
131 Q9 Rockville Ag & B
35 L7 Rockwell End Bucks
18 F10 Rockwell Green Somset
32 F4 Rodborough Gloucs
33 M7 Rodbourne Swindn
32 H8 Rodbourne Wilts
45 L2 Rodd Herefs
119 K6 Roddam Nthumb
11 N8 Rodden Dorset
103 N3 Roddymoor Dur
20 F4 Rode Somset
70 E3 Rode Heath Ches E
83 J11 Rode Heath Ches E
168 f9 Rodel W Isls
69 Q11 Roden Wrekin
18 D7 Rodhuish Somset
57 K2 Rodington Wrekin
57 K2 Rodington Heath Wrekin
32 D2 Rodley Gloucs
90 G3 Rodley Leeds
32 H5 Rodmarton Gloucs
25 K9 Rodmell E Susx
38 F9 Rodmersham Kent
38 F9 Rodmersham Green Kent
19 N5 Rodney Stoke Somset
71 N6 Rodsley Derbys
19 J6 Rodway Somset
97 N7 Roecliffe N York
83 L5 Roe Cross Tamesd
50 F9 Roe Green Herts
50 H4 Roe Green Herts
82 G4 Roe Green Salfd
36 F6 Roehampton Gt Lon
24 E4 Roffey W Susx
162 G6 Rogart Highld
23 M10 Rogate W Susx
101 L11 Roger Ground Cumb
31 J7 Rogerstone Newpt
168 f9 Roghadal W Isls
31 N7 Rogiet Mons
34 H6 Roke Oxon
113 P9 Roker Sundld
77 N8 Rollesby Norfk
73 J10 Rolleston Leics
85 M10 Rolleston Notts
71 N9 Rolleston on Dove Staffs
93 M2 Rolston E R Yk
19 L2 Rolstone N Som
26 D5 Rolvenden Kent
26 E5 Rolvenden Layne Kent
103 J6 Romaldkirk Dur
20 E2 Roman Baths & Pump Room BaNES
97 N2 Romanby N York
127 M8 Romanno Bridge Border
17 N7 Romansleigh Devon
26 E3 Romden Castle Kent
152 G7 Romesdal Highld
13 J3 Romford Dorset
37 M3 Romford Gt Lon
83 K6 Romiley Stockp
37 N8 Romney Street Kent
22 C10 Romsey Hants
57 P8 Romsley Shrops
58 E8 Romsley Worcs
153 L6 Rona Highld
123 M9 Ronachan Ag & B
20 G3 Rood Ashton Wilts
102 H2 Rookhope Dur
14 F10 Rookley IoW
14 F10 Rookley Green IoW
19 L4 Rooks Bridge Somset
18 E8 Rooks Nest Somset
97 K3 Rookwith N York
93 N4 Roos E R Yk
94 E7 Roose Cumb
94 F7 Roosebeck Cumb
61 N9 Roothams Green Bed
22 H8 Ropley Hants
22 H8 Ropley Dean Hants
23 J8 Ropley Soke Hants
73 P4 Ropsley Lincs
159 Q7 Rora Abers
56 E4 Rorrington Shrops
158 A7 Rosarie Moray
3 K3 Rose Cnwll
88 E3 Roseacre Lancs
17 P7 Rose Ash Devon
126 E8 Rosebank S Lans
41 L5 Rosebush Pembks
5 K2 Rosecare Cnwll
4 C10 Rosecliston Cnwll
105 K11 Rosedale Abbey N York
52 F6 Rose Green Essex
52 F4 Rose Green Suffk
52 G3 Rose Green Suffk
15 P7 Rose Green W Susx
162 B6 Rosehall Highld
159 M4 Rosehearty Abers
25 L7 Rose Hill E Susx
89 N4 Rose Hill Lancs
69 N11 Rosehill Shrops
157 L4 Roseisle Moray
25 P10 Roselands E Susx
41 J9 Rosemarket Pembks
156 C6 Rosemarkie Highld
10 D2 Rosemary Lane Devon
142 B9 Rosemount P & K
4 F8 Rosenannon Cnwll
3 L9 Rosenithon Cnwll
25 M6 Roser's Cross E Susx
4 G10 Rosevean Cnwll
3 M6 Rosevine Cnwll
2 G6 Rosewarne Cnwll
127 P5 Rosewell Mdloth
104 D6 Roseworth S on T
2 G6 Roseworthy Cnwll
101 P7 Rosgill Cumb
2 B9 Roskestal Cnwll
152 D9 Roskhill Highld
3 K9 Roskorwell Cnwll
110 F11 Rosley Cumb
127 P5 Roslin Mdloth
71 N11 Rosliston Derbys
132 B11 Rosneath Ag & B
108 D12 Ross D & G
119 M3 Ross Nthumb
69 L3 Rossett Wrexhm
97 L10 Rossett Green N York
91 Q11 Rossington Donc
125 L3 Rossland Rens
46 A10 Ross-on-Wye Herefs
167 N9 Roster Highld
82 F8 Rostherne Ches E
101 J8 Rosthwaite Cumb
71 L6 Roston Derbys
2 F8 Rosudgeon Cnwll
134 E11 Rosyth Fife
119 L10 Rothbury Nthumb
72 H7 Rotherby Leics
25 N5 Rotherfield E Susx
35 K8 Rotherfield Greys Oxon
35 K8 Rotherfield Peppard Oxon
84 F2 Rotherham Rothm
84 G2 Rotherham Crematorium Rothm
60 F9 Rothersthorpe Nhants
60 F9 Rothersthorpe Services Nhants
23 K3 Rotherwick Hants
157 P8 Rothes Moray
124 D5 Rothesay Ag & B
158 H10 Rothiebrisbane Abers
158 E8 Rothiemay Moray
148 H6 Rothiemurchus Lodge Highld
158 H10 Rothienorman Abers
72 F8 Rothley Leics
112 F3 Rothley Nthumb
158 G11 Rothmaise Abers
91 J5 Rothwell Leeds
93 K11 Rothwell Lincs
60 H4 Rothwell Nhants
99 M10 Rotsea E R Yk
142 F4 Rottal Lodge Angus
25 J10 Rottingdean Br & H
100 C8 Rottington Cumb
109 M5 Roucan D & G
109 M5 Roucan Loch Crematorium D & G
14 F10 Roud IoW
76 A7 Rougham Norfk
64 C9 Rougham Green Suffk
70 G7 Rough Close Staffs
39 K10 Rough Common Kent
89 N2 Roughlee Lancs
149 Q5 Roughpark Abers
86 H8 Roughton Lincs
77 J4 Roughton Norfk
57 P6 Roughton Shrops
37 P10 Roughway Kent
52 E11 Roundbush Essex
50 D11 Round Bush Herts
51 N8 Roundbush Green Essex
50 D6 Round Green Luton
11 J3 Roundham Somset
91 J3 Roundhay Leeds
58 E7 Rounds Green Sandw
37 Q7 Round Street Kent
24 C5 Roundstreet Common W Susx
21 K2 Roundway Wilts
142 F7 Roundyhill Angus
169 c3 Rousay Ork
10 F6 Rousdon Devon
48 E10 Rousham Oxon
47 K4 Rous Lench Worcs
124 F5 Routenburn N Ayrs
93 J2 Routh E R Yk
35 L5 Rout's Green Bucks
4 H6 Row Cnwll
95 K3 Row Cumb
102 B4 Row Cumb
110 F5 Rowanburn D & G
132 D8 Rowardennan Stirlg
83 M7 Rowarth Derbys
14 F4 Row Ash Hants
19 N3 Rowberrow Somset
14 E10 Rowborough IoW
21 J2 Rowde Wilts
8 F5 Rowden Devon
79 P10 Rowen Conwy
71 M5 Rowfield Derbys
111 N8 Rowfoot Nthumb
18 H9 Rowford Somset
52 B7 Row Green Essex
52 H7 Rowhedge Essex
24 D4 Rowhook W Susx
59 K11 Rowington Warwks
84 B6 Rowland Derbys
15 K4 Rowland's Castle Hants
113 J9 Rowland's Gill Gatesd
23 M6 Rowledge Surrey
112 G11 Rowley Dur
92 G4 Rowley E R Yk
56 E3 Rowley Shrops
90 F8 Rowley Hill Kirk
63 K8 Rowley Mile Services Suffk
58 E7 Rowley Regis Sandw
58 E7 Rowley Regis Crematorium Sandw
45 M9 Rowlstone Herefs
24 B2 Rowly Surrey
14 G6 Rowner Hants
58 F10 Rowney Green Worcs
22 C11 Rownhams Hants
22 C11 Rownhams Services Hants
100 E7 Rowrah Cumb
49 M11 Rowsham Bucks
84 C7 Rowsley Derbys
82 H9 Rows of Trees Ches E
34 E7 Rowstock Oxon
86 E9 Rowston Lincs
84 G8 Rowthorne Derbys
69 M2 Rowton Ches W
56 F2 Rowton Shrops
56 G8 Rowton Shrops
69 R11 Rowton Wrekin
36 B8 Row Town Surrey
118 C4 Roxburgh Border
92 F7 Roxby N Linc
105 L7 Roxby N York
61 Q10 Roxton Bed
51 P9 Roxwell Essex
36 E5 Royal Botanic Gardens Gt Lon
103 P6 Royal Oak Darltn
81 N4 Royal Oak Lancs
69 R6 Royal's Green Ches E
146 H11 Roy Bridge Highld
90 G8 Roydhouse Kirk
51 K8 Roydon Essex
64 G5 Roydon Norfk
75 P6 Roydon Norfk
51 K9 Roydon Hamlet Essex
91 K8 Royston Barns
51 J2 Royston Herts
89 Q9 Royton Oldham
11 c1 Rozel Jersey
69 K6 Ruabon Wrexhm
136 D6 Ruaig Ag & B
3 N6 Ruan High Lanes Cnwll
3 M5 Ruan Lanihorne Cnwll
3 J10 Ruan Major Cnwll
3 J10 Ruan Minor Cnwll
46 B11 Ruardean Gloucs
46 B11 Ruardean Hill Gloucs
46 B11 Ruardean Woodside Gloucs
58 E9 Rubery Birm
168 c16 Rubha Ban W Isls
101 P2 Ruckcroft Cumb
45 P7 Ruckhall Herefs
26 H5 Ruckinge Kent
87 K5 Ruckland Lincs
57 J4 Ruckley Shrops
104 E9 Rudby N York
112 H7 Rudchester Nthumb
72 F4 Ruddington Notts
32 C2 Ruddle Gloucs
3 Q3 Ruddlemoor Cnwll
46 E10 Rudford Gloucs
20 F4 Rudge Somset
32 B7 Rudgeway S Glos
24 C4 Rudgwick W Susx
46 B9 Rudhall Herefs
82 E10 Rudheath Ches W
82 F10 Rudheath Woods Ches E
52 D11 Rudley Green Essex
32 F10 Rudloe Wilts
30 H7 Rudry Caerph
99 M7 Rudston E R Yk
70 H3 Rudyard Staffs
118 B6 Ruecastle Border
88 F7 Rufford Lancs
98 A10 Rufforth C York
68 E6 Rug Denbgs
60 B5 Rugby Warwks
71 J11 Rugeley Staffs
19 J9 Ruishton Somset
36 C3 Ruislip Gt Lon
144 E8 Rùm Highld
158 A7 Rumbach Moray
134 C8 Rumbling Bridge P & K
65 L5 Rumburgh Suffk
103 N4 Rumby Hill Dur
4 D7 Rumford Cnwll
126 G2 Rumford Falk
30 H9 Rumney Cardif
18 G10 Rumwell Somset
81 Q8 Runcorn Halton
15 N6 Runcton W Susx
75 M9 Runcton Holme Norfk
23 N5 Runfold Surrey
76 F10 Runhall Norfk
77 P9 Runham Norfk
77 Q10 Runham Norfk
18 F10 Runnington Somset
52 C10 Runsell Green Essex
88 G7 Runshaw Moor Lancs
105 M7 Runswick N York
142 D4 Runtaleave Angus
38 C3 Runwell Essex
35 L9 Ruscombe Wokham
46 B7 Rushall Herefs
64 H5 Rushall Norfk
21 M3 Rushall Wilts
58 F4 Rushall Wsall
64 B9 Rushbrooke Suffk
57 J6 Rushbury Shrops
50 H4 Rushden Herts
61 L7 Rushden Nhants
38 F7 Rushenden Kent
25 P5 Rusher's Cross E Susx
8 C9 Rushford Devon
64 C5 Rushford Norfk
53 L8 Rush Green Essex
37 M3 Rush Green Gt Lon
50 F6 Rush Green Herts
82 E7 Rush Green Warrtn
25 P7 Rushlake Green E Susx
65 P4 Rushmere Suffk
53 L2 Rushmere St Andrew Suffk
23 N6 Rushmoor Surrey
45 L3 Rushock Herefs
58 C10 Rushock Worcs
83 J6 Rusholme Manch
69 Q2 Rushton Ches W
60 H4 Rushton Nhants
57 L3 Rushton Shrops
70 G2 Rushton Spencer Staffs
46 F4 Rushwick Worcs
103 Q5 Rushyford Dur
133 J7 Ruskie Stirlg
86 E10 Ruskington Lincs
94 G3 Rusland Cross Cumb
24 F3 Rusper W Susx
32 C2 Ruspidge Gloucs
52 B9 Russell Green Essex
35 K7 Russell's Water Oxon
65 K7 Russel's Green Suffk
24 F2 Russ Hill Surrey
25 N3 Rusthall Kent
24 B10 Rustington W Susx
99 K4 Ruston N York
99 M8 Ruston Parva E R Yk
105 N9 Ruswarp N York
57 K6 Ruthall Shrops
118 B4 Rutherford Border
125 Q5 Rutherglen S Lans
4 G8 Ruthernbridge Cnwll
68 F3 Ruthin Denbgs
151 N7 Ruthrieston C Aber
158 D8 Ruthven Abers
142 D8 Ruthven Angus
148 D8 Ruthven Highld
4 E9 Ruthvoes Cnwll
100 H3 Ruthwaite Cumb
109 N7 Ruthwell D & G
37 L6 Ruxley Corner Gt Lon
45 Q11 Ruxton Green Herefs
69 L10 Ruyton-XI-Towns Shrops
112 F6 Ryal Nthumb
11 J5 Ryall Dorset
46 G6 Ryall Worcs
37 Q8 Ryarsh Kent
35 J3 Rycote Oxon
101 L9 Rydal Cumb
14 G8 Ryde IoW
26 F7 Rye E Susx
69 P8 Ryebank Shrops
46 B10 Ryeford Herefs
26 E7 Rye Foreign E Susx
26 F8 Rye Harbour E Susx
93 M5 Ryehill E R Yk
35 K11 Ryeish Green Wokham
46 E7 Rye Street Worcs
73 Q8 Ryhall Rutlnd
91 K8 Ryhill Wakefd
113 P10 Ryhope Sundld
84 G7 Rylah Derbys
86 D5 Ryland Lincs
72 E3 Rylands Notts
96 E9 Rylstone N York
11 M2 Ryme Intrinseca Dorset
91 P3 Ryther N York
113 J8 Ryton Gatesd
98 F5 Ryton N York
57 P4 Ryton Shrops
59 P7 Ryton Warwks
59 N10 Ryton-on-Dunsmore Warwks
112 H8 Ryton Woodside Gatesd

S

89 M3 Sabden Lancs
51 M11 Sabine's Green Essex
50 H7 Sacombe Herts
50 H7 Sacombe Green Herts
113 K11 Sacriston Dur
104 B7 Sadberge Darltn
120 E5 Saddell Ag & B
60 E2 Saddington Leics
75 M7 Saddle Bow Norfk
24 G8 Saddlescombe W Susx
101 N9 Sadgill Cumb
51 M3 Saffron Walden Essex
41 L10 Sageston Pembks
76 C11 Saham Hills Norfk
76 B11 Saham Toney Norfk
69 M2 Saighton Ches W
129 N6 St Abbs Border
128 H7 St Agnes Border
3 J3 St Agnes Cnwll
2 b3 St Agnes IoS
50 D9 St Albans Herts
3 L3 St Allen Cnwll
10 b2 St Andrew Guern
135 N4 St Andrews Fife
135 N4 St Andrews Botanic Garden Fife
30 F10 St Andrew's Major V Glam
11 K6 St Andrews Well Dorset
88 C5 St Anne's Lancs
109 N2 St Ann's D & G
5 Q7 St Ann's Chapel Cnwll
6 H9 St Ann's Chapel Devon
3 K8 St Anthony Cnwll
25 P10 St Anthony's Hill E Susx
31 P5 St Arvans Mons
80 E10 St Asaph Denbgs
30 D11 St Athan V Glam
11 b2 St Aubin Jersey
3 Q3 St Austell Cnwll
100 C8 St Bees Cumb
3 R3 St Blazey Cnwll
3 R3 St Blazey Gate Cnwll
118 A4 St Boswells Border
11 a2 St Brelade Jersey
11 a2 St Brelade's Bay Jersey
4 F7 St Breock Cnwll
4 H6 St Breward Cnwll
31 Q4 St Briavels Gloucs
40 F8 St Brides Pembks
29 N10 St Bride's Major V Glam
31 M7 St Brides Netherwent Mons
30 E9 St Brides super-Ely V Glam
31 J8 St Brides Wentlooge Newpt
6 D7 St Budeaux C Plym
47 M7 Saintbury Gloucs
2 C8 St Buryan Cnwll
32 E11 St Catherine BaNES
131 N6 St Catherines Ag & B
32 F4 St Chloe Gloucs
41 Q7 St Clears Carmth
5 L8 St Cleer Cnwll
3 M5 St Clement Cnwll
11 c2 St Clement Jersey
5 L5 St Clether Cnwll
124 C4 St Colmac Ag & B
4 E9 St Columb Major Cnwll
4 C9 St Columb Minor Cnwll
4 E10 St Columb Road Cnwll
159 Q5 St Combs Abers
65 K5 St Cross South Elmham Suffk
143 N5 St Cyrus Abers
133 Q3 St David's P & K
40 E5 St David's Pembks
3 J5 St Day Cnwll
18 E6 St Decumans Somset
4 F10 St Dennis Cnwll
45 N8 St Devereux Herefs
42 C5 St Dogmaels Pembks
41 J5 St Dogwells Pembks
5 Q8 St Dominick Cnwll
29 P11 St Donats V Glam
21 J2 St Edith's Marsh Wilts
4 F6 St Endellion Cnwll
4 D10 St Enoder Cnwll
3 L4 St Erme Cnwll
5 P10 St Erney Cnwll
2 F6 St Erth Cnwll
2 F6 St Erth Praze Cnwll
4 D7 St Ervan Cnwll
4 D8 St Eval Cnwll
3 P4 St Ewe Cnwll

30 F9 **St Fagans** Cardif
30 F9 **St Fagans Welsh Life Museum** Cardif
159 Q7 **St Fergus** Abers
133 K3 **St Fillans** P & K
41 L10 **St Florence** Pembks
5 J2 **St Gennys** Cnwll
80 D9 **St George** Conwy
19 L2 **St Georges** N Som
30 F9 **St George's** V Glam
36 C8 **St George's Hill** Surrey
5 P10 **St Germans** Cnwll
17 J8 **St Giles in the Wood** Devon
5 P3 **St Giles-on-the-Heath** Devon
3 K7 **St Gluvia's** Cnwll
55 M10 **St Harmon** Powys
103 N5 **St Helen Auckland** Dur
100 D4 **St Helens** Cumb
26 D9 **St Helens** E Susx
14 H9 **St Helens** IoW
81 Q5 **St Helens** St Hel
81 P5 **St Helens Crematorium** St Hel
36 G7 **St Helier** Gt Lon
11 b2 **St Helier** Jersey
2 E7 **St Hilary** Cnwll
30 D10 **St Hilary** V Glam
10 B3 **Saint Hill** Devon
25 J3 **Saint Hill** W Susx
30 H4 **St Illtyd** Blae G
50 E5 **St Ippollitts** Herts
40 F9 **St Ishmael's** Pembks
4 E7 **St Issey** Cnwll
5 N8 **St Ive** Cnwll
62 D6 **St Ives** Cambs
2 E5 **St Ives** Cnwll
13 K4 **St Ives** Dorset
77 K7 **St James** Norfk
60 F8 **St James's End** Nhants
65 L5 **St James South Elmham** Suffk
4 E8 **St Jidgey** Cnwll
5 Q11 **St John** Cnwll
11 b1 **St John** Jersey
103 L4 **St Johns** Dur
80 c5 **St John's** IoM
37 M9 **St Johns** Kent
23 Q3 **St Johns** Surrey
46 F4 **St Johns** Worcs
17 J6 **St John's Chapel** Devon
102 G3 **St John's Chapel** Dur
75 K8 **St John's Fen End** Norfk
75 K8 **St John's Highway** Norfk
116 D3 **St John's Kirk** S Lans
108 D4 **St John's Town of Dalry** D & G
36 G4 **St John's Wood** Gt Lon
80 e2 **St Jude's** IoM
2 B7 **St Just** Cnwll
3 L6 **St Just-in-Roseland** Cnwll
159 J11 **St Katherines** Abers
3 K9 **St Keverne** Cnwll
4 G6 **St Kew** Cnwll
4 G6 **St Kew Highway** Cnwll
5 L9 **St Keyne** Cnwll
4 G8 **St Lawrence** Cnwll
52 G11 **St Lawrence** Essex
14 F11 **St Lawrence** IoW
11 b1 **St Lawrence** Jersey
39 Q8 **St Lawrence** Kent
35 P3 **St Leonards** Bucks
13 K4 **St Leonards** Dorset
26 D10 **St Leonards** E Susx
37 Q9 **St Leonard's Street** Kent
2 B9 **St Levan** Cnwll
30 F10 **St Lythans** V Glam
4 G7 **St Mabyn** Cnwll
134 F3 **St Madoes** P & K
45 M8 **St Margarets** Herefs
51 J8 **St Margarets** Herts
27 Q3 **St Margaret's at Cliffe** Kent
169 d7 **St Margaret's Hope** Ork
65 L5 **St Margaret South Elmham** Suffk
80 c7 **St Marks** IoM
3 J9 **St Martin** Cnwll
5 M10 **St Martin** Cnwll
10 b2 **St Martin** Guern
11 c1 **St Martin** Jersey
2 c1 **St Martin's** IoS
142 B11 **St Martin's** P & K
69 K7 **St Martins** Shrops
69 K7 **St Martin's Moor** Shrops
11 a1 **St Mary** Jersey
22 D4 **St Mary Bourne** Hants
7 N5 **St Marychurch** Torbay
30 D10 **St Mary Church** V Glam
37 L7 **St Mary Cray** Gt Lon
30 C9 **St Mary Hill** V Glam
27 J6 **St Mary in the Marsh** Kent
36 G3 **St Marylebone Crematorium** Gt Lon
2 c2 **St Mary's** IoS
169 d6 **St Mary's** Ork
27 J6 **St Mary's Bay** Kent
31 N11 **St Mary's Grove** N Som
38 D6 **St Mary's Hoo** Medway
45 P11 **St Maughans** Mons
45 P11 **St Maughans Green** Mons
3 L7 **St Mawes** Cnwll
4 D8 **St Mawgan** Cnwll
5 P8 **St Mellion** Cnwll
30 H8 **St Mellons** Cardif
4 D7 **St Merryn** Cnwll
3 P3 **St Mewan** Cnwll
3 P5 **St Michael Caerhays** Cnwll
19 K8 **St Michael Church** Somset
3 M5 **St Michael Penkevil** Cnwll
26 E4 **St Michaels** Kent
57 K11 **St Michaels** Worcs
88 F2 **St Michael's on Wyre** Lancs
65 L5 **St Michael South Elmham** Suffk
4 F6 **St Minver** Cnwll
135 N7 **St Monans** Fife
5 K8 **St Neot** Cnwll
61 Q8 **St Neots** Cambs
40 H3 **St Nicholas** Pembks
30 E10 **St Nicholas** V Glam
39 N8 **St Nicholas at Wade** Kent
133 M9 **St Ninians** Stirlg
65 P2 **St Olaves** Norfk
53 K8 **St Osyth** Essex
11 a1 **St Ouen** Jersey
45 Q10 **St Owens Cross** Herefs
37 L7 **St Pauls Cray** Gt Lon
50 E6 **St Paul's Walden** Herts
11 a1 **St Peter** Jersey
10 c2 **St Peter Port** Guern
10 b2 **St Peter's** Guern
39 Q8 **St Peter's** Kent
62 B6 **St Peter's Hill** Cambs
41 J11 **St Petrox** Pembks
5 L9 **St Pinnock** Cnwll
114 G3 **St Quivox** S Ayrs
3 J10 **St Ruan** Cnwll
10 c1 **St Sampson** Guern
10 b2 **St Saviour** Guern
11 b2 **St Saviour** Jersey
3 N3 **St Stephen** Cnwll
5 N4 **St Stephens** Cnwll
5 Q10 **St Stephens** Cnwll
4 H5 **St Teath** Cnwll
4 H6 **St Tudy** Cnwll
41 J11 **St Twynnells** Pembks
5 J10 **St Veep** Cnwll
143 L9 **St Vigeans** Angus
4 F9 **St Wenn** Cnwll
45 P10 **St Weonards** Herefs
30 E9 **St y-Nyll** V Glam
7 J11 **Salcombe** Devon
10 D7 **Salcombe Regis** Devon
52 F9 **Salcott-cum-Virley** Essex
82 G6 **Sale** Traffd
87 N5 **Saleby** Lincs
46 H3 **Sale Green** Worcs
26 C7 **Salehurst** E Susx
43 M9 **Salem** Carmth
54 F8 **Salem** Cerdgn
137 P7 **Salen** Ag & B
138 B5 **Salen** Highld
89 K4 **Salesbury** Lancs
49 P7 **Salford** C Beds
47 Q9 **Salford** Oxon
82 H5 **Salford** Salfd
47 L4 **Salford Priors** Warwks
36 G11 **Salfords** Surrey
77 L9 **Salhouse** Norfk
134 C9 **Saline** Fife
21 M9 **Salisbury** Wilts
21 M9 **Salisbury Cathedral** Wilts
21 N8 **Salisbury Crematorium** Wilts
21 L6 **Salisbury Plain** Wilts
101 P3 **Salkeld Dykes** Cumb
76 G7 **Salle** Norfk
87 K6 **Salmonby** Lincs
47 L10 **Salperton** Gloucs
61 N10 **Salph End** Bed
126 E5 **Salsburgh** N Lans
70 H9 **Salt** Staffs
109 N11 **Salta** Cumb
90 E3 **Saltaire** C Brad
6 C7 **Saltash** Cnwll
156 C3 **Saltburn** Highld
105 J6 **Saltburn-by-the-Sea** R & Cl
73 M5 **Saltby** Leics
110 C10 **Salt Coates** Cumb
100 E11 **Saltcoats** Cumb
124 G9 **Saltcoats** N Ayrs
88 D5 **Saltcotes** Lancs
25 J10 **Saltdean** Br & H
100 C5 **Salterbeck** Cumb
96 C11 **Salterforth** Lancs
82 D11 **Salterswall** Ches W
21 M7 **Salterton** Wilts
87 N2 **Saltfleet** Lincs
87 N2 **Saltfleetby All Saints** Lincs
87 N2 **Saltfleetby St Clement** Lincs
87 M3 **Saltfleetby St Peter** Lincs
32 C11 **Saltford** BaNES
76 F3 **Salthouse** Norfk
58 H7 **Saltley** Birm
31 K8 **Saltmarsh** Newpt
92 C6 **Saltmarshe** E R Yk
69 L2 **Saltney** Flints
98 E5 **Salton** N York
16 H7 **Saltrens** Devon
113 L8 **Saltwell Crematorium** Gatesd
113 J4 **Saltwick** Nthumb
27 L4 **Saltwood** Kent
24 D9 **Salvington** W Susx
46 G2 **Salwarpe** Worcs
11 K5 **Salway Ash** Dorset
47 L2 **Sambourne** Warwks
70 C10 **Sambrook** Wrekin
88 H4 **Samlesbury** Lancs
89 J5 **Samlesbury Bottoms** Lancs
18 F11 **Sampford Arundel** Somset
18 E6 **Sampford Brett** Somset
8 F4 **Sampford Courtenay** Devon
18 F11 **Sampford Moor** Somset
9 P2 **Sampford Peverell** Devon
6 E4 **Sampford Spiney** Devon
169 f4 **Samsonlane** Ork
53 J8 **Samson's Corner** Essex
128 D5 **Samuelston** E Loth
122 B5 **Sanaigmore** Ag & B
2 C8 **Sancreed** Cnwll
92 E3 **Sancton** E R Yk
19 M5 **Sand** Somset
145 M7 **Sandaig** Highld
100 H2 **Sandale** Cumb
91 J7 **Sandal Magna** Wakefd
144 G11 **Sandavore** Highld
169 f2 **Sanday** Ork
169 f2 **Sanday Airport** Ork
70 D2 **Sandbach** Ches E
70 D2 **Sandbach Services** Ches E
131 P11 **Sandbank** Ag & B
12 H7 **Sandbanks** Poole
158 E4 **Sandend** Abers
36 H8 **Sanderstead** Gt Lon
102 D7 **Sandford** Cumb
9 K4 **Sandford** Devon
12 F7 **Sandford** Dorset
13 L4 **Sandford** Hants
14 F10 **Sandford** IoW
19 M3 **Sandford** N Som
126 C9 **Sandford** S Lans
69 K10 **Sandford** Shrops
69 Q8 **Sandford** Shrops
34 F4 **Sandford-on-Thames** Oxon
20 B10 **Sandford Orcas** Dorset
48 D9 **Sandford St Martin** Oxon
27 M4 **Sandgate** Kent
159 N4 **Sandhaven** Abers
106 E8 **Sandhead** D & G
91 L11 **Sandhill** Rothm
11 M4 **Sandhills** Dorset
11 P2 **Sandhills** Dorset
91 K3 **Sand Hills** Leeds
34 G3 **Sandhills** Oxon
23 P7 **Sandhills** Surrey
112 E7 **Sandhoe** Nthumb
131 L8 **Sandhole** Ag & B
92 D3 **Sand Hole** E R Yk
92 D4 **Sandholme** E R Yk
74 F3 **Sandholme** Lincs
23 M2 **Sandhurst** Br For
46 F10 **Sandhurst** Gloucs
26 D6 **Sandhurst** Kent
26 C6 **Sandhurst Cross** Kent
97 N4 **Sandhutton** N York
98 D9 **Sand Hutton** N York
72 D3 **Sandiacre** Derbys
87 P4 **Sandilands** Lincs
82 D10 **Sandiway** Ches W
21 M11 **Sandleheath** Hants
34 E4 **Sandleigh** Oxon
20 E10 **Sandley** Dorset
38 C10 **Sandling** Kent
82 G11 **Sandlow Green** Ches E
169 n8 **Sandness** Shet
52 B11 **Sandon** Essex
50 H4 **Sandon** Herts
70 G9 **Sandon** Staffs
70 G9 **Sandon Bank** Staffs
14 G10 **Sandown** IoW
5 M10 **Sandplace** Cnwll
50 E8 **Sandridge** Herts
32 H11 **Sandridge** Wilts
75 N5 **Sandringham** Norfk
35 M6 **Sands** Bucks
105 N8 **Sandsend** N York
94 E4 **Sand Side** Cumb
95 K4 **Sandside** Cumb
92 B9 **Sandtoft** N Linc
38 E11 **Sandway** Kent
39 P10 **Sandwich** Kent
101 M7 **Sandwick** Cumb
169 r11 **Sandwick** Shet
168 j4 **Sandwick** W Isls
100 C8 **Sandwith** Cumb
100 C8 **Sandwith Newtown** Cumb
61 Q11 **Sandy** C Beds
87 J9 **Sandy Bank** Lincs
81 L11 **Sandycroft** Flints
25 N6 **Sandy Cross** E Susx
46 C3 **Sandy Cross** Herefs
110 D2 **Sandyford** D & G
7 M4 **Sandygate** Devon
80 e2 **Sandygate** IoM
40 G9 **Sandy Haven** Pembks
109 J9 **Sandyhills** D & G
95 J8 **Sandylands** Lancs
90 E3 **Sandy Lane** C Brad
70 C7 **Sandylane** Staffs
28 G7 **Sandylane** Swans
33 J11 **Sandy Lane** Wilts
69 M6 **Sandy Lane** Wrexhm
8 H7 **Sandy Park** Devon
110 G7 **Sandysike** Cumb
45 P9 **Sandyway** Herefs
165 K3 **Sangobeg** Highld
165 K3 **Sangomore** Highld
82 C7 **Sankey Bridges** Warrtn
57 P11 **Sankyn's Green** Worcs
137 L2 **Sanna Bay** Highld
168 j4 **Sanndabhaig** W Isls
124 C8 **Sannox** N Ayrs
115 Q6 **Sanquhar** D & G
100 F10 **Santon** Cumb
80 d7 **Santon** IoM
100 F10 **Santon Bridge** Cumb
63 P3 **Santon Downham** Suffk
59 Q6 **Sapcote** Leics
46 D2 **Sapey Common** Herefs
64 C6 **Sapiston** Suffk
62 B6 **Sapley** Cambs
71 M8 **Sapperton** Derbys
32 H4 **Sapperton** Gloucs
73 Q4 **Sapperton** Lincs
74 F5 **Saracen's Head** Lincs
167 P8 **Sarclet** Highld
14 F5 **Sarisbury** Hants
29 P8 **Sarn** Brdgnd
66 C8 **Sarn** Gwynd
55 M5 **Sarn** Powys
56 C6 **Sarn** Powys
42 F11 **Sarnau** Carmth
42 F4 **Sarnau** Cerdgn
68 C7 **Sarnau** Gwynd
44 E8 **Sarnau** Powys
68 H11 **Sarnau** Powys
66 E9 **Sarn Bach** Gwynd
45 M4 **Sarnesfield** Herefs
29 P8 **Sarn Park Services** Brdgnd
69 J11 **Sarn-wen** Powys
28 H2 **Saron** Carmth
42 G7 **Saron** Carmth
66 H3 **Saron** Gwynd
79 J11 **Saron** Gwynd
50 B11 **Sarratt** Herts
39 N8 **Sarre** Kent
47 Q10 **Sarsden** Oxon
22 B6 **Sarson** Hants
103 M2 **Satley** Dur
27 N4 **Satmar** Kent
102 H11 **Satron** N York
17 M7 **Satterleigh** Devon
94 G2 **Satterthwaite** Cumb
35 K8 **Satwell** Oxon
151 J5 **Sauchen** Abers
142 B11 **Saucher** P & K
143 M4 **Sauchieburn** Abers
32 D3 **Saul** Gloucs
85 N3 **Saundby** Notts
41 M10 **Saundersfoot** Pembks
35 L4 **Saunderton** Bucks
16 H4 **Saunton** Devon
87 L7 **Sausthorpe** Lincs
3 K4 **Saveock** Cnwll
70 H7 **Saverley Green** Staffs
90 G6 **Savile Town** Kirk
60 B7 **Sawbridge** Warwks
51 L8 **Sawbridgeworth** Herts
99 J4 **Sawdon** N York
72 D4 **Sawley** Derbys
96 A11 **Sawley** Lancs
97 K7 **Sawley** N York
62 G11 **Sawston** Cambs
61 Q4 **Sawtry** Cambs
73 L7 **Saxby** Leics
86 D3 **Saxby** Lincs
92 G7 **Saxby All Saints** N Linc
72 H6 **Saxelbye** Leics
64 F9 **Saxham Street** Suffk
85 Q5 **Saxilby** Lincs
76 E4 **Saxlingham** Norfk
65 J2 **Saxlingham Green** Norfk
65 J2 **Saxlingham Nethergate** Norfk
65 J2 **Saxlingham Thorpe** Norfk
65 M9 **Saxmundham** Suffk
72 H3 **Saxondale** Notts
63 L9 **Saxon Street** Cambs
65 K8 **Saxtead** Suffk
65 K9 **Saxtead Green** Suffk
65 J8 **Saxtead Little Green** Suffk
76 G5 **Saxthorpe** Norfk
91 M3 **Saxton** N York
24 G7 **Sayers Common** W Susx
98 C6 **Scackleton** N York
100 H9 **Scafell Pike** Cumb
85 L2 **Scaftworth** Notts
98 G6 **Scagglethorpe** N York
136 b3 **Scalasaig** Ag & B
92 D5 **Scalby** E R Yk
99 L2 **Scalby** N York
61 M9 **Scald End** Bed
60 G6 **Scaldwell** Nhants
110 H8 **Scaleby** Cumb
110 H8 **Scalebyhill** Cumb
111 L11 **Scale Houses** Cumb
94 F6 **Scales** Cumb
101 K5 **Scales** Cumb
110 H11 **Scalesceugh** Cumb
73 K6 **Scalford** Leics
105 K8 **Scaling** N York
105 K8 **Scaling Dam** R & Cl
169 r10 **Scalloway** Shet
153 L11 **Scalpay** Highld
87 J5 **Scamblesby** Lincs
90 D7 **Scammonden** Kirk
138 E3 **Scamodale** Highld
98 H5 **Scampston** N York
86 C5 **Scampton** Lincs
156 A10 **Scaniport** Highld
90 D7 **Scapegoat Hill** Kirk
130 D7 **Scarba** Ag & B
99 L3 **Scarborough** N York
3 N3 **Scarcewater** Cnwll
84 G7 **Scarcliffe** Derbys
91 K2 **Scarcroft** Leeds
167 N2 **Scarfskerry** Highld
103 L8 **Scargill** Dur
136 C7 **Scarinish** Ag & B
88 D8 **Scarisbrick** Lancs
100 H4 **Scarness** Cumb
76 D9 **Scarning** Norfk
73 J2 **Scarrington** Notts
88 E9 **Scarth Hill** Lancs
91 M3 **Scarthingwell** N York
93 N9 **Scartho** NE Lin
169 q6 **Scatsta Airport** Shet
92 G9 **Scawby** N Linc
91 N10 **Scawsby** Donc
91 P9 **Scawthorpe** Donc
98 A4 **Scawton** N York
25 J6 **Scayne's Hill** W Susx
44 G9 **Scethrog** Powys
70 E3 **Scholar Green** Ches E
90 E4 **Scholemoor Crematorium** C Brad
90 F5 **Scholes** Kirk
90 F9 **Scholes** Kirk
91 K3 **Scholes** Leeds
91 K11 **Scholes** Rothm
88 H9 **Scholes** Wigan
103 Q6 **School Aycliffe** Dur
90 E4 **School Green** C Brad
70 A2 **School Green** Ches W
35 K11 **Schoolgreen** Wokham
10 H4 **School House** Dorset
90 G8 **Scissett** Kirk
40 H4 **Scleddau** Pembks
85 K4 **Scofton** Notts
64 H6 **Scole** Norfk
134 E2 **Scone** P & K
153 J11 **Sconser** Highld
135 K7 **Scoonie** Fife
86 E9 **Scopwick** Lincs
160 G7 **Scoraig** Highld
99 L11 **Scorborough** E R Yk
3 J5 **Scorrier** Cnwll
7 J5 **Scorriton** Devon
95 L11 **Scorton** Lancs
103 Q10 **Scorton** N York
77 K7 **Sco Ruston** Norfk
110 H9 **Scotby** Cumb
103 P9 **Scotch Corner** N York
103 P9 **Scotch Corner Services** N York
95 K9 **Scotforth** Lancs
70 D5 **Scot Hay** Staffs
86 D5 **Scothern** Lincs
73 Q4 **Scotland** Lincs
113 L4 **Scotland Gate** Nthumb
134 F7 **Scotlandwell** P & K
89 J9 **Scot Lane End** Bolton
167 J5 **Scotscalder Station** Highld
110 G6 **Scotsdike** Cumb
112 F3 **Scot's Gap** Nthumb
150 F4 **Scotsmill** Abers
125 N4 **Scotstoun** C Glas
113 K8 **Scotswood** N u Ty
92 E10 **Scotter** Lincs
92 E10 **Scotterthorpe** Lincs
73 R6 **Scottlethorpe** Lincs
92 E11 **Scotton** Lincs
97 M9 **Scotton** N York
103 N11 **Scotton** N York
77 K7 **Scottow** Norfk
73 R3 **Scott Willoughby** Lincs
76 D11 **Scoulton** Norfk
71 K9 **Scounslow Green** Staffs
164 E8 **Scourie** Highld
164 D8 **Scourie More** Highld
169 q12 **Scousburgh** Shet
90 B9 **Scouthead** Oldham
167 K2 **Scrabster** Highld
118 C7 **Scraesburgh** Border
87 K7 **Scrafield** Lincs
119 J9 **Scrainwood** Nthumb
74 G2 **Scrane End** Lincs
72 G9 **Scraptoft** Leics
77 Q8 **Scratby** Norfk
98 E9 **Scrayingham** N York
26 C8 **Scrays** E Susx
74 A2 **Scredington** Lincs
87 M7 **Scremby** Lincs
129 Q10 **Scremerston** Nthumb
73 J2 **Screveton** Notts
87 J7 **Scrivelsby** Lincs
97 M9 **Scriven** N York
85 L2 **Scrooby** Notts
71 M8 **Scropton** Derbys
86 H9 **Scrub Hill** Lincs
97 L2 **Scruton** N York
110 H6 **Scuggate** Cumb
165 P4 **Scullomie** Highld
76 B5 **Sculthorpe** Norfk
92 E8 **Scunthorpe** N Linc
28 E7 **Scurlage** Swans
10 G2 **Sea** Somset
11 J3 **Seaborough** Dorset
70 E6 **Seabridge** Staffs
27 L4 **Seabrook** Kent
113 P9 **Seaburn** Sundld
81 L6 **Seacombe** Wirral
91 K3 **Seacroft** Leeds
87 Q8 **Seacroft** Lincs
74 F3 **Seadyke** Lincs
152 H9 **Seafield** Highld
127 J4 **Seafield** W Loth
127 P2 **Seafield Crematorium** C Edin
25 L11 **Seaford** E Susx
81 L5 **Seaforth** Sefton
72 G7 **Seagrave** Leics
33 J8 **Seagry Heath** Wilts
113 P11 **Seaham** Dur
119 P4 **Seahouses** Nthumb
37 N9 **Seal** Kent
23 N5 **Seale** Surrey
99 L4 **Seamer** N York
104 E8 **Seamer** N York
124 G8 **Seamill** N Ayrs
77 N6 **Sea Palling** Norfk
93 J9 **Searby** Lincs
39 J9 **Seasalter** Kent
100 D10 **Seascale** Cumb
100 H11 **Seathwaite** Cumb
100 H8 **Seathwaite** Cumb
94 H4 **Seatle** Cumb
100 H8 **Seatoller** Cumb
5 N11 **Seaton** Cnwll
100 D4 **Seaton** Cumb
10 E6 **Seaton** Devon
113 N11 **Seaton** Dur
99 P11 **Seaton** E R Yk
39 M10 **Seaton** Kent
113 M5 **Seaton** Nthumb
73 N11 **Seaton** RutInd
113 K6 **Seaton Burn** N Tyne
104 F5 **Seaton Carew** Hartpl
113 M5 **Seaton Delaval** Nthumb
92 C2 **Seaton Ross** E R Yk
113 M5 **Seaton Sluice** Nthumb
11 J6 **Seatown** Dorset
104 G10 **Seave Green** N York
14 H8 **Seaview** IoW
110 C10 **Seaville** Cumb
11 J2 **Seavington St Mary** Somset
19 M11 **Seavington St Michael** Somset
31 J5 **Sebastopol** Torfn
101 L2 **Sebergham** Cumb
59 L3 **Seckington** Warwks
95 P2 **Sedbergh** Cumb
31 P6 **Sedbury** Gloucs
96 C2 **Sedbusk** N York
47 K7 **Sedgeberrow** Worcs
73 M3 **Sedgebrook** Lincs
63 L4 **Sedge Fen** Suffk
104 C5 **Sedgefield** Dur
75 P3 **Sedgeford** Norfk
20 G9 **Sedgehill** Wilts
19 L4 **Sedgemoor Services** Somset
58 D6 **Sedgley** Dudley
82 H4 **Sedgley Park** Bury
95 L3 **Sedgwick** Cumb
26 C8 **Sedlescombe** E Susx
35 M2 **Sedrup** Bucks
38 F10 **Seed** Kent
20 H2 **Seend** Wilts
20 H2 **Seend Cleeve** Wilts
35 Q6 **Seer Green** Bucks
65 L2 **Seething** Norfk
81 M4 **Sefton** Sefton
81 L4 **Sefton Town** Sefton
113 L6 **Seghill** Nthumb
70 F9 **Seighford** Staffs
79 J11 **Seion** Gwynd
58 B5 **Seisdon** Staffs
69 J8 **Selattyn** Shrops
23 K8 **Selborne** Hants
91 Q4 **Selby** N York
23 P10 **Selham** W Susx
36 H7 **Selhurst** Gt Lon
117 P5 **Selkirk** Border
45 R9 **Sellack** Herefs
169 s4 **Sellafirth** Shet
2 C7 **Sellan** Cnwll
18 H11 **Sellick's Green** Somset
27 J4 **Sellindge** Kent
38 H10 **Selling** Kent
20 H2 **Sells Green** Wilts
58 F8 **Selly Oak** Birm
25 M9 **Selmeston** E Susx
37 J8 **Selsdon** Gt Lon
32 F4 **Selsey** Gloucs
15 N8 **Selsey** W Susx
24 H4 **Selsfield Common** W Susx
101 P11 **Selside** Cumb
96 A5 **Selside** N York
27 M3 **Selsted** Kent
84 G10 **Selston** Notts
18 B5 **Selworthy** Somset
52 G2 **Semer** Suffk
20 G2 **Semington** Wilts
20 G9 **Semley** Wilts
74 B4 **Sempringham** Lincs
36 B9 **Send** Surrey
36 B9 **Send Marsh** Surrey
30 F6 **Senghenydd** Caerph
2 B8 **Sennen** Cnwll
2 B8 **Sennen Cove** Cnwll
44 C9 **Sennybridge** Powys
85 K3 **Serlby** Notts
97 Q5 **Sessay** N York

75 M8 Setchey Norfk
13 P4 Setley Hants
128 C4 Seton Mains E Loth
96 B8 Settle N York
98 G6 Settrington N York
18 G8 Seven Ash Somset
47 K10 Sevenhampton Gloucs
33 P6 Sevenhampton Swindn
53 M3 Seven Hills Crematorium Suffk
37 L3 Seven Kings Gt Lon
37 M9 Sevenoaks Kent
37 M10 Sevenoaks Weald Kent
29 M3 Seven Sisters Neath
47 J11 Seven Springs Gloucs
52 F6 Seven Star Green Essex
31 P8 Severn Beach S Glos
46 G6 Severn Stoke Worcs
31 Q7 Severn View Services S Glos
61 N10 Sevick End Bed
26 H3 Sevington Kent
51 N3 Sewards End Essex
51 J11 Sewardstonebury Essex
49 Q10 Sewell C Beds
99 P7 Sewerby E R Yk
3 J7 Seworgan Cnwll
73 M6 Sewstern Leics
104 E9 Sexhow N York
47 N8 Sezincote Gloucs
168 k1 Sgiogarstaigh W Isls
35 J3 Shabbington Bucks
57 Q3 Shackerley Shrops
72 B9 Shackerstone Leics
72 C4 Shacklecross Derbys
23 P5 Shackleford Surrey
89 Q6 Shade Calder
168 i2 Shader W Isls
104 B2 Shadforth Dur
65 N5 Shadingfield Suffk
26 G4 Shadoxhurst Kent
91 J3 Shadwell Leeds
64 C5 Shadwell Norfk
51 K3 Shaftenhoe End Herts
20 G10 Shaftesbury Dorset
91 P9 Shaftholme Donc
91 K8 Shafton Barns
91 K8 Shafton Two Gates Barns
82 E4 Shakerley Wigan
22 B2 Shalbourne Wilts
14 C9 Shalcombe IoW
23 J6 Shalden Hants
23 K6 Shalden Green Hants
7 N4 Shaldon Devon
14 D9 Shalfleet IoW
52 B6 Shalford Essex
36 B11 Shalford Surrey
52 B6 Shalford Green Essex
70 F9 Shallowford Staffs
39 J11 Shalmsford Street Kent
48 H7 Shalstone Bucks
24 B2 Shamley Green Surrey
142 H5 Shandford Angus
132 B10 Shandon Ag & B
156 F2 Shandwick Highld
73 J11 Shangton Leics
113 L5 Shankhouse Nthumb
14 G10 Shanklin IoW
101 Q7 Shap Cumb
169 e5 Shapinsay Ork
12 F4 Shapwick Dorset
19 M7 Shapwick Somset
59 J7 Shard End Birm
72 C4 Shardlow Derbys
58 D3 Shareshill Staffs
91 K7 Sharlston Wakefd
91 K7 Sharlston Common Wakefd
58 H9 Sharman's Cross Solhll
38 C7 Sharnal Street Medway
61 L9 Sharnbrook Bed
89 P6 Sharneyford Lancs
59 Q6 Sharnford Leics
11 Q3 Sharnhill Green Dorset
88 G4 Sharoe Green Lancs
97 M6 Sharow N York
50 C4 Sharpenhoe C Beds
119 J10 Sharperton Nthumb
77 M7 Sharp Green Norfk
32 C4 Sharpness Gloucs
25 J4 Sharpthorne W Susx
5 M7 Sharptor Cnwll
58 E11 Sharpway Gate Worcs
76 E4 Sharrington Norfk
57 P8 Shatterford Worcs
39 N10 Shatterling Kent
84 B4 Shatton Derbys
6 E6 Shaugh Prior Devon
11 J5 Shave Cross Dorset
70 B4 Shavington Ches E
90 C3 Shaw C Brad
89 Q9 Shaw Oldham
33 M7 Shaw Swindn
34 E11 Shaw W Berk
32 G11 Shaw Wilts
57 L2 Shawbirch Wrekin
168 h3 Shawbost W Isls
69 Q10 Shawbury Shrops
89 P8 Shawclough Rochdl
46 C9 Shaw Common Gloucs
119 L8 Shawdon Hill Nthumb
60 B4 Shawell Leics
22 E9 Shawford Hants
89 P6 Shawforth Lancs
50 H4 Shaw Green Herts
88 G7 Shaw Green Lancs
97 L10 Shaw Green N York
109 J5 Shawhead D & G
97 L8 Shaw Mills N York
126 D7 Shawsburn S Lans
20 G6 Shear Cross Wilts
109 M7 Shearington D & G
60 D2 Shearsby Leics
19 J8 Shearston Somset
16 G10 Shebbear Devon
70 D9 Shebdon Staffs
166 H4 Shebster Highld
125 P6 Sheddens E Rens
14 G4 Shedfield Hants
71 L2 Sheen Staffs
84 E6 Sheepbridge Derbys
113 J9 Sheep Hill Dur
90 F7 Sheepridge Kirk
91 J4 Sheepscar Leeds
32 G2 Sheepscombe Gloucs
6 F5 Sheepstor Devon
8 C3 Sheepwash Devon
113 L3 Sheepwash Nthumb
31 N9 Sheepway N Som
72 A10 Sheepy Magna Leics
72 A10 Sheepy Parva Leics
51 M8 Sheering Essex
38 F7 Sheerness Kent
36 B8 Sheerwater Surrey
23 L10 Sheet Hants
2 D8 Sheffield Cnwll
84 E3 Sheffield Sheff
34 H11 Sheffield Bottom W Berk
84 E3 Sheffield City Road Crematorium Sheff
25 K5 Sheffield Green E Susx
50 D3 Shefford C Beds
164 E4 Sheigra Highld
57 L4 Sheinton Shrops
56 G9 Shelderton Shrops
58 J8 Sheldon Birm
83 Q11 Sheldon Derbys
10 C3 Sheldon Devon
38 H10 Sheldwich Kent
38 H10 Sheldwich Lees Kent
90 E5 Shelf Calder
64 G5 Shelfanger Norfk
47 M2 Shelfield Warwks
58 F4 Shelfield Wsall
47 M2 Shelfield Green Warwks
72 H2 Shelford Notts
59 P7 Shelford Warwks
118 G2 Shellacres Nthumb
51 N9 Shelley Essex
90 G8 Shelley Kirk
52 H4 Shelley Suffk
90 G8 Shelley Far Bank Kirk
34 B6 Shellingford Oxon
51 P9 Shellow Bowells Essex
46 D2 Shelsley Beauchamp Worcs
46 D2 Shelsley Walsh Worcs
61 M7 Shelton Bed
65 J3 Shelton Norfk
73 K2 Shelton Notts
56 H2 Shelton Shrops
65 J3 Shelton Green Norfk
72 B4 Shelton Lock C Derb
70 E7 Shelton Under Harley Staffs
56 E5 Shelve Shrops
45 Q6 Shelwick Herefs
51 P11 Shenfield Essex
48 C6 Shenington Oxon
50 E10 Shenley Herts
49 M7 Shenley Brook End M Keyn
50 E10 Shenleybury Herts
49 M7 Shenley Church End M Keyn
45 M7 Shenmore Herefs
107 K5 Shennanton D & G
58 H4 Shenstone Staffs
58 C10 Shenstone Worcs
58 H4 Shenstone Woodend Staffs
72 B11 Shenton Leics
149 N2 Shenval Moray
74 F8 Shepeau Stow Lincs
50 G6 Shephall Herts
36 F4 Shepherd's Bush Gt Lon
35 K8 Shepherd's Green Oxon
32 D4 Shepherds Patch Gloucs
27 N2 Shepherdswell Kent
90 F9 Shepley Kirk
32 B5 Shepperdine S Glos
36 C7 Shepperton Surrey
36 C7 Shepperton Green Surrey
62 E11 Shepreth Cambs
72 D7 Shepshed Leics
19 M11 Shepton Beauchamp Somset
20 B6 Shepton Mallet Somset
20 C8 Shepton Montague Somset
38 C11 Shepway Kent
104 D3 Sheraton Dur
20 B11 Sherborne Dorset
33 N2 Sherborne Gloucs
19 Q3 Sherborne Somset
22 H3 Sherborne St John Hants
47 Q2 Sherbourne Warwks
104 B2 Sherburn Dur
99 K5 Sherburn N York
104 B2 Sherburn Hill Dur
91 M4 Sherburn in Elmet N York
36 C11 Shere Surrey
76 B6 Shereford Norfk
21 Q10 Sherfield English Hants
23 J3 Sherfield on Loddon Hants
89 M5 Sherfin Lancs
7 K10 Sherford Devon
12 F6 Sherford Dorset
57 P2 Sheriffhales Shrops
98 D7 Sheriff Hutton N York
76 H3 Sheringham Norfk
49 N5 Sherington M Keyn
24 F7 Shermanbury W Susx
75 P4 Shernborne Norfk
21 J7 Sherrington Wilts
32 G7 Sherston Wilts
72 F2 Sherwood C Nott
85 K9 Sherwood Forest Notts
85 L7 Sherwood Forest Crematorium Notts
125 Q5 Shettleston C Glas
88 G9 Shevington Wigan
88 G8 Shevington Moor Wigan
88 G9 Shevington Vale Wigan
5 P10 Sheviock Cnwll
90 D5 Shibden Head C Brad
14 F9 Shide IoW
118 F3 Shidlaw Nthumb
146 A4 Shiel Bridge Highld
153 Q7 Shieldaig Highld
109 M3 Shieldhill D & G
126 F2 Shieldhill Falk
116 E2 Shieldhill House Hotel S Lans
126 D6 Shields N Lans
138 B3 Shielfoot Highld
142 G6 Shielhill Angus
124 G3 Shielhill Inver
34 C4 Shifford Oxon
57 N3 Shifnal Shrops
119 N9 Shilbottle Nthumb
103 P5 Shildon Dur
125 M6 Shillford E Rens
18 C10 Shillingford Devon
34 G6 Shillingford Oxon
9 M7 Shillingford Abbot Devon
9 M7 Shillingford St George Devon
12 D2 Shillingstone Dorset
50 D4 Shillington C Beds
118 G9 Shillmoor Nthumb
33 Q3 Shilton Oxon
59 P8 Shilton Warwks
64 H5 Shimpling Norfk
64 B11 Shimpling Suffk
64 B11 Shimpling Street Suffk
103 Q2 Shincliffe Dur
113 M10 Shiney Row Sundld
35 K11 Shinfield Wokham
62 D11 Shingay Cambs
53 Q3 Shingle Street Suffk
7 K6 Shinnersbridge Devon
162 C4 Shinness Highld
37 N10 Shipbourne Kent
76 D10 Shipdham Norfk
19 M3 Shipham Somset
7 M5 Shiphay Torbay
35 L9 Shiplake Oxon
35 K9 Shiplake Row Oxon
19 L3 Shiplate N Som
90 F3 Shipley C Brad
72 C2 Shipley Derbys
57 Q5 Shipley Shrops
24 D6 Shipley W Susx
24 H2 Shipley Bridge Surrey
26 H4 Shipley Hatch Kent
65 M3 Shipmeadow Suffk
63 K4 Shippea Hill Station Cambs
34 E5 Shippon Oxon
47 Q6 Shipston on Stour Warwks
49 L9 Shipton Bucks
47 K11 Shipton Gloucs
98 B9 Shipton N York
57 K6 Shipton Shrops
21 P5 Shipton Bellinger Hants
11 K6 Shipton Gorge Dorset
15 M7 Shipton Green W Susx
32 G7 Shipton Moyne Gloucs
48 E11 Shipton-on-Cherwell Oxon
92 E2 Shiptonthorpe E R Yk
47 Q11 Shipton-under-Wychwood Oxon
35 J5 Shirburn Oxon
88 D8 Shirdley Hill Lancs
102 B3 Shire Cumb
84 H7 Shirebrook Derbys
84 E2 Shiregreen Sheff
31 P9 Shirehampton Bristl
113 M6 Shiremoor N Tyne
31 N6 Shirenewton Mons
58 G4 Shire Oak Wsall
85 J4 Shireoaks Notts
26 F4 Shirkoak Kent
84 F9 Shirland Derbys
57 L5 Shirlett Shrops
14 D4 Shirley C Sotn
71 N6 Shirley Derbys
37 J7 Shirley Gt Lon
58 H9 Shirley Solhll
45 N3 Shirl Heath Herefs
14 G4 Shirrell Heath Hants
123 Q3 Shirvan Ag & B
17 L4 Shirwell Devon
120 H6 Shiskine N Ayrs
103 K3 Shittlehope Dur
45 N2 Shobdon Herefs
13 L3 Shobley Hants
9 L4 Shobrooke Devon
72 H6 Shoby Leics
69 M5 Shocklach Ches W
69 M5 Shocklach Green Ches W
38 F4 Shoeburyness Sthend
39 Q11 Sholden Kent
14 E4 Sholing C Sotn
56 G2 Shoot Hill Shrops
4 D7 Shop Cnwll
16 C9 Shop Cnwll
15 N5 Shopwyke W Susx
89 Q7 Shore Rochdl
36 H4 Shoreditch Gt Lon
18 H10 Shoreditch Somset
37 M8 Shoreham Kent
24 F9 Shoreham Airport W Susx
24 F9 Shoreham-by-Sea W Susx
129 N10 Shoreswood Nthumb
22 G9 Shorley Hants
33 K5 Shorncote Gloucs
37 Q6 Shorne Kent
5 M10 Shorta Cross Cnwll
25 L6 Shortbridge E Susx
23 M6 Shortfield Common Surrey
25 L7 Shortgate E Susx
58 G6 Short Heath Birm
23 L7 Shortheath Hants
58 E4 Short Heath Wsall
3 L4 Shortlanesend Cnwll
125 L10 Shortlees E Ayrs
61 N11 Shortstown Bed
14 E10 Shorwell IoW
20 D3 Shoscombe BaNES
65 J2 Shotesham Norfk
38 C3 Shotgate Essex
53 M4 Shotley Suffk
112 G10 Shotley Bridge Dur
112 G10 Shotleyfield Nthumb
53 M5 Shotley Gate Suffk
53 M4 Shotley Street Suffk
38 H11 Shottenden Kent
23 N8 Shottermill Surrey
47 N4 Shottery Warwks
48 D5 Shotteswell Warwks
53 P3 Shottisham Suffk
71 Q5 Shottle Derbys
71 Q5 Shottlegate Derbys
104 C5 Shotton Dur
104 D3 Shotton Dur
81 L11 Shotton Flints
113 K5 Shotton Nthumb
118 F4 Shotton Nthumb
104 C2 Shotton Colliery Dur
126 F6 Shotts N Lans
81 L10 Shotwick Ches W
157 N6 Shougle Moray
75 N9 Shouldham Norfk
75 N9 Shouldham Thorpe Norfk
46 F3 Shoulton Worcs
25 Q4 Shover's Green E Susx
70 D5 Shraleybrook Staffs
69 L11 Shrawardine Shrops
57 Q11 Shrawley Worcs
36 B4 Shreding Green Bucks
59 K11 Shrewley Warwks
56 H2 Shrewsbury Shrops
21 L6 Shrewton Wilts
15 P6 Shripney W Susx
33 P7 Shrivenham Oxon
64 D3 Shropham Norfk
52 G7 Shrub End Essex
46 A6 Shucknall Herefs
51 P2 Shudy Camps Cambs
130 F6 Shuna Ag & B
46 H11 Shurdington Gloucs
35 M10 Shurlock Row W & M
47 K2 Shurnock Worcs
166 H5 Shurrery Highld
166 H5 Shurrery Lodge Highld
18 H6 Shurton Somset
59 K6 Shustoke Warwks
9 L4 Shute Devon
10 F5 Shute Devon
48 C6 Shutford Oxon
70 F10 Shut Heath Staffs
46 G7 Shuthonger Gloucs
49 K5 Shutlanger Nhants
9 N9 Shutterton Devon
58 C3 Shutt Green Staffs
59 L3 Shuttington Warwks
84 G6 Shuttlewood Derbys
89 N7 Shuttleworth Bury
168 h3 Siabost W Isls
168 i2 Siadar W Isls
60 E4 Sibbertoft Nhants
56 G8 Sibdon Carwood Shrops
48 C7 Sibford Ferris Oxon
48 C7 Sibford Gower Oxon
52 C5 Sible Hedingham Essex
51 P5 Sibley's Green Essex
5 L7 Siblyback Cnwll
87 L10 Sibsey Lincs
87 K10 Sibsey Fenside Lincs
74 A11 Sibson Cambs
72 B10 Sibson Leics
167 P6 Sibster Highld
85 M6 Sibthorpe Notts
85 N11 Sibthorpe Notts
65 M8 Sibton Suffk
64 B9 Sicklesmere Suffk
97 N11 Sicklinghall N York
19 J9 Sidbrook Somset
10 C6 Sidbury Devon
57 M7 Sidbury Shrops
91 K9 Sid Cop Barns
19 M3 Sidcot N Som
37 L6 Sidcup Gt Lon
100 D4 Siddick Cumb
82 H10 Siddington Ches E
33 K5 Siddington Gloucs
58 E10 Sidemoor Worcs
77 K4 Sidestrand Norfk
10 C6 Sidford Devon
15 N7 Sidlesham W Susx
15 N7 Sidlesham Common W Susx
26 B10 Sidley E Susx
10 C7 Sidmouth Devon
56 H8 Siefton Shrops
7 K4 Sigford Devon
99 P11 Sigglesthorne E R Yk
30 C10 Sigingstone V Glam
33 P2 Signet Oxon
22 H2 Silchester Hants
72 G7 Sileby Leics
94 C4 Silecroft Cumb
64 G2 Silfield Norfk
43 L4 Silian Cerdgn
22 D10 Silkstead Hants
90 H9 Silkstone Barns
90 H10 Silkstone Common Barns
73 R2 Silk Willoughby Lincs
109 P10 Silloth Cumb
99 K2 Silpho N York
96 F11 Silsden C Brad
50 C3 Silsoe C Beds
20 E9 Silton Dorset
127 N5 Silverburn Mdloth
95 K6 Silverdale Lancs
70 E5 Silverdale Staffs
52 D8 Silver End Essex
159 J5 Silverford Abers
76 H6 Silvergate Norfk
65 L9 Silverlace Green Suffk
65 K6 Silverley's Green Suffk
49 J6 Silverstone Nhants
38 E9 Silver Street Kent
19 P8 Silver Street Somset
9 N4 Silverton Devon
3 J4 Silverwell Cnwll
57 L9 Silvington Shrops
89 N9 Simister Bury
83 M6 Simmondley Derbys
112 C6 Simonburn Nthumb
17 P4 Simonsbath Somset
18 F11 Simonsburrow Devon
89 M4 Simonstone Lancs
96 C2 Simonstone N York
129 L11 Simprim Border
49 N7 Simpson M Keyn
40 G7 Simpson Cross Pembks
129 J9 Sinclair's Hill Border
115 J4 Sinclairston E Ayrs
97 M4 Sinderby N York
112 B10 Sinderhope Nthumb
82 F7 Sinderland Green Traffd
35 L11 Sindlesham Wokham
72 A4 Sinfin C Derb
49 L8 Singleborough Bucks
37 K9 Single Street Gt Lon
26 H3 Singleton Kent
88 D3 Singleton Lancs
15 N4 Singleton W Susx
37 Q6 Singlewell Kent
26 D3 Sinkhurst Green Kent
150 D5 Sinnarhard Abers
98 E3 Sinnington N York
46 F2 Sinton Worcs
46 F2 Sinton Green Worcs
36 G5 Sipson Gt Lon
30 F2 Sirhowy Blae G
26 C4 Sissinghurst Kent
32 C9 Siston S Glos
5 P3 Sitcott Devon
2 G8 Sithney Cnwll
2 G8 Sithney Common Cnwll
2 G8 Sithney Green Cnwll
38 F9 Sittingbourne Kent
57 P7 Six Ashes Shrops
30 H4 Six Bells Blae G
86 G3 Sixhills Lincs
63 J9 Six Mile Bottom Cambs
27 K3 Sixmile Cottages Kent
21 J11 Sixpenny Handley Dorset
11 b1 Six Rues Jersey
95 K3 Sizergh Castle Cumb
65 P9 Sizewell Suffk
169 e6 Skaill Ork
115 K4 Skares E Ayrs
151 N9 Skateraw Abers
129 J5 Skateraw E Loth
152 G8 Skeabost Highld
103 N10 Skeeby N York
73 J10 Skeffington Leics
93 Q7 Skeffling E R Yk
84 G8 Skegby Notts
85 N7 Skegby Notts
87 Q8 Skegness Lincs
162 H7 Skelbo Highld
162 H8 Skelbo Street Highld
91 N8 Skelbrooke Donc
74 F3 Skeldyke Lincs
86 B6 Skellingthorpe Lincs
83 K8 Skellorn Green Ches E
91 N8 Skellow Donc
90 G8 Skelmanthorpe Kirk
88 F9 Skelmersdale Lancs
124 F4 Skelmorlie N Ayrs
166 B5 Skelpick Highld
108 H3 Skelston D & G
98 B9 Skelton C York
101 M3 Skelton Cumb
92 C5 Skelton E R Yk
97 N7 Skelton N York
103 L10 Skelton N York
105 J7 Skelton R & Cl
101 K10 Skelwith Bridge Cumb
87 M7 Skendleby Lincs
151 K5 Skene House Abers
45 P10 Skenfrith Mons
99 L9 Skerne E R Yk
165 Q4 Skerray Highld
164 F6 Skerricha Highld
95 K8 Skerton Lancs
59 P6 Sketchley Leics
28 H6 Sketty Swans
29 K5 Skewen Neath
98 C6 Skewsby N York
77 J6 Skeyton Norfk
77 K6 Skeyton Corner Norfk
166 H3 Skiall Highld
87 M2 Skidbrooke Lincs
93 R11 Skidbrooke North End Lincs
92 H4 Skidby E R Yk
168 k1 Skigersta W Isls
18 C9 Skilgate Somset
73 M5 Skillington Lincs
109 P9 Skinburness Cumb
133 Q11 Skinflats Falk
152 C8 Skinidin Highld
34 D11 Skinners Green W Berk
105 K7 Skinningrove R & Cl
123 R8 Skipness Ag & B
110 G4 Skipper's Bridge D & G
110 G11 Skiprigg Cumb
99 P10 Skipsea E R Yk
99 P10 Skipsea Brough E R Yk
96 E10 Skipton N York
97 N5 Skipton-on-Swale N York
91 R3 Skipwith N York
93 K3 Skirlaugh E R Yk
116 F3 Skirling Border
35 L6 Skirmett Bucks
98 E9 Skirpenbeck E R Yk
102 B4 Skirwith Cumb
95 Q6 Skirwith N York
167 Q3 Skirza Highld
110 H7 Skitby Cumb
35 L4 Skittle Green Bucks
40 D10 Skokholm Island Pembks
40 D9 Skomer Island Pembks
145 L3 Skulamus Highld
56 D10 Skyborry Green Shrops
52 E7 Skye Green Essex
148 H3 Skye of Curr Highld
96 G8 Skyreholme N York
90 B5 Slack Calder
90 B9 Slackcote Oldham
95 K5 Slack Head Cumb
87 P6 Slackholme End Lincs
159 K8 Slacks of Cairnbanno Abers
32 G3 Slad Gloucs
10 C3 Slade Devon
17 J2 Slade Devon
17 Q6 Slade Devon
34 G6 Slade End Oxon
37 M5 Slade Green Gt Lon
58 D3 Slade Heath Staffs
84 H3 Slade Hooton Rothm
4 G7 Sladesbridge Cnwll
46 F8 Slades Green Worcs
111 N10 Slaggyford Nthumb
95 Q10 Slaidburn Lancs
90 D8 Slaithwaite Kirk
84 C9 Slaley Derbys
112 E9 Slaley Nthumb
126 F3 Slamannan Falk
49 P10 Slapton Bucks
7 L9 Slapton Devon
48 H5 Slapton Nhants
89 P9 Slattocks Rochdl
24 G5 Slaugham W Susx
32 F10 Slaughterford Wilts
60 G2 Slawston Leics
23 M7 Sleaford Hants
86 E11 Sleaford Lincs
101 Q7 Sleagill Cumb
69 N9 Sleap Shrops
70 A11 Sleapford Wrekin
50 E9 Sleapshyde Herts
162 E7 Sleasdairidh Highld
41 K7 Slebech Pembks
46 F8 Sledge Green Worcs
99 J8 Sledmere E R Yk
111 K5 Sleetbeck Cumb
12 G5 Sleight Dorset
103 J8 Sleightholme Dur
105 N9 Sleights N York
12 F6 Slepe Dorset
167 N3 Slickly Highld
120 H7 Sliddery N Ayrs
144 G2 Sligachan Highld
131 P9 Sligrachan Ag & B
32 D4 Slimbridge Gloucs
70 E8 Slindon Staffs
15 Q5 Slindon W Susx
24 D4 Slinfold W Susx
79 L11 Sling Gwynd
98 D6 Slingsby N York
50 C7 Slip End C Beds
50 G3 Slip End Herts
61 L5 Slipton Nhants
71 J11 Slitting Mill Staffs
130 G8 Slockavullin Ag & B

77 K7 Sloley Norfk
8 H7 Sloncombe Devon
87 N6 Sloothby Lincs
35 Q9 Slough Slough
35 Q8 Slough Crematorium Bucks
19 J11 Slough Green Somset
24 G5 Slough Green W Susx
154 A10 Slumbay Highld
23 Q4 Slyfield Green Surrey
95 K7 Slyne Lancs
118 B3 Smailholm Border
89 Q7 Smallbridge Rochdl
9 L5 Smallbrook Devon
31 Q4 Smallbrook Gloucs
77 L7 Smallburgh Norfk
83 N9 Smalldale Derbys
83 Q8 Smalldale Derbys
24 F8 Small Dole W Susx
72 C2 Smalley Derbys
72 C2 Smalley Common Derbys
72 C2 Smalley Green Derbys
24 H2 Smallfield Surrey
58 H7 Small Heath Birm
26 E5 Small Hythe Kent
10 G4 Smallridge Devon
70 F4 Smallthorne C Stke
103 M8 Smallways N York
70 E2 Smallwood Ches E
94 H11 Small Wood Hey Lancs
64 E5 Smallworth Norfk
22 C5 Smannell Hants
102 D9 Smardale Cumb
26 E3 Smarden Kent
26 E3 Smarden Bell Kent
25 M2 Smart's Hill Kent
119 L3 Smeafield Nthumb
138 A2 Smearisary Highld
10 D2 Smeatharpe Devon
27 J4 Smeeth Kent
60 E2 Smeeton Westerby Leics
97 J8 Smelthouses N York
167 L10 Smerral Highld
58 C6 Smestow Staffs
58 F7 Smethwick Sandw
70 E2 Smethwick Green Ches E
72 A7 Smisby Derbys
14 F8 Smitheclose IoW
46 E4 Smith End Green Worcs
110 H7 Smithfield Cumb
95 K9 Smith Green Lancs
91 K9 Smithies Barns
9 Q2 Smithincott Devon
51 K3 Smith's End Herts
51 N6 Smith's Green Essex
51 Q2 Smith's Green Essex
160 B11 Smithstown Highld
156 C8 Smithton Highld
89 Q7 Smithy Bridge Rochdl
82 F10 Smithy Green Ches E
83 J7 Smithy Green Stockp
84 E11 Smithy Houses Derbys
59 Q7 Smockington Leics
165 K3 Smoo Highld
52 F8 Smythe's Green Essex
108 H3 Snade D & G
56 F4 Snailbeach Shrops
63 K7 Snailwell Cambs
99 J4 Snainton N York
91 Q6 Snaith E R Yk
83 P6 Snake Pass Inn Derbys
97 L4 Snape N York
65 M10 Snape Suffk
88 D8 Snape Green Lancs
65 M10 Snape Street Suffk
37 K3 Snaresbrook Gt Lon
72 A9 Snarestone Leics
86 D4 Snarford Lincs
26 G6 Snargate Kent
26 H6 Snave Kent
46 H4 Sneachill Worcs
56 E6 Snead Powys
64 H4 Sneath Common Norfk
105 N9 Sneaton N York
105 P9 Sneatonthorpe N York
86 E4 Snelland Lincs
82 H10 Snelson Ches E
71 M6 Snelston Derbys
64 D3 Snetterton Norfk
75 N4 Snettisham Norfk
72 C8 Snibston Leics
46 E9 Snig's End Gloucs
119 K10 Snitter Nthumb
86 C2 Snitterby Lincs
47 P3 Snitterfield Warwks
84 C8 Snitterton Derbys
57 K9 Snitton Shrops
26 F3 Snoadhill Kent
45 L6 Snodhill Herefs
38 B9 Snodland Kent
37 Q11 Snoll Hatch Kent
90 H10 Snowden Hill Barns
67 L4 Snowdon Gwynd
67 Q9 Snowdonia National Park
51 K4 Snow End Herts
47 L8 Snowshill Gloucs
64 F5 Snow Street Norfk
15 J4 Soake Hants
30 E8 Soar Cardif
7 J11 Soar Devon
44 D8 Soar Powys
144 F5 Soay Highld
22 H11 Soberton Hants
14 H4 Soberton Heath Hants
101 N5 Sockbridge Cumb
104 B9 Sockburn Darltn
80 F10 Sodom Denbgs
69 K7 Sodylt Bank Shrops
63 J6 Soham Cambs
63 J5 Soham Cotes Cambs
168 d10 Solas W Isls
40 G8 Solbury Pembks
16 E9 Soldon Devon
16 E9 Soldon Cross Devon
23 J7 Soldridge Hants
27 J2 Sole Street Kent
37 Q7 Sole Street Kent
59 J9 Solihull Solhll
45 N3 Sollers Dilwyn Herefs
46 B8 Sollers Hope Herefs
88 F7 Sollom Lancs
40 F6 Solva Pembks
110 F5 Solwaybank D & G
73 K8 Somerby Leics
93 J9 Somerby Lincs
84 F10 Somercotes Derbys
13 L6 Somerford Dorset
33 K5 Somerford Keynes Gloucs
15 M7 Somerley W Susx
65 P2 Somerleyton Suffk
71 L7 Somersal Herbert Derbys
87 K6 Somersby Lincs
62 E5 Somersham Cambs
53 J2 Somersham Suffk
48 E9 Somerton Oxon
19 N9 Somerton Somset
63 P10 Somerton Suffk
57 K2 Somerwood Shrops
24 E9 Sompting W Susx
35 L9 Sonning Wokham
35 K8 Sonning Common Oxon
35 K9 Sonning Eye Oxon
69 K5 Sontley Wrexhm
13 L5 Sopley Hants
32 F7 Sopworth Wilts
107 M8 Sorbie D & G
167 K4 Sordale Highld
136 H3 Sorisdale Ag & B
115 L2 Sorn E Ayrs
167 N4 Sortat Highld
86 H5 Sotby Lincs
86 F8 Sots Hole Lincs
65 N5 Sotterley Suffk
81 J11 Soughton Flints
49 N9 Soulbury Bucks
101 N5 Soulby Cumb
102 D8 Soulby Cumb
48 F8 Souldern Oxon
61 L8 Souldrop Bed
70 A5 Sound Ches E
157 R7 Sound Muir Moray
32 C9 Soundwell S Glos
8 D6 Sourton Devon
94 E4 Soutergate Cumb
75 N8 South Acre Norfk
27 M3 South Alkham Kent
36 D5 Southall Gt Lon
7 K11 South Allington Devon
133 P9 South Alloa Falk
47 J9 Southam Gloucs
48 D2 Southam Warwks
23 P10 South Ambersham W Susx
14 D4 Southampton C Sotn
22 E11 Southampton Airport Hants
22 D11 Southampton Crematorium Hants
84 H4 South Anston Rothm
35 P11 South Ascot W & M
26 H3 South Ashford Kent
14 C7 South Baddesley Hants
139 K6 South Ballachulish Highld
98 B10 South Bank C York
104 F6 South Bank R & Cl
20 B9 South Barrow Somset
36 G8 South Beddington Gt Lon
5 N3 South Beer Cnwll
38 C4 South Benfleet Essex
15 P6 South Bersted W Susx
13 L5 South Bockhampton Dorset
37 K7 Southborough Gt Lon
25 N2 Southborough Kent
13 K6 Southbourne Bmouth
15 L5 Southbourne W Susx
11 J5 South Bowood Dorset
91 Q8 South Bramwith Donc
6 H6 South Brent Devon
20 D7 South Brewham Somset
31 Q11 South Bristol Crematorium Bristl
119 P11 South Broomhill Nthumb
76 E10 Southburgh Norfk
77 M10 South Burlingham Norfk
99 K10 Southburn E R Yk
20 B9 South Cadbury Somset
86 B5 South Carlton Lincs
85 J4 South Carlton Notts
92 F4 South Cave E R Yk
33 K5 South Cerney Gloucs
25 J7 South Chailey E Susx
10 G3 South Chard Somset
119 N6 South Charlton Nthumb
20 C10 South Cheriton Somset
103 P5 South Church Dur
38 F4 Southchurch Sthend
103 M7 South Cleatlam Dur
92 E3 South Cliffe E R Yk
85 P6 South Clifton Notts
87 L3 South Cockerington Lincs
29 M8 South Cornelly Brdgnd
5 K2 Southcott Cnwll
8 D5 Southcott Devon
9 J8 Southcott Devon
16 G8 Southcott Devon
21 N3 Southcott Wilts
35 M2 Southcourt Bucks
65 P5 South Cove Suffk
76 B4 South Creake Norfk
90 E8 South Crosland Kirk
72 H8 South Croxton Leics
99 K11 South Dalton E R Yk
37 N7 South Darenth Kent
25 J9 South Downs National Park
92 A4 South Duffield N York
25 K9 Southease E Susx
87 J3 South Elkington Lincs
91 M8 South Elmsall Wakefd
120 C10 Southend Ag & B
93 Q7 South End E R Yk
21 M11 South End Hants
46 D6 South End Herefs
93 K6 South End N Linc
64 D3 South End Norfk
33 N10 Southend Wilts
38 E4 Southend Airport Essex
38 E4 Southend Crematorium Sthend
38 E4 Southend-on-Sea Sthend
101 L3 Southernby Cumb
26 E2 Southernden Kent
29 N10 Southerndown V Glam
109 L10 Southerness D & G
153 N3 South Erradale Highld
10 B6 Southerton Devon
63 K2 Southery Norfk
37 N3 South Essex Crematorium Gt Lon
38 E3 South Fambridge Essex
34 C8 South Fawley W Berk
92 G6 South Ferriby N Linc
92 H5 South Field E R Yk
126 E3 Southfield Falk
37 P6 Southfleet Kent
14 F11 Southford IoW
36 G2 Southgate Gt Lon
75 N4 Southgate Norfk
76 B4 Southgate Norfk
76 G7 Southgate Norfk
28 G7 Southgate Swans
37 J11 South Godstone Surrey
13 L2 South Gorley Hants
113 K7 South Gosforth N u Ty
37 Q2 South Green Essex
52 H8 South Green Essex
38 E9 South Green Kent
76 F9 South Green Norfk
64 H6 South Green Suffk
127 M3 South Gyle C Edin
38 B2 South Hanningfield Essex
23 L11 South Harting W Susx
15 K7 South Hayling Hants
119 L4 South Hazelrigg Nthumb
35 P4 South Heath Bucks
25 K10 South Heighton E Susx
113 N11 South Hetton Dur
91 K8 South Hiendley Wakefd
5 N7 South Hill Cnwll
19 N9 South Hill Somset
34 F4 South Hinksey Oxon
16 C7 South Hole Devon
24 E2 South Holmwood Surrey
37 M4 South Hornchurch Gt Lon
19 Q5 South Horrington Somset
6 H10 South Huish Devon
86 B8 South Hykeham Lincs
113 N9 South Hylton Sundld
50 E2 Southill C Beds
22 F5 Southington Hants
92 H11 South Kelsey Lincs
156 B8 South Kessock Highld
93 K7 South Killingholme N Linc
97 P4 South Kilvington N York
60 D4 South Kilworth Leics
91 L8 South Kirkby Wakefd
7 L4 South Knighton Devon
86 G11 South Kyme Lincs
126 B6 South Lanarkshire Crematorium S Lans
10 E6 Southleigh Devon
34 C3 South Leigh Oxon
85 N4 South Leverton Notts
47 L5 South Littleton Worcs
36 G7 South London Crematorium Gt Lon
64 E5 South Lopham Norfk
73 N10 South Luffenham Rutlnd
25 K8 South Malling E Susx
33 N7 South Marston Swindn
36 G10 South Merstham Surrey
119 J6 South Middleton Nthumb
91 M4 South Milford N York
6 J10 South Milton Devon
50 F10 South Mimms Herts
50 F10 South Mimms Services Herts
38 G2 Southminster Essex
17 N6 South Molton Devon
113 J10 South Moor Dur
34 C5 Southmoor Oxon
34 G7 South Moreton Oxon
142 F7 Southmuir Angus
15 N6 South Mundham W Susx
85 N9 South Muskham Notts
92 F3 South Newbald E R Yk
48 D8 South Newington Oxon
21 L8 South Newton Wilts
84 F9 South Normanton Derbys
36 H7 South Norwood Gt Lon
36 H11 South Nutfield Surrey
37 N4 South Ockendon Thurr
61 Q8 Southoe Cambs
64 H8 Southolt Suffk
87 L5 South Ormsby Lincs
74 A10 Southorpe C Pete
90 H7 South Ossett Wakefd
97 N3 South Otterington N York
11 N6 Southover Dorset
25 Q5 Southover E Susx
86 E2 South Owersby Lincs
90 E6 Southowram Calder
36 F11 South Park Surrey
11 K3 South Perrott Dorset
19 M11 South Petherton Somset
5 N5 South Petherwin Cnwll
76 B11 South Pickenham Norfk
5 Q10 South Pill Cnwll
7 K10 South Pool Devon
11 L5 South Poorton Dorset
88 C7 Southport Sefton
88 D8 Southport Crematorium Lancs
127 L2 South Queensferry C Edin
17 N5 South Radworthy Devon
86 D11 South Rauceby Lincs
76 B7 South Raynham Norfk
83 J6 South Reddish Stockp
77 K4 Southrepps Norfk
87 M4 South Reston Lincs
86 F7 Southrey Lincs
169 d8 South Ronaldsay Ork
33 N4 Southrop Gloucs
23 J6 Southrope Hants
75 M9 South Runcton Norfk
85 P8 South Scarle Notts
15 J7 Southsea C Port
69 K4 Southsea Wrexhm
138 G9 South Shian Ag & B
113 N7 South Shields S Tyne
113 M8 South Shields Crematorium S Tyne
88 C4 South Shore Bpool
103 M5 Southside Dur
87 M2 South Somercotes Lincs
97 M8 South Stainley N York
37 N5 South Stifford Thurr
20 D2 South Stoke BaNES
34 G8 South Stoke Oxon
24 B9 South Stoke W Susx
26 H4 South Stour Kent
37 P8 South Street Kent
39 J10 South Street Kent
39 K8 South Street Kent
127 J7 South Tarbrax S Lans
8 G6 South Tawton Devon
2 H5 South Tehidy Cnwll
87 M5 South Thoresby Lincs
103 M8 South Thorpe Dur
23 J7 South Town Hants
77 Q10 Southtown Norfk
19 K11 Southtown Somset
168 d14 South Uist W Isls
110 H11 Southwaite Cumb
110 H11 Southwaite Services Cumb
77 M9 South Walsham Norfk
36 H5 Southwark Gt Lon
23 K5 South Warnborough Hants
24 E5 Southwater W Susx
24 D5 Southwater Street W Susx
19 P6 Southway Somset
37 N2 South Weald Essex
11 P10 Southwell Dorset
85 L10 Southwell Notts
36 D6 South West Middlesex Crematorium Gt Lon
35 K5 South Weston Oxon
5 L3 South Wheatley Cnwll
14 H5 Southwick Hants
61 M2 Southwick Nhants
19 L5 Southwick Somset
113 N9 Southwick Sundld
24 F9 Southwick W Susx
20 F3 Southwick Wilts
19 Q3 South Widcombe BaNES
72 F11 South Wigston Leics
26 H3 South Willesborough Kent
86 G4 South Willingham Lincs
104 D4 South Wingate Dur
84 E9 South Wingfield Derbys
73 N7 South Witham Lincs
65 Q6 Southwold Suffk
22 E7 South Wonston Hants
77 M10 Southwood Norfk
19 Q8 Southwood Somset
38 D2 South Woodham Ferrers Essex
75 M6 South Wootton Norfk
20 F2 South Wraxall Wilts
8 G6 South Zeal Devon
90 C6 Sowerby Calder
97 P4 Sowerby N York
90 D6 Sowerby Bridge Calder
101 L2 Sowerby Row Cumb
88 D2 Sower Carr Lancs
18 A10 Sowerhill Somset
31 J4 Sowhill Torfn
63 M10 Sowley Green Suffk
90 D7 Sowood Calder
6 E5 Sowton Devon
9 N6 Sowton Devon
90 C6 Soyland Town Calder
77 K5 Spa Common Norfk
51 Q3 Spain's End Essex
74 D6 Spalding Lincs
92 C4 Spaldington E R Yk
61 P6 Spaldwick Cambs
85 P7 Spalford Notts
74 A3 Spanby Lincs
23 J3 Spanish Green Hants
76 F8 Sparham Norfk
76 F8 Sparhamill Norfk
94 G4 Spark Bridge Cumb
101 M5 Sparket Cumb
20 B9 Sparkford Somset
58 H8 Sparkhill Birm
6 F7 Sparkwell Devon
76 C9 Sparrow Green Norfk
83 N8 Sparrowpit Derbys
25 P4 Sparrows Green E Susx
22 D8 Sparsholt Hants
34 B7 Sparsholt Oxon
112 C11 Spartylea Nthumb
71 K7 Spath Staffs
98 E3 Spaunton N York
18 H7 Spaxton Somset
146 G11 Spean Bridge Highld
24 D7 Spear Hill W Susx
22 B9 Spearywell Hants
35 M5 Speen Bucks
34 E11 Speen W Berk
99 P6 Speeton N York
81 N8 Speke Lpool
25 N2 Speldhurst Kent
51 L7 Spellbrook Herts
26 B4 Spelmonden Kent
48 B10 Spelsbury Oxon
90 F5 Spen Kirk
35 K11 Spencers Wood Wokham
70 E2 Spen Green Ches E
96 H3 Spennithorne N York
103 Q4 Spennymoor Dur
47 L2 Spernall Warwks
46 G4 Spetchley Worcs
12 F4 Spetisbury Dorset
65 M5 Spexhall Suffk
157 R4 Spey Bay Moray
149 J2 Speybridge Highld
157 P9 Speyview Moray
87 M7 Spilsby Lincs
119 N4 Spindlestone Nthumb
84 G5 Spinkhill Derbys
162 F9 Spinningdale Highld
85 J7 Spion Kop Notts
33 J9 Spirthill Wilts
81 L8 Spital Wirral
85 K2 Spital Hill Donc
86 C2 Spital in the Street Lincs
25 K7 Spithurst E Susx
128 D4 Spittal E Loth
98 F10 Spittal E R Yk
167 L6 Spittal Highld
129 Q9 Spittal Nthumb
41 J6 Spittal Pembks
141 R9 Spittalfield P & K
149 Q10 Spittal of Glenmuick Abers
141 R4 Spittal of Glenshee P & K
118 A7 Spittal-on-Rule Border
77 J8 Spixworth Norfk
4 E6 Splatt Cnwll
5 L4 Splatt Cnwll
8 F3 Splatt Devon
25 K6 Splayne's Green E Susx
30 H9 Splottlands Cardif
97 N10 Spofforth N York
72 C3 Spondon C Derb
69 J2 Spon Green Flints
64 F2 Spooner Row Norfk
76 A9 Sporle Norfk
128 H4 Spott E Loth
128 G10 Spottiswoode Border
60 F7 Spratton Nhants
23 M6 Spreakley Surrey
8 G5 Spreyton Devon
6 E8 Spriddlestone Devon
86 D4 Spridlington Lincs
125 Q4 Springburn C Glas
110 F7 Springfield D & G
52 B10 Springfield Essex
135 J5 Springfield Fife
58 E4 Springhill Staffs
58 G3 Springhill Staffs
108 H6 Springholm D & G
125 K10 Springside N Ayrs
85 Q3 Springthorpe Lincs
90 H10 Spring Vale Barns
113 L9 Springwell Sundld
81 N7 Springwood Crematorium Lpool
93 L4 Sproatley E R Yk
82 F11 Sproston Green Ches W
91 N10 Sprotbrough Donc
53 K3 Sproughton Suffk
118 E3 Sprouston Border
77 K9 Sprowston Norfk
73 M6 Sproxton Leics
98 C4 Sproxton N York
69 M8 Spunhill Shrops
69 Q3 Spurstow Ches E
11 L6 Spyway Dorset
40 F4 Square & Compass Pembks
57 P5 Stableford Shrops
70 E7 Stableford Staffs
84 C2 Stacey Bank Sheff
96 B7 Stackhouse N York
41 J11 Stackpole Pembks
64 F3 Stacksford Norfk
89 P6 Stacksteads Lancs
6 E8 Staddiscombe C Plym
92 D5 Staddlethorpe E R Yk
83 N10 Staden Derbys
34 H5 Stadhampton Oxon
168 c14 Stadhlaigearraidh W Isls
101 P2 Staffield Cumb
152 H4 Staffin Highld
70 G10 Stafford Staffs
70 H10 Stafford Crematorium Staffs
70 F8 Stafford Services (northbound) Staffs
70 F8 Stafford Services (southbound) Staffs
49 Q5 Stagsden Bed
91 J10 Stainborough Barns
100 D5 Stainburn Cumb
97 L11 Stainburn N York
73 N6 Stainby Lincs
91 J8 Staincross Barns
103 M6 Staindrop Dur
36 B6 Staines Surrey
74 A6 Stainfield Lincs
86 F6 Stainfield Lincs
91 Q8 Stainforth Donc
96 B7 Stainforth N York
88 C3 Staining Lancs
90 D7 Stainland Calder
105 P9 Stainsacre N York
84 G7 Stainsby Derbys
95 L3 Stainton Cumb
101 N5 Stainton Cumb
110 G9 Stainton Cumb
85 J2 Stainton Donc
103 L7 Stainton Dur
104 E8 Stainton Middsb
103 M11 Stainton N York
86 E5 Stainton by Langworth Lincs
105 Q11 Staintondale N York
86 G2 Stainton le Vale Lincs
94 E6 Stainton with Adgarley Cumb
100 H6 Stair Cumb
114 H3 Stair E Ayrs
91 K9 Stairfoot Barns
106 H7 Stairhaven D & G
105 L7 Staithes N York
113 L3 Stakeford Nthumb
95 J11 Stake Pool Lancs
15 J5 Stakes Hants
20 D11 Stalbridge Dorset
20 D11 Stalbridge Weston Dorset
77 M6 Stalham Norfk
77 M7 Stalham Green Norfk
38 G11 Stalisfield Green Kent
64 E2 Stalland Common Norfk
20 B11 Stallen Dorset
93 L8 Stallingborough NE Lin
96 D3 Stalling Busk N York
70 G7 Stallington Staffs
94 H11 Stalmine Lancs
94 H11 Stalmine Moss Side Lancs
83 L5 Stalybridge Tamesd
52 B4 Stambourne Essex
51 Q3 Stambourne Green Essex
73 Q9 Stamford Lincs
119 P7 Stamford Nthumb
81 P11 Stamford Bridge Ches W
98 E9 Stamford Bridge E R Yk
112 G6 Stamfordham Nthumb
36 H3 Stamford Hill Gt Lon
88 D2 Stanah Lancs
50 F8 Stanborough Herts
49 Q10 Stanbridge C Beds
12 H4 Stanbridge Dorset
90 C3 Stanbury C Brad
89 M9 Stand Bury
126 D4 Stand N Lans
126 G3 Standburn Falk
58 D3 Standeford Staffs
26 E3 Standen Kent
26 D5 Standen Street Kent
20 F4 Standerwick Somset
23 M8 Standford Hants
100 E4 Standingstone Cumb
32 E3 Standish Gloucs
88 H8 Standish Wigan
88 H9 Standish Lower Ground Wigan
34 C4 Standlake Oxon
22 D9 Standon Hants
51 J6 Standon Herts
70 E7 Standon Staffs
51 J7 Standon Green End Herts
64 G8 Standwell Green Suffk
126 F6 Stane N Lans
76 C7 Stanfield Norfk
50 E2 Stanford C Beds
27 K4 Stanford Kent
56 E2 Stanford Shrops

46 C4 **Stanford Bishop** Herefs
57 N11 **Stanford Bridge** Worcs
70 C10 **Stanford Bridge** Wrekin
34 G10 **Stanford Dingley** W Berk
34 B6 **Stanford in the Vale** Oxon
37 Q4 **Stanford le Hope** Thurr
60 C5 **Stanford on Avon** Nhants
72 E6 **Stanford on Soar** Notts
57 N11 **Stanford on Teme** Worcs
51 M10 **Stanford Rivers** Essex
84 G6 **Stanfree** Derbys
105 J7 **Stanghow** R & Cl
74 D11 **Stanground** C Pete
89 L5 **Stanhill** Lancs
75 R3 **Stanhoe** Norfk
116 G5 **Stanhope** Border
103 J3 **Stanhope** Dur
26 H3 **Stanhope** Kent
71 P10 **Stanhope Bretby** Derbys
61 K3 **Stanion** Nhants
58 C10 **Stanklin** Worcs
72 C2 **Stanley** Derbys
113 J10 **Stanley** Dur
84 G8 **Stanley** Notts
141 R11 **Stanley** P & K
57 N8 **Stanley** Shrops
70 G4 **Stanley** Staffs
91 J6 **Stanley** Wakefd
72 C2 **Stanley Common** Derbys
103 N3 **Stanley Crook** Dur
91 K6 **Stanley Ferry** Wakefd
88 E9 **Stanley Gate** Lancs
70 G4 **Stanley Moor** Staffs
47 K8 **Stanley Pontlarge** Gloucs
24 H9 **Stanmer** Br & H
36 E2 **Stanmore** Gt Lon
22 E9 **Stanmore** Hants
34 E9 **Stanmore** W Berk
111 P3 **Stannersburn** Nthumb
64 B10 **Stanningfield** Suffk
90 G4 **Stanningley** Leeds
113 K5 **Stannington** Nthumb
84 C3 **Stannington** Sheff
113 K4 **Stannington Station** Nthumb
45 L2 **Stansbatch** Herefs
63 N10 **Stansfield** Suffk
71 L4 **Stanshope** Staffs
52 D2 **Stanstead** Suffk
51 J8 **Stanstead Abbotts** Herts
37 P8 **Stansted** Kent
51 M6 *Stansted Airport* Essex
51 M5 **Stansted Mountfitchet** Essex
71 P11 **Stanton** Derbys
47 L8 **Stanton** Gloucs
45 L10 **Stanton** Mons
112 H2 **Stanton** Nthumb
71 L5 **Stanton** Staffs
64 D7 **Stanton** Suffk
72 B5 **Stanton by Bridge** Derbys
72 D3 **Stanton by Dale** Derbys
19 Q2 **Stanton Drew** BaNES
33 N6 **Stanton Fitzwarren** Swindn
34 D3 **Stanton Harcourt** Oxon
84 G8 **Stanton Hill** Notts
84 B8 **Stanton in Peak** Derbys
56 H9 **Stanton Lacy** Shrops
84 C8 **Stanton Lees** Derbys
57 K6 **Stanton Long** Shrops
72 G4 **Stanton on the Wolds** Notts
20 C2 **Stanton Prior** BaNES
21 L2 **Stanton St Bernard** Wilts
34 G3 **Stanton St John** Oxon
32 H9 **Stanton St Quintin** Wilts
64 D8 **Stanton Street** Suffk
72 D8 **Stanton under Bardon** Leics
69 Q10 **Stanton upon Hine Heath** Shrops
20 B2 **Stanton Wick** BaNES
32 D2 **Stantway** Gloucs
69 M10 **Stanwardine in the Field** Shrops
69 M9 **Stanwardine in the Wood** Shrops
52 F7 **Stanway** Essex
47 L8 **Stanway** Gloucs
52 G7 **Stanway Green** Essex
65 J7 **Stanway Green** Suffk
36 C6 **Stanwell** Surrey
36 B6 **Stanwell Moor** Surrey
61 L6 **Stanwick** Nhants
110 H9 **Stanwix** Cumb
168 c14 **Staoinebrig** W Isls
98 F2 **Stape** N York
13 J4 **Stapehill** Dorset
70 B5 **Stapeley** Ches E
71 P10 **Stapenhill** Staffs
39 N10 **Staple** Kent
18 D10 **Staple Cross** Devon
26 C7 **Staple Cross** E Susx
24 G5 **Staplefield** W Susx
19 J11 **Staple Fitzpaine** Somset
62 G10 **Stapleford** Cambs
50 H7 **Stapleford** Herts
73 L7 **Stapleford** Leics
85 Q9 **Stapleford** Lincs
72 D3 **Stapleford** Notts
21 L7 **Stapleford** Wilts
37 M2 **Stapleford Abbotts** Essex
51 M11 **Stapleford Tawney** Essex
18 H9 **Staplegrove** Somset
18 H10 **Staplehay** Somset
58 E10 **Staple Hill** Worcs
26 C3 **Staplehurst** Kent
14 F9 **Staplers** IoW
39 J9 **Staplestreet** Kent
111 K6 **Stapleton** Cumb
56 E11 **Stapleton** Herefs
72 C11 **Stapleton** Leics
103 Q8 **Stapleton** N York
56 H4 **Stapleton** Shrops
19 N10 **Stapleton** Somset
10 D2 **Stapley** Somset
61 Q8 **Staploe** Bed
46 C6 **Staplow** Herefs
135 J7 **Star** Fife
41 P4 **Star** Pembks
19 M3 **Star** Somset
97 M9 **Starbeck** N York
96 E6 **Starbotton** N York
9 N8 **Starcross** Devon
59 M10 **Stareton** Warwks
84 D9 **Starkholmes** Derbys
51 L4 **Starlings Green** Essex
26 C8 **Starr's Green** E Susx
65 J5 **Starston** Norfk
7 L10 **Start** Devon
103 K7 **Startforth** Dur
32 H8 **Startley** Wilts
39 P10 **Statenborough** Kent
82 E7 **Statham** Warrtn
19 L9 **Stathe** Somset
73 K4 **Stathern** Leics
104 D3 **Station Town** Dur
61 P7 **Staughton Green** Cambs
61 P8 **Staughton Highway** Cambs
31 Q2 **Staunton** Gloucs
46 E9 **Staunton** Gloucs
73 L2 **Staunton in the Vale** Notts
45 M2 **Staunton on Arrow** Herefs
45 M6 **Staunton on Wye** Herefs
94 H3 **Staveley** Cumb
101 N11 **Staveley** Cumb
84 F6 **Staveley** Derbys
97 N8 **Staveley** N York
7 K6 **Staverton** Devon
46 G10 **Staverton** Gloucs
60 B8 **Staverton** Nhants
20 G2 **Staverton** Wilts
46 G10 **Staverton Bridge** Gloucs
19 L7 **Stawell** Somset
18 E10 **Stawley** Somset
167 Q6 **Staxigoe** Highld
99 L5 **Staxton** N York
54 E7 **Staylittle** Cerdgn
55 K6 **Staylittle** Powys
88 D2 **Staynall** Lancs
85 N10 **Staythorpe** Notts
96 H11 **Stead** C Brad
96 G6 **Stean** N York
98 C6 **Stearsby** N York
19 J5 **Steart** Somset
51 Q6 **Stebbing** Essex
51 Q6 **Stebbing Green** Essex
58 H7 **Stechford** Birm
26 E4 **Stede Quarter** Kent
23 N10 **Stedham** W Susx
112 D9 **Steel** Nthumb
25 M4 **Steel Cross** E Susx
134 C9 **Steelend** Fife
111 K4 **Steele Road** Border
94 D5 **Steel Green** Cumb
69 P7 **Steel Heath** Shrops
45 Q3 **Steen's Bridge** Herefs
23 K9 **Steep** Hants
14 F11 **Steephill** IoW
90 C6 **Steep Lane** Calder
12 F8 **Steeple** Dorset
52 F11 **Steeple** Essex
20 H3 **Steeple Ashton** Wilts
48 E9 **Steeple Aston** Oxon
48 D10 **Steeple Barton** Oxon
51 Q2 **Steeple Bumpstead** Essex
49 K9 **Steeple Claydon** Bucks
61 P4 **Steeple Gidding** Cambs
21 K7 **Steeple Langford** Wilts
50 G2 **Steeple Morden** Cambs
90 C2 **Steeton** C Brad
152 D6 **Stein** Highld
113 J8 **Stella** Gatesd
27 K2 **Stelling Minnis** Kent
19 M10 **Stembridge** Somset
4 G10 **Stenalees** Cnwll
115 R9 **Stenhouse** D & G
133 P11 **Stenhousemuir** Falk
86 H4 **Stenigot** Lincs
152 H9 **Stenscholl** Highld
72 A4 **Stenson Fields** Derbys
128 G5 **Stenton** E Loth
168 j4 **Steornabhagh** W Isls
41 M9 **Stepaside** Pembks
109 J4 **Stepford** D & G
37 J4 **Stepney** Gt Lon
83 K7 **Stepping Hill** Stockp
50 B3 **Steppingley** C Beds
126 B4 **Stepps** N Lans
65 M9 **Sternfield** Suffk
21 K3 **Stert** Wilts
63 K9 **Stetchworth** Cambs
50 F5 **Stevenage** Herts
26 B8 **Steven's Crouch** E Susx
124 H9 **Stevenston** N Ayrs
22 F5 **Steventon** Hants
34 E6 **Steventon** Oxon
51 N2 **Steventon End** Essex
49 Q4 **Stevington** Bed
50 B2 **Stewartby** Bed
125 Q6 **Stewartfield** S Lans
125 L8 **Stewarton** E Ayrs
49 N9 **Stewkley** Bucks
19 K11 **Stewley** Somset
87 L3 **Stewton** Lincs
14 H9 **Steyne Cross** IoW
24 E8 **Steyning** W Susx
40 H9 **Steynton** Pembks
16 C9 **Stibb** Cnwll
76 D6 **Stibbard** Norfk
16 G9 **Stibb Cross** Devon
21 P2 **Stibb Green** Wilts
74 A11 **Stibbington** Cambs
118 D3 **Stichill** Border
3 P3 **Sticker** Cnwll
87 L8 **Stickford** Lincs
8 F6 **Sticklepath** Devon
18 D7 **Sticklepath** Somset
51 L4 **Stickling Green** Essex
87 K9 **Stickney** Lincs
76 D3 **Stiffkey** Norfk
46 D5 **Stifford's Bridge** Herefs
38 E9 **Stiff Street** Kent
26 C2 **Stile Bridge** Kent
19 N6 **Stileway** Somset
168 c14 **Stilligarry** W Isls
91 P2 **Stillingfleet** N York
98 B7 **Stillington** N York
104 C6 **Stillington** S on T
61 Q3 **Stilton** Cambs
32 D5 **Stinchcombe** Gloucs
11 Q6 **Stinsford** Dorset
56 F4 **Stiperstones** Shrops
58 G8 **Stirchley** Birm
57 M3 **Stirchley** Wrekin
159 R9 **Stirling** Abers
133 M9 **Stirling** Stirlg
133 N10 **Stirling Services** Stirlg
61 Q7 **Stirtloe** Cambs
96 E10 **Stirton** N York
52 D7 **Stisted** Essex
33 P11 **Stitchcombe** Wilts
3 J6 **Stithians** Cnwll
5 N8 **St Ive Cross** Cnwll
59 M9 **Stivichall** Covtry
86 G7 **Stixwould** Lincs
81 N10 **Stoak** Ches W
116 H3 **Stobo** Border
12 F7 **Stoborough** Dorset
12 F7 **Stoborough Green** Dorset
117 Q9 **Stobs Castle** Border
119 P11 **Stobswood** Nthumb
51 Q11 **Stock** Essex
19 N2 **Stock** N Som
22 C7 **Stockbridge** Hants
126 D10 **Stockbriggs** S Lans
38 D9 **Stockbury** Kent
34 D11 **Stockcross** W Berk
110 G11 **Stockdalewath** Cumb
38 G11 **Stocker's Hill** Kent
73 L11 **Stockerston** Leics
47 J3 **Stock Green** Worcs
46 B8 **Stocking** Herefs
59 M6 **Stockingford** Warwks
51 L5 **Stocking Pelham** Herts
10 E4 **Stockland** Devon
18 H6 **Stockland Bristol** Somset
25 N2 **Stockland Green** Kent
9 L3 **Stockleigh English** Devon
9 L4 **Stockleigh Pomeroy** Devon
33 J11 **Stockley** Wilts
45 M7 **Stockley Hill** Herefs
19 L11 **Stocklinch** Somset
45 M4 **Stockmoor** Herefs
83 J6 **Stockport** Stockp
83 K7 **Stockport Crematorium** Stockp
90 H11 **Stocksbridge** Sheff
112 G8 **Stocksfield** Nthumb
45 Q2 **Stockton** Herefs
65 M3 **Stockton** Norfk
56 D4 **Stockton** Shrops
57 N5 **Stockton** Shrops
48 D2 **Stockton** Warwks
21 J7 **Stockton** Wilts
70 D11 **Stockton** Wrekin
70 G4 **Stockton Brook** Staffs
82 D7 **Stockton Heath** Warrtn
104 D7 **Stockton-on-Tees** S on T
57 N11 **Stockton on Teme** Worcs
98 D9 **Stockton on the Forest** C York
32 H2 **Stockwell** Gloucs
58 C4 **Stockwell End** Wolves
71 K10 **Stockwell Heath** Staffs
32 B11 **Stockwood** Bristl
11 M3 **Stockwood** Dorset
47 K3 **Stock Wood** Worcs
95 K9 **Stodday** Lancs
39 M9 **Stodmarsh** Kent
76 F4 **Stody** Norfk
164 B11 **Stoer** Highld
11 M2 **Stoford** Somset
21 L7 **Stoford** Wilts
18 E7 **Stogumber** Somset
18 H6 **Stogursey** Somset
59 N9 **Stoke** Covtry
16 C7 **Stoke** Devon
15 K6 **Stoke** Hants
22 D4 **Stoke** Hants
38 D7 **Stoke** Medway
11 K4 **Stoke Abbott** Dorset
60 H3 **Stoke Albany** Nhants
64 G7 **Stoke Ash** Suffk
72 G2 **Stoke Bardolph** Notts
46 C2 **Stoke Bliss** Worcs
49 K5 **Stoke Bruerne** Nhants
52 B3 **Stoke by Clare** Suffk
52 G4 **Stoke-by-Nayland** Suffk
9 M5 **Stoke Canon** Devon
22 E7 **Stoke Charity** Hants
5 P7 **Stoke Climsland** Cnwll
46 B4 **Stoke Cross** Herefs
36 D9 **Stoke D'Abernon** Surrey
61 M3 **Stoke Doyle** Nhants
73 M11 **Stoke Dry** Rutlnd
46 B6 **Stoke Edith** Herefs
59 J5 **Stoke End** Warwks
21 L9 **Stoke Farthing** Wilts
75 P10 **Stoke Ferry** Norfk
7 M9 **Stoke Fleming** Devon
12 E7 **Stokeford** Dorset
7 M7 **Stoke Gabriel** Devon
32 B9 **Stoke Gifford** S Glos
72 B11 **Stoke Golding** Leics
49 M5 **Stoke Goldington** M Keyn
35 Q8 **Stoke Green** Bucks
85 N5 **Stokeham** Notts
49 N9 **Stoke Hammond** Bucks
70 B9 **Stoke Heath** Shrops
58 D11 **Stoke Heath** Worcs
77 J11 **Stoke Holy Cross** Norfk
7 N4 **Stokeinteignhead** Devon
46 B5 **Stoke Lacy** Herefs
48 G9 **Stoke Lyne** Oxon
35 M2 **Stoke Mandeville** Bucks
35 L5 **Stokenchurch** Bucks
36 H3 **Stoke Newington** Gt Lon
7 L10 **Stokenham** Devon
70 F5 **Stoke-on-Trent** C Stke
46 H9 **Stoke Orchard** Gloucs
35 Q8 **Stoke Poges** Bucks
58 E11 **Stoke Pound** Worcs
45 Q3 **Stoke Prior** Herefs
58 D11 **Stoke Prior** Worcs
17 L4 **Stoke Rivers** Devon
73 N5 **Stoke Rochford** Lincs
35 J8 **Stoke Row** Oxon
19 K9 **Stoke St Gregory** Somset
19 J10 **Stoke St Mary** Somset
20 C5 **Stoke St Michael** Somset
57 K8 **Stoke St Milborough** Shrops
56 G8 **Stokesay** Shrops
56 G8 **Stokesay Castle** Shrops
77 N9 **Stokesby** Norfk
104 F9 **Stokesley** N York
19 N11 **Stoke sub Hamdon** Somset
35 J5 **Stoke Talmage** Oxon
20 D9 **Stoke Trister** Somset
70 A9 **Stoke upon Tern** Shrops
70 F5 **Stoke-upon-Trent** C Stke
12 C3 **Stoke Wake** Dorset
58 E11 **Stoke Wharf** Worcs
18 H5 **Stolford** Somset
51 N10 **Stondon Massey** Essex
35 L2 **Stone** Bucks
32 C5 **Stone** Gloucs
26 F6 **Stone** Kent
37 N6 **Stone** Kent
85 J3 **Stone** Rothm
19 Q8 **Stone** Somset
70 G8 **Stone** Staffs
58 C9 **Stone** Worcs
62 G2 **Stonea** Cambs
19 L4 **Stone Allerton** Somset
20 B4 **Ston Easton** Somset
19 L3 **Stonebridge** N Som
64 C3 **Stonebridge** Norfk
59 K8 **Stonebridge** Warwks
74 E10 **Stone Bridge Corner** C Pete
84 F9 **Stonebroom** Derbys
90 E5 **Stone Chair** Calder
25 M5 **Stone Cross** E Susx
25 P10 **Stone Cross** E Susx
25 P4 **Stone Cross** E Susx
25 M3 **Stone Cross** Kent
26 H4 **Stone Cross** Kent
39 P10 **Stone Cross** Kent
64 A10 **Stonecross Green** Suffk
26 B5 **Stonecrouch** Kent
31 N10 **Stone-edge-Batch** N Som
93 K4 **Stoneferry** C KuH
123 Q5 **Stonefield Castle Hotel** Ag & B
25 Q5 **Stonegate** E Susx
105 L9 **Stonegate** N York
98 D5 **Stonegrave** N York
46 G5 **Stonehall** Worcs
111 Q5 **Stonehaugh** Nthumb
151 M10 **Stonehaven** Abers
21 M6 **Stonehenge** Wilts
92 A9 **Stone Hill** Donc
6 D8 **Stonehouse** C Plym
95 R3 **Stone House** Cumb
32 F3 **Stonehouse** Gloucs
111 N9 **Stonehouse** Nthumb
126 D8 **Stonehouse** S Lans
59 M10 **Stoneleigh** Warwks
69 R4 **Stoneley Green** Ches E
61 P7 **Stonely** Cambs
23 K9 **Stoner Hill** Hants
73 L6 **Stonesby** Leics
48 C11 **Stonesfield** Oxon
53 L6 **Stones Green** Essex
37 N10 **Stone Street** Kent
52 G4 **Stone Street** Suffk
52 H3 **Stone Street** Suffk
65 M5 **Stone Street** Suffk
27 J4 **Stonestreet Green** Kent
101 J8 **Stonethwaite** Cumb
157 P4 **Stonewells** Moray
37 N6 **Stonewood** Kent
168 c14 **Stoneybridge** W Isls
58 D9 **Stoneybridge** Worcs
126 H5 **Stoneyburn** W Loth
13 N2 **Stoney Cross** Hants
72 G10 **Stoneygate** C Leic
38 G2 **Stoneyhills** Essex
106 E7 **Stoneykirk** D & G
84 B5 **Stoney Middleton** Derbys
59 Q6 **Stoney Stanton** Leics
20 D8 **Stoney Stoke** Somset
20 C7 **Stoney Stratton** Somset
56 F3 **Stoney Stretton** Shrops
151 M5 **Stoneywood** C Aber
133 M11 **Stoneywood** Falk
64 G10 **Stonham Aspal** Suffk
58 G4 **Stonnall** Staffs
35 K7 **Stonor** Oxon
73 J11 **Stonton Wyville** Leics
46 D5 **Stony Cross** Herefs
57 J11 **Stony Cross** Herefs
22 B11 **Stonyford** Hants
84 G7 **Stony Houghton** Derbys
49 L6 **Stony Stratford** M Keyn
58 G2 **Stonywell** Staffs
17 M5 **Stoodleigh** Devon
18 B11 **Stoodleigh** Devon
27 K4 **Stop 24 Services** Kent
24 B7 **Stopham** W Susx
50 D6 **Stopsley** Luton
4 E6 **Stoptide** Cnwll
81 L8 **Storeton** Wirral
46 D6 **Storeyard Green** Herefs
168 j4 **Stornoway** W Isls
168 j4 *Stornoway Airport* W Isls
46 E5 **Storridge** Herefs
24 C8 **Storrington** W Susx
95 K5 **Storth** Cumb
92 B2 **Storwood** E R Yk
157 N3 **Stotfield** Moray
50 F3 **Stotfold** C Beds
57 M8 **Stottesdon** Shrops
72 G10 **Stoughton** Leics
23 Q4 **Stoughton** Surrey
15 M4 **Stoughton** W Susx
46 H5 **Stoulton** Worcs
58 C8 **Stourbridge** Dudley
58 C8 **Stourbridge Crematorium** Dudley
12 E3 **Stourpaine** Dorset
57 Q10 **Stourport-on-Severn** Worcs
20 E10 **Stour Provost** Dorset
20 F10 **Stour Row** Dorset
91 J4 **Stourton** Leeds
58 C8 **Stourton** Staffs
47 Q7 **Stourton** Warwks
20 E8 **Stourton** Wilts
20 D11 **Stourton Caundle** Dorset
19 M8 **Stout** Somset
169 r11 **Stove** Shet
65 N5 **Stoven** Suffk
117 P2 **Stow** Border
85 Q4 **Stow** Lincs
75 M9 **Stow Bardolph** Norfk
64 D2 **Stow Bedon** Norfk
75 M9 **Stowbridge** Norfk
62 H8 **Stow-cum-Quy** Cambs
31 Q3 **Stowe** Gloucs
56 E10 **Stowe** Shrops
71 J9 **Stowe by Chartley** Staffs
60 D9 **Stowehill** Nhants
20 C10 **Stowell** Somset
19 Q3 **Stowey** BaNES
8 B5 **Stowford** Devon
8 B7 **Stowford** Devon
10 C7 **Stowford** Devon
17 M3 **Stowford** Devon
64 D8 **Stowlangtoft** Suffk
61 P6 **Stow Longa** Cambs
38 D2 **Stow Maries** Essex
64 E10 **Stowmarket** Suffk
47 N9 **Stow-on-the-Wold** Gloucs
27 K3 **Stowting** Kent
27 K3 **Stowting Common** Kent
64 F9 **Stowupland** Suffk
148 H4 **Straanruie** Highld
150 H9 **Strachan** Abers
131 M7 **Strachur** Ag & B
65 J7 **Stradbroke** Suffk
20 H4 **Stradbrook** Wilts
63 N10 **Stradishall** Suffk
75 N9 **Stradsett** Norfk
86 B10 **Stragglethorpe** Lincs
72 H3 **Stragglethorpe** Notts
34 B10 **Straight Soley** Wilts
127 P4 **Straiton** Mdloth
114 G7 **Straiton** S Ayrs
151 M3 **Straloch** Abers
141 P5 **Straloch** P & K
71 K7 **Stramshall** Staffs
80 e6 **Strang** IoM
82 H5 **Strangeways** Salfd
46 A9 **Strangford** Herefs
106 E5 **Stranraer** D & G
54 G11 **Strata Florida** Cerdgn
23 J2 **Stratfield Mortimer** W Berk
23 J2 **Stratfield Saye** Hants
23 J3 **Stratfield Turgis** Hants
61 Q11 **Stratford** C Beds
37 J4 **Stratford** Gt Lon
65 M9 **Stratford St Andrew** Suffk
52 H5 **Stratford St Mary** Suffk
21 M8 **Stratford sub Castle** Wilts
21 L9 **Stratford Tony** Wilts
47 P3 **Stratford-upon-Avon** Warwks
160 B11 **Strath** Highld
160 H2 **Strathan** Highld
165 N4 **Strathan** Highld
126 C9 **Strathaven** S Lans
125 P2 **Strathblane** Stirlg
161 K6 **Strathcanaird** Highld
154 B9 **Strathcarron** Highld
138 B11 **Strathcoil** Ag & B
150 B5 **Strathdon** Abers
135 M4 **Strathkinness** Fife
126 G3 **Strathloanhead** W Loth
147 P9 **Strathmashie House** Highld
134 G6 **Strathmiglo** Fife
155 N6 **Strathpeffer** Highld
141 M7 **Strathtay** P & K
121 K4 **Strathwhillan** N Ayrs
166 D4 **Strathy** Highld
166 D3 **Strathy Inn** Highld
132 H4 **Strathyre** Stirlg
16 C10 **Stratton** Cnwll
11 P6 **Stratton** Dorset
33 K4 **Stratton** Gloucs
48 H9 **Stratton Audley** Oxon
20 C4 **Stratton-on-the-Fosse** Somset
33 N7 **Stratton St Margaret** Swindn
65 J3 **Stratton St Michael** Norfk
77 J7 **Stratton Strawless** Norfk
18 E7 **Stream** Somset
25 J7 **Streat** E Susx
36 H6 **Streatham** Gt Lon
50 C5 **Streatley** C Beds
34 G8 **Streatley** W Berk
10 D7 **Street** Devon
95 L10 **Street** Lancs
105 K10 **Street** N York
19 N7 **Street** Somset
59 Q8 **Street Ashton** Warwks
69 K7 **Street Dinas** Shrops
25 P6 **Street End** E Susx
39 K11 **Street End** Kent
15 N7 **Street End** W Susx
113 K9 **Street Gate** Gatesd
58 H2 **Streethay** Staffs
98 A11 **Street Houses** N York
104 B11 **Streetlam** N York
84 E11 **Street Lane** Derbys
58 G5 **Streetly** Wsall
58 G5 **Streetly Crematorium** Wsall
63 K11 **Streetly End** Cambs
20 B7 **Street on the Fosse** Somset
56 G7 **Strefford** Shrops
142 B10 **Strelitz** P & K
72 E2 **Strelley** Notts
98 C8 **Strensall** C York
46 H6 **Strensham** Worcs
46 G6 **Strensham Services (northbound)** Worcs
46 H6 **Strensham Services (southbound)** Worcs
19 J6 **Stretcholt** Somset
7 L9 **Strete** Devon
45 N3 **Stretford** Herefs
45 Q3 **Stretford** Herefs
82 G6 **Stretford** Traffd
51 L3 **Strethall** Essex
62 H6 **Stretham** Cambs
15 N5 **Strettington** W Susx
69 M4 **Stretton** Ches W
84 E8 **Stretton** Derbys
73 N7 **Stretton** Rutlnd
58 C2 **Stretton** Staffs
71 P9 **Stretton** Staffs
82 D8 **Stretton** Warrtn
59 M2 **Stretton en le Field** Leics
46 B6 **Stretton Grandison** Herefs
59 P10 **Stretton-on-Dunsmore** Warwks
47 P7 **Stretton on Fosse** Warwks
45 P6 **Stretton Sugwas** Herefs
59 Q8 **Stretton under Fosse** Warwks
57 K5 **Stretton Westwood** Shrops
159 M6 **Strichen** Abers
83 L7 **Strines** Stockp
18 G6 **Stringston** Somset
61 K8 **Strixton** Nhants
31 Q5 **Stroat** Gloucs
167 Q1 **Stroma** Highld
153 R11 **Stromeferry** Highld
169 b6 **Stromness** Ork
132 E5 **Stronachlachar** Stirlg
131 L11 **Stronafian** Ag & B
161 L3 **Stronchrubie** Highld
131 P11 **Strone** Ag & B
146 E11 **Strone** Highld
147 N2 **Strone** Highld

146 G11 Stronenaba Highld
131 P2 Stronmilchan Ag & B
169 f4 Stronsay Ork
169 f4 *Stronsay Airport Ork*
138 E5 Strontian Highld
26 E5 Strood Kent
38 B8 Strood Medway
36 F11 Strood Green Surrey
24 B6 Strood Green W Susx
32 G3 Stroud Gloucs
23 K10 Stroud Hants
36 B7 Stroude Surrey
38 E3 Stroud Green Essex
32 F3 Stroud Green Gloucs
73 N4 Stroxton Lincs
152 E10 Struan Highld
141 K4 Struan P & K
87 N4 Strubby Lincs
77 L10 Strumpshaw Norfk
126 D8 Strutherhill S Lans
135 K6 Struthers Fife
155 M9 Struy Highld
78 E8 Stryd-y-Facsen IoA
69 J5 Stryt-issa Wrexhm
159 N8 Stuartfield Abers
58 F4 Stubbers Green Wsall
14 G6 Stubbington Hants
89 M7 Stubbins Lancs
65 K2 Stubbs Green Norfk
12 F2 Stubhampton Dorset
84 D5 Stubley Derbys
82 C5 Stubshaw Cross Wigan
85 Q11 Stubton Lincs
13 L2 Stuckton Hants
96 B7 Studfold N York
35 N9 Stud Green W & M
50 B7 Studham C Beds
110 E9 Studholme Cumb
11 H8 Studland Dorset
47 L2 Studley Warwks
33 J10 Studley Wilts
47 L2 Studley Common Warwks
97 L7 Studley Roger N York
97 L6 Studley Royal N York
63 J5 Stuntney Cambs
25 P8 Stunts Green E Susx
70 E8 Sturbridge Staffs
85 Q3 Sturgate Lincs
51 Q2 Sturmer Essex
12 C2 Sturminster Common Dorset
12 G4 Sturminster Marshall Dorset
12 C2 Sturminster Newton Dorset
39 L9 Sturry Kent
92 G10 Sturton N Linc
85 Q4 Sturton by Stow Lincs
85 N4 Sturton le Steeple Notts
64 G6 Stuston Suffk
91 M2 Stutton N York
53 L5 Stutton Suffk
82 H8 Styal Ches E
89 K3 Stydd Lancs
157 Q5 Stynie Moray
85 K2 Styrrup Notts
132 B6 Succoth Ag & B
46 D4 Suckley Worcs
46 D4 Suckley Green Worcs
61 L4 Sudborough Nhants
65 N11 Sudbourne Suffk
73 P2 Sudbrook Lincs
31 P7 Sudbrook Mons
86 D5 Sudbrooke Lincs
71 M8 Sudbury Derbys
36 E3 Sudbury Gt Lon
52 E3 Sudbury Suffk
89 P8 Sudden Rochdl
46 F2 Suddington Worcs
32 H3 Sudgrove Gloucs
99 K2 Suffield N York
77 J5 Suffield Norfk
69 R11 Sugdon Wrekin
70 D8 Sugnall Staffs
45 P6 Sugwas Pool Herefs
145 J4 Suisnish Highld
80 e3 Sulby IoM
48 G6 Sulgrave Nhants
48 G5 Sulgrave Manor Nhants
34 H10 Sulham W Berk
34 H11 Sulhamstead W Berk
34 H11 Sulhamstead Abbots W Berk
34 H11 Sulhamstead Bannister W Berk
24 C8 Sullington W Susx
169 q6 Sullom Shet
169 r6 Sullom Voe Shet
30 G11 Sully V Glam
169 q12 *Sumburgh Airport Shet*
97 K8 Summerbridge N York
4 D10 Summercourt Cnwll
75 Q3 Summerfield Norfk
58 B10 Summerfield Worcs
35 K6 Summer Heath Bucks
41 N9 Summerhill Pembks
58 G3 Summerhill Staffs
69 K4 Summer Hill Wrexhm
103 P7 Summerhouse Darltn
95 L3 Summerlands Cumb
84 E5 Summerley Derbys
15 N5 Summersdale W Susx
89 M8 Summerseat Bury
34 F3 Summertown Oxon
89 Q9 Summit Oldham
89 Q7 Summit Rochdl
102 C9 Sunbiggin Cumb
36 D7 Sunbury Surrey
108 H4 Sundaywell D & G
122 B7 Sunderland Ag & B
100 G3 Sunderland Cumb
95 J9 Sunderland Lancs
113 N9 Sunderland Sundld
103 Q3 Sunderland Bridge Dur
113 N9 Sunderland Crematorium Sundld
117 L5 Sundhope Border
50 C5 Sundon Park Luton
37 L9 Sundridge Kent
93 N7 Sunk Island E R Yk
35 Q11 Sunningdale W & M
35 P11 Sunninghill W & M
34 E4 Sunningwell Oxon
103 M3 Sunniside Dur
113 K9 Sunniside Gatesd
103 N4 Sunny Brow Dur
72 A4 Sunnyhill C Derb
89 K6 Sunnyhurst Bl w D
133 M8 Sunnylaw Stirlg
34 F3 Sunnymead Oxon
21 P4 Sunton Wilts
36 E7 Surbiton Gt Lon
74 E5 Surfleet Lincs
74 E5 Surfleet Seas End Lincs
77 L10 Surlingham Norfk
52 E7 Surrex Essex
24 G3 Surrey & Sussex Crematorium W Susx
76 H4 Sustead Norfk
92 D10 Susworth Lincs
16 E9 Sutcombe Devon
16 E9 Sutcombemill Devon
64 F2 Suton Norfk
87 L6 Sutterby Lincs
74 E3 Sutterton Lincs
62 B11 Sutton C Beds
74 A11 Sutton C Pete
62 F5 Sutton Cambs
7 J10 Sutton Devon
8 H4 Sutton Devon
91 P8 Sutton Donc
25 L11 Sutton E Susx
36 G8 Sutton Gt Lon
27 P2 Sutton Kent
91 M5 Sutton N York
77 M7 Sutton Norfk
73 K3 Sutton Notts
34 D3 Sutton Oxon
40 H7 Sutton Pembks
57 J2 Sutton Shrops
57 N7 Sutton Shrops
69 L9 Sutton Shrops
70 B8 Sutton Shrops
82 B6 Sutton St Hel
70 D10 Sutton Staffs
53 P2 Sutton Suffk
23 Q11 Sutton W Susx
36 D11 Sutton Abinger Surrey
37 N7 Sutton at Hone Kent
60 G2 Sutton Bassett Nhants
32 H9 Sutton Benger Wilts
11 L2 Sutton Bingham Somset
72 E6 Sutton Bonington Notts
75 J6 Sutton Bridge Lincs
72 C10 Sutton Cheney Leics
58 H5 Sutton Coldfield Birm
58 H5 Sutton Coldfield Crematorium Birm
34 F6 Sutton Courtenay Oxon
74 H6 Sutton Crosses Lincs
85 L4 Sutton cum Lound Notts
72 D5 Sutton Fields Notts
36 B10 Sutton Green Surrey
69 M5 Sutton Green Wrexhm
97 M5 Sutton Howgrave N York
84 G9 Sutton in Ashfield Notts
90 C2 Sutton-in-Craven N York
60 B2 Sutton in the Elms Leics
83 K10 Sutton Lane Ends Ches E
57 N4 Sutton Maddock Shrops
19 L7 Sutton Mallet Somset
21 J9 Sutton Mandeville Wilts
81 Q6 Sutton Manor St Hel
45 R6 Sutton Marsh Herefs
20 B10 Sutton Montis Somset
93 K4 Sutton-on-Hull C KuH
87 P4 Sutton on Sea Lincs
98 B8 Sutton-on-the-Forest N York
71 N8 Sutton on the Hill Derbys
85 N7 Sutton on Trent Notts
11 Q8 Sutton Poyntz Dorset
74 G8 Sutton St Edmund Lincs
74 G7 Sutton St James Lincs
45 Q5 Sutton St Nicholas Herefs
22 E7 Sutton Scotney Hants
22 E6 Sutton Scotney Services Hants
38 D10 Sutton Street Kent
48 B7 Sutton-under-Brailes Warwks
97 Q4 Sutton-under-Whitestonecliffe N York
98 E11 Sutton upon Derwent E R Yk
26 D2 Sutton Valence Kent
20 H6 Sutton Veny Wilts
20 G11 Sutton Waldron Dorset
82 B9 Sutton Weaver Ches W
19 Q3 Sutton Wick BaNES
34 E6 Sutton Wick Oxon
87 L5 Swaby Lincs
71 P11 Swadlincote Derbys
75 R9 Swaffham Norfk
63 J8 Swaffham Bulbeck Cambs
63 J8 Swaffham Prior Cambs
77 K5 Swafield Norfk
104 E10 Swainby N York
45 P6 Swainshill Herefs
77 J11 Swainsthorpe Norfk
32 E11 Swainswick BaNES
48 C7 Swalcliffe Oxon
39 K8 Swalecliffe Kent
93 L10 Swallow Lincs
86 B7 Swallow Beck Lincs
21 J9 Swallowcliffe Wilts
23 K2 Swallowfield Wokham
84 G3 Swallow Nest Rothm
51 P11 Swallows Cross Essex
22 D4 Swampton Hants
12 H9 Swanage Dorset
49 M9 Swanbourne Bucks
30 G11 Swanbridge V Glam
57 N6 Swancote Shrops
82 F10 Swan Green Ches W
92 G5 Swanland E R Yk
37 M7 Swanley Kent
37 M7 Swanley Village Kent
22 G11 Swanmore Hants
72 C7 Swannington Leics
76 G8 Swannington Norfk
86 C7 Swanpool Garden Suburb Lincs
37 P6 Swanscombe Kent
29 J6 Swansea Swans
28 G6 *Swansea Airport Swans*
29 J5 Swansea Crematorium Swans
28 H5 Swansea West Services Swans
52 E6 Swan Street Essex
77 K6 Swanton Abbot Norfk
76 E8 Swanton Morley Norfk
76 E5 Swanton Novers Norfk
38 E10 Swanton Street Kent
58 E6 Swan Village Sandw
84 F10 Swanwick Derbys
14 F5 Swanwick Hants
73 Q2 Swarby Lincs
77 J11 Swardeston Norfk
72 B5 Swarkestone Derbys
119 N10 Swarland Nthumb
22 G7 Swarraton Hants
96 G11 Swartha C Brad
94 F5 Swarthmoor Cumb
74 B3 Swaton Lincs
62 E7 Swavesey Cambs
13 N5 Sway Hants
73 P6 Swayfield Lincs
22 D11 Swaythling C Sotn
46 B2 Sweet Green Worcs
9 L5 Sweetham Devon
25 M5 Sweethaws E Susx
26 C2 Sweetlands Corner Kent
5 K2 Sweets Cnwll
4 H9 Sweetshouse Cnwll
65 L9 Swefling Suffk
72 B8 Swepstone Leics
48 C8 Swerford Oxon
82 H11 Swettenham Ches E
30 H5 Swffryd Blae G
26 E3 Swift's Green Kent
64 H11 Swilland Suffk
88 F4 Swillbrook Lancs
91 K4 Swillington Leeds
17 L5 Swimbridge Devon
17 L5 Swimbridge Newland Devon
33 Q2 Swinbrook Oxon
90 G5 Swincliffe Kirk
97 K9 Swincliffe N York
17 M3 Swincombe Devon
96 C10 Swinden N York
85 Q8 Swinderby Lincs
46 H9 Swindon Gloucs
119 J11 Swindon Nthumb
58 C6 Swindon Staffs
33 M8 Swindon Swindn
93 K3 Swine E R Yk
92 C6 Swinefleet E R Yk
32 C11 Swineford S Glos
61 N7 Swineshead Bed
74 D2 Swineshead Lincs
74 D2 Swineshead Bridge Lincs
167 M9 Swiney Highld
60 C5 Swinford Leics
34 D3 Swinford Oxon
27 M3 Swingfield Minnis Kent
27 M3 Swingfield Street Kent
52 G2 Swingleton Green Suffk
119 P5 Swinhoe Nthumb
93 M11 Swinhope Lincs
96 F3 Swinithwaite N York
46 C6 Swinmore Common Herefs
71 L5 Swinscoe Staffs
100 H6 Swinside Cumb
73 Q6 Swinstead Lincs
86 E4 Swinthorpe Lincs
129 L10 Swinton Border
97 K5 Swinton N York
98 F6 Swinton N York
91 M11 Swinton Rothm
82 G4 Swinton Salfd
72 F8 Swithland Leics
155 Q4 Swordale Highld
145 N9 Swordland Highld
166 B4 Swordly Highld
82 E8 Sworton Heath Ches E
54 F11 Swyddffynnon Cerdgn
35 J6 Swyncombe Oxon
70 F7 Swynnerton Staffs
11 L7 Swyre Dorset
68 H9 Sycharth Powys
55 M9 Sychnant Powys
55 M3 Sychtyn Powys
69 K3 Sydallt Wrexhm
33 J2 Syde Gloucs
37 J6 Sydenham Gt Lon
35 K4 Sydenham Oxon
5 Q6 Sydenham Damerel Devon
23 Q8 Sydenhurst Surrey
76 A5 Syderstone Norfk
11 N5 Sydling St Nicholas Dorset
22 E3 Sydmonton Hants
57 Q3 Sydnal Lane Shrops
85 M11 Syerston Notts
67 L5 Sygun Copper Mine Gwynd
89 P7 Syke Rochdl
91 Q7 Sykehouse Donc
65 J6 Syleham Suffk
28 F3 Sylen Carmth
169 s7 Symbister Shet
125 K11 Symington S Ayrs
116 D3 Symington S Lans
11 J6 Symondsbury Dorset
45 R11 Symonds Yat Herefs
90 F3 Sympson Green C Brad
10 H4 Synderford Dorset
42 H4 Synod Inn Cerdgn
165 Q8 Syre Highld
47 K10 Syreford Gloucs
48 H6 Syresham Nhants
72 G8 Syston Leics
73 N2 Syston Lincs
58 B11 Sytchampton Worcs
60 H7 Sywell Nhants

T

82 F9 Tabley Hill Ches E
48 E11 Tackley Oxon
64 G2 Tacolneston Norfk
91 M2 Tadcaster N York
83 P10 Taddington Derbys
47 L8 Taddington Gloucs
16 H8 Taddiport Devon
22 H2 Tadley Hants
62 C11 Tadlow Cambs
48 C7 Tadmarton Oxon
32 D10 Tadwick BaNES
36 F9 Tadworth Surrey
30 F2 Tafarnaubach Blae G
41 L4 Tafarn-y-bwlch Pembks
68 G2 Tafarn-y-Gelyn Denbgs
30 F8 Taff's Well Rhondd
55 K4 Tafolwern Powys
29 L7 Taibach Neath
162 H10 Tain Highld
167 M3 Tain Highld
168 g7 Tairbeart W Isls
44 D9 Tai'r Bull Powys
51 N6 Takeley Essex
51 M6 Takeley Street Essex
44 F8 Talachddu Powys
80 G8 Talacre Flints
9 Q5 Talaton Devon
40 F8 Talbenny Pembks
30 D8 Talbot Green Rhondd
13 J6 Talbot Village Bmouth
10 B5 Taleford Devon
55 L4 Talerddig Powys
42 H4 Talgarreg Cerdgn
44 H8 Talgarth Powys
152 E11 Talisker Highld
70 E4 Talke Staffs
70 E4 Talke Pits Staffs
111 L9 Talkin Cumb
154 B3 Talladale Highld
116 G6 Talla Linnfoots Border
114 H8 Tallaminnock S Ayrs
69 M6 Tallarn Green Wrexhm
100 F3 Tallentire Cumb
43 M8 Talley Carmth
74 A9 Tallington Lincs
69 J5 Tallwrn Wrexhm
165 N4 Talmine Highld
42 F9 Talog Carmth
43 K3 Talsarn Cerdgn
67 L7 Talsarnau Gwynd
4 E8 Talskiddy Cnwll
78 H9 Talwrn IoA
69 L5 Talwrn Wrexhm
54 F7 Tal-y-bont Cerdgn
79 P11 Tal-y-Bont Conwy
67 K10 Tal-y-bont Gwynd
79 L10 Tal-y-bont Gwynd
44 G10 Talybont-on-Usk Powys
79 P10 Tal-y-Cafn Conwy
45 N11 Tal-y-coed Mons
30 D9 Tal-y-garn Rhondd
54 G3 Tal-y-llyn Gwynd
66 H4 Talysarn Gwynd
31 J4 Tal-y-Waun Torfn
55 J4 Talywern Powys
82 D4 Tamer Lane End Wigan
6 D6 Tamerton Foliot C Plym
59 K4 Tamworth Staffs
74 G2 Tamworth Green Lincs
59 K4 Tamworth Services Warwks
97 Q9 Tancred N York
40 G5 Tancredston Pembks
37 J10 Tandridge Surrey
113 J9 Tanfield Dur
113 J10 Tanfield Lea Dur
41 J7 Tangiers Pembks
22 B4 Tangley Hants
15 P5 Tangmere W Susx
168 b17 Tangusdale W Isls
102 G9 Tan Hill N York
169 e6 Tankerness Ork
91 J11 Tankersley Barns
39 K8 Tankerton Kent
167 P7 Tannach Highld
151 K11 Tannachie Abers
142 H6 Tannadice Angus
58 G10 Tanner's Green Worcs
65 J8 Tannington Suffk
126 C5 Tannochside N Lans
84 D9 Tansley Derbys
61 N2 Tansor Nhants
113 J10 Tantobie Dur
104 F8 Tanton N York
58 D10 Tanwood Worcs
58 H10 Tanworth in Arden Warwks
67 M6 Tan-y-Bwlch Gwynd
68 C2 Tan-y-fron Conwy
69 J4 Tan-y-fron Wrexhm
67 M5 Tan-y-grisiau Gwynd
42 E5 Tan-y-groes Cerdgn
168 e9 Taobh Tuath W Isls
35 P8 Taplow Bucks
123 L9 Tarbert Ag & B
123 Q6 Tarbert Ag & B
168 g7 Tarbert W Isls
132 C7 Tarbet Ag & B
145 N9 Tarbet Highld
164 E7 Tarbet Highld
81 P7 Tarbock Green Knows
114 H2 Tarbolton S Ayrs
127 J6 Tarbrax S Lans
58 E11 Tardebigge Worcs
142 H2 Tarfside Angus
150 D7 Tarland Abers
88 F6 Tarleton Lancs
88 E8 Tarlscough Lancs
33 J5 Tarlton Gloucs
19 L4 Tarnock Somset
109 P11 Tarns Cumb
95 J2 Tarnside Cumb
69 Q2 Tarporley Ches W
17 R5 Tarr Somset
12 F4 Tarrant Crawford Dorset
12 F2 Tarrant Gunville Dorset
12 F2 Tarrant Hinton Dorset
12 F4 Tarrant Keyneston Dorset
12 F3 Tarrant Launceston Dorset
12 F3 Tarrant Monkton Dorset
12 F3 Tarrant Rawston Dorset
12 F3 Tarrant Rushton Dorset
25 K10 Tarring Neville E Susx
46 B6 Tarrington Herefs
145 J5 Tarskavaig Highld
159 L11 Tarves Abers
81 P11 Tarvin Ches W
81 P11 Tarvin Sands Ches W
64 H2 Tasburgh Norfk
57 M6 Tasley Shrops
48 C10 Taston Oxon
71 N10 Tatenhill Staffs
49 M5 Tathall End M Keyn
95 N7 Tatham Lancs
87 K4 Tathwell Lincs
37 K9 Tatsfield Surrey
69 N3 Tattenhall Ches W
76 B6 Tatterford Norfk
76 A6 Tattersett Norfk
86 H9 Tattershall Lincs
86 G9 Tattershall Bridge Lincs
86 H9 Tattershall Thorpe Lincs
53 K4 Tattingstone Suffk
53 K4 Tattingstone White Horse Suffk
10 G3 Tatworth Somset
157 R8 Tauchers Moray
18 H10 Taunton Somset
18 H10 Taunton Deane Crematorium Somset
18 G10 Taunton Deane Services Somset
76 H9 Taverham Norfk
51 N7 Taverners Green Essex
41 N8 Tavernspite Pembks
6 D4 Tavistock Devon
8 G5 Taw Green Devon
17 K6 Tawstock Devon
83 M9 Taxal Derbys
131 L3 Taychreggan Hotel Ag & B
141 J5 Tay Forest Park P & K
123 L10 Tayinloan Ag & B
46 D10 Taynton Gloucs
33 P2 Taynton Oxon
139 J11 Taynuilt Ag & B
135 M2 Tayport Fife
130 E10 Tayvallich Ag & B
86 G2 Tealby Lincs
142 G10 Tealing Angus
113 K9 Team Valley Gatesd
145 L6 Teangue Highld
155 Q5 Teanord Highld
102 B10 Tebay Cumb
102 B9 Tebay Services Cumb
49 Q9 Tebworth C Beds
9 K6 Tedburn St Mary Devon
47 J8 Teddington Gloucs
36 E6 Teddington Gt Lon
46 C3 Tedstone Delamere Herefs
46 C3 Tedstone Wafer Herefs
104 F6 Teesport R & Cl
104 E7 Teesside Crematorium Middsb
104 E7 Teesside Park S on T
60 E6 Teeton Nhants
21 J8 Teffont Evias Wilts
21 J8 Teffont Magna Wilts
41 P4 Tegryn Pembks
73 M7 Teigh Rutlnd
8 G7 Teigncombe Devon
7 M4 Teigngrace Devon
7 N4 Teignmouth Devon
117 N9 Teindside Border
57 M3 Telford Wrekin
57 N2 Telford Crematorium Wrekin
57 N3 Telford Services Shrops
20 F3 Tellisford Somset
25 K10 Telscombe E Susx
25 K10 Telscombe Cliffs E Susx
140 G6 Tempar P & K
109 N3 Templand D & G
5 J7 Temple Cnwll
127 Q6 Temple Mdloth
59 K9 Temple Balsall Solhll
43 K4 Temple Bar Cerdgn
20 B3 Temple Cloud BaNES
20 D10 Templecombe Somset
63 L10 Temple End Suffk
27 N3 Temple Ewell Kent
47 M3 Temple Grafton Warwks
47 L9 Temple Guiting Gloucs
91 Q6 Temple Hirst N York
84 F7 Temple Normanton Derbys
151 L11 Temple of Fiddes Abers
102 B5 Temple Sowerby Cumb
9 L2 Templeton Devon
41 M8 Templeton Pembks
112 H10 Templetown Dur
61 Q10 Tempsford C Beds
57 K11 Tenbury Wells Worcs
41 M10 Tenby Pembks
53 K7 Tendring Essex
53 K6 Tendring Green Essex
53 K6 Tendring Heath Essex
75 L11 Ten Mile Bank Norfk
53 J7 Tenpenny Heath Essex
26 E5 Tenterden Kent
52 C8 Terling Essex
69 R11 Tern Wrekin
70 A8 Ternhill Shrops
109 K5 Terregles D & G
98 D6 Terrington N York
75 L6 Terrington St Clement Norfk
75 K8 Terrington St John Norfk
58 H10 Terry's Green Warwks
38 B11 Teston Kent
14 C4 Testwood Hants
32 G6 Tetbury Gloucs
32 G5 Tetbury Upton Gloucs
69 L8 Tetchill Shrops
5 N2 Tetcott Devon
87 K6 Tetford Lincs
93 P10 Tetney Lincs
93 P10 Tetney Lock Lincs
35 J4 Tetsworth Oxon
58 C4 Tettenhall Wolves
58 C5 Tettenhall Wood Wolves
84 G8 Teversal Notts
62 G9 Teversham Cambs
117 N9 Teviothead Border
50 G8 Tewin Herts
50 G7 Tewin Wood Herts
46 G8 Tewkesbury Gloucs
38 G9 Teynham Kent
90 F3 Thackley C Brad
100 F6 Thackthwaite Cumb
101 M5 Thackthwaite Cumb
24 D7 Thakeham W Susx
35 K3 Thame Oxon
36 E7 Thames Ditton Surrey
37 L4 Thamesmead Gt Lon
39 Q8 Thanet Crematorium Kent
39 K10 Thanington Kent
116 D3 Thankerton S Lans
64 H3 Tharston Norfk
34 F11 Thatcham W Berk
81 Q6 Thatto Heath St Hel
51 P4 Thaxted Essex
97 M3 Theakston N York
92 E7 Thealby N Linc
19 N5 Theale Somset
34 H10 Theale W Berk
93 J3 Thearne E R Yk
70 E3 The Bank Ches E
57 L5 The Bank Shrops
33 K4 The Beeches Gloucs
65 N8 Theberton Suffk
71 J9 The Blythe Staffs
56 F5 The Bog Shrops
47 J3 The Bourne Worcs
153 J11 The Braes Highld
58 C6 The Bratch Staffs
45 P2 The Broad Herefs
128 H5 The Brunt E Loth

80 e4 The Bungalow IoM
57 Q11 The Burf Worcs
46 G11 The Butts Gloucs
32 H3 The Camp Gloucs
69 N6 The Chequer Wrexhm
61 P9 The City Bed
35 L5 The City Bucks
47 Q9 The Common Oxon
21 P8 The Common Wilts
33 K7 The Common Wilts
26 B3 The Corner Kent
60 F9 The Counties Crematorium Nhants
80 d2 The Cronk IoM
60 E3 Theddingworth Leics
87 N3 Theddlethorpe All Saints Lincs
87 N3 Theddlethorpe St Helen Lincs
125 J7 The Den N Ayrs
32 B2 The Forest of Dean Crematorium Gloucs
45 L3 The Forge Herefs
26 H4 The Forstal Kent
70 B8 The Fouralls Shrops
38 E8 The Garden of England Crematorium Kent
94 D4 The Green Cumb
52 C8 The Green Essex
105 L9 The Green N York
20 G8 The Green Wilts
46 G6 The Grove Worcs
24 C4 The Haven W Susx
46 F9 The Haw Gloucs
104 F4 The Headland Hartpl
94 D4 The Hill Cumb
35 M9 The Holt Wokham
45 Q2 The Hundred Herefs
9 J2 Thelbridge Cross Devon
26 G5 The Leacon Kent
35 P4 The Lee Bucks
80 e1 The Lhen IoM
125 P6 The Linn Crematorium E Rens
64 E6 Thelnetham Suffk
157 Q5 The Lochs Moray
64 H5 Thelveton Norfk
82 E7 Thelwall Warrtn
82 H6 The Manchester Crematorium Manch
56 E5 The Marsh Powys
76 F7 Themelthorpe Norfk
113 K10 The Middles Dur
26 C6 The Moor Kent
28 H7 The Mumbles Swans
125 Q7 The Murray S Lans
46 G8 The Mythe Gloucs
31 P3 The Narth Mons
151 J8 The Neuk Abers
48 F6 Thenford Nhants
33 K11 Theobald's Green Wilts
23 N5 The Park Crematorium Hants
32 D5 The Quarry Gloucs
26 E3 The Quarter Kent
46 H10 The Reddings Gloucs
50 H3 Therfield Herts
44 H8 The Rhôs Powys
91 Q10 The Rose Hill Crematorium Donc
133 M3 The Ross P & K
23 N5 The Sands Surrey
32 F10 The Shoe Wilts
57 M5 The Smithies Shrops
62 G11 The Spike Cambs
59 L10 The Spring Warwks
31 J5 The Square Torfn
37 P11 The Stair Kent
26 F6 The Stocks Kent
23 L7 The Straits Hants
20 H3 The Strand Wilts
64 B5 Thetford Norfk
63 P3 Thetford Forest Park
101 L2 Thethwaite Cumb
2 F6 The Towans Cnwll
50 D6 The Vale Crematorium Luton
45 Q5 The Vauld Herefs
57 N3 The Wyke Shrops
51 K11 Theydon Bois Essex
92 A2 Thicket Priory N York
32 F10 Thickwood Wilts
86 H6 Thimbleby Lincs
104 D11 Thimbleby N York
81 K8 Thingwall Wirral
97 Q5 Thirkleby N York
97 Q4 Thirlby N York
128 F10 Thirlestane Border
97 K3 Thirn N York
97 P4 Thirsk N York
93 L4 Thirtleby E R Yk
88 E3 Thistleton Lancs
73 N7 Thistleton Rutlnd
63 L5 Thistley Green Suffk
98 G8 Thixendale N York
112 E5 Thockrington Nthumb
74 H9 Tholomas Drove Cambs
97 Q7 Tholthorpe N York
41 M9 Thomas Chapel Pembks
101 M2 Thomas Close Cumb
158 E10 Thomastown Abers
47 L2 Thomas Town Warwks
64 C2 Thompson Norfk
37 Q6 Thong Kent
96 F3 Thoralby N York
85 K6 Thoresby Notts
87 N5 Thoresthorpe Lincs
93 L11 Thoresway Lincs
93 M11 Thorganby Lincs
92 A2 Thorganby N York
105 K11 Thorgill N York
65 N7 Thorington Suffk
52 H4 Thorington Street Suffk
96 E10 Thorlby N York
51 L7 Thorley Herts
14 C9 Thorley IoW
51 L6 Thorley Houses Herts
14 C9 Thorley Street IoW
97 Q6 Thormanby N York
104 E7 Thornaby-on-Tees S on T
76 F4 Thornage Norfk
49 K8 Thornborough Bucks
97 L5 Thornborough N York
90 F4 Thornbury C Brad
16 G10 Thornbury Devon
46 B3 Thornbury Herefs
32 B6 Thornbury S Glos
110 E10 Thornby Cumb
60 E5 Thornby Nhants
71 J3 Thorncliff Staffs
94 D6 Thorncliffe Crematorium Cumb
10 H4 Thorncombe Dorset
23 Q6 Thorncombe Street Surrey
61 Q11 Thorncott Green C Beds
14 D10 Thorncross IoW
64 G8 Thorndon Suffk
8 D6 Thorndon Cross Devon
92 A8 Thorne Donc
19 P11 Thorne Coffin Somset
7 K5 Thornecroft Devon
16 G8 Thornehillhead Devon
91 K2 Thorner Leeds
58 G4 Thornes Staffs
91 J7 Thornes Wakefd
18 F10 Thorne St Margaret Somset
36 B5 Thorney Bucks
74 E10 Thorney C Pete
85 Q6 Thorney Notts
19 M10 Thorney Somset
13 M5 Thorney Hill Hants
15 L6 Thorney Island W Susx
74 F10 Thorney Toll Cambs
19 J10 Thornfalcon Somset
11 N2 Thornford Dorset
111 Q7 Thorngrafton Nthumb
19 L8 Thorngrove Somset
93 M5 Thorngumbald E R Yk
75 P2 Thornham Norfk
64 G7 Thornham Magna Suffk
64 G7 Thornham Parva Suffk
73 R10 Thornhaugh C Pete
14 E4 Thornhill C Sotn
30 G8 Thornhill Caerph
100 D9 Thornhill Cumb
116 B11 Thornhill D & G
83 Q8 Thornhill Derbys
90 H7 Thornhill Kirk
133 K7 Thornhill Stirlg
30 G8 Thornhill Crematorium Cardif
90 G7 Thornhill Lees Kirk
90 F6 Thornhills Calder
99 N8 Thornholme E R Yk
12 E4 Thornicombe Dorset
118 G4 Thornington Nthumb
103 M3 Thornley Dur
104 C3 Thornley Dur
112 B9 Thornley Gate Nthumb
125 P6 Thornliebank E Rens
63 M9 Thorns Suffk
83 M7 Thornsett Derbys
82 G8 Thorns Green Ches E
100 H5 Thornthwaite Cumb
97 J9 Thornthwaite N York
142 F8 Thornton Angus
49 K7 Thornton Bucks
90 D4 Thornton C Brad
98 F11 Thornton E R Yk
134 H8 Thornton Fife
88 C2 Thornton Lancs
72 D9 Thornton Leics
86 H7 Thornton Lincs
104 E8 Thornton Middsb
129 P10 Thornton Nthumb
40 H9 Thornton Pembks
81 L4 Thornton Sefton
93 J7 Thornton Curtis N Linc
81 L4 Thornton Garden of Rest Crematorium Sefton
125 P6 Thorntonhall S Lans
36 H7 Thornton Heath Gt Lon
81 L8 Thornton Hough Wirral
96 D11 Thornton-in-Craven N York
95 P6 Thornton in Lonsdale N York
97 N2 Thornton-le-Beans N York
98 D7 Thornton-le-Clay N York
98 G4 Thornton le Dale N York
92 H11 Thornton le Moor Lincs
97 N3 Thornton-le-Moor N York
81 N10 Thornton-le-Moors Ches W
97 P3 Thornton-le-Street N York
129 K5 Thorntonloch E Loth
96 E3 Thornton Rust N York
97 J3 Thornton Steward N York
97 K3 Thornton Watlass N York
51 L10 Thornwood Common Essex
128 G10 Thornydykes Border
101 L6 Thornythwaite Cumb
73 K2 Thoroton Notts
97 P11 Thorp Arch Leeds
71 M4 Thorpe Derbys
99 K11 Thorpe E R Yk
87 N4 Thorpe Lincs
96 F8 Thorpe N York
65 N2 Thorpe Norfk
85 N11 Thorpe Notts
36 B7 Thorpe Surrey
64 H6 Thorpe Abbotts Norfk
72 E7 Thorpe Acre Leics
73 K6 Thorpe Arnold Leics
91 M7 Thorpe Audlin Wakefd
98 H6 Thorpe Bassett N York
38 F4 Thorpe Bay Sthend
73 M11 Thorpe by Water Rutlnd
91 K11 Thorpe Common Rothm
59 L3 Thorpe Constantine Staffs
77 K9 Thorpe End Norfk
53 L7 Thorpe Green Essex
88 H6 Thorpe Green Lancs
64 C11 Thorpe Green Suffk
91 K11 Thorpe Hesley Rothm
91 P8 Thorpe in Balne Donc
60 F2 Thorpe Langton Leics
104 C5 Thorpe Larches Dur
36 B6 Thorpe Lea Surrey
86 B4 Thorpe le Fallows Lincs
53 L7 Thorpe-le-Soken Essex
92 D2 Thorpe le Street E R Yk
60 H5 Thorpe Malsor Nhants
48 F6 Thorpe Mandeville Nhants
77 J4 Thorpe Market Norfk
76 H8 Thorpe Marriot Norfk
64 C11 Thorpe Morieux Suffk
65 P10 Thorpeness Suffk
91 J5 Thorpe on the Hill Leeds
86 B7 Thorpe on the Hill Lincs
36 B7 Thorpe Park Surrey
77 K10 Thorpe St Andrew Norfk
87 N8 Thorpe St Peter Lincs
84 H4 Thorpe Salvin Rothm
73 J8 Thorpe Satchville Leics
104 C6 Thorpe Thewles S on T
86 F9 Thorpe Tilney Lincs
97 Q9 Thorpe Underwood N York
60 G4 Thorpe Underwood Nhants
61 M4 Thorpe Waterville Nhants
91 P4 Thorpe Willoughby N York
75 M9 Thorpland Norfk
53 J8 Thorrington Essex
9 M4 Thorverton Devon
50 D7 Thrales End C Beds
64 G6 Thrandeston Suffk
61 L5 Thrapston Nhants
100 G3 Threapland Cumb
96 E8 Threapland N York
69 M6 Threapwood Ches W
71 J6 Threapwood Staffs
71 J6 Threapwood Head Staffs
114 F6 Threave S Ayrs
108 F8 Threave Castle D & G
45 Q10 Three Ashes Herefs
24 G3 Three Bridges W Susx
3 J4 Three Burrows Cnwll
26 D4 Three Chimneys Kent
44 H7 Three Cocks Powys
52 C6 Three Counties Crematorium Essex
28 G6 Three Crosses Swans
25 P6 Three Cups Corner E Susx
46 C2 Three Gates Worcs
77 L8 Threehammer Common Norfk
5 L4 Three Hammers Cnwll
75 K10 Three Holes Norfk
74 A3 Threekingham Lincs
25 Q4 Three Leg Cross E Susx
13 J3 Three Legged Cross Dorset
35 K11 Three Mile Cross Wokham
3 K4 Threemilestone Cnwll
127 K2 Three Miletown W Loth
26 D9 Three Oaks E Susx
101 K5 Threlkeld Cumb
51 L9 Threshers Bush Essex
96 E8 Threshfield N York
77 P9 Thrigby Norfk
102 H6 Thringarth Dur
72 C7 Thringstone Leics
97 M2 Thrintoft N York
62 F11 Thriplow Cambs
84 H3 Throapham Rothm
74 G9 Throckenhalt Lincs
50 H4 Throcking Herts
113 J7 Throckley N u Ty
47 J4 Throckmorton Worcs
13 K5 Throop Bmouth
12 D6 Throop Dorset
112 H3 Throphill Nthumb
119 K10 Thropton Nthumb
133 P9 Throsk Stirlg
32 H3 Througham Gloucs
109 J4 Throughgate D & G
8 G6 Throwleigh Devon
38 G10 Throwley Kent
38 G11 Throwley Forstal Kent
72 E4 Thrumpton Notts
85 M4 Thrumpton Notts
167 P7 Thrumster Highld
93 P9 Thrunscoe NE Lin
119 L8 Thrunton Nthumb
33 Q5 Thrup Oxon
32 G4 Thrupp Gloucs
48 E11 Thrupp Oxon
8 B7 Thrushelton Devon
72 H7 Thrussington Leics
21 Q5 Thruxton Hants
45 N8 Thruxton Herefs
91 M11 Thrybergh Rothm
72 C4 Thulston Derbys
38 C4 Thundersley Essex
72 F8 Thurcaston Leics
84 G3 Thurcroft Rothm
16 D9 Thurdon Cnwll
76 H5 Thurgarton Norfk
85 L11 Thurgarton Notts
90 H10 Thurgoland Barns
72 E11 Thurlaston Leics
59 Q10 Thurlaston Warwks
19 J10 Thurlbear Somset
74 A7 Thurlby Lincs
86 B8 Thurlby Lincs
87 N5 Thurlby Lincs
61 P9 Thurleigh Bed
6 H10 Thurlestone Devon
19 J8 Thurloxton Somset
90 G10 Thurlstone Barns
65 N2 Thurlton Norfk
70 E3 Thurlwood Ches E
72 G9 Thurmaston Leics
72 G10 Thurnby Leics
77 N8 Thurne Norfk
38 D10 Thurnham Kent
61 N4 Thurning Nhants
76 F6 Thurning Norfk
91 M9 Thurnscoe Barns
37 N5 Thurrock Services Thurr
110 F10 Thursby Cumb
89 Q4 Thursden Lancs
76 D5 Thursford Norfk
23 P7 Thursley Surrey
167 K3 Thurso Highld
81 J8 Thurstaston Wirral
64 C8 Thurston Suffk
90 B9 Thurston Clough Oldham
110 F9 Thurstonfield Cumb
90 F8 Thurstonland Kirk
64 C9 Thurston Planch Suffk
77 L11 Thurton Norfk
71 N7 Thurvaston Derbys
76 E10 Thuxton Norfk
102 G11 Thwaite N York
64 G8 Thwaite Suffk
94 G2 Thwaite Head Cumb
90 D2 Thwaites C Brad
65 L2 Thwaite St Mary Norfk
90 D2 Thwaites Brow C Brad
99 L6 Thwing E R Yk
134 C3 Tibbermore P & K
116 B11 Tibbers D & G
46 E10 Tibberton Gloucs
46 H3 Tibberton Worcs
70 B10 Tibberton Wrekin
117 J6 Tibbie Shiels Inn Border
64 G4 Tibenham Norfk
84 F8 Tibshelf Derbys
99 K9 Tibthorpe E R Yk
25 Q4 Ticehurst E Susx
22 G8 Tichborne Hants
73 P9 Tickencote Rutlnd
31 N10 Tickenham N Som
49 N6 Tickford End M Keyn
85 J2 Tickhill Donc
56 H6 Ticklerton Shrops
72 B6 Ticknall Derbys
93 J2 Tickton E R Yk
58 H9 Tidbury Green Solhll
21 Q3 Tidcombe Wilts
34 H4 Tiddington Oxon
47 P3 Tiddington Warwks
32 G9 Tiddleywink Wilts
25 P4 Tidebrook E Susx
5 P10 Tideford Cnwll
5 N9 Tideford Cross Cnwll
31 Q5 Tidenham Gloucs
83 Q9 Tideswell Derbys
34 H10 Tidmarsh W Berk
47 Q7 Tidmington Warwks
21 L11 Tidpit Hants
21 P5 Tidworth Wilts
40 H8 Tiers Cross Pembks
49 K4 Tiffield Nhants
143 J5 Tigerton Angus
168 c10 Tigh a Ghearraidh W Isls
168 c10 Tigharry W Isls
124 B3 Tighnabruaich Ag & B
7 K6 Tigley Devon
61 N7 Tilbrook Cambs
37 P5 Tilbury Thurr
52 B3 Tilbury Green Essex
52 C3 Tilbury Juxta Clare Essex
59 J7 Tile Cross Birm
59 L9 Tile Hill Covtry
59 J9 Tilehouse Green Solhll
35 J10 Tilehurst Readg
23 N6 Tilford Surrey
24 G4 Tilgate W Susx
24 G4 Tilgate Forest Row W Susx
19 Q7 Tilham Street Somset
46 C8 Tillers Green Gloucs
133 Q8 Tillicoultry Clacks
126 E8 Tillietudlem S Lans
52 G11 Tillingham Essex
45 P6 Tillington Herefs
23 Q10 Tillington W Susx
45 P5 Tillington Common Herefs
150 H6 Tillybirloch Abers
150 G5 Tillyfourie Abers
151 M3 Tillygreig Abers
134 E6 Tillyrie P & K
39 P11 Tilmanstone Kent
75 L7 Tilney All Saints Norfk
75 L7 Tilney High End Norfk
75 K8 Tilney St Lawrence Norfk
21 K5 Tilshead Wilts
69 P7 Tilstock Shrops
69 N4 Tilston Ches W
69 Q3 Tilstone Bank Ches W
69 Q2 Tilstone Fearnall Ches W
49 Q10 Tilsworth C Beds
73 J9 Tilton on the Hill Leics
32 F5 Tiltups End Gloucs
51 N5 Tilty Essex
86 F9 Timberland Lincs
70 F2 Timbersbrook Ches E
18 C6 Timberscombe Somset
97 J10 Timble N York
18 C9 Timewell Devon
110 F6 Timpanheck D & G
82 G7 Timperley Traffd
20 C3 Timsbury BaNES
22 B10 Timsbury Hants
168 f4 Timsgarry W Isls
168 f4 Timsgearraidh W Isls
64 B8 Timworth Suffk
64 B8 Timworth Green Suffk
12 C6 Tincleton Dorset
111 M9 Tindale Cumb
103 N5 Tindale Crescent Dur
49 J8 Tingewick Bucks
90 H5 Tingley Leeds
50 B4 Tingrith C Beds
169 r9 Tingwall Airport Shet
5 P4 Tinhay Devon
22 D5 Tinker's Hill Hants
84 C8 Tinkersley Derbys
84 F2 Tinsley Sheff
24 G3 Tinsley Green W Susx
4 H4 Tintagel Cnwll
4 G4 Tintagel Castle Cnwll
31 P4 Tintern Abbey Mons
31 P4 Tintern Parva Mons
19 N11 Tintinhull Somset
83 M5 Tintwistle Derbys
109 M4 Tinwald D & G
73 Q9 Tinwell Rutlnd
17 P2 Tippacott Devon
75 K11 Tipp's End Norfk
13 N5 Tiptoe Hants
58 E6 Tipton Sandw
58 E6 Tipton Green Sandw
10 B6 Tipton St John Devon
52 E8 Tiptree Essex
52 E8 Tiptree Heath Essex
44 B6 Tirabad Powys
136 C7 Tiree Ag & B
136 C7 Tiree Airport Ag & B
123 M7 Tiretigan Ag & B
46 F9 Tirley Gloucs
30 F4 Tirphil Caerph
101 P5 Tirril Cumb
69 J3 Tir-y-fron Flints
20 H9 Tisbury Wilts
24 C4 Tisman's Common W Susx
71 M4 Tissington Derbys
16 C6 Titchberry Devon
14 F5 Titchfield Hants
14 F5 Titchfield Common Hants
61 M5 Titchmarsh Nhants
75 Q2 Titchwell Norfk
72 H3 Tithby Notts
45 L2 Titley Herefs
50 F5 Titmore Green Herts
37 K10 Titsey Surrey
16 C11 Titson Cnwll
70 F7 Tittensor Staffs
76 B7 Tittleshall Norfk
58 B11 Titton Worcs
69 Q2 Tiverton Ches W
9 N2 Tiverton Devon
64 H4 Tivetshall St Margaret Norfk
64 H4 Tivetshall St Mary Norfk
18 B5 Tivington Somset
90 H9 Tivy Dale Barns
70 H10 Tixall Staffs
73 P10 Tixover Rutlnd
169 q12 Toab Shet
84 E9 Toadhole Derbys
84 D10 Toadmoor Derbys
137 N4 Tobermory Ag & B
130 E6 Toberonochy Ag & B
168 c14 Tobha Mor W Isls
158 G11 Tocher Abers
158 D4 Tochieneal Moray
33 K9 Tockenham Wilts
33 K8 Tockenham Wick Wilts
104 H7 Tocketts R & Cl
89 K6 Tockholes Bl w D
32 B7 Tockington S Glos
97 Q10 Tockwith N York
20 E11 Todber Dorset
119 M11 Todburn Nthumb
50 B5 Toddington C Beds
47 K8 Toddington Gloucs
50 B5 Toddington Services C Beds
50 F5 Todds Green Herts
47 P7 Todenham Gloucs
142 G10 Todhills Angus
110 G8 Todhills Cumb
103 P4 Todhills Dur
110 G8 Todhills Services Cumb
89 Q6 Todmorden Calder
84 G4 Todwick Rothm
62 E9 Toft Cambs
82 G9 Toft Ches E
73 R7 Toft Lincs
169 r6 Toft Shet
59 Q10 Toft Warwks
103 N5 Toft Hill Dur
86 H8 Toft Hill Lincs
65 N3 Toft Monks Norfk
86 D3 Toft next Newton Lincs
76 B6 Toftrees Norfk
76 D9 Toftwood Norfk
119 P10 Togston Nthumb
145 K5 Tokavaig Highld
35 K9 Tokers Green Oxon
168 k3 Tolastadh W Isls
4 E10 Toldish Cnwll
18 F8 Tolland Somset
21 J11 Tollard Farnham Dorset
20 H11 Tollard Royal Wilts
91 P9 Toll Bar Donc
59 N9 Tollbar End Covtry
11 M5 Toller Fratrum Dorset
11 M5 Toller Porcorum Dorset
97 R8 Tollerton N York
72 G4 Tollerton Notts
11 L4 Toller Whelme Dorset
52 G9 Tollesbury Essex
52 F9 Tolleshunt D'Arcy Essex
52 F9 Tolleshunt Knights Essex
52 F9 Tolleshunt Major Essex
12 C6 Tolpuddle Dorset
168 k3 Tolsta W Isls
36 E7 Tolworth Gt Lon
148 E2 Tomatin Highld
146 H5 Tomchrasky Highld
146 F7 Tomdoun Highld
147 J2 Tomich Highld
155 P8 Tomich Highld
156 B3 Tomich Highld
162 E5 Tomich Highld
149 M4 Tomintoul Moray
48 E2 Tomlow Warwks
155 P9 Tomnacross Highld
149 N2 Tomnavoulin Moray
70 G4 Tompkin Staffs
31 K4 Ton Mons
31 L5 Ton Mons
37 N11 Tonbridge Kent
29 N8 Tondu Brdgnd
18 F10 Tonedale Somset
54 D4 Ton fanau Gwynd
90 G4 Tong C Brad
38 G10 Tong Kent
57 P3 Tong Shrops
72 C6 Tonge Leics
38 G11 Tong Green Kent
23 N5 Tongham Surrey
108 E10 Tongland D & G
57 P3 Tong Norton Shrops
165 N5 Tongue Highld
74 C7 Tongue End Lincs
30 F8 Tongwynlais Cardif
29 M5 Tonmawr Neath
29 L5 Tonna Neath
30 E7 Ton-teg Rhondd
50 H7 Tonwell Herts
30 C6 Tonypandy Rhondd
30 D7 Tonyrefail Rhondd
34 G4 Toot Baldon Oxon
51 M10 Toot Hill Essex
22 C11 Toothill Hants
33 M8 Toothill Swindn
36 G6 Tooting Gt Lon
36 G6 Tooting Bec Gt Lon
97 N5 Topcliffe N York
65 K3 Topcroft Norfk
65 K3 Topcroft Street Norfk
61 M8 Top End Bed
91 Q7 Topham Donc
89 P9 Top of Hebers Rochdl
52 B4 Toppesfield Essex
89 L8 Toppings Bolton
64 H2 Toprow Norfk
9 N7 Topsham Devon
69 J3 Top-y-rhos Flints
120 G6 Torbeg N Ayrs
162 H7 Torboll Highld
156 A9 Torbreck Highld
7 L5 Torbryan Devon
139 L2 Torcastle Highld
7 L10 Torcross Devon
155 R7 Tore Highld
5 J11 Torfrey Cnwll
123 P7 Torinturk Ag & B
85 P5 Torksey Lincs
32 E9 Tormarton S Glos
120 G5 Tormore N Ayrs
156 D7 Tornagrain Highld
150 G6 Tornaveen Abers
147 P2 Torness Highld
103 N4 Toronto Dur
100 H3 Torpenhow Cumb
126 H3 Torphichen W Loth
150 G7 Torphins Abers

6 C7 Torpoint Cnwll
7 N6 Torquay Torbay
7 N5 Torquay Crematorium Torbay
128 C10 Torquhan Border
6 F8 Torr Devon
153 K8 Torran Highld
125 Q3 Torrance E Duns
125 K9 Torranyard N Ayrs
18 D7 Torre Somset
154 B6 Torridon Highld
153 R6 Torridon House Highld
145 J3 Torrin Highld
120 E4 Torrisdale Ag & B
165 Q4 Torrisdale Highld
163 M3 Torrish Highld
95 K8 Torrisholme Lancs
162 D6 Torrobull Highld
151 N6 Torry C Aber
134 C10 Torryburn Fife
10 a2 Torteval Guern
109 M5 Torthorwald D & G
24 B10 Tortington W Susx
58 B10 Torton Worcs
32 D6 Tortworth S Glos
152 H9 Torvaig Highld
94 F2 Torver Cumb
133 N10 Torwood Falk
117 P3 Torwoodlee Border
85 L3 Torworth Notts
16 D7 Tosberry Devon
153 N10 Toscaig Highld
62 B8 Toseland Cambs
95 R9 Tosside Lancs
64 D9 Tostock Suffk
152 C7 Totaig Highld
152 G8 Tote Highld
153 J5 Tote Highld
23 N10 Tote Hill W Susx
22 G7 Totford Hants
87 M4 Tothill Lincs
13 P7 Totland IoW
84 D5 Totley Sheff
84 D4 Totley Brook Sheff
7 L6 Totnes Devon
72 E4 Toton Notts
136 F4 Totronald Ag & B
152 F4 Totscore Highld
36 H2 Tottenham Gt Lon
75 M8 Tottenhill Norfk
36 F2 Totteridge Gt Lon
49 Q10 Totternhoe C Beds
89 M8 Tottington Bury
89 L4 Tottleworth Lancs
14 C4 Totton Hants
35 N9 Touchen End W & M
91 M2 Toulston N York
18 G8 Toulton Somset
163 K10 Toulvaddie Highld
38 C11 Tovil Kent
3 Q4 Towan Cnwll
4 D7 Towan Cnwll
124 E4 Toward Ag & B
124 E4 Toward Quay Ag & B
49 J5 Towcester Nhants
2 D6 Towednack Cnwll
35 K3 Towersey Oxon
150 C5 Towie Abers
103 M3 Tow Law Dur
74 H11 Town End Cambs
95 J4 Town End Cumb
101 K9 Town End Cumb
102 B5 Town End Cumb
125 K2 Townend W Duns
111 K11 Towngate Cumb
74 B8 Towngate Lincs
88 E9 Town Green Lancs
77 M9 Town Green Norfk
83 Q4 Townhead Barns
100 E3 Townhead Cumb
101 M10 Town Head Cumb
102 B4 Townhead Cumb
109 M3 Townhead D & G
96 B9 Town Head N York
108 F8 Townhead of Greenlaw D & G
134 E10 Townhill Fife
104 C3 Town Kelloe Dur
5 Q7 Townlake Devon
82 E5 Town Lane Wigan
25 K7 Town Littleworth E Susx
82 D5 Town of Lowton Wigan
25 N4 Town Row E Susx
22 G3 Towns End Hants
10 H2 Townsend Somset
2 F7 Townshend Cnwll
63 N3 Town Street Suffk
32 D6 Townwell S Glos
118 F5 Town Yetholm Border
98 C9 Towthorpe C York
98 H8 Towthorpe E R Yk
91 M3 Towton N York
80 D9 Towyn Conwy
81 M7 Toxteth Lpool
87 L8 Toynton All Saints Lincs
87 L8 Toynton Fen Side Lincs
87 M8 Toynton St Peter Lincs
37 L10 Toy's Hill Kent
114 H3 Trabboch E Ayrs
115 J3 Trabbochburn E Ayrs
3 J9 Traboe Cnwll
18 E10 Tracebridge Somset
156 F6 Tradespark Highld
44 D9 Trallong Powys
84 D9 Tramway Museum Derbys
128 C5 Tranent E Loth
81 L7 Tranmere Wirral
166 E6 Trantelbeg Highld
166 E6 Trantlemore Highld
113 J4 Tranwell Nthumb
43 N11 Trapp Carmth
128 F4 Traprain E Loth
58 H11 Trap's Green Warwks
22 C2 Trapshill W Berk
117 L4 Traquair Border
35 J11 Trash Green W Berk
89 Q3 Trawden Lancs
54 F10 Trawscoed Cerdgn
67 N7 Trawsfynydd Gwynd
30 D6 Trealaw Rhondd
88 E4 Treales Lancs
78 D9 Trearddur Bay IoA
152 F7 Treaslane Highld
4 E6 Treator Cnwll
30 D10 Tre Aubrey V Glam
30 D6 Trebanog Rhondd
29 K4 Trebanos Neath
5 M6 Trebartha Cnwll
4 H4 Trebarwith Cnwll
5 M4 Trebeath Cnwll
4 E6 Trebetherick Cnwll
18 D7 Treborough Somset
4 D9 Trebudannon Cnwll
5 N6 Trebullett Cnwll
4 H6 Treburgett Cnwll
5 P6 Treburley Cnwll
4 D7 Treburrick Cnwll
4 H9 Trebyan Cnwll
44 B9 Trecastle Powys
5 N5 Trecogo Cnwll
8 F4 Trecott Devon
41 J4 Trecwn Pembks
30 C4 Trecynon Rhondd
5 L5 Tredaule Cnwll
2 D8 Tredavoe Cnwll
30 F3 Tredegar Blae G
4 H7 Tredethy Cnwll
46 H9 Tredington Gloucs
47 Q6 Tredington Warwks
4 E7 Tredinnick Cnwll
4 G10 Tredinnick Cnwll
5 K8 Tredinnick Cnwll
5 L10 Tredinnick Cnwll
5 M10 Tredinnick Cnwll
44 G8 Tredomen Powys
41 L2 Tredrissi Pembks
4 F6 Tredrizzick Cnwll
31 L6 Tredunnock Mons
44 G8 Tredustan Powys
2 B9 Treen Cnwll
2 C6 Treen Cnwll
4 H10 Treesmill Cnwll
84 F3 Treeton Rothm
40 G3 Trefasser Pembks
78 G10 Trefdraeth IoA
44 G8 Trefecca Powys
55 M6 Trefeglwys Powys
54 F11 Trefenter Cerdgn
41 J6 Treffgarne Pembks
40 G5 Treffgarne Owen Pembks
30 E7 Trefforest Rhondd
40 G5 Treffynnon Pembks
30 F2 Trefil Blae G
43 K3 Trefilan Cerdgn
40 F4 Trefin Pembks
69 J9 Treflach Wood Shrops
68 H11 Trefnannau Powys
80 F10 Trefnant Denbgs
69 J9 Trefonen Shrops
66 F5 Trefor Gwynd
78 F8 Trefor IoA
5 J5 Trefrew Cnwll
67 P2 Trefriw Conwy
5 M5 Tregadillett Cnwll
31 P3 Tre-gagle Mons
78 H8 Tregaian IoA
31 M2 Tregare Mons
3 K9 Tregarne Cnwll
43 N3 Tregaron Cerdgn
79 L11 Tregarth Gwynd
4 D9 Tregaswith Cnwll
4 H4 Tregatta Cnwll
4 G8 Tregawne Cnwll
5 L4 Tregeare Cnwll
68 G8 Tregeiriog Wrexhm
78 F6 Tregele IoA
4 G6 Tregellist Cnwll
3 M5 Tregenna Cnwll
2 B7 Tregeseal Cnwll
3 L7 Tregew Cnwll
30 C3 Tre-Gibbon Rhondd
3 K9 Tregidden Cnwll
3 Q4 Tregiskey Cnwll
40 F5 Treglemais Pembks
5 K2 Tregole Cnwll
3 J6 Tregolls Cnwll
4 E7 Tregonce Cnwll
4 F9 Tregonetha Cnwll
3 N5 Tregony Cnwll
5 J5 Tregoodwell Cnwll
3 Q3 Tregorrick Cnwll
4 F9 Tregoss Cnwll
44 H7 Tregoyd Powys
3 Q3 Tregrehan Mills Cnwll
42 H6 Tre-groes Cerdgn
4 H9 Tregullon Cnwll
4 F7 Tregunna Cnwll
5 L5 Tregunnon Cnwll
4 D8 Tregurrian Cnwll
55 P5 Tregynon Powys
42 H11 Tre-gynwr Carmth
30 D6 Trehafod Rhondd
5 Q10 Trehan Cnwll
30 E5 Treharris Myr Td
4 G6 Treharrock Cnwll
4 D7 Trehemborne Cnwll
43 L5 Treherbert Carmth
29 P5 Treherbert Rhondd
5 N9 Trehunist Cnwll
5 N6 Trekenner Cnwll
4 H4 Treknow Cnwll
3 J10 Trelan Cnwll
3 K5 Trelash Cnwll
3 M3 Trelassick Cnwll
5 L11 Trelawne Cnwll
80 F9 Trelawnyd Flints
3 K9 Treleague Cnwll
3 K10 Treleaver Cnwll
41 Q4 Trelech Carmth
42 F9 Trelech a'r Betws Carmth
40 E5 Treleddyd-fawr Pembks
3 L6 Trelew Cnwll
30 F5 Trelewis Myr Td
4 G5 Treligga Cnwll
4 F6 Trelights Cnwll
4 G6 Trelill Cnwll
5 N5 Trelinnoe Cnwll
3 N3 Trelion Cnwll
3 L6 Trelissick Cnwll
3 L6 Trelissick Garden Cnwll
31 P3 Trellech Mons
31 N4 Trelleck Grange Mons
80 G8 Trelogan Flints
4 E8 Trelow Cnwll
3 J9 Trelowarren Cnwll
5 M10 Trelowia Cnwll
3 M6 Treluggan Cnwll
56 D4 Trelystan Powys
67 K7 Tremadog Gwynd
5 K4 Tremail Cnwll
42 D5 Tremain Cerdgn
5 L4 Tremaine Cnwll
5 M8 Tremar Cnwll
5 P10 Trematon Cnwll
5 M8 Trembraze Cnwll
80 F10 Tremeirchion Denbgs
2 C7 Tremethick Cross Cnwll
4 G9 Tremore Cnwll
80 G9 Tre-Mostyn Flints
3 L9 Trenance Cnwll
4 D8 Trenance Cnwll
4 E7 Trenance Cnwll
3 Q4 Trenarren Cnwll
57 M2 Trench Wrekin
35 J9 Trench Green Oxon
3 M3 Trendeal Cnwll
2 D6 Trendrine Cnwll
4 F7 Treneague Cnwll
2 H7 Trenear Cnwll
5 L4 Treneglos Cnwll
2 G6 Trenerth Cnwll
5 K11 Trenewan Cnwll
4 H6 Trenewth Cnwll
5 K3 Trengune Cnwll
4 C9 Treninnick Cnwll
4 B10 Trenowah Cnwll
3 K7 Trenoweth Cnwll
19 Q11 Trent Dorset
70 F6 Trentham C Stke
17 L2 Trentishoe Devon
72 D4 Trentlock Derbys
85 P4 Trent Port Lincs
70 F6 Trent Vale C Stke
2 G7 Trenwheal Cnwll
29 P9 Treoes V Glam
30 C5 Treorchy Rhondd
4 G6 Trequite Cnwll
54 F6 Tre'r-ddol Cerdgn
30 D9 Trerhyngyll V Glam
5 N10 Trerulefoot Cnwll
42 E4 Tresaith Cerdgn
3 M4 Tresawle Cnwll
2 b2 Tresco IoS
2 b2 Tresco Heliport IoS
58 C5 Trescott Staffs
2 F7 Trescowe Cnwll
4 B10 Tresean Cnwll
32 E6 Tresham Gloucs
136 G7 Treshnish Isles Ag & B
3 M4 Tresillian Cnwll
5 J5 Tresinney Cnwll
5 L2 Treskinnick Cross Cnwll
5 L4 Tresmeer Cnwll
5 J3 Tresparrett Cnwll
141 K5 Tressait P & K
169 q8 Tresta Shet
169 t4 Tresta Shet
85 N5 Treswell Notts
2 G5 Treswithian Cnwll
54 F6 Tre Taliesin Cerdgn
4 H4 Trethevey Cnwll
2 B9 Trethewey Cnwll
30 G7 Trethomas Caerph
3 N3 Trethosa Cnwll
4 G10 Trethurgy Cnwll
40 E5 Tretio Pembks
45 Q10 Tretire Herefs
44 H10 Tretower Powys
69 J3 Treuddyn Flints
5 M6 Trevadlock Cnwll
4 H3 Trevalga Cnwll
69 L3 Trevalyn Wrexhm
4 F6 Trevanger Cnwll
4 F7 Trevanson Cnwll
2 D7 Trevarrack Cnwll
4 E9 Trevarren Cnwll
4 D8 Trevarrian Cnwll
3 P5 Trevarrick Cnwll
3 J5 Trevarth Cnwll
41 P7 Trevaughan Carmth
42 G10 Tre-Vaughan Carmth
2 D5 Treveal Cnwll
4 B10 Treveal Cnwll
4 H6 Treveighan Cnwll
3 J3 Trevellas Downs Cnwll
5 L9 Trevelmond Cnwll
4 C10 Trevemper Cnwll
3 P5 Treveor Cnwll
3 M4 Treverbyn Cnwll
4 G10 Treverbyn Cnwll
3 K7 Treverva Cnwll
2 B9 Trevescan Cnwll
31 J4 Trevethin Torfn
4 H5 Trevia Cnwll
5 N8 Trevigro Cnwll
3 L6 Trevilla Cnwll
4 C10 Trevilson Cnwll
4 E10 Treviscoe Cnwll
3 N5 Treviskey Cnwll
3 P4 Trevithick Cnwll
4 D9 Trevithick Cnwll
4 C10 Trevoll Cnwll
4 D6 Trevone Cnwll
69 J6 Trevor Wrexhm
2 C8 Trevorgans Cnwll
4 E7 Trevorrick Cnwll
4 D6 Trevose Cnwll
2 G8 Trew Cnwll
4 H5 Trewalder Cnwll
44 H8 Trewalkin Powys
4 H4 Trewarmett Cnwll
5 J4 Trewassa Cnwll
2 F8 Trewavas Cnwll
5 L5 Treween Cnwll
2 B7 Trewellard Cnwll
5 M5 Trewen Cnwll
2 H8 Trewennack Cnwll
41 K11 Trewent Pembks
56 D2 Trewern Powys
4 G5 Trewetha Cnwll
4 G6 Trewethern Cnwll
5 M10 Trewidland Cnwll
3 K10 Trewillis Cnwll
5 L5 Trewint Cnwll
5 M9 Trewint Cnwll
3 M6 Trewithian Cnwll
5 N7 Trewoodloe Cnwll
2 H10 Trewoon Cnwll
3 P3 Trewoon Cnwll
3 M5 Treworga Cnwll
3 L4 Treworgan Cnwll
3 M6 Treworlas Cnwll
5 J3 Treworld Cnwll
3 M6 Treworthal Cnwll
45 L10 Tre-wyn Mons
4 D7 Treyarnon Cnwll
23 M11 Treyford W Susx
13 J4 Trickett's Cross Dorset
111 L7 Triermain Cumb
41 J6 Triffleton Pembks
5 M4 Trillacott Cnwll
104 C4 Trimdon Dur
104 C3 Trimdon Colliery Dur
104 C3 Trimdon Grange Dur
77 K4 Trimingham Norfk
53 N4 Trimley Lower Street Suffk
53 N4 Trimley St Martin Suffk
53 N4 Trimley St Mary Suffk
57 P9 Trimpley Worcs
28 E4 Trimsaran Carmth
51 L7 Trims Green Herts
17 J3 Trimstone Devon
140 H5 Trinafour P & K
30 H5 Trinant Caerph
35 P2 Tring Herts
35 P2 Tringford Herts
35 P2 Tring Wharf Herts
143 L5 Trinity Angus
11 b1 Trinity Jersey
134 B4 Trinity Gask P & K
18 G7 Triscombe Somset
139 K3 Trislaig Highld
3 L3 Trispen Cnwll
113 K2 Tritlington Nthumb
4 D10 Troan Cnwll
141 N9 Trochry P & K
30 F4 Troedrhiwfuwch Caerph
42 F5 Troedyraur Cerdgn
30 E4 Troedyrhiw Myr Td
80 B10 Trofarth Conwy
11 b1 Trois Bois Jersey
2 H6 Troon Cnwll
125 J11 Troon S Ayrs
91 J3 Tropical World Roundhay Park Leeds
132 G6 Trossachs Stirlg
132 F6 Trossachs Pier Stirlg
64 B7 Troston Suffk
5 M3 Troswell Cnwll
46 G3 Trotshill Worcs
37 P8 Trottiscliffe Kent
23 M10 Trotton W Susx
112 C2 Troughend Nthumb
89 P6 Trough Gate Lancs
101 L5 Troutbeck Cumb
101 M10 Troutbeck Cumb
101 M10 Troutbeck Bridge Cumb
84 E5 Troway Derbys
20 G3 Trowbridge Wilts
72 D3 Trowell Notts
72 D2 Trowell Services Notts
20 F3 Trowle Common Wilts
50 C8 Trowley Bottom Herts
77 J10 Trowse Newton Norfk
90 G3 Troy Leeds
20 D6 Trudoxhill Somset
18 H10 Trull Somset
91 Q8 Trumfleet Donc
152 C5 Trumpan Highld
46 C7 Trumpet Herefs
62 F10 Trumpington Cambs
35 Q11 Trumpsgreen Surrey
77 K5 Trunch Norfk
88 C2 Trunnah Lancs
3 L5 Truro Cnwll
3 L5 Truro Cathedral Cnwll
5 M4 Truscott Cnwll
9 L8 Trusham Devon
71 P7 Trusley Derbys
87 P4 Trusthorpe Lincs
58 C6 Trysull Staffs
34 D5 Tubney Oxon
7 L7 Tuckenhay Devon
57 P7 Tuckhill Shrops
2 H5 Tuckingmill Cnwll
20 H9 Tuckingmill Wilts
13 K6 Tuckton Bmouth
3 P4 Tucoyse Cnwll
53 L2 Tuddenham Suffk
63 M6 Tuddenham Suffk
37 P11 Tudeley Kent
103 Q3 Tudhoe Dur
46 A10 Tudorville Herefs
66 C7 Tudweiliog Gwynd
23 Q6 Tuesley Surrey
32 F2 Tuffley Gloucs
22 E5 Tufton Hants
41 K5 Tufton Pembks
73 K10 Tugby Leics
57 K7 Tugford Shrops
119 P5 Tughall Nthumb
133 P8 Tullibody Clacks
147 Q2 Tullich Highld
156 F2 Tullich Highld
141 P7 Tulliemet P & K
159 K11 Tulloch Abers
131 K8 Tullochgorm Ag & B
147 K11 Tulloch Station Highld
142 B7 Tullymurdoch P & K
150 F4 Tullynessle Abers
36 H6 Tulse Hill Gt Lon
28 F2 Tumble Carmth
52 D6 Tumbler's Green Essex
86 H9 Tumby Lincs
87 J9 Tumby Woodside Lincs
141 J6 Tummel Bridge P & K
25 N3 Tunbridge Wells Kent
110 C4 Tundergarth D & G
77 K6 Tungate Norfk
20 C3 Tunley BaNES
70 F4 Tunstall C Stke
93 P4 Tunstall E R Yk
38 E9 Tunstall Kent
95 N6 Tunstall Lancs
103 P11 Tunstall N York
77 N10 Tunstall Norfk
70 D9 Tunstall Staffs
65 M10 Tunstall Suffk
113 N10 Tunstall Sundld
83 P10 Tunstead Derbys
77 K7 Tunstead Norfk
83 M8 Tunstead Milton Derbys
23 J5 Tunworth Hants
45 Q6 Tupsley Herefs
23 J3 Turgis Green Hants
47 M11 Turkdean Gloucs
60 F2 Tur Langton Leics
20 F2 Turleigh Wilts
57 P7 Turleygreen Shrops
89 N7 Turn Lancs
45 M7 Turnastone Herefs
114 D6 Turnberry S Ayrs
6 D8 Turnchapel C Plym
71 P5 Turnditch Derbys
89 J4 Turner Green Lancs
25 P7 Turner's Green E Susx
59 J11 Turner's Green Warwks
24 H3 Turner's Hill W Susx
12 D6 Turners Puddle Dorset
51 J10 Turnford Herts
127 M3 Turnhouse C Edin
12 D3 Turnworth Dorset
158 H7 Turriff Abers
89 L7 Turton Bottoms Bl w D
74 F11 Turves Cambs
49 P4 Turvey Bed
35 L6 Turville Bucks
35 K6 Turville Heath Bucks
48 H7 Turweston Bucks
117 L7 Tushielaw Inn Border
71 N9 Tutbury Staffs
58 E10 Tutnall Worcs
31 P6 Tutshill Gloucs
77 J6 Tuttington Norfk
5 P6 Tutwell Cnwll
85 M6 Tuxford Notts
169 b4 Twatt Ork
169 q8 Twatt Shet
126 B2 Twechar E Duns
117 Q4 Tweedbank Border
129 P9 Tweedmouth Nthumb
116 G6 Tweedsmuir Border
3 K5 Twelveheads Cnwll
25 Q6 Twelve Oaks E Susx
82 G11 Twemlow Green Ches E
74 C6 Twenty Lincs
20 D2 Twerton BaNES
36 E6 Twickenham Gt Lon
46 F10 Twigworth Gloucs
24 G7 Twineham W Susx
24 G6 Twineham Green W Susx
20 E3 Twinhoe BaNES
52 E4 Twinstead Essex
17 P5 Twitchen Devon
56 F9 Twitchen Shrops
39 N10 Twitham Kent
6 G4 Two Bridges Devon
84 C8 Two Dales Derbys
59 K4 Two Gates Staffs
7 L5 Two Mile Oak Cross Devon
17 J3 Two Pots Devon
50 C9 Two Waters Herts
72 A10 Twycross Leics
59 M3 Twycross Zoo Leics
49 J9 Twyford Bucks
22 E10 Twyford Hants
73 J8 Twyford Leics
73 N6 Twyford Lincs
76 E7 Twyford Norfk
35 L9 Twyford Wokham
45 Q7 Twyford Common Herefs
30 F3 Twyn-carno Caerph
108 E10 Twynholm D & G
46 H7 Twyning Green Gloucs
43 Q10 Twynllanan Carmth
30 F10 Twyn-yr-Odyn V Glam
31 M3 Twyn-y-Sheriff Mons
61 L5 Twywell Nhants
45 M7 Tyberton Herefs
58 H6 Tyburn Birm
28 H2 Tycroes Carmth
68 F11 Tycrwyn Powys
75 J7 Tydd Gote Lincs
74 H7 Tydd St Giles Cambs
74 H7 Tydd St Mary Lincs
15 K6 Tye Hants
51 M6 Tye Green Essex
51 N3 Tye Green Essex
52 C7 Tye Green Essex
90 F4 Tyersal C Brad
82 E4 Tyldesley Wigan
39 K9 Tyler Hill Kent
35 P6 Tylers Green Bucks
51 M9 Tyler's Green Essex
37 J10 Tylers Green Surrey
30 D5 Tylorstown Rhondd
55 M8 Tylwch Powys
68 C6 Ty-nant Conwy
68 B9 Ty-nant Gwynd
139 Q11 Tyndrum Stirlg
68 H6 Ty'n-dwr Denbgs
113 N7 Tynemouth N Tyne
113 M7 Tynemouth Crematorium N Tyne
29 P5 Tynewydd Rhondd
128 G4 Tyninghame E Loth
115 R9 Tynron D & G
31 P10 Tyntesfield N Som
30 D7 Ty'n-y-bryn Rhondd
30 G7 Ty'n-y-coedcae Caerph
79 J8 Tynygongl IoA
54 F11 Tynygraig Cerdgn
79 P10 Ty'n-y-Groes Conwy
30 E7 Tyn-y-nant Rhondd
49 N5 Tyringham M Keyn
58 H8 Tyseley Birm
29 N9 Tythegston Brdgnd
83 K9 Tytherington Ches E
32 C7 Tytherington S Glos
20 E6 Tytherington Somset
20 H6 Tytherington Wilts
10 G4 Tytherleigh Devon
32 H10 Tytherton Lucas Wilts
50 E9 Tyttenhanger Herts
4 H11 Tywardreath Cnwll
4 H10 Tywardreath Highway Cnwll
79 P9 Tywyn Conwy
54 D4 Tywyn Gwynd

U

65 L7 Ubbeston Green Suffk
19 P3 Ubley BaNES
103 P10 Uckerby N York
25 L6 Uckfield E Susx
46 G7 Uckinghall Worcs
46 H10 Uckington Gloucs
57 K2 Uckington Shrops
126 B5 Uddingston S Lans
116 B4 Uddington S Lans
26 E8 Udimore E Susx
151 M2 Udny Green Abers
151 N3 Udny Station Abers
33 M9 Uffcott Wilts
9 Q2 Uffculme Devon
73 R9 Uffington Lincs
34 B7 Uffington Oxon
57 J2 Uffington Shrops
74 A10 Ufford C Pete
65 K11 Ufford Suffk
48 C2 Ufton Warwks
34 H11 Ufton Nervet W Berk
120 E6 Ugadale Ag & B
6 H7 Ugborough Devon
65 N5 Uggeshall Suffk
105 N9 Ugglebarnby N York
84 C2 Ughill Sheff
51 M5 Ugley Essex
51 M5 Ugley Green Essex
105 L8 Ugthorpe N York
168 d14 Uibhist A Deas W Isls
168 c10 Uibhist A Tuath W Isls
136 F5 Uig Ag & B

152 B7 Uig Highld
152 F5 Uig Highld
168 f4 Uig W Isls
152 G8 Uigshader Highld
137 K12 Uisken Ag & B
167 P8 Ulbster Highld
101 M6 Ulcat Row Cumb
87 M6 Ulceby Lincs
93 K8 Ulceby N Linc
93 K7 Ulceby Skitter N Linc
26 D2 Ulcombe Kent
100 H3 Uldale Cumb
32 E5 Uley Gloucs
113 K2 Ulgham Nthumb
161 J8 Ullapool Highld
58 H11 Ullenhall Warwks
46 H11 Ullenwood Gloucs
91 N3 Ulleskelf N York
60 B3 Ullesthorpe Leics
84 G3 Ulley Rothm
46 A5 Ullingswick Herefs
152 E10 Ullinish Lodge Hotel Highld
100 E6 Ullock Cumb
101 M6 Ullswater Cumb
94 D2 Ulpha Cumb
95 K4 Ulpha Cumb
99 P9 Ulrome E R Yk
169 r5 Ulsta Shet
52 D10 Ulting Wick Essex
137 K7 Ulva Ag & B
58 H8 Ulverley Green Solhll
94 F5 Ulverston Cumb
12 H8 Ulwell Dorset
115 Q6 Ulzieside D & G
17 L7 Umberleigh Devon
164 F10 Unapool Highld
95 K2 Underbarrow Cumb
111 J4 Under Burnmouth Border
90 F4 Undercliffe C Brad
57 J2 Underdale Shrops
26 C2 Underling Green Kent
37 N10 Under River Kent
84 G10 Underwood Notts
63 L4 Undley Suffk
31 M7 Undy Mons
80 e6 Union Mills IoM
26 B5 Union Street E Susx
169 s3 Unst Shet
84 E5 Unstone Derbys
84 E5 Unstone Green Derbys
101 N3 Unthank Cumb
102 B2 Unthank Cumb
110 G11 Unthank Cumb
84 D5 Unthank Derbys
129 P10 Unthank Nthumb
21 M4 Upavon Wilts
11 P4 Up Cerne Dorset
38 D8 Upchurch Kent
17 P6 Upcott Devon
45 L4 Upcott Herefs
63 M9 Upend Cambs
9 M4 Up Exe Devon
76 G8 Upgate Norfk
64 F3 Upgate Street Norfk
65 K3 Upgate Street Norfk
11 M4 Uphall Dorset
127 K3 Uphall W Loth
9 L3 Upham Devon
22 F10 Upham Hants
45 M2 Uphampton Herefs
46 F2 Uphampton Worcs
19 K3 Uphill N Som
88 G9 Up Holland Lancs
125 L6 Uplawmoor E Rens
46 E9 Upleadon Gloucs
104 H7 Upleatham R & Cl
38 H9 Uplees Kent
11 L6 Uploders Dorset
18 D11 Uplowman Devon
10 G6 Uplyme Devon
15 L4 Up Marden W Susx
37 N3 Upminster Gt Lon
19 Q11 Up Mudford Somset
23 J4 Up Nately Hants
10 E3 Upottery Devon
56 G7 Upper Affcot Shrops
162 E9 Upper Ardchronie Highld
57 P8 Upper Arley Worcs
48 H11 Upper Arncott Oxon
48 F7 Upper Astrop Nhants
34 G9 Upper Basildon W Berk
90 C5 Upper Batley Kirk
24 E8 Upper Beeding W Susx
61 L3 Upper Benefield Nhants
58 E11 Upper Bentley Worcs
166 E5 Upper Bighouse Highld
84 F8 Upper Birchwood Derbys
30 F7 Upper Boat Rhondd
48 E4 Upper Boddington Nhants
54 F7 Upper Borth Cerdgn
48 B7 Upper Brailes Warwks
145 L3 Upper Breakish Highld
45 P6 Upper Breinton Herefs
46 F3 Upper Broadheath Worcs
72 H5 Upper Broughton Notts
34 F11 Upper Bucklebury W Berk
21 N11 Upper Burgate Hants
37 Q7 Upper Bush Medway
110 H10 Upperby Cumb
61 Q11 Upper Caldecote C Beds
19 L3 Upper Canada N Som
13 N2 Upper Canterton Hants
60 B9 Upper Catesby Nhants
58 E10 Upper Catshill Worcs
44 E6 Upper Chapel Powys
18 H9 Upper Cheddon Somset
21 J9 Upper Chicksgrove Wilts
21 Q4 Upper Chute Wilts
36 H3 Upper Clapton Gt Lon
22 C6 Upper Clatford Hants
47 J11 Upper Coberley Gloucs
24 E9 Upper Cokeham W Susx
71 K5 Upper Cotton Staffs
57 K3 Upper Cound Shrops
91 K9 Upper Cudworth Barns
90 G9 Upper Cumberworth Kirk
157 R5 Upper Dallachy Moray
39 Q11 Upper Deal Kent
61 M7 Upper Dean Bed
90 G9 Upper Denby Kirk
111 M7 Upper Denton Cumb
25 N9 Upper Dicker E Susx
56 H8 Upper Dinchope Shrops
166 H3 Upper Dounreay Highld
53 M5 Upper Dovercourt Essex
133 K6 Upper Drumbane Stirlg
97 P8 Upper Dunsforth N York
23 Q6 Upper Eashing Surrey
156 D5 Upper Eathie Highld
46 B6 Upper Egleton Herefs
71 K3 Upper Elkstone Staffs
71 L6 Upper Ellastone Staffs
83 N9 Upper End Derbys
22 C4 Upper Enham Hants
57 P6 Upper Farmcote Shrops
23 K7 Upper Farringdon Hants
32 E2 Upper Framilode Gloucs
23 L6 Upper Froyle Hants
152 E7 Upperglen Highld
19 N6 Upper Godney Somset
50 D3 Upper Gravenhurst C Beds
45 M11 Upper Green Mons
63 M8 Upper Green Suffk
22 C2 Upper Green W Berk
45 R9 Upper Grove Common Herefs
84 C8 Upper Hackney Derbys
23 M5 Upper Hale Surrey
36 C11 Upper Halliford Surrey
37 Q8 Upper Halling Medway
73 N9 Upper Hambleton Rutlnd
39 K10 Upper Harbledown Kent
39 L11 Upper Hardres Court Kent
45 N3 Upper Hardwick Herefs
25 L4 Upper Hartfield E Susx
84 E10 Upper Hartshay Derbys
46 H10 Upper Hatherley Gloucs
70 E7 Upper Hatton Staffs
91 L11 Upper Haugh Rothm
57 J8 Upper Hayton Shrops
90 F7 Upper Heaton Kirk
98 D9 Upper Helmsley N York
45 K4 Upper Hergest Herefs
60 E9 Upper Heyford Nhants
48 E9 Upper Heyford Oxon
45 P4 Upper Hill Herefs
37 M7 Upper Hockenden Kent
90 F7 Upper Hopton Kirk
46 E5 Upper Howsell Worcs
71 J2 Upper Hulme Staffs
24 B4 Upper Ifold Surrey
33 P5 Upper Inglesham Swindn
32 E7 Upper Kilcott Gloucs
28 G6 Upper Killay Swans
131 P2 Upper Kinchrackine Ag & B
34 B8 Upper Lambourn W Berk
58 E3 Upper Landywood Staffs
19 N3 Upper Langford N Som
84 H7 Upper Langwith Derbys
135 L7 Upper Largo Fife
71 J7 Upper Leigh Staffs
19 Q2 Upper Littleton N Som
150 H8 Upper Lochton Abers
58 G2 Upper Longdon Staffs
50 E4 Upper & Lower Stondon C Beds
57 Q5 Upper Ludstone Shrops
167 N9 Upper Lybster Highld
46 B11 Upper Lydbrook Gloucs
45 P6 Upper Lyde Herefs
56 F11 Upper Lye Herefs
45 L8 Upper Maes-coed Herefs
90 G11 Upper Midhope Sheff
90 B9 Uppermill Oldham
57 Q10 Upper Milton Worcs
33 K6 Upper Minety Wilts
47 J5 Upper Moor Worcs
90 G4 Upper Moor Side Leeds
157 R7 Upper Mulben Moray
57 L6 Upper Netchwood Shrops
71 J7 Upper Nobut Staffs
23 P11 Upper Norwood W Susx
84 B5 Upper Padley Derbys
13 P5 Upper Pennington Hants
35 K2 Upper Pollicott Bucks
98 B10 Upper Poppleton C York
47 N5 Upper Quinton Warwks
22 B10 Upper Ratley Hants
47 P11 Upper Rissington Gloucs
57 L11 Upper Rochford Worcs
108 C8 Upper Ruscoe D & G
46 C2 Upper Sapey Herefs
32 H8 Upper Seagry Wilts
49 Q6 Upper Shelton C Beds
76 G3 Upper Sheringham Norfk
124 G4 Upper Skelmorlie N Ayrs
47 N10 Upper Slaughter Gloucs
32 C2 Upper Soudley Gloucs
45 L4 Upper Spond Herefs
27 M3 Upper Standen Kent
61 P9 Upper Staploe Bed
77 K11 Upper Stoke Norfk
60 D9 Upper Stowe Nhants
21 N11 Upper Street Hants
64 H6 Upper Street Norfk
77 L8 Upper Street Norfk
77 M8 Upper Street Norfk
53 K5 Upper Street Suffk
63 N10 Upper Street Suffk
64 G11 Upper Street Suffk
46 G7 Upper Strensham Worcs
50 B5 Upper Sundon C Beds
47 N9 Upper Swell Gloucs
91 J11 Upper Tankersley Barns
65 J2 Upper Tasburgh Norfk
71 J7 Upper Tean Staffs
90 E9 Upperthong Kirk
84 G4 Upperthorpe Derbys
92 C10 Upperthorpe N Linc
69 M5 Upper Threapwood Ches W
23 Q10 Upperton W Susx
71 N4 Upper Town Derbys
84 D8 Uppertown Derbys
103 L3 Upper Town Dur
46 A5 Upper Town Herefs
167 Q1 Uppertown Highld
31 P11 Upper Town N Som
64 C8 Upper Town Suffk
28 F2 Upper Tumble Carmth
48 B6 Upper Tysoe Warwks
65 K11 Upper Ufford Suffk
33 K5 Upperup Gloucs
33 P9 Upper Upham Wilts
38 C7 Upper Upnor Medway
143 J10 Upper Victoria Angus
20 D5 Upper Vobster Somset
48 E5 Upper Wardington Oxon
49 M7 Upper Weald M Keyn
60 D9 Upper Weedon Nhants
46 E6 Upper Welland Worcs
25 K8 Upper Wellingham E Susx
32 D11 Upper Weston BaNES
65 J6 Upper Weybread Suffk
46 F4 Upper Wick Worcs
22 H7 Upper Wield Hants
35 K2 Upper Winchendon Bucks
84 C9 Upperwood Derbys
21 M7 Upper Woodford Wilts
22 G4 Upper Wootton Hants
32 F10 Upper Wraxall Wilts
46 E6 Upper Wyche Worcs
9 M3 Uppincott Devon
73 M11 Uppingham Rutlnd
12 H3 Uppington Dorset
57 K3 Uppington Shrops
97 Q3 Upsall N York
129 M10 Upsettlington Border
51 K10 Upshire Essex
22 C8 Up Somborne Hants
39 M9 Upstreet Kent
11 N4 Up Sydling Dorset
64 D7 Upthorpe Suffk
35 L2 Upton Bucks
74 B10 Upton C Pete
61 Q5 Upton Cambs
81 N11 Upton Ches W
5 M7 Upton Cnwll
16 C11 Upton Cnwll
101 K3 Upton Cumb
7 J10 Upton Devon
10 B4 Upton Devon
12 B8 Upton Dorset
12 G6 Upton Dorset
99 N10 Upton E R Yk
81 P7 Upton Halton
22 C11 Upton Hants
22 C3 Upton Hants
72 B11 Upton Leics
85 Q3 Upton Lincs
60 F9 Upton Nhants
77 M9 Upton Norfk
85 M10 Upton Notts
85 M5 Upton Notts
33 P2 Upton Oxon
34 F7 Upton Oxon
41 K10 Upton Pembks
105 K7 Upton R & Cl
35 Q9 Upton Slough
18 C9 Upton Somset
19 N9 Upton Somset
91 M8 Upton Wakefd
47 M3 Upton Warwks
20 G8 Upton Wilts
81 K7 Upton Wirral
46 C9 Upton Bishop Herefs
32 C10 Upton Cheyney S Glos
57 M6 Upton Cressett Shrops
46 B9 Upton Crews Herefs
5 M7 Upton Cross Cnwll
50 D4 Upton End C Beds
23 J5 Upton Grey Hants
81 N11 Upton Heath Ches W
9 K4 Upton Hellions Devon
20 H6 Upton Lovell Wilts
57 K2 Upton Magna Shrops
20 D7 Upton Noble Somset
9 M5 Upton Pyne Devon
46 G11 Upton St Leonards Gloucs
20 G5 Upton Scudamore Wilts
46 H4 Upton Snodsbury Worcs
2 F5 Upton Towans Cnwll
46 G6 Upton upon Severn Worcs
58 D11 Upton Warren Worcs
15 P4 Upwaltham W Susx
62 H6 Upware Cambs
75 J10 Upwell Norfk
11 P7 Upwey Dorset
51 L6 Upwick Green Herts
62 C4 Upwood Cambs
21 K3 Urchfont Wilts
45 Q5 Urdimarsh Herefs
97 M6 Ure Bank N York
104 D8 Urlay Nook S on T
82 G6 Urmston Traffd
157 P5 Urquhart Moray
104 G10 Urra N York
155 P7 Urray Highld
143 N7 Usan Angus
103 P2 Ushaw Moor Dur
31 L4 Usk Mons
86 E2 Usselby Lincs
113 M9 Usworth Sundld
82 B11 Utkinton Ches W
90 D2 Utley C Brad
9 K5 Uton Devon
87 K2 Utterby Lincs
71 K8 Uttoxeter Staffs
66 B9 Uwchmynydd Gwynd
36 C4 Uxbridge Gt Lon
169 s3 Uyeasound Shet
41 J8 Uzmaston Pembks

V

10 c1 Vale Guern
54 G9 Vale of Rheidol Railway Cerdgn
78 D9 Valley IoA
23 Q2 Valley End Surrey
4 H5 Valley Truckle Cnwll
153 J5 Valtos Highld
168 f4 Valtos W Isls
38 B4 Vange Essex
31 J3 Varteg Torfn
169 s5 Vatsetter Shet
152 D9 Vatten Highld
30 D2 Vaynor Myr Td
10 b2 Vazon Bay Guern
169 r9 Veensgarth Shet
44 H7 Velindre Powys
18 E7 Vellow Somset
16 D7 Velly Devon
16 F9 Venngreen Devon
56 E3 Vennington Shrops
10 B6 Venn Ottery Devon
9 K5 Venny Tedburn Devon
5 P7 Venterdon Cnwll
14 G11 Ventnor IoW
6 F7 Venton Devon
22 B3 Vernham Dean Hants
22 B3 Vernham Street Hants
56 H8 Vernolds Common Shrops
13 J3 Verwood Dorset
3 N6 Veryan Cnwll
3 N5 Veryan Green Cnwll
10 E7 Vicarage Devon
94 D7 Vickerstown Cumb
90 F9 Victoria Barns
30 G3 Victoria Blae G
4 F9 Victoria Cnwll
169 r7 Vidlin Shet
157 P5 Viewfield Moray
126 C5 Viewpark N Lans
37 P8 Vigo Kent
10 c2 Village de Putron Guern
11 a1 Ville la Bas Jersey
10 b2 Villiaze Guern
26 C7 Vinehall Street E Susx
25 N7 Vines Cross E Susx
38 C10 Vinters Park Crematorium Kent
36 B7 Virginia Water Surrey
5 P3 Virginstow Devon
20 D5 Vobster Somset
169 r7 Voe Shet
45 M7 Vowchurch Herefs
82 C6 Vulcan Village St Hel

W

94 C2 Waberthwaite Cumb
103 N6 Wackerfield Dur
64 H3 Wacton Norfk
46 H5 Wadborough Worcs
49 K11 Waddesdon Bucks
7 M7 Waddeton Devon
81 M5 Waddicar Sefton
92 G11 Waddingham Lincs
89 L2 Waddington Lancs
86 C8 Waddington Lincs
9 L9 Waddon Devon
11 N7 Waddon Dorset
4 F7 Wadebridge Cnwll
10 G2 Wadeford Somset
61 M4 Wadenhoe Nhants
51 J7 Wadesmill Herts
25 P4 Wadhurst E Susx
84 D6 Wadshelf Derbys
32 F11 Wadswick Wilts
91 P11 Wadworth Donc
68 C2 Waen Denbgs
80 G11 Waen Denbgs
68 H11 Waen Powys
68 H11 Waen Fach Powys
79 K11 Waen-pentir Gwynd
79 K11 Waen-wen Gwynd
56 F4 Wagbeach Shrops
31 J4 Wainfelin Torfn
87 N9 Wainfleet All Saints Lincs
87 N9 Wainfleet Bank Lincs
87 N9 Wainfleet St Mary Lincs
65 L3 Wainford Norfk
5 K2 Wainhouse Corner Cnwll
38 B7 Wainscott Medway
31 L10 Wain's Hill N Som
90 C5 Wainstalls Calder
102 E9 Waitby Cumb
93 N10 Waithe Lincs
91 J6 Wakefield Wakefd
91 J7 Wakefield Crematorium Wakefd
58 G8 Wake Green Birm
73 P11 Wakerley Nhants
52 E6 Wakes Colne Essex
65 P7 Walberswick Suffk
15 Q5 Walberton W Susx
113 J7 Walbottle N u Ty
108 F7 Walbutt D & G
110 H8 Walby Cumb
19 Q5 Walcombe Somset
73 R3 Walcot Lincs
92 E6 Walcot N Linc
56 E7 Walcot Shrops
57 K2 Walcot Shrops
33 N8 Walcot Swindn
47 M3 Walcot Warwks
60 C4 Walcote Leics
64 G5 Walcot Green Norfk
86 F9 Walcott Lincs
77 M5 Walcott Norfk
96 F4 Walden N York
96 E4 Walden Head N York
91 P7 Walden Stubbs N York
38 C9 Walderslade Medway
15 L4 Walderton W Susx
11 K6 Walditch Dorset
71 L7 Waldley Derbys
113 L11 Waldridge Dur
53 N2 Waldringfield Suffk
25 M7 Waldron E Susx
84 G4 Wales Rothm
19 Q10 Wales Somset
86 F2 Walesby Lincs
85 L6 Walesby Notts
46 A10 Walford Herefs
56 F10 Walford Herefs
69 M10 Walford Shrops
70 E8 Walford Staffs
69 M11 Walford Heath Shrops
70 B5 Walgherton Ches E
60 H6 Walgrave Nhants
13 P5 Walhampton Hants
82 F4 Walkden Salfd
113 L8 Walker N u Ty
117 M3 Walkerburn Border
89 K2 Walker Fold Lancs
85 N2 Walkeringham Notts
85 N2 Walkerith Lincs
50 G5 Walkern Herts
45 Q5 Walker's Green Herefs
58 G9 Walker's Heath Birm
134 G7 Walkerton Fife
13 M6 Walkford Dorset
6 E5 Walkhampton Devon
92 G3 Walkington E R Yk
84 D3 Walkley Sheff
89 P5 Walk Mill Lancs
47 K2 Walkwood Worcs
112 D7 Wall Nthumb
58 H3 Wall Staffs
114 E7 Wallacetown S Ayrs
114 F3 Wallacetown S Ayrs
25 K8 Wallands Park E Susx
81 K6 Wallasey Wirral
94 E4 Wall End Cumb
45 N3 Wall End Herefs
38 E6 Wallend Medway
46 C7 Waller's Green Herefs
111 J8 Wallhead Cumb
58 C7 Wall Heath Dudley
112 F7 Wall Houses Nthumb
34 H7 Wallingford Oxon
36 G8 Wallington Gt Lon
14 G5 Wallington Hants
50 G4 Wallington Herts
58 E4 Wallington Heath Wsall
41 K5 Wallis Pembks
13 J6 Wallisdown Poole
24 D3 Walliswood Surrey
169 p9 Walls Shet
113 L7 Wallsend N Tyne
101 L5 Wallthwaite Cumb
57 J6 Wall under Haywood Shrops
128 B5 Wallyford E Loth
39 Q11 Walmer Kent
88 F6 Walmer Bridge Lancs
89 N8 Walmersley Bury
39 N10 Walmestone Kent
58 H6 Walmley Birm
58 H6 Walmley Ash Birm
87 L5 Walmsgate Lincs
19 K6 Walpole Somset
65 M7 Walpole Suffk
75 K7 Walpole Cross Keys Norfk
75 K8 Walpole Highway Norfk
75 K7 Walpole St Andrew Norfk
75 K7 Walpole St Peter Norfk
19 K5 Walrow Somset
58 F5 Walsall Wsall
58 F4 Walsall Wood Wsall
89 Q6 Walsden Calder
59 N8 Walsgrave on Sowe Covtry
64 E7 Walsham le Willows Suffk
89 M8 Walshaw Bury
97 P10 Walshford N York
75 J8 Walsoken Norfk
127 K8 Walston S Lans
50 E4 Walsworth Herts
35 M5 Walter's Ash Bucks
25 M2 Walters Green Kent
30 E10 Walterston V Glam
45 L9 Walterstone Herefs
27 K2 Waltham Kent
93 N10 Waltham NE Lin
51 J10 Waltham Abbey Essex
14 G4 Waltham Chase Hants
51 J10 Waltham Cross Herts
73 L6 Waltham on the Wolds Leics
35 M9 Waltham St Lawrence W & M
51 Q4 Waltham's Cross Essex
37 J3 Walthamstow Gt Lon
74 C10 Walton C Pete
111 K8 Walton Cumb
84 E7 Walton Derbys
97 P11 Walton Leeds
60 C3 Walton Leics
49 N7 Walton M Keyn
45 K3 Walton Powys
56 H9 Walton Shrops
19 N7 Walton Somset
70 F8 Walton Staffs
70 F9 Walton Staffs
53 N4 Walton Suffk
15 M6 Walton W Susx
91 K7 Walton Wakefd
47 Q4 Walton Warwks
69 Q11 Walton Wrekin
46 H8 Walton Cardiff Gloucs
41 K6 Walton East Pembks
20 E11 Walton Elm Dorset
48 F8 Walton Grounds Nhants
31 M10 Walton-in-Gordano N Som
82 D7 Walton Lea Crematorium Warrtn
88 H5 Walton-le-Dale Lancs
36 D7 Walton-on-Thames Surrey
70 H10 Walton-on-the-Hill Staffs
36 F9 Walton on the Hill Surrey
53 N7 Walton on the Naze Essex
72 F7 Walton on the Wolds Leics
71 N11 Walton-on-Trent Derbys
31 M10 Walton Park N Som
40 G8 Walton West Pembks
96 E10 Waltonwrays Crematorium N York
80 G9 Walwen Flints
80 H10 Walwen Flints
81 J9 Walwen Flints
112 D6 Walwick Nthumb
103 P7 Walworth Darltn
36 H5 Walworth Gt Lon
103 P6 Walworth Gate Darltn
40 G8 Walwyn's Castle Pembks
10 F3 Wambrook Somset
110 D10 Wampool Cumb
23 P5 Wanborough Surrey
33 P8 Wanborough Swindn
50 D6 Wandon End Herts
36 G6 Wandsworth Gt Lon
65 P6 Wangford Suffk
72 F8 Wanlip Leics
116 B8 Wanlockhead D & G
25 N10 Wannock E Susx
73 R11 Wansford C Pete
99 M9 Wansford E R Yk
26 C2 Wanshurst Green Kent
37 K3 Wanstead Gt Lon
20 D6 Wanstrow Somset
32 C4 Wanswell Gloucs
34 C7 Wantage Oxon
46 E3 Wants Green Worcs
32 D9 Wapley S Glos
59 N11 Wappenbury Warwks
48 H5 Wappenham Nhants
25 P7 Warbleton E Susx
34 G6 Warborough Oxon
62 D4 Warboys Cambs
88 C3 Warbreck Bpool
5 L3 Warbstow Cnwll
82 F7 Warburton Traffd
102 D7 Warcop Cumb
38 H7 Warden Kent
112 D7 Warden Nthumb
58 H7 Ward End Birm
50 D2 Warden Street C Beds
64 E9 Ward Green Suffk
89 J3 Ward Green Cross Lancs
50 C3 Wardhedges C Beds
48 E5 Wardington Oxon
69 R3 Wardle Ches E

89 Q7 Wardle Rochdl
113 M8 Wardley Gatesd
73 L10 Wardley Rutlnd
82 G4 Wardley Salfd
83 Q10 Wardlow Derbys
83 K8 Wardsend Ches E
62 G4 Wardy Hill Cambs
51 J8 Ware Herts
12 F7 Wareham Dorset
26 G5 Warehorne Kent
119 M5 Warenford Nthumb
119 M4 Waren Mill Nthumb
119 M4 Warenton Nthumb
51 J7 Wareside Herts
62 C10 Waresley Cambs
58 B10 Waresley Worcs
38 C10 Ware Street Kent
35 N10 Warfield Br For
7 M8 Warfleet Devon
74 D4 Wargate Lincs
35 L9 Wargrave Wokham
45 P7 Warham Herefs
76 D3 Warham All Saints Norfk
76 C3 Warham St Mary Norfk
112 C5 Wark Nthumb
118 F3 Wark Nthumb
17 L7 Warkleigh Devon
61 J5 Warkton Nhants
48 E6 Warkworth Nhants
119 P9 Warkworth Nthumb
97 M2 Warlaby N York
89 Q6 Warland Calder
5 K8 Warleggan Cnwll
20 E2 Warleigh BaNES
90 D6 Warley Town Calder
37 J9 Warlingham Surrey
71 P4 Warmbrook Derbys
91 K6 Warmfield Wakefd
70 C2 Warmingham Ches E
61 N2 Warmington Nhants
48 D5 Warmington Warwks
20 G5 Warminster Wilts
32 C10 Warmley S Glos
91 N10 Warmsworth Donc
12 C7 Warmwell Dorset
46 G3 Warndon Worcs
22 H10 Warnford Hants
24 E4 Warnham W Susx
24 E4 Warnham Court W Susx
24 B9 Warningcamp W Susx
24 F5 Warninglid W Susx
83 J10 Warren Ches E
40 H11 Warren Pembks
104 G5 Warrenby R & Cl
116 C3 Warrenhill S Lans
35 M8 Warren Row W & M
50 G5 Warren's Green Herts
38 F11 Warren Street Kent
49 N4 Warrington M Keyn
82 D7 Warrington Warrtn
127 P2 Warriston C Edin
127 P2 Warriston Crematorium C Edin
14 E5 Warsash Hants
71 K3 Warslow Staffs
84 H7 Warsop Vale Notts
98 H10 Warter E R Yk
97 K5 Warthermaske N York
98 D9 Warthill N York
25 Q9 Wartling E Susx
73 J6 Wartnaby Leics
88 E5 Warton Lancs
95 K6 Warton Lancs
119 K10 Warton Nthumb
59 L4 Warton Warwks
59 L11 Warwick Warwks
111 J9 Warwick Bridge Cumb
47 Q2 Warwick Castle Warwks
111 J9 Warwick-on-Eden Cumb
48 B3 Warwick Services Warwks
111 J5 Warwicksland Cumb
169 c3 Wasbister Ork
100 G9 Wasdale Head Cumb
83 N8 Wash Derbys
51 K4 Washall Green Herts
4 G8 Washaway Cnwll
7 K8 Washbourne Devon
19 M4 Washbrook Somset
53 K3 Washbrook Suffk
18 B11 Washfield Devon
103 L10 Washfold N York
18 E6 Washford Somset
9 K2 Washford Pyne Devon
86 D6 Washingborough Lincs
113 M9 Washington Sundld
24 D8 Washington W Susx
113 L9 Washington Services Gatesd
58 H7 Washwood Heath Birm
22 G2 Wasing W Berk
112 F11 Waskerley Dur
47 Q3 Wasperton Warwks
86 E8 Wasps Nest Lincs
98 B5 Wass N York
18 E6 Watchet Somset
33 P6 Watchfield Oxon
19 K5 Watchfield Somset
101 P11 Watchgate Cumb
100 G2 Watchill Cumb
7 N5 Watcombe Torbay
101 J7 Watendlath Cumb
9 J8 Water Devon
89 N5 Water Lancs
62 G7 Waterbeach Cambs
15 N5 Waterbeach W Susx
110 D5 Waterbeck D & G
76 B4 Waterden Norfk
34 F2 Water Eaton Oxon
58 D2 Water Eaton Staffs
61 P10 Water End Bed
61 P11 Water End Bed
50 C3 Water End C Beds
100 F6 Waterend Cumb
92 C3 Water End E R Yk
51 N2 Water End Essex
50 B8 Water End Herts
50 F10 Water End Herts
71 K4 Waterfall Staffs
125 P6 Waterfoot E Rens
50 H8 Waterford Herts
91 M5 Water Fryston Wakefd
5 J5 Watergate Cnwll
101 L10 Waterhead Cumb
127 N7 Waterheads Border
103 N2 Waterhouses Dur
71 K4 Waterhouses Staffs
37 Q10 Wateringbury Kent
32 H4 Waterlane Gloucs
5 J7 Waterloo Cnwll
84 F8 Waterloo Derbys
45 L5 Waterloo Herefs
145 L3 Waterloo Highld
126 E7 Waterloo N Lans
77 J8 Waterloo Norfk
141 Q10 Waterloo P & K
41 J10 Waterloo Pembks
12 H6 Waterloo Poole
81 L5 Waterloo Sefton
9 Q2 Waterloo Cross Devon
66 H2 Waterloo Port Gwynd
15 J5 Waterlooville Hants
101 M6 Watermillock Cumb
74 B11 Water Newton Cambs
59 J6 Water Orton Warwks
34 H3 Waterperry Oxon
18 E9 Waterrow Somset
24 B7 Watersfield W Susx
89 L6 Waterside Bl w D
35 Q4 Waterside Bucks
110 D11 Waterside Cumb
91 R8 Waterside Donc
114 H6 Waterside E Ayrs
125 M9 Waterside E Ayrs
126 B3 Waterside E Duns
89 K6 Water's Nook Bolton
152 A8 Waterstein Highld
34 H3 Waterstock Oxon
40 H9 Waterston Pembks
49 J8 Water Stratford Bucks
29 M8 Water Street Neath
70 A11 Waters Upton Wrekin
94 F3 Water Yeat Cumb
50 D11 Watford Herts
60 D7 Watford Nhants
60 D7 Watford Gap Services Nhants
96 H7 Wath N York
97 M5 Wath N York
91 L10 Wath upon Dearne Rothm
75 M8 Watlington Norfk
35 J6 Watlington Oxon
84 H11 Watnall Notts
167 M6 Watten Highld
64 E7 Wattisfield Suffk
64 E11 Wattisham Suffk
11 K6 Watton Dorset
99 L10 Watton E R Yk
76 C11 Watton Norfk
50 H7 Watton-at-Stone Herts
76 C11 Watton Green Norfk
51 M11 Wattons Green Essex
126 D3 Wattston N Lans
30 D6 Wattstown Rhondd
30 H6 Wattsville Caerph
92 G5 Wauldby E R Yk
150 G9 Waulkmill Abers
28 H5 Waunarlwydd Swans
54 E8 Waunfawr Cerdgn
67 J3 Waunfawr Gwynd
28 G4 Waungron Swans
30 G3 Waunlwyd Blae G
49 P7 Wavendon M Keyn
110 D11 Waverbridge Cumb
69 N2 Waverton Ches W
110 D11 Waverton Cumb
93 J3 Wawne E R Yk
77 N6 Waxham Norfk
93 P5 Waxholme E R Yk
39 P8 Way Kent
7 K4 Waye Devon
11 J3 Wayford Somset
11 K5 Waytown Dorset
9 L2 Way Village Devon
19 L2 Way Wick N Som
18 F6 Weacombe Somset
34 B4 Weald Oxon
36 E3 Wealdstone Gt Lon
90 H2 Weardley Leeds
19 M4 Weare Somset
16 H7 Weare Giffard Devon
102 G3 Wearhead Dur
19 M9 Wearne Somset
103 Q4 Wear Valley Crematorium Dur
102 C10 Weasdale Cumb
76 A7 Weasenham All Saints Norfk
76 B7 Weasenham St Peter Norfk
82 H5 Weaste Salfd
58 G10 Weatheroak Hill Worcs
82 D10 Weaverham Ches W
71 L11 Weaverslake Staffs
99 K6 Weaverthorpe N York
19 L3 Webbington Somset
32 C10 Webb's Heath S Glos
58 F11 Webheath Worcs
45 N7 Webton Herefs
159 L11 Wedderlairs Abers
96 D11 Wedding Hall Fold N York
39 N10 Weddington Kent
59 N6 Weddington Warwks
21 L3 Wedhampton Wilts
19 M5 Wedmore Somset
58 E5 Wednesbury Sandw
58 D4 Wednesfield Wolves
85 P7 Weecar Notts
49 M11 Weedon Bucks
60 D9 Weedon Nhants
48 H5 Weedon Lois Nhants
58 H4 Weeford Staffs
7 K6 Week Devon
17 K6 Week Devon
17 N8 Week Devon
9 J3 Weeke Devon
22 E8 Weeke Hants
61 J4 Weekley Nhants
5 L2 Week St Mary Cnwll
93 J3 Weel E R Yk
53 K7 Weeley Essex
53 K7 Weeley Crematorium Essex
53 L7 Weeley Heath Essex
141 K8 Weem P & K
70 G10 Weeping Cross Staffs
47 L3 Weethley Warwks
63 N3 Weeting Norfk
93 Q6 Weeton E R Yk
88 D4 Weeton Lancs
97 L11 Weeton N York
90 H3 Weetwood Leeds
89 P5 Weir Lancs
69 K10 Weirbrook Shrops
6 C5 Weir Quay Devon
169 q8 Weisdale Shet
76 F9 Welborne Norfk
86 C10 Welbourn Lincs
98 E7 Welburn N York
104 C10 Welbury N York
73 P3 Welby Lincs
62 G3 Welches Dam Cambs
16 C8 Welcombe Devon
119 M11 Weldon Bridge Nthumb
60 D4 Welford Nhants
34 D10 Welford W Berk
47 M4 Welford-on-Avon Warwks
60 G2 Welham Leics
85 M4 Welham Notts
50 F9 Welham Green Herts
23 L5 Well Hants
87 M6 Well Lincs
97 L4 Well N York
46 E6 Welland Worcs
142 H10 Wellbank Angus
35 N7 Well End Bucks
50 F11 Well End Herts
47 Q3 Wellesbourne Warwks
47 Q3 Wellesbourne Mountford Warwks
50 E5 Well Head Herts
37 L8 Well Hill Kent
34 F10 Wellhouse W Berk
37 L5 Welling Gt Lon
61 J7 Wellingborough Nhants
76 B7 Wellingham Norfk
86 C9 Wellingore Lincs
100 E10 Wellington Cumb
45 P5 Wellington Herefs
18 F10 Wellington Somset
57 M2 Wellington Wrekin
46 D6 Wellington Heath Herefs
45 P5 Wellington Marsh Herefs
20 D3 Wellow BaNES
14 C9 Wellow IoW
85 L7 Wellow Notts
51 K6 Wellpond Green Herts
19 P5 Wells Somset
72 B10 Wellsborough Leics
70 B4 Wells Green Ches E
90 D4 Wells Head C Brad
76 C3 Wells-next-the-sea Norfk
51 P7 Wellstye Green Essex
9 M3 Well Town Devon
134 B3 Welltree P & K
134 D10 Wellwood Fife
62 H2 Welney Norfk
69 M7 Welshampton Shrops
46 A11 Welsh Bicknor Herefs
69 P7 Welsh End Shrops
69 L8 Welsh Frankton Shrops
40 H5 Welsh Hook Pembks
45 Q11 Welsh Newton Herefs
56 C3 Welshpool Powys
30 D9 Welsh St Donats V Glam
101 L2 Welton Cumb
92 G5 Welton E R Yk
86 D5 Welton Lincs
60 C7 Welton Nhants
87 N7 Welton le Marsh Lincs
87 J3 Welton le Wold Lincs
93 P6 Welwick E R Yk
50 F7 Welwyn Herts
50 F8 Welwyn Garden City Herts
69 P9 Wem Shrops
19 J7 Wembdon Somset
36 E3 Wembley Gt Lon
6 E9 Wembury Devon
17 M10 Wembworthy Devon
124 F4 Wemyss Bay Inver
54 F10 Wenallt Cerdgn
51 M3 Wendens Ambo Essex
48 G11 Wendlebury Oxon
76 C9 Wendling Norfk
35 N3 Wendover Bucks
2 H7 Wendron Cnwll
62 D11 Wendy Cambs
4 H6 Wenfordbridge Cnwll
65 N6 Wenhaston Suffk
62 B5 Wennington Cambs
37 M4 Wennington Gt Lon
95 N7 Wennington Lancs
84 C8 Wensley Derbys
96 G3 Wensley N York
91 M7 Wentbridge Wakefd
56 F6 Wentnor Shrops
62 G5 Wentworth Cambs
91 K11 Wentworth Rothm
91 J10 Wentworth Castle Barns
30 F10 Wenvoe V Glam
45 N4 Weobley Herefs
45 N4 Weobley Marsh Herefs
24 B9 Wepham W Susx
75 N10 Wereham Norfk
58 C4 Wergs Wolves
67 J7 Wern Gwynd
44 G11 Wern Powys
56 D2 Wern Powys
69 J8 Wern Shrops
83 L6 Werneth Low Tamesd
28 F6 Wernffrwd Swans
81 J11 Wern-y-gaer Flints
74 C10 Werrington C Pete
5 N4 Werrington Cnwll
70 G5 Werrington Staffs
81 N10 Wervin Ches W
88 E4 Wesham Lancs
22 E11 Wessex Vale Crematorium Hants
84 E9 Wessington Derbys
30 D11 West Aberthaw V Glam
75 Q7 West Acre Norfk
129 P10 West Allerdean Nthumb
7 J10 West Alvington Devon
21 M6 West Amesbury Wilts
17 R6 West Anstey Devon
97 K2 West Appleton N York
87 J6 West Ashby Lincs
15 M5 West Ashling W Susx
20 G3 West Ashton Wilts
103 N5 West Auckland Dur
99 K4 West Ayton N York
18 G8 West Bagborough Somset
30 H3 West Bank Blae G
81 Q8 West Bank Halton
86 G4 West Barkwith Lincs
105 M8 West Barnby N York
128 H4 West Barns E Loth
76 C5 West Barsham Norfk
11 K6 West Bay Dorset
76 G4 West Beckham Norfk
36 C6 West Bedfont Surrey
39 L9 Westbere Kent
52 G6 West Bergholt Essex
34 F11 West Berkshire Crematorium W Berk
11 L7 West Bexington Dorset
75 P7 West Bilney Norfk
24 G9 West Blatchington Br & H
113 N8 West Boldon S Tyne
73 M2 Westborough Lincs
13 J6 Westbourne Bmouth
15 L5 Westbourne W Susx
20 E9 West Bourton Dorset
90 F4 West Bowling C Brad
27 J3 West Brabourne Kent
76 C10 West Bradenham Norfk
89 L2 West Bradford Lancs
19 Q7 West Bradley Somset
90 H8 West Bretton Wakefd
72 F3 West Bridgford Notts
103 J7 West Briscoe Dur
58 F6 West Bromwich Sandw
58 F6 West Bromwich Crematorium Sandw
39 P7 Westbrook Kent
34 D10 Westbrook W Berk
33 J11 Westbrook Wilts
17 M5 West Buckland Devon
18 G10 West Buckland Somset
96 F3 West Burton N York
15 Q4 West Burton W Susx
48 H7 Westbury Bucks
56 F3 Westbury Shrops
20 G4 Westbury Wilts
20 G5 Westbury Leigh Wilts
32 D2 Westbury on Severn Gloucs
31 Q9 Westbury-on-Trym Bristl
19 P5 Westbury-sub-Mendip Somset
103 M2 West Butsfield Dur
92 D9 West Butterwick N Linc
88 D4 Westby Lancs
36 B8 West Byfleet Surrey
106 F11 West Cairngaan D & G
77 Q9 West Caister Norfk
127 J5 West Calder W Loth
19 Q10 West Camel Somset
12 C8 West Chaldon Dorset
34 C7 West Challow Oxon
7 K10 West Charleton Devon
11 L3 West Chelborough Dorset
119 P11 West Chevington Nthumb
24 C7 West Chiltington W Susx
11 K2 West Chinnock Somset
21 M4 West Chisenbury Wilts
36 B10 West Clandon Surrey
27 P3 West Cliffe Kent
38 E4 Westcliff-on-Sea Sthend
11 L2 West Coker Somset
7 K6 West Combe Devon
20 C7 Westcombe Somset
19 Q6 West Compton Somset
11 M6 West Compton Abbas Dorset
47 P10 Westcote Gloucs
48 D9 Westcote Barton Oxon
49 K11 Westcott Bucks
9 P4 Westcott Devon
36 D11 Westcott Surrey
92 A2 West Cottingwith N York
21 P2 Westcourt Wilts
91 Q6 West Cowick E R Yk
28 H7 West Cross Swans
5 M3 West Curry Cnwll
110 F11 West Curthwaite Cumb
25 M11 Westdean E Susx
15 N4 West Dean W Susx
21 Q9 West Dean Wilts
74 B9 West Deeping Lincs
81 M6 West Derby Lpool
75 N10 West Dereham Norfk
119 M6 West Ditchburn Nthumb
17 J3 West Down Devon
21 K5 Westdown Camp Wilts
4 H5 Westdowns Cnwll
36 C5 West Drayton Gt Lon
85 M6 West Drayton Notts
167 M2 West Dunnet Highld
37 M7 Wested Kent
92 H5 West Ella E R Yk
49 Q4 West End Bed
35 N10 West End Br For
30 H5 West End Caerph
62 D7 West End Cambs
110 F9 West End Cumb
92 F4 West End E R Yk
93 L4 West End E R Yk
93 N5 West End E R Yk
32 E3 Westend Gloucs
14 E4 West End Hants
22 H7 West End Hants
50 G9 West End Herts
50 H9 West End Herts
89 L5 West End Lancs
90 G3 West End Leeds
93 Q11 West End Lincs
31 N11 West End N Som
91 N2 West End N York
76 C10 West End Norfk
77 Q9 West End Norfk
34 G7 West End Oxon
32 D7 West End S Glos
20 C8 West End Somset
23 P2 West End Surrey
36 D8 West End Surrey
35 M9 West End W & M
24 F7 West End W Susx
20 H10 West End Wilts
21 J10 West End Wilts
33 J9 West End Wilts
23 J2 West End Green Hants
111 Q7 Westend Town Nthumb
27 K4 Westenhanger Kent
167 K6 Westerdale Highld
105 J9 Westerdale N York
53 L2 Westerfield Suffk
15 P5 Westergate W Susx
37 K10 Westerham Kent
113 J7 Westerhope N u Ty
7 M6 Westerland Devon
32 C9 Westerleigh S Glos
32 D9 Westerleigh Crematorium S Glos
127 J3 Wester Ochiltree W Loth
135 P6 Wester Pitkierie Fife
160 F11 Wester Ross Highld
15 N5 Westerton W Susx
143 M7 Westerton of Rossie Angus
169 p9 Westerwick Shet
36 F8 West Ewell Surrey
38 B11 West Farleigh Kent
48 F4 West Farndon Nhants
69 K9 West Felton Shrops
20 C4 Westfield BaNES
100 C5 Westfield Cumb
26 D8 Westfield E Susx
167 J4 Westfield Highld
126 C3 Westfield N Lans
76 D10 Westfield Norfk
126 G3 Westfield W Loth
12 B3 Westfields Dorset
45 P6 Westfields Herefs
142 B8 Westfields of Rattray P & K
38 C9 Westfield Sole Kent
99 M5 West Flotmanby N York
18 F10 Westford Somset
102 H3 Westgate Dur
92 C9 Westgate N Linc
76 D3 Westgate Norfk
90 G5 Westgate Hill C Brad
39 P7 Westgate on Sea Kent
76 H7 Westgate Street Norfk
34 D7 West Ginge Oxon
21 P2 West Grafton Wilts
23 K3 West Green Hants
21 P9 West Grimstead Wilts
24 E6 West Grinstead W Susx
91 P5 West Haddlesey N York
60 D6 West Haddon Nhants
34 F7 West Hagbourne Oxon
58 D8 West Hagley Worcs
65 N5 Westhall Suffk
72 C2 West Hallam Derbys
72 C2 West Hallam Common Derbys
92 F6 West Halton N Linc
11 P9 Westham Dorset
25 P10 Westham E Susx
37 J4 West Ham Gt Lon
19 M5 Westham Somset
15 N5 Westhampnett W Susx
84 E5 West Handley Derbys
34 D6 West Hanney Oxon
38 B2 West Hanningfield Essex
21 M9 West Harnham Wilts
19 Q3 West Harptree BaNES
23 L10 West Harting W Susx
19 J10 West Hatch Somset
20 H9 West Hatch Wilts
143 K10 West Haven Angus
19 M6 Westhay Somset
88 E9 Westhead Lancs
75 L9 West Head Norfk
58 F9 West Heath Birm
22 G3 West Heath Hants
163 N3 West Helmsdale Highld
34 D7 West Hendred Oxon
50 D10 West Hertfordshire Crematorium Herts
99 J5 West Heslerton N York
19 L2 West Hewish N Som
46 A6 Westhide Herefs
151 L6 Westhill Abers
9 Q6 West Hill Devon
25 J4 West Hoathly W Susx
12 E7 West Holme Dorset
19 Q6 Westholme Somset
45 P4 Westhope Herefs
56 H7 Westhope Shrops
37 P3 West Horndon Essex
48 F4 Westhorp Nhants
74 D4 Westhorpe Lincs
64 E8 Westhorpe Suffk
19 Q5 West Horrington Somset
36 C10 West Horsley Surrey
119 K4 West Horton Nthumb
27 N3 West Hougham Kent
89 K9 Westhoughton Bolton
95 P6 Westhouse N York
84 F9 Westhouses Derbys
13 J5 West Howe Bmouth
18 B8 West Howetown Somset
36 E10 Westhumble Surrey
134 D3 West Huntingtower P & K
19 K6 West Huntspill Somset
50 D7 West Hyde C Beds
36 B2 West Hyde Herts
27 K5 West Hythe Kent
17 N2 West Ilkerton Devon
34 E8 West Ilsley W Berk
15 L6 West Itchenor W Susx
87 L8 West Keal Lincs
33 M11 West Kennett Wilts
124 G8 West Kilbride N Ayrs
37 N8 West Kingsdown Kent
32 F9 West Kington Wilts
81 J7 West Kirby Wirral
98 H5 West Knapton N York
12 B7 West Knighton Dorset
20 G8 West Knoyle Wilts
119 L2 West Kyloe Nthumb
6 G8 Westlake Devon
19 M11 West Lambrook Somset
51 K6 Westland Green Herts
27 P2 West Langdon Kent
23 N10 West Lavington W Susx
21 K4 West Lavington Wilts
103 M8 West Layton N York
72 E5 West Leake Notts
118 F3 West Learmouth Nthumb
104 E10 West Lees N York
8 G3 West Leigh Devon
16 H6 Westleigh Devon
18 E11 Westleigh Devon
18 F8 West Leigh Somset
65 N8 Westleton Suffk
76 A8 West Lexham Norfk
56 F3 Westley Shrops
63 P8 Westley Suffk
63 K9 Westley Waterless Cambs
98 C8 West Lilling N York
35 L2 Westlington Bucks
127 M7 West Linton Border
110 G8 Westlinton Cumb
32 E9 West Littleton S Glos
34 D7 West Lockinge Oxon
36 F4 West London Crematorium Gt Lon
12 D8 West Lulworth Dorset
99 J7 West Lutton N York
19 Q8 West Lydford Somset
17 N2 West Lyn Devon
19 K9 West Lyng Somset
75 M6 West Lynn Norfk
37 Q9 West Malling Kent
46 E5 West Malvern Worcs
15 L4 West Marden W Susx

85 M6 West Markham Notts
39 N9 Westmarsh Kent
93 N9 West Marsh NE Lin
75 R5 West Marton N York
96 C10 West Marton N York
20 G10 West Melbury Dorset
91 L10 West Melton Rothm
22 H10 West Meon Hants
23 J9 West Meon Hut Hants
22 H9 West Meon Woodlands Hants
52 H9 West Mersea Essex
24 H8 Westmeston E Susx
112 G8 West Mickley Nthumb
57 Q9 West Midland Safari Park Worcs
50 H7 Westmill Herts
51 J5 Westmill Herts
11 L5 West Milton Dorset
36 G5 Westminster Gt Lon
38 F7 West Minster Kent
36 D7 West Molesey Surrey
19 J9 West Monkton Somset
13 J4 West Moors Dorset
12 F5 West Morden Dorset
118 B2 West Morriston Border
90 D2 West Morton C Brad
19 Q10 West Mudford Somset
142 F7 Westmuir Angus
98 D5 West Ness N York
104 C7 West Newbiggin Darltn
100 F2 Westnewton Cumb
93 M3 West Newton E R Yk
75 N5 West Newton Norfk
19 J9 West Newton Somset
36 H6 West Norwood Gt Lon
36 H6 West Norwood Crematorium Gt Lon
113 N7 Westoe S Tyne
7 L4 West Ogwell Devon
32 D11 Weston BaNES
70 C4 Weston Ches E
10 C4 Weston Devon
10 D7 Weston Devon
11 P10 Weston Dorset
81 Q8 Weston Halton
23 K10 Weston Hants
45 M3 Weston Herefs
50 G4 Weston Herts
74 E6 Weston Lincs
97 J11 Weston N York
48 G5 Weston Nhants
85 N7 Weston Notts
56 E10 Weston Shrops
57 L6 Weston Shrops
69 J9 Weston Shrops
70 H9 Weston Staffs
34 C10 Weston W Berk
46 A6 Weston Beggard Herefs
32 G7 Westonbirt Gloucs
60 G2 Weston by Welland Nhants
22 F7 Weston Colley Hants
63 K10 Weston Colville Cambs
23 J5 Weston Corbett Hants
70 G6 Weston Coyney C Stke
60 G8 Weston Favell Nhants
63 K10 Weston Green Cambs
57 P2 Weston Heath Shrops
74 E6 Weston Hills Lincs
59 N7 Weston in Arden Warwks
50 B4 Westoning C Beds
31 M10 Weston-in-Gordano N Som
50 B4 Westoning Woodend C Beds
70 D10 Weston Jones Staffs
76 G8 Weston Longville Norfk
69 M10 Weston Lullingfields Shrops
6 D7 Weston Mill Crematorium C Plym
47 N4 Weston-on-Avon Warwks
48 F11 Weston-on-the-Green Oxon
23 J5 Weston Patrick Hants
69 J7 Weston Rhyn Shrops
47 M6 Weston-sub-Edge Gloucs
19 K2 Weston-super-Mare N Som
19 L2 Weston-super-Mare Crematorium N Som
35 N2 Weston Turville Bucks
57 Q2 Weston-under-Lizard Staffs
46 B10 Weston under Penyard Herefs
69 Q9 Weston-under-Redcastle Shrops
59 N11 Weston under Wetherley Warwks
71 P6 Weston Underwood Derbys
49 N4 Weston Underwood M Keyn
72 C5 Weston-upon-Trent Derbys
19 L8 Westonzoyland Somset
20 F11 West Orchard Dorset
33 M11 West Overton Wilts
98 F7 Westow N York
5 N3 West Panson Devon
151 K8 West Park Abers
13 J5 West Parley Dorset
37 P10 West Peckham Kent
5 N3 West Peeke Devon
113 K10 West Pelton Dur
19 P7 West Pennard Somset
4 B9 West Pentire Cnwll
61 P7 West Perry Cambs
17 R2 West Porlock Somset
19 L10 Westport Somset
11 Q3 West Pulham Dorset
16 F8 West Putford Devon
18 F6 West Quantoxhead Somset
126 G2 Westquarter Falk
30 F10 Westra V Glam
9 L4 West Raddon Devon
113 M11 West Rainton Dur
86 E3 West Rasen Lincs
93 M11 West Ravendale NE Lin
169 d2 Westray Ork
169 d1 Westray Airport Ork
76 B6 West Raynham Norfk
85 L4 West Retford Notts
34 G9 Westridge Green W Berk
126 G4 Westrigg W Loth
113 K7 West Road Crematorium N u Ty
33 P6 Westrop Swindn

104 D10 West Rounton N York
63 L5 West Row Suffk
75 R5 West Rudham Norfk
76 H3 West Runton Norfk
128 G10 Westruther Border
74 H11 Westry Cambs
128 D6 West Saltoun E Loth
9 K4 West Sandford Devon
169 r5 West Sandwick Shet
96 G4 West Scrafton N York
113 L4 West Sleekburn Nthumb
77 P7 West Somerton Norfk
11 Q7 West Stafford Dorset
92 C11 West Stockwith Notts
15 M5 West Stoke W Susx
102 G10 West Stonesdale N York
19 M5 West Stoughton Somset
20 E10 West Stour Dorset
39 N9 West Stourmouth Kent
63 P6 West Stow Suffk
21 M2 West Stowell Wilts
22 F6 West Stratton Hants
38 F11 West Street Kent
39 P11 West Street Kent
38 B6 West Street Medway
64 D7 West Street Suffk
63 P7 West Suffolk Crematorium Suffk
97 L5 West Tanfield N York
5 J9 West Taphouse Cnwll
123 P6 West Tarbert Ag & B
24 D10 West Tarring W Susx
119 N11 West Thirston Nthumb
15 L6 West Thorney W Susx
84 G5 Westthorpe Notts
72 G5 West Thorpe Notts
37 N5 West Thurrock Thurr
37 Q5 West Tilbury Thurr
23 J9 West Tisted Hants
86 F4 West Torrington Lincs
19 P2 West Town BaNES
15 K7 West Town Hants
45 N2 West Town Herefs
31 N11 West Town N Som
19 P7 West Town Somset
20 D6 West Town Somset
21 Q9 West Tytherley Hants
75 J8 West Walton Norfk
75 J8 West Walton Highway Norfk
101 J2 Westward Cumb
16 G6 Westward Ho! Devon
26 G2 Westwell Kent
33 P3 Westwell Oxon
26 G2 Westwell Leacon Kent
21 Q11 West Wellow Hants
6 E9 West Wembury Devon
135 J9 West Wemyss Fife
62 F7 Westwick Cambs
103 L7 Westwick Dur
19 L2 West Wick N Som
77 K6 Westwick Norfk
63 K11 West Wickham Cambs
37 J7 West Wickham Gt Lon
41 K9 West Williamston Pembks
20 H3 West Wiltshire Crematorium Wilts
75 M7 West Winch Norfk
21 P8 West Winterslow Wilts
15 L7 West Wittering W Susx
96 G3 West Witton N York
9 P5 Westwood Devon
37 P6 Westwood Kent
39 Q8 Westwood Kent
84 G10 Westwood Notts
111 Q7 Westwood Nthumb
20 F7 Westwood Wilts
112 C3 West Woodburn Nthumb
22 C2 West Woodhay W Berk
59 L9 Westwood Heath Covtry
20 E6 West Woodlands Somset
92 B10 Westwoodside N Linc
23 K7 West Worldham Hants
24 D10 West Worthing W Susx
63 K10 West Wratting Cambs
35 M6 West Wycombe Bucks
112 H8 West Wylam Nthumb
32 G9 West Yatton Wilts
37 P7 West Yoke Kent
16 D8 West Youlstone Cnwll
38 D7 Wetham Green Kent
111 J10 Wetheral Cumb
97 P11 Wetherby Leeds
64 E9 Wetherden Suffk
64 G8 Wetheringsett Suffk
52 B5 Wethersfield Essex
64 G9 Wetherup Street Suffk
70 H5 Wetley Rocks Staffs
69 R2 Wettenhall Ches E
71 L3 Wetton Staffs
99 J9 Wetwang E R Yk
70 D8 Wetwood Staffs
21 Q3 Wexcombe Wilts
35 Q8 Wexham Slough
35 Q8 Wexham Street Bucks
76 G3 Weybourne Norfk
23 N5 Weybourne Surrey
65 J5 Weybread Suffk
65 J6 Weybread Street Suffk
36 C8 Weybridge Surrey
10 G5 Weycroft Devon
167 L4 Weydale Highld
22 B5 Weyhill Hants
11 P9 Weymouth Dorset
11 P9 Weymouth Crematorium Dorset
49 M8 Whaddon Bucks
62 E11 Whaddon Cambs
32 F2 Whaddon Gloucs
20 G2 Whaddon Wilts
21 N9 Whaddon Wilts
101 P6 Whale Cumb
84 H6 Whaley Derbys
83 M8 Whaley Bridge Derbys
84 H6 Whaley Thorns Derbys
167 P8 Whaligoe Highld
89 L3 Whalley Lancs
89 L3 Whalley Banks Lancs
169 s7 Whalsay Shet
112 H4 Whalton Nthumb
74 F6 Whaplode Lincs
74 F8 Whaplode Drove Lincs
48 D4 Wharf Warwks
96 A7 Wharfe N York
88 E3 Wharles Lancs
49 P6 Wharley End C Beds
84 C2 Wharncliffe Side Sheff
98 H7 Wharram-le-Street N York

82 E11 Wharton Ches W
45 Q3 Wharton Herefs
103 N9 Whashton N York
95 L4 Whasset Cumb
47 Q6 Whatcote Warwks
59 K5 Whateley Warwks
52 H2 Whatfield Suffk
10 H3 Whatley Somset
20 D5 Whatley Somset
32 C8 Whatley's End S Glos
26 C8 Whatlington E Susx
27 K3 Whatsole Street Kent
84 D10 Whatstandwell Derbys
73 J3 Whatton Notts
107 M8 Whauphill D & G
103 J10 Whaw N York
65 P3 Wheal Rose Cnwll
35 J7 Wheatacre Norfk
50 E8 Wheathampstead Herts
57 L8 Wheathill Shrops
19 Q8 Wheathill Somset
90 D5 Wheatley Calder
23 L6 Wheatley Hants
34 G3 Wheatley Oxon
104 C3 Wheatley Hill Dur
91 P10 Wheatley Hills Donc
89 N3 Wheatley Lane Lancs
58 C2 Wheaton Aston Staffs
69 K4 Wheatsheaf Wrexhm
18 B7 Wheddon Cross Somset
27 K2 Wheelbarrow Town Kent
35 M6 Wheeler End Bucks
35 L10 Wheeler's Green Wokham
26 D3 Wheeler's Street Kent
23 P6 Wheelerstreet Surrey
70 D3 Wheelock Ches E
70 D3 Wheelock Heath Ches E
89 J6 Wheelton Lancs
91 M5 Wheldale Wakefd
92 A2 Wheldrake C York
33 N5 Whelford Gloucs
35 Q4 Whelpley Hill Bucks
101 K3 Whelpo Cumb
81 J9 Whelston Flints
50 H6 Whempstead Herts
98 C7 Whenby N York
64 A10 Whepstead Suffk
53 L3 Wherstead Suffk
22 C6 Wherwell Hants
83 P9 Wheston Derbys
37 Q11 Whetsted Kent
36 G2 Whetstone Gt Lon
72 F11 Whetstone Leics
110 C11 Wheyrigg Cumb
94 C4 Whicham Cumb
48 B8 Whichford Warwks
113 K8 Whickham Gatesd
8 C5 Whiddon Devon
8 G6 Whiddon Down Devon
53 K3 Whight's Corner Suffk
142 H9 Whigstreet Angus
60 D8 Whilton Nhants
16 F11 Whimble Devon
9 P5 Whimple Devon
77 M6 Whimpwell Green Norfk
76 E10 Whinburgh Norfk
88 D2 Whin Lane End Lancs
108 F10 Whinnie Liggate D & G
110 F10 Whinnow Cumb
159 Q11 Whinnyfold Abers
104 C7 Whinny Hill S on T
14 F8 Whippingham IoW
50 B7 Whipsnade C Beds
50 B7 Whipsnade Wild Animal Park C Beds
9 M6 Whipton Devon
84 D4 Whirlow Sheff
86 B7 Whisby Lincs
73 L8 Whissendine Rutlnd
76 C7 Whissonsett Norfk
131 Q9 Whistlefield Ag & B
131 N9 Whistlefield Inn Ag & B
35 L10 Whistley Green Wokham
81 P6 Whiston Knows
60 H8 Whiston Nhants
84 F3 Whiston Rothm
58 C2 Whiston Staffs
71 J5 Whiston Staffs
57 P4 Whiston Cross Shrops
71 J5 Whiston Eaves Staffs
59 L6 Whitacre Fields Warwks
94 C4 Whitbeck Cumb
46 D3 Whitbourne Herefs
113 P8 Whitburn S Tyne
126 G5 Whitburn W Loth
81 M9 Whitby Ches W
105 N8 Whitby N York
81 M10 Whitbyheath Ches W
129 J8 Whitchester Border
32 B11 Whitchurch BaNES
49 M10 Whitchurch Bucks
30 G9 Whitchurch Cardif
6 D4 Whitchurch Devon
22 E5 Whitchurch Hants
45 R11 Whitchurch Herefs
34 H9 Whitchurch Oxon
40 F5 Whitchurch Pembks
69 P6 Whitchurch Shrops
10 H5 Whitchurch Canonicorum Dorset
34 H9 Whitchurch Hill Oxon
11 Q7 Whitcombe Dorset
56 F6 Whitcot Shrops
56 D8 Whitcott Keysett Shrops
27 K2 Whiteacre Kent
59 K6 Whiteacre Heath Warwks
52 C5 Whiteash Green Essex
18 F11 White Ball Devon
147 M4 Whitebridge Highld
31 P3 Whitebrook Mons
151 N4 Whitecairns Abers
88 H4 Whitechapel Lancs
30 H4 Whitechapel Gt Lon
88 H2 White Chapel Lancs
41 N3 Whitechurch Pembks
31 Q3 Whitecliffe Gloucs
52 E6 White Colne Essex
89 J7 White Coppice Lancs
127 Q3 Whitecraig E Loth
32 B3 Whitecroft Gloucs
106 G6 Whitecrook D & G
2 E7 Whitecross Cnwll
2 H11 White Cross Cnwll
4 F7 Whitecross Cnwll
126 H2 Whitecross Falk
162 E8 Whiteface Highld
120 G3 Whitefarland N Ayrs
114 G6 Whitefaulds S Ayrs
89 N9 Whitefield Bury

17 N4 Whitefield Devon
18 E9 Whitefield Somset
81 P7 Whitefield Lane End Knows
151 Q2 Whiteford Abers
82 D11 Whitegate Ches W
23 K4 Whitehall Hants
169 f4 Whitehall Ork
24 D6 Whitehall W Susx
100 C7 Whitehaven Cumb
38 H10 Whitehill Kent
72 C8 Whitehill Leics
23 L8 Whitehill and Bordon Hants
158 G4 Whitehills Abers
150 G5 Whitehouse Abers
123 P7 Whitehouse Ag & B
58 H5 Whitehouse Common Birm
128 F3 Whitekirk E Loth
103 K3 White Kirkley Dur
11 Q5 White Lackington Dorset
19 L11 Whitelackington Somset
46 H4 White Ladies Aston Worcs
35 M4 Whiteleaf Bucks
113 J10 White-le-Head Dur
14 F5 Whiteley Hants
14 G10 Whiteley Bank IoW
83 K9 Whiteley Green Ches E
36 C8 Whiteley Village Surrey
24 H5 Whitemans Green W Susx
43 J10 White Mill Carmth
156 H7 Whitemire Moray
72 E2 Whitemoor C Nott
4 F10 Whitemoor Cnwll
84 E11 Whitemoor Derbys
70 F2 Whitemoor Staffs
169 q9 Whiteness Shet
52 C8 White Notley Essex
34 B2 Whiteoak Green Oxon
20 D3 White Ox Mead BaNES
21 P10 Whiteparish Wilts
87 L5 White Pit Lincs
151 M3 Whiterashes Abers
51 N8 White Roding Essex
167 Q7 Whiterow Highld
157 J6 Whiterow Moray
32 F3 Whiteshill Gloucs
25 M8 Whitesmith E Susx
88 G5 White Stake Lancs
10 F2 Whitestaunton Somset
9 L6 Whitestone Devon
45 R6 White Stone Herefs
9 L6 Whitestone Cross Devon
52 G4 Whitestreet Green Suffk
98 F7 Whitewall Corner N York
35 M9 White Waltham W & M
20 D2 Whiteway BaNES
32 H2 Whiteway Gloucs
95 P11 Whitewell Lancs
6 G4 Whiteworks Devon
27 P2 Whitfield Kent
48 H7 Whitfield Nhants
111 Q9 Whitfield Nthumb
32 C6 Whitfield S Glos
111 Q9 Whitfield Hall Nthumb
10 F5 Whitford Devon
80 G9 Whitford Flints
92 D6 Whitgift E R Yk
70 G9 Whitgreave Staffs
107 M9 Whithorn D & G
121 K6 Whiting Bay N Ayrs
91 K4 Whitkirk Leeds
41 N7 Whitland Carmth
117 Q8 Whitlaw Border
114 G3 Whitletts S Ayrs
91 P6 Whitley N York
35 K10 Whitley Readg
84 D2 Whitley Sheff
32 G11 Whitley Wilts
113 N6 Whitley Bay N Tyne
113 M6 Whitley Bay Crematorium N Tyne
112 D9 Whitley Chapel Nthumb
70 E9 Whitley Heath Staffs
90 E9 Whitley Lower Kirk
37 L10 Whitley Row Kent
58 H9 Whitlock's End Solhll
32 E3 Whitminster Gloucs
13 J3 Whitmore Dorset
70 E6 Whitmore Staffs
28 D11 Whitnage Devon
48 B2 Whitnash Warwks
45 K5 Whitney-on-Wye Herefs
100 H3 Whitrigg Cumb
110 D9 Whitrigg Cumb
110 D9 Whitrigglees Cumb
21 M11 Whitsbury Hants
129 M9 Whitsome Border
31 L8 Whitson Newpt
39 K8 Whitstable Kent
5 M2 Whitstone Cnwll
119 L8 Whittingham Nthumb
56 G7 Whittingslow Shrops
84 E5 Whittington Derbys
47 K10 Whittington Gloucs
95 N5 Whittington Lancs
75 P11 Whittington Norfk
69 K8 Whittington Shrops
58 C8 Whittington Staffs
59 J3 Whittington Staffs
59 L5 Whittington Warwks
46 G4 Whittington Worcs
84 E6 Whittington Moor Derbys
49 J6 Whittlebury Nhants
88 H6 Whittle-le-Woods Lancs
74 E11 Whittlesey Cambs
62 G11 Whittlesford Cambs
89 L7 Whittlestone Head Bl w D
92 F6 Whitton N Linc
119 L10 Whitton Nthumb
56 D11 Whitton Powys
104 C6 Whitton S on T
57 K10 Whitton Shrops
53 K2 Whitton Suffk
33 Q10 Whittonditch Wilts
112 Q9 Whittonstall Nthumb
22 E3 Whitway Hants
84 H3 Whitwell Derbys
50 E6 Whitwell Herts
14 F11 Whitwell IoW
97 Q11 Whitwell N York
73 N9 Whitwell Rutlnd
98 E7 Whitwell-on-the-Hill N York
76 G7 Whitwell Street Norfk

72 C7 Whitwick Leics
91 L6 Whitwood Wakefd
89 P7 Whitworth Lancs
69 P8 Whixall Shrops
97 P9 Whixley N York
103 M8 Whorlton Dur
104 E10 Whorlton N York
45 R2 Whyle Herefs
36 H9 Whyteleafe Surrey
31 Q5 Wibdon Gloucs
90 E4 Wibsey C Brad
59 Q7 Wibtoft Warwks
46 E2 Wichenford Worcs
38 F10 Wichling Kent
13 L6 Wick Bmouth
10 D4 Wick Devon
167 Q6 Wick Highld
32 D10 Wick S Glos
18 H6 Wick Somset
29 M9 Wick Somset
29 P10 Wick V Glam
24 B10 Wick W Susx
21 N10 Wick Wilts
45 M5 Wick Worcs
167 Q6 Wick Airport Highld
63 J6 Wicken Cambs
49 K7 Wicken Nhants
51 L4 Wicken Bonhunt Essex
86 E4 Wickenby Lincs
49 Q4 Wick End Bed
76 A5 Wicken Green Village Norfk
84 G2 Wickersley Rothm
52 G3 Wicker Street Green Suffk
38 B3 Wickford Essex
14 G4 Wickham Hants
34 C10 Wickham W Berk
52 D9 Wickham Bishops Essex
39 M10 Wickhambreaux Kent
63 N10 Wickhambrook Suffk
47 L6 Wickhamford Worcs
64 F8 Wickham Green Suffk
34 D10 Wickham Green W Berk
64 F8 Wickham Heath W Berk
65 L10 Wickham Market Suffk
77 N10 Wickhampton Norfk
52 D4 Wickham St Paul Essex
64 F8 Wickham Skeith Suffk
64 G10 Wickham Street Suffk
64 F8 Wickham Street Suffk
76 F11 Wicklewood Norfk
76 H5 Wickmere Norfk
31 L11 Wick St Lawrence N Som
25 M9 Wickstreet E Susx
32 D7 Wickwar S Glos
51 M4 Widdington Essex
89 Q4 Widdop Calder
119 Q11 Widdrington Nthumb
113 K2 Widdrington Station Nthumb
8 H9 Widecombe in the Moor Devon
5 M10 Widegates Cnwll
16 C11 Widemouth Bay Cnwll
113 K6 Wide Open N Tyne
51 Q10 Widford Essex
51 K7 Widford Herts
33 L7 Widham Wilts
15 J5 Widley Hants
35 N5 Widmer End Bucks
72 G5 Widmerpool Notts
37 K7 Widmore Gt Lon
81 Q8 Widnes Halton
81 Q7 Widnes Crematorium Halton
10 E5 Widworthy Devon
88 H9 Wigan Wigan
82 C4 Wigan Crematorium Wigan
19 M11 Wigborough Somset
10 C6 Wiggaton Devon
75 L8 Wiggenhall St Germans Norfk
75 L8 Wiggenhall St Mary Magdalen Norfk
75 L8 Wiggenhall St Mary the Virgin Norfk
51 Q2 Wiggens Green Essex
71 K2 Wiggenstall Staffs
69 K7 Wiggington Shrops
92 C9 Wigginton C York
35 P2 Wigginton Herts
48 C8 Wigginton Oxon
59 K3 Wigginton Staffs
35 P3 Wigginton Bottom Herts
96 B9 Wigglesworth N York
110 E10 Wiggonby Cumb
24 C7 Wiggonholt W Susx
97 Q11 Wighill N York
76 C4 Wighton Norfk
58 C5 Wightwick Wolves
84 D6 Wigley Derbys
22 B11 Wigley Hants
56 G11 Wigmore Herefs
38 C9 Wigmore Medway
85 Q6 Wigsley Notts
61 M4 Wigsthorpe Nhants
72 G11 Wigston Leics
72 G10 Wigston Fields Leics
59 Q7 Wigston Parva Leics
85 J4 Wigthorpe Notts
74 E3 Wigtoft Lincs
110 E11 Wigton Cumb
107 M6 Wigtown D & G
90 G11 Wigtwizzle Sheff
91 J2 Wike Leeds
60 H3 Wilbarston Nhants
98 E10 Wilberfoss E R Yk
62 G5 Wilburton Cambs
61 J7 Wilby Nhants
64 E4 Wilby Norfk
65 J7 Wilby Suffk
21 M2 Wilcot Wilts
69 L11 Wilcott Shrops
31 M7 Wilcrick Newpt
84 D6 Wildgay Green Derbys
83 L11 Wildboarclough Ches E
61 N9 Wilden Bed
58 B10 Wilden Worcs
63 M5 Wilde Street Suffk
14 H4 Wildern Hants
50 G9 Wildhill Herts
126 E7 Wildmanbridge S Lans
58 E9 Wildmoor Worcs
92 D11 Wildsworth Lincs
72 F3 Wilford C Nott
72 F3 Wilford Hill Crematorium Notts
70 A6 Wilkesley Ches E